British Columbia Securities Act and Regulation Annotated

with Policy Statements, Blanket Orders and Rulings, and Notices and Interpretation Notes

1996

Jeffrey A. Read, B.A., LL.B.

of Fraser & Beatty

James L. Heppell, B.Sc., LL.B.

of Hanna Heppell Bell & Visosky

members of the British Columbia Bar

CARSWELL

Thomson Professional Publishing

⊗ The acid-free paper used in this publication meets the minimum requirements of American National Standard for Information Sciences – Permanence of Paper for Printed Library Materials, ANSI Z39.48-1984.

ISBN 0-459-54768-2

CARSWELL
Thomson Professional Publishing

Introduction

The *British Columbia Securities Act and Regulation Annotated 1996* is a compendium of British Columbia securities legislation, regulations, forms, local, national and uniform policies, blanket orders, and notices and interpretation notes as at July 1, 1995. Legislative provisions which have passed Third Reading but were not in force at the time of publication appear in shaded print following the provisions that they will replace, if any. It is our intention to update this book on an annual basis to provide an easy-to-use and up-to-date reference source of the legislation and policies affecting securities practice in British Columbia.

The *Securities Act* and the Regulation have been annotated by the editors to provide a summary of the British Columbia Superintendent of Brokers, Securities Commission and court decisions which interpret the legislation. We have also annotated the materials to provide helpful cross-referencing and notes on practice points. While the annotations are based on our experience with the securities regulators, our review of decisions issued by them and a review of all available sources, they do not necessarily correspond to the position of the Commission, the Superintendent of Brokers or their staff. We would appreciate comments from practitioners as to other practice points which they would like to see covered in upcoming editions.

The editors would like to thank Susan Adams of the Policy and Legislation Department of the British Columbia Securities Commission for her able assistance in making this publication possible.

Every effort has been made to provide an accurate compilation of the legislation of, and the policies issued under, the British Columbia *Securities Act*. The text of the materials has been left unchanged in the interests of accuracy.

Vancouver, British Columbia
July, 1995

JAR (604) 443-7107
JLH (604) 688-6905

Table of Contents

Local Policy Statements

Table of Contents ix

Blanket Orders and Rulings

Table of Contents   xi

Table of Cases

References are to page numbers.

SECURITIES ACT

TABLE OF CONTENTS

PART 1

INTERPRETATION

PART 2

THE COMMISSION

PART 2.1

[Repealed]

PART 2.2

FINANCIAL ADMINISTRATION

PART 3

SELF REGULATORY BODIES AND STOCK EXCHANGES

PART 4

REGISTRATION

PART 5

EXEMPTION FROM REGISTRATION REQUIREMENTS

PART 6

TRADING IN SECURITIES GENERALLY

PART 7

PROSPECTUS

Act

PART 15

INVESTIGATIONS AND AUDITS

PART 16

ENFORCEMENT

PART 17

REVIEWS AND APPEALS

SECURITIES ACT

S.B.C. 1985, c. 83; as amended by 1987, cc. 42, 59; 1988, c. 58;
1989, cc. 30, 40, 47, 78; 1990, cc. 3, 11, 25; 1992, cc. 52, 55;
1993, c. 35; 1994, c. 51; 1995, cc. 15, 45

PART 1

INTERPRETATION

Further definitions are found in ss. 3 (Special Relationships), 29(1) (Exemption from Registration Requirements), 74 (Takeover Bids and Issuer Bids), 100 (Proxies) and 104(1) (Self Dealing) of the Act and ss. 1 (Interpretation), 2 (Finance Issuer), 11 (Registration), 72.1 (Registrant), 116 (Exchanged Security), 164 (Proxies – Rights of Beneficial Owner of Securities), 167.1 (Conflicts of Interest) and 184 (Prospecting Syndicates) of the Regulation.

Interpretation

1. (1) In this Act

"adviser" means a person engaging in, or holding himself out as engaging in, the business of advising another with respect to investment in or the purchase or sale of securities;

"adviser" means a person engaging in, or holding himself out as engaging in, the business of advising another with respect to investment in or the purchase or sale of securities or exchange contracts;

[S. 1(1) "adviser" am. 1990, c. 25, s. 1(a) (nyif).]

"associate" means, where used to indicate a relationship with any person,

(a) a partner, other than a limited partner, of that person,

(b) a trust or estate in which that person has a substantial beneficial interest or for which that person serves as trustee or in a similar capacity,

(c) an issuer in respect of which that person beneficially owns or controls, directly or indirectly, voting securities carrying more than 10% of the voting rights attached to all outstanding voting securities of the issuer, or

(d) a relative, including the spouse, of that person or a relative of that person's spouse, where the relative has the same home as that person,

and for the purpose of this definition "spouse" includes a man or woman not married to that person but who is living with that person and has lived with that person as husband or wife for a period of not less than 6 months;

"associate" means, where used to indicate a relationship with any person,

(a) a partner, other than a limited partner, of that person,

(b) a trust or estate in which that person has a substantial beneficial interest or for which that person serves as trustee or in a similar capacity,

(c) an issuer in respect of which that person beneficially owns or controls, directly or indirectly, voting securities carrying more than 10% of the voting rights attached to all outstanding voting securities of the issuer, or

(d) a relative, including the spouse, of that person or a relative of that person's spouse, where the relative has the same home as that person,

[S. 1(1) "associate" am. 1995, c. 45, s. 1(a) (nyif).]

"business day" means a day other than Saturday or a holiday;

"class of exchange contracts" includes a series of a class of exchange contracts;

[S. 1(1) "class of exchange contracts" en. 1990, c. 25, s. 1(b) (nyif).]

"class of securities" includes a series of a class of securities;

"clearing agency" means

(a) a person that

(i) in connection with trades in securities, acts as an intermediary in paying funds, in delivering securities or in doing both of those things, and

(ii) provides centralized facilities for the clearing of trades in securities, or

(b) a person that provides centralized facilities as a depository in connection with trades in securities;

[S. 1(1) "clearing agency" en. 1989, c. 78, s. 1(b).]

"clearing agency" means a person that

(a) in connection with trades in securities, acts as an intermediary in paying funds, in delivering securities or in doing both of those things,

(b) provides centralized facilities through which trades in securities or exchange contracts are cleared, or

(c) provides centralized facilities as a depository of securities;

[S. 1(1) "clearing agency" re-en. 1990, c. 25, s. 1(c) (nyif).]

"commission" means the British Columbia Securities Commission continued under Part 2;

[S. 1(1) "commission" am. 1995, c. 15, s. 1.]

"commission rule" means a rule made or deemed to be made by the commission under section 159.1;

[S. 1(1) "commission rule" en. 1995, c. 45, s. 2 (nyif).]

[S. 1(1) "commodity contract" repealed 1989, c. 78, s. 1(a).]

[S. 1(1) "commodity option" repealed 1989, c. 78, s. 1(a).]

"contract" includes a trust agreement, declaration of trust or other similar instrument;

"contractual plan" means a contract or other arrangement for the purchase of securities of a mutual fund by payments over a specified period or by a specified number of payments where the amount deducted from any one of the payments as sales charges is larger than the amount that would have been deducted from that payment for sales charges if deductions had been made from each payment at a constant rate for the duration of the plan;

"control person" means

(a) a person who holds a sufficient number of the voting rights attached to all outstanding voting securities of an issuer, or

(b) each person in a combination of persons, acting in concert by virtue of an agreement, arrangement, commitment or understanding, which holds in total a sufficient number of the voting rights attached to all outstanding voting securities of an issuer

to affect materially the control of the issuer, and, where a person or combination of persons holds more than 20% of the voting rights attached to all outstanding voting securities of an issuer, the person or combination of persons shall, in the absence of evidence to the contrary, be deemed to hold a sufficient number of the voting rights to affect materially the control of the issuer;

"dealer" means a person who trades in securities as principal or agent;

"dealer" means a person who trades in securities or exchange contracts as principal or agent;

[S. 1(1) "dealer" am. 1990, c. 25, s. 1(a) (nyif).]

"decision" means a direction, decision, order, ruling or requirement made under a power or right conferred by this Act or the regulations;

"designated organization" means an organization that is authorized under section 159(2)(a) to exercise a power or perform a duty of the superintendent;

"designated organization" means an organization that is authorized under section 159.1(2)(e) to exercise a power or perform a duty of the executive director;

[S. 1(1) "designated organization" re-en. 1995, c. 45, s. 3 (nyif).]

"designated security", as used in the definition of "private issuer", means

(a) voting securities, or

(b) securities that are not debt securities and that carry a residual right to participate in the earnings of the issuer or, upon the liquidation or winding up of the issuer, in its assets;

[S. 1(1) "designated security" en. 1990, c. 25, s. 1(d).]

"director" means a director of a corporation or an individual occupying or performing, with respect to a corporation or any other person, a similar position or similar functions;

Re Aatra Resources Ltd., Victor J. Meunier, Paul A. Quinn, Ralph A.A. Simpson, Joel Machtinger, Henry P.M. Huber, Alex Pancer, David J. Foster and Durham Securities Corp. Ltd. (1993), 3 C.C.L.S. 51 (B.C. Sec. Comm.).

A person is a promoter and a *de facto* director if he, and not the directors of record, makes all the significant business decisions, conducts negotiations and directs counsel.

"distribution" means, where used in relation to trading in securities,

(a) a trade in a security of an issuer that has not been previously issued,

(b) a trade by or on behalf of an issuer in a previously issued security of that issuer that has been redeemed or purchased by or donated to that issuer,

(c) a trade in a previously issued security of an issuer from the holdings of a control person,

(d) a trade by or on behalf of an underwriter in a security which was acquired by that underwriter, acting as underwriter, before the coming into force of this section, if that security continues, on the day this section comes into force, to be owned by or on behalf of that underwriter so acting,

(e) a trade deemed to be a distribution

(i) in an order made under section 59 by the commission or the superintendent, or

(i) in an order made under section 59 by the commission or the executive director, or

[Subpara. (i) am. 1995, c. 45, s. 1(b) (nyif).]

(ii) in the regulations,

[Para. (e) re-en. 1988, c. 58, s. 1(a).]

(f) a transaction or series of transactions involving further purchases and sales in the course of or incidental to a distribution, and

(g)   a prescribed class of trade or transaction;

See ss. 133 and 134 of the Regulation with respect to deemed distributions.

"distribution contract" means a contract under which a mutual fund or its legal representative grants to a person the right to purchase the securities of the mutual fund for distribution or to distribute the securities of the mutual fund on behalf of the mutual fund;

[S. 1(1) "equity security" repealed 1989, c. 78, s. 1(a).]

"exchange contract" means a futures contract or an option that meets both of the following requirements:

(a)   its performance is guaranteed by a clearing agency;

(b)   it is traded on an exchange pursuant to standardized terms and conditions set forth in that exchange's bylaws, rules or regulatory instruments, at a price agreed on when the futures contract or option is entered into on the exchange,

and includes another instrument or class of instruments that meets both of those requirements and is designated as an exchange contract in an order the commission may make for the purpose of this definition;

[S. 1(1) "exchange contract" en. 1990, c. 25, s. 1(d) (nyif).]

"exchange issuer" means an issuer whose securities are listed and posted for trading on a stock exchange recognized for the purpose of this definition by the commission but does not include

"exchange issuer" means an issuer whose securities are listed and posted for trading on an exchange recognized for the purpose of this definition by the commission but does not include

[S. 1(1) "exchange issuer" am. 1990, c. 25, s. 1(e) (nyif).]

(a)   an issuer, or

(b)   a class of issuers

described in an order which the commission may make for the purpose of this definition.

[S. 1(1) "exchange issuer" en. 1988, c. 58, s. 1(b).]

The Vancouver Stock Exchange has been recognized by the Commission as a stock exchange for the purposes of this definition; see Local Policy Statement 3-44 "Recognition of Stock Exchanges and Jurisdictions". See BOR 88/2 "The Definition of Exchange Issuer", which excludes all issuers whose securities are listed on the Vancouver Stock Exchange and are listed or quoted on any other stock exchange or quotation system in Canada from the definition of "exchange issuer."

"executive director" means the executive director appointed under section 7;

[S. 1(1) "executive director" en. 1995, c. 45, s. 2 (nyif).]

"futures contract" means a contract to make delivery or take delivery on a specified date or during a specified period of

(a)   a specified cash equivalent of the subject matter of the contract, or

(b)   a specified asset;

[S. 1(1) "futures contract" en. 1990, c. 25, s. 1(f) (nyif).]

"Federal Business Development Bank" means the Federal Business Development Bank incorporated under the *Federal Business Development Bank Act* (Canada);

"holder in the Province" means, in respect of a security of an issuer, a holder of the security of the issuer whose last address as shown on the books of the issuer is in the Province;

"individual" means a natural person, but does not include

(a) a partnership, unincorporated association, unincorporated syndicate, unincorporated organization or trust, or

(b) a natural person in his capacity as a trustee, executor, administrator or personal or other legal representative;

"insider" means, where used in relation to an issuer,

(a) a director or senior officer of the issuer,

(b) a director or senior officer of a person that is itself an insider or subsidiary of the issuer,

(c) a person that has

(i) direct or indirect beneficial ownership of,

(ii) control or direction over, or

(iii) a combination of direct or indirect beneficial ownership of and of control or direction over

securities of the issuer carrying more than 10% of the voting rights attached to all the issuer's outstanding voting securities, excluding, for the purpose of the calculation of the percentage held, any securities held by the person as underwriter in the course of a distribution, or,

[Para. (c) re-en. 1990, c. 25, s. 1(g).]

(d) the issuer itself, where it has purchased, redeemed or otherwise acquired any securities of its own issue, for so long as it continues to hold those securities;

See NIN 95/15 "Disclosure of Securities under 'Control or Direction' " for guidance as to the meaning of the phrase "control or direction".

United Services Funds (Trustees of) v. Lazzell, 28 B.C.L.R. (2d) 26, additional reasons at [1989] 1 W.W.R. 445, 30 B.C.L.R. (2d) 103 (S.C.).

This was an action by the trustees of a Texas mutual fund against a number of defendants, including two who were undisclosed insiders of a reporting issuer. The court reviewed the definitions of "insider" and "promoter" found in the former Securities Act (R.S.B.C. 1979, c. 380) and concluded that it is obvious from the defintions that the law considers that investors have a right to know who has control and who is an insider. By the very nature of these sections, these are material matters. It commented further, regarding the duties of directors, that not every director of every company who knows that someone is in breach of the insider reporting sections of the Securities Act is necessarily himself guilty of an offence. However, here the directors had a duty to the fund as a principal shareholder to apprise it of the relevant facts as to control and illegal trading, whether or not they had, as directors, a duty to inform the fund of the scheme of bribery itself.

"insurer" means an insurance company;

[S. 1(1) "insurer" am. 1989, c. 47, s. 397(a).]

"issuer" means a person who

(a) has a security outstanding,

(b) is issuing a security, or

(c) proposes to issue a security;

"investor relations activities" means any activities or oral or written communications, by or on behalf of an issuer or security holder of the issuer, that promote or reasonably could be expected to promote the purchase or sale of securities of the issuer, but does not include

(a) the dissemination of information provided, or records prepared, in the ordinary course of the business of the issuer

(i) to promote the sale of products or services of the issuer, or

(ii) to raise public awareness of the issuer,

that cannot reasonably be considered to promote the purchase or sale of securities of the issuer,

(b) activities or communications necessary to comply with the requirements of

(i) this Act or the regulations, or

(ii) the bylaws, rules or other regulatory instruments of a self regulatory body or exchange,

(c) communications by a publisher of, or writer for, a bona fide newspaper, news magazine or business or financial publication, that is of general and regular paid circulation, distributed only to subscribers to it for value or to purchasers of it, where

(i) the communication is only through the newspaper, magazine or publication, and

(ii) the publisher or writer receives no commission or other consideration other than for acting in the capacity of publisher or writer, or

(d) activities or communications that may be prescribed for the purpose of this definition;

[S. 1(1) "investor relations activities" en. 1995, c. 45, s. 2 (nyif).]

"management contract" means a contract under which a mutual fund is provided with investment advice;

"material change" means, where used in relation to the affairs of an issuer, a change in the business, operations, assets or ownership of the issuer that would reasonably be expected to have a significant effect on the market price or value of any of the securities of the issuer and includes a decision to implement that change made by

(a) senior management of the issuer who believe that confirmation of the decision by the directors is probable, or

(b) the directors of the issuer;

See s. 67 of the Act with respect to the definition of "material change" as discussed in the *Pezim* decision.

"material fact" means, where used in relation to securities issued or proposed to be issued, a fact that significantly affects, or could reasonably be expected to significantly affect, the market price or value of those securities;

Pezim v. British Columbia (Superintendent of Brokers) (1992), 66 B.C.L.R. (2d) 257, (sub nom. *Pezim v. British Columbia Securities Commission)* 96 D.L.R. (4th) 137, 13 B.C.A.C. 1, 24 W.A.C. 1, reversed [1994] 2 S.C.R. 577, 4 C.C.L.S. 114, [1994] 7 W.W.R. 1, 92 B.C.L.R. (2d) 145, 14 B.L.R. (2d) 217, 22 Admin. L.R. (2d) 1, 114 D.L.R. (4th) 385, 168 N.R. 321, 46 B.C.A.C. 1, 75 W.A.C. 1.

The definition of "material fact" is broader than that of "material change". It encompasses any fact that can "reasonably be expected to significantly affect" the market price or value of the securities of an issuer, and not only changes "in the business, operations, assets or ownership of the issuer" that would reasonably be expected to have such an effect.

Re Fraser Bow Securities Inc. and Trading In Securities Consisting of Units of Homesavers Equity Fund Limited Partnership and Blackshine Mines Limited Partnership, [1988] 84 B.C.S.C. Weekly Summary (B.C. Supt. of Brokers).

Where an offering memorandum contained misleading disclosure due to the fact that the allocation of administration and selling commissions was improperly disclosed, the Superintendent of Brokers held that the definitions of "misrepresentation" and "material fact" should not be narrowly construed. Despite the fact that the aggregate of the fees was properly disclosed, their allocation would be a material fact to the investor, as it may affect not just the value of his investment, but his decision as to whether to purchase at all.

"misrepresentation" means

(a) an untrue statement of a material fact, or

(b) an omission to state a material fact that is

(i) required to be stated, or

(ii) necessary to prevent a statement that is made from being false or misleading in the circumstances in which it was made;

Re Axagon Resources Ltd., Stephen Jeffery Greenwald and Jay Robin Greenwald (1993), 1 C.C.L.S. 75 (B.C. Sec. Comm.).

A security agreement which grants a security interest over all of a company's intangibles and inventory to another company controlled by the secretary, Chief Financial Officer and director of the first company may be a material fact. The omission to disclose it, as required in the statement of material facts, may be a misrepresentation. Press releases of a company that contain false and misleading financial information can reasonably be expected to significantly affect the market price of the company's shares and therefore such press releases will be considered to contain misrepresentations.

"mutual fund" includes an issuer of a security that entitles the holder to receive on demand, or within a specified period after demand, an amount computed by reference to the value of a proportionate interest in the whole or in a part of the net assets, including a separate fund or trust account, of the issuer of the security;

"mutual fund distributor" means a person distributing a security under a distribution contract;

"mutual fund in the Province" means a mutual fund that is

(a) a reporting issuer, or

(b) organized under the laws of the Province,

but does not include a private mutual fund;

"mutual fund manager" means a person who provides investment advice under a management contract;

[S. 1(1) "offering memorandum" repealed 1989, c. 78, s. 1(a).]

"officer" means the chairman or a vice chairman of the board of directors, the president, a vice president, the secretary, an assistant secretary, the treasurer, an assistant treasurer, the general manager and any other individual appointed an officer of a corporation or acting in a capacity similar to those specified offices on behalf of an issuer or a registrant;

"officer" means the chair or a vice chair of the board of directors, the president, a vice president, the secretary, an assistant secretary, the treasurer, an assistant treasurer, the general manager and any other individual appointed an officer of a corporation or acting in a capacity similar to those specified offices on behalf of an issuer or a registrant;

[S. 1(1) "officer" am. 1995, c. 45, s. 1(c) (nyif).]

"person" includes an individual, corporation, partnership, party, trust, fund, association and any other organized group of persons and the personal or other legal representative of a person to whom the context can apply according to law;

"portfolio manager" means an adviser who manages the investment portfolio of clients through discretionary authority granted by one or more clients;

"portfolio security" means, where used in relation to a mutual fund, a security held or proposed to be purchased by the mutual fund;

"private issuer" means a person that

(a) is not a reporting issuer or a mutual fund,

(b) is an issuer all of whose issued and outstanding securities that are designated securities

    (i) are subject to restrictions on transfer contained in

        (A) the constating documents of the issuer, or

        (B) one or more agreements between the issuer and the holders of its designated securities, and

    (ii) are beneficially owned, directly or indirectly, by not more than 50 persons, counting any 2 or more joint registered owners as one beneficial owner, exclusive of persons

        (A) that are employed by the issuer or an affiliate of it, or

        (B) that beneficially owned, directly or indirectly, designated securities of the issuer while employed by it or by an affiliate of it and, at all times since ceasing to be so employed, have continued to beneficially own, directly or indirectly, at least one designated security of the issuer, and

(c) has not distributed to the public after October 31, 1989 any of its designated securities or any securities convertible into or exchangeable for its designated securities;

[S. 1(1) "private issuer" re-en. 1990, c. 25, s. 1(h).]

See NIN 89/29 "Meaning of 'the Public'" and BOR 91/4 "Trades of Securities of Private Issuers".

"private mutual fund" means a mutual fund that is

(a) operated as an investment club, where

    (i) its securities are held by not more than 50 persons and it has never sought to borrow money from the public,

    (ii) it does not pay or give any remuneration for investment, management or administration advice in respect of trades in securities, except normal brokerage fees, and

    (iii) all of its members are required to make contributions in proportion to the securities each holds for the purpose of financing its operations, or

(a) operated as an investment club, where

    (i) the securities issued by it are held by not more than 50 persons and it has never sought to borrow money from the public,

    (ii) it does not pay or give any remuneration for investment, management or administration advice in respect of trades in securities or exchange contracts, except normal brokerage fees, and

    (iii) all of its members are required to make contributions, for the purpose of financing its operations, in proportion to the securities issued by it that each member holds, or

[Para. (a) re-en. 1990, c. 25, s. 1(i) (nyif).]

(b) administered by a trust company but which has no promoter or manager other than

    (i) a trust company,

    (ii) an affiliate of a trust company, or

    (iii) a person who

        (A) is registered as a portfolio manager, or

        (B) but for an exemption under this Act or the regulations, is required to be registered as a portfolio manager,

and consists of

    (iv) a pooled fund that is maintained solely to serve registered retirement savings plans, retirement income plans, deferred profit sharing plans, pension plans or other similar plans registered under the *Income Tax Act* (Canada),

[Subpara. (iv) am. 1990, c. 25, s. 1(j).]

    (v) a common trust fund as defined by the *Financial Institutions Act* or

[Subpara. (v) am. 1989, c. 47, s. 397(b).]

    (vi) a pooled fund that is maintained by a trust company in which money, belonging to various estates and trusts in its care, is commingled, with the authority of the settlor, testator or trustee, for the purpose of facilitating investment where no general solicitations are made to sell securities in the fund;

"private mutual fund" means a mutual fund that is

(a) operated as an investment club, where

    (i) the securities issued by it are held by not more than 50 persons and it has never sought to borrow money from the public,

    (ii) it does not pay or give any remuneration for investment, management or administration advice in respect of trades in securities or exchange contracts, except normal brokerage fees, and

    (iii) all of its members are required, for the purpose of financing its operations, to make contributions in proportion to the securities issued by it that each member holds, or

(b) administered by a trust company but which has no promoter or manager other than a trust company, and consists of

    (i) a pooled fund that is maintained solely to serve registered retirement savings plans, retirement income plans, deferred profit sharing plans, pension plans or other similar plans registered under the *Income Tax Act* (Canada),

    (ii) a common trust fund as defined by the *Financial Institutions Act*, or

    (iii) a pooled fund that is maintained by a trust company in which money, belonging to various estates and trusts in its care, is commingled, with the authority of the settlor, testator or trustee, for the purpose of facilitating investment where no general solicitations are made to sell securities in the fund;

[S. 1(1) "private mutual fund" re-en. 1995, c. 45, s. 3 (nyif).]

"promoter" means, where used in relation to an issuer, a person who

(a) acting alone or in concert with one or more other persons, directly or indirectly, takes the initiative in founding, organizing or substantially reorganizing the business of the issuer, or

(b) in connection with the founding, organization or substantial reorganization of the business of the issuer, directly or indirectly receives, in consideration of services or property or both, 10% or more of a class of the issuer's own securities or 10% or more of the proceeds from the sale of a class of the issuer's own securities of a particular issue

but does not include a person who

(c) receives securities or proceeds referred to in paragraph (b) solely

(i) as underwriting commissions, or

(ii) in consideration for property, and

(d) does not otherwise take part in founding, organizing or substantially reorganizing the business;

"registrant" means a person registered or required to be registered under this Act or the regulations;

"regulation", except in sections 138(1)(e) and sections 159, 159.1, 159.3, 159.5 and 159.6, includes a commission rule;

[S. 1(1) "regulation" en. 1995, c. 45, s. 2 (nyif).]

"reporting issuer" means an issuer that

(a) has issued securities in respect of which

(i) a prospectus was filed and a receipt was issued,

(ii) a statement of material facts was filed and accepted, or

(ii) an exchange offering prospectus was filed and accepted, or

[Subpara. (ii) am. 1990, c. 25, s. 1(k) (nyif).]

(iii) a securities exchange take over bid circular was filed,

under a former enactment,

(b) has filed a prospectus or statement of material facts and obtained a receipt for it under this Act or the regulations,

(b) has filed a prospectus or exchange offering prospectus and obtained a receipt for it under this Act or the regulations,

[Para. (b) am. 1990, c. 25, s. 1(l) (nyif).]

(c) has any securities which have been at any time listed and posted for trading on any stock exchange in the Province, regardless of when the listing and posting for trading began,

(c) has any securities which have been at any time listed and posted for trading on any exchange in the Province, regardless of when the listing and posting for trading began,

[Para. (c) am. 1990, c. 25, s. 1(m) (nyif).]

(d) [Repealed 1989, c. 78, s. 1(c).]

(e) is a corporation that has exchanged its securities with another corporation or with the holders of the securities of that other corporation in connection with an amalgamation, merger, reorganization or arrangement where one of the parties to the amalgamation, merger, reorganization or arrangement was a reporting issuer at the time of the amalgamation, merger, reorganization or arrangement, and the corporation that has exchanged its securities shall be deemed to have been a reporting issuer as at the date of the amalgamation, merger, reorganization or arrangement, for the longest period of time that one of the parties to the amalgamation, merger, reorganization or arrangement had been a reporting issuer at the date of the amalgamation, merger, reorganization or arrangement,

(f) is designated as a reporting issuer in an order which the commission may make for the purpose of this definition, or

[Para. (f) re-en. 1988, c. 58, s. 1(c).]

(g) has filed a securities exchange take over bid circular under this Act or the regulations,

unless the commission orders under section 72 that it has ceased to be a reporting issuer;

See Local Policy Statement 3-45 "Designation as a Reporting Issuer". See BOR 89/8 "Reporting Companies under the British Columbia Company Act and the definition of 'Reporting Issuer'." See also NIN 89/17 "Local Policy Statement 3-45 – Designation as a Reporting Issuer and Business Investor Offerings."

Re Richmond Cabs Ltd. and Gill and Others, [1990] 27 B.C.S.C. Weekly Summary (B.C. Sec. Comm.).

The Securities Act gives the Commission the power to designate an issuer as a reporting issuer. As a matter of policy, the Commission only grants such an order to an issuer that has similar status in another jurisdiction and wishes to become a reporting issuer in British Columbia without filing a prospectus and where the Commission is satisfied that the issuer is in good standing in the other jurisdiction, has a satisfactory base of disclosure available and would not be refused a receipt for a prospectus if one was filed.

"salesman" means an individual employed by a dealer to make trades in securities on the dealer's behalf;

"salesman" means an individual employed by a dealer to make trades in securities or exchange contracts on the dealer's behalf;

[S. 1(1) "salesman" am. 1990, c. 25, s. 1(a) (nyif); repealed 1995, c. 45, s. 3 (nyif).]

"salesperson" means an individual employed by a dealer to make trades on the dealer's behalf in securities, exchange contracts or both;

[S. 1(1) "salesperson" en. 1995, c. 45, s. 3 (nyif).]

"security" includes

(a) a document, instrument or writing commonly known as a security,

(b) a document evidencing title to, or an interest in, the capital, assets, property, profits, earnings or royalties of a person,

(c) a document evidencing an option, subscription or other interest in or to a security,

(d) a bond, debenture, note or other evidence of indebtedness, share, stock, unit, unit certificate, participation certificate, certificate of share or interest, preorganization certificate or subscription other than

(i) a contract of insurance issued by an insurer, and

(ii) an evidence of deposit issued by a savings institution,

(e) an agreement under which the interest of the purchaser is valued, for the purposes of conversion or surrender, by reference to the value of a proportionate interest in a specified portfolio of assets but does not include a contract issued by an insurer which provides for payment at maturity of an amount not less than 3/4 of the premiums paid by the purchaser for a benefit payable at maturity,

(f) an agreement providing that money received will be repaid or treated as a subscription to shares, stock units or interests at the option of the recipient or of any person,

(g) a profit sharing agreement or certificate,

(h) a certificate of interest in an oil, natural gas or mining lease, claim or royalty voting trust certificate,

(i) an oil or natural gas royalty or lease or a fractional or other interest in either,

(j) a collateral trust certificate,

(k) an income or annuity contract, other than one made by

 (i) an insurer,

[Subpara. (ii) repealed 1987, c. 59, s. 20(a).]

(l) an investment contract,

[Para. (l) am. 1987, c. 59, s. 20(b).]

(m) a document evidencing an interest in a scholarship or educational plan or trust,

(n) a commodity contract that is not

 (i) traded on a commodity exchange recognized by the commission, or

 (ii) in a form accepted by the superintendent,

under the *Commodity Contract Act*, or

(n) an instrument that is a futures contract or an option but is not an exchange contract, or

[Para. (n) re-en. 1990, c. 25, s. 1(n) (nyif).]

(o) an exploration permit under the *Petroleum and Natural Gas Act*,

whether or not any of the above relate to an issuer;

whether or not any of the above relate to an issuer, but does not include an exchange contract;

[S. 1(1) "security" am. 1990, c. 25, s. 1(o) (nyif).]

Re Boulder Creek Development Limited and Lester Gene Chapman, [1988] 73 B.C.S.C. Weekly Summary (B.C. Supt. of Brokers).

The definition of "security" includes "participation agreements" which entitle the purchaser, upon payment of a certain amount of money, to a percentage working interest in an oil and gas lease held by a company.

Re Pac Industries, Inc., Flint Mines, Inc. and Certain Securities Issued by Them Consisting of Mineral Aggregate Units In The Thibert Creek Placer Project Near Dease Lake, British Columbia, [1987] 35 B.C.S.C. Weekly Summary (B.C. Supt. of Brokers).

The decision dealt with whether "mineral aggregate units" were securities and provides a good general review, at pp. 9 to 14, of the meaning in British Columbia of "investment contract". This discussion is summarized as follows.

The definition of securities in the Act includes an "investment contract". The basic test adopted by the Supreme Court of Canada in *Pacific Coast Coin Exchange of Canada v. Ontario (Securities Commission)*, [1978] 2 S.C.R. 112, 2 B.L.R. 212, 80 D.L.R. (3d) 529, 18 N.R. 52, of what constitutes an investment contract is the "common enterprise test", which is based on the decision of *Securities and Exchange Commission v. W.J. Howey Co.*, 328 U.S. 293, 90 L. Ed. 1244 (1945). For an investment contract to exist, there must be:

(i) an investment of money;

(ii) in a common enterprise between the investor and those seeking the investment;

(iii) with profits to come from the efforts of others.

The Supreme Court of Canada and the British Columbia Court of Appeal have also applied the "risk capital test". That test was formulated in 1971 in *State of Hawaii, Court of Securities v. Hawaii Market Center, Inc.*, 485 P. 2d 105. The test provides that an investment contract is created whenever:

(1) an offeree furnishes initial value to an offeror;

(2) a portion of this initial value is subjected to the risk of the enterprise;

(3) the furnishing of the initial value is induced by the offeror's promises or representations which give rise to a reasonable understanding that a valuable benefit of some kind, over and above the initial value, will accrue to the offeree as a result of the operation of the enterprise; and

(4) the offeree does not receive the right to exercise practical and actual control over the managerial decisions of the enterprise.

The overriding principles applicable to both tests were enunciated in the *Pacific Coast Coin Exchange* case, where it was stated that securities legislation is remedial legislation which must be construed broadly and be read in the context of the economic realities to which it is addressed. Substance, not form, is the governing factor.

Re Yuen Chow International Group, Yuen Way Hang Lung International Foreign Exchange Co., Yuen Chow Equities Limited, Hang Lung Market Data Information Services, Inc., Sonny Tat Wong and John Lai, [1995] 22 B.C.S.C. Weekly Summary 26 (B.C. Sec. Comm.).

Foreign exchange contracts are investment contracts and therefore securities within the meaning of the Act. Persons trading in foreign exchange contracts are required to be registered pursuant to s. 20 of the Act and trades may only be made in accordance with s. 42 of the Act by way of a prospectus or in reliance on a prospectus exemption.

"senior officer" means

(a)   the chairman or a vice chairman of the board of directors, the president, a vice president, the secretary, the treasurer or the general manager of a corporation,

(b)   any individual who performs functions for a person similar to those normally performed by an individual occupying any office specified in paragraph (a), and

(c)   the 5 highest paid employees of an issuer, including any individual referred to in paragraph (a) or (b) and excluding a commissioned salesman who does not act in a managerial capacity;

"senior officer" means

(a)   the chair or a vice chair of the board of directors, the president, a vice president, the secretary, the treasurer or the general manager of a corporation,

(b)   any individual who performs functions for a person similar to those normally performed by an individual occupying any office specified in paragraph (a), and

(c)   the 5 highest paid employees of an issuer, including any individual referred to in paragraph (a) or (b) and excluding a commissioned salesperson who does not act in a managerial capacity;

[S. 1(1) "senior officer" am. 1995, c. 45, s. 1(c), (d) (both nyif).]

"spouse" means a person who

(a) is married to another person and is not living separate and apart, within the meaning of the *Divorce Act* (Canada), from the other person, or

(b) is living with another person in a marriage-like relationship,

and, for the purpose of this definition, the marriage or marriage-like relationship may be between members of the same sex;

[S. 1(1) "spouse" en. 1995, c. 45, s. 2 (nyif).]

"subsidiary" means an issuer that is controlled by another issuer;

"superintendent" means the Superintendent of Brokers appointed under section 7;

[S. 1(1) "superintendent" repealed 1995, c. 45, s. 1(e) (nyif).]

"trade" includes

(a) a disposition of a security for valuable consideration whether the terms of payment be on margin, instalment or otherwise, but does not include a purchase of a security or a transfer, pledge, mortgage or other encumbrance of a security for the purpose of giving collateral for a debt,

[Para. (a) re-en. 1988, c. 58, s. 1(d).]

(a.1) entering into an exchange contract,

[Para. (a.1) en. 1990, c. 25, s. 1(p) (nyif).]

(b) participation as a floor trader in a transaction in a security on the floor of a stock exchange,

(c) the receipt by a registrant of an order to buy or sell a security,

(b) participation as a trader in a transaction in a security or exchange contract made on the floor of or through the facilities of an exchange,

(c) the receipt by a registrant of an order to buy or sell a security or exchange contract,

[Paras. (b) and (c) re-en. 1990, c. 25, s. 1(p) (nyif).]

(d) a transfer of beneficial ownership of a security to a transferee, pledgee, mortgagee or other encumbrancer under a realization on collateral given for a debt, and

[Para. (d) re-en. 1988, c. 58, s. 1(d).]

(e) any act, advertisement, solicitation, conduct or negotiation directly or indirectly in furtherance of any of the activities specified in paragraphs (a) to (d);

The definition of "trade" includes an advertisement of a security. The rules regarding advertisements are set out in Interim National Policy Statement 42 "Advertising of Securities on Radio or Television", Local Policy Statement 3-39 "Guidelines for Advertising Issues of Securities and for Promotional Activities During the Course of a Distribution", and Draft National Policy Statement 43 "Advertisement of Securities". Draft National Policy Statement 43 was the subject of a great deal of criticism when it was originally issued for comment in November, 1989. The policy is in the process of being substantially rewritten.

Re Morgan-Taylor International Inc. and Paul Kevin Groat and James Morris Durward, [1989] 107 B.C.S.C. Weekly Summary (B.C. Sec. Comm.).

The word "trade" is given a very broad definition, intended to encompass a wide range of activities related to the selling of securities. Where calls are made to induce an interest in purchasing shares, it is irrelevant whether or not specific offers to sell or specific representations as to future prices were made. If the callers clearly convey a message that is intended to induce a purchase of securities then the message is an act or solicitation that falls squarely within the meaning of the term "trade" as defined in the Act.

R. v. Thiemer (May 27, 1987), Doc. CC870457, Fisher Co. Ct. J., [1988] B.C.W.L.D. 127 (Co. Ct.) (unreported).

A promoter was convicted in Provincial Court for unlawful "trading in securities" under the previous Securities Act. Promotional material had been distributed headed with the question "Would you be open to an investment sometime in the future?", followed by text that indicated that further information would be sent if the answer was in the affirmative. On appeal, it was held that the document did not constitute "trading" as the word is defined in the former Securities Act (R.S.B.C. 1979, c. 380), because the solicitation contained no "terms of payment".

Smith v. Hamelin, 75 B.C.L.R. (2d) 360, [1993] 3 W.W.R. 285 (S.C.).

The B.C. Supreme Court held that a cease trading order issued by the Securities Commission does not prevent corporate shares from being used as security for the payment of a law firm's legal fees. This is because the transaction comes directly within the words of the exception in (2) of the definition "... but does not include ... a transfer, pledge, mortgage or other encumbrance of a security for the purpose of giving collateral for a debt ..." The court went on to hold that the cease trading order prevents a law firm from realizing upon the shares held as security because this would constitute a "trade". Clauses (a) and (d) of the definition should be read together and consequently (d) cannot be read as being subject to (a).

The court was not of the opinion that this would leave a security holder in an impossible position because the security holder could maintain possession of the pledged security until the advances were repaid, it could apply to the Securities Commission under s. 153 of the Securities Act for a revocation order or it could appeal the Commission's decision under s. 149 of the Act.

[S. 1(1) "trust company" repealed 1989, c. 47, s. 397(c).]

"underwriter" means a person who,

(a) as principal, agrees to purchase a security for the purpose of distribution,

(b) as agent, offers for sale or sells a security in connection with a distribution, or

(c) participates directly or indirectly in a distribution described in paragraph (a) or (b),

but does not include

(d) a person whose interest in the transaction is limited to receiving the usual and customary distribution or sales commission payable by an underwriter or issuer,

[Para. (d) re-en. 1990, c. 25, s. 1(q).]

(e) a mutual fund that accepts its securities for surrender and resells them,

(f) a corporation that purchases shares of its own issue and resells them, or

(g) a bank with respect to securities described in section 32 and to prescribed banking transactions;

"voting security" means a security of an issuer that

(a) is not a debt security, and

(b) carries a voting right either under all circumstances or under some circumstances that have occurred and are continuing.

[S. 1(1) "voting security" re-en. 1989, c. 78, s. 1.]

(2) For the purposes of this Act, an issuer is affiliated with another issuer where

(a) one of them is the subsidiary of the other, or

(b) each of them is controlled by the same person.

(3) For the purposes of this Act, an issuer is controlled by a person where

(a) voting securities of the issuer are held, other than by way of security only, by or for the benefit of that person, and

(b) the voting rights attached to those voting securities are entitled, if exercised, to elect a majority of the directors of the issuer.

(4) For the purposes of this Act, a person beneficially owns securities that are beneficially owned by

(a) an issuer controlled by that person, or

(b) an affiliate of that person or an affiliate of any issuer controlled by that person.

Insiders

2. (1) The following persons are insiders of a mutual fund that is a reporting issuer:

(a) a mutual fund manager for the mutual fund;

(b) a mutual fund distributor for the mutual fund;

(c) an insider of a manager or distributor described in paragraph (a) or (b).

(2) Where an issuer becomes an insider of a reporting issuer, every director or senior officer of the issuer shall be deemed to have been an insider of the reporting issuer for the previous 6 months or for the shorter period that he was a director or senior officer of the issuer.

(3) Where a reporting issuer becomes an insider of another reporting issuer, every director or senior officer of the latter reporting issuer shall be deemed to have been an insider of the former reporting issuer for the previous 6 months or for the shorter period that he was a director or senior officer of the latter reporting issuer.

Definition of special relationships

3. For the purposes of sections 68 and 119, a person is in a special relationship with a reporting issuer where the person

(a) is an insider, affiliate or associate of

(i) the reporting issuer,

(ii) a person that is proposing to make a take over bid, as defined in section 74, for the securities of the reporting issuer, or

(iii) a person that is proposing to become a party to a reorganisation, amalgamation, merger, arrangement or similar business combination with the reporting issuer or is proposing to acquire a substantial portion of the property of the reporting issuer,

(b) is engaging in or is proposing to engage in any business or professional activity with or on behalf of the reporting issuer or with or on behalf of a person described in paragraph (a)(ii) or (iii),

(c) is a director, officer or employee of the reporting issuer or of a person described in paragraph (a)(ii) or (iii) or (b),

(d) knows of a material fact or of a material change with respect to the reporting issuer, having acquired the knowledge while in a relationship described in paragraph (a), (b) or (c) with the reporting issuer, or

(e) knows of a material fact or of a material change with respect to the reporting issuer, having acquired the knowledge from another person at a time when

(i) that other person was in a special relationship with the reporting issuer, whether under this paragraph or any of paragraphs (a) to (d), and

(ii) the person that acquired knowledge of the material fact or material change from that other person knew or reasonably ought to have known of the special relationship referred to in subparagraph (i).

[S. 3 re-en. 1989, c. 78, s. 2.]

PART 2

THE COMMISSION

Commission

4. (1) The British Columbia Securities Commission is continued under the same name, and, by this subsection, is constituted as a corporation consisting of its members appointed under subsection (3), whether appointed before or after the commission's incorporation.

[S. 4(1) re-en. 1995, c. 15, s. 2.]

(1.1) The commission is responsible for the administration of this Act.

[S. 4(1.1) en. 1995, c. 15, s. 2.]

(2) The commission shall consist of not more than 9 members appointed by the Lieutenant Governor in Council.

[S. 4(2) am. 1989, c. 78, s. 3.]

(2) The commission consists of not more than 11 members appointed by the Lieutenant Governor in Council.

[S. 4(2) re-en. 1995, c. 45, s. 4 (nyif).]

(3) The Lieutenant Governor in Council may fix the terms and conditions of the appointments of the members of the commission including, but not limited to, appointing members of the commission for different terms of office, or for limited, specified purposes or functions or for all purposes or functions of the commission.

(4) The Lieutenant Governor in Council shall designate one member of the commission to be chairman and chief executive officer of the commission and may designate one member of the commission to be vice chairman of the commission.

(4) The Lieutenant Governor in Council must designate one member of the commission to be chair and chief executive officer of the commission and may designate one or 2 vice chairs of the commission from among its members.

[S. 4(4) re-en. 1995, c. 45, s. 4 (nyif).]

(5) The members of the commission shall be reimbursed for any reasonable expenses necessarily incurred by them in the performance of their duties.

(6) Where a member of the commission is appointed for a limited, specified purpose or function of the commission, the member shall not be considered a member of the commission for any other purpose or function than that specified nor shall he participate in any aspect of the commission's business outside the limited, specified purpose or function for which he was appointed.

(7) When the chairman is absent or incapable of acting, the powers and duties of the chairman shall be exercised and performed by

(a) the vice chairman, or

(b) where there is no vice chairman, a person appointed by the minister.

(7) When the chair is absent or incapable of acting, the powers and duties of the chair must be exercised and performed by

(a) a vice chair, or

(b) where there is no vice chair, a person appointed by the minister.

[S. 4(7) re-en. 1995, c. 45, s. 4 (nyif).]

(8) The commission may hold hearings in or outside the Province in conjunction with any other body empowered by law to administer or regulate trading in securities and may consult with that other body during the course of a hearing.

(8) The commission may hold hearings in or outside the Province in conjunction with any other body empowered by law to administer or regulate trading in securities or exchange contracts and may consult with that other body during the course of a hearing.

[S. 4(8) am. 1990, c. 25, s. 2 (nyif).]

(9) The chairman, vice chairman or any other member of the commission may exercise the powers and shall perform the duties delegated to him by the commission under section 6.

(9) A person who is the chair, a vice chair or a member of the commission may exercise the powers and must perform the duties delegated to that person by the commission under section 6.

[S. 4(9) re-en. 1995, c. 45, s. 4 (nyif).]

See NIN 92/2 "Communication with the Securities Commission".

Bennett v. British Columbia (Securities Commission) (1991), 82 D.L.R. (4th) 129, affirmed 69 B.C.L.R. (2d) 171, [1992] 5 W.W.R. 481, 94 D.L.R. (4th) 339, 18 B.C.A.C. 191, 31 W.A.C. 191, leave to appeal to S.C.C. refused [1992] 6 W.W.R. lvii, 70 B.C.L.R. (2d) xxxii, 143 N.R. 396, 20 B.C.A.C. 80, 35 W.A.C. 80, 97 D.L.R. (4th) vii.

The Securities Commission and Superintendent of Brokers are not, in essence, delegates or agents of the Crown. The very fabric of the Securities Act is the establishment of an independent knowledgeable Commission responsible for the administration of the Act itself. Neither the Commission nor the Superintendent of Brokers are "government officials" in a way that would make them part of government in the sense that a prosecutor, employed by the Ministry of the Attorney General, is an agent of the Crown.

Bennett v. British Columbia (Securities Commission) (1992), 69 B.C.L.R. (2d) 171, [1992] 5 W.W.R. 481, 94 D.L.R. (4th) 339, 18 B.C.A.C. 191, 31 W.A.C. 191, affirming (1991), 82 D.L.R. (4th) 129, leave to appeal to S.C.C. refused [1992] 6 W.W.R. lvii, 70 B.C.L.R. (2d) xxxii, 143 N.R. 396, 20 B.C.A.C. 80, 35 W.A.C. 80, 97 D.L.R. (4th) vii.

The chambers judge's decision was appealed on a number of grounds. The Court of Appeal upheld the chambers judge's decision in finding that the proposed Securities Commission hearing was not an abuse of process by virtue of any "fundamental principles of justice", bias, delay or given the multiplicity of proceedings. Further, the Securities Commission's action in continuing with its own investigation and hearing into allegations of insider trading against the petitioners, after criminal charges arising from the same circumstances were dismissed, did not amount to issue estoppel. The court based its decision primarily upon the fact that the Securities Commission was not a party to the criminal proceedings and it would not be a party to the hearing it conducts. The fact that the Commission authorized or allowed members of its staff to assist in the Offence Act prosecution did not bar the Commission from exercising its adjudicative functions through the medium of a hearing. The Court of Appeal went on to deal with and dismiss arguments with respect to the application of s. 7 of the Charter and whether the prohibition under s. 68 of the Act is within the constitutional powers of the British Columbia legislature.

See discussion of a further appeal of this hearing on the basis of the apprehension of bias of one of the panel members at s. 144.

Bennett v. British Columbia (Superintendent of Brokers) and British Columbia (Securities Commission), [1994] 40 B.C.S.C. Weekly Summary 75 (C.A.), affirmed (sub nom. *Bennett v. British Columbia (Superintendent of Brokers)*) 5 C.C.L.S. 93, 96 B.C.L.R. (2d) 274, 118 D.L.R. (4th) 449, (sub nom. *Bennett v. British Columbia Securities Commission (No. 4)*) 51 B.C.A.C. 81, 84 W.A.C. 81 (C.A.).

In a subsequent action the applicants sought leave to appeal a decision by the Commission not to disqualify two members of its panel on the basis of alleged bias by reason of their participation in the dismissal of certain preliminary objections when the two members were members of a previous panel. The applicants intended to renew the preliminary objection before the reconstituted panel. Taylor J.A., in Chambers, dismissed the application for leave to appeal because no basis could possibly be established for apprehension of bias and the issue could have been brought before the court as part of the previous year's appeal. The Court further commented that were it to grant leave to appeal from a ruling made during the course of a hearing before the completion of the hearing, this would inevitably call for a stay of the proceedings or place the continuation of the proceedings under a grave cloud of uncertainty. The applicants applied to the Court of Appeal to vary or discharge the decision of Taylor J.A. The Court of Appeal dismissed the application.

Rak v. British Columbia (Superintendent of Brokers) (1990), 51 B.C.L.R. (2d) 27, 47 Admin. L.R. 243, 74 D.L.R. (4th) 725 (C.A.).

A decision of the Commission was appealed on the basis of the degree of proof that should be imposed on the Superintendent of Brokers and whether that test had been met. The Court of Appeal held that it would be difficult if not impossible to articulate a degree of proof that the Commission requires in any particular case, provided that the Commission is mindful of the common law principles of standards and degrees or proof as they apply to each case before it.

Re Marathon Minerals Inc. and Earl MacRae, J. Keith Judd, Michael D. Judd, Neil W. Humphery, Cathryn J. Garcia, B.J. Illingby, Marvin L. Judd, Buxton Placer Exploration Ltd., Douglas R.G. Harris, George Krueckl, Corcoran & Co. Ltd. Partnership and Piers Vanziffle, [1989] 112 B.C.S.C. Weekly Summary (B.C. Sec. Comm.).

In considering whether the investigative and enforcement provisions of the Act are retrospective in application the Commission held that the presumption against retrospectivity does not apply where the intention of a statutory provision is regulatory and protective. The primary purpose of those provisions is to protect the public who would be vulnerable if a person held the office of a director or officer. The section's purpose is not to punish or penalize the person who is prohibited from holding it. The Commission must consider the public interest and, in determining what is in the public interest, must be able to consider all the relevant facts, including activities before and after the effective date of the amendment.

Chromex Nickel Mines Ltd. v. British Columbia (Securities Commission) (1992), 70 B.C.L.R. (2d) 186, 6 Admin. L.R. (2d) 268 (S.C.).

After four weeks of a hearing the appointment of one of the commissioners expired. He was not re-appointed and the Commission established a new panel to recommence the hearing. The petitioners applied for judicial review to prevent the hearing from beginning again. Sanders J. held that the tribunal had acted within its statutory mandate in deciding to recommence the hearing and that there was no denial of fairness or natural justice.

Agent of the government

4.1 (1) The commission is an agent of the government.

(2) The commission has the power and capacity of a natural person of full capacity.

(3) The *Company Act* does not apply to the commission, but the Lieutenant Governor in Council may order that one or more of the provisions of that Act apply.

(4) The commission is not liable to taxation, except insofar as the government is liable.

[S. 4.1 en. 1995, c. 15, s. 3.]

Panels

5. (1) The chairman may establish one or more panels of the commission, and, in matters referred to a panel by the chairman, a panel has the powers of the commission.

(2) The chairman may refer a matter that is before the commission to a panel or a matter that is before a panel to the commission or another panel.

(3) A panel shall consist of 2 or more members of the commission appointed by the chairman.

(4) The chairman may terminate an appointment to a panel and may fill a vacancy on a panel before the commencement of a hearing.

5. (1) The chair may establish one or more panels of the commission, and, in matters referred to a panel by the chair, a panel has the powers of the commission.

(2) The chair may refer a matter that is before the commission to a panel or a matter that is before a panel to the commission or another panel.

(3) A panel shall consist of 2 or more members of the commission appointed by the chair.

(4) The chair may terminate an appointment to a panel and may fill a vacancy on a panel before the commencement of a hearing.

[S. 5 am. 1995, c. 45, s. 5 (nyif).]

Delegation

6. (1) Subject to subsection (2), the commission may delegate its powers and duties under this Act, the regulations or another enactment to the chairman, vice chairman, a member of the commission or the superintendent.

[S. 6(1) am. 1992, c. 52, s. 1.]

6. (1) Subject to subsections (2) and (2.1), the commission may delegate its powers and duties under this Act or another enactment to the chair, a vice chair, a member of the commission or the executive director.

[S. 6(1) re-en. 1995, c. 45, s. 6(a) (nyif).]

(2) The commission shall not delegate a power or duty referred to in section 96(1), 121, 126, 127, 129, 132 to 136, 140, 144.1, 144.2 or 147 to the superintendent.

[S. 6(2) am. 1989, c. 78, s. 4(a).]

(2) The commission shall not delegate a power or duty referred to in section 96(1), 121, 126, 127, 129, 132 to 136, 140, 144.1, 144.2 or 147 to the executive director.

[S. 6(2) am. 1995, c. 45, s. 7 (nyif).]

(2.1) The commission must not delegate the power to make rules under section 159.1.

[S. 6(2.1) en. 1995, c. 45, s. 6(b) (nyif).]

(3) A member of the commission shall not sit on any hearing required to be held by the commission with respect to any matter in relation to which he exercised a power or performed a duty referred to in section 126, 127, 129 or 132 to 136 and which was delegated to him under subsection (1).

[S. 6(3) am. 1989, c. 78, s. 4(b).]

For a discussion of the scope of the delegation and the process for appeals from a single commissioner see *Greenwell* under s. 147 and *Simonyi-Gindele* under s. 135.

Superintendent

7. (1) The commission must appoint a person to be the Superintendent of Brokers.

[S. 7(1) re-en. 1995, c. 15, s. 4.]

(2) The superintendent is the chief administrative officer of the commission and shall obey the policy directives given by the commission.

(3) The superintendent may exercise the powers and shall perform the duties vested in or imposed on

(a) him under this Act or the regulations, and

(b) the commission under this Act or the regulations that are delegated to him by the commission.

(4) The superintendent may by conditional or unconditional written authority, delegate the superintendent's powers and duties under this Act, the regulations or another enactment to any person employed under subsection (1).

[S. 7(4) en. 1987, c. 42, s. 95; re-en. 1992, c. 52, s. 2.]

(5) Notwithstanding subsection (4), the superintendent shall not delegate

(a) powers or duties of the commission that are delegated to him by the commission, or

(b) a power or duty referred to in section 64, 73, 144, 148(3) or 158 of this Act.

[S. 7(5) en. 1987, c. 42, s. 95; am. 1989, c. 78, s. 5(b); 1990, c. 25, s. 3.]

(6) A person to whom the superintendent, by a written authority under subsection (4), delegates his powers and duties may exercise the powers and shall perform the duties in accordance with the written authority.

[S. 7(6) en. 1987, c. 42, s. 95.]

Executive director

7. (1) The commission must appoint a person to be the executive director.

(2) The executive director is the chief administrative officer of the commission and must obey the policy directives given by the commission.

(3) The executive director may exercise the powers and must perform the duties vested in or imposed on

(a) the executive director under this Act, and

(b) the commission under this Act that are delegated to the executive director by the commission.

(4) The executive director, by conditional or unconditional written authority, may delegate the executive director's powers and duties under this Act or another enactment to any person employed under section 7.1.

(5) Despite subsection (4), the executive director must not delegate

(a) powers or duties of the commission that are delegated to the executive director by the commission, or

(b) a power or duty referred to in section 64, 73, 144, 148(3) or 158.

(6) A person to whom the executive director, by written authority under subsection (4), delegates powers and duties may exercise the powers and must perform the duties in accordance with the written authority.

(7) Persons employed in the office of the executive director as directors are deputies of the executive director.

[S. 7 re-en. 1995, c. 45, s. 8 (nyif).]

Kripps v. Touche Ross & Co. (1990), 52 B.C.L.R. (2d) 291, affirmed 69 B.C.L.R. (2d) 62, 94 D.L.R. (4th) 284, 15 B.C.A.C. 184, 27 W.A.C. 184, leave to appeal to S.C.C. refused [1993] 2 S.C.R. viii, 78 B.C.L.R. (2d) xxxiv, 101 D.L.R. (4th) vii, 156 N.R. 239, 32 B.C.A.C. 239, 53 W.A.C. 239.

The plaintiffs in this action sued the Superintendent of Brokers for negligence in failing to scrutinize a prospectus for plain disclosure of all material facts. The Superintendent applied under R. 19 to strike out the plaintiffs' claims for disclosing no reasonable cause of action. Madam Justice Boyd held that the former Securities Act (R.S.B.C. 1979, c. 380) does not state that the superintendent is under a duty to determine whether every prospectus filed should be investigated, with a view to uncovering any infraction of the Securities Act. There is no clear legislative intent in the former Securities Act to impose any duty upon the Superintendent to protect individual investors. Rather, the legislation reflects an attempt to bring order and regulation to the securities industry which will inure to the protection of investors. This case provides guidance as to the role of the Superintendent under the present Securities Act.

On appeal, Taylor J.A. upheld the decision of Madam Justice Boyd.

Officers and employees

7.1 The commission may appoint officers and employees of the commission necessary to enable the commission and the superintendent to perform their duties and exercise their powers under this Act and may define the duties and, subject to the prior approval of the Treasury Board, determine the remuneration and classification of the officers and employees.

[S. 7.1 en. 1995, c. 15, s. 5.]

7.1 The commission may appoint officers and employees of the commission necessary to enable the commission and the executive director to perform their duties and exercise their powers under this Act and may define the duties and, subject to the prior approval of the Treasury Board, determine the remuneration and classification of the officers and employees.

[S. 7.1 am. 1995, c. 45, s. 7 (nyif).]

Benefits

7.2 (1) The *Public Service Benefit Plan Act* applies to the commission and to the officers and employees.

(2) The Lieutenant Governor in Council may order that the *Pension (Public Service) Act* applies to a member of the commission who is named in the order, and in that case subsection (3) applies in respect of a member so named.

(3) The *Pension (Public Service) Act* applies to the officers and employees of the commission and

(a) the commission is deemed to be an employer and the officers and employees of the commission are deemed to be employees within the meaning of that Act,

(b) the commission must make deductions from the salaries of the officers and employees as required under that Act and pay the money to the superannuation commissioner under that Act, and

(c) the commission must, in addition, pay to the superannuation commissioner, employer's contributions in the amounts equivalent to the amounts required under that Act.

[S. 7.2 en. 1995, c. 15, s. 5.]

Confidentiality

8. (1) Every person acting under the authority of this Act shall keep confidential all facts, information and records obtained or furnished under this Act or the regulations, or under a former enactment, except so far as his public duty requires or this Act permits him to make disclosure of them or to report or take official action on them.

> See the *Stallwood* decision at s. 126 of the Act.

(2) Subject to subsections (3) and (4), the facts, information and records referred to in subsection (1) shall be released to the Ombudsman at his request.

(3) All facts, information and records which are obtained

(a) from a law enforcement agency, or

(b) pursuant to an investigation under this Act,

shall only be released to the Ombudsman if he first produces the written consent of

(c) the law enforcement agency, or

(d) the person from whom the facts, information or records were obtained pursuant to the investigation,

to release the facts, information or records.

(4) All facts, information and records which could lead to the identification of an informant under this Act shall only be released to the Ombudsman if the person to whom the Ombudsman makes his request first obtains the written consent of the informant to release the facts, information or records.

B.C. Securities Commission Securities Policy Advisory Committee

8.1 (1) The minister may establish a B.C. Securities Commission Securities Policy Advisory Committee consisting of members appointed by the minister.

(2) The purpose of the advisory committee is to provide to the commission advice on administrative, regulatory and legislative matters relating to trading in securities and to the securities industry.

[S. 8.1 en. 1995, c. 45, s. 9 (nyif).]

Appointment of experts

9. (1) The commission may appoint an expert to assist it in any way it considers expedient.

(2) The commission may submit any record or thing for examination to an expert appointed under subsection (1), and the commission has the same power as is vested in an investigator under section 128(1) to summon and enforce the attendance of witnesses before the expert and to compel them to give evidence under oath or in any other manner, and to produce records and things or classes of records and things.

[S. 9(2) am. 1992, c. 52, s. 3.]

(3) Where an expert has made an examination or conducted an investigation under this section, the commission may require the person whose records or things were examined or investigated to pay prescribed fees or charges for the costs of the examination or investigation.

PART 2.1

[Part 2.1 (s. 9.1) repealed 1995, c. 15, s. 6.]

PART 2.2

[Part 2.2 en. 1995, c. 15, s. 7.]

FINANCIAL ADMINISTRATION

Definition

9.11 In this Part "Minister of Finance" has the same meaning as in the *Financial Administration Act*.

Revenue and expenditure

9.2 (1) Revenue received under this Act and the *Commodity Contract Act*, including but not limited to revenue from administrative penalties under section 144.1 of this Act and any cost recoveries under either Act, but not including revenue from fines referred to in section 138 of this Act or section 47 of the *Commodity Contract Act*, must be paid to the commission.

> **9.2** (1) Revenue received under this Act, including, but not limited to, revenue from administrative penalties under section 144.1 and any cost recoveries under this Act, but not including revenue from fines referred to in section 138, or from any payments to the minister under an order referred to in section 140(1)(b), must be paid to the commission,

[S. 9.2(1) re-en. 1995, c. 45, s. 10(a) (nyif).]

(2) Subject to subsection (3), money received by the commission may be expended for any costs involved in the administration and enforcement of this Act and of the *Commodity Contract Act* and for any costs involved in operating the commission.

> (2) Subject to subsection (3), money received by the commission may be expended for any costs involved in the administration and enforcement of this Act and for any costs involved in operating the commission.

[S. 9.2(2) am. 1995, c. 45, s. 10(b) (nyif).]

(3) Money received by the commission as revenue from administrative penalties under section 144.1 of this Act may be expended only for the purpose of promoting knowledge of participants in the securities market of the legal, regulatory and ethical standards that govern the operation of the securities market in British Columbia.

(4) This section applies notwithstanding section 9 of the *Financial Administration Act*.

Appropriation

9.3 At the request of the commission, but subject to approval of the Treasury Board, the Minister of Finance may pay to the commission out of the consolidated revenue fund amounts not exceeding $5.5 million over the period ending March 31, 1998.

Administrative services

9.4 The Lieutenant Governor in Council may designate administrative services that the commission must obtain from the government or from any government corporation, agency, branch, department or other government organization or entity that is specified in the order making the designation.

Fiscal agent

9.5 The Minister of Finance is the fiscal agent of the commission.

Investment

9.6 (1) The commission must place with the Minister of Finance, for investment, any money the commission receives but does not immediately require for carrying out the purposes of this Act.

(2) Money placed with the Minister of Finance under this section is to be treated for all purposes as money placed with the Minister of Finance pursuant to section 36(3) of the *Financial Administration Act.*

Borrowing powers

9.7 Subject to the approval of the Lieutenant Governor in Council and the Minister of Finance, the commission, for the purpose of carrying out any power, right, function or duty conferred or imposed on the commission under this or any other Act, may borrow the sums of money the commission considers necessary or advisable.

Accounting

9.8 (1) The commission must establish and maintain accounting policies and systems satisfactory to the Minister of Finance.

(2) The commission, whenever required by the Minister of Finance, must render detailed accounts of the commission's revenues and expenditures for the period or to the day the Minister of Finance designates.

(3) All books or records of account and other financial records must at all times be open for inspection by the Minister of Finance or a person designated by the Minister of Finance.

(4) The chair of the Treasury Board may direct the Comptroller General to examine and report to Treasury Board on any or all of the financial and accounting operations of the commission.

(5) At least once in every fiscal year, the accounts of the commission must be audited and reported on by an auditor appointed by the Lieutenant Governor in Council, and the costs of the audit must be paid by the commission.

(6) The fiscal year for the commission is a period of 12 months beginning on April 1 in each year and ending on March 31 in the next year.

Business plan

9.9 At least once in every fiscal year of the commission and as directed by the Treasury Board, the commission must submit to the Treasury Board, for review and approval, a business plan that includes

(a) a proposed budget for the subsequent 3 fiscal years,

(b) management objectives for the next 3 years, and

(c) other information that the Treasury Board may specify.

Annual report

9.91 (1) The commission must prepare and submit to the minister, within 90 days after the end of each fiscal year of the commission, a report for that fiscal year.

(2) The report must be laid before the Legislative Assembly by the minister as soon as practicable.

(3) The report must contain

(a) a summary of the commission's operations for the fiscal year of the report,

(b) a financial statement in the form required by the Minister of Finance showing the revenues, expenditures, assets and liabilities of the commission for the fiscal year of of the report, and

(c) any other information that the minister may specify.

(4) The financial statement referred to in subsection (3)(b) must be prepared in accordance with generally accepted accounting principles.

PART 3

SELF REGULATORY BODIES AND
STOCK EXCHANGES

SELF REGULATORY BODIES AND EXCHANGES

[Part 3 heading re-en. 1990, c. 25, s. 4 (nyif).]

Interpretation

10. A reference in sections 13 to 18 to a self regulatory body or a stock exchange is a reference to a self regulatory body or stock exchange, as the case may be, which has been recognized by the commission under section 11.

10. A reference in sections 13 to 18 to a self regulatory body or an exchange is a reference to a self regulatory body or an exchange, as the case may be, which has been recognized by the commission under section 11.

[S. 10 am. 1990, c. 25, s. 5 (nyif).]

Recognition of self regulatory bodies and stock exchanges

11. (1) On the application of an association representing registrants, the commission may recognize the applicant as a self regulatory body.

> The Investment Dealers' Association has been recognized by way of a private letter issued by the Commission.

(2) On application, the commission may recognize a person as a stock exchange in the Province.

(2) On application, the commission may recognize a person as an exchange in the Province.

[S. 11(2) am. 1990, c. 25, s. 6 (nyif).]

> The Vancouver Stock Exchange has been recognized; see Local Policy Statement 3-44 "Recognition of Stock Exchanges and Jurisdictions".

Stock exchange required to be recognized

12. No person shall carry on business as a stock exchange in the province unless he is recognized by the commission under section 11(2).

Exchange required to be recognized

12. No person shall carry on business as an exchange in the Province unless recognized by the commission under section 11(2).

[S. 12 re-en. 1990, c. 25, s. 7 (nyif).]

Duty of self regulatory body and stock exchange

13. (1) Subject to this Act, the regulations and any decision made by the commission, every self regulatory body and every stock exchange shall regulate the standards of practice and business conduct of its members.

13. (1) Subject to this Act, the regulations and any decision made by the commission, every self regulatory body and every exchange shall regulate the standards of practice and business conduct of its members.

[S. 13(1) am. 1990, c. 25, s. 8(a) (nyif).]

Re Edward Joseph Kirby, [1993] 14 B.C.S.C. Weekly Summary 6 (B.C. Sec. Comm.).

An application was made for a review of a decision of the Vancouver Stock Exchange on the basis that the hearing committee held a reasonable apprehension of bias. The Commission held that there was in this case, no reasonable apprehension of bias with the hearing committee of the Exchange, notwithstanding some comments made by the executive committee of the Exchange in a letter to Kirby. The Commission confirmed that the Exchange must conduct its hearings in such a way that there is no apprehension of bias.

(2) A self regulatory body or stock exchange shall provide to the commission or to the superintendent, at the request of the commission or the superintendent, any information or record in its possession relating to

(a) a registrant or a client of a registrant,

(b) an issuer, or

(c) trading in securities.

(2) A self regulatory body or exchange shall provide to the commission or to the superintendent, at the request of the commission or the superintendent, any information or record in its possession relating to

(a) a registrant or a client of a registrant,

(b) an issuer, or

(c) trading in securities or exchange contracts.

[S. 13 am. 1989, c. 78, s. 6; s. 13(2) am. 1990, c. 25, s. 8 (nyif).]

Duty of self regulatory body and exchange

13. (1) Subject to this Act, the regulations and any decision made by the commission, every self regulatory body and every exchange must regulate the standards of practice and business conduct of its members.

(2) A self regulatory body or exchange must provide to the commission or to the executive director, at the request of the commission or the executive director,

(a) a copy, or a partial copy as specified in the request, of the charter, as defined in section 1 of the *Financial Institutions Act*, of the self regulatory body or exchange, or

(b) any information or record in the possession of the self regulatory body or exchange relating to

    (i) a registrant or former registrant,

    (ii) a client or former client of a registrant or of a former registrant,

    (iii) an issuer,

    (iv) trading in securities or exchange contracts,

    (v) any of the self regulatory body's or exchange's

        (A) bylaws, rules, other regulatory instruments or policies, or

        (B) directions, decisions, orders or rulings that are made under any of its bylaws, rules, other regulatory instruments or policies,

    (vi) the charter, as defined in section 1 of the *Financial Institutions Act*, of the self regulatory body or exchange, or

    (vii) this Act or the regulations.

[S. 13 re-en. 1995, c. 45, s. 11 (nyif).]

Regulation of self regulatory bodies and stock exchanges

14. (1) The commission may, where it considers it to be in the public interest, make any decision respecting

   (a) a bylaw, rule or other regulatory instrument or policy, or a direction, decision, order or ruling made under a bylaw, rule or other regulatory instrument or policy, of a self regulatory body or stock exchange,

   (b) the procedures or practices of a self regulatory body or stock exchange,

[Para. (b) am. 1989, c. 78, s. 7.]

   (c) the manner in which a stock exchange carries on business,

   (d) the trading of securities on or through the facilities of a stock exchange,

   (e) a security listed and posted for trading on a stock exchange, and

   (f) issuers, whose securities are listed and posted for trading on a stock exchange, to ensure that they comply with this Act and the regulations.

14. (1) The commission may, where it considers it to be in the public interest, make any decision respecting

   (a) a bylaw, rule or other regulatory instrument or policy, or a direction, decision, order or ruling made under a bylaw, rule or other regulatory instrument or policy, of a self regulatory body or exchange,

   (b) the procedures or practices of a self regulatory body or exchange,

   (c) the manner in which an exchange carries on business,

   (d) the trading of securities or exchange contracts on or through the facilities of an exchange,

   (d.1) an exchange contract trading on an exchange,

   (e) a security listed and posted for trading on an exchange, and

   (f) issuers, whose securities are listed and posted for trading on an exchange, to ensure that they comply with this Act and the regulations.

[S. 14(1) am. 1990, c. 25, s. 9 (nyif).]

(2) A person affected by a decision made by the commission under subsection (1) shall act in accordance with it.

Hearing and review

15. (1) A person directly affected by a direction, decision, order or ruling made under a bylaw, rule or other regulatory instrument or policy of a self regulatory body or of a stock exchange may apply to the commission for a hearing and review of the matter under Part 17 of this Act, and section 147(3) to (5) applies.

15. (1) A person directly affected by a direction, decision, order or ruling made under a bylaw, rule or other regulatory instrument or policy of a self regulatory body or of an exchange may apply to the commission for a hearing and review of the matter under Part 17 of this Act, and section 147(3) to (5) applies.

[S. 15(1) am. 1990, c. 25, s. 10(a) (nyif).]

Kadlec and Reynolds v. Optima Energy Ltd., British Columbia Securities Commission, and Vancouver Stock Exchange (September 27, 1988), Vancouver Doc. CA009589, Taggart J.A., [1988] B.C.W.L.D. 3430 (C.A.) (unreported).

The combined effect of ss. 15 and 147(3) of the Securities Act is to give 30 days to appeal from an order of the Vancouver Stock Exchange.

Re George Dengin, [1990] 36 B.C.S.C. Weekly Summary (B.C. Sec. Comm.).

It is clear that the Commission has no jurisdiction to extend the time for filing a notice requesting a hearing and review under s. 147(3) of the Act.

GHZ Resource Corp. v. Vancouver Stock Exchange (May 12, 1992), Vancouver Doc. C923165, Mackoff J., [1992] 46 B.C.S.C. Weekly Summary 42 (S.C.) (not yet reported).

Mackoff J. dismissed the application of the plaintiff who sought to appeal a decision of the Vancouver Stock Exchange directly to the Supreme Court instead of the B.C. Securities Commission on the ground that the Supreme Court would be usurping the function of the B.C. Securities Commission.

Re GHZ Resource Corp. and Vancouver Stock Exchange, [1992] 27 B.C.S.C. Weekly Summary 18 (B.C. Sec. Comm.).

The Securities Commission held that the shareholders of GHZ did not have standing in a hearing to review a decision of the Vancouver Stock Exchange. While they may be incidentally affected by the decision, they are not directly affected by the decision for the purposes of s. 15 of the Securities Act. The Commission permitted the shareholders to present relevant evidence under s. 154.1(b) of the Act.

GHZ Resource Corp. and GHZ Resource Corp. Shareholders' Group v. Vancouver Stock Exchange and British Columbia (Securities Commission) (1993), 1 C.C.L.S. 229, affirmed 1 C.C.L.S. 246 (B.C.C.A.).

The decision of the Securities Commission was appealed on a number of grounds. The court did not consider the shareholders' claim for standing as "the shareholders, whatever their legal status, were given a full opportunity to be heard." Leave to appeal was not granted.

Re Merlin Resources Inc., [1994] 30 B.C.S.C. Weekly Summary 6 (B.C. Sec. Comm.).

The Securities Commission will only interfere with a decision of the Vancouver Stock Exchange if it finds that the Exchange has proceeded on an incorrect principle, erred in law or overlooked material evidence, or if new and compelling evidence is presented to the Commission that was not presented to the Exchange.

Re Andrew Sim Katz and Barry Reagh, [1995] 19 B.C.S.C. Weekly Summary 5 (B.C. Sec. Comm.).

An application was made for a review of a decision made by a hearing panel established under a by-law of the Vancouver Stock Exchange. The Commission concluded that s. 15 of the Act is sufficiently broad to encompass the review of the appointment of the Exchange hearing panel. However, the Commission concluded that the process by which the Exchange appoints hearing panels may be reasonably perceived to be independent.

(2) An applicant under subsection (1) shall send a copy of the notice requesting a hearing and review to the superintendent and the affected self regulatory body or stock exchange.

[S. 15(2) am. 1989, c. 78, s. 8.]

(2) An applicant under subsection (1) shall send a copy of the notice requesting a hearing and review to the superintendent and the affected self regulatory body or exchange.

[S. 15(2) am. 1990, c. 25, s. 10(b) (nyif).]

Hearing and review

15. (1) The executive director or a person directly affected by a direction, decision, order or ruling made under a bylaw, rule or other regulatory instrument or policy of a self regulatory body or of an exchange may apply by notice to the commission for a hearing and review of the matter under Part 17, and section 147(3) to (5) applies.

(2) An applicant under subsection (1), other than the executive director, must send a copy of the notice requesting a hearing and review to the executive director and the affected self regulatory body or exchange.

(3) If the executive director applies under subsection (1), the executive director must send a copy of the notice requesting a hearing and review to

(a) the affected self regulatory body or exchange, and

(b) the persons directly affected by the direction, decision, order or ruling referred to in subsection (1).

[S. 15 re-en. 1995, c. 45, s. 11 (nyif).]

See Local Policy Statement 3-12 "Rules for Proceedings".

Compliance review of self regulatory body or exchange

15.1 (1) The executive director may appoint in writing a person to review the business and conduct of a self regulatory body or exchange for the purpose of determining whether the self regulatory body or exchange is

(a) complying, or has complied, with

(i) this Act and the regulations,

(ii) any decision made under this Act or the regulations, or

(iii) the charter, as defined in section 1 of the *Financial Institutions Act*, of the self regulatory body or exchange, or

(b) enforcing or administering its bylaws, rules, other regulatory instruments or policies.

(2) On production of the appointment, a person conducting a review under this section may

(a) enter the business premises of a self regulatory body or exchange, during business hours,

(b) examine the records referred to in section 13(2)(b),

(c) examine property, assets or things of the self regulatory body or exchange,

(d) make copies of the records referred to in section 13(2)(b), and

(e) make inquiries of the self regulatory body or exchange, or persons employed by the self regulatory body or exchange, concerning the operations and procedures of the self regulatory body or exchange.

(3) In exercising the power to make copies under subsection (2)(d), the person conducting the review under this section may

(a) carry out the copying at the business premises of the self regulatory body or exchange, or

(b) on giving an appropriate receipt, remove records for the purpose of copying them at other premises specified in the receipt.

(4) Records removed under subsection (3)(b) for copying must be promptly returned to the person from which they were received.

(5) The executive director may require a self regulatory body or exchange that is the subject of a review under this section to pay prescribed fees or prescribed charges for the costs of the review.

(6) A person must not

(a) withhold, destroy, conceal or refuse to give any information, or

(b) withhold, destroy, conceal or refuse to produce any record or thing

reasonably required for a review under this section.

[S. 15.1 en. 1995, c. 45, s. 12 (nyif).]

Records of transactions on stock exchanges

16. (1) A stock exchange shall keep a record showing the time and date when each transaction on the exchange was recorded.

16. (1) An exchange shall keep a record showing the time and date when each transaction on the exchange was recorded.

[S. 16(1) am. 1990, c. 25, s. 11(a) (nyif).]

(2) Where a client of a member of a stock exchange produces to the stock exchange a written confirmation of a transaction between himself and the member, the stock exchange shall supply to the client

(a) particulars of the time at which the transaction was recorded, and

(b) verification or otherwise of the matters set out in the confirmation.

[S. 16(2) am. 1989, c. 78, s. 9.]

(2) Where a client of a member of an exchange produces to the exchange a written confirmation of a transaction between the client and the member, the exchange shall supply to the client

(a) particulars of the time at which the transaction was recorded, and

(b) verification or otherwise of the matters set out in the confirmation.

[S. 16(2) re-en. 1990, c. 25, s. 11(b) (nyif).]

Stock exchange and self regulatory body auditors

17. (1) A stock exchange and, where the commission determines it is appropriate, a self regulatory body shall appoint an auditor.

17. (1) An exchange and, where the commission determines it is appropriate, a self regulatory body shall appoint an auditor.

[S. 17(1) am. 1990, c. 25, s. 12 (nyif).]

The Commission has determined that it is appropriate that the Investment Dealers' Association appoint an auditor.

(2) An auditor appointed under subsection (1) shall

(a) be practising as an auditor in Canada, and

(b) first be approved by the commission.

The Commission has approved, by way of a private letter, Coopers & Lybrand as the auditor of the Vancouver Stock Exchange and Clarkson Gordon, now Ernst & Young, as the auditor of the Investment Dealers' Association.

Audits of members of stock exchanges and self regulatory bodies

18. (1) A stock exchange and, where the commission determines it is appropriate, a self regulatory body shall appoint a panel of auditors from auditors who are practising as auditors in Canada.

18. (1) An exchange and, where the commission determines it is appropriate, a self regulatory body shall appoint a panel of auditors from auditors who are practising as auditors in Canada.

[S. 18(1) am. 1990, c. 25, s. 13(a) (nyif).]

> The Commission has determined that it is appropriate that the Investment Dealers' Association shall appoint a panel of auditors from auditors who are practising as auditors in Canada.

(2) Each member of a stock exchange and of a self regulatory body, as the case may be, shall appoint an auditor from a panel appointed under subsection (1).

(2) Each member of an exchange and of a self regulatory body, as the case may be, shall appoint an auditor from a panel appointed under subsection (1).

[S. 18(2) am. 1990, c. 25, s. 13(b) (nyif).]

(3) An auditor appointed under subsection (2) shall

(a) examine the financial affairs of the member

    (i) as required by the bylaws, rules or other regulatory instruments of policies of the self regulatory body or stock exchange, and

    (ii) in a manner satisfactory to the commission, and

(b) report on each examination to the auditor of the stock exchange or of the self regulatory body, as the case may be, appointed under section 17.

(3) An auditor appointed under subsection (2) shall

(a) examine the financial affairs of the member

    (i) as required by the bylaws, rules or other regulatory instruments of policies of the self regulatory body or exchange, and

    (ii) in a manner satisfactory to the commission, and

(b) report on each examination to the auditor of the exchange or of the self regulatory body, as the case may be, appointed under section 17.

[S. 18(3) am. 1990, c. 25, s. 13(c) (nyif).]

(b) report on each examination to the self regulatory body or exchange, as the case may be.

[Para. (b) re-en. 1995, c. 45, s. 13(a) (nyif).]

(4) A bylaw, rule or regulation referred to in subsection (3) respecting the practice and procedure of examinations does not come into force until it has been approved by the commission.

(4) A bylaw, rule or regulatory instrument referred to in subsection (3) respecting the practice and procedure of examinations does not come into force until it has been approved by the commission.

[S. 18(4) am. 1995, c. 45, s. 13(b) (nyif).]

The Commission has approved, by way of a private letter, Rule G.3.00 of the Vancouver Stock Exchange as the rule respecting the practice and procedure of examinations to be performed by the auditor of a member of the Vancouver Stock Exchange. The Commission has also approved, by way of a private letter, by-laws No. 16 and 17 and Regulation No. 300 of the Investment Dealers' Association as the by-laws and regulations respecting the practice and procedure of examinations to be performed by the auditor of a member of the Investment Dealers' Association under section 18(3) of the Act.

Filing of financial statements

19. A registrant, other than a salesman, whose financial affairs are not subject to examination under section 18 shall

(a) keep all records necessary for the proper recording of his business transactions and financial affairs,

(b) file annually, and at any other time that the commission may require, a financial statement as to his financial position that is

(i) in a form satisfactory to the commission,

(ii) certified by him or his officer or partner, and

(iii) reported on by his auditor, and

(c) file other information in a form, and at the times, required by the commission.

[S. 19 repealed 1989, c. 78, s. 10 (nyif).]

Exemption order by commission

19.1 On application by an interested person or on the commission's own motion, the commission, if the commission considers that to do so would not be prejudicial to the public interest, may order that an exchange or self regulatory body or class of exchanges or regulatory bodies is exempt from one or more of the requirements of this Part or of the regulations relating to this Part.

[S. 19.1 en. 1995, c. 45, s. 14 (nyif).]

PART 4

REGISTRATION

Requirement of registration

20. (1) No person shall

(a) trade in a security unless he is registered as

(i) a dealer, or

(ii) a salesman, partner, director or officer of a registered dealer and is acting on behalf of that dealer,

(a) trade in a security or exchange contract unless he is registered as

(i) a dealer, or

(ii) a salesman, partner, director or officer of a registered dealer and is acting on behalf of that dealer,

[Para. (a) am. 1990, c. 25, s. 14 (nyif).]

(b) act as an underwriter unless he is registered as an underwriter, or

(c) act as an adviser unless he is registered as

(i) an adviser, or

(ii) a partner, director or officer of a registered adviser and is acting on behalf of that adviser

in accordance with the regulations.

Re Aatra Resources Ltd., Victor J. Meunier, Paul A. Quinn, Ralph A.A. Simpson, Joel Machtinger, Henry P.M. Huber, Alex Pancer, David J. Foster and Durham Securities Corp. Ltd. (1993), 3 C.C.L.S. 92 (B.C. Sec. Comm.).

A registered dealer holds a special position in the securities market and regulatory system as, subject to certain exemptions, trading in securities can only be done by or through a registered dealer. A registered salesman of a dealer is required to meet educational requirements and to conduct business in accordance with the regulatory standards. The purpose of the registration requirement in the Act was described by Fauteux J. in the Supreme Court of Canada case *Gregory & Co. v. Quebec (Securities Commission)*, [1961] S.C.R. 584, 28 D.L.R. (2d) 721, as follows at p. 588:

> The paramount object of the Act is to ensure that persons who, in the province, carry on the business of trading in securities or acting as investment counsel, shall be honest and of good repute and, in this way, to protect the public, in the province or elsewhere, from being defrauded as a result of certain activities . . .

An individual who is a registrant, an experienced securities salesman and a partner in a registered dealer, had an obligation to prevent the manipulation scheme in which he participated. This scheme defrauded investors, prejudiced the public interest in a fair and efficient securities market and contributed to bringing the market into disrepute.

Refer to NIN 95/7 "Duties of Registrants in the Supervision of Accounts Operating under Powers of Attorney or Trading Authorities" for guidance as to the responsibilities of a registrant to exercise care and diligence in supervising and accepting orders for accounts operated under powers of attorney or trading authorities.

Re Robert Anthony Donas, [1995] 14 B.C.S.C. Weekly Summary 39 (B.C. Sec. Comm.).

This decision provides guidance as to what constitutes acting as an "adviser" under s. 20(1)(c) of the Act. The key factor in determining whether a person is advising with respect to the purchase or sale of securities is the nature of the information given or offered by that person. An individual who does nothing more than provide factual information about an issuer and its business activities is not advising in securities. An individual who offers an opinion on the investment merits of an issuer or an issuer's securities or who recommends an investment in an issuer or the purchase or sale of an issuer's securities is advising in securities. If a person advising in securities is distributing or offering the advice in a way that reflects a business purpose, then that person must be registered under the Act.

---

(2) An application for registration or for renewal or reinstatement of registration or for an amendment to registration shall be made to the superintendent in the required form and shall be accompanied by the prescribed fee.

[S. 20(2) am. 1989, c. 78, s. 11.]

The required forms are as follows:

Form 3 –   Application for Registration as Dealer, Advisor or Underwriter.

Form 4 –   Uniform Application for Registration/Approval.

Form 4A – (Abbreviated Application for Registration/Approval – Mutual Funds Salesman of Financial Institution).

Form 5 –   Uniform Application for Renewal of Licence or Registration.

Form 7 – Application for Amendment of Registration as Dealer, Advisor or Underwriter.

Form 7A – Application for Transfer/Change of Status.

(3) A person applying for registration under this section shall not trade in a security or act as an underwriter or adviser until he has received written confirmation of his registration from the superintendent.

(3) A person applying for registration under this section shall not trade in a security or exchange contract or act as an underwriter or adviser until he has received written confirmation of his registration from the superintendent.

[S. 20(3) am. 1990, c. 25, s. 14 (nyif).]

Requirement of registration

20. (1) A person must not

(a) trade in a security or exchange contract unless the person is registered in accordance with the regulations as

    (i) a dealer, or

    (ii) a salesperson, partner, director or officer of a registered dealer and is acting on behalf of that dealer,

(b) act as an underwriter unless the person is registered in accordance with the regulations as an underwriter, or

(c) act as an adviser unless the person is registered in accordance with the regulations as

    (i) an adviser, or

    (ii) an advising employee, partner, director or officer of a registered adviser and is acting on behalf of that adviser.

(2) An application for registration or for renewal or reinstatement of registration or for an amendment to registration must be made to the executive director in the required form and must be accompanied by the prescribed fee.

(3) A person applying for registration under this section must not

(a) trade in a security or exchange contract,

(b) act as an underwriter, or

(c) act as an adviser

until the person has received written confirmation of the registration from the executive director.

[S. 20 re-en. 1995, c. 45, s. 15 (nyif).]

See Canadian Securities Administrators Notice 93/2 "Bought Deals", Canadian Securities Administrators Notice 93/3 "Pre-Marketing Activities in the Context of Bought Deals", and Canadian Securities Administrators Notice 93/4 "Bought Deals" for information on bought deal financing.

Granting registration

21. (1) Subject to subsection (2), where an applicant

(a) is considered by the superintendent to be suitable for registration in the capacity applied for, and

(b) pays the prescribed fee,

the superintendent shall grant the applicant registration or renewal or reinstatement of registration or an amendment to registration, as the case may be.

(2) Where an applicant or an officer or director of an applicant is not a resident of the Province on the date of application, the superintendent may refuse to register the applicant unless, at the time of application, the applicant or his officer or director

(a) is registered in a capacity corresponding to that of a dealer, underwriter, adviser, salesman, partner or officer under the law of the jurisdiction respecting trading in securities in which he last resided, and

(b) has been so registered for at least one year immediately before the date of application.

(2) Where an applicant or partner, officer or director of an applicant is not a resident of the Province on the date of application, the superintendent may refuse to register the applicant unless, at the time of application, the applicant or the applicant's partner, officer or director

(a) is registered in a capacity corresponding to that of a dealer, underwriter, adviser, salesman, partner, officer or director under the law of the jurisdiction respecting trading in securities or exchange contracts, as the case may be, in which the applicant last resided, and

(b) has been so registered for at least one year immediately before the date of application.

[S. 21(2) re-en. 1990, c. 25, s. 15 (nyif).]

(3) The superintendent shall not refuse to grant, renew, reinstate or amend a registration without giving the applicant an opportunity to be heard.

Granting registration

21. (1) Subject to subsection (2), if an applicant

(a) is considered by the executive director to be suitable for registration in the capacity applied for, and

(b) pays the prescribed fee,

the executive director must grant the applicant registration or renewal or reinstatement of registration or an amendment to registration, as the case may be.

(2) If an applicant or partner, director or officer of an applicant is not a resident of the Province on the date of application, the executive director may refuse to register the applicant unless, at the time of application, the applicant meets the requirements of subsection (1) and, in addition, the applicant or the applicant's partner, director or officer

(a) is registered in a capacity corresponding to that of a dealer, underwriter, adviser, salesperson, advising employee, partner, director or officer under the law of the jurisdiction respecting trading in securities or exchange contracts, as the case may be, in which the applicant last resided, and

(b) has been so registered for at least one year immediately before the date of application.

(3) The executive director must not refuse to grant, renew, reinstate or amend a registration without giving the applicant an opportunity to be heard.

[S. 21 re-en. 1995, c. 45, s. 15 (nyif).]

See the Registration Transfer Regulation, Amended National Policy Statement 17 "Violations of Securities Laws of Other Jurisdictions – Conduct Affecting Fitness for Continued Registration", and National Policy Statement 18 "Conflict of Interest – Registrants Acting as Corporate Directors".

Re First Vancouver Securities Inc., [1989] 103 B.C.S.C. Weekly Summary, leave to appeal refused (B.C. Sec. Comm.).

In making a s. 21 determination that applicants are suitable for registration, the Superintendent reviews information provided by the applicant on its shareholders and directors and must be satisfied that granting registration would not be prejudicial to the public interest. The legislation sets no limits on the use of the Superintendent's power to require, within a specified time, further information or records to be submitted by a registrant. Where the key issue in considering the public interest with respect to the continued registration of a firm was the suitability of the firm's owners, then their identity had to be known, which in turn implied that information concerning their affairs had to be readily available.

Stenner v. British Columbia (Securities Commission) (1993), 23 Admin. L.R. (2d) 247 (B.C. S.C.).

The Commission has no original power over the registration of an applicant under the Securities Act. Only the Superintendent has the original power under s. 21. The Commission's powers are by way of appeal under s. 147. The Commission cannot, and does not purport under Local Policy 3-22 "Requirements for Registration for Trading in Securities" to, delegate powers of registration to the V.S.E. Instead, it authorizes the V.S.E. to carry out that power under the authority of s. 159(2)(a)(i) of the Act. To the extent clause 1.3.1 of Local Policy 3-22 states that the Commission has delegated some of its registration authority to the V.S.E., the policy is wrong. The Commission had no such authority in the first place. To the extent the Local Policy refers to a delegated power, it leaves the impression that there is a residue of that power left in the original holder, in this case the Superintendent. One who delegates may still exercise the delegated power himself.

Conditions imposed on registration

22. (1) The superintendent may restrict a registration or renewal or reinstatement of registration by imposing conditions on it and, without limiting this power, may restrict

(a) the duration of the registration, and

(b) the registration to trades in specified securities or a specified class of securities.

(b) the scope of the registration to trades in specified securities or exchange contracts or to a specified class of securities or class of exchange contracts.

[Para. (b) re-en. 1990, c. 25, s. 16 (nyif).]

(2) The superintendent shall not impose a condition on a registration under subsection (1) without giving the applicant an opportunity to be heard.

(3) A registrant shall comply with a condition imposed on his registration under the regulations or by the superintendent under subsection (1).

Conditions imposed on registration and registrants

22. (1) The executive director may restrict a registration or a renewal or reinstatement of registration and may impose conditions of registration on the registrant, and, without limiting these powers, may

(a) restrict the duration of the registration,

(b) restrict the registration to trades in specified securities or exchange contracts or a specified class of securities or class of exchange contracts, and

(c) direct that any or all of the registration exemptions described in sections 30 to 32 or any of the registration exemptions set out in the regulations do not apply to the registrant.

(2) The executive director acting under subsection (1) must not restrict a registration or impose a condition of registration on a registrant without giving the registrant or intended registrant an opportunity to be heard.

(3) A registrant must comply with a restriction or condition imposed under the regulations or, under subsection (1), by the executive director.

[S. 22 re-en. 1995, c. 45, s. 15 (nyif).]

See Local Policy Statement 3-38 "Registration of Non-residents – Securities Act", Local Policy Statement 3-42 "Registered Representatives Continued Fitness for Registration", National Policy Statement 25 "Registrants: Advertising: Disclosure of Interest", and NIN 92/8 "Ontario Securities Commission Policy No. 4.8, Non-resident Advisers".

Stenner v. British Columbia (Securities Commission) (1993), 23 Admin. L.R. (2d) 247 (B.C. S.C.).

Section 22 of the Act provides that no conditions can be imposed without giving the applicant an opportunity to be heard. While this section only speaks about an applicant for registration, it should be interpreted so as to apply to an existing registrant upon whom it is proposed to impose further conditions. There cannot be a proper hearing unless the applicant is told what conditions are proposed to be imposed on him by the Superintendent, and given adequate time to prepare his case to meet them. What is considered to be proper notice will depend on the nature of the hearing in each particular case.

In this case, the informal hearings between the applicant and the Superintendent did not satisfy the rules of natural justice and did not afford the applicant the sort of hearing required by s. 22(2). The Superintendent was, however, found to have acted in good faith and was without knowledge that the applicant objected to the lack of notice of the hearing. The Superintendent thought the applicant was satisfied with the informal hearing when the conditions on his registration were imposed and the applicant did nothing to disabuse him of that impression.

Subsequent application

23. A person may reapply for registration or for renewal of, reinstatement of or an amendment to registration where

    (a)   he intends to use information not previously submitted, or

    (b)   material circumstances described in his previous application have changed.

Further information

24. The superintendent may require

24. The executive director may require

    (a)   within a specified time, further information or records to be submitted by an applicant,

    (b)   at any time, verification by affidavit or otherwise of any information or records submitted by an applicant, or

    (c)   an examination under oath, to be conducted by a person designated in writing by the superintendent, of

    (c)   an examination under oath, to be conducted by a person designated in writing by the executive director, of

        (i)   the applicant,

        (ii)   a partner, officer, director, governor or trustee of, or any person performing a like function for, the applicant, or

(iii) an employee of the applicant.

[S. 24 am. 1989, c. 78, s. 12; 1995, c. 45, s. 7 (nyif).]

See *Re First Vancouver Securities* under s. 21 of the Act.

Compliance review of registrant

24.1 (1) The executive director may appoint in writing a person to review the business and conduct of a registered dealer, underwriter or adviser, or of a former registrant in any of those categories, for the purpose of determining whether the registrant is complying, or has complied, or former registrant has complied while registered, with

(a) this Act and the regulations,

(b) any decision made under this Act or the regulations, or

(c) the bylaws, rules, other regulatory instruments or policies of the self regulatory body or exchange, if any, of which the registrant is a member.

(2) On production of the appointment, a person conducting a review under this section may

(a) enter the business premises of a registered dealer, underwriter or adviser, or of a former registrant in any of those categories, during business hours,

(b) examine the records of the registrant or of the former registrant that are required to be kept under this Act or the regulations,

(c) make copies of the records referred to in paragraph (b), and

(d) make inquiries of the registrant or the former registrant, or of persons employed by the registrant or former registrant, concerning the operations and procedures of the registrant or of the former registrant.

(3) In exercising the power to make copies under subsection (2)(c), the person conducting the review under this section may

(a) carry out the copying at the business premises of the registrant or former registrant, or

(b) on giving an appropriate receipt, remove records for the purpose of copying them at other premises specified in the receipt.

(4) Records removed under subsection (3)(b) for copying must be promptly returned to the person from which they were received.

(5) The executive director may require a registrant or former registrant that is the subject of a review under this section to pay prescribed fees or prescribed charges for the costs of the review.

(6) A person must not withhold, destroy, conceal or refuse to give any information, or produce any record or thing reasonably required for a review under this section.

[S. 24.1 en. 1995, c. 45, s. 16 (nyif).]

Suspension of salesman registration

25. Where the employment of a salesman with a registered dealer is terminated or suspended, the registration of the salesman is immediately suspended until the superintendent

(a) receives written notice of

(i) the reinstatement of employment of the salesman from the registered dealer, or

(ii) the employment of the salesman from another registered dealer, and

(b) approves the reinstatement of registration of the salesman.

Suspension of salesperson's registration

25. If the employment of a salesperson with a registered dealer is terminated or suspended, the registration of the salesperson is immediately suspended until the executive director

(a) receives written notice of

  (i) the reinstatement of employment of the salesperson from the registered dealer, or

  (ii) the employment of the salesperson from another registered dealer, and

(b) approves the reinstatement of registration of the salesperson.

[S. 25 re-en. 1995, c. 45, s. 17 (nyif).]

26. [Repealed 1990, c. 25, s. 17.]

Surrender of registration

27. The superintendent may accept the surrender of the registration of a person where he is satisfied that

27. The executive director may accept the surrender of the registration of a person where he is satisfied that

[S. 27 am. 1995, c. 45, s. 7 (nyif).]

(a) the financial obligations of the person to his clients have been discharged, and

(b) the surrender of the registration is not prejudicial to the public interest.

> See Uniform Act Policy Statement 2-07 "Surrender of Registration – Other Than Salesman".

Notice of change

28. (1) Subject to the regulations, a registered dealer shall file in the required form a notice of

(a) the opening or closing of a branch office, in the Province, of the registered dealer,

(b) a change in the directors or officers of the registered dealer and, in the case of termination of employment or of office by any means, the reason for termination,

(c) commencement or termination of the employment of a registered salesman and, in the case of termination of employment by any means, the reason for termination, or

(d) a change in

  (i) the address for service, in the Province, of the registered dealer,

  (ii) any business address of the registered dealer,

  (iii) the holders of any of the voting securities issued by the registered dealer,

  (iv) the partners of the registered dealer, or

  (v) the name and address of the person in charge of any branch office, in the Province, of the registered dealer.

> The required form is Form 7 "Application for Amendment of Registration as a Dealer, Adviser or Underwriter".

(2) Subject to the regulations, a registered adviser or a registered underwriter shall file in the required form a notice of a change in

(a)   the directors or officers of the registered adviser or registered underwriter and, in the case of termination of employment or of office by any means, the reason for termination,

(b)   the address for service, in the Province, of the registered adviser or registered underwriter,

(c)   any business address of the registered adviser or registered underwriter,

(d)   the holders of any of the voting securities issued by the registered adviser or registered underwriter, or

(e)   the partners of the registered adviser or registered underwriter.

> The required form is Form 7 "Application for Amendment of Registration as a Dealer, Adviser or Underwriter".

(3) Subject to the regulations, a registered salesman shall file in the required form a notice of a change in

(a)   the address for service, in the Province, of the registered salesman,

(b)   any business address of the registered salesman, or

(c)   the employment of the registered salesman by a registered dealer.

[S. 28(1) to (3) re-en. 1990, c. 25, s. 18(a).]

> The required form is Form 7A "Application for Transfer/Change of Status".

(4) The superintendent may require the person giving notice under this section to apply for an amendment of his registration.

(5) Where the superintendent considers that it is not prejudicial to the public interest, he may exempt a registrant who is a reporting issuer from subsection (1)(d)(iii) or (2)(d).

[S. 28(5) am. 1990, c. 25, s. 18(b).]

Notice of change

28. (1) Subject to the regulations, a registered dealer must immediately file in the required form a notice of

(a)   the opening or closing of a branch office, in the Province, of the dealer,

(b)   a change in the partners, directors or officers of the dealer and, in the case of termination of employment or of office by any means, the reason for termination,

(c)   commencement or termination of the employment of a registered salesperson and, in the case of termination of employment by any means, the reason for termination,

(d)   a change in

(i)   the address for service, in the Province, of the dealer,

(ii)   any business address of the dealer,

(iii)   the holders of any of the voting securities issued by the dealer,

(iv)   the name and address of the person in charge of any branch office, in the Province, of the dealer, or

(v)   the name of the dealer or the name of any partner, director or officer of the dealer, or

(e)   a material change in other information previously filed, including

(i)   a charge or indictment against, or a conviction of, the dealer or a partner, director or officer of the dealer for an offence under the law,

    (ii) a finding, made against the dealer or a partner, director or officer of the dealer in a civil proceeding, of fraud, theft, deceit, misrepresentation or similar conduct,

   (iii) bankruptcy of the dealer or a partner, director or officer of the dealer, or

   (iv) the appointment of a receiver or receiver manager to hold the assets of the dealer or a partner, director or officer of the dealer.

(2) Subject to the regulations, a registered adviser or a registered underwriter must immediately file in the required form a notice of

(a) a change in the partners, directors or officers of the adviser or underwriter and, in the case of termination of employment or of office by any means, the reason for termination,

(b) commencement or termination of the employment of a registered advising employee and, in the case of termination of employment by any means, the reason for termination,

(c) a change in

    (i) the address for service, in the Province, of the adviser or underwriter,

   (ii) any business address of the adviser or underwriter,

   (iii) the holders of any of the voting securities issued by the adviser or underwriter, or

   (iv) the name of the adviser or underwriter or the name of any partner, director or officer of the adviser or underwriter, or

(d) a material change in other information previously filed, including

    (i) a charge or indictment against, or a conviction of, the adviser or underwriter or a partner, director or officer of the adviser or underwriter for an offence under the law,

   (ii) a finding, made against the adviser or underwriter or a partner, director or officer of the adviser or underwriter in a civil proceeding, of fraud, theft, deceit, misrepresentation or similar conduct,

   (iii) bankruptcy of the adviser or underwriter or a partner, director or officer of the adviser or underwriter, or

   (iv) the appointment of a receiver or receiver manager to hold the assets of the adviser or underwriter or a partner, director or officer of the adviser or underwriter.

(3) Subject to the regulations, a registered salesperson or a registered advising employee must immediately file in the required form a notice of

(a) a change in

    (i) the address for service, in the Province, of the salesperson or advising employee,

   (ii) any business address of the salesperson or advising employee,

   (iii) the employment of the salesperson by a registered dealer or of the advising employee by a registered adviser, or

   (iv) the name of the salesperson or advising employee, or

(b) a material change in other information previously filed, including

    (i) a charge or indictment against, or a conviction of, the salesperson or advising employee for an offence under the law,

   (ii) a finding, made against the salesperson or advising employee in a civil proceeding, of fraud, theft, deceit, misrepresentation or similar conduct,

(iii) bankruptcy of the salesperson or advising employee, or

(iv) the appointment of a receiver or receiver manager to hold the assets of the salesperson or advising employee.

(4) The executive director may require the person giving notice under this section to apply for an amendment of the person's registration.

(5) If the executive director considers that it is not prejudicial to the public interest, the executive director may exempt a registrant that is a reporting issuer from subsection (1)(d)(iii) or (2)(c)(iii).

(6) On any change in the name of a registrant, the registrant must

(a) promptly apply for a replacement certificate, and

(b) if the registrant is a dealer, underwriter or adviser, promptly apply for a replacement certificate for each individual registered to act on the registrant's behalf.

[S. 28 re-en. 1995, c. 45, s. 17 (nyif).]

PART 5

EXEMPTION FROM REGISTRATION REQUIREMENTS

Interpretation

29. (1) For the purposes of this Part,

(a) a trust company or an insurer shall be deemed to be acting as principal when it purchases or sells as an agent or trustee for accounts that are fully managed by it, and

(b) a portfolio manager shall be deemed to be acting as principal when he purchases or sells as an agent for accounts that are fully managed by him.

(2) In this Part

(a) "contract" and "policy" have the meanings defined in section 1 of the *Insurance Act*,

(b) "group insurance" has the meaning defined in section 122 of the *Insurance Act*, and

(c) "life insurance" has the meaning defined in section 1 of the *Financial Institutions Act*.

[S. 29(2) re-en. 1989, c. 47, s. 398.]

Advisers

30. (1) For purposes of this section, "accountant" means an individual who is a member in good standing of a corporation having statutory authority to regulate its members in the practice of accountancy.

(2) Subject to subsection (3), the following persons may act as advisers without registration under section 20(1)(c):

(a) an insurer or a savings institution;

(b) the Federal Business Development Bank;

(c) a barrister and solicitor or an accountant;

(d) a person whom the superintendent considers has suitable educational qualifications or relevant experience;

(e) a registered dealer or a partner, officer, director or employee of a registered dealer,

[Para. (e) am. 1990, c. 25, s. 19(a).]

(f) a publisher of, or writer for, a *bona fide* newspaper, news magazine or business or financial publication, that is of general and regular paid circulation, distributed only to subscribers to it for value or to purchasers of it, who

   (i) gives advice as an adviser only through the newspaper, magazine or publication,

   (ii) has no direct or indirect interest in any of the securities in respect of which he gives advice, and

   (ii) has no direct or indirect interest in any of the securities or exchange contracts in respect of which he gives advice, and

[Subpara. (ii) am. 1990, c. 25, s. 19(b) (nyif).]

   (iii) receives no commission or other consideration for giving the advice other than for acting in his capacity as a publisher or writer;

  (g) a person or class of persons designated by the regulations.

  (3) A person is exempted under subsection (2)(a), (b), (c), (e) or (f) so long as the performance of the service as an adviser is solely incidental to his principal business or occupation as stated in those paragraphs.

Advisers

  30. (1) In this section, "accountant" means an individual who is a member in good standing, other than a student member, of a corporation having statutory authority to regulate its members in the practice of accountancy in the Province.

  (2) Subject to subsection (3), the following persons may act as advisers without registration under section 20(1)(c):

  (a) an insurer or a savings institution;

  (b) the Federal Business Development Bank;

  (c) a barrister and solicitor or an accountant;

  (d) a registered dealer, with respect to research reports or similar analysis prepared by an employee of the dealer and distributed by the dealer;

  (e) a registered dealer or a person that is registered under this Act as a partner, director, officer or salesperson of a registered dealer;

  (f) a publisher of, or writer for, a bona fide newspaper, news magazine or business or financial publication, that is of general and regular paid circulation distributed only to subscribers to it for value or to purchasers of it, where the publisher or writer

   (i) gives advice as an adviser only through the newspaper, magazine or publication,

   (ii) has no direct or indirect interest in any of the securities or exchange contracts in respect of which the person gives advice, and

   (iii) receives no commission or other consideration for giving the advice other than for acting in the person's capacity as a publisher or writer;

  (g) a person or class of persons designated by the regulations.

  (3) Despite subsection (2), a person described in that subsection is not exempted from the requirement to register under section 20(1)(c) as an adviser if,

  (a) in the case of a person described in subsection (2)(a), (b), (c), (d) or (f), the person acts as an adviser where

   (i) the advice the person gives is not solely incidental to the person's principal business contemplated by the relevant paragraph in subsection (2), or

   (ii) if the person advertises its business, advising is featured in the advertisements, or

  (b) in the case of a person described in subsection (2)(e), the advice the person gives is not reasonably in fulfillment of the person's duty to ensure the suitability of a proposed purchase or sale for a client.

[S. 30 re-en. 1995, c. 45, s. 17 (nyif).]

Exemption of trades

31. (1) In this section "issuer bid", "offeree issuer", "offeror" and "take over bid" have the meanings defined in section 74.

(2) Subject to the regulations, registration under section 20(1) is not required for the following trades in securities:

[S. 31(2) am. 1990, c. 25, s. 20(a).]

(2) Subject to the regulations, registration under section 20(1)(a) is not required for the following trades in securities:

[S. 31(2) am. 1995, c. 45, s. 18(a) (nyif).]

> The corresponding prospectus exemptions are found in s. 55(2) of the Act. Additional registration exemptions are found in s. 76 of the Regulation.

(1) a trade in a security by

(i) an executor, administrator, guardian or committee of an estate,

(i) an executor, administrator, guardian or substitute decision maker or guardian appointed under the *Adult Guardianship Act* with authority to manage the financial affairs, business or assets of the owner of the security,

[Subpara. (i) am. 1993, c. 35, s. 97 (nyif).]

(ii) an authorized trustee or assignee, interim or official receiver or a custodian under the *Bankruptcy Act* (Canada),

(iii) a receiver under the *Supreme Court Act*,

[Subpara. (iii) am. 1989, c. 40, s. 192.]

(iv) a receiver, receiver manager or a liquidator under the *Company Act*, the *Law and Equity Act*, the *Personal Property Security Act*, the *Business Corporations Act* (Canada), the *Winding-up Act* (Canada) or this Act,

[Subpara. (iv) am. 1990, c. 11, s. 107.]

(v) a vendor conducting a judicial sale, or

(vi) a sheriff conducting a sale under the *Court Order Enforcement Act* in his official capacity;

(2) a trade where the person purchasing as principal, but not as underwriter, is

(i) the Federal Business Development Bank,

(ii) a savings institution,

(iii) an insurer,

(iv) a subsidiary of a person referred to in subparagraphs (i) to (iii) where that person owns beneficially all of the voting securities of the subsidiary, except the voting securities required by law to be owned by directors of that subsidiary,

(v) Her Majesty in right of Canada or a province, or

(vi) a municipal corporation, public board or commission in Canada;

(3) a trade in a security by or on behalf of the owner, for his account, or by or on behalf of the issuer of the security, for the issuer's account, if the trade is

(i) isolated

(ii) not made in the course of continued and successive transactions of a like nature, and

(iii) not made by a person whose usual business is trading in securities;

Although there is a registration exemption for an owner making an isolated sale of his securities, there is no matching exemption from the prospectus requirements. Exemption from the prospectus requirements is limited to an issuer's sale of its own securities.

(4) a trade where the person purchases as principal, is not an individual and is designated as an exempt purchaser in an order that the superintendent may make for the purpose of this paragraph;

[Para. (4) re-en. 1989, c. 78, s. 14(a).]

(4) a trade where the person purchases as principal, is not an individual and is designated as an exempt purchaser in an order that the executive director may make for the purpose of this paragraph;

[Para. (4) am. 1995, c. 45, s. 7 (nyif).]

See Local Policy Statement 3-15 "Exempt Purchaser Status".

(5) a trade where a person purchases as principal, and the trade is in a security which has an aggregate acquisition cost to the purchaser of not less than a prescribed amount;

The prescribed amount is $97,000; see s. 77(1) of the Regulation. An offering memorandum must be utilized if the distribution is advertised; see s. 127 of the Regulation.

(6) a trade by an issuer in a security of its own issue as consideration for part or all of another person's assets, so long as the fair value of the purchased assets is not less than a prescribed amount;

The prescribed amount is $100,000; see s. 77(2) of the Regulation. See also Local Policy Statement 3-07 "Policy Guidelines Respecting Trading Shares, Performance Shares and Other Consideration".

(7) a trade in a security by a person acting solely through a registered dealer;

(8) a trade by an issuer in

(i) a right granted by the issuer to holders of its securities to purchase additional securities of its own issue, or

[Subpara. (i) am. 1990, c. 25, s. 20(b).]

(ii) a security of a reporting issuer held by the issuer and transferred or issued through the exercise of a right to purchase, convert or exchange previously granted by the issuer,

so long as the issuer gives the superintendent written notice stating the date, amount, nature and conditions of the proposed trade, including the approximate net proceeds to be derived by the issuer on the basis of the additional securities being fully taken up and paid for, and the superintendent

so long as the issuer gives the executive director written notice stating the date, amount, nature and conditions of the proposed trade, including the approximate net proceeds to be derived by the issuer on the basis of the additional securities being fully taken up and paid for, and the executive director

[Para. (8) am. 1995, c. 45, s. 7 (nyif).]

(iii) has not informed the issuer in writing within 10 days of the giving of the notice that he objects to the trade, or

(iv) has withdrawn any objection he has to the proposed trade;

The Superintendent routinely informs the issuer in writing within 10 days of the giving of the notice that he objects to the trade. See Local Policy Statement 3-05 "Rights Offerings to Shareholders", Uniform Act Policy 2-05 "Applications under Sections 34(1)14 and 71(1)(h) of the Securities Act, R.S.O. 1980, c. 466 by a Company Wishing to Sell Additional Securities to its Security Holders", BOR 91/5 "Resale of Rights Acquired Under a Rights Offering", and NIN 90/13 "Rights Offerings".

(9) a trade in a security of an issuer that is exchanged by or for the account of the issuer with the issuer's security holders, with one or more other issuers or with the security holders of the other issuers in connection with an amalgamation, merger, reorganization or arrangement where

　　(i) an information circular in the required form, proxy statement or similar disclosure record in respect of the amalgamation, merger, reorganization or arrangement is prepared and delivered to each of the security holders whose approval of the amalgamation, merger, reorganization or arrangement is required under applicable legislation before it can proceed, and

　　(ii) the amalgamation, merger, reorganization or arrangement is approved by the security holders referred to in subparagraph (i) in accordance with the requirements of the applicable legislation;

[Para. *(9)* re-en. 1992, c. 52, s. 4(a).]

(9) a trade in a security of

　　(i) an issuer, in this paragraph called the "first issuer", that is exchanged by or for the account of the first issuer with one or more of

　　　　(A) the first issuer's security holders,

　　　　(B) one or more other issuers, in this paragraph called the "other issuers", and

　　　　(C) the security holders of the other issuers,

　　(ii) the first issuer by a holder of that security to one or more of the first issuer and the other issuers, or

　　(iii) any of the other issuers by the holder of that security to one or more of the first issuer and the other issuers

in connection with an amalgamation, merger, reorganization or arrangement where

　　(iv) an information circular in the required form, proxy statement or similar disclosure record in respect of the amalgamation, merger, reorganization or arrangement is prepared and delivered to each of the security holders whose approval of the amalgamation, merger, reorganization or arrangement is required under applicable legislation before it can proceed, and

　　(v) the amalgamation, merger, reorganization or arrangement is approved by the security holders referred to in subparagraph (iv) in accordance with the requirements of the applicable legislation;

[Para. *(9)* re-en. 1995, c. 45, s. 18(b) (nyif).]

Issuers often desire to rely on this exemption to carry out a reverse takeover as the securities issued under this exemption will not be subject to a hold period or seasoning period if the issuer is an "exchange issuer". However, this exemption may not generally be relied upon to issue securities pursuant to a reverse takeover unless the reverse takeover involves an amalgamation, merger, reorganization or arrangement.

(10) a trade by an issuer in a security of its own issue with

  (i) its employee, senior officer or director or an employee, senior officer or director of an affiliate of the issuer so long as that person is not induced to purchase by expectation of employment or continued employment,

  (ii) a trustee on behalf of a person referred to in subparagraph (i), or

  (iii) an issuer all of the voting securities of which are beneficially owned by one or more of the persons referred to in subparagraph (i);

[Para. *(10)* am. 1989, c. 78, s. 14(a).]

See BOR 90/2 "Trades in shares issued in accordance with the Employee Investment Act".

---

(11) a trade by an issuer in a security under a plan made available by that issuer to the holders of a class of publicly traded securities of the issuer, and which plan

  (i) permits the holder to direct that dividends or interest paid in respect of securities of the issuer's own issue be applied to the purchase from the issuer of

[Subpara. (i) am. 1989, c. 78, s. 14(c).]

  (A) publicly traded securities of the issuer's own issue, or

  (B) other securities of the issuer's own issue not referred to in clause (A) that are redeemable at the option of the holder, and

  (ii) may include an option permitting a holder to purchase by cash payment securities of the issuer referred to in subparagraph (i) so long as the aggregate number of securities issued under the option in any financial year of the issuer does not exceed 2% of the outstanding securities of that class at the commencement of that financial year;

[Para. *(11)* am. 1992, c. 52, s. 4(b) and (c).]

(12) a trade by an issuer in a security,

  (i) of its own issue that is distributed by it to its security holders as a stock dividend or other distribution out of earnings or surplus,

  (ii) that is distributed by it to its security holders under a dissolution or winding up of the issuer, or

  (iii) of its own issue transferred or issued through the exercise of a right

  (A) of the holder to purchase, convert or exchange or otherwise acquire, or

  (B) of the issuer to require the holder to purchase, convert or exchange,

  in accordance with the terms and conditions of a previously issued security of the issuer,

provided that no commission or other remuneration is paid or given to others in respect of the trade except for administrative or professional services or for services performed by a registered dealer;

[Para. *(12)* am. 1989, c. 78, s. 14(d)-(f).]

(13) a trade that is the transfer of beneficial ownership of a security to a transferee, pledgee, mortgagee or other encumbrancer under a realization on collateral given for a debt;

[Para. *(13)* re-en. 1988, c. 58, s. 3(a).]

A purchase of a security or a transfer, pledge, mortgage or other encumbrance of a security is specifically exempted from the definition of a "trade".

(14) a trade by an issuer in a security of a reporting issuer held by the issuer that is distributed by it to its security holders as a dividend in specie so long as the issuer gives the superintendent written notice stating the date, amount, nature and conditions of the proposed trade and the superintendent

(14) a trade by an issuer in a security of a reporting issuer held by the issuer that is distributed by it to its security holders as a dividend in specie so long as the issuer gives the executive director written notice stating the date, amount, nature and conditions of the proposed trade and the executive director

[Para. (14) am. 1995, c. 45, s. 7 (nyif).]

    (i) has not informed the issuer in writing within 10 days of the giving of the notice that he objects to the trade, or

    (ii) has withdrawn any objection he has to the proposed trade;

(15) a trade by an issuer in a security of its own issue where the trade is reasonably necessary to facilitate its incorporation or organization and the security is traded

    (i) for a nominal consideration to not more than 5 incorporators of organizers, or

    (ii) where the law under which the issuer is incorporated or organized requires the trade to be for a greater consideration or to a larger number of incorporators or organizers, for that greater consideration or to that larger number of incorporators or organizers;

(16) a trade by

    (i) a person to an underwriter acting as purchaser, or

    (ii) an underwriter to another underwriter;

(17) a trade by

    (i) an issuer in a security of its own issue to a promoter of that issuer, or

    (ii) a promoter of an issuer in a security issued by that issuer to another promoter of that issuer;

(18) a trade in a security of an issuer where each party to the trade is a control person of that issuer;

(19) a trade by or for the account of a lender, pledgee, mortgagee or other encumbrancer for the purpose of liquidating a bona fide debt by selling or offering for sale a security pledged, mortgaged or otherwise encumbered as collateral for the debt;

(20) the execution of an order to purchase or sell through a registered dealer by a bank or a trust company as agent for a person and the trade by that person made by placing the order with the bank or trust company so long as

    (i) the order of the person to purchase or sell is unsolicited, and

    (ii) the bank or trust company does not actively promote or market an order execution access service;

(21) a trade by an issuer in a security of its own issue as consideration for the acquisition of mining, petroleum or natural gas properties or any interest in them so long as the seller of those properties enters into an escrow or pooling agreement in the required form when ordered by

    (i) the superintendent, or

    (ii) a stock exchange in the Province authorized to so order by the superintendent;

(21) a trade by an issuer in a security of its own issue as consideration for the acquisition of mining, petroleum or natural gas properties or any interest in them

[Para. (21) am. 1990, c. 25, s. 20(c) (nyif).]

> No form is specified. See Local Policy Statement 3-07 "Policy Guidelines Respecting Trading Shares, Performance Shares and Other Consideration".

(22) a trade in a security of a mutual fund to a purchaser, other than the initial trade in a security of the mutual fund to that purchaser, where

    (i) the initial trade in a security of the mutual fund to that purchaser was made under the exemption described in paragraph *(5)*, and

    (ii) either the net asset value or the aggregate acquisition cost, whichever is applicable, of the securities in the mutual fund held by the purchaser as at the date of the trade is not less than a prescribed amount;

> The prescribed amount is $100,000; see s. 77(3) of the Regulation.

(23) a trade made on or through the facilities of a stock exchange recognized by the commission for the purposes of this paragraph where

    (i) the trade is effected in whole or part by means of telephone or other telecommunications equipment linking the facilities of that stock exchange with the facilities of another stock exchange recognized by the commission for the purposes of this paragraph, and

    (ii) the purchase and sale is effected by or through persons each of whom is registered as a dealer, or in a similar capacity, under the law of a province;

(23) a trade made on or through the facilities of an exchange recognized by the commission for the purposes of this paragraph where

    (i) the trade is effected in whole or part by means of telephone or other telecommunications equipment linking the facilities of that exchange with the facilities of another exchange recognized by the commission for the purposes of this paragraph, and

    (ii) the purchase and sale is effected by or through persons each of whom is registered as a dealer, or in a similar capacity, under the law of a province;

[Para. *(23)* am. 1990, c. 25, s. 20(d), (e) (both nyif).]

> No stock exchange has been recognized by the Commission.

(24) [Repealed 1988, c. 58, s. 3(b).]

(25) a trade in a security of an offeree issuer to an offeror under a take over bid or issuer bid;

(26) a trade to a holder of a security in a mutual fund under provisions in the instrument constituting the mutual fund that permit or require dividends or distributions of income or capital gains attributable to the securities to be reinvested in additional securities of the mutual fund of

    (i) the same class of securities, or

    (ii) of a class of securities having the same attributes as that class,

so long as no sales or other acquisition charges are levied;

[Para. *(26)* am. 1990, c. 25, s. 20(f).]

(26.1) a trade by an issuer in a security of its own issue to a registered dealer or registered underwriter as consideration for services performed by the registered dealer or registered underwriter in connection with a distribution of securities of the issuer;

[Para. *(26.1)* en. 1989, c. 78, s. 14(g).]

See Local Policy Statement 3-21 "Share and Unit Offerings of Unlisted Issuers and Options and Warrants Available to Registrants Participating in Such Offerings", NIN 92/22 "Fiscal Agency Agreements – Request for Comment", NIN 93/18 "Fiscal Agency Agreements – Restrictions on Exemption Orders", and NIN 93/21 "Fiscal Agency Agreements – Applications for Discretionary Exemption Orders".

(27) a trade in a bond or debenture by way of an order given to a bank or trust company where

    (i) the order to purchase or sell is unsolicited,

    (ii) the bank or trust company is acting as principal, and

    (iii) the bond or debenture is

        (A) acquired by the bank or trust company from a registered dealer for purposes of the trade, or

        (B) sold by the bank or trust company to a registered dealer following the trade;

(28) a trade in a security of an offeror that is exchanged by or for the account of the offeror with the security holders of an offeree issuer under a take over bid or issuer bid;

[Para. *(28)* am. 1992, c. 52, s. 4(d).]

(29) a trade in a security to the issuer of the security pursuant to the purchase, redemption or acquisition of the security by the issuer;

[Para. *(29)* re-en. 1988, c. 58, s. 3(c).]

(29.1) a trade resulting from an unsolicited order placed with an individual who is not a resident of and does not carry on business in the Province;

[Para. *(29.1)* en. 1990, c. 25, s. 20(g) (nyif).]

(30) a trade designated by regulation or a trade within a class of trade designated by regulation.

Further exemptions from registration are set out in s. 76 of the Regulation.

(3) Subject to the regulations, for purposes of subsection (2)*(8)* or *(14)*, the superintendent shall not object to the trade unless he considers it to be in the public interest to do so.

(3) Subject to the regulations, for purposes of subsection (2)*(8)* or *(14)*, the executive director shall not object to the trade unless he considers it to be in the public interest to do so.

[S. 31(3) am. 1995, c. 45, s. 7 (nyif).]

(4) The superintendent shall not object to a trade referred to in subsection (2)*(8)* or *(14)* without giving the person who filed the written notice an opportunity to be heard.

[S. 31(4) am. 1989, c. 78, s. 15.]

(4) The executive director shall not object to a trade referred to in subsection (2)*(8)* or *(14)* without giving the person who filed the written notice an opportunity to be heard.

[S. 31(4) am. 1995, c. 45, s. 7 (nyif).]

Exemption when trading in certain securities

> The corresponding prospectus exemptions are found in s. 58(1)(a) of the Act.

32. Subject to the regulations, a person may trade in the following securities without being registered under section 20(1):

[S. 32 am. 1990, c. 25, s. 21(a).]

32. Subject to the regulations, a person may trade in the following securities without being registered under section 20(1)(a):

[S. 32 am. 1995, c. 45, s. 19(a) (nyif).]

(a) bonds, debentures or other evidence of indebtedness

    (i) of or guaranteed by the government of Canada or by a province of Canada,

    (i.1) of or guaranteed by

        (A) a country, or

        (B) a political division of a country

    recognized in an order the commission may make for the purpose of this subparagraph,

[Subpara. (i) re-en. 1990, c. 25, s. 21(b).]

    (ii) of a municipal corporation in Canada, including debentures

        (A) issued for public, separate, secondary or vocational school purposes,

        (B) guaranteed by any municipal corporation in Canada, or

        (C) secured by or payable out of rates or taxes levied under the law of a province on property in that province and collectible by or through the municipality where the property is situated,

    (iii) of or guaranteed by an insurer or a savings institution, other than bonds, debentures or other evidence of indebtedness which are subordinate in right of payment to deposits held by the issuer or guarantor of those bonds, debentures or other evidence of indebtedness,

    (iv) of or guaranteed by the International Bank for Reconstruction and Development established by the Agreement for an International Bank for Reconstruction and Development approved by the *Bretton Woods Agreements Act* (Canada), where the bonds, debentures or other evidences of indebtedness are payable in the currency of Canada or of the United States of America, or

    (v) of or guaranteed by the Asian Development Bank or the Inter-American Development Bank, where the bonds, debentures or other evidences of indebtedness are payable in the currency of Canada or of the United States of America and where, with respect to those securities, the certificates, records or other information required by the commission are filed;

> See BOR 91/6 with respect to recognition of foreign jurisdictions. See BOR 90/1 "Trades of Government Warrants" and BOR 91/6 "Recognition of Certain Countries and Political Divisions of Countries Issuing Bonds, Debentures or Other Evidence of Indebtedness", and Interim Local Policy Statement 3-43 "Government Strip Bonds".

(b) or receipts issued by a trust company or a credit union for money received for guaranteed investment,

(c) securities issued by a private mutual fund;

See s. 78 of the Regulation for the limitation on this exemption.

(d) negotiable promissory notes or commercial paper maturing not more than 12 months from the date of issue so long as

(i) each note or commercial paper is not convertible or exchangeable into or accompanied by a right to purchase another security other than a security described in this section, and

(ii) each note or commercial paper traded to an individual has a denomination or principal amount of not less than a prescribed amount;

(ii) the purchaser is not an individual;

[Subpara. (ii) re-en. 1995, c. 45, s. 19(b) (nyif).]

The prescribed amount is $50,000; see s. 77(4) of the Regulation.

(e) mortgages or other encumbrances on property that are

(i) not contained in or secured by a bond, debenture or similar obligation or in a trust deed or other instrument to secure bonds or debentures or similar obligations, and

(ii) offered for sale by a person who is registered or exempted from registration under the *Mortgage Brokers Act*;

(f) securities that evidence indebtedness due under a conditional sales contract or other title retention contract, that provide for the acquisition of personal property, and that are not offered for sale to an individual;

(g) securities issued by an issuer organized exclusively for educational, benevolent, fraternal, charitable, religious or recreational purposes and not for profit, where

(i) no part of the net earnings of the issuer accrue to the benefit of a security holder,

(ii) no commission or other remuneration is paid in connection with the sale of the securities,

(iii) if the trade is made by the issuer, an information statement in the required form is delivered to the purchaser before an agreement of purchase and sale is entered into, and

(iv) if the trade is made by the issuer, the information statement is filed not later than 10 days after the trade;

[Para. (g) am. 1992, c. 52, s. 5(a).]

(h) securities issued by an association to which the *Cooperative Association Act* applies;

(i) shares or deposits of a credit union;

(j) securities of a private issuer where the securities are not offered for sale to the public;

See NIN 89/29 "Meaning of 'the Public'".

(k) securities issued and sold by a prospector for the purpose of financing a prospecting expedition;

(l) securities issued by a prospecting syndicate that has filed a prospecting syndicate agreement for which the superintendent has issued a receipt, where

(i) the securities are sold by the prospector or one of the prospectors who staked claims that belong to or are the subject of a declaration of trust in favour of the prospecting syndicate, and

    (ii) the prospector delivers a copy of the prospecting syndicate agreement to the person purchasing the security before accepting payment for the security;

(m) securities issued by a prospecting syndicate that has filed a prospecting syndicate agreement for which the superintendent has issued a receipt, where the securities are not offered for sale to the public and are sold to not more than 50 persons;

[S. 32(k), (l), (m) repealed 1995, c. 45, s. 19(c) (nyif).]

(n) securities issued by a cooperative corporation as defined in the *Real Estate Act* for the purpose of evidencing a right to use or occupy a part of the land owned by the cooperative corporation where the securities cannot be dealt with apart from the right to use or occupy so long as a prospectus or disclosure statement has been filed and accepted under the *Real Estate Act*;

[S. 32(n) am. 1992, c. 52, s. 5(b).]

(o) variable insurance contracts issued by an insurer where the variable insurance contract is

    (i) a contract of group insurance,

    (ii) a whole life insurance contract providing for the payment at maturity of an amount no less than 3/4 of the premium paid up to the age of 75 for a benefit payable at maturity,

    (iii) an arrangement for the investment of policy dividends and policy proceeds in a separate and distinct fund to which contributions are made only from policy dividends and policy proceeds, or

    (iv) a variable life annuity;

(p) securities designated by regulation or securities within a class of securities designated by regulation.

No other securities or securities within a class of securities have been designated by regulation.

Exemption of trades in exchange contracts

32.1 Subject to the regulations, registration under section 20(1) is not required for the following trades in exchange contracts:

(a) a trade in an exchange contract by a person acting solely through a registered dealer;

(b) a trade resulting from an unsolicited order placed with an individual who is not a resident of and does not carry on business in the Province;

(c) a trade designated by regulation or a trade within a class of trades designated by regulation.

[S. 32.1 en. 1990, c. 25, s. 22 (nyif).]

Exemption order by commission or superintendent

33. On application by an interested person or on the commission's or the superintendent's own motion, the commission or the superintendent may order that a trade, intended trade, security, exchange contract or person or class of trades, intended trades, securities, exchange contracts or persons is exempt from one or more of the requirements of Part 4 or the regulations related to Part 4 where the commission or the superintendent considers that to do so would not be prejudicial to the public interest.

[S. 33 re-en. 1992, c. 52, s. 6.]

Exemption order by commission or executive director

33. On application by an interested person or on the commission's or the executive director's own motion, the commission or the executive director may order that a trade, intended trade, security, exchange contract or person or class of trades, intended trades, securities, exchange contracts or persons is exempt from one or more of the requirements of Part 4 or the regulations related to Part 4 where the commission or the executive director considers that to do so would not be prejudicial to the public interest.

[S. 33 am. 1995, c. 45, s. 7 (nyif).]

See NIN 88/5 "Guideline for Applications to the Securities Commission or the Superintendent of Brokers for Decisions or Orders", which sets out the procedure for applying for discretionary exemptions under this section, and Local Policy Statement 3-24 "Statutory Orders and Exemptions Made under Sections 33 and 59 of the Securities Act". Exemptions are issued by the Superintendent or the Commission in respect of specific applications submitted to them or in respect of certain types of transactions. Rulings regarding certain types of transactions are called blanket orders, and are reproduced in this book under the heading "Blanket Orders and Rulings".

PART 6

TRADING IN SECURITIES GENERALLY

Calling at or telephoning residence

34. (1) In this section "residence" includes a building or part of building in which the occupant resides permanently or temporarily and any appurtenant premises.

(2) No person shall

(a) attend at any residence, or

(b) telephone from within the Province to any residence within or outside the Province

for the purpose of trading in a security.

(2) No person shall

(a) attend at any residence, or

(b) telephone from within the Province to any residence within or outside the Province

for the purpose of trading in a security or exchange contract.

[S. 34(2) am. 1990, c. 25, s. 24(a) (nyif).]

(3) Subsection (2) does not apply where

(a) the person calls at or telephones the residence

(i) of a close personal friend, a business associate or a client with whom or on whose behalf the person calling or telephoning has been in the habit of trading in securities, or

[Subpara. (i) am. 1989, c. 78, s. 9.]

(i) of a close personal friend, a business associate or a client with whom or on whose behalf the person calling or telephoning has been in the habit of trading in securities or exchange contracts, or

[Subpara. (i) am. 1990, c. 25, s. 24(b) (nyif).]

    (ii) of a person who

        (A) has received a copy of a prospectus filed under this Act, and

        (B) has requested that information respecting a security offered in that prospectus be furnished to him by the person calling or telephoning,

        and the person calling or telephoning refers only to the request for information respecting that security, or

(b) the person is trading in a security in respect of which he is exempted under sections 31 and 32 from registration.

(b) the person is making a trade in respect of which the person is exempted from registration under section 31 or 32.1 or is trading in a security in respect of which the person is exempted from registration under section 32.

[Para. (b) re-en. 1990, c. 25, s. 24(c) (nyif).]

(4) For purposes of this section, a person shall be conclusively deemed to have called or telephoned where a partner, officer, director or salesman of the person calls or telephones on that person's behalf.

[S. 34(4) am. 1990, c. 25, s. 24(d).]

(4) For the purposes of this section, a person is conclusively deemed to have called or telephoned if a salesperson, advising employee, partner, director, officer or agent of the person calls or telephones on the person's behalf.

[S. 34(4) re-en. 1995, c. 45, s. 20 (nyif).]

(5) The commission may exempt from subsection (2) a person or class of persons trading in securities generally or trading in a specific security or class of securities.

(5) The commission may exempt from subsection (2) a person or class of persons trading in

(a) securities or exchange contracts generally,

(b) a specific security or exchange contract, or

(c) a class of securities or a class of exchange contracts.

[S. 34(5) re-en. 1990, c. 25, s. 24(e) (nyif).]

Re Boulder Creek Development Ltd. and Lester Gene Chapman, [1988] 73 B.C.S.C. Weekly Summary (B.C. Supt. of Brokers).

With respect to s. 34(2)(b), solicitations made by a company to persons outside of the province come within the purview of the Act.

Representations prohibited

35. (1) No person, with the intention of effecting a trade in a security,

(a) other than a security that carries an obligation of the issuer to redeem or purchase or a right of the owner to require redemption or purchase, shall make any representation, written or oral, that he or any person will

    (i) resell or repurchase, or

    (ii) refund all or any of the purchase price of

    that security,

(b) shall give an undertaking, written or oral, relating to the future value or price of that security, or

(c) shall, except with the written permission of the superintendent, make any representation, written or oral, that

(i) the security will be listed and posted for trading on a stock exchange, or

(ii) application has been or will be made to list and post the security for trading on a stock exchange.

The Commission interprets this prohibition broadly and is of the view that it is inappropriate to make a statement that an issuer may in the future apply to be listed and posted for trading on a stock exchange. The Commission has adopted the practice of the Ontario Securities Commission, namely to require evidence of conditional listing of a security before permitting representations about applications for listing.

NIN 94/22 "Permission Under Section 35(1)(c) of the Securities Act" provides that the prohibition against representations as to securities being listed on a stock exchange which is found in s. 35(1) does not apply with respect to securities for which at least a preliminary short form prospectus has been filed in accordance with the Memorandum of Understanding for Expedited Review of Short Form Prospectuses and Renewal AIFS, found after NIN 94/21, provided certain requirements are met.

---

(2) Subsection (1)(a) does not apply to a representation contained in an enforceable written agreement where the security involved has an aggregate acquisition cost in excess of a prescribed amount.

The prescribed amount is $50,000; see s. 82 of the Regulation. See also National Policy Statement 21 "National Advertising – Warnings", National Policy Statement 22 "Use of Information and Opinion re Mining and Oil Properties by Registrants and Others", Interim National Policy Statement 42 "Advertising of Securities on Radio or Television", and Local Policy Statement 3-39 "Guidelines for Advertising Issues of Securities and for Promotional Activities During the Course of a Distribution".

Representations prohibited

35. (1) No person, with the intention of effecting a trade in a security,

(a) shall represent that the person or another person will

(i) resell or repurchase the security, or

(ii) refund all or any of the purchase price of the security,

(b) shall give an undertaking relating to the future value or price of the security, or

(c) shall represent, unless the person obtains the written permission of the superintendent,

(i) that the security will be listed and posted for trading on an exchange, or

(ii) that application has been or will be made to list and post the security for trading on an exchange.

(2) Subsection (1)(a) does not apply to a representation

(a) in respect of a security that carries an obligation of the issuer to redeem or purchase or a right of the owner to require redemption or purchase, or

(b) contained in a written agreement where the security involved has an aggregate acquisition cost in excess of a prescribed amount.

(3) No person, with the intention of effecting a trade in an exchange contract,

(a) shall represent that the person or another person will

    (i) refund all or part of any margin put up or premium paid in respect of the exchange contract, or

    (ii) assume all or part of the obligation under the exchange contract, or

(b) shall give an undertaking relating to the future value of the exchange contract.

[S. 35 re-en. 1990, c. 25, s. 25 (nyif).]

Representations prohibited

35. (1) A person, while engaging in investor relations activities or with the intention of effecting a trade in a security, must not

(a) represent that the person or another person will

    (i) resell or repurchase the security, or

    (ii) refund all or any of the purchase price of the security,

(b) give an undertaking relating to the future value or price of the security,

(c) represent, without obtaining the prior written permission of the executive director,

    (i) that the security will be listed and posted for trading on an exchange, or

    (ii) that application has been or will be made to list and post the security for trading on an exchange, or

(d) make a statement that the person knows, or ought reasonably to know, is a misrepresentation.

(2) Subsection (1)(a) does not apply to a representation

(a) in respect of a security that carries an obligation of the issuer to redeem or purchase, or a right of the owner to require redemption or purchase, or

(b) contained in a written agreement if the security involved has an aggregate acquisition cost in excess of a prescribed amount.

(3) A person, with the intention of effecting a trade in an exchange contract, must not

(a) represent that the person or another person will

    (i) refund all or part of any margin put up or premium paid in respect of the exchange contract, or

    (ii) assume all or part of the obligation under the exchange contract,

(b) give an undertaking relating to the future value of the exchange contract, or

(c) make a statement that the person knows, or ought reasonably to know, is a misrepresentation.

[S. 35 re-en. 1995, c. 45, s. 21 (nyif).]

Registered dealer acting as principal

36. (1) This section does not apply to a trade referred to in section 31 or a trade in a security described in section 32.

(2) Where a registered dealer

(a) intends, as principal, to effect a trade in a security with a person who is not a registered dealer, and

(b) issues, publishes or sends a notice, circular, pamphlet, letter, advertisement, telegram or some other record to that person to effect that trade, he shall not contract for the sale or purchase of the security unless before contracting, and before accepting payment or receiving any security or other consideration under or in anticipation of the contract, he has stated in the record issued, published or sent to that person under paragraph (b) that he proposes to act as principal in the trade.

See s. 122(1) of the Act with respect to the results of not complying with this requirement.

(3) A statement made in compliance with this section or the regulations that a registered dealer proposes to act or has acted as principal in respect of a trade in a security does not prevent that dealer from acting as agent in respect of a trade of that security.

See National Policy Statement 25 "Registrants Advertising Disclosure of Interest".

Disclosure of investor relations activities

36.1 (1) An issuer that knows, or an issuer's security holder that knows, that a person is engaged in investor relations activities on behalf of the issuer or a security holder of the issuer must disclose

(a) the fact of the engagement, and

(b) on whose behalf the person is engaged

to any person who inquires.

(2) A person engaged in investor relations activities, and an issuer or security holder on whose behalf investor relations activities are undertaken, must ensure that every record disseminated, as part of the investor relations activities, by the person engaged in those activities clearly and conspicuously discloses that the record is issued by or on behalf of the issuer or security holder.

[S. 36.1 en. 1995, c. 45, s. 22 (nyif).]

Use of name of another registrant

37. A registrant shall not use the name of another registrant on letterheads, forms, advertisements or signs, as a correspondent or otherwise, unless he is a partner, officer or agent of, or is authorized in writing by, the other registrant.

Representation of registration

38. A person shall not represent that the person is registered under this Act unless

(a) the representation is true, and

(b) in making the representation, the person specifies the person's category of registration under this Act and the regulations.

[S. 38 re-en. 1990, c. 25, s. 26.]

Holding out by unregistered person

39. A person who is not registered shall not, directly or indirectly, hold himself out as being registered.

Approval by commission not to be advertised

40. A person shall not represent, orally or in writing, that the commission or the superintendent has in any way approved the financial standing, fitness, or conduct of any registrant or passed on the merits of any security or issuer.

Approval of commission or superintendent not to be represented

40. A person shall not represent that the commission or the superintendent has approved the financial standing, fitness or conduct of any registrant or passed on the merits of any security, exchange contract or issuer.

[S. 40 re-en. 1990, c. 25, s. 27 (nyif).]

Approval of commission or executive director not to be represented

40. A person shall not represent that the commission or the executive director has approved the financial standing, fitness or conduct of any registrant or passed on the merits of any security, exchange contract or issuer.

[S. 40 am. 1995, c. 45, s. 7 (nyif).]

Declaration as to short position

41. (1) A person who places an order for the sale of a security through a registered dealer acting on his behalf and who

(a) does not own the security, or

(b) if he is acting as agent knows his principal does not own the security,

shall, at the time of placing the order to sell, declare to the registered dealer that he or his principal, as the case may be, does not own the security, and that fact shall be disclosed by the dealer in the written confirmation of sale.

(2) Subject to the regulations, for the purposes of subsection (1), a person does not own a security that

(a) has been borrowed by that person,

(b) is subject to any restriction on its sale, or

(c) may be acquired by that person on the exercise of a right to acquire the security by purchase, conversion, exchange or any other means.

[S. 41 am. 1989, c. 78, s. 16(b).]

See Uniform Act Policy 2-08 "Declaration as to Short Position – Listed and Unlisted Securities".

Prohibited transaction or scheme

41.1 No person, directly or indirectly, shall engage in or participate in a transaction or scheme relating to a trade or acquisition of a security if the person knows or ought reasonably to know that the transaction or scheme

(a) creates or results in a misleading appearance of trading activity in, or an artificial price for, any security listed on a stock exchange in the Province,

(b) perpetrates a fraud on any person in the Province, or

(c) perpetrates a fraud on any person anywhere in connection with the securities of a reporting issuer.

[S. 41.1 en. 1989, c. 78, s. 17.]

41.1 No person, directly or indirectly, shall engage in or participate in a transaction or scheme relating to a trade in or acquisition of a security or a trade in an exchange contract if the person knows or ought reasonably to know that the transaction or scheme

(a) creates or results in an misleading appearance of trading activity in, or an artificial price for, any security listed, or exchange contract traded, on an exchange in the Province,

(b) perpetrates a fraud on any person in the Province, or

(c) perpetrates a fraud on any person anywhere in connection with

(i) the securities of a reporting issuer, or

(ii) trading in exchange contracts on an exchange in the Province.

[S. 41.1 am. 1990, c. 25, s. 28 (nyif).]

See NIN 95/5 "Principles of Fair Trading" for guidance as to what constitutes abusive trading practices.

PART 6.1

[Part 6.1 en. 1990, c. 25, s. 29 (nyif).]

TRADING IN EXCHANGE CONTRACTS

Trading on an exchange in the Province

41.2 (1) No person shall trade in an exchange contract on an exchange in the Province unless

(a) the exchange is recognized by the commission under section 11(2), and

(b) the form of the exchange contract has been accepted by the commission.

(2) On application by an exchange in the Province, the commission by order may accept a form of exchange contract for the purpose of subsection (1)(b).

(3) The commission shall not refuse to accept a form of exchange contract under subsection (2) without giving the applicant an opportunity to be heard.

Trading on an exchange outside the Province

41.3 (1) A registrant shall not trade in an exchange contract on behalf of another person on an exchange outside the Province unless the exchange is recognized by the commission.

(2) On application by an exchange outside the Province or on the commission's own motion, the commission by order may recognize an exchange outside the Province for the purposes of subsection (1).

(3) The commission shall not refuse to recognize an exchange under subsection (2) without giving the applicant an opportunity to be heard.

Exemption order by commission or executive director

41.4 On application by an interested person or on the commission's or the executive director's own motion, the commission or the executive director, if the commission or the executive director considers that to do so would not be prejudicial to the public interest, may order that a trade, intended trade, exchange contract or person or class of trades, intended trades, exchange contracts or persons is exempt from one or more of the requirements of this Part or the regulations relating to this Part.

[S. 41.4 en. 1995, c. 45, s. 23 (nyif).]

PART 7

PROSPECTUS

Prospectus required

42. (1) Unless exempted under this Act or the regulations, a person shall not distribute a security unless a preliminary prospectus and a prospectus respecting that security

(a) have been filed with, and

(b) receipts obtained for them from,

the superintendent.

the executive director.

[S. 42(1) am. 1995, c. 45, s. 7 (nyif).]

See Local Policy Statement 3-02 "Prospectus Filing Requirements" with respect to the documentation that must be filed with a preliminary prospectus or a prospectus. See also National Policy Statement 45 "Multijurisdictional Disclosure System", and NIN 91/22 "Guide for Use of the Multijurisdictional Disclosure System by Canadian Issuers in the U.S. Market".

(2) A preliminary prospectus and a prospectus shall be in the required form.

The required forms are set out in Forms 12, 12A, 13, 14, 14A and 15. See s. 114(1) of the Act with respect to liability for misrepresentation in a prospectus. See NIN 95/17 "Form 14A – Information Required in Prospectus of a Natural Resource Issuer", which prescribes Form 14A as the form for natural resource issuers effective August 1, 1995. See also s. 90 of the Regulation with respect to the discretion of the superintendent in requiring additional disclosure.

Form 12A specifies disclosure in greater detail. Other jurisdictions have accepted a Form 12A prospectus for filing in a national offering, so long as it satisfies the requirements of their designated form.

See BOR 95/1 "Form 12A Summary Prospectus Disclosure System".

Re Aatra Resources Ltd., Victor J. Meunier, Paul A. Quinn, Ralph A.A. Simpson, Joel Machtinger, Henry P.M. Huber, Alex Pancer, David J. Foster and Durham Securities Corp. Ltd. (1993), 3 C.C.L.S. 51 (B.C. Sec. Comm.).

A prospectus in the required Form 14 is false and misleading if it fails to disclose that a person is a promoter and *de facto* director of a company or that the shares and options held in the names of third parties were beneficially held by that person.

(3) A short form of preliminary prospectus and a short form of prospectus, each in the required form, may, if permitted by the regulations, be filed under this section.

(3) A simplified preliminary prospectus and a simplified prospectus, each in the required form, may, if permitted by the regulations, be filed under this section.

[S. 42(3) am. 1995, c. 45, s. 24 (nyif).]

Applies to a statement of material facts; see s. 122 of the Regulation. The required form of a short form of prospectus for a mutual fund is Form 50.

Voluntary filing of prospectus

43. A preliminary prospectus and a prospectus may be filed in accordance with this Part to enable the issuer to become a reporting issuer even though no distribution under that prospectus is contemplated.

Contents

44. (1) A prospectus shall provide full, true and plain disclosure of all material facts relating to the securities issued or proposed to be distributed.

See National Policy Statement 13 "Disclaimer Clause on Prospectus", National Policy Statement 32 "Prospectus Warning re: Scope of Distribution", and National Policy Statement 35 "Purchaser's Statutory Rights".

(2) A preliminary prospectus shall substantially comply with the requirements of this Act and the regulations respecting the content of a prospectus.

[S. 44(2) re-en. 1988, c. 58, s. 5(a).]

(3) A prospectus, other than a prospectus filed under section 43, shall contain statements that

(a)   a purchaser has

(i)   a right of withdrawal from an agreement of purchase and sale, and

(ii) where a prospectus contains a misrepresentation, a right of rescission or damages, and

(b) these rights must be exercised within limited time periods.

> The right of withdrawal is set out in s. 66(3) of the Act. The right of rescission or damages is set out in s. 114 of the Act. The time periods are set out in s. 124 of the Act.

(4) In addition to the requirements of subsection (3), a prospectus of a mutual fund in the Province shall contain a statement of the rights given to a purchaser under section 123.

(5) [Repealed 1988, c. 58, s. 5(b).]

Superintendent's discretion

45. (1) Before issuing a receipt for a preliminary prospectus or for a prospectus, the superintendent may impose additional filing requirements and conditions if the superintendent considers that it is in the public interest to do so.

[S. 45(1) re-en. 1989, c. 78, s. 18(a).]

> **45.** (1) Before issuing a receipt for a preliminary prospectus or for a prospectus, the executive director may impose additional filing requirements and conditions if the executive director considers that it is in the public interest to do so.

[S. 45(1) am. 1995, c. 45, s. 7 (nyif).]

> Applies to a statement of material facts; see s. 122 of the Regulation.

(2) The superintendent may accept a form of prospectus or preliminary prospectus that is in accordance with the law of another jurisdiction if it contains full, true and plain disclosure of all material facts relating to the security to be distributed.

[S. 45(2) am. 1989, c. 78, s. 18(b).]

> (2) The executive director may accept a form of prospectus or preliminary prospectus that is in accordance with the law of another jurisdiction if it contains full, true and plain disclosure of all material facts relating to the security to be distributed.

[S. 45(2) am. 1995, c. 45, s. 7 (nyif).]

> This section has been used by the Commission to accept disclosure documents having similar content. An example is a prospectus of a Nova Scotia issuer prepared pursuant to that province's form.

Receipts

46. (1) Subject to section 45(1), the superintendent shall issue a receipt for a preliminary prospectus as soon as practicable after it has been filed under this Part.

[S. 46(1) am. 1989, c. 78, s. 19(a).]

> **46.** (1) Subject to section 45(1), the executive director shall issue a receipt for a preliminary prospectus as soon as practicable after it has been filed under this Part.

[S. 46(1) am. 1995, c. 45, s. 7 (nyif).]

> A receipt for a preliminary prospectus is generally dated the date the preliminary prospectus was filed and is usually delivered on that day or the business day next following.

(2) Subject to the regulations, the superintendent shall issue a receipt for a prospectus filed under this Part unless he considers it to be prejudicial to the public interest to do so.

(2) Subject to the regulations, the executive director shall issue a receipt for a prospectus filed under this Part unless he considers it to be prejudicial to the public interest to do so.

[S. 46(2) am. 1995, c. 45, s. 7 (nyif).]

> See s. 115 of the Regulation which sets out the circumstances in which the superintendent will not issue a receipt.

(3) The superintendent shall not refuse to issue a receipt for a prospectus without giving the person who filed the prospectus an opportunity to be heard.

[S. 46(3) am. 1989, c. 78, s. 19(b).]

(3) The executive director shall not refuse to issue a receipt for a prospectus without giving the person who filed the prospectus an opportunity to be heard.

[S. 46(3) am. 1995, c. 45, s. 7 (nyif).]

> Applies to a statement of material facts; see s. 122 of the Regulation.

Amendment to preliminary prospectus

47. (1) Where an adverse material change occurs in the affairs of an issuer after a receipt is issued for a preliminary prospectus but before a receipt is issued for a prospectus, the person who intends to make the distribution shall file an amendment to the preliminary prospectus disclosing the change, as soon as practicable and in any event no later than 10 days after the change occurs.

> It is unclear why one must file an amendment with respect to an adverse material change while an amendment with respect to a positive material change need only be filed voluntarily.

(2) An amendment to a preliminary prospectus may be filed under subsection (1) that discloses a material change other than an adverse material change.

(3) The superintendent shall issue, as soon as practicable, receipt for an amendment to a preliminary prospectus filed under subsection (1).

(3) The executive director shall issue, as soon as practicable, receipt for an amendment to a preliminary prospectus filed under subsection (1).

[S. 47(3) am. 1995, c. 45, s. 7 (nyif).]

(4) The person filing the amendment under subsection (1) shall send, as soon as it has been filed, the amendment to the preliminary prospectus to each recipient of the preliminary prospectus according to the record maintained under section 63.

Amendment to prospectus

48. (1) Where, after a receipt is issued for a prospectus but before the completion of the distribution under it, a material change occurs in the affairs of an issuer, the person who is making the distribution shall file an amendment to the prospectus disclosing the change, as soon as practicable, and in any event no later than 10 days after the change occurs.

> Note that the amendment must be filed whether the material change is adverse or positive. See Local Policy Statement 3-25 "Re: Natural Resource Issuer – 'Best Efforts' Prospectus and Amendments to Prospectus Arising from Market Conditions".

(2) Where, after a receipt is issued for a prospectus but before the completion of the distribution under it, additional securities of the same class of securities previously disclosed in the prospectus are to be distributed, the person making the distribution shall file an amendment to the prospectus disclosing the additional securities.

[S. 48(2) am. 1988, c. 58, s. 6(a).]

(2) Where, after a receipt is issued for a prospectus but before the completion of the distribution under it, additional securities of the same class of securities previously disclosed in the prospectus are to be distributed, the person making the distribution shall file an amendment to the prospectus disclosing the additional securities, as soon as practicable, and in any event no later than 10 days after the decision to increase the number of securities offered is made.

[S. 48(2) am. 1995, c. 45, s. 25(a) (nyif).]

(3) Where, after a receipt is issued for the prospectus but before the completion of the distribution under it, the terms or conditions of the offering disclosed in the prospectus are to be altered, the person making the distribution shall file an amendment to the prospectus disclosing the change.

(3) Where, after a receipt is issued for the prospectus but before the completion of the distribution under it, the terms or conditions of the offering disclosed in the prospectus are to be altered, the person making the distribution shall file an amendment to the prospectus disclosing the change, as soon as practicable, and in any event no later than 10 days after the decision to alter the terms or conditions is made.

[S. 48(3) am. 1995, c. 45, s. 25(b) (nyif).]

(4) The superintendent shall issue a receipt for an amendment to a prospectus filed under this section and section 46(2) and (3) applies.

(4) The executive director shall issue a receipt for an amendment to a prospectus filed under this section and section 46(2) and (3) applies.

[S. 48(4) am. 1995, c. 45, s. 7 (nyif).]

(5) Except with the written permission of the superintendent, a distribution or an additional distribution shall not proceed until a receipt for an amendment to a prospectus that is required to be filed under this section is issued by the superintendent.

[S. 48(5) am. 1988, c. 58, s. 6(b).]

(5) Except with the written permission of the executive director, a distribution or an additional distribution shall not proceed until a receipt for an amendment to a prospectus that is required to be filed under this section is issued by the executive director.

[S. 48(5) am. 1995, c. 45, s. 7 (nyif).]

Certificate of issuer

49. (1) The issuer shall ensure that a prospectus contains a certificate that states

(a) where the prospectus is filed under section 42 or 51,

"The foregoing constitutes full, true and plain disclosure of all material facts relating to the securities offered by this prospectus as required by the *Securities Act* and its regulations.", and

[S. 49(1)(a) am. 1989, c. 78, s. 20(a).]

Applies to a statement of material facts; see s. 122 of the Regulation. See para. 3.2(B) of Local Policy Statement 3-02 "Prospectus Filing Requirements", which deals with the dating of the certificates.

See BOR 95/1 "Form 12A Summary Prospectus Disclosure System".

(b) where the prospectus is filed under section 43,

"The foregoing constitutes full, true and plain disclosure of all material facts relating to the securities previously issued by the issuer as required by the *Securities Act* and its regulations."

[S. 49(1)(b) am. 1988, c. 58, s. 7.]

(2) Subject to subsections (3) to (5), the certificate required under subsection (1) shall be signed

(a) by the issuer's chief executive officer and chief financial officer,

(b) on behalf of the directors of the issuer by any 2 directors, other than the persons referred to in paragraph (a), who are duly authorized to sign, and

(c) by each person who is a promoter of the issuer.

[S. 49(2)(c) re-en. 1989, c. 78, s. 20(b).]

Applies to a statement of material facts; see s. 122 of the Regulation.

(3) Where the issuer has only 3 directors, 2 of whom are the chief executive officer and the chief financial officer, the number of directors required to sign the certificate under subsection (2)(b) shall be one.

Applies to a statement of material facts; see s. 122 of the Regulation.

(4) Where the superintendent is satisfied on evidence or submissions made to him that the chief executive officer or the chief financial officer of the issuer, or both, is not available to sign a certificate in a prospectus, he may allow any other responsible officer of the issuer to sign it instead.

(4) Where the executive director is satisfied on evidence or submissions made to him that the chief executive officer or the chief financial officer of the issuer, or both, is not available to sign a certificate in a prospectus, he may allow any other responsible officer of the issuer to sign it instead.

[S. 49(4) am. 1995, c. 45, s. 7 (nyif).]

Applies to a statement of material facts; see s. 122 of the Regulation.

(5) The superintendent may, with respect to the certificate required by subsection (1),

(5) The executive director may, with respect to the certificate required by subsection (1),

[S. 49(5) am. 1995, c. 45, s. 7 (nyif).]

(a) exempt a promoter from signing it,

(b) allow a promoter's agent, who is duly authorized in writing, to sign it on behalf of the promoter, or

(c) on conditions he imposes, require any person who has been a promoter of the issuer within the preceding 2 years to sign it.

Applies to a statement of material facts; see s. 122 of the Regulation.

Certificate of underwriter

50. (1) Where an underwriter is in a contractual relationship with the issuer or holder of the securities offered by a prospectus, the prospectus shall contain a certificate signed by the underwriter that states:

> "To the best of our knowledge, information and belief, the foregoing constitutes full, true and plain disclosure of all material facts relating to the securities offered by this prospectus as required by the *Securities Act* and its regulations."

See BOR 95/1 "Form 12A Summary Prospectus Disclosure System".

(2) The superintendent may allow an underwriter's agent, who is duly authorized in writing, to sign the certificate required by subsection (1) on behalf of the underwriter.

(2) The executive director may allow an underwriter's agent, who is duly authorized in writing, to sign the certificate required by subsection (1) on behalf of the underwriter.

[S. 50(2) am. 1995, c. 45, s. 7 (nyif).]

Applies to a statement of material facts; see s. 122 of the Regulation.

Lapse of prospectus

50.1 (1) Subject to subsection (3), no person shall distribute a security under a prospectus after the lapse date of the prospectus.

(2) The lapse date of a prospectus is the earlier of

(a) the prescribed date, or

(b) a date designated by the superintendent.

(b) a date designated by the executive director.

[Para. (b) am. 1995, c. 45, s. 7 (nyif).]

(3) A person may distribute a security under a prospectus after the lapse date of the prospectus on prescribed terms and conditions.

(4) A purchaser may, in prescribed circumstances, cancel a trade that was completed after the lapse date in reliance on subsection (3).

[S. 50.1 en. 1992, c. 52, s. 7 (nyif).]

Lapse of prospectus

51. (1) In this section "lapse date" means the date determined under subsections (2) and (3) on which a prospectus ceases to be valid for the distribution of the securities for which the prospectus was filed.

(2) No person shall distribute a security under a prospectus filed under section 42 or this section after 12 months have elapsed from the later of

(a) the date of the issue of the receipt for the preliminary prospectus relating to the security, or

(b) the date of the last prospectus filed under this section, unless a new prospectus is filed under this section and the superintendent has issued a receipt for it.

[S. 51(2) re-en. 1989, c. 78, s. 21(a).]

See BOR 91/10 "First Renewal Prospectuses Filed by Mutual Funds under National Policy Statement #36".

---

(3) Notwithstanding subsection (2), the superintendent may shorten the period of time under subsection (2) to less than 12 months in respect of a distribution under a prospectus that is filed under section 42 or this section.

[S. 51(3) re-en. 1989, c. 78, s. 21(a).]

See paras. 9.3 and 10.5 of Local Policy Statement 3-02 "Prospectus Filing Requirements", which deal with restricted offering periods.

---

(4) Notwithstanding subsection (2), a distribution may be continued for a further 12 months beyond the lapse date of a prospectus if

    (a)   a pro forma prospectus prepared in the required form is filed not less than 30 days before the lapse date,

    (b)   a new prospectus is filed within 10 days following the lapse date, and

    (c)   a receipt for the new prospectus referred to in paragraph (b) is issued by the superintendent within the 20 days following the lapse date.

(5) A trade completed after the lapse date in reliance on subsection (4) may be cancelled at the election of the purchaser if any condition under subsection (4) is not met

    (a)   within the applicable time set out in subsection (4)(a), (b) or (c), or

    (b)   within the extended time, if any, permitted under subsection (7) by the superintendent.

[S. 51(5) re-en. 1989, c. 78, s. 21(a).]

(6) Where a purchaser elects to cancel a purchase under subsection (5), he shall do so within 90 days from the day on which he became aware that a condition under subsection (4) was not complied with.

(7) On the application of a reporting issuer made before or after the expiry of a time limit under subsection (4)(a), (b) or (c), if the superintendent considers that the extension would not be prejudicial to the public interest, the superintendent may order that any of the time limits under subsection (4)(a), (b) or (c) be extended.

  [S. 51(7) re-en. 1989, c. 78, s. 21(a).]

See BOR 91/10 "First Renewal Prospectuses Filed by Mutual Funds under National Policy Statement 36", NIN 88/5 "Guidelines for Applications to the Securities Commission or the Superintendent of Brokers for Decisions or Orders", and Canadian Securities Administrators Notice 92/2 "Applications for Discretionary Orders".

---

(8) An order made under subsection (7) after the expiry of a time limit under subsection (4)(a), (b) or (c) does not affect a purchaser's right under subsection (5) to cancel a trade made before the date of the order.

[S. 51(8) en. 1989, c. 78, s. 21(b).]

Distribution of securities may be continued

51. (1) A person who distributed securities under a prospectus filed under section 42 or this section may, on prescribed terms and conditions, continue to distribute securities under a new prospectus by filing the new prospectus with, and obtaining a receipt for the new prospectus from, the superintendent under this section.

(2) Notwithstanding section 42(1), a person may file a new prospectus under subsection (1) without filing a preliminary prospectus with, and obtaining a receipt for the preliminary prospectus from, the superintendent.

(3) A short form of prospectus in the required form may, if permitted by the regulations, be filed under this section.

[S. 51 re-en. 1992, c. 52, s. 7 (nyif).]

51. (1) A person who distributed securities under a prospectus filed under section 42 or this section may, on prescribed terms and conditions, continue to distribute securities under a new prospectus by filing the new prospectus with, and obtaining a receipt for the new prospectus from, the executive director under this section.

(2) Notwithstanding section 42(1), a person may file a new prospectus under subsection (1) without filing a preliminary prospectus with, and obtaining a receipt for the preliminary prospectus from, the executive director.

(3) A short form of prospectus in the required form may, if permitted by the regulations, be filed under this section.

[S. 51 am. 1995, c. 45, s. 7 (nyif).]

Order to furnish information re distribution

52. (1) Where a person proposing to make a distribution of previously issued securities of an issuer is unable to obtain from the issuer information or material that is necessary to enable the person to comply with this Part or the regulations, the superintendent may order the issuer to furnish to that person the information and material that the superintendent considers necessary.

52. (1) Where a person proposing to make a distribution of previously issued securities of an issuer is unable to obtain from the issuer information or material that is necessary to enable the person to comply with this Part or the regulations, the executive director may order the issuer to furnish to that person the information and material that the executive director considers necessary.

[S. 52(1) am. 1995, c. 45, s. 7 (nyif).]

(2) The information and material supplied under subsection (1) may be used by the person to whom it is furnished for the purpose of complying with this Part and the regulations.

(3) Where a person proposing to make a distribution of previously issued securities of an issuer is unable

    (a) to obtain any or all of the signatures to the certificates required by, or

    (b) to comply otherwise with,

this Part and the regulations, the superintendent may, on being satisfied that

this Part and the regulations, the executive director may, on being satisfied that

[S. 52(3) am. 1995, c. 45, s. 7 (nyif).]

    (c) the person has made all reasonable efforts to comply, and

    (d) no person is likely to be prejudicially affected by the failure to comply,

make an order exempting that person from any of the provisions of this Part or the regulations.

Applies to a statement of material facts; see s. 122 of the Regulation.

PART 8

EXEMPTIONS FROM PROSPECTUS REQUIREMENTS

Interpretation

53. In this Part "issuer bid", "offeree issuer", "offeror" and "take over bid" have the meanings defined in section 74.

54. [Repealed 1989, c. 78, s. 22.]

Exemptions

55. (1) In this section

(a) a trust company or an insurer shall be deemed to be acting as principal when it purchases or sells as an agent or trustee for accounts that are fully managed by it, and

(b) a portfolio manager shall be deemed to be acting as principal when he purchases or sells as an agent for accounts that are fully managed by him.

(2) Subject to the regulations, section 42 does not apply to a distribution where

[S. 55(2) am. 1990, c. 25, s. 30(a).]

> The corresponding registration exemptions are found in s. 31(2) of the Act. Additional prospectus exemptions are found in s. 117 of the Regulation. The resale restrictions applicable to securities issued under these exemptions are set out in ss. 133 (other than exchange issuers) and 134 (exchange issuers) of the Regulation. The requirement to file a Form 20 not later than 10 days after the distribution pursuant to certain of these exemptions is set out in s. 132 of the Regulation.

(1) the purchaser of the security is

     (i) the Federal Business Development Bank,

     (ii) a savings institution,

     (iii) an insurer,

     (iv) a subsidiary of a person referred to in subparagraphs (i) to (iii) where that person owns beneficially all of the voting securities of the subsidiary, except the voting securities required by law to be owned by directors of that subsidiary,

     (v) Her Majesty in right of Canada or a province, or

     (vi) a municipal corporation, public board or commission in Canada,

who purchases as principal,

(2) the trade is made by or on behalf of an issuer in a specific security of its own issue for the issuer's account and is

     (i) isolated,

     (ii) not made in the course of continued and successive transactions of a like nature, and

     (iii) not made by a person whose usual business is trading in securities,

> Note that this exemption may only be used by the issuer and may not be used by a person who has purchased securities of an issuer.

(3) the person is purchasing as principal, is not an individual and is designated as an exempt purchaser in an order that the superintendent may make for the purpose of this paragraph,

[S. 55(2)*(3)* re-en. 1989, c. 78, s. 23(a).]

(3) the person is purchasing as principal, is not an individual and is designated as an exempt purchaser in an order that the executive director may make for the purpose of this paragraph,

[S. 55(2)*(3)* am. 1995, c. 45, s. 7 (nyif).]

See Local Policy Statement 3-15 "Exempt Purchaser Status" regarding the procedure to become qualified as an exempt purchaser.

(4) the person is purchasing as principal, and the trade is in a security which has an aggregate acquisition cost to the purchaser of not less than a prescribed amount,

The prescribed amount is $97,000; see s. 118(1) of the Regulation. See Local Policy Statement 3-24 "Statutory Orders and Exemptions made under Sections 33 and 59 of the Securities Act" with respect to guidelines regarding the use of this exemption. An offering memorandum must be utilized if the distribution is advertised; see s. 127 of the Regulation.

(5) the trade is made by an issuer in a security of its own issue as consideration for part or all of another person's assets, so long as the fair value of the purchased assets is not less than a prescribed amount,

The prescribed amount is $100,000; see s. 118(2) of the Regulation. See Local Policy Statement 3-07 "Policy Guidelines Respecting Trading Shares, Performance Shares and Other Consideration", and NIN 92/3 "Waivers Consequential to Local Policy Statement 3-07".

(6) the trade is made from one registered dealer to another registered dealer where the registered dealer making the purchase is acting as principal,

(7) the trade is made by an issuer in

(i) a right granted by the issuer to holders of its securities to purchase additional securities of its own issue, or

[Subpara. (i) am. 1990, c. 25, s. 30(b).]

(ii) a security of a reporting issuer held by the issuer and transferred or issued through the exercise of a right to purchase, convert or exchange previously granted by the issuer,

so long as the issuer gives the superintendent written notice stating the date, amount, nature and conditions of the proposed trade, including the approximate net proceeds to be derived by the issuer on the basis of the additional securities being fully taken up and paid for, and the superintendent

so long as the issuer gives the executive director written notice stating the date, amount, nature and conditions of the proposed trade, including the approximate net proceeds to be derived by the issuer on the basis of the additional securities being fully taken up and paid for, and the executive director

[S. 55(2)*(7)* am. 1995, c. 45, s. 7 (nyif).]

(iii) has not informed the issuer in writing within 10 days of the giving of the notice that he objects to the trade, or

(iv) has withdrawn any objections he has to the proposed trade,

The Superintendent routinely informs the issuer in writing within 10 days of the giving of the notice that he objects to the trade. See BOR 91/5 "Resale of Rights acquired under a Rights Offering" and NIN 90/13 "Rights Offerings".

(8) the trade is in a security of an issuer that is exchanged by or for the account of the issuer with the issuer's security holders, with one or more other issuers or with the security holders of the other issuers in connection with an amalgamation, merger, reorganization or arrangement where

    (i) an information circular in the required form, proxy statement or similar disclosure record in respect of the amalgamation, merger, reorganization or arrangement is prepared and delivered to each of the security holders whose approval of the amalgamation, merger, reorganization or arrangement is required under applicable legislation before it can proceed, and

    (ii) the amalgamation, merger, reorganization or arrangement is approved by the security holders referred to in subparagraph (i) in accordance with the requirements of the applicable legislation,

[S. 55(2)*(8)* re-en. 1992, c. 52, s. 8(a).]

(8) a trade in a security of

    (i) an issuer, in this paragraph called the "first issuer", that is exchanged by or for the account of the first issuer with one or more of

        (A) the first issuer's security holders,

        (B) one or more other issuers, in this paragraph called the "other issuers", and

        (C) the security holders of the other issuers,

    (ii) the first issuer by a holder of that security to one or more of the first issuer and the other issuers, or

    (iii) any of the other issuers by the holder of that security to one or more of the first issuer and the other issuers

in connection with an amalgamation, merger, reorganization or arrangement where

    (iv) an information circular in the required form, proxy statement or similar disclosure record in respect of the amalgamation, merger, reorganization or arrangement is prepared and delivered to each of the security holders whose approval of the amalgamation, merger, reorganization or arrangement is required under applicable legislation before it can proceed, and

    (v) the amalgamation, merger, reorganization or arrangement is approved by the security holders referred to in subparagraph (iv) in accordance with the requirements of the applicable legislation,

[S. 55(2)*(8)* re-en. 1995, c. 45, s. 26 (nyif.).]

> Issuers often desire to rely on this exemption to carry out a reverse takeover as the securities issued under this exemption will not be subject to a hold period or seasoning period if the issuer is an "exchange issuer". However, this exemption may not generally be relied upon to issue securities pursuant to a reverse takeover unless the reverse takeover involves an amalgamation, merger, reorganization or arrangement.

(9) a trade is made by an issuer in a security of its own issue with

    (i) its employee, senior officer or director or an employee, senior officer or director of an affiliate of the issuer so long as that person is not induced to purchase by expectation of employment or continued employment,

    (ii) a trustee on behalf of a person referred to in subparagraph (i), or

    (iii) an issuer all of the voting securities of which are beneficially owned by one or more of the persons referred to in subparagraph (i),

[S. 55(2)*(9)* am. 1989, c. 78, s. 23(b).]

See Local Policy Statement 3-31 "Incentive Options to Directors and Employees – Unlisted Issuers", BOR 90/2 "Trades in Shares Issued in Accordance with the Employee Investment Act".

(10) the trade is made by an issuer in a security under a plan made available by that issuer to the holders of a class of publicly traded securities of the issuer, and which plan

> (i) permits the holder to direct that dividends or interest paid in respect of securities of the issuer's own issue be applied to the purchase from the issuer of

>> (A) publicly traded securities of the issuer's own issue, or

>> (B) other securities of the issuer's own issue not referred to in clause (A) that are redeemable at the option of the holder, and

> (ii) may include an option permitting a holder to purchase by cash payment securities of the issuer referred to in subparagraph (i) so long as the aggregate number of securities issued under the option in any financial year of the issuer does not exceed 2% of the outstanding securities of that class at the commencement of that financial year,

[S. 55(2)*(10)* am. 1992, c. 52, s. 8(b), (c).]

(11) the trade is made by an issuer in a security,

> (i) of its own issue that is distributed by it to its security holders as a stock dividend or other distribution out of earnings or surplus,

> (ii) that is distributed by it to its security holders under a dissolution or winding up of the issuer, or

> (iii) of its own issue that is transferred or issued through the exercise of a right

>> (A) of the holder to purchase, convert or exchange or otherwise acquire, or

>> (B) of the issuer to require the holder to purchase, convert or exchange

>> in accordance with the terms and conditions of a previously issued security of the issuer,

> provided that no commission or other remuneration is paid or given to others in respect of the trade except for administrative or professional services or for services performed by a registered dealer,

[S. 55(2)*(11)* am. 1989, c. 78, s. 23(c) and (d).]

(12) the trade is the transfer of beneficial ownership of a security to a transferee, pledgee, mortgagee or other encumbrancer under a realization on collateral given for a debt,

[S. 55(2)*(12)* re-en. 1988, c. 58, s. 10(a).]

A purchase of a security or a transfer, pledge, mortgage or other encumbrance of a security for the purpose of giving collateral for a debt is specifically excluded from the definition of "trade" in s. 1(1) of the Act.

(13) the trade is made by an issuer in a security of a reporting issuer held by the issuer that is distributed by it to its security holders as a dividend in specie so long as the issuer gives the superintendent written notice stating the date, amount, nature and conditions of the proposed trade and the superintendent

(13) the trade is made by an issuer in a security of a reporting issuer held by the issuer that is distributed by it to its security holders as a dividend in specie

so long as the issuer gives the executive director written notice stating the date, amount, nature and conditions of the proposed trade and the executive director

[S. 55(2)*(13)* am. 1995, c. 45, s. 7 (nyif).]

     (i) has not informed the issuer in writing within 10 days of the giving of the notice that he objects to the trade, or

     (ii) has withdrawn any objection he has to the proposed trade,

(14) the trade is made by an issuer in a security of its own issue where the trade is reasonably necessary to facilitate its incorporation or organization and the security is traded

     (i) for a nominal consideration to not more than 5 incorporators or organizers, or

     (ii) where the law under which the issuer is incorporated or organized requires the trade to be for a greater consideration or to a larger number of incorporators or organizers, for that greater consideration or to that larger number of incorporators or organizers,

(15) the trade is made by

     (i) a person to an underwriter acting as purchaser, or

     (ii) an underwriter to another underwriter,

(16) the trade is made by

     (i) an issuer in a security of its own issue to a promoter of that issuer, or

     (ii) a promoter of an issuer in a security issued by that issuer to another promoter of that issuer,

(17) the trade is in the security of an issuer where each party to the trade is a control person of that issuer,

(18) the trade is made by an issuer in a security of its own issue as consideration for the acquisition of mining, petroleum or natural gas properties or any interest in them so long as the seller of those properties enters into an escrow or pooling agreement in the required form when ordered by

     (i) the superintendent, or

     (ii) a stock exchange in the Province authorized to so order by the superintendent,

(18) the trade is made by an issuer in a security of its own issue as consideration for the acquisition of mining, petroleum or natural gas properties or any interest in them

[Para. *(18)* am. 1990, c. 25, s. 30(c) (nyif).]

No form is specified and no stock exchange has been authorized by the Superintendent. There is an amendment proposed to this section which has not yet been brought into force. See Local Policy Statement 3-07 "Policy Guidelines Respecting Trading Shares, Performance Shares and Other Consideration".

(19) the trade is in a security of a mutual fund to a purchaser, other than the initial trade in a security of the mutual fund to that purchaser, where

     (i) the initial trade in a security of the mutual fund to that purchaser was made under the exemption described in paragraph *(4)*, and

     (ii) either the net asset value or the aggregate acquisition cost, whichever is applicable, of the securities in the mutual fund held by the purchaser as at the date of the trade is not less than a prescribed amount,

The prescribed amount is $100,000; see s. 118(3) of the Regulation.

(20) the trade is made on or through the facilities of a stock exchange recognized by the commission for the purposes of this paragraph where

(i) the trade is effected in whole or part by means of telephone or other telecommunications equipment linking the facilities of that stock exchange with the facilities of another stock exchange recognized by the commission for the purposes of this paragraph, and

(ii) the purchase and sale is effected by or through persons each of whom is registered as a dealer, or in a similar capacity, under the law of a province,

(20) the trade is made on or through the facilities of an exchange recognized by the commission for the purposes of this paragraph where

(i) the trade is effected in whole or part by means of telephone or other telecommunications equipment linking the facilities of that exchange with the facilities of another exchange recognized by the commission for the purposes of this paragraph, and

(ii) the purchase and sale is effected by or through persons each of whom is registered as a dealer, or in a similar capacity, under the law of a province,

[Para. (20) am. 1990, c. 25, s. 30(d), (e) (both nyif).]

(21) [Repealed 1988, c. 58, s. 10(b).]

(22) the trade is made in a security of an offeree issuer to an offeror under a take over bid or issuer bid,

(23) the trade is made to a holder of a security in a mutual fund under provisions in the instrument constituting the mutual fund that permit or require dividends or distributions of income or capital gains attributable to the securities to be reinvested in additional securities of the mutual fund of

(i) the same class of securities, or

(ii) of a class of securities having the same attributes as that class,

so long as no sales or other acquisition charges are levied,

[S. 55(2)(23) am. 1990, c. 25, s. 30(f).]

(24) a trade by an issuer in a security of its own issue to a registered dealer or registered underwriter as consideration for services performed by the registered dealer or registered underwriter in connection with a distribution of securities of the issuer,

[S. 55(2)(24) re-en. 1989, c. 78, s. 23(e).]

This exemption is utilized for the distribution of shares to a registered dealer or registered underwriter paid as a sponsorship fee or corporate finance fee to such dealer or underwriter pursuant to a reverse takeover, even if a financing is not carried out in conjunction with the reverse takeover. See Local Policy Statement 3-21 "Share and Unit Offerings of Unlisted Issuers and Options and Warrants Available to Registrants Participating in Such Offerings", NIN 92/22 "Fiscal Agency Agreements – Request for Comment", NIN 93/18 "Fiscal Agency Agreements – Restrictions on Exemption Orders", and NIN 93/21 "Fiscal Agency Agreements – Applications for Discretionary Exemption Orders".

(25) the trade is made in a security of an offeror that is exchanged by or for the account of the offeror with the security holders of an offeree issuer under a take over bid that under section 80(1)(a), (b), (e) or (f) is exempted from sections 87 to 92,

[S. 55(2)*(25)* am. 1989, c. 78, s. 23(f).]

(26) the trade is made in a security of an offeror that is exchanged by or for the account of the offeror with the security holders of an offeree issuer under a take over bid that under section 80(1)(c) or (d) is exempted from sections 87 to 92,

[S. 55(2)*(26)* am. 1989, c. 78, s. 23(g).]

(27) the trade is made in a security of an offeror under a take over bid or an issuer bid where a securities exchange take over bid circular or securities exchange issuer bid circular in respect of the security was filed by the offeror,

[S. 55(2)*(27)* re-en. 1992, c. 52, s. 8(d).]

(28) the trade is made in a security to the issuer of the security pursuant to the purchase, redemption or acquisition of the security by the issuer, or

[S. 55(2)*(28)* re-en. 1988, c. 58, s. 10(c).]

(28) the trade is made in a security to the issuer of the security pursuant to the purchase, redemption or acquisition of the security by the issuer,

[Para. *(28)* am. 1990, c. 25, s. 30(g) (nyif).]

(28.1) a trade resulting from an unsolicited order placed with an individual who is not a resident of and does not carry on business in the Province, or

[Para. *(28.1)* en. 1990, c. 25, s. 30(g) (nyif).]

(29) the trade is designated by regulation or the trade is within a class of trades designated by regulation.

Section 117 of the Regulation sets out additional classes of trades exempt from requirements of s. 42.

---

(3) Subject to the regulations, for purposes of subsection (2)*(7)* or *(13)*, the superintendent shall not object to the trade unless he considers it in the public interest to do so.

(3) Subject to the regulations, for purposes of subsection (2)*(7)* or *(13)*, the executive director shall not object to the trade unless he considers it in the public interest to do so.

[S. 55(3) am. 1995, c. 45, s. 7 (nyif).]

(4) The superintendent shall not object to a trade referred to in subsection (2)*(7)* or *(13)* without giving the person who filed the written notice an opportunity to be heard.

(4) The executive director shall not object to a trade referred to in subsection (2)*(7)* or *(13)* without giving the person who filed the written notice an opportunity to be heard.

[S. 55(4) am. 1995, c. 45, s. 7 (nyif).]

56. [Repealed 1988, c. 58, s. 11.]

57. [Repealed 1988, c. 58, s. 11.]

Exemption from prospectus requirements

58. (1) Section 42 does not apply to a distribution

(a) of a security described in section 32 excluding paragraph (p),

---

See BOR 90/1 "Trades of Government Warrants".

(b) consisting of options to sell or purchase securities known as "puts" and "calls" which permit the holder of the option to sell or purchase from the writer of the option a specified amount of securities at a specific price, on or before a specified date or the occurrence of a specified event, provided that

    (i) the option has been written by or the performance under the option is guaranteed by a member of a stock exchange recognized by the commission for this purpose,

    (i) the option has been written by or the performance under the option is guaranteed by a member of an exchange recognized by the commission for this purpose,

    (ii) the securities that are the subject of the option are listed and posted for trading on a stock exchange recognized by the commission for this purpose, and

    (ii) the securities that are the subject of the option are listed and posted for trading on an exchange recognized by the commission for this purpose, and

[Subparas. (i) and (ii) am. 1990, c. 25, s. 31(a) (nyif).]

    (iii) the option is in the required form, or

[S. 58(1)(b)(iii) am. 1988, c. 58, s. 12.]

> Form 25 is the required form for a put/option contract and Form 26 is the required form for a call/option contract.

(c) of a security that is

    (i) listed and posted for trading on a stock exchange recognized for purposes of this subsection by the commission, and

    (ii) made on or through the facilities of the stock exchange referred to in subparagraph (i) in accordance with the rules of the stock exchange or the requirements of the commission,

so long as a statement of material facts has been filed as prescribed.

(c) of a security that is

    (i) listed and posted for trading on an exchange recognized for purposes of this subsection by the commission, and

    (ii) made on or through the facilities of the exchange referred to in subparagraph (i) in accordance with the rules of the exchange or the requirements of the commission,

so long as an exchange offering prospectus has been filed as prescribed.

[Para. (c) am. 1990, c. 25, s. 31(a), (b), (c) (all nyif).]

> Form 24 sets out the required form of a statement of material facts and Local Policy Statement 3-26 sets out the procedure for filing a statement of material facts. The Vancouver Stock Exchange has been so recognized; see Local Policy Statement 3-44 "Recognition of Stock Exchanges and Jurisdictions".

(2) Notwithstanding subsection (1)(c), for the purposes of sections 66 and 114,

(a) a distribution referred to in subsection (1)(c) shall be conclusively deemed to be a distribution to which section 42 applies, and

(b) a statement of material facts referred to in subsection (1)(c) shall be conclusively deemed to be a prospectus.

(b) an exchange offering prospectus referred to in subsection (1)(c) shall be conclusively deemed to be a prospectus.

[S. 58 am. 1987, c. 42, s. 96; s. 58(2)(b) am. 1990, c. 25, s. 31(d) (nyif).]

Exemption from prospectus requirements

58. Section 42 does not apply to a distribution

(a) of a security described in section 32(a) to (o), or

(b) consisting of options to sell or purchase securities known as "puts" and "calls" which permit the holder of the option to sell or purchase from the writer of the option a specified amount of securities at a specified price, on or before a specified date or the occurrence of a specified event, provided that

    (i) the option has been written by or the performance under the option is guaranteed by a member of an exchange recognized by the commission for this purpose,

    (ii) the securities that are the subject of the option are listed and posted for trading on an exchange recognized by the commission for this purpose, and

    (iii) the option is in the required form.

[S. 58 re-en. 1992, c. 52, s. 9 (nyif).]

Exemption order by superintendent

59. (1) On application by an interested person or on the commission's or the superintendent's own motion, the commission or the superintendent may, where the commission or the superintendent considers that to do so would not be prejudicial to the public interest, order that

59. (1) On application by an interested person or on the commission's or the executive director's own motion, the commission or the executive director may, where the commission or the executive director considers that to do so would not be prejudicial to the public interest, order that

[S. 59(1) am. 1995, c. 45, s. 7 (nyif).]

(a) a trade, intended trade, security or person or class of trades, intended trades, securities or persons is exempt from one or more of the requirements of Part 7 or the regulations related to Part 7, and

(b) a trade or intended trade or class of trades or intended trades is deemed to be a distribution.

[S. 59(1) re-en. 1992, c. 52, s. 10.]

Refer to NIN 88/5 "Guidelines for Applications to the Securities Commission or Superintendent of Brokers for Decisions or Orders" and Local Policy Statement 3-24 "Statutory Orders and Exemptions made under Sections 33 and 59 of the Securities Act" with respect to the procedure to be followed in making an application for an order under this section. Exemptions are issued by the Superintendent or the Commission in respect of specific applications submitted to them or in respect of certain types of transactions. Rulings regarding certain types of transactions are commonly called blanket orders and are reproduced in this book under the heading "Blanket Orders and Rulings".

(2) On application of an interested person, the commission or the superintendent may determine whether the distribution of a security has been concluded or is currently in progress.

[S. 59(2) am. 1988, c. 58, s. 13(b).]

(2) On application of an interested person, the commission or the executive director may determine whether the distribution of a security has been concluded or is currently in progress.

[S. 59(2) am. 1995, c. 45, s. 7 (nyif).]

Certificates respecting status of reporting issuers

60. (1) On application, the superintendent may issue a certificate that an issuer is a reporting issuer.

60. (1) On application, the executive director may issue a certificate that an issuer is a reporting issuer.

[S. 60(1) am. 1995, c. 45, s. 7 (nyif).]

(2) The commission shall maintain a list of defaulting reporting issuers for public inspection during normal business hours in the commission's offices.

(3) On application, the superintendent may issue a certificate that a reporting issuer is not in default of

(3) On application, the executive director may issue a certificate that a reporting issuer is not in default of

[S. 60(3) am. 1995, c. 45, s. 7 (nyif).]

(a)   filing financial statements required by this Act or the regulations, or

(b)   paying prescribed fees and charges.

[S. 60(3) re-en. 1992, c. 52, s. 11(a).]

See NIN 94/27 "New Form of Certificate Under Section 60(3) of the Securities Act".

(4) A person

(a)   may rely on a certificate issued under subsection (1) to determine that an issuer is a reporting issuer, and

(b)   subject to subsection (5), may rely on the list maintained under subsection (2) or a certificate issued under subsection (3) to determine that a reporting issuer is not in default of filing financial statements required by this Act or the regulations or paying prescribed fees and charges.

[Para. (b) am. 1992, c. 52, s. 11(b).]

(5) Subsection 4(b) does not apply to a person that knows or reasonably ought to know that a reporting issuer that is not named in the list maintained under subsection (2) or that is named in a certificate issued under subsection (3), as the case may be, is in default of filing financial statements required by this Act or the regulations or paying prescribed fees and charges.

[S. 60 re-en. 1989, c. 78, s. 24; s. 60(5) am. 1992, c. 52, s. 11(b).]

PART 9

CIRCULATION OF MATERIALS

Waiting period

61. (1) In this section "waiting period" means the interval between the issue of a receipt by the superintendent for a preliminary prospectus and the issue of a receipt by him for the prospectus in respect of the same distribution.

61. (1) In this section "waiting period" means the interval between the issue of a receipt by the executive director for a preliminary prospectus and the issue of a receipt by him for the prospectus in respect of the same distribution.

[S. 61(1) am. 1995, c. 45, s. 7 (nyif).]

(2) Notwithstanding section 42, but subject to Part 6, during the waiting period for distribution of a security, a dealer or the issuer of the security may

(a) communicate with a person

   (i) identifying the security proposed to be distributed,

   (ii) stating the price of the security, if determined,

   (iii) stating the name and address of a person from whom purchases of the security may be made, and

   (iv) stating further information permitted or required by the regulations,

   so long as the dealer or issuer states the name and address of a person from whom a preliminary prospectus may be obtained,

(b) give out a preliminary prospectus, and

(c) solicit expressions of interest from a prospective purchaser so long as before the solicitation, or as soon as practicable after the prospective purchaser indicates an interest in purchasing the security, a copy of the preliminary prospectus is sent to him.

> Refer to Local Policy Statement 3-39 "Guidelines for Advertising Issues of Securities and for Promotional Activities during the Course of a Distribution" and Uniform Act Policy 2-13 "Advertising During Waiting Period Between Preliminary and Final Prospectuses" with respect to advertising that may be carried out during the waiting period.

Distribution of preliminary prospectus

62. Where a dealer or an issuer takes any action under section 61, he shall send a copy of the preliminary prospectus to each person who, without solicitation, indicates an interest in purchasing the security and requests a copy of the preliminary prospectus.

> The preliminary prospectus is filed by Commission staff in the company's public file.

Distribution list

63. Where a dealer or an issuer takes any action under section 61, he shall maintain a record of the names and addresses of all persons to whom the preliminary prospectus has been sent.

Defective preliminary prospectus

64. Where the superintendent considers that a preliminary prospectus does not substantially comply with section 44(1), he may, without giving notice, order that trading which is permitted by section 61(2) in the security to which the preliminary prospectus relates cease until a revised preliminary prospectus satisfactory to the superintendent is filed and sent to each recipient of the defective preliminary prospectus according to the record maintained in section 63.

64. Where the executive director considers that a preliminary prospectus does not substantially comply with section 44(1), he may, without giving notice, order that trading which is permitted by section 61(2) in the security to which the preliminary prospectus relates cease until a revised preliminary prospectus satisfactory to the executive director is filed and sent to each recipient of the defective preliminary prospectus according to the record maintained in section 63.

[S. 64 am. 1995, c. 45, s. 7 (nyif).]

Material given on distribution

65. From the date of issue of a receipt for a prospectus relating to a security, a person distributing the security may give out

(a) the prospectus,

(b) any record filed with or referred to in the prospectus, and

(c) any record used in section 61(2)(a).

Obligation to send prospectus

66. (1) A dealer, not acting as agent of the purchaser, who receives an order or subscription for a security offered in a distribution to which section 42 applies shall send to the purchaser

(a) before entering into the written confirmation of the sale agreement resulting from the order or subscription, or

(b) not later than midnight on the second business day after entering into the agreement,

the latest prospectus filed respecting the security.

66. (1) A dealer, not acting as agent of the purchaser, who receives an order or subscription for a security offered in a distribution to which section 42 applies must send to the purchaser

(a) before entering into the written confirmation of the agreement of purchase and sale resulting from the order or subscription, or

(b) not later than midnight on the second business day after entering into the agreement,

the latest prospectus filed or required to be filed, with respect to the security, and any amendment to that prospectus, filed or required to be filed, under this Act.

[S. 66(1) re-en. 1995, c. 45, s. 27 (nyif).]

(2) Notwithstanding subsection (1), a dealer shall not be required to send an amendment to a prospectus to a purchaser where the agreement of purchase and sale of the security has been entered into before filing the amendment.

(2) Despite subsection (1), a dealer is not required to send an amendment to a prospectus to a purchaser if the agreement of purchase and sale of the security has been entered into before the obligation to file the amendment arises under section 48.

[S. 66(2) re-en. 1995, c. 45, s. 27 (nyif).]

(3) A sale agreement referred to in subsection (1) is not binding on the purchaser if the dealer from whom the purchaser purchases the security receives, not later than 2 business days after receipt by the purchaser of the latest prospectus that the purchaser is entitled to receive under this Act, written notice evidencing the intention of the purchaser not to be bound by the agreement.

[S. 66(3) am. 1992, c. 52, s. 12.]

(3) An agreement of purchase and sale referred to in subsection (1) is not binding on the purchaser if the dealer from whom the purchaser purchases the security receives, not later than 2 business days after receipt by the purchaser of the latest prospectus, and any amendment to the prospectus, that the purchaser is entitled to receive under this Act, written notice sent by the purchaser, evidencing the intention of the purchaser not to be bound by the agreement.

[S. 66(3) re-en. 1995, c. 45, s. 27 (nyif).]

(4) Subsection (3) does not apply if the purchaser

(a) is a registrant, or

(b) disposes of the beneficial ownership of the security referred to in subsection (3), otherwise than to secure indebtedness, before the expiration of the time referred to in subsection (3).

(5) For the purposes of this section, subject to subsection (7), receipt of the latest prospectus by a dealer who

(a) is acting as agent of, or

(b) after receipt commences to act as agent of,

the purchaser with respect to the purchase of a security referred to in subsection (1) is deemed to be receipt by the purchaser on the date on which the dealer received the prospectus.

(5) For the purposes of this section, subject to subsection (7), receipt of the latest prospectus, and any amendment to the prospectus, that the purchaser is entitled to receive under this Act, by a dealer who

(a) is acting as agent of the purchaser, or

(b) after receipt commences to act as agent of the purchaser,

with respect to the purchase of a security referred to in subsection (1), is deemed to be receipt by the purchaser on the date on which the dealer received the prospectus and any amendment to that prospectus.

[S. 66(5) re-en. 1995, c. 45, s. 27 (nyif).]

(6) For the purposes of this section, receipt of the notice referred to in subsection (3) by a dealer who acted as agent of the seller with respect to the sale of the security referred to in subsection (1) is deemed to be receipt by the seller on the date on which the dealer received the notice.

(7) For the purposes of this section, a dealer does not act as agent of the purchaser unless he is acting solely as agent of the purchaser with respect to the sale in question and has not received and has no agreement to receive compensation from or on behalf of the seller with respect to that sale.

(8) The onus of providing that the time for giving notice under subsection (3) has expired is on the dealer from whom the purchaser has agreed to purchase the security.

(9) Where the issuer acts as his own dealer in respect of a trade, this section applies to the issuer as if he were a dealer.

Applies to a statement of material facts; see s. 58(2)(b) of the Act.

Exemption order by commission or executive director

66.1 On application by an interested person or on the commission's or the executive director's own motion, the commission or the executive director, if the commission or the executive director considers that to do so would not be prejudicial to the public interest, may order that a person or class of persons is exempt from one or more of the requirements of this Part or of the regulations relating to this Part.

[S. 66.1 en. 1995, c. 45, s. 28 (nyif).]

PART 10

CONTINUOUS DISCLOSURE

See National Policy Statement 49 "Self Regulatory Organization Membership".

Publication of material change

67. (1) Where a material change occurs in the affairs of a reporting issuer, the reporting issuer shall

(a) as soon as practicable issue and file a press release that is authorized by a senior officer and that discloses the nature and substance of the change, and

(b) file a required report, as soon as practicable, but in any event no later than 10 days after the date on which the change occurs.

Form 27 is the required form. See s. 144 of the Regulation with respect to further filing procedures, National Policy Statement 40 "Timely Disclosure", and NIN 89/35 "Disclosure of Promotional or Investor Relations Arrangements".

---

(2) Subsection (1) does not apply to a reporting issuer which immediately files the report required under subsection (1)(b) marked "confidential" together with written reasons why there should not be a press release under subsection (1)(a) so long as

(a) in the opinion of the reporting issuer, the disclosure required by subsection (1) would be unduly detrimental to its interests, or

(b) the material change in the affairs of the reporting issuer

(i) consists of a decision to implement a change made by senior management of the issuer who believe that confirmation of the decision by the directors is probable, and

(ii) senior management of the issuer has no reason to believe that persons with knowledge of the material change have made use of that knowledge in purchasing or selling securities of the issuer.

The Superintendent takes the position that he may require disclosure of a confidential material change even if, in the opinion of the reporting issuer, the disclosure would be unduly detrimental to its interest.

---

(3) Where a report has been filed under subsection (2), the reporting issuer shall advise the commission in writing, within 10 days of the date of filing the initial report and every 10 days after that, that it believes the report should continue to remain confidential until

(a) the material change is generally disclosed in the manner referred to in subsection (1)(a), or

(b) if the material change consists of a decision of the type referred to in subsection (2)(b), that decision has been rejected by the directors of the issuer.

Re Harry Claude Faulkner (1994), 4 C.C.L.S. 192 (B.C. Sec. Comm.).

Unauthorized payments by a company to its management company which were the company's most significant financial activities and would reasonably have been expected to have a significant effect on the market price of the company's shares will be considered to be a material change under s. 67(1) of the Act.

Pezim v. British Columbia (Superintendent of Brokers) (1992), 66 B.C.L.R. (2d) 257, (sub nom. *Pezim v. British Columbia Securities Commission*) 96 D.L.R. (4th) 137, 13 B.C.A.C. 1, 24 W.A.C. 1, reversed [1994] 2 S.C.R. 557, 4 C.C.L.S. 117, [1994] 7 W.W.R. 1, 92 B.C.L.R. (2d) 145, 14 B.L.R. (2d) 217, 22 Admin. L.R. (2d) 1, 114 D.L.R. (4th) 385, 168 N.R. 321, 46 B.C.A.C. 1, 75 W.A.C. 1.

In this case, the Commission concluded that the respondents had contravened s. 67 of the Act by failing to disclose "material changes" with respect to assay results of a drilling program in the Eskay Creek area of northwestern British Columbia. The Court of Appeal took an extremely narrow approach as to what constituted a "material change" in allowing the appeal and setting aside the orders of the Commission. The Supreme Court of Canada allowed the appeal, set aside the judgment of the Court of Appeal and substituted therefore the findings and orders of the Commission.

The Supreme Court of Canada stated that the determination of what constitutes a "material change" for the purposes of general disclosure under s. 67 of the Act is a matter which falls squarely within the regulatory mandate and expertise of the Commission. In order for a change to be a "material change", it must be:

(a) "in relation to the affairs of the issuer";

(b) "in the business, operations, assets or ownership of the issuer"; and

(c) "material, i.e., would reasonably be expected to have a significant effect on the market price or value of the securities of the issuer".

Not all changes are material changes. The determination of what information should be disclosed is an issue which goes to the heart of the regulatory expertise and mandate of the Commission, i.e., regulating the securities market in the public interest. The timeliness of disclosure required by material changes being disclosed to the public "as soon as practicable" falls within the Commission's regulatory jurisdiction.

Although the duty to inquire is not expressly stated in s. 67 of the Act, such an interpretation contextualizes the general obligation to disclose material changes and guarantees the fairness of the market, which is the underlying goal of the Act. Such a duty is not incompatible with the insider trading provisions of s. 68 of the Act. If an issuer wishes to engage in a securities transaction, its directors must inquire about all material changes in the issuer's affairs. Consequently, the directors will have, at one point in time, knowledge of undisclosed material facts and material changes which constitute inside information. However, as long as the material facts and material changes are adequately disclosed prior to the transaction, there will be no possibility of insider trading. The erecting of a Chinese wall, which prevents directors of a company from having inside information, does not erase the duty imposed on directors to inquire about material changes, as the disclosure requirement under s. 67 is on the issuer.

Trading or informing where undisclosed change

68. (1) No person that

(a) is in a special relationship with a reporting issuer, and

(b) knows of a material fact or material change with respect to that reporting issuer, which material fact or material change has not been generally disclosed,

shall purchase or sell

(c) securities of that reporting issuer,

(d) a put, a call, an option or another right or obligation to purchase or sell securities of the reporting issuer, or

(e) a security, the market price of which varies materially with the market price of any securities of the reporting issuer.

(2) No reporting issuer and no person in a special relationship with a reporting issuer shall inform another person of a material fact or material change with respect to the reporting issuer before the material fact or material change has been generally disclosed, unless giving the information is necessary in the course of business of the reporting issuer or of the person in the special relationship with the reporting issuer.

(3) No person that proposes to

(a) make a take over bid, as defined in section 74, for the securities of a reporting issuer,

(b) become a party to a reorganization, amalgamation, merger, arrangement or similar business combination with a reporting issuer, or

(c) acquire a substantial portion of the property of a reporting issuer

shall inform another person of a material fact or material change with respect to the reporting issuer before the material fact or material change has been generally disclosed, unless giving the information is necessary to effect the take over bid, business combination or acquisition, as the case may be.

(4) A person does not contravene subsection (1), (2) or (3) if the person proves on the balance of probabilities that at the time of the purchase or sale referred to in subsection (1) or at the time of giving the information under subsection (2) or (3), as

the case may be, the person reasonably believed that the material fact or material change had been generally disclosed.

[S. 68 re-en. 1989, c. 78, s. 25.]

See s. 3 of the Act for the definition of a person in a special relationship with a reporting issuer. See s. 152.3 of the Regulation with respect to defences to an action originating under this section.

Re Harry Claude Faulkner (1994), 4 C.C.L.S. 192 (B.C. Sec. Comm.).

Faulkner, a director of International Shasta Resources Ltd. and the person responsible for managing Shasta's day-to-day affairs, was found to have contravened s. 68(1) of the Act. Over a 17-month period, Faulkner actively purchased and sold Shasta shares when he had knowledge of undisclosed payments made by Shasta to him and his company. The Commission found that the payments were undisclosed material changes.

Re Aatra Resources Ltd., Victor J. Meunier, Paul A. Quinn, Ralph A.A. Simpson, Joel Machtinger, Henry P.M. Huber, Alex Pancer, David J. Foster and Durham Securities Corp. Ltd. (1993), 3 C.C.L.S. 51 (B.C. Sec. Comm.).

The defendant, Huber was engaged in business activities with Aatra Resources Ltd., namely acting as agent on its public offering. He also knew that a third party was attempting to corner the market for the securities of Aatra. The Commission determined that this fact could certainly be expected to significantly affect the market price of Aatra's shares. While Huber had this knowledge, he sold 40,000 Aatra shares from his own and his family's accounts. The Commission found that in selling these shares Huber contravened s. 68 of the Act.

Bennett v. British Columbia Securities Commission (1991), 82 D.L.R. (4th) 129, affirmed 69 B.C.L.R. (2d) 171, [1992] 5 W.W.R. 481, 94 D.L.R. (4th) 339, 18 B.C.A.C. 191, 31 W.A.C. 191, leave to appeal to S.C.C. refused [1992] 6 W.W.R. lvii, 70 B.C.L.R. (2d) xxxii, 143 N.R. 396, 20 B.C.A.C. 80, 35 W.A.C. 80, 97 D.L.R. (4th) vii.

The petitioners made an application to have the Securities Commission prohibited from holding a hearing into alleged insider trading in the shares of Doman Industries Ltd. by arguing that s. 68 of the Securities Act is *ultra vires* the province.

Section 68 of the Securities Act is central to the entire role of the Commission, as well as the Act itself. The aim and purpose of s. 68 is clearly to lay down specific ethical standards for those engaged in the trading of the securities of reporting issuers and for those individuals in a special relationship with a reporting issuer. It is to promote a level playing field for those engaged in the buying and selling of shares. The Securities Act is concerned in pith and substance with the conduct of trading from an ethical and not a mechanical point of view. Those are the "dominant aspects" of the Act in general and s. 68 in particular.

Any overlap or encroachment of British Columbia into this sphere of federal powers, under either interprovincial/international trade and commerce under s. 91(2) or interprovincial works or undertakings under s. 92(10)(a), is merely incidental to the ethical regulation that is the pith and substance of s. 68. The overall aim of the Securities Act is to regulate the trading of securities in the province.

Bennett v. British Columbia (Securities Commission) (1992), 69 B.C.L.R. (2d) 171, [1992] 5 W.W.R. 481, 94 D.L.R. (4th) 339, 18 B.C.A.C. 191, 18 W.A.C. 191, affirming (1991), 82 D.L.R. (4th) 129, leave to appeal to S.C.C. refused [1992] 6 W.W.R. lvii, 70 B.C.L.R. (2d) xxxii, 143 N.R. 396, 20 B.C.A.C. 80, 35 W.A.C. 80, 97 D.L.R. (4th) vii.

The decision of the B.C.S.C. was upheld by the B.C.C.A. which concluded that the Securities Act and, more particularly, section 68 are within the legislative competence of the Province of British Columbia.

Leave to appeal to the Supreme Court of Canada was refused on August 27, 1992.

Re Greenwell Resources Corp. and Harold Dale Baker and Thomas Rodney Irving,
[1989] 125 B.C.S.C. Weekly Summary (B.C. Sec. Comm.).

Section 68(1) is one of the key provisions of the Act. It is intended to make the market operate more fairly by prohibiting trading in securities by certain persons having possession of certain information that has not been disclosed to the public.

69. [Repealed 1989, c. 78, s. 25.]

Interpretation

69.1 For the purpose of reporting under section 70,

(a) ownership passes when

(i) an offer to sell is accepted by the purchaser or the purchaser's agent, or

(ii) an offer to buy is accepted by the seller or the seller's agent, and

(b) a security or class of securities, including a put, call option or other right or obligation to purchase or sell securities of a reporting issuer, must be reported as prescribed in the regulations.

[S. 69.1 en. 1995, c. 45, s. 29 (nyif).]

Insider reports

70. (1) In this section "reporting issuer" does not include a mutual fund.

(2) A person who is an insider of a reporting issuer shall, within 10 days of becoming an insider, file an insider report in the required form effective the date on which he became an insider, disclosing any direct or indirect beneficial ownership of, or control or direction over, securities of the reporting issuer.

The required form is Form 36. See BOR 88/6 "Filing of Insider Reports by Control Persons". Refer also to NIN 95/14 "Amendments to the Insider Report Form (Form 36)". These amendments were effective April 17, 1995.

(3) Where a person who is an insider of a reporting issuer does not have any direct or indirect beneficial ownership of, or control or direction over, securities of the reporting issuer, the person is not required to file a report under subsection (2) merely to state that fact.

(4) Where a person

(a) has filed or is required to file an insider report under subsection (2) or under a former enactment, and

(b) whose direct or indirect beneficial ownership of, or control or direction over, securities of the reporting issuer changes from that shown or required to be shown in the latest insider report filed by him,

he shall, within 10 days after the end of the month in which the change takes place, file an insider report in the required form disclosing

(c) his direct or indirect beneficial ownership of, or control or direction over, securities of the reporting issuer at the end of that month, and

[S. 70 (4)(c) am. 1992, c. 52, s. 13.]

(d) the change or changes in his ownership in securities of the reporting issuer that occurred during the month

so long as he was an insider of the reporting issuer at any time that month.

See NIN 95/14 "Amendments to the Insider Report Form (Form 36)". These amendments were effective April 17, 1995.

(5) Where a director or senior officer

(a) of an issuer is deemed under section 2(2) to have been an insider of a reporting issuer, or

(b) of a reporting issuer is deemed under section 2(3) to have been an insider of another reporting issuer,

then within 10 days after the date on which that deeming occurs, that director or senior officer shall file the insider reports referred to in subsections (2) and (4), for the period for which the director or senior officer is deemed to have been an insider.

[S. 70(5) re-en. 1989, c. 78, s. 26.]

The required form is Form 36. See NIN 95/15 "Disclosure of Securities under 'Control or Direction' " for guidance as to the meaning of the phrase "control or direction".

See the annotations under s. 1(1) "insider", and Uniform Act Policy 2-09 "Insider Trading Reports – Loan and Trust Companies", Uniform Act Policy 2-10 "Insider Trading Reports – Persons Required to Report in More Than One Capacity", BOR 88/6 "Filing of Insider Reports by Control Persons", BOR 91/7 "Multijurisdictional Disclosure System", and NIN 91/19 "New Computer System for Insider Reports". See also ss. 148 to 152.2 of the Regulation with respect to insider trading reports.

Re Seven Mile High Group Inc. and Maurice Hamelin and Craig Harrison, [1991] 47 B.C.S.C. Weekly Summary 7 (B.C. Sec. Comm.).

The information provided by insider reports is important market information, as it discloses to market participants the trading activities of the persons most closely connected to, and therefore in a position to be most knowledgeable about, a reporting issuer. Timely reporting is particularly important where, as in this case, the insider is an active trader.

Report of a transfer

71. Where voting securities are registered in the name of a person other than the beneficial owner and the person knows that

(a) the securities are beneficially owned by an insider, and

(b) the insider has failed to file an insider report as required by section 70,

that person shall file a report of the transfer in the required form, unless the transfer to the person was for the purpose of giving collateral for a bona fide debt.

[S. 71 repealed 1995, c. 45, s. 30 (nyif).]

The required form is Form 38.

Order relieving reporting issuer

72. Where the commission considers that it would not be prejudicial to the public interest to do so, it may, on the application of a reporting issuer, order that the reporting issuer is deemed to have ceased to be a reporting issuer.

See Local Policy Statement 3-34 "Application for Non-reporting Status", NIN 88/5 "Guidelines for Applications to the Securities Commission or the Superintendent of Brokers for Decisions or Orders", and Canadian Securities Administrators Notice 92/2 "Applications for Discretionary Orders".

Halt trading order

73. (1) Where

(a) the commission or the superintendent

(a) the commission or the executive director

[Para. (a) am. 1995, c. 45, s. 7 (nyif).]

    (i) considers that there are unexplained and unusual fluctuations in the volume of trading in, or market price of, a security,

    (i) considers that there are unexplained and unusual fluctuations in the volume of trading in, or market price of, a security or exchange contract,

    (ii) becomes aware of information, other than information filed under this Act, which when disclosed to the public may cause or is likely to cause unusual fluctuations in the volume of trading in, or market price of, a security,

    (ii) becomes aware of information, other than information filed under this Act, which when disclosed to the public may cause or is likely to cause unusual fluctuations in the volume of trading in, or market price of, a security or exchange contract,

    (iii) considers that there may have been a material change in the business or operations of an issuer that, when disclosed, could significantly affect the market price of a security issued by it, or

    (iv) considers that circumstances exist or are about to occur that could result in other than an orderly trading of a security, and

    (iv) considers that circumstances exist or are about to occur that could result in other than an orderly trading of a security or exchange contract, and

[Subparas. (i), (ii) and (iv) am. 1990, c. 25, s. 32(a) (nyif).]

(b) the commission or the superintendent considers it to be in the public interest,

(b) the commission or the executive director considers it to be in the public interest,

[Para. (b) am. 1995, c. 45, s. 7 (nyif).]

it or he may, without a hearing, order that all trading in that security be halted for a specified period, not to exceed 3 business days.

it or he may, without a hearing, order that all trading in that security or exchange contract be halted for a specified period, not to exceed 3 business days.

[S. 73(1) am. 1990, c. 25, s. 32(b) (nyif).]

(2) Notice of every order made under subsection (1) shall be sent immediately to the issuer whose securities are affected by it.

(3) Where a security affected by an order made under subsection (1) is listed and posted for trading on a stock exchange in the Province, the commission or superintendent shall immediately advise the stock exchange of the order, by sending a notice by electronic means that produce a printed copy, and, in that event, the order becomes effective, for all purposes and in respect of all persons, as soon as the stock exchange is advised.

(3) Where

(a) a security affected by an order made under subsection (1) is listed and posted for trading on an exchange in the Province, or

(b) an exchange contract affected by an order made under subsection (1) is traded on an exchange in the Province,

the commission or superintendent shall immediately advise the exchange of the order, by sending a notice by electronic means that produce a printed copy, and, in that event, the order becomes effective, for all purposes and in respect of all persons, as soon as the exchange is advised.

[S. 73(3) re-en. 1990, c. 25, s. 32(c) (nyif).]

(3) Where

(a) a security affected by an order made under subsection (1) is listed and posted for trading on an exchange in the Province, or

(b) an exchange contract affected by an order made under subsection (1) is traded on an exchange in the Province,

the commission or executive director must immediately send written notice of the order to the exchange, and the order becomes effective, for all purposes and in respect of all persons, as soon as the exchange receives the notice.

[S. 73(3) re-en. 1995, c. 45, s. 31 (nyif).]

Personal information form

73.1 The commission or the superintendent may require the directors, officers, promoters or control persons of an issuer or a class of issuers, within the time it or he specifies, to file personal information in the required form.

[S. 73.1 en. 1988, c. 58, s. 14.]

73.1 The commission or the executive director may require the directors, officers, promoters or control persons of an issuer or a class of issuers, within the time it or he specifies, to file personal information in the required form.

[S. 73.1 am. 1995, c. 45, s. 7 (nyif).]

The required form, Form 4B, is set out in NIN 92/18 "Required Form of Personal Information". The Commission and the superintendent do not currently place Form 4Bs in the issuer's public file.

Exemption order by commission or superintendent

73.2 On application by an interested person or on the commission's or the superintendent's own motion, the commission or the superintendent may order that a person or class of persons is exempt from one or more of the requirements of this Part or the regulations related to this Part where

(a) the requirement in respect of which an exemption is to be granted conflicts with a similar requirement of the law of the jurisdiction in which the reporting issuer is incorporated, organized or continued, or

(b) the commission or the superintendent considers that to do so would not be prejudicial to the public interest.

[S. 73.2 en. 1992, c. 52, s. 14 (nyif).]

Exemption order by commission or executive director

73.2 On application by an interested person or on the commission's or the executive director's own motion, the commission or the executive director may order that a person or class of persons is exempt from one or more of the requirements of this Part or the regulations related to this Part where

(a) the requirement in respect of which an exemption is to be granted conflicts with a similar requirement of the law of the jurisdiction in which the reporting issuer is incorporated, organized or continued, or

(b) the commission or the executive director considers that to do so would not be prejudicial to the public interest.

[S. 73.2 am. 1995, c. 45, s. 32 (nyif).]

PART 11

TAKE OVER BIDS AND ISSUER BIDS

[Part 11 re-en. 1989, c. 78, s. 27.]

Re Beringer Properties Inc., Beringer Acquisitions Ltd., Parallel Research Inc., Sean Francis Kehoe, James Morris Durward and Trian Equities Ltd., [1993] 18 B.C.S.C. Weekly Summary 18 (B.C. Sec. Comm.).

Part 11 of the Act provides for a comprehensive code of conduct for all parties involved in a take over bid. The purpose of the take over legislation is to ensure the protection of the *bona fide* interests of the shareholders of target companies. One of the ways this purpose is achieved is by establishing regulatory requirements so that shareholders of a target company receive any information which would reasonably be expected to affect their decision to accept or reject the take over bid.

Division 1 — Interpretation

Interpretation

74. (1) In this Part

"equity security" means any security of an issuer that carries a residual right to participate in the earnings of the issuer and, upon the liquidation or winding up of the issuer, in its assets;

"formal bid" means

(a) a take over bid or an issuer bid to which section 87 applies, or

(b) a take over bid that is exempted from sections 87 to 92 or an issuer bid that is exempted from sections 87 to 90 and 92

(i) by reason of an exemption under section 80(1)(a) or 81(e), if the offeror is required to deliver to every holder in the Province of securities subject to the bid a disclosure document of the type contemplated by section 115(12), or

(ii) by reason of an exemption under section 80(1)(e) or 81(h), if the offeror is required to deliver disclosure material relating to the bid to holders of the class of securities subject to the bid;

"issuer bid" means an offer to acquire or redeem securities of an issuer made by the issuer to any person who is in the Province or to any holder in the Province of securities of the issuer and includes a purchase, redemption or other acquisition of securities of the issuer by the issuer from any such person, but does not include an offer to acquire or redeem debt securities that are not convertible into securities other than debt securities;

"offer to acquire" includes

(a)　an offer to purchase, or a solicitation of an offer to sell, securities, or

(b)　an acceptance of an offer to sell securities, whether or not such offer to sell has been solicited,

or any combination thereof, and the person accepting an offer to sell shall be deemed to be making an offer to acquire to the person that made the offer to sell;

"offeree issuer" means an issuer whose securities are the subject of a take over bid, an issuer bid or an offer to acquire;

"offeror" means a person who makes a take over bid, issuer bid or offer to acquire and, for the purposes of section 93, includes a person who acquires a security, whether or not by way of a take over bid, issuer bid or offer to acquire;

"offeror's securities" means securities of an offeree issuer beneficially owned, or over which control or direction is exercised, on the date of an offer to acquire, by an offeror or any person acting jointly or in concert with the offeror;

"published market" means, as to any class of securities, any market on which the securities are traded, if the prices at which they have been traded on that market are regularly published in a bona fide newspaper or business or financial publication of general and regular paid circulation;

"take over bid" means an offer to acquire outstanding voting or equity securities of a class made to any person who is in the Province or to any holder in the Province of securities subject to the offer to acquire, where the securities subject to the offer to acquire, together with the offeror's securities, constitute in the aggregate 20% or more of the outstanding securities of that class of securities at the date of the offer to acquire.

With respect to take over bids, see National Policy Statement 37 "Take Over Bids: Reciprocal Cease Trading Orders".

---

(2) In sections 96 and 97 "interested person" means

(a)　an offeree issuer,

(b)　a security holder, director or officer of an offeree issuer,

(c)　an offeror,

(d)　the superintendent, and

(d)　the executive director, and

[Para. (d) am. 1995, c. 45, s. 7 (nyif).]

(e)　any person not referred to in subsections (a) to (d) who in the opinion of the commission or the Supreme Court, as the case may be, is a proper person to make an application under section 96 or 97, as the case may be.

Computation of time; expiry of bid

75. For the purposes of this Part,

(a)　a period of days shall be computed as commencing on the day next following the event which began the period and terminating at midnight on the last day of the period, except that if the last day of the period does not fall on a business day, the period terminates at midnight on the next business day, and

(b)　a take over bid or an issuer bid expires at the later of

(i)　the end of the period, including any extension, during which securities may be deposited pursuant to the bid, and

(ii)　the time at which the offeror becomes obligated by the terms of the bid to take up or reject securities deposited thereunder.

Convertible securities

76. For the purposes of this Part,

(a) a security shall be deemed to be convertible into a security of another class if, whether or not on conditions, it is or may be convertible into or exchangeable for, or if it carries the right or obligation to acquire, a security of the other class, whether of the same or another issuer, and

(b) a security that is convertible into a security of another class shall be deemed to be convertible into a security or securities of each class into which the second mentioned security may be converted, either directly or through securities of one or more other classes of securities that are themselves convertible.

Deemed beneficial ownership

77. (1) For the purposes of this Part, in determining the beneficial ownership of securities of an offeror or of any person acting jointly or in concert with the offeror, at any given date, the offeror or the person shall be deemed to have acquired and be the beneficial owner of a security, including an unissued security, if the offeror or the person

(a) is the beneficial owner of any security convertible within 60 days following such date into the security, or

(b) has the right or obligation, whether or not on conditions, to acquire within 60 days following such date beneficial ownership of the security whether through the exercise of an option, warrant, right or subscription privilege or otherwise.

(2) Where 2 or more offerors acting jointly or in concert make one or more offers to acquire securities of a class, the securities subject to any such offer or offers to acquire shall be deemed to be securities subject to the offer to acquire of each such offeror for the purpose of determining whether any such offeror is making a take over bid.

(3) Where an offeror or any person acting jointly or in concert with the offeror is deemed because of subsection (1) to be the beneficial owner of unissued securities, the securities shall be deemed to be outstanding for the purpose of calculating the number of outstanding securities of that class in respect of that offeror's offer to acquire.

Acting jointly or in concert

78. (1) For the purposes of this Part, it is a question of fact as to whether a person is acting jointly or in concert with an offeror and, without limiting the generality of the foregoing, the following shall be presumed to be acting jointly or in concert with an offeror:

(a) every person who, as a result of any agreement, commitment or understanding, whether formal or informal, with the offeror or with any other person acting jointly or in concert with the offeror, acquires or offers to acquire securities of the issuer of the same class as those subject to the offer to acquire;

(b) every person who, as a result of any agreement, commitment or understanding, whether formal or informal, with the offeror or with any other person acting jointly or in concert with the offeror, intends to exercise jointly or in concert with the offeror or with any other person acting jointly or in concert with the offeror any voting rights attaching to any securities of the offeree issuer;

(c) every associate or affiliate of the offeror.

(2) Notwithstanding subsection (1), a registered dealer acting solely in an agency capacity for the offeror in connection with a take over bid or an issuer bid and not executing principal transactions for its own account in the class of securities subject to the offer to acquire or performing services beyond customary dealer's functions shall not be presumed solely by reason of such agency relationship to be acting jointly or in concert with the offeror in connection with the bid.

Re Frank Herbert Mirgon and Annie Mirgon, [1991] 9 B.C.S.C. Weekly Summary (Statement of Facts and Undertaking).

Under s. 78 of the Act, there is a rebuttable presumption that the spouse of an offeror acts jointly or in concert with the offeror for the purposes of Pt. 11 of the Act.

Re Eugenio Sirianni and Francesco Sirianni and Montreux Development Corp., [1991] 40 B.C.S.C. Weekly Summary 7 (B.C. Sec. Comm.).

In the context of a take over bid or an issuer bid, s. 78 of the Act states that it is a question of fact whether a person is acting jointly or in concert with an offeror and, without limiting the generality of the foregoing, a person is presumed to be acting jointly or in concert with an offeror where there is an agreement, commitment or understanding, whether formal or informal, with the offeror. In this decision the Commission looked at a number of factors including the fact that they were brothers, the time of their respective involvement, the parties with whom they dealt and how intertwined their activities were to decide that the Siriannis were acting jointly or in concert.

Trian Equities Ltd. v. Beringer Acquisitions Ltd. (December 24, 1992), Vancouver Doc. A910605, Trainor J., [1993] B.C.W.L.D. 483 (S.C.) (not yet reported).

Trian petitioned the court for an order under the Securities Act that Beringer Acquisitions Ltd., Beringer Properties Inc., Sean Kehoe and James Durward contravened the provisions of the Securities Act in making a take over bid for the common shares of Trian. One of the issues to be considered was whether all of the respondents were proper parties to the proceeding. Beringer Acquisition Ltd. and Beringer Properties Inc. have registered offices at the same address and have the same President and Director, Sean Kehoe, who was also the sole shareholder of Beringer Acquisitions Ltd. James Durward conceived of the idea of a take over bid and prepared the bid documents. If the bid were successful, Durward, as compensation, would have a right to exercise an option to acquire a 50% interest in certain of the common shares of Beringer Acquisitions Ltd. which would have given him a 50% voting interest.

The court held that the Securities Act does not limit or restrict the proper parties to the nominal offeror (the person who makes a take over bid, in this case Beringer Acquisitions Ltd.) but looks to the persons found to be acting jointly or in concert with an offeror as a result of s. 78(1) of the Securities Act. This decision is a question of fact. Trainor J. found all the respondents to be proper parties to the proceedings based on the particular facts of the case.

Application to direct and indirect offers

79. For the purposes of this Part, a reference to an offer to acquire or to the acquisition or ownership of securities or to control or direction over securities shall be construed to include a direct or indirect offer to acquire or the direct or indirect acquisition or ownership of securities, or the direct or indirect acquisition or ownership of securities, or the direct or indirect control or direction over securities, as the case may be.

Division 2 — Exemptions

Exempt take over bids

80. (1) Subject to the regulations, a take over bid is exempt from sections 87 to 92 if

   (a) the bid is made through the facilities of a stock exchange recognized by the commission for the purposes of this paragraph,

   (a) the bid is made through the facilities of an exchange recognized by the commission for the purposes of this paragraph,

[Para. (a) am. 1990, c. 25, s. 33 (nyif).]

> The Vancouver Stock Exchange, the Alberta Stock Exchange, The Toronto Stock Exchange and the Montreal Exchange have been so recognized – See Local Policy Statement 3-44 "Recognition of Stock Exchanges and Jurisdictions".

  (b) the bid is for not more than 5% of the outstanding securities of a class of securities of the issuer and,

     (i) the aggregate number of securities acquired by the offeror and any person acting jointly or in concert with the offeror within any period of 12 months in reliance upon the exemption provided by this paragraph does not, when aggregated with acquisitions otherwise made by the offeror and any person acting jointly or in concert with the offeror within the same 12 month period, constitute in excess of 5% of the outstanding securities of that class of the issuer at the commencement of the 12 month period, and

     (ii) if there is a published market for the securities acquired, the value of the consideration paid for any of the securities acquired is not in excess of the market price at the date of acquisition, determined in accordance with the regulations, plus reasonable brokerage fees or commissions actually paid,

  (c) the bid meets all of the following conditions:

     (i) purchases are made from not more than 5 persons in the aggregate, including persons outside of the Province;

     (ii) the bid is not made generally to security holders of the class of securities that is the subject of the bid;

     (iii) the value of the consideration paid for any of the securities, including brokerage fees or commissions, does not exceed 115% of the market price of securities of that class at the date of the bid, determined in accordance with the regulations,

> "Market price" is defined in s. 154 of the Regulation.

  (d) the offeree issuer is not a reporting issuer, there is not a published market in respect of the securities that are the subject of the bid, and the number of holders of securities of that class is not more than 50, exclusive of holders who

     (i) are in the employment of the offeree issuer or an affiliate of the offeree issuer, or

     (ii) were formerly in the employment of the offeree issuer or an affiliate of the offeree issuer and who while in that employment were, and have continued after that employment to be, security holders of the offeree issuer,

  (e) the bid meets all of the following conditions:

     (i) the number of holders in the Province of securities of the class subject to the bid is fewer than 50;

     (ii) the securities held by such holders constitute, in the aggregate, less than 2% of the outstanding securities of that class;

     (iii) the bid is made in compliance with the laws of a jurisdiction that is recognized for the purposes of this subparagraph by the commission;

     (iv) all material relating to the bid that is sent by the offeror to holders of securities of the class that is subject to the bid is concurrently sent to all holders in the Province of such securities and is filed, or

> The Commission recognizes Alberta, Manitoba, Ontario, Quebec and Saskatchewan and the United States, where the bid complies with, and is not exempt from, the requirements of the Securities and Exchange Commission; see Local Policy Statement 3-44 "Recognition of Stock Exchanges and Jurisdictions".

(f)   the bid is exempted by the regulations.

> See s. 155 of the Regulation.

(2) For the purposes of subsection (1)(c), where an offeror makes an offer to acquire securities from a person and the offeror knows or ought to know after reasonable enquiry that,

(a)   one or more other persons on whose behalf that person is acting as nominee, agent, trustee, executor, administrator or other legal representative has a direct beneficial interest in those securities, then each of such others shall be included in the determination of the number of persons to whom the offer to acquire has been made, but, where an inter vivos trust has been established by a single settlor or where an estate has not vested in all persons beneficially entitled thereto, the trust or estate shall be considered a single security holder in such determination, or

(b)   the person acquired the securities in order that the offeror might make use of the exemption provided by subsection (1)(c), then each person from whom those securities were acquired shall be included in the determination of the number of persons to whom the offer to acquire has been made.

Exempt issuer bids

81. Subject to the regulations, an issuer bid is exempt from sections 87 to 90 and 92 if

(a)   the securities are purchased, redeemed or otherwise acquired in accordance with terms and conditions attaching thereto that permit the purchase, redemption or acquisition of the securities by the issuer without the prior agreement of the owners of the securities, or where the securities are acquired to meet sinking fund or purchase fund requirements,

(b)   the purchase, redemption or other acquisition is required by the instrument creating or governing the class of securities or by the statute under which the issuer was incorporated, organized or continued,

(c)   the securities carry with them or are accompanied by a right of the owner of the securities to require the issuer to redeem or repurchase the securities and the securities are acquired pursuant to the exercise of such right,

(d)   the securities are acquired from a current or former employee of the issuer or of an affiliate of the issuer, and if there is a published market in respect of the securities,

   (i)   the value of the consideration paid for any of the securities acquired does not exceed the market price of the securities at the date of the acquisition, determined in accordance with the regulations, and

   (ii)   the aggregate number or, in the case of convertible debt securities, the aggregate principal amount of securities acquired by the issuer within a period of 12 months in reliance on the exemption provided by this paragraph does not exceed 5% of the securities of that class issued and outstanding at the commencement of the period,

(e)   the bid is made through the facilities of a stock exchange recognized by the commission for the purpose of this paragraph,

(e)   the bid is made through the facilities of an exchange recognized by the commission for the purpose of this paragraph,

[Para. (e) am. 1990, c. 25, s. 33 (nyif).]

> The Vancouver Stock Exchange, the Alberta Stock Exchange, The Toronto Stock Exchange and the Montreal Exchange have been so recognized; see Local Policy Statement 3-44 "Recognition of Stock Exchanges and Jurisdictions".

(f)   following the publication of a notice of intention in the required form and in the manner prescribed by the regulations, the issuer purchases securities in the normal course in the open market, including through the facilities of a stock exchange, if the aggregate number, or, in the case of convertible debt securities, the aggregate principal amount, of securities acquired by the issuer within a period of 12 months in reliance on the exemption provided by this paragraph does not exceed 5% of the securities of that class issued and outstanding at the commencement of the period,

(f) following the publication of a notice of intention in the required form and in the manner prescribed by the regulations, the issuer purchases securities in the normal course in the open market, including through the facilities of an exchange, if the aggregate number, or, in the case of convertible debt securities, the aggregate principal amount, of securities acquired by the issuer within a period of 12 months in reliance on the exemption provided by this paragraph does not exceed 5% of the securities of that class issued and outstanding at the commencement of the period,

[Para. (f) am. 1990, c. 25, s. 33 (nyif).]

See s. 158 of the Regulation with respect to timely requirements for the notice of intention and the press release. The required form is Form 31.

(g) the issuer is not a reporting issuer, there is not a published market in respect of the securities that are the subject of the bid and the number of holders of securities of the issuer is not more than 50, exclusive of holders who

(i) are in the employment of the issuer or an affiliate of the issuer, or

(ii) were formerly in the employment of the issuer or an affiliate of the issuer and who while in that employment were, and have continued after the employment to be, security holders of the issuer,

(h) the bid meets all of the following conditions:

(i) the number of holders in the Province of securities of the class subject to the bid is fewer than 50;

(ii) the securities held by such holders constitute, in the aggregate, less than 2% of the outstanding securities of that class;

(iii) the bid is made in compliance with the laws of a jurisdiction that is recognized for the purposes of this subparagraph by the commission;

(iv) all material relating to the bid that is sent by the offeror to holders of securities of the class that is subject to the bid is concurrently sent to all holders in the Province of such securities and is filed, or

The Commission recognizes Alberta, Manitoba, Ontario, Quebec and Saskatchewan and the United States, where the bid complies with, and is not exempt from, the requirements of the Securities and Exchange Commission; see Local Policy Statement 3-44 "Recognition of Stock Exchanges and Jurisdictions".

(i) the bid is exempted by the regulations.

Stock exchange requirements

82. A bid that is made in reliance upon any exemption in sections 80 or 81 through the facilities of a stock exchange shall be made in accordance with the bylaws, rules and other regulatory instruments or policies of the exchange.

82. A bid that is made in reliance upon any exemption in sections 80 or 81 through the facilities of an exchange shall be made in accordance with the bylaws, rules and other regulatory instruments or policies of the exchange.

[S. 82 am. 1990, c. 25, s. 33 (nyif).]

Division 3 — Restrictions on Acquisitions or Sales

Restrictions on acquisitions during take over bid

83. (1) In this Division "offeror" means

(a) an offeror making a formal bid other than a bid referred to in section 80(1)(e) or 81(h),

(b) a person acting jointly or in concert with an offeror referred to in paragraph (a), or

(c) a control person of an offeror referred to in paragraph (a) or an associate or affiliate of such control person.

(2) An offeror shall not offer to acquire or make, or enter into, an agreement, commitment or understanding to acquire beneficial ownership of any securities of the class that are subject to a take over bid otherwise than pursuant to the bid on and from the day of the announcement of the offeror's intention to make the bid until its expiry.

(3) Notwithstanding subsection (2), an offeror making a take over bid may purchase, through the facilities of a stock exchange recognized by the commission for the purpose of section 80(1)(a), securities of the class that are subject to the bid and securities convertible into securities of that class commencing on the third business day following the date of the bid until the expiry of the bid if

(3) Notwithstanding subsection (2), an offeror making a take over bid may purchase, through the facilities of an exchange recognized by the commission for the purpose of section 80(1)(a), securities of the class that are subject to the bid and securities convertible into securities of that class commencing on the third business day following the date of the bid until the expiry of the bid if

[S. 83(3) am. 1990, c. 25, s. 33 (nyif).]

(a) the intention to make such purchases is stated in the take over bid circular,

(b) the aggregate number of securities acquired under this subsection does not constitute in excess of 5% of the outstanding securities of that class as at the date of the bid, and

(c) the offeror issues and files a press release forthwith after the close of business of the exchange on each day on which securities have been purchased under this subsection disclosing the information prescribed by the regulations.

> See s. 156 of the Regulation with respect to exemptions from these requirements. See s. 159 of the Regulation with respect to the disclosure required in the press release.

Restrictions on acquisitions during issuer bid

84. An offeror making an issuer bid shall not offer to acquire, or make or enter into any agreement, commitment or understanding to acquire, beneficial ownership of any securities of the class that are subject to the bid otherwise than pursuant to the bid on and from the day of the announcement of the offeror's intention to make the bid until the bid's expiry, but this section does not apply so as to prevent the offeror from purchasing, redeeming or otherwise acquiring any such securities during such period in reliance on an exemption under section 81(a), (b) or (c).

Restrictions on pre-bid and post-bid acquisitions

85. (1) Where a take over bid that is a formal bid is made by an offeror and, within the period of 90 days immediately preceding the bid, the offeror acquired beneficial ownership of securities of the class subject to the bid pursuant to a transaction not generally available on identical terms to holders of that class of securities,

(a) the offeror shall offer consideration for securities deposited under the bid at least equal to and in the same form as the highest consideration that was paid on a per security basis under any of such prior transactions or the offeror shall offer at least the cash equivalent of such consideration, and

(b) the offeror shall offer to acquire under the bid that percentage of securities of the class subject to the bid that is at least equal to the highest percentage that the number of securities acquired from a seller in such a prior transaction was of the total number of securities of that class beneficially owned by such seller at the time of the prior transaction.

> See s. 157 of the Regulation with respect to an exemption from this requirement.

(2) During the period beginning with the expiry of a take over bid that is a formal bid and ending at the end of the 20th business day thereafter, whether or not any securities are taken up under the bid, an offeror shall not acquire beneficial ownership of securities of the class that was subject to the bid except by way of a transaction that is generally available to holders of that class of securities on terms identical to those under the bid.

(3) Subsections (1) and (2) do not apply to trades effected in the normal course on a published market, so long as

(a) any broker acting for the purchaser or seller does not perform services beyond the customary broker's function and does not receive more than reasonable fees or commissions,

(b) the purchaser or any person acting for the purchaser does not solicit or arrange for the solicitation of offers to sell securities of the class subject to the bid, and

(c) the seller or any person acting for the seller does not solicit or arrange for the solicitation of offers to buy securities of the class subject to the bid.

Sales during bid prohibited

86. (1) An offeror shall not, except pursuant to a bid, sell or make or enter into any agreement, commitment or understanding to sell any securities of the class subject to the bid on and from the day of the announcement of the offeror's intention to make the bid until its expiry.

(2) Notwithstanding subsection (1), an offeror, before the expiry of a bid, may make or enter into an arrangement, commitment or understanding to sell securities that may be taken up by the offeror pursuant to the bid, after the expiry of the bid, if the intention to sell is disclosed in the take over bid circular or issuer bid circular, as the case may be.

Division 4 — Rules for Bids

Division 4 — Requirements for Bids

[Division 4 heading re-en. 1995, c. 45, s. 33 (nyif).]

General provisions

87. Subject to the regulations, the following rules apply to every take over bid and issuer bid:

87. Subject to the regulations, the following requirements apply to every take over bid and issuer bid:

[S. 87 am. 1995, c. 45, s. 34 (nyif).]

(a) *Delivery of bid.*—The bid shall be made to all holders of securities of the class that is subject to the bid who are in the Province, and delivered by the offeror to all holders in the Province of securities of that class and of securities that, before the expiry of the bid, are convertible into securities of that class;

(b) *Minimum deposit period.*—The offeror shall allow securities to be deposited pursuant to the bid for at least the prescribed period;

> The prescribed period is 21 days from the date of the bid; see s. 163.8(a) of the Regulation.

(c) *When taking up prohibited.*—No securities deposited pursuant to the bid shall be taken up by the offeror until the expiration of the prescribed period;

> The prescribed period is 21 days from the date of the bid; see s. 163.8(a) of the Regulation.

(d) *Withdrawal.*—Securities deposited pursuant to the bid may be withdrawn by or on behalf of a depositing security holder,

    (i) at any time before the expiration of the prescribed period from the date of the bid,

> The prescribed period from the date of the bid is 21 days; see s. 163.8(b) of the Regulation.

    (ii) at any time before the expiration of the prescribed period from the date of a notice of change or variation under section 90, and

> The prescribed period from the date of a notice of change or variation under s. 90 of the Act is 10 days; see s. 163.8(c) of the Regulation.

    (iii) where the securities have not been taken up and paid for by the offeror, after the expiry of the prescribed period;

> The prescribed period is 45 days from the date of the bid; see s. 163.8(d) of the Regulation.

(e) *Exception.*—The right of withdrawal conferred by paragraph (d)(ii) does not apply

    (i) where the securities have been taken up by the offeror at the date of the notice,

    (ii) where a variation in the terms of a bid consists solely of an increase in the consideration offered for the securities subject to the bid and the time for deposit is not extended for a period greater than that required by section 90(5), or

    (iii) in the circumstances described in section 90(6);

(f) *Notice of withdrawal.*—Notice of withdrawal of any securities under paragraph (d) shall be made by or on behalf of the depositing security holder by a method that provides the depository designated under the bid with a written or printed copy and, to be effective, the notice must be actually received by the depository and, where notice is given in accordance with this paragraph, the offeror shall return the securities to the depositing security holder;

(g) *Pro rata take up.*—Where the bid is made for less than all of the class of securities subject to the bid and where a greater number of securities is deposited pursuant thereto than the offeror is bound or willing to acquire under the bid, the securities shall be taken up and paid for by the offeror, as nearly as may be pro rata, disregarding fractions, according to the number of securities deposited by each depositing security holder;

(h) *Effect of market purchases.*—Where an offeror purchases securities as permitted by section 83(3), the securities so purchased shall be counted in the determination of whether a condition as to the minimum number of securities to be deposited in the bid has been fulfilled, but shall not reduce the number of securities the offeror is bound under the bid to take up;

(i) *When securities must be taken up and paid for.*—Subject to paragraphs (j) and (k), the offeror shall take up and pay for securities deposited under the bid, where all the terms and conditions of the bid have been complied with or waived, not later than the prescribed period after the expiry of the bid;

> The prescribed period after the expiry of the bid is 10 days; see s. 163.8(e) of the Regulation.

(j) *Idem.*—Any securities that are taken up by the offeror under the bid shall be paid for by the offeror as soon as possible, and in any event not more than 3 days, after the taking up of the securities;

(k) *Idem.*—Any securities deposited pursuant to the bid subsequent to the date on which the offeror first takes up securities deposited under the bid shall be taken up and paid for by the offeror within 10 days of the deposit of the securities;

(l) *Extension restricted.*—A bid may not be extended by the offeror, where all the terms and conditions thereof have been complied with except those waived by the offeror, unless the offeror first takes up and pays for all securities deposited thereunder and not withdrawn;

(m) *Press release.*—Where all the terms and conditions of the bid have been complied with or waived, the offeror shall forthwith issue a notice by press release to that effect, which press release shall disclose the approximate number of securities deposited and the approximate number that will be taken up.

> See National Policy Statement 45 "Multijurisdictional Disclosure System" with respect to disclosure requirements for bids involving a U.S. issuer, and NIN 91/12 "Ontario Securities Commission Policy Statement 9.1" – disclosure, valuation, review and approval requirements and recommendations for insider bids, going private transactions and related party transactions.
>
> *Re Slocan Forest Products Ltd. and Canfor Corporation*, [1995] 2 B.C.S.C. Weekly Summary 26 (B.C. Sec. Comm.), affirmed (sub nom. *Slocan Forest Products Ltd. v. Canfor Corp.*) 4 B.C.L.R. (3d) 243 (C.A.).
>
> The issuance of deposit receipts, which may only be exchanged for the shares of a target corporation after certain events have taken place, does not violate s. 87 of the Securities Act as the issuance of such deposit receipts constitutes the taking up and paying for the target corporation's shares. No withdrawal rights would arise under s. 87(d)(iii) 45 days after the date of the offer. The Court of Appeal granted leave to appeal the decision of the Commission and dismissed the appeal.

Financing of bid

88. Where a take over bid or issuer bid provides that the consideration for the securities deposited pursuant to the bid is to be paid in cash or partly in cash, the offeror shall make adequate arrangements prior to the bid to ensure that the required funds are available to effect payment in full for all securities that the offeror has offered to acquire.

Consideration in bids

89. (1) Subject to the regulations, where a take over bid or issuer bid is made, all holders of the same class of securities shall be offered identical consideration.

(2) If an offeror makes or intends to make a take over bid or issuer bid, neither the offeror nor any person acting jointly or in concert with the offeror shall enter into any collateral agreement, commitment or understanding with any holder or beneficial owner of securities of the offeree issuer that has the effect of providing to the holder or owner a consideration of greater value than that offered to the other holders of the same class of securities.

(3) Where a variation in the terms of the take over bid or issuer bid before the expiry of the bid increases the value of the consideration offered for the securities subject to the bid, the offeror shall pay such increased consideration to each person whose securities are taken up pursuant to the bid, whether or not such securities were taken up by the offeror before the variation.

Division 5 — Bid Circulars

Offeror's circular

90. (1) An offeror shall deliver, with or as part of a take over bid or issuer bid, a take over bid circular or issuer bid circular, as the case may be.

(2) Where, before the expiry of a take over bid or issuer bid or after the expiry of the bid but before the expiry of all rights to withdraw the relevant securities, a change has occurred in the information contained in a take over bid circular or issuer bid circular or in any notice of change or notice of variation that would reasonably be expected to affect the decision of the holders of the securities of the offeree issuer to accept or reject the bid, a notice of the change shall be delivered to every person to whom the circular was required to be delivered and whose securities were not taken up at the date of the occurrence of the change.

> See s. 160 of the Regulation with respect to the disclosure required in the notice of change.

(3) Subsection (2) does not apply to a change that is not within the control of the offeror or of an affiliate of the offeror unless it is a change in a material fact relating to the securities being offered in exchange for securities of the offeree issuer.

(4) Where there is a variation in the terms of a take over bid or issuer bid, including any extension of the period during which securities may be deposited thereunder, and whether or not the variation results from the exercise of any right contained in the bid, a notice of the variation shall be delivered to every person to whom the take over bid circular or issuer bid circular was required to be delivered and whose securities were not taken up at the date of the variation.

> See s. 160(2) of the Regulation with respect to the disclosure required in the notice of variation. See s. 161(2) of the Regulation with respect to an exemption from this requirement.

(5) Subject to subsection (6), where there is a variation in the terms of a take over bid or issuer bid, the period during which securities may be deposited pursuant to the bid shall not expire before the prescribed period after the notice of variation has been delivered.

> The prescribed period after the notice of variation has been delivered is 10 days; see s. 163.8(f) of the Regulation.

(6) Subsection (5) does not apply to a variation in the terms of a bid consisting solely of the waiver of a condition in the bid where the consideration offered for the securities that are subject to the bid consists solely of cash.

(7) A take over bid circular and an issuer bid circular shall be in the required form.

> The required forms are, respectively, Forms 32 and 33. See s. 115 of the Act with respect to liability for misrepresentation in a circular.
>
> *Trian Equities Ltd. v. Beringer Acquisitions Ltd.* (December 24, 1992), Vancouver Doc. A910605, Trainor J., [1993] B.C.W.L.D. 483 (S.C.) (not yet reported).
>
> Trian Equities Ltd. petitioned the Supreme Court for an order that the respondents distributed a take over bid offer and circular which was in breach of the Securities Act. Trainor J. held that the respondents did not meet their obligations to make disclosure of all material facts at a prospectus level of disclosure because the respondents did not comply with the requirements of Form 32 relating to the circular. In not so complying, information items which could be considered reasonably important to a shareholder in deciding how to vote was not provided. Furthermore, Trainor J. refused to accept the submission of counsel for the respondents that the fact that there is no evidence before the court that a shareholder of Trian

was misled by the take over bid offer and circular establishes that there was no contravention. The court held that an order pursuant to s. 97 of the Act was justified because the take over bid offer and circular distributed by the respondents were in breach of the Act.

Re Beringer Properties Inc., Beringer Acquisitions Ltd., Parallel Research Inc., Sean Francis Kehoe, James Morris Durward and Trian Equities Ltd., [1993] 18 B.C.S.C. Weekly Summary 18 (B.C. Sec. Comm.).

The regulatory requirements for a take over bid circular are specific. In this case, the deficiencies in the take over bid circular were significant and, as a consequence, the disclosure in the circular fell far short of meeting the regulatory requirements in s. 90(7) of the Act and Forms 32 and 12. The failure to meet these disclosure requirements resulted in the take over bid being cease traded and withdrawn. It is the responsibility of the management of a company to ensure that the company's take over bid complies with the regulatory requirements.

(8) A notice of change and a notice of variation shall contain the information required by this Part and the regulations.

Directors' circular

91. (1) Where a take over bid has been made, a directors' circular shall be prepared and delivered by the board of directors of an offeree issuer to every person to whom a take over bid must be delivered under section 87(a), not later than the prescribed period after the date of the bid.

The prescribed period after the date of the bid is 10 days; see s. 163.8(g) of the Regulation.

(2) The board of directors shall include in a directors' circular either a recommendation to accept or to reject a take over bid and the reasons for their recommendation, or a statement that they are unable to make or are not making a recommendation and, if no recommendation is made, the reasons for not making a recommendation.

See National Policy Statement 38 "Take-over Bids – Defensive Tactics".

(3) An individual director or officer may recommend acceptance or rejection of a take over bid if the director or officer delivers with the recommendation a circular prepared in accordance with the regulations.

(4) Where a board of directors is considering recommending acceptance or rejection of a take over bid, it shall, at the time of sending or delivering a directors' circular, advise the security holders of this fact and may advise them not to tender their securities until further communication is received from the directors.

(5) Where subsection (4) applies, the board of directors shall deliver the recommendation or the decision not to make a recommendation at least the prescribed number of days before the scheduled expiry of the period during which securities may be deposited under the bid.

(6) Where, before the expiry of a take over bid or after the expiry of the bid but before the expiry of all rights to withdraw the securities that have been deposited under the bid,

(a) a change has occurred in the information contained in a directors' circular or in any notice of change to a directors' circular that would reasonably be expected to affect the decision of the holders of the securities to accept or reject the bid, the board of directors of the offeree issuer shall forthwith deliver a notice of the change to every person to whom the circular was required to be sent disclosing the nature and substance of the change, or

(b) a change has occurred in the information contained in an individual director's or officer's circular or any notice of change thereto that would reasonably be expected to affect the decision of the holders of the securities to accept or reject the bid, other than a change that is not within the control of the individual director or officer, as the case may be, the individual director or officer, as the case may be, shall forthwith deliver a notice of change in relation thereto to the board of directors.

See s. 160(3) of the Regulation with respect to the required disclosure in the notice of change.

(7) Where an individual director or officer submits a circular under subsection (3) or a notice of change under subsection (6)(b) to the board of directors, the board, at the offeree issuer's expense, shall deliver a copy of the circular or notice to the persons referred to in subsection (1).

(8) A directors' circular and a director's or officer's circular shall be in the required form.

The required forms are, respectively, Forms 34 and 35.

(9) A notice of change shall contain the information required by this Part and the regulations.

Delivery to offeree issuer

92. (1) A take over bid and any notice of change or variation shall be filed and shall be delivered to the offeree issuer at its principal office and an issuer bid and any notice of change or variation shall be filed on the day such bid or notice is delivered to holders of securities of the offeree issuer, or as soon as practicable thereafter.

(2) Every directors' circular and every individual director's or officer's circular or any notice of change in relation thereto that is delivered to security holders of an offeree issuer shall be filed and shall be delivered to the offeror at its principal office on the day the directors' circular or individual director's or officer's circular or the notice of change is delivered to the holders of securities of the offeree issuer, or as soon as practicable thereafter.

(3) A take over bid or issuer bid, a take over bid circular, an issuer bid circular, a directors' circular, an individual director's or officer's circular and every notice of change or variation in any such bid or circular shall be mailed by prepaid first class mail or delivered by personal delivery or in such other manner as the superintendent may approve to the intended recipient and any bid, circular or notice so mailed or delivered shall be deemed to have been delivered and such bid, circular or notice shall be deemed conclusively for the purposes of sections 87, 90 and 91 and this section to have been dated as of the date on which it was so mailed or delivered to all or substantially all of the persons entitled to receive it.

(3) A take over bid or issuer bid, a take over bid circular, an issuer bid circular, a directors' circular, an individual director's or officer's circular and every notice of change or variation in any such bid or circular shall be mailed by prepaid first class mail or delivered by personal delivery or in such other manner as the executive director may approve to the intended recipient and any bid, circular or notice so mailed or delivered shall be deemed to have been delivered and such bid, circular or notice shall be deemed conclusively for the purposes of sections 87, 90 and 91 and this section to have been dated as of the date on which it was so mailed or delivered to all or substantially all of the persons entitled to receive it.

[S. 92(3) am. 1995, c. 45, s. 7 (nyif).]

Division 6 — Special Reporting and Limitations on Acquisitions

Reports of acquisitions

93. (1) Every offeror that, except pursuant to a formal bid, acquires beneficial ownership of, or the power to exercise control or direction over, or securities convertible into, voting or equity securities of any class of a reporting issuer that, together with such offeror's securities of that class, would constitute 10% or more of the outstanding securities of that class,

93. (1) Every offeror that, except pursuant to a formal bid, acquires beneficial ownership of, or the power to exercise control or direction over, or securities convertible into, voting or equity securities of any class of a reporting issuer that, together with such offeror's securities of that class, would constitute 5% or more of the outstanding securities of that class,

[S. 93(1) am. 1990, c. 25, s. 34 (nyif) (repealed 1995, c. 45, s. 59 (nyif)).]

(a) shall issue and file forthwith a press release containing the information prescribed by the regulations, and

(b) within 2 business days, shall file a report containing the same information as is contained in the press release issued under paragraph (a).

(2) Where an offeror is required to file a report under subsection (1) or a further report under this subsection and the offeror or any person acting jointly or in concert with the offeror acquires beneficial ownership of, or the power to exercise control or direction over, or securities convertible into, an additional 2% or more of the outstanding securities of the class or there is a change in any other material fact in such a report, the offeror,

(a) shall issue and file forthwith a press release containing the information prescribed by the regulations, and

(b) within 2 business days, shall file a report containing the same information as is contained in the press release issued under paragraph (a).

(3) During the period commencing on the occurrence of an event in respect of which a report or further report is required to be filed under this section and terminating on the expiry of one business day after the date that the report or further report is filed, neither the offeror nor any person acting jointly or in concert with the offeror shall acquire or offer to acquire beneficial ownership of any securities of the class in respect of which the report or further report is required to be filed or any securities convertible into securities of that class.

(4) Subsection (3) does not apply to an offeror that is the beneficial owner of, or has the power to exercise control or direction over, securities that, together with such offeror's securities of that class, constitute 20% or more of the outstanding securities of that class.

> See s. 163.1 of the Regulation with respect to the required disclosure in the press release. There is no prescribed form for the report required under s. 93(1)(b). The Commission prefers to see the report in typed form, dealing with the issues raised in s. 163.1 of the Regulation, and certified by an officer of the offeror. See also NIN 89/13 "Statutory Filings".

Acquisitions during bid by other offeror

94. (1) Where, after a formal bid has been made for voting or equity securities of an offeree issuer that is a reporting issuer and before the expiry of the bid, an offeror, other than the person making the bid, acquires beneficial ownership of, or the power to exercise control or direction over, securities of the class subject to the bid which, when added to such offeror's securities of that class, constitute 5% or more of the outstanding securities of that class, the offeror shall, not later than the opening of trading on the next business day, issue a press release containing the information prescribed by the regulations and, forthwith, the offeror shall file a copy of the press release.

(2) Where an offeror that has filed or is required to file a press release under subsection (1) or a further press release under this subsection or any person acting jointly or in concert with the offeror acquires beneficial ownership of, or control or direction over, securities of the class subject to the bid which, when added to the securities of that class acquired after the filing of the press release by the offeror and any person acting jointly or in concert with the offeror, aggregates an additional 2% or more of the class of outstanding securities, the offeror shall, not later than the opening of trading on the next business day, issue a further press release containing the information prescribed by the regulations and, forthwith, the offeror shall file a copy of the press release.

> See s. 163.2 of the Regulation with respect to the required disclosure in the press release or further press release. There is no required form for the report required under s. 93(2)(b). The Commission prefers to see the report in typed form, dealing with the issues raised in s. 163.2 of the Regulation, and certified by an officer of the offeror. See also NIN 89/13 "Statutory Filings".

No duplication of reports

95. Where the facts required to be reported or in respect of which a press release is required to be filed under sections 93 and 94 are identical, a report or press release is required only under the provision requiring the earlier report or press release, as the case may be.

Division 7 — Special Applications

Applications to the commission

96. (1) Where, on the application by an interested person or on the commission's own motion, the commission considers that a person has not complied or is not complying with this Part or the regulations related to this Part, the commission may make an order,

(a) restraining the distribution of any record used or issued in connection with a take over bid or issuer bid,

(b) requiring an amendment to or variation of any record used or issued in connection with a take over bid or issuer bid and requiring the distribution of any amended, varied or corrected record, and

(c) directing any person to comply with this Part or the regulations related to this Part or restraining any person from contravening this Part or the regulations related to this Part and directing the directors and senior officers of the person to cause the person to comply with or to cease contravening this Part or the regulations related to this Part.

(2) On an application by an interested person or on the commission's own motion, the commission may

(2) On an application by an interested person or on the commission's own motion, if the commission considers that to do so would not be prejudicial to the public interest, the commission may

(a) decide for the purposes of section 89(2) that an agreement, commitment or understanding with a selling security holder is made for reasons other than to increase the value of the consideration paid to the selling security holder for the securities of the selling security holder and that the agreement, commitment or understanding may be entered into notwithstanding that subsection,

(b) vary any time period set out in this Part and the regulations related to this Part, and

(c) order that a person or class of persons is exempt from one or more of the requirements of this Part or the regulations related to this Part where the commission considers that to do so would not be prejudicial to the public interest.

(c) order that a person or class of persons is exempt from one or more of the requirements of this Part or the regulations related to this Part.

[S. 96 am. 1992, c. 52, s. 15; s. 96(2) am. 1995, c. 45, s. 35(a), (b) (both nyif.)]

> See National Policy Statement 37 "Take-over Bids: Reciprocal Cease Trading Orders", BOR 91/7 "Multijurisdictional Disclosure System" which deals with take over bids involving U.S. issuers, NIN 88/5 "Guidelines for Applications to the Securities Commission or the Superintendent of Brokers for Decisions or Orders", and Canadian Securities Administrators Notice 92/2 "Applications for Discretionary Orders."

Applications to the Supreme Court

97. (1) An interested person may apply to the Supreme Court for an order under this section.

(2) Where, on an application under subsection (1), the Supreme Court is satisfied that a person has not complied with this Part or the regulations related to this Part, the Supreme Court may make such interim or final order as the Supreme Court thinks fit, including, without limiting the generality of the foregoing,

(a) an order compensating any interested person who is a party to the application for damages suffered as a result of a contravention of this Part or the regulations related to this Part,

(b) an order rescinding a transaction with any interested person, including the issue of a security or a purchase and sale of a security,

(c) an order requiring any person to dispose of any securities acquired pursuant to or in connection with a take over bid or an issuer bid,

(d) an order prohibiting any person from exercising any or all of the voting rights attaching to any securities, and

(e) an order requiring the trial of an issue.

Transition

98. This Part and Part 11 of the Securities Regulation, B.C. Reg. 270/86, as each read immediately before the coming into force of this section, continue to apply in respect of every take over bid and issuer bid commenced before the coming into force of this section.

99. [Repealed 1989, c. 78, s. 27.]

PART 12

PROXIES

Interpretation

100. In this Part

"form of proxy" means a written or printed form that, on completion and execution by or on behalf of a security holder, becomes a proxy;

"proxy" means a completed and executed form of proxy by which a security holder has appointed a person as his nominee to attend and act for him and on his behalf at a meeting of security holders;

"security holder" means a holder in the Province of a voting security of a reporting issuer;

"solicit" includes

(a) a request for a proxy whether or not it is accompanied by or included in a form of proxy,

(b) a request to execute or not to execute a form of proxy or to revoke a proxy,

(c) the sending of a form of proxy or other communication to a security holder under circumstances reasonably calculated to result in the procurement, withholding or revocation of a proxy of that security holder, or

(d) the sending, along with a notice of a meeting, of a form of proxy to a security holder by management of a reporting issuer,

but does not include

(e) the sending of a form of proxy to a security holder in response to an unsolicited request made by him or on his behalf, or

(f) the performance by any person of ministerial acts or professional services on behalf of a person soliciting a proxy.

Solicitation of proxies

101. (1) If the management of a reporting issuer gives or intends to give notice of a meeting to its security holders, the management shall, in accordance with the regulations, at the same time as or before giving that notice, send to each security holder who is entitled to notice of the meeting a required form of proxy for use at the meeting.

> No form is specified. See s. 103(1) of the Act for exemptions from this requirement. See s. 166 of the Regulation with respect to filing requirements. Although no form is specified as the required form of proxy, Items 1 and 2 of Form 30 set forth certain required information. See also National Policy Statement 41 "Shareholder Communication", Local Policy Statement 3-37 "Restricted Shares (Uncommon Equities) Distributions and Disclosure", and Local Policy Statement 3-41 "Lawyer's Conflict of Interest".
>
> *Ambassador Industries Ltd. v. Camfrey Resources Ltd.* (February 1, 1991), Vancouver Doc. A902996, Owen-Flood J., [1991] B.C.W.L.D. 1414 (S.C.) (unreported).
>
> Part 12 of the Securities Act applies only to security holders and solicitations in the province. The Company Act applies to security holders and solicitations both within and outside the province. Consequently, proxy solicitations are governed by both the Securities Act and the Company Act for security holders within the province. Solicitations which are defective under both Acts can be cured under s. 230 of the Company Act.

(2) No person shall solicit proxies from security holders unless,

(a) in the case of a solicitation by or on behalf of the management of a reporting issuer, the management sends to each security holder whose proxy is solicited an information circular in the required form as an appendix to the notice of the meeting or as a separate document accompanying the notice, or

(b) in the case of a solicitation by a person other than a person by or on behalf of the management of a reporting issuer, that person, concurrently with or before the solicitation, sends an information circular in the required form to each security holder whose proxy is solicited.

(b) in the case of any other solicitation, the person soliciting the proxies, concurrently with or before the solicitation, sends an information circular in the required form to each security holder whose proxy is solicited.

[Para. (b) am. 1995, c. 45, s. 36 (nyif).]

> See s. 167(1) of the Regulation with respect to a requirement to file a copy of the information circular with the Commission. The required form is Form 30.

(3) Subsection (2) does not apply to a solicitation

(a) where the total number of security holders whose proxies are solicited is not more than 15, unless the solicitation is made by or on behalf of the management of a reporting issuer,

(b) prescribed by regulation, or

(c) by a person in respect of securities of which he is the beneficial owner.

(4) For the purposes of subsection (3)(a), 2 or more persons who are joint registered owners of one or more securities shall be considered one security holder.

(5) [Repealed 1990, c. 25, s. 35.]

Voting where proxies

102. (1) The chairman at a meeting has the right not to conduct a vote by way of ballot on any matter where the form of proxy used at the meeting provides for a means by which the security holder whose proxy is solicited may specify how the securities registered in his name are to be voted.

102. (1) The chair at a meeting has the right not to conduct a vote by way of ballot on any matter where the form of proxy used at the meeting provides for a means by which the security holder whose proxy is solicited may specify how the securities registered in his name are to be voted.

[S. 102(1) am. 1995, c. 45, s. 5 (nyif).]

(2) Subsection (1) does not apply where

(a) a poll is demanded by a security holder present at the meeting in person or represented at it by proxy, or

(b) more than 5% of all voting rights attached to all the securities, that are entitled to be voted and to be represented at the meeting, are represented by proxies who are required to vote against what would otherwise be the meeting's decision on the matters referred to in subsection (1).

(3) Voting securities of an issuer that are

(a) registered in the name of

(i) a registrant or his nominee, or

(ii) a custodian or his nominee, and

(b) not beneficially owned by the registrant or the custodian, as the case may be,

shall not be voted by the registrant or custodian at any meeting of the issuer's security holders except in accordance with the regulations.

> See s. 165 of the Regulation, Pt. V, s. III, 2 of National Policy Statement 41, and s. 176 of the British Columbia Company Act.

(4) Subsection (3) does not apply to a registrant or custodian who is a trustee of securities held under a trust instrument that regulates how those securities are to be voted.

Exemptions

103. (1) This Part does not apply to a reporting issuer who complies with the requirements of the law of the jurisdiction in which the reporting issuer carries on business or is incorporated, organized or continued so long as those requirements are substantially similar to the requirements of this Part.

> Paragraph (F) of Ontario Securities Commission Policy 7-1 sets out Ontario's list of jurisdictions with laws "substantially similar to the requirements of this Part". As the Commission does not have a policy with respect to this issue, it is suggested that the Ontario policy be reviewed for guidance regarding this matter.

(2) On application by an interested person or on the commission's own motion, the commission may order that a person or class of persons is exempt from one or more of the requirements of this Part or the regulations related to this Part where

(a) the requirement in respect of which an exemption is to be granted conflicts with a similar requirement of the law of the judrisdiction in which the reporting issuer is incorporated, organized or continued, or

(b) the commission considers that to do so would not be prejudicial to the public interest.

[S. 103 am. 1992, c. 52, s. 16.]

> An application would only be made under this subsection if the applicant was uncertain of whether it fitted within subs. (1) and wanted the comfort of a ruling. See NIN 88/5 "Guidelines for Applications to the Securities Commission or the Superintendent of Brokers for Decisions or Orders", and Canadian Securities

Administrators Notice 92/2 "Applications for Discretionary Orders". See BOR 91/7 "Multijurisdictional Disclosure System" with respect to exemptions provided in respect of proxy solicitations by an American issuer.

PART 13

SELF DEALING

Interpretation

104. (1) In this Part

"investment" means a purchase of a security of an issuer or a loan or advance to a person, but does not include a loan or advance, whether secured or unsecured, that is

(a) made by a mutual fund, its mutual fund manager or its mutual fund distributor, and

(b) merely ancillary to the main business of the mutual fund, its manager or its distributor;

"investment" means a purchase of a security, a trade in an exchange contract, or a loan or advance to a person, but does not include a loan or advance that

(a) is made by a mutual fund, its mutual fund manager or its mutual fund distributor, and

(b) is merely ancillary to the main business of the mutual fund, its mutual fund manager or its mutual fund distributor;

[S. 104(1) "investment" re-en. 1990, c. 25, s. 36 (nyif).]

"mutual fund" means a mutual fund in the Province;

"person responsible for the management of a mutual fund" includes a person that has a legal power or right to control, or that is in fact able to control, a mutual fund;

[S. 104(1) "person responsible for the management of a mutual fund" en. 1995, c. 45, s. 37 (nyif).]

"related mutual funds" includes more than one mutual fund under common management;

"related person" means, in relation to a mutual fund, a person in whom the mutual fund, its mutual fund manager or its mutual fund distributor are prohibited by this Part from making an investment.

"responsible person" means

(a) a person responsible for the management of a mutual fund or its portfolio or advising the mutual fund with respect to its portfolio and every individual who is a partner, director or officer of that person,

(b) a related mutual fund,

(c) every associate or affiliate of a person that is a responsible person,

(d) every individual who is a partner, director or officer of an associate or affiliate of a person who, in relation to a mutual fund is a responsible person, if the individual

(i) participates in the formulation of investment decisions made on behalf of the mutual fund, or

(ii) before implementation of investment decisions made on behalf of the mutual fund, has access to those decisions or to advice given to the mutual fund relating to those decisions, and

(e) every individual who is an employee of a person who, in relation to a mutual fund, is a responsible person, if the individual

(i) participates in the formulation of investment decisions made on behalf of the mutual fund, or

(ii) before implementation of investment decisions made on behalf of the mutual fund, has access to those decisions or to advice given to the mutual fund relating to those decisions.

[S. 104(1) "responsible person" en. 1995, c. 45, s. 37 (nyif).]

(2) For the purposes of this Part,

(a) an issuer in which

(i) a mutual fund holds voting securities carrying more than 10% of the voting rights attached to all outstanding voting securities of the issuer, or

(ii) a mutual fund and related mutual funds hold voting securities carrying more than 20% of the voting rights attached to all outstanding voting securities of the issuer

is a related person of that mutual fund or of each of those mutual funds,

(b) a person or a group of persons has a significant interest in an issuer if, in the case of

(i) one person, he owns beneficially, directly, or indirectly, more than 10%, or

(ii) a group of persons, the group owns beneficially, directly or indirectly, individually or collectively, more than 50%,

of the outstanding securities of the issuer, and

(c) a person or a group of persons is a substantial security holder of an issuer if that person or group of persons owns beneficially, directly or indirectly, individually or collectively, voting securities carrying more than 20% of the voting rights attached to all outstanding voting securities of the issuer.

(3) For the purposes of this Part, where a person or a group of persons owns beneficially, directly or indirectly, voting securities of an issuer, that person or group of persons shall be deemed to own beneficially a proportion of voting securities of any other issuer that are owned beneficially, directly or indirectly, by the first mentioned issuer, which proportion shall equal the proportion of the voting securities of the first mentioned issuer that are owned beneficially, directly or indirectly, by that person or group of persons.

(4) For the purposes of subsection (2)(c), when computing the percentage of voting rights attached to voting securities owned by an underwriter, there shall be excluded any voting securities acquired by him as underwriter in a distribution of the securities, but the exclusion ceases to have effect on completion or cessation of the distribution by him.

(5) Notwithstanding subsection (3), a mutual fund is not prohibited from making an investment in an issuer only because a person or a group of persons, who own beneficially, directly, or indirectly, voting securities of the mutual fund, its mutual fund manager or its mutual fund distributor, is by reason of that ownership deemed under subsection (3) to own beneficially voting securities of the issuer.

Investments of mutual funds

105. (1) A mutual fund shall not knowingly make or hold an investment by way of loan to or in

(a) an officer or director of the mutual fund, its mutual fund manager or its mutual fund distributor or an associate of any of them, or

(b) an individual where the individual or an associate of the individual is a substantial security holder of the mutual fund, its mutual fund manager or its mutual fund distributor.

(2) A mutual fund shall not knowingly make or hold an investment to or in

(a) a person who is a substantial security holder of the mutual fund, its mutual fund manager or its mutual fund distributor,

(b) a person in which the mutual fund, alone or together with one or more related mutual funds, is a substantial security holder, or

(c) an issuer in which

    (i) an officer or director of the mutual fund, its mutual fund manager or its mutual fund distributor or an associate of any of them, or

    (ii) a person who is a substantial security holder of the mutual fund, its mutual fund manager or its mutual fund distributor,

has a significant interest.

(3) No mutual fund manager or mutual fund distributor shall knowingly hold an investment made after the coming into force of this Act, where the investment is an investment described in this section.

> See National Policy Statement 39 "Mutual Funds".

Indirect investment

106. (1) A mutual fund, its mutual fund manager or its mutual fund distributor shall not knowingly enter into a contract or other arrangement that results in its being directly or indirectly liable or contingently liable in respect of an investment in or to a person to whom it is prohibited by section 105 from making an investment.

(2) For the purposes of the application of this section to section 105, a contract or other arrangement referred to in subsection (1) of this section shall be deemed to be an investment.

Relieving orders

107. On application of an interested person, the commission, where it is satisfied that

(a) a class of investment, a particular investment, a contract or other arrangement represents the business judgment of responsible persons uninfluenced by considerations other than the best interests of a mutual fund, or

(b) a particular investment, contract or other arrangement is in the best interest of a mutual fund,

may order that section 105 or 106 does not apply to that class of investment, particular investment, contract or other arrangement.

> See NIN 88/5 "Guidelines for Applications to the Securities Commission or the Superintendent of Brokers for Decisions or Orders", and Canadian Securities Administrators Notice 92/2 "Applications for Discretionary Orders".

Fees on investment for mutual fund

108. A mutual fund shall not make an investment in consequence of which a related person of the mutual fund will receive a fee or other compensation unless

(a) the fees are paid under a contract which is disclosed in a preliminary prospectus or prospectus filed by the mutual fund and accepted by the superintendent, or

(a) the fees are paid under a contract which is disclosed in a preliminary prospectus or prospectus filed by the mutual fund and accepted by the executive director, or

[S. 108(a) am. 1995, c. 45, s. 7 (nyif.)]

(b) on the application of the mutual fund, the commission, where it considers that it would not be prejudicial to the public interest to do so, otherwise orders.

See NIN 88/5 "Guidelines for Applications to the Securities Commission or the Superintendent of Brokers for Decisions or Orders", and Canadian Securities Administrators Notice 92/2 "Applications for Discretionary Orders".

Standard of care for management of mutual fund

108.1 Every person responsible for the management of a mutual fund and every person that performs a similar function in relation to a mutual fund as that person or who occupies a position or office with such a responsibility must

(a) exercise the powers and discharge the duties related to that responsibility, function, position or office, in good faith and in the best interests of the mutual fund, and

(b) exercise the degree of care, diligence and skill that a reasonably prudent person would exercise in the circumstances.

[S. 108.1 en. 1995, c. 45, s. 38 (nyif).]

Report of mutual fund manager

109. A mutual fund manager shall file a report in the required form for each mutual fund to which he provides services or advice respecting

(a) a purchase or sale of securities between the mutual fund and any related person,

(b) a loan received by the mutual fund from, or made by the mutual fund to, any of its related persons,

(c) a purchase or sale effected by the mutual fund through any related person for which the related person received a fee from the mutual fund or from the other person to the transaction, or from both, and

(d) a transaction in which the mutual fund, by arrangement other than an arrangement relating to insider trading in portfolio securities, is a joint participant with one or more of its related persons,

within 30 days after the end of the month in which the purchase, sale, loan or transaction occurs.

109. A mutual fund manager shall file a report in the required form for each mutual fund to which he provides services or advice respecting

(a) a purchase or sale of securities or a trade in exchange contracts between the mutual fund and any related person,

(b) a loan received by the mutual fund from, or made by the mutual fund to, any of its related persons,

(c) a purchase or sale of a security or a trade in an exchange contract effected by the mutual fund through any related person for which the related person received a fee from the mutual fund or from the other person to the transaction, or from both, and

(d) a transaction in which the mutual fund, by arrangement other than an arrangement relating to insider trading in portfolio securities, is a joint participant with one or more of its related persons,

within 30 days after the end of the month in which the purchase, sale, trade, loan or transaction occurs.

[S. 109 am. 1990, c. 25, s. 37 (nyif).]

The required form is Form 39.

110. [Repealed 1988, c. 58, s. 11.]

Responsible person

110.1 (1) A mutual fund or responsible person must not knowingly cause the mutual fund to

(a) invest in any issuer in which a responsible person is a partner, officer or director unless that fact is disclosed to the mutual fund security holders before the purchase,

(b) purchase or sell the securities of any issuer from or to the account of a responsible person, or

(c) make a loan to a responsible person.

(2) A mutual fund or a responsible person must not knowingly enter into a contract or other arrangement that results in the mutual fund being directly or indirectly liable or contingently liable in respect of a transaction that is prohibited by this section.

[S. 110.1 en. 1995, c. 45, s. 38 (nyif).]

Trades by mutual fund insiders

111. A person who has access to information concerning the investment program of a mutual fund or the investment portfolio managed by a portfolio manager shall not purchase or sell securities of an issuer for his account where

(a) the portfolio securities of the mutual fund or the investment portfolio include securities issued by that issuer, and

(b) the information is used by the person for his benefit or advantage.

Trades by insiders

111. A person who has access to information concerning the investment program of a mutual fund or the investment portfolio managed for a client by a portfolio manager or by a registered dealer acting as a portfolio manager shall not use that information to purchase or sell securities or to trade exchange contracts for the person's benefit or advantage.

[S. 111 re-en. 1990, c. 25, s. 38 (nyif).]

Filing in other jurisdiction

112. Where the law of the jurisdiction in which the reporting issuer carries on business or is incorporated, organized or continued requires substantially the same reports in that jurisdiction as are required by this Part, the filing requirements of this Part may be complied with by filing the reports which are required by the law of the other jurisdiction and which are manually signed or certified.

[S. 112 am. 1990, c. 25, s. 39; 1992, c. 52, s. 17.]

112. Where the law of the jurisdiction in which the reporting issuer carries on business or is incorporated, organized or continued requires substantially the same reports in that jurisdiction as are required by this Part, the filing requirements of this Part may be complied with by filing the reports which are required by the law of the other jurisdiction and which are signed or certified.

[S. 112 am. 1995, c. 45, s. 39 (nyif).]

Exemptions

113. On application by an interested person or on the commission's own motion, the commission may order that a person or transaction or a class of persons or transactions is exempt from one or more of the requirements of this Part or the regulations related to this Part where

(a) the requirement in respect of which an exemption is to be granted conflicts with a similar requirement of the law of the jurisdiction in which the reporting issuer is incorporated, organized or continued, or

(b) the commission considers that to do so would not be prejudicial to the public interest.

[S. 113 re-en. 1992, c. 52, s. 18.]

See NIN 88/5 "Guidelines for Applications to the Securities Commission or the Superintendent of Brokers for Decisions or Orders", and Canadian Securities Administrators Notice 92/2 "Applications for Discretionary Orders".

PART 14

CIVIL LIABILITY

Liability for misrepresentation in prospectus

114.(1) Where a prospectus contains a misrepresentation, a person who purchases a security offered by the prospectus during the period of distribution

(a) shall be deemed to have relied on the misrepresentation if it was a misrepresentation at the time of purchase, and

(b) has a right of action for damages against

(i) the issuer or a selling security holder on whose behalf the distribution is made,

(ii) every underwriter of the securities who is required under section 50 to sign the certificate in the prospectus,

(iii) every director of the issuer at the time the prospectus was filed,

(iv) every person whose consent has been filed as prescribed, and

(v) every person who signed the prospectus.

(2) A person referred to in subsection (1)(b)(iv) is liable only with respect to a misrepresentation contained in a report, opinion or statement made by him.

(3) Where the person referred to in subsection (1) purchased the security from a person or underwriter referred to in subsection (1)(b)(i) or (ii) or from another underwriter of the securities, the purchaser may elect to exercise a right of rescission against that person or underwriter, in which case the purchaser shall have no right of action for damages against that person under subsection (1).

(4) No person is liable under subsection (1) if he proves that the person who purchased the securities had knowledge of the misrepresentation.

(5) No person is liable under subsection (1) if he proves that

(a) the prospectus was filed without his knowledge or consent and that, on becoming aware of its filing, he gave reasonable general notice that it was so filed,

(b) after the issue of a receipt for the prospectus and before the purchase of the securities by the purchaser, on becoming aware of any misrepresentation in the prospectus, he withdrew his consent to it and gave reasonable general notice of his withdrawal and the reason for it,

(c) with respect to any part of the prospectus purporting

(i) to be made on the authority of an expert, or

(ii) to be a copy of, or an extract from, a report, opinion or statement of an expert,

he had no reasonable grounds to believe and did not believe that

(iii) there had been a misrepresentation, or

(iv) the relevant part of the prospectus,

(A) did not fairly represent the report, opinion or statement of the expert, or

(B) was not a fair copy of, or an extract from, the report, opinion or statement of the expert,

(d) with respect to any part of the prospectus purporting

(i) to be made on his own authority as an expert, or

(ii) to be a copy of, or an extract from, his own report, opinion or statement as an expert,

but that contained a misrepresentation attributable to failure to fairly represent his report, opinion or statement as an expert,

(iii) he had, after reasonable investigation, reasonable grounds to believe and did believe that the relevant part of the prospectus fairly represented his report, opinion or statement as an expert, or

(iv) on becoming aware that the relevant part of the prospectus did not fairly represent his report, opinion or statement as an expert, he, as soon as practicable, advised the commission and gave reasonable general notice that

(A) his report, opinion or statement was not fairly represented, and

(B) he would not be responsible for that part of the prospectus, or

(e) with respect to a false statement

(i) purporting to be a statement made by an official person, or

(ii) contained in what purports to be a copy of, or an extract from, a public official document,

it was a correct and fair representation of the statement or copy of, or an extract from, the document, and he had reasonable grounds to believe and did believe that the statement was true.

(6) No person is liable under subsection (1) with respect to any part of the prospectus purporting

(a) to be made on his own authority as an expert, or

(b) to be a copy of, or an extract from, his own report, opinion or statement as an expert

unless he

(c) failed to conduct a reasonable investigation to provide reasonable grounds for a belief that there had been no misrepresentation, or

(d) believed that there had been a misrepresentation.

(7) No person is liable under subsection (1) with respect to any part of the prospectus not purporting

(a) to be made on the authority of an expert, and

(b) to be a copy of, or an extract from, a report, opinion or statement of an expert

unless he

(c) failed to conduct a reasonable investigation to provide reasonable grounds for a belief that there had been no misrepresentation, or

(d) believed that there had been a misrepresentation.

(8) Subsections (5) to (7) do not apply to the issuer or a selling security holder.

(9) An underwriter is not liable for more than the total public offering price represented by the portion of the distribution underwritten by him.

(10) In an action for damages under subsection (1), the defendant is not liable for all or any part of the damages that he proves does not represent the depreciation in value of the security resulting from the misrepresentation.

(11) The liability of all persons referred to in subsection (1)(b) is joint and several as between themselves with respect to the same cause of action.

(12) A defendant who is found liable to pay a sum in damages may recover a contribution, in whole or in part, from a person who is jointly and severally liable under this section to make the same payment in the same cause of action unless, in all the circumstances of the case, the court is satisfied that it would not be just and equitable.

(13) In no case shall the amount recoverable by a plaintiff under this section exceed the price at which the securities he purchased were offered to the public.

(14) The right of action for rescission or damages conferred by this section is in addition to and not in derogation from any other right the purchaser may have.

(15) Where a misrepresentation is contained in a summary statement of a mutual fund filed with a prospectus, the misrepresentation shall be deemed to be contained in the prospectus.

(16) Where a misrepresentation is contained in an annual information form filed with a short form of prospectus, the misrepresentation shall be deemed to be contained in the short form of prospectus.

[S. 114(16) en. 1987, c. 42, s. 98.]

(16) Where a misrepresentation is contained in an annual information form filed with a simplified prospectus, the misrepresentation shall be deemed to be contained in the simplified prospectus.

[S. 114(16) am. 1995, c. 45, s. 24 (nyif).]

Applies to a statement of material facts; see s. 58(2)(b) of the Act. See s. 124 of the Act with respect to the statutory limitation periods applicable to such actions. The burden of proof under this section is a balance of probability.

Liability for misrepresentation in circular

115. (1) Where a take over bid circular, issuer bid circular, notice of change or notice of variation sent under Part 11 contains a misrepresentation, a person to whom the circular or notice was sent shall be deemed to have relied on the misrepresentation, and has a right of action for

(a) rescission against the offeror, or

(b) damages against

    (i) each person who signed the certificate in the circular or notice,

    (ii) every director of the offeror at the time the circular or notice was signed,

    (iii) every person whose consent has been filed as prescribed, and

    (iv) the offeror.

[S. 115(1) re-en. 1992, c. 52, s. 19(a).]

(2) A person referred to in subsection (1)(b)(iii) is liable only with respect to a misrepresentation contained in a report, opinion or statement made by him.

(3) Where a directors' circular or a director's or officer's circular or a notice of change in respect of a directors' circular or a director's or officer's circular sent under Part 11 contains a misrepresentation, a person to whom the circular or notice was sent shall be deemed to have relied on the misrepresentation and has a right of action for damages against every director or officer who signed the circular or notice.

[S. 115(3) re-en. 1992, c. 52, s. 19(b).]

(4) No person is liable under subsection (1) or (3) if he proves that the person exercising the right of action had knowledge of the misrepresentation.

(5) No person is liable under subsection (1) or (3) if he proves that

(a) the circular or notice was sent without his knowledge or consent and that, on becoming aware of that fact, he gave, as soon as practicable, reasonable general notice that it was so sent,

(b) after sending of the circular or notice and on becoming aware of any mis-representation in the circular or notice, he withdrew his consent to it and gave reasonable general notice of the withdrawal and the reason for it,

(c) with respect to any part of the circular or notice purporting

    (i) to be made on the authority of an expert, or

    (ii) to be a copy of, or an extract from, a report, opinion or statement of an expert,

he had no reasonable grounds to believe and did not believe that

    (iii) there had been a misrepresentation, or

    (iv) the relevant part of the circular or notice

        (A) did not fairly represent the report, opinion or statement of the expert, or

        (B) was not a fair copy of, or extract from, the report, opinion or statement of the expert,

(d) with respect to any part of the circular or notice purporting

    (i) to be made on his own authority as an expert, or

    (ii) to be a copy of, or an extract from, his own report, opinion or statement as an expert,

but that contained a misrepresentation attributable to failure to fairly represent his report, opinion or statement as an expert,

    (iii) he had, after reasonable investigation, reasonable grounds to believe and did believe that the relevant part of the circular or notice fairly represented his report, opinion or statement as an expert, or

    (iv) on becoming aware that the relevant part of the circular or notice did not fairly represent his report, opinion or statement as an expert, he, as soon as practicable, advised the commission and gave reasonable general notice that

        (A) his report, opinion or statement was not fairly represented, and

        (B) he would not be responsible for that part of the circular or notice, or

(e) with respect to a false statement,

    (i) purporting to be a statement made by an official person, or

    (ii) contained in what purports to be a copy of, or extract from, a public official document,

it was a correct and fair representation of the statement or copy of, or extract from, the document, and he had reasonable grounds to believe and did believe that the statement was true.

[S. 115(5) am. 1992, c. 52, s. 19(c).]

(6) No person is liable under subsection (1) or (3) with respect to any part of the circular or notice purporting

(a) to be made on his own authority as an expert, or

(b) to be a copy of, or an extract from, his own report, opinion or statement as an expert

unless he

(c) failed to conduct a reasonable investigation to provide reasonable grounds for a belief that there had been no misrepresentation, or

(d) believed there had been a misrepresentation.

[S. 115(6) am. 1992, c. 52, s. 19(c).]

(7) No person is liable under subsection (1) or (3) with respect to any part of the circular or notice not purporting

(a) to be made on the authority of an expert, and

(b) to be a copy of, or an extract from, a report, opinion or statement of an expert

unless he

(c) failed to conduct a reasonable investigation to provide reasonable grounds for a belief that there had been no misrepresentation, or

(d) believed there had been a misrepresentation.

[S. 115(7) am. 1992, c. 52, s. 19(c).]

(8) Subsections (5) to (7) do not apply to the offeror.

(9) The liability of

(a) all persons referred to in subsection (1)(b), or

(b) all directors and officers referred to in subsection (3),

is joint and several as between themselves with respect to the same cause of action.

(10) A defendant who is found liable to pay a sum in damages may recover a contribution, in whole or in part, from a person who is jointly and severally liable under this section to make the same payment in the same cause of action unless, in all the circumstances of the case, the court is satisfied that it would not be just and equitable.

(11) In an action for damages under subsection (1) or (3) based on a misrepresentation affecting a security offered by the offeror in exchange for securities of the offeree issuer, the defendant is not liable for all or any part of the damages that he proves does not represent the depreciation in value of the security resulting from the misrepresentation.

(12) For purposes of this section, where the offeror in a take over bid or an issuer bid described in section 80(1)(a) or 81(e) is required by the bylaws, rules or other regulatory instruments or policies of the stock exchange, on or through the facilities of which the bid is made, to file a disclosure record with the stock exchange or to deliver a disclosure record, the disclosure record is deemed to be a take over bid circular, issuer bid circular, notice of change or notice of variation, as the case may be, sent as required by Part 11.

[S. 115(12) am. 1989, c. 78, s. 28; 1992, c. 52, s. 19(d).]

(12) For purposes of this section, where the offeror in a take over bid or an issuer bid described in section 80(1)(a) or 81(e) is required by the bylaws, rules or other regulatory instruments or policies of the exchange, on or through the facilities of which the bid is made, to file a disclosure record with the exchange or to deliver a disclosure record, the disclosure record is deemed to be a take over bid circular, issuer bid circular, notice of change or notice of variation, as the case may be, sent as required by Part 11.

[S. 115(12) am. 1990, c. 25, s. 40 (nyif).]

(13) The right of action for rescission or damages conferred by this section is in addition to and not in derogation from any other right available.

See s. 124 of the Act with respect to the statutory limitation periods applicable to such actions.

Standard of reasonableness

116. In determining what is a reasonable investigation or what are reasonable grounds for belief for the purposes of sections 114 and 115, the standard of reasonableness shall be that required of a prudent person in the circumstances of the particular case.

Liability in margin contracts

117.(1) Where a registered dealer makes a contract with a client to buy and carry on margin the securities of any issuer, and

(a) while the contract continues, the dealer sells securities of the same issuer for any account in which the dealer, his director, his firm, or a partner in his firm has a direct or indirect interest, and

(b) the effect of the sale is to reduce the amount of those securities in the hands of the dealer or under his control in the ordinary course of business to below the amount of those securities that the dealer should be carrying for all his clients,

the dealer shall immediately disclose those facts to the client, and the contract with the client is voidable at the election of the client.

(2) If a client elects under subsection (1) to void the contract, he may, in respect of that contract, recover from the dealer

(a) all money paid by the client to the dealer with interest, and

(b) any securities deposited by the client with the dealer.

(3) The client shall make an election under subsection (1) by sending written notice to the registered dealer within 30 days after the disclosure made to the client under subsection (1).

(4) A dealer is not liable under subsection (1) if he proves that the reduction of the amount of securities to below the amount he should be carrying was unintentional.

[S. 117(1) to (3) am. 1989, c. 78, s. 9.]

Right of action for failure to deliver documents

118. A person who is

(a) a purchaser of a security to whom a prospectus was required under section 66(1) to be sent but which prospectus was not sent, or

(a) a purchaser of a security to whom a prospectus or any amendment to a prospectus was required under section 66 to be sent but which prospectus or amendment was not sent or was not filed under the Act, or

[S. 118(a) re-en. 1995, c. 45, s. 40 (nyif).]

(b) a person to whom a take over bid circular, issuer bid circular, notice of change or notice of variation was required under Part 11 to be delivered but which circular or notice was not delivered,

has a right of action for damages or rescission against the dealer or offeror who failed to comply with the applicable requirement.

[S. 118 re-en. 1992, c. 52, s. 20.]

Liability in special relationship where material fact or material change undisclosed

119. (1) For the purposes of subsection (2) and (3), "securities of the reporting issuer" or "securities of a reporting issuer" includes

(a) a put, a call, an option or another right or obligation to purchase or sell securities of the reporting issuer, or

(b) a security, the market price of which varies materially with the market price of any securities of the reporting issuer.

(2) Where any person purchases or sells securities of a reporting issuer at any time when the person

(a) is in a special relationship with the reporting issuer, and

(b) knows of a material fact or material change with respect to the reporting issuer, which material fact or material change has not been generally disclosed,

the person is liable to compensate the seller or purchaser, as the case may be, of the securities of the reporting issuer for damages as a result of the purchase or sale unless the person proves that, at the time of the purchase or sale,

(c)   the person reasonably believed that the material fact or material change had been generally disclosed, or

(d)   the material fact or material change was known or ought reasonably to have been known to the seller or purchaser, as the case may be.

(3) Where any person (the "first person") that is

(a)   a reporting issuer,

(b)   a person in a special relationship with a reporting issuer, or

(c)   a person that proposes to

    (i)   make a take over bid, as defined in section 74, for the securities of a reporting issuer,

    (ii) become a party to a reorganization, amalgamation, merger, arrangement or similar business combination with a reporting issuer, or

    (iii) acquire a substantial portion of the property of a reporting issuer

informs another person of a material fact or material change with respect to the reporting issuer before the material fact or material change has been generally disclosed, the first person is liable to compensate for damages any person that thereafter sells securities of the reporting issuer to or purchases securities of the reporting issuer from the person that received the information unless the first person proves that,

(d)   at the time of giving the information, the first person reasonably believed the material fact or material change had been generally disclosed,

(e)   at the time of the sale or purchase, as the case may be, the person who sold securities of the reporting issuer to or purchased securities of the reporting issuer from the person who received the information knew or reasonably ought to have known of the material fact or material change,

(f)   in the case of an action against a reporting issuer or a person in a special relationship with a reporting issuer, the information was given in the course of business of the reporting issuer or of the person in a special relationship with a reporting issuer, or

(g)   in the case of an action against a person described in paragraph (c), the giving of the information was necessary to effect the take over bid, business combination or acquisition, as the case may be.

(4) Where any person

(a)   has access to information concerning the investment program of a mutual fund in the Province or the investment portfolio managed for a client by a portfolio manager or by a registered dealer acting as a portfolio manager, and

(b)   uses that information for the person's direct benefit or advantage to purchase or sell securities of an issuer for the person's own account where the portfolio securities of the mutual fund or the investment portfolio managed for the client by the portfolio manager or registered dealer include securities of that issuer,

(b)   uses that information to purchase or sell securities or to trade exchange contracts for the person's benefit or advantage,

[Para. (b) re-en. 1990, c. 25, s. 41(a) (nyif).]

the person is liable to account to the mutual fund or the client of the portfolio manager or registered dealer, as the case may be, for any benefit or advantage received or receivable by the person as a result of the purchase or sale.

the person is liable to account to the mutual fund or the client of the portfolio manager or registered dealer, as the case may be, for any benefit or advantage received or receivable by the person as a result of the purchase or sale of securities or the trade in exchange contracts.

[S. 119(4) am. 1990, c. 25, s. 41(b) (nyif).]

(5) Where any person (the "first person") that is an insider, affiliate or associate of a reporting issuer

(a) sells or purchases securities of the reporting issuer with knowledge of a material fact or material change with respect to the reporting issuer, which material fact or material change has not been generally disclosed, or

(b) informs another person of a material fact or material change with respect to the reporting issuer before the material fact or material change has been generally disclosed, unless giving the information is necessary in the course of business of the reporting issuer or the insider, affiliate or associate of the reporting issuer,

the first person is liable to account to the reporting issuer for any benefit or advantage received or receivable by the first person or the other person as a result of the purchase, sale or giving of information, as the case may be, unless the first person proves that, at the time of the purchase, sale or giving of information, the first person reasonably believed that the material fact or material change had been generally disclosed.

(6) Where 2 or more persons in a special relationship with a reporting issuer are liable under subsection (2) or (3) as to the same transaction or series of transactions, their liability is joint and several.

(7) In assessing damages under subsection (2) or (3), the court shall consider,

(a) if the plaintiff is

(i) a purchaser, the price that the plaintiff paid for the security less the average market price of the security over the 20 trading days immediately following general disclosure of the material fact or material change, or

(ii) a seller, the average market price of the security over the 20 trading days immediately following general disclosure of the material fact or material change less the price that the plaintiff received for the security, and

(b) any other measure of damages the court considers relevant in the circumstances.

[S. 119 re-en. 1989, c. 78, s. 29.]

See s. 3 of the Act for the definition of a person in a special relationship with a reporting issuer. See s. 152.3 of the Regulation with respect to defences to an action under this section.

120. [Repealed 1989, c. 78, s. 29.]

Action by commission on behalf of issuer

121.(1) On application by

(a) the commission, or

(b) any person who

(i) was, at the time of a transaction referred to in section 119(2) or (3), or

[Subpara. (i) am. 1989, c. 78, s. 30(a).]

(ii) is, at the time of the application,

a security holder of the reporting issuer,

the Supreme Court may, if satisfied that

(c) the applicant has reasonable grounds for believing that the reporting issuer has a cause of action under section 119(5), and

(d) the reporting issuer has

(i) refused or failed to commence an action under section 119(5) within 60 days after receipt of a written request from the applicant to do so, or

(ii) failed to prosecute diligently an action commenced by it under section 119(5), make an order, on any terms as to security for costs or otherwise that it considers proper, requiring the commission or authorizing the person or the commission to commence or continue an action in the name of, and on behalf of, the reporting issuer to enforce the liability created by section 119(5).

[S. 121(1) am. 1989, c. 78, s. 30(b).]

(2) On application by

(a) the commission, or

(b) any person who

(i) was, at the time of a transaction referred to in section 119(4), or

(ii) is, at the time of the application,

a security holder of the mutual fund,

the Supreme Court may, if satisfied that

(c) the applicant has reasonable grounds for believing that the mutual fund has a cause of action under section 119(4), and

(d) the mutual fund has

(i) refused or failed to commence an action under section 119(4) within 60 days after receipt of a written request from the applicant to do so, or

(ii) failed to prosecute diligently an action commenced by it under section 119(4),

make an order, on any terms as to security for costs or otherwise that it considers proper, requiring the commission or authorizing the person or the commission to commence or continue an action in the name of, and on behalf of, the mutual fund to enforce the liability created by section 119(4).

[S. 121(2) am. 1989, c. 78, s. 30(c).]

(3) Where an action under section 119(4) or (5) is commenced or continued by the directors of the reporting issuer, the Supreme Court may order the reporting issuer to pay all costs properly incurred by the directors in commencing or continuing the action, as the case may be, if it is satisfied that the action is in the best interests of the reporting issuer and its security holders.

(4) Where an action under section 119(4) or (5) is commenced or continued by a person who is a security holder of the reporting issuer, the Supreme Court may order the reporting issuer to pay all costs properly incurred by the security holder in commencing or continuing the action, as the case may be, if it is satisfied that

(a) the reporting issuer refused or failed to commence the action or, having commenced it, failed to prosecute it diligently, and

(b) the action is in the best interests of the reporting issuer and its security holders.

(5) Where an action under section 119(4) or (5) is commenced or continued by the commission, the Supreme Court shall order the reporting issuer to pay all costs properly incurred by the commission in commencing or continuing the action, as the case may be.

[S. 121(3) to (5) am. 1989, c. 78, s. 30(d).]

(6) In determining whether an action or its continuance is in the best interests of a reporting issuer and its security holders, the court shall consider the relationship between the potential benefit to be derived from the action by the reporting issuer and its security holders and the cost involved in the prosecution of the action.

(7) Notice of every application under subsection (1) or (2) shall be sent to the commission and the reporting issuer, or the mutual fund, as the case may be, and each of them may appear and be heard.

(8) Every order made under subsection (1) or (2) requiring or authorizing the commission to commence or continue an action shall provide that the reporting issuer or mutual fund, as the case may be,

(a) cooperate fully with the commission in the commencement or continuation of the action, and

(b) make available to the commission all records and other material or information relevant to the action and known to, or reasonably ascertainable by, the reporting issuer or mutual fund.

Rescission of contract

122. (1) Where section 36(2) applies to a contract and is not complied with, a person who has entered into the contract may rescind it by sending a written notice of rescission to the registered dealer within 60 days of the date of the delivery of the security to the person or by the person if he is, at the time the notice of rescission is given, the beneficial owner of the security purchased.

(2) Where a registered dealer

(a) is required by the regulations to give to a client a written confirmation of a trade in a security setting out that he has acted as principal in the transaction, and

(b) has failed to comply with that requirement,

a person who has entered into the contract may rescind it by sending a written notice of rescission to the registered dealer within 7 days of the date of the delivery of the written confirmation of the contract.

[S. 122(2)(a) am. 1989, c. 78, s. 9.]

(3) In an action for rescission to which this section applies, the onus of proving compliance with section 36 or the regulations is on the registered dealer.

(4) No action for rescission shall be commenced under this section after the expiration of 90 days from the date of sending the notice under subsection (1) or (2).

Rescission of purchase of mutual fund security

123. (1) Every purchaser of a security of a mutual fund in the Province may, where the amount of the purchase does not exceed a prescribed amount, rescind the purchase by sending a written notice to the registered dealer from whom the purchase was made, in the case of

(a) a lump sum purchase, within 48 hours after receipt of the confirmation, or

(b) a contractual plan, within 60 days after receipt of the confirmation of the initial payment.

(2) Subject to subsection (4), the amount a purchaser may recover on exercise of a right to rescind under subsection (1) shall not exceed the net asset value, at the time the right is exercised, of the securities purchased.

(3) The right to rescind a purchase made under a contractual plan may be exercised only with respect to payments scheduled to be made within the time specified in subsection (1) for rescinding a purchase made under a contractual plan.

(4) Every registered dealer from whom the purchase of a security of a mutual fund was made shall reimburse the purchaser who has exercised his right of rescission in accordance with this section for the amount of sales charges and fees relevant to the investment of the purchaser in the mutual fund in respect of the securities for which the written notice of rescission was given.

Limitation period

124. Unless otherwise provided in this Act or in the regulations, no action to enforce a civil remedy created by this Part or by the regulations shall be commenced more than, in the case of

(a) an action for rescission, 180 days after the date of the transaction that gave rise to the cause of action, or

(b) an action other than for rescission, the earlier of

    (i) 180 days after the plaintiff first had knowledge of the facts giving rise to the cause of action, or

(ii) 3 years after the date of the transaction that gave rise to the cause of action.

PART 15

INVESTIGATIONS AND AUDITS

125. [Repealed 1988, c. 58, s. 24.]

Provision of information to superintendent

125.1(1) The superintendent, by an order applicable generally or to one or more persons or entities named or otherwise described in the order, may require a

(a) clearing agency,

(b) registrant,

(c) reporting issuer,

(d) custodian of assets of a mutual fund, or

(e) custodian of securities issued by a mutual fund and held under a custodial agreement or other arrangement with a person engaged in the distribution of those securities,

to provide information or to produce records specified or otherwise described in the order within the time or at the intervals specified in the order.

(2) The superintendent may require verification by affidavit of information provided or records produced pursuant to an order under subsection (1).

[S. 125.1 re-en. 1989, c. 78, s. 31.]

Provision of information to executive director

125.1 (1) The executive director, by an order applicable generally or to one or more persons or entities named or otherwise described in the order, may require,

(a) for the administration of this Act,

(b) to assist in the administration of the securities laws of another jurisdiction,

(c) in respect of matters relating to trading in securities in the Province, or

(d) in respect of matters in the Province relating to trading in securities in another jurisdiction,

any of the following persons to provide information or to produce records or classes of records specified or otherwise described in the order within the time or at the intervals specified in the order:

(e) a clearing agency;

(f) a registrant;

(g) a person exempted from the requirement to be registered under section 20 by an order under section 33;

(h) a reporting issuer;

(i) a manager or custodian of assets, shares or units of a mutual fund;

(j) a general partner of a person referred to in paragraph (f), (g), (h), (k), (n) or (o);

(k) a person purporting to distribute securities in reliance on an exemption

(i) described in section 55(2), or

(ii) in an order issued under section 59;

(l) a transfer agent or registrar for securities of a reporting issuer;

(m) a director or officer of a reporting issuer;

(n) a promoter or control person of a reporting issuer;

(o) a person engaged in investor relations activities on behalf of a reporting issuer or security holder of a reporting issuer;

(p) the Canadian Investor Protection Fund.

(2) The executive director may require verification by affidavit of information provided or records or classes of records produced pursuant to an order under subsection (1).

[S. 125.1 re-en. 1995, c. 45, s. 41 (nyif).]

Investigation order by commission

126. (1) The commission may, by order, appoint a person to make an investigation the commission considers expedient

(a) for the administration of this Act,

(b) to assist in the administration of the securities laws of another jurisdiction,

(c) in respect of matters relating to trading in securities in the Province, or

(d) in respect of matters in the Province relating to trading in securities in another jurisdiction.

(b) to assist in the administration of the securities or exchange contracts laws of another jurisdiction,

(c) in respect of matters relating to trading in securities or exchange contracts in the Province, or

(d) in respect of matters in the Province relating to trading in securities or exchange contracts in another jurisdiction.

[S. 126(1) re-en. 1988, c. 58, s. 16; s. 126(1)(b) to (d) am. 1990, c. 25, s. 42 (nyif).]

(2) The commission shall, in its order, specify the scope of an investigation to be carried out under subsection (1).

British Columbia Securities Commission v. Meunier (December 24, 1991), Vancouver Doc. A914153, Houghton J., [1992] B.C.W.L.D. 364 (S.C.) (unreported).

A person is liable to attend for examination and produce documents notwithstanding the fact that the Superintendent is proceeding against him.

British Columbia (Securities Commission) v. Stallwood, [1995] B.C.W.L.D. 1840, [1995] 23 B.C.S.C. Weekly Summary 16 (S.C.).

Seven petitioners sought a declaration that ss. 8(1), 126, 127, 128 and 132 of the Act violate ss. 7 and 8 of the Charter. The Court held that none of the grounds argued by the petitioners were sufficient to declare the sections invalid.

The Court found that ss. 126, 127 and 128 do not violate ss. 7 and 8 of the Charter by virtue of the sections not having a relevancy requirement. It would be unrealistic to restrict the scope of an investigation when many of the facts were solely with the witnesses and not known to the Commission. Sections 8(1) and 127 are not invalid by reason of a lack of a requirement to minimize the intrusion of an investigation as the expectation of privacy of a person in the securities market is low. Further, s. 128 does not encroach on the federal jurisdiction to enact criminal law as the predominant purpose of including any penal consequences in s. 128 is the regulation of the securities industry. The overlap into criminal law is incidental and insufficient to invalidate the statute. Sections 126 and 132 do not violate the principles of fundamental justice by reason of vagueness. Furthermore, ss. 8(1) and 132 do not deny the petitioners' procedural fairness and the right to full answer and defence as none of the petitioners were in jeopardy and a sufficient level of disclosure of particulars was made to the petitioners. Finally, the Court ruled that the Commission did not delegate its statutory duty to the investigator pursuant to ss. 6 and 126 of the Act, in contravention of administrative law principles.

Power of investigator

127. (1) An investigator appointed under section 126 or 131 may, with respect to the person who is the subject of the investigation, investigate, inquire into, inspect and examine

 (a) the affairs of that person,

 (b) any records, negotiations, transactions, investigations, investments, loans, borrowings and payments to, by, on behalf of, in relation to or connected with that person,

[S. 127(1)(b) am. 1989, c. 78, s. 32(b); 1992, c. 52, s. 21.]

 (c) any property, assets or things owned, acquired or disposed of in whole or in part by that person or by a person acting on behalf of or as agent for that person,

 (d) the assets at any time held by, the liabilities, debts, undertakings and obligations at any time existing and the financial or other conditions at any time prevailing in respect of that person, and

 (e) the relationship that may at any time exist or have existed between that person and any other person by reason of

  (i) investments made,

  (ii) commissions promised, secured or paid,

  (iii) interests held or acquired,

  (iv) the lending or borrowing of money, securities or other property,

  (v) the transfer, negotiation or holding of securities,

  (v) the transfer, negotiation or holding of securities or exchange contracts,

[Subpara. (v) am. 1990, c. 25, s. 2 (nyif).]

  (vi) interlocking directorates,

  (vii) common control,

  (viii) undue influence or control, or

  (ix) any other relationship.

[S. 127(1) am. 1989, c. 78, s. 32(a).]

(2) On application by the commission and on being satisfied by information on oath that it is necessary and in the public interest for any purpose relating to an investigation ordered by the commission under section 126, the Supreme Court may make an order authorizing a person named in the order

 (a) to enter into the premises or on the land of a person at any reasonable time, for the purpose of carrying out an inspection, examination or analysis,

 (b) to require the production of any records, property, assets or things and to inspect, examine or analyze them, and

 (c) on giving a receipt, to remove any records, property, assets or things inspected, examined or analyzed under paragraph (a) for the purpose of further inspection, examination or analysis.

(3) The Supreme Court's power to make an order under subsection (2) does not include the power to authorize the person named in it to enter into any room or place actually being used as a residence without the consent of the occupant.

(4) An application for an order under subsection (2) shall be made in the prescribed manner.

(5) An application for an order under subsection (2) may be

 (a) made ex parte, and

(b) heard in camera

unless the Supreme Court otherwise directs.

[S. 127(2) to (5) re-en. 1989, c. 78, s. 32(c).]

(6) Inspection, examination or analysis under this section shall be completed as soon as practical and the records, property, assets or things shall be promptly returned to the person who produced them.

(7) On an inspection, examination or analysis under this section, the authorized person named in the order or a person acting under his direction may

(a) mark the records, property, assets or things for identification, or

(b) use or alter the records, property, assets or things to the extent reasonably necessary to facilitate the inspection, examination or analysis,

and does not incur any liability because of doing so.

(8) No person shall withhold, destroy, conceal or refuse to give any information or produce any record or thing reasonably required under this section by the investigator or person named in an order under subsection (2).

[S. 127(6) to (8) en. 1989, c. 78, s. 32(c).]

(2) On being satisfied that it is necessary and in the public interest, the commission, by order, may authorize an investigator appointed under section 126

(a) to enter the business premises of

(i) a registrant specified in the order,

(ii) a self regulatory body recognized under section 11(1), or

(iii) an exchange recognized under section 11(2),

during business hours for the purpose of carrying out an inspection, examination or analysis of records, property, assets or things that are used in the business of that person and that may reasonably relate to the order made under section 126,

(b) to require the production of the records, property, assets or things referred to in paragraph (a) and to inspect, examine or analyze them, and

(c) on giving a receipt, to remove the records, property, assets or things inspected, examined or analyzed under paragraph (a) or (b) for the purpose of further inspection, examination or analysis.

(3) On application by the commission and on being satisfied by information on oath that there are reasonable and probable grounds to believe that there may be anything that may reasonably relate to an order made under section 126,

(a) in a business premise, or

(b) in a building, receptacle or place, other than a room or place actually being used as a residence,

the Supreme Court may make an order authorizing a person named in the order

(c) to enter into that business premise, building or receptacle at any reasonable time, for the purpose of carrying out an inspection, examination or analysis of records, property, assets or things that may reasonably relate to the order made under section 126,

(d) to require the production of the records, property, assets or things referred to in paragraph (c) and to inspect, examine or analyze them, and

(e) on giving a receipt, to remove the records, property, assets or things referred to in paragraph (c) for the purpose of further inspection, examination or analysis.

(4) An application for an order under subsection (3) must be made in the prescribed manner and, unless the Supreme Court otherwise directs, may be

(a) made without notice, and

(b) heard in the absence of the public.

(5) Inspection, examination or analysis under this section must be completed as soon as practical and the records, property, assets or things must be returned promptly to the person who produced them.

(6) On an inspection, examination or analysis under this section, an investigator appointed under section 126 and authorized under subsection (2) of this section, a person named in an order under subsection (3) of this section or a person acting under the direction of either of them may

(a) mark the records, property, assets or things for identification, or

(b) use or alter the records, property, assets or things to the extent reasonably necessary to facilitate the inspection, examination or analysis,

and does not incur any liability because of doing so.

(7) A person must not

(a) withhold, destroy, conceal or refuse to give any information, or

(b) withhold, destroy, conceal or refuse to produce any record or thing

reasonably required under subsection (2) or (3) by

(c) an investigator appointed under section 126 and authorized under subsection (2) of this section, or

(d) a person named in an order under subsection (3) of this section.

[S. 127(2) to (7) re-en. 1995, c. 45, s. 42 (nyif); s. 127(8) repealed 1995, c. 45, s. 42 (nyif).]

Section 171.1 of the Regulation states that an application for an order under s. 127(2) of the Act shall be made in accordance with the Supreme Court Rules.

See the *Stallwood* decision at s. 126 of the Act.

Investigator's power at hearing

128. (1) An investigator appointed under section 126 or 131 has the same power

(a) to summon and enforce the attendance of witnesses,

(b) to compel witnesses to give evidence on oath or in any other manner, and

(c) to compel witnesses to produce records and things and classes of records and things

as the Supreme Court has for the trial of civil actions, and the failure or refusal of a witness

[S. 128(1)(c) am. 1992, c. 52, s. 22 (a).]

(d) to attend,

(e) to take an oath,

(f) to answer questions, or

(g) to produce the records and things or classes of records and things in the custody, possession or control of the witness

[S. 128(1)(g) re-en. 1992, c. 52, s. 22(b).]

makes the witness, on application to the Supreme Court, liable to be committed for contempt as if in breach of an order or judgment of the Supreme Court.

(2) Section 38 of the *Evidence Act* does not exempt any financial institution, as defined in section 37 of that Act, or any officer or employee of the institution from the operation of this section.

(3) A witness giving evidence at an investigation conducted under section 126 or 131 may be represented by counsel.

See s. 169 of the Regulation with respect to the requirements for personal service and the fees and allowances to be paid.

British Columbia (Securities Commission) v. Palm (1991), 82 D.L.R. (4th) 758 (B.C.S.C.).

Pursuant to s. 128 of the Act, the failure or refusal of a witness to attend in accordance with a summons issued pursuant to this section makes the witness liable to be committed for contempt "as if in breach of an order or judgment of the Supreme Court".

British Columbia (Securities Commission) v. Branch, 43 B.C.L.R. (2d) 286, 68 D.L.R. (4th) 347, affirmed 63 B.C.L.R. (2d) 331, [1992] 3 W.W.R. 165, 88 D.L.R. (4th) 381, affirmed [1995] 5 W.W.R. 129, 4 B.C.L.R. (3d) 1, 7 C.C.L.S. 1 (S.C.C.).

In the course of an investigation of a company by the Commission, the appellants who were two of the company's officers were served with summonses pursuant to s. 128(1) of the Securities Act. The summonses compelled the officers' attendance for examination under oath and required them to produce all information and records in their possession relating to the company. The officers refused to appear and the Commission petitioned the British Columbia Supreme Court for an order citing the officers for contempt. In response, the officers applied for a declaration that s. 128(1) violates ss. 7 and 8 of the Charter. The Court dismissed the officers' application. Wood J. rejected the appellants' claims in respect of privilege against self-incrimination and of a right to remain silent under s. 7. He further held that the seizure authorized by s. 128(1)(c) of the Act is not "unreasonable" within the meaning of s. 8. Wood J. ordered the appellants to comply with the summonses, or, in default, to show cause or be held in contempt. The British Columbia Court of Appeal dismissed an appeal.

The Supreme Court of Canada dismissed the appeal of the Court of Appeal decision. The majority held that s. 128(1) does not violate s. 7 of the Charter. The purpose of the Act, which is to protect the economy and the public from unscrupulous trading practices, justifies limited inquiries. As the Act is concerned with obtaining evidence to regulate the securities industry, which is a goal of significant public importance, an inquiry such as the one at hand legitimately compels testimony. The central purpose of the Commission's inquiry in this case is to obtain the relevant evidence for the purpose of the instant proceedings, and not to incriminate the appellants. Further, as in this case, if the person subpoenaed is compelled to testify, then all communications including those arising from the production of documents are also compellable.

The majority further held that s. 128(1) does not violate s. 8 of the Charter. Persons involved in the securities market, which is a highly regulated industry, do not have a high expectation of privacy with respect to regulatory needs that have been expressed in the legislation. Securities legislation, which has important implications for the nation's prosperity, is dependent on the willing compliance of participants with the defined standards of conduct. The social utility of the legislation justifies the minimal intrusion that the appellants may face. Moreover, the appellants' expectation of privacy is limited as documents produced in the course of a regulated business are associated with a lesser privacy right than are strictly personal documents.

See the *Stallwood* decision at s. 126 of the Act.

British Columbia (Securities Commission) v. Steven Simonyi-Gindele and Robert Andrew McNeilly (June 12, 1992), Doc. A921540 (S.C.) (not yet reported).

The Supreme Court held that the Commission's investigators were legally entitled to compel someone to give evidence under s. 129 of the Act despite the fact that the person had been charged with criminal offences dealing with the same subject matter as the Commission was investigating, the Commission and the R.C.M.P. were co-operating in a joint investigation and the police could not compel the person to testify.

In the *Meunier* decision of the B.C. Supreme Court, discussed at s. 126, the Supreme Court held that the issuance of a Notice of Hearing does not bar subsequent investigations by the Superintendent.

Appointment of expert

129. Where an investigation is ordered under section 126, the commission may appoint an expert to examine the affairs, records and properties of the person being investigated.

Report to commission

130. Every person appointed under section 126 or 129 shall provide the commission with a complete report of the investigation or examination made including any transcript of evidence and material in his possession relating to the investigation or examination.

Report to commission

130. Every person appointed under section 126 to 129 must provide, at the request of the commission or a member of the commission involved in making the appointment, a complete report of the investigation, examination or analysis made, including any transcript of evidence and material in the person's possession relating to the investigation or examination.

[S. 130 re-en. 1995, c. 45, s. 42 (nyif).]

Investigation order by minister

131.(1) The minister may, by order, appoint a person to make an investigation the minister considers expedient

    (a) for the administration of this Act,

    (b) to assist in the administration of the securities laws of another jurisdiction,

    (c) in respect of matters relating to trading in securities in the Province, or

    (d) in respect of matters in the Province relating to trading in securities in another jurisdiction.

    (b) to assist in the administration of the securities or exchange contracts laws of another jurisdiction,

    (c) in respect of matters relating to trading in securities or exchange contracts in the Province, or

    (d) in respect of matters in the Province relating to trading in securities or exchange contracts in another jurisdiction.

[S. 131(1) re-en. 1988, c. 58, s. 17; s. 131(1)(b) to (d) am. 1990, c. 25, s. 42 (nyif).]

(2) The minister shall, in his order, specify the scope of an investigation to be carried out under subsection (1).

Evidence not be disclosed

132. No person, without the consent of the commission, shall disclose, except to his counsel, any information or evidence obtained or the name of any witness examined or sought to be examined under section 127, 128 or 129.

See the discussion under s. 128.

See the *Stallwood* decision at s. 126 of the Act.

Report to minister

133. Where an investigation has been made under section 126 or 131, then, if requested to do so by the minister, the commission or the investigator, as the case may be, shall make a complete report to the minister including, if so requested, the evidence, findings, comments, recommendations and any material in its or his possession relating to it, and the minister may publish all or part of the report in any way he considers proper.

[S. 133 am. 1989, c. 78, s. 33.]

Costs

134. The commission may require a person whose affairs are investigated under this Part to pay prescribed fees or charges for the costs of the investigation.

Order to freeze property

135. (1) The commission may, where

  (a) it proposes to order an investigation in respect of a person under section 126 or during or after an investigation in respect of a person under section 126 or 131,

  (b) it or the superintendent proposes to make or has made an order under section 144 in respect of a person,

[Para. (b) re-en. 1990, c. 25, s. 43(a).]

  (b) it or the executive director proposes to make or has made an order under section 144 in respect of a person,

[Para. (b) am. 1995, c. 45, s. 7 (nyif).]

  (c) [Repealed 1990, c. 25, s. 43(a).]

  (d) criminal proceedings or proceedings in respect of a contravention of this Act or the regulations are about to be or have been instituted against a person and the commission considers the proceedings to be connected with or to arise out of a security or a matter relating to trading in securities, or out of any business conducted by the person, or

[Para. (d) am. 1988, c. 58, s. 18(a).]

  (d) criminal proceedings or proceedings in respect of a contravention of this Act or the regulations are about to be or have been instituted against a person and the commission considers the proceedings to be connected with or to arise out of a security or exchange contract or a matter relating to trading in securities or exchange contracts, or out of any business conducted by the person, or

[Para. (d) am. 1990, c. 25, s. 43(b) (nyif).]

  (e) a person fails or neglects to comply with financial conditions applicable to him under the Act or the regulations,

direct, in writing, a person

  (f) having on deposit, under control or for safekeeping any funds, securities, or other property of the person referred to in paragraph (a), (b), (c), (d) or (e), to hold those funds, securities or other property, and

(f) having on deposit, under control or for safekeeping any funds, securities, exchange contracts or other property of the person referred to in paragraph (a), (b), (d) or (e), to hold those funds, securities, exchange contracts or other property, and

[Para. (f) re-en. 1990, c. 25, s. 43(c) (nyif).]

(g) referred to in paragraph (a), (b), (d) or (e)

(i) to refrain from withdrawing any funds, securities or other property from any person having them on deposit, under control or for safekeeping, or

(ii) to hold all funds, securities or other property of clients or others in his possession or control in trust for an interim receiver, custodian, trustee, receiver manager, receiver or liquidator appointed pursuant to the *Bankruptcy Act* (Canada), the *Company Act*, the *Law and Equity Act*, the *Personal Property Security Act*, the *Winding-up Act* (Canada), the *Supreme Court Act* or this Act.

[Para. (g) am. 1989, c. 78, s. 34(b), (c); 1990, c. 25, s. 43(d); subpara. (ii) am. 1988, c. 58, c. 18(b); 1989, c. 40, s. 193; 1990, c. 11, s. 107.]

(g) referred to in paragraph (a), (b), (d) or (e)

(i) to refrain from withdrawing any funds, securities, exchange contracts or other property from any person having them on deposit, under control or for safekeeping, or

(ii) to hold all funds, securities, exchange contracts or other property of clients or others in his possession or control in trust for an interim receiver, custodian, trustee, receiver manager, receiver or liquidator appointed pursuant to the *Bankruptcy Act* (Canada), the *Company Act*, the *Law and Equity Act*, the *Personal Property Security Act*, the *Winding-up Act* (Canada), the *Supreme Court Act* or this Act.

[Para. (g) am. 1990, c. 25, s. 43(e) (nyif).]

(2) In the case of a savings institution, a direction of the commission under subsection (1) applies only to the offices, branches or agencies of the savings institution that are named in the direction.

(3) A direction of the commission under subsection (1) does not apply to funds, securities or other property in a clearing agency or to securities in process of transfer by a transfer agent unless the direction expressly so states.

[S. 135(3) am. 1989, c. 78, s. 34(d).]

(3) A direction of the commission under subsection (1) does not apply to funds, securities, exchange contracts or other property in a clearing agency or to securities in process of transfer by a transfer agent unless the direction expressly so states.

[S. 135(3) am. 1990, c. 25, s. 43(f) (nyif).]

(4) In any of the circumstances referred to in subsection (1)(a) to (e), the commission may, in writing, notify a land title office or gold commissioner that proceedings are being or are about to be taken that may affect land or mining claims belonging to the affected person.

(5) A notice sent under subsection (4) or a copy of a written revocation or modification under subsection (6) shall be registered or recorded against the lands or claims mentioned in it and has the same effect as the registration or recording of a certificate of *lis pendens* or a caveat.

(5) A notice sent under subsection (4) or a copy of a written revocation or modification under subsection (6) shall be registered or recorded against the lands or claims mentioned in it and has the same effect as the registration or recording of a certificate of pending litigation or a caveat.

[S. 135(5) am. 1992, c. 55, Sched. 1 (nyif).]

(6) The commission may, in writing, revoke or modify a notice given under subsection (4) and where a notice is revoked or modified, the commission shall send a copy of the written revocation or modification to the land title office or gold commissioner, as the case may be.

Simonyi-Gindele v. British Columbia (Attorney General) (1991), (sub nom. *Simonyi-Gindele v. British Columbia (Securities Commission)*) 9 B.C.A.C. 237, 19 W.A.C. 237 (C.A.)

The Commission is entitled to determine whether or not s. 135 of the Act is not unconstitutional. Assuming there was a right to appeal from the decision of a single commissioner, it would be unsatisfactory to permit the appeal to proceed without the Commission having had a full opportunity to deal with the issue. The Commission then went on to determine that the section was not unconstitutional.

Re Amswiss Scientific Inc. and Ramcross Capital Corporation, 354397 B.C. Ltd., Geneva Capital Corp., Robert Andrew McNeilly, Toni Cross, Robert W. Dingee, Robin Wakefield and Steven Simonyi-Gindele, [1992] 7 B.C.S.C. Weekly Summary 12 (B.C. Sec. Comm.).

The purpose of s. 135(1) is to preserve property for persons who may have claims to or interests in it, for example, by way of rescission or damages under Pt. 14 of the Act. Like a s. 144(1) temporary cease trade order or a s. 73 halt order, a freeze order enables the Commission to respond immediately to information that, in its opinion, warrants regulatory intervention to prevent or minimize prejudice to the public interest.

By reading ss. 135 and 136 together, it is clear that the Commission itself has no authority to manage or otherwise deal with the frozen property. That authority rests exclusively with the Supreme Court and its appointees, and the Commission can only apply to the court to seek the appointment of a receiver, receiver-manager or trustee. As such, the Commission itself does not come into possession of any of the frozen property. On the plain reading of ss. 135(1) and 136, a freeze order is not a seizure, and even if it was held to be a seizure within the meaning of s. 8 of the Charter, it would not be an unreasonable seizure. The consequences of orders under s. 135(1), like those under s. 144, are economic and do not impact on the physical liberty and security of the person.

Appointment of receiver, etc.

136. (1) The commission may, where any of the circumstances referred to in section 135(1)(a) to (e) exist, apply to the Supreme Court for the appointment of a receiver, receiver manager or a trustee of all or any part of the property of the person.

(2) On an application under subsection (1), the court may, where it is satisfied that the appointment of a receiver, receiver manager or a trustee of all or any part of the property of the person is in the best interests of

(a)   that person's creditors,

(b)   persons, any of whose property is in the possession or under the control of that person, or

(c)   the security holders of or subscribers to the person,

by order, appoint a receiver, receiver manager or a trustee of all or any part of the property of that person.

(3) The commission may make an ex parte application under this section and in that event the court may make a temporary order under subsection (2) appointing a receiver, receiver manager or a trustee for a period not exceeding 15 days.

Act

(4) A receiver, receiver manager or trustee appointed under this section shall be the receiver, receiver manager or trustee of all or any part of the property belonging to the person or held by the person on behalf of or in trust for any other person, and the receiver, receiver manager or trustee may, if authorized by the court, wind up or manage the business and affairs of the person and may exercise powers necessary or incidental to the winding up or management.

(5) [Repealed 1990, c. 11, s. 108.]

> See discussion under s. 135 of the Act.

Audits

137. (1) Notwithstanding sections 17 and 18, where the commission considers it to be in the public interest, the commission may appoint in writing a person to

  (a)   conduct an examination and inspection of the financial affairs and records of

        (i)   a self regulatory body or a stock exchange, as the case may be, which has been recognized by the commission under section 11,

        (i)   a self regulatory body or an exchange, as the case may be, which has been recognized by the commission under section 11,

[Subpara. (i) am. 1990, c. 25, s. 44(a) (nyif).]

        (ii)   a clearing agency,

        (iii)   a registrant,

        (iv)   a reporting issuer,

        (v)   a custodian of assets of a mutual fund, or

        (vi)   a custodian of securities issued by a mutual fund and held under a custodial agreement or other arrangement with a person engaged in the distribution of those securities, and

  (b)   prepare financial or other statements and reports required by the commission.

[S. 137(1) re-en. 1989, c. 78, s. 35.]

(2) A person appointed under subsection (1) may inquire into and examine all securities, cash and records of every description of the person whose financial affairs are being examined.

(2) A person appointed under subsection (1) may inquire into and examine all trades, securities, exchange contracts, cash and records of every description of the person whose financial affairs are being examined.

[S. 137(2) am. 1990, c. 25, s. 44(b) (nyif).]

(3) No person shall withhold, destroy, conceal or refuse to give any information, record or thing reasonably required for an examination under this section.

(4) The commission may require the person whose affairs are examined under this section to pay prescribed fees or charges for the examination.

Exchange of information

137.1 Where the commission considers it would not be prejudicial to the public interest, it may authorize disclosure of facts, information and records obtained under this Part to any body empowered by the laws of another jurisdiction to administer or regulate trading in securities in that jurisdiction.

[S. 137.1 en. 1988, c. 58, s. 19; am. 1992, c. 52, s. 23.]

137.1 Where the commission considers it would not be prejudicial to the public interest, it may authorize disclosure of facts, information and records obtained under this Part to any body empowered by the laws of another jurisdiction to administer or regulate trading in securities or exchange contracts in that jurisdiction.

[S. 137.1 am. 1990, c. 25, s. 2 (nyif).]

PART 16

ENFORCEMENT

Offences generally

138. (1) Every person who

(a)　makes a statement in evidence or information submitted or given under this Act or the regulations to the commission, the superintendent or any person appointed to make an investigation or audit under this Act or the regulations that, at the time and in light of the circumstances under which it is made, is a misrepresentation,

(a)　makes a statement in evidence or information submitted or given under this Act or the regulations to the commission, the executive director or any person appointed to make an investigation or audit under this Act or the regulations that, at the time and in light of the circumstances under which it is made, is a misrepresentation,

[Para. (a) am. 1995, c. 45, s. 7 (nyif).]

(a.1) fails to file, furnish, deliver or send a record that

(i)　is required to be filed, furnished, delivered or sent under this Act or the regulations, or

(ii)　is required to be filed, furnished, delivered or sent under this Act or the regulations within the time required under this Act or the regulations,

[Para. (a.1) en. 1989, c. 78, s. 36(a).]

(b)　makes a statement in any record required to be filed, furnished, delivered or sent under this Act or the regulations that, at the time and in light of the circumstances under which it is made, is a misrepresentation,

[Para. (b) am. 1989, c. 78, s. 36(b).]

(c)　contravenes any of section 20, 34 to 42, 51(2), 67 to 70, 82 to 94, 101(1) and (2), 105, 106, 108, 111, 127(8), 132 or 137(3) of this Act,

[Para. (c) am. 1988, c. 58, s. 20; 1989, c. 78, s. 36(c).]

(c)　contravenes any of section 20, 34 to 42, 50.1(1), 67 to 70, 82 to 94, 101(1) and (2), 105, 106, 108, 111, 127(8), 132 or 137(3) of this Act,

[Para. (c) am. 1992, s. 52, s. 24 (nyif).]

(c)　contravenes any of section 15.1(6), 20, 24.1(6), 34 to 41.3, 42, 50.1(1), 67 to 70, 82 to 94, 101(1) and (2), 105, 106, 108, 108.1, 110.1, 111, 127(7), 132 or 137(3) of this Act,

[Para. (c) am. 1995, c. 45, s. 43(a) (nyif).]

(d)　fails to observe or to comply with a decision made under this Act, or

(e)　contravenes any of the provisions of the regulations that are specified by regulation for the purpose of this paragraph,

(d) fails to observe or to comply with a decision made under this Act,

(e) contravenes any of the provisions of the regulations that are specified by regulation for the purpose of this paragraph, or

[Paras. (d) and (e) am. 1995, c. 45, s. 43(b) (nyif).]

(f) contravenes any of the provisions of the commission rules that are specified by regulation for the purpose of this paragraph,

[Para. (f) en. 1995, c. 45, s. 43(b) (nyif).]

commits an offence and is liable, in the case of a person other than an individual, to a fine of not more than $1 million and, in the case of an individual, to a fine of not more than $1 million or to imprisonment for not more than 3 years or to both.

[S. 138(1) am. 1989, c. 78, s. 36(d) and (e).]

(2) A person does not commit an offence under subsection (1)(a) or (b) where the person

(a) did not know, and

(b) in the exercise of reasonable diligence, could not have known,

that the statement was a misrepresentation.

[S. 138(2) am. 1989, c. 78, s. 36(f).]

(3) Where a person, other than an individual, commits an offence under subsection (1), an employee, officer, director or agent of that person who authorizes, permits or acquiesces in the offence commits the same offence whether or not that person is convicted of the offence.

[S. 138(3) re-en. 1989, c. 78, s. 36(g).]

(4) Notwithstanding subsection (1), if a person has contravened section 68(1), the fine to which that person is liable shall be

(a) not less than any profit made by that person because of the contravention of section 68(1), and

(b) not more than the greater of

(i) $1 million, or

(ii) an amount equal to triple any profit made by that person because of the contravention of section 68(1).

(5) Notwithstanding subsection (1), if a person has contravened section 68(2) or (3), the fine to which that person is liable shall be

(a) not less than any profit made by that person because of the contravention of section 68(2) or (3), and

(b) not more than the greatest of

(i) $1 million,

(ii) an amount equal to triple any profit made by that person because of the contravention of section 68(2) or (3), or

(iii) an amount equal to triple any profit made by one or more other persons who

(A) were informed by that person of the material fact or material change in contravention of section 68(2) or (3), and

(B) with knowledge of the material fact or material change, purchased or sold securities in contravention of section 68(1).

(6) For the purposes of subsections (4) and (5), "profit",

(a) of a person that purchased securities in contravention of section 68(1), means the amount determined by

    (i) ascertaining the average market price of the security over the 20 trading days immediately following general disclosure of the material fact or material change, and

    (ii) subtracting from that average market price the amount paid by that person for the securities,

(b) of a person that sold securities in contravention of section 68(1), means the amount determined by

    (i) ascertaining the amount received by that person for the securities, and

    (ii) subtracting from that amount the average market price of the securities over the 20 trading days immediately following general disclosure of the material fact or material change, and

(c) of a person that informed one or more other persons of a material fact or material change in contravention of section 68(2) or (3) and received any direct or indirect consideration for the information, means the value of the consideration received by that person.

[S. 138(4) to (6) en. 1989, c. 78, s. 36(h).]

The burden of proof under this section is beyond a reasonable doubt.

Re Chromex Nickel Mines Ltd., Kleena Kleene Gold Mines Ltd. and Michael Hretchka, [1991] 29 B.C.S.C. Weekly Summary 9 (B.C. Sec. Comm.).

The provisions of the Act are not in truth retrospective, since the real aim of the law is prospective and aimed at protecting the public.

Execution of warrant issued in another province

139. (1) Where a court of another province issues a warrant for the arrest of a person on a charge of contravening the provisions of an Act or regulations of that province that are similar to the provisions of this Act or the regulations, a court of the Province, within whose territorial jurisdiction that person is or is suspected to be, may, on satisfactory proof of the handwriting of the person who issued the warrant, make an endorsement on the warrant in the required form.

The required form is Form 40.

---

(2) A warrant endorsed under subsection (1) is sufficient authority to

(a) the person bringing the warrant,

(b) all other persons to whom it was originally directed, and

(c) all peace officers within the territorial jurisdiction of the court of the Province so endorsing the warrant,

to execute the warrant within that jurisdiction, to take the person arrested under the warrant out of, or anywhere in, the Province and to rearrest that person anywhere in the Province.

(3) A peace officer

(a) of the Province, or

(b) of any other province who is passing through the Province,

having in his custody a person arrested in another province under a warrant endorsed under subsection (1), is entitled to hold, take and rearrest the person anywhere in the Province under the warrant without proof of the warrant or the endorsement.

Order for compliance

140. (1) Where the commission considers that a person has failed to comply with or is violating a decision or a provision of this Act or the regulations, the commission may, in addition to any other powers it may have, apply to the Supreme Court for an order directing

(a) the person to comply with or to cease violating the decision or provision, and

(b) the directors and senior officers of the person to cause the person to comply with or to cease violating the decision or provision.

140. (1) Where the commission considers that a person has failed to comply with or is violating a provision of this Act or of the regulations or has failed to comply with or is violating a decision, the commission, in addition to any other powers it may have, may apply to the Supreme Court for one or both of the following:

(a) an order that

    (i) the person comply with or cease violating the provision or decision, and

    (ii) the directors and senior officers of the person cause the person to comply with or to cease violating the provision or decision;

(b) an order that the person pay to the minister for payment into the consolidated revenue fund one or both of the following:

    (i) any moneys obtained by the person directly or indirectly as a result of the failure to comply or the violation;

    (ii) the amount of any payments or losses avoided by the person directly or indirectly as a result of the failure to comply or the violation.

[S. 140(1) re-en. 1995, c. 45, s. 44 (nyif).]

(2) On an application under subsection (1), the Supreme Court may make the order applied for and any other order the court considers appropriate, including, without limiting the generality of this power, an order

(a) setting aside a transaction relating to trading in securities or exchange contracts,

(b) requiring the issuance or cancellation of a security or the purchase, disposition or exchange of a security or exchange contract,

(c) prohibiting the voting of a security or the exercise of a right attaching to a security or exchange contract, and

(a) setting aside a transaction relating to trading in securities or exchange contracts,

(b) requiring the issuance or cancellation of a security or the purchase, disposition or exchange of a security or exchange contract,

(c) prohibiting the voting of a security or the exercise of a right attaching to a security or exchange contract, and

[Paras. (a) to (c) re-en. 1990, c. 25, s. 45 (nyif).]

(d) appointing a director of the person that is the subject of the application.

[S. 140(2) re-en. 1989, c. 78, s. 37.]

(3) An order may be made under this section notwithstanding that a penalty has already been imposed on that person in respect of the same non-compliance or violation.

Section 5 of the Offence Act

141. Section 5 of the *Offence Act* does not apply to this Act or the regulations.

Limitation period

142. No proceedings under this Act, other than an action referred to in section 124, shall be commenced more than 6 years after the date of the events that give rise to the proceedings.

[S. 142 re-en. 1989, c. 78, s. 38; am. 1990, c. 25, s. 46.]

Re D.N.I. Holdings Inc. and Gino Cicci, [1993] 38 B.C.S.C. Weekly Summary 6 (B.C. Sec. Comm.), leave to appeal to C.A. refused (sub nom. *British Columbia (Securities Commission) v. Cicci*) 2 C.C.L.S. 117, 39 B.C.A.C. 126, 64 W.A.C. 126 (C.A.).

In December 1988, the Commission retained an outside party to review D.N.I.'s promotional material and news releases which had been arranged and distributed by Cicci during the periods from July, 1988 to December, 1988. A report was provided to the Commission in January, 1989 and a Notice of Hearing was issued by the Superintendent on December 4, 1991. During this period of inactivity, there were some changes in the Commission's staff, heavy workload and other "pressing priorities". The hearing was initially set for January 12, 1992 but did not commence until March 1, 1993 at which Cicci made a motion to have the proceedings stayed, arguing an abuse of process due to the length of delay.

The Commission refused the motion. When considering an abuse of process based on an argument of length of delay, the Commission will balance the interest of the person being charged with "the interest of the community in being assured that the trading of securities is carried out with the propriety which they have a right to expect under the Securities Act". In light of all the circumstances in this case and the "fundamental principles of justice which underlay the community sense of fair play and decency", the Commission in this case rejected Cicci's abuse of process argument. Further, s. 11(b) of the Canadian Charter of Rights and Freedoms has no application to proceedings of the Commission as they are of "an administrative nature instituted for the protection of the public in accordance with the policy of a statute".

On a separate issue, the Commission considered the change in the limitation period for initiating proceedings under the Act which was effective on November 1, 1989. The limitation period was changed from "2 years after the facts on which the proceedings are based first come to the knowledge of the Commission" to "6 years after the date of the events giving rise to the proceedings". The law is clear that, unless the amendment adversely affects vested rights, amending a statute to change a limitation period is a procedural change and hence retrospective. (See *R. v. Chandra Darma*, [1905] 2 K.B. 335, *Sommers v. R.*, [1959] S.C.R. 678, 31 C.R. 36, 124 C.C.C. 241 [B.C.].)

The Court of Appeal dismissed the application for leave to appeal from the Commission's decision as the proposed appeal lacked merit. While there was unquestionably a substantial delay from the time the facts were known by the regulatory authorities to the date the Notice of Hearing was issued, the notice had been issued within the applicable six-year limitation period. At the time of the application for leave to appeal, the limitation period had not yet expired. Furthermore, the Commission had given an explanation for the delay. Although other comments might be made about the lack of diligence displayed in pursuing the matter, there was no suggestion that the delay was occasioned by any ulterior purpose. Determining the possible prejudice to the applicant as a result of the delay was not properly the subject of preliminary determination.

Costs of investigation

143. (1) A person convicted of an offence against this Act or the regulations is liable, after the review and filing of a certificate under this section, for the costs of the investigation of the offence.

[S. 143(1) am. 1989, c. 30, s. 47.]

(2) The superintendent may prepare a certificate setting out the costs of the investigation of an offence including the cost of the time spent by himself, his staff and any fees paid to an expert, investigator or witness.

(2) The executive director may prepare a certificate setting out the costs of the investigation of an offence including the cost of the time spent by himself, his staff and any fees paid to an expert, investigator or witness.

[S. 143(2) am. 1995, c. 45, s. 7 (nyif).]

(3) The superintendent may apply to a master or registrar of a court to review the certificate under the rules of court as if the certificate were a bill of costs, and on the review the master or registrar shall review the costs and may vary them if he considers that they are unreasonable or not related to the investigation.

[S. 143(3) am. 1989, c. 30, s. 47(b).]

(3) The executive director may apply to a master or registrar of a court to review the certificate under the rules of court as if the certificate were a bill of costs, and on the review the master or registrar shall review the costs and may vary them if he considers that they are unreasonable or not related to the investigation.

[S. 143(3) am. 1995, c. 45, s. 7 (nyif).]

(4) The tariff of costs in the rules of court does not apply to a certificate reviewed under this section.

[S. 143(4) am. 1989, c. 30, s. 47(c).]

(5) On the review the master or registrar shall take into account any fees already paid by the defendant under sections 9(3) and 134 in respect of the same investigation.

[S. 143(5) am. 1989, c. 30, s. 47(d).]

(6) After review the certificate may be filed in the court in which the proceedings were heard and may be enforced against the person convicted as if it were an order of the court.

[S. 143(6) am. 1989, c. 30, s. 47(e).]

Enforcement orders

144. (1) Where the commission or the superintendent considers it to be in the public interest, the commission or the superintendent, after a hearing, may order

144. (1) Where the commission or the executive director considers it to be in the public interest, the commission or the executive director, after a hearing, may order

[S. 144(1) am. 1995, c. 45, s. 45(a) (nyif).]

(a)   that a person comply with or cease contravening, and that the directors and senior officers of the person cause the person to comply with or cease contravening,

   (i) a provision of this Act or the regulations,

   (ii) a decision, whether or not the decision has been filed under section 144.2, or

   (iii) a bylaw, rule, or other regulatory instrument or policy or a direction, decision, order or ruling made under a bylaw, rule or other regulatory instrument or policy of a self regulatory body or stock exchange, as the case may be, which has been recognized by the commission under section 11,

   (iii) a bylaw, rule, or other regulatory instrument or policy or a direction, decision, order or ruling made under a bylaw, rule or other regulatory instrument or policy of a self regulatory body or exchange, as the case may be, which has been recognized by the commission under section 11,

[Subpara. (iii) am. 1990, c. 25, s. 47(a) (nyif).]

(b)   that

   (i) all persons

(ii) the person or persons named in the order, or

(iii) one or more classes of persons

cease trading in a specified security or in a class of security,

cease trading in a specified security or exchange contract or in a class of security or a class of exchange contract,

[Para. (b) am. 1990, c. 25, s. 47(b) (nyif).]

(b) that

(i) all persons,

(ii) the person or persons named in the order, or

(iii) one or more classes of persons

cease trading in, or be prohibited from purchasing, a specified security or exchange contract or a specified class of securities or class of exchange contracts,

[Para. (b) re-en. 1995, c. 45, s. 45(b) (nyif).]

(c) that any or all of the exemptions described in any of sections 30 to 32, 55, 58, 80 or 81 do not apply to a person,

(c) that any or all of the exemptions described in any of sections 30 to 32.1, 55, 58, 80 or 81 do not apply to a person,

[Para. (c) am. 1990, c. 25, s. 47(c) (nyif).]

(d) that a person

(i) resign any position that the person holds as a director or officer of an issuer, and

(ii) is prohibited from becoming or acting as a director or officer of any issuer,

(i) resign any position that the person holds as a director or officer of an issuer,

(ii) is prohibited from becoming or acting as a director or officer of any issuer, or

[Subparas. (i) and (ii) am. 1995, c. 45, s. 45(c) (nyif).]

(iii) is prohibited from engaging in investor relations activities,

[Subpara. (iii) en. 1995, c. 45, s. 45(c) (nyif).]

(e) that a registrant or issuer

(e) that a registrant, issuer or person engaged in investor relations activities

[Para. (e) am. 1995, c. 45, s. 45(d) (nyif).]

(i) is prohibited from disseminating to the public, or authorizing the dissemination to the public, of any information or record of any kind that is described in the order,

(ii) is required to disseminate to the public, by the method described in the order, any information or record relating to the affairs of the registrant or issuer that the commission or the superintendent considers must be disseminated, or

> (ii) is required to disseminate to the public, by the method described in the order, any information or record relating to the affairs of the registrant or issuer that the commission or the executive director considers must be disseminated, or

[Subpara. (ii) am. 1995, c. 45, s. 45(a) (nyif).]

> (iii) is required to amend, in the manner specified in the order, any information or record of any kind described in the order before disseminating the information or record to the public or authorizing its dissemination to the public, or

(f) that a registrant be reprimanded or that a person's registration be suspended, cancelled or restricted.

> (f) that a registrant be reprimanded, that a person's registration be suspended, cancelled or restricted or that conditions be imposed on a registrant.

[Para. (f) re-en. 1995, c. 45, s. 45(e) (nyif).]

Re Aatra Resources Ltd., Victor J. Meunier, Paul A. Quinn, Ralph A.A. Simpson, Joel Machtinger, Henry P.M. Huber, Alex Pancer, David J. Foster and Durham Securities Corp. Ltd. (1993), 3 C.C.L.S. 51 (B.C. Sec. Comm.).

The Commission requires a high standard of proof, within the civil standard of proof on a balance of probabilities, for any findings that would lead to the cancellation of a person's registration under the Act.

[S. 144(1) am. 1990, c. 25, s. 47(d).]

See NIN 89/21 "Removal of Trading Exemptions".

Re Mervin Derrick Holoboff (a.k.a. Derrick Mervin Constance Holoboff), Jane Elizabeth Holoboff and Katheryn Elizabeth Louise McKinney, [1993] 29 B.C.S.C. Weekly Summary 7 (B.C. Sec. Comm.).

The Alberta Securities Commission had previously ordered that Holoboff and McKinney cease trading in securities in Alberta and removed their exemptions under the Securities Act (Alberta) for life. Holoboff and McKinney were also each convicted under the Securities Act (Alberta) of seven counts of trading without registration and seven counts of distributing securities without having filed a prospectus. The Commission was asked to issue an order restricting access by the respondents to the British Columbia capital markets. The Commission found that on the basis of this evidence and the respondents' intention to carry on a similar business in British Columbia, the respondents represented a threat to investors in British Columbia. It was therefore in the public interest to restrict the participation of these persons in the British Columbia securities market by preventing them from raising capital for, or managing the business and affairs of, issuers in British Columbia for a period of 25 years.

---

(2) Where the commission or the superintendent considers that the length of time required to hold a hearing under subsection (1), other than under subsection (1)(e)(ii) or (iii), could be prejudicial to the public interest, the commission or the superintendent may make a temporary order, without a hearing, to have effect for not longer than 15 days after the date the temporary order is made.

> (2) Where the commission or the executive director considers that the length of time required to hold a hearing under subsection (1), other than under subsection (1)(e)(ii) or (iii), could be prejudicial to the public interest, the commission or the

executive director may make a temporary order, without a hearing, to have effect for not longer than 15 days after the date the temporary order is made.

[S. 144(2) am. 1995, c. 45, s. 7 (nyif).]

> See NIN 88/11 "The Effect of Criminal and Civil Litigation on Trading Rights and Registration".

(3) Where the commission or the superintendent considers it necessary and in the public interest, the commission or the superintendent may, without a hearing, make an order extending a temporary order until a hearing is held and a decision is rendered.

(3) Where the commission or the executive director considers it necessary and in the public interest, the commission or the executive director may, without a hearing, make an order extending a temporary order until a hearing is held and a decision is rendered.

[S. 144(3) am. 1995, c. 45, s. 7 (nyif).]

> See the discussion of *Pessl* at s. 149 with respect to temporary orders when leave to appeal a decision of the Commission has been granted.
>
> *Re Robert G. Reid*, [1992] 45 B.C.S.C. Weekly Summary 9 (B.C. Sec. Comm.).
>
> Reid was subject to securities related criminal charges in Alabama and the Superintendent of Brokers issued temporary orders withdrawing Reid's statutory exemptions and prohibiting him from becoming or acting as a director of any reporting issuer or any issuer that provides management, administrative, promotional or consulting services to a reporting issuer. The Commission extended the temporary orders on the ground that their mandates under the Securities Act are to regulate the trading of securities in the province and to protect the public interest. The Commission held that to permit Reid to continue to trade in securities may affect the integrity of the local capital markets and erode investor confidence which is not in the public interest. The Commission also held that NIN 88/11 indicates that the Superintendent will generally issue temporary orders, withdrawing a person's statutory exemption, when someone is charged with a securities related offence.
>
> *Reid v. British Columbia (Securities Commission)*, Hinds J.A., Vancouver Doc. CA016318, November 27, 1992, [1993] B.C.W.L.D. 226, 21 B.C.A.C. 75 at 79, 37 W.A.C. 75 at 79 (C.A.).
>
> Hinds J.A. granted leave to appeal and ordered a stay of the temporary orders against Reid subject to the terms that Reid not act as a director or officer of any reporting issuer in B.C. until the disposition of the appeal and Reid report in writing to the Commission on Friday of each and every week all of his trading activities for the previous week ending on the previous Friday. The court made this order on the ground that it was not satisfied that it was necessary for the suspension of Reid's rights to continue. This decision was upheld by the Court of Appeal (*Reid v. British Columbia (Securities Commission)*, Vancouver Doc. CA016318, January 7, 1993, [1993] B.C.W.L.D. 482, 21 B.C.A.C. 75, 37 W.A.C. 75 (C.A.)).
>
> *Re Harvey S. Wish*, [1992] 50 B.C.S.C. Weekly Summary 28 (B.C. Sec. Comm.).
>
> On the basis of facts substantially the same as in the case of Reid, the Commission held that in light of Mr. Justice Hinds' decision in Reid, they would not extend the temporary orders against Wish.

Re Axagon Resources Ltd., Stephen Jeffery Greenwald and Jay Robin Greenwald (1993), 1 C.C.L.S. 75 (B.C. Sec. Comm.).

It is damaging to the integrity of the market and prejudicial to the public interest when a reporting issuer issues shares for no or for inadequate consideration. The adequacy of the consideration paid for a company's shares is not solely a private matter. Where there is *prima facie* evidence that the company's shares were issued for no or for inadequate consideration, it is necessary and in the public interest to extend a temporary order prohibiting any trading of these shares until an investigation is completed, a hearing under s. 144(1) of the Act is held and a decision is rendered.

(4) The commission or the superintendent, as the case may be, shall send written notice of every order made under this section to any person that is directly affected by the order.

(4) The commission or the executive director, as the case may be, shall send written notice of every order made under this section to any person that is directly affected by the order.

[S. 144(4) am. 1995, c. 45, s. 7 (nyif).]

(5) Where notice of a temporary order is sent under subsection (4), the notice shall be accompanied by a notice of hearing.

[S. 144 re-en. 1989, c. 78, s. 39.]

See the discussion of the role of the Commission under s. 4 of the Act. See also NIN 89/21 "Orders Pursuant to Section 145 (sic) of the Securities Act – Removal of Trading Exemptions".

Re Aatra Resources Ltd., Victor J. Meunier, Joanne S. McClusky, Paul A. Quinn, Ralph A.A. Simpson, Joel Machtinger, Henry P.M. Huber, Alex Pancer, David J. Foster and Durham Securities Corp. Ltd. [1992] 3 B.C.S.C. Weekly Summary 16 (B.C. Sec. Comm.).

The Commission can consider evidence of breaches of Vancouver Stock Exchange by-laws, rules and policies in determining whether it is in the public interest to make orders under s. 144 of the Act. The Exchange does not need to be granted standing in such hearings because of the fact that actions by or involving the Exchange might come under scrutiny during the hearing.

Re Toodoggone Gold Inc. and Algo Resources Ltd. and Errol Hemingson, Margaret Alexa Hemingson and Aggressive Resource Management Ltd., [1991] 29 B.C.S.C. Weekly Summary 24 (B.C. Sec. Comm.).

The discretion granted to the Commission is not, by anything found in s. 144(1), confined to circumstances in which a breach of the Act, the Regulation or a policy statement occurs.

Re Eugenio Sirianni and Francesco Sirianni and Montreux Development Corp., [1991] 40 B.C.S.C. Weekly Summary 7 (B.C. Sec. Comm.).

In determining whether it is in the public interest to make an order under s. 144(1) of the Act, the Commission does not need to find a specific breach of the Act, the Regulation or a policy statement of the Commission. To suggest otherwise would be contrary to the plain wording of s. 144(1) and would mean that the Commission would fail to carry out its mandate.

With respect to s. 154.1(c), hearsay is clearly admissible before the Commission. In admitting it the Commission must observe the rules of natural justice, but this does not mean that it must be tested by cross-examination.

Re Russell James Bennett, William Richards Bennett and Harbanse Singh Doman, [1992] 11 B.C.S.C. Weekly Summary 6 (B.C. Sec. Comm.).

In the absence of specific rules laid down by the Act or the Regulation, the Commission controls the procedures for holding a hearing under s. 144(1), subject only to the proviso that they exercise their discretion in accordance with the rules of natural justice. The Commission's mandate under the Act is to regulate trading in securities and to protect the public interest. The Commission must act in the public interest in performing its duty to hold a hearing under s. 144(1).

The public interest that the Commission must consider in exercising its duty to hold a hearing under s. 144(1) is not necessarily the same as the public interest it must consider in making orders under s. 144(1). The Commission does, however, have a duty under s. 144(1) to hold hearings expeditiously, as part of its mandate under the Act to act in the public interest.

When a hearing is held and a decision is rendered, an application may be made for leave to appeal under s. 149 of the Act. Only at that time, if leave is granted, can the Commission's ruling be reviewed and then only if their ruling results in the decision being voidable as having been made without complying with the requirements of natural justice.

Bennett v. British Columbia (Superintendent of Brokers) (1993), 77 B.C.L.R. (2d) 145, (sub nom. *Doman v. British Columbia (Securities Commission)*) 22 B.C.A.C. 300, 38 W.A.C. 300, additional reasons (April 2, 1993), Vancouver Docs. CA016670, CA016671, CA016672, [1993] B.C.W.L.D. 1197 (not yet reported), reversed in part (1993), 21 C.P.C. (3d) 387 (B.C.C.A.).

The Commission dismissed an objection that the participation of Commissioner Devine resulted in a reasonable apprehension of bias because Mr. Devine was a director, shareholder, chairman of the audit committee and a member of the executive compensation committee of one of Doman Industries, major competitors. On January 25, 1993 an application for leave to appeal the decision on the apprehension of bias and an application for a stay of proceedings was made to the Court of Appeal. Lambert J.A. granted leave to appeal and granted a stay of proceedings of the Commission, including the delivery of any reasons for any ruling made by the panel on the hearing.

Hamouth v. British Columbia (Securities Commission) (1991), 57 B.C.L.R. (2d) 363, 1 B.C.A.C. 116, 1 W.A.C. 116 (C.A.).

In exercising the power conferred by this section to make and extend orders withdrawing trading privileges, the Superintendent or the Commission need not strictly adhere to the specific requirements of s. 144(4) and (5) in cases concerned with a *lis inter partes* and not a matter concerning the public interest. Substantial compliance is sufficient. There is no reason to restrict s. 144(3) to authorizing the making of only one order of extension. The legislation contemplates an action until a hearing is held.

British Columbia (Securities Commission) v. Manager of Canadian Broadcasting Corp. Pension Plan (1994), 3 C.C.L.S. 174 (C.A.).

Section 144 does not give the Commission the power to issue letters of request in aid of the Commission with respect to evidence to be tendered at a hearing under s. 144.

Administrative penalty

144.1 Where the commission, after a hearing,

(a) determines that a person has contravened

   (i) a provision of this Act or of the regulations, or

   (ii) a decision, whether or not the decision has been filed under section 144.2, and

(b) considers it to be in the public interest to make the order the commission may order the person to pay the commission an administrative penalty of not more than $100,000.

[S. 144.1 en. 1989, c. 78, s. 40.]

Enforcement of commission orders

144.2 (1) Where the commission has made a decision after a hearing, the commission may file the decision at any time in a Supreme Court registry by filing a copy of the decision certified by the chairman of the commission.

144.2 (1) Where the commission has made a decision after a hearing, the commission may file the decision at any time in a Supreme Court registry by filing a copy of the decision certified by the chair of the commission.

[S. 144.2(1) am. 1995, c. 45, s. 5 (nyif).]

(2) On being filed under subsection (1), a decision of the commission has the same force and effect, and all proceedings may be taken on it, as if it were a judgment of the Supreme Court.

[S. 144.2 en. 1989, c. 78, s. 40.]

No Commission decisions have been filed in the Supreme Court Registry as at the date of this edition.

---

145. [Repealed 1989, c. 78, s. 39.]

145.1 [Repealed 1989, c. 78, s. 39.]

Failure to comply with filing requirements

146. (1) For the reasons set out in subsection (2), the commission or the superintendent, without a hearing, may order that all persons, the person or persons named in the order or one or more specified persons or classes of persons cease trading in a specified security or exchange contract or in a class of security or class of exchange contract.

146. (1) For the reasons set out in subsection (2), the commission or the executive director, without a hearing, may order that all persons, the person or persons named in the order or one or more specified persons or classes of persons cease trading in a specified security or exchange contract or in a class of security or class of exchange contract.

[S. 146(1) am. 1995, c. 45, s. 7 (nyif).]

(2) The commission or the superintendent may make an order under subsection (1) where the issuer of the security, the exchange on which the exchange contract is traded or the person in respect of which the order is made

(2) The commission or the executive director may make an order under subsection (1) where the issuer of the security, the exchange on which the exchange contract is traded or the person in respect of which the order is made

[S. 146(2) am. 1995, c. 45, s. 7 (nyif).]

(a)   fails to file a record required to be filed under this Act or the regulations, provided that the order is revoked as soon as practicable after the record referred to in the order, completed in accordance with this Act and the regulations, is filed, or

(b)   files a record required to be filed under this Act or the regulations which record has not been completed in accordance with this Act or the regulations, provided that the order is revoked as soon as practicable after the record referred to in the order, completed in accordance with this Act and the regulations, is filed.

(3) The commission or the superintendent, as the case may be, shall send to any person directly affected by an order made under subsection (1)

(3) The commission or the executive director, as the case may be, shall send to any person directly affected by an order made under subsection (1)

[S. 146(3) am. 1995, c. 45, s. 7 (nyif).]

(a) written notice of the order, and

(b) written notice of a revocation of the order, if any.

[S. 146 re-en. 1992, c. 52, s. 25.]

See Local Policy Statement 3-35 "Reactivation of Dormant Issuers".

PART 17

REVIEWS AND APPEALS

Review of decision of superintendent

147. (1) The superintendent shall notify the commission of every decision he makes

147. (1) The executive director shall notify the commission of every decision he makes

[S. 147(1) am. 1995, c. 45, s. 7 (nyif).]

(a) refusing registration of any person,

(b) suspending, terminating, restricting or imposing conditions on registration of any person,

(c) refusing to permit a distribution or additional distribution to proceed until a receipt for an amendment to a prospectus is issued,

[S. 147(1)(c) re-en. 1989, c. 78, s. 42(b).]

(d) refusing to issue a receipt for a prospectus under section 46,

(e) ordering trading to halt under section 73,

(f) ordering trading to cease under section 146,

[S. 147(1)(f) am. 1989, c. 78, s. 42(a).]

(g) refusing to exempt a person or class of persons under section 33 from registration requirements or under section 59(1) from prospectus requirements, and

[S. 147(1)(g) re-en. 1987, c. 42, s. 99; am. 1992, c. 52, s. 26(a).]

(h) under section 144, and

[S. 147(1)(h) re-en. 1989, c. 78, s. 42(b).]

at the same time as he notifies the person directly affected by his decision.

(2) The commission may review a decision referred to in subsection (1) and where it intends to do so shall, within 30 days of the date of the decision, notify the superintendent and any person directly affected by the superintendent's decision of its intention.

(2) The commission may review a decision referred to in subsection (1) and where it intends to do so shall, within 30 days of the date of the decision, notify the executive director and any person directly affected by the superintendent's decision of its intention.

[S. 147(2) am. 1995, c. 45, s. 7 (nyif).]

(3) Except where otherwise expressly provided, any person directly affected by a decision of the superintendent may, by a notice in writing sent to the commission

within 30 days after the date on which the superintendent sent the notice of the decision to the person, request and be entitled to a hearing and a review of the decision of the superintendent.

[S. 147(3) am. 1989, c. 78, s. 42(c); 1992, c. 52, s. 26(b).]

(3) Except where otherwise expressly provided, any person directly affected by a decision of the executive director may, by a notice in writing sent to the commission within 30 days after the date on which the executive director sent the notice of the decision to the person, request and be entitled to a hearing and a review of the decision of the executive director.

[S. 147(3) am. 1995, c. 45, s. 7 (nyif).]

Advance Capital Services v. The British Columbia Securities Commission, The Superintendent of Brokers, Gordon D. Mulligan, The Deputy Superintendent of Brokers, Greenwell Resources Corporation and Supreme Resources Inc. (January 18, February 9, 1993), Vancouver Doc. A902296, Holmes J. (S.C.) (not yet reported).

Section 147(3) of the Act does not offer a hearing *de novo* except to a person "directly affected" and to one whom the Superintendent of Brokers has mailed a notice of his decision. The section is worded in such a way that if the superintendent did not mail notice of the decision to a person then that person has no status to request a hearing *de novo*.

(4) On a hearing and review, the commission may confirm or vary the decision under review or make another decision it considers proper.

(5) The commission may grant a stay of the decision under review until disposition of the hearing and review.

(6) The superintendent is a party to a hearing and review under this section of any decision.

(6) The executive director is a party to a hearing and review under this section of any decision.

[S. 147(6) am. 1995, c. 45, s. 7 (nyif).]

(7) A designated organization is a party to a hearing and review under this section of its decision.

(8) A self regulatory body or stock exchange is a party to a hearing and review under this section of its decision.

(8) A self regulatory body or exchange is a party to a hearing and review under this section of its decision.

[S. 147(8) am. 1990, c. 25, s. 49 (nyif).]

See Local Policy Statement 3-12 "Rules for Proceedings".

Re Greenwell Resources Corp. and Supreme Resources Inc. and Advance Capital Services Corp., Jason Dallas, Robert Palm, Michael Doherty and David Lyon, [1992] 8 B.C.S.C. Weekly Summary 5 (B.C. Sec. Comm.).

Section 147(3) gives the right of a hearing and review to any person directly affected by an order of the Superintendent. Section 148(1), by reference to s. 147(3), gives the right of a hearing and review to any person directly affected by an order of a member of the Commission acting under authority delegated under s. 6. Section 147(3) entitles applicants who are directly affected by cease trade orders to a hearing and review of those orders. There is no suggestion that shareholders of an issuer must always be considered to be directly affected by a decision directly affecting the issuer.

A decision of a member to whom the Commission has delegated authority is a decision of the Commission. The only distinction in the Act between a decision of a member and a decision of the Commission or a panel established by the chairman under s. 5 is that a decision of a member is subject to review under s. 148. Section 153 gives the Commission the power to revoke or vary a decision made by a member to whom the Commission has delegated authority.

A person directly affected by a decision may apply to the Commission at any time under s. 153 for an order revoking or varying the decision. The Commission may make such an order, with or without holding a hearing, where it considers it would not be prejudicial to the public interest.

There is no requirement in the Act to give notice or hold a hearing before an investigation order is issued. This is because the issuance of an investigation order does not involve an adjudication of rights. Once the investigation has concluded, the person subject to the investigation is entitled to a hearing in respect of any orders proposed under s. 144(1). The plain words of the Act require that a notice of hearing accompany a temporary order. There is no requirement in the Act that a notice of hearing accompany the extension of a temporary order.

See also the decisions under s. 15(1) of the Act.

Review of decision of person acting under delegated authority

148. (1) A designated organization and a person acting under authority delegated to him by the commission under section 6 shall immediately notify the commission and the superintendent of every decision it or he makes, and section 147(2) to (5) applies to that decision.

148. (1) A designated organization and a person acting under authority delegated to him by the commission under section 6 shall immediately notify the commission and the executive director of every decision it or he makes, and section 147(2) to (5) applies to that decision.

[S. 148(1) am. 1995, c. 45, s. 7 (nyif).]

(2) A person referred to in subsection (1) shall not sit on a hearing and review by the commission of his decision.

(3) The superintendent may request and is entitled to a hearing and a review of a decision of a designated organization and section 147(2) to (5) applies to that decision.

(3) The executive director may request and is entitled to a hearing and a review of a decision of a designated organization and section 147(2) to (5) applies to that decision.

[S. 148(3) am. 1995, c. 45, s. 7 (nyif).]

Re Vancouver Stock Exchange and Bankit Resource Corp., Caliente Resources Ltd., Draw International Resources Corp., Flow Resources Ltd., High Rise Resources Ltd., Longboat Resources Inc., Midnapore (1979) Resources Inc., Nu-Start Resource Corp., and Shallow Resources Inc., [1988] 101 B.C.S.C. Weekly Summary (B.C. Sec. Comm.).

In dealings with appeals from the Vancouver Stock Exchange, the Commission will not interfere with a decision of the Exchange unless the Exchange has proceeded on some incorrect principle, has erred in law, or has overlooked some material evidence or some new and compelling evidence that is presented to the Commission.

148.1 [Repealed 1988, c. 58, s. 24.]

148.2 [Repealed 1988, c. 58, s. 24.]

Appeal of decision of commission

149. (1) A person directly affected by a decision of the commission, other than

(a) a decision under section 33 or 59,

(b) a decision under section 147 in connection with the review of a decision of the superintendent under section 33 or 59, or

(b) a decision under section 147 in connection with the review of a decision of the executive director under section 33 or 59, or

[Para. (b) am. 1995, c. 45, s. 7 (nyif).]

(c) a decision by a person acting under authority delegated by the commission under section 6,

[S. 149(1)(c) en. 1992, c. 52, s. 27(a).]

may appeal to the Court of Appeal with leave of a justice of that court.

[S. 149(1) re-en. 1989, c. 78, s. 43.]

Maurice Hamlin and Craig Harrison v. British Columbia Securities Commission (1993), 2 C.C.L.S. 68 (C.A.).

Issues of fact alone or issues which relate to matters which the legislature has authorized the Commission to deal with because of its expertise in such matters are not issues which merit review by the Court of Appeal. Based upon this, the court refused an application for leave to appeal on grounds for appeal including findings of fact by the Commission, whether certain transactions amounted to material changes, whether the Commission erred in law when they found that the appellants were not entitled to rely upon the auditors, whether a failure to disclose amounted to a misrepresentation, and whether the Commission was wrong in law in reference to its findings on certain advertisements by use of references to National Policy Statement 40 and National Policy Statement 22.

British Columbia (Securities Commission) v. Marino John Ignatius Specogna, Marino John Ignatius Specogna, and Efrem Mario Maurizio Specogna Lucia Specogna, [1994] 33 B.C.S.C. Weekly Summary 5 (C.A.).

The issuance of a notice of hearing by the Commission does not constitute a decision of the Commission which would be appealable pursuant to s. 149 of the Securities Act.

Delmas v. Vancouver Stock Exchange, 98 B.C.L.R. (2d) 212, 5 C.C.L.S. 209, [1995] 1 W.W.R. 738, 119 D.L.R. (4th) 136 (S.C.).

In this case the petitioner applied for judicial review of the dismissal by a Vancouver Stock Exchange disciplinary panel of his objections to the panel's jurisdiction. The plaintiff sought prohibition and certiorari, pursuant to provisions of the Judicial Review Procedure Act, alleging that the Exchange lacked legal competence to proceed against the petitioner for the alleged wrongdoing. The Court refused to grant the petitioner the prerogative relief sought, holding that it would not be in accordance with the expressed legislative intent, as taken from the provisions of the Securities Act. The legislative scheme in place relative to the regulation of securities matters in British Columbia contemplates that matters within the jurisdiction of the Vancouver Stock Exchange will be dealt with in the first instance by that body, with a right to appeal to the Securities Commission. Thereafter, with leave, there is provision for an appeal to the Court of Appeal. This legislative scheme ensures that relatively specialized bodies will deal with matters at earlier stages but also provides a clear route of appeal to a judicial tribunal. Applications for relief should follow this route and should not be made under the Judicial Review Procedure Act.

---

(2) The commission or the Court of Appeal may grant a stay of the decision appealed from until the disposition of the appeal.

Frances David Balfour v. Superintendent of Brokers, the British Columbia Securities Commission, Peter Cox, Leonard E. Tinkler (1993), 32 B.C.A.C. 35, 53 W.A.C. 35 (C.A.) (in Chambers).

Whether an applicant's right to remain silent will be infringed if a Commission hearing is not adjourned until after the conclusion of a criminal proceeding against the applicant is an arguable issue such that leave to appeal a decision of the Commission refusing to adjourn such hearing will be granted. An order to stay the continuation of the Commission's hearing pending the hearing of the appeal will be granted if irreparable prejudice to the applicant may otherwise result.

(3) [Repealed 1992, c. 52, s. 27(b).]

(4) Where an appeal is taken under this section, the Court of Appeal may direct the commission to make a decision or to perform an act that the commission is authorized and empowered to do.

(5) Notwithstanding an order of the Court of Appeal in a particular matter, the commission may make a further decision on new material or where there is a significant change in the circumstances, and that decision is also subject to this section.

(6) The commission is a party to an appeal under this section.

[S. 149(6) en. 1987, c. 42, s. 101.]

Pezim v. British Columbia (Superintendent of Brokers) (1992), 66 B.C.L.R. (2d) 257, (sub nom. *Pezim v. British Columbia Securities Commission*) 96 D.L.R. (4th) 137, 13 B.C.A.C. 1, 24 W.A.C. 1, reversed [1994] 2 S.C.R. 557, 4 C.C.L.S. 117, [1994] 7 W.W.R. 1, 92 B.C.L.R. (2d) 145, 14 B.L.R. (2d) 217, 22 Admin. L.R. (2d) 1, 114 D.L.R. (4th) 385, 168 N.R. 321, 46 B.C.A.C. 1, 75 W.A.C. 1.

The appeal to the Supreme Court of Canada dealt mainly with the appropriate standard of review for an appellate court reviewing a decision of a securities commission which is not protected by a privative clause, where there exists a statutory right of appeal and where the case turns on a question of statutory interpretation. The central question in ascertaining this standard is to determine the legislative intent in conferring jurisdiction on the administrative tribunal. The courts have developed a spectrum in determining the applicable standard that ranges from the standard of reasonableness to that of correctness. The courts have also enunciated a principal of deference that applies not just to the facts as found by the tribunal, but also to the legal questions before the tribunal in light of its role and expertise. At the reasonableness end of the spectrum, where deference is at its highest, are those cases where a tribunal protected by a true privative clause is deciding a matter within its jurisdiction and where there is no statutory right of appeal. At the correctness end of the spectrum, where deference in terms of legal questions is at its lowest, are those cases where the issues concern the interpretation of provisions limiting the tribunal's jurisdiction (jurisdictional error) or where the statutory right of appeal allows the reviewing court to substitute its opinion for that of the tribunal and where the tribunal has no greater expertise than the court on the issue in question, as for example in the area of human rights. Even where there is no privative clause and where there is a statutory right of appeal, the concept of the specialization of duties requires that deference be shown to decisions of specialized tribunals on matters which fall squarely within the tribunal's expertise.

Section 144 of the Securities Act gives the Commission a broad discretion to make orders that it considers to be in the public interest. Thus, a reviewing court should not disturb the Commission's order unless the Commission has made some error in principle in exercising its discretion or has exercised its discretion in a capricious or vexatious manner.

Hemsworth v. British Columbia (Securities Commission) (1992), 7 C.P.C. (3d) 382 (C.A.).

In determining whether to grant leave to appeal a decision of the Commission the court unanimously confirmed that an application for leave to appeal is not confined to questions of law. Questions of fact may also be considered in such an appeal and an affidavit tendered in chambers may be introduced to establish those facts.

Pessl v. British Columbia (Securities Commission) (December 7, 1992), Vancouver Doc. CA016309, [1993] B.C.W.L.D. 339 (C.A.) (not yet reported).

The court held that it was sufficient for the applicants, in a leave to appeal application, to propose to argue issues such as procedural fairness, fundamental justice and the evidentiary threshold necessary to make a public interest order in determining that leave to appeal should be granted.

The court went on to review the evidence alleged by the Commission and the effect of the temporary order on the applicant, and examined the tests of "balance of convenience" and "irreparable harm", in determining that the temporary orders issued against the applicants should be lifted.

Huber v. British Columbia (Securities Commission) (1993), 3 C.C.L.S. 88 (B.C. C.A.).

An application for leave to appeal a decision of the Commission will not be heard where better economies of time and cost would be achieved by waiting until the decision of the Commission is final in all respects. In this case, there had been a determination by the Commission that provisions of the Act have been contravened but there was still outstanding the remaining step of determining the appropriate penalty for such contraventions. The Court of Appeal adjourned the leave to appeal application until the Commission had made such a determination. The principles to be applied to a stay application at the appellate level are found in the judgment of the Supreme Court of Canada in *Manitoba (Attorney General) v. Metropolitan Stores (MTS) Ltd.*, [1987] 1 S.C.R. 110, [1987] 3 W.W.R. 1, 87 C.L.L.C. 14,015, 38 D.L.R. (4th) 321, 73 N.R. 341 (sub nom. *Metropolitan Stores (MTS) Ltd. v. Manitoba Food & Commercial Workers, Local 832*), 18 C.P.C. (2d) 273, 46 Man. R. (2d) 241, 25 Admin. L.R. 20, which set forth three tests to be applied:

> The first test is a preliminary and tentative assessment of the merits of the case. The traditional way consists in asking whether the litigant who seeks the interlocutory injunction can make out a *prima facie* case. A more recent formulation holds that all that is necessary is to satisfy the court that there is a serious question to be tried as opposed to a frivolous or vexatious claim. The "serious question" test is sufficient in a case involving the constitutional challenge of a law where the public interest must be taken into consideration in the balance of convenience. The second test addresses the question of irreparable harm. The third test, called the balance of convenience, is a determination of which of the two parties will suffer the greater harm from the grant or refusal of an interlocutory injunction, pending a decision on the merits.

The headnote further stated that when the stay is sought against a statutory body, the public interest is a factor to be taken into account when weighing the balance of convenience. In this case, the Court of Appeal only applied the irreparable harm and balance of convenience tests and left any conclusions as to the merits of the proposed appeal to the chambers judge before whom the leave application would be ultimately set down.

Henry Huber v. British Columbia Securities Commission and the Vancouver Stock Exchange (1994), 3 C.C.L.S. 98 (B.C.C.A.).

In determining whether to grant or refuse leave to appeal from a decision of a statutory tribunal, such as the Commission, consideration may be given by a justice of the Court of Appeal to one or more of the following matters:

1. whether the proposed appeal raises a question of general importance as to the extent of jurisdiction of the tribunal appealed from;
2. whether the appeal is limited to questions of law involving:
    (a) the application of statutory provisions;
    (b) a statutory interpretation that was particularly important to the litigants; or
    (c) the interpretation of standard wording which appears in many statutes;
3. whether there was a marked difference of opinion of the decisions below and sufficient merit in the issue put forward;
4. whether there is some prospect of the appeal succeeding on its merits;
5. whether there is any clear benefit to be derived from the appeal; and
6. whether the issue on appeal has been considered by a number of appellate bodies.

(See *Queens Plate Development Ltd. v. Vancouver Assessor, Area 9* (1987), 16 B.C.L.R. (2d) 104, 22 C.P.C. (2d) 265 (C.A.)).

Also see the discussion of the *Bennett* decisions under s. 144.

PART 18

GENERAL PROVISIONS

Admissibility in evidence of certified statement

150. A statement concerning

(a) the registration or non-registration of a person under this Act or by the regulations,

(b) the filing or non-filing of a record or material required or permitted to be filed under this Act or the regulations,

(c) any other matter or information arising out of the registration or non-registration of a person or the filing or non-filing of a record or material, whichever is the case, or

(d) the date on which the facts on which any proceedings are to be based first came to the knowledge of the commission,

purporting to be certified by the commission, a member of it or the superintendent is, without proof of the office or signature of the person certifying, admissible in evidence, so far as it is relevant, for all purposes in any action, proceeding or prosecution.

purporting to be certified by the commission, a member of it or the executive director is, without proof of the office or signature of the person certifying, admissible in evidence, so far as it is relevant, for all purposes in any action, proceeding or prosecution.

[S. 150 am. 1995, c. 45, s. 7 (nyif).]

Filing and inspection of records

151.(1) Unless otherwise indicated, records required by this Act or by the regulations to be filed shall be filed by depositing them with the commission.

(1.1) Subject to the regulations, records required by this Act or by the regulations to be filed may be filed electronically in any form specified by the executive director.

[S. 151(1.1) en. 1995, c. 45, s. 46 (nyif).]

(2) All records filed under this Act or the regulations shall, subject to subsection (3), be made available for public inspection during normal business hours.

(3) The commission may hold in confidence a record or any class of record required to be filed under this Act or the regulations so long as it considers that

    (a) the record or class of record discloses intimate financial, personal or other information, and

    (b) the desirability of avoiding disclosure of the information, in the interests of any person affected, outweighs the desirability of adhering to the principle of public disclosure.

Immunity of commission and others

152. (1) No action or other proceeding for damages lies and no application for judicial review under the *Judicial Review Procedure Act* shall be instituted against the commission, a member of the commission, an officer, servant or agent of the commission, a designated organization, a member of a designated organization, an officer, servant or agent of a designated organization, an employee appointed to administer this Act or any person proceeding under

    (a) an order, a written or oral direction or the consent of the commission, or

    (b) an order of the minister made under this Act,

for any act done in good faith in the

    (c) performance or intended performance of any duty, or

    (d) exercise or the intended exercise of any power,

under this Act or the regulations, or for any neglect or default in the performance or exercise in good faith of that duty or power.

Stenner v. British Columbia (Securities Commission) (1993), 23 Admin. L.R. (2d) 247 (B.C. S.C.).

There is a defence at common law to an action for damages against the quasi judicial official who makes a wrong decision in the course of his duties in good faith. This same defence is codified under s. 152(1)(c) of the Act. The expressions "intended performance" and "intended exercise" refer to an act which is intended to be done but has not yet been done. It covers anything done as a preliminary step in the performance of a duty or the exercise of a power which is not carried to completion. It does not refer to an act which an official has done and which he intended to be in the performance of a duty or power but which was found not to be. If an act is outside the official's jurisdiction, it is unlikely that this section protects the official simply because he thought, and therefore intended, that it should be within that jurisdiction. The official, however, was in this case protected by the common law defence of good faith.

---

(2) No person has any remedies and no proceedings lie or shall be brought against any person for any act done or omission made as a result of compliance with this Act, the regulations or any decision rendered under this Act or the regulations.

Kripps v. Touche Ross & Co. (1990), 48 B.C.L.R. (2d) 171 (C.A.).

This was an appeal from an order dismissing an application by the Commission and the Crown to strike out a statement of claim and third party notice. The claim was based on the Commission's alleged negligence and lack of good faith in carrying out its statutory duties. In dismissing the appeal the court stated that s. 152 has done nothing more than put into statutory form the law as it was under the old s. 142. Section 152 has substantially the same component of good faith as had s. 142 of the prior Act (R.S.B.C. 1979, c. 380). Both sections require facts from which a finding of bad faith can be made before a plaintiff can succeed in maintaining an action against the Commission. The common thread of bad faith in both sections leads to the conclusion that the rights of potential plaintiffs under s. 152 of the new Act are in effect substantially the same as if they were under s. 142 of the old Act. That being so, s. 152 should be construed as having retrospective effect.

Discretion to revoke or vary decision

153. The commission, the superintendent or a designated organization may, where it or he considers it would not be prejudicial to the public interest, make an order revoking in whole or in part or varying a decision it or he has made under this Act, the regulations, another enactment or a former enactment, whether or not the decision has been filed under section 144.2.

[S. 153 am. 1989, c. 78, s. 44; 1992, c. 52, s. 28.]

153. The commission, the executive director or a designated organization may, where it or he considers it would not be prejudicial to the public interest, make an order revoking in whole or in part or varying a decision it or he has made under this Act, the regulations, another enactment or a former enactment, whether or not the decision has been filed under section 144.2.

[S. 153 am. 1995, c. 45, s. 7 (nyif).]

See also NIN 88/5 "Guidelines for Applications to the Securities Commission or the Superintendent of Brokers for Decisions or Orders", and Canadian Securities Administrators Notice 92/2 "Applications for Discretionary Orders".

See *Re Greenwell Resources Corp.* under s. 147 of the Act.

Conditions on decisions

154. The commission or the superintendent may impose any conditions it or he considers necessary in respect of any decision made by it or him.

154. The commission or the executive director may impose any conditions it or he considers necessary in respect of any decision made by it or him.

[S. 154 am. 1995, c. 45, s. 7 (nyif).]

See NIN 89/34 "Settlements with the British Columbia Securities Commission".

Authority of persons presiding at hearings

154.1 The person presiding at a hearing required or permitted under this Act or the regulations

(a) has the same power that an investigator appointed under section 126 or 131 has under section 128,

(b) shall receive all relevant evidence submitted by a person to whom notice has been given and may receive relevant evidence submitted by any person, and

(c) is not bound by the rules of evidence.

[S. 154.1 en. 1988, c. 58, s. 25.]

Four Star Management Ltd. v. British Columbia (Securities Commission) (1990), 46 B.C.L.R. (2d) 195, 71 D.L.R. (4th) 317, (sub nom. *O.E.X. Electromagnetic Inc. v. British Columbia (Securities Commission)*) 43 Admin. L.R. 274, leave to appeal to S.C.C. refused 51 B.C.L.R. (2d) xxxv, 1 Admin L.R. (2d) 264, 74 D.L.R. (4th) viii, (sub nom. *Williams v. British Columbia Securities Commission*) 130 N.R. 319.

The admission of evidence in the form of depositions of United States proceedings, without the cross-examination of the deposition evidence, does not lead to a denial of a fair hearing or a denial of natural justice where the Commission is aware of the limited weight to be attached to such evidence and where all the deponents were United States residents and beyond the power of the Commission to compel their attendance.

See also *Sirianni* under s. 144 of the Act, *Marathon Minerals* under s. 4 of the Act, and *GHZ* under s. 15.

prescribed fees or charges for the costs of or related to the hearing that are incurred by or on behalf of the commission or the superintendent including, without limiting this,

    (a) costs of matters preliminary to the hearing,

    (b) costs for time spent by the commission or the superintendent or the staff of either of them,

    (c) fees paid to an expert or witness, and

    (d) costs of legal services.

[S. 154.2 en. 1988, c. 58, s. 25.]

154.2 The person presiding at a hearing required or permitted under this Act or the regulations may order a person whose affairs are the subject of the hearing to pay prescribed fees or charges for the costs of or related to the hearing that are incurred by or on behalf of the commission or the executive director including, without limiting this,

    (a) costs of matters preliminary to the hearing,

    (b) costs for time spent by the commission or the executive director or the staff of either of them,

    (c) fees paid to an expert or witness, and

    (d) costs of legal services.

[S. 154.2 am. 1995, c. 45, s. 7 (nyif).]

Pezim v. British Columbia (Superintendent of Brokers), (sub nom. *Re Calpine Resources Inc. and Prime Resources Corp., now known as Prime Resources Group Inc., Murray Pezim, Lawrence Page and John Ivany)* [1990] 50 B.C.S.C. Weekly Summary, reversed (1992), 66 B.C.L.R. (2d) 257, (sub nom. *Pezim v. British Columbia Securities Commission)* 96 D.L.R. (4th) 137, 13 B.C.A.C. 1, 24 W.A.C. 1, reversed [1994] 2 S.C.R. 557, 4 C.C.L.S. 117, [1994] 7 W.W.R. 1, 92 B.C.L.R. (2d) 145, 14 B.L.R. (2d) 217, 22 Admin. L.R. (2d) 1, 114 D.L.R. (4th) 385, 168 N.R. 321, 46 B.C.A.C. 1, 75 W.A.C. 1.

Section 154.2 power relates only to the recovery of the costs to the public of holding the hearing. It is not a power to award costs as between parties. The purpose of ordering payment of costs under s. 154.2 is not to penalize the persons affected but to require those persons, rather than the general public, to bear the costs of a regulatory proceeding necessitated by their conduct.

On appeal, the appellant argued a reasonable apprehension of bias pursuant to s. 154.2. It was argued that the discretion towards costs, as conferred by s. 154.2, would not be exercised by a Commission which has a financial interest in the proceedings because of financial self-interest. The Court of Appeal rejected this argument and held that the members of the Commission are in no different position insofar as financial benefit than any member of the tax-paying public. The statute authorizes a decision that the costs are to be paid, if circumstances warrant, by those who occasioned the expense. There is no injustice in this and no reasonable apprehension of bias.

Re D.N.I. Holdings Inc. and Gino Cicci, [1993] 38 B.C.S.C. Weekly Summary 6 (B.C. Sec. Comm.).

Cicci argued that the Commission's ability, under s. 154.2 of the Act, to assess costs against him to offset costs incurred by the Commission in relation to the hearing raises an apprehension of bias. The Commission rejected this argument, relying on the principle enunciated in *Brosseau v. Alberta (Securities Commission)*, [1989] 1 S.C.R. 301, [1989] 3 W.W.R. 456, 65 Alta. L.R. (2d) 97, (sub nom. *Barry v. Alberta*

(Securities Commission)) 35 Admin. L.R. 1, 93 N.R. 1, 57 D.L.R. (4th) 458, 96 A.R. 241. Where the legislature has expressly conferred on the Commission a statutory power to collect costs related to a hearing required to be held under the Act, this legislative provision in and of itself cannot be said to give rise to a reasonable apprehension of bias.

Re Rainforest Mushrooms Ltd. and G. Gerry Hargitai, John Czinege, [1993] 48 B.C.S.C. Weekly Summary 20 (B.C. Sec. Comm.).

The process by which the Commission may order a person whose affairs are the subject of the hearing to pay the Commission's costs is specifically provided for under s. 154.2 of the Act. The Supreme Court of Canada considered this type of scheme in *Pearlman v. Law Society (Manitoba)*, [1991] 2 S.C.R. 869, (sub nom. *Pearlman v. Manitoba Law Society Judicial Committee*) [1991] 6 W.W.R. 289, 2 Admin. L.R. (2d) 185, 84 D.L.R. (4th) 105, 130 N.R. 121, 75 Man. R. (2d) 81, 6 W.A.C. 81, 6 C.R.R. (2d) 259, and found that it did not give rise to a reasonable apprehension of bias. On this basis, the respondent's argument was rejected.

Extrajurisdictional evidence

154.3 (1) Where it appears to the Supreme Court, on an application made by the commission, that a person outside of the Province may have evidence that may be relevant to

(a) an investigation ordered by the commission under section 126, or

(b) a hearing required or permitted under this Act or the regulations,

the Supreme Court may issue a letter of request directed to the judicial authority of the jurisdiction in which the person to be examined is believed to be located.

[S. 154.3(1) re-en. 1994, c. 51, s. 10(a).]

(2) The letter of request referred to in subsection (1) shall

(a) be signed by the judge hearing the application or another judge of the Supreme Court, and

(b) be provided to the commission for disposition under subsection (4).

(3) A letter of request issued under subsection (1) may request the judicial authority to which it is directed to

(a) order the person referred to in the letter of request to be examined under oath in the manner, at the place and by the date referred to in the letter of request,

(a.1) order, in the case of an examination for the purposes of a hearing referred to in subsection (1)(b), that a person who is a party to the hearing is entitled to

(i) be present or represented by counsel during the examination, and

(ii) examine the person referred to in paragraph (a),

[Para. (a.1) en. 1994, c. 51, s. 10(b).]

(b) appoint a person as the examiner to conduct the examination,

(c) order the person to be examined to produce at the examination the records and things or classes of records and things specified in the letter of request,

(d) direct that the evidence obtained by the examination be recorded and certified in the manner specified by the letter of request, and

(e) take any further or other action that the Supreme Court considers appropriate.

(3.1) The failure of the person entitled under subsection (3)(a.1) to be present or represented by counsel during the examination or to examine the person referred to in subsection (3)(a) does not prevent the commission from reading in the evidence at the hearing if the examination has otherwise been conducted in accordance with the order made under that subsection.

[S. 154.3(3.1) en. 1994, c. 51, s. 10(c).]

(4) The commission shall send the letter of request,

(a) if the examination is to be held in Canada, to the Deputy Attorney General for the Province of British Columbia, or

(b) if the examination is to be held outside Canada, to the Under Secretary of State for External Affairs of Canada.

(5) The letter of request shall have attached to it

(a) any interrogatories to be put to the person to be examined,

(b) if known, a list of the names, addresses and telephone numbers of

    (i) the solicitors or agents of the commission,

    (ii) the person to be examined, and

    (iii) where applicable, the person entitled under subsection (3)(a.1) to be present or represented by counsel during the examination and to examine the person referred to in paragraph (3)(a),

both in the Province and in the other jurisdiction, and

[Para. (b) re-en. 1994, c. 51, s. 10(d).]

(c) a translation of the letter of request and any interrogatories into the appropriate official language of the jurisdiction where the examination is to take place, along with a certificate of the translator, bearing the full name and address of the translator, that the translation is a true and complete translation.

(6) The commission shall file with the Under Secretary of State for External Affairs of Canada or with the Deputy Attorney General for the Province of British Columbia, as the case may be, an undertaking to be responsible for all of the charges and expenses incurred by the Under Secretary or the Deputy Attorney General, as the case may be, in respect of the letter of request and to pay them on receiving notification of the amount.

(7) This section does not limit any power the commission may have to obtain evidence outside of the Province by any other means.

(8) The making of an order by a judicial authority referred to in subsection (1) pursuant to a letter of request issued under that subsection does not determine whether evidence obtained pursuant to the order is admissible in evidence in a hearing before the commission.

(9) Except where otherwise provided by this section, the practice and procedure in connection with appointing a person, conducting an examination and certifying and returning the appointment under this section, as far as possible, are the same as those that govern similar matters in civil proceedings in the Supreme Court.

[S. 154.3 en. 1992, c. 52, s. 29; s. 154.3(8), (9) en. 1994, c. 51, s. 10(e).]

Extrajurisdictional request for evidence

154.4 (1) In this section "qualifying letter of request" means a letter of request that

(a) is issued by a court or tribunal of competent jurisdiction in a jurisdiction other than the Province,

(b) is issued on behalf of the body that is, in the jurisdiction from which the letter is issued, empowered by the laws of that jurisdiction to administer or regulate the trading of securities or exchange contracts in that jurisdiction,

(c) is issued in relation to

    (i) a matter under investigation by the body referred to in paragraph (b), or

(ii) a matter that is the subject of a hearing before the body referred to in paragraph (b), and

[Para. (c) re-en. 1994, c. 51, s. 11(a).]

(d) requests that evidence in relation to a matter referred to in paragraph (c) be obtained from a person believed to be located in the Province.

[Para. (d) am. 1994, c. 51, s. 11(b).]

(2) On receipt of a qualifying letter of request, the Supreme Court may make the order it considers appropriate and may, without limitation

(a) order that the person referred to in subsection (1)(d) be examined under oath in the manner, at the place and by the date requested by the foreign court or tribunal,

(a.1) order, in the case of an examination for the purposes of a hearing referred to in subsection (1)(c)(ii), that a person who is a party to the hearing is entitled to

(i) be present or represented by counsel during the examination, and

(ii) examine the person referred to in paragraph (a),

[Para. (a.1) en. 1994, c. 51, s. 11(c).]

(b) appoint a person as the examiner to conduct the examination,

(c) order that the person referred to in subsection (1)(d) produce at the examination any records and things or classes of records and things specified in the request,

(d) direct that the evidence obtained by the examination be recorded and certified in the manner requested, and

(e) make any further or other order that the Supreme Court considers appropriate.

(3) An order under subsection (2) may be enforced in the same manner as if the order were made in or in respect of a proceeding brought in the Supreme Court and where the person referred to in subsection (1) (d) fails without lawful excuse to comply with the order, the person is in contempt of the Supreme Court and is subject to the penalty that the Supreme Court imposes.

(4) A person ordered to give evidence under subsection (2) has the same rights

(a) to receive conduct money or any other money that the person would have had if the examination were held in relation to a proceeding in the Supreme Court, and

(b) to refuse to answer questions and produce records and things or classes of records and things that the person would have in a proceeding in the Supreme Court.

(5) The person appointed by the Supreme Court as the examiner has the authority to administer an oath or affirmation to the person to be examined.

(6) Except where otherwise provided by this section, the practice and procedure in connection with appointing a person, conducting an examination and certifying and returning the appointment under this section, as far as possible, are the same as those that govern similar matters in civil proceedings in the Supreme Court.

[S. 154.4 en. 1992, c. 52, s. 29; s. 154.4(6) en. 1994, c. 51, s. 11(d).]

Contempt

154.5 On application by the commission to the Supreme Court, a person is liable to be committed for contempt as if the person were in breach of an order or judgment of the Supreme Court, if the person's conduct in, or in relation to, a hearing required or permitted under this Act would be a contempt of the Supreme Court if done in, or in relation to, a hearing of that court.

[S. 154.5 en. 1995, c. 45, s. 47 (nyif).]

Refunds

155. Where

   (a)   an application for registration or renewal or reinstatement of registration is abandoned, or

   (b)   a prospectus or similar record is withdrawn,

the superintendent may, on application of an affected person, refund the fee or part of the fee paid in accordance with section 13 of the *Financial Administration Act*.

the executive director may, on application of an affected person, refund the fee or part of the fee paid in accordance with section 13 of the *Financial Administration Act*.

[S. 155 am. 1995, c. 45, s. 7 (nyif).]

Review of fees and charges

155.1(1) If a person is ordered to pay prescribed fees or prescribed charges for the costs of, or related to,

   (a)   an examination or investigation by a person appointed under section 9,

   (b)   a review under section 15.1 or 24.1,

   (c)   an investigation, examination or inspection under Part 15, or

   (d)   a hearing required or permitted under this Act or the regulations,

the person ordered to pay the fees or charges may apply within 30 days after the date of the order to a master or registrar of the Supreme Court to review the order.

(2) On a review under this section, the master or registrar may vary the total amount of the fees and charges, within the limits, if any, set out in the regulations, after considering all of the circumstances, including

   (a)   the complexity, difficulty or novelty of the issues involved,

   (b)   the skill, specialized knowledge and responsibility required of the person or persons who conducted the examination, review, investigation, or hearing referred to in subsection (1)(a) to (d),

   (c)   the total amount of the fees and charges set out in the order referred to in subsection (1), and

   (d)   the time reasonably expended.

(3) On application for a review under this section of an order to pay prescribed fees or prescribed charges, the applicant must give notice of the application to the maker of the order that is to be reviewed.

(4) The Supreme Court Rules relating to taxation of costs apply to a review of the total amount of fees and charges made under this section.

[S. 155.1 en. 1995, c. 45, s. 47 (nyif).]

Notices generally

156. (1) Unless otherwise provided by this Act or ordered by the commission or superintendent, a record required to be sent under this Act or the regulations shall be

   (a)   personally delivered,

   (b)   mailed, or

   (c)   transmitted by electronic means that produce a printed copy,

to the person to whom the record is required to be sent.

156. (1) Unless otherwise provided by this Act or ordered by the commission or executive director, a record that under this Act or the regulations is sent or is required to be sent must be

(a) personally delivered,

(b) mailed, or

(c) transmitted by electronic means

to the person that under this Act or the regulations is the intended recipient of the record.

[S. 156(1) re-en. 1995, c. 45, s. 48 (nyif).]

(2) A record sent to a person by means referred to in subsection (1)(b) or (c) shall be sent to that person

(a) at the latest address known for that person by the sender of the record, or

(b) at the address for service in the Province filed by that person with the commission.

(3) A record is deemed to have been personally delivered to the commission where the record is deposited at the office of the commission during normal business hours.

(4) A record is deemed to have been received by the person to whom it was sent, where mailed

(a) by ordinary mail, on the seventh day after mailing, or

(b) by registered mail, on the earlier of the seventh day after mailing or the day its receipt was acknowledged in writing by the person to whom it was sent or by a person accepting it on that person's behalf.

(5) If, on 3 consecutive occasions, the records sent by an issuer to a security holder in accordance with subsection (2) are returned, the issuer is not required to send any further records to the security holder until the security holder informs the issuer in writing of the security holder's new address.

[S. 156(5) en. 1992, c. 52, s. 30.]

Reference to record includes amendment

157. Unless the context indicates otherwise, a reference to a specific record includes a reference to any amendment, variation or modification of it that is permitted or required under this Act or the regulations.

Required records

158. (1) Subject to the further requirements of this Act or the regulations, where this Act or the regulations provide that a record is to be prepared, filed, furnished or sent in a required form, the superintendent may specify the form, content and other particulars relating to the record including specifying

158. (1) Subject to the further requirements of this Act or the regulations, where this Act or the regulations provide that a record is to be prepared, filed, furnished or sent in a required form, the executive director may specify the form, content and other particulars relating to the record including specifying

[S. 158(1) am. 1995, c. 45, s. 7 (nyif).]

(a) the principles to be applied in its preparation, and

(b) accompanying records to be filed with it.

See NIN 90/22 "Filing of Specified Forms".

(2) Where this Act or the regulations provide that a record is to be prepared, filed, furnished or sent in a required form, the superintendent may, for different classes of a particular kind of record, specify a different form, content and other particulars relating to the record including specifying

(2) Where this Act or the regulations provide that a record is to be prepared, filed, furnished or sent in a required form, the executive director may, for different classes of a particular kind of record, specify a different form, content and other particulars relating to the record including specifying

[S. 158(2) am. 1995, c. 45, s. 7 (nyif).]

(a) the principles to be applied in its preparation, and

(b) accompanying records to be filed with it.

Regulations

159. (1) The Lieutenant Governor in Council may make regulations respecting trading in securities or the securities industry and for the purpose of regulating trading in securities or the securities industry, including regulations

159. (1) The Lieutenant Governor in Council may make regulations for the purpose of regulating trading in securities or exchange contracts, or regulating the securities industry or exchange contracts industry, including regulations

[S. 159(1) am. 1990, c. 25, s. 50(a) (nyif).]

159. The Lieutenant Governor in Council may make regulations for the purpose of regulating trading in securities or exchange contracts, or regulating the securities industry or exchange contracts industry, including regulations

[S. 159(1) renumbered as s. 159 1995, c. 45, s. 49(a) (nyif).]

(1) regulating the listing and trading of securities and records relating to them,

(2) regulating the trading of securities other than on a stock exchange recognized by the commission,

(1) regulating the listing and trading of securities, and the trading of exchange contracts, on an exchange recognized by the commission under section 11(2),

(2) regulating the trading of securities and exchange contracts other than on an exchange recognized by the commission under section 11(2),

[Paras. *(1)* and *(2)* re-en. 1990, c. 25, s. 50(b) (nyif).]

(3) prescribing rules governing conflict of interest for members of the commission, its employees, the superintendent, employees in his office and persons engaged by the commission or the superintendent to act as advisers or to perform duties under this Act or the regulations,

[Para. *(3)* am. 1987, c. 42, s. 102.]

(3) governing conflict of interest for members of the commission, its employees, the executive director, employees in his office and persons engaged by the commission or the executive director to act as advisers or to perform duties under this Act, the regulations or the commission rules,

[Para. *(3)* am. 1995, c. 45, ss. 7, 49(b), (c) (all nyif).]

(4) requiring the commission to publish a periodical containing specified information filed with the commission,

(5) providing for the referral of a question of policy or interpretation to the commission for a hearing and determination,

(6) respecting registration under this Act including, but not limited to, prescribing

(i) categories for persons for purposes of registration and otherwise, (i.1) the duration of registration, and permitting the commission to determine the duration of registration and to determine different periods of duration of registration for different categories of registrants,

(ii) the manner of allocating persons to categories, and permitting the superintendent to make these allocations, and

(ii) the manner of allocating persons to categories, and permitting the executive director to make these allocations,

[Subpara. (ii) am. 1995, c. 45, s. 49(d) (nyif).]

(iii) conditions to be met by persons in these categories,

(iii) conditions to be met by persons in the categories,

[Subpara. (iii) am. 1995, c. 45, s. 49(e) (nyif).]

(iv) standards of conduct to be met by registrants and practices to be carried out by registrants, and

(v) requirements that are necessary or advisable for the prevention or regulation of conflicts of interest,

[Subparas. (iv) and (v) en. 1995, c. 45, s. 49(f) (nyif).]

(7) authorizing the superintendent to require an applicant for registration or a registrant to be bonded,

(7) authorizing the executive director to require an applicant for registration or a registrant to be bonded,

[Para. (7) am. 1995, c. 45, s. 7 (nyif).]

(8) respecting the suspension or cancellation of a registration under this Act,

(9) governing trust arrangements for the holding of securities and funds of a client by a registrant,

(10) prescribing the practice and procedure by which the superintendent recognizes exempt purchasers under sections 31 and 55,

(10) prescribing the practice and procedure by which the executive director designates exempt purchasers under sections 31 and 55,

[Para. (10) re-en. 1995, c. 45, s. 49(g) (nyif).]

(11) respecting the transfer and pledging of securities through a clearing agency,

[Para. (11) am. 1989, c. 78, s. 45(a).]

(11) respecting the transfer and pledging of securities or the transfer of exchange contracts,

[Para. (11) re-en. 1990, c. 25, s. 50(c) (nyif).]

(12) respecting annual information forms, prospectuses, preliminary prospectuses, pro forma prospectuses, short forms of prospectuses and preliminary prospectuses and summary statements including amending, modifying or varying this Act as may be necessary for the purpose of permitting the use of annual information forms, short forms of prospectuses and preliminary prospectuses,

[Para. (12) am. 1987, c. 42, s. 103; 1989, c. 78, s. 45(b).]

(12) respecting annual information forms, prospectuses, preliminary prospectuses, pro forma prospectuses, simplified prospectuses and preliminary prospectuses and summary statements including amending, modifying or varying this Act as may be necessary for the purpose of permitting the use of annual information forms, simplified prospectuses and preliminary prospectuses,

[Para. *(12)* am. 1995, c. 45, s. 49(h) (nyif).]

(13) respecting disclosure documents; respecting their use in connection with any distribution made in the circumstances described in section 55(2) or with any distribution referred to in section 58(1); governing their form and content, including, without limiting this power, requiring content that has the effect of conferring on each purchaser under the distribution a contractual right of action, a contractual right of withdrawal from an agreement of purchase and sale, or both,

[Para. *(13)* re-en. 1989, c. 78, s. 45(c); am. 1990, c. 25, s. 50(d).]

(13) respecting disclosure documents; respecting their use in connection with any distribution made in the circumstances described in section 55(2) or with any distribution referred to in section 58; governing their form and content, including, without limiting this power, requiring content that has the effect of conferring on each purchaser under the distribution a contractual right of action, a contractual right of withdrawal from an agreement of purchase and sale, or both,

[Para. *(13)* am. 1992, c. 52, s. 31(a) (nyif).]

(14) prescribing the circumstances under which a class or classes of trades of securities, acquired under an exemption from section 42 granted under this Act or the regulations, shall be deemed to be a distribution,

[Para. *(14)* am. 1988, c. 58, s. 26(a).]

(14) prescribing the circumstances under which a class or classes of trades of securities, acquired under an exemption from section 42 granted under this Act, the regulations or the commission rules, shall be deemed to be a distribution,

[Para. *(14)* am. 1995, c. 45, s. 49(c) (nyif).]

(14.1) respecting the lapse date of a prospectus and the continuation of a distribution under a new prospectus including, without limitation,

    (i) prescribing the terms and conditions under which a distribution may be continued after the lapse date,

    (ii) prescribing the circumstances in which cancellation rights are available to certain purchasers after the lapse date,

    (iii) authorizing the superintendent to order an extension of the prescribed period of time within which a distribution may be continued after the lapse date, and

    (iii) authorizing the executive director to order an extension of the prescribed period of time within which a distribution may be continued after the lapse date, and

[Subpara. (iii) am. 1995, c. 45, s. 7 (nyif).]

    (iv) prescribing the terms and conditions under which a new prospectus may be receipted,

[S. 159(1) *(14.1)* en. 1992, c. 52, s. 31(b).]

(15) prescribing terms that shall be contained in an escrow or pooling agreement with respect to securities issued for consideration other than cash,

(16) respecting prospecting syndicates and including the liability of members to a syndicate agreement and the contents and filing of a syndicate agreement,

[Para. *(16)* repealed 1995, c. 45, s. 49(i) (nyif).]

(17) amending, modifying or varying the regulations as may be necessary for the purpose of regulating exchange issuers,

[Para. *(17)* am. 1988, c. 58, s. 26(b).]

(17) respecting any matter necessary or advisable to regulate exchange issuers,

[Para. *(17)* re-en. 1995, c. 45, s. 49(j) (nyif).]

(18) prescribing the information required or permitted to be distributed under section 61(2),

(19) requiring any issuer or class of issuers to comply with Part 10 or any provision of it,

(19) respecting any matter necessary or advisable to carry out effectively the intent and purpose of Part 10, including, but not limited to,

    (i) requiring any issuer or class of issuers to comply with Part 10 or any provision of it,

    (ii) prescribing how a security or class of securities, including a put, call, option or other right or obligation to purchase or sell securities of a reporting issuer, must be reported in an insider report filed under section 70, and

    (iii) prescribing standards for determining when a material fact or material change has been generally disclosed,

[Para. *(19)* re-en. 1995, c. 45, s. 49(j) (nyif).]

(19.1) respecting any matter the Lieutenant Governor in Council considers to be necessary or advisable to carry out effectively the intent and purpose of sections 68 and 119 including, without restricting the generality of the foregoing,

    (i) exempting any class or classes of persons, of trades or of securities from any of the requirements of section 68 and from liability under section 119,

    (ii) prescribing circumstances and conditions for the purpose of an exemption under subparagraph (i), and

    (iii) prescribing standards for determining when a material fact or material change has been generally disclosed,

[Para. *(19.1)* en. 1989, c. 78, s. 45(d); repealed 1995, c. 45, s. 49(j) (nyif).]

(20) respecting any matter necessary or advisable to carry out effectively the intent and purpose of Part 11 including, without restricting generality of the foregoing,

    (i) providing for exemptions in addition to those set out in sections 80 and 81,

    (ii) providing for exemptions for sections 83 to 86,

    (iii) restricting any exemption set out in sections 80 and 81 or 83 to 86,

    (iv) prescribing rules in addition to those in section 87 and varying any rule set out in that section,

    (v) prescribing rules relating to the conduct or management of the affairs of an offeree issuer during or in anticipation of a take over bid, and

(vi) prescribing the form and content of any circular, report or other document required to be delivered or filed,

[Para. *(20)* re-en. 1989, c. 78, s. 45(e).]

(20) respecting any matter necessary or advisable to carry out effectively the intent and purpose of section 119, including, but not limited to,

    (i) exempting any class of persons, trades, securities or exchange contracts from liability under section 119,

    (ii) prescribing circumstances and conditions for the purpose of an exemption under subparagraph (i), and

    (iii) prescribing standards for determining when a material fact or material change has been generally disclosed,

[Para. *(20)* re-en. 1995, c. 45, s. 49(j) (nyif).]

(21) prescribing a penalty for the early redemption of securities of a mutual fund,

(21) respecting any matter necessary or advisable to carry out effectively the intent and purpose of Part 11, including, but not limited to,

    (i) restricting any exemption set out in sections 80 and 81 or 83 to 86,

    (ii) prescribing requirements in addition to those set out in section 87 and varying any requirement set out in that section,

    (iii) prescribing requirements relating to the conduct or management of the affairs of an offeree issuer during or in anticipation of a take over bid, and

    (iv) prescribing the form and content of any circular, report or other document required to be delivered or filed,

[Para. *(21)* re-en. 1995, c. 45, s. 49(j) (nyif).]

(22) respecting sales charges imposed by a mutual fund distributor or contractual plan service corporation under a contractual plan on purchasers of securities of a mutual fund, and commissions to be paid to salesmen of securities of a mutual fund,

(22) respecting any matter necessary or advisable to carry out effectively the intent and purpose of Part 12, including, but not limited to,

    (i) prescribing requirements for the solicitation and voting of proxies, and

    (ii) prescribing requirements relating to communication with registered holders or beneficial owners of securities and relating to other persons, including depositories and registrants, that hold securities on behalf of beneficial owners,

[Para. *(22)* re-en. 1995, c. 45, s. 49(j) (nyif).]

(23) prescribing a standard of care for a person responsible for the management of a mutual fund,

(23) respecting any matter necessary or advisable to regulate mutual funds or non-redeemable investment funds, including commodity pools, and the distribution and trading of the securities of the funds, including, but not limited to,

    (i) prescribing disclosure requirements in respect of funds, including the use of particular forms or of particular types of documents,

    (ii) prescribing permitted investment policy and investment practices for the funds and prohibiting or restricting certain types of investments or investment practices for the funds,

(iii) prescribing requirements governing the custodianship of assets for funds,

(iv) prescribing matters requiring approval of the security holders of the funds, the commission or the executive director, and defining for specified types of matters what constitutes approval by the security holders,

(v) respecting fees, commissions or compensation payable by a fund, a purchaser of securities of a fund or a holder of securities of a fund relating to

(A) sales charges, commissions or sales incentives, and

(B) investment advice or administrative or management services provided to the fund,

(vi) prescribing procedures relating to

(A) sales and redemptions of fund securities, and

(B) payments for sales and redemptions, and

(vii) designating a mutual fund or a class of mutual funds as a private mutual fund or class of private mutual funds, as the case may be,

[Para. *(23)* re-en. 1995, c. 45, s. 49(j) (nyif).]

(24) respecting

(i) fees payable by a mutual fund to a mutual fund manager for investment advice or administrative or management services, and

(ii) the principles on which and the manner in which an investment counsel may charge clients,

(24) prescribing the principles for determining the market value, market price or closing price of a security or exchange contract, or the net asset value of a security, and authorizing the commission to make that determination,

[Para. *(24)* re-en. 1995, c. 45, s. 49(j) (nyif).]

(25) designating a mutual fund or a class of mutual funds as a private mutual fund,

(25) prescribing standards in relation to the suitability for certain investors of certain securities and exchange contracts,

[Para. *(25)* re-en. 1995, c. 45, s. 49(j) (nyif).]

(26) prescribing the principles for determining the market value, the market price or closing price of a security, and authorizing the commission to make that determination,

(26) prescribing the principles for determining the market value, the market price or closing price of a security or exchange contract, and authorizing the commission to make that determination,

[Para. *(26)* am. 1990, c. 25, s. 50(e) (nyif).]

(26) prescribing the practice and procedure for investigations, examinations or inspections under Part 15,

[Para. *(26)* re-en. 1995, c. 45, s. 49(j) (nyif).]

(27) prescribing the practice and procedure for, and establishing fees and charges which may be levied by the commission for, investigations and examinations under Part 15,

[Para. *(27)* am. 1989, c. 78, s. 45(f).]

(27) establishing fees and charges, or limits on fees and charges, for the purpose of Part 15 or of section 9, 15.1, 24.1 or 154.2,

[Para. *(27)* re-en. 1995, c. 45, s. 49(j) (nyif).]

(27.1) establishing the fees and charges for the purpose of section 154.2,

[Para. *(27.1)* en. 1988, c. 58, s. 26(c); repealed 1995, c. 45, s. 49(j) (nyif).]

(28) prescribing those decisions made under the regulations which shall be subject to an appeal under Part 17,

(28) prescribing those decisions made under the regulations or the commission rules which shall be subject to an appeal under Part 17,

[Para. *(28)* am. 1995, c. 45, s. 49(k) (nyif).]

(29) prescribing the rules and procedures to be followed in any hearing required or permitted by this Act,

(30) providing for the collection by a designated organization of fees payable to the commission or superintendent and for their remission to the commission or superintendent,

(30) providing for the collection by a designated organization of fees payable to the commission or executive director and for their remission to the commission or executive director,

[Para. *(30)* am. 1995, c. 45, s. 7 (nyif).]

(31) determining what constitutes approval of a person's records for which approval is required under this Act or the regulations,

(31) determining what constitutes approval of a person's records for which approval is required under this Act, the regulations or the commission rules,

[Para. *(31)* am. 1995, c. 45, s 49(c) (nyif).]

(32) incorporating by reference and adopting codes and standards as they are amended from time to time before or after the making of the regulations,

(33) governing the furnishing or distribution of information or records by a person, including the commission and the superintendent, or class of persons to any person, including the commission and the superintendent, the payment of fees for furnishing that information or records and including authorizing the superintendent to regulate and control the use of advertising and sales literature for securities,

(33) governing the furnishing or distribution of information or records by a person, including the commission and the superintendent, or class of persons to any person, including the commission and the superintendent, the payment of fees for furnishing that information or records and including authorizing the superintendent to regulate and control the use of advertising and sales literature for securities or exchange contracts,

[Para. *(33)* am. 1990, c. 25, s. 50(f) (nyif).]

(33) governing the furnishing or distribution of information or records by a person, including the commission and the executive director, or class of persons to any person, including the commission and the executive director, the payment of fees for furnishing that information or records and including authorizing the executive director to regulate and control the use of advertising and sales literature for securities or exchange contracts,

[Para. *(33)* am. 1995, c. 45, s. 7 (nyif).]

(34) respecting the keeping and furnishing of accounts and records, and the preparation, filing and furnishing or distributing of financial statements, annual reports and other records by any person or class of persons,

(35) prescribing the fees payable in connection with the administration of this Act or the regulations or the activities carried out by the commission or the superintendent under another enactment or a policy statement,

[S. 159(1)(*35*) am. 1992, c. 52, s. 31(c).]

(35) prescribing the fees payable in connection with the administration of this Act, the regulations or the commission rules or the activities carried out by the commission or the executive director under another enactment or a policy statement,

[S. 159(1)(*35*) am. 1995, c. 45, ss. 7, 49(c) (both nyif).]

(35.1) authorizing the commission to recognize a stock exchange for any purpose under this Act or the regulations,

[Para. *(35.1)* en. 1988, c. 58, s. 26(c).]

(35.1) authorizing the commission to recognize an exchange for any purpose under this Act or the regulations,

[Para. *(35.1)* am. 1990, c. 25, s. 50(g) (nyif).]

(35.1) authorizing the commission to recognize an exchange for any purpose under this Act, the regulations or the commission rules,

[Para. *(35.1)* am. 1995, c. 45, s. 49(c) (nyif).]

(36) authorizing the commission or the superintendent to vary the provisions of the regulations, excluding regulations made under paragraph *(3)*, as they apply to any person or class of persons,

(36) authorizing the commission or the executive director to vary the provisions of the regulations, excluding regulations made under paragraph *(3)*, as they apply to any person, trade, security or exchange contract or class of persons, trades, securities or exchange contracts,

[Para. *(36)* am. 1995, c. 45, ss. 7, 49(l) (both nyif).]

(36.1) providing that any or all of the exemptions in this Act or the regulations do not apply to a class of persons; and prescribing circumstances in which or conditions on which the exemption is or the exemptions are disapplied under this paragraph,

[Para. *(36.1)* en. 1989, c. 78, s. 45(g).]

(36.1) providing that any or all of the exemptions in this Act, the regulations or the commission rules do not apply to a class of persons, trades, securities or exchange contracts, and prescribing circumstances in which or conditions on which the exemption is or the exemptions are disapplied under this paragraph,

[Para. *(36.1)* am. 1995, c. 45, s. 49(c), (m) (both nyif).]

(37) authorizing the commission or the superintendent to order that any or all of the provisions of this Act or the regulations do not apply to a particular person or class of persons,

(37) authorizing the commission or the executive director to order that any or all of the provisions of this Act or the regulations do not apply to a particular person, trade, security or exchange contract or class of persons, trades, securities or exchange contracts,

[Para. *(37)* am. 1995, c. 45, ss. 7, 49(1) (both nyif).]

(37.1) exempting a class of persons, trades, securities or exchange contracts from one or more of the provisions of Parts 3, 4, 6, 6.1, 7, 9, 10, 11, 12 and 13, of the regulations relating to any of those Parts or of the commission rules relating to any of those Parts,

(37.2) prescribing circumstances and conditions for the purpose of an exemption under paragraph (37.1),

[Paras. *(37.1)* and *(37.2)* en. 1995, c. 45, s. 49(n) (nyif).]

(38) authorizing the commission or the superintendent to order that any or all of the provisions of this Act or the regulations, excluding regulations made under paragraph *(3)*, do not apply to a particular person or class of persons,

(38) authorizing the commission or the executive director to order that any or all of the provisions of this Act or the regulations, excluding regulations made under paragraph *(3)*, do not apply to a particular person, trade, security or exchange contract or class of persons, trades, securities or exchange contracts,

[Para. *(38)* am. 1995, c. 45, ss. 7, 49(1) (both nyif).]

(39) respecting those matters for which this Act provides that regulations be made or requirements prescribed,

(39) respecting those matters for which this Act provides that regulations or commission rules be made or requirements prescribed,

[Para. *(39)* am. 1995, c. 45, s. 49(o) (nyif).]

(40) respecting the filing of records under this Act and the regulations,

(40) respecting the filing of records under this Act, the regulations and the commission rules,

[Para. *(40)* am. 1995, c. 45, s. 49(p) (nyif).]

(40.1) prescribing that any of the requirements of section 70, 71 or 93 do not apply to a particular person or class of persons,

[Para. *(40.1)* en. 1988, c. 58, s. 26(c); repealed 1995, c. 45, s. 49(q) (nyif).]

(41) respecting

(i) the amendment or modification of a record and the effect of that amendment or modification,

(ii) the use of codes and symbols for the identification of persons on records,

(iii) the use of records, prepared in accordance with similar laws of another jurisdiction, to satisfy the requirements of this Act or the regulations, and

(iv) the certification of a record required in this Act or the regulations,

  (iii) the use of records, prepared in accordance with similar laws of another jurisdiction, to satisfy the requirements of this Act, the regulations or the commission rules,

  (iv) the certification of a record required in this Act, the regulations or the commission rules, and

[Subparas. (iii) and (iv) am. 1995, c. 45, s. 49(c), (r) (both nyif).]

  (v) the filing of records by electronic means,

[Subpara. (v) en. 1995, c. 45, s. 49(r) (nyif).]

(41.1) defining words and expressions used but not defined in this Act,

[Para. *(41.1)* en. 1990, c. 25, s. 50(h).]

(42) to meet any difficulties that may arise by reason of the repeal of the *Securities Act*, R.S.B.C. 1979, c. 380, and the substitution of this Act,

(43) for the purpose of section 138(1)(e), specifying provisions of the regulations, the contravention of any of which constitutes an offence under section 138(1)(e).

[Para. *(43)* en. 1989, c. 78, s. 45(g).]

(44) for the purpose of section 138(1)(f), specifying provisions of the commission rules, the contravention of any of which constitutes an offence under section 138(1)(f),

(45) governing the procedures that are to be followed by the commission in making and repealing commission rules including, but not limited to, prescribing requirements with which the commission must comply before depositing a commission rule with the registrar of regulations,

(46) prescribing a regulation made by the Lieutenant Governor in Council under this Act to be a commission rule,

(47) amending or repealing any commission rule.

[Paras. *(44)* to *(47)* en. 1995, c. 45, s. 49(s) (nyif).]

(2) The commission may make regulations

(a) authorizing one or more of the Vancouver Stock Exchange, the Pacific District of the Investment Dealers Association of Canada or any other organization on terms and conditions prescribed by the commission, to exercise any of the superintendent's powers or to perform any of his duties under Part 4 including, but not limited to, the power

  (i) to grant, renew or reinstate registration, to refuse to grant, renew or reinstate registration or to attach terms, conditions or restrictions to registration, reinstatement or renewal of registration,

  (ii) to suspend or cancel registration,

  (iii) to satisfy itself of any matter that is a condition precedent to the exercise of a power under this section,

  (iv) to require an applicant or registrant to submit to examination under oath, and

  (v) to require delivery of a bond,

Act

Stenner v. British Columbia (Securities Commission) (1993), 23 Admin. L.R. (2d) 247 (B.C. S.C.).

The powers and duties under Part 4 of the Act include those of registering salespeople. The Commission had authorized the V.S.E. to perform that duty and exercise that power by the Registration Transfer Regulation, B.C. Reg. 286/86. In addressing this issue of jurisdiction between the Commission and the V.S.E., the court's attention was drawn to the use of the word "delegate" in s. 7 of the Act as opposed to the word "authorize" in s. 159(2). In the court's opinion, nothing turns upon that difference. In s. 7 the Superintendent is enabled to cede his own powers to others. The word "delegate" is properly used to describe the disposition of one's own powers. One cannot delegate what one does not have and, therefore, the word "authorize" is properly used in s. 159(2) which enables the Commission to vest powers which it does not itself have in the V.S.E. With respect to the question of whether the authorization excludes the Superintendent from his powers under Part 4, the court stated that there is no explicit exclusion provided by the Act. The meaning of its words must be gained from the consideration of its scheme as a whole. Section 159(3) gives the Commission power to withdraw a matter from the V.S.E. before a hearing and refer it to the Superintendent for decision. That includes a hearing into registration and the conditions to be imposed. Withdrawal may prove to be the device by which the concurrent exercise of power over the same subject matter by both the V.S.E. and the Superintendent is avoided. That does not necessarily mean that there is no concurrent jurisdiction until the matter is withdrawn; but the fact that the section goes on to provide that it may then be referred to the Superintendent, suggests that the legislature meant there should not be a concurrent power once the V.S.E. is authorized under s. 159(2). If the Superintendent had a concurrent power, there would be no need to refer it to him after withdrawing it from the V.S.E. Simply to withdraw it from the V.S.E. would leave him alone in the field to exercise his power. The confusion that might well result from concurrent jurisdiction persuaded the court that the legislation never intended that the Superintendent's powers should survive a transfer to the V.S.E.

(b) establishing criteria to be applied and procedures to be followed by a designated organization in making a direction, decision, order or ruling under this section,

(c) requiring

(i) applications for registration, reinstatement or renewal of registration to be made to a designated organization, and

(ii) any notification referred to in section 28 or any other thing to be delivered to the designated organization,

(d) requiring a designated organization

(i) to provide the superintendent with reports and information respecting any matter that is before the designated organization or any decision made by it under this section,

(ii) to notify applicants, registrants or other persons of registrations granted or decisions made by the designated organization under this section, and

(iii) to keep records, including records of decisions made by the designated organization under this section and to permit public inspection of classes of records prescribed by the commission,

(e) empowering a designated organization to delegate any power or duty conferred on it under this section to a committee of the designated organization, and deeming the decisions of the committee to be the decisions of the designated organization, and

(f) respecting the custody and use of the superintendent's seal of office and of any device for affixing a facsimile of his signature.

[S. 159(2) repealed 1995, c. 45, s. 50 (nyif).]

See the Registration Transfer Regulation.

---

(3) Where a designated organization is authorized to exercise a power under this section, the commission may, before a hearing is held, withdraw from the designated organization any matter that is before it for its decision, and the commission may refer the matter to the superintendent for decision.

[S. 159(3) repealed 1995, c. 45, s. 50 (nyif).]

Commission may make rules

159.1(1) Subject to subsections (4) to (7), the commission may make rules for the purpose of regulating trading in securities or exchange contracts, or regulating the securities industry or exchange contracts industry.

(2) Without limiting subsection (1) but subject to subsections (4) to (7), the commission may make rules as follows:

(a) respecting those matters for which this Act provides that commission rules be made;

(b) respecting those matters for which this Act provides that requirements be prescribed, except for those matters referred to in sections 9(3), 15.1(5), 20(2), 21(1)(b), 24.1(5), 127(4), 134, 137(4), 154.2, 155.1(1) and (3), 159(45) and (46) and subsections (5) to (8) of this section;

(c) with respect to the same matters with respect to which the Lieutenant Governor in Council may make regulations under section 159(1), (2), (6) to (25), (30), (31), (33), (34), (35.1), (36.1), (37.1), (37.2), (40) and (41) and to the same extent;

(d) incorporating by reference and adopting codes and standards as they are amended from time to time before or after the making of the rules;

(e) authorizing one or more organizations, on specified terms and conditions, to exercise any of the executive director's powers under Part 4 or to perform any of the executive director's duties under Part 4, including, but not limited to, the power

(i) to grant, renew or reinstate registration, to refuse to grant, renew or reinstate registration or to attach terms, conditions or restrictions to any grant, renewal or reinstatement of registration,

(ii) to suspend or cancel registration,

(iii) to satisfy itself of any matter that is a condition precedent to the exercise of a power it is authorized under this paragraph to exercise,

(iv) to require an applicant or registrant to submit to examination under oath, and

(v) to require delivery of a bond;

(f) establishing criteria to be applied and procedures to be followed by a designated organization in making a direction, decision, order or ruling it is authorized under paragraph (e) to make;

(g) requiring

(i) applications for registration or for renewal or reinstatement of registration to be made to a designated organization, and

(ii) any notification referred to in section 28 or any other thing to be delivered to the designated organization;

    (h) requiring a designated organization

        (i) to provide the executive director with reports and information respecting any matter that is before the designated organization or any decision made by it under an authority given to it under paragraph (e),

        (ii) to notify applicants, registrants or other persons of registrations granted or decisions made by the designated organization under an authority given to it under paragraph (e), and

        (iii) to keep records, including records of decisions made by the designated organization under an authority given to it under paragraph (e) and to permit public inspection of classes of records specified by the commission;

    (i) empowering a designated organization to delegate any power or duty conferred on it under paragraph (e) to a committee of the designated organization, and deeming the decisions of the committee to be the decisions of the designated organization;

    (j) respecting the custody and use of the executive director's seal of office and of any device for affixing a facsimile of the executive director's signature.

(3) Where a designated organization is exercising or intends to exercise a power provided to it under subsection (2)(e) to make a decision, the commission may withdraw from the designated organization any matter that is before the designated organization for its decision, and the commission may refer the matter to the executive director for decision.

(4) Unless the power to do so is expressly provided to the commission under this section, the commission must not make rules under this section with respect to the matters with respect to which the Lieutenant Governor in Council may make regulations under section 159(3) to (5), (26) to (29), (32), (35), (36), (37), (38), (39) and (41.1) to (47).

(5) The commission must, before making or repealing a rule under this section, obtain the consent of the minister in accordance with the regulations and comply with any other prescribed procedures and requirements.

(6) Without limiting subsection (5), the commission must not deposit with the registrar of regulations any rule made by the commission under this section unless the commission has complied with the prescribed procedures and requirements.

(7) Despite subsections (5) and (6), the commission may deposit with the registrar of regulations a rule made by the commission under this section without complying with the prescribed procedures and requirements where

    (a) the commission considers it necessary and in the public interest to deposit the rule without delay, and

    (b) the minister consents

        (i) to the making of the rule, and

        (ii) to the rule being deposited without the commission's compliance with the prescribed procedures and requirements.

(8) Unless earlier revoked, a rule made under subsection (7) is revoked on the day that is the prescribed number of days following the day on which the rule is deposited with the registrar of regulations.

(9) The Lieutenant Governor in Council may, by regulation, designate a regulation made under section 159, whether made before or after the coming into force of this section, to be a rule of the commission and the designated regulation is deemed for all purposes to be a rule of the commission made under this section.

(10) The Lieutenant Governor in Council may, by regulation, repeal or amend any of the rules made by the commission under this section.

[S. 159.1 en. 1995, c. 45, s. 50 (nyif).]

Regulations Act applies to commission rules

159.2 The *Regulations Act* applies to a commission rule.

[S. 159.2 en. 1995, c. 45, s. 51 (nyif).]

Conflicts

159.3 Where a commission rule conflicts with a regulation made by the Lieutenant Governor in Council under section 159, the regulation prevails.

[S. 159.3 en. 1995, c. 45, s. 51 (nyif).]

Administrative powers respecting commission rules

159.4 The commission may

(a) vary the provisions of the commission rules as they apply to any person, trade, security or exchange contract or class of persons, trades, securities or exchange contracts,

(b) order that any or all of the exemptions in the commission rules do not apply to a person, trade, security or exchange contract or class of persons, trades, securities or exchange contracts,

(c) order that any or all of the provisions of the commission rules do not apply to a person, trade, security or exchange contract or class of persons, trades, securities or exchange contracts, and

(d) authorize the executive director to exercise a power given to the commission under paragraphs (a) to (c).

[S. 159.4 en. 1995, c. 45, s. 51 (nyif).]

Policy statements

159.5 (1) The commission may issue policy statements, and other instruments the commission considers advisable, to facilitate the exercise of its powers and the performance of its duties under this Act, the regulations and the commission rules.

(2) A policy statement or other instrument referred to in subsection (1) is not a commission rule or a regulation within the meaning of the *Regulations Act*.

[S. 159.5 en. 1995, c. 45, s. 51 (nyif).]

Transitional – commission regulations

159.6 Any regulations enacted by the commission under section 159(2) as it read before the coming into force of section 159.1 are deemed to be commission rules.

[S. 159.6 en. 1995, c. 45, s. 51 (nyif).]

Transitional

160. (1) Every registration made and receipt for a prospectus issued under the *Securities Act*, R.S.B.C. 1979, c. 380, and in effect immediately before this Act comes into force, continues in force in the same manner as if the registration was made or the receipt was issued under this Act.

(2) An issuer shall be conclusively deemed to have been a reporting issuer from the date it met the condition of the appropriate paragraph in the definition of "reporting issuer" in section 1 whether or not that date is before or after the coming into force of this Act.

(3) Every registration made under the *Commodity Contract Act*, R.S.B.C. 1979, c. 56, and in effect upon repeal of that Act, continues in force in the same manner as if the registration was made under this Act.

[S. 160(3) en. 1990, c. 25, s. 51 (nyif).]

Appropriation

161. [Spent.]

Consequential amendments and repeal

162-212. [Spent.]

Commencement

213. This Act comes into force by regulation of the Lieutenant Governor in Council.

SECURITIES REGULATION

TABLE OF CONTENTS

Regulation

Regulation

PART 12 — PROXIES

Division (1) — Rights of Beneficial Owner of Securities

PART 13 — SELF DEALING

There are no regulations under this Part.

PART 13.1 — CONFLICTS OF INTEREST

PART 14 — CIVIL LIABILITY

PART 15 — INVESTIGATIONS AND AUDITS

PART 16 — ENFORCEMENT

PART 17 — REVIEWS AND APPEALS

PART 18 — GENERAL PROVISIONS

Division (1) — Miscellaneous

Division (2) — Prospecting Syndicates

REGISTRATION TRANSFER REGULATION

TABLE OF CONTENTS

Regulation

SECURITIES REGULATION

B.C. Reg. 270/86, as amended by B.C. Regs. 24/87; 94/88; 245/88; 305/88; 306/88; 307/88; 378/88; 66/89; 163/89; 316/89; 134/91; 130/92; 39/94; 417/94; 97/95

PART 1

INTERPRETATION

Interpretation

1. In this regulation

"Act" means the *Securities Act*, S.B.C. 1985, c. 83;

"auditor" means a person who is qualified under section 4(4.1) to make an auditor's report referred to in section 4(4);

[S. 1 "auditor" en. B.C. Reg. 316/89, s. 1.]

"debt security" means a bond, debenture, note or similar instrument representing indebtedness, whether secured or unsecured;

[S. 1 "exchange issuer" and "government incentive security" repealed B.C. Reg. 305/88, s. 1(a).]

"industrial issuer" includes an issuer designated by the superintendent as an industrial issuer;

"investment issuer" means an issuer whose principal business is or will be the acquisition of or investment in securities and includes an issuer that issues any of the following:

(a) investment certificates;

(b) savings certificates;

(c) savings contracts;

(d) investment contracts;

(e) other similar securities;

[S. 1 "investment issuer" am. B.C. Reg. 305/88, s. 1(b).]

"natural resource issuer" means a mining, gas, oil or exploration issuer designated by the superintendent as a natural resource issuer.

"sophisticated purchaser" means a purchaser who

(a) in connection with a distribution of a security makes the acknowledgment and gives the undertaking referred to in section 128, and

(b) by virtue of his net worth and investment experience or his consultation with or advice from a person who is not an insider of the issuer, but who is a registered adviser or a registered dealer, is able to evaluate the prospective investment on the basis of information respecting the investment provided by the issuer;

"spouse" includes a man or woman not married to a person but who is living with that person and has lived with that person as husband or wife for a period of not less than 6 months.

[S. 1 "sophisticated purchaser" and "spouse" en. B.C. Reg. 305/88, s. 1(c).]

Finance issuer defined

2. (1) In subsection (2) "issuer" includes its subsidiaries and affiliates.

(2) Subject to subsection (3), in this regulation "finance issuer" means an issuer

(a) who, as a material part of its business activities,

(i) acquires or discounts acceptances, accounts receivable, bills of sale, chattel mortgages, conditional sales contracts, drafts and promissory notes and other obligations representing part or all of the sales price of merchandise or services,

    (ii) acts as a factor or purchases or leases personal property for the purpose of conducting conditional sales or similar transactions, or

    (iii) makes secured or unsecured loans, or both, and

(b) who

    (i) issued securities for which a prospectus was filed and a receipt was obtained or issued under the Act or a former enactment, or

    (ii) distributes securities of its own issue in the Province without filing a prospectus, in reliance on section 32(d) of the Act.

(3) In this regulation "finance issuer" does not include a savings institution, the Federal Business Development Bank, an insurer, an underwriter, a dealer, an industrial issuer, a natural resource issuer or an investment issuer.

Generally accepted principles and standards

3. (1) Subject to any contrary provision of the Act or this regulation, the principles, reports and standards that are recommended in the Handbook of the Canadian Institute of Chartered Accountants, as amended from time to time in that Handbook, are incorporated by reference as part of this regulation.

(2) A reference in this regulation to "generally accepted accounting principles", "auditor's report" and "generally accepted auditing standards" is a reference to the principles, report and standards, respectively, that are recommended in the Handbook and incorporated by reference under subsection (1).

(3) Subject to section 107(2), where an issuer is incorporated or organized in a jurisdiction other than Canada or one of its provinces, "generally accepted accounting principles" may mean, at the option of the issuer, either

(a) the principles that are required in the incorporating or organizing jurisdiction under the applicable legislation, or

(b) where a recommendation has been made by an association in the incorporating or organizing jurisdiction that is the equivalent of the Canadian Institute of Chartered Accountants, the principles recommended by that equivalent association.

> Regulation s. 107(2) states that the option set out under s. 3(3) shall only be exercised with the consent of the Superintendent, subject to any conditions that he may impose. It is the practice of the Superintendent's office to require the request for consent to be made prior to the filing of the financial statements. This pre-approval requirement is particularly important when filing financial statements with the preliminary prospectus, as the lack of pre-approval may result in the entire application being held up or returned.

(4) Where an option is exercised under subsection (3), the notes to the issuer's financial statements shall state which option has been applied in the choice of generally accepted accounting principles.

Preparation of financial statements

4. (1) For the purposes of subsection (2), "joint regulatory bodies" means the Alberta Stock Exchange, the Montreal Exchange, the Toronto Stock Exchange, the Vancouver Stock Exchange and the Investment Dealers' Association of Canada.

(2) Subject to any contrary provision of the Act or this regulation, the interpretations, statements, schedules, notes and instructions approved and issued by the joint regulatory bodies for the purpose of their members completing a Joint Regulatory Financial Questionnaire and Report, as amended from time to time, are incorporated by reference as part of this regulation.

(3) Subject to subsections (6) and (8), the financial statements required by the Act and this regulation shall be prepared in accordance with generally accepted accounting principles and with any applicable provision of the Act or this regulation.

(4) Subject to sections 92, 96(2), 105(3), 113(1) and (2), 135(4) and 140(3) of this regulation, a person who is required to file a financial statement under the Act or this regulation shall include an auditor's report on it prepared by a person who is qualified under subsection (4.1) to make the auditor's report.

[S. 4(4) re-en. B.C. Reg. 316/89, s. 2.]

(4.1) A person is qualified to make an auditor's report referred to in subsection (4) only if

    (a) the person is a member, or is a partnership whose partners are members, in good standing of, and is authorized to carry on the practice of public accounting by the institute of chartered accountants of a province of Canada,

    (b) the person is a member, or is a partnership whose partners are members, in good standing of, and is authorized to carry on the practice of public accounting by the Certified General Accountants' Association of British Columbia,

    (c) the person is certified as an auditor by the Auditor Certification Board established under section 205 of the Company Act, or

    (d) the person

        (i) has qualifications as an auditor in a jurisdiction other than a province of Canada that the superintendent considers are similar to the qualifications for membership in the Institute of Chartered Accountants of British Columbia, and

        (ii) is authorized to carry on the practice of public accounting by the appropriate authority in that jurisdiction.

[S. 4(4.1) en. B.C. Reg. 316/89, s. 2(b).]

Financial statement requirements are found in a number of places. See NIN 89/30 "Qualifications of Auditors Filing Reports", NIN 91/17 "Section 203(3)(b) of the Company Act – Consent by the Superintendent of Brokers to the Waiver of the Appointment of an Auditor for a Subsidiary Corporation", NIN 91/18 "Auditor's Report on Comparative Financial Statements", NIN 91/21 "Accounting for Business Combinations and Corporate Reorganizations", Canadian Securities Administrators Notice 90/1 "Audit Committees", National Policy Statement 3 "Unacceptable Auditors", National Policy Statement 31 "Change of Auditor of a Reporting Issuer", National Policy Statement 14 "Acceptability of Currencies in Material Filed with Securities Regulatory Authorities", and National Policy Statement 27 "Canadian Generally Accepted Accounting Principles".

---

(5) Where an auditor reports on a financial statement permitted or required by the Act or this regulation, the report shall be prepared in accordance with generally accepted auditing standards as well as with any applicable provision of the Act or this regulation and the auditor shall make the necessary examinations to enable him to make the report.

(6) Subsection (3) does not apply to an insurer that is an insurer undertaking and transacting life insurance or that is a bank, so long as the insurer prepares its financial statements in accordance with

    (a) the statute incorporating, continuing or governing it, and

    (b) any applicable generally accepted accounting principles.

(7) Notwithstanding any other section of this regulation, it is not necessary

    (a) to designate any financial statement referred to in the Act or this regulation as the income statement, the statement of surplus, the statement of change in financial position, the balance sheet, the statement of investment portfolio, the statement of portfolio transactions or the statement of changes in net assets, or

    (b) to state in any financial statement any matter that, in all the circumstances, is of relative insignificance.

(8) Where a financial statement is not prepared in accordance with generally accepted accounting principles, the superintendent shall accept it for the purposes for which it is to be filed if

    (a) he is satisfied that it is not reasonable and practicable for the issuer to revise the presentation in the financial statement to conform to generally accepted accounting principles,

(b) the commission, by order, accepts the financial statement

   (i) after giving the interested parties an opportunity to be heard, and

   (ii) after concluding in all the circumstances of the case that the variation from generally accepted accounting principles is supported or justified by considerations that outweigh the desirability of uniform adherence to those principles,

   and publishes its reasons in writing for making the order, or

(c) by an order under paragraph (b)

   (i) the commission has previously accepted a financial statement of the same issuer with a corresponding variation from generally accepted accounting principles, and

   (ii) the superintendent is satisfied that there has been no material change in the circumstances on which the decision of the commission was based.

(9) Where applicable, and where the period or date reported on is a financial year or financial year end, there shall be referred to in or by way of a note to the financial statements,

(a) in the case of a finance issuer, or an issuer engaged primarily in investing, an analysis of shares, bonds, debentures and other investments showing separately

   (i) the name of each issuer of the securities owned,

   (ii) the class or designation of each security held,

   (iii) the number of each class of shares or aggregate face value of each class of other securities held, and

   (iv) the cost and market value of each class of securities held and, if the carrying value is other than average cost, the basis of valuation, and

(b) where an industrial or natural resource issuer is in the promotional, exploratory or developmental stage, an analysis, if material, of

   (i) shares, bonds, debentures and other investments owned by the issuer showing separately each item listed and required under paragraph (a)(i) to (iv), and

   (ii) deferred charges for the period covered by the income statement or statement of changes in financial position, segregating, year by year, expenditures for development and exploration of each material property held from expenditures for administration and showing the total for each.

Disclosure of securities beneficially owned

5. (1) Where the Act or this regulation requires the disclosure of the number or percentage of securities beneficially owned by a person and, under section 1(4) of the Act, one or more corporations will also have to be shown as beneficially owning the securities, a statement

(a) disclosing all the securities beneficially owned by the person or deemed to be beneficially owned, and

(b) indicating whether the ownership is direct or indirect and, if indirect, indicating

   (i) the name of the controlled corporation or corporation affiliated with the controlled corporation through which the securities are indirectly owned, and

   (ii) the number or percentage of the securities so owned by the corporation,

is sufficient disclosure without disclosing the name of any other corporation which is deemed to beneficially own the same securities.

(2) Where the Act or this regulation requires the disclosure of the number or percentage of securities beneficially owned by a corporation and, under section 1(4) of the Act, one or more other corporations will also have to be shown as beneficially owning the securities, a statement

(a) disclosing all securities beneficially owned or deemed to be beneficially owned by the parent corporation, and

(b) indicating whether the ownership is direct or indirect and, if indirect, indicating

     (i) the name of the subsidiary through which the securities are indirectly owned, and

    (ii) the number or percentage of the securities so owned,

shall be deemed sufficient disclosure without disclosing the name of any other corporation which is deemed to beneficially own the same securities.

PART 2

THE COMMISSION

Conflict of Interest Rules

Application

6. (1) This Part only applies to

(a) each member of the commission,

(b) the superintendent, and

(c) each officer, clerk or other person who is employed or who holds office or an appointment under the Act or this regulation, other than an appointment under section 136 or 137 of the Act.

(2) Sections 8 and 9 do not apply to transactions in

(a) personal promissory notes, or

(b) securities referred to in section 32(a) to (j) and (n) to (p) of the Act.

(3) Section 8 does not apply to an associate within the meaning of paragraph (d) of the definition of "associate" in section 1 of the Act where that associate effects the purchase or trade in his sole discretion and, where applicable, provides the necessary funds from his personal resources.

General conduct

7. No person to whom this Part applies shall

(a) engage directly or indirectly in any personal business transaction or private arrangement for personal profit which accrues from or is based upon his official position or authority or upon confidential or non-public information which he gains by reason of such position or authority,

(b) act in a manner that might result in or create the appearance of

     (i) a public office being used for private benefit, gain or profit,

    (ii) a person receiving preferential treatment,

   (iii) government efficiency or economy being impeded,

    (iv) loss of independence or impartiality, or

Re Russell James Bennett, William Richards Bennett and Harbanse Singh Doman, [1993] 43 B.C.S.C. Weekly Summary 4 (B.C. Sec. Comm.).

The proper test to be applied to determine whether there is a reasonable apprehension of bias on the part of a panel member of the Commission is as follows:

What would an informed person, viewing the matter realistically and practically and having thought the matter through conclude. Would he think that it is more likely than not that [a panel member], consciously or unconsciously, would not decide fairly on whether an order should be made prohibiting [a person] from being a director and officer of [a company which is in competition with a second company of which the panel member is a director].

Whether there is a reasonable apprehension of bias depends on the facts.

Bennett v. British Columbia (Superintendent of Brokers), [1994] 3 W.W.R. 687, 87 B.C.L.R. (2d) 22, 2 C.C.L.S. 14, 17 Admin. L.R. (2d) 222, 109 D.L.R. (4th) 717, (sub nom. *Bennett v. British Columbia Securities Commission (No. 2)*) 37 B.C.A.C. 313, 60 W.A.C. 313 (C.A.), leave to appeal to S.C.C. refused 91 B.C.L.R. (2d) xxxvi, 5 C.C.L.S. 281, [1994] 6 W.W.R. lxx, 24 Admin. L.R. (2d) 80, 112 D.L.R. (4th) vii, 176 N.R. 76, 176 N.R. 77, 52 B.C.A.C. 240, 86 W.A.C. 240 (S.C.C.).

On appeal from the ruling of the Commission that a panel member was not disqualified by reason of an apprehension of bias, the Court of Appeal posed a similar question to be applied to determine whether there is a reasonable apprehension of bias on the part of such a panel member:

Would a reasonable person think it just that a director of a company in a certain industry should sit on such an inquiry as this into the conduct of a director of another company in the same industry if the result of that inquiry might be that the director whose conduct is in issue and who is of substantial importance to his own company may be barred from the management of his company and that company may be seriously harmed by his non-participation in the management?

      (v) loss of public confidence in the integrity of the commission,

(c) divulge or release, in advance or otherwise, confidential, non-public or official information to a person unless authorized under the Act or this regulation,

(d) act as an official in a matter in which he has a personal interest,

(e) be involved, directly or indirectly, in any business or financial affairs or matters which may conflict with his official duties or responsibilities, or

(f) without the written permission of the minister, hold office in or be a director of a reporting issuer, other than

      (i) an extra-provincial issuer whose securities are exempt from registration under section 32(a) to (j) or (n) to (p) of the Act, or

      (ii) a non-profit or charitable corporation in the Province.

Transactions

8. No person to whom this Part applies shall, whether directly or through an associate,

(a) purchase or trade in a security of an issuer with knowledge of a material fact or material change in respect of that issuer that he knows or ought reasonably to know has not been generally disclosed,

(b) where he knows a fact or change in the affairs of an issuer and that the fact or change is a material fact or change, inform other than in the necessary course of duty another person of that material fact or change before it has been generally disclosed,

(c) purchase or trade in a security of an issuer when, in respect of any security held or issued by that issuer,

      (i) a filing by way of prospectus or preliminary prospectus or amended prospectus is being processed,

      (ii) 60 days have not elapsed since the date a receipt for the prospectus or preliminary prospectus was issued,

      (iii) an application is pending for a ruling or opinion under the Act or this regulation, or

      (iv) 60 days have not elapsed since the date on which the ruling or opinion was given, or

(d) purchase or trade in securities of

      (i) an issuer whose status is, under the Act or this regulation, being investigated or otherwise considered to determine the application of a provision of the Act or this regulation, or

    (ii) a person who is involved in a pending investigation, formal or otherwise, by the commission or the superintendent or who is involved in a proceeding before either of them or in a proceeding to which either of them is a party.

Reporting to minister or to commission

9. (1) At the time of taking office or employment with the commission, a new member of the commission shall provide the minister, and every other person referred to in section 6(1)(b) or (c) shall provide the commission, with a report disclosing his direct or indirect beneficial ownership of, or control or direction over, securities.

(2) Each member of the commission shall report to the minister, and every other person referred to in section 6(1)(b) or (c) shall report to the commission, within 10 days following the end of the month in which a change occurs in his direct or indirect beneficial ownership of, or control or direction over, securities, disclosing

(a) his direct or indirect beneficial ownership of, or control or direction over, securities at the end of that month, and

(b) the change or changes in his ownership in securities that occurred during the month.

(3) The minister may require a person to dispose of a security acquired as a result of an intentional or accidental violation of section 10.

Disclosure of interest

10. (1) Every person referred to in section 6(1)(c) shall advise the superintendent if

(a) he has any interest in a security, or any personal interest in an issuer or project that is the subject or part of the subject of any matter assigned to him as part of his duties, or

(b) his prior employment or relationship to any person or project may prejudice or affect his work on the assignment.

(2) In the event of a personal interest of the superintendent or of a member of the commission, the superintendent or member shall advise the chairman of the commission.

(3) In the event of a personal interest of the chairman of the commission, he shall report the matter to the minister.

[Ss. 6-10 re-en. B.C. Reg. 305/88, s. 2.]

PART 3

SELF REGULATORY BODIES AND STOCK EXCHANGES

There are no regulations under this Part.

PART 4

REGISTRATION

Division (1)
General

Interpretation

11. In this Part

"Canadian Investment Finance Course" means a course prepared and conducted by the Canadian Securities Institute and so designated by that institute;

> The Canadian Investment Finance Course is now called the Canadian Investment Management Course.

"Canadian Investment Funds Course" means a course prepared and conducted by the Education Division of The Investment Funds Institute of Canada and so designated by that institute;

"Canadian Securities Course" means a course prepared and conducted by the Canadian Securities Institute and so designated by that institute;

"capital" means money raised through issuing bonds, certificates, debentures, long-term notes or other long-term obligations, or shares, and includes contributed surplus, earned surplus and reserves;

"Chartered Financial Analysts Course" means a course prepared and conducted by the Institute of Chartered Financial Analysts and so designated by that institute;

"client's trust account" means an account designated and maintained by a registrant as a client's trust account with a bank or a trust company registered under the Trust Company Act or under similar federal or provincial legislation;

"free credit balance" includes money received or held by a registrant from or for the account of a client

(a) for investing in and paying for securities to be purchased by the client from or through the registrant where, at the time of payment by the client, the registrant

  (i) does not own the securities, or

  (ii) has not yet purchased the securities on behalf of the client, and

(b) as proceeds of securities

  (i) purchased from the client by the registrant, or

  (ii) sold by the registrant for the account of the client,

where the securities have been delivered by the client to the registrant;

"market value" means,

(a) where used with reference to a commodity futures contract, the settlement price on the relevant date or last trading day before the relevant date,

(b) where used with reference to a security that is listed and posted for trading on a stock exchange, the bid price or, if sold short, the ask price, as shown on the exchange quotation sheets at the close of business on the relevant date or last trading day before the relevant date, subject to an appropriate adjustment where an unusually large or unusually small quantity of securities is being valued, and

(c) where used with reference to a security that is not listed and posted for trading on a stock exchange, a value determined in accordance with section 12;

"minimum net free capital means the amount determined under section 20, 21 or 22, as appropriate;

"Partners', Directors' and Officers' Qualifying Examination" means an examination prepared and conducted by the Canadian Securities Institute and so designated by that institute;

"Registered Representative Examination" means an examination based on the Manual for Registered Representatives prepared and conducted by the Canadian Securities Institute and so designated by that institute.

The Registered Representative Examination is now called the Conduct and Practices Handbook Exam.

Market value

12. (1) Subject to subsection (2), the market value of a security that is not listed and posted for trading on a stock exchange shall be determined by assigning to it

(a) a reasonable value on the basis of values shown in published market reports or inter-dealer quotation sheets on the relevant date or last trading day before the relevant date, or

(b) a value that would be more appropriate than the value assigned under paragraph (a) when all the prevailing circumstances are taken into account.

(2) The commission may determine

  (a) a different market value from one determined under subsection (1) if it is of the opinion that the value determined under this subsection is more appropriate in light of all the circumstances, and

  (b) the market value of a security as zero where no published market report or inter-dealer quotation sheet exists with respect to that security.

Division (2)
Categories of Registrants and Related Provisions

Dealer categories

13. (1) In this section "real estate security" means a security of an issuer whose assets, that are the principal subject of its business, consist of real property, a partnership interest in real property or documents evidencing an interest in real property.

(2) Every person registered as a dealer under the Act shall be classified in one or more of the following categories according to qualification:

  (a) *broker* – a person who is a member of a stock exchange in the Province recognized by the commission and who trades in securities in the capacity of agent or principal;

> The Vancouver Stock Exchange has been so recognized. See Local Policy Statement 3-44 "Recognition of Stock Exchanges and Jurisdictions".

  (b) *investment dealer* – a person who is a member, a branch office member or an associate member of the Pacific District of the Investment Dealers' Association of Canada and who is engaged all or part of his time in trading in securities in the capacity of agent or principal;

  (c) *mutual fund dealer* – a person who trades exclusively in the securities of mutual funds;

  (d) *scholarship plan dealer* – a person who trades exclusively in securities of a scholarship or educational plan or trust;

  (e) *securities dealer* – a person who trades in securities generally and who is engaged all or part of his time in trading in securities in the capacity of agent or principal;

  (f) *security issuer* – an issuer who trades in securities for purposes of distributing securities of its own issue, exclusively for its own account;

  (g) [Repealed B.C. Reg. 306/88, First Sched., s. 1.]

  (h) *real estate securities dealer* – a person who trades in the capacity of agent or principal exclusively in real estate securities.

[S. 13(2) am. B.C. Reg. 306/88, First Sched., s. 1.]

> See Interim Local Policy Statement 3-22 "Requirements for Registration for Trading in Securities", and NIN 88/40 "Sale of Mutual Funds by Financial Institutions – Principles of Regulation".

Underwriter

13.1 Every person registered as a dealer in the category of broker, investment dealer or securities dealer shall also be deemed to have been granted registration as an underwriter.

[S. 13.1 en. B.C. Reg. 306/88, First Sched., s. 2.]

Adviser categories

14. Every person registered as an adviser under the Act shall be classified in one or more of the following categories according to qualification:

  (a) *investment counsel* – a person who engages in or holds himself out as engaging in the business of advising others as to the investing in or buying or selling of specific securities or who is primarily engaged in giving continuous advice on the investment of funds on the basis of the particular objectives of each client;

(b) *portfolio manager* – a person who is managing the investment portfolio of clients through discretionary authority granted by them;

(c) *securities adviser* – a person who engages in or holds himself out as engaging in the business of advising others through direct advice or through publications as to the investing in or buying or selling of specific securities, not purporting to be tailored to the needs of specific clients.

[S. 14 am. B.C. Reg. 306/88, First Sched., s. 3.]

Broker or investment dealer acting as portfolio manager

15. The provisions of this Part that apply to a portfolio manager do not apply to one who is an investment dealer or broker and is, by the operation of section 73 or 74, exempt from registration under 20(1)(c) of the Act as an adviser with respect to his acting as a portfolio manager.

Division (3)
Conditions of Registration — General

Compliance a continuing condition of registration

16. Each registrant shall comply with the applicable requirements of this regulation and failure to do so shall be considered by the superintendent on any application for registration, renewal or reinstatement of registration or an amendment to registration under Part 4 of the Act or in any proceedings under section 26 of the Act.

[S. 16 am. B.C. Reg. 306/88, First Sched., s. 4.]

See Local Policy Statement 3-42 "Registered Representatives Continued Fitness for Registration", Amended National Policy Statement 17 "Violations of Securities Laws of Other Jurisdictions – Conduct Affecting Fitness for Continued Registration", National Policy Statement 18 – "Conflict of Interest – Registrants Acting as Corporate Directors", and Uniform Act Policy 2-06 "Use of Shareholders' Lists by Registrants".

Jurisdiction of incorporation or formation of registrants

16.1 (1) A person that is not an individual shall not be registered as an adviser, dealer or underwriter unless incorporated, formed or created under the laws of Canada or a province.

(2) Subsection (1) does not apply to a security issuer.

(3) Where the superintendent considers that it would not be prejudicial to the public interest to do so, he may exempt a person from the requirements of this section.

[S. 16.1 en. B.C. Reg. 306/88, First Sched., s. 5.]

Registrant's interest in other registrants

17. (1) No registrant or partner, officer or associate of a registrant shall have a direct or indirect interest in any other registrant without the approval of the superintendent.

(2) For the purposes of subsection (1), affiliated persons shall be treated as one person.

Superintendent's conditions of registration

18. (1) The superintendent may impose conditions of registration on a registrant or group of registrants in place of some or all of the conditions of registration in sections 23 to 58, 60 to 64 and 70 to 72.

(2) Before exercising his powers under subsection (1) the superintendent shall

(a) give prior notice of the proposed conditions and an opportunity to be heard to registrants affected, and

(b) publish the notice in the publication referred to in section 152.

Summons for examination under oath

19. A summons for an examination under section 24(c) of the Act shall be in the required form.

The required form is Form 8.

Division (4)
Conditions of Registration re Capital, Bonding and Insurance

Minimum net free capital

20. (1) A broker and an investment dealer shall maintain a minimum net free capital computed in accordance with the Joint Regulatory Financial Questionnaire and Report referred to in section 4(2).

(2) A securities dealer shall maintain a minimum net free capital computed in accordance with the Joint Regulatory Financial Questionnaire and Report referred to in section 4(2), but he shall include the capital requirement on adjusted liabilities to a minimum of $50 000 instead of the minimum of $75 000 set out in that questionnaire and report.

(3) A mutual fund dealer, scholarship plan dealer and real estate securities dealer shall maintain a minimum free capital consisting of

    (a) the maximum amount that is deductible under a bond that is required to be held under section 23, and

    (b) the amount of working capital set out in subsection (4), calculated in accordance with generally accepted accounting principles.

[S. 20(3) am. B.C. Reg. 306/88, First Sched., s. 6(a).]

(4) For the purposes of subsection (3)(b), the amount of working capital required for

    (a) a mutual fund dealer is $25 000,

    (b) a scholarship plan dealer is $25 000, and

    (c) [Repealed B.C. Reg. 306/88, First Sched., s. 6(b).]

    (d) a real estate securities dealer is $25 000.

See NIN 90/29 "Proposals for Securities Firms".

Adviser's minimum free capital

21. (1) An adviser shall maintain a minimum free capital consisting of

    (a) the maximum amount that is deductible under a bond that is required to be held by him under section 23, and

    (b) $5 000 of working capital calculated in accordance with generally accepted accounting principles.

(2) Subsection (1) does not apply to an adviser who provides written or published advice if

    (a) the adviser exercises no control over clients' funds or securities, and

    (b) no investment advice is, or purports to be, tailored to the needs of specific clients.

Underwriter's minimum free capital

22. An underwriter shall maintain a minimum free capital consisting of

    (a) the maximum amount that is deductible under a bond that is required to be held by him under section 23, and

    (b) $10 000 of net free capital calculated in accordance with the required form.

No form has been specified.

Bonding requirement

23. The superintendent may require an applicant for registration or a registrant to be bonded in any amount the superintendent considers necessary.

Notice of change in or claim under bond

24. A registrant shall give, without delay, written notice to the superintendent of any change in or claim made under a bond maintained as required by the superintendent.

Compensation or contingency trust fund

25. (1) A dealer, other than a security issuer, shall participate in and contribute to a compensation fund or contingency trust fund approved by the superintendent established by

    (a) a self regulatory body or a stock exchange recognized under section 11 of the Act, or

> The Vancouver Stock Exchange has been recognized under s. 11 of the Act.

    (b) a trust company.

> The form of trust agreement is prescribed by Form 53.

(2) The amount contributed by the dealer to a fund referred to in subsection (1) shall, subject to subsection (3), be the amount required by the self regulatory body, stock exchange, or in the case of a fund established by a trust company, the superintendent, as the case may be.

(3) The commission may vary the amount required to be contributed by any participant in a fund under subsection (1) if it considers it would not be prejudicial to the public interest to do so and a notice of the variation is published in the publication referred to in section 152.

Subordination agreement

26. At the request of the superintendent, a registrant shall enter into a subordination agreement in the required form.

> The required form is Form 60.

Division (5)
Conditions of Registration re Record Keeping and Reporting

Record keeping by registrant

27. A registrant shall maintain at its head office or, where its head office is out of the Province, at its chief place of business in the Province

    (a) records that clearly and competently record all of its business transactions and financial affairs that are conducted

        (i) in the Province if its head office is out of the Province, and

        (ii) in or out of the Province if its head office is in the Province, and

    (b) records that are required to be maintained by the registrant under section 29.

> See National Policy Statement 16 "Maintenance of Provincial Trading Records".

Adequate precautions and access

28. A registrant may only record or store information using mechanical, electronic or other devices if

    (a) the method used is not prohibited by law,

    (b) he takes adequate precautions, appropriate to the methods used, to guard against falsification of the information recorded or stored, and

(c)   he provides a means for making the information available in an accurate and intelligible form within a reasonable time to any person lawfully entitled to examine the information.

Record keeping

29. (1) A registrant shall maintain the records referred to in sections 30 to 39 in accordance with those sections.

(2) Where the superintendent considers that it would not be appropriate to the business of a registrant, a class of registrants or registrants generally to require the keeping of a record referred to in subsection (1), he may, in writing, make an order exempting a particular registrant, a class of registrants or registrants generally from maintaining all or some of those records.

Blotters

30. Blotters or other records of original entry shall contain an itemized daily record of

(a)   all purchases and sales of securities,

(b)   all receipts and deliveries of securities including certificate numbers,

(c)   all receipts and disbursements of cash,

(d)   all other debits and credits,

(e)   the account for which each transaction was effected,

(f)   the name of the securities, their class or designation and their number or value,

(g)   the unit and aggregate purchase or sale price, if any, and

(h)   the trade date and the name or other designation of the person from whom the securities were purchased or received or to whom they were sold or delivered.

Ledgers

31. Ledgers or other records shall reflect

(a)   in detail, the assets, liability and capital accounts and the income and expenditure accounts,

(b)   securities in transfer,

(c)   dividends and interest received,

(d)   securities borrowed and securities loaned,

(e)   money borrowed and money loaned, together with a record of related collateral and substitutions in the collateral, and

(f)   securities that the registrant has failed to receive and failed to deliver.

Ledger accounts

32. Ledger accounts or other records shall be itemized separately showing

(a)   each cash and margin account of each client,

(b)   all purchases, sales, receipts and deliveries of securities and commodities for the account, and

(c)   all other debits and credits to the account.

Securities record

33. A securities record shall show separately for each security, as at the trade date or settlement date,

(a)   all long and short positions, including securities in safekeeping, carried for the registrant's account or for the account of clients,

(b)   the location of all securities long and the position offsetting securities sold short, and

(c)   in all cases, the name or designation of the account in which each position is carried.

Orders and instructions

34. A record of each order and any other instruction, given or received for the purchase or sale of securities, whether executed or not, shall show with respect to each order and instruction

(a) its terms and conditions,

(b) any modification or cancellation of it,

(c) the account to which it relates,

(d) where it is placed by an individual, other than

    (i) the person in whose name the account is operated, or

    (ii) the individual who is duly authorized to place orders or instructions on behalf of a client that is a corporation,

the name, sales number or designation of the individual placing it,

[Subpara. (ii) am B.C. Reg. 316/89, s. 3.]

(e) its time of entry and, where applicable, a statement that it is entered under the exercise of a discretionary power of the registrant or registrant's employee,

(f) the price at which it was executed, and

(g) the time of its execution or cancellation, where practicable.

Confirmations and notices

35. A confirmations and notices record shall consist of

(a) a copy of every confirmation for each purchase and sale of securities required by section 80, and

(b) a copy of every notice of all other debits and credits of securities, cash and other items for the accounts of clients.

Cash and margin accounts

36. (1) Subject to section 43(2), a record of cash and margin accounts shall show, with respect to each cash account and margin account for each client,

(a) the name and address of the beneficial owner of the account and of the guarantor, if any,

(b) where the trading instructions are accepted from a person other than the client, written authorization or ratification from the client naming that person, and

(c) in the case of a margin account, an executed margin agreement containing the signature of the beneficial owner and the guarantor, if any, and any additional information required under sections 43 to 45,

but in the case of a joint account or an account of a corporation, the record is required only in respect of the person duly authorized to transact business for the account.

Options records

37. An options record shall show

(a) all puts, calls, spreads, straddles and other options granted or guaranteed by the registrant or in which he has any direct or indirect interest,

(b) the identification of the security and the underlying security, and

(c) the number of underlying securities to which the put, call, spread, straddle or other option relates.

Monthly record

38. A record prepared for each month shall show

(a) the proof of money balances of all ledger accounts in the form of trial balances, and

(b) a reasonable calculation of the minimum net free capital required under section 20(1) or (2)

within a reasonable time following the end of each month.

Time for record keeping

39. Registrants shall keep records of

(a) unexecuted orders and instructions under section 34 and confirmation under section 3 for a period of at least 2 years, and

(b) executed orders and instructions under section 34 for a period of at least 5 years, the first 2 years of that period in a readily accessible location.

Division (6)
Conditions of Registration re Client
Accounts and Statements of Account and Portfolio

Dealer's and adviser's business procedures

40. Every dealer or adviser shall establish prudent business procedures for dealing with clients and shall ensure that those procedures are adequately supervised.

Broker's and investment dealer's guidelines

41. It is sufficient compliance with section 40 if a person acting as a broker or an investment dealer observes guidelines on client account supervision that are

(a) published by the Vancouver Stock Exchange or the Investment Dealers' Association of Canada,

(b) submitted to the commission before they take effect, and

(c) not objected to by the commission.

> See Local Policy Statement 3-33 "R.R.S.P.'s Administered by Brokers on Behalf of Authorized Trustees".
>
> The Commission has received, and does not object to, the publication entitled "Internal Control Guidelines", prepared by the Investment Dealers' Association of Canada. These are guidelines on client account supervision to be observed by brokers and investment dealers.

Responsibility for opening new accounts and supervising

42. Subject to sections 44 and 45, a registrant shall record in writing the procedures established under section 40 and shall designate a partner or director and, in the case of a branch office, a manager reporting directly to the designated partner or director, to be responsible for approving the opening of new client accounts and supervising of trades made for or to that client.

Enquiries concerning each client

43. (1) For the purposes of section 40 and subject to sections 44 and 45, every dealer, investment counsel and portfolio manager shall make enquiries concerning each client

(a) to establish the identity and, where applicable, credit worthiness of the client and the reputation of the client if information known to the dealer, investment counsel or portfolio manager causes doubt as to whether the client is of good reputation, and

(b) to determine the general investment needs and objectives of the client and the suitability of a proposed purchase or sale for that client.

(2) Subsection (1)(b) does not apply to a dealer in respect of a trade executed by him on the instructions of an investment counsel, portfolio manager, another dealer, a bank, a trust company or an insurer.

Executing orders in own name or by code

44. Where an investment counsel or portfolio manager opens and trades an account on behalf of a client and executes the client's orders in its own name or identifies the client by means of a code or symbols, a dealer who transacts business with the investment counsel or portfolio manager concerning those orders shall establish the credit worthiness of the investment counsel or portfolio manager, but need not otherwise determine the suitability of a trade for the client of the investment counsel or portfolio manager.

Executing orders without payment guarantee

45. Where an investment counsel or a portfolio manager opens and trades an account on behalf of a client and executes the client's orders in the name of the client without an agreement under which payment of the account is guaranteed by the investment counsel or portfolio manager, the dealer transacting business with the investment counsel or portfolio manager concerning those orders shall

(a) obtain full information to establish the credit worthiness of the client in whose name the orders are executed, or

(b) obtain a letter of undertaking from the investment counsel or portfolio manager that contains

(i) a statement that the investment counsel or portfolio manager is familiar with the provisions of this Part concerning account supervision, and

(ii) a covenant from the investment counsel or portfolio manager to make the inquiries required by this Division and, where known, to advise the dealer if the client in whose name the orders are executed is an insider or an employee, director or officer of a corporation, or an employee or partner in a firm, engaged in the securities business,

but the dealer need not otherwise determine the suitability of a trade in that account.

Standards of investment to be filed

46. (1) An investment counsel and a portfolio manager shall each develop written policies that maintain standards ensuring fairness in the allocation of investment opportunities among its clients.

(2) The investment counsel and the portfolio manager shall each file a copy of its policies under subsection (1) and shall give a copy of those policies to each client.

[S. 46 am. B.C. Reg. 305/88, ss. 3, 4.]

Charges for services

47. An investment counsel and a portfolio manager shall each charge clients directly for its services and may base those charges on the dollar value of the client's portfolio, but may not base them

(a) on the value or volume of the transactions initiated for the client, or

(b) except with the written agreement of the client, contingently on profits or performance.

[S. 47 am. B.C. Reg. 305/88, s. 3.]

Separate supervision of accounts and pooling

48. (1) Subject to subsection (2), an investment counsel and a portfolio manager shall ensure that

(a) the account of each client is supervised separately and distinctly from the accounts of other clients, and

(b) except in the case of a mutual fund or pension fund, an order placed on behalf of one client is not pooled with that of another client.

[S. 48(1) B.C. Reg. 305/88, s. 5(a).]

(2) A portfolio manager may, subject to the bylaws and rules of the Vancouver Stock Exchange with respect to commission rate structure, pool an order placed on behalf of one account with an order placed on behalf of another account.

[S. 48(2) re-en. B.C. Reg. 305/88, s. 5(b).]

Change in ownership or sale of account

49. (1) Where there has been a material change in the ownership or control of an investment counsel or a portfolio manager, the investment counsel or portfolio manager shall immediately give each of its clients

(a) a written statement explaining the change, and

(b) advice of the right to withdraw the account.

(2) Where it is proposed that an investment counsel or a portfolio manager sell or assign the account of a client in whole or in part to another registrant, the investment counsel or portfolio manager shall before the sale or assignment give to that client

(a) a written statement explaining the proposed sale or assignment, and

(b) advice of the right to withdraw the account.

[S. 49 am. B.C. Reg. 305/88, s. 6.]

50. [Repealed B.C. Reg. 306/88, First Sched., s. 7.]

Unencumbered securities held under safekeeping agreement

51. A registrant who holds unencumbered securities for a client under a written safekeeping agreement shall

(a) keep them apart from all other securities,

(b) identify them in his security position record, client's ledger and statement of account as being held in safekeeping for a client, and

(c) release the securities from the safekeeping agreement only on instructions of the client.

Unencumbered securities not held under safekeeping agreement

52. (1) Subject to subsection (3), a registrant who, other than under a written safekeeping agreement holds unencumbered securities for a client that are either fully paid for or are excess margin securities shall

(a) segregate and identify the securities as being held in trust for the client, and

(b) describe them in his security position record, client's ledger and statement of account as being held in segregation.

(2) A registrant may, in accordance with a written agreement between himself and a client, sell or loan securities held in trust and segregated under subsection (1) if the client becomes indebted to him, but shall only sell or loan the securities to the extent reasonably necessary to cover the indebtedness.

(3) Bulk segregation of securities described in subsection (1) is permissible.

Clients' free credit balances

53. A registrant shall, on receiving clients' free credit balances, immediately and clearly identify them as free credit balances and deposit them in a trust account for clients.

[S. 53 am. B.C. Reg. 305/88, s. 7.]

Brokers and Investment Dealers have been exempted from these requirements pursuant to s. 57 of the Regulation by way of a private letter issued by the Superintendent.

Connor Financial Corp. v. British Columbia (Superintendent of Brokers) (1994), 5 C.C.L.S. 276 (B.C. S.C.).

This decision clarified that registrants are under a trust obligation with respect to funds received by them. This obligation continues until the securities are held in trust or the client has irrevocably received the funds.

Clients' subscriptions or prepayments

54. Where a registrant holds subscriptions or prepayments for a client pending investment, it shall

(a) hold the subscriptions or prepayments in a trust account for the client, and

(b) ensure that the subscriptions or prepayments are segregated from its own assets.

[S. 54 am. B.C. Reg. 305/88, s. 8.]

Brokers and Investment Dealers have been exempted from these requirements pursuant to s. 57 of the Regulation by way of a private letter issued by the Superintendent.

See the *Connor Financial Corp.* decision at s. 53 of the Regulation.

Transfers between securities accounts and commodity account of same client

55. (1) In this section "free credit balance" does not include money in a client's securities account that is committed to be used on a specific settlement date as payment for securities where the registrant who maintains the securities account prepares financial statements on a settlement date basis.

(2) Where a registrant maintains for a client

(a) a securities account containing a free credit balance, and

(b) a commodity account containing a debit balance of $5 000 or more,

he shall transfer from the securities account to the commodity account

(c) all of the free credit balance if it is less in amount than the debit balance, or

(d) a portion of the free credit balance, if it is equal to or greater in amount than the debit balance, sufficient to eliminate the debit balance.

Transfer of funds between accounts where no debit balance

56. A registrant who maintains a securities account and a commodity account for the same client may make a transfer of any amount of a free credit balance from the securities account to the commodity account of the client so long as the transfer

(a) is made in accordance with a written agreement between the registrant and the client, and

(b) is not a transfer referred to in section 55,

unless the client otherwise directs him in writing, or orally, if later confirmed in writing.

Exemption from sections 51 to 56

57. The superintendent may, in writing, exempt a particular registrant or class of registrants, where the registrant or registrants are members of the Pacific District of the Investment Dealers' Association of Canada or the Vancouver Stock Exchange from one or more of sections 51 to 56 if he considers that

(a) the requirements of the organization of which the registrant or registrants are members provide equivalent protection for clients to that provided under sections 51 to 56, and

(b) the registrant or registrants being exempted comply with those equivalent requirements.

[S. 57 re-en. B.C. Reg. 305/88, s. 9.]

Statement of account

58. (1) Subject to subsection (4), where a client has a debit or credit balance with a dealer or a dealer is holding a client's securities, the dealer shall send a statement of account to that client at the end of each month in which the client effects a transaction.

(2) Subject to subsections (1) and (4), where a dealer is holding a client's funds or securities on a continuing basis, the dealer shall forward, not less than once every 3 months, a statement of account to the client showing any debit or credit balance and the details of any securities held.

(3) A statement of account sent under subsection (1) or (2) shall indicate clearly which securities are held for safekeeping or in segregation.

(4) Subsections (1) and (2) do not apply to a mutual fund dealer who sends a statement of account to each client at least once every 12 months showing

(a) the number and market value at the date of purchase or redemption of securities purchased or redeemed during the period since the date of the last statement sent under this subsection, and

(b) the total market value of all securities of the mutual fund held by the client at the date of the statement.

(5) Except where a client has expressly directed otherwise, a portfolio manager shall send to each client at least once every 3 months a statement of the client's portfolio.

(6) The superintendent may, if he considers that it would not be harmful to the public interest, vary the requirements of subsection (1) as it applies to any dealer.

Division (7)
Proficiency and Qualification Requirements

Salesmen

59. (1) Subject to subsection (2), no individual shall be granted registration as a salesman of a dealer unless he

(a) has been registered previously as a dealer or as a partner or officer of a dealer, or

(b) successfully completes the Canadian Securities Course.

(2) An individual may be granted registration as a salesman of a mutual fund dealer if he successfully completes the Canadian Investment Funds Course.

(3) No individual may be granted registration as a salesman of a broker, investment dealer or securities dealer unless, in addition to meeting the requirements of subsection (1), he

(a) has been registered previously as a salesman, or

(b) successfully completes the Registered Representative Examination.

> The Registered Representative Examination is now called the Conduct and Practices Handbook Exam.

[S. 59(3) am. B.C. Reg. 306/88, First Sched., s. 8.]

Securities adviser

60. (1) No individual shall be granted registration as a securities adviser or as a partner or officer of a securities adviser unless he has

(a) successfully completed the Canadian Securities Course and the Canadian Investment Finance Course, and

> The Canadian Investment Finance Course is now called the Canadian Investment Management Course.

(b) performed research involving the financial analysis of investments for at least 5 years under the supervision of an adviser.

(2) No corporation shall be granted registration as a securities adviser unless

(a) an individual who meets the requirements of subsection (1) is appointed an officer of the corporation, and

(b) the individual so appointed is the officer responsible for discharging the corporation's obligations.

Investment counsel and portfolio manager

61. (1) No individual shall be granted registration as an investment counsel or a portfolio manager or as a partner or officer of an investment counsel or a portfolio manager unless he has

(a) successfully completed the Canadian Securities Course, the Canadian Investment Finance Course and the first year of the Chartered Financial Analysts Course, and

> The Canadian Investment Finance Course is now called the Canadian Investment Management Course.

(b) been employed performing research involving the financial analysis of investments for at least 5 years, with at least 3 of those years under the supervision of an adviser responsible for the management or supervision of investment portfolios having an aggregate value of at least $1 million.

(2) No corporation shall be granted registration as an investment counsel or a portfolio manager unless

(a) an individual who meets the requirements of subsection (1) is appointed an officer of the corporation, and

(b) the individual so appointed is responsible for discharging the corporation's obligations.

[S. 61 am. B.C. Reg. 305/88, s. 10.]

Broker and dealer

62. (1) No individual shall be granted registration as a broker, an investment dealer or a securities dealer, or as a partner or officer of a broker, an investment dealer or securities dealer, unless he has successfully completed the Partners', Directors' and Officers' Qualifying Examination.

(2) No corporation shall be granted registration as a broker, an investment dealer or securities dealer unless

(a) an individual who meets the requirements of subsection (1) is appointed an officer of the corporation, and

(b) the individual so appointed is responsible for discharging the corporation's obligations.

Exemption from sections 59 to 62

63. The superintendent may, in writing, exempt a person from compliance in whole or in part from sections 59 to 62 on any conditions he considers necessary if he considers that the person has the educational qualifications and experience equivalent to the requirements of those sections.

Salesman employed other than full time

64. (1) Subject to subsections (2) and (3), no individual shall be granted registration, renewal or reinstatement of registration as a salesman unless he is or will be employed full time as a salesman.

> *Re Rodger Lutz and a Referral Question under Section 180 of the Securities Regulation* (1993), 1 C.C.L.S. 264 (B.C. Sec. Comm.).
>
> Lutz was registered as a mutual funds salesman under the Act. He also held licenses as a real estate agent and as a life insurance agent. A condition attached to his securities registration precluded him from any real estate related activity without the written consent of the Superintendent. Lutz applied for an exemption to permit him to pursue all employment options for which he was licensed or registered. The Commission denied the application. The proposal to allow real estate licensees to obtain registration for trading in securities, other than real estate securities, would not be justified on the basis of the existing exemptions from full-time employment. Dual licensing for securities and insurance is specifically permitted. Also in very limited circumstances, dual employment in financial institutions and their dealer subsidiaries is permitted. It would be inappropriate to create this further exemption without a thorough analysis and consultation.

(2) Subsection (1) does not apply to an individual who

(a) is a part time student enrolled in a business, commercial or financial course,

(b) is employed other than as a salesman for 6 months or less during the calendar year,

(c) holds a licence as an insurance agent under the Insurance Act and is employed, appointed, authorized or sponsored by the dealer who employs him or proposes to employ him, or

[Para. (c) am. B.C. Reg. 305/88, s. 11.]

(d) is registered under the Commodity Contract Act.

(3) The superintendent may exempt an individual from subsection (1) where the individual

(a) is a full time student enrolled in a business, commercial or financial course and who intends to continue a career in the investment business,

(b) carries on a hobby or a recreational or cultural activity that will not interfere with his duties and responsibilities as a salesman,

(c) is employed as a salesman by a mutual fund dealer in an area that is so remote and sparsely populated that full time employment as a salesman in that area is not economically feasible,

(d) with the written consent of the dealer employing him as a salesman, is employed outside the normal working hours and there is no conflict of interest arising from his duties as a salesman and his outside employment, or

(e) is carrying on an outside activity which will not, in the circumstances, interfere with his duties and responsibilities as a salesman and there is no conflict of interest arising from his duties as a salesman and his outside activity.

See Local Policy Statement 3-16 "Registration for Securities and Insurance".

---

65. [Repealed B.C. Reg. 305/88, s. 12.]

Division (8)
Registration and Amendments to Registration

Application for registration

66. (1) An applicant for registration shall file the financial statements required under section 136, made up as at a date not more than 90 days before the date of the application.

[S. 66(1) am. B.C. Reg. 305/88, s. 13(a).]

(2) The superintendent may accept other supporting documents in lieu of the financial statements referred to in subsection (1).

(3) The superintendent may exempt an applicant for registration as a salesman of a dealer, as a partner or officer of a dealer or of an adviser or as an adviser from applying on the required form where the information required in that form has previously been filed by the applicant and is current and accurate for the date of application.

[S. 66(3) am. B.C. Reg. 305/88, s. 13(b).]

Period of registration

67. (1) Unless earlier suspended or cancelled and subject to section 22(1) of the Act, a registration and a renewal of registration remains valid for the period of duration determined by the commission.

(2) For purposes of subsection (1), the commission may determine different periods of duration for different classes of registrants.

Renewal of registration

68. An application for renewal of a registration shall be filed no later than 30 days before the date on which the registration expires.

Insider trading exemptions are found in s. 152.3 of the Regulation.

Notice under section 28 of Act

69. A notice under section 28 of the Act shall be filed within 5 business days of the change to which it relates.

Division (9)
Financial Statements and Annual Reports

Financial statement under section 19 of Act

70. The annual financial statement under section 19(b) of the Act shall be filed within 90 days of the financial year end of the registrant.

Audits under section 18 of Act

71. It is a condition of his registration that no registrant shall withhold, destroy or conceal any information or documents or otherwise fail to cooperate with a reasonable request made by the auditor of the registrant in the course of an audit under section 18 of the Act.

Registrant's direction to auditor

72. (1) An applicant for registration who is not a member in good standing of a self regulatory body or stock exchange recognized under section 11(1) or (2) of the Act shall

(a) issue a written direction to his auditor, and submit a copy of the direction to the superintendent, instructing that auditor to conduct, at the applicant's expense, any audit requested by the superintendent during the applicant's registration, and

(b) immediately notify the superintendent in writing of any change in its auditor and shall issue a written direction to his auditor, and submit a copy of the direction to the superintendent, instructing that auditor to conduct, at the registrant's expense, any audit required by the superintendent during the registrant's registration.

[S. 72(1) re-en. B.C. Reg. 305/88, s. 14.]

(2) Where the commission makes a request for an audit and the registrant issues a direction under subsection (1), the registrant shall pay the cost of the audit.

Division (9.1)

[Division (9.1) en. B.C. Reg. 306/88, First Sched., s. 9.]

Registrant Ownership and Diversification Requirements

Interpretation

72.1 In this Division, "registrant" means a registered adviser, dealer or underwriter, but does not include a security issuer.

Notice of ownership

72.2 (1) Subject to subsection (2), a registrant that knows or has reason to believe that any person, either alone or in combination with one or more other persons and whether directly or indirectly,

(a) is about to acquire beneficial ownership of or exercise control or direction over, or

(b) has acquired beneficial ownership of or is exercising control or direction over

securities of the registrant that, together with the person's or persons' securities, constitute in the aggregate 10% or more of the outstanding securities of any class or series of voting securities of the registrant, shall forthwith give written notice of that fact to the superintendent together with the name of each person involved.

(2) Notice is not required to be given under subsection (1)(b) respecting an acquisition or exercise of control or direction

(a) of which notice has previously been given under subsection (1)(a), or

(b) if the acquisition occurred or the exercise of control or direction commenced before June 30, 1987.

Regulation

Notice of diversification

72.3 (1) A registrant that intends to carry on, directly or indirectly, through one or more persons, any other business than that of adviser, dealer or underwriter, as the case may be, shall give written notice of that intention to the superintendent at least 30 days before the registrant commences carrying on the other business.

(2) If, within the 30 days immediately after receipt of the notice referred to in subsection (1), the superintendent gives a written notice of objection to the registrant, the registrant shall not commence carrying on the other business unless the superintendent gives his written approval.

(3) After giving the registrant an opportunity to be heard, the superintendent may, where he considers it to be in the public interest,

(a) refuse to allow the registrant to carry on the other business, or

(b) allow the registrant to carry on the other business on the conditions, if any, imposed by the superintendent.

Exemption

72.4 Where the superintendent considers that it would not be prejudicial to the public interest to do so, he may exempt any person from any requirement of this Division.

Division (10)
Suspension and Cancellation

No regulations under this Division.

PART 5

EXEMPTION FROM REGISTRATION REQUIREMENTS

Investment dealer acting as portfolio manager

73. An investment dealer is exempt from registration under section 20(1)(c) of the Act as an adviser with respect to his acting as a portfolio manager where the investment dealer is a member and is subject to the discipline of the Investment Dealers' Association of Canada and that association has

(a) passed bylaws or regulations that

(i) govern its members' activities as portfolio managers,

(ii) impose conditions and standards applicable to all of its members who manage investment portfolios through discretionary authority granted by clients, and

(iii) are substantially equivalent to the requirements for registration as portfolio managers under this regulation,

(b) notified the superintendent that it recognizes the investment dealer as acting as a portfolio manager, and

(c) notified the superintendent of the names of the partners, directors, officers or employees of the investment dealer who are

(i) designated or approved under its applicable bylaws or regulations to make investment decisions on behalf of or to offer advice to clients, and

(ii) resident in the Province and registered under section 20 of the Act to trade in securities.

Broker acting as portfolio manager

74. A broker is exempt from registration under section 20(1)(c) of the Act as an adviser with respect to his acting as a portfolio manager where the broker is a member of a stock exchange, approved by the commission, which is the self regulatory body to whose discipline the broker is subject, and that stock exchange has

(a) passed bylaws or regulations that

(i) govern its members' activities as portfolio managers,

(ii) impose conditions and standards applicable to all of its members who manage investment portfolios through discretionary authority granted by clients, and

(iii) are substantially equivalent to the requirements for registration as portfolio managers under this regulation, and

(b) notified the superintendent that it recognizes the broker as acting as a portfolio manager, and

(c) notified the superintendent of the names of the partners, directors, officers or employees of the broker who are

(i) designated or approved under its applicable bylaws or regulations to make investment decisions on behalf of or to offer advice to clients, and

(ii) resident in the Province and registered under section 20 of the Act to trade in securities.

> The Vancouver Stock Exchange has been so recognized. See Local Policy Statement 3-44 "Recognition of Stock Exchanges and Jurisdictions".

Application for recognition as exempt purchaser

75. (1) An applicant for as an exempt purchaser under section 31(2)*(4)* or 55(2)*(3)* of the Act shall apply in the required form.

[S. 75(1) am. B.C. Reg. 24/87, Sch., s. 1.]

> The required form is Form 11. See Local Policy Statement 3-15 "Exempt Purchaser Status".

(2) The superintendent shall not grant a person recognition as an exempt purchaser for a period longer than one year.

(3) An exempt purchaser who wishes to maintain continuity of his recognition as an exempt purchaser shall apply for renewal of that recognition no later than 30 days before his current recognition expires.

Exemptions

76. Registration under section 20 of the Act is not required for a trade in the following circumstances:

> The corresponding prospectus exemptions are found in s. 117 of the Regulation. Additional registration exemptions are found in s. 31(2) of the Act.

(a) *50 purchasers* — the trade is made by an issuer in a security of its own issue where

(i) during the 12 month period preceding the trade, sales under this paragraph have been made to not more than 49 different purchasers,

(ii) the purchaser is

(A) a sophisticated purchaser,

(B) a spouse, parent, brother, sister or child of a senior officer or director of the issuer, or of an affiliate of the issuer, or

(C) a company, all the voting securities of which are beneficially owned by one or more of a spouse, parent, brother, sister or child of a senior officer or director of the issuer, or of an affiliate of the issuer,

(iii) the purchaser purchases as principal,

(iv) the offer and sale of the security is not accompanied by an advertisement and no selling or promotional expenses have been paid or incurred in connection with the offer and sale, except for professional services or for services performed by a registered dealer or a person referred to in paragraph (d)(ii), and

    (v) an offering memorandum is delivered to the purchaser in compliance with section 126;

See Local Policy Statement 3-24 "Statutory Exemptions and Orders Made Under Section 33 and Section 59 of the Securities Act" which, in para. 4.2, sets forth the Commission's views on the calculation of the number of offerees under two predecessor exemptions to this exemption.

  (b) *$25 000* — the trade is made by an issuer in a security of its own issue where

    (i) the purchaser purchases as principal,

    (ii) the purchaser is a sophisticated purchaser,

    (iii) the aggregate acquisition cost to the purchaser is not less than $25 000, and

    (iv) an offering memorandum is delivered to the purchaser in compliance with section 126;

It is generally understood that the guidance provided as to determining the "aggregate acquisition cost to the purchaser" under ss. 31(2)(5) and 55(2)(4) of the Act also applies to this exemption.

  (c) *Securities for debt* — the trade is made by an exchange issuer in a security of its own issue to settle a bona fide debt;

  (d) *Bonus or finder's fee* — the trade is made by an exchange issuer in a security of its own issue as consideration for

    (i) a loan or loan guarantee, or

    (ii) services performed by a person, not an insider or an associate of an insider of the issuer, in connection with

      (A) the acquisition or disposition of assets, or

      (B) a distribution by the issuer to persons not resident in the Province where the distribution is under section 55(2) of the Act;

  (e) *Management company employee* — the trade is made by an exchange issuer in a security of its own issue to an individual employed by a person providing management services to the issuer where the individual is not induced to purchase by expectation of employment or continued employment with either the issuer or the person providing the management services;

  (f) *Friends and relatives* — trade is made by an exchange issuer in a security of its own issue where

    (i) during the 12 month period preceding the trade, sales under this paragraph have been made to not more than 24 different purchasers,

    (ii) the amount paid for the security of the issuer in respect of the trade, together with the amount paid for the securities of the issuer in respect of all trades under this paragraph during the 12 month period preceding the trade, does not exceed $250 000,

    (iii) the purchaser purchases as principal,

    (iv) the purchaser is

      (A) a spouse, parent, brother, sister, child or close personal friend of a senior officer or director of the issuer, or of an affiliate of the issuer, or

      (B) a company, all voting securities of which are beneficially owned by one or more of a spouse, parent, brother, sister, child or close personal friend of a senior officer or director of the issuer, or of an affiliate of the issuer,

(v) the offer and sale of the security is not accompanied by an advertisement and no selling or promotional expenses have been paid or incurred in connection with the offer and sale, and

(vi) if an offering memorandum is delivered to the purchaser, the offering memorandum is delivered to the purchaser in compliance with section 126.

[S. 76 re-en. B.C. Reg. 305/88, s. 15.]

Prescribed amounts for exemptions

77. (1) For the purpose of section 31(2)*(5)* of the Act, the aggregate acquisition cost to the purchaser is not less than $97 000.

(2) For the purpose of section 31(2)*(6)* of the Act, the fair value of the purchased assets is not less than $100 000.

(3) For the purpose of section 31(2)*(22)* of the Act, the net asset value or the aggregate acquisition cost, whichever is applicable, is not less than $100 000.

(4) For the purpose of section 32(d) of the Act, the denomination or principal amount of the note or commerical paper is not less than $50 000.

[S. 77 re-en. B.C. Reg. 305/88, s. 16.]

Restriction on exemption

78. The exemption under section 32(c) of the Act does not apply to a person making a trade in a security of a private mutual fund administered by a trust company where the promoter or manager of the private mutual fund is a person other than the trust company.

[S. 78 re-en. B.C. Reg. 305/88, s. 17.]

Restriction on exemption

78.1 The exemption under section 32(g) of the Act does not apply to a person making a trade of securities unless

(a) the person making the trade is the issuer,

(b) the purchaser is the issuer or a security holder of the issuer, or

(c) the person making the trade is not the issuer and, before the trade is made, the person

(i) notifies the issuer of the proposed trade, and

(ii) furnishes the purchaser with a copy of any applicable information statement and financial and other information concerning the issuer's affairs that the issuer provided to the person during the 2 years immediately preceding the date of the proposed trade.

[S. 78.1 en. B.C. Reg. 417/94.]

79. [Renumbered as s. 181 B.C. Reg. 305/88, s. 39.]

PART 6

TRADING IN SECURITIES GENERALLY

Division (1)
General Trading

Confirmation of trade

80. (1) Where a registered dealer conducts a transaction for a client, he shall promptly send to the client a written confirmation of the transaction setting out the required information in accordance with subsections (2) to (5).

(2) Where a trade is made in a security, the confirmation shall set out

(a) the quantity and description of the security,

(b) the consideration,

(c) whether or not the registered dealer acted as principal or agent,

(d) if acting as agent in a trade, the name of the person from, to or through whom the security was bought or sold,

(e) the date on which the trade took place,

(f) the name of the stock exchange, if any, where the trade took place,

(g) the commission charged for the trade,

(h) the name of any salesman involved in the trade, and

(i) the information required by section 167.6(1), if applicable.

[Para. (i) en. B.C. Reg. 306/88, First Sched., s. 10.]

(3) For the purposes of subsection (2), a person or a salesman may be identified in a written confirmation by means of a code or symbols if the written confirmation also contains a statement that the name of the person or salesman will be furnished to the client on request.

[S. 80(3) am. B.C. Reg. 316/89, s. 3.]

(4) Where a person uses a code or symbols for identification in a confirmation required by subsection (2), the person shall forthwith file the code or symbols and their meaning, and shall notify the commission within 5 days of any change in or addition to the code or symbols or their meaning.

(5) A registered dealer who has acted as agent for a trade in a security shall promptly disclose to the commission or superintendent on its or his request

(a) the name of the person from, to or through whom the security was bought or sold, and

(b) to the extent of his knowledge after having made due enquiry, sufficient further particulars to identify that person.

Confirmation of trade respecting mutual funds

81. (1) In this section "charges" means sales charges, service charges and any other amount charged to the client.

(2) Where a trade is made in a security of a mutual fund, in addition to the requirements of section 80(2), the confirmation shall set out

(a) the price for each security at which the trade was effected, and

(b) any amount deducted for charges.

(3) Where a trade is made in a security of a mutual fund under a contractual plan, in addition to the requirements of section 80(2) and subsection (1), the confirmation shall set out,

(a) where an initial payment is made under a contractual plan that requires the prepayment of charges, a statement of the initial payment and the part of the charges that is allocated to subsequent payments in the mutual fund and the manner of its allocation to them,

(b) where a subsequent payment is made under a contractual plan that requires the prepayment of charges, a statement of the part of the charges that is allocated to the payment which is the subject of the confirmation,

(c) where an initial purchase is made under a contractual plan which permits the deduction of charges from the first and subsequent instalments, a brief statement of the charges to be deducted from subsequent purchases, and

(d) where a subsequent purchase is made under a contractual plan, a statement of the total number of securities of the mutual fund acquired and the amount of charges paid under the contractual plan up to the date on which the confirmation is sent.

(4) The confirmation of a trade made in a security of a mutual fund under a contractual plan need not contain the information described in subsection (3)(d) where

(a) the contractual plan was entered into before the coming into force of the Act, or

(b) the holder of the contractual plan has, in addition to any rights to which he may be entitled under section 123 of the Act or otherwise, rights under the plan in accordance with subsection (5).

[Para. (b) am. B.C. Reg. 305/88, s. 18(a).]

(5) For the purposes of subsection (4)(b), the holder of the plan shall be permitted

(a) to receive on demand, at any time within 365 days after the date on which the contractual plan was entered into, the sum of

  (i) a refund of the net asset value of the securities credited to him before the date of demand, and

  (ii) a refund of that portion of sales charges, excluding insurance premiums and fees to trustees of registered retirement savings plans, that is in excess of 30% of the scheduled payments under the plan that were made before the date of demand, but not including voluntary prepayments of instalments, or

(b) to have and to exercise the rights described in section 123 of the Act, at any time within 180 days after the date on which the contractual plan was entered into.

(6) Where a right is given under subsection (5), the registered dealer required under section 80 to confirm the transaction shall send to the investor a notice, approved by the superintendent, that describes the rights under subsection (5) and section 123 of the Act and sets out a table of charges and other information relevant to a decision of the investor as to whether he will exercise those rights, and the notice shall be sent

(a) where a right is given under subsection (5)(a),

  (i) with each confirmation, other than for reinvested dividends or income, during the first 365 days after the date on which the contractual plan was entered into, and

  (ii) not less than 15 days and not more than 45 days before the end of that 365 day period, and

(b) where a right is given under subsection (5)(b),

  (i) with each confirmation, other than for reinvested dividends or income, during the first 180 days after the date on which the contractual plan was entered into, and

  (ii) not less than 15 days and not more than 45 days before the end of that 180 day period.

[S. 81(6) re-en. B.C. Reg. 305/88, s. 18(b).]

(7) Where a client advises a registered dealer in writing before a trade in a security of a mutual fund of the client's participation in an automatic payment plan, automatic withdrawal plan or contractual plan that provides for systematic trading in the securities of the mutual fund no less frequently than monthly, the registered dealer shall provide the confirmation of that trade as required by section 80, and thereafter during the continued existence of the plan and the client's participation in it the registered dealer, in lieu of the confirmations of trade required by section 80, may send to the client, no less frequently than half yearly, written summaries of trades containing the information required by section 80 to be disclosed to the client, with respect to all trades of the security of the mutual fund by the client since the last confirmation or summary of trade was prepared.

(8) A registered dealer who complies with subsection (7) need not comply with section 80(2) if the confirmation or summary of trades contains a statement that the name of the person from, to or through whom the security of the mutual fund was bought or sold will be furnished to the client upon request.

Representations prohibited

82. For the purpose of section 35(2) of the Act the prescribed amount is $50 000.

83. [Repealed B.C. Reg. 306/88, First Sched., s. 11.]

84. [Repealed B.C. Reg. 306/88, First Sched., s. 11.]

85. [Repealed B.C. Reg. 306/88, First Sched., s. 11.]

Financial information to customer by dealer

86. (1) Subject to subsection (2), a registered dealer shall

(a) when requested by a client, provide to that client

    (i) a copy of the most recently prepared annual statement of the dealer's financial condition, as filed with the commission or with the self regulatory body of which the dealer is a member, made up and certified, as required by section 182, and

    (ii) a list of the names of the partners or directors and senior officers of the dealer, made up and certified as of a date not more than 30 days before the request, and

[S. 86(1)(a) am. B.C. Reg. 316/89, s. 3.]

(b) inform its clients on every statement of account or by other means approved by the commission that the information referred to in paragraph (a) is available on request.

(2) Where the superintendent determines that a dealer or a class of dealers is subject to conditions of registration or to regulations imposed by a self regulatory body or a stock exchange that require provision of other appropriate information to clients similar to the information required under subsection (1), the superintendent may, on terms he considers appropriate, exempt the dealer or class of dealers from the need to comply with subsection (1).

[S. 86 am. B.C. Reg. 316/89, s. 4.]

Division (2)
Advertising Materials

Submission of advertising

87. (1) Where the superintendent has given a dealer, adviser, underwriter or issuer an opportunity to be heard, and is satisfied that his past conduct in the use of advertising and sales literature makes it necessary for the protection of the public, the superintendent may order him to deliver to the superintendent copies of all advertising and sales literature that the dealer, adviser, underwriter or issuer proposes to use in connection with trading in securities at least 7 days before the advertising and sales literature is used.

[S. 87(1) re-en. B.C. Reg. 305/88, s. 19.]

(2) Where an order is made under subsection (1), the superintendent may, after examining the advertising and literature delivered to him, prohibit their use or require that deletions or changes be made in them.

> See Local Policy Statement 3-39 "Guidelines for Advertising Issues of Securities and for Promotional Activities During the Course of a Distribution".

PART 7

PROSPECTUS

Division (1)
Filing Documents

Variation of requirements

88. The superintendent may vary a provision of this Part in respect of a particular issuer's preliminary prospectus and prospectus if the variation

(a) does not inhibit full, true and plain disclosure, and

(b) is necessary for full, true and plain disclosure.

Applies to a statement of material facts; see s. 122 of the Regulation.

Preliminary prospectus

89. (1) A preliminary prospectus need not include

(a) information concerning the price to the underwriter, the offering price of the securities or other matters dependent on or relating to those prices,

(b) an auditor's report, or

(c) an accountant's report.

(2) Every preliminary prospectus shall have the following printed in red ink on the outside front cover:

"This is a preliminary prospectus relating to these securities, a copy of which has been filed with the British Columbia Securities Commission but which has not yet become final for the purpose of a distribution. Information contained herein is subject to completion or amendment. These securities may not be sold nor may offers to buy be accepted prior to the time a receipt is obtained from the British Columbia Securities Commission for the final prospectus."

Disclosure called for by prospectus form

90. (1) Where in one of the required forms calling for prospectus disclosure, or in one of the items of the prospectus forms, the disclosure called for could, in the opinion of the superintendent, properly be made applicable to an issuer, the superintendent may require the issuer to comply with that prospectus required form or that item in the prospectus required form.

(2) Reference need not be made in a prospectus to items contained in the prospectus required form required under the Act or this regulation that are inapplicable or answered in the negative.

(3) The superintendent may exempt a person from disclosing information in answer to any item of a prospectus required form where the superintendent considers it is immaterial information in the circumstances.

Applies to a statement of material facts; see s. 122 of the Regulation. The prescribed prospectus forms are Forms 12, 13 and 14. For policies and notices affecting disclosure in prospectuses, see National Policy Statement 12 "Disclosure of 'Market Out' Clauses in Underwriting Agreements and Prospectuses", National Policy Statement 13 "Disclaimer Clause on Prospectus", National Policy Statement 32 "Prospectus Warning re: Scope of Distribution", National Policy Statement 35 "Purchaser's Statutory Rights", NIN 89/36 "Disclosure of Experience of Directors, Officers, Promoters and Control Persons", and NIN 92/4 "Draft National Policy Statement No. 46 – Index and Commodity Warrants and Other Derivative Securities".

The Canadian Securities Administrators have released for comment a draft policy with respect to foreign issuer prospectuses and continuous disclosure which sets forth the Canadian Securities Administrators' view that it is in the public interest to implement a national policy to facilitate world-class foreign issuers offering securities in Canada as part of an international offering. See NIN 93/16 "Draft National Policy Statement No. 53 – Foreign Issuer Prospectus and Continuous Disclosure System".

Presentation of content of prospectus

91. (1) Every preliminary prospectus and every prospectus shall have the following printed on the outside front cover:

"No securities commission or similar authority in Canada has in any way passed upon the merits of the securities offered hereunder and any representation to the contrary is an offence."

(2) Subject to subsection (3), the body of a printed prospectus shall be in roman type at least as large as 10 point modern type.

(3) Financial statements, statistical or tabular data and accompanying notes contained in the printed prospectus shall be in roman type at least as large as 8 point modern type, to the extent necessary for convenient presentation.

(4) The type in a printed prospectus shall be leaded at least 2 points.

(5) Where the superintendent determines that to permit the inclusion of specific graphs, photographs or maps would not be misleading or detract from the readability of the prospectus, the prospectus may contain

(a) graphs that are relevant to matters dealt with in the text,

(b) photographs, if they depict only the product of the issuer, and

(c) maps for the purpose of indicating the locations for property or operations present or proposed of the issuer.

(6) The information contained in a prospectus may be

(a) set out other than in the order of items contained in the required form,

(b) expressed in a condensed or summarized manner that does not obscure required information or other information necessary for preventing the required information from being incomplete or misleading, and

(c) set out only once where it is in fact required by more than one applicable item of a prospectus form.

(7) The information contained in a prospectus shall

(a) be presented in narrative form,

(b) where required to be presented in tabular form, be substantially presented in the form required,

(c) be set out under appropriate headings or captions reasonably indicative of the principal subject matter set out under them, and

(d) contain a reasonably detailed table of contents.

Pro forma prospectus

92. Every pro forma prospectus shall substantially comply with the requirements of the Act and this regulation governing the form and content of a prospectus except that the certificates required in respect of that pro forma prospectus under sections 49 and 50 of the Act and the auditors' reports may be omitted.

Mutual fund prospectus

93. (1) A mutual fund may file either

(a) a prospectus under section 42 or 51 of the Act, or

(b) a short form of prospectus system of disclosure under subsection (2).

(2) The short form of prospectus system of disclosure is comprised of

(a) a short form of prospectus,

(b) an annual information form in the required form, and

(c) other information as is required to be filed by the mutual fund, including

(i) the financial information required by section 96,

(ii) any material change report filed under section 67(1)(b) of the Act, and

(iii) the information circular required under section 101(2) of the Act or the annual filing made in lieu thereof.

The required form for a prospectus of a mutual fund issuer is Form 15, the required form for a short form mutual fund prospectus is Form 50, and the required form for an Annual Information Form of a mutual fund prospectus is Form 51. For a discussion of these requirements see National Policy Statement 29 "Mutual Funds Investing in Mortgages", National Policy Statement 36 "Mutual Funds: Simplified Prospectus Qualification System", National Policy Statement No. 39 "Mutual Funds", and NIN 90/4 "National Policy No. 39 – Mutual Funds Distributor's Report and Auditor's Letter".

(3) The information referred to in subsection (2)(b) and (c) shall be known collectively as the permanent information record.

(4) The consents given under section 99 are required in all respects for the purposes of the short form of prospectus system of disclosure.

(5) Where 2 or more mutual funds have the same mutual fund manager and their affairs are conducted in a similar manner, the mutual funds may file one annual information form and one short form of prospectus to qualify for distribution the securities of the related mutual funds.

(6) The superintendent may refuse to accept for filing the annual information form and the short form of prospectus submitted under subsection (5) on the basis that the disclosure contained in them is unduly complex or unclear.

Annual information form of a mutual fund

94. (1) Every annual information form of a mutual fund shall be submitted to the superintendent for filing and, on acceptance of such filing, the superintendent shall notify the mutual fund of the acceptance.

(2) The annual information form shall be accompanied by an undertaking of the mutual fund manager or, if the mutual fund has no manager, of the mutual fund, to the superintendent, to provide to any person without charge, upon request to the mutual fund, one copy of the permanent information record of the mutual fund.

(3) A mutual fund that files an annual information form shall file concurrently therewith a preliminary or pro forma short form of prospectus.

[Ss. 93 and 94 re-en. B.C. Reg. 305/88, s. 20.]

See National Policy Statement 36 "Mutual Funds: Simplified Prospectus Qualification System" for the requirements of an Annual Information Form.

Short form of prospectus of a mutual fund

95. (1) Every preliminary, but not pro forma, short form of prospectus of a mutual fund shall have printed in red ink on the outside front cover page the following statement or a variation of it that the superintendent permits:

"This is a preliminary short form of prospectus relating to these securities, a copy of which has been filed with [insert names of provinces and territories in which the preliminary short form of prospectus has been filed] but which has not yet become final for the purpose of a distribution. Information contained herein is subject to completion or amendment. These securities may not be sold to, nor may offers to buy be accepted from, residents of such jurisdictions prior to the time a receipt for the final short form of prospectus is obtained from the appropriate securities commission or other regulatory authority."

(2) Every preliminary short form of prospectus and short form of prospectus of a mutual fund shall be submitted to the superintendent for filing, and no person shall distribute the securities offered under it until a receipt has been obtained from the superintendent.

Financial statements required under sections 94 and 95

96. (1) Every annual information form and short form of prospectus filed under section 94 or 95 shall be accompanied by, or there shall have been previously filed,

(a) an income statement,

(b) a balance sheet,

(c) a statement of investment portfolio,

(d) a statement of portfolio transactions, and

(e) a statement of changes in net assets

of the mutual fund each for, or as at the end of, as appropriate, its last financial year with, except for paragraphs (c) and (d), comparative figures for its next preceding financial year, or for any period or periods permitted or required by the superintendent, together with an auditors' report thereon.

(2) Notwithstanding subsection (1), a statement of portfolio transactions need not be reported on by an auditor and need not be sent or delivered to a purchaser if the statement of portfolio transactions

(a) contains a certificate signed by the chief executive officer and chief financial officer of the mutual fund, or the person or persons temporarily carrying out the responsibilities of either of them, that the statement of portfolio transactions presents fairly the required information, and

(b) forms part of the mutual fund's permanent information record and is forwarded to a person who requests a copy of the permanent information record.

[S. 96 re-en. B.C. Reg. 305/88, s. 20.]

Sending short form of prospectus of a mutual fund

97. (1) Where a short form of prospectus of a mutual fund has been filed and a receipt has been issued, a dealer may send the short form of prospectus to a purchaser of securities instead of the prospectus as required by section 66 of the Act and, where a dealer so elects, sections 66 and 118 of the Act apply to the short form of prospectus.

(2) Where a short form of prospectus is sent to a purchaser under subsection (1) it shall be accompanied by

(a) a copy of the financial statements referred to in section 96(1), and

[Para. (a) am. B.C. Reg. 305/88, s. 21.]

(b) where one or more financial statements for periods subsequent to those covered by the financial statements described in paragraph (a) have been filed with the commission, a copy of the financial statements that were filed most recently before the day the short form of prospectus is sent.

Request for prospectus

98. A short form of prospectus of a mutual fund sent to a purchaser shall contain a statement informing the purchaser that a copy of the permanent information record will be provided to the purchaser on request.

[S. 98 am. B.C. Reg. 305/88, s. 22.]

Written consent of professional to be named

99. (1) In this section "professional person" means a person whose profession gives authority to a statement made by him in his professional capacity and includes a barrister and solicitor, an accountant, an appraiser, an auditor, an engineer and a geologist.

(2) Where a professional person is named in a prospectus, short form of prospectus, annual information form or in any record used in connection with or accompanying the prospectus, short form of prospectus or annual information form as having prepared or certified any part or all of it, including a report or valuation used in or in connection with it, the written consent of that person to be named and as authorizing the use of the report or valuation shall be filed no later than when the prospectus, short form of prospectus or annual information form is filed, unless the superintendent considers that obtaining the written consent is impracticable or involves undue hardship.

(3) In his written consent an accountant or an auditor shall

(a) refer to his report, stating the date of it and the dates of the financial statements on which the report is made, and

(b) include a statement to the effect that he has read the prospectus, short form of prospectus or annual information form and has no reason to believe that there are any misrepresentations in it that

(i) may be derived from the financial statements on which he reported, or

(ii) are within his knowledge as a result of his audit of the financial statements.

> Applies to a statement of material facts; see s. 122 of the Regulation. See Uniform Act Policy 2-04 "Consent of Solicitors – Disclosure of Interest".

Disclosure in prospectus where professional person has interest

100. Where the consent of the professional person referred to in section 99(2) is required to be filed under that section and that person

(a) has received or expects to receive an interest, direct or indirect, in the property of the issuer or of an associate or affiliate of the issuer,

(b) beneficially owns, directly or indirectly, a security of the issuer or of an associate or affiliate of the issuer, or

(c) is expected to be or is elected, appointed or employed as a director, officer or employee of the issuer or of an associate or affiliate of the issuer,

the issuer shall disclose in the prospectus, short form of prospectus or annual information form the interest, ownership or expectation or fact, as the case may be.

> See Local Policy Statement 3-41 "Lawyer's Conflict of Interest".

Further consents

101. Where a change is proposed to be made in a prospectus, short form of prospectus or annual information form that, in the opinion of the superintendent, materially affects a consent given under section 99, he may require a further written consent to be obtained and filed under that section before accepting the prospectus, short form of prospectus or annual information form for filing.

[Ss. 99-101 re-en. B.C. Reg. 305/88, s. 23.]

Property report for natural resource issuer

102. A natural resource issuer shall, when it files a prospectus or preliminary prospectus, file a full and up to date report in the required form made by a mining engineer, geologist or other qualified individual acceptable to the superintendent, on its major properties or on properties on which the issuer intends to spend a material part of the proceeds of the issue of securities.

> See Local Policy Statement 3-01 "Factors to be Considered in Arriving at a Decision that a Natural Resource Property has Sufficient Merit to Justify an Expenditure Thereon of Risk Capital Derived from Public Subscription", National Policy Statement 2A "Guide for Engineers, Geologists, and Prospectors Submitting Reports on Mining Properties to Canadian Provincial Securities Administrators", National Policy Statement 2B "Guide for Engineers and Geologists Submitting Oil and Gas Reports to Canadian Provincial Securities Administrators", and NIN 87/45 "Technical Reports on Mining Properties Accompanying Prospectuses Submitted for Acceptance by the Superintendent of Brokers". Either of Form 54 or Form 55 is the required form.

Property report certificate concerning natural resource issuer

103. A property report filed under section 102 shall be accompanied by a certificate on the report that states

(a) the address and occupation of the individual making the report,

(b) the qualifications of that individual,

(c) whether or not the report is based on personal examination,

(d) the date of personal examination, if any,

(e) where the report is not based on personal examination, the source of the information contained in the report, and

(f) whether or not the individual making the report

(i) has received or expects to receive any direct or indirect interest in the property of the natural resource issuer or any associate or affiliate of that issuer, or

(ii) has a direct or indirect interest in or beneficially owns directly or indirectly any securities of the natural resource issuer or any associate or affiliate of that issuer,

together with the particulars of the interest or ownership, if any.

Applies to a statement of material facts; see s. 122 of the Regulation.

Division (2)
Financial Statements

Financial statements — prospectus — issuer other than mutual fund

104. (1) Subject to subsection (3), a prospectus of an issuer other than a mutual fund shall contain

(a) an income statement of the issuer for

(i) each of its last 5 financial years, and

(ii) any part of a subsequent financial year to the date at which the balance sheet required by paragraph (d) is made up,

(b) a statement of surplus of the issuer for each financial year and part of a financial year covered by the income statement required by paragraph (a),

(c) subject to subsection (3), a statement of changes in financial position of the issuer for each financial year and part of a financial year covered by the income statement required by paragraph (a),

(d) a balance sheet of the issuer

(i) as at a date not more than 120 days before a receipt is issued for the preliminary prospectus or for a new prospectus referred to in section 51 of the Act, as the case may be, and

(ii) subject to subsection (2), as at the corresponding date of the previous financial year, and

(e) where the issuer is a natural resource issuer or industrial issuer in the promotional, exploratory or developmental stage, an analysis of deferred charges, segregating separately year by year, or by part year where applicable, expenditures for promotion, exploration and development from expenditures for administration and showing the total for each.

(2) Where the balance sheet required by subsection (1)(d)(i) is as at a date other than a financial year end, the balance sheet required by subsection (1)(d)(ii) may be omitted if the prospectus contains a balance sheet as at

(a) the most recent financial year end, and

(b) the financial year end immediately preceding the most recent financial year end.

(3) Every prospectus of an issuer engaged primarily in the business of investing shall include a statement of changes in net assets instead of the statement of changes in financial position required by subsection (1)(c).

(4) Where the securities to which a prospectus relates are debt securities and the payment of principal or interest is guaranteed, the prospectus shall contain the financial statements required by subsection (1) with respect to the guarantor.

(5) Where the financial statements required by subsection (1) relate to part of a financial year, the prospectus shall contain an income statement, a statement of surplus and a statement of changes in financial position for the comparable period in the preceding financial year.

(6) The superintendent may exempt an issuer from including in a prospectus any record required by this section if he considers that it is not contrary to the public interest to do so.

> Local Policy Statement 3-02 "Prospectus Filing Requirements" contains additional requirements relating to financial statements to be filed with a prospectus. See NIN 88/5 "Guidelines for Applications to the Securities Commission or the Superintendent of Brokers for Decisions or Orders", and Canadian Securities Administrators Notice 92/2 "Applications for Discretionary Orders".

Financial statements — prospectus — mutual fund

105. (1) The financial statements of a mutual fund shall include

(a) a balance sheet,

(b) a statement of investment portfolio,

(c) a statement of portfolio transactions,

(d) a statement of changes in net assets, and

(e) an income statement

each as at the end of its last financial year or for the year ended that date, as the case may be, prepared in accordance with the required form.

> The required form is Form 52.

(2) A mutual fund shall include in every prospectus the financial statements referred to in subsection (1).

(3) Notwithstanding subsection (1), a statement of portfolio transactions need not be reported on by an auditor and need not be sent or delivered to a purchaser if the statement of portfolio transactions

(a) contains a certificate signed by the chief executive officer and chief financial officer of the mutual fund or the person or persons temporarily carrying out the responsibilities of either of them, that the statement of portfolio transactions presents fairly the required information, and

(b) forms part of the mutual fund's permanent information record and is forwarded to a person who requests a copy of the permanent information record.

Additional contents of a prospectus and acquisition of a business

106. (1) The superintendent may permit or require a prospectus to contain, as part of the financial statements, a pro forma balance sheet of the issuer and of all its subsidiaries

(a) as at the date on which the balance sheet required by section 104(1)(d)(i) is made up, and

(b) giving effect to

(i) the issue and sale or redemption or other retirement of securities issued or to be issued by the issuer, and

(ii) other transactions that the superintendent permits or requires.

(2) Where the proceeds of the securities offered by a prospectus are to be applied in whole or in part, directly or indirectly, to finance the acquisition of a business by a purchase of assets or shares, the superintendent may permit or require the inclusion in the prospectus of

(a) the financial statements

(i) referred to in section 104(1)(a), (b), (c) and (d)(i) for the respective periods or as at the dates specified in those paragraphs of that section, and

(ii) referred to in section 104(5) for the period or as at the date specified in that section,

of the business that is to be acquired, and

(b) a pro forma balance sheet combining the assets and liabilities of the issuer and the business that is to be acquired as shown by their respective balance sheets as at the date referred to in section 104(1)(d)(i) or at the other date that the superintendent permits or requires.

(3) Subject to subsection (6), where

(a) the proceeds of the securities offered by a prospectus are to be applied in whole or in part, directly or indirectly, to finance the acquisition of a business by a purchase of assets or shares, and

(b) the superintendent is satisfied that it would be meaningful to investors and necessary for full, true and plain disclosure of all material facts relating to the securities,

the superintendent shall require pro forma financial statements to be included in the prospectus for a period of not more than one year immediately before the date referred to in section 104(1)(d)(i) and may permit or require pro forma financial statements to be included in the prospectus for a period of not more than 5 years before that date.

(4) An auditor's report prepared in connection with the pro forma financial statements referred to in subsection (2) or (3) need only report on the manner in which those statements are compiled.

(5) Where, under subsection (2), the superintendent permits or requires one or more of the financial statements of a business that is to be acquired to be included in a prospectus, sections 107 to 109 apply, as appropriate, to the financial statements of the business to be acquired.

(6) The pro forma financial statements shall combine, year by year,

(a) the income or losses of the issuer with the income or losses of the business to be acquired, and

(b) the changes in financial position of the issuer with the changes in financial position of the business to be acquired.

Financial statements of foreign issuer

107. (1) Subject to subsection (2), where a prospectus contains financial statements

(a) of an issuer incorporated or organized in a jurisdiction other than Canada or one of its provinces, and

(b) the financial statements are prepared in accordance with the generally accepted accounting principles chosen by the issuer pursuant to the option given to him by section 3(3),

the notes to the financial statements shall explain and quantify any significant differences between the principles applied and the principles referred to in section 3.

(2) With respect to financial statements referred to in subsection (1), the option of the issuer under section 3(3) shall only be exercised with the consent of the superintendent and subject to any conditions that he may impose.

Statements of asset coverage and earnings coverage in a prospectus

108. (1) Subject to subsection (2), a prospectus relating to

(a) an issue of debt securities having a term to maturity in excess of one year, or

(b) an issue of preferred shares,

shall contain statements of asset coverage and earnings coverage.

(2) Subsection (1) does not apply to a prospectus relating to securities of a newly organized issuer.

(3) The superintendent may, where he considers that it would not be harmful to the public interest, order that subsection (1) does not apply to the prospectus of an issuer.

Estimates of future earnings in a prospectus

109. (1) In this section

"distributing firm" means a registrant that is an underwriter with respect to a distribution and includes the issuer of the securities being distributed if the issuer is registered as a security issuer;

"forecast" means a written estimate of the most probable results of operations of an issuer, alone or together with one or more of its affiliates, that contains any or all of,

(a) an estimate of earnings or a range of earnings,

(b) an estimate of the most probable financial position,

(c) an estimate of changes in financial position,

for one or more periods that are future periods not completed when the estimate is made, but does not include

(d) an estimate that is prepared in the ordinary course of business and without reference to a specific distribution of securities, and

(e) an estimate that appears in a compendium of estimates relating to a number of issuers or in a publication that is distributed regularly to investors or prospective investors, who are not selected because of their potential interest in a specific issue of securities.

(2) The superintendent may permit the inclusion of a forecast in a prospectus and where he does so,

(a) the forecast shall be identified as such in the prospectus, and

(b) the prospectus shall include the written comments of an accountant qualified to engage in public practice concerning the accountant's review of the forecast.

(3) No distributing firm, during the course of a distribution of securities for which a prospectus is required to be filed under the Act, shall disseminate a forecast with respect to the issuer of those securities, unless the forecast is set out in the prospectus and what is disseminated by the distributing firm consists solely of that forecast or a reasonable extract from it or summary of it.

See National Policy Statement 48 and NIN 93/6 "Amendment to National Policy No. 48 – Future-Oriented Financial Information".

Financial statements — subsidiary

110. The superintendent may direct that separate financial statements of a subsidiary of an issuer be included in a prospectus of the issuer, whether or not the financial statements of the subsidiary are consolidated with the financial statements of the issuer contained in the prospectus.

Financial statements — unconsolidated

111. The superintendent may permit unconsolidated financial statements to be included in a prospectus as supplementary information.

Approval of financial statements in a prospectus

112. (1) Where an issuer, whose financial statements are included in a prospectus, has or is required to have an audit committee of his directors, each financial statement included in the prospectus shall be submitted for review by the committee before approval is given to it by the directors.

[S. 112(1) am. B.C. Reg. 305/88, s. 24.]

(2) The statements referred to in subsection (1) shall be approved by the directors and signed manually by 2 of them who are duly authorized to signify approval.

Financial statements not requiring an audit report

113.(1) A financial statement that is included in a prospectus and which relates to any part of a financial year subsequent to the last audited financial year of the issuer need not be reported on by an auditor where

(a) that part of the financial year ended

  (i) not more than 90 days before the date on which a receipt was issued for the preliminary prospectus, and

  (ii) not more than 12 months after the last audited financial year, and

(b) the issuer's balance sheet as at the end of the latest audited financial year is included in the prospectus.

(2) An auditor need not report on

(a) the balance sheet referred to in section 104(1)(d)(ii),

(b) the income statement, the statement of surplus and the statement of changes in financial position that are required by section 104(5),

(c) the financial statements and the pro forma balance sheet, for the same period for an acquired business, referred to in section 106(2).

(3) Where, under this section, a financial statement contained in a prospectus is not reported on by an auditor, there shall be filed

(a) the auditor's communication that is suggested for these circumstances by the Handbook of the Canadian Institute of Chartered Accountants, or

(b) where the auditor is unable to provide the communication referred to in paragraph (a), the communication the superintendent reasonably requires.

(4) The commission or the superintendent may vary the period of time specified in subsection (1).

[S. 113(4) re-en. B.C. Reg. 305/88, s. 25.]

Preliminary prospectus not containing auditor's report

114. (1) An issuer who files a preliminary prospectus that does not contain his auditor's report shall at the same time file with the preliminary prospectus a letter written and signed by his auditor and addressed to the superintendent.

(2) Subject to subsection (3), the auditor shall include in his letter

(a) a statement relating to his examination as may be appropriate in the circumstances,

(b) a statement that he has no reason to believe, on the basis of available information, that the financial statements included in the preliminary prospectus do not provide a fair representation of the earnings and financial position of the issuer, and

(c) specified dates, years or periods of time as may be appropriate relating to his examination.

(3) Where the auditor's examination of the accounts of the issuer has not progressed sufficiently for him to properly make the statements in the letter required by subsection (2), the auditor may make such other statements as the circumstances require and that the superintendent considers acceptable in the circumstances.

Applies to a statement of material facts; see s. 58 of the Regulation.

Division (3)
Receipts on Filing

Refusal to issue a receipt for prospectus

115. (1) In this section "underwriter" means an underwriter who has signed a certificate included in a prospectus under section 50 of the Act.

(2) The superintendent shall not issue a receipt for a prospectus if he considers that

(a) the prospectus or any record required to be filed with it

　(i) does not comply substantially with the appropriate requirements of the Act and this regulation, or

　(ii) contains a misrepresentation or a statement, promise, estimate or forecast that is misleading, false or deceptive,

(b) an unconscionable consideration has been paid or given or is intended to be paid or given for any services or promotional purposes or for the acquisition of property,

(c) the aggregate of

　(i) the proceeds from the sale of the securities under the prospectus that are to be paid into the treasury of the issuer, and

　(ii) the other resources of the issuer

is insufficient to accomplish the purpose of the issue stated in the prospectus,

(d) the issuer cannot reasonably be expected to be financially responsible in the conduct of its business because of the financial condition of the issuer or that of its officers, directors, promotors or control persons,

(e) because of the past conduct of the issuer or that of its officers, directors, promoters or control persons, the business of the issuer will not be conducted with integrity and in the best interests of the security holders of the issuer,

(f) the escrow or pooling agreement in the required form that he considers necessary or advisable with respect to the securities has not been entered into or the rights or restrictions that he considers necessary or advisable with respect to the securities have not been attached to the securities,

(g) in the case of a prospectus filed by a finance issuer,

　(i) the plan for distribution of the securities offered is not acceptable,

　(ii) the securities offered are not secured in the way, on the terms and by the means required by this regulation,

　(iii) the issuer does not meet the requirements of this regulation, or

　(iv) the security offered relates to a debt security not issued under a trust indenture, or

(h) a person who has prepared or certified any part of the prospectus or, who is named as having prepared or certified a report or valuation used in or with a prospectus, is not acceptable.

Applies to a statement of material facts; see s. 122 of the Regulation.

---

(3) Subject to subsection (6), the following general rules apply to the issuing of receipts for a prospectus:

(a) the superintendent shall not issue a receipt for a prospectus where he is aware that the issuer is in default in filing any document required under the Act or this regulation or under the statute by or under which it is incorporated or organized unless he considers there is sufficient justification for the failure to file;

(b) where a receipt for a prospectus is not issued within 75 days from the date of a receipt for a preliminary prospectus due to the inaction of the person filing the preliminary prospectus, the superintendent shall not issue a final receipt for that prospectus;

(c) where

　(i) a preliminary prospectus names an issuer's underwriter who proposes to act as underwriter in the Province and who is not a registrant, or

　(ii) a distribution is to be effected by the issuer and the issuer is not a registrant,

the superintendent shall not issue the receipt for the preliminary prospectus until the underwriter or issuer, as appropriate, is registered under section 21 of the Act;

(d) the superintendent shall not issue a receipt for a prospectus relating to securities underwritten on a firm commitment basis, other than securities to be distributed continuously, unless the prospectus indicates that the securities are to be taken up by the underwriter, if at all, on or before a date not later than 10 days from the date on which the final receipt is issued;

(e) where there is no trading market for the securities offered and none is expected to develop as a consequence of the distribution, except for mutual funds, a notice to this effect must be included on the cover page of the prospectus together with a statement that purchasers may not be able to resell securities purchased under the prospectus;

(f) where a minimum amount of funds is required by an issuer, the superintendent shall not issue the receipt for a prospectus relating to securities proposed to be distributed on a best efforts basis unless the prospectus indicates that the offering will cease if the minimum amount of funds is not subscribed within the number of days permitted by the superintendent.

> The superintendent will not issue a receipt for a prospectus of an issuer listing on the Canadian Dealers Network.

(4) The superintendent shall not issue a receipt for a prospectus of an issuer doing business primarily as an industrial issuer, natural resource issuer or mutual fund if the issuer has as part of its name any of the following words: "Acceptance"; "Credit"; "Finance"; "Loan"; "Trust".

(5) Subsection (4) does not apply to

(a) a trust company,

(b) an issuer that had "investment trust" as part of its name before July 1, 1968, or

(c) an issuer that includes on the outside front cover page of the prospectus a statement, approved by the superintendent, indicating the nature of the business that it actually carries on.

(6) Where the superintendent is satisfied that there is sufficient justification he may permit or require that the provisions of subsection (3) be amended or waived as they apply to a particular person or class of persons.

[S. 120 renumbered as s. 115 and am. B.C. Reg. 305/88, s. 27.]

> All issuers intending to list their securities on the Vancouver Stock Exchange must apply to the Pre-Listing Advisory Committee ("PLAC") prior to submitting their preliminary prospectus to the Superintendent. The PLAC will review the application, paying particular attention to the previous conduct of the principals of the issuer and their professionals. The Superintendent has agreed not to issue a receipt for submissions which the PLAC has rejected or has not yet approved.
>
> There are a number of notices, blanket orders, local policy statements, national policy statements and uniform policy statements dealing with the filing of and review procedures involving prospectuses. Refer to the tables of contents at the beginning of each section for a complete listing.

PART 8

[Pt. 8 re-en. B.C. Reg. 305/88, s. 28.]

EXEMPTION FROM PROSPECTUS REQUIREMENTS

Divison (1)
Interpretation

Interpretation

116. In this Part "exchanged security" means, in relation to a security, another security issued under section 55(2)*(8)* or *(11)*(iii) of the Act that is derived from the security through a trade or series of trades that are made under section 55(2)*(8)* or *(11)*(iii) of the Act.

Division (2)
Exemptions

Exemptions

117. Section 42 of the Act does not apply to a distribution in the following circumstances:

> The corresponding registration exemptions are found in s. 76 of the Regulation. Additional prospectus exemptions are found in s. 55 of the Act.

(a) *50 purchasers*—the trade is made by an issuer in a security of its own issue where

　(i) during the 12 month period preceding the trade, sales under this paragraph have been made to not more than 49 different purchasers,

　(ii) the purchaser is

　　(A) a sophisticated purchaser,

　　(B) a spouse, parent, brother, sister or child of a senior officer or director of the issuer, or of an affiliate of the issuer, or

　　(C) a company, all the voting securities of which are beneficially owned by one or more of a spouse, parent, brother, sister or child of a senior officer or director of the issuer, or of an affiliate of the issuer,

　(iii) the purchaser purchases as principal,

　(iv) the offer and sale of the security is not accompanied by an advertisement and no selling or promotional expenses have been paid or incurred in connection with the offer and sale, except for professional services or for services performed by a registered dealer or a person referred to in paragraph (g)(ii), and

　(v) an offering memorandum is delivered to the purchaser in compliance with section 126;

> See Local Policy Statement 3-24 "Statutory Exemptions and Orders Made Under Section 33 and Section 59 of the Securities Act" which, in paragraph 4.2, sets forth the Commission's views on the calculation of the number of offerees under two predecessor exemptions to this exemption.
>
> Where a generally worded advertisement was placed in a local newspaper for the sale of pre-prospectus and primary stock, the Commission held that use of an advertisement, whether intended to sell the exempt securities or not, precluded the use of the exemption in s. 122(b) of the former Securities Regulation, an earlier exemption with some similarities to the present s. 117(a). See the *Fraser Bow Securities* decision at s. 1(1) of the Act, "material fact".

(b) *$25 000* — the trade is made by an issuer in a security of its own issue where

　(i) the purchaser purchases as principal,

　(ii) the purchaser is a sophisticated purchaser,

　(iii) the aggregate acquisition cost to the purchaser is not less than $25 000, and

　(iv) an offering memorandum is delivered to the purchaser in compliance with section 126;

> It is generally understood that the guidance provided as to determining the "aggregate acquisition cost to the purchaser" under ss. 31(2)(5) and 55(2)(4) of the Act also applies to this exemption.

(c) *Control person — other than exchange issuer* — the trade is in a security of an issuer that is not an exchange issuer from the holdings of a control person where

> (i) the issuer of the security is a reporting issuer, has been a reporting issuer for the 12 months preceding the trade and is not in default of any requirement of the Act or this regulation,
>
> (ii) 6 months have elapsed from the date the control person acquired the security or, if the security is an exchanged security that was issued in relation to a security held by the control person, 6 months have elapsed from the date the control person acquired the security in relation to which the exchanged security was issued,
>
> (iii) if the control person has acquired the security to be distributed
>
>> (A) under section 55(2)(1) to (6), (18), (19), (24) or (26) of the Act or section 117(a) or (b) of this regulation, a 12 month period has elapsed from the later of the date of the issue of the security and the date the issuer became a reporting issuer, or
>>
>> (B) in the circumstances referred to in section 133(3)(a) or (b), the 12 month period referred to in section 133(3)(e)(iii) has elapsed,

See s. 120 of the Regulation regarding legending requirements.

> (iv) the control person has filed a notice of intention to sell and declaration in compliance with section 129,
>
> (v) no unusual effort is made to prepare the market or create a demand for the security, and
>
> (vi) no extraordinary commission or other consideration is paid in respect of the trade;

(d) *Control person — exchange issuer* — the trade is in a security of an exchange issuer from the holdings of a control person where

> (i) the issuer of the security has been a reporting issuer for the 12 months preceding the trade and is not in default of any requirement of the Act or this regulation,
>
> (ii) 6 months have elapsed from the date the control person acquired the security or, if the security is an exchanged security that was issued in relation to a security held by the control person, 6 months have elapsed from the date the control person acquired the security in relation to which the exchanged security was issued,
>
> (iii) if the security to be distributed was issued before the issuer became an exchange issuer, or is an exchanged security issued in relation to a security that was issued before the issuer became an exchange issuer,
>
>> (A) the security to be distributed, or a security in relation to which that security was issued, has been distributed under a prospectus or a statement of material facts,
>>
>> (B) an escrow agreement in the required form or a pooling agreement in the required form has been entered into or the requirement to enter into an escrow or pooling agreement has been waived by the superintendent, or

See NIN 92/3 "Waivers Consequential to Local Policy Statement 3-07". The required form of escrow agreement is Form 16. No form has been specified for the pooling agreement. The superintendent does not require securities to be pooled; however, brokerage houses participating in an initial public offering will often require that some or all shares issued prior to the initial public offering be placed in pool with the issuer's transfer agent. The schedule for the release of the shares from pool is a matter of negotiation between the holders of such shares and the brokerage house.

>> (C) the 12 month period referred to in section 133(2)(c) or (3)(e)(iii), whichever would be applicable if the seller were not a control person and the issuer had not become an exchange issuer, has elapsed,

(iv) subject to paragraph (iii), if the security to be distributed was issued after the issuer became an exchange issuer and acquired by the control person

    (A) under section 55(2)(1), (2), (4), (6), (19) or (26) of the Act or section 117(a), (b) or (i) of this regulation, a 12 month period has elapsed from the earlier of the date of issue of the security and the date a written agreement committing the control person to acquire the security, subject only to any required regulatory approval, has been executed by all parties to the agreement,

    (B) under section 55(2)(5) of the Act, section 134(2)(b) of this regulation is satisfied, or

    (C) in the circumstances referred to in section 134(3)(a) or (b), section 134(3)(e)(ii) or (iii), whichever would be applicable if the seller were not a control person, is satisfied,

> See s. 120 of the Regulation regarding legending requirements.

(v) the control person has filed a notice of intention to sell and declaration in compliance with section 129,

(vi) no unusual effort is made to prepare the market or create a demand for the security, and

(vii) no extraordinary commission or other consideration is paid in respect of the trade;

(e) *Control person — exchange issuer — 5% free trading* —the trade is in a security of an exchange issuer from the holdings of a control person where

(i) the security was acquired by the control person on or through the facilities of the Vancouver Stock Exchange,

(ii) the trade is made on or through the facilities of the Vancouver Stock Exchange, and

(iii) the security traded, together with the securities of the same class traded by the control person under this paragraph during the 90 day period preceding the trade, do not exceed 5% of the securities of the class outstanding at the date of the trade;

> This exemption was put in place to allow control persons of exchange issuers sufficient flexibility to be able to establish an orderly market in the issuer's securities.

(f) *Securities for debt* — the trade is made by an exchange issuer in a security of its own issue to settle a bona fide debt;

(g) *Bonus or finder's fee* — the trade is made by an exchange issuer in a security of its own issue as consideration for

(i) a loan or loan guarantee, or

(ii) services performed by a person, not an insider or an associate of an insider of the issuer, in connection with

    (A) the acquisition or disposition of assets, or

    (B) a distribution by the issuer to persons not resident in the Province where the distribution is under section 55(2) of the Act;

(h) *Management company employee* — the trade is made by an exchange issuer in a security of its own issue to an individual employed by a person providing management services to the issuer where the individual is not induced to purchase by expectation of employment or continued employment with either the issuer or the person providing the management services;

(i) *Friends and relatives* — the trade is made by an exchange issuer in a security of its own issue where

(i) during the 12 month period preceding the trade, sales under this paragraph have been made to not more than 24 different purchasers,

(ii) the amount paid for the security of the issuer in respect of the trade, together with the amount paid for the securities of the issuer in respect of all trades under this paragraph during the 12 month period preceding the trade, does not exceed $250 000,

(iii) the purchaser purchases as principal,

(iv) the purchaser is

(A) a spouse, parent, brother, sister, child or close personal friend of a senior officer or director of the issuer, or of an affiliate of the issuer, or

(B) a company, all the voting securities of which are beneficially owned by one or more of a spouse, parent, brother, sister, child or close personal friend of a senior officer or director of the issuer, or of an affiliate of the issuer,

(v) the offer and sale of the security is not accompanied by an advertisement and no selling or promotional expenses have been paid or incurred in connection with the offer and sale, and

(vi) if an offering memorandum is delivered to a purchaser, the offering memorandum is delivered to the purchaser in compliance with section 126.

See Local Policy Statement 3-24 "Statutory Exemptions and Orders Made Under Section 33 and Section 59 of the Securities Act" which, in paragraph 4.2, sets forth the Commission's views on the calculation of the number of offerees under two predecessor exemptions to this exemption.

Where a generally worded advertisement was placed in a local newspaper for the sale of pre-prospectus and primary stock, the Commission held that use of an advertisement, whether intended to sell the exempt securities or not, precluded the use of the exemption in s. 122(b) of the former Securities Regulation, an earlier exemption with some similarities to the present s. 117(a). See the *Fraser Bow Securities* decision at s. 1(1) of the Act, "material fact".

Prescribed amounts for exemptions

118. (1) For the purpose of section 55(2)*(4)* of the Act, the aggregate acquisition cost to the purchaser is not less than $97 000.

(2) For the purpose of section 55(2)*(5)* of the Act, the fair value of the purchased assets is not less than $100 000.

(3) For the purpose of section 55(2)*(19)* of the Act, the net asset value or the aggregate acquisition cost, whichever is applicable, is not less than $100 000.

Restriction on exemption

119. The exemption under section 58(1)(a) of the Act, where the security is described in section 32(c) of the Act, does not apply to a person making a distribution of a security of a private mutual fund administered by a trust company where the promoter or manager of the private mutual fund is a person other than the trust company.

Restriction on exemption

119.1 The exemption under section 58(1)(a) of the Act does not apply to a person making a distribution of securities described in section 32(g) of the Act unless

(a) the person making the distribution is the issuer,

(b) the purchaser is the issuer or a security holder of the issuer, or

(c) the person making the distrubution is not the issuer and, before the distribution is made, the person

(i) notifies the issuer of the proposed distribution, and

(ii) furnishes the purchaser with a copy of any applicable information statement and financial and other information concerning the issuer's affairs that the issuer provided to the person during the 2 years immediately preceding the date of the proposed distribution.

[S. 119.1 en. B.C. Reg. 417/94.]

Certificate legend

120. (1) In this section "hold period" means any 12 month period specified in section 117(c)(iii), (d)(iii) or (iv), 133(2)(c) or (3)(e), or 134(2)(a) or (b) or (3)(e).

(2) Where a security, at the date of its issue, is subject to a hold period, the issuer shall endorse the certificate representing the security

(a) with a statement that the security represented by the certificate is subject to a hold period and may not be traded in British Columbia until the expiry of the hold period except as permitted by the *Securities Act* (British Columbia) and regulations made under the Act, and

(b) if the issuer is a reporting issuer at the date of issue, with a statement that specifies the date the hold period expires.

(3) On the application of an issuer or on the commission's own motion, the commission may order that subsection (2) does not apply to a particular issuer or class of issuers.

See BOR 88/5 "Legending of Certificates".

Division (3)
Statement of Material Facts

Requirements

121. A statement of material facts under section 58(1)(c) of the Act shall

(a) provide full, true and plain disclosure of all material facts relating to the security proposed to be offered,

(b) be in the required form,

The required form is Form 24.

(c) be filed with the superintendent and a stock exchange recognized by the commission for the purposes of section 58(1)(c) of the Act, and

(d) be accepted by the superintendent unless he considers that it would be prejudicial to the public interest to do so.

See Local Policy Statement 3-26 "Statement of Material Facts Submitted to the Superintendent of Brokers and the Vancouver Stock Exchange for Vetting".

See discussion at s. 1 "misrepresentation" of the Securities Act for a Commission decision that found a security agreement to be a material fact that required disclosure in the statement of material facts.

Application of other provisions

122. Sections 44(3), 45(1), 46(3), 49(1)(a) and (2) to (5), 50 and 52 of the Act and sections 88, 90, 99 to 103 and 115(2) of this regulation apply, with the necessary modifications, to a statement of material facts.

[S. 122 am. B.C. Reg. 316/89, s. 5.]

Amendment

123. (1) Where, after a statement of material facts has been filed and accepted but before the completion of the distribution under it, a material change occurs in the affairs of an issuer, the person making the distribution shall file an amendment to the statement of material facts disclosing the change as soon as practicable and, in any event, no later than 10 days after the change occurs.

(2) Where, after a statement of material facts has been filed and accepted but before the completion of the distribution under it, the terms or conditions of the offering disclosed in the statement of material facts are to be altered, the person making the distribution shall file an amendment to the statement of material facts disclosing the change.

(3) A distribution under a statement of material facts shall not proceed until an amendment to the statement of material facts that is required to be filed under this section is filed with and accepted by the superintendent and each stock exchange with which the statement of material facts has been filed.

Exemption

124. Where a person proposing to distribute securities under a statement of material facts is unable to comply with a provision of this regulation relating to statements of material facts, the superintendent may exempt the person from that provision where he considers that

    (a) all reasonable efforts have been made to comply, and

    (b) it would not be prejudicial to the public interest to do so.

See NIN 88/5 "Guidelines for Applications to the Securities Commission or the Superintendent of Brokers for Decisions or Orders", and Canadian Securities Administrators Notice 92/2 "Applications for Discretionary Orders".

Division (4)
Offering Memorandum

125. [Repealed B.C. Reg. 316/89, s. 6.]

Contractual right of action and delivery

126. An offering memorandum required to be delivered in connection with a distribution under section 55(2)*(4)* of the Act or section 117(a), (b) or (i) of this regulation shall

    (a) be delivered to the purchaser before an agreement of purchase and sale is entered into,

    (b) contain a right of action against the issuer for rescission or damages that

        (i) is available to a purchaser to whom an offering memorandum containing a misrepresentation has been delivered,

        (ii) is enforceable on notice being given to the issuer not later than 90 days after the date

            (A) on which payment was made for the securities, or

            (B) on which the initial payment was made for the securities, where payments subsequent to the initial payment are made under a contractual commitment entered into prior to, or concurrently with, the initial payment,

        (iii) reasonably corresponds to the rights provided in section 114 of the Act applicable to a prospectus,

        (iv) is subject to the defence that the purchaser had knowledge of the misrepresentation, and

        (v) is in addition to and not in derogation from any other right the purchaser may have, and

    (c) be in the required form.

[S. 126 am. B.C. Reg. 316/89, s. 7.]

The required form is Form 43 with respect to an offering memorandum required under s. 55(2)(4) of the Act or s. 117(a), (b) or (i) of the Regulation. For offering memoranda under the immigrant investor program Form 43A sets out that the offering memorandum must be in the form required by the Federal and Provincial Immigration departments. See BOR 89/10 "Required Form of Offering Memorandum", and NIN 89/32 "Required Form of Offering Memorandum".

Distribution through advertisement

127. Where a person advertises in connection with a distribution of a security under section 55(2)(4) of the Act, the person shall deliver to each purchaser an offering memorandum in compliance with section 126.

Division (5)
Filings

Acknowledgment

128. Where a person distributes a security under section 117(a), (b) or (i), the person shall file an acknowledgment and undertaking by the purchaser in the required form not later than 10 days after the distribution.

The required form is Form 20A. See NIN 88/43 "Form 20A – Clarification of Requirements".

Notice by control person

129. (1) A notice of intention to sell and declaration in connection with a distribution under section 117(c) or (d) shall be

(a)   in the required form,

(b)   certified as follows:

"The seller for whose account the securities to which this certificate relates are to be sold hereby represents that he has no knowledge of any material change that has occurred in the affairs of the issuer of the securities which has not been generally disclosed and reported to the Commission, nor has he any knowledge of any other material adverse information in regard to the current and prospective operations of the issuer which have not been generally disclosed.",

(c)   signed by the control person not more than 24 hours prior to its filing, and

(d)   filed with the commission and with each stock exchange in Canada on which the security is listed, at least 7 days and not more than 14 days before the initial trade of the securities specified in the notice.

(2) A notice of intention to sell and declaration filed under section 117(c) or (d) shall be renewed by filing the form referred to in subsection (1) with the commission and with each stock exchange in Canada on which the security is listed not later than 60 days after the filing referred to in subsection (1) and thereafter not later than 28 days after the latest filing under this subsection until a notice has been filed with the commission and with each stock exchange in Canada on which the security is listed stating the number of securities specified in the notice referred to in subsection (1) that have been sold and, if any of the securities specified in the notice referred to in subsection (1) have not been sold, that these securities are no longer for sale.

The required form is Form 23.

Report by control person

130. Where a person distributes a security under section 117(c) or (d), the person shall file a report in the required form not later than 3 days after the distribution.

The required form is Form 36. See NIN 95/14 "Amendments to the Insider Report Form (Form 36)". These amendments were effective April 17, 1995. See also BOR 88/6 "Filing of Insider Reports by Control Persons".

Offering memorandum

131. Where a person delivers an offering memorandum to a purchaser, the person shall file a copy of the offering memorandum not later than 10 days after the distribution.

Note that the requirement to file arises any time an offering memorandum is delivered, even if the applicable exemption did not require such delivery.

Report on distribution

132. (1) Subject to subsections (2) and (3), where an issuer distributes a security under section 55(2)*(1)* to *(5)*, *(8)* to *(10)*, *(11)*(i), *(14)*, *(16)*(i), *(18)*, *(19)* or *(24)* to *(27)* of the Act or section 117(a), (b) or (f) to (i) of this regulation, the issuer shall file a report in the required form not later than 10 days after the distribution.

[S. 132(1) am. B.C. Reg. 97/95, s. 1(a).]

(2) Where a person distributes a security through a purchase plan or purchase arrangement under section 55(2)*(9)* or *(10)* of the Act, the person shall file the report required under subsection (1) at the time the plan or arrangement commences and at least once a year thereafter and, in addition, where the number of securities distributed in one month exceeds 1% of the securities of the same class outstanding at the beginning of the month, the person shall file, in respect of the securities distributed in that month, the report required under subsection (1) not later than 10 days after the end of the month.

[S. 132(2) am. B.C. Reg. 316/89, s. 8.]

(3) Where an issuer distributes a security under section 55(2)(19) of the Act, the issuer shall file the report required under subsection (1) not later than 10 days after the end of the calendar year in which the distribution took place.

[S. 132(3) en. B.C. Reg. 97/95, s. 1(b).]

The required form is Form 20. Note that a Form 20 is required only when it is an issuer that distributes the security. See NIN 89/13 "Statutory Filings" which states that the Commission will step up its review and enforcement procedures on all statutory filings.

Division (6)
Deemed Distributions

Deemed distributions — other than exchange issuers

133. (1) This section does not apply to securities of an exchange issuer.

(2) Subject to subsection (3), a trade in a security acquired by the seller under section 55(2)*(1)* to *(6)*, *(18)*, *(19)*, *(24)* or *(26)* of the Act or section 117(a) or (b) of this regulation is deemed to be a distribution unless

(a) the issuer of the security is a reporting issuer,

(b) if the seller is an insider of the issuer of the security, the issuer is not in default of any requirement of the Act or this regulation,

(c) a 12 month period has elapsed from the later of the date of the issue of the security and the date the issuer became a reporting issuer,

See s. 120 of the Regulation regarding legending requirements.

(d) the trade is not a distribution from the holdings of a control person,

(e) no unusual effort is made to prepare the market or create a demand for the security, and

(f) no extraordinary commission or other consideration is paid in respect of the trade.

(3) Where a security, which for the purposes of this subsection is called the "primary security", has been traded under an exemption referred to in subsection (2) and

(a) the primary security was then traded under section 55(2)*(11)*(ii), *(12)* or *(13)* of the Act, or

(b) an exchanged security was then issued in relation to the primary security,

each subsequent trade of the primary security or exchanged security is deemed to be a distribution

(c) unless the security that is the subject of the trade was acquired by the seller under section 55(2)*(22)* of the Act,

(d) unless the security that is the subject of the trade, an earlier exchanged security or the primary security has been distributed under a prospectus or statement of material facts, or

(e) unless

    (i) the issuer of the security that is the subject of the trade is a reporting issuer,

    (ii) if the seller is an insider of the issuer of the security that is the subject of the trade, the issuer is not in default of any requirement of the Act or this regulation,

    (iii) a 12 month period has elapsed from the later of the date of issue of the primary security and the date the issuer of the security that is the subject of the trade became a reporting issuer,

> See s. 120 of the Regulation regarding legending requirements.

    (iv) the trade is not a distribution from the holdings of a control person,

    (v) no unusual effort is made to prepare the market or create a demand for the security that is the subject of the trade, and

    (vi) no extraordinary commission or other consideration is paid in respect of the trade.

(4) Subject to subsection (3), a trade

(a) in a security acquired by the seller under

    (i) section 55(2)*(7)* to *(11)*, *(13)*, *(23)* or *(25)* of the Act, other than a security acquired by the seller under section 55(2)*(11)*(iii) of the Act in accordance with the terms and conditions of a previously issued security where that previously issued security was distributed under a prospectus or a statement of material facts, or

    (ii) section 58(1)(a) of the Act where at the time the seller acquired the security it was described in section 32(j) of the Act,

(b) in a previously issued security of an issuer held by the seller upon the coming into force of the Act where the issuer was not a reporting issuer at that time, or

(c) in a security that

    (i) was acquired by a person under a trade referred to in paragraph (a) or (b), and used by that person for the purpose of giving collateral for a debt, and

    (ii) was then acquired by the seller under a realization on that collateral under section 55(2)*(12)* of the Act,

is deemed to be a distribution unless

(d) the issuer of the security is a reporting issuer and has been a reporting issuer for the 12 months preceding the trade,

(e) if the seller is an insider of the issuer of the security, the issuer is not in default of any requirement of the Act or this regulation,

(f) the trade is not a distribution from the holdings of a control person,

(g) no unusual effort is made to prepare the market or create a demand for the security, and

(h) no extraordinary commission or other consideration is paid in respect of the trade.

(5) A trade

(a) in a security acquired by the seller under section 55(2)(14) of the Act, or in an exchanged security issued to the seller in relation to that security, is deemed to be a distribution unless the purchaser is a promoter of the issuer,

(b) in a security acquired by a promoter in the circumstances referred to in paragraph (a), or in an exchanged security issued to the promoter in relation to that security, is deemed to be a distribution, or

(c) in a security acquired by the seller under section 55(2)(15) or (16) of the Act, or in an exchanged security issued to the seller in relation to that security, is deemed to be a distribution.

Deemed distributions — exchange issuers

134. (1) This section applies only to securities of an exchange issuer.

(2) Subject to subsection (3), a trade in a security issued after the issuer became an exchange issuer and acquired by the seller under section 55(2)(1) to (6), (19) or (26) of the Act or section 117(a), (b) or (i) of this regulation is deemed to be a distribution unless

(a) with respect to a security acquired by the seller under section 55(2)(1) to (4), (6), (19) or (26) of the Act or section 117(a), (b) or (i) of this regulation, a 12 month period has elapsed from the earlier of the date of issue of the security and the date a written agreement committing the seller to acquire the security, subject only to any required regulatory approval, has been executed by all parties to the agreement, or

(b) with respect to a security acquired by the seller under section 55(2)(5) of the Act

(i) an escrow agreement in the required form or a pooling agreement in the required form has been entered into or the requirement to enter into an escrow or pooling agreement has been waived by the superintendent, or

---

See NIN 92/3 "Waivers Consequential to Local Policy Statement 3-07". The required form of escrow agreement is Form 16. No form of pooling agreement has been prescribed. The superintendent does not require securities to be pooled; however, brokerage houses participating in an initial public offering will often require that some or all shares issued prior to the initial public offering be placed in pool with the issuer's transfer agent. The schedule for the release of the shares from pool is a matter of negotiation between the holders of such shares and the brokerage house.

(ii) a 12 month period has elapsed from the date of the issue of the security,

---

See s. 120 of the Regulation regarding legending requirements.

---

and

(c) if the seller is an insider of the issuer of the security, the issuer is not in default of any requirement of the Act or this regulation,

(d) the trade is not a distribution from the holdings of a control person,

(e) no unusual effort is made to prepare the market or create a demand for the security, and

(f) no extraordinary commission or other consideration is paid in respect of the trade.

(3) Where a security issued after the issuer became an exchange issuer, which for the purposes of this subsection is called the "primary security", has been traded under an exemption referred to in subsection (2), and

(a) the primary security was then traded under section 55(2)*(11)*(ii), *(12)* or *(13)* of the Act, or

(b) an exchanged security was then issued in relation to the primary security,

each subsequent trade of the primary security or exchanged security is deemed to be a distribution

(c) unless the security that is the subject of the trade was acquired by the seller under section 55(2)*(22)* of the Act,

(d) unless the security that is the subject of the trade, an earlier exchanged security or the primary security has been distributed under a prospectus or a statement of material facts, or

(e) unless

(i) if the seller is an insider of the issuer of the security that is the subject of the trade, the issuer is not in default of any requirement of the Act or this regulation,

(ii) if the primary security was traded under section 55(2)*(1)* to *(4)*, *(6)*, *(19)* or *(26)* of the Act or section 117(a), (b) or (i) of this regulation, a 12 month period has elapsed from the earlier of the date of issue of the primary security and the date a written agreement committing the seller to acquire the primary security, subject only to any required regulatory approval, has been executed by all parties to the agreement,

(iii) if the primary security was traded under section 55(2)*(5)* of the Act

(A) an escrow agreement in the required form or a pooling agreement in the required form has been entered into or the requirement to enter into an escrow or pooling agreement has been waived by the superintendent, or

See NIN 92/3 "Waivers Consequential to Local Policy Statement 3-07". The required form of escrow agreement is Form 16. No form has been specified for the pooling agreement. The superintendent does not require securities to be pooled; however, brokerage houses participating in an initial public offering will often require that some or all shares issued prior to the initial public offering be placed in pool with the issuer's transfer agent. The schedule for the release of the shares from pool is a matter of negotiation between the holders of such shares and the brokerage house.

(B) a 12 month period has elapsed from the date of issue of the primary security,

See s. 120 of the Regulation regarding legending requirements.

(iv) the trade is not a distribution from the holdings of a control person,

(v) no unusual effort is made to prepare the market or create a demand for the security that is the subject of the trade, and

(vi) no extraordinary commission or other consideration is paid in respect of the trade.

(4) Subject to subsections (3) and (6), a trade in a security issued after the issuer became an exchange issuer and acquired by the seller under

(a) section 55(2)*(7)* to *(11)*, *(13)*, *(18)* or *(23)* to *(25)* of the Act, other than a security acquired by the seller under section 55(2)*(11)*(iii) of the Act in accordance with the terms and conditions of a previously issued security where that previously issued security was distributed under a prospectus or a statement of material facts, or

   (b) section 117(f) to (h) of this regulation

is deemed to be a distribution unless

   (c) if the seller is an insider of the issuer of the security, the issuer is not in default of any requirement of the Act or this regulation,

   (d) the trade is not a distribution from the holdings of a control person,

   (e) no unusual effort is made to prepare the market or create a demand for the security, and

   (f) no extraordinary commission or other consideration is paid in respect of the trade.

(5) A trade in a security issued after the issuer became an exchange issuer and acquired by the seller under section 55(2)*(15)* or *(16)* of the Act, or in an exchanged security issued to the seller in relation to that security, is deemed to be a distribution.

(6) A trade in a security issued before the issuer became an exchange issuer, or in an exchanged security issued in relation to that security after the issuer became an exchange issuer, is deemed to be a distribution

   (a) unless

      (i) the security that is the subject of the trade, or a security in relation to which that security was issued, has been distributed under a prospectus or a statement of material facts, and

      (ii) the trade is not a distribution from the holdings of a control person,

   (b) unless

      (i) an escrow agreement in the required form or a pooling agreement in the required form has been entered into or the requirement to enter into an escrow or pooling agreement has been waived by the superintendent, and

      (ii) the trade is not a distribution from the holdings of a control person, or

   (c) unless the conditions referred to in section 133 that would have applied had the issuer not become an exchange issuer are satisfied.

[S. 134 am. B.C. Reg. 163/89.]

See NIN 92/3 "Waivers Consequential to Local Policy Statement 3-07". The required form of escrow agreement is Form 16. No form has been specified for the pooling agreement. The superintendent does not require securities to be pooled; however, brokerage houses participating in an initial public offering will often require that some or all shares issued prior to the initial public offering be placed in pool with the issuer's transfer agent. The schedule for the release of the shares from pool is a matter of negotiation between the holders of such shares and the brokerage house.

PART 9

CIRCULATION OF MATERIALS

There are no regulations under this Part.

PART 10

CONTINUOUS DISCLOSURE

Divison (1)
Financial Disclosure

See NIN 88/10 "Full Disclosure in Financial Statements" and National Policy Statement 51 "Changes in the Ending Date of a Financial Year and in Reporting Status".

Interim financial statements

135. (1) A reporting issuer other than a mutual fund shall file, within 60 days of the date to which it is made up, an interim financial statement,

(a) where the reporting issuer has not completed its first financial year, for the period commencing with the beginning of that financial year and ending 9, 6 and 3 months respectively before the date on which that financial year ends, or

(b) where the reporting issuer has completed its first financial year, for the periods commencing after the end of its last completed financial year and ending 3, 6 and 9 months after that date and a comparative financial statement to the end of each of the corresponding periods in the last financial year.

[S. 135(1) am. B.C. Reg. 316/89, s. 9]

The initial filing of interim financial statements by a reporting issuer relates to the quarterly period of the issuer ending immediately subsequent to the date it became a reporting issuer.

(2) A mutual fund in the Province shall file, within 60 days of the date to which it is made up, an interim financial statement,

(a) where the fund has not completed its first financial year, for the period commencing with the beginning of that financial year and ending 6 months before the date on which that financial year ends, and

(b) where the fund has completed its first financial year, for the 6 month period of the current financial year that commenced immediately following the last financial year.

(3) No interim financial statement need be filed

(a) under subsection (1), for any period that is less than 3 months, and

(b) under subsection (2), if the first financial year is less than 6 months.

(4) The interim financial statements filed under subsections (1) and (2) need not include an auditor's report, but if an auditor has been associated with those statements, his audit report or his comments on the unaudited financial information shall accompany the statements.

(5) The interim financial statements filed under subsection (1) shall include

(a) subject to subsection (6), a statement of changes in financial position, and

(b) an income statement.

(6) An issuer primarily engaged in the business of investing shall file a statement of changes in net assets for each period instead of a statement of changes in financial position.

(7) [Repealed B.C. Reg. 305/88, s. 29.]

See NIN 91/20 "Comparative Interim Financial Statements".

Comparative financial statements

136. (1) A reporting issuer, other than a mutual fund, and a mutual fund in the Province shall file annually a comparative financial statement relating separately to

(a) the period that commenced on the date of incorporation or organization and ended as at the close of the first financial year or, if the reporting issuer or mutual fund has completed a financial year, the last financial year, as the case may be, and

(b) the period covered by the financial year next preceding the last financial year, if any.

(2) A statement required to be filed under subsection (1) shall

(a) be filed within 140 days from the end of the latest financial year, and

    (b)   include, where it is to be filed by a reporting issuer other than a mutual fund in the Province,

        (i) an income statement,

        (ii) a statement of surplus,

        (iii) subject to subsection (4), a statement of changes in financial position if the issuer is not primarily engaged in the business of investing, and

        (iv) a balance sheet.

    (3) Where a change has been made in the ending date of a financial year, the issuer shall provide the superintendent with a notice of the change and the reasons for it on or before the earlier of

    (a)   the new date elected for the financial year end, or

    (b)   360 days from the end of the latest financial year reported on.

    (4) Every issuer primarily engaged in the business of investing shall file a statement of changes in net assets for each period instead of a statement of changes in financial position.

    (5) Each financial statement required to be filed under subsection (1) shall be approved by the directors of the reporting issuer, and the approval shall be evidenced by the manual or facsimile signatures of 2 directors duly authorized to signify the approval.

Interim financial statement to be filed under section 135(2)

    137. Subject to sections 139 and 140, a mutual fund in the Province shall include in every interim financial statement required to be filed under section 135(2)

    (a)   an income statement,

    (b)   a statement of investment portfolio,

    (c)   a statement of portfolio transactions, and

    (d)   a statement of changes in net assets,

prepared for or as at the end of the period, as appropriate.

Comparative financial statement to be filed under section 136

    138. Subject to sections 139 and 140, a mutual fund in the Province shall file the comparative financial statements required under section 136 in the required form prepared for or as at the end of the period, as appropriate.

The required form is Form 52.

Modification of sections 137 and 138

    139. Where a mutual fund invests exclusively in the shares or units of another mutual fund, it shall include the statements referred to in sections 137 and 138 for that other mutual fund, together with its own interim or annual financial statements for the same period.

Omission of statement of portfolio transactions

    140. (1) Notwithstanding sections 105, 137 and 138, but subject to subsection (4), a statement of portfolio transactions may be omitted from any interim or annual financial statements of a mutual fund if a copy of the statement that would otherwise be required to be included therein is filed prior to or concurrently with the filing of the financial statements from which that statement has been omitted.

    (2) Notwithstanding section 105, but subject to subsection (4), a statement of portfolio transactions may be omitted from a prospectus of a mutual fund if a copy of the statement that would otherwise be required to be included therein is filed concurrently with the filing of the prospectus or has previously been filed with the commission under subsection (1).

    (3) A statement of portfolio transactions filed under this section need not be reported upon by an auditor, but shall contain a certificate signed by the chief executive officer and chief financial officer, or the person temporarily carrying out the

responsibilities of either of them, that the statement of portfolio transactions presents fairly the required information.

(4) Where a statement of portfolio transactions is omitted from interim or annual financial statements under subsection (1) or from a prospectus under subsection (2), the published financial statements or prospectus shall contain a statement indicating that additional information as to portfolio transactions will be provided without charge on request to a specified address and

(a) the omitted information shall be sent promptly and without charge to each person that requests it in compliance with the indication, and

(b) where a person requests that such omitted information be sent routinely to that person the request shall be carried out while the information continues to be omitted from subsequent financial statements or prospectuses until the person requests, or agrees to, termination of the arrangement.

Delivery of financial statement to security holders

141.A person who is required to file a financial statement under section 135 or 136 shall concurrently

(a) send it to each holder of its securities, other than holders of debt instruments, whose latest address as shown on the books of the reporting issuer is in the Province, and

(b) file written confirmation of compliance with paragraph (a).

[S. 141 re-en. B.C. Reg. 305/88, s. 30.]

> See BOR 89/2 "Requirement to Send Interim Financial Statements to Shareholders of a Reporting Issuer".

Financial statements — finance issuer

142. (1) A finance issuer, not otherwise required to file financial statements in accordance with sections 135 and 136, shall file, in duplicate, the financial statements required under those sections as if those sections applied.

(2) Subject to subsection (3), a finance issuer, whether or not otherwise required to file financial statements under sections 135 and 136, shall file, annually, within 140 days after the end of its financial year, a report in the required form.

> The required form is Form 29.

(3) A finance issuer is exempt from subsection (2) where

(a) the Association of Canadian Financial Corporations, after consultation with the Investment Dealers' Association of Canada, has passed a bylaw setting a standard of continuous disclosure for its members considered by the commission to be an appropriate alternative to the disclosure requirement of subsection (2), and

(b) the finance issuer, whether it is a member of the Association of Canadian Financial Corporations or an agreeing non-member,

(i) complies with the bylaw referred to in paragraph (a),

(ii) files copies of each report required by the bylaw with

(A) the Association of Canadian Financial Corporations under the bylaw, and

(B) the commission and the Vancouver Stock Exchange under subsection (8), and

(iii) agrees that it will, as soon as possible on the request of the Association of Canadian Financial Corporations or of an interested party, add the name of an interested party to its mailing list for distribution of such reports until the interested party requests or agrees to the removal of his name from the mailing list.

Regulation

(4) For purposes of subsection (3), an "agreeing non-member" is a finance issuer that is not a member of the Association of Canadian Financial Corporations but has filed an undertaking with the commission that it will comply with the bylaw of the Association of Canadian Financial Corporations relating to continuous disclosure.

(5) Where the commission, on application by a finance issuer, considers that the method of operation of the applicant is such that the reporting requirements of subsections (1) and (2) are not appropriate, the commission may order that some or all of the reporting requirements of subsection (1) or (2) do not apply to the finance issuer.

(6) A report filed under subsection (2) shall be accompanied by a report of the auditor of the finance issuer stating that he has

(a) read the report, and

(b) no reason to believe that there are any misrepresentations in the information contained in it based upon

   (i) the financial statements upon which he reported, or

   (ii) his knowledge arising from his audit of the financial statements.

(7) Copies of the report required by subsection (2) or prepared under subsection (3), including exhibits and all records required in support of it, shall be filed

(a) with the commission, and

(b) where any security of the finance issuer is listed on the Vancouver Stock Exchange, with the Vancouver Stock Exchange.

(8) Any reports filed with the commission and the Vancouver Stock Exchange shall be manually signed by a senior financial officer of the finance issuer.

(9) A finance issuer shall, on the request of its debt security holder, provide the holder with a copy of its financial statements most recently filed under section 135 or 136 or under subsection (1).

Relief from certain requirements

143. (1) On the application of a reporting issuer or on the commission's own motion, the commission may make an order, where it considers it is not harmful to the public interest, exempting, in whole or in part,

(a) a reporting issuer from the reporting in the financial statements that are required to be filed under this Part of

   (i) comparative financial statements for specified periods,

   (ii) sales or gross operating revenue, if the commission is satisfied that the disclosure of that information would be unduly detrimental to the interests of the reporting issuer, or

   (iii) basic earnings per share or fully diluted earnings per share, or

(b) a reporting issuer or class of reporting issuers from a specific requirement of this Part where

   (i) the requirement conflicts with the laws of the jurisdiction in which the issuer or class of issuers are incorporated, organized or continued,

   (ii) the issuer or class of issuers ordinarily distribute financial information to its security holders in a form, or at times, different from those required by this Part, or

   (iii) in the circumstances of the particular case, it is satisfied that there is adequate justification for the exemption.

Re Inter Cable Communications Inc. (1994), 4 C.C.L.S. 309 (B.C. Sec. Comm.).

Section 143 of the Regulation gives the Commission the discretion to make an order exempting a reporting issuer from the reporting obligations that are required to be filed including comparative financial statements for specified periods where the Commission considers it is not harmful to the public interest or, in the circumstances of the particular case, where the Commission is satisfied that there is adequate justification for the exemption. In this case, the applicant company applied for relief, arguing that the preparation of audited financial statements would put the company out of business and it was in the public interest for the company to survive. The Commission dismissed the application. The Commission was not convinced that granting the exemption would not be harmful to the public interest or that there was adequate justification for exempting the company from the reporting requirements in ss. 135 and 136 of the Regulation. Further, it was not in the public interest to permit trading (limited or otherwise) in the company's securities until the company complied with the reporting requirements.

(2) In subsections (3) and (4) "non-Canadian issuer" means an issuer incorporated under the law of a jurisdiction, other than Canada or a province of Canada, that is or will be a reporting issuer because one or more of its securities is or will be listed on a stock exchange recognized by the commission for the purposes of this subsection and subsections (3) and (4).

[S. 143(2) am. B.C. Reg. 24/87, Sched., s. 4.]

The Vancouver Stock Exchange has been so recognized; see Local Policy Statement 3-44 "Recognition of Stock Exchanges and Jurisdictions". See also BOR 89/2 "Requirement to Send Interim Financial Statements to Shareholders of a Reporting Issuer", BOR 91/7 "Multijurisdictional Disclosure System", NIN 88/5 "Guidelines for Applications to the Securities Commission or the Superintendent of Brokers for Decisions or Orders", and Canadian Securities Administrators Notice 92/2 "Applications for Discretionary Orders".

(3) On the application of a non-Canadian issuer or on the commission's own motion, the commission may make an order, where it considers it is not harmful to the public interest, exempting, in whole or in part,

(a) a non-Canadian issuer from the reporting, in the financial statements that are required to be filed under this Part of

(i) comparative financial statements for specified periods,

(ii) sales or gross operating revenue, if the commission is satisfied that the disclosure of that information would be unduly detrimental to the interests of the reporting issuer, or

(iii) basic earnings per share or fully diluted earnings per share,

(b) a non-Canadian issuer or class of non-Canadian issuers from a specific requirement of this Part where

(i) the requirement conflicts with the laws of the jurisdiction in which the issuer or class of issuers are incorporated, organized or continued,

(ii) the issuer or class of issuers ordinarily distribute financial information to its security holders in a form, or at times, different from those required by this Part, or

(iii) in the circumstances of the particular case, it is satisfied that there is adequate justification for the exemption.

(4) The commission may vary any of the provisions of this Part as they apply or would, but for an exemption under subsection (3), apply to a non-Canadian issuer or class of non-Canadian issuers.

Division (2)
Filing

Publication of material change

144. (1) Subject to subsection (2), a report required to be filed under section 67(1)(b) of the Act shall be filed in the required form in an envelope marked "Continuous Disclosure".

(2) A reporting issuer who files

(a) the report required by section 67(1)(b) of the Act in reliance on section 67(2) of the Act, or

(b) the notification required by section 67(3) of the Act,

shall mark the report or notification "Confidential" and file it in an envelope marked "Confidential — section 67 of the Act".

> The required form is Form 27.

Filing — quarterly report

145. An exchange issuer shall file a quarterly report in the required form with the commission and the Vancouver Stock Exchange.

> The required form is Form 61. See BOR 89/2 "Requirement to Send Interim Financial Statements to Shareholders of a Reporting Issuer".

Filing of material sent to security holders or filed in other jurisdictions

146. (1) Every reporting issuer shall file in duplicate

(a) a copy of all material sent by the reporting issuer to its security holders, and

(b) subject to subsection (2), all information not already filed with the commission, whether in the same or a different form, that it files with a government of another jurisdiction, or an agency thereof, or with a stock exchange of another jurisdiction, under the securities or corporation law of that jurisdiction or under the bylaws, rules or regulations of the stock exchange, on the basis that it is material to investors although the information is not specifically required to be filed by the terms of the applicable statute or regulation or of the applicable bylaws, rules or regulations of the stock exchange.

(2) No information is required to be filed with the commission under subsection (1)(b) where the information filed in the other jurisdiction is information that is specifically required to be filed in the other jurisdiction by the terms of the applicable statute or regulation or of the bylaws, rules or regulations of the stock exchange.

(3) Information required to be filed with the commission under subsection (1) shall be sent to the commission within 24 hours after

(a) sending the information referred to in subsection (1)(a) to its security holders, or

(b) filing in another jurisdiction the information referred to in subsection (1)(b).

(4) Information that is filed with the commission pursuant to subsection (1)(b) and that has been filed on a confidential basis in all other jurisdictions in which it is filed, shall be kept confidential so long as it remains confidential in all those other jurisdictions.

Filing of records filed in another jurisdiction

147. Where the laws of the jurisdiction in which the reporting issuer carries on business or in which it was incorporated, organized or continued require the reporting issuer to file substantially the same information in that jurisdiction as is required by this regulation, the reporting issuer may comply with the filing requirements of this regulation by filing copies of the press release, timely disclosure report, information circular or financial statements and auditor's report, as the case may be, required by that jurisdiction provided that such records are manually signed and certified in accordance with section 182.

[S. 147 am. B.C. Reg. 305/88, s. 31.]

Division (3)
Insider Reporting

Interpretation

148. For purposes of this Division,

(a) the acquisition or disposition of a put, call or other transferable option respecting a security is a change in the beneficial ownership of that security, and

(b) when filing an insider report, ownership passes when

    (i) an offer to sell is accepted by the purchaser or his agent, or

    (ii) an offer to buy is accepted by the seller or his agent.

Report deemed filed by affiliate or controlled corporation

149. Where a person files a report under sections 70, 71 or 93 of the Act and the report includes details of

(a) securities beneficially owned or deemed to be beneficially owned by a corporation controlled by that person, or owned by an affiliate of that person or of the controlled corporation, or

(b) changes in the controlled corporation's or affiliate's beneficial ownership or deemed beneficial ownership of the securities,

the controlled corporation, its affiliate and the affiliate of the person who files the report, as the case may be, are not required to file a separate report.

[S. 149 am. B.C. Reg. 305/88, s. 32.]

Report by executor and co-executor

150. (1) In this section "executor" includes an administrator, trustee or other personal representative of an estate and "co-executor" has a corresponding meaning.

(2) Subject to subsection (3), where the executor or a co-executor of an estate files a report under section 70 or 93 of the Act in respect of securities owned by the estate,

(a) a co-executor, and

(b) the directors and senior officers of the executor or a co-executor are not required to file a separate report.

(3) Subsection (2) only applies to reporting requirements that arise solely from the capacity of a person as a co-executor or as a director or senior officer of an executor or co-executor.

[S. 150 re-en. B.C. Reg. 305/88, s. 33.]

Transfer report of insider

151. A report required to be filed under section 71 of the Act shall be filed in the required form.

The required form is Form 38.

Publication of summaries of reports

152. The commission shall summarize the information contained in every report filed under sections 70 and 93 of the Act in or as part of a periodical available to the public on payment of the appropriate fee set out in section 183.

Filing in other jurisdiction

152.1 Where the laws of the jurisdiction in which the reporting issuer carries on business or in which it was incorporated, organized or continued require substantially the same reports in that jurisdiction as are required by section 70 of the Act, the filing requirements of section 70 may be complied with by filing the reports which are required by the laws of the other jurisdiction and which are manually signed or certified in the required form.

No form has been specified.

Exemptions

152.2 On the application of an interested person or on its or his own motion, the commission or the superintendent may make an order exempting, in whole or in part, a person or a class of persons from all or some of the requirements of section 70 of the Act where

(a) a requirement of section 70 conflicts with a similar requirement of the laws of the jurisdiction in which the reporting issuer carries on business or in which he is incorporated, organized or continued with which the reporting issuer is required to comply, or

(b) it or he is satisfied in the circumstances of the particular case that

   (i) there is adequate justification for so doing, and

   (ii) it would not be prejudicial to the public interest to do so.

> See Local Policy Statement 3-14 "Applications for Insider Reporting Exemption" for circumstances where the Commission or Superintendent will generally grant discretionary exemption orders for directors and senior officers of affiliates of a reporting issuer and of affiliates of corporate insiders of a reporting issuer.

[Ss. 152.1 and 152.2 re-en. B.C. Reg. 305/88, s. 34.]

Division (4)
Insider Trading Exemptions

Exemptions

152.3 (1) In this section "securities" of a reporting issuer includes

(a) a put, a call, an option or another right or obligation to purchase or sell securities of the reporting issuer, or

(b) a security, the market price of which varies materially with the market price of any securities of the reporting issuer.

(2) A person that purchases or sells securities of a reporting issuer with knowledge of a material fact or material change with respect to the reporting issuer, which material fact or material change has not been generally disclosed, is exempt from section 68(1) of the Act and from liability under section 119 of the Act if the person proves on the balance of probabilities that

(a) the person had knowledge of the material fact or material change by reason only that the material fact or material change was known to one or more of that person's directors, officers, partners, employees or agents,

(b) the decision to purchase or sell the securities was made by one or more of the person's directors, officers, partners, employees or agents and none of those persons who participated in that decision had actual knowledge of the material fact or material change, and

(c) with respect to the purchase or sale of the securities, none of the person's directors, officers, partners, employees or agents who had actual knowledge of the material fact or material change gave any advice based on that actual knowledge to that person's directors, officers, partners, employees or agents who made or participated in the decision to purchase or sell the securities.

(3) A person that purchases or sells securities of a reporting issuer with knowledge of a material fact or material change with respect to the reporting issuer, which material fact or material change has not been generally disclosed, is exempt from section 68(1) of the Act and from liability under section 119 of the Act if the person proves on the balance of probabilities that

(a) the person purchased or sold the securities

   (i) as agent for another person pursuant to a specific unsolicited order to purchase or sell given by that other person and did not, before completion of the purchase or sale, give any advice to that other person based on the knowledge of that material fact or material change,

   (ii) as agent for another person pursuant to a specific solicited order to purchase or sell given by that other person prior to the person that acted as agent having knowledge of the material fact or material change,

   (iii) as agent or trustee for another person pursuant to that other person's participation in an automatic dividend reinvestment plan, an automatic purchase plan or another similar automatic plan, or

(iv) as agent or trustee for another person to fulfill in whole or in part a legal obligation of that other person,

(b) the person purchased or sold the securities pursuant to the person's participation in an automatic dividend reinvestment plan, an automatic purchase plan or another similar automatic plan that the person entered into prior to having knowledge of the material fact or material change, or

(c) the person purchased or sold the securities pursuant to a legal obligation that the person had entered into prior to having knowledge of the material fact or material change.

(4) A person is exempt from section 68(1) (2) and (3) of the Act if the person proves on the balance of probabilities that at the time of the purchase or sale referred to in section 68(1) of the Act or at the time of giving the information under section 68(2) or (3) of the Act, as the case may be, the person reasonably believed that

(a) the other party to the purchase or sale, or

(b) the person who received the information of the material fact or material change,

as the case may be, had knowledge of the material fact or material change.

[S. 152.3 en. B.C. Reg. 316/89, s. 10]

See BOR 88/6 "Filing of Insider Reports by Control Persons", BOR 91/7 "Multijurisdictional Disclosure System", NIN 88/5 "Guidelines for Application to the Securities Commission or the Superintendent of Brokers for Decisions or Orders", and Canadian Securities Administrators Notice 92/2 "Applications for Discretionary Orders".

PART 11

[Pt. 11 re-en. as ss. 153 to 163.8 B.C. Reg. 316/89, s. 11.]

TAKE OVER BIDS AND ISSUER BIDS

Divison (1)
Financial Disclosure

Valuation requirements

153. (1) In this section

"formal valuation" means a valuation of participating securities that

(a) is prepared by a qualified and independent valuer,

(b) is based on appropriate techniques and on relevant assumptions including going concern and liquidation assumptions if both types of assumptions are relevant or including whichever of those 2 types of assumptions are relevant if only one of them is relevant, and

(c) contains the valuer's opinion as to a value or range of values for the participating securities, without any downward adjustments in value on account of any of the participating securities not being part of a controlling interest;

"going private transaction" means an amalgamation, arrangement, consolidation or other transaction

(a) proposed to be carried out by an issuer of a participating security, and

(b) of which one consequence is that a holder's interest in that participating security may be terminated without the holder's consent and without the substitution for that interest of an interest of equivalent value in another participating security

(i) of that issuer,

(ii) of a successor to the business of that issuer, or

(iii) of another issuer that controls that issuer,

but does not include the acquisition of participating securities pursuant to a statutory right of acquisition;

"insider bid" means a take over bid made

(a) by an insider of the offeree issuer whose securities are the subject of the bid, or

(b) by any associate or affiliate of an insider of that offeree issuer;

"participating security" means an equity security and includes a security that is convertible within the meaning of section 76 of the Act into an equity security.

(2) Every

(a) take over bid circular that is required by the Act

(i) in respect of an insider bid, or

(ii) where the offeror anticipates that a going private transaction will follow the take over bid, or

(b) issuer bid circular that is required by the Act

shall contain

(c) a summary of a formal valuation of the offeree issuer,

(d) an outline of any other independent or material non-independent valuation of the offeree issuer or of its material assets or securities that was made within the 24 months immediately preceding the date of the bid, and

(e) a description of

(i) the source of any valuation that under paragraph (d) is required to be outlined, and

(ii) the circumstances under which that valuation was made.

(3) On application by the offeror under a take over bid or issuer bid, the superintendent, if satisfied that

(a) disclosure of information under any of the requirements of subsection (2) would cause a detriment to the offeree issuer or to the security holders of the offeree issuer that would outweigh the benefit of the information to the prospective recipients,

(b) the offeror lacks access to information enabling the offeror to comply with subsection (2), or

(c) the variation would not be prejudicial to the public interest,

may vary the provisions of this section as they apply to the offeror under that bid by waiving any or all of the requirements of subsection (2).

(4) Subject to subsection (5), a formal valuation required by subsection (2) to be summarized in a take over bid circular or issuer bid circular shall be as of a date that is not more than 120 days before the date of the take over bid or issuer bid and shall contain appropriate adjustments for material events that occurred after the date of the formal valuation and before the date of the circular.

(5) A formal valuation required by subsection (2) to be summarized in a take over bid circular or issuer bid circular may be as of a date that is more than 120 days before the date of the take over bid or issuer bid if the formal valuation is accompanied by a letter confirming that the valuer has no reasonable ground to believe that any event that occurred after the date of the formal valuation and before the date of the letter has materially affected the value or range of values determined in the formal valuation or, if there has been an event that has had that effect, describing the event and stating the resultant change in the value or range of values in the formal valuation.

(6) Subject to subsection (7), a formal valuation and any letter of confirmation required under subsection (5) to accompany it shall be filed concurrently with the filing of the circular in which reference to the formal valuation is made.

(7) On application by the offeror under a take over bid or issuer bid, the superintendent may vary the provisions of this section as they apply to the offeror under that bid by waiving the filing requirements of subsection (6).

See NIN 88/5 "Guidelines for Application to the Securities Commission or the Superintendent of Brokers for Decisions or Orders", and Canadian Securities Administrators Notice 92/2 "Applications for Discretionary Orders".

Market price

154. (1) For the purposes of Part 11 of the Act, "market price" of a class of securities for which there is a published market, at any date, is an amount equal to the simple average of the closing price of securities of that class for each of the business days on which there was a closing price falling not more than 20 business days before that date.

(2) Where a published market does not provide a closing price, but provides only the highest and lowest prices of securities traded on a particular day, the market price of the securities, at any date, is an amount equal to the average of the simple averages of the highest and lowest prices for each of the business days on which there were highest and lowest prices falling not more than 20 business days before that date.

(3) Where there is more than one published market for a security, the market price for the purposes of subsections (1) and (2) shall be determined as follows:

(a) if only one of the published markets is in Canada, the market price shall be determined solely by reference to that market;

(b) if there is more than one published market in Canada, the market price shall be determined solely by reference to the published market in Canada on which the greatest volume of trading in the particular class of securities occurred during the 20 business days immediately preceding the date as of which the market price is being determined;

(c) if there is no published market in Canada, the market price shall be determined solely by reference to the published market on which the greatest volume of trading in the particular class of securities occurred during the 20 business days immediately preceding the date as of which the market price is being determined.

(4) Where there has been trading of securities in a published market for fewer than 10 of the 20 business days immediately preceding the date as of which the market price of the securities is being determined, the market price shall be the average of the following prices established for each day of the 20 business days immediately preceding that date

(a) the average of the bid and ask prices for each day on which there was no trading;

(b) the closing price of securities of the class for each day that there has been trading, if the published market provides a closing price;

(c) the average of the highest and lowest prices of securities of that class for each day that there has been trading, if the published market provides only the highest and lowest prices of securities traded on a particular day.

(5) Notwithstanding subsection (1), (2), (3) or (4), for the purpose of section 80(1)(b) of the Act, where an offeror acquires securities on a published market, the market price for those securities shall be the price of the last board lot of securities of that class purchased, before the acquisition by the offeror, by a person that was not acting jointly or in concert with the offeror.

Exempt take over bid

155. A take over bid for securities in respect of which there is no published market is exempt from sections 87 to 92 of the Act if

(a) purchases are made from not more than 5 persons in the aggregate, including persons outside of the Province, and

(b) the bid is not made generally to security holders of the class of securities that is the subject of the bid.

Restrictions on acquisitions or sales during bid

156. (1) Section 83(2) of the Act does not apply to an offeror in respect of an agreement between a security holder and the offeror to the effect that the security holder, in accordance with the terms and conditions of a take over bid that is a formal bid made by the offeror, will deposit the security holder's securities pursuant to the bid.

(2) Section 86(1) of the Act does not apply to an offeror under an issuer bid in respect of the issue by it of securities pursuant to a dividend plan, dividend reinvestment plan, purchase plan or another similar plan.

(3) Sections 83(2) to 86 of the Act do not apply to an associate of a control person referred to in section 83(1)(c) of the Act who is not acting jointly or in concert with the control person in respect of the formal bid referred to in section 83(1)(a) of the Act.

Pre-bid private transactions

157. In the circumstances set out in subsection (1) of section 85 of the Act, that subsection does not apply to an offeror under a take over bid if the transaction that occurred within 90 days immediately preceding the bid was

    (a)   a trade in a security of the issuer that had not been previously issued, or

    (b)   a trade by or on behalf of the issuer in a previously issued security of that issuer that had been redeemed or purchased by or donated to that issuer.

Notice of intention

158. A notice of intention referred to in section 81(f) of the Act shall be filed and a press release in respect of the issuer bid that is the subject of the notice shall be issued at least 5 days before the commencement of the issuer bid.

Information required in press release

159. A press release required under section 83(3)(c) of the Act shall disclose, in respect of the class of securities subject to the take over bid and of each class of securities convertible within the meaning of section 76 of the Act into securities of that class purchased through the facilities of the stock exchange,

    (a)   the name of the purchaser,

    (b)   where the purchaser is a person referred to in section 83(1)(b) or (c) of the Act, the relationship of the purchaser and the offeror,

    (c)   the number of securities purchased by the purchaser on the day for which the press release is required,

    (d)   the highest price paid for the securities by the purchaser on the day for which the press release is required,

    (e)   the aggregate number of securities purchased through the facilities of the stock exchange by the purchaser during the currency of the bid,

    (f)   the average price paid for the securities that were purchased by the purchaser through the facilities of the stock exchange during the currency of the bid, and

    (g)   the total number of securities owned by the purchaser as of the close of business of the stock exchange on the day for which the press release is required.

Content of notice of change or notice of variation

160. (1) A notice of change required under section 90(2) of the Act shall contain

    (a)   a description of the change in the information contained in

        (i)   the take over bid circular,

        (ii)   the issuer bid circular,

        (iii)   any notice of change previously delivered under section 90(2) of the Act, or

        (iv)   any notice of variation previously delivered under section 90(4) of the Act,

(b) the date of the change,

(c) the date up to which securities may be deposited,

(d) the date by which securities deposited must be taken up by the offeror,

(e) a description of the rights of withdrawal that are available to security holders, and

(f) a signed certificate in the same form as is required to be contained in a take over bid circular or issuer bid circular, amended to refer to the initial circular and to all subsequent notices of change or notices of variation.

(2) A notice of variation required under section 90(4) of the Act shall contain

(a) a description of the variation in the terms of the take over bid or issuer bid,

(b) the date of the variation,

(c) the date up to which securities may be deposited,

(d) the date by which securities deposited must be taken up by the offeror,

(e) a description of the rights of withdrawal that are available to security holders, and

(f) a signed certificate in the same form as is required to be contained in a take over bid circular or issuer bid circular, amended to refer to the initial circular and to all subsequent notices of change or notices of variation.

(3) A notice of change required under section 91(6)(a) or (b) of the Act shall contain

(a) a description of the change in the information contained in

    (i) the directors' circular,

    (ii) any notice of change previously delivered under section 91(6)(a) of the Act,

    (iii) the director's or officer's circular, or

    (iv) any notice of change previously delivered under section 91(6)(b) of the Act, and

(b) a signed certificate in the same form as is required to be contained in a directors' circular or director's or officer's circular, amended to refer to the initial circular and to all subsequent notices of change or notices of variation.

Restriction on variations in terms of bids

161. (1) No variation in the terms of a take over bid or issuer bid, other than a variation that is the waiver by the offeror of a condition that is specifically stated in the bid as being waivable at the sole option of the offeror, shall be made after the expiry of the period, including any extension of the period, during which securities may be deposited pursuant to the bid.

(2) Where there is a variation in the terms of a take over bid or issuer bid that is the waiver by the offeror of a condition that is specifically stated in the bid as being waivable at the sole option of the offeror, section 90(4) of the Act does not apply in respect of that bid if

(a) the waiver occurs, and the offeror has issued a press release announcing the waiver, during the 5 days immediately following the expiry of the period, including any extension of the period, during which securities may be deposited pursuant to the bid, and

(b) the consideration offered for the securities consists solely of cash.

Consent of expert to use of name

162. (1) In this section "expert" means

(a) a professional person as defined in section 99, and

(b) a person whose business gives authority to a statement given by the person related to that business.

(2) Where a report, appraisal or statement of an expert is included in or accompanies

(a) a take over bid circular, issuer bid circular, directors' circular or director's or officer's circular, or

(b) a notice of change or notice of variation in respect of a take over bid or issuer bid,

the written consent of the expert to the use of the report, appraisal or statement shall be filed concurrently with the circular or notice.

Definition for sections 163.1 and 163.2

163. In sections 163.1 and 163.2 "securities of the offeree issuer" means

(a) voting or equity securities issued by the offeree issuer that are of the class of securities acquired in an acquisition described in section 93(1) or (2) of the Act, and

(b) securities of each class of voting or equity securities that is convertible within the meaning of section 76 of the Act into securities of the class described in paragraph (a).

Press release concerning acquisitions by offeror

163.1(1) A press release required under section 93 of the Act shall be authorized by a senior officer of the offeror and shall set out

(a) the name of the offeror,

(b) the number of securities of the offeree issuer that were acquired in the acquisition that gave rise to the requirement under section 93(1)(a) or (2)(a) of the Act to issue the press release,

(c) the beneficial ownership of, and the control and direction over, any of the securities of the offeree issuer, by the offeror and all persons acting jointly or in concert with the offeror, immediately after the acquisition described in paragraph (b),

(d) the name of the market in which the acquisition described in paragraph (b) took place,

(e) the purpose of the offeror and all persons acting jointly or in concert with the offeror in making the acquisition described in paragraph (b), including any intention of the offeror and all persons acting jointly or in concert with the offeror to increase the beneficial ownership of, or control or direction over, any of the securities of the offeree issuer,

(f) where applicable, a description of any change in a material fact set out in a previous press release issued under section 93(1)(a) or (2)(a) of the Act, and

(g) the names of all persons acting jointly or in concert with the offeror in connection with the securities of the offeree issuer.

(2) A report required under section 93(1)(b) or 2(b) of the Act shall be signed by the offeror and shall include the information required by subsection (1).

Press release by person other than the offeror under a formal bid

163.2(1) In this section "offeror" means the offeror referred to in section 94 of the Act that makes the acquisition that gives rise to the requirement under section 94 of the Act to issue a press release or further press release.

(2) A press release or further press release required under section 94 of the Act shall be authorized by a senior officer of the offeror and shall set out

(a) the name of the offeror,

(b) the number of securities of the offeree issuer that were acquired in the acquisition that gave rise to the requirement under section 94 of the Act to issue the press release or further press release,

(c) the beneficial ownership of, and the control and direction over, any of the securities of the offeree issuer, by the offeror and all persons acting jointly or in concert with the offeror, immediately after the acquisition described in paragraph (b),

(d) the name of the market in which the acquisition described in paragraph (b) took place, and

(e) the purpose of the offeror and all persons acting jointly or in concert with the offeror in making the acquisition described in paragraph (b), including any intention of the offeror and all persons acting jointly or in concert with the offeror to increase the beneficial ownership of, or control or direction over, any of the securities of the offeree issuer.

No duplicationof report or press release

163.3 Where

(a) an offeror and one or more persons acting jointly or in concert with the offeror are required to issue and file a press release or report under section 93 of the Act or a press release or further press release under section 94 of the Act, and

(b) a press release, report or further press release issued and filed by the offeror discloses the information required by section 163.1 or 163.2 as to a person acting jointly or in concert with the offeror,

that person need not issue and file a separate press release, report or further press release, as the case may be.

Statement of rights

163.4 (1) A take over bid circular, issuer bid circular, directors' circular, director's or officer's circular, or any notice of change or notice of variation that is required under Part 11 of the Act, shall contain a statement of the rights provided by section 115 of the Act relating to that circular or notice.

(2) If a take over bid or issuer bid is made in the Province and in another province or territory of Canada, inclusion of the following statement in each of any circulars or notices required under Part 11 of the Act shall be deemed to be compliance with subsection (1):

"Securities legislation in certain of the provinces and territories of Canada provides security holders of the offeree issuer with, in addition to any other rights they may have at law, rights of rescission or to damages, or both, if there is a misrepresentation in a circular or notice that is required to be delivered to such security holders. However, such rights must be exercised within prescribed time limits. Security holders should refer to the applicable provisions of the securities legislation of their province or territory for particulars of those rights or consult with a lawyer."

(3) If the take over bid or issuer bid is made in the Province only, inclusion of the following statement in each of any circulars or notices required under Part 11 of the Act shall be deemed to be compliance with subsection (1):

"Securities legislation in British Columbia provides security holders of the offeree issuer with, in addition to any other rights they may have at law, rights of rescission or to damages, or both, if there is a misrepresentation in a circular or notice that is required to be delivered to such security holders. However, such rights must be exercised within prescribed time limits. Security holders should refer to the applicable provisions of the British Columbia securities legislation for particulars of those rights or consult with a lawyer."

Disclosure

163.5 (1) The information contained in a circular or notice required under Part 11 of the Act shall be clearly presented and the statements made in the circular or notice shall be divided into groups according to subject matter and the various groups of statements shall be preceded by appropriate headings.

(2) The order of items in the appropriate form need not be followed.

(3) Where practical and appropriate, information in a circular or notice shall be presented in tabular form.

(4) All amounts required in a circular or notice shall be stated in figures.

(5) Information required by more than one applicable item in the appropriate form need not be repeated.

(6) No statement need be made in response to any item in the appropriate form that is inapplicable and negative answers to any item may be omitted except where expressly required by the applicable form.

Alternate signing authority

163.6 Where the superintendent is satisfied on evidence or submissions made to the superintendent that a chief executive officer or chief financial officer is, for adequate cause, not available to sign a certificate required under Part 11 of the Act, the superintendent may permit the certificate or notice to be signed by another responsible officer or director.

Timely filing of circular or notice

163.7 A circular or notice required under Part 11 of the Act shall be filed on the same date that it is first sent to security holders of the offeree issuer.

Prescribed time periods

163.8 For the purpose of

(a) both of paragraphs (b) and (c) of section 87 of the Act, the prescribed period is 21 days from the date of the bid,

(b) section 87(d)(i) of the Act, the prescribed period from the date of the bid is 21 days,

(c) section 87(d)(ii) of the Act, the prescribed period from the date of a notice of change or variation under section 90 of the Act is 10 days,

(d) section 87(d)(iii) of the Act, the prescribed period is 45 days from the date of the bid,

(e) section 87(i) of the Act, the prescribed period after the expiry of the bid is 10 days,

(f) section 90(5) of the Act, the prescribed period after the notice of variation has been delivered is 10 days, and

(g) section 91(1) of the Act, the prescribed period after the date of the bid is 10 days.

PART 12

PROXIES

Divison (1)
Rights of Beneficial Owner of Securities

Interpretation

164. (1) In this Part "security holder" and "solicit" have the same meanings as in section 100 of the Act.

(2) In section 165

"custodian" means a custodian of securities issued by a mutual fund and held for the benefit of plan holders under a custodial agreement or other arrangement;

"record date" means the date determined under section 73 of the Company Act.

Meeting information and voting instructions

165. (1) In this section "other relevant material" includes a bid circular, a director's circular and a director's or officer's circular within the meaning of Part 11 of the Act.

(2) Subject to subsections (3) and (4), where

(a) a registrant or custodian receives a notice of a meeting of an issuer's security holders or other relevant material,

(b) the registrant or custodian, or its nominee, as the case may be, is a registered security holder of that issuer at the record date for notice of that meeting or at the date of the other relevant material, as the case may be,

(c) the security is not beneficially owned by the registrant or custodian, and

(d) the registrant or custodian knows the name and address of the beneficial owner of the security,

the registrant or custodian shall send, without delay, a copy of any notice, financial statement, information circular or other relevant material received from the reporting issuer or its agent to the beneficial owner.

(3) Subsection (2) does not apply to a registrant or custodian where neither the issuer nor the beneficial owner of the security referred to in subsection (2) has agreed to pay the reasonable costs of sending the material under that subsection.

(4) On request, the reporting issuer or its agent shall, at its own expense, send the required number of copies of the notice, statement, circular or other relevant material referred to in subsection (2) to the registrant or custodian, as the case may be.

(5) Where the beneficial owner instructs or requests the registrant or custodian to do so, the registrant or custodian shall, in accordance with the instructions or request,

(a) vote the security or give a proxy requiring a nominee to vote the security, or

(b) where requested in the instructions, give the beneficial owner or his nominee a proxy enabling one of them, as specified in the request, to vote the security.

[S. 165(5) am. B.C. Reg. 305/88, s. 36.]

Filing of copies of proxy

166. (1) A person who sends a form of proxy or an information circular to security holders shall, without delay, file a copy of the form of proxy or the information circular, or both, together with all other material sent by him in connection with the meeting to which the form of proxy or information circular relates.

(2) An information circular filed under subsection (1) shall be certified by the manual or facsimile signature of an officer or director.

Filing copies of information circular

167. (1) Where the management of a reporting issuer is required to send an information circular under section 101(2)(a) of the Act, the reporting issuer shall, without delay, file a copy of the information circular certified in accordance with subsection (3).

(2) In any case where subsection (1) is not applicable, the reporting issuer shall file annually, within 140 days from the end of its financial year, a report in the required form certified in accordance with subsection (3).

The required form is Form 28.

---

(3) The circular and report required in this section shall be certified by the manual or facsimile signature of an officer or director.

PART 13

SELF DEALING

There are no regulations under this Part.

PART 13.1

[Pt. 13.1 en. B.C. Reg. 306/88, First Sched., s. 12.]

CONFLICTS OF INTEREST

Interpretation

167.1(1) In this Part

"associated party of the registrant" means

(a) a related party of the registrant,

(b) a partner of the registrant,

   (c)   a director, officer, salesman or employee of the registrant or a director, officer, partner, salesman or employee of a related party of the registrant if

      (i) in the case described in section 167.5(1)(b), he participates in the trade or purchase,

      (ii) in the case described in section 167.7(1)(b), he participates in the formulation or giving of the advice,

      (iii) in the case described in section 167.8(1)(b), he participates in the formulation of the investment decision, or

      (iv) in the case described in section 167.9(1)(b) or section 167.9(2)(b), he participates in the formulation or making of the recommendation or statement, or

   (d)   an associate of any of the above persons, other than an associate within the meaning of paragraph (a) or (c) of the definition of "associate" in section 1(1) of the Act;

"connected party" means, in respect of a registrant,

   (a)   a person that has any indebtedness to, or other relationship with,

      (i) the registrant,

      (ii) a related party of the registrant,

      (iii) a director, officer or partner of the registrant or of a related party of the registrant, or

   (b)   any related party of the person first referred to in paragraph (a),

if, in respect of an initial distribution of securities issued by or held by the person first referred to in paragraph (a) or the related party referred to in paragraph (b), the indebtedness or other relationship may under the circumstances lead a reasonable prospective purchaser of the securities to question whether the registrant and the person or the registrant and the related party, as the case may be, are independent of each other, whether or not the indebtedness or other relationship is a material fact, or

   (c)   a person designated under section 167.2 to be a connected party;

"fully registered dealer" means a registered dealer described in section 13(2)(a), (b) or (e);

"initial distribution" means

   (a)   a distribution within the meaning of paragraph (a), (b), (c) or (d) of the definition of "distribution" in section 1(1) of the Act,

   (b)   a deemed distribution within the meaning of section 133(5)(c) or 134(5), where

      (i) the security was acquired by the seller under section 55(2)(15) of the Act, or

      (ii) if the security is an exchanged security as defined in section 116, the security was issued in relation to a security aquired by the seller under section 55(2)(15) of the Act, or

   (c)   a transaction or series of transactions involving further purchases and sales in the course of or incidental to a distribution referred to in paragraph (a), or in the course of or incidental to a deemed distribution referred to in paragraph (b);

"registrant" means a registered adviser, dealer or underwriter, but does not include a security issuer;

"related party" means, in respect of a person, any other person that is

   (a)   related to that person under subsections (2) to (4);

   (b)   deemed to be a related party under subsection (5), or

   (c)   designated under section 167.2 to be a related party;

"security" includes, in respect of an issuer,

(a) a put, call, option or other right or obligation to purchase or sell securities of the issuer, and

(b) a security of any other issuer all or substantially all of whose assets are securities of the issuer.

(2) For the purposes of this Part, each of 2 persons is related to the other if

(a) cither influences the other,

(b) both influence the same third person, or

(c) both are influenced by the same third person.

(3) For the purposes of subsection (2), a person influences another person if, through the beneficial ownership of or exercise of control or direction over, or through a combination of such ownership of or control or direction over,

(a) voting securities of that other person,

(b) securities currently convertible or exchangeable into voting securities of that other person, or

(c) securities carrying a currently exercisable right to acquire voting securities of that other person or to acquire convertible or exchangeable securities referred to in paragraph (b),

whether direct or indirect and whether alone or in combination with one or more persons, he exercises a controlling influence over the management and policies of that other person.

(4) For the purposes of subsection (2) and without limiting the generality of subsection (3), a person shall, in the absence of evidence to the contrary, be deemed to influence another person if he

(a) beneficially owns or exercises control or direction over securities which constitute in the aggregate more than 20% of the outstanding securities of any class or series of voting securities of that other person, or

(b) would, upon conversion, exchange or exercise of any security or right referred to in subsection (3)(b) or (c), beneficially own or exercise control or direction over securities which would constitute in the aggregate more than 20% of the outstanding securities of any class or series of voting securities of that other person,

whether directly or indirectly and whether alone or in combination with one or more other persons.

(5) For the purposes of this Part, if any 2 persons are related parties of the same other person, those 2 persons are deemed to be related parties of each other.

(6) Notwithstanding the definition of "connected party" or "related party" in subsection (1), a person is not a connected party of a registrant or a related party of a registrant only because the registrant, acting as an underwriter and in the ordinary course of its business, owns securities issued by the person in the course of an initial distribution.

Superintendent's discretion

167.2 (1) On the application of an interested person or on the superintendent's own motion, the superintendent may vary the provisions of this Part as they apply to a person by designating the person to be a related party or a connected party of a registrant

(a) if the superintendent considers the designation appropriate because of the manner in which the person carries on its business with the registrant or with any related party of the registrant, or

(b) in any other case if the superintendent considers the designation to be in the public interest.

(2) The superintendent shall not make a designation under subsection (1) without first giving the registrant and the other person affected an opportunity to be heard.

Conflict of interest rules statement

167.3 (1) Every registrant shall prepare and file a conflict of interest rules statement in the required form.

> The required form is Form 69.

(2) A registrant shall provide free of charge a copy of its current conflict of interest rules statement to each of its clients at the time he becomes a client of the registrant or by October 15, 1988, whichever is later.

(3) In the event of any significant change in the information required to be contained in the conflict of interest rules statement, the registrant shall

    (a) forthwith prepare and file a revised version of the conflict of interest rules statement containing the information required by subsection (1), and

    (b) provide to each of its clients a copy of the revised version within 45 days of the filing.

(4) Notwithstanding subsection (1), a registrant that does not engage in activities as an adviser, dealer or underwriter in respect of a security in the circumstances set out in sections 167.4, 167.5, 167.7, 167.8 or 167.9 is not required to prepare, file or provide to its clients a conflict of interest rules statement if it files in the required form

    (a) a statement that it does not engage in such activities, and

    (b) an undertaking that it will not engage in such activities except in compliance with this Part.

> The required form is Form 70. See NIN 89/3 "Conflict of Interest Rules Statement – Clarification of Filing Requirements", BOR 91/7 "Multijurisdictional Disclosure System", Local Policy Statement 3-30 "Underwriter's Conflict of Interest", and National Policy Statement 4 "Conditions for Dealer Sub-underwritings".

Limitations on underwriting

167.4 (1) In this section

"independent underwriter" means, in connection with an initial distribution of securities issued by a registrant or issued by or held by a related party or connected party of a registrant, another registrant who is acting as underwriter and in respect of which the issuer is not a related party or connected party;

"special selling group member" means, in connection with an initial distribution of securities, a registrant who

    (a) would be an underwriter but for the exclusion set out in paragraph (d) of the definition of "underwriter" in section 1(1) of the Act, and

    (b) entered into an agreement or understanding with the issuer or an underwriter to participate directly or indirectly in the initial distribution

        (i) in the case of an initial distribution made under a prospectus or a statement of material facts, before the filing of the prospectus or statement of material facts, or

        (ii) in any other case, before the commencement of the initial distribution of the securities.

(2) No registrant shall act as an underwriter or special selling group member in connection with an initial distribution of securities issued by the registrant or issued by or held by a related party or connected party of the registrant unless

    (a) a prospectus is prepared, filed and sent in accordance with the Act, or some other document that contains the same disclosure relating to the provisions of this Part as is required by the form for a prospectus is delivered by the registrant to the purchaser, or to a dealer acting as the purchaser's agent, before entering into an agreement of purchase and sale respecting the securities,

    (b) in the case of an initial distribution made under a prospectus or under a statement of material facts, except in the circumstances described in paragraph (c), the portion of the initial distribution underwritten by at least one independent underwriter is not less than the aggregate of the portions of the initial distribution underwritten by or, in the capacity of special selling group member, sold by the registrant and each other registrant in respect of which the issuer is a related party or a connected party,

(c) in the case of an initial distribution made under a prospectus or under a statement of material facts where every registrant acting as underwriter or special selling group member agrees to act as agent and no such registrant is obligated under any circumstances to act as principal, a portion of the initial distribution is sold by at least one independent underwriter, and

(d) in the case of an initial distribution referred to in paragraphs (b) or (c), the certificate required under section 50 of the Act to be contained in the prospectus or the certificate required under section 122 to be contained in the statement of material facts, as the case may be, is signed by the independent underwriter or underwriters referred to in those paragraphs.

(3) Subsection (2)(a) does not apply to

(a) an initial distribution

(i) that is not made under a prospectus or under a statement of material facts, and

(ii) in which all of the purchasers are related parties of the registrant and are purchasing as principal but not as underwriter, or

(b) an initial distribution exempted from section 42 of the Act under section 117(c), (d) or (e).

(4) Subsection (2)(b) to (d) does not apply to

(a) an initial distribution in which all of the purchasers are related parties of the registrant and are purchasing as principal but not as underwriter, or

(b) an initial distribution where the person issuing the securities is not a related party of the registrant and is a connected party of the registrant only because the registrant, in connection with its agreement with the person to underwrite the securities, makes or guarantees a loan to the person subsequent to the preliminary prospectus being filed under section 42(1) of the Act or subsequent to the statement of material facts being filed under section 121, as the case may be.

(5) Subsection (2) does not apply in respect of a trade or purchase where the registrant neither solicits the trade or purchase nor advises the client in respect of it.

> See BOR 92/2 "Limitations on a Registrant Underwriting Securities of a Related Party or Connected Party of the Registrant".

Limitations on trading

167.5 (1) No registrant shall,

(a) as principal or agent, trade in or purchase a security with, from or on behalf of any client where the security is issued by the registrant or a related party of the registrant or is being issued in the course of an initial distribution by a connected party of the registrant, or

(b) as principal or agent, trade in or purchase a security with, from or on behalf of any client where any director, officer, partner, salesman or employee of the registrant who participates in the trade or purchase actually knows that the security will directly or indirectly be

(i) purchased from or sold to the registrant or an associated party of the registrant, or

(ii) purchased from a person who is a connected party of the registrant and who is a control person of the issuer of the security,

unless

(c) the registrant has, before entering into an agreement of purchase and sale respecting the security, delivered the current conflict of interest rules statement of the registrant to the client, or has informed the client orally or by some other means of substantially all the information and all changes in such information required by section 167.3(1) and (3)(a) to be included in the conflict of interest rules statement, and

(d) the registrant complies with the requirements of sections 80 and 167.6.

(2) Subsection (1) does not apply if

(a) the client is purchasing as principal and is either a fully registered dealer or is a related party of the registrant, or

(b) the registrant neither solicits the trade or purchase nor advises the client in respect of it.

[S. 167.5 am. B.C. Reg. 306/88, Second Sched., s. 1; B.C. Reg. 378/88.]

See BOR 88/11 "Conflict of Interest Rules Statement – Confirmation and Reporting of Transactions by Registrants".

Confirmation and reporting of transactions

167.6 (1) The written confirmation of the transaction required by section 80 to be sent by a registered dealer to a client shall,

(a) in the case of a security issued by a related party of the registrant or, in the course of an initial distribution, a security issued by a connected party of the registrant, state that the security was issued by a related party or a connected party of the registrant, as the case may be, and

(b) where any director, officer, partner, salesman or employee of the registrant who participated in the transaction actually knew at the time of the transaction that the security would directly or indirectly be

(i) purchased from or sold to an associated party of the registrant, or

(ii) purchased from a person who at the time of the transaction was a connected party of the registrant and was a control person of the issuer of the security,

state that the security was directly or indirectly purchased from or sold to such a person.

(2) Any report, other than the written confirmation required by section 80, sent or delivered by a registrant to a client respecting any trade or purchase of a security made by the registrant with, from or on behalf of the client, including a trade or purchase of a security for an account or portfolio of the client over which the registrant has discretionary authority, shall,

(a) in the case of a security issued by a related party of the registrant or, in the course of an initial distribution, a security issued by a connected party of the registrant, state that the security was issued by a related party or a connected party of the registrant, as the case may be, and

(b) where any director, officer, partner, salesman or employee of the registrant who participated in the transaction actually knew at the time of the transaction that the security would directly or indirectly be

(i) purchased from or sold to the registrant or an associated party of the registrant, or

(ii) purchased from a person who was a connected party of the registrant and who at the time of the transaction was a control person of the issuer of the security,

state that the security was directly or indirectly purchased from or sold to such a person.

See BOR 88/11 "Conflict of Interest Rules Statement – Confirmation and Reporting of Transactions by Registrants".

Limitations on advising

167.7 (1) No registrant shall act as an adviser in respect of a security where

(a) the security is issued by a related party of the registrant or is being issued in the course of an initial distribution by a connected party of the registrant, or

(b) any director, officer, partner, salesman or employee of the registrant who participates in the formulation or giving of the advice actually knows, or it is reasonable for any such person to expect in the circumstances, that wholly or partly as a result of the advice given the security will directly or indirectly be

(i) purchased from or sold to the registrant or an associated party of the registrant, or

(ii) purchased from a person who is a connected party of the registrant and who is a control person of the issuer of the security,

unless the registrant before advising the client makes to the client a concise statement either in writing or orally, confirmed promptly to the client in writing,

(c) in the case of paragraph (a), disclosing the relationship between the registrant and the issuer of the security, and

(d) in the case of paragraph (b), disclosing

(i) that the registrant knows or expects that the security will or may be directly or indirectly purchased from or sold to the registrant or an associated party of the registrant or directly or indirectly purchased from a connected party of the registrant, and

(ii) the relationship between the registrant and such person or persons.

(2) Subsection (1) does not apply if

(a) the client is a fully registered dealer or a related party of the registrant, or

(b) the advice is given by a registered dealer and

(i) is solely incidental to a trade or purchase of the security carried out by the registered dealer, and

(ii) no fee is charged for the advice other than the usual and customary commission for the trade or purchase.

(3) Subsection (1)(a) does not apply if section 167.8(1)(a) applies.

(4) Subsection (1)(b) does not apply if section 167.8(1)(b) applies.

Limitations on the exercise of discretion

167.8 (1) No registrant shall, in respect of any account or portfolio of a client over which it has discretionary authority,

(a) purchase for or sell from such account or portfolio a security where the security is issued by the registrant or a related party of the registrant or is being issued in the course of an initial distribution by a connected party of the registrant,

(b) purchase for or sell from such account or portfolio a security where any director, officer, partner, salesman or employee of the registrant who participates in the formulation of the investment decision made by the registrant on behalf of the client actually knows, or it is reasonable for any such person to expect in the circumstances, that the security will directly or indirectly be

(i) purchased from or sold to the registrant or an associated party of the registrant, or

(ii) purchased from a person who is a connected party of the registrant and who is a control person of the issuer of the security, or

(c) purchase for such account or portfolio a security being issued in the course of an initial distribution where

(i) any director, officer, partner, salesman or employee of the registrant or of a related party of the registrant, who participates in the formulation of the investment decision made by the registrant on behalf of the client, is a director or officer of the issuer of the security, or

    (ii) an associate of any of the persons referred to in paragraph (c)(i), other than an associate within the meaning of paragraph (a), (b) or (c) of the definition of "associate" in section 1(1) of the Act, is a director or officer of the issuer of the security,

unless prior to such purchase or sale the registrant has disclosed to the client all relevant facts in respect of the matters referred to in paragraph (a), (b) or (c), as the case may be, and has obtained the client's specific and informed written consent to purchase or sell the security for or from his account or portfolio.

    (2) Subsection (1) does not apply if the client is a fully registered dealer or a related party of the registrant.

    (3) No registrant shall make a loan from any account or portfolio of a client over which it has discretionary authority to

    (a) the registrant,

    (b) a related party of the registrant,

    (c) a partner of the registrant,

    (d) a director, officer, salesman or employee of the registrant or of a related party of the registrant, or

    (e) an associate of any of the above persons, other than an associate within the meaning of paragraph (a) or (c) of the definition of "associate" in section 1(1) of the Act.

Limitations on recommendations

    167.9 (1) No registrant shall make a recommendation, or cooperate with any other person in the making of a recommendation, that a security be sold, exchanged, purchased or held where

    (a) the security is issued by the registrant or a related party of the registrant or is being issued in the course of an initial distribution by a connected party of the registrant,

    (b) any director, officer, partner, salesman or employee of the registrant who participates in the formulation or making of the recommendation actually knows, or it would be reasonable for any such person to expect in the circumstances, that wholly or partly as a result of the recommendation the security will directly or indirectly be

        (i) purchased from or sold to the registrant or an associated party of the registrant, or a trade, purchase or holding of the security will result in a material direct or indirect financial benefit to such person, other than the usual and customary commission payable to a registered dealer, or

        (ii) purchased from a person who is a connected party of the registrant and who is a control person of the issuer of the security, or

    (c) the registrant is a dealer or underwriter who has at any time during the past 12 months

        (i) assumed an underwriting liability respecting the security, or

        (ii) provided financial advice to the issuer of the security for consideration,

unless the recommendation is contained in a circular, pamphlet or similar publication that is published, issued or sent by the registrant and is of a type distributed with reasonable regularity in the ordinary course of the registrant's business, and includes in a conspicuous position, in type not less legible than is used in the body of such publication, a statement

    (d) in the case described in paragraph (a), except where the security is issued by the registrant, disclosing the relationship between the registrant and the issuer of the security including, in the case of a related party, the nature and extent of the ownership of, or the control or direction over, the securities of the other person, and in the case of a connected party, the nature of the indebtedness or other relationship,

    (e) in the case described in paragraph (b), disclosing, as the case may be, either or both of the following:

(i) that the registrant knows or expects that the security will or may be directly or indirectly purchased from or sold to the registrant or an associated party of the registrant, or directly or indirectly purchased from a connected party of the registrant, and the relevant facts on which such knowledge or expectation is based;

(ii) that the registrant knows or expects that a trade, purchase or holding of the security will or may result in the registrant or an associated party of the registrant receiving a financial benefit, and the nature and extent of such benefit,

and disclosing the relationship between the registrant and such person or persons referred to in either or both of subparagraph (i) or (ii), as the case may be, and

(f) in the case described in paragraph (c), disclosing that the registrant has, during the past 12 months,

(i) assumed an underwriting liability respecting the security, or

(ii) provided financial advice to the issuer of the security for consideration,

as the case may be.

(2) No registrant, with the intention of effecting a purchase of or trade in a security, shall alone or in cooperation with any other person publish, issue or send a circular, pamphlet, advertisement or other statement, other than a recommendation, promoting the security where

(a) the security is issued by the registrant or a related party of the registrant or is being issued in the course of an initial distribution by a connected party of the registrant, or

(b) any director, officer, partner, salesman or employee of the registrant who participates in the formulation or making of the statement actually knows, or it would be reasonable for any such person to expect in the circumstances, that wholly or partly as a result of the statement the security will directly or indirectly be

(i) purchased from or sold to the registrant or an associated party of the registrant, or

(ii) purchased from a person who is a connected party of the registrant and who is a control person of the issuer of the security,

unless the statement discloses in a conspicuous position, in type not less legible than is used in the body of such statement,

(c) that it is published, issued or sent by the registrant,

(d) in the case described in paragraph (a), except where the security is issued by the registrant, the relationship between the registrant and the issuer of the security, and

(e) in the case described in paragraph (b),

(i) that the registrant knows or expects that the security will or may be directly or indirectly purchased from or sold to the registrant or an associated party of the registrant or directly or indirectly purchased from a connected party of the registrant, and

(ii) the relationship between the registrant and such person or persons.

(3) Subsections (1) and (2) do not apply to a recommendation or statement that is not written and that is not made in a public medium of communication.

Limitations on networking

167.10 (1) In this section "networking arrangement" means an arrangement between a registrant and a savings institution or an insurer, whether or not the savings institution or insurer is a registrant, under which the registrant

(a) offers for sale or sells to the public a combination of securities and goods or services, a portion of which consists of securities, goods or services issued or provided by the savings institution or insurer or

    (b)   cooperates with the savings institution or insurer in the joint offering for sale or sale of securities and goods or services, including by paying the savings institution or insurer or its employees a commission for referring to the registrant a client to whom the registrant sells securities and goods or services,

but does not include trades in or purchases by the registrant of securities issued by the savings institution or insurer on the same basis on which the registrant trades in or purchases securities issued by persons other than savings institutions or insurers.

(2) A registrant that intends to enter into a networking arrangement shall, at least 30 days before entering into the networking arrangement, give written notice of its intention to the superintendent providing all relevant facts relating to the networking arrangement.

(3) If, within the 30 days immediately after receipt of the notice referred to in subsection (2), the superintendent gives a written notice of objection to the registrant, the registrant shall not enter into the networking arrangement unless the superintendent gives his written approval.

(4) After giving the registrant an opportunity to be heard, the superintendent may, where he considers it to be in the public interest,

    (a)   refuse to allow the registrant to enter into the networking arrangement, or

    (b)   allow the registrant to enter into the networking arrangement on conditions, if any, imposed by the superintendent.

See NIN 88/40 "Sale of Mutual Funds by Financial Institutions – Principles of Regulation", NIN 88/48 "Full Service and Discount Brokerage Activities by Financial Institutions – Principles of Regulation", NIN 90/7 "Dual Employment of Individuals Employed by Financial Institutions and Securities Registrants", and NIN 90/16 "Principles of Regulation re: Activities of Registrants Related to Financial Institutions" with respect to Regulatory Guidelines.

Exceptions

167.11(1) Section 167.4 does not apply to a registrant in respect of an initial distribution of securities issued by a mutual fund.

(2) Sections 167.5(1)(a), 167.6(1)(a) and (2)(a), 167.7(1)(a), 167.8(1)(a), 167.9(1)(a) and (2)(a), except as those sections apply to initial distributions of securities of related parties, and section 167.4 do not apply to any trading in or purchasing of, or advising, exercising discretion, or making recommendations or statements in respect of, securities described in section 32 of the Act.

Exemption

167.12 Where the superintendent considers that it would not be prejudicial to the public interest to do so, he may exempt a registrant from any provision of this Part.

See BOR 88/11 "Conflict of Interest Rules Statement Confirmation and Reporting of Transactions by Registrants", BOR 93/4 "Networking Arrangements Governed by the Principles of Regulation", and NIN 93/24 "Exemption for Filing Notice of Networking Arrangements Governed by the Principles of Regulation".

PART 14

CIVIL LIABILITY

Amount prescribed for section 123 of the Act

167.13 For the purpose of section 123(1) of the Act, the prescribed amount is $50 000.

[S. 167.13 en. B.C. Reg. 316/89, s. 12.]

PART 15

INVESTIGATIONS AND AUDITS

Application

168. The practices and procedures set out in this Part shall apply to every investigation and audit conducted under Part 15 of the Act.

Personal service

169. (1) A summons issued by a person under section 128 of the Act shall be served personally on the individual summoned.

(2) A person summoned under section 128 of the Act shall be paid the fees and allowances for his attendance before the investigator to which a witness summoned to attend before the Supreme Court is entitled.

Form of summons

170. A summons to a person to appear before an investigator under section 128 of the Act shall be in the required form.

The required form is Form 1.

Affidavit

171. The service of a summons, the payment or tender of fees and allowances to a person summoned and the service of a notice on a witness may be proved by an affidavit in the required form.

[S. 171 am. B.C. Reg. 305/88, s. 37.]

The required form is Form 2.

Application to Supreme Court to enter premises and obtain information

171.1 An application for an order under section 127(2) of the Act shall be made in accordance with the Supreme Court Rules.

[S. 171.1 en. B.C. Reg. 316/89, s. 13.]

PART 16

ENFORCEMENT

Reactivation of dormant issuer

171.2 Where an order of the commission or superintendent under section 146(1) of the Act that all trading cease in a specified security or class of security of an issuer has been in effect for more than 90 days, then the issuer, concurrently with filing the required record or information referred to in the order, shall file additional records or additional information about the business and affairs of the issuer that the commission or the superintendent considers necessary to determine whether trading in the specified security or class of securities, as the case may be, is prejudicial to the public interest.

[S. 171.2 en. B.C. Reg. 316/89, s. 14.]

See Local Policy Statement 3-35 "Reactivation of Dormant Issuers". *Re Chromex Nickel Mines Ltd., Kleena Kleene Gold Mines Ltd. and Michael Hretchka*, [1991] 29 B.C.S.C. Weekly Summary 9 (B.C. Sec. Comm.). In a decision dealing with an application relating to the validity of policy statements and regulations, it was submitted that Local Policy Statement 3-35 did not need to be complied with because it does not have retrospective effect. The Commission held that the requirements of s. 171.2 of the Regulation are designed to ensure that those issuers whose securities have been cease traded for more than 90 days file records and information about their business and affairs so that the public will not be prejudiced when the securities are trading again. This is a measure de-

signed to protect the public, and it is in keeping with the general regulatory role of the Commission. Since s. 171.2 is designed to protect the public, the presumption against the retrospective affect of statutes is effectively rebutted. Local Policy Statement 3-35 is issued as a guideline for those issuers who must comply with s. 171.2 of the Regulation. The policy, like all policies, is not binding on the Commission or the Superintendent and therefore it is not a fettering of the discretion of the Commission or the Superintendent. Similarly, national policies are issued as a guideline.

PART 17

REVIEWS AND APPEALS

Application

172. This Part applies to a hearing required or permitted to be held under the Act or this regulation other than a hearing held under Part 15 of the Act.

Notice

173. In addition to any other person to whom notice is required to be given, notice in writing of the time, place and purpose of a hearing shall be given to any person considered by the person presiding to be directly affected by it.

174. [Repealed B.C. Reg. 305/88, s. 38.]

Receiving evidence

175. (1) and (2) [Repealed B.C. Reg. 305/88, s. 38.]

(3) All oral evidence received at the hearing may be taken down in writing or preserved as the person presiding directs.

(4) The oral evidence recorded, the documentary evidence and things received in evidence shall form the record.

Representation by counsel

176. A person attending a hearing or submitting evidence at a hearing under this Part may be represented by counsel.

Decision

177. (1) After a hearing, where the decision made at it adversely affects the right of a person to trade in securities, at the request of the person affected, the person presiding shall issue written reasons for the decision.

(2) The person presiding shall give notice of every decision and accompanying written reasons as soon as practicable to every person to whom notice of the hearing was given and to every person who is, in the opinion of the person presiding, directly affected by the decision.

When hearing public

178. (1) A hearing shall be open to the public.

(2) Where the person presiding considers that a public hearing would be unduly prejudicial to a party or a witness and that it would not be contrary to the public interest, it may order that the public be excluded for all or part of the hearing.

Sufficiency of notice

179. Any notice required under this Part is sufficiently given if sent to the required person in accordance with section 156 of the Act or to an address directed by the person presiding.

Referral of question to commission

180. (1) If the superintendent is of the opinion that a material question affecting the public interest or a novel question of policy or interpretation is raised because of

(a)   an application made to him,

(b)   a record filed with him, or

(c) a matter arising out of the exercise or performance by him of an authorized power or duty,

he may refer the question to the commission for determination.

(2) Where a question is referred under subsection (1), the superintendent shall

(a) state the question in writing, setting out the facts on which it is based, and

(b) file with the commission the written question together with additional information he considers relevant.

(3) The commission shall, without delay, send the material filed under subsection (2)(b) to the person who made the application or who filed the document out of which the question arose.

[S. 180(2)(b) and (3) am. B.C. Reg. 24/87, Sch., s. 8.]

(4) Notice of any hearing to be held by the commission under this section shall be

(a) given to all persons who the commission considers or who, in the opinion of the superintendent, are interested parties, and

(b) sufficiently given if published in the periodical referred to in section 152.

(5) The commission shall consider and determine a question referred to it under this section by holding a hearing, and may remit any matter to the superintendent for a decision in accordance with its determination.

See Local Policy Statement 3-12 "Rules for Proceedings".

PART 18

GENERAL PROVISIONS

Division (1)
Miscellaneous

Escrow agent

181. No person shall act as escrow agent with respect to any agreement filed with the superintendent without the permission of the superintendent.

[S. 79 renumbered as s. 181 B.C. Reg. 305/88, s. 39.]

Transition authorization

181.1 The commission is authorized to vary the provisions of this regulation as they apply to any person or class of persons to provide transition provisions respecting amendments to this regulation other than amendments made under section 159(1)(3) of the Act.

[S. 181.1 en. B.C. Reg. 305/88, s. 40.]

See BOR 88/3 "Transitional rules respecting securities traded prior to September 1, 1988 under an exemption from Section 42 of the Securities Act".

Execution and certification of documents

182. Except as otherwise provided in the Act or this regulation,

(a) where a record is required or permitted to be filed by an individual and required to be signed or certified, it shall be manually signed by the individual immediately above his typewritten or printed name,

(b) subject to paragraphs (c) and (d), where a record is required or permitted to be filed by a person other than an individual and required to be signed or certified, it shall be manually signed by an officer or director of that person or, subject to paragraph (e), by the attorney or agent of that person, immediately above the typewritten or printed name of the officer, director, attorney or agent signing it,

(c) where a partner signs or certifies on behalf of a professional partnership, he is not required to sign his name,

    (d)   where an individual other than a partner signs or certifies on behalf of a professional partnership, he shall manually sign his name immediately above his typewritten or printed name, and

    (e)   where a record required or permitted to be filed by a person has been executed by an attorney or agent of that person, a duly completed power of attorney or document of authority authorizing the signing of the record shall be filed with the record.

Fees and filing

    183.(1) There shall be paid to the superintendent for a matter itemized in Column 1 the fee prescribed for that item.

    [Fee schedule re-en. B.C. Reg. 94/88, Sched. 1, s. 2.]

See BOR 92/1 with respect to reduced fees to be paid by members of the press for a subscription to the Weekly Summary and to search a file, and NIN 94/2 "Filing Requirements for Annual Information Forms".

Cheques for fees should be made payable to the "British Columbia Securities Commission" pursuant to NIN 95/24 "Fee Payments under the Securities Act and the Commodity Contract Act".

Item	Column 1	Column 2

1. For registration or renewal of registration as a dealer, excluding security issuers, regardless of the number of categories to which the application relates for a 2 year period

    (a)   for the dealer's chief place of business in the Province $5 000

    (b)   for each branch office of the dealer in the Province   100

    [Item 1 am. B.C. Reg. 66/89, Sched., s. 1(a).]

2. For registration or renewal of registration as a security issuer, for a one year period   2 500

    [Item 2 am. B.C. Reg. 66/89, Sched., s. 1(b).]

3. For registration or renewal of registration as a salesman, partner, director or officer of a dealer in the Province, other than as a salesman of a security issuer, for a 2 year period   500

4. For registration or renewal of registration as a salesman of a security issuer, for a one year period   500

5. For registration or renewal of registration as an underwriter, for a 2 year period   5 000

    [Item 5 am. B.C. Reg. 66/89, Sched., s. 1(c).]

6. For registration or renewal of registration as an adviser, regardless of the number of categories to which the application relates, for a 2 year period

    (a)   for the adviser's chief place of business in the Province   3 000

    (b)   for each branch office of the adviser in the Province   100

7. For registration or renewal of registration as a partner, director or officer of an adviser in the Province, for a 2 year period   500

8. For reinstatement of the registration of a salesman, partner, director or officer from one dealer to another dealer   100

9. For reinstatement of the registration of a partner, director or officer from one adviser to another   100

10. For notification of change under section 28(1) or (2) of the Act   100

    [Item 10 am. B.C. Reg. 66/89, Sched., s. 1(d).]

11. For recognition as an exempt purchaser   2 000

12. In addition to any fees paid under item 13,

   (a) for filing a preliminary prospectus or pro forma prospectus

      (i) where that preliminary prospectus or pro forma prospectus relates to only one type, class or series of security   2 500

      (ii) where that preliminary prospectus or pro forma prospectus relates to more than one type, class or series of security,

         (A) the fee set out in subparagraph (i) for each issuer, and

         (B) for each additional type, class or series of security for each issuer   500

    or

   (b) for filing a preliminary prospectus where no distribution is contempleted   2 500

[Item 12 re-en. B.C. Reg. 39/94, Sched., s. 1(a).]

13. In addition to any fees paid under item 12, for filing a preliminary prospectus or pro forma prospectus where both an issuer and a security holder are proposing to distribute securities   1 000

[Item 13 re-en. B.C. Reg. 39/94, Sched., s. 1(b).]

14. For filing a prospectus, the amount, if any, by which

   (a) .03% or

   (b) in the case of a money market mutual fund, 0.01%

of the proceeds realized by the issuer or security holder from the distribution under the prospectus to purchasers in the Province exceeds the aggregate of the fees paid under items 12 and 13, which amount shall be paid in accordance with subsections (3) and (4)

[Item 14 re-en. B.C. Reg. 66/89, Sched., s. 1(f).]

15. For filing a statement of material facts   1 500

[Item 15 am. B.C. Reg. 134/91, Sched., s. 1(a).]

16. For filing an annual information form by an issuer other than a mutual fund   1 000

17. For filing an amendment to a preliminary prospectus, prospectus, annual information form or statement of material facts   250

18. For filing a technical or engineering report with

   (a) a preliminary prospectus, pro forma prospectus, prospectus, annual information form, amendment to a preliminary prospectus or prospectus   500

   (b) an application under section 153 of the Act for revocation or variation of a decision in respect of the reactivation of a dead or dormant company   500

[Item 18 re-en. B.C. Reg. 66/89, Sched., s. 1(g).]

19. For filing a notice by an issuer of its intention to offer securities under section 55(2)(7) and (13) of the Act   500

19.1 For filing a notice by a registrant of its intention to enter into a networking arrangement under section 167.10 of this regulation   750

[Item 19.1 en. B.C. Reg. 130/92, Sched., s. 1(a).]

20. Subject to item 21, for filing an application to the commission or the superintendent for a decision under the Act, this regulation, another enactment or a policy statement, where no other fee for that filing is prescribed   750

[Item 20 re-en. B.C. Reg. 39/94, Sched., s. 1(c).]

21. In addition to the fee paid under item 20, where the applicant requests an application filed under item 20 be expedited, or where the commission or the superintendent determines that an application filed under item 20 is complex, an additional fee   1 250

[Item 21 am. B.C. Reg. 134/91, Sched., s. 1(c).]

22. For filing a report

(a) under section 132 of this regulation, other than for a distribution under section 55(2)*(8)* or *(11)*(i) of the Act, or pursuant to the terms of an order made under section 59 of the Act, the greater of

(i) $100, or

(ii) .03% or, in the case of a money market mutual fund, .01% of the proceeds realized by the issuer from the distribution of the securities described in the report to purchasers in the Province, or

(b) under section 132 of this regulation, for a distribution under section 55(2)*(8)* or *(11)*(i) of the Act   100

[Item 22 re-en. B.C. Reg. 66/89, Sched., s. 1(h); am. B.C. Reg. 97/95, s. 2.]

23. For filing an annual financial statement by a reporting issuer, as required under section 136 of this regulation, where the statement is filed

(a) by an exchange issuer

(i) within the prescribed time period   850

(ii) outside the prescribed time period   1 050

(iii) outside the prescribed time period and the commission or superintendent has ordered that trading in the securities of the issuer cease and the order has not been revoked   1 350

(b) by a reporting issuer other than an exchange issuer

(i) within the prescribed time period   600

(ii) outside the prescribed time period   800

(iii) outside the prescribed time period and the commission or superintendent has ordered that trading in the securities of the issuer cease and the order has not been revoked   1 100

[Item 23 re-en. B.C. Reg. 39/94, Sched., s. 1(d).]

23.1 For filing an interim financial statement by a reporting issuer, as required under section 135 of this regulation, where the statement is filed

(a) within the prescribed time period, no fee is payable,

(b) outside the prescribed time period   200

(c) outside the prescribed time period and the commission or superintendent has ordered that trading in the securities of the issuer cease and the order has not been revoked   500

[Item 23.1 re-en. B.C. Reg. 39/94, Sched., s. 1(e).]

24. For filing a take over bid circular or issuer bid circular   750

25. For filing an application under section 153 of the Act for revocation or variation of a decision in respect of the reactivation of a dead or dormant company   2 500

[Item 25 re-en. B.C. Reg. 66/89, Sched., s. 1(k).]

26. For filing a prospecting syndicate agreement   250

Regulation

27. Where no other fee is prescribed, for filing, under the Act or this regulation, a record other than

   (a) a press release under section 67(1)(a), 83(3)(c), 93(1)(a) or (2)(a), 94(1) or (2) of the Act or section 147 of this regulation,

   (b) a report under section 67(1)(b) of the Act,

   (c) personal information under section 73.1 of the Act,

   (d) an acknowledgment and undertaking under section 128 of this regulation, or

   (e) a copy of an offering meorandum under section 131 of this regulation   25

   [Item 27 re-en. B.C. Reg. 39/94, Sched., s. 1(f).]

28. For search of a file   6

29. For a copy of a record in the public file of the commission, for each page   50¢

30. For the certification of a record

   (a) for the number of pages, up to and including 10, included in the record   10

   (b) for each additional page over 10 included in the record   1

   [Item 30 re-en. B.C. Reg. 39/94, Sched., s. 1(g).]

31. The fees and charges for an examination or investigation by a person appointed under section 9 or 137 of the Act are an amount equal to the amount paid by the commission for the examination or investigation, not exceeding fees of $1 000 for each day of the examination or investigation plus all charges for the costs of the examination or investigation

32. The fees and charges for an investigation by a person appointed under section 126 or 131 of the Act are an amount equal to the amount paid by the commission or the minister for the investigation, not exceeding fees of $1 000 for each day of the investigation plus all charges for the costs of the investigation

33. The fees and charges for the costs of or related to a hearing may include

   (a) administrative costs, in the amount of $1 000 for each day or partial day of hearing,

   (b) costs for time spent on investigation and on other matters preliminary to the hearing by the commission or the superintendent or the staff of either of them, in the amount of $50 per hour for each person involved,

   (c) disbursements properly incurred by the commission or the superintendent or the staff of either of them,

   (d) fees paid to an expert or witness, in the amount of the actual fees paid to a maximum of $200 per hour for each person involved,

   (e) disbursements properly incurred by an expert,

   (f) costs for legal services in the amount of the actual fees paid to a maximum of $200 per hour for each person involved, and

   (g) disbursements properly incurred in connection with the provision of legal services

34. For filing an application for a certificate confirming that a reporting issuer is not in default of any requirement of the Act or regulations   100

   [Items 31 and 32 re-en. as items 31-34 B.C. Reg. 307/88, Sched. 1.]

34.1 For filing a report under section 67(2) of the Act   100

   [Item 34.1 en. B.C. Reg. 39/94, Sched., s. 1(h).]

35. For filing a report required under section 70 of the Act, where the report is filed

    (a) within the required time period, no fee is payable,

    (b) outside the required time period   50

[Item 35 en. B.C. Reg. 66/89, Sch., s. 1(m).]

36. For an annual subscription to the periodical referred to in section 152,

    (a) where picked up by the subscriber from the commission   300

    (b) where mailed by the commission by first class mail to anywhere in Canada or the United States   350

    (c) where mailed by the commission overseas   500

[Item 36 en. B.C. Reg. 130/92, Sched., s. 1(a).]

37. For an approval of a waiver of the appointment of an auditor under section 203(3)(b) of the *Company Act*   100

[Item 37 en. B.C. Reg. 39/94, Sched., s. 1(h).]

38. For a consent to the restoration of a company or extraprovincial company to the register under section 286(4)(d) of the *Company Act*   100

[Item 38 en. B.C. Reg. 39/94, Sched., s. 1(h).]

39. For filing a listing application under Local Policy Statement 3-19   1 500

[Item 39 en. B.C. Reg. 39/94, Sched., s. 1(h).]

40. For a waiver under Part XII of National Policy Statment No. 41   100

[Item 40 en. B.C. Reg. 39/94, Sched., s. 1(h).]

(1.1) Where the commission considers it to be in the public interest the commission may order that any or all of items 28, 29 and 36 of subsection (1)

    (a) be varied by reducing the fee payable, or

    (b) do not apply

in respect of a person who is a representative of the media or any class of persons who are representatives of the media.

[S. 183 (1.1) en. B.C. Reg. 130/92, s. 1(b).]

(2) Where a record is filed with the commission, the superintendent or a designated organization and the record has not been completed in accordance with the Act or this regulation, the commission, the superintendent or the designated organization may return the record to the person by whom it has been filed, and no refund of the fee or any part of it paid upon the filing of the record shall be made unless the commission, the superintendent or the designated organization otherwise directs.

[S. 183(2) re-en. B.C. Reg. 94/88, Sched. 1, s. 2.]

(3) For the purposes of the fee payable under item 14 of subsection (1),

    (a) where the prospectus relates to securities that are not distributed continuously, the issuer or security holder must file

        (i) with the prospectus, an estimate of the proceeds that will be realized from the distribution under the prospectus to purchasers in the Province, accompanied by,

            (A) if the superintendent so requires, an advance of the prescribed fee based on the estimate of the proceeds, or

            (B) in any other case, an undertaking to pay the prescribed fee not more than 30 days after the completion of the distribution under the prospectus, and

        (ii) not more than 30 days after the completion of the distribution under the prospectus, a notice of the proceeds realized from the distribution under the prospectus to purchasers in the Province and, subject to subsection (4), the notice must be accompanied by the prescribed fee, or

(b) where the prospectus relates to securities that are distributed continuously, the issuer or security holder must file a notice of the proceeds realized from the distribution under the prospectus to purchasers in the Province, accompanied by the prescribed fee, on the earlier of

(i) the date a new prospectus relating to the securities is filed under section 51 of the Act, or

(ii) 13 months from the date of the prospectus.

[S. 183(3) re-en. B.C. Reg. 66/89, Sched., s. 2; am. B.C. Reg. 39/94, Sched., s. 2.]

(4) Where an advance was paid as required under subsection (3) (a) (i) (A), the notice filed under subsection (3)(a)(ii) shall be accompanied by

(a) the amount by which the prescribed fee exceeds the advance, or

(b) a request for a refund of the amount by which the advance exceeds the prescribed fee.

[S. 183(4) re-en. B.C. Reg. 66/89, Sched., s. 3.]

(5) A designated organization that is authorized under the Registration Transfer Regulation to exercise a power or perform a duty of the superintendent in respect of which a fee is payable to the superintendent under items 1, 3, 8, 10 and 27 to 29 of subsection (1) shall collect the fee and, subject to the Retention of Fees by Self Regulatory Organizations Regulation made by the Treasury Board, remit the fee to the superintendent within 7 business days after the last day of the month in which the power was exercised or the duty was performed.

[S. 183(5) am. B.C. Reg. 94/88, Sched. 1, s. 4.]

(6) In this section

"cash equivalents" means cash or evidences of deposit issued or fully guaranteed by a bank or by a loan corporation or trust company registered under applicable federal or provincial legislation, where the bank, loan corporation or trust company has obtained, from rating agencies approved by the commission, a credit rating for its short term indebtedness that meets or exceeds the credit rating required by the commission;

"money market mutual fund" means a mutual fund that has

(a) all of its assets invested in one or more of the following:

(i) cash equivalents or evidences of indebtedness maturing in 13 months or less;

(ii) government indebtedness maturing in 25 months or less;

(iii) floating rate indebtedness where the principal amounts of the indebtedness have a market value of approximately par at the time of each change in the rate to be paid to the holders of the indebtedness,

(b) a portfolio with a dollar-weighted average term to maturity not exceeding the period specified by the commission,

(c) not less than 95% of its assets invested in cash equivalents or securities, which assets are denominated in the same currency as the units of the mutual fund, and

(d) not less than 95% of its assets invested in cash equivalents or evidences of indebtedness of issuers that have obtained, from rating agencies approved by the commission, a credit rating for their commercial paper that meets or exceeds the credit rating required by the commission.

[S. 183(6) en. B.C. Reg. 66/89, Sched., s. 4; re-en. B.C. Reg. 39/94, Sched., s. 3.]

Division (2)
Prospecting Syndicates

Interpretation

184. In this Division

"agreement" means prospecting syndicate agreement;

"member" means a member of a syndicate;

"syndicate" means prospecting syndicate;

"vendor unit" means a unit of the syndicate issued in consideration for the transfer to the syndicate of mining properties.

185. Limitation of liability.—Where an agreement is filed and a receipt issued for it, the liability of the members under it or of the parties to it is limited to the extent provided by its terms where

    (a) the sole purpose of the syndicate is to finance prospecting expeditions, to develop preliminary mining or to acquire mining properties, or to do any combination of those things,

    (b) the agreement clearly sets out the terms that are set out in section 186, and

[S. 185(b) am. B.C. Reg. 305/88, s. 41.]

    (c) the agreement limits the capital of the syndicate to $250,000.

186. Terms of the agreement.—For the purposes of section 185, the terms of an agreement shall clearly set out

    (a) the purpose of the syndicate,

    (b) the particulars of any transaction, effected or contemplated, which involves the issue of units in the syndicate for consideration other than cash,

    (c) the maximum amount that may be charged or taken by a person as commission on the sale of units in the syndicate,

    (d) that the maximum amount that may be charged or taken by a person as commission on the sale of units in the syndicate will not exceed 25% of the sale price,

    (e) the maximum number of vendor units in the syndicate that may be issued,

    (f) that the maximum number of vendor units in the syndicate will not exceed 1/3 of the total number of units of the syndicate,

    (g) the location of the principal office of the syndicate,

    (h) that the principal office will at all times be maintained in the Province,

    (i) that the superintendent and the members of the syndicate will be notified immediately of any change in the location of the principal office,

    (j) that a person holding mining properties for the syndicate will execute a declaration of trust in favour of the syndicate for those mining properties,

    (k) that, after the sale for cash of any issued units of the syndicate, no mining properties will be acquired by the syndicate, other than by staking, without the approval of those members holding at least 2/3 of the issued units of the syndicate that have been sold for cash,

    (l) that the administrative expenditures of the syndicate, including salaries, office expenses, advertising and commissions paid by the syndicate with respect to the sale of its units, will be limited to 1/3 of the total amount received by the syndicate from the sale of its units,

    (m) that a statement of the receipts and disbursements of the syndicate will be sent to the superintendent and to each member yearly,

    (n) that 90% of the vendor units will be escrowed units that may be released with the consent of the superintendent,

    (o) that any release of vendor units will not be in excess of one vendor unit for each unit of the syndicate sold for cash, and

    (p) that no securities, other than those of the syndicate, and no mining properties owned by or held in trust for the syndicate, will be disposed of without the approval of those members holding at least 2/3 of the issued units, other than escrowed units, of the syndicate.

[S. 186 am. B.C. Reg. 305/88, s. 42.]

Receipt for filed agreement

187. (1) The superintendent may, in his discretion, issue a receipt for an agreement that is filed with him.

(2) The superintendent is not required to determine whether the agreement conforms to each provision of section 186 when issuing the receipt.

Copies of filed agreement

188. The prospector shall send a copy of the filed agreement to each person purchasing units in the syndicate before he accepts payment for the units.

Prohibition of trading by dealer

189. No dealer shall trade, as agent for a syndicate or as a principal, in a security that is issued by the syndicate.

Hearing required if receipt refused

190. The superintendent shall not refuse to issue a receipt under section 187 without first giving the person who filed the agreement an opportunity to be heard.

[S. 190 am. B.C. Reg. 305/88, s. 43.]

REGISTRATION TRANSFER REGULATION

B.C. Reg. 286/86

> See s. 159(2) of the Act with respect to application.

Interpretation

1. In this regulation

"Act" means the *Securities Act*, S.B.C. 1985, c. 83;

"prescribed fee" means the fee prescribed in the Securities Regulation.

Delegation of powers and duties of the superintendent

2. For the purpose of the definition of "designated organization" in section 1 of the Act and for the purposes of section 159 of the Act, the Vancouver Stock Exchange and the Pacific District of the Investment Dealers' Association of Canada are each given authority by sections 5 to 8 to exercise the superintendent's powers and to perform his duties, as specifically set out in sections 5 to 8, and each of those organizations is referred to in this regulation as a designated organization.

Application

3. (1) An application

(a) by a member of a designated organization for registration or renewal of registration as a broker, or investment dealer or as a salesman of one of them,

(b) by an individual for permission under section 62(1) of the Securities Regulation to trade as a partner or officer of a member of a designated organization, or

(c) for approval under section 59(1) of the Securities Regulation of the employment of a salesman by a member of a designated organization

shall, subject to subsections (2) and (3) and to section 159(2) of the Act, be made to the designated organization instead of to the superintendent.

(2) An applicant who is a member of both designated organizations may, subject to subsections (3) and (5), make an application under subsection (1) to either designated organization.

(3) On filing an application with one designated organization, a broker, or investment dealer or an applicant for registration as one of them may not, without the written consent of the superintendent, make an application under subsection (1) to the other designated organization in the same or a subsequent year.

(4) An application under subsection (1) for registration or renewal of registration

as a salesman, or for approval of the employment of a salesman, shall be made to the designated organization to which the employer or prospective employer made application.

(5) Notwithstanding subsection (4), all applications under subsection (1) for

(a) registration or renewal of registration as a salesman, or

(b) approval of the employment of a salesman

who is to be restricted to trading on the floor of the Vancouver Stock Exchange shall be made to the Vancouver Stock Exchange.

Further applications

4. Where

(a) an application by a member of a designated organization under section 2 for registration is refused by the designated organization, and

(b) there are new facts pertinent to the application or circumstances material to the application have changed,

another application may be made, pursuant to section 23 of the Act, to the designated organization instead of to the superintendent.

Powers and duties under sections 20 to 22 of the Act

5. (1) A designated organization is authorized, on application by an applicant who is a member of the designated organization and on payment of the prescribed fee,

(a) to grant registration as a broker or investment dealer or as a salesman, partner, director or officer of either a broker or investment dealer, where, in the opinion of the designated organization, the applicant is suitable for registration and the proposed registration is not objectionable,

(b) after giving the applicant an opportunity to be heard, to refuse to grant a registration referred to in paragraph (a) where, in the opinion of the designated organization, the applicant is not suitable for registration and the proposed registration is objectionable,

(c) to grant renewal of a registration referred to in paragraph (a),

(d) to attach to a registration or renewal of registration under paragraph (a) or (c), the terms, conditions or restrictions the designated organization deems necessary, and

(e) for the purpose of section 25 of the Act, to approve the employment of a salesman by a person where the person is registered for trading in securities and is a member of the designated organization.

(2) The powers a designated organization is authorized to exercise under subsection (1)(c) and (e) do not include the power to refuse

(a) to grant renewal of a registration, or

(b) to approve the employment of a salesman by a person registered for trading in securities.

(3) Where a designated organization grants registration to an applicant, it is authorized to give a written notice of the registration to the applicant for the purposes of section 20(3) of the Act.

Power under section 23

6. A designated organization is, with respect to its members, authorized to grant leave to an applicant pursuant to section 23 of the Act.

Powers under section 24 of the Act

7. A designated organization is, with respect to its members, authorized to exercise the superintendent's powers under section 24 of the Act.

Powers under section 21(2) of the Act

8. (1) A designated organization is authorized to refuse registration, pursuant to section 21(2) of the Act, where an applicant or an officer or director of an applicant is not a resident of the Province on the date of application, unless, at the time of application, the applicant or his officer or director

(a) is registered in a capacity corresponding to that of a dealer, underwriter, adviser, salesman, partner or officer under the law of the jurisdiction respecting trading in securities in which he last resided, and

(b) has been so registered for at least one year immediately before the date of application.

(2) The designated organization shall not refuse to grant, renew, reinstate or amend a registration without giving the applicant an opportunity to be heard.

Notices

9. Where a registered broker, investment dealer or salesman is a member of a designated organization, he shall, instead of notifying the superintendent, notify the designated organization within 5 business days after any event in respect of which a broker, investment dealer or salesman is required to notify the superintendent pursuant to section 28 of the Act and section 68 of the Securities Regulation.

Records

10. (1) A designated organization shall keep

(a) every application made to it under this regulation,

(b) a copy of every certificate of registration granted by it under this regulation,

(c) records of every decision made by the designated organization under this regulation respecting registration including the reasons for the decision where reasons are provided,

(d) a copy of every approval under section 5(1)(e), and

(e) every notice delivered under section 9.

(2) A designated organization shall permit the public to inspect at the designated organization's place of business any document required to be kept under subsection (1).

[Provisions of the *Securities Act* relevant to the enactment of this regulation: section 159(2)]

SECURITIES ACT

INDEX OF FORMS

Effective June 30, 1995

Form #	Title	Securities Act or Regulation Section or Form
1	Summons to attend before an investigator under section 128 of the Act	Reg 170
2	Affidavit of service	Reg 171
3	Application for registration as dealer, advisor or underwriter	Act 20(2)
4	Uniform application for registration/approval	Act 20(2) & 73.1
4A	(Abbreviated application for registration/approval – mutual fund salesman of financial institution)	Act 20(2)
4B	Personal information for directors, officers, promoters, & control persons	Act 73.1
5	Uniform application for renewal of licence or registration	Act 20(2)
6	Reserved	
7	Application for amendment of registration as dealer, advisor or underwriter	Act 20(2), 28(1) & (2)
7A	Application for transfer/change of status	Act 20(2) & 28(3)
8	Summons for an examination under section 24(c) of the Act	Reg 19
9-10	Reserved	
11	Application for exempt purchaser status	Reg 75
12	Information required in prospectus of industrial issuer	Act 42(2) See NIN#93/23
12A	Information required in prospectus of junior industrial issuer	Act 42(2) see NIN#94/18 effective 01/06/95
13	Information required in prospectus of finance issuer	Act 42(2) See NIN#93/23
14	Information required in prospectus of natural resource issuer	Act 42(2) See NIN#93/23
14A	Information required in prospectus of natural resource issuer	Act 42(2) See NIN#95/17 effective 08/01/95
15	Information required in prospectus of mutual fund	Act 42(2) See NIN#93/23
16	Escrow agreement (relating to performance shares)	Reg 117(d)(iii)(B) & 134(6)(b)(i)

Form #	Title	Securities Act or Regulation Section or Form
17	Revoked (03/01/90)	
18	Revoked (09/01/88)	
19	Reserved	
20	Report of exempt distribution	Reg 132
20A	Acknowledgement and undertaking Draft Form 20A (IP and NIP) - see NIN#94/15	Reg 128
21, 21A & 22	Revoked (09/01/88)	
23	Notice of intention to sell and declaration pursuant to section 117(c) and (d) of the Securities Regulation	Reg 129
24	Statement of material facts	Reg 121(b) (formerly Reg 116)
25	Put option contract	Act 58(1)(b)(iii) (formerly Act 58(b))
26	Call option contract	Act 58(1)(b)(iii) (formerly Act 58(b))
27	Material change report under section 67(1) of the Act	Act 67(1) & Reg 144
28	Annual filing of reporting issuer	Reg 167(2) (formerly Reg 146) See NIN#93/23
29	Finance company questionnaire and financial report	Reg 142
30	Information circular	Act 31(2)(9)(i), 55(2)(8)(i), 101(2)(a) & (b) & 101(5) see NIN#93/23 and NIN#95/16 (amendment effective 07/01/95)
31	Notice of intention to make an issuer bid	Act 81(f)
32	Take over bid circular	Act 90(7)
33	Issuer bid circular	Act 90(7)
34	Directors' circular	Act 91(8)
35	Director's or officer's circular	Act 91(8)
36	Insider report	Act 70(2) & (4) & Reg 130 see NIN#95/14 and NIN#95/15
37	Reserved	
38	Report by a registered owner of securities beneficially owned by an insider required under section 71 of the Act	Act 71 & Reg 151

Form #	Title	Securities Act or Regulation Section or Form
39	Report of a mutual fund manager required under section 109 of the Act	Act 109
40	Endorsement of warrant	Act 139(1)
41	Statement of executive compensation	Form 30, Item 6 see NIN#93/23
42	Reserved	
43	Offering memorandum	Reg 126(c)
43A	Offering memorandum – immigrant investor program	Reg 126(c)
44-49	Reserved	
50	Short form of prospectus of a mutual fund	Act 42(3) (formerly Reg 95)
51	Annual information form of a mutual fund	Reg 93(2)(b) (formerly Reg 94)
52	Financial statements of a mutual fund	Reg 105(1) & 138 (formerly Reg 104(1))
53	Trust agreement	Reg 25
54	Technical report on mineral properties excluding oil and gas	Reg 102
55	Technical report on oil and gas properties	Reg 102
56-57	Reserved	NIN#94/26
58	Information Statement required under section 32(g) of the Act For Not-For-Profit Organizations	Act 32(g)
59	Reserved	
60	Subordination agreement	Reg 26
61	Quarterly report	Reg 145 see NIN#89/5 and NIN#95/19 (amendment effective 07/31/95)
62-68	Reserved	
69	Conflict of interest rules statement	Reg 167.3(1)
70	Statement and undertaking pursuant to section 167.3(4) of the Securities Regulation	Reg 167.3(4)
	Fee Checklist – Securities Regulation	Reg 183(1)

INDEX OF REFERENCES TO A
REQUIRED FORM WHERE NO FORM IS SPECIFIED

Effective June 30, 1995

Securities Act or Regulation Section or Form	Form or Requirement	Title
Act 31(2)(21) 55(2)(18) & Reg 117(d)(iii)(B) 134(2)(b)(i)	No form specified	Escrow agreement (relating to property shares)

Securities Act or Regulation Section or Form	Form or Requirement	Title
Act 31(2)(21) 55(2)(18) & Reg 117(d)(iii)(B) 134(2)(b)(i) 134(6)(b)(i)	No form specified	Pooling agreement
Act 101(1)	No form specified but must comply with items 1 and 2 of Form 30	Form of proxy
Reg 22(b)	No form specified	Underwriter's calculation of net free capital
Reg 152.1	No form specified	Form of signature and certification

This is the form required under section 170 of the Securities Regulation for a summons to a person to attend before an investigator under section 128 of the Securities Act.

FORM 1

Securities Act

IN THE MATTER OF THE SECURITIES ACT
S.B.C. 1985, c. 83

AND

IN THE MATTER OF

SUMMONS TO ATTEND BEFORE AN INVESTIGATOR
UNDER SECTION 128

TO: [NAME]
              [ADDRESS]

      TAKE NOTICE that I have been appointed by order of the [British Columbia Securities Commission/Minister of Finance and Corporate Relations] dated the _____ day of _____, 19__ to make an investigation in the matter noted above. In connection with that investigation you are required to attend before me to give evidence on oath at the time, date and place set out below. You are also required to bring with you all records and things in your possession or power relating to _____ [including:].

      TIME:

      DATE:

      PLACE:

DATED AT Vancouver, British Columbia this _____ day of _____ 19 ____.

_____
Investigator

Please note the provisions of the Securities Act attached hereto.

Securities Act S.B.C. 1985, c. 83

Investigation order by commission

126(1) The commission may, by order, appoint a person to make an investigation the commission considers expedient

    (a) for the administration of this Act,

    (b) to assist in the administration of the securities laws of another jurisdiction,

    (c) in respect of matters relating to trading in securities in the Province, or

    (d) in respect of matters in the Province relating to trading in securities in another jurisdiction.

  (2) The commission shall, in its order, specify the scope of an investigation to be carried out under subsection (1).

Investigator's power at hearing

128(1) An investigator appointed under section 126 or 131 has the same power

    (a) to summon and enforce the attendance of witnesses,

    (b) to compel witnesses to give evidence on oath or in any other manner, and

    (c) to compel witnesses to produce records and things

as the Supreme Court has for the trial of civil actions, and the failure or refusal of a witness

    (d) to attend,

(e) to take an oath,

(f) to answer questions, or

(g) to produce the records and things in his custody or possession

makes the witness, on application to the Supreme Court, liable to be committed for contempt as if in breach of an order or judgment of the Supreme Court.

(2) Section 38 of the *Evidence Act* does not exempt any financial institution, as defined in section 37 of that Act, or any officer or employee of the institution from the operation of this section.

(3) A witness giving evidence at an investigation conducted under section 126 or 131 may be represented by counsel.

Investigation order by minister

131(1) The minister may, by order, appoint a person to make an investigation the minister considers expedient

(a) for the administration of this Act,

(b) to assist in the administration of the securities laws of another jurisdiction,

(c) in respect of matters relating to trading in securities in the Province, or

(d) in respect of matters in the Province relating to trading in securities in another jurisdiction.

(2) The minister shall, in his order, specify the scope of an investigation to be carried out under subsection (1).

Evidence not to be disclosed

132   No person, without the consent of the commission, shall disclose, except to his counsel, any information or evidence obtained or the name of any witness examined or sought to be examined under section 127, 128 or 129.

Note: You are entitled to be paid the same personal allowances for your attendance at the investigation as are paid for the attendance of a witness summoned to attend before the Supreme Court.

This is the form required under section 171 of the Securities Regulation for an affidavit of service.

FORM 2
Securities Act
IN THE MATTER OF THE SECURITIES ACT
S.B.C. 1985, c. 83
AND
IN THE MATTER OF
AFFIDAVIT OF SERVICE

I, [name], [occupation], of [address], Province of British Columbia, MAKE OATH AND SAY AS FOLLOWS:

1.   On [day], the _____ day of _____, 19__, at the hour of _____ o'clock in the ____ noon, I served [name of individual/company] with the following: [list documents served]

(a) [e.g. a true copy of a summons]

(b) [etc.]

(c) [conduct money in the amount of a $]

by leaving the said documents [and the conduct money] with [name], [position with company, where applicable], at [address], in the Province of British Columbia.

2.   True copies of the [list documents served] are attached hereto and marked as Exhibits ["A", "B", "C", etc.] respectively.

SWORN BEFORE ME at the City of   )
Vancouver, in the Province of   )
British Columbia, this   day   )
of , 199 .   )
)
)
)
)
_____   )
A Commissioner for taking   )
Affidavits for British Columbia   )
)
)

_____

Form 3

**Province of
British Columbia**
BC Securities Commission

Check
One
(√) | Securities Act ☐
Commodity
Contract Act ☐

Application for Registration as Dealer, Adviser or Underwriter

Note: Should any space be insufficient for your answers, a statement may be attached and marked as an exhibit cross-referencing each statement to the item to which it pertains providing it is initialled by the applicant and the Commissioner taking the affidavit.

Application is made for registration under the ....Act.

in the category of ....

1. (a) Name of Applicant ....

  (b) Head Office Business Address ....

     Telephone No. ....   Postal Code ....

  (c) Address for service in British Columbia ....

     Telephone No. ....   Postal Code ....

2. The applicant maintains accounts at the following bank(s): (State bank and branches through which business is transacted)

....

....Fiscal Year End:..

3. Is applicant applying for registration of any branch offices? If so, state addresses: ....

....

  INSTRUCTION: Answer "Yes" or "No" to the following questions. If "Yes" give particulars.

4. Has the applicant, or to the best of the applicant's information and belief has any affiliate of the applicant,

  (a) been registered in any capacity under the Securities Act/Commodity Contract Act of British Columbia?........................

....

  (b) applied for registration, in any capacity, under the Securities Act/Commodity Contract Act of British Columbia? ....

....

5. Is the applicant, or to the best of the applicant's information and belief is any affiliate of the applicant, now, or has any such person or company been,

  (a) registered or licensed in any capacity in any other province, state or country which requires registration or licensing to deal or trade in securities? ....

....

  (b) registered or licensed in any other capacity in British Columbia or any other province, state or country under any legislation which requires registration or licensing to deal with the public in any capacity? (e.g. as an insurance agent, real estate agent, private investigator, mortgage broker, etc.) ....

....

  (c) refused registration or a licence mentioned in 5(a) or (b) above or has any registration or licence been suspended or cancelled in any category mentioned in 5(a) or (b) above? ....

....

(d) denied the benefit of any exemption from registration provided by the Securities Act/Commodity Contract Act of British Columbia, or similar exemption provided by securities acts or regulations of any other province, state or country?

....

6. Is the applicant, or to the best of the applicant's information and belief is any affiliate of the applicant, now, or has any such person or company been,

(a) a member of any Stock Exchange, Investment Dealers Association, Investment Bankers, or similar organization, in any province, state or country? ....

....

(b) refused membership in any Stock Exchange, Investment Dealers Association, Investment Bankers, or similar organization, in any province, state or country? ....

....

(c) suspended as member of any Stock Exchange, Investment Dealers Association, Investment Bankers, or similar organization, in any province, state or country? ....

....

7. Has the applicant, or to the best of the applicant's information and belief has any affiliate of the applicant, operated under, or carried on business under, any name other than the name shown in this application? ....

....

8. Has the applicant, or to the best of the applicant's information and belief, has any affiliate of the applicant,

(a) ever been convicted under the law of any province, state or country, excepting minor traffic violations?

....

Is there currently an outstanding charge or indictment against the applicant or affiliate? ....
INSTRUCTION: Question 8(a) refers to all laws, e.g. Criminal, Immigration, Customs, Liquor, etc. of any province, state or country, in any part of the world. You are not required to disclose any convictions for which a pardon has been granted under the Criminal Records Act (Canada), and which pardon has not been revoked.

(b) ever been the defendant or respondent in any proceedings in any civil court in any jurisdiction in any part of the world wherein fraud was alleged? ....

(c) at any time declared bankruptcy, or made a voluntary assignment in bankruptcy? (If "Yes", give particulars and also attach a certified copy of discharge). ....

(d) ever been refused a fidelity / surety bond? ....

9. Set out in the space provided, the name of the applicant, or the name of and position held by each director, officer or partner of the applicant seeking or holding registration.
NOTE: an underwriter may not trade with the public.

Names of persons who will act (In addition to last name, give full first and middle names)	Office Held	Names of persons who will act (In addition to last name, give full first and middle names)	Office Held
1.		5.	
2.		6.	
3.		7.	
4.		8.	

10. Attach and mark as an exhibit:

(a) a completed Form 4 for each director, officer or partner of the applicant seeking or holding registration.

FIN 2003 (2) 87/7

(b) for each person or company who is a director, officer or partner of the applicant and not referred to in clause (a), the information required by Form 4.

(c) In the case of applicants for registration as investment counsel only, a letter from each person who, on behalf of the applicant will give investment advice, outlining directly related experience of such person so as to justify designation by the Director of such person to so act.

11.   A — Capitalization of a Company:

Other than a Security Issuer, complete below or attach marked as an exhibit to the application a statement containing the information called for below, to provide information with respect to the financial structure and control of the applicant company.

(a) The authorized and issued capital of the company, stating:

Preferred Shares: Number................................ $ Value ....

Common Shares: Number................................ $ Value ....

(1) authorized capital ....

(2) issued ....

(3) total dollar value
    of other securities:

    (i) Bonds ....

    (ii) Debentures ....

    (iii) Any other loans, state source and
          maturity dates ....

                                        TOTAL $ ....

(b) The names, addresses and usual place of residence of registered, and direct, and indirect, beneficial owners of each class of security or obligation issued, and, if a trust is the beneficial owner, the names, addresses and usual place of residence of each person or company having a beneficial interest in the trust, and the nature and extent of the holdings and percentage of interest attributable to each security holder, lender or cestui que trust (beneficiary).

(c) State name and address of every depository holding any of the assets of the company:

INSTRUCTIONS: Answer "Yes" or "No" to the following questions. If "Yes" give particulars.

(d) Has any person or company undertaken to act as a guarantor in relation to the financial or other undertakings of the applicant?

....

(e) Has a Subordination Agreement been executed by the creditor(s) in relation to loans owing by the applicant?

....

(f) Is there any person or company whose name is not disclosed in the statement called for by (b) above who has any direct or indirect interest in the applicant, either beneficially or otherwise?

B — Capitalization of a Partnership or Proprietorship:

Attach, marked as an exhibit to the application, a statement containing the information called for below with respect to the assets of the partnership or proprietorship, and demonstrate therein the degree of control (voting power) of each of the participants in the applicant.

(a) Amount of paid-in capital $ ....

(b) Description of the assets:

FIN 2003 (3) 87/7

Forms

(c) State name and address of every depository holding any of the assets:

(d) Source, amount and maturity date of any obligations owing by the partnership, if any:
(Where applicable, give names and addresses of creditors).

INSTRUCTION: Answer "Yes" or "No" to the following questions. If "Yes" give particulars.

(e) Has any person or company undertaken to act as a guarantor in relation to the financial or other undertakings of applicant?

....

(f) Has a Subordination Agreement been executed by the creditor(s) in relation to loans owing by the applicant?

....

(g) Is there any person or company whose name is not disclosed above who has any interest in the applicant, either beneficially or otherwise?.

....

....

DATED at ....
                                                    (Name of Applicant)

this .... day of .... 19 .... By ....
                                             (Signature of applicant, director, officer or partner)

                                             ....
                                                (Official capacity)

AFFIDAVIT
In the matter of the Securities Act / Commodity Contract Act

Province of British Columbia   I, ...
                                                   (Name in full)

.... of ....   }   of the ....

To Wit: in the Province of ....

MAKE OATH AND SAY:

1. I am the applicant (or a director, officer or partner of the applicant) herein for registration and I signed the application.

2. The statements of fact made in the application are true.

SWORN before me at the ....

in the .... of ....

this .... day of .... 19 ....   }   ....
                                                     (Signature of Deponent)

....
        (A Commissioner, etc.)

It is an offence under the Securities Act/Commodity Contract Act to file an application containing a statement that, at the time and in light of the circumstances in which it is made, is a misrepresentation.

FIN 2003 (4) 87/7

Province of
British Columbia
BC Securities Commission

Check one (√) | Securities Act ☐
Commodity
Contract Act ☐

Form 4
Uniform Application for
Registration/Approval

INSTRUCTIONS

1. This form is to be used by every individual seeking registration or approval from a Canadian Securities Commission or similar authority and/or a self-regulatory organization, or submitting an application for registration or approval as a partner, director or officer of a dealer, broker, adviser or underwriter to a Canadian Securities Commission or similar authority.

2. This form may also be used by any individual submitting an application for registration as a dealer, broker or adviser to a Canadian Securities Commission or similar authority.

3. All applicable questions must be answered. Failure to do so may cause delays in the processing of the application.

4. This form and all attachments added thereto **must be** typewritten. Any form or attachment completed by any other means may be considered not properly filed.

5. All attachments pertaining to any question must be made exhibits to the form and each one must be so marked. All **signatures must be originals.** The Commissioner of Oaths before whom the application is sworn, as well as the applicant, is required to initial all attachments.

6. In completing the application, applicants should seek advice from an authorized officer of the sponsoring firm or from a legal adviser, if necessary.

7. Number of originally-signed copies of the form to be filed with the self-regulatory organization and/or Securities Commission or similar authority varies from province to province. If unsure of the procedure, please consult the Registration Department of the self-regulatory organization through which you are applying or the applicable Securities Commission, or similar authority.

8. Applicants for registration in Quebec need only disclose information for the past 10 years in respect of Questions 15(B), 15(D), 17(A), 17(B), 18 and 19.

FOR INTERNAL USE ONLY

Application approved by	Date

1. APPLICANT:

Last Name	First, Second & Third Names

Residential address (with postal code)	Area Code: Telephone:

Address for service in British Columbia (with postal code)	Social Insurance Number (not required for applications in Ontario)

Present position in the firm	Commenced employment on Year Month Day

2. FIRM:

Name	Area Code: Telephone:

Address where applicant will be working (with postal code)	

FIN 2004 (5) 90/7

3. **TYPE OF REGISTRATION OR APPROVAL REQUESTED:**

INSTRUCTION: Check **ALL** applicable boxes to indicate the registration or approval requested. The "Types of Registration or Approval Requested" have the meaning attributed to them in the applicable securities act, commodity contract act, or regulation and in by-laws, rules and regulations of exchanges, the Investment Dealers Association of Canada and other self-regulatory organizations. Applicants filing for restricted registration should file under OTHER, specifying the nature of the restricted registration applied for.

REGISTERED REPRESENTATIVE OR SALESPERSON REGISTRATION:

☐ Securities
☐ Commodity Futures
☐ Commodity Futures Options
☐ Options
☐ Mutual Funds
☐ Floor Trader — Securities ☐
           — Commodity Futures ☐
☐ Individual Member
☐ Scholarship Plans
☐ Government Incentive Securities
☐ Real Estate Securities
☐ Other (specify) _____

OTHERS:

☐ Partner
☐ Director
☐ Officer (title) _____
           — Trading ☐
           — Non-Trading ☐
           — Counselling ☐
☐ Branch manager
☐ Director, Investor, or Officer of approved affiliated company (delete designation not applicable)
☐ Industry Investor
☐ Non-Industry Investor
☐ Portfolio Manager
☐ Designated/Alternate Registered Options Principal
☐ Designated/Alternate Registered Futures Principal
☐ Designated/Alternate Registered Futures Options Principal
☐ Other (specify) _____

4. **APPLYING FOR REGISTRATION/APPROVAL FROM THE FOLLOWING:**

INSTRUCTION: Check all appropriate boxes to indicate the Canadian Securities Commissions or similar authority and/or self-regulatory organizations with which the applicant is seeking registration or approval.

SECURITIES COMMISSIONS OR SIMILAR AUTHORITIES

☐ Alberta   ☐ New Brunswick   ☐ Nova Scotia   ☐ Quebec
☐ British Columbia   ☐ Newfoundland   ☐ Ontario   ☐ Saskatchewan
☐ Manitoba   ☐ NorthwestTerritories   ☐ Prince Edward Island   ☐ Yukon Territory

SELF-REGULATORY ORGANIZATIONS

☐ Alberta Stock Exchange   ☐ Toronto Stock Exchange
☐ Investment Dealers Association of Canada   ☐ Vancouver Stock Exchange
☐ Montreal Exchange   ☐ Winnipeg Commodity Exchange
☐ Toronto Futures Exchange   ☐ Winnipeg Stock Exchange
     ☐ Other (specify) _____

5. **PERSONAL DESCRIPTION OF APPLICANT:**

(A)

DATE OF BIRTH			PLACE OF BIRTH				Sex
Year	Month	Day	City		Province	Country	
Height	Weight		Colour of eyes	Colour of hair	Name of spouse & nature of his/her employment		
Citizenship			If **NOT** a Canadian Citizen, answer question 5(B) below.				

(B)

Are you a permanent resident?	Number of years of continuous residence in Canada		Passport			
		Country	Place of issue	Date of issue	Number	

FIN 2004 (4) 90/7

6. PHOTOGRAPH:

   INSTRUCTION: Attach hereto two copies of a black and white photograph, full face, showing a true likeness of the applicant as the applicant now appears and *taken within the last 6 months;* they must measure 2" x 2", be of passport quality and bear on the back the date on which the photographs were taken, *the signature of the applicant and that of the Commissioner of Oaths or that of an officer, director, partner or branch manager of the sponsoring firm.*

7. EDUCATION.

   (A)
INSTRUCTION: State the last school attended in each level.	Degree or Diploma	Date Obtained
High School or Secondary Level		
Post-Secondary, College, CEGEP or University		
Professional Education		
Other		

   Have you successfully completed:

	Yes	No	Exempt*	Date Completed
Canadian Securities Course	☐	☐	☐	_____
Examination based on Manual for Registered Representatives	☐	☐	☐	_____
Partners/Directors/Officers Qualifying Examination	☐	☐	☐	_____
Canadian Investment Finance (course 2): Part I	☐	☐	☐	_____
Part II	☐	☐	☐	_____
F.C.S.I.	☐	☐	☐	_____
Chartered Financial Analyst Course	☐	☐	☐	_____
Qualifying Examination for Registered Options Principal	☐	☐	☐	_____
Canadian Options Course	☐	☐	☐	_____
Canadian Investment Funds Course	☐	☐	☐	_____
National Commodity Futures Examination	☐	☐	☐	_____
Canadian Commodity Futures Examination	☐	☐	☐	_____
Canadian Futures Examination	☐	☐	☐	_____
Commodity Supervisors Examination	☐	☐	☐	_____
Branch Manager's Examination	☐	☐	☐	_____
Other (specify) _____				_____

   * If you have been granted exemption, attach full particulars.

   (B) Have you **ever** applied for and been refused exemptions from any of the above listed examination requirements? (If so, give particulars as an attachment). _____

8. EMPLOYMENT HISTORY:

   (A) The following information constitutes full disclosure of your business activities, including any periods of self-employment and unemployment, for 10 years immediately prior to the date of this application, excluding any summer employment while a full-time student, but including **all** securities or commodities industry employment during and prior to the ten-year period.

Name and address of employer	Name and title of immediate superior	Nature of employment and duties of applicant	Reasons for leaving	FROM Yr. Mo.	TO Yr. Mo.
PRESENT:					
PREVIOUS:					

FIN 2004 (6) 90/7

3-14   B.C.S.A. Forms

(B)

Have you *ever* been discharged by an employer for cause? _____
(If so, give particulars as an attachment).

_____
_____

9. **RESIDENTIAL HISTORY:** (give all home addresses for the past 10 years)

Include street, city, province & postal code	FROM yr. mo.	TO yr. mo.
PRESENT:		
PREVIOUS:		

10. **REFERENCES:**
Give three names as references, excluding relatives and persons associated with the sponsoring firm. References must include a bank or trust company at which you have an account (give account number)

Name	Firm Name	Business Address (with postal code) and Telephone (with area code)	Occupation

Account No. at reference bank or trust co.: _____

Note: Account No. need not be given if this form is accompanied by a written reference from a bank or trust co. with which the applicant has an account.

FIN 2004 (3) 90/7

ANSWER "YES" OR "NO" TO EACH OF QUESTIONS 11 TO 20 INCLUSIVE.
IF THE ANSWER TO ANY OF THE FOLLOWING QUESTIONS IS "YES",
COMPLETE DETAILS *MUST BE* ATTACHED BY WAY OF EXHIBIT.

YES/NO

11. **CHANGE OF NAME:**

INSTRUCTION: Name changes resulting from marriage, divorce, court order or any other process must be listed here giving appropriate dates.

Have you *ever* had, used, operated under, or carried on business under any name other than the name mentioned in Question 1 of this form, or have you ever been known under any other name?

Previous Name: _____ Date: _____   _____

12. **PRIOR REGISTRATION OR LICENSING:**

(A) Are you now or have you *ever* been registered or licensed, or applied for registration or a licence in any capacity under any act or regulation thereof, regulating trading in securities, commodities or commodity futures contracts of any province, territory, state or country? List all authorities with whom you were registered and the dates of registration. State whether the registration is currently in effect.

　　Authority: _____ Date: _____

　　Authority: _____ Date: _____

(B) Are you now, or have you *ever* been a partner, shareholder, director or officer of any company or of a partnership which has been registered or licensed, or is now registered or licensed (except as an issuer if you are or have been solely a shareholder) in any capacity under any act or regulation thereof, regulating trading in securities, commodities or commodity futures contracts of any province, territory, state or country?

(C) Are you now or have you ever been registered or licensed, or applied for registration or a licence, under any legislation which requires registration or licensing to deal with the public in any capacity *other than trading in securities, commodities or commodity futures contracts* in any province, territory, state or country?

QUESTIONS 13 TO 18 INSTRUCTION: In answering Question 13 to 18, and particularly Question 15, you may need assistance from an authorized officer of the sponsoring firm or from a legal adviser. Full details are required as attachments in respect of any question to which the applicant answers "yes". These details must include the circumstances, the relevant dates, the names of the parties involved and the final determination if known.

13. **REFUSAL, SUSPENSION, CANCELLATION OR DISCIPLINARY MEASURE**

(A) Have you *ever* been refused registration or a licence, or has your registration or licence been suspended or cancelled, under any act or regulation thereof, regulating trading in securities, commodities or commodity futures contracts of any province, territory, state or country?

(B) Are you now or have you *ever* been a partner, shareholder, director or officer of a company or of a partnership which has, during the time of your association with it, been refused registration (except a registration as an issuer if you are or have been solely a shareholder) or a licence, or whose registration has been suspended or cancelled under the act, or regulation thereof, regulating trading in securities, commodities or commodity futures contracts of any province, territory, state or country?

(C) Have you *ever* been refused registration or a licence, or has your registration or licence been suspended or cancelled, under any legislation which requires registration or licensing to deal with the public in any capacity *other than trading in securities, commodities or commodity futures contracts* in any province, territory, state or country?

(D) Have you been denied the benefit of any exemption from registration or licensing provided by any act or regulation thereof regulating trading in securities, commodities or any commodity futures contracts of any province, territory, state or country?

(E) Has any prior or current registration or licensing to deal or trade in securities, commodities or commodity futures contracts held by you or any partnership or company of which you were at the time of such event a partner, officer or director or holder of voting securities carrying more than 5 percent of the votes carried by all outstanding voting securities *ever* been the subject of disciplinary action undertaken by any authority regulating or supervising trading in securities, commodities, or commodity futures contracts?

FIN 2004 (7) 90/7

B.C.S.A. Forms

14. **SELF-REGULATORY ORGANIZATIONS:**

Have you or has any partnership or company of which you are or were at the time of such event a partner, director, officer or holder of voting securities carrying more than 5% of the votes carried by all outstanding voting securities:

   (A) *Ever* been a member of any stock exchange, commodities exchange, commodity futures exchange, association of investment dealers, investment bankers, brokers, broker-dealers, mutual fund dealers, commodity futures dealers, investment counsel, other professional association or any similar organization in any province, territory, state or country?

   (B) *Ever* been refused registration or licensing or approval for membership or approval in any other capacity by/in any of the institutions or associations described in Question 14A?

   (C) *Ever* been the subject of disciplinary action undertaken by any authority as described in question 14(A)?

15. **OFFENCES UNDER THE LAW**

INSTRUCTION: Offences under such federal statutes as the *Income Tax Act (Canada)* and the *Immigration Act (Canada)* constitute criminal offences and must be disclosed when answering this question. It should be noted that pleas or findings of guilt for impaired driving are *Criminal Code (Canada)* matters and must be disclosed. Where you have pleaded guilty or been found guilty of an offence, such offence must be reported even though an absolute or conditional discharge has been granted.

You are not required to disclose any offence for which a pardon has been granted under the *Criminal Records Act (Canada)* and such pardon has not been revoked. Under such circumstances, the appropriate response would be "No".

If you are in doubt as to previous dealings you have had with law enforcement agencies and the applicability of this question with respect to such encounters, you should obtain the advice of an authorized officer of your sponsor or a legal adviser.

   (A) Past Offences Involving Securities or Commodities —
   Have you *ever* pleaded guilty or been found guilty under any law of any province, territory, state or country of any offence relating to trading in securities, commodities, commodity futures contracts or options or with the theft thereof, or with any related offence, or been a party to any proceedings taken on account of fraud arising out of any trade in or advice in respect thereof?

   (B) Past Offences Involving Other Criminal Offences or Contraventions —
   Have you *ever* pleaded guilty or been found guilty under any law of any province, territory, state or country for contraventions or other criminal offences not noted in (A) above?

   (C) Current Charges or Indictments —
   Are you *currently the subject of a charge or indictment,* under any law of any province, territory, state or country for contraventions, criminal offences or other conduct of the type described in (A) or (B) above?

   (D) Partnership or Company Offences or Current Charges or Indictments —
   Has any partnership or company of which you are or were at the time of such event a partner, officer, director or a holder of voting securities carrying more than 5% of the votes carried by all outstanding voting securities, *ever* pleaded guilty or been found guilty, or is any such partnership or company currently the subject of *a charge or indictment,* under any law of any province, territory, state or country for contraventions, criminal offences or other conduct of the type described in (A) or (B) above?

16. **CIVIL PROCEEDINGS**

Has any claim been made successfully or, to your knowledge, is any claim pending in any civil proceedings before a court or other tribunal in any province, territory, state or country which was, or is, based in whole or in part on fraud, theft, deceit, misrepresentation or similar conduct?

   (A) Against you?

   (B) Against any partnership or company of which you are or were at the time of such event, or at the time such proceedings were commenced, a partner, director, officer or holder of voting securities carrying more than 5% of the votes carried by all outstanding voting securities?

17. BANKRUPTCY

    (A) Under the law of any province, territory, state or country have you **ever**:

        (a) been declared bankrupt or made a voluntary assignment in bankruptcy? _____

        (b) made a proposal under any legislation relating to bankruptcy or insolvency? _____

        (c) been subject to or instituted any proceedings, arrangement or compromise with creditors including, without limitation, produced a declaration under the Quebec Voluntary Deposit of Salary Wages Law or had a receiver and/or manager appointed to hold your assets? _____

        If yes, and if applicable, attach copy of any discharge, release or document with similar effect.

    (B) Has any partnership or corporation of which you are or were at the time of such event a partner, director, officer or holder of voting securities carrying more than 5% of the votes carried by all outstanding voting securities **ever**:

        (a) been declared bankrupt or made a voluntary assignment in bankruptcy? _____

        (b) made a proposal under any legislation relating to bankruptcy or insolvency? _____

        (c) been subject to proceedings under any legislation relating to the winding up, dissolution or companies' creditors arrangements? _____

        (d) been subject to or instituted any proceedings, arrangement or compromise with creditors or had a receiver and/or manager appointed to hold its assets? _____

        If yes, and if applicable, attach copy of any discharge, release or document with similar effect.

18. JUDGEMENT OR GARNISHMENT:

Has any judgement or garnishment **ever** been rendered against you or is any judgement or garnishment outstanding against you, in any civil court in any province, state or country for damages or other relief in respect of a fraud or for any reason whatsoever? _____

19. SURETY BOND OR FIDELITY BOND

    (A) Have you **ever** applied for a surety bond or fidelity bond and been refused? _____

    If yes, attach name and address of bonding company, and when and why the bond was refused.

    (B) Are you presently bonded? _____

20. BUSINESS ACTIVITIES

    (A) Will you be actively engaged in the business of the firm with which you are now applying and devote the major portion of your time thereto? _____

    (B) Are you engaged in any other business or have any other employment for gain except your occupation with the firm with which you are now applying? _____

    If so, **attach full details** including the full name and address of the business, the nature of the business, your title or position and the amount of time you devote to the business.

    (C) Are you a partner, director, officer, shareholder or other contributor of capital of a partnership or of a company having as its principal business that of a broker, dealer or adviser in securities, commodities, commodity futures contracts or options other than the firm with which you are now applying? If so, **attach full details**. _____

21. (A) State the number, value, class and percentage of shares or the amount of partnership interest you own or propose to acquire upon approval. If acquiring shares upon approval, state source, i.e. treasury shares, or if upon transfer, state name of transferor.

    (B) State the value of subordinated debentures or bonds of the firm to be held by you or any other subordinated loan to be made by you to the firm.

    (C) Are you or will you upon approval be the beneficial owner of the shares, bonds, debentures, partnership interest or other notes held by you? If not, state name, residential address and occupation of the beneficial owner.

> **CAUTION**
> FILING OF ANY FALSE INFORMATION OR FAILURE TO DISCLOSE FULL INFORMATION REQUIRED BY OR ON THIS APPLICATION MAY RESULT IN ITS REJECTION OR IN DISCIPLINARY ACTION TAKEN AGAINST THE APPLICANT AND/OR THE SPONSORING FIRM WITHIN THE PROVISIONS OF THE APPLICABLE SECURITIES AND/OR COMMODITY FUTURES LEGISLATION, REGULATIONS AND POLICY STATEMENTS OF THE SECURITIES REGULATORY AUTHORITIES AND WITHIN THE TERMS OF THE BY-LAWS, RULINGS, RULES AND/OR REGULATIONS OF ANY ONE OF THE SELF-REGULATORY ORGANIZATIONS TO WHICH THIS APPLICATION IS SUBMITTED, OR MAY RESULT IN A REFUSAL TO REGISTER THE APPLICANT.

CERTIFICATE AND AGREEMENT OF APPLICANT AND SPONSORING FIRM

The undersigned hereby certify that the forgoing statements are true and correct to the best of our knowledge, information and belief and hereby undertake to notify the self-regulatory organization in writing of any material change therein as prescribed by any by-law or rule of the respective self-regulatory organization

We agree that we are conversant with the by-laws, rulings, rules and regulations of the self-regulatory organizations listed in Question 4.

We agree to be bound by and to observe and comply with them as they are from time to time amended or supplemented, and we agree to keep ourselves fully informed about them as so amended and supplemented. We submit to the jurisdiction of the self-regulatory organizations and, wherever applicable, the Governors, Directors and committees thereof, and we agree that any approval granted pursuant to this application may be revoked, terminated or suspended at any time in accordance with the then applicable by-laws, rulings, rules and regulations. In the event of any such revocation or termination, the undersigned applicant agrees forthwith to terminate his/her association with the undersigned sponsoring firm and thereafter not to accept employment with or perform services of any kind for any member or member house of the self-regulatory organizations or any approved affiliated company or other affiliate of any such member or member house, in each case if and to the extent provided in the then applicable by-laws, rulings, rules and regulations of the self-regulatory organizations. Our obligations above are joint and several.

We agree to the transfer of this application form, without amendment, to another of the self-regulatory organizations listed in Question 4 of this application form in the event that at some time in the future the undersigned applicant applies to such other self-regulatory organization.

The undersigned applicant has discussed the questions in this application and in particular Question 15 and 16 with an officer or branch manager of this firm. The undersigned authorized officer is satisfied that the applicant fully understands the questions, and further certifies on behalf of the sponsoring firm that the applicant will be engaged as registered or approved.

The undersigned applicant acknowledges and consents that any of the self-regulatory organizations may obtain any information whatsoever from any source, as permitted by law in any jurisdiction in Canada or elsewhere.

Dated at _____ this _____ day of _____ 19 _____

_____   _____
(Signature of Applicant)   *(Name of Sponsoring Firm)*

By _____
(Partner or Authorized Officer)

AFFIDAVIT

I, the undersigned applicant, do depose and say that I have read and understand the questions in this application form as well as the answers made by myself thereto and the Caution set out above, and that statements of fact made therein and in the attachments, if any, are true.

Sworn before me _____   _____
(Commissioner of Oaths, etc.)   *(Signature of Deponent)*

at the city of _____ , Province of _____

this _____ day of _____ 19 _____

The Province of Saskatchewan & Manitoba require this affidavit to be sworn before a notary public or barrister or solicitor where the applicant is outside the province at the time of application.

It is an offence under applicable Canadian securities and commodity futures legislation to file an application which contains a statement that, at the time and in light of the circumstances in which it is made, is false or misleading, or which fails to state any material fact.

FIN 2004 (1) 90/7

Province of
British Columbia

BRITISH COLUMBIA SECURITIES COMMISSION

**Form 4A (Draft)
Abbreviated application
for registration/approval-
mutual fund salesman of
financial institution**

General Instructions

1. This form is only to be used by individuals seeking registration from the British Columbia Securities Commission as a mutual fund salesperson while employed by a financial institution.

2. Should any space be insufficient for your answers, complete Schedule A.

3. This form and attachments must be typed. All signatures must be originals. The number of originally signed copies of the form to be filed varies from province to province. Please consult the applicable securities commission.

1. APPLICANT:

	Docket #

Last Name	First, Second & Third Names

Residential Address (with postal code)	Area Code: Work Telephone:
Address for service in province of registration (with postal code)	Social Insurance No. (Not Required in Ont.)
Present position with the dealer	Commenced Employment on Day Month Year

2. DEALER:

Name	Area Code: Telephone:
Address where applicant will be working (street, city, province, postal code)	

3. PERSONAL DESCRIPTION OF APPLICANT

Date of Birth Day Month Year	Place of Birth City Province Country		Sex
Height	Weight	Colour of Eyes	Colour of Hair	For Applicant of Foreign Origin: Place of Entry Date
Citizenship			Father's Name

4. EDUCATION: HAVE YOU SUCCESSFULLY COMPLETED:

	Yes	No	Date Completed
Canadian Investment Funds Course (IFIC)	___	___	_____
Investment Funds in Canada (ICB)	___	___	_____
Principles of Mutual Fund Investment (TCI)	___	___	_____
Other (Specify) _____	___	___	_____

IFIC - Investment Funds Institute of Canada   TCI - Trust Companies Institute
ICB - Institute of Canadian Bankers

5.   EMPLOYMENT HISTORY:

(Yes or No)

   A)   Have you been employed by the sponsoring financial institu-
        tion for less than five years?   _____

        If YES, please disclose fully on Schedule A all business
        activities for the ten-year period immediately before the date
        of this application, including periods when unemployed. Ex-
        clude any summer employment while a full-time student.

   B)   Have you ever been discharged by an employer for cause?   (Yes or No)
        (If YES, give particulars on Schedule A.)   _____

ANSWER "YES" OR "NO" TO ALL OF THE FOLLOWING QUESTIONS. IF THE
ANSWER TO ANY QUESTION (except Question 13) IS "YES", PLEASE GIVE COM-
PLETE DETAILS ON SCHEDULE A.

6.   CHANGE OF NAME: Have you ever had, used, operated under or
     carried on business under any name other than the name men-
     tioned in Question 1, or have you ever been known under any other   (Yes or No)
     name?   _____
     INSTRUCTION: Name changes resulting from marriage, divorce,
     court order or any other process should be listed on Schedule A
     giving appropriate dates.

7.   PRIOR REGISTRATION OR LICENSING:

   A)   Have you ever been registered or licensed in any capacity in
        any province, territory, state or country to deal or trade in
        securities OR to deal with the public in any capacity?   _____

   B)   Have you ever been refused registration or a licence men-
        tioned in A) or has any such registration or license been
        cancelled or suspended for cause?   _____

   C)   Have you ever been denied the benefit of any exemption from
        registration or licensing provided by any legislation regulat-
        ing trading in securities in any province, territory, state or
        country?   _____

   D)   Have you ever been the subject of disciplinary action under-
        taken by any authority regulating or supervising trading in
        securities?   _____

8.   SELF-REGULATORY ORGANIZATIONS:

   A)   Have you ever been a member of any stock exchange, as-
        sociation of investment dealers, brokers, mutual fund
        dealers, investment counsel, other professional association or
        any similar organization of any province, territory, state or
        country?   _____

   B)   Have you ever been refused membership in or approval by
        any of the institutions or associations described in question
        A) above?   _____

   C)   Have you ever been the subject of disciplinary action under-
        taken by any institution or association described in question
        A) above?   _____

9.   OFFENCES UNDER THE LAW: Have you ever been charged,
     indicted or convicted, under the law of any province, territory,
     state or country?   _____
     INSTRUCTION: This question refers to all laws, i.e. Criminal
     Code, income tax, immigration, liquor, etc. of any province, ter-
     ritory, state or country in any part of the world. Minor traffic
     violations need not be disclosed.

10. CIVIL PROCEEDINGS: Have you ever been the defendant or respondent in any proceedings in any civil court in any jurisdiction in any part of the world where fraud, theft, deceit, misrepresentation or similar conduct was alleged against you? _____

11. BANKRUPTCY:

Under the law of any province, territory, state or country have you

A) ever been declared bankrupt or made a voluntary assignment in bankruptcy? _____

B) made a proposal under any legislation relating to bankruptcy or insolvency? _____

C) been subject to or instituted any proceedings, arrangement or compromise with creditors including, without limitation, produced a declaration under the Quebec Voluntary Deposit of Salary Wages Law or had a receiver and/or manager appointed to hold your assets? _____

If YES, and if applicable, attach copy of any discharge, release or document with similar effect.

12. SURETY BOND OR FIDELITY BOND: Have you ever applied for a surety bond or fidelity bond and been refused? _____

13. BUSINESS ACTIVITIES: Will you be employed full time in the business of the firm with which you are now applying and its sponsoring financial institution? If NO, give details on Schedule A of any other business or employment for gain that you are engaged in. _____

CERTIFICATE OF APPLICANT AND SPONSORING DEALER

The undersigned hereby certify that the foregoing statements are true and correct to the best of our information and belief.

The undersigned applicant acknowledges and agrees that any Canadian securities commission may obtain any information whatsoever from any source as permitted by law in any jurisdiction in Canada or elsewhere.

Dated at _____ this _____ day of _____ 19 __

_____   _____
Signature of Applicant   Name of Sponsoring Firm

By: _____
(Partner or Authorized Officer)

AFFIDAVIT OF APPLICANT

I, the undersigned applicant do depose and say that I have read and understand the questions in this application form as well as the answers that I have made, and that the statements of fact that I have made in this application form and in the attachments, if any, are true.

Sworn before me at _____

in the Province of _____

this _____ day of _____, 19 ____

_____   _____
(A Commissioner for Oaths, etc.)   Signature of Applicant

(This affidavit may not be required in all provinces)

The Provinces of British Columbia, Saskatchewan, Manitoba and the Northwest Territories require this Affidavit to be sworn before a notary public or barrister or solicitor, where the applicant is outside the province or territory at the time of application.

It is an offence under applicable Canadian securities legislation to file an application which contains a misrepresentation.

SCHEDULE A TO FORM 4A

APPLICANT'S NAME _____

DATE _____

1. This schedule is to report details of answers to questions on Form 4A.

2. Please initial the form.

QUESTION NUMBER	ANSWER

Province of
British Columbia
BC Securities Commission

FORM 4B

PERSONAL INFORMATION FOR DIRECTORS,
OFFICERS, PROMOTERS & CONTROL PERSONS

FOR INTERNAL USE ONLY

DATE	
DISCLOSURE	☐ YES ☐ NO
FOREIGN ENQUIRY	☐
UPDATE	☐

CAUTION

A person who makes a false statement by statutory declaration commits an indictable offence under the Criminal Code that is punishable by imprisonment for a term not exceeding fourteen years.

INSTRUCTIONS:

1. *Application* Every director, officer, promoter and control person of an issuer must file this form when required to do so pursuant to section 73.1 of the Securities Act or any local policy statement issued by the Commission.

2. *Completion of form* This form and any attachment to it must be typewritten or printed legibly in ink. Enter "N/A" ("not applicable") where appropriate.

3. *Solemn declaration and attachments* The official before whom this form is declared must mark as exhibits and initial any attachments to this form. Persons completing this form must also initial any attachments. This form and any attachments must contain original signatures or initials as appropriate.

4. *Legal advice* Persons required to complete this form should consider seeking legal advice.

5. *Where to file* On completion of this form, file it with:

   British Columbia Securities Commission
   1100 – 865 Hornby Street
   Vancouver, B.C.
   V6Z 2H4

DEFINITIONS:

Unless otherwise indicated, terms used in this form have the same meaning as in the Securities Act, S.B.C. 1985, c. 83 and the Securities Regulation, B.C. Reg. 270/86.

In this form:

"director" includes a director of a general partner of a limited partnership;

"issuer" includes a general partner of a limited partnership;

"officer" includes an officer of a general partner of a limited partnership.

In questions 8 to 12 inclusive of this form:

"guilty", in relation to a plea or a finding, includes an absolute or conditional discharge;

"offence" means

a) a summary conviction or indictable offence under the **Criminal Code (Canada),**

b) a misdemeanour or felony under the criminal legislation of the United States of America or of any state or territory of the United States of America,

c) an offence under the criminal legislation of any jurisdiction other than Canada, the United States of America or a state or territory of the United States of America,

d) a quasi-criminal offence, for example under the **Income Tax Act (Canada)** or the tax legislation of any other jurisdiction, the **Immigration Act (Canada)** or the immigration legislation of any other jurisdiction, or the Securities Act (British Columbia) or the securities legislation of any other jurisdiction,

and excludes

e) an offence for which a pardon has been granted and has not been revoked under the **Criminal Records Act (Canada)** or the comparable legislation of any other jurisdiction, and

f) an offence under the motor vehicle legislation of any jurisdiction;

"securities regulatory authority" means a body created by statute in any jurisdiction to administer securities law and policy but does not include a stock exchange or other self regulatory organization.

"self regulatory organization" means

a) a stock, commodities, futures or options exchange,

b) an association of investment, securities, mutual fund, commodities, or futures dealers,

c) an association of investment counsel or portfolio managers,

d) an association of other professionals, for example legal, accounting, engineering, and

e) any other self regulatory organization.

FOR INTERNAL USE ONLY

REVIEWED BY	DATE REVIEWED Y M D

1. IDENTIFICATION

LAST NAME   FIRST, SECOND AND THIRD NAMES

ADDRESS FOR SERVICE IN BRITISH COLUMBIA - Include postal code

ISSUER'S NAME

PRESENT POSITION WITH THE ISSUER - check (✓) as applicable

☐ DIRECTOR   ☐ PROMOTER
☐ OFFICER   ☐ CONTROL PERSON

IF DIRECTOR/OFFICER
DATE ELECTED/APPOINTED
Y   M   D

IF OFFICER - TITLE

2. EDUCATIONAL HISTORY - Provide your educational history starting with the most recent. Include secondary education.

SCHOOL	LOCATION	DEGREE OR DIPLOMA	DATE OBTAINED Y M D

PROFESSIONAL DESIGNATION - Provide any professional designations held, for example, Barrister & Solicitor, C.A., C.M.A., C.G.A., P.Eng., P. Geol., and F.G.A.C., and indicate by whom and the date the designations were granted.

PROFESSIONAL DESIGNATION	GRANTER OF DESIGNATION	DATE GRANTED Y M D	IN EFFECT - YES OR NO

FIN 2004/5(1) Rev 92 / 2 / 25

3. EMPLOYMENT HISTORY - Provide your employment history for the 10 years immediately prior to the date of this form starting with your current employment.

EMPLOYER NAME	EMPLOYER ADDRESS	POSITION HELD	FROM Y M	TO Y M

Provide any legal names, other than the name given in 1, and assumed names under which you have carried on business or otherwise been known.

	FROM Y M	TO Y M

4. PHOTOGRAPH

Attach to this form two identical black and white photographs, full face, taken within the last 6 months showing a true likeness of yourself as you now appear. The photographs must measure 2" x 2", be of passport quality and bear on the back the date on which they were taken, your signature and the signature of a Commissioner of Oaths, Notary Public or other official authorized by law to administer oaths.

5. PERSONAL INFORMATION

RESIDENTIAL TELEPHONE NUMBER area code	BUSINESS TELEPHONE NUMBER area code	FAX NUMBER area code
DATE OF BIRTH Y M D	PLACE OF BIRTH - CITY PROVINCE/STATE	COUNTRY

SEX ☐ MALE ☐ FEMALE	HEIGHT	WEIGHT	COLOUR OF EYES	COLOUR OF HAIR	DISTINGUISHING CHARACTERISTICS - If any
MARITAL STATUS	FULL NAME OF SPOUSE - Include common - law			OCCUPATION OF SPOUSE	

CITIZENSHIP

If you are not a Canadian citizen, are you a permanent resident of Canada? ☐ YES ☐ NO   Number of years of continuous residence in Canada: *Years*

PASSPORT COUNTRY OF ISSUE	NAME OF CITY WHERE PASSPORT WAS ISSUED	DATE PASSPORT ISSUED Y M D	PASSPORT NUMBER
DRIVER'S LICENCE NUMBER	PROVINCE/STATE WHERE DRIVER'S LICENCE WAS ISSUED	SOCIAL INSURANCE/SECURITY NUMBER	

6. RESIDENTIAL HISTORY - Provide all residential addresses for the past 10 years starting with your current principal residential address.

STREET ADDRESS, CITY, PROVINCE/STATE, COUNTRY & POSTAL/ZIP CODE	FROM Y M	TO Y M

7. POSITIONS IN OTHER ISSUERS

Provide the names of reporting issuers in British Columbia and of issuers with continuous disclosure obligations in other jurisdictions of which you are now, or within the past five years have been, a director, officer, promoter or control person, the positions you held and the periods during which you held those positions. Use attachment if necessary.

NAMES OF (REPORTING) ISSUERS	POSITIONS HELD WITH ISSUER	FROM Y	M	TO Y	M

INSTRUCTIONS for Questions 8 to 12 inclusive – answer "yes" or "no" in the space provided. Refer to the definitions on the first page of this form. If your answer to any of questions 8 to 12 is "yes", you must, in an attachment, give complete details including the circumstances, relevant dates, names of the parties involved and final disposition, if known.

8. OFFENCES

YES / NO

A. OFFENCES

Have you pleaded guilty to or been found guilty of an offence?

B. CURRENT CHARGES, INDICTMENTS OR PROCEEDINGS

Are you the subject of a current charge, indictment or proceeding for an offence?

9. ADMINISTRATIVE PROCEEDINGS

A. PROCEEDINGS BY SECURITIES REGULATORY AUTHORITY

Has a securities regulatory authority:

a) prohibited or disqualified you under securities or corporate legislation from acting as a director or officer of an issuer?

b) refused to register or license you to trade securities or restricted, suspended or cancelled your registration or licence?

c) refused to issue a receipt for a prospectus or other offering document solely or partially as a result of your being associated with that issuer?

d) issued a cease trading or similar order against you?

e) issued an order that denied you the right to use any statutory exemptions?

f) taken any other proceeding against you?

B. PROCEEDINGS BY SELF REGULATORY ORGANIZATION

Have you been reprimanded, suspended, fined or otherwise disciplined, in any jurisdiction, by a self regulatory organization?

C. CURRENT PROCEEDINGS BY SECURITIES REGULATORY AUTHORITY OR SELF REGULATORY ORGANIZATION

Are you now the subject, in any jurisdiction, of:

a) a notice of hearing or similar notice issued by a securities regulatory authority?

b) a proceeding by a self regulatory organization?

D. SETTLEMENT AGREEMENT

Have you entered into a settlement agreement with a securities regulatory authority, a self regulatory organization or an attorney general or comparable official in any jurisdiction in a matter that involved actual or alleged fraud, theft, deceit, misrepresentation, insider trading, unregistered trading, unregistered distributions, failure to disclose material facts or changes or similar conduct by you, or involved any other violation of securities legislation or a self regulatory organization's rules?

E. SUSPENSION OR TERMINATION OF EMPLOYMENT

Has a registered dealer, in any jurisdiction, suspended or terminated your employment with the dealer for cause?

10. CIVIL PROCEEDINGS

A. JUDGMENT, GARNISHMENT AND INJUNCTIONS

Has a civil court in any jurisdiction:

a) rendered a judgment or ordered garnishment against you in a civil claim based in whole or in part on fraud, theft, deceit, misrepresentation, insider trading, unregistered trading, unregistered distributions, failure to disclose material facts or changes or similar conduct?

b) issued an injunction or similar ban against you by consent or otherwise in a civil claim described in question a)?

B. CURRENT CLAIMS

Are you now the subject, in any jurisdiction, of a civil claim that is based in whole or in part on actual or alleged fraud, theft, deceit, misrepresentation, insider trading, unregistered trading, unregistered distributions, failure to disclose material facts or changes or similar conduct?

C. SETTLEMENT AGREEMENT

Have you entered into a settlement agreement, in any jurisdiction, in a civil action that involved actual or alleged fraud, theft, deceit, misrepresentation, insider trading, unregistered trading, unregistered distributions, failure to disclose material facts or changes or similar conduct on your part?

Forms

11. PERSONAL BANKRUPTCY

Have you in any jurisdiction:

a) had a petition in bankruptcy issued against you or made a voluntary assignment in bankruptcy? _____

b) made a proposal under any legislation relating to bankruptcy or insolvency? _____

c) been subject to or instituted any proceeding, arrangement or compromise with creditors? _____

d) had a receiver, receiver manager or trustee appointed to hold your assets? _____

Are you now an undischarged bankrupt? _____

If you answered "yes" to any of questions a) to d), and if applicable, attach a copy of any discharge, release or other document that has a similar effect.

12. PROCEEDINGS AGAINST ISSUER

To the best of your knowledge, were you a director, officer, promoter, or control person of an issuer, in any jurisdiction, at the time of events that led to:

a) the issuer pleading guilty to, or being found guilty of, an offence based in whole or in part on fraud, theft, deceit, misrepresentation, insider trading, unregistered trading, unregistered distributions, failure to disclose material facts or changes or similar conduct? _____

b) a pending charge, indictment or proceeding against the issuer, for an offence described in question a)? _____

c) a securities regulatory authority:

    i)   refusing, restricting, suspending or cancelling the registration or licencing of the issuer to trade securities? _____

    ii) issuing a cease trading or similar order against the issuer, other than an order for failure to file financial statements that was revoked within 30 days of its issuance? _____

    iii) issuing an order that denied the issuer the right to use any statutory exemptions? _____

    iv) taking any other proceeding against the issuer? _____

    v)   issuing a current notice of hearing or similar notice against the issuer? _____

d) a reprimand, suspension, fine or disciplinary action of the issuer by a self regulatory organization? _____

e) a current proceeding against the issuer by a self regulatory organization? _____

f) a civil court:

    i)   rendering a judgment or ordering garnishment in a claim against the issuer based in whole or in part on fraud, theft, deceit, misrepresentation, insider trading, unregistered trading, unregistered distributions, failure to disclose material facts or changes or similar conduct? _____

    ii) issuing an injunction or similar ban against the issuer by consent or otherwise in a claim described in question i)? _____

g) a current civil claim against the issuer that is based in whole or in part on actual or alleged fraud, theft, deceit, misrepresentation, insider trading, unregistered trading, unregistered distributions, failure to disclose material facts or changes or similar conduct? _____

h) the issuer entering a settlement agreement with a securities regulatory authority, a self regulatory organization or an attorney general or comparable official in any jurisdiction in a matter that involved actual or alleged fraud, theft, deceit, misrepresentation, insider trading, unregistered trading, unregistered distributions, failure to disclose material facts or changes or similar conduct by the issuer, or involved any other violation of securities legislation or a self regulatory organization's rules? _____

i) the issuance of a petition in bankruptcy against the issuer or a voluntary assignment in bankruptcy? _____

j) a proposal by the issuer under any legislation relating to bankruptcy or insolvency? _____

k) proceedings against the issuer under any legislation relating to winding up, dissolution or companies' creditors arrangements? _____

l) a proceeding, arrangement or compromise by the issuer with creditors? _____

m) the appointment of a receiver, receiver manager or trustee to hold the issuer's assets? _____

Is an issuer in any jurisdiction of which you are now a director, officer, promoter or control person, now an undischarged bankrupt? _____

If you answered "yes" to any of questions i) to m), and if applicable, attach a copy of any discharge, release or other document that has a similar effect.

CAUTION

A person who makes a false statement by statutory declaration commits an indictable offence under the Criminal Code that is punishable by imprisonment for a term not exceeding fourteen years. Steps will be taken to verify the answers you have given in this form, including verification of information relating to any previous criminal record.

STATUTORY DECLARATION

I, _____ solemnly declare that
        Name of director, officer, promoter or control person

a) I have read and understand the questions and caution in this form;

b) the answers I have given to the questions in this form and in any attachments to it are true except where stated to be to the best of my knowledge in which case I believe the answers to be true; and

c) I make this solemn declaration conscientiously believing it to be true and knowing it is of the same legal force and effect as if made under oath.

Declared before me _____   _____
        Name of Commissioner of Oaths, Notary Public or other official authorized by law to administer oaths   Signature of maker of the statutory declaration

at _____ ,   _____
        City   Province/State

on _____ , 19 _____   _____
        Signature of Commissioner of Oaths, Notary Public or other official authorized by law to administer oaths

FIN 2004/8(4) Rev 92 / 2 / 25   HB 1513

Province of British Columbia

	FOR OFFICE USE ONLY
FILE NUMBER	REGISTRATION/LICENCE NO.
APPROVED BY	DATE OF APPROVAL
KEYED BY	DATE KEYED
RESTRICTION	

UNIFORM APPLICATION FOR RENEWAL
OF LICENCE OR REGISTRATION (FORM 3-4)

APPLICANT TO COMPLETE ALL SHADED AREAS. CHECK (**O**) APPROPRIATE BOXES SHOWN.
IF INFORMATION HAS CHANGED, ATTACH AN EXHIBIT GIVING DETAILS.

		AS NOTED	CHANGED
APPLICANT NAME OR TRADE NAME	①	☐	☐
EMPLOYER NAME	②	☐	☐
BUSINESS ADDRESS	③	☐	☐

REGISTRATION/LICENCE OF THE ABOVE IS DUE FOR RENEWAL ON

UNDER LICENCE FEE   COUNCIL FEE   ACT, AS ④ TOTAL FEE REQUIRED   ④ ☐ ☐

APPLICANT LEGAL NAME ⑤   ⑤ ☐ ☐

BUSINESS TELEPHONE ⑥   ⑥ ☐ ☐

SERVICE ADDRESS IN B.C. ⑦   ⑦ ☐ ☐

CLASSES OF INSURANCE ⑧
EMPLOYER FILE NUMBER
SPONSOR FILE NUMBER   ⑧ ☐ ☐

SPONSOR NAME ⑨   ⑨ ☐ ☐

RESIDENCE

ADDRESS

☐ (**O**) I REQUEST RENEWAL OF THE ABOVE REGISTRATION/LICENCE

☐ (**O**) I DO NOT DESIRE RENEWAL OF THE ABOVE REGISTRATION/LICENCE   SEE REVERSE FOR INSTRUCTIONS

AMENDMENTS TO INFORMATION – INDIVIDUAL APPLICANT
SINCE THE DATE OF THE LAST APPLICATION:

	YES	NO
A) HAVE YOU BEEN CHARGED OR INDICTED, OR HAVE YOU BEEN CONVICTED WITHOUT PARDON, UNDER ANY LAW OF ANY PROVINCE, STATE OR COUNTRY, EXCEPTING FOR MINOR TRAFFIC VIOLATIONS?	☐	☐
B) HAVE YOU PERSONALLY, OR HAS ANY BUSINESS OF WHICH YOU ARE OR WERE AN OFFICER, DIRECTOR OR PARTNER, BEEN SUBJECT TO BANKRUPTCY PROCEEDINGS?	☐	☐
C) ARE THERE ANY PENDING LEGAL PROCEEDINGS AGAINST YOU OR AGAINST ANY BUSINESS OF WHICH YOU WERE AT THE TIME AN OFFICER, DIRECTOR OR PARTNER IN ANY CIVIL COURT IN BRITISH COLUMBIA OR ELSEWHERE, FOR ANY REASON WHATSOEVER?	☐	☐
D) HAS ANY JUDGEMENT, WHICH IS UNSATISFIED, BEEN RENDERED AGAINST YOU PERSONALLY OR AGAINST ANY BUSINESS OF WHICH YOU WERE AT THE TIME AN OFFICER, DIRECTOR OR PARTNER IN ANY CIVIL COURT IN BRITISH COLUMBIA OR ELSEWHERE, FOR ANY REASON WHATSOEVER? ____	☐	☐
E) HAVE YOU CHANGED ANY OTHER REGISTRATION INFORMATION FROM THAT PREVIOUSLY SUBMITTED? ____	☐	☐

AMENDMENTS TO INFORMATION – CORPORATE, PARTNERSHIP APPLICANT
SINCE THE DATE OF THE LAST APPLICATION, HAS THE APPLICANT:

	YES	NO
A) BEEN SUBJECT TO PROCEEDINGS IN BANKRUPTCY? ____	☐	☐
B) HAD A JUDGEMENT OF A COURT RENDERED AGAINST THEM IN ANY CIVIL COURT IN BRITISH COLUMBIA OR ELSEWHERE, FOR ANY REASON WHATSOEVER, WHICH IS UNSATISFIED? ____	☐	☐
C) BEEN SUBJECT TO ANY LEGAL PROCEEDINGS WHICH ARE NOW PENDING? ____	☐	☐
D) HAD ANY CHANGE IN OFFICERS, DIRECTORS OR PARTNERS? ____	☐	☐
E) CHANGED ANY OTHER REGISTRATION INFORMATION FROM THAT PREVIOUSLY SUBMITTED? ____	☐	☐

IF THE ANSWER TO ANY OF THE ABOVE QUESTIONS IS YES, ATTACH AN EXHIBIT GIVING DETAILS

APPLICANT'S SIGNATURE	DATE
CERTIFICATE OF APPROVAL BY INTENDED EMPLOYER OR SPONSOR (SIGNATURE OF EMPLOYER OR SPONSOR)	DATE

TITLE OF SIGNING AUTHORITY (SEE REVERSE FOR INSTRUCTIONS)

THIS FORM MUST BE COMPLETED AND RETURNED TO THE ABOVE ADDRESS WITH REQUIRED FEE, 30 DAYS PRIOR TO DUE DATE. RETURN TOP COPY ONLY. RETAIN BOTTOM COPY FOR YOUR RECORDS.

WARNING

ANY APPLICATION CONTAINING A FALSE STATEMENT MAY RESULT IN REFUSAL, SUSPENSION OR CANCELLATION OF ANY LICENCE OR REGISTRATION

FIN 850 REV. 87/1

SUBMIT THIS COPY

This form is computer generated only. The Registration Department of the Commission automatically sends it to the Registrant at the renewal time.

Form 7

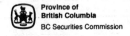 **Province of
British Columbia**
BC Securities Commission

 Check One (✓) | Securities Act ☐
Commodity
Contract Act ☐

Application for Amendment of Registration as Dealer, Adviser or Underwriter

INSTRUCTIONS

1. This form is the form required under Section 28 of the Securities Act and Section 20 of the Commodity Contract Act.

2. All applicable questions must be answered. Failure to do so may cause delays in the processing of the application.

3. This form and all attachments added thereto must be typewritten or hand printed. Any form or attachment completed by any other means may be considered not properly filed.

4. All attachments pertaining to any question must be made exhibits to the form and each one must be so marked. All signatures must be originals. The Commissioner of Oaths before whom the application is sworn, as well as the applicant, is required to initial all attachments.

5. Please attach the applicable fee.

Name of Registrant ....

Application is made for amendment to our existing registration as ....

....

under the ....Act and the following statements of fact are made in respect thereof:

ANSWER **"YES"** OR **"NO"** TO EACH OF QUESTIONS 1 TO 8 INCLUSIVE.
IF THE ANSWER TO ANY OF THE FOLLOWING QUESTIONS IS **"YES"**,
COMPLETE DETAILS **MUST BE** ATTACHED BY WAY OF EXHIBIT.

A. HAS THERE BEEN A CHANGE IN THE FOLLOWING: **YES/NO**

1. The name of the applicant.   _____

2. Address for service or any business address.   _____

3. Partners, officers or directors and the reason
    for any such person's resignation, dismissal,
    severance or termination of employment or office.   _____

4. Trading officials of the applicant.   _____

5. Holders of voting securities of the applicant.   _____

6. Branch offices in British Columbia.   _____

7. The person in charge of any branch office in British Columbia.   _____

8. Other significant changes pertaining to the applicant.   _____

FIN 2007 (1) 87/11

B. Attached hereto and marked as an exhibit to the application for amendment is:

1. The name of each new partner, officer or director of the applicant.

2. A completed Form 4 (or Form 1-U-85) for each new partner, officer or director of the applicant.

} This information **MUST** be provided if you have answered YES to A.3. or A.4.

C. Attached hereto and marked as an exhibit to the application for amendment is a statement of changes which have ocurred in the financial structure and control of the applicant, which would make the information previously given by the applicant pursuant to this or any previous Regulation, false or misleading.

DATED at ....

....
(Name of Applicant)

this .... day of .... 19 ....

By ....
(Signature of applicant, director, officer or partner)

....
(Official capacity)

AFFIDAVIT

In the matter of the Securities Act / Commodity Contract Act

Province of British Columbia

.... of ....

To Wit:

}

I, ...
(Name in full)

of the ....

in the Province of ....

MAKE OATH AND SAY:

1. I am the applicant (or a director, officer or partner of the applicant) herein for amendment of registration and I signed the application.

2. The statements of fact made in the application for amendment of registration are true.

SWORN before me at the ....

in the .... of ....

this .... day of .... 19 ....

....
(A Commissioner, etc.)

}

....
(Signature of Deponent)

It is an offence under the Securities Act/Commodity Contract Act to file an application containing a statement that, at the time and in light of the circumstances in which it is made, is a misrepresentation.

Forms

Province of British Columbia
BC SECURITIES COMMISSION

Check One (✔)

| Securities Act ☐ |
| Commodity Contract Act ☐ |

Form 7A
Application for Transfer/ Change of Status
FOR INTERNAL USE ONLY

| APPLICATION APPROVED BY | DATE APPROVED |

Name of Applicant: ....

Residential address *(Include Postal Code)*: ....

Name of employer: ....

Address where Applicant will be working *(Include Postal Code)*: ....

Address for service in the Province *(Include Postal Code)*: ....

Applying for registration as: ....

☐ TRANSFER   ☐ CHANGE OF STATUS

A. TRANSFER

Name of previous employer: ....

Date of termination: ....

B. CHANGE OF STATUS

CURRENT REGISTRATION: ....

Applicable examination written *(Attach proof of passing)*:   Date passed:

HAVE THERE BEEN CHANGES IN THE INFORMATION GIVEN IN QUESTIONS 11 THROUGH 20 (SEE REVERSE) OF THE UNIFORM APPLICATION FOR REGISTRATION/APPROVAL PREVIOUSLY FILED BY YOU AND APPROVED? CIRCLE ONE: YES/NO. IF YES, ATTACH FULL PARTICULARS.

The undersigned hereby certify that the foregoing statements are true and correct to the best of our knowledge, information and belief (after having seen the Uniform Application for Registration/Approval and all subsequent Applications for Transfer/Change of Status previously filed by the applicant) and we hereby undertake to notify the British Columbia Securities Commission in writing, of any change therein within the period prescribed by the British Columbia Securities Act, Commodity Contract Act or regulations of either Act.

_____   _____
Date Signed   *Signature of Applicant*

_____   _____
Print Name of Partner, Director or Officer of the Dealer,   *Signature of Partner, Director of Officer*
Adviser or Underwriter that employs the Applicant

♻ Recycled Paper

DK-1190   FIN 2007A Rev. 90/6/6

NOTE: The following areas are addressed in the Uniform Application and constitute questions 11 through 20 respectively:

CHANGE OF NAME
PRIOR REGISTRATION OR LICENSING
REFUSAL, SUSPENSION, CANCELLATION OR DISCIPLINARY MEASURE
SELF-REGULATORY ORGANIZATIONS
OFFENCES UNDER THE LAW
CIVIL PROCEEDINGS
BANKRUPTCY
JUDGMENT OR GARNISHMENT
SURETY BOND OR FIDELITY BOND
BUSINESS ACTIVITIES

This is the form required under section 19 of the Securities Regulation for a summons for an examination under oath under section 24(c) of the Securities Act.

FORM 8

Securities Act

IN THE MATTER OF THE SECURITIES ACT
S.B.C. 1985, c. 83

AND

IN THE MATTER OF

SUMMONS FOR AN EXAMINATION UNDER SECTION 24(c)

TO: [NAME]
 [ADDRESS]

TAKE NOTICE that you are required to attend an examination under oath to be conducted by [name] at the time, date and place set out below. You are also required to bring with you all information and records in your possession or power relating _____ [including:].

TIME:

DATE:

PLACE:

DATED AT Vancouver, British Columbia this _____ day of _____, 19 ____.

_____
Superintendent of Brokers

Please note the provision of the Securities Act attached hereto.

Securities Act, S.B.C. 1985, c. 83

Further information

24 The superintendent may require,

   (a) within a specified time, further information or records to be submitted by an applicant,

   (b) at any time, verification by affidavit or otherwise of any information or records submitted by an applicant, or

   (c) an examination under oath, to be conducted by a person designated in writing by the superintendent, of

      (i) the applicant,

      (ii) a partner, officer, director, governor or trustee of, or any person performing a like function for, the applicant, or

      (iii) an employee of the applicant.

November 1, 1989

This is the form required under section 75 of the Securities Regulation for an application for exempt purchaser status under sections 31(2)(4) and 55(2)(3) of the Securities Act.

FORM 11

Securities Act

APPLICATION FOR EXEMPT PURCHASER STATUS

1. State the name, address for service and telephone number of the applicant.

_____

_____

2.   State the jurisdiction and date of incorporation, organization or continuation of the applicant.

_____

_____

3.   State the jurisdiction in which the applicant is authorized to carry on business as a financial institution, and provide a copy of the applicant's charter or license issued by the appropriate regulatory authority.

_____

_____

4.   Name all persons that are insiders of the applicant, or that would be insiders of the applicant were it a reporting issuer under the British Columbia Securities Act, and state their relationship to the applicant.

_____

_____

5.   Name all individuals who are officers, directors, trustees, partners or representatives, as the case may be, of the applicant, and state the occupations of each of them for the past five years.

_____

_____

6.   State any other relevant facts and reasons why the applicant should be designated as an exempt purchaser.

_____

_____

If the space provided in any item is insufficient, additional pages may be used and must be cross referenced to the item, and signed by the applicant.

The undersigned hereby acknowledge that this application is true and accurate in all respects.

Dated at _____ this _____ day of _____, 19___.
            (insert city and country)

                                   _____
                                     (insert name of applicant)

_____   _____
(signature of authorized signatory)   (signature of authorized signatory)

_____   _____
(name and official capacity)   (name and official capacity)

IT IS AN OFFENCE FOR A PERSON TO MAKE A STATEMENT IN A DOCUMENT REQUIRED TO BE FILED OR FURNISHED UNDER THE SECURITIES ACT OR THE SECURITIES REGULATION THAT, AT THE TIME AND IN THE LIGHT OF THE CIRCUMSTANCES UNDER WHICH IT IS MADE, IS A MISREPRESENTATION.

The prospectus for an industrial issuer required by Section 42(2) of the Act shall be in the following form.

FORM 12

Securities Act

INFORMATION REQUIRED IN PROSPECTUS OF INDUSTRIAL ISSUER

Item 1 - Distribution Spread:

The information called for by the following Table shall be given, in substantially the tabular form indicated, on the first page of the prospectus as to all securities being offered for cash (estimate amounts, if necessary).

TABLE

	Column 1	Column 2	Column 3
	Price to Public	Underwriting discounts or commissions	Proceeds to issuer or selling security-holder
Per unit	....	....	....
Total	....	....	....

INSTRUCTIONS:

1.   Only commissions paid or payable in cash by the issuer or selling security holder or discounts granted are to be included in the table. Commissions or other consideration paid or payable in cash or otherwise by other persons and consideration other than discounts granted and other than cash paid or payable by the issuer or selling security holder shall be set out following the table with a reference thereto in the second column of the table. Any finder's fees or similar payments shall be appropriately disclosed.

2.   The table should set out separately those securities which are underwritten, those under option and those to be sold on a "best efforts" basis.

3.   If the presentation of information in the form contemplated herein results in unnecessary complication, the tabular form may, with the consent of the Superintendent, be varied.

4.   If it is impracticable to state the offering price, the method by which it is to be determined shall be explained. In addition, if the securities are to be offered at the market, indicate the market involved and the market price as of the latest practicable date.

5.   If any of the securities offered are to be offered for the account of existing security holders, refer on the first page of the prospectus to the information called for by Instruction 4 to Item 26. State the portion of the expenses of distribution to be borne by the selling security holder.

6.   If debt securities are to be offered at a premium or a discount, state in bold face type the effective yield if held to maturity.

Item 2 - Plan of Distribution:

(a)   If the securities being offered are to be sold through underwriters, give the names of the underwriters. State briefly the nature of the underwriters' obligation to take up and pay for the securities. Indicate the date by which the underwriters are to purchase the securities.

(b)   where the prospectus discloses a plan of distribution not involving a firm underwriting or other subscription guarantee it must also disclosure the amount of a minimum subscription. The face page shall contain the following disclosure or a reasonable paraphrase thereof:

"This offering is subject to a minimum subscription being received by the issuer within 180 days of the effective date of .... (date of receipt of prospectus). Further particulars of the minimum subscription are disclosed on page .... under the caption use of proceeds."

INSTRUCTIONS:

1. All that is required as to the nature of the underwriters' obligation is whether the underwriters are or will be committed to take up and pay for all of the securities if any are taken up, or whether the underwriting is merely an agency or "best efforts" arrangement under which the underwriters are required to take up and pay for only such securities as they may sell.

2. Where an underwriting is subject to a "market out" clause, a statement in the prospectus under Plan of Distribution should be made with respect to the "market out" clause.

A sample paragraph is as follows:
Plan of Distribution:

"Under an agreement dated .... 19.... between the issuer and .... as underwriter, the issuer has agreed to sell and the underwriter has agreed to purchase on .... 19.... the .... at a price of $........, payable in cash to the issuer against delivery. The obligations of the underwriter under the agreement may be terminated at its discretion on the basis of its assessment of the state of the financial markets and may also be terminated upon the occurrence of certain stated events. The underwriter is however, obligated to take up and pay for all of the .... if any of the .... are purchased under the agreement."

3. Where a minimum subscription is required by the superintendent, which will normally be that amount which together with uncommitted funds on hand will suffice to finance the minimum program disclosed in the prospectus plus the issuer's estimated administration costs over the ensuing current period then:

    (a) All funds raised during the 180 days must be deposited in an account at a bank or trust company designated as a trust account until the full minimum amount has been received;

    (b) An agreement must be entered into with the trustee of such trust account whereby the trustee undertakes:

        (i) where within the 180-day period the minimum subscription has been received, to release the subscription funds to the issuer and to notify the Superintendent of such release; and

        (ii) where the minimum amount is not raised within the 180-day period to refund the subscription in full with interest accruing thereon to the shareholders.

4. The Superintendent contemplates granting no extension for a minimum subscription beyond the 180-day period.

Item 3 - Market for Securities:

Where no *bona fide* market exists, or will exist after the distribution, state in bold face type on the first page: "There is no market through which these securities may be sold". Disclose how the price paid to the issuer was established, whether by negotiation with the underwriter, arbitrarily by the issuer, or otherwise.

Item 4 - Summary of Prospectus:

Give a synopsis near the beginning of the prospectus of that information in the body of the prospectus which in the opinion of the issuer or selling security holder would be most likely to influence the investor's decision to purchase the security.

INSTRUCTION:

1. This summary should highlight in condensed form the information, both favourable and adverse, including risk factors in item 10, particularly pertinent to a decision to purchase the securities offered, including information about both the issuer and the securities.

2.   Appropriate cross references may be made to items in the prospectus where information is difficult to summarize accurately, but this shall not detract from the necessity to have the salient points summarized in the summary.

Item 5 - Use of Proceeds to Issuer:

(a)   State the estimated net proceeds to be derived by the issuer from the sale of the securities to be offered, the principal purposes for which the net proceeds are intended to be used and the approximate amount intended to be used for each purpose.

(b)   State the particulars of any provisions or arrangements made for holding any part of the net proceeds of the issue in trust or subject to the fulfilment of any conditions.

INSTRUCTIONS:

1.   Statements as to the principal purposes to which the proceeds are to be applied are to be reasonably specific although details of the particulars of proposed expenditures are not to be given except as otherwise required hereunder. The phrase "for general corporate purposes" is, in most cases, not sufficient.

2.   Where a minimum subscription is required by the superintendent a separate columnar allocation of this minimum amount of proceeds shall be shown in addition to a columnar allocation of the maximum amount proposed to be raised by this prospectus.

3.   Include a statement regarding the proposed use of the actual proceeds if they should prove insufficient to accomplish the purposes set out, and the order of priority in which they will be applied. However, the statement need not be made if the underwriting arrangements are such that, if any securities are sold, it can be reasonably expected that the actual proceeds of the issue will not be substantially less than the estimated aggregate proceeds to the issuer as shown under item 1.

4.   If any material amounts of other funds are to be used in conjunction with the proceeds, state the amounts and sources of the other funds. If any material part of the proceeds is to be used to reduce or retire indebtedness, this item is to be answered as to the use of the proceeds of that indebtedness if the indebtedness was incurred within the two preceding years.

5.   If any material amount of the proceeds is to be used directly or indirectly to acquire assets, otherwise than in the ordinary course of business, briefly describe the assets, and, where known, the particulars of the purchase price being paid for or being allocated to the respective categories of assets (including intangible assets) that are being acquired and, where practicable and meaningful, give the name of the person from whom the assets are to be acquired. State the cost of the assets to the issuer and the principle followed in determining the cost. State briefly the nature of the title to or interest in the assets to be acquired by the issuer. If any part of the consideration for the acquisition of any of the assets consists of securities of the issuer, give brief particulars of the designation, number or amount, voting rights (if any) and other appropriate information relating to the class of securities, including particulars of any allotment or issuance of any such securities within the two preceding years.

Item 6 - Sales Otherwise than for Cash:

If any of the securities being offered are to be offered otherwise than for cash, state briefly the general purposes of the issue, the basis upon which the securities are to be offered, the amount of compensation paid or payable to any person and any other expenses of distribution, and by whom they are to be borne.

INSTRUCTION:

If the offer is to be made pursuant to a plan of acquisition, describe briefly the general effect of the plan and state when it became or is to become operative.

Item 7 - Share and Loan Capital Structure:

Furnish in substantially the tabular form indicated, or where appropriate in notes thereto:

(1) particulars of the share and loan capital of the issuer;

(2) particulars of the loan capital of each subsidiary of the issuer (other than loan capital owned by the issuer or its wholly-owned subsidiaries) whose financial statements are contained in the prospectus on either a consolidated or individual basis;

(3) the aggregate amount of the minority interest in the preference shares, if any, and the aggregate amount of the minority interest in the common shares and surplus of all subsidiaries whose financial statements are contained in the prospectus on a consolidated basis; and

(4) the aggregate amount of the minority interest in the preference shares, if any, and the aggregate amount of minority interest in the common shares and surplus of all subsidiaries whose financial statements are contained in the prospectus on an individual basis and not included in the consolidated financial statements.

TABLE

Column 1	Column 2	Column 3	Column 4	Column 5
Designation of security	Amount authorized or to be authorized	Amount outstanding as of the date of the most balance sheet contained in the prospectus	Amount outstanding as of a specific date within 30 days	Amount to be outstanding if all securities being issued are sold

....

INSTRUCTIONS:

1. Include all indebtedness for borrowed money as to which a written understanding exists that the indebtedness may extend beyond one year. Do not include other indebtedness classified as current liabilities unless secured.

2. Include in the table the amount of obligations under financial leases capitalized in accordance with generally accepted accounting principles. Set out in a note to the table a cross reference to any note in the financial statements containing information concerning the extent of obligations arising by virtue of other leases on real property.

3. Individual items of indebtedness which are not in excess of 3% of total assets as shown in the balance sheet referred to in Column 3 may be set out in a single aggregate amount under an appropriate caption such as "Sundry Indebtedness".

4. Where practicable, state in general terms the respective priorities of the indebtedness shown in the table.

5. Give particulars of the amount, general description of and security for any substantial indebtedness proposed to be created or assumed by the issuer or its subsidiaries, other than indebtedness offered by the prospectus.

6. Set out in a note the amount of contributed surplus and retained earnings as of the date of the most recent balance sheet contained in the prospectus.

7. Set out in a note the number of shares subject to rights, options and warrants.

8. No information need be given under Column 2 with respect to the common and preference shares of subsidiaries.

9. For the purposes of Column 3, in computing the amount of the minority interest in the subsidiaries whose financial statements are contained in the prospectus on an individual basis and not included in the consolidated financial statements, such computation may be based on the financial statements of each such subsidiary contained in the prospectus.

10. In computing the minority interest in the subsidiaries for the purpose of Column 4, the amount set out in Column 3 may be used provided that appropriate adjustment is made to such amount to reflect any change in the percentage of ownership in the capital and surplus of any subsidiary by the minority interest.

11. The thirty-day period referred to in Column 4 is to be calculated within thirty days of the date of the preliminary prospectus or the date of the *pro forma* prospectus. Where more than thirty days have elapsed from the date of the preliminary or *pro forma* prospectus, the information included in the prospectus shall, if feasible, be updated to a date within thirty days of the prospectus.

12. The information to be set out in Column 5 may be based upon the information contained in Column 4, adjusted to take into account any amounts set out in Column 4 to be retired out of the issue.

Item 8 - Name and Incorporation of Issuer:

State the full corporate name of the issuer and the address of its head office and principal office. State the laws under which the issuer was incorporated and whether incorporated by articles of incorporation or otherwise and the date the corporation came into existence. If material state whether these have been amended.

INSTRUCTIONS:

1. Particulars of the documents need to be set out only if material to the securities offered by the prospectus. See Item 17.

2. If the issuer is not a company, give material details of its form of organization and structure.

Item 9 - Description of Business:

Briefly describe the business carried on and intended to be carried on by the issuer and its subsidiaries and the general development of the business within the five preceding years. If the business consists of the production or distribution of different kinds of products or the rendering of different kinds of services, indicate, in so far as practicable, the principal products or services.

INSTRUCTIONS:

1. The description shall not relate to the powers and objects specified in the incorporating instruments, but to the actual business carried on and intended to be carried on. Include the business of subsidiaries of the issuer only in so far as is necessary to understand the character and development of the business conducted by the combined enterprise.

2. In describing developments, information shall be given as to matters such as the following: the nature and results of any bankruptcy, receivership or similar proceedings with respect to the issues or any of its subsidiaries; the nature and results of any other material reorganization of the issuer or any of its subsidiaries; the acquisition or disposition of any material amount of assets otherwise than in the ordinary course of business; material changes in the types of products produced or services rendered by the issuer and its subsidiaries; and any material changes in the mode of conducting the business of the issuer or its subsidiaries.

Item 10- Risk Factors:

(a) Where appropriate to a clear understanding by investors of the risk factors and speculative nature of the enterprise or the securities being offered, an introductory statement shall be made on the first page or in the summary of the prospectus summarizing the factors which make the purchase a risk or speculation. Include such matters as the pro forma dilution of the investment based on net tangible assets and a comparison, in percentages, of the securities being offered for cash and those issued or to be issued to promoters, directors, officers, substantial securityholders as defined in section 104(2) of the Act, and underwriters for cash, property and services. The information may be given in the body of the prospectus if an appropriate reference is made on the first page or in the summary of the prospectus to the risks and the speculative or promotional nature of the enterprise and a cross reference is made to the place in the prospectus where the information is contained.

(b) Where there is a risk that purchasers of the securities offered may become liable to make an additional contribution beyond the price of the security, disclose any information or facts that may bear on the security holder's assessment of risk associated with the investment.

Item 11- Acquisitions:

Briefly describe all material acquisitions and dispositions whether of shares or assets by the issuer and its subsidiaries during the past two years and to the extent reasonably practicable the impact of these acquisitions or dispositions on the operating results and financial position of the issuer.

Item 12 - Description of Property:

State briefly the location and general character of the principal properties, including buildings and plants, of the issuer and its subsidiaries. If any property is not freehold property or is held subject to any major encumbrance, so state and briefly describe the nature of the title or encumbrance, as the case may be.

INSTRUCTION:

What is required is information essential to an investor's appraisal of the securities being offered. Such information should be furnished as will reasonably inform investors as to the suitability, adequacy, productive capacity and extent of utilization of the facilities used in the enterprise. Detailed descriptions of the physical characteristics of individual properties or legal descriptions by metes and bounds are not required and should not be given.

Item 13 - Variations in Operating Results:

Explain to the extent reasonably practicable any substantial variations, both favourable; and adverse, in the operating results of the issuer over the last three years, but the Superintendent may permit or require an explanation of such substantial variations over a longer period not to exceed five years.

INSTRUCTION:

The explanation should be in narrative form. However, where ratios are used to illustrate variations, a table may be used to supplement the narrative.

Item 14 - Asset and Earnings Coverage:

Disclose asset and earnings coverage in an appropriate and reasonable form where required by section 111 of the Regulation.

Item 15 - Promoters:

If any person is or has been a promoter of the issuer or of any of its subsidiaries within the five years immediately preceding the date of the preliminary prospectus or pro forma prospectus, furnish the following information:

(a) State the names of the promoters, the nature and amount of anything of value (including money, property, contracts, options or rights of any kind) received or to be received by each promoter directly or indirectly from the issuer, or from any of its subsidiaries, and the nature and amount of any assets, services or other consideration therefor received or to be received by the issuer or subsidiary.

(b) As to any assets acquired within the past two years or to be acquired by the issuer or by any of its subsidiaries from a promoter, state the amount at which acquired or to be acquired and the principle followed or to be followed in determining the amount. Identify the person making the determination and state his relationship, if any, with the issuer, any subsidiary or any promoter. State the date that the assets were acquired by the promoter and the cost thereof to the promoter.

Item 16 - Legal Proceedings:

Briefly describe any legal proceedings material to the issuer to which the .issuer or any of its subsidiaries is a party or of which any of their property is the subject. Make a similar statement as to any such proceedings known to be contemplated.

INSTRUCTION:

Include the name of the court or agency, the date instituted, the principal parties thereto, the nature of the claim, the amount claimed, if any, whether the proceedings are being contested, and the present status of the proceedings.

Item 17 - Issuance of Shares:

(a) If shares are being offered, state the description or the designation of the class of shares offered and furnish all material attributes and characteristics including, without limiting the generality of the foregoing, the following information:

    (i) dividend rights;

    (ii) voting rights;

    (iii) liquidation or distribution rights;

    (iv) pre-emptive rights;

    (v) conversion rights;

    (vi) redemption, purchase for cancellation or surrender provisions;

    (vii) sinking or purchase fund provisions;

    (viii) liability to further calls or to assessment by the issuer; and

    (ix) provisions as to modification, amendment or variation of any such rights or provisions.

(b) If the rights of holders of such shares may be modified otherwise than in accordance with the provisions attaching to such shares or the provisions of the governing Act relating thereto, so state and explain briefly.

INSTRUCTIONS:

1. This item requires only a brief summary of the provisions that are material from an investment standpoint. Do not set out verbatim the provisions attaching to the shares; only a succinct resume is required.

2. If the rights attaching to the shares being offered are materially limited or qualified by the rights of any other class of securities, or if any other class of securities (other than obligations covered in Item 18), ranks ahead of or equally with the shares being offered, include information regarding such other securities that will enable investors to understand the rights attaching to the shares being offered. If any shares being offered are to be offered in exchange for other securities, an appropriate description of the other securities shall be given. No information need be given, however, as to any class of securities that is to be redeemed or otherwise retired, provided appropriate steps to assure redemption or retirement have been or will be taken prior to or contemporaneously with the delivery of the shares being offered.

3. In addition to the summary referred to in instruction 1, the issuer may set out verbatim in a schedule to the prospectus the provisions attaching to the shares being offered.

Item 18 - Issuance of Obligations:

If obligations are being offered, give a brief summary of the material attributes and characteristics of the indebtedness and the security therefor including, without limiting the generality of the foregoing:

Forms

(a)   Provisions with respect to interest rate, maturity, redemption or other retirement, sinking fund and conversion rights.

(b)   The nature and priority of any security for the obligations, briefly identifying the principal properties subject to lien or charge.

(c)   Provisions permitting or restricting the issuance of additional securities, the incurring of additional indebtedness and other material negative covenants, (including restrictions against payment of dividends, restrictions against giving security on the assets of the issuer or its subsidiaries and the like) and provisions as to the release or substitution of assets securing the obligations, the modification of the terms of the security and similar provisions.

(d)   The name of the trustee under any indenture relating to the obligations and the nature of any material relationship between the trustee and the issuer or any of its affiliates.

(e)   Indicate any financial arrangements between the issuer and any of its affiliates or among its affiliates that could affect the security for the indebtedness.

INSTRUCTION:

The instructions to Item 17 apply to this item with due alteration for point of detail.

Item 19 - Issuance of Other Securities:

If securities other than shares or obligations are being offered, outline briefly the rights evidenced thereby. If subscription warrants or rights are being offered or issued, state the description and amount of securities covered thereby, the period during which, and the price at which, the warrants or rights are exercisable, and the principal terms and conditions by which they may be exercised.

INSTRUCTION:

The instructions to Item 17 apply to this item with due alteration for point of detail.

Item 20 - Dividend Record:

State the amount of dividends or other distributions, if any, paid by the issuer during its last five completed financial years preceding the date of the preliminary prospectus or *pro forma* prospectus.

INSTRUCTION:

Dividends should be set out on a per share basis, shown separately for each class of shares in respect of each of the financial years. Appropriate adjustments shall be made to reflect changes in capitalization during the period.

Item 21 - Directors and Officers:

List the names and home addresses in full or, alternatively, solely the municipality of residence or postal address, of all directors and officers of the issuer and indicate all positions and offices with the issuer hold by each person named, and the principal occupations within the five preceding years, of each director and officer.

INSTRUCTIONS:

1.   Where the municipality of residence or postal address is listed, the Director may request that the home address in full be furnished to the Commission.

2.   Where the principal occupation of a director or officer is that of an officer of a company other than the issuer, state the principal business in which such company is engaged.

3. Where a director or officer has held more than one position in the issuer, or a parent or subsidiary thereof, state only the first and last position held.

Item 22 - Executive Compensation:

Complete and attach to or include in this Form a Statement of Executive Compensation in Form 41, provided however, that the disclosure required by Items V, VIII, IX and X of Form 41 may be omitted for purposes of this Form.

> See NIN 93/23 "Executive Compensation".

Item 23 – Indebtedness of Directors, Executive Officers and Senior Officers:

    (a)   The information required by this Item must be provided for each individual who is or, at any time during the most recently completed financial year, was a director, executive officer or senior officer of the issuer, each proposed nominee for election as a director of the issuer, and each associate of any such director, officer or proposed nominee,

        (i)   who is, or at any time since the beginning of the most recently completed financial year of the issuer has been, indebted to the issuer or any of its subsidiaries, or

        (ii) whose indebtedness to another entity is, or at any time since the beginning of the most recently completed financial year of the issuer has been, the subject of a guarantee, support agreement, letter of credit or other similar arrangement or understanding provided by the issuer or any of its subsidiaries.

    (b)   State in the tabular form under the caption set out, for any indebtedness referred to in paragraph (a) of this Item that was entered into in connection with a purchase of securities of the issuer or any of its subsidiaries:

        (i)   The name of the borrower (column (a)).

        (ii) If the borrower is a director, executive officer or senior officer, the principal position of the borrower. If the borrower was, during the year, but no longer is a director or officer, include a statement to that effect. If the borrower is a proposed nominee for election as a director, include a statement to that effect. If the borrower is included as an associate describe briefly the relationship of the borrower to an individual who is or, during the year, was a director, executive officer or senior officer or who is a proposed nominee for election as a director, name that individual and provide the information required by this subparagraph for that individual (column (a)).

        (iii) Whether the issuer or a subsidiary of the issuer is the lender or the provider of a guarantee, support agreement, letter of credit or similar arrangement or understanding (column (b)).

        (iv) The largest aggregate amount of the indebtedness outstanding at any time during the last completed financial year (column (c)).

        (v) The aggregate amount of indebtedness outstanding as at a date within thirty days of certification of the prospectus (column (d)).

        (vi) Separately for each class or series of securities, the sum of the number of securities purchased during the last completed financial year with the financial assistance (column (e)).

        (vii) The security for the indebtedness, if any, provided to the issuer, any of its subsidiaries or the other entity (column (f)).

TABLE OF INDEBTEDNESS OF DIRECTORS, EXECUTIVE OFFICERS AND SENIOR OFFICERS UNDER SECURITIES PURCHASE PROGRAMS

Name and Principal Position (a)	Involvement of Issuer or Subsidiary (b)	Largest Amount Outstanding During [Last Completed Financial Year] ($) (c)	Amount Outstanding as at [current date] ($) (d)	Financially Assisted Securities Purchases During [Last Completed Financial Year] (#) (e)	Security for Indebtedness (f)

(c)   State in the introduction immediately preceding the table required by paragraph (b) of this Item, for indebtedness entered into in connection with a purchase of securities of the issuer or any of its subsidiaries, separately, the aggregate indebtedness,

   (i) to the issuer or any of its subsidiaries, and

   (ii) to another entity if the indebtedness is the subject of a guarantee, support agreement, letter of credit or other similar arrangement or understanding provided by the issuer or any of its subsidiaries,

of all officers, directors, employees and former officers, directors and employees of the issuer or any of its subsidiaries outstanding as at a date within thirty days of certification of the prospectus.

(d)   State in the tabular form under the caption set out, for any indebtedness referred to in paragraph (a) of this Item that was not entered into in connection with a purchase of securities of the issuer or any of its subsidiaries, the information referred to in subparagraphs (b) (i) through (v) of this Item.

TABLE OF INDEBTEDNESS OF DIRECTORS, EXECUTIVE OFFICERS AND SENIOR OFFICERS [insert if the issuer has a securities purchase program "OTHER THAN UNDER SECURITIES PURCHASE PROGRAMS"]

Name and Principal Position (a)	Involvement of Issuer or Subsidiary (b)	Largest Amount Outstanding During [Last Completed Financial Year] ($) (c)	Amount Outstanding as at [current date] ($) (d)

(e)   State in the introduction immediately preceding the table required by paragraph (d) of this Item, for indebtedness not entered into in connection with a purchase of securities of the issuer or any of its subsidiaries, separately, the aggregate indebtedness,

   (i) to the issuer or any of its subsidiaries, and

   (ii) to another entity if the indebtedness is the subject of a guarantee, support agreement, letter of credit or other similar arrangement or understanding provided by the issuer or any of its subsidiaries,

of all officers, directors, employees and former officers, directors and employees of the issuer or any of its subsidiaries outstanding as at a date within thirty days of certification of the prospectus.

(f)   Disclose in a footnote to, or a narrative accompanying, each table required by this Item,

   (i) the material terms of each incidence of indebtedness and, if applicable, of each guarantee, support agreement, letter of credit or other similar arrangement or understanding, including without limitation the term to maturity, rate of interest and any understanding, agreement or intention to limit recourse, and for the table required by paragraph (d) only, any security for the indebtedness and the nature of the transaction in which the indebtedness was incurred,

(ii) any material adjustment or amendment made during the most recently completed financial year to the terms of the indebtedness and, if applicable, the guarantee, support agreement, letter of credit or similar arrangement or understanding, and

(iii) the class or series of the securities purchased with financial assistance or held as security for the indebtedness and, if the class or series of securities is not publicly traded, all material terms of the securities, including but not limited to provisions for exchange, conversion, exercise, redemption, retraction and dividends.

(g) No disclosure need be made under this Item of an incidence of indebtedness that has been entirely repaid on or before the date of certification of the prospectus or of routine indebtedness.

"Routine indebtedness" means indebtedness described in any of the following:

(i) If an issuer makes loans to employees generally, whether or not in the ordinary course of business, loans are considered routine indebtedness if made on terms, including those as to interest rate and security, no more favourable to the borrower than the terms on which loans are made by the issuer to employees generally, but the amount at any time during the last completed financial year remaining unpaid under the loans to any one director, executive officer, senior officer or proposed nominee together with his or her associates that are treated as routine indebtedness under this clause must not exceed $25,000.

(ii) Whether or not the issuer makes loans in the ordinary course of business, a loan to a director, executive officer or senior officer is considered routine indebtedness if,

A. the borrower is a full-time employee of the issuer,

B. the loan is fully secured against the residence of the borrower, and

C. the amount of the loan does not exceed the annual salary of the borrower.

(iii) If the issuer makes loans in the ordinary course of business, a loan is considered routine indebtedness if made to a person or company other than a full-time employee of the issuer, and if the loan,

A. is made on substantially the same terms, including those as to interest rate and security, as are available when a loan is made to other customers of the issuer with comparable credit ratings, and

B. involves no more than usual risks of collectibility.

(iv) Indebtedness arising by reason of purchases made on usual trade terms or of ordinary travel or expense advances, or for similar reasons is considered routine indebtedness if the repayment arrangements are in accord with usual commercial practice.

(h) For purposes of this Item, "executive officer" has the same meaning as in Form 41 and "support agreement" includes, but is not limited to, an agreement to provide assistance in the maintenance or servicing of any indebtedness and an agreement to provide compensation for the purpose of maintaining or servicing any indebtedness of the borrower.

See NIN 93/23 "Executive Compensation".

Item 24 - Options to Purchase Securities:

Furnish (in tabular form, if possible) the information referred to in Instruction 1, as at a specified date not more than thirty days before the date of the preliminary prospectus or pro forma prospectus, as the case may be, and as at the date of the filing of the prospectus, as to options to purchase securities of the issuer or any of its subsidiaries that are held or proposed to be held:

(i) by all executive officers as a group and all directors who are not also executive officers as a group, indicating the aggregate number of executive officers and the aggregate number of directors to whom the information applies, without naming them;

(ii) by all executive officers of all subsidiaries of the issuer as a group and all directors of such subsidiaries who are not also executive officers as a group, without naming them, excluding individuals referred to in clause (i);

(iii) by all other employees of the issuer as a group, without naming them;

(iv) by all other employees of the subsidiaries of the issuer as a group, without naming them; and

(v) by any other person or company, naming each such person or company.

INSTRUCTIONS:

1. Describe the options, stating the material provisions of each class or type of option including,

(i) the designation and number of the securities under option;

(ii) the purchase price of the securities under option or the formula by which the purchase price will be determined, and the expiration dates of such options;

(iii) if reasonably ascertainable, the market value of the securities under option on the date of grant; and

(iv) if reasonably ascertainable, the market value of the securities under option on the specified date.

2. For the purposes of this Item,

(i) "executive officer" means the chairman and any vice-chairman of the board of directors of an issuer who performs the functions of such office on a full-time basis, the president, any vice-president in charge of a principal business unit such as sales, finance or production, and any officer of the issuer or of a subsidiary who performs a policy-making function in respect of the issuer, whether or not such officer is also a director of the issuer or the subsidiary;

(ii) "options" includes all options, share purchase warrants or rights other than those shares issued on a pro rata basis, to all security holders of the same class resident in Canada and an extension of an option shall be deemed to be a granting of an option.

3. Options that are proposed to be held are those where there is an approval or understanding or commitment of the issuer or a subsidiary in respect of the granting of such options.

4. In the disclosure made under this Item 24, do not include options granted or proposed to be granted that are otherwise disclosed in Item 1 or 2, including options granted or to be granted to the underwriter in respect of the distribution under the prospectus.

Item 25 - Escrowed Shares:

State as of a specified date within thirty days prior to the date of the preliminary prospectus or pro forma prospectus, in substantially the tabular form indicated, the number of shares of each class of voting securities of the issuer to the knowledge of the issuer held in escrow, disclosing the name of the depositary, if any, the date of and the conditions governing the release of the shares from escrow;

TABLE

Column 1	Column 2	Column 3
Designation of class	Number of securities held in escrow	Percentage of class
....	....	....
....	....	....

Item 26 - Principal Holders of Securities:

Furnish the following information as of a specified date within thirty days prior to the date of the preliminary prospectus or pro forma prospectus, in substantially the tabular form indicated.

(a) The number of securities of each class of voting securities of the issuer owned of record or beneficially, directly or indirectly, by each person who owns of record, or is known by the issuer to own beneficially, directly or indirectly, more than 10 per cent of any class of such securities. Show in Column 3 whether the securities are owned both or record and beneficially, of record only, or beneficially only, and show in Columns 4 and 5 the respective amounts and percentages known by the issuer to be owned in each such manner.

TABLE

Column 1	Column 2	Column 3	Column 4	Column 5
Name and address	Designation of class	Type of ownership	Number of securities owned	Percentage of class
....	....	....	....	....

(b) The percentage of securities of each class of voting securities of the issuer or any of its parents or its subsidiaries, beneficially owned, directly or indirectly, by all directors and senior officers of the issuer, as a group, without naming them:

TABLE

Column 1	Column 2
Designation of Class	Percentage of Class
....	....
....	....

INSTRUCTIONS:

1. Where a person is shown by the issuer as owning directly or indirectly more than 10 per cent of any class of such securities, the Superintendent may require the disclosure of such additional information as is necessary to identify any individual who, through his direct or indirect ownership of voting securities in the person owns directly or indirectly more than 10 percent of any class of such securities. The name of such an individual should be disclosed in a foot note to the table described in paragraph (a).

2. For purposes of paragraph (a), securities owned beneficially, directly or indirectly, and of record shall be aggregated in determining whether any person owns more than 10 per cent of the securities of any class.

3. If voting securities are being offered in connection with, or pursuant to, a plan of acquisition, amalgamation or reorganization, indicate as far as practicable, the respective holdings of voting securities that will exist after giving effect to the plan.

4. If any of the securities being offered are to be offered for the account of a securityholder name such security holder and state the number or amount of the securities owned by him, the number or amount to be offered for his account, and the number or amount to be owned by him after the offering.

5. If, to the knowledge of the issuer or the underwriter of the securities being offered, more than 10 per cent of any class of voting securities of the issuer are held or are to be held subject to any voting trust or other similar agreement, other than an escrow arrangement referred to in Item 24, state the designation of such securities, the number or amount held or to be held and the duration of the agreement. Give the names and addresses of the voting trustees and outline briefly their voting rights and other powers under the agreement.

6. If, to the knowledge of the issuer, the parent or the underwriter of the securities being offered, any person named in answer to paragraph (a) is an associate or affiliate of any other person named therein, disclose, in so far as known, the material facts of such relationship, including any basis for influence over the issuer enjoyed by the person other than the holding of the voting securities of the issuer.

Item 27 - Intercorporate Relationships:

(a) Furnish a list of each subsidiary, other than inactive subsidiaries, of the issuer. As to each such subsidiary indicate the jurisdiction under the laws of which it was organized, and the percentage of voting securities owned by its parent.

(b) Clearly illustrate by way of a diagram or otherwise the intercorporate relationships of the issuer, its parent and those subsidiaries listed pursuant to paragraph (a).

(c) Where one of the primary businesses of the issuer is investing, reinvesting, owning, holding or trading in securities, give in substantially the tabular form indicated the following information as at a date within thirty days of the date of the preliminary prospectus or pro forma prospectus, with respect to each company 5 per cent or more of whose securities of any class are owned directly or indirectly by the issuer or its affiliates.

TABLE

Name and address of company	Nature of its principal business	Percentage of securities of any class beneficially owned, directly or indirectly	Percentage of book value of of issuer's assets invested therein
....	....	....	....
....	....	....	....

INSTRUCTIONS:

1. If the securities being issued are to be issued in connection with, or pursuant to, a plan of acquisition, reorganization, readjustment, or succession, indicate insofar as practicable the status to exist upon consummation of the plan.

2. The name of any particular subsidiary may be omitted if

(a) - the assets of the subsidiary, or
     - the investment in and advances to the subsidiary by its parent and the parent's other subsidiaries

if any, do not exceed 10 per cent of the assets of the parent and its subsidiaries on a consolidated basis;

(b)   the sales and operating revenue of the subsidiary do not exceed 10 per cent of the sales and operating revenues of its parent and the parent's subsidiaries on a consolidated basis; and

(c)   the unnamed subsidiaries considered in the aggregate as a single subsidiary would satisfy the conditions in (a) and (b) if the reference therein to 10 per cent were replaced by 20 per cent.

Item 28 - Prior Sales:

(a)   State the prices at which securities of the class offered by the prospectus have been sold within the twelve months prior to the date of the preliminary prospectus or pro forma prospectus, or are to be sold, by the issuer or selling security holder if such prices differ from those at which the securities are offered by the prospectus. State the number of securities sold or to be sold at each price.

(b)   Where the class of securities offered are listed on a Canadian stock exchange or solely on a foreign stock exchange, give price ranges and volume traded on such stock exchange on a monthly basis for each month or, if applicable, part month, of the current quarter and the immediately preceding quarter and on a quarterly basis for the next preceding seven quarters provided that the Superintendent may permit the omission of the information regarding trading volume.

INSTRUCTION:

In the case of sales by a selling securityholder, the information required by paragraph (a) may be given in the form of price ranges for each calendar month.

Item 29 - Interest of Management and Other in Material Transactions:

Describe briefly, and where practicable state the approximate amount of any material interest, direct or indirect, of any of the following persons in any transaction within the three years prior to the date of the preliminary prospectus or pro forma prospectus, or in any proposed transaction which has materially affected or will materially affect the issuer or any of its subsidiaries:

(i)   any director or senior officer of the issuer;

(ii) any securityholder named in answer to paragraph (a) of Item 26; and

(iii) associate or affiliate of any of the foregoing persons.

INSTRUCTIONS:

1.   Give a brief description of the material transaction. Include the name and address of each person whose interest in any transaction is described and the nature of the relationship by reason of which such interest is required to be described.

2.   As to any transaction involving the purchase or sale of assets by or to the issuer or any subsidiary, state the cost of the assets to the purchaser and the cost thereof to the seller if acquired by the seller within two years to the transaction.

3.   This item does not apply to any interest arising from the ownership of securities of the issuer where the securityholder receives no extra or special benefit or advantage not shared on an equal basis by all other holders of the same class of securities or all other holders of the same class of securities who are resident in Canada.

4.   Information shall be included as to any material underwriting discounts or commissions upon the sale of securities by the issuer where any of the specified persons was or is to be an underwriter or is an associate, affiliate or partner of a person, or partnership that was or is to be an underwriter.

5.   No information need be given in answer to this item as to any transaction or any interest therein, where,

(i)   the rates or charges involved in the transaction are fixed by law or determined by competitive bids;

(ii) the interest of a specified person in the transaction is solely that of a director of another issuer that is a party to the transaction;

(iii) the transaction involves services as a bank or other depository of funds, transfer agent, registrar, trustee under a trust indenture or other similar services;

(iv) the interest of a specified person, including all periodic instalments in the case of any lease or other agreement providing for periodic payments or instalments, does not exceed $50,000; or

(v)   the transaction does not, directly or indirectly, involve remuneration for services, and,

(a) the interest of the specified person arose from the beneficial ownership, direct or indirect, of less than 10 per cent of any class of voting securities of another company that is a party to the transaction,

(b) the transaction is in the ordinary course of business of the issuer or its subsidiaries, and

(c) the amount of the transaction or series of transactions is less than 10 per cent of the total sales or purchases, as the case may be, of the issuer and its subsidiaries for the last completed financial year.

6.   Information shall be furnished in answer to this item with respect to transactions not excluded above that involve remuneration, directly or indirectly, to any of the specified persons for services in any capacity unless the interest of the person arises solely from the beneficial ownership, direct or indirect, of less than 10 per cent of any class of voting securities of another company furnishing the services to the issuer or its subsidiaries.

7.   This item does not require the disclosure of any interest in any transaction unless such interest and transaction are material.

Item 30 - Auditors, Transfer Agents and Registrars:

(a)   State the name and address of the auditor of the issuer.

(b)   Where shares are offered, state the names of the issuer's transfer agents and registrars and the location (by municipalities) of the registers of transfers of each class of shares of the issuer. Where securities other than shares are offered, state the location (by municipalities) of each register on which transfers of such securities may be recorded.

Item 31 - Material Contracts:

Give particulars of every material contract entered into within the two years prior to the date of the preliminary prospectus or pro forma prospectus, by the issuer or any of its subsidiaries and state a reasonable time and place at which any such contract or a copy thereof may be inspected during distribution of the securities being offered.

INSTRUCTIONS:

1.   The term "material contract" for this purpose means any contract that can reasonably be regarded as presently material to the proposed investor in the securities being offered.

2.   Set out a complete list of all material contracts, indicating those which are disclosed elsewhere in the prospectus and provide particulars with respect to those material contracts about which particulars are not given elsewhere in the prospectus. This item does not require disclosure of contracts entered into in the ordinary course of business of the issuer or its subsidiaries as the case may be.

3.   Particulars of contracts should include the dates of, parties to, consideration and general nature of the contracts, succinctly described.

4. Particulars of contracts need not be disclosed, or copies of such contracts made available for inspection, if the Superintendent determines that such disclosure or making- available would impair the value of the contract and would not be necessary for the protection of investors.

Item 32 - Other Material Facts:

Give particulars of any other material facts relating to the securities proposed to be offered and not disclosed pursuant to the foregoing items.

IT IS AN OFFENCE FOR A PERSON TO MAKE A STATEMENT IN A DOCU- MENT REQUIRED TO BE FILED OR FURNISHED UNDER THE ACT OR THIS REGULATION THAT, AT THE TIME AND IN THE LIGHT OF THE CIRCUMSTANCES UNDER WHICH IT IS MADE, IS A MISREPRESEN- TATION.

January 15, 1987

FORM 12A

INFORMATION REQUIRED IN PROSPECTUS OF JUNIOR INDUSTRIAL ISSUER

TABLE OF CONTENTS

Forms

19.   AUDITOR

20.   REGISTRAR AND TRANSFER AGENT

21.   MATERIAL CONTRACTS

    21.1   Particulars of material contracts

    21.2   Inspection of material contracts

22.   OTHER MATERIAL FACTS

23.   PURCHASERS' STATUTORY RIGHTS

24.   FINANCIAL STATEMENTS, REPORTS AND OTHER EXHIBITS

25.   CERTIFICATES

The prospectus required under Section 42(2) of the Securities Act for an industrial issuer where, under Local Policy Statement 3-17, the underwriter is required to obtain an assessment report, or would have been required to obtain an assessment report if the Superintendent had not waived the requirement, shall be in the following form.

Forms

FORM 12A

Securities Act

INFORMATION REQUIRED IN PROSPECTUS OF A JUNIOR INDUSTRIAL ISSUER

GENERAL INSTRUCTIONS

1.   This form provides a guideline to issuers in determining the extent of disclosure that is required to provide investors with full, true and plain disclosure of all material facts. Depending on the circumstances of the particular issuer, additional disclosure may be necessary.

2.   All disclosure contained in the prospectus must be factual and non-promotional. Prospectuses are required to contain material facts. Statements of opinions, beliefs or views must not be made unless the statements are made on the authority of experts and consents are obtained and filed. The Superintendent may require verification of disclosure.

3.   The disclosure contained in the prospectus must be understandable to readers and, in particular, should avoid the use of jargon. If technical terms are required, these terms shall be defined in a glossary that must be included in the prospectus.

4.   This form may be used as a base disclosure document where the issuer elects to use a summary prospectus as permitted by Local Policy Statement 3-02. In that case, references to "prospectus" in this form are to be replaced by references to "base disclosure document".

5.   Except where the context otherwise requires, "prospectus" refers to preliminary or final prospectus as appropriate.

6.   In specific items, the instructions indicate that "issuer" includes the issuer's subsidiaries and proposed subsidiaries. In other circumstances, "issuer" may include the issuer's subsidiaries and proposed subsidiaries if the context reasonably requires. An entity can only be considered a proposed subsidiary if the entity will be a subsidiary on completion of the offering.

7.   Where information as to the identity of a person is disclosed, disclose whether the person is at **Arm's Length** to the issuer or, if not, the relationship of the person to the issuer. Where the person is not at **Arm's Length** and is not an individual, disclose the name of any individual who is an insider of the person by virtue of paragraph (c) of the definition of insider in the Act.

8.   Whenever disclosure is required to be made of costs paid or to be paid by the issuer, disclose the portion of the costs paid or to be paid to insiders or holders of performance shares.

9.   When disclosure is required as of a specific date and there has been a significant or material change in the information subsequent to the date the information must be presented as of a date that reflects this change.

10. Each item outlines disclosure requirements. Instructions to assist you in providing this disclosure are printed in smaller type.

11. Certain terms used in this Form are defined in the Securities Act, S.B.C. 1985, c. 83 (the **"Act"**), Securities Regulation, B.C. Reg. 270/86 (the **"Regulation"**) and the Interpretation Act, R.S.B.C 1979, c. 206. Certain terms defined in specific sections of this Form are in bold. Other defined terms used in this Form, which are capitalized and in bold, are as follows:

"Agent" means agent or underwriter, as applicable.

"Arm's Length" is defined in Local Policy Statement 3-07 in relation to an arm's length transaction.

"Breakdown of Costs" means a schedule of costs associated with the specific classification, separately itemizing each component that represents 10% or more of the total costs, with all other costs being grouped together under the heading "miscellaneous costs".

"Development Costs" means costs incurred by the issuer, its subsidiaries and proposed subsidiaries relating to product research and development, material acquisitions of plant, equipment, technology, and marketing rights, and does not include general and administrative costs.

"Funds Available" means the aggregate of

(a)   the net proceeds to be derived by the issuer from the sale of the securities offered under the prospectus,

(b)   the estimated minimum working capital available to the issuer, its subsidiaries and proposed subsidiaries as of the Most Recent Month End, and

(c)   the amounts and sources of other funds that will be available to the issuer, its subsidiaries and proposed subsidiaries prior to or concurrently with the completion of the offering.

"Management" means all directors, officers, employees and contractors whose expertise is critical to the issuer, its subsidiaries and proposed subsidiaries in providing the issuer with a reasonable opportunity to achieve its stated business objectives.

"Most Recent Month End" means the latest month end prior to the date of the prospectus or revised preliminary prospectus or, where the date of the prospectus or revised preliminary prospectus is within ten days of the end of the latest month, the month end prior to the end of that month.

"Product" means any product, service or technology of the issuer

(a)   that has a net book value representing more than 10% of the issuer's total assets,

(b)   that generates more than 10% of the issuer's gross revenues,

(c)   on which more than 10% of the proceeds of the offering will be spent, or

(d)   that is or will be the focus of the issuer's stated business objectives.

"Stub Period" means the period between the issuer's most recently completed financial year and the **Most Recent Month End**.

1.   FACE PAGE DISCLOSURE

1.1 *Required language* - State in bold print at the top of the face page of the prospectus the following:

> **THIS PROSPECTUS CONSTITUTES A PUBLIC OFFERING OF THESE SECURITIES ONLY IN THOSE JURISDICTIONS WHERE THEY MAY BE LAWFULLY OFFERED FOR SALE AND THEREIN ONLY BY PERSONS PERMITTED TO SELL SUCH SECURITIES. NO SECURITIES COMMISSION OR SIMILAR AUTHORITY IN CANADA HAS IN ANY WAY PASSED UPON THE MERITS OF THE SECURITIES OFFERED HEREUNDER AND ANY REPRESENTATION TO THE CONTRARY IS AN OFFENCE.**

1.2 *Preliminary prospectus disclosure* - State in red ink on the left hand side of the face page of the preliminary prospectus the following legend or any variation that may be permitted:

> This is a preliminary prospectus relating to these securities, a copy of which has been filed with the British Columbia Securities Commission but which has not yet become final for the purpose of a distribution. Information contained herein is subject to completion or amendment. The securities may not be sold nor may offers to buy be accepted prior to the time a receipt is obtained from the British Columbia Securities Commission for the final prospectus.

1.3 *Basic disclosure about the offering* - Provide the following information:

INITIAL PUBLIC OFFERING [or] NEW ISSUE [and/or] SECONDARY OFFERING

DATE

[PRELIMINARY] PROSPECTUS

[Name of Issuer
Head Office Address
Telephone Number]

[total number and type of securities qualified for distribution under this prospectus, including any options or warrants, and price per security]

1.4 *Distribution spread* - Provide details of all securities offered for cash in substantially the following form:

	Price to Public	Agents' discounts or commissions	Proceeds to issuer or selling security-holder
Per security	. . . .	. . . .	. . . .
Total	. . . .	. . . .	. . . .

1. Where amounts are not known to the issuer at the date of the preliminary prospectus, the issuer must estimate the amounts in the table provided a notation to that effect is made under the table.

2. Only commissions paid or payable in cash by the issuer or selling security holder and discounts granted are to be included in the table. Other commissions or consideration, including warrants, options, finders fees, sponsorship fees, fiscal agency payments or other similar payments, shall be set out as a note to the table.

3. Where the issuer has granted the **Agent** a "greenshoe" option, disclose the number of additional securities that may be issued if the option is exercised as a note to the table.

4. Where the prospectus discloses a plan of distribution not involving an underwriting or other subscription guarantee, the closing of the distribution under the prospectus must be subject to a minimum subscription and, where the prospectus also discloses a maximum subscription that differs from the minimum subscription, totals must be provided for both the minimum and maximum subscriptions.

5. If any of the securities being offered are for the account of a security holder, provide a cross reference to "Plan of Distribution - Secondary Offering".

1.5 *Market for securities*

    (a)   In a preliminary prospectus, state the following:

> An application has been made to conditionally list the securities offered under this prospectus on the _____ Exchange. Listing is subject to the issuer fulfilling all the listing requirements of the Exchange.

(b)   In a final prospectus, state the following:

    The _____ Exchange has conditionally listed the securities being offered under this prospectus. The listing is subject to the issuer fulfilling all of the listing requirements of the _____ Exchange, including prescribed distribution and financial requirements, on or before _____.

• Where the preliminary prospectus is also being filed in another jurisdiction and that jurisdiction will not permit disclosure that a conditional listing application has been made, the statement required by (a) may be omitted provided the issuer confirms in writing to the Superintendent that a conditional listing application has been made with a stock exchange.

1.6   *Risk factors* - State the following in bold type:

    INVESTMENTS IN SMALL BUSINESSES INVOLVE A HIGH DEGREE OF RISK AND INVESTORS SHOULD NOT INVEST ANY FUNDS IN THIS OFFERING UNLESS THEY CAN AFFORD TO LOSE THEIR ENTIRE INVESTMENT. REFER TO "RISK FACTORS".

1.7   *Public and insider ownership* - Disclose the aggregate number of voting securities that will be held by the public and the aggregate number of voting securities that will be held by promoters, insiders, holders of performance shares and **Agents** as a group, each as a percentage of the total issued and outstanding voting securities of the issuer upon the completion of the offering.

1.8   *Foreign issuers* - If the **issuer** is incorporated or continued under the laws of a jurisdiction other than Canada or a province or territory of Canada, state the following (with the bracketed information completed as appropriate):

    [All of] [Certain of] the directors and officers of the issuer and [all of] [certain of] the experts named herein reside outside of Canada. [[Substantially] all of the assets of these persons and of the Issuer may be located outside of Canada.] Although the Issuer has appointed [insert name and address of agent for service] as its agent for service of process in British Columbia, it may not be possible for investors to effect service of process within British Columbia upon the directors, officers and experts referred to above. It may also not be possible to enforce against the Issuer, [certain of] its directors and officers and [certain of] the experts named herein judgments obtained in Canadian courts predicated upon the civil liability provisions of applicable securities laws in Canada.

• In this subsection, **"issuer"** includes the issuer's subsidiaries, proposed subsidiaries and predecessor(s).

1.9   *Agent* - State the name and address of the **Agent**. If the **issuer** or selling security holder is a related or connected party of the **Agent**, summarize the nature of the relationship and provide a cross reference to "Relationship between Issuer or Selling Security Holder and **Agent**".

• In this subsection, **"issuer"** includes the issuer's subsidiaries and proposed subsidiaries.

2.   TABLE OF CONTENTS

Include a table of contents setting out the headings of each section in the prospectus and the page number on which each section starts.

3.   SUMMARY OF PROSPECTUS

State:

    The following is a summary of the principal features of this Offering. More detailed information is contained in the body of the Prospectus.

Provide a brief description of the following items:

(a)   the principal business of the issuer, its subsidiaries and proposed subsidiaries,

(b)   the securities offered by the issuer, including the offering price and the net proceeds expected to be realized by the issuer,

(c) the intended use of the **Funds Available**, including the amount allocated for each use,

(d) the stated business objectives that the issuer expects to accomplish using the **Funds Available**,

(e) the specific risks relating to the business disclosed in paragraph (a), and

(f) any other information considered appropriate under the circumstances.

1. Where this document is a base disclosure document used in connection with a summary prospectus, this section is not required in the base disclosure document.

2. Appropriate cross references must be made to items and page numbers in the prospectus.

3. Normally, the summary should not exceed two pages in length.

4. CORPORATE STRUCTURE

4.1 *Name and incorporation* - Provide

(a) the full name of the issuer and the address of its registered office and its address for service in Canada;

(b) the laws under which the issuer was incorporated or organized and the date the issuer came into existence;

(c) the full name of each of the issuer's subsidiaries or proposed subsidiaries, the laws under which they were incorporated or organized and the date they came into existence;

(d) if applicable, that the issuer has been a party to any amalgamation, arrangement or continuance or has changed its name, and the laws governing the event; and

(e) relevant details of the issuer's form of organization and structure, where the issuer is not a company.

4.2 *Intercorporate relationships* - Illustrate by way of a diagram or otherwise the intercorporate relationships among the issuer, its parent, subsidiaries and proposed subsidiaries. For each subsidiary and proposed subsidiary, state the percentage of voting securities owned or to be owned by its parent.

If the securities offered under the prospectus are being issued in connection with, or pursuant to, an amalgamation, merger, reorganization or arrangement, illustrate by way of a diagram or otherwise the intercorporate relationships both before and after the completion of the proposed transaction.

5. BUSINESS OF THE ISSUER

5.1 *Description and general development* - Describe the business carried on and intended to be carried on by the **issuer**, including **Products** that the **issuer** is or will be developing or producing, and the stage of development of each of the **Products**.

Disclose the year of commencement of operations and summarize the general development of the business of the **issuer** during the five preceding financial years and the **Stub Period**, or such shorter period as the **issuer** may have been in existence. Provide disclosure for earlier periods if material to an understanding of the development of the business.

1. In describing developments, include disclosure of the following: the nature and results of any bankruptcy, receivership or similar proceedings; the nature and results of any material reorganization; material prior litigation (including any series of proceedings based on similar causes of action); the nature and date of any prior trading suspensions or cease trade orders made against the **issuer** by any regulatory authority; material changes in the types of **Products** produced or services rendered; and any material changes in the method of conducting the business.

2. Where this document will be used as a base disclosure document, the disclosure in this section should be in sufficient detail so that when it is extracted to the summary prospectus from the base disclosure document it will provide investors with a reasonable understanding of the **issuer's** business.

Forms

3. In this section, **"issuer"** includes the issuer's subsidiaries, proposed subsidiaries and predecessor(s).

5.2   *Summary and analysis of financial operations* - Provide the information indicated in the table set out below with respect to the issuer's financial operations during the last two financial years and any period subsequent to the most recent financial year end for which financial statements are included in the prospectus.

TABLE

	* Month Period Ending *	Year Ending *	Year Ending *
Sales			
Gross profit			
Research and Development Expenses			
Sales and Marketing Expenses			
General and Administrative Expenses			
Net Income (Loss)			
Working Capital			
Property, Plant and Equipment			
Deferred Research and Development			
Other Intangibles			
Long Term Liabilities			
Shareholders' equity Dollar amount Number of securities			

State the following as a note to the number of shares in the table (with the bracketed information completed as appropriate):

There are [* shares] issued and outstanding as of the date of this prospectus, of which [*] are performance shares that will be released from escrow at the rate of one share for each $[*] of cumulative cash flow generated by the Issuer from its operations. Upon the successful completion of this offering, a total of [* shares] will be issued and outstanding.

Discuss and compare the issuer's results of operations, including the reasons for any substantial variations, for the periods included in the table, and the anticipated impact of these historical operations on the future activities of the issuer. Include, to the extent reasonably practicable, a description of the impact of acquisitions or dispositions disclosed in section 5.5 on the operating results and financial position of the issuer.

Also, include a discussion of liquidity on an historical and prospective basis in the context of the issuer's business and focus on the ability of the issuer to generate adequate amounts of cash and cash equivalents when needed. This discussion, at a minimum, should identify and describe the following,

(a)   any known trends or expected fluctuations in the issuer's liquidity, taking into account known demands, commitments, events or uncertainties, and where a deficiency is identified indicate the course of action that has been taken or is proposed to be taken to remedy the deficiency;

(b)   those balance sheet conditions or income or cash flow items that may be indicators of the issuer's liquidity condition;

(c)   the requirements relating to working capital items (e.g. where significant quantities of inventory are required to be carried to meet rapid delivery requirements of customers or where extended payment terms have been provided to customers);

(d)   the nature and extent of legal or practical restrictions on the ability of subsidiaries to transfer funds to the issuer and the impact such restrictions have had or are expected to have on the ability of the issuer to meet its obligations;

(e)   whether the issuer is in arrears on the payment of dividends, interest, or principal payment on borrowing; and

(f)   whether the issuer is in default on any debt covenants at the present time or was in default during the most recently completed financial year and any period subsequent to the most recent financial year end for which financial statements are included in the prospectus.

1. The sales and gross profit disclosed in the table must be separately presented by industry and geographic segment.

2. Net income disclosed in the table is net income after tax.

3. Where it would be meaningful to an investor, include in the table any prior periods covered by the financial statements included in the prospectus and provide an analysis of the issuer's results of operations for those periods.

4. Where the closing of the distribution under the prospectus is subject to a minimum subscription, adjust the required statement as appropriate.

5. Where the issuer has not had significant sales, the analysis must discuss all material expenditures. Related or similar types of expenditures representing in the aggregate greater than 10% of total expenditures would generally be considered material.

6. In the discussion identify any unusual or extraordinary events or transactions or any significant economic changes that materially affect income from continuing operations and describe the extent to which income from continuing operations was affected.

7. Describe in the discussion the extent to which any changes in net sales or revenues are attributable to changes in selling prices or to changes in the volume or quantity of goods or services being sold or to the introduction of new **Products** or services. Where the issuer knows of events that are expected to materially affect costs or revenues, describe the event(s).

8. Where there has been a significant or material change in operations from the date of the information in the table, the analysis of operations and variations in operations must discuss the change.

5.3   *Stated business objectives* - State the business objectives that the **issuer** expects to accomplish using the **Funds Available** and the time period in which these business objectives are expected to be achieved.

1. The **issuer's** stated business objectives must not include any prospective financial information with respect to sales, whether expressed in terms of dollars or units, unless the information is prepared in accordance with National Policy Statement No. 48. Where sales performance is considered to be an important objective, it must be stated in general terms. For example, the **issuer** may state that it anticipates generating sufficient cash flow from sales to pay its operating costs for a specified period following completion of the offering.

2. Where the closing of the distribution under the prospectus is subject to a minimum subscription, the description of the **issuer's** stated business objectives should reflect both the minimum and maximum net proceeds to be derived by the **issuer**.

3. In this section, **"issuer"** includes the issuer's subsidiaries and proposed subsidiaries.

5.4   *Milestones* - Describe each significant event that must occur for the business objectives to be accomplished and state the specific time period in which each event is expected to occur and the costs related to each event.

1. Examples of significant events would include hiring of key personnel, making major capital acquisitions, obtaining necessary regulatory approvals, implementing marketing plans and strategies and commencing production and sales.

2. The milestones must be cross referenced to the related items in the prospectus.

5.5　*Acquisitions and dispositions* - Disclose any material acquisitions and dispositions relating to the **issuer's** current business made by the **issuer** during the five preceding financial years and the **Stub Period**, or such shorter period as the **issuer** may have been in existence, and any intended material acquisitions or dispositions, including particulars of

(a)　the nature of the assets acquired or disposed of or to be acquired or disposed of,

(b)　the actual or proposed date of each acquisition or disposition,

(c)　the name of the vendor or purchaser and whether the transaction was or will be at **Arm's Length**,

(d)　for an acquisition or disposition not at **Arm's Length**, the vendor's out of pocket costs as described in Local Policy Statement No. 3-07,

(e)　the consideration, both monetary and non-monetary, paid or to be paid to or by the **issuer**,

(f)　any material obligations that must be complied with in order to keep any acquisition or disposition agreement in good standing,

(g)　how the consideration was determined (e.g. limited to out of pocket costs, valuation opinion or **Arm's Length** negotiations), and

(h)　any valuation opinion required by a policy of a securities regulatory authority or a stock exchange to support the value of the consideration paid in connection with a transaction not previously approved by the Superintendent or the Vancouver Stock Exchange, or that has been approved within the preceding financial year and the **Stub Period**, including the name of the author, the date of the opinion, the assets to which the opinion relates and the value attributed to the assets.

1. Out of pocket costs must be supported by either audited financial statements or an audited statement of costs.

2. The granting or acquiring of any material licence agreement by the **issuer** or any predecessor is considered to be an acquisition or disposition for purposes of this section.

3. In this section, **"issuer"** includes the issuer's subsidiaries, proposed subsidiaries and predecessor[s].

5.6　*Management* - Provide the following information for each member of **Management**:

(a)　state the individual's name, age, position and responsibilities with the **issuer** and relevant educational background,

(b)　state whether the individual works full time for the **issuer** or what proportion of the individual's time will be devoted to the **issuer**,

(c)　state whether the individual is an employee or independent contractor of the **issuer**,

(d)　state the individual's principal occupations or employment during the five years prior to the date of the prospectus, disclosing with respect to each organization as of the time such occupation or employment was carried on:

(i)　its name and principal business,

(ii)　if applicable, that the organization was an affiliate of the **issuer**,

(iii)　positions held by the individual,

(iv)　whether it is still carrying on business, if known to the individual,

(e) describe the individual's experience in the **issuer's** industry, and

(f) state whether the individual has entered into a non-competition or non-disclosure agreement with the **issuer**.

1. The description of the principal occupation of a member of **Management** must be specific. The terms "businessman" or "entrepreneur" are not sufficiently specific.

2. The disclosure in (d)(iv) is only required where the individual was or is an officer or director of the organization.

3. In this section, **"issuer"** includes the issuer's subsidiaries and proposed subsidiaries.

5.7 *Organizational structure* - Provide a chart setting out the number of full and part time employees currently in each department and the approximate number of full and part time employees or contractors in each department required to meet the issuer's stated business objectives.

5.8 *Products* - Describe

(a) the **Products** developed or to be developed as part of the **issuer's** stated business objectives,

(b) the history of development of the **Products**, including estimated **Development Costs** to the **Most Recent Month End**,

(c) the stage of development of the **Products**, including whether they are at the design, prototype, market test or commercial production stage,

(d) if the **Products** are not at the commercial production stage or if part of the **Funds Available** will be used for research and development,

 (i) the stage of development that **Management** anticipates will be reached using the **Funds Available**,

 (ii) the major components of the proposed development program that will be funded using the **Funds Available** and provide a **Breakdown of Costs**, and

 (iii) whether the **issuer** is conducting its own research and development, is subcontracting out the research and development or is using a combination of those methods,

(e) any material regulatory approvals that are required for the **issuer** to achieve its stated business objectives,

(f) where the development of documentation is considered to be necessary in the **issuer's** industry, the stage of development of documentation, including manuals, relating to the **Products**, and

(g) the potential impact of any laws, such as industry or environmental regulations or controls on ownership or profit repatriation, or economic or political conditions that may materially affect the **issuer's** operations.

1. The disclosure in (g) need only summarize the potential impact.

2. In this section, **"issuer"** includes the issuer's subsidiaries and proposed subsidiaries.

5.9 *Future developments* - If the **Products** are not at the commercial production stage or if the **Products** will not be in commercial production at conclusion of the proposed development program, describe the additional steps required to get to commercial production and provide an estimate of the **Development Costs** and time periods, to the extent known, and describe any uncertainties relating to the completion of the steps, the estimate of the costs or the time periods.

1. The disclosure in this section must identify any material regulatory approvals that are required for the **issuer's Products** to be in commercial production.

2. In this section, **"issuer"** includes the issuer's subsidiaries and proposed subsidiaries.

5.10 *Proprietary protection* - Where proprietary protection is normally obtained for products similar to the **Products**, describe

(a)   the proprietary protection of the **Products** including the duration of all material patents, copyrights and trade marks,

(b)   if no proprietary protection has been obtained, the steps **Management** intends to take to secure proprietary protection and, if known, the time periods for completing these steps, or explain why this proprietary protection has not or will not be obtained, and

(c)   the steps taken by the issuer, its subsidiaries and proposed subsidiaries to protect their respective know how, trade secrets and other intellectual property, including physical possession of source codes and any use of confidentiality or non-competition agreements.

• Where the issuer, its subsidiaries and proposed subsidiaries are the licensees under any material licence agreement, provide the information required by this section, where known after reasonable investigation, with respect to the licensor.

5.11 *Operations* - If the **issuer** is currently marketing its **Products** or will be marketing its **Products** as part of its stated business objectives, provide the following information regarding the production and sales of its **Products**:

(a)   describe the actual or proposed method of production of the **Products** or, if the **Products** are services, the method of providing the services,

(b)   state whether the **issuer** is producing the **Products** itself, is subcontracting out production, is purchasing the **Products** or is using a combination of these methods,

(c)   disclose the location of existing property, plant and equipment, indicating whether the property, plant or equipment is owned or leased by the **issuer**,

(d)   state the payment terms, expiration dates and the terms of any renewal options of any material leases or mortgages, whether the leases or mortgages are in good standing and, if applicable, that the landlord or mortgagee is not at **Arm's Length** with the **issuer**,

(e)   disclose any specialized skill or knowledge requirements necessary for the **Products** to be produced and describe the extent that this skill or knowledge is available to the **issuer**,

(f)   disclose sources and availability of raw materials, component parts, or finished products including factors that may have a material impact on the **issuer's** operations such as:

   (i) dependence on a limited number of suppliers for essential raw materials, component parts, or finished products,

   (ii) potential shortages of raw materials, component parts or finished products, or

   (iii) any unusual payment terms under any agreements or other arrangements with the **issuer's** principal suppliers, that may impact on the **issuer's** cash flow,

(g)   where any principal supplier of raw materials, component parts or finished products is not at **Arm's Length** with the **issuer**, disclose its name, relationship with the **issuer** and the material terms of any existing contract or arrangement with the **issuer**,

(h)   disclose the extent to which the **issuer's** business is dependent upon a single or a limited number of customers,

(i)   where any existing or proposed principal customer is not at **Arm's Length** with the **issuer**, disclose its name, relationship with the **issuer**, the material terms of any contract or arrangement with the **issuer** and the proportion of the **issuer's** total net sales made to that customer during the preceding financial year and the **Stub Period**,

(j)   describe any unusual payment terms under any agreements or other arrangements with the **issuer's** principal customers that may impact on the **issuer's** cash flow, and

(k) disclose any proposed material changes to plant, property and equipment, manpower or sources of supply required to enable the **issuer** to meet its stated business objectives and provide a **Breakdown of Costs** for the major components of the proposed material changes that will be funded using the **Funds Available**.

• In this section, **"issuer"** including the issuer's, its subsidiaries and proposed subsidiaries.

5.12 *Market* - Provide the following information regarding the market for the **Products**:

(a) describe the market segment and specific geographical area in which the **issuer** is selling or expects to sell its **Products** as contemplated by its stated business objectives or intends to sell its **Products** upon completion of its product development,

(b) describe material industry trends within the market segments and specific geographical areas referred to in paragraph (a) that may impact on the **issuer's** ability to meet the **issuer's** stated business objectives,

(c) describe the competition within the market segments and specific geographical areas referred to in paragraph (a) including, to the extent known after reasonable investigation by the **issuer**,

    (i) names of the **issuer's** principal competitors,

    (ii) a comparison of the principal aspects of competition (e.g. price, service, warranty or product performance) between the **issuer** and its principal competitors, and

    (iii) potential sources of significant new competition,

(d) disclose the extent of market acceptance of the **Products** and the method used to determine whether market acceptance exists (e.g. market testing or surveys), including the names of the parties who performed the appropriate procedures and, if not at **Arm's Length** with the **issuer**, their relationship with the **issuer**,

(e) if applicable, state that obsolescence is a factor in the **issuer's** industry and describe how the **issuer** intends to maintain its competitive position,

(f) describe the effect of any material market controls or regulations within the market segment and specific geographical area referred to in paragraph (a) that may affect the marketing of the **Products** (e.g. marketing boards or export quotas), and

(g) describe the effect of any seasonal variation within the market segment and specific geographical area referred to in paragraph (a) that may affect the sales of the **Products**.

1. In this section, **"issuer"** means the issuer, its subsidiaries and proposed subsidiaries.

2. In discussing competition, consideration must be given to substitute or alternative products that may impact on the **issuer's** ability to meet its stated business objectives.

5.13 *Marketing plans and strategies* - If the **issuer** is currently marketing its **Products** or will be marketing its **Products** in order to achieve its stated business objectives, provide the following information regarding the **issuer's** marketing plans and strategies:

(a) describe when, how and by whom the **Products** are or will be marketed and, if not at **Arm's Length** with the **issuer**, their relationship with the **issuer**,

(b) disclose any marketing programs actual or proposed to meet the **issuer's** stated business objectives and the major components of the marketing programs (e.g. trade shows, magazines, television or radio advertising),

(c) provide a **Breakdown of Costs** for major components of the marketing programs,

(d)   disclose the **issuer's** pricing policy (e.g. at market, discount or premium), and

(e)   where after sales service, maintenance or warranties are a significant competitive factor, describe the differences between the **issuer's** policies and those of its principal competitors.

• In this section, **"issuer"** means the issuer, its subsidiaries and proposed subsidiaries.

5.14 *Administration* - Provide

(a)   the estimated aggregate monthly and total administration costs that will be incurred in order for the issuer to achieve its stated business objectives, the time period during which these costs will be incurred and any anticipated variations in the monthly amounts during that period, and

(b)   a **Breakdown of Costs** of the monthly administration costs disclosed in paragraph (a), including any anticipated variations.

• Administrative support includes professional fees, transfer agent fees, management fees, rent, travel, investor relations and other administrative costs, such as those costs required to maintain a reporting issuer in good standing, whether incurred by the issuer or its subsidiaries.

6.   USE OF PROCEEDS

6.1 *Funds Available* - Provide a breakdown of **Funds Available** as follows:

(a)   the net proceeds to be derived by the issuer from the sale of the securities offered under the prospectus,

(b)   the estimated working capital available to the issuer, its subsidiaries and proposed subsidiaries as of the **Most Recent Month End**, and

(c)   the amounts and sources of other funds that will be available to the issuer, its subsidiaries and proposed subsidiaries prior to or concurrently with the completion of the offering.

1. In each prospectus and revised preliminary prospectus, the amount of working capital must be updated to the **Most Recent Month End**.

2. Where other sources of funds will be available to the issuer, identify the material terms, including the timing, and identity of the person providing the funds.

6.2 *Principal purposes* - Provide, in tabular form, a description of each of the principal purposes, with amounts, for which the **Funds Available** will be used. Where the closing of the distribution under the prospectus is subject to a minimum subscription, provide separate columns disclosing the use of proceeds for the minimum and maximum subscriptions.

State the following (with the bracketed information completed as appropriate):

The Issuer will spend the funds available to it on the completion of this offering to further the Issuer's stated business objectives set out in "Business of the Issuer". There may be circumstances where, for sound business reasons, a reallocation of funds may be necessary in order for the Issuer to achieve its stated business objectives.

1. If there is a maximum subscription that differs from the minimum subscription, identify the order of priority for the principal purposes.

2. Statements as to principal purposes for which the **Funds Available** are to be used must be specific and be cross referenced to the estimated costs disclosed in Item 5. Where the issuer has had no sales or limited sales, the table must include the administrative costs required for the issuer to achieve its stated business objectives.

3. **Funds Available** not allocated to one of the principal purposes must be identified as "Working Capital To Fund Ongoing Operations" and must be sufficient to fund the issuer's operations during the offering period and, following completion of the offering, to maintain the issuer as a reporting issuer during the time frame contemplated by its stated business objectives.

4. Where **Funds Available** will be paid to an insider or holder of performance shares,

identify, either in the table or by way of a note to the table, the person, amount of the payments and principal purposes to which the payments relate.

5. Where more than 10% of the **Funds Available** will be used to reduce or retire indebtedness and where the indebtedness was incurred within the two preceding years, the principal purposes for which the indebtedness was used must be disclosed and where the creditor is an insider to the issuer or is a holder of performance shares, identify the creditor and the nature of the relationship to the issuer.

6. Where the prospectus is used in connection with a special warrant or similar transaction, the principal purposes for which the funds raised in such transaction must be disclosed. Where all or a portion of these funds have been spent provide a cross reference to the detail discussion in Item 5 and explain how the funds were spent. The **Funds Available** must include the balance of the funds, if any, raised by the special warrant or similar transaction that have not been spent.

6.3 *Conflicts of interest* - Where the issuer is a related party or connected party of the **Agent**, or where the securities to be offered are out of the holdings of a selling security holder who is a related party or connected party of the **Agent**, provide a summary of the nature of the relationship between the **Agent** and the issuer, or the **Agent** and the selling security holder, as the case may be.

State the extent to which the proceeds of the distribution will be applied, directly or indirectly, for the benefit of the **Agent** or any related party of the **Agent**. Where the proceeds will not be applied for the benefit of the **Agent** or any related party of the **Agent**, so state. Provide a cross-reference to the information required by Item 16.

1. For example, disclosure would be required in most cases where the issuer received a loan from the **Agent** and thus would be a connected party of the **Agent**. Reference should be made to section 167.4 of the **Regulation** for further requirements.

2. For the purposes of this section, reference to an **Agent** includes a special selling group member, as defined in section 167.4 of the **Regulation**.

7. RISK FACTORS

List the risks that could be considered to be material to an investor as follows:

(a) risks relating to the nature of the business of the **issuer**,

(b) risks relating to the nature of the offering, and

(c) any other risks.

1. Risk factors may include but are not limited to such matters as cash flow and liquidity problems, inexperience of **Management** in start up operations, inexperience of **Management** in the particular industry in which the **issuer** operates, dependence of the **issuer** on an unproven **Product**, environmental regulations, economic or political conditions, absence of an existing market for the **Product**, absence of an operating history, absence of profitable operations in recent periods, an erratic financial history, significant competition, conflicts of interest with **Management**, reliance on the efforts of a single individual, the arbitrary establishment of the offering price and any material differences between the laws governing the incorporation, continuance or organization of the issuer and the B.C. Company Act relating to security holders' rights and remedies.

2. With respect to (a), the most significant risk factors should be disclosed at the top of the list.

3. In this Item, **"issuer"** means the issuer, its subsidiaries and proposed subsidiaries.

8. DIRECTORS, OFFICERS AND PROMOTERS

1. In this Item, **"issuer"** includes the issuer's subsidiaries and proposed subsidiaries.

2. In sections 8.3 through 8.6, the Superintendent may require information for periods prior to those indicated in the section depending upon the materiality of the events.

3. Provide the information required by this Item for each proposed nominee for election as a director of the **issuer** and indicate clearly that the individual is a proposed nominee.

8.1 *Name, address, occupation and security holding* - List the names and the municipality of residence of all directors, officers and promoters of the **issuer** and, for
each person, disclose

    (a)   the current positions and offices with the **issuer**,

    (b)   the principal occupations during the five years prior to the date of the
prospectus and, where the principal occupation is that of an officer of a
company other than the **issuer**, state the name of the company and the
principal business in which it was engaged, and

    (c)   the number of securities of the **issuer** beneficially owned, directly or
indirectly, indicating the number of performance shares held in escrow and
the percentage of the class to be held on conclusion of the offering.

Where a director, officer or promoter is an associate of another director, officer or
promoter, disclose as a footnote the relationships.

1. The Superintendent may waive the disclosure required by this section where the
operations of a subsidiary or a proposed subsidiary are not material to the **issuer's**
operations.

2. The description of the principal occupation of a director, officer or promoter must be
specific. The terms "businessman" or "entrepreneur" are not sufficiently specific.

3. Where the director, officer or promoter is a member of **Management**, the information in (b), other than a current occupation, may be disclosed by a cross reference to
the page on which the information required by section 5.6 is disclosed.

4. If there is a maximum subscription that differs from the minimum subscription,
disclose the percentage of the class held by the directors, officers and promoters on
both a minimum and maximum basis.

8.2 *Aggregate ownership of securities* - State the aggregate number of each class of
voting securities of the issuer that at the completion of the offering are beneficially owned, directly or indirectly, by all directors, officers and promoters of the
issuer, as a group, as of the completion of the offering and then state the
percentage that number will represent of the total issued and outstanding voting
securities of the issuer upon the completion of the offering.

    • In this section, "issuer" does not include the issuer's subsidiaries and proposed
subsidiaries.

8.3 *Other reporting issuers* - Where any director, officer or promoter of the **issuer** is,
or within the five years prior to the date of the prospectus has been, a director,
officer or promoter of any other reporting issuer, state the name of the individual,
the number of reporting issuers for which the individual acted, the names of
those issuers and the periods during which the individual has so acted.

8.4 *Corporate cease trade orders or bankruptcies* - Where any director, officer or
promoter of the **issuer** is, or within the five years prior to the date of the
prospectus has been, a director, officer or promoter of any other issuer that, while
that person was acting in that capacity,

    (a)   was the subject of a cease trade or similar order or an order that denied the
issuer access to any statutory exemptions for a period of more than 30
consecutive days, state the fact and describe the reasons and whether the
order is still in effect, or

    (b)   was declared bankrupt or made a voluntary assignment in bankruptcy,
made a proposal under any legislation relating to bankruptcy or insolvency
or been subject to or instituted any proceedings, arrangement, or compromise with creditors or had a receiver, receiver manager or trustee
appointed to hold the assets of that person, state the fact.

8.5 *Penalties or sanctions* - Where any director, officer or promoter of the **issuer** has,
within the ten years prior to the date of the prospectus, been subject to any
penalties or sanctions imposed by a court or securities regulatory authority
relating to trading in securities, promotion or management of a publicly traded
issuer, or theft or fraud, describe the penalties or sanctions imposed.

1. Penalties or sanctions include charges that have been laid or notices of hearing that have been issued as of the date of the prospectus.

2. The Superintendent may require information relating to other penalties and sanctions depending on the materiality of the events.

8.6 *Individual bankruptcies* - Where any director, officer or promoter of the **issuer** has, within the five years prior to the date of the prospectus, been declared bankrupt or made a voluntary assignment in bankruptcy, made a proposal under any legislation relating to bankruptcy or insolvency or been subject to or instituted any proceedings, arrangement, or compromise with creditors or had a receiver, receiver manager or trustee appointed to hold the assets of that individual, state the fact.

8.7 *Conflicts of interest* - Disclose particulars of any existing or potential conflicts of interest of any of the directors, officers or promoters of the **issuer** as a result of their outside business interests.

9. INDEBTEDNESS OF DIRECTORS, OFFICERS, PROMOTERS AND OTHER MANAGEMENT

State the name of each director, officer, promoter and member of **Management** and each of their respective associates or affiliates who is or has been indebted to the **issuer** at any time during the preceding financial year and the **Stub Period** and state, for each person,

(a) the largest amount of indebtedness outstanding at any time,

(b) the nature of the indebtedness and the purpose for which it was incurred,

(c) the amount presently outstanding,

(d) the rate of interest paid or charged,

(e) the terms of repayment,

(f) the nature of any security granted to the **issuer**, and

(g) if the person is an associate or affiliate of a director, officer or member of **Management**, the person's relationship to the director, officer or member of **Management** of the **issuer**.

1. In this Item, **"issuer"** includes the issuer's subsidiaries and proposed subsidiaries.

2. Provide the information required by this Item for each proposed nominee for election as a director of the **issuer** and indicate clearly that the individual is a proposed nominee.

10. PAYMENTS TO INSIDERS AND PROMOTERS

• In this Item, **"issuer"** includes the issuer's subsidiaries and proposed subsidiaries.

10.1 *Executive compensation* - Provide the information required by Form 41 with the following changes:

(a) disclosure must be provided for each of the **issuer's** four most highly compensated executive officers, in addition to the CEO, regardless of the amount of their compensation, and

(b) in addition to the periods required under Form 41, disclosure must be provided for the **Stub Period**.

• The Superintendent may require disclosure of compensation paid to persons other than executive officers.

10.2 *Related party transactions* - Where, during the five preceding financial years and the **Stub Period**, or such shorter period as the **issuer** may have been in existence, the **issuer** has acquired assets or services from an insider, promoter or member of **Management** and their respective associates or affiliates, disclose the following for each acquisition:

(a) the name of the individual,

(b) the nature of the assets or services,

(c)   the form and value of the consideration, and

(d)   where the issuer has acquired assets,

    (i) the cost of the assets to the seller, and

    (ii) where the consideration referred to in paragraph (c) above exceeds the seller's out-of-pocket costs, a cross reference to the valuation opinion disclosed in section 5.5.

1. Information with respect to executive compensation need not be disclosed in this section.

2. Any debt settlement made by the **issuer** to any insider or promoter must be disclosed in this section.

3. For acquisitions where the consideration is not in excess of the greater of 10% of the aggregate compensation or consideration paid to the individual under sections 10.1 and 10.2 or $5,000, the information required by this item may be aggregated together and classified as "miscellaneous".

4. As an alternative to the disclosure required in (b), provide a cross reference to the page(s) of the prospectus where the required disclosure is made.

10.3 *Proposed compensation* - Where known, provide the information required by Form 41 as modified by section 10.1 with respect to the amounts that the **issuer** anticipates it will pay during the 12 month period following completion of the offering.

• The amounts referred to in this section include the forms of compensation referred to in sections 10.1 and 10.2 above.

11.   SHARE CAPITAL

11.1 *Existing and proposed share capital* - Provide, in the tabular form indicated or, where appropriate, in notes to the table, particulars of the share capital of the issuer.

TABLE

	Column 1	Column 2	Column 3
	Number of issued securities	Price per security	Total consideration
(a) Prior sales of securities	____		____
(b) Issued as of [the **Most Recent Month End**]			
(c) Offering	____		____
(d) To be issued if all securities being offered are sold		[N/A]	

1. Where the consideration for any of the prior sales included in the table is other than cash, describe in a note cross referenced to the prior sale set out in (a) of the table the method of determining the value of the consideration (e.g. out of pocket costs, valuation opinion, **Arm's Length** negotiation or, in the case of services, determination by directors based on estimated fair market value).

2. Set out in the table or a note thereto the number of securities of each class authorized to be issued.

3. In columns 1 and 3 of the table, (b) is equal to the total of (a), and (d) is equal to the total of (b) and (c).

4. The information shall be updated to the **Most Recent Month End**.

5. In (a) of the table list prior sales aggregated on the basis of the same price per security and type of consideration.

6. If there is a minimum subscription, disclose the number of securities that are offered and that would be issued on both a minimum and maximum basis.

7. A separate table shall be prepared for each class or kind of securities that the issuer has issued or will have issued upon completion of the offering.

8. As a note to the table, indicate whether there are any restrictions on the transferability of the securities (e.g. hold periods, escrow or pooling agreement) and summarize the nature of the restrictions. Where the information is provided elsewhere the disclosure may be provided by a cross-reference to the page in the prospectus where the disclosure is contained.

11.2 *Options and other rights to purchase securities*

(a) Disclose, as of the **Most Recent Month End** prior to the date of the prospectus, the following information respecting each **option** that is held or will be held upon completion of the offering by any person:

    (i) the name of each person and the reasons that the **option** was granted,

    (ii) the name of the grantor and the nature of the **option** granted to each person (e.g. options, **Agent's** warrants or other warrants),

    (iii) the designation and number of the securities subject to the **option**,

    (iv) the purchase price of the securities subject to the **option** or the formula by which the purchase price will be determined,

    (v) the expiration date of the **option**, and

    (vi) if there is a published market for the securities, the market value of the securities subject to the **option** as of the date of grant and the **Most Recent Month End**.

(b) State the aggregate number of each class or kind of securities that are subject to **options** described in paragraph (a)(iii) above.

(c) State the following:

There are no assurances that the options, warrants or other rights described above will be exercised in whole or in part.

1. In this section, **"option"** means option, warrant or other right to purchase securities of the **issuer**, granted by the **issuer**, selling security holder, insider, promoter, control person or holder of performance shares.

2. In this section, **"issuer"** includes the issuer's subsidiaries and proposed subsidiaries.

3. The information shall be updated to the **Most Recent Month End**.

11.3 *Fully diluted share capital* - Provide the information indicated in the table set out below for each class of securities of the issuer.

TABLE

	Number of securities	Percentage of Total
(a) Issued as of the **Most Recent Month End**		
(b) Offered under the prospectus		
(c) Securities reserved for future issue as of the **Most Recent Month End**		
Total		100

Forms

1. (a) is the amount indicated in (b) of column 1 of the table in section 11.1.

2. If there is a minimum subscription, disclose the number of securities offered and total on both a minimum and maximum basis.

3. (c) is the amount indicated in paragraph (b) from section 11.2

4. A separate table shall be prepared for each class or kind of securities that the issuer has issued or will have issued upon completion of the offering.

5. The information shall be updated to the **Most Recent Month End**.

11.4 *Principal holders of voting securities* - Provide as of the **Most Recent Month End**, the information indicated in the table set out below for each person who has, or is known by the issuer to have:

    (a)   direct or indirect beneficial ownership of,

    (b)   control or direction over, or

    (c)   a combination of direct or indirect beneficial ownership of and of control or direction over

voting securities that will constitute more than 10 per cent of any class of such securities upon completion of the offering.

TABLE

Column 1	Column 2	Column 3	Column 4
Name and municipality of residence	Number of securities	Percentage of class prior to the offering	Percentage of class after the offering

1. Where a person that is not an individual is shown by the issuer as owning directly or indirectly more than 10 per cent of any class of such securities, identify the individual shareholders of the person as required by General Instruction 7. The name of such individuals should be disclosed in a note to the table.

2. If voting securities will be issued prior to, concurrently with or immediately following the offering, indicate as far as practicable the respective holding of voting securities that will exist after giving effect to the issue.

3. If there is a maximum subscription that differs from the minimum subscription, disclose the percentage of the class held by the principal holders on both a minimum and maximum basis.

4. If, to the knowledge of the issuer or the **Agent**, more than 10 per cent of any class of voting securities of the issuer are held or are to be held subject to any voting trust or other similar agreement/arrangement, state the designation of such securities, the number or amount held or to be held and the duration of the agreement. Give the names and addresses of the voting trustees and outline briefly their voting rights and other powers under the agreement.

5. Where a person identified in the table is a control person of the issuer and is not a director, officer or promoter of the issuer, provide the disclosure required for sections 8.3 - 8.6 for the control person. If the control person is a corporation, the disclosure must be provided for the control persons of the corporation.

6. A separate table shall be prepared for each class or kind of voting securities that the issuer has issued or will have issued upon completion of the offering.

7. The information shall be updated to the **Most Recent Month End**.

11.5 *Performance shares or escrow securities* - Where the issuer has performance shares or escrow securities issued as of the date of the prospectus, state

    (a)   the number of performance shares or escrow securities,

    (b)   the estimated percentage that the performance shares or escrow securities will represent of the total issued and outstanding voting securities of the issuer, upon the completion of the offering,

(c)   the names of the beneficial owners of the performance shares or escrow securities and the number of performance shares or escrow securities owned by each and why the person is a principal as defined in Local Policy Statement No. 3-07,

(d)   the name of the escrow agent,

(e)   the date of the escrow agreement and the conditions governing the transfer, release and cancellation of the performance shares or escrow securities, and

(f)   the rights or obligations of a person who ceases to be a principal, dies or becomes bankrupt to retain, transfer or surrender to the issuer for cancellation the performance shares or escrow securities.

• If there is a maximum subscription that differs from the minimum subscription, disclose the percentage that the performance shares or escrow securities will represent on both a minimum and maximum basis.

12.   PLAN OF DISTRIBUTION

12.1 *Terms of the distribution agreement* - With respect to the agreement entered into between the issuer and the **Agents**, state

(a)   the names of the **Agents**,

(b)   the date of the agreement,

(c)   the nature of the **Agents'** obligation to take up and pay for any of the securities being offered,

(d)   the number of securities expected to be sold by each of the **Agents**,

(e)   the number of additional securities that may be issued, if the issuer has granted the **Agent** a "greenshoe" option,

(f)   the conditions, if any, under which the **Agent** may "market out",

(g)   the nature of the consideration to be paid to the **Agent**,

(h)   the conditions, if any, under which any of the proceeds are to be held in trust or escrow pending completion of the offering, and

(i)   the number of days following the completion of the offering by which issuer will receive the net proceeds of the offering from the **Agents** or the date by which the **Agents** are to purchase the securities.

12.2 *Minimum and maximum subscription* - Where the prospectus discloses a plan of distribution not involving a firm underwriting or other subscription guarantee, it must also disclose the amount of the minimum and maximum subscriptions.

12.3 *Secondary offering* - If any of the securities being offered are for the account of a security holder, name the security holder and state the number of the securities owned by that security holder, the number to be offered and the number to be owned by that security holder after the completion of the distribution. State the portion of the expenses of distribution to be borne by the selling security holder.

12.4 *Extraprovincial offerings* - Disclose whether there are any agreements or arrangements to sell any portion of the offering outside of British Columbia. If so, disclose in what other jurisdictions the offering may be sold, the identity of the person who will be selling the securities in the other jurisdictions and the estimated portion of the offering, if any, to be sold outside of Canada.

• Agreements or arrangements include those made with a selling group outside of the British Columbia or with clients of the **Agents** who are not residents of British Columbia.

13.   DESCRIPTION OF SECURITIES OFFERED

13.1 *Terms* - Describe the securities being offered and summarize their material attributes and characteristics, including, if applicable:

(a)   dividend rights;

(b)   voting rights;

(c)   liquidation or distribution rights;

(d)   pre-emptive rights;

(e)   conversion rights;

(f)   if the securities are subscription warrants or rights, the period during which, and the price at which, the warrants or rights are exercisable;

(g)   redemption, purchase for cancellation or surrender provisions;

(h)   sinking or purchase fund provisions; and

(i)   provisions as to modification, amendment or variation of any such rights or provisions.

• If the rights attaching to the securities being offered are materially limited or qualified by the rights of any other class of securities, or if any other class of ranks ahead of or equally with the securities being offered, include information regarding such other securities in order to enable investors to understand the rights attaching to the securities being offered.

13.2 *Modification of terms* - If the rights of holders of the securities may be modified otherwise than pursuant to a mechanism provided for by governing legislation relating to the securities, briefly describe the method by which those rights may be modified.

14.   SPONSORSHIP AND FISCAL AGENCY AGREEMENTS

If the issuer has entered into any agreement with any registrant to sponsor the issuer or to provide corporate finance services for the issuer or its securities, either now or in the future, disclose the following information regarding these services:

(a)   the date of the agreement,

(b)   the name of the registrant,

(c)   the consideration, both monetary and non-monetary, paid or to be paid by the issuer, and

(d)   a summary of the nature of the services to be provided, including the period during which the services will be provided, activities to be carried out and, where market making services will be provided, whether the registered broker or dealer will commit its own funds to the purchase of securities of the issuer or whether the registered broker or dealer will act as agent for others to do so.

15.   INVESTOR RELATIONS ARRANGEMENTS

If the issuer has entered into any written or oral agreement or understanding with any person to provide any promotional or investor relations services for the issuer or its securities, either now or in the future, disclose the following information regarding these services:

(a)   the date of the agreement and the anticipated date that the services will commence,

(b)   the name, principal business and place of business of the person providing the services,

(c)   the background of the person providing the services,

(d)   whether the person has, or is known by the issuer to have:

(i) direct or indirect beneficial ownership of,

(ii) control or direction over, or

(iii) a combination of direct or indirect beneficial ownership of and of control or direction over

securities of the issuer,

(e)   whether the person has any right to acquire securities of the issuer, either in full or partial compensation for services,

(f)   the consideration both monetary and non-monetary paid or to be paid by the issuer, including whether any payments will be made in advance of services being provided,

(g)   if the issuer does not have sufficient funds to pay for the services, how the issuer intends to pay for the services, and

(h)   the nature of the services to be provided, including the period during which the services will be provided.

1. Include any arrangements made by the issuer or any other person on behalf of the issuer or on the person's own initiative where the issuer knows, after reasonable enquiry, that such an arrangement exists.

2. The disclosure in (c) and (h) need only summarize the background and nature of services.

3. If there are no promotional or investor relations arrangements, so state.

16.   RELATIONSHIP BETWEEN ISSUER OR SELLING SECURITY HOLDER AND AGENT

Where the **issuer** is a related party or connected party, as defined in the **Regulation**, of an **Agent** or where the securities to be offered are out of the holdings of a selling security holder who is a related party or connected party of the **Agent**, describe

(a)   the nature of the relationship or connection between the **issuer** and the **Agent** or the selling security holder and the **Agent**, as the case may be, including

    (i)   the basis on which the **issuer** or selling security holder is a related party or connected party of the **Agent**,

    (ii) the name of each relevant related party of the **Agent**,

    (iii) the details of the ability of the **Agent** or any related party of the **Agent** to affect materially the operations of the **issuer**, and

    (iv) whether the **issuer** is indebted to the **Agent** or any related party of the **Agent** and, if so, provide particulars of such indebtedness, and

(b)   the extent to which the proceeds of the issue will be applied, directly or indirectly, for the benefit of the **Agent** or any related party of the **Agent**. (For example, where the issuer has received a loan from the **Agent**, the issuer would be a connected party of the **Agent** and would have to comply with section 167.4 of the **Regulation**.)

1. For the purpose of this item, reference to an **Agent** includes a special selling group member as defined in section 167.4(1) of the **Regulation**.

2. In this item, "**issuer**" means the issuer, its subsidiaries and proposed subsidiaries.

17.   RELATIONSHIP BETWEEN ISSUER AND PROFESSIONAL PERSONS

Disclose the nature and extent of any beneficial interest, direct or indirect, in any securities or property, of the **issuer** or of an associate or affiliate of the **issuer**, held by a professional person referred to in section 99(2) of the **Regulation**, or any associate of the professional person. Also, disclose whether the professional person or any associate of the professional person, is or is expected to be elected, appointed or employed as a director, senior officer or employee of the **issuer**, or of an associate or affiliate of the **issuer**, or is a promoter of the **issuer**, or of an associate or affiliate of the **issuer**.

1. The interest of a professional person and all associates of that professional person may be shown in the aggregate. Disclosure of the interest in or position with the **issuer** or an associate or affiliate of the **issuer** held by an associate of the professional person is only required where known by the professional person after reasonable inquiry.

Forms

2. In this section, **"issuer"** includes the issuer's subsidiaries and proposed subsidiaries.

18. LEGAL PROCEEDINGS

Describe any outstanding and, if known, contemplated legal proceedings that are material to the business and affairs of the issuer.

• Include the name of the court or agency, the date the proceedings were instituted, the principal parties to the proceedings, the nature of the proceedings, the amount claimed, if any, whether the proceedings are being contested, the present status of the proceedings and, if a legal opinion is referred to in the prospectus, the name of counsel providing that opinion.

19. AUDITOR

State the name and address of the auditor of the issuer.

20. REGISTRAR AND TRANSFER AGENT

State the name of the issuer's registrar and transfer agent. Where the issuer has branch registers for transfers of its securities, state the location (by municipalities) of the registers.

21. MATERIAL CONTRACTS

21.1 *Particulars of material contracts* - Disclose all material contracts to which the issuer is a party, including

(a)   the date of each contract,

(b)   the parties to each contract,

(c)   the consideration paid or payable by or to the issuer, and

(d)   the general nature of each contract.

• As an alternative to the disclosure required in this section, provide a cross reference to the page(s) of the prospectus where the required disclosure with respect to a particular contract is made.

21.2 *Inspection of material contracts* - State a reasonable time and place in the Province at which a copy of any material contract may be inspected during distribution of the securities being offered under the prospectus.

22. OTHER MATERIAL FACTS

Give particulars of any other material facts relating to the securities proposed to be offered and not disclosed elsewhere in the prospectus.

23. PURCHASERS' STATUTORY RIGHTS

State the following:

The British Columbia Securities Act provides purchasers with the right to withdraw from an agreement to purchase securities within two days after receipt or deemed receipt of a prospectus and any amendment. The Securities Act further provides a purchaser with remedies for rescission or damages where the prospectus and any amendment contains a misrepresentation or is not delivered to the purchaser, provided that such remedies for rescission or damages are exercised by the purchaser within the time limit prescribed by the Securities Act. The purchaser should refer to sections 66, 114, 118 and 124 of the Securities Act for the particulars of these rights or consult with a legal advisor.

Where the distribution involves a distribution of securities to be issued pursuant to the exercise of special warrants (or in connection with a similar type of transaction), state the following (with bracketed information completed as appropriate):

In the event that a holder of a special warrant, who acquires a [identify underlying securities] of the issuer upon the exercise of a special warrant as provided for in this prospectus, is or becomes entitled under applicable securities legislation to the remedy of rescission by reason of this prospectus or any amendment thereto containing a misrepresentation, such holder shall be entitled to rescission not only of the holder's exercise of the special warrant(s) but also of the [private placement or other exempt transaction] pursuant to which the special warrant(s) were initially acquired, and shall be entitled in connection with such rescission to a full refund of all consideration paid on the acquisition of the special warrant(s). In the event such holder is a permitted assignee of the interest of the original special warrant subscriber, such permitted assignee shall be entitled to exercise the rights of rescission and refund granted hereunder as if such permitted assignee was such original subscriber. The foregoing is in addition to any other right or remedy available to a holder of special warrants under section 114 of the Securities Act or otherwise at law.

• Where this document is a base disclosure document used in connection with a summary prospectus, this section is not required in the base disclosure document because it is contained in the summary prospectus.

24. FINANCIAL STATEMENTS, REPORTS AND OTHER EXHIBITS

Include the financial statements, reports and other exhibits required by applicable local policy statements or by the **Act** and **Regulation**.

25. CERTIFICATES

Provide the certificates of the issuer, **Agent** and promoter as required by the **Act** and **Regulation**.

****

IT IS AN OFFENCE FOR A PERSON TO MAKE A STATEMENT IN A DOCUMENT REQUIRED TO BE FILED OR FURNISHED UNDER THE ACT OR THE REGULATION THAT, AT THE TIME AND IN THE LIGHT OF THE CIRCUMSTANCES UNDER WHICH IT IS MADE, IS A MISREPRESENTATION.

The summary prospectus for an industrial issuer where the issuer is required to file a prospectus on Form 12A shall be in the following form. The summary prospectus may be filed under Section 42(2) of the Securities Act with a base disclosure document that complies with Form 12A.

FORM 12A - SUMMARY PROSPECTUS
Securities Act
INFORMATION REQUIRED IN SUMMARY PROSPECTUS OF A JUNIOR INDUSTRIAL ISSUER

GENERAL INSTRUCTIONS

1. The summary prospectus prepared in accordance with this form is a verbatim extract of those sections of the base disclosure document identified below, except where otherwise indicated below.

2. References to "base disclosure document" in the sections required to be extracted from the base disclosure document must be replaced by references to "summary prospectus".

3. Where cross references are included in the sections extracted from the base disclosure document and the item referred to is not included in the summary prospectus, the cross reference should be deleted.

1. FACE PAGE DISCLOSURE

1.1 Extract sections 1.1, 1.2 and 1.3 verbatim from the base disclosure document.

1.2 State in substantially the following form:

This [preliminary] summary prospectus extracts certain material information from the [preliminary] base disclosure document. The [preliminary] base disclosure document dated [*], including financial statements and any reports on them [specify the dates of the financial statements and reports on the financial statements] and other reports [specify the type, date and author of report], filed with the British Columbia Securities Commission is specifically incorporated by reference into this [preliminary] summary prospectus. Copies of the [preliminary] base disclosure document may be obtained on request without charge from the issuer at the address and telephone number set out on the face page of this [preliminary] summary prospectus. The table of contents of the [preliminary] base disclosure document dated * is included as an appendix to this [preliminary] summary prospectus.

Securities laws in British Columbia provide certain rights for security holders that are described in this [preliminary] summary prospectus. These rights are based on the disclosure made in the base disclosure document, which is incorporated into this summary prospectus by reference, and the disclosure contained in this summary prospectus. All of these rights are available to you even though you may only receive this summary prospectus.

1.3 Extract sections 1.4, 1.5, 1.6, 1.7 and 1.9 verbatim from the base disclosure document.

2. NAME AND INCORPORATION

Extract section 4.1 verbatim from the base disclosure document.

3. BUSINESS OF ISSUER AND USE OF PROCEEDS

3.1 Extract section 5.1 verbatim from the base disclosure document.

3.2 Extract all of section 5.2 verbatim from the base disclosure document excluding the analysis discussion.

3.3 Extract sections 5.3, 5.4, 6.1, 6.2, 6.3, 5.14(a) and 5.6 verbatim from the base disclosure document.

4. RISK FACTORS

Extract section 7(a) verbatim from the base disclosure document.

5. DIRECTORS, OFFICERS AND PROMOTERS AND PAYMENTS TO INSIDERS AND PROMOTERS

Extract sections 8.1(a) and (c), 8.3, 8.4, 8.5, 10.1, 10.2(a)-(c), 10.2(d)(i) and 10.3 verbatim from the base disclosure document.

6. SHARE CAPITAL

6.1 Extract section 11.2(b) verbatim from the base disclosure document.

6.2 If a principal holder is other than a director, officer or promoter, extract section 11.4 verbatim from the Form 12A base disclosure document.

7. PLAN OF DISTRIBUTION AND DESCRIPTION OF SECURITIES OFFERED

7.1 Extract section 12.3 verbatim from the base disclosure document.

7.2 Where the securities to be offered are not common shares, extract sections 13.1 and 13.2 verbatim from the base disclosure document.

8. INVESTOR RELATIONS ARRANGEMENTS

Extract item 15 verbatim from the base disclosure document.

9. LEGAL PROCEEDINGS

Extract item 18 verbatim from the base disclosure document.

10. INSPECTION OF MATERIAL CONTRACTS

Extract section 21.2 verbatim from the base disclosure document.

11. OTHER MATERIAL FACTS

Extract item 22 verbatim from the base disclosure document.

12. PURCHASERS' STATUTORY RIGHTS

Extract item 23 verbatim from the base disclosure document.

13. CERTIFICATES

13.1 The preliminary summary prospectus and summary prospectus must include a certificate in the following form signed by the chief executive officer, the chief financial officer and, on behalf of the board of directors of the issuer, any two directors of the issuer, other than the chief executive officer and chief financial officer, duly authorized to sign and any person who is a promoter of the issuer:

> The foregoing, together with the documents incorporated by reference, constitutes full, true and plain disclosure of all material facts relating to the securities offered by this summary prospectus as required by the Securities Act and its regulations.

13.2 Where an underwriter is in a contractual relationship with the issuer or holder of securities offered by the summary prospectus, the preliminary summary prospectus and summary prospectus must include a certificate in the following form signed by the underwriter:

> To the best of our knowledge, information and belief, the foregoing, together with the documents incorporated by reference, constitutes full, true and plain disclosure of all material facts relating to the securities offered by this summary prospectus as required by the Securities Act and its regulations.

14. APPENDIX

Attach the table of contents from the base disclosure document as an appendix.

****

IT IS AN OFFENCE FOR A PERSON TO MAKE A STATEMENT IN A DOCUMENT REQUIRED TO BE FILED OR FURNISHED UNDER THE ACT OR THE REGULATION THAT, AT THE TIME AND IN THE LIGHT OF THE CIRCUMSTANCES UNDER WHICH IT IS MADE, IS A MISREPRESENTATION.

FORM 13

Securities Act

INFORMATION REQUIRED IN PROSPECTUS OF FINANCE ISSUER

Item 1 - Distribution Spread:

The information called for by the following Table shall be given, in substantially the tabular form indicated, on the first page of the prospectus as to all securities being offered for cash (estimate amounts, if necessary).

TABLE

	Column 1	Column 2	Column 3
	Price to Public	Underwriting discounts or commissions	Proceeds to issuer or selling securityholder
Per unit	....	....	....
Total	....	....	....

INSTRUCTIONS:

1. Only commissions paid or payable in cash by the issuer or selling securityholder or discounts granted are to be included in the table. Commissions or other consideration paid or payable in cash or otherwise by other persons and consideration other than discounts granted and other than cash paid or payable by

the issuer or selling securityholder shall be set out following the table with a reference thereto in the second column of the table. Any finder's fees or similar payments shall be appropriately disclosed. Where debt securities are offered, the price to the public, the underwriting discounts and commission and the proceeds to the finance company, except with the consent of the Superintendent, shall be expressed as a percentage.

2.   The table should set out separately those securities which are underwritten, those under option and those to be sold on a "best efforts" basis.

3.   If the presentation of information in the form contemplated herein results in unnecessary complication, the tabular form may, with the consent of the Superintendent, be varied.

4.   If it is impracticable to state the offering price, the method by which it is to be determined shall be explained. In addition, if the securities are to be offered at the market, indicate the market involved and the market price as of the latest practicable date.

5.   If any of the securities offered are to be offered for the account of existing securityholders, refer on the first page of the prospectus to the information called for by Instruction 4 to Item 30. State the portion of the expenses of distribution to be borne by the selling securityholder.

6.   If debt securities are to be offered at a premium or a discount, state in bold face type the effective yield if held to maturity.

7.   Where debt securities are to be issued but are not subject to a trust indenture this fact must be clearly stated on the outside front cover.

Item 2 - Plan of Distribution

(a)   If the securities being offered are to be sold through underwriters, give the names of the underwriters. State briefly the nature of the underwriters' obligation to take up and pay for the securities. Indicate the date by which the underwriters are to purchase the securities.

(b)   Outline briefly the plan of distribution of any securities being offered that are to be offered otherwise than through underwriters. Where there is a "best efforts" offering, indicate, where practicable, on the first page the minimum amount, if any, required to be raised, and also indicate, where practicable, the maximum amount that could be raised and the latest date that the offering is to remain open.

INSTRUCTIONS:

1.   All that is required as to the nature of the underwriters' obligation is whether the underwriters are or will be committed to take up and pay for all of the securities if any are taken up, or whether the underwriting is merely an agency or "best efforts" arrangement under which the underwriters are required to take up and pay for only such securities as they may sell.

2.   Where an underwriting is subject to a "market out" clause, a statement in the prospectus under Plan of Distribution should be made with respect to the "market out" clause.

A sample paragraph is as follows:

Plan of Distribution:

"Under an agreement dated ....19....between the issuer and .... as underwriter, the issuer has agreed to sell and the underwriter has agreed to purchase on ....19.... the ....at a price of $........, payable in cash to the issuer against delivery. The obligations of the underwriter under the agreement may be terminated at its discretion on the basis of its assessment of the state of the financial markets and may also be terminated upon the occurrence of certain stated events. The underwriter is however, obligated to take up and pay for all of the ....if any of the .... are purchased under the agreement."

Item 3 - Market for Securities:

Where no *bona fide* market exists, or will exist after the distribution, state in bold face type on the first page: "There is no market through which these securities may be sold". Disclose how the price paid to the issuer was established, whether by negotiation with the underwriter, arbitrarily by the issuer, or otherwise.

Item 4 - Summary of Prospectus:

Give a synopsis near the beginning of the prospectus of that information in the body of the prospectus which in the opinion of the issuer or selling security holder would be most likely to influence the investor's decision to purchase the security.

INSTRUCTION:

1. This summary should highlight in condensed form the information, both favourable and adverse, including risk factors in Item 14, particularly pertinent to a decision to purchase the securities offered, including information about both the issuer and the securities.

2. Appropriate cross references may be made to items in the prospectus where information is difficult to summarize accurately, but this shall not detract from the necessity to have the salient points summarized in the summary.

Item 5 - Use of Proceeds to Issuer:

    (a)   State the estimated net proceeds to be derived by the issuer from the sale of the securities to be offered, the principal purposes for which the net proceeds are intended to be used and the approximate amount intended to be used for each purpose.

    (b)   State the particulars of any provisions or arrangements made for holding any part of the net proceeds of the issue in trust or subject to the fulfillment of any conditions.

INSTRUCTIONS:

1. Statements as to the principal purposes to which the proceeds are to be applied are to be reasonably specific although details of the particulars of proposed expenditures are not to be given except as otherwise required hereunder. The phrase "for general corporate purposes" is, in most cases, not sufficient.

2. Include a statement regarding the proposed use of the actual proceeds if they should prove insufficient to accomplish the purposes set out, and the order of priority in which they will be applied. However, the statement need not be made if the underwriting arrangements are such that, if any securities are sold, it can be reasonably expected that the actual proceeds of the issue will not be substantially less than the estimated aggregate proceeds to the issuer as shown under item 1.

3. If any material amounts of other funds are to be used in conjunction with the proceeds, state the amounts and sources of the other funds. If any material part of the proceeds is to be used to reduce or retire indebtedness, this item is to be answered as to the use of the proceeds of that indebtedness if the indebtedness was incurred within the two preceding years.

4. If any material amount of the proceeds is to be used directly or indirectly to acquire assets, otherwise than in the ordinary course of business, briefly describe the assets, and, where known, the particulars of the purchase price being paid for or being allocated to the respective categories of assets (including intangible assets) that are being acquired and, where practicable and meaningful, give the name of the person from whom the assets are to be acquired. State the cost of the assets to the issuer and the principle followed in determining the cost. State briefly the nature of the title to or interest in the assets to be acquired by the issuer. If any part of the consideration for the acquisition of any of the assets consists of securities of the issuer, give brief particulars of the designation, number or amount, voting rights (if any) and other appropriate information relating to the class of securities, including particulars of any allotment or issuance of any such securities within the two preceding years.

Item 6 - Sales Otherwise than for Cash:

If any of the securities being offered are to be offered otherwise than for cash, state briefly the general purposes of the issue, the basis upon which the securities are to be offered, the amount of compensation paid or payable to any person and any other expenses of distribution, and by whom they are to be borne.

INSTRUCTION:

If the offer is to be made pursuant to a plan of acquisition, describe briefly the general effect of the plan and state when it became or is to become operative.

Item 7 - Share and Loan Capital Structure:

Furnish in substantially the tabular form indicated, or where appropriate in notes thereto:

(1)   particulars of the share and loan capital of the issuer;

(2)   particulars of the loan capital of each subsidiary of the issuer (other than loan capital owned by the issuer or its wholly-owned subsidiaries) whose financial statements are contained in the prospectus on either a consolidated or individual basis;

(3)   the aggregate amount of the minority interest in the preference shares, if any, and the aggregate amount of the minority interest in the common shares and surplus of all subsidiaries whose financial statements are contained in the prospectus on a consolidated basis; and

(4)   the aggregate amount of the minority interest in the preference shares, if any, and the aggregate amount of minority interest in the common shares and surplus of all subsidiaries whose financial statements are contained in the prospectus on an individual basis and not included in the consolidated financial statements.

(5)   Disclose any potential dilution of the assets per share and earnings per share in a computation, giving effect to the current issue and to all existing options, warrants and conversion rights in relation to any capital security of the finance issuer.

TABLE

Column 1	Column 2	Column 3	Column 4	Column 5
Designation of security	Amount authorized or to be authorized	Amount outstanding as of the date of the most balance sheet contained in the prospectus	Amount outstanding as of a specific date within 30 days	Amount to be outstanding if all securities being issued are sold

INSTRUCTIONS:

1.   Include all indebtedness for borrowed money as to which a written understanding exists that the indebtedness may extend beyond one year. Include as an aggregate amount and by classes indebtedness payable within one year from the date of the balance sheet which is evidenced by drafts, bills of exchange, banker's acceptances or promissory notes.

2.   Include in the table the amount of obligations under financial leases capitalized in accordance with generally accepted accounting principles. Set out in a note to the table a cross reference to any note in the financial statements containing information concerning the extent of obligations arising by virtue of other leases on real property.

3. Individual items of indebtedness which are not in excess of 3% of total assets as shown in the balance sheet referred to in Column 3 may be set out in a single aggregate amount under an appropriate caption such as "Sundry Indebtedness".

4. Where practicable, state in general terms the respective priorities of the indebtedness shown in the table.

5. Give particulars of the amount, general description of and security for any substantial indebtedness proposed to be created or assumed by the issuer or its subsidiaries, other than indebtedness offered by the prospectus.

6. Set out in a note the amount of contributed surplus and retained earnings as of the date of the most recent balance sheet contained in the prospectus.

7. Set out in a note the number of shares subject to rights, options and warrants.

8. No information need be given under Column 2 with respect to the common and preference shares of subsidiaries.

9. For the purposes of Column 3, in computing the amount of the minority interest in the subsidiaries whose financial statements are contained in the prospectus on an individual basis and not included in the consolidated financial statements, such computation may be based on the financial statements of each such subsidiary contained in the prospectus.

10. In computing the minority interest in the subsidiaries for the purpose of Column 4, the amount set out in Column 3 may be used provided that appropriate adjustment is made to such amount to reflect any change in the percentage of ownership in the capital and surplus of any subsidiary by the minority interest.

11. The thirty-day period referred to in Column 4 is to be calculated within thirty days of the date of the preliminary prospectus or the date of the pro forma prospectus. Where more than thirty days have elapsed from the date of the preliminary or pro forma prospectus, the information included in the prospectus shall, if feasible, be updated to a date within thirty days of the prospectus.

12. The information to be set out in Column 5 may be based upon the information contained in Column 4, adjusted to take into account any amounts set out in Column 4 to be retired out of the issue.

13. Where the amount outstanding as of a specific date within thirty days cannot be precisely calculated, so state; an estimated figure should be used, with a note indicating the basis of calculation and the reasons therefor.

14. In the case of short term notes issued on an agency basis, column 5, may, with the consent of the Director, be omitted.

Item 8 - Operations of the Issuer:

Employing tabular form where appropriate, with such explanatory notes as are essential to an investor's appraisal of the securities being offered, set forth the following information in respect of the issuer, its subsidiaries and affiliates;

Maturity of Receivables

(a) Set out a schedule of receivables showing receivables:

    (i) due in the current financial year;

    (ii) due within the next subsequent financial year;

    (iii) due within the two years next thereafter; and

    (iv) due at any later date.

Analysis of Outstanding Receivables

(b) Give in tabular form, including, for example, wholesale, retail industrial, consumer loans, mortgages, leasing, business loans, dealer capital loans and any other type of loan constituting a significant class of business. Indicate the approximate amount and percentage of sales finance receivables covered by dealer endorsement or repurchase agreements.

Funding Requirements

(c)   Show the aggregate current sinking fund requirements and maximum purchase fund requirements for the succeeding five years. Segregate this information according to the class and series of security covered. Do not repeat details given in the prospectus relating to the rights, privileges and preferences of each class of security ranking prior to or equally with such security. In addition, provide an analysis setting forth commitments which must be met both as to sinking fund requirements and the maturing of long term debt indicating the amount due within,

      (i)   one year;

      (ii)   one year to two years;

      (iii)   two years to three years;

      (iv)   three years to five years;

      (v)   five years to ten years; and

      (vi)   over ten years.

Schedule of Current Position

(d)   Show the finance issuer's liquid capital position based on the financial position as of the date of the balance sheet in the prospectus both before and after giving effect to the proposed issue. Include assets which will be due within the next twelve months and the liabilities payable within the same period. Where there is a deficiency in liquid capital, explain the significance thereof having regard to the financial structure, the mode of operation of the issuer, and the prior experience of the issuer.

(e)   If the effective tax rate is significantly less than is normally paid by finance issuers generally, explain the principal reasons for such tax rate.

(f)   Indicate those subsidiaries and operations which have produced material operating losses within the preceding two financial years, giving details thereof.

(g)   Set out the amounts of the finance issuer's credit losses for each of the preceding five financial years and show such amounts as a percentage of liquidations, and of average outstandings.

INSTRUCTIONS:

In answering this item, give appropriate details of the quality, collectibility and arrears of receivables and include an age analysis of accounts receivable, and the percentage of receivables refinanced after being in arrears for periods from three months to in excess of eighteen months.

Item 9 - Asset and Earnings Coverage:

Disclose asset and earnings coverage in an appropriate and reasonable form where required by section 111 of the Regulation.

Item 10 - Name and Incorporation of Issuer:

State the full corporate name of the issuer and the address of its head office and principal office. State the laws under which the issuer was incorporated and whether incorporated by articles of incorporation or otherwise and the date the corporation came into existence. If material state whether these have been amended.

INSTRUCTIONS:

1.   Particulars of the documents need to be set out only if material to the securities offered by the prospectus. See Item 21.

2.   If the issuer is not a company, give material details of its form of organization and structure.

Item 11 - Relationship with Other Person:

Where the issuer has a parent, or one or more dominant interests exist, indicate the nature of the relationship between the issuer and the parent or dominant interest including,

(a) Whether the issuer operates as an adjunct to the primary business of the parent or dominant interest.

(b) What percentage of the voting securities of the issuer is owned by its parent, or by any dominant interest.

(c) Whether the parent of, or dominant interest in, the issuer intends to make loans to the issuer.

(d) Whether the issuer makes loans to or invests in securities of any affiliate or associate.

(e) Any other basis of influence by the parent or dominant interest.

INSTRUCTIONS:

1. A dominant interest exists in a specified person when,

   (i) that company is controlled by another person;

   (ii) that person is an affiliate of another person other than a person controlled by it;

   (iii) a person owns, directly or indirectly, more than 10 percent of the voting securities of that person; or

   (iv) another person is customarily able to direct the operations of the person by virtue of:

      a. management contracts,

      b. licensing or franchise agreements,

      c. options on voting securities,

      d. escrow or pooling or voting trust agreements,

      e. any other means.

2. Where any parent is a resident of, or a corporation or other organization formed under the laws of, any foreign country, give the name of such country for each such foreign parent, and, if the parent is a corporation or other organization, state briefly the nature of the organization.

3. If the existence of a dominant influence is open to reasonable doubt in any instance, the issuer may disclaim the existence of a dominant influence and any admission thereof; in such case, however, the issuer shall state the material facts pertinent to the possible existence of a dominant influence.

Item 12 - Intercorporate Relationships

(a) Furnish a list of each subsidiary, other than inactive subsidiaries, of the issuer. As to each such subsidiary indicate the jurisdiction under the laws of which it was organized, and the percentage of voting securities owned by its parent.

(b) Clearly illustrate by way of a diagram or otherwise the intercorporate relationships of the issuer, its parent and those subsidiaries listed pursuant to paragraph (a).

(c) Where one of the primary businesses of the issuer is investing, reinvesting, owning, holding or trading in securities, give in substantially the tabular form indicated the following information as at a date within thirty days of the date of the preliminary prospectus or pro forma prospectus, with respect to each company 5 per cent or more of whose securities of any class are owned directly or indirectly by the issuer or its affiliates.

TABLE

Name and address of company	Nature of its principal business	Percentage of securities of any class beneficially owned, directly or indirectly	Percentage of book value of issuer's assets invested therein
....	....	....	....

INSTRUCTIONS:

1. If the securities being issued are to be issued in connection with, or pursuant to, a plan of acquisition, reorganization, readjustment, or succession, indicate insofar as practicable the status to exist upon consummation of the plan.

2. The name of any particular subsidiary may be omitted if

   (a)   - the assets of the subsidiary, or

        - the investment in and advances to the subsidiary by its parent and the parent's other subsidiaries

        if any, do not exceed 10 per cent of the assets of the parent and its subsidiaries on a consolidated basis;

   (b) the sales and operating revenue of the subsidiary do not exceed 10 per cent of the sales and operating revenues of its parent and the parent's subsidiaries on a consolidated basis; and

   (c) the unnamed subsidiaries considered in the aggregate as a single subsidiary would satisfy the conditions in (a) and (b) if the reference therein to 10 per cent were replaced by 20 per cent.

Item 13 - Description of Business:

   (a) Briefly describe the business carried on and intended to be carried on by the issuer and its subsidiaries and the general development of the business within the five preceding years. Where a material proportion of the assets of the issuer and its subsidiaries is invested in or is derived from,

        (i) financial services;

        (ii) other services;

        (iii) the distribution of products;

        (iv) the production of products;

        (v) real estate development;

        (vi) investment in securities of companies other than subsidiaries; or

        (vii) any other specific branch of the business,

   furnish in substantially the tabular form indicated, as at the date of the last balance sheet,

        (viii) the percentage of the consolidated assets of the issuer and its subsidiaries employed in each separate operation;

        (ix) the percentage of the consolidated gross revenues of the issuer and its subsidiaries derived from each separate operation.

TABLE

Column 1	Column 2	Column 3
Separate operation in which a material proportion of assets are invested	Percentage of Consolidated Assets, at book value, devoted thereto	Percentage of Gross Revenue derived therefrom
1. Finance Company Service	....	....
2. Other Services	....	....
3. Distribution of Products	....	....
4. Production of Products	....	....
5. Real Estate development	....	....
6. Investment in securities of companies other than subsidiaries	....	....
7. Any other specific branch of the business	....	....

(b) If the issuer has carried on any business other than that of a finance issuer during the past five years, state the nature of such other business and give the approximate date on which the issuer commenced to operate principally as a finance issuer. If the issuer's name was changed during the period, state its former name and the date on which the name was changed.

(c) If during the past two years any affiliate or associate of the issuer or its subsidiaries had any material interest, direct or indirect, in any transaction involving the purchase of any substantial amount of assets presently held by the issuer or any of its subsidiaries, describe the interest of the affiliate or associate in such transaction and state the cost of such assets to the purchaser and to the seller.

(d) Where a material proportion of the consolidated assets or consolidated gross revenues of the issuer is invested in, or is derived from real property, state briefly the location and general character of the principal properties, including buildings and plants of the issuer and its subsidiaries. If any such property is not freehold property or is held subject to any major encumbrance, so state and briefly describe the nature of the title or any such encumbrance, as the case may be.

(e) Where the primary business of the issuer, or of any subsidiary or affiliate, in investing, reinvesting, owning, holding or trading in securities, indicate whether such business is carried on by the issuer itself or by a subsidiary or affiliate, naming such subsidiary or affiliate together with a brief outline of its corporate history and structure and

   (i) describe the policy or proposed policy with respect to each of the following types of activities, outlining the extent, if any, to which the issuer has engaged in such activities during the last five years and indicate which of such policies may not be changed without shareholder action;

   a. the issuance of securities other than the securities offered,

   b. the borrowing of money,

   c. the underwriting of securities of other issuers;

   d. the concentration of investments in a particular class or kind of industry;

   e. the purchase and sale of real estate;

   f. the purchase and sale of commodities or commodity future contracts,

    g. the making of loans, whether secured or unsecured, and

    h. any other policy which the issuer deems fundamental.

INSTRUCTION:

For the purpose of clause g, the purchase of debt securities for investment purposes is not to be considered the making of a loan by the issuer.

    (ii) describe the investment policy of the issuer with respect to each of the following matters which is not described as a fundamental policy of the issuer under subparagraph (i) of this paragraph, indicating which of such investment policies may not be changed without shareholder action:

    a. the type of securities (for example, bonds, preferred shares, common shares) in which it may invest, indicating the proportion of the assets which may be invested in each such type of security,

    b. the percentage of assets which it may invest in the securities of any one issuer,

    c. the percentage of securities of any one issuer which it may acquire,

    d. investment in securities of issuers for the purpose of exercising control or management,

    e. investment in securities of mutual fund issuers or other investment issuers, and

    f. any other investment policy not specified above or in subparagraph (i) of this paragraph which is set out in the issuer's articles of incorporation, other constating documents, by-laws or regulations.

1.   The description shall not relate to the powers and objects specified in the incorporating instruments, but to the actual business carried on and intended to be carried on. Include the business of subsidiaries of the issuer only in so far as is necessary to understand the character and development of the business conducted by the combined enterprise.

2.   Outline such material facts as are essential to an investor's appraisal of the securities being offered. Where applicable, such information should be furnished as well reasonably inform investors as to the suitability, adequacy, productive capacity and extent of utilization of the facilities used in the enterprise. Detailed descriptions of the physical characteristics of individual properties or legal descriptions by metes and bounds are not required and shall not be given.

3.   In describing developments, information shall be given as to matters such as the nature and results of any bankruptcy, receivership or similar proceedings with respect to the issuer or any of its subsidiaries, the nature and results of any other material reorganization of the issuer or any of its subsidiaries and any material changes in the mode of conducting the business of the issuer or its subsidiaries.

4.   In answering paragraph (c) of this item, transactions between the issuer and a wholly-owned subsidiary need not be disclosed.

5.   The words "wholly-owned subsidiary" as used in this item include a subsidiary where directors and officers are beneficial owners of voting securities to the extent necessary to qualify as directors.

6.   Indicate who or what group of persons is responsible for investment decisions, the granting of loans, and the establishing of bad-debt allowances.

7.   Indicate whether the approval of the board of directors of the issuer is required for loans and acquisitions and whether the board of directors is comprised of nominees of the dominant interest in the finance issuer.

8.   Instruction 1 to Item 11 applies to this item with due alteration for points of detail.

Item 14 - Risk Factors:

(a) Where appropriate to a clear understanding by investors of the risk factors and speculative nature of the enterprise or the securities being offered, an introductory statement shall be made on the first page or in the summary of the prospectus summarizing the factors which make the purchase a risk or speculation. Include such matters as the pro forma dilution of the investment based on net tangible assets and a comparison, in percentages, of the securities being offered for cash and those issued or to be issued to promoters, directors, officers, substantial securityholders as defined in section 104(2) of the Act, and underwriters for cash, property and services. The information may be given in the body of the prospectus if an appropriate reference is made on the first page or in the summary of the prospectus to the risks and the speculative or promotional nature of the enterprise and a cross reference is made to the place in the prospectus where the information is contained.

(b) Where there is a risk that purchasers of the securities offered may become liable to make an additional contribution beyond the price of the security, disclose any information or facts that may bear on the security holder's assessment of risk associated with the investment.

Item 15 - Acquisitions:

Briefly describe all material acquisitions and dispositions whether of shares or assets by the issuer and its subsidiaries during the past two years and to the extent reasonably practicable the impact of these acquisitions or dispositions on the operating results and financial position of the issuer.

Item 16 - Variations in Operating Results:

Explain to the extent reasonably practicable any substantial variations, both favourable ;and adverse, in the operating results of the issuer over the last three years, but the Superintendent may permit or require an explanation of such substantial variations over a longer period not to exceed five years.

INSTRUCTION:

The explanation should be in narrative form. However, where ratios are used to illustrate variations, a table may be used to supplement the narrative.

Item 17 - Tax Status of Issuer:

State in general terms the bases upon which the income and capital receipts of the issuer are taxed.

Item 18 - Tax Status of Securityholder:

State in general terms the income tax consequences to the holders of the securities offered hereby of any distribution to such holders in the form of dividends or otherwise.

Item 19 - Promoters:

If any person is or has been a promoter of the issuer or of any of its subsidiaries within the five years immediately preceding the date of the preliminary prospectus or *pro forma* prospectus, furnish the following information:

(a) State the names of the promoters, the nature and amount of anything of value (including money, property, contracts, options or rights of any kind) received or to be received by each promoter directly or indirectly from the issuer, or from any of its subsidiaries, and the nature and amount of any assets, services or other consideration therefor received or to be received by the issuer or subsidiary.

(b) As to any assets acquired within the past two years or to be acquired by the issuer or by any of its subsidiaries from a promoter, state the amount at which acquired or to be acquired and the principle followed or to be followed in determining the amount. Identify the person making the determination and state his relationship, if any, with the issuer, any subsidiary or any promoter. State the date that the assets were acquired by the promoter and the cost thereof to the promoter.

Forms

Item 20 - Legal Proceedings:

Briefly describe any legal proceedings material to the issuer to which the issuer or any of its subsidiaries is a party or of which any of their property is the subject. Make a similar statement as to any such proceedings known to be contemplated.

INSTRUCTION:

Include the name of the court or agency, the date instituted, the principal parties thereto, the nature of the claim, the amount claimed, if any, whether the proceedings are being contested, and the present status of the proceedings.

Item 21 - Issuance of Shares:

(a)   If shares are being offered, state the description or the designation of the class of shares offered and furnish all material attributes and characteristics including, without limiting the generality of the foregoing, the following information:

   (i) dividend rights;

   (ii) voting rights;

   (iii) liquidation or distribution rights;

   (iv) pre-emptive rights;

   (v) conversion rights;

   (vi) redemption, purchase for cancellation or surrender provisions;

   (vii) sinking or purchase fund provisions;

   (viii) liability to further calls or to assessment by the issuer; and

   (ix) provisions as to modification, amendment or variation of any such rights or provisions.

(b)   If the rights of holders of such shares may be modified otherwise than in accordance with the provisions attaching to such shares or the provisions of the governing Act relating thereto, so state and explain briefly.

INSTRUCTIONS:

1.   This item requires only a brief summary of the provisions that are material from an investment standpoint. Do not set out verbatim the provisions attaching to the shares; only a succinct resume is required.

2.   If the rights attaching to the shares being offered are materially limited or qualified by the rights of any other class of securities, or if any other class of securities (other than obligations covered in Item 18), ranks ahead of or equally with the shares being offered, include information regarding such other securities that will enable investors to understand the rights attaching to the shares being offered. If any shares being offered are to be offered in exchange for other securities, an appropriate description of the other securities shall be given. No information need be given, however, as to any class of securities that is to be redeemed or otherwise retired, provided appropriate steps to assure redemption or retirement have been or will be taken prior to or contemporaneously with the delivery of the shares being offered.

3.   In addition to the summary referred to in instruction 1, the issuer may set out verbatim in a schedule to the prospectus the provisions attaching to the shares being offered.

Item 22 - Issuance of Obligations:

If obligations are being offered, give a brief summary of the material attributes and characteristics of the indebtedness and the security therefor including, without limiting the generality of the foregoing:

(a)   Provisions with respect to interest rate, maturity, redemption or other retirement, sinking fund and conversion rights.

(b)   The nature and priority of any security for the obligations, briefly identifying the principal properties subject to lien or charge.

(c)   Provisions permitting or restricting the issuance of additional securities, the incurring of additional indebtedness and other material negative covenants, (including restrictions against payment of dividends, restrictions against giving security on the assets of the issuer or its subsidiaries and the like) and provisions as to the release or substitution of assets securing the obligations, the modification of the terms of the security and similar provisions.

(d)   The name of the trustee under any indenture relating to the obligations and the nature of any material relationship between the trustee and the issuer or any of its affiliates.

(e)   Indicate any financial arrangements between the issuer and any of its affiliates or among its affiliates that could affect the security for the indebtedness.

INSTRUCTION:

The instructions to Item 17 apply to this item with due alteration for point of detail.

Item 23 - Issuance of Other Securities:

If securities other than shares or obligations are being offered, outline briefly the rights evidenced thereby. If subscription warrants or rights are being offered or issued, state the description and amount of securities covered thereby, the period during which, and the price at which, the warrants or rights are exercisable, and the principal terms and conditions by which they may be exercised.

INSTRUCTION:

The instructions to Item 17 apply to this item with due alteration for point of detail.

Item 24 - Dividend Record:

State the amount of dividends or other distributions, if any, paid by the issuer during its last five completed financial years preceding the date of the preliminary prospectus or *pro forma* prospectus.

INSTRUCTION:

Dividends should be set out on a per share basis, shown separately for each class of shares in respect of each of the financial years. Appropriate adjustments shall be made to reflect changes in capitalization during the period.

Item 25 - Directors and Officers

List the names and home addresses in full or, alternatively, solely the municipality of residence or postal address, of all directors and officers of the issuer and indicate all positions and offices with the issuer held by each person named, and the principal occupations within the five preceding years, of each director and officer.

INSTRUCTIONS:

1.   Where the municipality of residence or postal address is listed, the Superintendent may request that the home address in full be furnished to the Commission.

2.   Where the principal occupation of a director or officer is that of an officer of a company other than the issuer, state the principal business in which such company is engaged.

3.   Where a director or officer has held more than one position in the issuer, or a parent or subsidiary thereof, state only the first and last position held.

Item 26 - Executive Compensation

Complete and attach to or include in this Form a Statement of Executive Compensation in Form 41, provided however, that the disclosure required by Items V, VIII, IX and X of Form 41 may be omitted for purposes of this Form.

See NIN 93/23 "Executive Compensation".

ITEM 27 - Indebtedness of Directors, Executive Officers and Senior Officers

(a) The information required by this Item must be provided for each individual who is or, at any time during the most recently completed financial year, was a director, executive officer and senior officer of the issuer, each proposed nominee for election as a director of the issuer, and each associate of any such director, officer or proposed nominee,

(i) who is, or at any time since the beginning of the most recently completed financial year of the issuer has been, indebted to the issuer or any of its subsidiaries, or

(ii) whose indebtedness to another entity is, or at any time since the beginning of the most recently completed financial year of the issuer has been, the subject of a guarantee, support agreement, letter of credit or other similar arrangement or understanding provided by the issuer or any of its subsidiaries.

(b) State in the tabular form under the caption set out, for any indebtedness referred to in paragraph (a) of this Item that was entered into in connection with a purchase of securities of the issuer or any of its subsidiaries:

(i) The name of the borrower (column (a)).

(ii) If the borrower is a director, executive officer or senior officer, the principal position of the borrower. If the borrower was, during the year, but no longer is a director or officer, include a statement to that effect. If the borrower is a proposed nominee for election as a director, include a statement to that effect. If the borrower is included as an associate describe briefly the relationship of the borrower to an individual who is or, during the year, was a director, executive officer or senior officer or who is a proposed nominee for election as a director, name that individual and provide the information required by this subparagraph for that individual (column (a)).

(iii) Whether the issuer or a subsidiary of the issuer is the lender or the provider of a guarantee, support agreement, letter of credit or similar arrangement or understanding (column (b)).

(iv) The largest aggregate amount of the indebtedness outstanding at any time during the last completed financial year (column (c)).

(v) The aggregate amount of indebtedness outstanding as at a date within thirty days of certification of the prospectus (column (d)).

(vi) Separately for each class or series of securities, the sum of the number of securities purchased during the last completed financial year with the financial assistance (column (e)).

(vii) The security for the indebtedness, if any, provided to the issuer, any of its subsidiaries or the other entity (column (f)).

TABLE OF INDEBTEDNESS OF DIRECTORS, EXECUTIVE OFFICERS AND SENIOR OFFICERS UNDER SECURITIES PURCHASE PROGRAMS

Name and Principal Position (a)	Involvement of Issuer or Subsidiary (b)	Largest Amount Outstanding During [Last Completed Financial Year] ($) (c)	Amount Outstanding as at [current date] ($) (d)	Financially Assisted Securities Purchases During [Last Completed Financial Year] (#) (e)	Security for Indebtedness (f)

(c) State in the introduction immediately preceding the table required by paragraph (b) of this Item, for indebtedness entered into in connection with a purchase of securities of the issuer or any of its subsidiaries, separately, the aggregate indebtedness,

    (i) to the issuer or any of its subsidiaries, and

    (ii) to another entity if the indebtedness is the subject of a guarantee, support agreement, letter of credit or other similar arrangement or understanding provided by the issuer or any of its subsidiaries,

of all officers, directors, employees and former officers, directors and employees of the issuer or any of its subsidiaries outstanding as at a date within thirty days of certification of the prospectus.

(d) State in the tabular form under the caption set out, for any indebtedness referred to in paragraph (a) of this Item that was not entered into in connection with a purchase of securities of the issuer or any of its subsidiaries, the information referred to in subparagraphs (b) (i) through (v) of this Item.

TABLE OF INDEBTEDNESS OF DIRECTORS, EXECUTIVE OFFICERS AND SENIOR OFFICERS [insert if the issuer has a securities purchase program "OTHER THAN UNDER SECURITIES PURCHASE PROGRAMS"]

Name and Principal Position (a)	Involvement of Issuer or Subsidiary (b)	Largest Amount Outstanding During [Last Completed Financial Year] ($) (c)	Amount Outstanding as at [current date] ($) (d)

(e) State in the introduction immediately preceding the table required by paragraph (d) of this Item, for indebtedness not entered into in connection with a purchase of securities of the issuer or any of its subsidiaries, separately, the aggregate indebtedness,

    (i) to the issuer or any of its subsidiaries, and

    (ii) to another entity if the indebtedness is the subject of a guarantee, support agreement, letter of credit or other similar arrangement or understanding provided by the issuer or any of its subsidiaries,

of all officers, directors, employees and former officers, directors and employees of the issuer or any of its subsidiaries outstanding as at a date within thirty days of certification of the prospectus.

(f) Disclose in a footnote to, or a narrative accompanying, each table required by this Item,

    (i) the material terms of each incidence of indebtedness and, if applicable, of each guarantee, support agreement, letter of credit or other similar arrangement or understanding, including without limitation the term to maturity, rate of interest and any understanding, agreement or intention to limit recourse, and for the table required by paragraph (d) only, any security for the indebtedness and the nature of the transaction in which the indebtedness was incurred,

    (ii) any material adjustment or amendment made during the most recently completed financial year to the terms of the indebtedness and, if applicable, the guarantee, support agreement, letter of credit or similar arrangement or understanding, and

    (iii) the class or series of the securities purchased with financial assistance or held as security for the indebtedness and, if the class or series of securities is not publicly traded, all material terms of the securities, including but not limited to provisions for exchange, conversion, exercise, redemption, retraction and dividends.

Forms

(g)   No disclosure need be made under this Item of an incidence of indebtedness that has been entirely repaid on or before the date of certification of the prospectus or of routine indebtedness.

"Routine indebtedness" means indebtedness described in any of the following:

(i)   If an issuer makes loans to employees generally, whether or not in the ordinary course of business, loans are considered routine indebtedness if made on terms, including those as to interest rate and security, no more favourable to the borrower than the terms on which loans are made by the issuer to employees generally, but the amount at any time during the last completed financial year remaining unpaid under the loans to any one director, executive officer, senior officer or proposed nominee together with his or her associates that are treated as routine indebtedness under this clause must not exceed $25,000.

(ii) Whether or not the issuer makes loans in the ordinary course of business, a loan to a director, executive officer or senior officer is considered routine indebtedness if,

A.   the borrower is a full-time employee of the issuer,

B.   the loan is fully secured against the residence of the borrower, and

C.   the amount of the loan does not exceed the annual salary of the borrower.

(iii) If the issuer makes loans in the ordinary course of business, a loan is considered routine indebtedness if made to a person or company other than a full-time employee of the issuer, and if the loan,

A.   is made on substantially the same terms, including those as to interest rate and security, as are available when a loan is made to other customers of the issuer with comparable credit ratings, and

B.   involves no more than usual risks of collectibility.

(iv) Indebtedness arising by reason of purchases made on usual trade terms or of ordinary travel or expense advances, or for similar reasons is considered routine indebtedness if the repayment arrangements are in accord with usual commercial practice.

(h)   For purposes of this Item, "executive officer" has the same meaning as in Form 41 and "support agreement" includes, but is not limited to, an agreement to provide assistance in the maintenance or servicing of any indebtedness and an agreement to provide compensation for the purpose of maintaining or servicing any indebtedness of the borrower.

See NIN 93/23 "Executive Compensation".

Item 28 - Options to Purchase Securities:

Furnish (in tabular form, if possible) the information referred to in Instruction 1, as at a specified date not more than thirty days before the date of the preliminary prospectus or pro forma prospectus, as the case may be, and as at the date of the filing of the prospectus, as to options to purchase securities of the issuer or any of its subsidiaries that are held or proposed to be held,

(i)   by all executive officers as a group and all directors who are not also executive officers as a group, indicating the aggregate number of executive officers and the aggregate number of directors to whom the information applies, without naming them;

(ii) by all executive officers of all subsidiaries of the issuer as a group and all directors of such subsidiaries who are not also executive officers as a group, without naming them, excluding individuals referred to in clause (i);

    (iii) by all other employees of the issuer as a group, without naming them;

    (iv) by all other employees of the subsidiaries of the issuer as a group, without naming them; and

    (v) by any other person or company, naming each such person or company.

INSTRUCTIONS:

1. Describe the options, stating the material provisions of each class or type of option including,

    (i) the designation and number of securities under option;

    (ii) the purchase price of the securities under option or the formula by which the purchase price will be determined, and the expiration dates of such options;

    (iii) if reasonably ascertainable, the market value of the securities under option on the date of grant; and

    (iv) if reasonably ascertainable, the market value of the securities under option on the specified date.

2. For the purposes of this Item,

    (i) "executive officer" means the chairman and any vice-chairman of the board of directors of an issuer who performs the functions of such office on a full-time basis, the president, any vice-president in charge of a principal business unit such as sales, finance or production, and any officer of the issuer or of a subsidiary who performs a policy-making function in respect of the issuer, whether or not such officer is also a director of the issuer or the subsidiary;

    (ii) "options" includes all options, share purchase warrants or rights other than those shares issued on a pro rata basis, to all security holders of the same class resident in Canada and an extension of an option shall be deemed to be a granting of an option.

3. Options that are proposed to be held are those where there is an approval or understanding or commitment of the issuer or a subsidiary in respect of the granting of such options.

4. In the disclosure made under this Item 28, do not include options granted or proposed to be granted that are otherwise disclosed in Item 1 or 2, including options granted or to be granted to the underwriter in respect of the distribution under the prospectus.

Item 29 - Escrowed Shares:

State as of a specified date within thirty days prior to the date of the preliminary prospectus or pro forma prospectus, in substantially the tabular form indicated, the number of shares of each class of voting securities of the issuer to the knowledge of the issuer held in escrow, disclosing the name of the depositary, if any, the date of and the conditions governing the release of the shares from escrow;

TABLE

Column 1	Column 2	Column 3
Designation of class	Number of securities held in escrow	Percentage of class
....	....	....

Item 30 - Principal Holders of Securities:

Furnish the following information as of a specified date within thirty days prior to the date of the preliminary prospectus or pro forma prospectus, in substantially the tabular form indicated.

(a) The number of securities of each class of voting securities of the issuer owned of record or beneficially, directly or indirectly, by each person who owns of record, or is known by the issuer to own beneficially, directly or indirectly, more than 10 per cent of any class of such securities. Show in Column 3 whether the securities are owned both or record and beneficially, of record only, or beneficially only, and show in Columns 4 and 5 the respective amounts and percentages known by the issuer to be owned in each such manner.

TABLE

Column 1	Column 2	Column 3	Column 4	Column 5
Name and address	Designation of class	Type of ownership	Number of securities owned	Percentage of class
....	....	....	....	....

(b) The percentage of securities of each class of voting securities of the issuer or any of its parents or its subsidiaries, beneficially owned, directly or indirectly, by all directors and senior officers of the issuer, as a group, without naming them:

TABLE

Column 1	Column 2
Designation of Class	Percentage of Class
....	....
....	....

INSTRUCTIONS:

1. Where a company is shown by the issuer as owning directly or indirectly more than 10 per cent of any class of such securities, the Superintendent may require the disclosure of such additional information as is necessary to identify any individual who, through his direct or indirect ownership of voting securities in the company owns directly or indirectly more than 10 percent of any class of such securities. The name of such an individual should be disclosed in a foot note to the table described in paragraph (a).

2. For purposes of paragraph (a) , securities owned beneficially, directly or indirectly, and or record shall be aggregated in determining whether any person owns more than 10 per cent of the securities of any class.

3. If voting securities are being offered in connection with, or pursuant to, a plan of acquisition, amalgamation or reorganization, indicate as far as practicable, the respective holdings of voting securities that will exist after giving effect to the plan.

4. If any of the securities being offered are to be offered for the account of a securityholder name such security holder and state the number or amount of the securities owned by him, the number or amount to be offered for his account, and the number or amount to be owned by him after the offering.

5. If, to the knowledge of the issuer or the underwriter of the securities being offered, more than 10 per cent of any class of voting securities of the issuer are held or are to be held subject to any voting trust or other similar agreement, other than an escrow arrangement referred to in Item 24, state the designation of such securities, the number or amount held or to be held and the duration of the agreement. Give the names and addresses of the voting trustees and outline briefly their voting rights and other powers under the agreement.

6. If, to the knowledge of the issuer, the parent or the underwriter of the securities being offered, any person named in answer to paragraph (a) is an associate or affiliate of any other person named therein, disclose, in so far as known, the material facts of such relationship, including any basis for influence over the issuer enjoyed by the person other than the holding of the voting securities of the issuer.

7. The word "issuer" as used in this item and in the instructions thereto includes any subsidiary or affiliate of the issuer.

Item 31 - Prior Sales:

(a) State the prices at which securities of the class offered by the prospectus have been sold within the twelve months prior to the date of the preliminary prospectus or pro forma prospectus, or are to be sold, by the issuer or selling security holder if such prices differ from those at which the securities are offered by the prospectus. State the number of securities sold or to be sold at each price.

(b) Where the class of securities offered are listed on a Canadian stock exchange or solely on a foreign stock exchange, give price ranges and volume traded on such stock exchange on a monthly basis for each month or, if applicable, part month, of the current quarter and the immediately preceding quarter and on a quarterly basis for the next preceding seven quarters provided that the Superintendent may permit the omission of the information regarding trading volume.

INSTRUCTION:

In the case of sales by a selling securityholder, the information required by paragraph (a) may be given in the form of price ranges for each calendar month.

Item 32 - Interest of Management and Other in Material Transactions:

Describe briefly, and where practicable state the approximate amount of any material interest, direct or indirect, of any of the following persons in any transaction within the three years prior to the date of the preliminary prospectus or pro forma prospectus, or in any proposed transaction which has materially affected or will materially affect the issuer or any of its subsidiaries:

(i) any director or senior officer of the issuer;

(ii) any securityholder named in answer to paragraph (a) of Item 26; and

(iii) any associate or affiliate of any of the foregoing persons.

INSTRUCTIONS:

1. Give a brief description of the material transaction. Include the name and address of each person whose interest in any transaction is described and the nature of the relationship by reason of which such interest is required to be described.

2. As to any transaction involving the purchase or sale of assets by or to the issuer or any subsidiary, state the cost of the assets to the purchaser and the cost thereof to the seller if acquired by the seller within two years to the transaction.

3. This item does not apply to any interest arising from the ownership of securities of the issuer where the securityholder receives no extra or special benefit or advantage not shared on an equal basis by all other holders of the same class of securities or all other holders of the same class of securities who are resident in Canada.

4. Information shall be included as to any material underwriting discounts or commissions upon the sale of securities by the issuer where any of the specified persons was or is to be an underwriter or is an associate, affiliate or partner of a person, or partnership that was or is to be an underwriter.

5. No information need be given in answer to this item as to any transaction or any interest therein, where,

    (i)   the rates or charges involved in the transaction are fixed by law or determined by competitive bids;

    (ii) the interest of a specified person in the transaction is solely that of a director of another company that is a party to the transaction;

    (iii) the transaction involves services as a bank or other depository of funds, transfer agent, registrar, trustee under a trust indenture or other similar services;

    (iv) the interest of a specified person, including all periodic instalments in the case of any lease or other agreement providing for periodic payments or instalments, does not exceed $50,000; or

    (v)   the transaction does not, directly or indirectly, involve remuneration for services, and,

          a. the interest of the specified person arose from the beneficial ownership, direct or indirect, of less than 10 per cent of any class of voting securities of another company that is a party to the transaction,

          b. the transaction is in the ordinary course of business of the issuer or its subsidiaries, and

          c. the amount of the transaction or series of transactions is less than 10 per cent of the total sales or purchases, as the case may be, of the issuer and its subsidiaries for the last completed financial year.

6. Information shall be furnished in answer to this item with respect to transactions not excluded above that involve remuneration, directly or indirectly, to any of the specified persons for services in any capacity unless the interest of the person arises solely from the beneficial ownership, direct or indirect, of less than 10 per cent of any class of voting securities of another company furnishing the services to the issuer or its subsidiaries.

7. This item does not require the disclosure of any interest in any transaction unless such interest and transaction are material.

8. The word "issuer" as used in this item and in the instructions thereto includes any subsidiary or affiliate of the issuer.

Item 33 - Location of Assets Encumbered Under Trust Indenture and Custodian of Portfolio Securities:

    (a)   Where capital securities of, or capital securities constituting all or part of, the investment portfolio of the issuer are charged, deposited, pledged, hypothecated or otherwise encumbered under a trust indenture, state where such capital securities are physically situate. If, as a part of any scheme of financing of or by the issuer, any capital securities of, or capital securities constituting all or part of, the investment portfolio of the issuer are to be charged, deposited, pledged, hypothecated or otherwise encumbered, state where such capital securities will by physically situate and indicate the persons expected to be parties to the transaction.

    (b)   Where the primary business of the issuer, or of a subsidiary or affiliate of the issuer, is investing, reinvesting, owning, holding, or trading in securities, state the name, principal business address and the nature of the business of each person holding portfolio securities of the issuer, or of any subsidiary or affiliate of the issuer which is investing, reinvesting, owning, holding or trading in securities, as custodian and the jurisdiction in which the portfolio securities are physically situate.

(c)   The name of the company holding assets encumbered under a trust inden-
        ture, or the name of the company holding portfolio securities as custodian
        may be omitted if it is a bank or otherwise with the consent of the Director.

INSTRUCTIONS:

1.   The word "issuer" as used in this item and in the instructions thereto includes
        any subsidiary or affiliate of the issuer.

2.   The words "investment portfolio" as used in this item and in the instructions
        thereto include any security other than commercial paper acquired where a
        material activity of the issuer includes an activity referred to in subclause 2(2)(a)
        of the Regulation.

3.   Where the scheme of financing is not disclosed in answer to Instruction 4 of Item
        5, Item 6, or Instruction 5 of Item 7, indicate the purpose of the scheme of
        financing. Where the scheme of financing is undertaken or proposed to be under-
        taken in connection with a take-over bid, so indicate. The source of capital for,
        and the intended offeree of, the proposed take-over bid need not be disclosed,
        provided that the provisions of Part II of the Act are complied with when the
        contemplated take-over bid is made.

4.   Where the finance issuer is custodian of its portfolio securities, or where debt
        securities are issued without a trust indenture, describe

        (i)   provisions made for the safekeeping of portfolio and other securities and
              assets;

        (ii) bonding arrangements, if any, for employees or agents dealing with
              portfolio and other securities and assets; and

        (iii) corporate procedures for dealing with the purchase, sale and transfer of
              portfolio and other securities and assets.

Item 34 - Statement of Functions of Issuer:

(a)   Where the predominant business of the issuer is investing, reinvesting,
        owning, holding or trading in securities, give a concise statement of the
        manner in which the following functions of the issuer are performed and
        who is responsible therefor, stating how such functions are co-ordinated
        and to the extent that any such functions are not performed by bona fide
        employees of the issuer, the names and addresses of the persons respon-
        sible for performing such functions:

        (i)   management of the non-financial investment holdings of the issuer;

        (ii) providing supervision of lending policies;

        (iii) management of the issuer;

        (iv) providing collection policies;

        (v)   making investment decisions and supervising their execution; and

        (vi) purchase and sale of the investment portfolio and brokerage ar-
              rangements relating thereto.

(b)   Indicate whether the approval of the board of directors of the issuer is
        required for the acquisition of investments, and whether the board of
        directors of the issuer making the investment comprises nominees of the
        dominant interest in the finance issuer.

INSTRUCTIONS:

1.   The word "issuer" as used in this item and in the instructions thereto includes
        any subsidiary or affiliate of the issuer.

2.   In giving information regarding the purchase and sale of the investment portfolio
        and brokerage arrangements relating thereto the name and address of only the
        principal broker need be given.

3.   In giving information regarding purchase and sale of the investment portfolio and
        brokerage arrangements relating thereto give brief details of the following mat-
        ters:

    (i) the total cost during the last completed financial year of the issuer of securities acquired, distinguishing between,

        (a) securities of or guaranteed by the government of any country or any political subdivision thereof;

        (b) short term notes; and

        (c) other securities;

    (ii) the total cost of securities held at the beginning and at the end of the issuer's last completed financial year;

    (iii) the formula, method or criteria used in allocating brokerage business to persons engaged in the distribution of the securities of the issuer;

    (iv) the formula, method or criteria used in allocating brokerage business to persons furnishing statistical, research or other services to the issuer or to the manager of the issuer, and

    (v) the amount of brokerage paid to the principal broker for the last three completed financial years, giving the total amount paid in each year and expressing the amount paid in each year as a percentage of the total brokerage paid by the issuer.

4. As used in this Form:

    (a) "principal broker" includes,

        (i) a person through whom the investment portfolio of the issuer is purchased or sold pursuant to a contractual arrangement with the issuer or the manager of the issuer providing for an exclusive right to purchase or sell the investment portfolio of the issuer or any feature which gives or is intended to give a broker or dealer a material competitive advantage over other brokers or dealers in respect of the purchase or sale of the investment portfolio of the issuer; or

        (ii) a person together with any affiliate, by or through whom 15 per cent or more of the securities transactions of the issuer were carried out in the last completed financial year of the issuer; and

    (b) "brokerage arrangements" or "brokerage business" include all purchases and sales of the investment portfolio whether effected directly or through an agent.

5. If one or more persons or companies performs more than one of the functions referred to in this item, so state, giving details of all functions so performed.

6. Instruction 1 to item 11 applies to this item with due alteration for points of detail.

Item 35 - Associated Persons:

Furnish the following information as to each person or company named in answer to paragraph (a) of Item 34:

1. If a named person or company is associated with the issuer or is a director or senior officer of or is associated with any affiliate of the issuer or is a director or senior officer of or is associated with any company which is associated with the issuer so state, and give particulars of the relationship.

2. If the issuer is associated with a name person or company or is associated with any affiliate of a named company or is associated with any company which is associated with the named person or company so state, and give particulars of the relationship.

3. If any person or company associated with the issuer is also associated with a named person or company so state, and give particulars of the relationship.

4. If a named person or company has a contract or arrangement with the issuer, give a brief description of the contract or arrangement, including the basis for determining the remuneration of the named person or company and give the

amount of remuneration paid or payable by the issuer and its subsidiaries to such person or company during the last completed financial year of the issuer.

5. If a named person or company is associated with any other named person or company so state, and give particulars of the relationship.

6. Where and to the extent required by the Director, give the business experience of each named person or company and, in the case of a named company, the directors and officers thereof.

Item 36 - Auditors, Transfer Agents and Registrars:

(a) State the name and address of the auditor of the issuer.

(b) Where shares are offered, state the names of the issuer's transfer agents and registrars and the location (by municipalities) of the registers of transfers of each class of shares of the issuer. Where securities other than shares are offered, state the location (by municipalities) of each register on which transfers of such securities may be recorded.

INSTRUCTIONS:

1. the word "issuer" as used in this item includes, in addition to the issuer, any person directly or indirectly controlling or controlled by the issuer, or any person under direct or common control with the issuer.

2. Where the consolidated financial statements of the issuer are set out in the prospectus and the auditor of one or more subsidiaries is not the auditor of the issuer, set out the name and address of such auditor and the name and address of the company on which he reported and where such auditor has given a qualified report set out this fact in the prospectus. In addition, where an auditor of a subsidiary or affiliate makes a report in which the wording thereof has the effect of establishing a qualification of the report, file with the Commission the auditor's report, the financial statement reported on, and details applicable to the qualification.

3. Where any subsidiary or any affiliate of the issuer does not have the same financial year-end as the issuer, state the reasons for this policy.

Item 37 - Material Contracts:

Give particulars of every material contract entered into within the two years prior to the date of the preliminary prospectus or pro forma prospectus, by the issuer or any of its subsidiaries and state a reasonable time and place at which any such contract or a copy thereof may be inspected during distribution of the securities being offered.

INSTRUCTIONS:

1. The term "material contract" for this purpose means any contract that can reasonably be regarded as presently material to the proposed investor in the securities being offered.

2. Set out a complete list of all material contracts, indicating those which are disclosed elsewhere in the prospectus and provide particulars with respect to those material contracts about which particulars are not given elsewhere in the prospectus. This item does not require disclosure of contracts entered into in the ordinary course of business of the issuer or its subsidiaries as the case may be.

3. Particulars of contracts should include the dates of, parties to, consideration and general nature of the contracts, succinctly described.

4. Particulars of contracts need not be disclosed, or copies of such contracts made available for inspection, if the Superintendent determines that such disclosure or making- available would impair the value of the contract and would not be necessary for the protection of investors.

Item 38 - Other Material Facts:

Give particulars of any other material facts relating to the securities proposed to be offered and not disclosed pursuant to the foregoing items.

IT IS AN OFFENCE FOR A PERSON TO MAKE A STATEMENT IN A DOCU-MENT REQUIRED TO BE FILED OR FURNISHED UNDER THE ACT OR

THIS REGULATION THAT, AT THE TIME AND IN THE LIGHT OF THE CIRCUMSTANCES UNDER WHICH IT IS MADE, IS A MISREPRESENTATION.

The prospectus for a natural resource issuer required by Section 42(2) of the Act shall be in the following form.

FORM 14

Securities Act

INFORMATION REQUIRED IN PROSPECTUS OF A NATURAL RESOURCE ISSUER

Item 1 - Distribution Spread:

The information called for by the following Table shall be given, in substantially the tabular form indicated, on the first page of the prospectus as to all securities being offered for cash (estimate amounts, if necessary).

TABLE

	Column 1	Column 2	Column 3
	Price to Public	Underwriting discounts or commissions or mark-ups	Proceeds to issuer or selling securityholder
Per unit....	....	....	....
Total........	....	....	....

INSTRUCTIONS:

1. Only commissions paid or payable in cash or discounts granted by the issuer or selling security holder and mark- ups by whomever paid are to be included in the table. Commissions or other consideration paid or payable in cash or otherwise by other persons and consideration other than discounts granted and other than cash paid or payable by the issuer or selling security holder, except mark-ups, shall be set out following the table with a reference thereto in the second column of the table. Any finder's fee or similar payments shall be appropriately disclosed.

2. The table should set out separately those securities which are underwritten, those under option and those to be sold on a "best efforts" basis.

3. If the presentation of information in the form contemplated herein results in unnecessary complication, the tabular form may, with the consent of the Superintendent, be varied.

4. If it is impracticable to state the offering price, the method by which it is to be determined shall be explained. In addition, if the securities are to be offered at the market, indicate the market involved and the market price as of the latest practicable date.

5. If any of the securities offered are to be offered for the account of existing security holders, refer on the first page of the prospectus to the information called for by Instruction 4 to Item 26. State the portion of the expenses of distribution to be borne by the selling security holder. State that the securities of the selling security holder will not be sold until distribution of the issuer's securities is completed.

6. If debt securities are to be offered at a premium or a discount, state in bold face type the effective yield if held to maturity.

Item 2 - Plan of Distribution

(a) If the securities being offered are to be sold through underwriters, give the names of the underwriters. State briefly the nature of the underwriters' obligation to take up and pay for the securities. Indicate the date by which the underwriters are to purchase the securities.

(b) Furnish the following information, if possible in tabular form: rights under option and underwriting agreements to purchase securities from the issuer or any of its subsidiaries which are outstanding as of a specified date within thirty days prior to the date of the preliminary prospectus or pro forma prospectus, or which are proposed to be given and particulars of sub-option and sub-underwriting agreements outstanding or proposed to be given and particulars of any assignments or proposed assignments of any such agreements.

(c) State briefly the discounts, commissions and mark-ups to be allowed or paid to registrants, if not disclosed in Item 1, including all cash, securities, contracts or other consideration to be received by any registrant in connection with the sale of the securities.

(d) Where the prospectus discloses a plan of distribution not involving a firm underwriting or other subscription guarantee it must also disclose the amount of a minimum subscription. The face page shall contain the following disclosure or a reasonable paraphrase thereof:

> "This offering is subject to a minimum subscription being received by the issuer within 180 days of the effective date of ... ... (date of receipt of prospectus). Further particulars of the minimum subscription are disclosed on page ... under the caption Use of Proceeds."

INSTRUCTIONS:

1. All that is required as to the nature of the underwriters' obligation is whether the underwriters are or will be committed to take up and pay for all of the securities if any are taken up, or whether the underwriting is merely and agency or "best efforts" arrangement under which the underwriters are required to take up and pay for only such securities as they may sell.

2. Describe the options, stating the material provisions including:

   (i) the designation and number of the securities called for by such options;

   (ii) the purchase prices of the securities called for and the expiration dates of such options; and

   (iii) the market value of the securities called for by such options as of the latest practicable date.

3. Where an underwriting is subject to a "market out" clause, a statement in the prospectus under Plan of Distribution should be made with respect to the "market out" clause.

A sample paragraph is as follows:

Plan of Distribution:

"Under an agreement dated .... 19.... between the issuer and .... as underwriter, the issuer has agreed to sell and the underwriter has agreed to purchase on .... 19.... the .... at a price of $................., payable in cash to the issuer against delivery. The obligations of the underwriter under the agreement may be terminated at its discretion on the basis of its assessment of the state of the financial markets and may also be terminated upon the occurrence of certain stated events. The underwriter is however, obligated to take up and pay for all of the .... if any of the .... are purchased under the agreement."

4. Where a minimum subscription is required by the superintendent, which will normally be that amount which together with uncommitted funds on hand will suffice to finance the minimum program disclosed in the prospectus plus the issuer's estimated administration costs over the ensuing current period then:

(a)   All funds raised during the 180 days must be deposited in an account at a bank or trust company designated as a trust account until the full minimum amount has been received.

(b)   An agreement must be entered into with the trustee of such trust account whereby the trustee undertakes:

(i)   where within the 180-day period the minimum subscription has been received, to release the subscription funds to the issuer and to notify the Superintendent of such release; and

(ii)   where the minimum amount is not raised within the 180-day period to refund the subscription in full with interest accruing thereon to the shareholders.

5.   The Superintendent contemplates granting no extension for a minimum subscription beyond the 180-day period.

Item 3 - Market for Securities

Where no bona fide market exists, or will exist after the distribution, state in bold face type on the first page: "There is no market through which these securities may be sold". Disclose how the price paid to the issuer was established, whether by negotiation with the underwriter, arbitrarily by the issuer, or otherwise.

Item 4 - Summary of Prospectus:

Give a synopsis near the beginning of the prospectus of that information in the body of the prospectus which in the opinion of the issuer or selling security holder would be most likely to influence the investor's decision to purchase the security.

INSTRUCTIONS:

1.   This summary should highlight in condensed from the information, both favourable and adverse, including risk factors in item 10, particularly pertinent to a decision to purchase the securities offered, including information about both the issuer and the securities.

2.   Appropriate cross references may be made to items in the prospectus where information is difficult to summarize accurately, but this shall not detract from the necessity to have the salient points summarized in the summary.

Item 5 - Use of Proceeds to Issuer:

(a)   State the estimated net proceeds to be derived by the issuer from the sale of the securities to be offered, the principal purposes for which the net proceeds are intended to be used and the approximate amount intended to be used for each purpose.

(b)   State the particulars of any provisions or arrangements made for holding any part of the net proceeds of the issuer in trust or subject to the fulfillment of any conditions.

INSTRUCTIONS:

1.   Statements as to the principal purposes to which the proceeds are to be applied are to be reasonably specific although details of the particulars of proposed expenditures are not to be given except as otherwise required hereunder. The phrase "for general corporate purposes" is, in most cases, not sufficient. Specify whether unallocated funds will be placed in a trust or escrow account, invested or added to the working capital of the issuer. Give details of the arrangements made for, and the persons responsible for the supervision of the trust or escrow account or the investments of unallocated funds and the investment policy to be followed. Where the unallocated funds are to be added to working capital, indicate the reason for doing so.

2.   Where a minimum subscription is required by the superintendent a separate columnar allocation of this minimum amount of proceeds shall be shown in addition to a columnar allocation of the maximum amount proposed to be raised by this prospectus.

3. Include a statement regarding the proposed use of the actual proceeds if they should prove insufficient to accomplish the purposes set out, and the order of priority in which they will be applied. However, the statement need not be made if the underwriting arrangements are such that, if any securities are sold, it can be reasonably expected that the actual proceeds of the issue will not be substantially less than the estimated aggregate proceeds to the issuer as shown under item 1.

4. If any material amount of other funds are to be used in conjunction with the proceeds, state the amounts and sources of the other funds. If any material part of the proceeds is to be used to reduce or retire indebtedness, this item is to be answered as to the use of the proceeds of that indebtedness if the indebtedness was incurred within the two preceding years.

5. If any material amount of the proceeds is to be used directly or indirectly to acquire assets, otherwise than in the ordinary course of business, briefly describe the assets, and, where known, the particulars of the purchase price being paid for or being allocated to the respective categories of assets (including intangible assets) that are being acquired and, where practicable and meaningful, give name of the person from whom the assets are to be acquired. State the cost of the assets to the issuer and the principle followed in determining the cost. State briefly the nature of the title to or interest in the assets to be acquired by the issuer. If any part of the consideration for the acquisition of any of the assets consists of securities of the issuer, give brief particulars of the designation, number or amount, voting rights (if any) and other appropriate information relating to the class of securities, including particulars of any allotment or issuance of any such securities within the two preceding years.

Item 6 - Sales Otherwise than for Cash:

If any of the securities being offered are to be offered otherwise than for cash, state briefly the general purposes of the issue, the basis upon which the securities are to be offered, the amount of compensation paid or payable to any person and any other expenses of distribution, and by whom they are to be borne.

INSTRUCTION:

If the offer is to be made pursuant to a plan of acquisition, describe briefly the general effect of the plan and state when it became or is to become operative.

Item 7 - Share and Loan Capital Structure:

Furnish in substantially the tabular form indicated, or where appropriate in notes thereto:

(1) particulars of the share and loan capital of the issuer;

(2) particulars of the loan capital of each subsidiary of the issuer (other than loan capital owned by the issuer or its wholly-owned subsidiaries) whose financial statements are contained in the prospectus on either a consolidated or individual basis;

(3) the aggregate amount of the minority interest in the preference shares, if any, and the aggregate amount of the minority interest in the common shares and surplus of all subsidiaries whose financial statements are contained in the prospectus on a consolidated basis; and

(4) the aggregate amount of the minority interest in the preference shares, if any, and the aggregate amount of minority interest in the common shares and surplus of all subsidiaries whose financial statements are contained in the prospectus on an individual basis and not included in the consolidated financial statements.

Forms

TABLE

Column 1	Column 2	Column 3	Column 4	Column 5
Designation of security	Amount authorized or to be authorized	Amount outstanding as of the date of the most recent balance sheet contained in the prospectus	Amount outstanding as of a specific date within 30 days	Amount to be outstanding if all securities being issued are sold

INSTRUCTIONS:

1. Include all indebtedness for borrowed money as to which a written understanding exists that the indebtedness may extend beyond one year. Do not include other indebtedness classified as current liabilities unless secured.

2. Include in the table the amount of obligations under financial leases capitalized in accordance with generally accepted accounting principles. Set out in a note to the table a cross reference to any note in the financial statements containing information concerning the extent of obligations arising by virtue of other leases on real property.

3. Individual items of indebtedness which are not in excess of 3% of total assets as shown in the balance sheet referred to in column 3 may be set out in a single aggregate amount under an appropriate caption such as "Sundry Indebtedness".

4. Where practicable, state in general terms the respective priorities of the indebtedness shown in the table.

5. Give particulars of the amount, general description of and security for any substantial indebtedness proposed to be created or assumed by the issuer or its subsidiaries, other than indebtedness offered by the prospectus.

6. Set out in a note the amount of contributed surplus and retained earnings as of the date of the most recent balance sheet contained in the prospectus.

7. Set out in a note the number of shares subject to rights, options and warrants.

8. No information need be given under Column 2 with respect to the common and preference shares of subsidiaries.

9. For the purposes of Column 3, in computing the amount of the minority interest in the subsidiaries whose financial statements are contained in the prospectus on an individual basis and not included in the consolidated financial statements, such computation may be based on the financial statements of each such subsidiary contained in the prospectus.

10. In computing the minority interest in the subsidiaries for the purpose of Column 4, the amount set out in Column 3 may be used provided that appropriate adjustment is made to such amount to reflect any change in the percentage of ownership in the capital and surplus of any subsidiary by the minority interest.

11. The thirty-day period referred to in Column 4 is to be calculated within thirty days of the date of the preliminary prospectus or the date of the pro forma prospectus. Where more than thirty days have elapsed from the date of the preliminary or pro forma prospectus, the information included in the prospectus shall, if feasible, by updated to a date within thirty days of the prospectus.

12. The information to be set out in Column 5 may be based upon the information contained in Column 4, adjusted to take into account any amounts set out in Column 4 to be retired out of the issue.

Item 8 - Name and Incorporation of Issuer:

State the full corporate name of the issuer and the address of its head office and principal office. State the laws under which the issuer was incorporated and whether incorporated by articles of incorporation or otherwise and the date the corporation came into existence. If material state whether these have been amended.

INSTRUCTIONS:

1.　Particulars of the documents need to be set out only if material to the securities offered by the prospectus. See Item 17.

2.　If the issuer is not a company, give material details of its form of organization and structure.

Item 9 - Description of Business:

Briefly describe the business carried on and intended to be carried on by the issuer and its subsidiaries and the general development of the business within the five preceding years.

INSTRUCTIONS:

(a)　The description shall not relate to the powers and objects specified in the incorporating instruments, but to the actual business carried on and intended to be carried on. Include the business of subsidiaries of the issuer only in so far as is necessary to understand the character and development of the business conducted by the combined enterprise.

2.　In describing developments, information shall be given as to matters such as the following:　the nature and results of any bankruptcy, receivership or similar proceedings with respect to the issuer or any of its subsidiaries; the nature and results of any other material reorganization of the issuer or any of its subsidiaries; the acquisition or disposition of any material amount of assets otherwise than in the ordinary course of business; material changes in the types of products produced or services rendered by the issuer and its subsidiaries; and any material changes in the mode of conducting the business of the issuer or its subsidiaries.

9(b)　In the case of an issuer other than an oil and gas issuer furnish the following information as to each of the properties, mines, and plants presently owned, leased, held under option or operated, or presently intended to be owned, leased, held under option or operated by the issuer or its subsidiaries:

(1)　The location of, size of and means of access to the property;

(2)　A brief description of the title, claim or lease under which the issuer or subsidiary has or will have the right to hold or operate the property, indicating any conditions which the issuer or subsidiary must meet in order to obtain or retain the property;

(3)　　　(i) the names and addresses of all vendors of property purchased within the three years immediately preceding the date of the preliminary prospectus or the date of the pro forma prospectus and the property acquired from each and if any such vendor is or was an insider or promoter of the issuer or an associate or affiliate of any insider or promoter of the issuer, so indicate, and

(ii) the names and addresses in full of every person who has received within the three years immediately preceding the date of the preliminary prospectus, or pro forma prospectus, or is to receive from any vendor a greater than 5 per cent interest in the shares or other consideration received or to be received by the vendor;

(4)　A brief history of previous prospecting, exploration, development and operations, including the names of previous operators, in so far as known;

(5)　　　(i) a brief description of the character, extent and condition of any underground exploration and development and any underground plant and equipment, and, if none, so state, and

(ii) a brief description of the character, extent and condition of any surface exploration and development and any surface plant and equipment, and, if none, so state.

(6) A brief description of the mineral deposits on the property and their dimensions, including the identity of their principal metallic or other constituents, in so far as known. If the work done has established the existence of reserves of proven, probable or possible ore, state:

(i) the estimated tonnage and grade of such class of ore reserves; and

(ii) the name of the person making the estimates and the nature of his relationship to the issuer.

(7) Describe the work already done by the issuer under its present management on the property and the issuer's or subsidiary's proposed programme of exploration or development of the property. If the property is without a known body of commercial ore and the proposed programme is an exploratory search for ore, a statement to that effect shall be made.

INSTRUCTIONS:

3. The information called for shall only be given with respect to such of the properties of the issuer and its subsidiaries upon which, in whole or in part, the proceeds of the issuer are to be expended or which are major producing properties. Information with respect to the other properties of the issuer and its subsidiaries shall be given in summary form.

4. The information required by clause (6) of this item may be given in reliance upon the report relating to such property required to be filed with the Commission pursuant to section 100 of the Regulation made under the Act if a statement to such effect is made in the prospectus.

9(c) In the case of an oil or gas issuer furnish the following information as to the important oil and gas properties, plants, facilities and installations and other important properties presently owned, leased or held under option, or presently intended to be owned, leased or held under option, or presently intended to be owned, leased or held under option by the issuer or its subsidiaries:

(1) The location, by fields, if possible, of all producing wells and all non-unitized wells capable of producing in which the issuer or its subsidiaries have an interest, indicating the total number of wells in each such field or other area, the interest of the issuer and its subsidiaries therein expressed in terms of net wells, distinguishing separately oil wells and gas wells;

(2) With respect to interests in properties on which no producing wells have been drilled, the gross acreage in which the issuer or its subsidiaries have an interest and the interest of the issue rand its subsidiaries therein expressed in terms of net leasable acreage, and the location of such acreage by geographical area;

(3) If the exploration or development work is contemplated to be carried out so state and give the general nature and the proposed extent thereof;

(4) To the extent that such properties are not unitized and are capable of but are not producing, indicate the proximity of such properties to pipe lines or other means of transportation;

(5) The quantity and type of the estimated proved and developed reserves, proved undeveloped reserves, and probable additional reserves of crude oil, natural gas and natural gas liquids of the issuer and its subsidiaries together with particulars as to the accessibility of those reserves to gathering systems;

(6) The net crude oil, natural gas liquids and natural gas production of the issuer and its subsidiaries, including the interest of the issuer and its subsidiaries in the crude oil, natural gas liquids and natural gas production of any other person for each of the last five completed financial years preceding the date of the preliminary prospectus or pro forma prospectus, and for the current year as at a date not more than four months prior to the date of the preliminary prospectus or pro forma prospectus;

(7) The number of wells the issuer or its subsidiaries have drilled or have participated in the drilling of for each of the last five completed financial years preceding the date of the preliminary prospectus or pro forma prospectus, and for the current year as at a date not more than four months prior to the date of the preliminary prospectus or pro forma prospectus, the number of such wells completed as producing wells and as dry holes, and the amount expended by the issuer and its subsidiaries during the five completed financial years and the portion of the current year on drilling and exploration activities;

(8)   (i) If any properties of the issuer or its subsidiaries were acquired within the three years immediately preceding the date of the preliminary prospectus or pro forma prospectus or are intended to be acquired by the issuer or subsidiary from an insider or promoter of the issuer or an associate or affiliate of any insider or promoter, state the name and address of each such transferor, the relationship of each such transferor to the issuer or its subsidiaries and the consideration paid or intended to be paid to each such transferor; and

(ii) The names and addresses of every person who has received or is to receive greater than 5 per cent interest in the consideration received or to be received by any transferor referred to in clause (i).

INSTRUCTIONS:

4. In giving the information required by clauses (1) and (2) of this item include such ownership interests as fee interests, leasehold interests, royalty interests, interests in reservation and all other types of ownership interests and variations thereof.

5. The information required by clause (5) of them item may be given in reliance upon the report relating to such property required to be filed with the Commission pursuant to section 100 of the Regulation made under the Act if a statement to such effect is made in the prospectus.

6. In giving the information required by clause (7) of this item, do not include the amounts expended for payments made for and under leases or other similar interest, but state separately for the years and period referred to in clause (7) the amounts paid or payable for and under the leases or other similar interests.

Item 10 - Risk Factors:

(a) Where appropriate to a clear understanding by investors of the risk factors and speculative nature of the enterprise or the securities being offered, an introductory statement shall be made on the first page or in the summary of the prospectus summarizing the factors which make the purchase a risk or speculation. Include such matters as:

(i) the pro forma dilution of the investment based on net tangible assets;

(ii) a comparison, in percentages, of the securities being offered for cash and those issued or to be issued to promoters, directors, officers, substantial security holders as defined in section 104(2) of the Act, and underwriters for cash, property and services.

(iii) whether there is little probability of profit and little or no probability of resale of shares purchased;

(iv) the underwriter is not obligated to buy back shares except to the extent he may have oversold the offering and the buy-back price may be significantly lower than the original selling price;

The information may be given in the body of the prospectus if an appropriate reference is made on the first page or in the summary of the prospectus to the risks and the speculative or promotional nature of the enterprise and a cross reference is made to the place in the prospectus where the information is contained.

(b) Where there is a risk that purchasers of the securities offered may become liable to make and additional contribution beyond the price of the security, disclose any information or facts that may bear on the security holder's assessment of risk associated with the investment.

Item 11 - Incorporation Within One Year - Preliminary Expenses:

Where an issuer has not been incorporated for more than one year prior to the date to which the most recent balance sheet contained in the prospectus is drawn up, state the amount or estimated amount of preliminary expenses, showing administrative and development expenses separately, including the amount already expended and the estimated future expenditures in each case.

Item 12 - Acquisitions:

Briefly describe all material acquisitions and dispositions whether of shares or assets by the issuer and its subsidiaries during the past two years and to the extent reasonably practicable the impact of these acquisitions or dispositions on the operating results and financial position of the issuer.

Item 13 - Variations in Operating Results:

Explain to the extent reasonably practicable any substantial variations, both favourable; and adverse, in the operating results of the issuer over the last three years, but the Superintendent may permit or require an explanation of such substantial variations over a longer period not to exceed five years.

INSTRUCTION:

The explanation should be in narrative form. However, where ratios are used to illustrate variations, a table may be used to supplement the narrative.

Item 14 - Asset and Earnings Coverage:

Disclose asset and earnings coverage in an appropriate and reasonable form where required by section 111 of the Regulation.

Item 15 - Promoters:

If any person is or has been a promoter of the issuer or of any of its subsidiaries within the five years immediately preceding the date of the preliminary prospectus or pro forma prospectus, furnish the following information:

(a) State the names of the promoters, the nature and amount of anything of value (including money, property, contracts, options or rights of any kind) received or to be received by each promoter directly or indirectly from the issuer, or from any of its subsidiaries, and the nature and amount of any assets, services or other consideration therefor received or to be received by the issuer or subsidiary.

(b) As to any assets acquired within the past two years or to be acquired by the issuer or by any of its subsidiaries from a promoter, state the amount at which acquired or to be acquired and the principle followed or to be followed in determining the amount. Identify the person making the determination and state his relationship, if any, with the issuer, any subsidiary or any promoter. State the date that the assets were acquired by the promoter and the cost thereof to the promoter.

Item 16 - Legal Proceedings:

Briefly describe any legal proceedings material to the issuer to which the issuer or any of its subsidiaries is a party or of which any of their property is the subject. Make a similar statement as to any such proceedings known to be contemplated.

INSTRUCTION:

Include the name of the court or agency, the date instituted, the principal parties thereto, the nature of the claim, the amount claimed, if any, whether the proceedings are being contested, and the present status of the proceedings.

Item 17 - Issuance of Shares:

(a) If shares are being offered, state the description or the designation of the class of shares offered and furnish all material attributes and characteristics including, without limiting the generality of the foregoing, the following information:

(i) dividend rights;

(ii) voting rights;

(iii) liquidation or distribution rights;

(iv) pre-emptive rights;

(v) conversion rights;

(vi) redemption, purchase for cancellation or surrender provisions;

(vii) sinking or purchase fund provisions;

(viii) liability to further calls or to assessment by the issuer; and

(ix) provisions as to modification, amendment or variation of any such rights or provisions.

(b) If the rights of holders of such shares may be modified otherwise than in accordance with the provisions attaching to such shares or the provisions of the governing Act relating thereto, so state and explain briefly.

INSTRUCTIONS:

1. This item requires only a brief summary of the provisions that are material from an investment standpoint. Do not set out verbatim the provisions attaching to the shares; only a succinct resume is required.

2. If the rights attaching to the shares being offered are materially limited or qualified by the rights of any other class of securities, or if any other class of securities (other than obligations covered in Item 18), ranks ahead of or equally with the shares being offered, include information regarding such other securities that will enable investors to understand the rights attaching to the shares being offered. If any shares being offered are to be offered in exchange for other securities, an appropriate description of the other securities shall be given. No information need be given, however, as to any class of securities that is to be redeemed or otherwise retired, provided appropriate steps to assure redemption or retirement have been or will be taken prior to or contemporaneously with the delivery of the shares being offered.

3. In addition to the summary referred to in instruction 1, the issuer may set out verbatim in a schedule to the prospectus the provisions attaching to the shares being offered.

Item 18 - Issuance of Obligations:

If obligations are being offered, give a brief summary of the material attributes and characteristics of the indebtedness and the security therefor including, without limiting the generality of the foregoing:

(a) Provisions with respect to interest rate, maturity, redemption or other retirement, sinking fund and conversion rights.

(b) The nature and priority of any security for the obligations, briefly identifying the principal properties subject to lien or charge.

(c) Provisions permitting or restricting the issuance of additional securities, the incurring of additional indebtedness and other material negative covenants, (including restrictions against payment of dividends, restrictions against giving security on the assets of the issuer or its subsidiaries and the like) and provisions as to the release or substitution of assets securing the obligations, the modification of the terms of the security and similar provisions.

(d) The name of the trustee under any indenture relating to the obligations and

Forms

the nature of any material relationship between the trustee and the issuer or any of its affiliates.

(e) Indicate any financial arrangements between the issuer and any of its affiliates or among its affiliates that could affect the security for the indebtedness.

INSTRUCTION:

The instructions to Item 17 apply to this item with due alteration for point of detail.

Item 19 - Issuance of Other Securities:

If the securities other than shares or obligations are being offered, outline briefly the rights evidenced thereby. If subscription warrants or rights are being offered or issued, state the description and amount of securities covered thereby, the period during which, and the price at which, the warrants or rights are exercisable, and the principal terms and conditions by which they may be exercised.

INSTRUCTION:

The instructions to Item 17 apply to this item with due alteration for point of detail.

Item 20 - Dividend Record:

State the amount of dividends or other distributions, if any, paid by the issuer during its last five completed financial years preceding the date of the preliminary prospectus or pro forma prospectus.

INSTRUCTION:

Dividends should be set out on a per share basis, shown separately for each class of shares in respect of each of the financial years. Appropriate adjustment shall be made to reflect changes in capitalization during the period.

Item 21 - Directors and Officers

List the names and home addresses in full or, alternatively, solely the municipality of residence or postal address, of all directors and officers of the issuer and indicate all positions and offices with the issuer held by each person named, and the principal occupations within the five preceding years, of each director and officer.

INSTRUCTIONS:

1. Where the municipality of residence or postal address is listed, the Superintendent may request that the home address in full be furnished to the Commission.

2. Where the principal occupation of a director or officer is that of an officer of a company other than the issuer, state the principal business in which such company is engaged.

3. Where a director or officer has held more than one position in the issuer, or a parent or subsidiary thereof, state only the first and last position held.

Item 22 - Executive Compensation

Complete and attach to or include in this Form a Statement of Executive Compensation in Form 41, provided however, that the disclosure required by Items V, VIII, IX and X of Form 41 may be omitted for purposes of this Form.

See NIN 93/23 "Executive Compensation".

ITEM 23 - Indebtedness of Directors, Executive Officers and Senior Officers

(a) The information required by this Item must be provided for each individual who is or, at any time during the most recently completed financial year, was a director, executive officer and senior officer of the issuer, each proposed nominee for election as a director of the issuer, and each associate of any such director, officer or proposed nominee,

(i) who is, or at any time since the beginning of the most recently completed financial year of the issuer has been, indebted to the issuer or any of its subsidiaries, or

(ii) whose indebtedness to another entity is, or at any time since the beginning of the most recently completed financial year of the issuer has been, the subject of a guarantee, support agreement, letter of credit or other similar arrangement or understanding provided by the issuer or any of its subsidiaries.

(b) State in the tabular form under the caption set out, for any indebtedness referred to in paragraph (a) of this Item that was entered into in connection with a purchase of securities of the issuer or any of its subsidiaries:

(i) The name of the borrower (column (a)).

(ii) If the borrower is a director, executive officer or senior officer, the principal position of the borrower. If the borrower was, during the year, but no longer is a director or officer, include a statement to that effect. If the borrower is a proposed nominee for election as a director, include a statement to that effect. If the borrower is included as an associate describe briefly the relationship of the borrower to an individual who is or, during the year, was a director, executive officer or senior officer or who is a proposed nominee for election as a director, name that individual and provide the information required by this subparagraph for that individual (column (a)).

(iii) Whether the issuer or a subsidiary of the issuer is the lender or the provider of a guarantee, support agreement, letter of credit or similar arrangement or understanding (column (b)).

(iv) The largest aggregate amount of the indebtedness outstanding at any time during the last completed financial year (column (c)).

(v) The aggregate amount of indebtedness outstanding as at a date within thirty days of certification of the prospectus (column (d)).

(vi) Separately for each class or series of securities, the sum of the number of securities purchased during the last completed financial year with the financial assistance (column (e)).

(vii) The security for the indebtedness, if any, provided to the issuer, any of its subsidiaries or the other entity (column (f)).

TABLE OF INDEBTEDNESS OF DIRECTORS, EXECUTIVE OFFICERS
AND SENIOR OFFICERS UNDER SECURITIES PURCHASE PROGRAMS

Name and Principal Position (a)	Involvement of Issuer or Subsidiary (b)	Largest Amount Outstanding During [Last Completed Financial Year] ($) (c)	Amount Outstanding as at [current date] ($) (d)	Financially Assisted Securities Purchases During [Last Completed Financial Year] (#) (e)	Security for Indebtedness (f)

(c) State in the introduction immediately preceding the table required by paragraph (b) of this Item, for indebtedness entered into in connection with a purchase of securities of the issuer or any of its subsidiaries, separately, the aggregate indebtedness,

(i) to the issuer or any of its subsidiaries, and

(ii) to another entity if the indebtedness is the subject of a guarantee, support agreement, letter of credit or other similar arrangement or understanding provided by the issuer or any of its subsidiaries,

of all officers, directors, employees and former officers, directors and employees of the issuer or any of its subsidiaries outstanding as at a date within thirty days of certification of the prospectus.

(d)   State in the tabular form under the caption set out for any indebtedness referred to in paragraph (a) of this Item that was not entered into in connection with a purchase of securities of the issuer or any of its subsidiaries, the information referred to in subparagraphs (b) (i) through (v) of this Item.

TABLE OF INDEBTEDNESS OF DIRECTORS, EXECUTIVE OFFICERS AND SENIOR OFFICERS [insert if the issuer has a securities purchase program "OTHER THAN UNDER SECURITIES PURCHASE PROGRAMS"]

Name and Principal Position (a)	Involvement of Issuer or Subsidiary (b)	Largest Amount Outstanding During [Last Completed Financial Year] ($) (c)	Amount Outstanding as at [current date] ($) (d)

(e)   State in the introduction immediately preceding the table required by paragraph (d) of this Item, for indebtedness not entered into in connection with a purchase of securities of the issuer or any of its subsidiaries, separately, the aggregate indebtedness,

   (i)   to the issuer or any of its subsidiaries, and

   (ii) to another entity if the indebtedness is the subject of a guarantee, support agreement, letter of credit or other similar arrangement or understanding provided by the issuer or any of its subsidiaries,

of all officers, directors, employees and former officers, directors and employees of the issuer or any of its subsidiaries outstanding as at a date within thirty days of certification of the prospectus.

(f)   Disclose in a footnote to, or a narrative accompanying, each table required by this Item,

   (i)   the material terms of each incidence of indebtedness and, if applicable, of each guarantee, support agreement, letter of credit or other similar arrangement or understanding, including without limitation the term to maturity, rate of interest and any understanding, agreement or intention to limit recourse, and for the table required by paragraph (d) only, any security for the indebtedness and the nature of the transaction in which the indebtedness was incurred,

   (ii) any material adjustment or amendment made during the most recently completed financial year to the terms of the indebtedness and, if applicable, the guarantee, support agreement, letter of credit or similar arrangement or understanding, and

   (iii) the class or series of the securities purchased with financial assistance or held as security for the indebtedness and, if the class or series of securities is not publicly traded, all material terms of the securities, including but not limited to provisions for exchange, conversion, exercise, redemption, retraction and dividends.

(g)   No disclosure need be made under this Item of an incidence of indebtedness that has been entirely repaid on or before the date of certification of the prospectus or of routine indebtedness.

"Routine indebtedness" means indebtedness described in any of the following:

   (i)   If an issuer makes loans to employees generally, whether or not in the ordinary course of business, loans are considered routine indebtedness if made on terms, including those as to interest rate and security, no more favourable to the borrower than the terms on which loans are made by the issuer to employees generally, but the amount at any time during the last completed financial year remaining unpaid under the loans to any one director, executive officer, senior officer or proposed nominee together with his or her associates that are treated as routine indebtedness under this clause must not exceed $25,000.

   (ii) Whether or not the issuer makes loans in the ordinary course of business, a loan to a director, executive officer or senior officer is considered routine indebtedness if,

     A. the borrower is a full-time employee of the issuer,

     B. the loan is fully secured against the residence of the borrower, and

     C. the amount of the loan does not exceed the annual salary of the borrower.

   (iii) If the issuer makes loans in the ordinary routine indebtedness if made to a person or company other than a full-time employee of the issuer, and if the loan,

     A. is made on substantially the same terms, including those as to interest rate and security, as are available when a loan is made to other customers of the issuer with comparable credit ratings, and

     B. involves no more than usual risks of collectibility.

   (iv) Indebtedness arising by reason of purchases made on usual trade terms or of ordinary travel or expense advances, or for similar reasons is considered routine indebtedness if the repayment arrangements are in accord with usual commercial practice.

(h) For purposes of this Item, "executive officer" has the same meaning as in Form 41 and "support agreement" includes, but is not limited to, an agreement to provide assistance in the maintenance or servicing of any indebtedness and an agreement to provide compensation for the purpose of maintaining or servicing any indebtedness of the borrower.

See NIN 93/23 "Executive Compensation".

Item 24 - Options to Purchase Securities:

Furnish (in tabular form, if possible) the information referred to in Instruction 1, as at a specified date not more than thirty days before the date of the preliminary prospectus or pro forma prospectus, as the case may be, and as at the date as of the signing of the final prospectus, as to options to purchase securities of the issuer or any of its subsidiaries that are held or proposed to be held

   (i) by all executive officers as a group and all directors who are not also executive officers as a group, indicating the aggregate number of executive officers and the aggregate number of directors to whom the information applies, without naming them;

   (ii) by all executive officers of all subsidiaries of the issuer as a group and all directors of such subsidiaries who are not also executive officers as a group, without naming them, excluding individuals referred to in clause (i);

   (iii) by all other employees of the issuer as a group, without naming them;

   (iv) by all other employees of the subsidiaries of the issuer as a group, without naming them; and

   (v) by any other person, naming each such person.

INSTRUCTIONS:

1. Describe the options, stating the material provisions of each class or type of option including,

   (i) the designation and number of the securities under option;

  (ii) the purchase price of the securities under option or the formula by which the purchase price will be determined, and the expiration dates of such options;

 (iii) if reasonably ascertainable, the market value of the securities under option on the date of grant; and

 (iv) if reasonably ascertainable, the market value of the securities under option on the specified date.

2.   For the purposes of this Item,

   (i) "executive officer" means the chairman and any vice-chairman of the board of directors of an issuer who performs the functions of such office on a full-time basis, the president, any vice-president in charge of a principal business unit such as sales, finance or production, and any officer of the issuer or of a subsidiary who performs a policy-making function in respect of the issuer, whether or not such officer is also a director of the issuer or the subsidiary;

  (ii) "options" includes all options, share purchase warrants or rights other than those shares issued on a pro rate basis, to all security holders of the same class resident in Canada and an extension of an option shall be deemed to be a granting of an option.

3.   Options that are proposed to be held are those where there is an approval or understanding or commitment of the issuer or a subsidiary in respect of the granting of such options.

4.   In the disclosure made under this Item 24, do not include options granted or proposed to be granted that are otherwise disclosed in Item 1 or 2, including options granted or to be granted to the underwriter in respect of the distribution under the prospectus.

Item 25 - Escrowed Shares:

State as of a specified date within thirty days prior to the date of the preliminary prospectus or pro forma prospectus, in substantially the tabular form indicated, the number of shares of each class of voting securities of the issuer to the knowledge of the issuer held in escrow, disclosing the name of the depositary, if any, the date of the conditions governing the release of the shares from escrow;

TABLE

Column 1	Column 2	Column 3
Designation of class	Number of securities held in escrow	Percentage of class
....	....	....
....	....	....

Item 26 - Principal Holders of Securities:

Furnish the following information as of a specified date within thirty days prior to the date of the preliminary prospectus or pro forma prospectus, in substantially the tabular form indicated.

(a)   The number of securities of each class of voting securities of the issuer owned of record or beneficially, directly or indirectly, by each person who owns of record, or is known by the issuer to own beneficially, directly or indirectly, more than 10 per cent of any class of such securities. Shown in Column 3 whether the securities are owned both of record and beneficially, of record only, or beneficially only, and show in Columns 4 and 5 the respective amounts and percentages known by the issuer to be owned in each such manner.

TABLE

Column 1	Column 2	Column 3	Column 4	Column 5
Name and Address	Designation of class	Type of ownership	Number of securities owned	Percentage of class
....	....	....	....	....

(b) The percentage of securities of each class of voting securities of the issuer or any of its parents or its subsidiaries, beneficially owned, directly or indirectly, by all directors and senior officers of the issuer, as a group, without naming them:

TABLE

Column 1	Column 2
Designation of Class	Percentage of Class
....	....
....	....

INSTRUCTIONS:

1. Where a company is shown by the issuer as owning directly or indirectly more than 10 per cent of any class of such securities, the Superintendent may require the disclosure of such additional information as is necessary to identify any individual who, through his direct or indirect ownership of voting securities in the company owns directly or indirectly more than 10 per cent of any class of such securities. The name of such an individual should be disclosed in a foot note to the table described in paragraph (a).

2. For purposes of paragraph (a), securities owned beneficially, directly or indirectly, and of record shall be aggregated in determining whether any person owns more than 10 per cent of the securities of any class.

3. If voting securities are being offered in connection with, or pursuant to, a plan of acquisition, amalgamation or reorganization, indicate as far as practicable, the respective holdings of voting securities that will exist after giving effect to the plan.

4. If any of the securities being offered are to be offered for the account of a security holder, name such security holder and state the number or amount of the securities owned by him, the number or amount to be offered for his account, and the number or amount to be owned by him after the offering.

5. If, to the knowledge of the issuer or the underwriter of the securities being offered, more than 10 per cent of any class of voting securities of the issuer are hold or are to be held subject to any voting trust or other similar agreement, other than an escrow arrangement referred to in Item 24, state the designation of such securities, the number or amount held or to be held and the duration of the agreement. Give the names and addresses of the voting trustees and outline briefly their voting rights and other powers under the agreement.

6. If, to the knowledge of the issuer, the parent or the underwriter of the securities being offered, any person named in answer to paragraph (a) is an associate or affiliate of any other person named therein, disclose, insofar as known, the material facts of such relationship, including any basis for influence over the issuer enjoyed by the person other than the holding of the voting securities of the issuer.

Forms

Item 27 - Intercorporate Relationships

   (a)   Furnish a list of each subsidiary, other than inactive subsidiaries, of the issuer. As to each such subsidiary indicate the jurisdiction under the laws of which it was organized, and the percentage of voting securities owned by its parent.

   (b)   Clearly illustrate by way of a diagram or otherwise the intercorporate relationships of the issuer, its parent and those subsidiaries listed pursuant to paragraph (a).

   (c)   Where one of the primary businesses of the issuer is investing, reinvesting, owning, holding or trading in securities, give in substantially the tabular form indicated the following information as at a date within thirty days of the date of the preliminary prospectus or pro forma prospectus, with respect to each company 5 per cent or more of whose securities of any class are owned directly or indirectly by the issuer or its affiliates.

TABLE

Name and address of company	Nature of its principal business	Percentage of securities of any class beneficially owned, directly or indirectly	Percentage of book value of issuer's assets invested therein
....	....	....	....

INSTRUCTIONS:

1.   If the securities being issued are to be issued in connection with, or pursuant to, a plan of acquisition, reorganization, readjustment, or succession, indicate insofar as practicable the status to exist upon consummation of the plan.

2.   The name of any particular subsidiary may be omitted if:

   (a)   - the assets of the subsidiary, or

        - the investment in and advances to the subsidiary by its parent and the parent's other subsidiaries

        if any, do not exceed 10 per cent of the assets of the parent and its subsidiaries on a consolidated basis;

   (b)   the sales and operating revenue of the subsidiary do not exceed 10 per cent of the sales and operating revenues of its parent and the parent's subsidiaries on a consolidated basis; and

   (c)   the unnamed subsidiaries considered in the aggregate as a single subsidiary would satisfy the conditions in (a) and (b) if the reference therein to 10 per cent were replaced by 20 per cent.

Unit offerings should not be released in the pre-prospectus stage. If warrants are to be outstanding post acceptance they must comply with LPS #3-31.

Item 28 - Prior Sales:

   (a)   State the prices at which securities of the class offered by the prospectus have been sold within the twelve months prior to the date of the preliminary prospectus or pro forma prospectus, or are to be sold, by the issuer or selling security holder if such prices differ from those at which the securities are offered by the prospectus. State the number of securities sold or to be sold at each price.

   (b)   Where the class of securities offered are listed on a Canadian stock exchange or solely on a foreign stock exchange, give price ranges and volume traded on such stock exchange on a monthly basis for each month or, if applicable, part month, of the current quarter and the immediately preceding quarter and on a quarterly basis for the next preceding seven quarters provided that the Superintendent may permit the omission of the information regarding trading volume.

INSTRUCTION:

1. In the case of sales by a selling security holder, the information required by paragraph (a) may be given in the form of price ranges for each calendar month.

2. Where sales are made to insiders or their associates, or to employees under a stock option, or where stock options or warranties were granted to any person or company, indicate to whom and at what price such sales were made or to whom such stock options or warrants were granted.

Item 29 - Interest of Management and Others in Material Transactions:

Describe briefly, and where practicable state the approximate amount of any material interest, direct or indirect, of any of the following persons in any transaction within three years prior to the date of the preliminary prospectus or pro forma prospectus, or in any proposed transaction which has materially affected or will materially affect the issuer or any of its subsidiaries:

   (i) any director or senior officer of the issuer;

   (ii) any security holder named in answer to paragraph (a) of Item 26; and

   (iii) any associate or affiliate of any of the foregoing persons.

INSTRUCTIONS:

1. Give a brief description of the material transaction. Include the name and address of each person whose interest in any transaction is described and the nature of the relationship by reason of which such interest is required to be described.

2. As to any transaction involving the purchase or sale of assets by or to the issuer or any subsidiary, state the cost of the assets to the purchaser and the cost thereof to the seller if acquired by the seller within two years to the transaction.

3. This item does not apply to any interest arising from the ownership of securities of the issuer where the security holder receives no extra or special benefit or advantage not shares on an equal basis by all other holders of the same class of securities or all other holders of the same class of securities who are resident in Canada.

4. Information shall be included as to any material underwriting discounts or commissions upon the sale of securities by the issuer where any of the specified persons was or is to be an underwriter or is an associate, affiliate or partner of a person, or partnership that was or is to be an underwriter.

5. No information need be given in answer to this item as to any transaction or any interest therein, where,

   (i) the rate or charges involved in the transaction are fixed by law or determined by competitive bids;

   (ii) the interest of a specified person in the transaction is solely that of a director of another company that is a party to the transaction;

   (iii) the transaction involves services as a bank or other depository of funds, transfer agent, registrar, trustee under a trust indenture or other similar services;

   (iv) the transaction does not, directly or indirectly, involve remuneration for services; and

      (a) the interest of the specified person arose from the beneficial ownership, direct or indirect, of less than 10 per cent of any class of voting securities of another company that is a party to the transaction,

      (b) the transaction is in the ordinary course of business of the issuer or its subsidiaries, and

(c) the amount of the transaction or series of transactions is less than 10 per cent of the total sales or purchases, as the case may be, of the issuer and its subsidiaries for the last completed financial year.

6.   Information shall be furnished in answer to this item with respect to transactions not excluded above that involve remuneration, directly or indirectly, to any of the specified persons for services in any capacity unless the interest of the person arises solely from the beneficial ownership, direct or indirect, of less than 10 per cent of any class of voting securities of another company furnishing the services to the issuer or its subsidiaries.

7.   This item does not require the disclosure of any interest in any transaction unless such interest and transaction are material.

Item 30 - Auditors, Transfer Agents and Registrars:

(a)   State the name and address of the auditor of the issuer;

(b)   Where shares are offered, state the names of the issuer's transfer agents and registrars and the location (by municipalities) of the registers of transfers of each class of shares of the issuer. Where securities other than shares are offered, state the location (by municipalities) of each register on which transfer of such securities may be recorded.

Item 31 - Material Contracts:

Give particulars of every material contract entered into within the two years prior to the date of the preliminary prospectus or pro forma prospectus, by the issuer or any of its subsidiaries and state a reasonable time and place at which any such contract or a copy thereof may be inspected during distribution of the securities being offered.

INSTRUCTIONS:

1.   The term "material contract" for this purpose means any contract that can reasonably be regarded as presently material to the proposed investor in the securities being offered.

2.   Set out a complete list of all material contracts, indicating those which are disclosed elsewhere in the prospectus and provide particulars with respect to those material contracts about which particulars are not given elsewhere in the prospectus. This item does not require disclosure of contracts entered into in the ordinary course of business of the issuer or its subsidiaries as the case may be.

3.   Particulars of contracts should include the date of, parties to, consideration and general nature of the contracts, succinctly described.

4.   Particulars of contracts need not be disclosed, or copies of such contracts made available for inspection, if the Superintendent determines that such disclosure or making available would impair the value of the contract and would not be necessary for the protection of investors.

Item 32 - Other Material Facts

Give particulars of any other material facts relating to the securities proposed to be offered and not disclosed pursuant to the foregoing items.

IT IS AN OFFENCE FOR A PERSON TO MAKE A STATEMENT IN A DOCUMENT REQUIRED TO BE FILED OR FURNISHED UNDER THE ACT OR THIS REGULATION THAT, AT THE TIME AND IN THE LIGHT OF THE CIRCUMSTANCES UNDER WHICH IT IS MADE, IS A MISREPRESENTATION.

NIN 95/17 "Form 14A - Information Required in Prospectus of a Natural Resource Issuer" prescribes Form 14A as the form of prospectus for natural resource issuers that do not satisfy the listing requirements for the senior board of the Vancouver Stock Exchange. This form is effective for all preliminary prospectuses filed on or after August 1, 1995.

FORM 14A

INFORMATION REQUIRED IN PROSPECTUS OF A NATURAL RESOURCE ISSUER

TABLE OF CONTENTS

Forms

23. AUDITOR

24. REGISTRAR AND TRANSFER AGENT

25. MATERIAL CONTRACTS

    25.1 Particulars of material contracts

    25.2 Inspection of contracts and reports

26. OTHER MATERIAL FACTS

27. PURCHASERS' STATUTORY RIGHTS

28. FINANCIAL STATEMENTS, REPORTS AND OTHER EXHIBITS

29. CERTIFICATES

The prospectus required under Section 42(2) of the Securities Act for a Natural Resource issuer (1) distributing securities solely in British Columbia, (2) distributing securities in British Columbia but not meeting the minimum listing requirements for the senior board of the VSE, or (3) where otherwise required or permitted by the Superintendent, shall be in the following form.

FORM 14A

Securities Act

INFORMATION REQUIRED IN PROSPECTUS OF A NATURAL RESOURCE ISSUER

GENERAL INSTRUCTIONS

1. This form provides a guideline to issuers in determining the extent of disclosure that is required to provide investors with full, true and plain disclosure of all material facts. Depending on the circumstances of the particular issuer, additional disclosure may be necessary.

2. All disclosure contained in the prospectus must be factual and non-promotional. Prospectuses are required to contain material facts. Statements of opinions, beliefs or views must not be made unless the statements are made on the authority of experts and consents are obtained and filed. The Superintendent may require verification of disclosure.

3. The disclosure contained in the prospectus must be understandable to readers and, in particular, should avoid the use of jargon. If technical terms are required, these terms shall be defined in a glossary that must be included in the prospectus.

4. This form may be used as a base disclosure document where the issuer elects to use a summary prospectus as permitted by Local Policy Statement 3-02. In that case, references to "prospectus" in this form are to be replaced by references to "base disclosure document".

5. Except where the context otherwise requires, "prospectus" refers to preliminary or final prospectus as appropriate.

6. In specific items, the instructions indicate that "issuer" includes the issuer's subsidiaries and proposed subsidiaries. In other circumstances, "issuer" may include the issuer's subsidiaries and proposed subsidiaries if the context reasonably requires. An entity can only be considered a proposed subsidiary if the entity will be a subsidiary on completion of the offering.

7. Where information as to the identity of a person is disclosed, disclose whether the person is at **Arm's Length** to the issuer or, if not, the relationship of the person to the issuer. Where the person is not at **Arm's Length** and is not an individual, disclose the name of any individual who is an insider of the person by virtue of paragraph (c) of the definition of insider in the **Act**.

8. Whenever disclosure is required to be made of costs paid or to be paid by the issuer, disclose the portion of the costs paid or to be paid to insiders or holders of performance shares or escrow securities.

9. When disclosure is required as of a specific date and there has been a significant or material change in the requested information subsequent to that date, the information must be presented as of a date that reflects this change.

10. Upon application only, unless otherwise permitted by an instruction, the Superintendent may waive the extent of disclosure required under certain items where the distribution is not an initial public offering and the issuer has material operating revenues.

11. Each item outlines disclosure requirements. Instructions to assist you in providing this disclosure are printed in smaller type.

12. Certain terms used in this Form are defined in the Securities Act, S.B.C. 1985, c. 83 (the "Act"), Securities Regulation, B.C. Reg. 270/86 (the "Regulation"), Interpretation Act, R.S.B.C. 1979, c. 206, and National Policy Statements, Nos. 2-A and 2-B. Certain terms defined in specific sections of the form are in bold type. Other defined terms used in this Form, which are capitalized and in bold type, are as follows:

"Agent" means underwriter.

"Arm's Length" means in relation to an arm's length transaction, unless otherwise determined by the Superintendent, a transaction between the issuer and a person that, at any time from the date of the transaction until the date of completion of the transaction, or in the case of an initial public offering until the date of completion of the initial public offering, the person was not

(a) an insider, associate, affiliate or principal (as defined in Local Policy Statement No. 3-07) of the issuer,

(b) a person that

(i) has a control person, insider or promoter that is a control person, insider or promoter of the issuer, or

(ii) has a control person, insider or promoter that is an associate or affiliate of a control person, insider or promoter of the issuer

except where the person's insiders that are described in paragraphs (i) and (ii) hold in total less than 10% of the voting securities of the person.

"Breakdown of Costs" means a schedule of costs associated with the specific classification, separately itemizing each component that represents 10% or more of the total costs, with all other costs being grouped together under the heading "miscellaneous costs".

"Funds Available" means the aggregate of

(a) the net proceeds to be derived by the issuer from the sale of the securities offered under the prospectus,

(b) the estimated minimum working capital available to the issuer, its subsidiaries and proposed subsidiaries as of the Most Recent Month End, and

(c) the amounts and sources of other funds that will be available to the issuer, its subsidiaries and proposed subsidiaries prior to or concurrently with the completion of the offering.

"Management" means all directors, officers, employees and contractors whose expertise is critical to the issuer, its subsidiaries and proposed subsidiaries in providing the issuer with a reasonable opportunity to achieve its objectives.

"Most Recent Month End" means the latest month end prior to the date of the prospectus or revised preliminary prospectus or, where the date of the prospectus or revised preliminary prospectus is within ten days of the end of the latest month, the month end prior to the end of that month.

"Principal Properties" means the Properties on which the issuer intends to expend a material part of the Funds Available.

"Properties" includes all the properties, mines, plants, facilities, and installations presently owned, leased, held under option, or presently intended to be owned, leased, or held under option by the issuer, its subsidiaries and proposed subsidiaries.

"Stub Period" means the period between the issuer's most recently completed financial year and the Most Recent Month End.

1. FACE PAGE DISCLOSURE

1.1 *Required language*

State in bold print at the top of the face page of the prospectus the following:

THIS PROSPECTUS CONSTITUTES A PUBLIC OFFERING OF THESE SECURITIES ONLY IN THOSE JURISDICTIONS WHERE THEY MAY BE LAWFULLY OFFERED FOR SALE AND THEREIN ONLY BY PERSONS PERMITTED TO SELL SUCH SECURITIES. NO SECURITIES COMMISSION OR SIMILAR AUTHORITY IN CANADA HAS IN ANY WAY PASSED UPON THE MERITS OF THE SECURITIES OFFERED HEREUNDER AND ANY REPRESENTATION TO THE CONTRARY IS AN OFFENCE.

1.2 *Preliminary prospectus disclosure*

State in red ink on the left hand side of the face page of the preliminary prospectus the following legend or any variation that may be permitted:

This is a preliminary prospectus relating to these securities, a copy of which has been filed with the British Columbia Securities Commission but which has not yet become final for the purpose of a distribution. Information contained herein is subject to completion or amendment. The securities may not be sold nor may offers to buy be accepted prior to the time a receipt is obtained from the British Columbia Securities Commission for the final prospectus.

1.3 *Basic disclosure about the offering*

Provide the following information:

INITIAL PUBLIC OFFERING [or] NEW ISSUE [and/or] SECONDARY OFFERING

DATE

[PRELIMINARY] PROSPECTUS

[Name of Issuer
Head Office Address
Telephone Number]

[total number and type of securities qualified for distribution under this prospectus, including any options or warrants, and price per security]

- If it is impracticable to state the offering price, the method by which it is to be determined shall be explained. In addition, if the securities are to be offered at market price, indicate the market involved and the market price as of the latest practicable date.

1.4 *Distribution spread*

Provide details of all securities offered for cash in substantially the following form:

	Price to public	**Agents'** discounts or commissions	Proceeds to issuer or selling security holder
Per security	. . . .	. . . .	. . . .
Total	. . . .	. . . .	. . . .

1. Where amounts are not known to the issuer at the date of the preliminary prospectus, the issuer must estimate the amounts in the table provided a notation to that effect is made under the table.

2. Only commissions paid or payable in cash by the issuer or selling security holder and discounts granted are to be included in the table. Other commissions or consideration, including warrants, options, finders fees, sponsorship fees, fiscal

agency payments or other similar payments, shall be set out as a note to the table.

3.   Where the issuer has granted the **Agent** a "greenshoe" option, disclose the number of additional securities that may be issued if the option is exercised as a note to the table.

4.   Where the prospectus discloses a plan of distribution not involving an underwriting or other subscription guarantee, the closing of the distribution under the prospectus must be subject to a minimum subscription and, where the prospectus also discloses a maximum subscription that differs from the minimum subscription, totals must be provided for both the minimum and maximum subscriptions.

5.   If any of the securities being offered are for the account of a security holder, provide a cross-reference to "Plan of Distribution - Secondary Offering".

6.   Where the prospectus is used in connection with a special warrant or similar transaction, state the amount that has been received by the issuer in the sale of the special warrants or in a similar transaction as a note to the table. If the funds are held in a special trust disclose the conditions for release or whether the funds have already been released.

1.5   *Market for securities*

(a)   In a preliminary prospectus, state the following:

An application has been made to conditionally list the securities offered under this prospectus on the _____ Exchange. Listing is subject to the issuer fulfilling all the listing requirements of the Exchange.

(b)   In a final prospectus, state the following:

The _____ Exchange has conditionally listed the securities being offered under this prospectus. The listing is subject to the issuer fulfilling all of the listing requirements of the _____ Exchange, including prescribed distribution and financial requirements, on or before _____.

Disclose any intention to stabilize the market. Provide a cross-reference to the "Plan of Distribution".

- Where the preliminary prospectus is also being filed in another jurisdiction and that jurisdiction will not permit disclosure that a conditional listing application has been made, the statement required by (a) may be omitted provided the issuer confirms in writing to the Superintendent that a conditional listing application has been made with a stock exchange.

1.6   *Risk factors*

State the following in bold type:

AN INVESTMENT IN NATURAL RESOURCE ISSUERS INVOLVE A SIGNIFICANT DEGREE OF RISK. THE DEGREE OF RISK INCREASES SUBSTANTIALLY WHERE THE ISSUER'S PROPERTIES ARE IN THE EXPLORATION AS OPPOSED TO THE DEVELOPMENT STAGE. REFER TO "RISK FACTORS".

1.7   *Public and insider ownership*

Disclose the aggregate number of voting securities that will be held by the public and the aggregate number of voting securities that will be held by promoters, insiders, holders of performance shares or escrow securities and **Agents** as a group, each as a percentage of the total issued and outstanding voting securities, upon the completion of the offering.

1.8   *Foreign issuers*

If the **issuer** is incorporated, continued or otherwise governed under the laws of a jurisdiction other than Canada or a province or territory of Canada, state the following (with the bracketed information completed as appropriate):

[All of] [Certain of] the directors and officers of the issuer and [all of] [certain of] the experts named herein reside outside of Canada. [[Substantially] all of the assets of these persons and of the issuer may be located outside of Canada.] Although the issuer has appointed [insert name and address of agent for service] as its agent for service of process in British Columbia, it may not be possible for investors to effect service of process within British Columbia upon the directors, officers and experts referred to above. It may also not be possible to enforce against the issuer, [certain of] its directors and officers, and [certain of] the experts named herein judgments obtained in Canadian courts predicated upon the civil liability provisions of applicable securities laws in Canada.

1.9 *Agent*

State the name and address of the **Agent**. If the **issuer** or selling security holder is a related or connected party of the **Agent**, summarize the nature of the relationship and provide a cross-reference to "Relationship between Issuer or Selling Security Holder and Agent".

- In this subsection, **"issuer"** includes the issuer's subsidiaries and proposed subsidiaries.

2. TABLE OF CONTENTS

Include a table of contents setting out the headings of each section in the prospectus and the page number on which each section starts.

3. SUMMARY OF PROSPECTUS

State:

The following is a summary of the principal features of this offering. More detailed information is contained in the body of the prospectus.

Provide a brief description of the following items:

(a) the principal business of the issuer, its subsidiaries and proposed subsidiaries,

(b) the name and location of the **Principal Properties** and the natural resource(s) being targeted,

(c) the securities offered by the issuer, including the offering price and the net proceeds expected to be realized by the issuer,

(d) the intended use of the **Funds Available**, including the amount allocated for each use,

(e) the expertise and experience of **Management** with respect to the business of the issuer,

(f) the specific risks relating to the business and to the **Principal Properties** disclosed in paragraphs (a) and (b), and

(g) any other information considered appropriate under the circumstances.

1. Where this document is a base disclosure document used in connection with a summary prospectus, this section is not required in the base disclosure document.

2. Appropriate cross-references must be made to items and page numbers in the prospectus.

3. Normally, the summary should not exceed two pages in length.

4. CORPORATE STRUCTURE

4.1 *Name and incorporation*

Provide

(a) the full name of the issuer, the address of its registered office and its address for service in Canada,

(b) the laws under which the issuer was incorporated or organized, the laws under which the issuer is presently governed, and the date the issuer came into existence,

(c) the full name of each of the issuer's subsidiaries or proposed subsidiaries, the laws under which they were incorporated or organized, the laws under which they are presently governed, the date they came into existence and the date they became subsidiaries of the issuer,

(d) if applicable, that the issuer has been a party to any amalgamation, arrangement or continuance or has changed its name, the laws governing the event, any prior names of the issuer, and that the issuer has consolidated or split its share capital, the date of the share consolidation or split and the ratio,

(e) relevant details of the issuer's form of organization and structure, where the issuer is not a company, and

(f) if material, a summary of the differences, with respect to security holder rights and remedies, between the laws under which the issuer is presently governed and the British Columbia Company Act.

4.2 *Intercorporate relationships*

Illustrate by way of a diagram or otherwise the intercorporate relationships among the issuer, its parent, subsidiaries and proposed subsidiaries. For each subsidiary and proposed subsidiary, state the percentage of voting securities owned or to be owned by its parent.

If the securities offered under the prospectus are being issued in connection with, or pursuant to, an amalgamation, merger, reorganization or arrangement, illustrate by way of a diagram or otherwise the intercorporate relationships both before and after the completion of the proposed transaction.

5. BUSINESS OF THE ISSUER

5.1 *Description and general development*

Describe the nature of the business carried on and intended to be carried on by the **issuer**.

Disclose the year of commencement of operations and summarize the general development of the business of the **issuer** during the five preceding financial years and the **Stub Period**, or such shorter period as the **issuer** may have been in existence. Provide disclosure for earlier periods if material to an understanding of the development of the business.

1. In describing developments, include disclosure of the following: the nature and results of any bankruptcy, receivership or similar proceedings; the nature and results of any material reorganization; material prior litigation (including any series of proceedings based on similar causes of action); the nature and date of any prior trading, suspensions, or cease trade orders made against the **issuer** by any regulatory authority; and material changes in the type of business undertaken.

2. Where this document will be used as a base disclosure document, the disclosure in this section should be in sufficient detail so that when it is extracted to the summary prospectus from the base disclosure document it will provide investors with a reasonable understanding of the **issuer's** business.

3. In this section, **"issuer"** includes the issuer's subsidiaries, proposed subsidiaries and predecessor(s).

5.2 *Summary and analysis of financial operations*

Provide the information indicated in the table set out below with respect to the issuer's financial operations during the last two financial years and any period subsequent to the most recent financial year end for which financial statements are included in the prospectus. Provide a cross-reference to the financial statements included in the prospectus.

TABLE

	*Month Period Ending *	Year Ending *	Year Ending *
Revenues			
Gross Profit			
Exploration and Development Expenses			
General and Administrative Expenses			
Net Income (Loss)			
Working Capital			
Properties			
Deferred Exploration and Development			
Other Assets			
Long Term Liabilities			
Shareholders' Equity Dollar Amount Number of Securities			

State the following as a note to the number of securities in the table (with the bracketed information completed as appropriate):

There are [* shares] issued and outstanding as of the date of this prospectus, of which [*] are [performance shares or escrow securities] that will be released from escrow only upon obtaining the consent of the appropriate regulatory authority. Upon the successful completion of this offering, a total of [* shares] will be issued and outstanding.

Discuss and compare the results of the issuer's operations and activities, including the reasons for any substantial variations, for the periods included in the table, and the anticipated impact of these historical operations on the future activities of the issuer. Include, to the extent reasonably practicable, a description of the impact of acquisitions or dispositions of **Properties** disclosed in Item 6 on the operating results and financial position of the issuer.

Where an issuer has material operating revenues include a discussion of liquidity on a historical and prospective basis in the context of the issuer's business and focus on the ability of the issuer to generate adequate amounts of cash and cash equivalents when needed. This discussion, at a minimum, should identify and describe the following,

(a) any known trends or expected fluctuations in the issuer's liquidity, taking into account known demands, commitments, events or uncertainties, and where a deficiency is identified indicate the course of action that has been taken or is proposed to be taken to remedy the deficiency,

(b) those balance sheet conditions or income or cash flow items that may be indicators of the issuer's liquidity condition,

(c) the nature and extent of legal or practical restrictions on the ability of subsidiaries to transfer funds to the issuer and the impact such restrictions have had or are expected to have on the ability of the issuer to meet its obligations,

(d) whether the issuer is in arrears on the payment of dividends, interest, or principal payment on borrowing, and

(e) whether the issuer is in default on any debt covenants at the present time or was in default during the most recently completed financial year and any period subsequent to the most recent financial year end for which financial statements are included in the prospectus.

1. Net income disclosed in the table is net income after tax.

2. Where it would be meaningful to an investor, include in the table any prior periods covered by the financial statements included in the prospectus and provide an analysis of the issuer's results of operations for those periods.

3. Where the closing of the distribution under the prospectus is subject to a minimum subscription, adjust the required statement as appropriate.

4. In the discussion identify any unusual or extraordinary events or transactions or any significant economic changes that materially affect income from continuing operations and describe the extent to which income from continuing operations was affected.

5. Describe in the discussion the extent to which any changes in net sales or revenues are attributable to changes in selling prices or to changes in the volume or quantity of products being sold.

6. The analysis must discuss all significant expenditures. An expenditure would generally be considered significant where the expenditure represents 20% or more of the total expenditures included in a material classification, such as deferred or expensed exploration and development, properties, or general and administrative expenses.

7. Where there has been a significant or material change in operations from the date of the information in the table, the analysis of operations and variations in operations must discuss the change.

6. PROPERTIES OF THE ISSUER

1. Except where otherwise permitted by the Superintendent, the information required by this item shall be derived from or supported by information obtained from property reports required under section 102 of the Regulation and prepared in accordance with Form 54 or Form 55, as the case may be, and/or from material contracts to which the **issuer** is a party. Where information is based on property reports, identify the report title, author and date, and that they are available for inspection upon request (see section 25.2).

2. All information required in this item shall be presented on a property by property basis.

3. When disclosure is required for the **Properties** of the **issuer**, describe all **Principal Properties** first, identifying them as such, before discussing the remaining **Properties** of the **issuer**.

4. Sufficient detail should be included in this item, so as to provide an investor with an opportunity to adequately evaluate the geological merits and/or economic prospects of the **Principal Properties** without having to refer to the Form 54 or Form 55 property reports.

5. At a minimum, include a property location map and a property plan map. Additional maps that would facilitate an investor's evaluation of the **Properties** may be required by the Superintendent.

6. In this item, **"issuer"** includes the issuer's subsidiaries, proposed subsidiaries and predecessor[s].

6A MINERAL PROPERTIES

6.1 *Location, description and acquisition*

Provide the following information for each of the **Properties** of the **issuer**:

(a) the name of, the location of, the size of, and the number of claims and concessions of the **Property**,

(b)   the nature (claim, title, lease, option, or other interest) and status (patented, unpatented, etc.) of the interest under which the **issuer** has or will have the rights to hold or operate the **Property**, and the expiry date, if applicable, and

(c)   the details of the acquisition or proposed acquisition of the **Property** by the **issuer**, including particulars of·

    (i)   the actual or proposed date of each acquisition,

    (ii) the name of the vendor and whether the transaction was or will be at **Arm's Length**,

    (iii) for an acquisition not at **Arm's Length**, the vendor's out of pocket costs as described in Local Policy Statement No. 3-07,

    (iv) the consideration, both monetary and non-monetary, including securities, carried interest, royalties and finders fees, paid or to be paid by the **issuer**,

    (v)   any material obligations that must be complied with in order to keep any acquisition agreement and property in good standing, including work progress with stated due dates where applicable,

    (vi) how the consideration was determined (e.g. limited to out of pocket costs, valuation opinion, or **Arm's Length** negotiations), and

    (vii) any valuation opinion required by a policy of a securities regulatory authority or a stock exchange to support the value of the consideration paid in connection with a transaction not previously approved by the Superintendent or the stock exchange, or that has been approved within the preceding financial year and the **Stub Period**, including the name of the author, the date of the opinion, the assets to which the opinion relates and the value attributed to the assets.

1.   A description of the location of the **Properties** will include such things as the country, province, state, latitude and longitude, township and range, distance from a geographic marker, and elevation.

2.   In providing the information requested by (b), indicate the type of interest (e.g., fee simple, leasehold, royalty, reservation, option, farmout, farmin or other type of interest and any variation thereof), including the percentage interest in the **Properties** held by the **issuer**, as well as the date on which the **issuer** has the right to hold or operate the **Properties**. In addition, indicate whether or not a title report has been obtained. If so, disclose any material qualifications to the title report and the relationship to the **issuer** of the individual providing the title report.

3.   Out of pocket costs must be supported by either audited financial statements or an audited statement of costs.

4.   Where the distribution is not an initial public offering, the disclosure required by (c) need only be provided for all acquisitions within the last three years and for all acquisitions where material obligations under the terms of the acquisition are still outstanding.

6.2   *Exploration and development history*

Describe

(a)   all prospecting, exploration, development and operations previously done by operators other than the **issuer** on the **Principal Properties**, including the names of the previous operators, years during which the work was done and the results they achieved, in so far as known after reasonable inquiry, and

(b)   all prospecting, exploration, development and operations previously done by the **issuer** on the **Properties**, including a **Breakdown of Costs** for the work done, referring to section 5.2, where appropriate.

•   Where the distribution is not an initial public offering, the **Breakdown of Costs** need only be provided for **Principal Properties**.

6.3 *Geology, mineral deposits and reserves*

For each of the **Principal Properties**, describe:

(a) the general geology and structure of the **Principal Property**,

(b) the type of, dimensions of, and grade of any mineralization,

(c) the mineral deposits and their dimensions, including the identity of their principal metallic or other constituents, in so far as known, and where the work done has established the existence of reserves of proven, probable or possible ore, or other mineralization,

(i) the estimated tonnage and grade of such class of mineral reserves,

(ii) whether the reserve is mineable or *in situ*, and

(iii) the name of the person making the estimates, the nature of the person's relationship to the **issuer**, and the date the estimates were made,

(d) the current extent and condition of any underground exploration and development, and any underground plant and equipment,

(e) the current extent and condition of any surface exploration and development, and any surface plant and equipment, and

(f) any other results that would allow for a more accurate evaluation of the geological merits of each **Principal Property**.

1. In providing the disclosure requested in (a), include such information as the rock type, amount of alluvial cover, faults, fissures and alterations.

2. Disclose whether any of the **Principal Properties** are without a known body of commercial ore and whether the proposed program is an exploratory search for ore.

6.4 *Proposed exploration and development program*

Disclose the nature and extent of the proposed exploration and development program that is to be carried out by the **issuer** using the **Funds Available** or by third parties under farmout or option agreements. Additionally, provide:

(a) a timetable for this program, describing each significant component of the program, and identifying the planned commencement and completion date of each significant component,

(b) a **Breakdown of Costs** for this proposed program with reference to Item 8, and

(c) a description of the general topography, vegetation, climate, infrastructure, means of access, source of labour and power sources that may affect the program.

1. In (a) include approximate dates for commencing and completing the planned exploration program, for releasing exploration results, and for obtaining the necessary regulatory approvals.

2. Significant components of the program include geological mapping, trenching, drilling, underground works, bulk sampling, feasibility study, etc.

3. If the exploration and development program is divided into stages, indicate whether proceeding with a subsequent stage in the program is contingent upon the results achieved on an earlier stage.

4. Disclose the name and relationship to the **issuer** of the engineer on whose recommendation or report the **issuer** is relying in formulating its exploration and development program.

5. The disclosure in (c) is only required when these factors may be potential impediments to commercial exploration. Examples may include limitations on the exploration season due to climate or effects on operations due to environmental regulations.

6.5   *Other properties*

Describe the plans that the **issuer** has for the **Properties** other than **Principal Properties**.

6.6   *Dispositions*

Disclose any material dispositions of **Properties** made by the **issuer** as of the **Most Recent Month End**.   Provide details of the disposition including particulars of the consideration, how the consideration was determined and whether the vendor was at **Arm's Length**.

- Where the distribution is not an initial public offering, the disclosure required need only be provided for dispositions within the last three years and for dispositions where material obligations under the terms of the dispositions are still outstanding.

6B   OIL AND GAS PROPERTIES

- Where the distribution is not an initial public offering, the disclosure required under this item with respect to minor interests in **Properties** that are not material to the **issuer**, may be aggregated in summary form by geographical location provided that the interest and the consideration paid is set out for each of the **Properties** in which the minor interest is held.

6.7   *Location, description and acquisition*

Provide the following information for each of the **Properties** of the **issuer**:

(a)   the name and location by field (or geographical area if a field name has not been designated),

(b)   the nature (title, lease, option or other interest) and status of the interest under which the **issuer** has or will have the rights to hold or operate the **Property**, and the expiry date, if applicable,

(c)   the working interest, the net revenue interest (both before and after pay out), together with the gross area of the lease, the assigned petroleum and natural gas rights (all depths, certain depths or formation), the expiry date of the lease and the royalties payable,

(d)   the total number of wells, including producing, shut-in, disposal, suspended and abandoned (identifying separately oil and gas wells in each category), and the amount of acreage available for further exploration and/or development,

(e)   the proximity of the **Property** to pipelines or other means of transportation, and

(f)   the details of the acquisition or proposed acquisition of the **Property** by the **issuer**, including particulars of:

(i)   the actual or proposed date of each acquisition,

(ii)   the name of the vendor and whether the transaction was or will be at **Arm's Length**,

(iii)   for an acquisition not at **Arm's Length**, the vendor's out of pocket costs as described in Local Policy Statement No. 3-07,

(iv)   the consideration, both monetary and non-monetary, including securities, carried interest, royalties and finders fees, paid or to be paid by the **issuer**,

(v)   any material obligations that must be complied with in order to keep any acquisition agreement and property in good standing, including work progress with stated due dates where applicable,

(vi)   how the consideration was determined (e.g. limited to out of pocket costs, valuation opinion or **Arm's Length** negotiations), and

(vii)   any valuation opinion required by a policy of a securities regulatory authority or a stock exchange to support the value of the consideration paid in connection with a transaction not previously approved by the Superintendent or the stock exchange, or that has been approved within the preceding financial year and the **Stub Period**, including the name of the author, the date of the opinion, the assets to which the opinion relates and the value attributed to the assets.

1.   In providing the information requested by (b), indicate the type of interest (e.g. fee simple, leasehold, royalty, reservation or other types of interests and variations thereof) including the percentage interest in the **Properties** held by the **issuer**. In addition, indicate whether or not a title report has been obtained. If so, disclose any material qualifications to the title report and the relationship to the **issuer** of the individual providing the title report.

2.   Out of pocket costs must be supported by either audited financial statements or an audited statement of costs.

3.   Where the distribution is not an initial public offering, the disclosure required by (f) need only be provided for all acquisitions within the last three years and for all acquisitions where material obligations under the terms of the acquisition are still outstanding.

6.8 *Production history*

Provide details on the net crude oil, natural gas liquids, natural gas and sulphur production of the **issuer** for each of the last five completed financial years preceding the date of the preliminary prospectus, and for the current year as of the **Most Recent Month End**. The details should include the net cash flow to the **issuer** derived from the production.

•   The disclosure required in this section includes any production in which the **issuer** has had any type of interest.

6.9 *Drilling activity*

As of the **Most Recent Month End**, state:

(a) the number of wells the **issuer** has drilled or has participated in the drilling of,

(b) the number of such wells completed as producing wells and the number abandoned as dry holes, and

(c) the amount expended by the **issuer** and its subsidiaries on these drilling and exploration activities with reference to section 5.2.

•   In providing the information requested in (c), do not include the amounts expended for payments made for and under leases or other similar interest.

6.10 *Geology and reserve summaries*

For all **Principal Properties**, describe:

(a) the petroleum geology in the area using the available geophysical, geochemical, geological and production data,

(b) the net quantity (after the deduction of royalties) and type (crude oil, natural gas, natural gas liquids, sulphur, etc.) of the estimated **reserves** of the issuer, together with the value assigned to the **reserves** on a net cash flow basis, using discount rates at 0, 10, 15, and 20%, and

(c) any other relevant details that will be of assistance to a prospective investor in evaluating the geological merits of each **Principal Property**.

State in bold print that the values reported under paragraph (b) above may not necessarily be fair market value of the **reserves**. Indicate whether the values are before or after income tax. Provide disclosure regarding the degree of risk assigned to the values, particularly of probable additional **reserves**, including a statement in bold print disclosing the approximate amount, or alternatively the approximate average percentage, by which the volume of probable **reserves** or their values have been reduced to allow for the risk associated with obtaining production from probable **reserves**. Where no percentage or calculated amounts as contemplated in the preceding sentence have been used to allow for the risk, describe the method otherwise employed to allow for such risk.

1. In paragraph (b), **"reserves"** include reserves as defined in National Policy Statement No. 2-B.

2. The information required by (b) should be provided by jurisdiction, category (producing, non-producing, etc.) and type of **reserve**.

3. In accordance with National Policy Statement No. 2-B, dollar values must be calculated at current prices and costs, unless under contract as to price, to all future time.

4. Provide a summary table of the assumptions employed regarding prices, costs, inflation and other factors used. Identify the source of the data used in the estimates, including any comments the author of the report might have respecting the soundness of the data.

5. Provide the estimated total capital costs necessary to achieve the net cash flow and the amount of such costs estimated to be incurred in each of the first two years of cash flow estimates.

6.11 *Proposed exploration and development program*

Disclose the nature and extent of the proposed exploration and development program that is to be carried out by the **issuer** using the **Funds Available** or by third parties under farmout or option agreements. Additionally, provide:

(a) a timetable for this proposed program, describing each significant component of the program, and identifying the planned commencement and completion dates of each significant component,

(b) a **Breakdown of Costs** for this proposed program with reference to Item 8, and

(c) a description of the general topography, vegetation, climate, infrastructure (including pipelines), means of access, source of labour and power sources that may affect the program.

1. In (a) include approximate dates for commencing and completing the planned exploration program, for releasing exploration results, and for obtaining the necessary regulatory approvals.

2. If the exploration and development program is divided into stages, disclose whether proceeding with a subsequent stage in the program is contingent upon the results achieved on an earlier stage.

3. The disclosure in (c) is only required when these factors may be potential impediments to commercial exploration. Examples may include limitations on the exploration season due to climate or effects on operations due to environmental regulations.

4. Disclose the name and relationship to the **issuer** of the engineer on whose recommendation or report the **issuer** is relying in formulating its exploration and development program.

6.12 *Other properties*

Describe the plans that the **issuer** has for the **Properties** other than **Principal Properties**.

6.13 *Dispositions*

Disclose any material dispositions of **Properties** made by the **issuer** as of the **Most Recent Month End**. Provide details of the disposition including particulars of the consideration, how the consideration was determined and whether the vendor was at **Arm's Length**.

• Where the distribution is not an initial public offering, the disclosure required need only be provided for dispositions within the last three years and for dispositions where material obligations under the terms of the dispositions are still outstanding.

Forms

7.   ADMINISTRATION

      Provide:

      (a)   the estimated aggregate monthly and total administration costs that will be
            incurred in order for the issuer to carry out its proposed exploration and
            development program or that will be incurred over a period of twelve
            months (whichever is greater), the time period during which these costs
            will be incurred, and any anticipated variations in the monthly amounts
            during that period, and

      (b)   a **Breakdown of Costs** for the monthly administration costs disclosed in
            paragraph (a), including any anticipated variations.

      1.   Administrative support includes professional fees, transfer agent fees, manage-
            ment fees, rent, travel, investor relations and other administrative costs, such as
            those costs required to maintain a reporting issuer in good standing, whether
            incurred by the issuer or its subsidiaries.

      2.   The disclosure under this item is not required where the distribution is not an
            initial public offering and the issuer has material operating revenues.

8.   USE OF PROCEEDS

8.1   *Funds Available*

      Provide a breakdown of **Funds Available** as follows:

      (a)   the net proceeds to be derived by the issuer from the sale of the securities
            offered under the prospectus,

      (b)   the estimated working capital available to the issuer, its subsidiaries and
            proposed subsidiaries as of the **Most Recent Month End**, and

      (c)   the amounts and sources of other funds that will be available to the issuer,
            its subsidiaries and proposed subsidiaries prior to or concurrently with the
            completion of the offering.

      1.   In each prospectus and revised preliminary prospectus, the amount of working
            capital must be updated to the **Most Recent Month End**.

      2.   Where other sources of funds will be available to the issuer, identify the
            material terms, including the timing, and identity of the person providing the
            funds.

8.2   *Principal purposes*

      Provide in tabular form, a description of each of the principal purposes, with
      amounts, for which the **Funds Available** will be used. Where the closing of the
      distribution under the prospectus is subject to a minimum subscription, provide
      separate columns disclosing the use of proceeds for the minimum and maximum
      subscriptions.

      State the following:

            The issuer will spend the funds available on the completion of this offering
            to carry out its proposed exploration and development program set out in
            "Properties of the Issuer". There may be circumstances where, for sound
            business reasons, a reallocation of funds may be necessary. The issuer will
            only redirect the funds to other properties and will do so only on the basis
            of a written recommendation from an independent, professional geologist or
            engineer.

      Where the issuer does not have material operating revenues, state the following
      (with the bracketed information completed as appropriate):

            The issuer's working capital available to fund ongoing operations will be
            sufficient to meet its administration costs for [*] months.

      1.   If there is a maximum subscription that differs from the minimum subscription,
            identify the order of priority for the principal purposes.

      2.   Statements as to principal purposes for which the **Funds Available** are to be
            used must be specific and be cross-referenced to the estimated costs disclosed in

Items 6 and 7. Where the issuer has not had material operating revenues, the table must include the administration costs required for the issuer to achieve its objectives or that will be incurred over a period of 12 months, whichever is greater.

3.   When disclosing expenditures made on specific **Properties**, indicate whether they are **Principal Properties**, or not.

4.   **Funds Available** not allocated to one of the principal purposes must be identified as "Working Capital to Fund Ongoing Operations".

5.   Where **Funds Available** will be paid to an insider or holder of performance shares or escrow securities, identify, either in the table or by way of a note to the table, the person, amount of the payments and principal purposes to which the payments relate.

6.   Where more than 10% of the **Funds Available** will be used to reduce or retire indebtedness and where the indebtedness was incurred within the two preceding years, the principal purposes for which the indebtedness was used and to whom the money was paid must be disclosed, and where the creditor is an insider to the issuer or is a holder of performance shares or escrow securities, identify the creditor and the nature of the relationship to the issuer.

7.   Where the prospectus is used in connection with a special warrant or similar transaction, the principal purposes for which the funds were raised in such transaction must be disclosed. Where all or a portion of these funds have been spent, provide cross-reference to the detailed discussion in Item 6 and explain how the funds were spent. The **Funds Available** will include the balance of the funds, if any, raised by the special warrant or similar transaction that have not been spent.

8.3   *Conflicts of interest*

Where the issuer is a related party or connected party of the **Agent**, or where the securities to be offered are out of the holdings of a selling security holder who is a related party or connected party of the **Agent**, provide a summary of the nature of the relationship between the **Agent** and the issuer, or the **Agent** and the selling security holder, as the case may be.

State the extent to which the proceeds of the distribution will be applied, directly or indirectly, for the benefit of the **Agent** or any related party of the **Agent**. Where the proceeds will not be applied for the benefit of the **Agent** or any related party of the **Agent**, so state. Provide a cross-reference to the information required by Item 20.

1.   For example, disclosure would be required in most cases where the issuer received a loan from the **Agent** and thus would be a connected party of the **Agent**. Reference should be made to section 167.4 of the **Regulation** for further requirements.

2.   For the purposes of this section, reference to an **Agent** includes a special selling group member, as defined in section 167.4 of the **Regulation**.

9.   RISK FACTORS

List the risks that could be considered to be material to an investor as follows:

(a)   risks relating to the nature of the business of the **issuer**,

(b)   risks relating to the nature of the offering, and

(c)   any other risks.

1.   Risk factors may include but are not limited to such matters as cash flow and liquidity problems, inexperience of **Management** in start up operations, inexperience of **Management** in the natural resource industry, lack of financial expertise, general risks inherent in natural resource exploration, environmental regulations, economic or political conditions, unpredictability of resource prices, absence of an operating history, absence of profitable operations in recent periods, an erratic financial history, conflicts of interest with **Management**, reliance on the efforts of a single individual, possible land title conflicts (e.g. native land claims, title uncertainty), foreign property laws (e.g. limited rights to

property, susceptibility to expropriation, etc.), the arbitrary establishment of offering price and any material differences between the laws presently governing the issuer and the B.C. Company Act relating to security holders rights and remedies.

2.   With respect to (a), the most significant risk factors should be disclosed at the top of the list.

3.   In this Item, **"issuer"** means the issuer, its subsidiaries and proposed subsidiaries.

10.   DIRECTORS, OFFICERS, PROMOTERS AND OTHER MANAGEMENT

1.   In this Item, **"issuer"** means the issuer, its subsidiaries and proposed subsidiaries.

2.   In sections 10.3 through 10.6, the Superintendent may require information for periods prior to those indicated in the section depending upon the materiality of the events.

3.   Provide the information required by this Item for each proposed nominee for election or appointment as a director of the **issuer** and indicate clearly that the individual is a proposed nominee.

10.1 *Name, address, occupation and security holding*

List the name, age and the municipality of residence for all directors, officers, promoters and other members of **Management** of the **issuer**, and for each person, disclose

(a)   the current position and office with the **issuer**,

(b)   the nature of expertise and relevant educational background in the **issuer's** business,

(c)   the principal occupation during the five years prior to the date of the prospectus and, where the principal occupation is that of an officer of a company other than the **issuer**, state the name of the company and the principal business in which it was engaged, and

(d)   the number of securities (including options) of the **issuer** beneficially owned, directly or indirectly, indicating the number of performance shares or escrow securities held in escrow and the percentage of the class to be held on conclusion of the offering.

Where a director, officer, promoter or other member of **Management** is an associate of another director, officer, promoter or other member of **Management**, disclose as a footnote the relationships.

1.   The disclosure is to be provided separately for the issuer and each of its subsidiaries and proposed subsidiaries.

2.   Upon application, the Superintendent may waive the disclosure required by this section where the operations of a subsidiary or a proposed subsidiary are not material to the issuer's operations.

3.   The description of the principal occupation of a director, officer, promoter or other member of **Management** must be specific. The terms "businessman" or "entrepreneur" are not sufficiently specific.

4.   If there is a maximum subscription that differs from the minimum subscription, disclose the percentage of the class held by the principal holders on both a minimum and maximum basis.

10.2 *Aggregate ownership of securities*

State the aggregate number of each class of voting securities of the **issuer** that at the completion of the offering are beneficially owned, directly or indirectly, by all directors, officers, promoters and other members of **Management** of the **issuer**, as a group, and then state the percentage that number will represent of the total issued and outstanding voting securities of the **issuer** at the completion of the offering.

- In this section, **"issuer"** does not include the issuer's subsidiaries and proposed subsidiaries.

10.3 *Other reporting issuers*

Where any director, officer, promoter or other member of **Management** of the **issuer** is, or within the five years prior to the date of the prospectus has been, a director, officer or promoter of any other reporting issuer, state the name of the individual, the number of reporting issuers for which the individual acted, the names of those issuers and the periods during which the individual has so acted.

10.4 *Corporate cease trade orders or bankruptcies*

Where any director, officer, promoter or other member of **Management** of the **issuer** is, or within the five years prior to the date of the prospectus has been, a director, officer or promoter of any other issuer that, while that person was acting in that capacity,

(a)   was the subject of a cease trade or similar order or an order that denied the issuer access to any statutory exemptions for a period of more than 30 consecutive days, state the fact and describe the reasons and whether the order is still in effect, or

(b)   was declared bankrupt or made a voluntary assignment in bankruptcy, made a proposal under any legislation relating to bankruptcy or insolvency or been subject to or instituted any proceedings, arrangement or compromise with creditors or had a receiver, receiver manager or trustee appointed to hold the assets of that person, state the fact.

10.5 *Penalties or sanctions*

Where any director, officer, promoter or other member of **Management** of the **issuer** has, within the ten years prior to the date of the prospectus, been subject to any penalties or sanctions imposed by a court or securities regulatory authority relating to trading in securities, promotion or management of a publicly traded issuer, or theft or fraud, describe the penalties or sanctions imposed.

1.   Penalties or sanctions include charges that have been laid or notices of hearing that have been issued as of the date of the prospectus.

2.   The Superintendent may require information relating to other penalties and sanctions depending on the materiality of the events.

10.6 *Individual bankruptcies*

Where any director, officer, promoter or other member of **Management** of the **issuer** has, within the five years prior to the date of the prospectus, been declared bankrupt or made a voluntary assignment in bankruptcy, made a proposal under any legislation relating to bankruptcy or insolvency, or been subject to or instituted any proceedings, arrangement or compromise with creditors, or had a receiver, receiver manager or trustee appointed to hold the assets of that individual, state the fact.

10.7 *Conflicts of interest*

Disclose particulars of any existing or potential conflicts of interest of any director, officer, promoter or other member of **Management** of the **issuer** as a result of their outside business interests.

11.   INDEBTEDNESS OF DIRECTORS, OFFICERS, PROMOTERS AND OTHER MANAGEMENT

State the name of all directors, officers, promoters and other members of **Management** and each of their respective associates or affiliates who is or has been indebted to the **issuer** at any time during the preceding financial year and the **Stub Period** and state, for each person,

(a)   the largest amount of indebtedness outstanding at any time,

(b)   the nature of the indebtedness and the purpose for which it was incurred,

Forms

(c)   the amount presently outstanding,

(d)   the rate of interest paid or charged,

(e)   the terms of repayment,

(f)   the nature of any security granted to the **issuer**, and

(g)   if the person is an associate or affiliate of a director, officer or member of **Management**, the person's relationship to the director, officer or member of **Management** of the **issuer**.

1.   In this Item, **"issuer"** includes the issuer's subsidiaries and proposed subsidiaries.

2.   Provide the information required by this Item for each proposed nominee for election or appointment as a director of the **issuer** and indicate clearly that the individual is a proposed nominee.

12.   PAYMENTS TO INSIDERS AND PROMOTERS

•   In this Item, **"issuer"** includes the issuer's subsidiaries and proposed subsidiaries.

12.1 *Executive compensation*

Provide the information required by Form 41 with the following changes:

(a)   disclosure must be provided for each of the **issuer's** four most highly compensated executive officers, in addition to the CEO, regardless of the amount of their compensation, and

(b)   in addition to the periods required under Form 41, disclosure must be provided for the **Stub Period**.

1.   The Superintendent may require disclosure of compensation paid to persons other than executive officers.

2.   Where the **issuer** has material operating revenues, the **issuer** need only provide the information required by Form 41.

12.2 *Related party transactions*

Where, during the five preceding financial years and the **Stub Period**, or such shorter period as the **issuer** may have been in existence, the **issuer** has acquired assets or services from an insider, promoter or member of **Management** and their respective associates or affiliates, disclose the following for each acquisition:

(a)   the name of the individual,

(b)   the nature of the assets or services,

(c)   the form and value of the consideration, and

(d)   where the **issuer** has acquired assets,

(i) the cost of the assets to the seller, and

(ii) where the consideration referred to in paragraph (c) above exceeds the seller's out of pocket costs, a cross-reference to the valuation opinion disclosed in section 6.1(c)(vii) or 6.7(f)(vii).

1.   Information with respect to executive compensation need not be disclosed in this section.

2.   Any debt settlements made by the **issuer** to any insider or promoter must be disclosed in this section. The settlement need not be disclosed where the distribution is not an initial public offering, the settlement was entered into more than 2 years ago, is not subject to obtaining regulatory or security holder's approval, and there are no obligations under the settlement still outstanding.

3.   For acquisitions where the consideration is not in excess of the greater of 10% of the aggregate compensation or consideration paid to the individual under sections 12.1 and 12.2 or $5,000, the information required by this item may be aggregated together and classified as "miscellaneous".

4.   As an alternative to the disclosure required in (b), provide a cross-reference to the page(s) of the prospectus where the required disclosure is made.

12.3 *Proposed compensation*

Where known, provide the information required by Form 41 as modified by section 12.1 with respect to the amounts that the **issuer** anticipates it will pay during the 12 month period following completion of the offering.

1. The amounts referred to in this section include the forms of compensation referred to in sections 12.1 and 12.2 above.

2. Where the **issuer** has material operating revenues, the **issuer** need only provide the information required by Form 41.

13. SHARE CAPITAL

13.1 *Existing and proposed share and long-term debt capital*

Provide, in the tabular form indicated or, where appropriate, in notes to the table, particulars of the share and long-term debt capital of the issuer.

TABLE

	Column 1	Column 2	Column 3
	Number of issued securities	Price per security	Total consideration
(a) Prior issuances of securities	_____		_____
(b) Issued as of [the **Most Recent Month End**]		[N/A]	
(c) Offering	_____		_____
(d) To be issued if all securities being offered are sold		[N/A]	

1. A separate table shall be prepared for each class or kind of securities that the issuer has issued or will have issued upon completion of the offering.

2. Set out in the table or a note thereto the number of securities of each class authorized to be issued.

3. If there is a minimum subscription, disclose the number of securities that are offered and that would be issued on both a minimum and maximum basis.

4. The information shall be updated to the **Most Recent Month End**.

5. In (a) of the table list prior issuances aggregated on the basis of the same price per security and type of consideration. Where the distribution is not an initial public offering, the disclosure required by (a) may be omitted.

6. Where the consideration for any of the prior issuances included in the table is other than cash, describe in a note cross-referenced to the prior issuances set out in (a) of the table the method of determining the value of the consideration (e.g. out of pocket costs, valuation opinion, **Arm's Length** negotiation or, in the case of services, determination by directors based on estimated fair market value).

7. In columns 1 and 3 of the table, (b) is equal to the total of (a), and (d) is equal to the total of (b) and (c).

8. Where the issuer has outstanding long-term debt, the information required by Item 7 of Form 14 shall be provided.

9. As a note to the table, indicate whether there are any restrictions on the transferability of the securities (e.g. hold periods, escrow or pooling agreements) and summarize the nature of the restrictions (including the dates hold periods expire and shares are released, and the related number of shares). Where the information is provided elsewhere the disclosure may be provided by a cross-reference to the page in the prospectus where the disclosure is contained.

13.2 *Options and other rights to purchase shares*

(a) Disclose, as of the **Most Recent Month End** prior to the date of the prospectus, the following information respecting each **option** that is held or will be held upon completion of the offering by any person:

   (i) the name of each person and the reasons that the **option** was granted,

   (ii) the name of the grantor and the nature of the **option** granted to each person (e.g. options, **Agent's** warrants or other warrants),

   (iii) the designation, number of the securities subject to the **option** and any material anti-dilution provisions,

   (iv) the purchase price of the securities subject to the **option** or the formula by which the purchase price will be determined,

   (v) the expiration date of the **option**, and

   (vi) if there is a published market for the securities, the market value of the securities subject to the **option** as of the date of grant and the **Most Recent Month End**.

(b) State the aggregate number of each class or kind of securities that are subject to **options** described in paragraph (a)(iii) above.

(c) State the following:

There are no assurances that the options, warrants or other rights described above will be exercised in whole or in part.

1. In this section, "option" means option, warrant or other right to purchase securities of the **issuer** granted by the **issuer**, selling security holder, insider, promoter, control person or holder of performance shares.

2. In this section, **"issuer"** includes the issuer's subsidiaries and proposed subsidiaries.

3. The information shall be updated to the **Most Recent Month End**.

4. Where the issuer has material operating revenue the information required for directors, officers and employees under (a) may be aggregated for options of the same type, grant date, exercise price and expiry date on the basis of the following categories:

   (i) all members of management as a group and all directors who are not also members of management as a group, indicating the aggregate number of members of management and the aggregate number of directors to whom the information applies, without naming them,

   (ii) all members of management of all subsidiaries of the issuer as a group and all directors of such subsidiaries who are not also members of management as a group, without naming them, excluding individuals referred to in clause (i),

   (iii) by all other employees of the issuer as a group, without naming them, and

   (iv) by all other employees of the subsidiaries of the issuer as a group, without naming them.

13.3 *Fully diluted share capital*

Provide the information indicated in the table set out below for each class of securities of the issuer.

TABLE

	Number of Securities	Percentage of Total
(a) Issued as of the **Most Recent Month End**		
(b) Offered under the prospectus		
(c) Securities reserved for future issue as of the **Most Recent Month End**		
Total		**100**

1. (a) is the amount indicated in (b) of column 1 of the table in section 13.1.

2. If there is a minimum subscription, disclose the number of securities offered and total on both a minimum and maximum basis.

3. (c) is the amount indicated in paragraph (b) from section 13.2 (with respect to options on securities of the issuer granted by the issuer only).

4. A separate table shall be prepared for each class or kind of securities that the issuer has issued or will have issued upon completion of the offering.

5. The information shall be updated to the **Most Recent Month End**.

13.4 *Principal holders of voting securities*

Provide as of the **Most Recent Month End**, the information indicated in the table set out below for each person who has, or is known by the issuer to have:

(a) direct or indirect beneficial ownership of,

(b) control or direction over, or

(c) a combination of direct or indirect beneficial ownership of and of control or direction over,

voting securities that will constitute more than 10 per cent of any class of such securities upon completion of the offering.

TABLE

Column 1	Column 2	Column 3	Column 4
Name and municipality of residence	Number of securities	Percentage of class prior to the offering	Percentage of class after the offering

1. Where a person that is not an individual is shown by the issuer as owning directly or indirectly more than 10 per cent of any class of such securities, identify the individual shareholders of the person as required by General Instruction 7. The name of such individuals should be disclosed in a footnote to the table.

2. If voting securities will be issued prior to, concurrently with or immediately following the offering, indicate as far as practicable the respective holding of voting securities that will exist after giving effect to the issue.

3. If there is a maximum subscription that differs from the minimum subscription, disclose the percentage of the class held by the principal holders on both a minimum and maximum basis.

4. If, to the knowledge of the issuer or the **Agent**, more than 10 per cent of any class of voting securities of the issuer are held or are to be held subject to any voting trust or other similar agreement/arrangement, state the designation of such securities, the number or amount held or to be held and the duration of the agreement. Give the names and addresses of the voting trustees and outline briefly their voting rights and other powers under the agreement.

5. Where a person identified in the table is a control person of the issuer and is not a director, officer or promoter of the issuer, provide the disclosure required for sections 10.3 - 10.6 for the control person. If the control person is a corporation, the disclosure must be provided for the control persons of the corporation.

6. A separate table shall be prepared for each class or kind of voting securities that the issuer has issued or will have issued upon completion of the offering.

7. The information shall be updated to the **Most Recent Month End**.

13.5 *Performance shares or escrow securities*

Where the issuer has performance shares or escrow securities issued as of the date of the prospectus, state

(a)   the number of performance shares or escrow securities,

(b)   the estimated percentage that the performance shares or escrow securities will represent of the total issued and outstanding voting securities of the issuer, upon the completion of the offering,

(c)   the names of the beneficial owners of the performance shares or escrow securities and the number of performance shares or escrow securities owned by each and, with respect to owners of performance shares, why the person is a principal as defined in Local Policy Statement No. 3-07,

(d)   the name of the escrow agent,

(e)   the date of the escrow agreement and the conditions governing the transfer, release and cancellation of the performance shares or escrow securities, and

(f)   the rights or obligations of a person who ceases to be a principal, dies or becomes bankrupt to retain, transfer or surrender to the issuer for cancellation the performance shares or escrow securities.

•   If there is a maximum subscription that differs from the minimum subscription, disclose the percentage that the performance shares or escrow securities will represent on both a minimum and maximum basis.

14.   DIVIDEND RECORD

State the amount of dividends or other distributions, if any, paid by the issuer during its last five preceding financial years and the **Stub Period**, or such shorter period as the issuer may have been in existence. Where dividends have been paid in the past, indicate the issuers present policy regarding future dividend payments.

•   Dividends should be set out on a per share basis, shown separately for each class of shares in respect of each of the financial years and the **Stub Period**. Appropriate adjustments shall be made to reflect changes in capitalization during the period.

15.   PRIOR SALES AND TRADING INFORMATION

Where the distribution is not an initial public offering, state the prices at which securities of the class offered by the prospectus have been sold within the 12 months prior to the date of the preliminary prospectus, or are to be sold, by the issuer or selling security holder where such prices differ from those at which the securities are offered by the prospectus. State the number of securities sold or to be sold at each price.

For each exchange or quotation system upon which the securities offered are listed or quoted, provide a weekly trading history (high, low and volume) for at least six weeks prior to the date of the prospectus and monthly for the preceding 12 months.

16.   PLAN OF DISTRIBUTION

16.1   *Terms of the distribution agreement*

With respect to the agreement entered into between the issuer and the **Agents**, state

(a)   the names of the **Agents**,

(b)   the date of the agreement,

(c)   the nature of the **Agents'** obligation to take up and pay for any of the securities being offered,

(d)   the number of securities expected to be sold by each of the **Agents** and whether any arrangements have been made for selling group participation,

(e)   the number of additional securities that may be issued, if the issuer has granted the **Agents** a "greenshoe" option,

(f)   the conditions, if any, under which the **Agents** may "market out",

(g) the nature of the consideration to be paid to the **Agents**,

(h) the conditions, if any, under which any of the proceeds are to be held in trust or escrow pending completion of the offering,

(i) the number of days following the completion of the offering by which the issuer will receive the net proceeds of the offering from the **Agents** or the date by which the **Agents** are to purchase the securities, and

(j) whether there is any intention to stabilize the market.

- Where the prospectus is used in connection with a special warrant or similar transaction and the funds are held in a special trust disclose the conditions for release or whether the funds have been released.

16.2 *Minimum and maximum subscription*

Where the prospectus discloses a plan of distribution not involving a firm under-writing or other subscription guarantee, it must also disclose the amount of the minimum and maximum subscriptions.

16.3 *Secondary offering*

If any of the securities being offered are for the account of a security holder, name the security holder and state the number of the securities owned by that security holder, the number to be offered and the number to be owned by that security holder after the completion of the distribution. Disclose the date the security holder acquired the securities and the cost to the security holder in the aggregate and on a per security basis. State that the securities of the selling security holder will not be sold until the distribution of the issuer is complete and the portion of the expenses of the distribution to be borne by the selling security holder.

16.4 *Extraprovincial offerings*

Disclose whether there are any agreements or arrangements to sell any portion of the offering outside of British Columbia. If so, disclose in what other jurisdictions the offering may be sold, the identity of the person who will be selling the securities in the other jurisdictions and the estimated portion of the offering, if any, to be sold outside of Canada.

- Agreements or arrangements include those made with a selling group outside of British Columbia or with clients of the **Agents** who are not residents of British Columbia.

17. DESCRIPTION OF SECURITIES OFFERED

17.1 *Terms*

Describe the securities being offered and summarize their material attributes and characteristics, including, if applicable:

(a) dividend rights,

(b) voting rights,

(c) liquidation or distribution rights,

(d) pre-emptive rights,

(e) conversion rights,

(f) if the securities are subscription warrants or rights, the period during which, and the price at which, the warrants or rights are exercisable,

(g) redemption, purchase for cancellation or surrender provisions,

(h) sinking or purchase fund provisions,

(i) if the securities are obligations, provisions with respect to interest rates, maturity, nature and priority of any security for the obligations, permis-sible substitutions for security, negative covenants, name of the trustee under any indenture relating to the obligations and the nature of any material relationship between the trustee and the issuer or any of its affiliates, and

(j)   provisions as to modification, amendment or variation of any such rights or provisions.

•   If the rights attaching to the securities being offered are materially limited or qualified by the rights of any other class of securities, or if any other class of securities ranks ahead of or equally with the securities being offered, include information regarding such other securities in order to enable investors to understand the rights attaching to the securities being offered.

17.2 *Modification of terms*

If the rights of holders of the securities may be modified otherwise than pursuant to a mechanism provided for by governing legislation relating to the securities, briefly describe the method by which those rights may be modified.

18. SPONSORSHIP AND FISCAL AGENCY AGREEMENTS

If the issuer has entered into any agreement with any registrant to sponsor the issuer or to provide corporate finance services for the issuer or its securities, either now or in the future, disclose the following information regarding these services:

(a)   the date of the agreement,

(b)   the name of the registrant,

(c)   the consideration, both monetary and non-monetary, paid or to be paid by the issuer, and

(d)   a summary of the nature of the services to be provided, including the period during which the services will be provided, activities to be carried out and, where market making services will be provided, whether the registered broker or dealer will commit its own funds to the purchase of securities of the issuer or whether the registered broker or dealer will act as **Agent** for others to do so.

19. INVESTOR RELATIONS ARRANGEMENTS

If the issuer has entered into any written or oral agreement or understanding with any person to provide any promotional or investor relations services for the issuer or its securities, or to engage in activities for the purpose of stabilizing the market, either now or in the future, disclose the following information regarding these services:

(a)   the date of the agreement and the anticipated date that the services will commence,

(b)   the name, principal business and place of business of the person providing the services,

(c)   the background of the person providing the services,

(d)   whether the person has, or is known by the issuer to have:

  (i) direct or indirect beneficial ownership of,

  (ii) control or direction over, or

  (iii) a combination of direct or indirect beneficial ownership of and of control or direction over,

  securities of the issuer,

(e)   whether the person has any right to acquire securities of the issuer, either in full or partial compensation for services,

(f)   the consideration both monetary and non-monetary paid or to be paid by the issuer, including whether any payments will be made in advance of services being provided,

(g)   if the issuer does not have sufficient funds to pay for the services, how the issuer intends to pay for the services, and

(h)   the nature of the services to be provided, including the period during which the services will be provided.

1. Include any arrangements made by the issuer or any other person on behalf of the issuer or on the person's own initiative where the issuer knows, after reasonable enquiry, that such an arrangement exists.

2. The disclosure in (c) and (h) need only summarize the background and nature of services.

3. If there are no promotional or investor relations arrangements, or arrangements to stabilize the market, so state.

20. RELATIONSHIP BETWEEN ISSUER OR SELLING SECURITY HOLDER AND AGENT

Where the **issuer** is a related party or connected party, as defined in the **Regulation**, of an **Agent** or where the securities to be offered are out of the holdings of a selling security holder who is a related party or connected party of the **Agent**, describe

(a) the nature of the relationship or connection between the **issuer** and the **Agent** or the selling security holder and the **Agent**, as the case may be, including,

(i) the basis on which the **issuer** or selling security holder is a related party or connected party of the **Agent**,

(ii) the name of each relevant related party of the **Agent**,

(iii) the details of the ability of the **Agent** or any related party of the **Agent** to affect materially the operations of the issuer, and

(iv) whether the **issuer** is indebted to the **Agent** or any related party of the **Agent** and, if so, provide particulars of such indebtedness, and

(b) the extent to which the proceeds of the issue will be applied, directly or indirectly, for the benefit of the **Agent** or any related party of the **Agent**.

(For example, where the **issuer** has received a loan from the **Agent**, the **issuer** would be a connected party of the **Agent** and would have to comply with section 167.4 of the Regulation.)

1. For the purpose of this item, reference to an **Agent** includes a special selling group member as defined in section 167.4(1) of the **Regulation**.

2. In this item, **"issuer"** means the issuer, its subsidiaries and proposed subsidiaries.

21. RELATIONSHIP BETWEEN ISSUER AND PROFESSIONAL PERSONS

Disclose the nature and extent of any beneficial interest, direct or indirect, in any securities or property, of the **issuer** or of an associate or affiliate of the **issuer**, held by a professional person referred to in section 99(2) of the **Regulation**, a **responsible solicitor** or any partner of a **responsible solicitor's** firm. Also, disclose whether the professional person, the **responsible solicitor** or any partner of the **responsible solicitor's** firm is, or is expected to be elected, appointed or employed as a director, senior officer or employee of the **issuer** or of an associate or affiliate of the **issuer**, or is a promoter of the **issuer** or of an associate or affiliate of the **issuer**.

1. The interest of a **responsible solicitor** and all partners of that **responsible solicitor's** firm may be shown in the aggregate. Disclosure regarding the interest of or position with the **issuer** or an associate or affiliate of the **issuer** held by any partner of the **responsible solicitor's** firm is only required where known by the **responsible solicitor** after reasonable inquiry.

2. In this section, **"responsible solicitor"** means the solicitor who is primarily responsible for the preparation of or for advice to the **issuer**, selling security holder or **Agent** with respect to the contents of the prospectus.

3. In this section, **"issuer"** includes the **issuer's** subsidiaries and proposed subsidiaries.

22. LEGAL PROCEEDINGS

Describe any outstanding and, if known, contemplated legal proceedings that are material to the business and affairs of the issuer.

- Include the name of the court or agency, the date the proceedings were instituted, the principal parties to the proceedings, the nature of the proceedings, the amount claimed, if any, whether the proceedings are being contested, the present status of the proceedings and, if a legal opinion is referred to in the prospectus, the name of counsel providing that opinion.

23. AUDITOR

State the name and address of the auditor of the issuer.

24. REGISTRAR AND TRANSFER AGENT

State the name of the issuer's registrar and transfer agent where the issuer has branch registers for transfers of its securities, state the location (by municipalities) of the registers.

25. MATERIAL CONTRACTS

25.1 *Particulars of material contracts*

Disclose all material contracts to which the issuer is a party, including

(a) the date of each contract,

(b) the parties to each contract,

(c) the consideration paid or payable by or to the issuer, and

(d) the general nature of each contract.

- As an alternative to the disclosure required in this section, provide a cross-reference to the page(s) of the prospectus where the required disclosure with respect to a particular contract is made.

25.2 *Inspection of contracts and reports*

State a reasonable time and place in the Province at which a copy of any material contract or report may be inspected during distribution of the securities being offered under the prospectus.

26. OTHER MATERIAL FACTS

Give particulars of any other material facts relating to the securities proposed to be offered and not disclosed elsewhere in the prospectus.

27. PURCHASERS' STATUTORY RIGHTS

State the following:

The British Columbia Securities Act provides purchasers with the right to withdraw from an agreement to purchase securities within two business days after receipt or deemed receipt of a prospectus and any amendment. The Securities Act further provides a purchaser with remedies for rescission or damages where the prospectus and any amendment contains a misrepresentation or is not delivered to the purchaser, provided that such remedies for rescission or damages are exercised by the purchaser within the time limit prescribed by the Securities Act. The purchaser should refer to sections 66, 114, 118 and 124 of the Securities Act for the particulars of these rights or consult with a legal advisor.

Where the distribution involves a distribution of securities to be issued pursuant to the exercise of special warrants (or in connection with a similar type of transaction), state the following (with bracketed information completed as appropriate):

In the event that a holder of a special warrant, who acquires a [identify underlying securities] of the issuer upon the exercise of a special warrant as provided for in this prospectus, is or becomes entitled under applicable securities legislation to the remedy of rescission by reason of this prospectus or any amendment thereto containing a misrepresentation, such holder shall be entitled to rescission not only of the holder's exercise of the special warrant(s) but also of the [private placement or other exempt transaction] pursuant to which the special warrant(s) were initially acquired, and shall be entitled in connection with such rescission to a full refund of all consideration paid on the acquisition of the special warrant(s). In the event such holder is a permitted assignee of the interest of the original special warrant subscriber, such permitted assignee shall be entitled to exercise the rights of rescission and refund granted hereunder as if such permitted assignee was such original subscriber. The foregoing is in addition to any other right or remedy available to a holder of special warrants under section 114 of the Securities Act or otherwise at law.

- Where this document is a base disclosure document used in connection with a summary prospectus, this section is not required in the base disclosure document because it is contained in the summary prospectus.

28.   FINANCIAL STATEMENTS, REPORTS AND OTHER EXHIBITS

Include the financial statements, reports and other exhibits required by applicable local policy statements or by the **Act** and **Regulation**.

29.   CERTIFICATES

Provide the certificates of the issuer, **Agent** and promoter as required by the **Act** and **Regulation**.

****

IT IS AN OFFENCE FOR A PERSON TO MAKE A STATEMENT IN A DOCUMENT REQUIRED TO BE FILED OR FURNISHED UNDER THE ACT OR THE REGULATION THAT, AT THE TIME AND IN THE LIGHT OF THE CIRCUMSTANCES UNDER WHICH IT IS MADE, IS A MISREPRESENTATION.

The prospectus for a mutual fund required by Section 42(2) of the Act shall be in the following form.

FORM 15

Securities Act

INFORMATION REQUIRED IN PROSPECTUS OF A MUTUAL FUND

Item 1 - Price of Securities on Sale or Redemption:

(a)   Describe briefly the method followed or to be followed by the issuer in determining the price at which its securities will be offered for sale and redeemed.

INSTRUCTIONS:

1.   State the frequency with which the offering or redemption price is determined and the time when the price becomes effective.

2.   Describe the rules used for the valuation of the issuer's assets and liabilities for the purpose of calculating net asset value and disclose all instances, within the past three years, when the discretion to deviate from these rules, if any, was exercised.

3.   Explain fully any difference in the price at which securities are offered for sale and the redemption price.

(b)   State the sales charge expressed as a percentage of the total amount paid by the purchaser and as a percentage of the net amount invested in securities of the issuer. State the redemption charge, if any, expressed as a percentage of the redemption price.

INSTRUCTIONS:

1.   If the sales or redemption charge varies on a quantity basis give particulars thereof indicating the quantities and the respective charges applicable thereto.

2. Indicate briefly any difference in the sales charge imposed upon the sale of securities in connection with the conversion or exchange of securities or the reinvestment of dividends and similar distributions.

3. In this form, "sales charge" includes all service charges including charges relating to such matters as cost of the establishment of a contractual plan and the cost of the continuing administration and maintenance of such a plan.

4. When giving particulars of the sales charge with respect to a contractual plan indicate when during the term of the plan the sales charge will be deducted.

5. Give particulars of the entitlement of the purchaser of a contractual plan to a refund of any sales charge incurred if the contractual plan is terminated during the term of such plan.

   (c) Describe briefly any specific authorization or requirement to reinvest the proceeds of dividends or similar distributions in the issuer's securities.

   (d) State the penalty, if any, for early redemption.

Item 2 - Method of Distribution:

Outline briefly the method of distribution of the securities being offered. If sales of securities are to be effected through an arrangement with a principal distributor, give brief details of any arrangements made with the principal distributor. See Items 22 and 23.

INSTRUCTIONS:

1. State whether it is the intention of the issuer to engage in the continuous sale of the securities of the issuer.

2. If the securities being offered are to be sold by way of a contractual plan whereby the purchaser agrees to make regular periodic payments for the securities offered, give brief particulars of the contractual plan, including,

   (i) minimum initial investment;

   (ii) subsequent minimum investment;

   (iii) sales charge deductions from such minimum investments; and

   (iv) sales charges as a percentage of the amount paid by the purchaser and as a percentage of the net amount invested in securities of the issuer.

   (v) the total amount invested contrasted to the amount paid by the purchaser.

3. As used in this Form, "principal distributor" includes,

   (i) a person through whom securities of the issuer are distributed pursuant to a contractual arrangement with the issuer or the manager providing for an exclusive right to distribute the securities in a particular area or any feature which gives or is intended to give a distributor a material competitive advantage over other distributors in respect of the securities offered, or

   (ii) a person, together with any affiliate, by or through whom 25 per cent or more of the securities of the issuer which were distributed during the last completed financial year of the issuer, were distributed.

4. With the consent of a person who would otherwise be a principal distributor may, with respect to any one or more of the items of disclosure required by this Form be treated as not coming within the definition of a principal contributor.

5. See Instruction 3 to Item 1(b).

Item 3 - Summary of Prospectus:

Give a synopsis near the beginning of the prospectus of that information in the body of the prospectus which in the opinion of the issuer would be most likely to influence the investor's decision to purchase the security.

INSTRUCTION:

1. This summary should highlight in condensed form the information, both favourable and adverse, including risk factors in item 6, particularly pertinent to

a decision to purchase the securities offered, including information about both the issuer and the securities.

2. Appropriate cross references may be made to items in the prospectus where information is difficult to summarize accurately, but this shall not detract from the necessity to have the salient points summarized in the summary.

Item 4 - Name and Incorporation of Issuer:

State the full name of the issuer and the address of its head office and principal office. State the laws under which the issuer was formed, and whether by articles of incorporation, trust indenture or otherwise and the date the issuer came into existence. If material, state whether the documents have been amended.

INSTRUCTION:

Particulars of any such documents need to be set out only if material to the securities offered by the prospectus. See Item 15.

Item 5 - Description of Business:

(a) Briefly describe the business of the issuer.

(b) If the issuer has engaged in any business other than that of a mutual fund during the past five years, state the nature of the other business and give the approximate date on which the issuer commenced to operate as a mutual fund. If the issuer's name was changed during the period, state its former name and the date on which it was changed. Indicate briefly the nature and results of any bankruptcy, receivership or similar proceedings or any other material reorganization of the issuer during the period.

(c) If during the past two years any affiliate of the issuer had any material interest, direct or indirect, in any transaction involving the purchase of any substantial amount of assets presently held by the issuer, describe the interest of the affiliate in such transaction and state the cost of such assets to the purchaser and to the seller.

Item 6 - Risk Factors:

(a) Where appropriate to a clear understanding by investors of the risk factors and speculative nature of the enterprise or the securities being offered, an introductory statement shall be made on the first page or in the summary of the prospectus summarizing the factors which make the purchase a risk or speculation. The information may be given in the body of the prospectus if an appropriate reference is made on the first page or in the summary of the prospectus to the risks and the speculative or promotional nature of the enterprise and a cross reference is made to the place in the prospectus where the information is contained.

(b) Where there is a risk that purchasers of the securities offered may become liable to make an additional contribution beyond the price of the security, disclose any information or facts that may bear on the security holder's assessment of risk associated with the investment.

Item 7 - Investment Objectives

Precisely state the investment objectives of the issuer.

INSTRUCTION:

Aims such as long-term capital appreciation or current income and the types of securities in which the issuer will invest should be described.

Item 8 - Investment Practices and Restrictions:

Where it is the policy or proposed policy of the issuer to engage in any of the following types of activities state the policy and the activity. Outline the extent, if any, to which the issuer has engaged in each of the activities during the last five years. Indicate which of the policies may not be changed without securityholder approval,

(a) the issuance of securities other than the securities offered;

(b)   the borrowing of money;

(c)   the underwriting of securities of other issuers;

(d)   the concentration of investments in a particular class or kind of industry;

(e)   the purchase and sale of real estate;

(f)   the purchase and sale of commodities or commodity future contracts;

(g)   the making of loans, whether secured or unsecured;

(h)   the investment of a specific proportion of assets of the issuer in a specific type of security (for example, bonds, preferred shares, money market instruments);

(i)   the investment of more than 10 per cent of the assets of the issuer in the securities of any one company;

(j)   the investment in more than 10 per cent of the securities of any one company;

(k)   the investment in securities of companies for the purpose of exercising control or management;

(l)   the investment in securities of investment companies or other mutual funds;

(m)   the purchase or sale of mortgages;

(n)   the purchase of securities on margin or selling short;

(o)   the investment in securities which are not fully paid;

(p)   the investment in illiquid securities and securities subject to restriction on resale;

(q)   the investment in foreign securities;

(r)   the investment in gold or gold certificates;

(s)   the pledging, mortgaging or hypothecating of the issuer's assets;

(t)   the sale or purchase of portfolio securities to or from directors or officers of the issuer or of the manager;

(u)   the guaranteeing of securities or obligations of any issuer;

(v)   the purchase of options, rights and warrants;

(w)   the writing of covered or uncovered clearing corporation options;

(x)   the investment in a security which may require the purchaser to make an additional contribution beyond the price of the security;

(y)   any investment other than in securities.

INSTRUCTIONS:

1.   It is not necessary to state the policy or list an activity in which the issuer has not and does not propose to be engaged.

2.   For the purposes of clause (g), the purchase of debt securities for investment purposes is not to be considered the making of a loan by the issuer.

3.   For the purposes of clause (p), where the issuer invests in securities subject to restriction on resale, describe how the securities are to be valued in the determination of net asset value of the fund.

Item 9 - Diversification of Assets:

Furnish in substantially the tabular form indicated the following information as at a date within thirty days of the date of the preliminary prospectus or pro forma prospectus with respect to each issuer 5 per cent or more of whose securities of any class are beneficially owned directly or indirectly by the mutual fund or any of its subsidiaries.

TABLE

Name and Address of company	Nature of its principal business	Percentage of securities of and class owned by issuer	Percentage of value of issuer's assets invested therein

INSTRUCTION:

>Where no material change has occurred in the information required by this item since the date of the financial statements included in the prospectus, the information may be given as at the date of the financial statements.

Item 10 - Management Fees:

(a) Indicate the method of determining the amount of management fees and, distinguishing between those charged to the issuer and those charged directly to security holders, other expenses, if any, and make a cross reference to the financial statements for details as to the amount of management fees and other expenses, if any, which have been charged to the issuer.

(b) Set out in tabular form a record of management expense ratio comprising the aggregate of all fees and other expenses paid or payable by the issuer during each of the last five completed financial years as a percentage of average net assets under administration during each of those periods. Such disclosure should also include a brief description of the method of calculating the percentage and a statement that the management expense ratio may vary from mutual fund to mutual fund.

INSTRUCTIONS:

1. Where management fees are changed or are proposed to be changed and where such change would have had an effect on the management expense ratio for the most recent financial year, if the change had been in effect throughout that year, the effect of such change should be disclosed.

2. Where the financial year is other than a full year, the management expense ratio should be annualized, the period covered specified and a statement made that the management expense ratio is annualized.

3. For the purposes of this item, "average net assets" should be calculated to be the average of the net assets determined at each valuation date of the issuer and before the deduction of management fees and other expenses, and the term "other expenses" means all other expenses incurred in the course of ordinary business relating to the organization, management and operation of the issuer with exception of commissions and brokerage fees on the purchase and sale of portfolio securities and taxes of all kinds, other than penalties, to which the issuer is subject.

4. Where an issuer invests in another mutual fund the management expense ratio shall be calculated on the basis of those assets of the issuer on which a management fee is charged.

5. The financial statements should set out in appropriate detail the amounts of the management fee and other expenses, if any, which have been charged to the issuer.

6. The basis or rates of charges levied against security holders rather than the issuer for special services such as trustee fees for registered retirement savings plans, redemption fees, conversion of investments from one fund to another within related mutual funds, or any other specific service charge to a class of investors, should be disclosed separately, in a single table, and should not be included as part of the management expense ratio.

Forms

Item 11 - Tax Status of Issuer:

State in general terms the bases upon which the income and capital receipts of the issuer are taxed.

Item 12 - Tax Status of Securityholder:

State in general terms the income tax consequences to the holders of the securities offered hereby of:

(a)   any distribution to such holders in the form of dividends or otherwise, including amounts beneficially received by way of reinvestment;

(b)   redemption;

(c)   sale;

(d)   transfer to another mutual fund, if applicable.

Item 13 - Promoters:

If any person is or has been a promoter of the issuer or of any of its subsidiaries within the five years immediately preceding the date of the preliminary prospectus or pro forma prospectus, furnish the following information:

(a)   State the names of the promoters, the nature and amount of anything of value (including money, property, contracts, options or rights of any kind) received or to be received by each promoter directly or indirectly from the issuer, or from any of its subsidiaries, and the nature and amount of any assets, services or other consideration therefor received or to be received by the issuer or subsidiary.

(b)   As to any assets acquired within the past two years or to be acquired by the issuer or by any of its subsidiaries from a promoter, state the amount at which acquired or to be acquired and the principle followed or to be followed in determining the amount. Identify the person making the determination and state his relationship, if any, with the issuer, any subsidiary or any promoter. State the date that the assets were acquired by the promoter and the cost thereof to the promoter.

Item 14 - Legal Proceedings:

Briefly describe any legal proceedings material to the issuer to which the issuer or any of its subsidiaries is a party or of which any of their property is the subject. Make a similar statement as to any such proceedings known to be contemplated.

INSTRUCTION:

Include the name of the court or agency, the date instituted, the principal parties thereto, the nature of the claim, the amount claimed, if any, whether the proceedings are being contested, and the present status of the proceedings.

Item 15 - Description of Shares or Units Offered:

(a)   If shares are being offered, state the description or the designation of the class of shares or units offered and furnish all material attributes and characteristics including, without limiting the generality of the foregoing, the following information:

   (i) dividend rights;

   (ii) voting rights;

   (iii) liquidation or distribution rights;

   (iv) pre-emptive rights;

   (v) conversion rights;

   (vi) redemption, purchase for cancellation or surrender provisions;

   (vii) liability to further calls or to assessment by the issuer; and

   (viii) provisions as to modification, amendment or variation of any such rights or provisions.

(b)   If the rights of holders of such shares may be modified otherwise than in accordance with the provisions attaching to such shares or units or the provisions of the governing Act relating thereto, so state and explain briefly.

INSTRUCTIONS:

1.   This item requires only a brief summary of the provisions that are material from an investment standpoint. Do not set out verbatim the provisions attaching to the shares; only a succinct resume is required.

2.   If the rights attaching to the shares being offered are materially limited or qualified by the rights of any other class of securities, or if any other class of securities ranks ahead of or equally with the shares being offered, include information regarding such other securities that will enable investors to understand the rights attaching to the shares being offered. If any shares being offered are to be offered in exchange for other securities, an appropriate description of the other securities shall be given. No information need be given, however, as to any class of securities that is to be redeemed or otherwise retired, provided appropriate steps to assure redemption or retirement have been or will be taken prior to or contemporaneously with the delivery of the shares being offered.

3.   In addition to the summary referred to in instruction 1, the issuer may set out verbatim in a schedule to the prospectus the provisions attaching to the shares being offered.

Item 16 - Issuance of Other Securities:

If securities other than shares are being offered, outline briefly the rights evidenced thereby.

INSTRUCTION:

The instructions to Item 15 apply to this item with due alteration for points of detail.

Item 17 - Dividend Record:

State the amount of dividends or other distributions, if any, paid by the issuer including income beneficially received by way of dividend reinvestment, during its last five completed financial years preceding the date of the preliminary prospectus or pro forma prospectus.

INSTRUCTION:

Dividends should be set on a per security basis, shown separately for each class of security in respect of each of the financial years. Appropriate adjustments shall be made to reflect changes in capitalization during the period.

Item 18 - Directors and Officers

List the names and home addresses in full or, alternatively, solely the municipality of residence or postal address, of all directors and officers of the issuer and indicate all positions and offices with the issuer held by each person named, and the principal occupations within the five preceding years, of each director and officer.

INSTRUCTIONS:

1.   Where the municipality of residence or postal address is listed, the Superintendent may request that the home address in full be furnished to the Commission.

2.   Where the principal occupation of a director or officer is that of an officer of a company other than the issuer, state the principal business in which such company is engaged.

3.   Where a director or officer has held more than one position in the issuer, or a parent or subsidiary thereof, state only the first and last position held.

Forms

Item 19 - Executive Compensation

Complete and attach to or include in this Form a Statement of Executive Compensation in Form 41, provided however, that the disclosure required by Items V, VIII, IX and X of Form 41 may be omitted for purposes of this Form.

See NIN 93/23 "Executive Compensation".

ITEM 20 - Indebtedness of Directors, Executive Officers and Senior Officers

(a) The information required by this Item must be provided for each individual who is or, at any time during the most recently completed financial year, was a director, executive officer and senior officer of the issuer, each proposed nominee for election as a director of the issuer, and each associate of any such director, officer or proposed nominee,

(i) who is, or at any time since the beginning of the most recently completed financial year of the issuer has been, indebted to the issuer or any of its subsidiaries, or

(ii) whose indebtedness to another entity is, or at any time since the beginning of the most recently completed financial year of the issuer has been, the subject of a guarantee, support agreement, letter of credit or other similar arrangement or understanding provided by the issuer or any of its subsidiaries.

(b) State in the tabular form under the caption set out, for any indebtedness referred to in paragraph (a) of this Item:

(i) The name of the borrower (column (a)).

(ii) If the borrower is a director, executive officer or senior officer, the principal position of the borrower. If the borrower was, during the year, but no longer is a director or officer, include a statement to that effect. If the borrower is a proposed nominee for election as a director, include a statement to that effect. If the borrower is included as an associate describe briefly the relationship of the borrower to an individual who is or, during the year, was a director, executive officer or senior officer or who is a proposed nominee for election as a director, name that individual and provide the information required by this subparagraph for that individual (column (a)).

(iii) Whether the issuer or a subsidiary of the issuer is the lender or the provider of a guarantee, support agreement, letter of credit or similar arrangement or understanding (column (b)).

(iv) The largest aggregate amount of the indebtedness outstanding at any time during the last completed financial year (column (c)).

(v) The aggregate amount of indebtedness outstanding as at a date within thirty days of certification of the prospectus (column (d)).

TABLE OF INDEBTEDNESS OF DIRECTORS, EXECUTIVE OFFICERS
AND SENIOR OFFICERS

Name and Principal Position (a)	Involvement of Issuer or Subsidiary (b)	Largest Amount Outstanding During [Last Completed Financial Year] ($) (c)	Amount Outstanding as at [current date] ($) (d)

(c) State in the introduction immediately preceding the table required by paragraph (b) of this Item, separately, the aggregate indebtedness,

(i) to the issuer or any of its subsidiaries, and

    (ii) to another entity if the indebtedness is the subject of a guarantee, support agreement, letter of credit or other similar arrangement or understanding provided by the issuer or any of its subsidiaries,

of all officers, directors, employees and former officers, directors and employees of the issuer or any of its subsidiaries outstanding as at a date within thirty days of certification of the prospectus.

(d)   Disclose in a footnote to, or a narrative accompanying, the table required by this Item,

    (i) the material terms of each incidence of indebtedness and, if applicable, of each guarantee, support agreement, letter of credit or other similar arrangement or understanding, including without limitation the term to maturity, rate of interest and any understanding, agreement or intention to limit recourse, any security for the indebtedness and the nature of the transaction in which the indebtedness was incurred, and

    (ii) any material adjustment or amendment made during the most recently completed financial year to the terms of the indebtedness and, if applicable, the guarantee, support agreement, letter of credit or similar arrangement or understanding.

(e)   No disclosure need be made under this Item of an incidence of indebtedness that has been entirely repaid on or before the date of certification of the prospectus or of routine indebtedness.

"Routine indebtedness" means indebtedness described in any of the following:

    (i) If an issuer makes loans to employees generally, whether or not in the ordinary course of business, loans are considered routine indebtedness if made on terms, including those as to interest rate and security, no more favourable to the borrower than the terms on which loans are made by the issuer to employees generally, but the amount at any time during the last completed financial year remaining unpaid under the loans to any one director, executive officer, senior officer or proposed nominee together with his or her associates that are treated as routine indebtedness under this clause must not exceed $25,000.

    (ii) Whether or not the issuer makes loans in the ordinary course of business, a loan to a director, executive officer or senior officer is considered routine indebtedness if,

      A. the borrower is a full-time employee of the issuer,

      B. the loan is fully secured against the residence of the borrower, and

      C. the amount of the loan does not exceed the annual salary of the borrower.

    (iii) If the issuer makes loans in the ordinary course of business, a loan is considered routine indebtedness if made to a person or company other than a full-time employee of the issuer, and if the loan,

      A. is made on substantially the same terms, including those as to interest rate and security, as are available when a loan is made to other customers of the issuer with comparable credit ratings, and

      B. involves no more than usual risks of collectibility.

    (iv) Indebtedness arising by reason of purchases made on usual trade terms or of ordinary travel or expense advances, or for similar reasons is considered routine indebtedness if the repayment arrangements are in accord with usual commercial practice.

Forms

(f)   For purposes of this Item, "executive officer" has the same meaning as in Form 41 and "support agreement" includes, but is not limited to, an agreement to provide assistance in the maintenance or servicing of any indebtedness and an agreement to provide compensation for the purpose of maintaining or servicing any indebtedness of the borrower.

See NIN 93/23 "Executive Compensation".

Item 21 - Custodian of Portfolio Securities:

(a)   State the name, principal business address and the nature of the business of each person holding portfolio securities of the issuer as custodian and the jurisdiction in which the portfolio securities are physically situate. The name of the custodian may be omitted if it is a bank, or otherwise with the consent of the Superintendent.

(b)   Give brief details of the contractual arrangements made with the custodian.

Item 22 - Statement of Functions of Issuer and Distribution of Securities:

(a)   Give a concise statement of the manner in which the following functions of the issuer are performed and who is responsible therefor, stating how such functions are co- ordinated and to the extent that any such functions are not performed by bona fide employees of the issuer, the names and addresses of the persons responsible for performing such functions:

    i) management of the issuer other than management of the investment portfolio;

    ii) management of the investment portfolio;

    iii) providing investment analysis;

    iv) providing investment recommendations;

    v) making investment decisions;

    vi) purchase and sale of the investment portfolio and brokerage arrangements relating thereto; and

    vii) distribution of the securities offered.

(b)   List the name and addresses in full, or, alternatively, solely the municipality of residence or portal address of all directors and officers of the named in answer to paragraph (a) of this item.

(c)   Indicate the method of determining the amount of management fees and state the total of such fees paid during each of the last five completed financial years and separately for the period from the last completed financial year to a date within thirty days of the preliminary prospectus or pro forma prospectus.

(d)   Indicate the circumstances under which the management agreement may be terminated.

(e)   Indicate conflicts of interest or potential conflicts of interest between the issuer and the persons named in answer to (a).

INSTRUCTIONS:

1.   Where an alternate address is listed, the Superintendent may request that the home address in full be furnished to the Commission.

2.   In giving the information regarding distribution of securities the name and address of only the principal distributor need be given.

3.   In giving information regarding the purchase and sale of the investment portfolio and brokerage arrangements relating thereto the name and address of only the principal broker need be given.

4.   In giving information regarding the purchase and sale of the investment portfolio and brokerage arrangements relating thereto give brief details of the following matters:

i) the total cost during the last completed financial year of the issuer of securities acquired, distinguishing between,

   (a) securities of or guaranteed by the government of any country, or any political subdivision thereof;

   (b) short-term notes; and

   (c) other securities;

ii) the total cost of securities held at the beginning and at the end of the issuer's last completed financial year;

iii) the formula, method or criteria used in allocating brokerage business to persons engaged in the distribution of the securities of the issuer;

iv) the formula, method or criteria used in allocating brokerage business to persons furnishing statistical, research or other services to the issuer or the manager of the issuer; and

v) the amount of brokerage paid to the principal broker for the last three completed financial years, giving the total amount paid in each year and expressing the amount paid in each year as a percentage of the total brokerage paid by the issuer.

5. If one or more persons performs more than one of the functions referred to in this item, so state, giving details of all functions so performed.

6. As used in this Form:

  (a) "principal broker" includes,

     (i) a person through whom the investment portfolio of the issuer is purchased or sold pursuant to a contractual arrangement with the issuer or the manager of the issuer providing for an exclusive right to purchase or sell the investment portfolio of the issuer or any feature which gives or is intended to give a broker or dealer a material competitive advantage over other brokers or dealers in respect of the purchase or sale of the investment portfolio of the issuer, or

     (ii) a person, together with any affiliate, by or through whom 15 per cent or more of the securities transactions of the issuer were carried out; and

  (b) "brokerage arrangements" or "brokerage business" include all purchases and sales of the investment portfolio, whether effected directly or through an agent.

7. With the consent of the Superintendent, a person who would otherwise be a principal broker may, with respect to any one or more of the items of disclosure required by this Form, be treated as not coming within the definition of a principal broker.

Item 23 - Associated Persons:

Furnish the following information as to each person named in answer to paragraph (a) of Item 22:

1. If a named person is associated with the issuer or is a director or senior officer of or is associated with any affiliate of the issuer or is a director or senior officer of or is associated with any person which is associated with the issuer, so state, and give particulars of the relationship.

2. If the issuer is associated with a named person or is associated with any affiliate of a named person or is associated with any company which is associated with the named person, so state, and give particulars of the relationship.

3. If any person associated with the issuer is also associated with a named person, so state, and give particulars of the relationship.

4. If a named person has a contract or arrangement with the issuer, give a brief description of the contract or arrangement, including the basis for determining

the remuneration of the named person and give the amount of remuneration paid or payable by the issuer and its subsidiaries to such person during the last completed financial year of the issuer.

5. If a named person is associated with any other named person, so state, and give particulars of the relationship.

6. Where and to the extent required by the Superintendent, give the business experience of each named person and, in the case of a named company, the directors and officers thereof.

Item 24 - Principal Holders of Securities:

Furnish the following information as of a specified date within thirty days prior to the date of the preliminary prospectus or pro forma prospectus, in substantially the tabular form indicated:

(a) The number of securities of each class of voting securities of:

   (i) the issuer; and

   (ii) the manager of the issuer;

owned of record or beneficially, directly or indirectly, by each person who owns of record, or is known by such issuer or manager to own beneficially, directly or indirectly, more than 10 per cent of any class of such securities. Show in Column 5 whether the securities are owned both of record and beneficially, of record only, or beneficially only, and show in Columns 6 and 7 the respective amounts and percentages known by the issuer or manager to be owned in each such manner.

TABLE

Column 1	Column 2	Column 3	Column 4	Column 5	Column 6	Column 7
Name and address	Name of company	Issuer or relationship thereto	Designation of class	Type of ownership	Number of securities owned	Percentage of class

(b) If any person named in answer to paragraph (a) owns of record or beneficially, directly or indirectly, more than 10 per cent of,

   (i) any class of voting securities of the principal distributor or the principal broker of the issuer or any parent of subsidiary thereof, or

   (ii) any proprietorship interest in the principal distributor or the principal broker of the issuer,

give the percentage of such securities or the percentage of such proprietorship interest so owned by such person.

(c) The percentage of securities of each class of voting securities beneficially owned, directly or indirectly, by all the directors, trustees and senior officers,

   (i) of the issuer in the issuer or in a parent or subsidiary thereof, and

   (ii) of the manager of the issuer in such manager or in a parent or subsidiary thereof,

in the case of each company as a group, without naming them.

TABLE

Column 1	Column 2	Column 3	Column 4
Name of company	Issuer or relationship thereto	Designation of class	Percentage of class

INSTRUCTIONS:

1. Where a person is shown by the issuer as owning directly or indirectly more than 10 per cent of any class of such securities, the Superintendent may require the disclosure of such additional information as is necessary to identify any individual who, through his direct or indirect ownership of voting securities in the person owns directly or indirectly more than 10 per cent of any class of such securities. The name of such an individual should be disclosed in a footnote to the table described in paragraph (a).

2. For the purposes of paragraph (a), securities owned beneficially, directly or indirectly, and of record shall be aggregated in determining whether any person owns more than 10 per cent of the securities of any class.

3. For the purposes of clause (i) of paragraph (a), where no material change has occurred in the information required by such clause since the date of the financial statements included in the prospectus, information may be given as of the date of the financial statements.

4. If voting securities are being offered in connection with, or pursuant to, a plan of acquisition, amalgamation or reorganization, indicate, as far as practicable, the respective holdings of voting securities that will exist after giving effect to the plan.

5. If, to the knowledge of the issuer, more than 10 per cent of any class of voting securities of the issuer or if, to the knowledge of the manager of the issuer, more than 10 per cent of any class of voting securities of such manager are held or are to be held subject to any voting trust or other similar agreement, state the designation of such securities, the number held or to be held and the duration of the agreement. Give the names and addresses of the voting trustees and outline briefly their voting rights and other powers under the agreement.

6. If, to the knowledge of the issuer, the parent of the issuer, the manager or the parent of the manager, any person named in answer to paragraph (a) is an associate or affiliate of any other person named therein, disclose, in so far as known, the material facts of such relationship, including any basis for influence over the issuer enjoyed by the person other than the holding of voting securities of the issuer.

Item 25 - Interest of Management and Others in Material Transactions:

Describe briefly, and where practicable state the approximate amount of any material interest, direct or indirect, of any of the following persons in any transaction within the three years prior to the date of the preliminary prospectus or pro forma prospectus, or in any proposed transaction which has materially affected or will materially affect the issuer:

(i) the manager of the issuer;

(ii) the principal distributor of the issuer;

(iii) the principal broker of the issuer;

(iv) any director or senior officer or trustee of the issuer or any person referred to in clauses (i), (ii) or (ii) hereof;

(v) any securityholder named in answer to paragraph (a) of Item 26; and

(vi) any associate or affiliate of any of the foregoing persons.

INSTRUCTIONS:

1. Give a brief description of the material transaction. Include the name and address of each person whose interest in any transaction is described and the nature of the relationship by reason of which such interest is required to be described.

2. As to any transaction involving the purchase or sale of assets by or to the issuer, state the cost of the assets to the purchaser and the cost thereof to the seller if acquired by the seller within two years to the transaction.

3. This item does not apply to any interest arising from the ownership of securities of the issuer where the securityholder receives no extra or special benefit or advantage not shared on an equal basis by all other holders of the same class of securities or all other holders of the same class of securities who are resident in Canada.

4. No information need be given in answer to this item as to any transaction or any interest therein, where,

   (i) the rates or charges involved in the transaction are fixed by law or determined by competitive bids;

   (ii) the interest of a specified person in the transaction is solely that of a director of another person that is a party to the transaction;

   (iii) the transaction involves services as a bank or other depository of funds, transfer agent, registrar, trustee under a trust indenture or other similar services;

   (iv) the interest of a specified person, including all periodic instalments in the case of any lease or other agreement providing for periodic payments or instalments, does not exceed $50,000; or

   (v) the transaction does not, directly or indirectly, involve remuneration for services, and,

      (a) the interest of the specified person arose from the beneficial ownership, direct or indirect, of less than 10 per cent of any class of voting securities of another person that is a party to the transaction,

      (b) the transaction is in the ordinary course of business of the issuer.

5. Information shall be furnished in answer to this item with respect to transactions not excluded above that involve remuneration, directly or indirectly, to any of the specified persons for services in any capacity unless the interest of the person arises solely from the beneficial ownership, direct or indirect, of less than 10 per cent of any class of voting securities of another person furnishing the services to the issuer or its subsidiaries.

6. This item does not require the disclosure of any interest in any transaction unless such interest and transaction are material.

Item 26 - Auditors, Transfer Agents and Registrars:

   (a) State the name and address of the auditor of the issuer.

   (b) Where shares are offered, state the names of the issuer's transfer agents and registrars and the location (by municipalities) of the registers of transfers of each class of shares of the issuer. Where securities other than shares are offered, state the location (by municipalities) of each register on which transfers of such securities may be recorded.

Item 27 - Material Contracts:

Give particulars of every material contract entered into within the two years prior to the date of the preliminary prospectus or pro forma prospectus, by the issuer or any of its subsidiaries and state a reasonable time and place at which any such contract or a copy thereof may be inspected during distribution of the securities being offered.

INSTRUCTIONS:

1. The term "material contract" for this purpose means any contract that can reasonably be regarded as presently material to the proposed investor in the securities being offered.

2. Set out a complete list of all material contracts, indicating those which are disclosed elsewhere in the prospectus and provide particulars with respect to those material contracts about which particulars are not given elsewhere in the prospectus. This item does not require disclosure of contracts entered into in the ordinary course of business of the issuer or its subsidiaries as the case may be.

3. Particulars of contracts should include the dates of, parties to, consideration and general nature of the contracts, succinctly described.

4. Particulars of contracts need not be disclosed, or copies of such contracts made available for inspection, if the Superintendent determines that such disclosure or making- available would impair the value of the contract and would not be necessary for the protection of investors.

Item 28 - Other Material Facts:

Give particulars of any other material facts relating to the securities proposed to be offered and not disclosed pursuant to the foregoing items.

IT IS AN OFFENCE FOR A PERSON TO MAKE A STATEMENT IN A DOCU-MENT REQUIRED TO BE FILED OR FURNISHED UNDER THE ACT OR THIS REGULATION THAT, AT THE TIME AND IN THE LIGHT OF THE CIRCUMSTANCES UNDER WHICH IT IS MADE, IS A MISREPRESEN-TATION.

January 19, 1987

FORM 16
Securities Act
ESCROW AGREEMENT

THIS AGREEMENT is dated for reference _____ , 19 ___ and made

AMONG:
      (the "Escrow Agent");

AND:
      (the "Issuer");

AND:
      EACH SHAREHOLDER, as defined in this Agreement

(collectively, the "Parties").

WHEREAS the Shareholder has acquired or is about to acquire shares of the Issuer;

AND WHEREAS the Escrow Agent has agreed to act as escrow agent in respect of the shares upon the acquisition of the shares by the Shareholder;

NOW THEREFORE in consideration of the covenants contained in this agreement and other good and valuable consideration (the receipt and sufficiency of which is acknowledged), the Parties agree as follows:

1. INTERPRETATION

In this agreement:

  (a) "Acknowledgement" means the acknowledgement and agreement to be bound in the form attached as Schedule A to this agreement;

  (b) "Act" means the Securities Act, S.B.C. 1985, c. 83;

  (c) "Exchange" means the Vancouver Stock Exchange;

  (d) "IPO" means the initial public offering of common shares of the Issuer under a prospectus which has been filed with, and for which a receipt has been obtained from, the Superintendent under section 42 of the Act;

  (e) "Local Policy Statement 3-07" means the Local Policy Statement 3-07 in effect as of the date of the reference of this agreement and attached as Schedule B to this agreement;

  (f) "Shareholder" means a holder of shares of the Issuer who executes this agreement or an Acknowledgement;

  (g) "Shares" means the shares of the Shareholder described in Schedule C to this agreement, as amended from time to time in accordance with section 9;

(h) "Superintendent" means the Superintendent of Brokers appointed under the Act; and

(i) "Superintendent or the Exchange" means the Superintendent, if the shares of the Issuer are not listed on the Exchange, or the Exchange, if the shares of the Issuer are listed on the Exchange.

2. PLACEMENT OF SHARES IN ESCROW

The Shareholder places the Shares in escrow with the Escrow Agent and shall deliver the certificates representing the Shares to the Escrow Agent as soon as practicable.

3. VOTING OF SHARES IN ESCROW

Except as provided by section 4(a), the Shareholder may exercise all voting rights attached to the Shares.

4. WAIVER OF SHAREHOLDER'S RIGHTS

The Shareholder waives the rights attached to the Shares

(a) to vote the Shares on a resolution to cancel any of the Shares,

(b) to receive dividends, and

(c) to participate in the assets and property of the Issuer on a winding up or dissolution of the Issuer.

5. ABSTENTION FROM VOTING AS A DIRECTOR

A Shareholder that is or becomes a director of the Issuer shall abstain from voting on a directors' resolution to cancel any of the Shares.

6. TRANSFER WITHIN ESCROW

(1) The Shareholder shall not transfer any of the Shares except in accordance with Local Policy Statement 3-07 and with the consent of the Superintendent or the Exchange.

(2) The Escrow Agent shall not effect a transfer of the Shares within escrow unless the Escrow Agent has received

(a) a copy of an Acknowledgement executed by the person to whom the Shares are to be transferred, and

(b) a letter from the Superintendent or the Exchange consenting to the transfer.

(3) Upon the death or bankruptcy of a Shareholder, the Escrow Agent shall hold the Shares subject to this agreement for the person that is legally entitled to become the registered owner of the Shares.

(4) [Set out in this subsection the rights and obligations of a Shareholder who ceases to be a principal, as that term is defined in Local Policy Statement 3-07, dies, or becomes bankrupt, to retain, transfer or surrender to the Issuer for cancellation any Shares held by the Shareholder.]

7. RELEASE FROM ESCROW

(1) The Shareholder irrevocably directs the Escrow Agent to retain the Shares until the Shares are released from escrow pursuant to subsection (2) or surrendered for cancellation pursuant to section 8.

(2) The Escrow Agent shall not release the Shares from escrow unless the Escrow Agent has received a letter from the Superintendent or the Exchange consenting to the release.

(3) The approval of the Superintendent or the Exchange to a release from escrow of any of the Shares shall terminate this agreement only in respect of the Shares so released.

8. SURRENDER FOR CANCELLATION

The Shareholder shall surrender the Shares for cancellation and the Escrow Agent shall deliver the certificates representing the Shares to the Issuer

(a) at the time of a major reorganization of the Issuer, if required as a condition of the consent to the reorganization by the Superintendent or the Exchange,

(b) where the Issuer's shares have been subject to a cease trade order issued under the Act for a period of 2 consecutive years,

(c) 10 years from the later of the date of issue of the Shares and the date of the receipt for the Issuer's prospectus on its IPO, or

(d) where required by section 6(4).

9. AMENDMENT OF AGREEMENT

(1) Subject to subsection (2), this agreement may be amended only by a written agreement among the Parties and with the written consent of the Superintendent or the Exchange.

(2) Schedule C to this agreement shall be amended upon

(a) a transfer of Shares pursuant to section 6,

(b) a release of Shares from escrow pursuant to section 7, or

(c) a surrender of Shares for cancellation pursuant to section 8,

and the Escrow Agent shall note the amendment on the Schedule C in its possession.

10. INDEMNIFICATION OF ESCROW AGENT

The Issuer and the Shareholders, jointly and severally, release, indemnify and save harmless the Escrow Agent from all costs, charges, claims, demands, damages, losses and expenses resulting from the Escrow Agent's compliance in good faith with this agreement.

11. RESIGNATION OF ESCROW AGENT

(1) If the Escrow Agent wishes to resign as escrow agent in respect of the Shares, the Escrow Agent shall give notice to the Issuer.

(2) If the Issuer wishes the Escrow Agent to resign as escrow agent in respect of the Shares, the Issuer shall give notice to the Escrow Agent.

(3) A notice referred to in subsection (1) and (2) shall be in writing and delivered to

(a) the Issuer at _____ , or

(b) the Escrow Agent at_____

and the notice shall be deemed to have been received on the date of delivery. The issuer or the Escrow Agent may change its address for notice by giving notice to the other party in accordance with this subsection.

(4) A copy of a notice referred to in subsection (1) or shall concurrently be delivered to the Superintendent or the Exchange.

(5) The resignation of the Escrow Agent shall be effective and the Escrow Agent shall cease to be bound by this agreement on the date that is 180 days after the date of receipt of the notice referred to in subsection (1) or (2) or on such other date as the Escrow Agent and the Issuer may agree upon (the "resignation date").

(6) The issuer shall, before the resignation date and with the written consent of the Superintendent or the Exchange, appoint another escrow agent and that appointment shall be binding on the Issuer and the Shareholders.

12. FURTHER ASSURANCES

The Parties shall execute and deliver any documents and perform any acts necessary to carry out the intent of this agreement.

13. TIME

Time is of the essence of this agreement.

14. GOVERNING LAWS

This agreement shall be construed in accordance with and governed by the laws of British Columbia and the laws of Canada applicable in British Columbia.

Forms

15. COUNTERPARTS

This agreement may be executed in two or more counterparts, each of which shall be deemed to be an original and all of which shall constitute one agreement.

16. LANGUAGE

Wherever a singular expression is used in this agreement, that expression is deemed to include the plural or the body corporate where required by the context.

17. ENUREMENT

This Agreement enures to the benefit of and is binding on the Parties and their heirs, executors, administrators, successors and permitted assigns.

The Parties have executed and delivered this agreement as of the date of reference of this agreement.

THE CORPORATE/COMMON SEAL of)
[Escrow Agent] was affixed in   )
the presence of:)
)
_____)
Authorized Signatory   )
)   C/S
_____)
Authorized Signatory   )

THE CORPORATE/COMMON SEAL of)
[Issuer] was affixed in the   )
presence of:)
)
_____)
Authorized Signatory   )
)   C/S
_____)
Authorized Signatory   )

Where the Shareholder is an individual

SIGNED, SEALED & DELIVERED by   )
[Shareholder] in the presence   )
of:)
)
_____)
Name   )
)   _____
_____)
Address   )   [Shareholder]
)
_____)
)
_____)
)
_____)
Occupation   )

Where the Shareholder is a company:

THE CORPORATE/COMMON SEAL of)
[Shareholder] was affixed in   )
the presence of:)
)
_____)
Authorized Signatory   )
)   C/S
_____)
Authorized Signatory   )

SCHEDULE A TO ESCROW AGREEMENT
ACKNOWLEDGEMENT AND AGREEMENT TO BE BOUND

To: Superintendent of Brokers   or   Vancouver Stock Exchange
#1100 - 865 Hornby Street   609 Granville Street
Vancouver, B.C.   Vancouver, B.C.
V6Z 2H4   V7Y 1H1

    (if the shares are not   (if the shares are listed
    listed on the Vancouver   on the Vancouver Stock
    Stock Exchange)   Exchange)

I acknowledge that

(a)   I have entered into an agreement with _____ under which _____ shares of _____ (the "Shares") will be transferred to me upon receipt of regulatory approval, and

(b)   the Shares are held in escrow subject to an escrow agreement dated for reference _____ , 19 ___ (the "Escrow Agreement"), a copy of which is attached as Schecule A to this acknowledgement.

In consideration of $1.00 and other good and valuable consideration (the receipt and sufficiency of which is acknowledged) I agree, effective upon receipt of regulatory approval of the transfer to me of the Shares, to be bound by the Escrow Agreement in respect of the Shares as if I were an original signatory to the Escrow Agreement.

Dated at _____ on _____ 19 ___ .

Where the transferee is an individual:

Signed, sealed and delivered by   )
[transferee] in the presence of:)
)
_____)
Name   )
)
_____)
Address   )   [transferee]
)
_____)
)
Occupation   )

Where the transferee is a company:

The Corporate/Common Seal of   )
[transferee] was affixed   )
in the presence of:)
)
_____)   C/S
Authorized signatory   )
)
_____)
Authorized signatory   )

SCHEDULE C TO ESCROW AGREEMENT

NAME OF SHAREHOLDER	NUMBER OF SHARES HELD IN ESCROW

This is the form required under section 132 of the Securities Regulation or, where required, under an order issued under section 59 of the Securities Act.

FORM 20

Securities Act

REPORT OF EXEMPT DISTRIBUTION

Report of a distribution under section 55(2)(1) to (5), (8) to (10), 11(i), (14), (16)(i), (18), (19) or (24) to (27) of the Securities Act, S.B.C. 1985, c.83 (the "Act"), section 117(a), (b) or (f) to (i) of the Securities Regulation, B.C. Reg. 270/86 (the "Regulation"), or, where required, under an order issued under section 59 of the Act.

1. Name, address and telephone number of the issuer of the security distributed (the "Issuer"):

   _____

   _____

2. State whether the Issuer is an exchange issuer.

   _____

3. Description of the security (the "Security") and the number distributed:

   _____

4. Section of the Act or Regulation under which the distribution was made:

   _____

5. Date of the distribution: _____

6. If the distribution was to 50 or fewer persons, complete clause (a) of this item. If the distribution was to more than 50 persons, circle clause (b) of this item.

   (a)

Full Name and Address of Purchaser(s)	Number of Securities Purchased	Purchase Price

   (b) The Issuer has prepared and certified a list comprising the information required by clause (a) of this section and a certified true copy of the list will be provided to the Commission upon request.

7. State the total proceeds derived in British Columbia by the Issuer from the distribution, i.e. the total value of the securities distributed to residents of British Columbia.

8. State the name and address of any person acting as agent in connection with the distribution and the compensation paid or to be paid to such agent, including discounts, commissions or other fees or payments of a similar nature. If the compensation includes securities of the Issuer, note that a separate Form 20 may be required to be filed under section 132 of the Regulation.

9. If the distribution was under section 117(a) of the Regulation, state the number of different purchasers who acquired securities of the Issuer under that exemption during the 12 month period preceding the distribution.

10. If the distribution was under section 117(i) of the Regulation, state

    (a) the number of different purchasers who acquired securities of the Issuer under that exemption during the 12 month period preceding the distribution, and

    (b) the total amount paid for securities of the Issuer issued under that exemption during the 12 month period preceding the distribution.

The undersigned hereby certifies that the statements made in this report are true and correct.

DATED at _____ this _____ day of _____ , 19 ___ .

_____
Name of Issuer

Per: _____
Signature of authorized signatory

_____

_____
Name and office of authorized signatory

IT IS AN OFFENCE FOR A PERSON TO MAKE A STATEMENT IN A DOCUMENT REQUIRED TO BE FILED OR FURNISHED UNDER THE SECURITIES ACT THAT, AT THE TIME AND IN THE LIGHT OF CIRCUMSTANCES UNDER WHICH IT IS MADE, IS A MISREPRESENTATION.

INSTRUCTIONS:

1. In answer to item 8, it is not necessary to include payments for services incidental to the distribution such as clerical, printing, legal or accounting services.

2. If the distribution was under section 117(a), (b) or (i) of the Regulation or if the filing of this report was required under an order issued under section 59 of the Act, the Issuer, at the time of filing this report, must file the completed undertaking and acknowledgement of the purchaser of the securities required by section 128 of the Regulation. The required form is Form 20A.

3. If the space provided for any answer is insufficient, additional sheets may be used. Each sheet must be cross referenced to the relevant item, properly identified and signed by the person whose signature appears on the report.

4. File this report with the required fee and completed Fee Checklist. In order to determine the fee payable, consult section 183 of the Regulation. Cheques should be made payable to the "Minister of Finance".

> Cheques for fees should no longer be made payable to the "Minister of Finance". They are now payable to the "British Columbia Securities Commission" pursuant to NIN 95/24 "Fee Payments under the Securities Act and the Commodity Contract Act".

This is the form required under section 128 of the Securities Regulation or, where required, under an order issued under section 59 of the Securities Act.

FORM 20A

Securities Act

ACKNOWLEDGEMENT AND UNDERTAKING

1. The undersigned, _____ (the "Purchaser"),
    [Name of the Purchaser]

    purchased from _____ (the "Issuer")
    [Name of the Issuer]

    _____ (the "Securities")
    [Number and description of securities]

    of the Issuer on _____
    [Date of distribution]

2.   The Purchaser acknowledges that he is the beneficial owner of the Securities.

3.   If the Securities were issued to the Purchaser under section 117(a) of the Securities Regulation, B.C. Reg. 270/86 (the "Regulation"), by circling (a), (b) or (c) and underlining the applicable relationship, the Purchaser acknowledges that:

  (a)   the Purchaser is by virtue of his net worth and investment experience or his consultation with or advice from a person who is not an insider of the Issuer, but who is a registered adviser or a registered dealer, is able to evaluate the prospective investment on the basis of information respecting the investment provided by the Issuer;

  (b)   the Purchaser is a spouse, parent, brother, sister or child of a senior officer or director of the Issuer, or of an affiliate of the Issuer; or

  (c)   the Purchaser is a company, all the voting securities of which are beneficially owned by one or more of a spouse, parent, brother, sister or child of a senior officer or director of the Issuer, or of an affiliate of the Issuer.

4.   If the securities were issued to the Purchaser under section 117(b) of the Regulation, the Purchaser, by circling this item 4, acknowledges that by virtue of his net worth and investment experience or his consultation with or advice from a person who is not an insider of the Issuer, but who is a registered adviser or a registered dealer, he is able to evaluate the prospective investment on the basis of information respecting the investment provided by the Issuer.

5.   If the Securities were issued to the Purchaser under section 117(i) of the Regulation, by circling (a) or (b) and *underlining* the applicable relationship, the Purchaser acknowledges that:

  (a)   the Purchaser is a spouse, parent, brother, sister, child or a close personal friend of a senior officer or director of the Issuer, or of an affiliate of the Issuer; or

  (b)   the Purchaser is a company, all of the voting securities of which are beneficially owned by one or more of a spouse, parent, brother, sister, child or close personal friend of a senior officer or director of the Issuer, or of an affiliate of the Issuer.

6.   The Purchaser further acknowledges that as a result of the Securities being distributed under an exemption from the requirements of Section 42 of the Securities Act, S.B.C. 1985, c.83 (the "Act"):

  (a)   the Purchaser is restricted from using most of the civil remedies available under the Act and the Regulation; and

  (b)   the Purchaser may not receive information that would otherwise be required to be provided to the Purchaser under the Act and the Regulation.

7.   If the Purchaser is a company, each of the undersigned shareholders of the Purchaser, being all the shareholders of the Company (the "Undersigned Shareholders"), undertakes not to effect a transfer of beneficial ownership of any shares of the Purchaser, except to an Undersigned Shareholder or to the Purchaser, and not to permit the Purchaser to issue additional shares of the Purchaser, except to an Undersigned Shareholder, for 12 months from the following date [circle appropriate provision]:

  (a)   if the Issuer is not an exchange issuer, from the later of the date of the issue of the Securities and the date the Issuer became a reporting issuer; or

  (b)   if the Issuer is an exchange issuer, from the earlier of the date of the issue of the Securities and the date a written agreement committing the Purchaser to acquire the Securities, subject only to any required regulatory approval, has been executed by all parties to the agreement.

The undersigned hereby certifies that the statements made in this report are true and correct.

DATED at _____ this _____ day of _____ , 19 ___

_____
Signature of the Purchaser
or, if the Purchaser is a
company, signature of
authorized signatory

_____

_____
Name of Purchaser, or if the
Purchaser is a company, name
and office of authorized
signatory

_____
Address of the Purchaser

IT IS AN OFFENCE FOR A PERSON TO MAKE A STATEMENT IN A DOCUMENT REQUIRED TO BE FILED OR FURNISHED UNDER THE SECURITIES ACT THAT, AT THE TIME AND IN THE LIGHT OF CIRCUMSTANCES UNDER WHICH IT IS MADE, IS A MISREPRESENTATION.

If the Undertaking in item 7 is applicable, the signatures of all shareholders of the Purchaser are required:

Relationship, if any, of
shareholder to senior
officer or director of the
Issuer or affiliate of the
Issuer

_____
Signature

_____   _____
Name

_____
Signature

_____   _____
Name

_____
Signature

_____   _____
Name

Forms

INSTRUCTIONS:

File this report with the required fee and completed Fee Checklist. In order to determine the fee payable, consult section 183 of the Regulation. Cheques should be made payable to the "Minister of Finance".

Cheques for fees should no longer be made payable to the "Minister of Finance". They are now payable to the "British Columbia Securities Commission" pursuant to NIN 95/24 "Fee Payments under the Securities Act and the Commodity Contract Act".

September 1, 1988

This is the form required under Section 129 of the Securities Regulation.

FORM 23

Securities Act

NOTICE OF INTENTION TO SELL AND DECLARATION PURSUANT TO SECTION 117(c) AND (d) OF THE SECURITIES REGULATION

1. Name and address of issuer _____

2. Name and address of selling control person _____

3. Number and description of securities of the issuer beneficially owned, directly or indirectly, by the control person

4. Number and description of securities proposed to be distributed by the control person

5. Date the issuer became a reporting issuer _____

6. Proposed method of distribution _____

7. Proposed commencement date and places of the distribution

8. If the securities are not to be distributed on or through the facilities of a stock exchange, provide the name and address of the purchaser(s) and the number of securities to be purchased, if known.

9. Where this form is a renewal of a previously filed Form 23 and is therefore being filed pursuant to Section 129(2) of the Securities Regulation, provide the following information:

    (a)   date of filing of original
          Form 23   _____

    (b)   date of most recent filing
          of a renewal Form 23   _____

    (c)   number of securities listed
          in item 4 of original Form 23   _____

(d) number of securities sold
     from date of original
     Form 23 to date of this
     Form 23   _____

(e) where all or a portion of
     the securities specified in
     item 4 of the original Form 23
     have not been sold and are
     no longer for sale, state the
     number of securities that
     are no longer for sale   _____

(f) number of securities
     remaining for sale   _____

Declaration, Certificate and Undertaking

The undersigned control person hereby represents that:

(a) any applicable hold periods relating to the securities referred to in item 4 of this
     Form will be satisfied on or before the date of the commencement of the distribu-
     tion; and

(b) that he has no knowledge of any material change that has occurred in the affairs
     of the issuer of the securities which has not been generally disclosed and reported
     to the Commission, nor has he any knowledge of any other material adverse
     information in regard to the current and prospective operations of the issuer
     which have not been generally disclosed.

The undersigned hereby certifies that the statements made in this notice are true and
correct.

DATED at _____ this _____ day of _____ , 19____.

                              _____
                              Signature of the control
                              person or, if the control
                              person is a company,
                              signature of authorized
                              signatory

                              _____
                              If the control person is
                              a company, name and
                              office of authorized
                              signatory

IT IS AN OFFENCE FOR A PERSON TO MAKE A STATEMENT IN A DOCUMENT
REQUIRED TO BE FILED OR FURNISHED UNDER THE SECURITIES ACT THAT,
AT THE TIME AND IN THE LIGHT OF CIRCUMSTANCES UNDER WHICH IT IS
MADE, IS A MISREPRESENTATION.

INSTRUCTIONS:

1.   If the space provided for any answer is insufficient, additional sheets may be
     used. Each sheet must be cross referenced to the relevant item, properly iden-
     tified and signed by the person whose signature appears in the notice.

2.   In item 7, if the place of the distribution is to be through the facilities of a stock
     exchange, a statement to that effect, with the name of the stock exchange, is
     sufficient.

3.   File this Form with the required fee and completed Fee Checklist. In order to
     determine the fee payable, consult section 183 of the Regulation. Cheques should
     be made payable to the "Minister of Finance".

Forms

> Cheques for fees should no longer be made payable to the "Minister of Finance". They are now payable to the "British Columbia Securities Commission" pursuant to NIN 95/24 "Fee Payments under the Securities Act and the Commodity Contract Act".

4. A Form must be filed with the British Columbia Securities Commission (the "Commission") and with each stock exchange in Canada on which the securities referred to in item 4 are listed at least seven days and not more than fourteen days before the initial trade of the securities referred to in item 4.

5. The Declaration, Certificate and Undertaking must be signed by the control person not more than 24 hours prior to the filing of this Form.

6. A Form 37 must be filed within 3 days after the completion of any trade in the securities proposed to be distributed.

7. A Form 23 must be renewed and filed not later than 60 days after the date of filing of the original Form 23 and thereafter not later than 28 days after the latest filing until a Form 23 has been filed with the Commission and with each stock exchange in Canada on which the security is listed stating the number of securities specified in the original Form 23 that have been sold and, if any of the securities specified in the original Form 23 have not been sold, that those securities are no longer for sale.

September 1, 1988

This is the form of Statement of Material Facts required by Section 116 of the regulations.

FORM 24

Securities Act

SUPERINTENDENT OF BROKERS

AND

VANCOUVER STOCK EXCHANGE

STATEMENT OF MATERIAL FACTS (# _____)

EFFECTIVE DATE: _____

NAME OF ISSUER, ADDRESS OF HEAD OFFICE AND TELEPHONE NUMBER
_____

ADDRESS OF REGISTERED AND RECORDS OFFICES OF ISSUER
_____

NAME AND ADDRESS OF REGISTRAR & TRANSFER AGENT FOR ISSUER'S SECURITIES IN BRITISH COLUMBIA
_____

OFFERING:

Agent / Underwriter:

Neither the Superintendent of Brokers nor the Vancouver Stock Exchange has in any way passed upon the merits of the securities offered hereunder and any representation to the contrary is an offence.

General Instructions

(1) The answers to the following items should be presented in narrative form, except where a tabular form is specifically required.

(2) "Issuer" shall include any subsidiary of the issuer.

(3) "Market maker" means a person who buys and sells securities of the issuer on a continuous basis with a view to creating and/or maintaining an orderly market for the securities of the issuer.

(4) "Year", except where the context otherwise requires, means a period of twelve months preceding the date of the certificate of the directors and promoters of the issuer.

(5) Financial statements and summaries of engineering reports, feasibility studies and market studies shall be incorporated in the statement of material facts and must precede the certificate of the directors and promoters of the issuer.

(6) When the answer to any item refers to an issuer other than the issuer whose securities are the subject of the distribution, disclose the name of any individual who is an insider or promoter of both of the issuers.

Cover Page

(1) Set out in tabular form, on the front cover of the statement of material facts: the description, designation and number of securities being offered by the issuer or selling shareholder; the price per security; the underwriting discount or commission; and the net proceeds or estimated net proceeds to the issuer or selling shareholder on both a per security and an aggregate basis. If it is not possible to state the price or the amount of the underwriting discount or commission, the method by which such amounts are to be calculated shall be explained.

(2) Where the securities offered are speculative in nature, the following statement shall be included on the front cover of the statement of material facts: "The securities offered hereunder are speculative in nature. Information concerning the risks involved may be obtained by reference to this document; further clarification, if required, may be sought from a broker."

1. Plan of Distribution

(1) State the manner in which the securities being offered are to be distributed, including the particulars of any underwriting or option agreements and sub-underwriting or suboption agreements outstanding or proposed to be given, the particulars of any assignments or proposed assignments of any such agreements and any rights of first refusal on future offerings.

(2) Give particulars of any payments in cash or securities or any other consideration made or to be made to a promoter, finder or any other person in connection with the offering.

(3) Where the issuer has a market maker, state name, address and the approximate number of securities of the issuer under his control.

(4) State the number of securities of the issuer beneficially owned, directly or indirectly, by the underwriter or agent, as the case may be.

(5) If any securities are offered by a selling security holder, state name, address, number of securities beneficially owned by him, directly or indirectly, number being offered and number to be owned by him after the offering. State that the securities of any selling security holder will not be sold until the distribution of the issuer's securities has been completed.

2. How the Net Proceeds of the Issue are to be Spent

(1) Set out in a tabular form the principal purposes for which the net proceeds and any material amounts of working capital on hand will be used and the estimated amount to be spent on each.

(2) In the case of a best efforts offering, include a statement regarding priority usage of the actual proceeds where the entire offering is not sold.

(3) In the event that proceeds from this offering will be insufficient to rectify any material working capital deficiency, explain how such working capital deficiency will be rectified so as to render the issuer solvent upon completion of the offering.

(4) State the particulars of any provisions or arrangements made for holding any part of the net proceeds in trust or subject to the fulfillment of any conditions howsoever imposed.

3. Material Natural Resource Properties

(1) Summary of Material Mining Properties - Furnish in substantially the tabular form indicated below the information specified for those mining properties which fall into Groups I, II and III as defined in the heading to the table. Include these definitions in the table heading in the statement of material facts.

SUMMARY OF MATERIAL MINING PROPERTIES

Group I - Properties for which regulatory approval has been obtained under this statement of material facts.

Group II - Presently held properties which are currently producing or being explored, or upon which exploration is planned within the next year.

Group III - Other presently held properties upon which the issuer's acquisition and exploration costs to date exceed $100,000.

Group	Property Name	Issuer's Acquisition and Exploration Costs to Date (in $)	Shares Issued To Date	Planned Expenditure from Funds Available upon Completion of the Offering
I				
II				
III				

Instructions for completing the above summary:

(a)   List properties in alphabetical order within each group.

(b)   Costs to date should be stated on an accrual basis (i.e. cash paid out as well as amounts currently due but not yet paid).

(c)   Include under "Planned Expenditure" only amounts included in Item 2(1). Do not include proceeds from the exercise of warrants or options.

(2)   Oil and Gas Properties with Undiscovered Reserves of over $1,000,000 - For issuers whose total undiscounted reserves of oil and gas exceed $1,000,000, provide the following information in substantially tabular form indicated below.

SUMMARY OF ESTIMATED NET RESERVES OF OIL AND GAS
PROPERTIES BY JURISDICTION AND CATEGORY

Jurisdiction	Category	Quantity OIL (BBLS)	GAS (MMCF)	Present Value of Net Cash Flow Undiscounted OIL	GAS	15% OIL	GAS
a) Canada	Proved – Producing Proved – Non-Producing Probable – Additional						
Subtotal							
b) U.S.A.	Proved – Producing Proved – Non-Producing Probable – Additional						
Subtotal							
c) _____ Other Jurisdiction	Proved – Producing Proved – Non-Producing Probable – Additional						
Subtotal							
Total							

Notes to the above table:

(a) The values reported above are _____ income tax.
(before, after)

(b) The values reported above may not necessarily be the fair market value of the reserves.

(3) Summary of Applicable to all Oil and Gas Properties Furnish in substantially the tabular form indicated in Appendix A the information specified for those oil and gas properties which fall into Groups I, II and III as defined in the heading to the table. Include these definitions in the table heading in the statement of material facts.

(4) Narrative Information:

(a) For each property listed in the summaries referred to in Items 3(1) and 3(3) above, provide the information specified in Item 3(4)(c) below. For Group I properties, also provide the information specified in Item 3(4)(d) below.

(b) Order of information:

i) The narrative information with respect to mining properties should follow the table referred to in Item 3(1) and the narrative information with respect to oil and gas properties should follow the table referred to in Item 3(3). The table referred to in Item 3(2), if applicable, should immediately precede the table referred to in Item 3(3).

ii) Properties should be described in the same order as listed on the tables and under the same headings (Group Properties for which regulatory approval has been obtained under this statement of material facts, etc. . . .)

(c) Information required for all properties listed:

i) Describe the interest owned or to be acquired by the issuer. The description should include the issuer's contribution to costs and share in revenues where these are not identical and should describe any applicable royalties, net smelter returns, carried interests, etc.

ii) Briefly describe any material exploration and development work carried out on the property to date, the results thereof and any exploration and development work which the issuer proposes to carry out on the property.

iii) Disclose any commitments respecting the property (such as installments of cash or shares required to maintain options, commitments to carry out exploration programs or drilling obligations required to maintain leases).

iv) Mining Properties – If work done on the property has established the existence and reserves of proven, probable or possible ore, disclose the estimated tonnage and grade of each such class of ore reserves as well as the name of the person making the estimates and the nature of his relationship to the issuer. If the property has no known ore reserves, so disclose.

Oil and Gas Properties – If reserves have been assigned in an independent engineering report acceptable to the regulatory authorities, identify the report by author and date, and state the category (proved producing, proved nonproducing, probable additional), type (crude oil, synthetic oil, natural gas, natural gas liquids, sulphur) and values assigned on a net cash-flow basis, using discount rates of 0% and 15%. If the property has no known reserves of oil and gas, so disclose.

v) For each property which is currently producing, state the total revenue generated, net to the issuer's interest, (a) in the latest complete fiscal year and (b) currently, on a monthly basis.

(d)   Additional information required for Group I properties:

    i) Disclose the name and address of the vendor.

    ii) If the property was acquired by the vendor within a year of the issuer's acquisition, state the cost of the property to the vendor.

    iii) If an insider or promoter of the issuer has held any interest in the property during the past three years, so disclose.

    iv) State the total consideration paid or payable by the issuer, including that information required by Item (3)(4)(c)(iii).

4.   *Particulars of Non-Resource Assets*

Where the issuer is engaged or proposes to engage, in whole or in part, in a business other than for the exploration and development of natural resources:

(1)   Briefly describe the business carried on or intended to be carried on by the issuer and the general development of such business within the past three years. Where applicable, provide a market or feasibility study or a summary thereof.

(2)   If the business consists of the production or distribution of various products or the rendering of various services, briefly describe the principal products or services.

(3)   State briefly the location and general character of any material properties, including buildings and plants, of the issuer. If any property is not freehold property, so state and briefly describe the nature of the title. If a property is subject to any material encumbrance, briefly describe the same.

(4)   If the issuer proposes to make a material acquisition of an asset, property or existing business, provide the following information:

    (a) Disclose the name and address of the vendor.

    (b) If the asset, property or business was acquired by the vendor within a year of the issuer's acquisition, state the cost thereof to the vendor.

    (c) If an insider or promoter of the issuer has held any interest in the asset, property or business during the past three years, so disclose.

    (d) State the total consideration paid or payable by the issuer.

    (e) Describe the interest owned or to be acquired by the issuer.

5.   *Corporation Information*

(1)   Give details of the place, date and method of incorporation, and of any change of name or reorganization which has taken place within the past three years. If the shares of the issuer have been consolidated or subdivided within the past three years, give the date and the ratio.

(2)   State the authorized and issued share capital of the issuer and outline briefly any material rights and restrictions attaching to the share capital, such as voting, preference, conversion or redemption rights.

(3)   Disclose details of any shares issued since the date of the latest financial statements included in the statement of material facts.

6.   *Directors, Officers, Promoters and Persons Holding More Than 10% of the Issued Voting Shares*

(1)   For each director, officer and promoter of the issuer, provide the following information:

    (a) State full name and residential or postal address.

    (b) Identify all positions held with the issuer (such as chairman, director, president, secretary, promoter).

    (c) State the number of voting shares of the issuer beneficially owned, directly or indirectly, separated by class into (a) escrowed, (b) pooled and (c) all other shares.

(d) State the name of each employer and give chief occupation in the previous five years. If the employer is a self-owned company, so state. Occupational descriptions should describe the function actually performed; vague descriptions such as "businessman" should be avoided.

(2) If any director, officer or promoter of the issuer is, or has been within the past three years, a director, officer or promoter of any other reporting issuer, provide the following information:

(a) State the number of such issuers of which he is currently a director, officer or promoter. Indicate that a list of the names of such issuers will be available for inspection at the location and during the times specified in Item 9(5).

(b) State the name of any such issuer which was, during the period he was a director, officer or promoter of the issuer, struck off the register of companies by the British Columbia Registrar of Companies, or other similar authority, or whose securities were the subject of a cease trade or suspension order for a period of more than thirty consecutive days. Describe as well the reasons for such striking, cease trade or suspension order.

(3) (a) If any director, officer, promoter or insider has received direct or indirect remuneration from the issuer within the past year, state particulars, including name of recipient, level of remuneration and duties performed.

(b) If any director, officer, promoter or insider has received anything of value from the issuer within the past year which has not been disclosed elsewhere in the statement of material facts, state particulars. Anything of value includes money, securities, property, contracts, options or rights of any kind, whether received directly or indirectly.

(4) Give the full name, residential or postal address and number of voting shares, separated by class into (a) escrowed, (b) pooled and (c) all other voting shares, beneficially owned by each person who is known by the signatories hereto to own beneficially, directly or indirectly, more than 10% of the voting shares of the issuer, other than those persons disclosed in Item 6(1). Where the beneficial owner is a corporation, provide the information required by General Instruction (8).

7. *Options to Purchase Securities of the Issuer*

(1) Disclose all options, share purchase warrants or rights, other than those disclosed in Items 1 and 3, granted to an insider or promoter of the issuer or by a present security holder.

(2) Options granted to employees may be shown in the aggregate.

8. *Securities of the Issuer Held in Escrow, in Pool or Subject to Hold Restrictions*

(1) Briefly describe the number of and the material terms governing release and cancellation of all escrow shares.

(2) Briefly describe the number of and the material terms governing release of all pooled shares.

(3) State the number of and briefly describe the material terms governing any other securities which are subject to an unexpired hold period originally imposed by the superintendent.

9. *Particulars of any Other Material Facts*

(1) Briefly describe any actual or pending material legal proceedings to which the issuer is or is likely to be a party or of which any of its property is or is likely to be the subject.

(2) Specify any properties proposed to be acquired for which regulatory approval is not being sought under the statement of material facts.

(3) If liabilities (including bonds, debentures, notes or other debt obligations) have significantly increased or altered subsequent to the date of the finan-

cial statements included in the statement of material facts, disclose particulars of such increase or alteration.

(4) Briefly state any other material facts not previously disclosed herein.

(5) State a reasonable time and place at which the following documents may be inspected during the distribution of the securities offered hereunder and for 30 days after completion of such distribution:

(a) all contracts referred to in the statement of material facts;

(b) all technical reports summarized or referred to in Items 3 and 4; and

(c) a list of the names of the reporting issuer referred to in Item 6(2)(a).

10. *The financial statements to be provided shall contain at least the undermentioned information:*

(1) An Emerging Growth Industrial Issuer is, for the purposes of this form, considered to be an issuer that is in the process of developing its productive capacity and requires the introduction of capital in order to sustain itself.

(2) Where the issuer is an emerging growth industrial issuer or a natural resource issuer not yet in production the following financial statements will be required for the latest financial year and any part of a subsequent financial year:

(a) a balance sheet;

(b) a statement of surplus or deficit:

(c) a statement of changes in financial position;

(d) an analysis of deferred charges, segregating where applicable expenditures for research, development and exploration, as the case may be, from expenditures for administration and showing the totals for each.

(3) The balance sheet of the Issuer shall be as at a date not more than 60 days before the date of the submission of the statement of material facts.

(4) Where the financial statements are prepared for part of a financial year:

(a) comparative figures for the comparable period in the prior year are not required; and

(b) may be prepared by a public accountant or by management, but if a public accountant has assisted in their preparation a copy of the auditor's communication suggested for these circumstances by the handbook of the Canadian Institute of Chartered Accountants shall be provided the Superintendent and the Exchange.

(5) Where the issuer is an industrial issuer having an acceptable sales base on which an income statement is meaningful or where the issuer is a natural resource issuer in production, the financial statements shall comprise of at least:

(a) an income statement;

(b) a statement of surplus or deficit;

(c) a statement of changes in financial position; and

(d) a balance sheet.

11. *Statutory Rights of Rescission*

Include only the following statement: "The British Columbia Securities Act provides purchasers with the right to rescind a contract for the purchase of securities where the statement of material facts and any existing amendments thereto either contain a misrepresentation or are not delivered to the purchaser before delivery of the written confirmation of sale. For further information concerning these rights, and the time limits within which they must be exercised, refer to Sections 66, 114 and 118 of the Securities Act or consult a lawyer."

12. *Close the Statement of Material Facts with the Following Certificates*

(1) Certificate of the directors and promoters of the issuer:

The foregoing constitutes full, true and plain disclosure of all material facts relating to the securities offered by this statement of material facts as required by the Securities Act and its regulations.

_____
Date

(a) This certificate must be signed in accordance with and subject to Section 49 of the Act.

(b) Identify each signature and signing capacity of the signatory.

(2) Certificate of the Underwriter(s)/Agent(s):

Where an underwriter is in a contractual relationship with the issuer or a security holder of the securities offered, the following certificate shall be signed by the underwriter or, where duly authorized in writing, the underwriter's agent.

To the best of our knowledge, information and belief, the foregoing constitutes full, true and plain disclosure of all material facts relating to the securities offered by this statement of material facts as required by the Securities Act and its regulations.

_____
Date

APPENDIX A

SUMMARY OF MATERIAL OIL AND GAS PROPERTIES

Group I - Properties for which regulatory approval has been obtained under this statement of material facts.

Group II - Presently held properties which are currently producing or being explored, upon which exploration is planned within the next year or which have undiscounted reserves in excess of $50,000 or current revenue in excess of $1,000 a month.

Group III - Other presently held properties upon which the issuer's acquisition and exploration costs to date exceed $100,000.

Group	Description	Undiscounted Value of Existing Reserves Net to the Issuer's Interest, as of Date of Report	Present Value of Existing Reserves (15% Discount Rate) Net to the Issuer's Interest, as of Date of Report
I			
II			
III			

Group	Issuer's Acquisition and Exploration Costs to Date (in $)	Shares Issued To Date	Issuer's Revenue To Date (in $)	Planned Expenditure from Funds Available upon Completion of the Offering
I				
II				
III				

Forms

Instructions for completing the above summary:

(a)   List properties in alphabetical order within each group.

(b)   Costs to date should be stated on an accrual basis (i.e. cash paid out as well as amounts currently due but not yet paid).

(c)   Include under "Planned Expenditure" only amounts included in Item 2(1). Do not include proceeds from the exercise of warrants or options.

This is the form of put option Contract required under Section 58(b) of the Securities Act.

FORM 25

Securities Act

PUT OPTION CONTRACT

_____, 19_____.

FOR VALUE RECEIVED, We agree to BUY from the Bearer _____ shares of the _____ stock of the _____ at _____ DOLLARS ($_____) per share AT ANY TIME WITHIN _____ days from date of contract.

THIS OPTION CONTRACT MAY BE EXERCISED BY PRESENTING IT TO THE UNDERSIGNED BEFORE THE EXACT EXPIRY DATE. IT WILL NOT BE ACCEPTED AFTER IT HAS EXPIRED AND CAN NOT BE EXERCISED BY TELEPHONE.

TERMS OF THIS CONTRACT PROVIDE:

(1)   On the day that the stock covered by this option sells ex-dividend, the contract price shall be reduced by the value of such cash dividend.

(2)   If the stock covered by this option is entitled to rights and/or warrants, the specified contract price shall be reduced by the value of such rights and/or warrants as fixed by the opening sale thereof on the day the stock sells ex-rights and/or ex-warrants. There will be no physical delivery of rights and/or warrants upon the exercise of this option.

(3)   In the event of a stock split or other similar action the share value of this option will become the equivalent in new securities when duly listed for trading and the total contract price shall not change.

(4)   Stock dividends shall be attached to the stock carried herewith when and if this option is exercised and the total contract price shall not be changed.

(5)   Upon presentation of this option to the undersigned within the time specified, the undersigned agrees to accept notice of the Bearer's exercise by acknowledging presentation of this option which shall constitute a contract and shall be controlling with respect to delivery of the stock and settlement in accordance with (recognized) Stock Exchange procedures.

THIS CONTRACT WILL EXPIRE AT EXACTLY 3:15 P.M. ON

_____ , 19_____.

If the (recognized) Stock Exchange is not in session at the expiry time due to a legal holiday, emergency closing or for any other reason, then this contract will expire at 3:15 p.m. at the next (recognized) Stock Exchange session following.

(Name of Member Firm or Member Corporation)

CONTRACT PRICE ADJUSTMENTS

Original Contract Price _____ $_____

	Date	Amount
Ex-Dividend	_____	_____
Ex-Dividend	_____	_____
NET CONTRACT PRICE		_____
		_____

This option contract has been presented for exercise on _____ , 19___ , by _____ in accordance with provisions as set out in this contract.

_____
(Name of Member Firm or Member Corporation)

This is the form of call option contract required under Section 58(b) of the Securities Act.

FORM 26

Securities Act

CALL OPTION CONTRACT

_____ , 19___.

FOR VALUE RECEIVED, We agree to SELL to the Bearer _____ shares of the _____ stock of the _____ at _____ DOLLARS ($_____) per share AT ANY TIME WITHIN _____ days from the date of contract.

THIS OPTION CONTRACT MAY BE EXERCISED BY PRESENTING IT TO THE UNDERSIGNED BEFORE THE EXACT EXPIRY DATE. IT WILL NOT BE ACCEPTED AFTER IT HAS EXPIRED AND CANNOT BE EXERCISED BY TELEPHONE.

TERMS OF THIS CONTRACT PROVIDE:

(1) On the day that the stock covered by this option sells ex-dividend, the contract price shall be reduced by the value of such cash dividend.

(2) If the stock covered by this option is entitled to rights and/or warrants the specified contract price shall be reduced by the value of such rights and/or warrants as fixed by the opening sale thereof on the day the stock sells ex-rights and/or ex-warrants. There will be no physical delivery of rights and/or warrants upon the exercise of this option.

(3) In the event of a stock split or other similar action the share value of this option will become the equivalent in new securities when duly listed for trading and the total contract price shall not change.

(4) Stock dividends shall be attached to the stock carried herewith when and if this option is exercised and the total contract price shall not change.

(5) Upon presentation of this option to the undersigned within the time specified the undersigned agrees to accept notice of the Bearer's exercise by acknowledging presentation of this option which shall constitute a contract and shall be controlling with respect to delivery of the stock and settlement in accordance with (recognized) Stock Exchange procedures.

THIS CONTRACT WILL EXPIRE AT EXACTLY 3:15 P.M. ON _____ , 19___.

If the (recognized) Stock Exchange is not in session at the expiry time due to a legal holiday, emergency closing or for any other reason, then this contract will expire at 3:15 p.m. at the next (recognized) Stock Exchange session following.

(Name of Member Firm or Member Corporation)

CONTRACT PRICE ADJUSTMENTS

Original Contract Price _____ $ _____

	Date	Amount
Ex-Dividend	_____	_____
Ex-Dividend	_____	_____
NET CONTRACT PRICE		_____

_____

This option contract has been presented for exercise on _____, 19___, by _____ in accordance with provisions as set out in this contract.

_____

(Name of Member Firm or Member Corporation)

This is the form of a material change report required under Section 67(1) of the Securities Act.

FORM 27

Securities Act

MATERIAL CHANGE REPORT UNDER SECTION 67(1) OF THE ACT

NOTE: This form is intended as a guideline. A letter or other document may be used if the substantive requirements of this form are complied with.

NOTE: Every report required to be filed under section 67(1) of the Act shall be sent to the Commission in an envelope addressed to the Commission and marked "Continuous Disclosure."

NOTE: WHERE THIS REPORT IS FILED ON A CONFIDENTIAL BASIS PUT AT THE BEGINNING OF THE REPORT IN BLOCK CAPITALS "CONFIDENTIAL SECTION 67", AND EVERYTHING THAT IS REQUIRED TO BE FILED SHALL BE PLACED IN AN ENVELOPE ADDRESSED TO THE SECRETARY OF THE COMMISSION MARKED "CONFIDENTIAL."

Item 1. *Reporting Issuer*

State the full name and address of the principal office in Canada of the reporting issuer.

Item 2. *Date of Material Change*

Item 3. *Press Release*

State the date and place of issuance of the press release issued pursuant to Section 67(1) of the Act.

Item 4. *Summary of Material Change*

Provide a brief but accurate summary of the nature and substance of the material change.

Item 5. *Full Description of Material Change*

Supplement the summary required under Item 4 with the disclosure which should be sufficiently complete to enable a reader to appreciate the significance of the material change without reference to other material. Management is in the best position to determine what facts are significant and must disclose those facts in a meaningful manner. See also Item 7.

This description of the significant facts relating to the material change will therefore include some or all of the following: dates, parties, terms and conditions, description of any assets, liabilities or capital affected, purpose, financial or dollar values, reasons for the change, and a general comment on the probable impact on the reporting issuer or its subsidiaries. Specific financial forecasts would not normally be required to comply with this form.

The above list merely describes examples of some of the facts which may be significant. The list is not intended to be inclusive or exhaustive of the information required in any particular situation.

Item 6. *Reliance on Section 67(2) of the Act*

If the report is being filed on a confidential basis in reliance on Section 67(2) of the Act, state the reasons for such reliance.

INSTRUCTION:

Refer to Section 67(3) of the Act concerning continuing obligations in respect of reports filed pursuant to this subsection.

Item 7. *Omitted Information*

In certain circumstances where a material change has occurred and a material change report has been or is about to be filed but Section 67(3) of the Act will no longer or will not be relied upon, a reporting issuer may nevertheless believe one or more significant facts otherwise required to be disclosed in the material change report should remain confidential and not be disclosed or not be disclosed in full detail in the material change report.

State whether any information has been omitted on this basis and provide the reasons for any such omission in sufficient detail to permit the Commission to exercise its discretion pursuant to Section 151(3) of the Act.

The reasons for the omission may be contained in a separate letter filed as provided in Section 146 of the Regulation.

Item 8. *Senior Officers*

To facilitate any necessary followup by the Commission, give the name and business telephone number of a senior officer of the reporting issuer who is knowledgeable about the material change and the report or an officer through whom such senior officer may be contacted by the Commission.

Item 9. *Statement of Senior Officer*

Include a statement in the following form signed by a senior officer of the reporting issuer:

"The foregoing accurately discloses the material change referred to herein."

Also include date and place of making the statement.

This is the form to be completed as required under Section 146 of the Securities Act Regulation.

FORM 28

Securities Act

ANNUAL FILING OF REPORTING ISSUER

NOTE: THIS FORM NEED NOT BE FILED WHERE THE MANAGEMENT OF A REPORTING ISSUER IS REQUIRED TO FILE AN INFORMATION CIRCULAR DURING ITS LAST FINANCIAL YEAR.

GENERAL INSTRUCTIONS:

1. The information contained in an information circular shall be clearly presented and the statements made therein shall be divided into groups according to subject matter and the various groups of statements shall be preceded by appropriate headings.

2. The order of items need not be followed.

3. Where practicable and appropriate, information required shall be presented in tabular form.

4. All amounts shall be stated figures.

5. Information required by more than one applicable item need not be repeated.

6. No statement need be made in response to any item that is inapplicable and negative answers to any item may be omitted.

Item 1   *Name of Reporting Issuer*

Item 2   *Jurisdiction under which Incorporated, Organized or Continued*

Item 3   *Financial Year End*

Item 4   *Voting Securities and Principal Holders of Voting Securities*

(a) State as to each class of voting securities of the reporting issuer, the number of securities outstanding and the voting rights for each security of each class.

(b) If, to the knowledge of the directors or senior officers of the reporting issuer, any person beneficially owns, directly or indirectly, or exercises control or direction over, voting securities carrying more than 10 per cent of the voting rights attached to any class of voting securities of the reporting issuer, name each such person, state the approximate number of the securities beneficially owned, directly or indirectly or over which control or direction is exercised, by each such person and the percentage of the class of outstanding voting securities of the reporting issuer represented by the number of voting securities so owned, controlled or directed.

Item 5   *Directors*

(a) Name each director of the reporting issuer and state the period or periods during which he has served as such.

(b) State when the term of office of each director will expire.

(c) State whether the reporting issuer has an executive committee of its board of directors or is required to have an audit committee of the board of directors and, if so, name those directors who are members of each such committee.

(d) State all other positions and offices with the reporting issuer held by each director.

(e) State the present principal occupation, business or employment of each director. Give the name and principal business of any person in which any such employment is carried on.

(f) State the number of securities of each class of voting securities of the reporting issuer or of any subsidiary of the reporting issuer beneficially owned, directly or indirectly, or over which control or direction is exercised by each director.

(g) If voting securities carrying 10 per cent of the voting rights attached to any class of voting securities of the reporting issuer or of a subsidiary of the reporting issuer are beneficially owned, directly or indirectly or controlled or directed by any director and his associates or affiliates, state the number of securities of each class of voting securities beneficially owned, directly or indirectly or controlled or directed by the associates or affiliates naming each associate or affiliate whose security holdings are 10 per cent or more.

Item 6   *Executive Compensation*

Complete and attach to or include in this form a Statement of Executive Compensation in Form 41.

Item 7   *Indebtedness of Directors, Executive Officers and Senior Officers*

(a) The information required by this Item must be provided for each individual who is, or at any time during the most recently completed financial year, was a director, executive officer and senior officer of the issuer, each proposed nominee for election as a director of the issuer, and each associate of any such director, officer or proposed nominee,

    (i) who is, or at any time since the beginning of the most recently completed financial year of the issuer has been, indebted to the issuer or any of its subsidiaries, or

    (ii) whose indebtedness to another entity is, or at any time since the beginning of the most recently completed financial year has been, the subject of a guarantee, support agreement, letter of credit or other similar arrangement or understanding provided by the issuer or any of its subsidiaries.

(b) State in the tabular form under the caption set out, for any indebtedness referred to in paragraph (a) of this Item that was entered into in connection with a purchase of securities of the issuer or any of its subsidiaries:

    (i) The name of the borrower (column (a)).

    (ii) If the borrower is a director, executive officer or senior officer, the principal position of the borrower. If the borrower was, during the year, but no longer is a director or officer, include a statement to that effect. If the borrower is a proposed nominee for election as a director, include a statement to that effect. If the borrower is included as an associate describe briefly the relationship of the borrower to an individual who is or, during the year, was a director, executive officer or senior officer or who is a proposed nominee for election as a director, name that individual and provide the information required by this subparagraph for that individual (column (a)).

    (iii) Whether the issuer or a subsidiary of the issuer is the lender or the provider of a guarantee, support agreement, letter of credit or similar arrangement or understanding (column (b)).

    (iv) The largest aggregate amount of the indebtedness outstanding at any time during the last completed financial year (column (c)).

    (v) The aggregate amount of indebtedness outstanding as at a date within thirty days of certification of the annual filing (column (d)).

    (vi) Separately for each class or series of securities, the sum of the number of securities purchased during the last completed financial year with the financial assistance (column (e)).

    (vii) The security for the indebtedness, if any, provided to the issuer, any of its subsidiaries or the other entity (column (f)).

TABLE OF INDEBTEDNESS OF DIRECTORS, EXECUTIVE OFFICERS AND SENIOR OFFICERS UNDER SECURITIES PURCHASE PROGRAMS

Name and Principal Position (a)	Involvement of Issuer or Subsidiary (b)	Largest Amount Outstanding During [Last Completed Financial Year] ($) (c)	Amount Outstanding as at [current date] ($) (d)	Financially Assisted Securities Purchases During [Last Completed Financial Year] (#) (e)	Security for Indebtedness (f)

(c) State in the introduction immediately preceding the table required by paragraph (b) of this Item, for indebtedness entered into in connection with a purchase of securities of the issuer or any of its subsidiaries, separately, the aggregate indebtedness,

(i) to the issuer or any of its subsidiaries, and

(ii) to another entity if the indebtedness is the subject of a guarantee, support agreement, letter of credit or other similar arrangement or understanding provided by the issuer or any of its subsidiaries,

of all officers, directors, employees and former officers, directors and employees of the issuer or any of its subsidiaries outstanding as at a date within thirty days of certification of the annual filing.

(d) State in the tabular form under the caption set out, for any indebtedness referred to in paragraph (a) of this Item that was not entered into in connection with a purchase of securities of the issuer or any of its subsidiaries, the information referred to in subparagraphs (b) (i) through (v) of this Item.

TABLE OF INDEBTEDNESS OF DIRECTORS, EXECUTIVE OFFICERS AND SENIOR OFFICERS [insert if the issuer has a securities purchase program "OTHER THAN UNDER SECURITIES PURCHASE PROGRAMS"]

Name and Principal Position (a)	Involvement of Issuer or Subsidiary (b)	Largest Amount Outstanding During [Last Completed Financial Year] ($) (c)	Amount Outstanding as at [current date] ($) (d)

(e) State in the introduction immediately preceding the table required by paragraph (d) of this Item, for indebtedness not entered into in connection with a purchase of securities of the issuer or any of its subsidiaries, separately, the aggregate indebtedness,

(i) to the issuer or any of its subsidiaries, and

(ii) to another entity if the indebtedness is the subject of a guarantee, support agreement, letter of credit or other similar arrangement or understanding provided by the issuer or any of its subsidiaries,

of all officers, directors, employees and former officers, directors and employees of the issuer or any of its subsidiaries outstanding as at a date within thirty days of certification of the annual filing.

(f) Disclose in a footnote to, or a narrative accompanying, each table required by this Item,

(i) the material terms of each incidence of indebtedness and, if applicable, of each guarantee, support agreement, letter of credit or other similar arrangement or understanding, including without limitation the term to maturity, rate of interest and any understanding, agreement or intention to limit recourse, and for the table required by paragraph (d) only, any security for the indebtedness and the nature of the transaction in which the indebtedness was incurred,

(ii) any material adjustment or amendment made during the most recently completed financial year to the terms of the indebtedness and, if applicable, the guarantee, support agreement, letter of credit or similar arrangement or understanding, and

(iii) the class or series of the securities purchased with financial assistance or held as security for the indebtedness and, if the class or series of securities is not publicly traded, all material terms of the securities, including but not limited to provisions for exchange, conversion, exercise, redemption, retraction and dividends.

(g) No disclosure need be made under this Item of an incidence of indebtedness that has been entirely repaid on or before the date of certification of the annual filing or of routine indebtedness.

"Routine indebtedness" means indebtedness described in any of the following clauses:

(i) If an issuer makes loans to employees generally, whether or not in the ordinary course of business, loans are considered routine indebtedness if made on terms, including those as to interest rate and security, no more favourable to the borrower than the terms on which loans are made by the issuer to employees generally, but the amount at any time during the last completed financial year remaining unpaid under the loans to any one director, executive officer, senior officer or proposed nominee together with his or her associates that are treated as routine indebtedness under this clause must not exceed $25,000.

(ii) Whether or not the issuer makes loans in the ordinary course of business, a loan to a director, executive officer or senior officer is considered routine indebtedness if,

A. the borrower is a full-time employee of the issuer,

B. the loan is fully secured against the residence of the borrower, and

C. the amount of the loan does not exceed the annual salary of the borrower.

(iii) If the issuer makes loans in the ordinary course of business, a loan is considered routine indebtedness if made to a person or company other than a full-time employee of the issuer, and if the loan,

A. is made on substantially the same terms, including those as to interest rate and security, as are available when a loan is made to other customers of the issuer with comparable credit ratings, and

B. involves no more than usual risks of collectibility.

(iv) Indebtedness arising by reason of purchases made on usual trade terms or of ordinary travel or expense advances, or for similar reasons is considered routine indebtedness if the repayment arrangements are in accord with usual commercial practice.

(h) For purposes of this Item, "executive officer" has the same meaning as in Form 41 and "support agreement" includes, but is not limited to, an agreement to provide assistance in the maintenance or servicing of any indebtedness and an agreement to provide compensation for the purpose of maintaining or servicing any indebtedness of the borrower.

See NIN 93/23 "Executive Compensation".

Item 8   *Interests of Insiders in Material Transactions*

Describe briefly and, where practicable, state the approximate amount of any material interest, direct or indirect, of any insider of the reporting issuer or any associate or affiliate of any insider of the reporting issuer in any transaction since the commencement of the reporting issuer's last financial year or in any proposed transaction which has materially affected or would materially affect the reporting issuer or any of its subsidiaries.

INSTRUCTIONS:

1. Give a brief description of the material transaction. Include the name and address of each person whose interest in any transaction is described and the nature of the relationship by reason of which such interest is required to be described.

2. As to any transaction involving the purchase or sale of assets by or to the reporting issuer or any of its subsidiaries, otherwise than in the ordinary course of business, state the cost of the assets to the purchaser and the cost thereof to the seller if acquired by the seller within two years to the transaction.

3. This item does not apply to any interest arising from the ownership of securities of the issuer where the securityholder receives no extra or special benefit or advantage not shared on an equal basis by all other holders of the same class of securities or all other holders of the same class of securities who are resident in Canada.

4. Information shall be included as to any material underwriting discounts or commissions upon the sale of securities by the reporting issuer where any of the specified persons was or is to be an underwriter who was or is to be in a contractual relationship with the reporting issuer with respect to securities of the reporting issuer or is an associate, affiliate or partner of a person, or partnership that was or is to be an underwriter.

5. No information need be given in answer to this item as to any transaction or any interest therein, where,

    (a) the rates or charges involved in the transaction are fixed by law or determined by competitive bids;

    (b) the interest of a specified person in the transaction is solely that of a director of another company that is a party to the transaction;

    (c) the transaction involves services as a bank or other depository of funds, transfer agent, registrar, trustee under a trust indenture or other similar services;

    (d) the transaction does not, directly or indirectly, involve remuneration for services, and,

         (i) the interest of the specified person arose from the beneficial ownership, direct or indirect, of less than 10 per cent of any class of voting securities of another company that is a party to the transaction,

         (ii) the transaction is in the ordinary course of business of the issuer or its subsidiaries, and

         (iii) the amount of the transaction or series of transactions is less than 10 per cent of the total sales or purchases, as the case may be, of the issuer and its subsidiaries for the last completed financial year.

6. Information shall be furnished in answer to this item with respect to transactions not excluded above that involve remuneration, directly or indirectly, to any of the specified persons for services in any capacity unless the interest of the person arises solely from the beneficial ownership, direct or indirect, of less than 10 per cent of any class of voting securities of another company furnishing the services to the issuer or its subsidiaries.

7. This item does not require the disclosure of any interest in any transaction unless such interest and transaction are material.

Item 9   *Auditor of the Reporting Issuer*

Name the auditor of the reporting issuer. If the auditor was first appointed within the last five years, state the date when the auditor was first appointed.

Item 10   *Management Contracts*

Where management functions of the reporting issuer or any subsidiary of the reporting issuer are to any substantial degree performed by a person other than the directors or senior officers of the reporting issuer or subsidiary:

    (i) give details of the agreement or arrangement under which the management functions are performed, including the name and address of any person who is a party to the agreement or arrangement or who is responsible for performing the management functions;

    (ii) give the names and home addresses in full or, alternatively, solely the municipality of residence or postal address, of the insiders of the person with which the reporting issuer or subsidiary has any such agreement or arrangement and, if the following information is known to the directors or senior officers of the reporting issuer, give the names and addresses of any person that would be an insider of any person with which the reporting issuer or subsidiary has any such agreement or arrangement if the person were a reporting issuer;

(iii) with respect to any person named in answer to paragraph (i), state the amounts paid or payable by the reporting issuer and its subsidiaries to the person since the commencement of the reporting issuer's last financial year and give particulars; and

(iv) with respect to any person named in answer to paragraph (i) or (ii) and their associates and affiliates, give particulars of,

(a) any indebtedness of the person, associate or affiliate to the reporting issuer or its subsidiaries that was outstanding, and

(b) any transaction or arrangement of the person, associate or affiliate with the reporting issuer or subsidiary,

at any time since the commencement of the reporting issuer's last financial year.

INSTRUCTIONS:

1. In giving the information called for by this item, it is not necessary to refer to any matter that in all the circumstances is relative insignificance.

2. In giving particulars of indebtedness, state the largest aggregate amount of indebtedness outstanding at any time during the period, the nature of the indebtedness and of the transaction in which it was incurred, the amount of indebtedness presently outstanding and the rate of interest paid or charged on the indebtedness.

3. It is not necessary to include as indebtedness amounts due from the particular person for purchases subject to usual trade terms, for ordinary travel and expense advances and for other like transactions.

The Finance Company Questionnaire and Financial Report required by Section 142 of the Securities Act Regulations shall be in the following form.

FORM 29

Securities Act

FINANCE COMPANY QUESTIONNAIRE AND FINANCIAL REPORT

INSTRUCTION:

The Finance Company Questionnaire and Financial Report shall be Form 29 required by the Ontario Securities Commission, amended as necessary for the change of jurisdiction.

January 19, 1987

The information circular required by Section 101 of the Act shall be in the following form.

FORM 30

Securities Act

INFORMATION CIRCULAR

GENERAL INSTRUCTIONS:

1. The information contained in an information circular shall be given for a specified date *not more than 30 days before the date on which the circular is first sent* to any security holder.

2. The information contained in an information circular shall be clearly presented and the statements made therein shall be divided into groups according to subject matter and the various groups of statements shall be preceded by appropriate headings.

3. The order of items need not be followed.

4. Where practicable and appropriate, information required shall be presented in tabular form.

5. All amounts shall be stated in figures.

6. Information required by more than one applicable item need not be repeated.

7. No statement need be made in response to any item that is inapplicable and negative answers to any item may be omitted.

8. Information that is not known to the person on whose behalf the solicitation is to be made and that is not reasonably within the power of the person to ascertain or procure may be omitted if a brief statement is made in the information circular of the circumstances rendering the information unavailable.

9. There may be omitted from the information circular any information contained in any other information circular, notice of meeting or form of proxy sent to the persons whose proxies were solicited in connection with the same meeting if reference is made to the particular document containing the information.

Item 1 – Revocability of Proxy

State whether the person giving the proxy has the power to revoke it. If any right of revocation is limited or is subject to compliance with any formal procedure, briefly describe the limitation or procedure.

Item 2 – Persons making the Solicitation

(a) If solicitation is made by or on behalf of the management of the reporting issuer, so state. Give the name of any director of the reporting issuer who has informed the management in writing that he intends to oppose any action intended to be taken by the management and indicate the action that he intends to oppose.

(b) If a solicitation is made otherwise than by or on behalf of the management of the reporting issuer, so state and give the name of the person on whose behalf it is made.

(c) If the solicitation is to be made otherwise than by mail, describe the method to be employed. If the solicitation is to be made by specially engaged employees or soliciting agents, state,

(i) the material features of any contract or arrangement for the solicitation and identify the parties to the contract or arrangement; and

(ii) the cost or anticipated cost thereof.

(d) State the name of the person by whom the cost of soliciting has been or will be borne, directly or indirectly.

INSTRUCTIONS:

1. Every form of proxy sent or delivered to a security holder of a reporting issuer by a person soliciting proxies shall indicate in bold-face type whether or not the proxy is solicited by or on behalf of the management of the reporting issuer provide a specifically designated blank space for dating the form of proxy and specify the meeting in respect of which the proxy is solicited.

2. An information circular or form of proxy shall indicate in bold-face type that the security holder has the right to appoint a person to represent him at the meeting other than the person, if any, designated in the form of proxy and shall contain instructions as to the manner in which the security holder may exercise the right.

3. If a form of proxy contains a designation of a named person as nominee, it shall provide a means whereby the security holder may designate in the form of proxy some other person as his nominee.

4. Every form of proxy shall provide a means for the security holder to specify that the securities registered in his name shall be voted for or against each matter or group of related matters identified therein or in the notice of meeting or in an information circular, other than the appointment of an auditor and the election of directors.

5. A proxy may confer discretionary authority with respect to each matter referred to in subsection (4) as to which a choice is not so specified in the form of proxy if the information circular states in bold-face type how the securities represented by the proxy will be voted in respect of each matter or group of related matters.

6. A proxy shall provide a means for the security holder to specify that the securities registered in the name of the security holder shall be voted or withheld from voting in respect of the appointment of an auditor or the election of directors.

7. A proxy or an information circular shall state that the securities represented by the proxy will be voted or withheld from voting in accordance with the instructions of the security holder on any ballot that may be called for and that, if the security holder specifies a choice under subsection (4) or (6), with respect to any matter to be acted upon, the securities shall be voted accordingly.

8. A proxy may confer discretionary authority with respect to,

    (a) amendments or variations to matters identified in the notice of meeting; and

    (b) other matters which may properly come before the meeting;

    where,

    (c) the person by whom or on whose behalf the solicitation is made is not aware within a reasonable time prior to the time the solicitation is made that any such amendment, variations or other matters are to be presented for action at the meeting; and

    (d) a specific statement is made in the information circular or in the form of proxy that the proxy is conferring such discretionary authority.

9. No proxy shall confer authority to vote,

    (a) for the election of any person or company as a director of a reporting issuer unless a bona fide proposed nominee for such election is named in the information circular; or

    (b) at any meeting other than the meeting specified in the notice of meeting or any adjournment thereof.

Item 3 – Interest of Certain Persons in Matters to be Acted Upon

Give brief particulars of any material interest, direct or indirect, by way of beneficial ownership of securities or otherwise, of each of the following persons or companies in any matter to be acted upon other than the election of directors or the appointment of auditors;

(a) if the solicitation is made by or on behalf of the management of the reporting issuer, each person who has been a director or senior officer of the reporting issuer at any time since the beginning of the last financial year of the reporting issuer;

(b) if the solicitation is made otherwise than by or on behalf of the management of the reporting issuer, each person on whose behalf, directly or indirectly, the solicitation is made;

(c) each proposed nominee for election as a director of the reporting issuer;

(d) each associate or affiliate of any of the foregoing persons.

INSTRUCTIONS:

1. The following persons shall be deemed to be persons by whom or on whose behalf the solicitation is made:

(a) any member of a committee or group that solicits proxies, and any person whether or not named as a member who, acting alone or with one or more other persons, directly or indirectly takes the initiative or engages in organizing, directing or financing any such committee or group;

(b) any person who finances or joins with another to finance the solicitations of proxies except a person who contributes not more than $250 and who is not otherwise a person by whom or on whose behalf the solicitation is made; or

(c) any person who lends money, provides credit or enters into any other arrangements, pursuant to any contract or understanding with a person by whom or on whose behalf a solicitation is made, for the purpose of financing or otherwise inducing the purchase, sale, holding or voting of securities of the reporting issuer, provided, that this clause does not include a bank or other lending institution or a dealer that, in the ordinary course of business, lends money or executes orders for the purchase or sale of securities and who is not otherwise a person on whose behalf a solicitation is made.

2. The following persons shall be deemed not to be persons by whom or on whose behalf a solicitation is made:

(a) any person retained or employed by a person by whom or on whose behalf a solicitation is made to solicit proxies and who is not otherwise a person by whom or on whose behalf a solicitation is made or any person who merely transmits proxy-soliciting material or performs ministerial or clerical duties;

(b) any person employed or retained by a person by whom or on whose behalf a solicitation is made in the capacity of lawyer, accountant, or advertising, public relations or financial adviser and whose activities are limited to the performance of his duties in the course of the employment or retainer;

(c) any person regularly employed as an officer or employee of the reporting issuer or any of its affiliates who is not otherwise a person by whom or on whose behalf a solicitation is made; or

(d) any officer or director of, or any person regularly employed by, any other person by whom or on whose behalf a solicitation is made, if the officer, director or employee is not otherwise a person by whom or on whose behalf a solicitation is made.

Item 4 – Voting Securities and Principal Holders of Voting Securities

(a) State as to each class of voting securities of the reporting issuer, entitled to be voted at the meeting, the number of securities outstanding and the voting rights for each security of each class.

(b) Give the record date as of which the security holders entitled to vote at the meeting will be determined or particulars as to the closing of the security transfer register, as the case may be, and, if the right to vote is not limited to security holders of record as of a specified record date, indicate the conditions under which security holders are entitled to vote.

(c) If, to the knowledge of the directors or senior officers of the reporting issuer, any person beneficially owns, directly or indirectly, or exercises control or direction over, voting securities carrying more than 10 per cent of the voting rights attached to any class of voting securities of the reporting issuer, name each such person, state the approximate number of the securities beneficially owned, directly or indirectly or over which control or direction is exercised, by each such person and the percentage of the class of outstanding voting securities of the reporting issuer represented by the number of voting securities so owned, controlled or directed.

Item 5 – Election of Directors

(a) If directors are to be elected, provide the following information, in tabular form to the extent practicable, for each person proposed to be nominated for election as a director and each other person whose term of office as a director will continue after the meeting:

(i) Name and identify as such each proposed director of the reporting issuer and name each director of the reporting issuer whose term of office will continue after the meeting.

(ii) State when the term of office for each director and proposed director will expire.

(iii) State whether the reporting issuer has an executive committee of its board of directors or is required to have an audit committee of the board of directors and, if so, name those directors who are members of each such committee.

(iv) Where a director or officer has held more than one position in the issuer, or a parent or subsidiary thereof, state only the first and last position held.

(v) State the present principal occupation, business or employment of each director and proposed director. Give the name and principal business of any person in which any such employment is carried on. Furnish similar information as to all of the principal occupations, businesses or employments of each proposed director within the five preceding years, unless he is now a director and was elected to his present term of office by a vote of security holders at a meeting, the notice of which was accompanied by an information circular.

(vi) If the proposed director is or has been a director of the reporting issuer, state the period or periods during which he has served as such.

(vii) State the number of securities of each class of voting securities of the reporting issuer or of any subsidiary of the reporting issuer beneficially owned, directly or indirectly, or over which control or direction is exercised by each director.

(viii) If voting securities carrying 10 per cent of the voting rights attached to any class of voting securities of the reporting issuer or of a subsidiary of the reporting issuer are beneficially owned, directly or indirectly or controlled or directed by any director and his associates or affiliates, state the number of securities of each class of voting securities beneficially owned, directly or indirectly or controlled or directed by the associates or affiliates naming each associate or affiliate whose security holdings are 10 per cent or more.

(b) If any proposed director is to be elected pursuant to any arrangement or understanding between the nominee and any other person, except the directors and senior officers of the reporting issuer acting solely in such capacity, name the other person and describe briefly the arrangement or understanding.

Item 6 – Executive Compensation

Complete and attach to or include in this form a Statement of Executive Compensation in Form 41.

The required form is Form 41.

Item 7 – Indebtedness of Directors, Executive Officers and Senior Officers

(a) The information required by this Item must be provided for each individual who is, or at any time during the most recently completed financial year was, a director, executive officer and senior officer of the issuer, each proposed nominee for election as a director of the issuer, and each associate of any such director, officer or proposed nominee,

   (i) who is, or at any time since the beginning of the most recently completed financial year of the issuer has been, indebted to the issuer or any of its subsidiaries, or

   (ii) whose indebtedness to another entity is, or at any time since the beginning of the most recently completed financial year has been, the subject of a guarantee, support agreement, letter of credit or other similar arrangement or understanding provided by the issuer or any of its subsidiaries.

(b)   State in the tabular form under the caption set out, for any indebtedness referred to in paragraph (a) of this Item that was entered into in connection with a purchase of securities of the issuer or any of its subsidiaries:

   (i) The name of the borrower (column (a)).

   (ii) If the borrower is a director, executive officer or senior officer, the principal position of the borrower. If the borrower was, during the year, but no longer is a director or officer, include a statement to that effect. If the borrower is a proposed nominee for election as a director, include a statement to that effect. If the borrower is included as an associate describe briefly the relationship of the borrower to an individual who is or, during the year, was a director, executive officer or senior officer or who is a proposed nominee for election as a director, name that individual and provide the information required by this subparagraph for that individual (column (a)).

   (iii) Whether the issuer or a subsidiary of the issuer is the lender or the provider of a guarantee, support agreement, letter of credit or similar arrangement or understanding (column (b)).

   (iv) The largest aggregate amount of the indebtedness outstanding at any time during the last completed financial year (column (c)).

   (v) The aggregate amount of indebtedness outstanding as at a date within thirty days of certification of the information circular (column (d)).

   (vi) Separately for each class or series of securities, the sum of the number of securities purchased during the last completed financial year with the financial assistance (column (e)).

   (vii) The security for the indebtedness, if any, provided to the issuer, any of its subsidiaries or the other entity (column (f)).

TABLE OF INDEBTEDNESS OF DIRECTORS, EXECUTIVE OFFICERS AND SENIOR OFFICERS UNDER SECURITIES PURCHASE PROGRAMS

Name and Principal Position (a)	Involvement of Issuer or Subsidiary (b)	Largest Amount Outstanding During [Last Completed Financial Year] ($) (c)	Amount Outstanding as at [current date] ($) (d)	Financially Assisted Securities Purchases During [Last Completed Financial Year] (#) (e)	Security for Indebtedness (f)

(c)   State in the introduction immediately preceding the table required by paragraph (b) of this Item, for indebtedness entered into in connection with a purchase of securities of the issuer or any of its subsidiaries, separately, the aggregate indebtedness,

   (i) to the issuer or any of its subsidiaries, and

   (ii) to another entity if the indebtedness is the subject of a guarantee, support agreement, letter of credit or other similar arrangement or understanding provided by the issuer or any of its subsidiaries, of all officers, directors, employees and former officers, directors and employees of the issuer or any of its subsidiaries outstanding as at a date within thirty days of certification of the information circular.

(d)   State in the tabular form under the caption set out for any indebtedness referred to in paragraph (a) of this Item that was not entered into in connection with a purchase of securities of the issuer or any of its subsidiaries, the information referred to in subparagraphs (b) (i) through (v) of this Item.

TABLE OF INDEBTEDNESS OF DIRECTORS, EXECUTIVE OFFICERS
AND SENIOR OFFICERS [insert if the issuer has a securities purchase program
"OTHER THAN UNDER SECURITIES PURCHASE PROGRAMS"]

Name and Principal Position (a)	Involvement of Issuer or Subsidiary (b)	Largest Amount Outstanding During [Last Completed Financial Year] ($) (c)	Amount Outstanding as at [current date] ($) (d)

(e)   State in the introduction immediately preceding the table required by paragraph (d) of this Item, for indebtedness not entered into in connection with a purchase of securities of the issuer or any of its subsidiaries, separately, the aggregate indebtedness,

    (i) to the issuer or any of its subsidiaries, and

    (ii) to another entity if the indebtedness is the subject of a guarantee, support agreement, letter of credit or other similar arrangement or understanding provided by the issuer or any of its subsidiaries,

of all officers, directors, employees and former officers, directors and employees of the issuer or any of its subsidiaries outstanding as at a date within thirty days of certification of the information circular.

(f)   Disclose in a footnote to, or a narrative accompanying, each table required by this Item,

    (i) the material terms of each incidence of indebtedness and, if applicable, of each guarantee, support agreement, letter of credit or other similar arrangement or understanding, including without limitation the term to maturity, rate of interest and any understanding, agreement or intention to limit recourse, and for the table required by paragraph (d) only, any security for the indebtedness and the nature of the transaction in which the indebtedness was incurred,

    (ii) any material adjustment or amendment made during the most recently completed financial year to the terms of the indebtedness and, if applicable, the guarantee, support agreement, letter of credit or similar arrangement or understanding, and

    (iii) the class or series of the securities purchased with financial assistance or held as security for the indebtedness and, if the class or series of securities is not publicly traded, all material terms of the securities, including but not limited to provisions for exchange, conversion, exercise, redemption, retraction and dividends.

(g)   No disclosure need be made under this Item of an incidence of indebtedness that has been entirely repaid on or before the date of certification of the information circular or of routine indebtedness.

"Routine indebtedness" means indebtedness described in any of the following clauses:

    (i) If an issuer makes loans to employees generally, whether or not in the ordinary course of business, loans are considered routine indebtedness if made on terms, including those as to interest rate and security, no more favourable to the borrower than the terms on which loans are made by the issuer to employees generally, but the amount at any time during the last completed financial year remaining unpaid under the loans to any one director, executive officer, senior officer or proposed nominee together with his or her associates that are treated as routine indebtedness under this clause must not exceed $25,000.

(ii) Whether or not the issuer makes loans in the ordinary course of business, a loan to a director, executive officer or senior officer is considered routine indebtedness if,

A. the borrower is a full-time employee of the issuer,

B. the loan is fully secured against the residence of the borrower, and

C. the amount of the loan does not exceed the annual salary of the borrower.

(iii) If the issuer makes loans in the ordinary course of business, a loan is considered routine indebtedness if made to a person or company other than a full-time employee of the issuer, and if the loan,

A. is made on substantially the same terms, including those as to interest rate and security, as are available when a loan is made to other customers of the issuer with comparable credit ratings, and

B. involves no more than usual risks of collectibility.

(iv) Indebtedness arising by reason of purchases made on usual trade terms or of ordinary travel or expense advances, or for similar reasons is considered routine indebtedness if the repayment arrangements are in accord with usual commercial practice.

(h) For purposes of this Item, "executive officer" has the same meaning as in Form 41 and "support agreement" includes, but is not limited to, an agreement to provide assistance in the maintenance or servicing of any indebtedness and an agreement to provide compensation for the purpose of maintaining or servicing any indebtedness of the borrower.

See NIN 93/23 "Executive Compensation".

Item 8 – Interest of Insiders in Material Transactions

Where not previously disclosed in an information circular, describe briefly, and where practicable, state the approximate amount of any material interest, direct or indirect, of any insider of the reporting issuer, any proposed nominee for election as a director of the reporting issuer or any associate or affiliate of such insider or proposed nominee in any transaction since the commencement of the reporting issuer's last financial year or in any proposed transaction which has materially affected or would materially affect the reporting issuer or any of its subsidiaries.

INSTRUCTIONS:

1. Give a brief description of the material transaction. Include the name and address of each person whose interest in any transaction is described and the nature of the relationship by reason of which such interest is required to be described.

2. As to any transaction involving the purchase or sale of assets by or to the issuer or any subsidiary, state the cost of the assets to the purchaser and the cost thereof to the seller if acquired by the seller within two years to the transaction.

3. This item does not apply to any interest arising from the ownership of securities of the issuer where the securityholder receives no extra or special benefit or

advantage not shared on an equal basis by all other holders of the same class of securities or all other holders of the same class of securities who are resident in Canada.

4. Information shall be included as to any material underwriting discounts or commissions upon the sale of securities by the issuer where any of the specified persons was or is to be an underwriter or is an associate, affiliate or partner of a person, or partnership that was or is to be an underwriter.

5. No information need be given in answer to this item as to any transaction or any interest therein, where,

    (a)   the rates or charges involved in the transaction are fixed by law or determined by competitive bids;

    (b)   the interest of a specified person in the transaction is solely that of a director of another issuer that is a party to the transaction;

    (c)   the transaction involves services as a bank or other depository of funds, transfer agent, registrar, trustee under a trust indenture or other similar services;

    (d)   the transaction does not, directly or indirectly, involve remuneration of services, and,

          (i)   the interest of the specified person arose from the beneficial ownership, direct or indirect, of less than 10 per cent of any class of voting securities of another issuer that is a party to the transaction;

          (ii) the transaction is in the ordinary course of business of the issuer or its subsidiaries; and

          (iii) the amount of the transaction or series of transactions is less than 10 per cent of the total sales or purchases, as the case may be, of the issuer and its subsidiaries for the last completed financial year.

6. Information shall be furnished in answer to this item with respect to transactions not excluded above that involve remuneration, directly or indirectly, to any of the specified persons for services in any capacity unless the interest of the person arises solely from the beneficial ownership, direct or indirect, of less than 10 per cent of any class of voting securities of another issuer furnishing the services to the issuer or its subsidiaries.

Item 9 – Appointment of Auditor

If action is to be taken with respect to the appointment of an auditor, name the auditor of the reporting issuer. If the auditor was first appointed within the last five years, state the date when the auditor was first appointed.

Item 10 – Management Contracts

Where management functions of the reporting issuer or any subsidiary of the reporting issuer are to any substantial degree performed by a person other than the directors or senior officers of the reporting issuer or subsidiary:

    (i)   give details of the agreement or arrangement under which the management functions are performed, including the name and address of any person who is a party to the agreement or arrangement or who is responsible for performing the management functions;

    (ii) give the names and home addresses in full or, alternatively, solely the municipality of residence or postal address, of the insiders of the person with which the reporting issuer or subsidiary has any such agreement or arrangement and, if the following information is known to the directors or senior officers of the reporting issuer, give the names and addresses of any person that would be an insider of any person with which the reporting issuer or subsidiary has any such agreement or arrangement if the person were a reporting issuer;

(iii) with respect to any person named in answer to paragraph (i), state the amounts paid or payable by the reporting issuer and its subsidiaries to the person since the commencement of the reporting issuer's last financial year and give particulars; and

(iv) with respect to any person named in answer to paragraph (i) or (ii) and their associates and affiliates, give particulars of,

(a) any indebtedness of the person, associate or affiliate to the reporting issuer or its subsidiaries that was outstanding, and

(b) any transaction or arrangement of the person, associate or affiliate with the reporting issuer or subsidiary,

at any time since the commencement of the reporting issuer's last financial year.

INSTRUCTIONS:

1.   In giving the information called for by this item, it is not necessary to refer to any matter that in all the circumstances is relative insignificance.

2.   In giving particulars of indebtedness, state the largest aggregate amount of indebtedness outstanding at any time during the period, the nature of the indebtedness and of the transaction in which it was incurred, the amount of indebtedness presently outstanding and the rate of interest paid or charged on the indebtedness.

3.   It is not necessary to include as indebtedness amounts due from the particular person for purchase subject to usual trade terms, for ordinary travel and expense advances and for other like transactions.

NIN 95/16 "Amendments to Form 30 (Information Circular)" provides that the following revised Item 11 of Form 30 is effective for information circulars dated on or after July 1, 1995.

Item 11 – Particulars of Matters to be Acted Upon

If action is to be taken on any matter to be submitted to the meeting of security holders, other than the approval of financial statements, the substance of the matter or related groups of matters should be described, except to the extent described pursuant to the foregoing items, in sufficient detail to permit security holders to form a reasoned judgement concerning the matter.

Without limiting the generality of the foregoing, such matters include alterations of share capital, charter amendments, property acquisitions or dispositions, amalgamations, mergers, arrangements, reorganizations or reverse take-overs.

Amalgamation, Merger, Arrangement or Reorganization

Where an information circular is prepared in connection with a meeting of security holders at which action is to be taken under applicable corporate legislation in respect of an amalgamation, merger, arrangement or reorganization, pursuant to which securities are to be issued, offered in exchange or otherwise distributed, the information circular shall include the information prescribed by the form of prospectus appropriate for each issuer whose securities are being issued, offered in exchange or otherwise distributed in connection with the amalgamation, merger, arrangement or reorganization with appropriate modifications; this requirement does not apply to a reorganization where the number of outstanding securities of an issuer is changed into a different number of securities of the same class and series.

In addition, where an amalgamation, arrangement, merger or reorganization would result in the acquisition of a business by an issuer and that acquisition is material to the issuer, the information circular of that issuer shall include the financial information about the business to be acquired that would be included in a prospectus if the proceeds of the offering under the prospectus were to be applied, in whole or in part, directly or indirectly, to finance the acquisition of a business by a purchase of assets or shares.

Reverse Take-over

The requirements set out under the caption "Amalgamation, Merger, Arrangement or Reorganization" do not apply to an information circular prepared in connection with a meeting of security holders at which action is to be taken in respect of one or more transactions resulting in a reverse take-over ("RTO") as contemplated by the Vancouver Stock Exchange ("VSE") policy on RTO transactions.

In the case of an RTO, reference should be made to the prospectus form applicable to the non-reporting issuer or business to be acquired for the applicable disclosure requirements. The information included in the information circular must permit security holders to form a reasoned judgement concerning the transaction. The relevant prospectus form is

(a) Form 12A, where the non-reporting issuer is a junior industrial issuer or the business to be acquired would create a junior industrial issuer; or

(b) Form 14A, where the non-reporting issuer is a natural resource issuer or the business to be acquired would create a natural resource issuer.

For greater certainty, and without limiting the generality of the foregoing, where the relevant form of prospectus is Form 12A, the information circular must contain, with appropriate modifications, the information relating to the non-reporting issuer or business to be acquired called for by the following items of Form 12A:

(a) item 4.1 (name and incorporation);

(b) items 5.1 (description and general development), 5.3 (stated business objectives), 5.4 (milestones), 5.5 (acquisitions and dispositions), 5.6 (management) and 5.14 (administration);

(c) item 7(a) (risks related to the nature of the business);

(d) item 8 (directors, officers and promoters);

(e) items 10.1 (executive compensation), 10.2 (a) to (c) and (d)(i) (related party transactions), and 10.3 (proposed compensation);

(f) item 11.2(b) (options and other rights to purchase securities);

(g) item 18 (legal proceedings); and

(h) item 22 (other material facts).

Similarly, where the relevant form of prospectus is Form 14A, the information circular must contain, with appropriate modifications, the information relating to the non-reporting issuer or the business to be acquired called for by the following items of Form 14A:

(a) item 4.1 (name and incorporation);

(b) item 5.1 (description and general development);

(c) for mineral properties, items 6.1 (location, description and acquisition), 6.2 (exploration and development history), 6.4 (proposed exploration and development program) and 6.5 (other properties);

(d) for oil and gas properties, items 6.7 (location, description and acquisition), 6.8 (production history), 6.9 (drilling activity), 6.11 (proposed exploration and development program) and 6.12 (other properties);

(e) item 7 (administration);

(f) item 9 (a) (risks related to the nature of the business);

(g) item 10 (directors, officers, promoters and other management);

(h) items 12.1 (executive compensation), 12.2(a) to (c) and (d) (i) (related party transactions), and 12.3 (proposed compensation);

(i) item 13.2(b) (options and other rights to purchase securities);

(j) item 22 (legal proceedings); and

(k) item 26 (other material facts).

In addition to the information required above under either Form 12A or Form 14A, the information circular must contain separate financial statements for the non-reporting issuer or for the business to be acquired prepared in accordance with Canadian generally accepted accounting principles and Local Policy Statement 3-02, except that financial statements need not be audited or reviewed. Interim financial statements are required to be included only where the date of the information circular is more than 120 days from the date of the most recent annual financial statements included in the information circular.

Any financial statements included in the information circular must be approved by

(a) the directors where the non-reporting issuer or the vendor of the business to be acquired is a corporation,

(b) the partners where the non-reporting issuer or the vendor of the business to be acquired is a partnership, or

(c) the sole proprietor where the non-reporting issuer or the vendor of the business to be acquired is a sole proprietorship.

The approval of the financial statements must be evidenced by the signature, or facsimile of the signature, of two directors or two partners duly authorized to evidence the approval, or of the sole proprietor, immediately above the typewritten or printed name of those directors or partners or that sole proprietor.

The information circular must disclose that a Filing Statement or a Statement of Material Facts with respect to the RTO containing full, true and plain disclosure of all material facts relating to the RTO, the listed issuer and the non-reporting issuer or the business to be acquired will be filed with the VSE.

The information circular must also disclose that a news release will be issued

(a) confirming that a Filing Statement or a Statement of Material Facts has been filed with the VSE with respect to the RTO and placed in the public file of the listed issuer,

(b) summarizing the information on the RTO, the listed issuer and the non-reporting issuer or the business to be acquired contained in the Filing Statement or Statement of Material Facts, and

(c) giving the name, address and telephone number of an officer of the listed issuer from whom a copy of the Filing Statement or Statement of Material Facts may be obtained free of charge.

February 1, 1987

This is the form required under section 81(f) of the Act for a notice of intention.

FORM 31

Securities Act

NOTICE OF INTENTION TO MAKE AN ISSUER BID

ITEM 1   Name of Issuer

ITEM 2   Securities Sought

State the class and number of securities or principal amount of debt securities sought.

ITEM 3   Time Period

State, where known, the dates on which the issuer bid will commence and close.

ITEM 4   Method of Acquisition

State the method by which the securities will be acquired.

ITEM 5   Consideration Offered

State the consideration to be offered.

ITEM 6   Payment for Securities

State the particulars of the method and time of payment of the consideration.

ITEM 7   Reasons for Bid

State the purpose and business reasons for the issuer bid.

ITEM 8   Acceptance of Bid

State the names of every director and every senior officer of the issuer who
intends to accept the issuer bid and, where their intention to accept the bid
is known after reasonable enquiry, state the names of

(a) every associate of every director and of every senior officer of the issuer;

(b) every person holding 10 per cent or more of any class of equity
securities of the issuer; and

(c) every person acting jointly or in concert with the issuer who intends to
accept the bid.

ITEM 9   Benefits from Bid

State the direct or indirect benefits to any of the persons named in item 8 of
accepting or refusing to accept the issuer bid.

ITEM 10   Material Changes in the Affairs of Issuer

Disclose the particulars of any plans or proposals for material changes in
the affairs of the issuer, including for example, any contract or agreement
under negotiation, any proposal to liquidate the issuer, to sell, lease or
exchange all or a substantial part of its assets, to amalgamate it with any
other business organization, or to make any material changes in its business, corporate structure (debt or equity), management or personnel.

ITEM 11   Signature

This notice must be signed by a director or senior officer of the issuer duly
authorized to sign.

ITEM 12   Date of Notice

November 1, 1989

This is the form required under section 90(7) of the Act for a take over bid circular.

FORM 32
Securities Act
TAKE OVER BID CIRCULAR

ITEM 1   Name of Offeror

ITEM 2   Name of Offeree Issuer

ITEM 3   Securities Subject to Bid

State the class of securities that are the subject of the bid and a description
of the rights of the holders of any other class of securities that have a right
to participate in the offer.

ITEM 4   Ownership of Securities of Offeree Issuer

State the number, designation and percentage of outstanding securities of
any class of securities of the offeree issuer beneficially owned or over which
control or direction is exercised by the offeror and by each director and
senior officer of the offeror, and, where known after reasonable enquiry, by

(a) each associate of a director or senior officer of the offeror;

(b) any person holding more than 10 per cent of any class of equity securities of the offeror; and

(c) any person acting jointly or in concert with the offeror

or, in each case where no securities are so owned, directed or controlled, a statement to that effect.

ITEM 5   Trading in Securities of Offeree Issuer

State, where known after reasonable enquiry has been made, the number and designation of any securities of the offeree issuer traded by the persons referred to in item 4 during the six- month period preceding the date of the take over bid, including the purchase or sale price and the date of each such transaction. If no such securities were traded, so state.

ITEM 6   Commitments to Acquire Securities of Offeree Issuer

Disclose all arrangements, agreements, commitments or understandings made by the offeror, and, where known after reasonable enquiry, by the persons referred to in item 4 to acquire equity securities of the offeree issuer, and the terms and conditions of any such commitments.

ITEM 7   Terms and Conditions of the Bid

State the terms of the take over bid. State, where the obligation of the offeror to take up and pay for securities under the take over bid is conditional, the particulars of each condition.

ITEM 8   Payment for Deposited Securities

State the particulars of the method and time of payment of the cash or other consideration to be paid for the securities of the offeree issuer.

ITEM 9   Right to Withdraw Deposited Securities

Describe the withdrawal rights of the security holders of the offeree issuer under the bid. State that notice of withdrawal of securities deposited must be given in a manner that provides the depository designated under the bid with a written or printed copy and must be actually received by the depository.

ITEM 10   Arrangements to Pay for Deposited Securities

State the source of any funds to be used for payment and, if such funds are to be borrowed, the terms of the loan, the circumstances under which it must be repaid and the proposed method of repayment.

ITEM 11   Trading in the Securities to be Acquired

State the principal market or markets for the securities of the offeree issuer sought to be acquired pursuant to the take over bid and indicate any change in a principal market that is planned following the bid, including but not limited to listing or de-listing on a stock exchange. Furnish, where reasonably ascertainable, a summary showing in reasonable detail the volume of trading and price range of the securities in the six- month period preceding the date of the take over bid. State the date that the take over bid to which this circular relates was announced to the public and the market price of the securities immediately before such announcement.

ITEM 12   Arrangements Between the Offeror and the Directors and Officers of Offeree Issuer

State the particulars of any arrangement, agreement, commitment or understanding made or proposed to be made between the offeror and any of the directors or senior officers of the offeree issuer, including particulars of any payment or other benefit proposed to be made or given by way of compensation for loss of office or as to their remaining in or retiring from office, if the take over bid is successful.

ITEM 13   Material Changes in Affairs of Offeree Issuer

State the particulars of any information known to the offeror that indicates any material change in the affairs of the offeree issuer since the date of the last published interim or annual financial statement of the offeree issuer.

ITEM 14   Valuation

Where a valuation is provided pursuant to a legal requirement or otherwise

(a) include a summary of the valuation disclosing the basis of computation, scope of review, relevant factors and their values, and the key assumptions on which the valuation is based; and

(b) advise where copies of the valuation are available for inspection and state that a copy of the valuation will be sent to any registered holder of securities of the offeree issuer sought to be acquired upon payment of a charge sufficient to cover copying and postage.

ITEM 15   Securities of an Offeror or Other Issuer to be Exchanged for Securities of Offeree Issuer

(1) Where a take over bid provides that the consideration for the securities of the offeree issuer is to be, in whole or in part, securities of an offeror or other issuer, include the information prescribed by the form of prospectus appropriate for the offeror or issuer whose securities are being offered in exchange for the securities of the offeree issuer.

(2) Where the form of prospectus so requires, include the financial statements of the offeror or other issuer required to be included in such prospectus, including, where the consideration is securities of the offeror,

(a) pro forma balance sheet and income statement of the offeror giving effect to the exchange of securities as at the date of the most recent balance sheet of the offeror that is included in the circular based on the information in the most recent audited financial statements of the offeree issuer;

(b) a description of the basis of preparation of the pro forma financial statements; and

(c) the basic and fully diluted earnings per share based on the pro forma financial statements.

(3) State the particulars of any information known to the offeror that indicates any material change in the affairs of the offeror or other issuer since the date of the last published interim or annual financial statement of the offeror or other issuer.

ITEM 16   Right of Appraisal and Acquisition

State any rights of appraisal the security holders of the offeree issuer have under the laws governing the offeree issuer and state whether or not the offeror intends to exercise any right of acquisition the offeror may have.

ITEM 17   Market Purchases of Securities

State whether or not the offeror intends to purchase in the market securities that are the subject of the take over bid.

ITEM 18   Material Changes in the Affairs of Offeree Issuer

Disclose the particulars of any plans or proposals of the offeror for material changes in the affairs of the offeree issuer, including for example, any proposal to liquidate the issuer, to sell, lease or exchange all or a substantial part of its assets, to amalgamate it with any other business organization or to make any material changes in its business, corporate structure (debt or equity), management or personnel.

Forms

ITEM 19   Other Material Facts

Describe

(a) any material facts concerning the securities of the offeree issuer; and

(b) any other matter not disclosed in the foregoing that has not previously been generally disclosed and is known to the offeror but which would reasonably be expected to affect the decision of the security holders of the offeree issuer to accept or reject the offer.

ITEM 20   Judicial Developments

Where the take over bid is an insider bid or where the offeror anticipates that a going private transaction will follow the take over bid, include reference to recent legal developments, if any, relating to the type of transaction or proposed transaction.

ITEM 21   Disclosure in Accordance with Form 33

In the case of a take over bid to which item 20 applies, include the disclosure required by Form 33, appropriately modified.

ITEM 22   Approval of Take Over Bid Circular

Where the take over bid is made by or on behalf of an offeror that has directors as defined in the Act, state that the take over bid circular has been approved by its board of directors and that the delivery of the take over bid circular to the security holders of the offeree issuer has been authorized by its board of directors.

ITEM 23   Solicitations

Disclose any person retained by or on behalf of the offeror to make solicitations in respect of the bid and the particulars of the compensation arrangements.

ITEM 24   Certificate

Include a certificate in the following form signed, where the take over bid is made by or on behalf of a person, other than an individual, by the chief executive officer, the chief financial officer and on behalf of the board of directors, by any two directors of the person other than the foregoing, all duly authorized to sign* and, where the take over bid is made by or on behalf of an individual, by the individual:

"The foregoing contains no untrue statement of a material fact and does not omit to state a material fact that is required to be stated or that is necessary to make a statement not misleading in the light of the circumstances in which it was made."

* Where the person has fewer than four directors and senior officers, the certificate must be signed by all of them.

ITEM 25   Date of Take Over Bid Circular

November 1, 1989

This is the form required under section 90(7) of the Act for an issuer bid circular.

FORM 33

Securities Act

ISSUER BID CIRCULAR

ITEM 1   Name of Issuer

ITEM 2   Securities Sought

State the class and number of securities or principal amount of debt securities sought.

ITEM 3   Time Period

State the dates on which the issuer bid will commence and close.

ITEM 4   Method of Acquisition

State the method by which the securities will be acquired.

ITEM 5   Consideration Offered

State the consideration to be offered.

ITEM 6   Payment for Deposited Securities

State the particulars of the method and time of payment of the consideration.

ITEM 7   Right to Withdraw Deposited Securities

Describe the rights to withdraw securities deposited pursuant to the bid. State that notice of withdrawal of securities deposited must be given in a manner that provides the depository designated under the bid with a written or printed copy and must be actually received by the depository.

ITEM 8   Source of Funds

State the source of any funds to be used for payment and, if such funds are to be borrowed, the terms of the loan, the circumstances under which it must be repaid and the proposed method of repayment.

ITEM 9   Participation

Where the issuer bid is for less than all of the outstanding securities of that class, state that if a greater number or principal amount of the securities are tendered than the issuer is bound or willing to take up and pay for, the issuer will take up as nearly as may be pro rata, disregarding fractions, according to the number or principal amount of the securities tendered.

ITEM 10   Reasons for Bid

State the purpose and business reasons for the issuer bid, and if it is anticipated that the issuer bid will be followed by a going private transaction, describe the proposed transaction.

ITEM 11   Trading in Securities to be Acquired

Furnish, where reasonably ascertainable, a summary showing

(a) the name of each stock exchange or other principal market on which the securities sought are traded;

(b) in reasonable detail for the twelve months preceding the date of the issuer bid, the volume of trading and price range of the class of the securities sought, or in the case of debt securities the prices quoted, on each principal market; and

(c) the date that the issuer bid to which the circular relates was announced to the public and the market price of the securities of the issuer immediately before such announcement.

Indicate any change in a principal market or markets that is planned following the bid.

ITEM 12   Ownership of Securities of Issuer

State the number, designation and the percentage of outstanding securities of any class of securities of the issuer beneficially owned or over which control or direction is exercised by each director and senior officer of the issuer, and, where known after reasonable enquiry, by

(a) each associate of a director or senior officer of the issuer;

(b) any person holding more than 10 per cent of any class of equity securities of the issuer; and

(c) any person acting jointly or in concert with the issuer,

or, in each case where no securities are so owned, directed or controlled, a statement to that effect.

ITEM 13   Commitments to Acquire Securities of Issuer

Disclose all arrangements, agreements, commitments or understandings made by the issuer and, where known after reasonable enquiry, by the persons referred to in item 12, to acquire equity securities of the issuer, and the terms and conditions of any such commitments.

ITEM 14   Acceptance of Bid

Where known after reasonable enquiry, state the name of every person named in item 12 who proposes to accept the issuer bid and the number of securities in respect of which the person proposes to accept the bid.

ITEM 15   Benefits from Bid

State the direct or indirect benefits to any of the persons named in item 12 of accepting or refusing to accept the issuer bid.

ITEM 16   Material Changes in the Affairs of Issuer

Disclose the particulars of any plans or proposals for material changes in the affairs of the issuer, including, for example, any contract or agreement under negotiation, any proposal to liquidate the issuer, to sell, lease or exchange all or a substantial part of its assets, to amalgamate it with any other business organization or to make any material changes in its business, corporate structure (debt or equity), management or personnel.

ITEM 17   Other Benefits to Insiders, Affiliates and Associates

If any material changes or subsequent transactions are contemplated, as described in item 10 or 16, state if known, any specific benefit, direct or indirect, as a result of such changes or transactions to any of the persons named in item 12.

ITEM 18   Arrangements Between Issuer and Security Holder

Provide the details of any arrangement, agreement, commitment or understanding, formal or informal, between the issuer and

(a) any security holder of the issuer with respect to the issuer bid; and

(b) any person with respect to any securities of the issuer in relation to the issuer bid.

ITEM 19   Previous Purchases and Sales

State the number and designation of any securities of the issuer purchased or sold by the issuer excluding securities purchased or sold pursuant to the exercise of employee stock options, warrants and conversion rights during the twelve months preceding the date of the issuer bid including the purchase or sale price, the date and purpose of each transaction.

ITEM 20   Financial Statements

(1) If the most recently available interim financial statements have not been delivered to security holders of the issuer, include the interim financial statements. If interim financial statements are not included, include a statement that the most recent interim financial statements will be sent without charge to anyone requesting them.

(2) Where interim financial statements are included, include a report of the chief financial officer of the offeree issuer, stating whether in the opinion of the chief financial officer, the financial statements present fairly the financial position of the offeree issuer and the results of its operations for the period under review.

ITEM 21   Valuation

Where a valuation is provided pursuant to a legal requirement or otherwise

(a) include a summary of the valuation disclosing the basis of computation, scope of review, relevant factors and their values, and the key assumptions on which the valuation is based; and

(b) advise where copies of the valuation are available for inspection and state that a copy of the valuation will be sent to any registered security holder upon payment of a charge sufficient to cover printing and postage.

ITEM 22   Securities of Issuer to be Exchanged for Others

Where an issuer bid provides that the consideration for the securities of the issuer is to be, in whole or in part, different securities of an issuer, include the information prescribed for the form of prospectus appropriate for the issuer.

ITEM 23   Approval of Bid

State that the issuer bid circular has been approved by the issuer's board of directors, disclosing the name of any director of the issuer who has informed the board of directors in writing of his opposition to the issuer bid and that the delivery of the issuer bid circular to the security holders of the issuer has been authorized by the issuer's board of directors.

Where the issuer bid is part of a transaction or to be followed by a transaction required to be approved by minority security holders, state the nature of the approval required.

ITEM 24   Previous Distribution

If the securities of the class subject to the issuer bid were distributed during the five years preceding the bid, state the distribution price per share and the aggregate proceeds received by the issuer or selling security holder.

ITEM 25   Dividend Policy

State the frequency and amount of dividends with respect to shares of the issuer during the two years preceding the date of the issuer bid, any restrictions on the issuer's ability to pay dividends and any plan or intention to declare a dividend or to alter the dividend policy of the issuer.

ITEM 26   Tax Consequences

Provide a general description of the consequences of the issuer bid under the Income Tax Act (Canada) to the issuer and to the security holders of any class affected.

ITEM 27   Expenses of Bid

Provide a statement of the expenses incurred or to be incurred in connection with the issuer bid.

ITEM 28   Judicial Developments

Include reference to recent legal developments if any, relating to the type of transaction or proposed transaction.

ITEM 29   Other Material Facts

Describe

(a) any material facts concerning the securities of the issuer; and

(b) any other matter not disclosed in the foregoing that has not previously been generally disclosed and is known to the issuer but which would reasonably be expected to affect the decision of the security holders of the issuer to accept or reject the offer.

ITEM 30   Solicitations

Disclose any person retained by or on behalf of the issuer to make solicitations in respect of the bid and the particulars of the compensation arrangements.

Forms

ITEM 31   Certificate

Include a certificate in the following form signed by the chief executive officer and the chief financial officer of the issuer, and on behalf of the board of directors, by any two directors of the issuer other than the foregoing, all duly authorized to sign*.

"The foregoing contains no untrue statement of a material fact and does not omit to state a material fact that is required to be stated or that is necessary to make a statement not misleading in the light of the circumstances in which it was made."

* Where the issuer has fewer than four directors and senior officers, the certificate must be signed by all of them.

ITEM 32   Date of Issuer Bid Circular

November 1, 1989

This is the form required under section 91(8) of the Act for a directors' circular.

FORM 34
Securities Act
DIRECTORS' CIRCULAR

ITEM 1   Name of Offeror

ITEM 2   Name of Offeree Issuer

ITEM 3   Names of Directors of the Offeree Issuer

ITEM 4   Ownership of Securities of Offeree Issuer

State the number, designation and the percentage of outstanding securities of any class of securities of the offeree issuer beneficially owned or over which control or direction is exercised by each director and senior officer of the offeree issuer, and, where known after reasonable enquiry, by,

(a) each associate of a director or senior officer of the offeree issuer;

(b) any person holding more than 10 per cent of any class of equity securities of the offeree issuer; and

(c) any person acting jointly or in concert with the offeree issuer,

or, in each case where no securities are so owned, directed or controlled, a statement to that effect.

ITEM 5   Acceptance of Take-Over Bid

Where known after reasonable enquiry, state the name of every person named in item 4 who has accepted or intends to accept the offer and the number of securities in respect of which such person has accepted or intends to accept the offer.

ITEM 6   Ownership of Securities of Offeror

Where a take over bid is made by or on behalf of an offeror that is an issuer, state the number, designation and percentage of outstanding securities of any class of securities of the offeror beneficially owned or over which control or direction is exercised by the offeree issuer, by each director and senior officer of the offeree issuer, and, where known after reasonable enquiry, by

(a) each associate of a director or senior officer of the offeree issuer;

(b) any person holding more than 10 per cent of any class of equity securities of the offeree issuer; and

(c) any person acting jointly or in concert with the offeree issuer,

or, in each case where no securities are so owned, directed or controlled, a statement to that effect.

ITEM 7   Relationship Between the Offeror and the Directors and Senior Officers of the Offeree Issuer

State the particulars of any arrangement, agreement, commitment or understanding made or proposed to be made between the offeror and any of the directors or senior officers of the offeree issuer, including particulars of any payment or other benefit proposed to be made or given by way of compensation for loss of office or as to their remaining in or retiring from office if the take over bid is successful. State also, whether any directors or senior officers of the offeree issuer are also directors or senior officers of the offeror or any subsidiary of the offeror and identify such persons.

ITEM 8   Agreement Between Offeree Issuer and Officers and Directors

State the particulars of any arrangement, agreement, commitment or understanding made or proposed to be made between the offeree issuer and any of the directors or senior officers of the offeree issuer, including particulars of any payment or other benefit proposed to be made or given by way of compensation for loss of office or as to their remaining in or retiring from office if the take over bid is successful.

ITEM 9   Interests of Directors and Senior Officers of the Offeree Issuer in Material Contracts of the Offeror

State whether any director or senior officer of the offeree issuer and their associates and, where known to the directors or senior officers after reasonable inquiry, whether any person who owns more than 10 per cent of any class of equity securities of the offeree issuer for the time being outstanding has any interest in any material contract to which the offeror is a party, and if so, state particulars of the nature and extent of such interest.

ITEM 10   Trading by Directors and Officers

(1) State the number of securities of the offeree issuer traded, the purchase or sale price and the date of each transaction during the six month period preceding the date of the directors' circular by the offeree issuer and each director and senior officer of the offeree issuer, and, where known after reasonable equity, by

(a)   each associate of a director or senior officer of the offeree issuer;

(b)   any person holding more than 10 per cent of a class of equity securities of the offeree issuer; and

(c)   any person acting jointly or in concert with the offeree issuer.

(2) Disclose the number and price of securities of the offeree issuer of the class of securities subject to the bid or convertible into securities of that class that have been issued to the directors and senior officers of the offeree issuer during the two-year period preceding the date of the circular.

ITEM 11   Additional Information

If any information required to be disclosed by the take over bid circular prepared by the offeror has been presented incorrectly or is misleading, supply any additional information within the knowledge of the offeree issuer which would make the information in the circular correct or not misleading.

ITEM 12   Material Changes in the Affairs of Offeree Issuer

State the particulars of any information known to any of the directors or senior officers of the offeree issuer that indicates any material change in the affairs of the offeree issuer since the date of the last published interim or annual financial statement of the offeree issuer.

ITEM 13   Other Information

State the particulars of any other information not disclosed in the foregoing but known to the directors which would reasonably be expected to affect the decision of the security holders of the offeree issuer to accept or reject the offer.

ITEM 14   Recommending Acceptance or Rejection of Bid

Include either a recommendation to accept or reject the take over bid and the reasons for such recommendation or a statement that the board of directors is unable to make or is not making a recommendation and if no recommendation is made, the reasons for not making a recommendation. Where a board of directors of an offeree issuer is considering recommending acceptance or rejection of a take over bid at the time of sending a directors' circular, state that fact and, if desired, advise the security holders of the offeree issuer not to tender their securities until a further communication is received from the directors.

ITEM 15   Response of Offeree Issuer

(1) Describe any transaction, board resolution, agreement in principle or signed contract of the offeree issuer in response to the bid.

(2) Disclose whether there are any negotiations underway in response to the bid which relate to or would result in

(a)   an extraordinary transaction such as a merger or reorganization involving the offeree issuer or a subsidiary;

(b)   the purchase, sale or transfer of a material amount of assets by the offeree issuer or a subsidiary;

(c)   an issuer bid for or other acquisition of securities by or of the offeree issuer; or

(d)   any material change in the present capitalization or dividend policy of the offeree issuer.

If there is an agreement in principle, give full particulars.

ITEM 16   Approval of Directors' Circular

State that the directors' circular has been approved by the directors of the offeree issuer and that the delivery of the directors' circular has been authorized by the directors of the offeree issuer.

ITEM 17   Financial Statements

Where unaudited financial statements of the offeree issuer are included in a directors' circular, include a report of the chief financial officer of the offeree issuer, stating whether in his opinion the financial statements present fairly the financial position of the offeree issuer and the results of its operations for the period under review.

ITEM 18   Certificate

Include a certificate in the following form signed by two directors of the issuer, duly authorized to sign on behalf of the board:

"The foregoing contains no untrue statement of a material fact and does not omit to state a material fact that is required to be stated or that is necessary to make a statement not misleading in the light of the circumstances in which it was made."

ITEM 19   Date of Directors' Circular

This is the form required under section 91(8) of the Act for a director's or officer's circular.

FORM 35

Securities Act

DIRECTOR'S OR OFFICER'S CIRCULAR

ITEM 1   Name of Offeror

ITEM 2   Name of Offeree Issuer

ITEM 3   Name of Director or Officer of Offeree Issuer

State the name of each director or officer delivering the circular.

ITEM 4   Ownership of Securities of Offeree Issuer

State the number, designation and percentage of outstanding securities of any class of securities of the offeree issuer beneficially owned or over which control or direction is exercised by the director or officer and, where known after reasonable enquiry, by the associates of the director or officer or, in each case where no securities are so owned, directed or controlled, a statement to that effect.

ITEM 5   Acceptance of Bid by Director or Officer

State whether the director or officer of the offeree issuer and whether any associate of such director or officer whose acceptance is known to the director or officer, after reasonable inquiry, has accepted or intends to accept the offer in respect of any securities of the offeree issuer sought to be acquired, and state the number of the securities in respect of which the director or officer, or where known after reasonable enquiry, any associate, has accepted or intends to accept the offer.

ITEM 6   Securities of Offeror Owned by Director or Officer

Where a take over bid is made by or on behalf of an issuer, state the number, designation and percentage of outstanding securities of any class of securities of the offeror beneficially owned or over which control or direction is exercised by the director or officer, or, where known after reasonable enquiry, by the associates of such director or officer.

ITEM 7   Arrangements between Offeror and Director or Officer

State the particulars of any arrangement, agreement, commitment or understanding made or proposed to be made between the offeror and the director or officer, including particulars of any payment or other benefit proposed to be made or given by way of compensation for loss of office or as to the director's or officer's remaining in or retiring from office if the take over bid is successful. State whether the director or officer is also a director or senior officer of the offeror or any subsidiary of the offeror.

ITEM 8   Arrangements between Offeree Issuer and Director or Officer

State the particulars of any arrangement, arrangement, commitment or understanding made or proposed to be made between the offeree issuer and the director or officer, including particulars of any payment or other benefit proposed to be made or given by way of compensation for loss of office or as to his or her remaining in or retiring from office if the take over bid is successful.

ITEM 9   Interests of Director or Officer in Material Contracts of Offeror

State whether or not the director or officer or the associates of the director or officer have any interest in any material contract to which the offeror is a party, and if so, state particulars of the nature and extent of such interest.

ITEM 10   Additional Information

If any information required to be disclosed by the take over bid circular prepared by the offeror has been presented incorrectly or is misleading, supply any additional information within the knowledge of the director or officer which would make the information in the circular correct or not misleading.

ITEM 11   Material Changes in the Affairs of Offeree Issuer

State the particulars of any information known to the director or officer that indicates any material change in the affairs of the offeree issuer since the date of the last published interim or annual financial statement of the offeree issuer and not previously generally publicly disclosed or in the opinion of the director or officer not adequately disclosed in the take over bid circular or directors' circular.

ITEM 12   Other Information

State the particulars of any other information not disclosed in the foregoing but known to the director or officer which would reasonably be expected to affect the decision of the security holders of the offeree issuer to accept or reject the offer.

ITEM 13   Recommendation

State the recommendation of the director or officer
and the reasons for the recommendation.

ITEM 14   Certificate

Include a certificate in the following form signed by or on behalf of each director or officer delivering the circular.

"The foregoing contains no untrue statement of a material fact and does not omit to state a material fact that is required to be stated or that is necessary to make a statement not misleading in the light of the circumstances in which it was made."

ITEM 15   Date of Director's or Officer's Circular

November 1, 1989

INSIDER REPORT

(See instructions on the back of this report)

Where freedom of information legislation is in force in the jurisdiction where this form is filed: The personal information requested on this form is collected under the authority and used for the purposes of administering the provincial securities Acts, Bank Act, Cooperative Credit Associations Act, Insurance Companies Act, Trust and Loan Companies Act and Canada Business Corporations Act. Under the CBCA the information provided satisfies the disclosure requirements of section 127. While the federal Privacy Act protects personal information provided, it also permits public disclosure pursuant to section 266 of the CBCA. All information contained in this form will be made available to the public. In British Columbia, if you have questions about how the Freedom of Information Act (number CCA-01-PU-002, In British Columbia, if you have questions about personal information collected on the form, call the Manager, Public Information and Records at (604) 660-4827 or write the Manager, 1100-865 Hornby Street, Vancouver, B.C. V6Z 2H4.

BOX 1. NAME OF THE REPORTING ISSUER (BLOCK LETTERS)

BOX 2. INSIDER DATA

RELATIONSHIP(S) TO REPORTING ISSUER

DATE OF LAST REPORT FILED   DAY   MONTH   YEAR

IF INITIAL REPORT, DATE ON WHICH YOU BECAME AN INSIDER   DAY   MONTH   YEAR

CHANGE IN RELATIONSHIP FROM LAST REPORT   YES   NO

BOX 3. NAME, ADDRESS AND TELEPHONE NUMBER OF THE INSIDER (BLOCK LETTERS)

FAMILY NAME OR CORPORATE NAME

GIVEN NAMES

NO.   STREET   APT

CITY

PROV.   POSTAL CODE

BUSINESS TELEPHONE NUMBER

BUSINESS FAX NUMBER

CHANGE IN NAME, ADDRESS OR TELEPHONE NUMBER FROM LAST REPORT   YES   NO

BOX 4. JURISDICTION(S) WHERE THE ISSUER IS A REPORTING ISSUER OR THE EQUIVALENT

- ALBERTA
- BRITISH COLUMBIA
- FEDERAL
  - BANK ACT
  - CCAA
  - ICA
  - TLCA
  - CBCA
- MANITOBA
- NEWFOUNDLAND
- NOVA SCOTIA
- ONTARIO
- QUEBEC
- SASKATCHEWAN
- UNITED STATES
- NASDAQ
- SEC

BOX 5. INSIDER HOLDINGS AND CHANGES (IF INITIAL REPORT, COMPLETE SECTIONS (A) (D) AND (F) ONLY. SEE ALSO INSTRUCTIONS TO BOX 5)

(A) DESIGNATION OF CLASS OF SECURITIES	(B) BALANCE OF CLASS OF SECURITIES ON LAST REPORT	(C) TRANSACTIONS						(D) PRESENT BALANCE OF CLASS OF SECURITIES HELD	(E) DIRECT/INDIRECT OWNERSHIP CONTROL OR DIRECTION	(F) IDENTIFY THE REGISTERED HOLDER WHOSE OWNERSHIP IS INDIRECT OR WHERE CONTROL OR DIRECTION IS EXERCISED
		DATE DAY MONTH YEAR	NATURE	NUMBER/VALUE ACQUIRED	NUMBER/VALUE DISPOSED OF	UNIT PRICE/ EXERCISE PRICE	$ US			

BOX 6. REMARKS

The undersigned certifies that the information given in this report is true and complete in every respect. It is an offence to file a report that, at the time and in the light of the circumstances in which it is made, contains a misrepresentation.

BOX 7. SIGNATURE

NAME (BLOCK LETTERS)   SIGNATURE

DATE OF THE REPORT   DAY   MONTH   YEAR

ATTACHMENT   YES   NO

This form is used as a uniform report for the insider reporting requirements under all provincial securities Acts, Bank Act, Cooperative Credit Associations Act, Insurance Companies Act, Trust and Loan Companies Act and Canada Business Corporations Act. The terminology used is generic to accommodate the various Acts.

CORRESPONDENCE   ENGLISH   FRENCH

KEEP A COPY FOR YOUR FILE

FIN 2026 Rev. 95 / 2 / 22 +E – 164   VERSION FRANÇAISE DISPONIBLE SUR DEMANDE

Forms

INSTRUCTIONS

Insider Reports in English and French are available from the Manitoba, Ontario, Québec and federal jurisdictions. If you are a corporate insider in the province of Québec, you will receive correspondence in French. Individuals in the province of Québec will receive, upon request, correspondence in English.

Where an insider of a reporting issuer does not own or have control or direction over securities of the reporting issuer, or where an insider's ownership or direction or control over securities of the reporting issuer remains unchanged from the last report filed, a report is not required. Insider reports are not required to be filed in New Brunswick, the Northwest Territories, Prince Edward Island or the Yukon.

"Reporting issuer" has the same meaning as the words "distributing bank" as defined in subsection 265(1) of the *Bank Act*; "distributing association" as defined in subsection 260(1) of the *Cooperative Credit Associations Act* (CCAA); and "distributing company" as defined in subsection 286(1) of the *Insurance Companies Act* (ICA) or subsection 270(1) of the *Trust and Loan Companies Act* (TLCA), "distributing corporation" as defined in subsection 126(1) of the *Canada Business Corporations Act* (CBCA).

"Debt securities" wherever it appears herein, has the same meaning as "debt obligation" as defined in subsection 2(1) of the CBCA.

BOX 1   Name of the reporting issuer
Provide the full legal name of the reporting issuer. Use a separate report for each reporting issuer.

BOX 2   Insider data
Indicate all of your relationship(s) to the reporting issuer using the following codes:

Reporting issuer that has acquired securities issued by itself (or by any of its affiliates - CBCA)   1

Subsidiary of the reporting issuer   2

Security holder who beneficially owns or who exercises control or direction over more than 10% of the securities of the reporting issuer (*Bank Act*, CCAA, ICA, TLCA, CBCA and Québec *Securities Act* – 10% of a class of shares) to which are attached voting rights or an unlimited right to a share of the profits and to its assets in case of winding up   3

Director of a reporting issuer   4

Senior officer of a reporting issuer   5

Director or senior officer of a security holder referred to in 3   6

Director or senior officer of an affiliate (*Bank Act*, CCAA, ICA, TLCA and CBCA) or of a subsidiary of the reporting issuer, other than in 4, 5 and 6   7

Deemed insider under the *Bank Act*, CCAA, ICA, TLCA and CBCA   8

If you have filed a report before, indicate whether your relationship to the reporting issuer has changed.

Specify the date of the last report you filed, and if it is an initial report, the date on which you became an insider.

BOX 3   Name, address and telephone number of the insider
Provide your name, address and business telephone number.

BOX 4   Jurisdiction
Indicate each jurisdiction where the issuer is a reporting issuer.

BOX 5   Insider holdings and changes
Show direct and indirect holdings in the initial report and where a transaction is reported. Indicate only one transaction per line.

For an initial report complete only:

(A) designation of class of securities held

(D) present balance of class of securities held

(E) nature of ownership (see List of Codes)

(F) identification of the registered holder where ownership is indirect

If you acquired or disposed of securities while an insider, complete sections (A) to (F):

(A) indicate a designation of the securities traded that is sufficient to identify the class, including yield, series, maturity.

(B) indicate the number of securities, or for debt securities, the aggregate nominal value, of the class held, directly and indirectly, before the transaction that is being reported.

(C) Indicate for each transaction:
- the date of the transaction (not the settlement date)
- the nature of the transaction (see List of Codes)
- the number of securities acquired or disposed of, or for debt securities, the aggregate nominal value
- the unit price paid or received on the day of the transaction, excluding the commission
- if the report is in American dollars, check the space under "$ US"

List of Codes

BOX 5 (C) Nature of transaction

Acquisition or disposition carried out in the market, excluding the:	
exercise of an option	10
Private placement (issuance from treasury)	11
Acquisition or disposition carried out privately	
(already issued securities)	20
Acquisition or disposition pursuant to a takeover bid or issuer bid	22
Change in the nature of ownership	25
Acquisition or disposition under a plan	30
Stock dividend	35
Acquisition or disposition of a call option	40
Acquisition or disposition of a put option	45
Expiration of an option	46
Acquisition or disposition by gift	50
Acquisition by inheritance or disposition by bequest	55
Short sale	60
Grant of warrants	65
Grant of rights	66
Exercise of warrants	70
Expiration of warrants	71
Expiration of rights	72
Exercise of rights	75
Exercise of options	76
Conversion or exchange	78
Stock split or consolidation	84
Redemption/retraction/cancellation/repurchase	85
Compensation for property	90
Compensation for services	95
Grant of options	96
Other than referred to above (please explain in Remarks)	97
Correction of information	99
(please explain in Remarks)	

(D) Indicate the number of securities, or for debt securities, the aggregate nominal value, of the class held, directly and indirectly, after the transaction that is being reported.

(E) Indicate the nature of ownership, control or direction of the class of securities held using the following codes:

Direct ownership	0
Indirect ownership (identify the registered holder)	1
Control or direction (identify the registered holder)	2

(F) For securities that are indirectly held, or over which control or direction is exercised, identify the registered holder

BOX 6   Remarks
Add any explanation necessary to make the report clearly understandable.

If space provided for any item is insufficient, additional sheets may be used. Additional sheets must refer to the appropriate Box and must be properly identified and signed.

Office staff are not permitted to alter a report.

BOX 7   Signature and filing
Sign and date the report.

File two copies of the report in each jurisdiction in which the issuer is reporting within the time limits prescribed by the applicable laws of that jurisdiction. British Columbia requires only one copy.

Manually sign one of the two copies.

Legibly print or type the name of each individual signing the report.

If the report is filed on behalf of a company, partnership, trust or other entity, legibly print or type the name of that entity after the signature.

If the report is signed on behalf of an individual by an agent, there shall be filed with each jurisdiction in which the report is filed a duly completed power of attorney.

Alberta Securities Commission
21st Floor
10025 Jasper Avenue
Edmonton, Alberta
T5J 3Z5

Office of the Superintendent of
Financial Institutions, Canada
13th Floor, Kent Square
255 Albert Street
Ottawa, Ontario
K1A 0H2

British Columbia Securities Commission
1100, 865 Hornby Street
Vancouver, British Columbia
V6Z 2H4

Director
Canada Business Corporations Act
9th Floor
Journal Tower South
365 Laurier Avenue West
Ottawa, Ontario
K1A 0C8

Manitoba Securities Commission
1128-405 Broadway
Winnipeg, Manitoba
R3C 3L6

Director of Securities
Department of Justice, Newfoundland
P.O. Box 8700
4th Floor, East Block
Confederation Building
St. John's, Newfoundland
A1B 4J6

Nova Scotia Securities Commission
Department of Attorney General
Joseph Howe Building, 2nd Floor
1690 Hollis Street
P.O. Box 458
Halifax, Nova Scotia
B3J 3J9

Ontario Securities Commission
Suite 800, Box 55
20 Queen Street West
Toronto, Ontario
M5H 3S8

Commission des valeurs
mobilières du Québec
C.P. 246, Tour de la Bourse
Montréal, (Québec)
H4Z 1G3

Saskatchewan Securities Commission
8th Floor
1914 Hamilton Street
Regina, Saskatchewan
S4P 3V7

FORM 38

Securities Act

THIS IS THE REPORT BY A REGISTERED OWNER OF SECURITIES BENEFI-CIALLY OWNED BY AN INSIDER REQUIRED UNDER SECTION 71 OF THE ACT

NOTE This report is only required where:

1. voting securities are transferred into the name of a person other than the beneficial owner;

2. the person knows that:

   (a) they are beneficially owned by an insider, and

   (b) the insider has failed to file a report of such ownership with the Securities Commission as required by Part 10 of the Act; and

3. the transfer was not for the purpose of giving collateral for a bona fide debt.

---

1. State the relationship between the undersigned and the insider.

2. Certificate (Instruction 1):

The undersigned hereby certifies that:

1. attached as an exhibit is an unexecuted insider trading report in respect of voting securities that are registered in the name of the undersigned but beneficially owned by the insider named in the report, and

2. the report has, in respect of such voting securities, been completed to the best of my information and belief.

_____   _____

Date of Report   Signature (Instruction 2)

INSTRUCTIONS:

1. Use as the exhibit the form of report the insider has failed to file as required by Part 10 of the Act. Complete the report only in respect of voting securities. If required information is not known by the person completing the attached report mark "Not known" or "Complete information not known".

2. Please print the name and office of the person executing this report or on whose behalf this report is executed.

February 1, 1987

FORM 39

Securities Act

THIS IS THE REPORT OF A MUTUAL FUND MANAGER REQUIRED UNDER SECTION 109 OF THE ACT

Name of the mutual fund for which the mutual fund manager provides services and advice

Name of the transaction

Category of the transaction (Instruction 1)

Parties to the transaction

Nature of the transaction (Instruction 2)

The undersigned hereby certifies that the information given in this report is true and complete in every respect.

Date of the Report

Name of Mutual Fund Manager

By _____
      Signature

_____
Official Capacity

INSTRUCTION 1

Categorize each transaction as being a transaction of purchase and sale of securities between the mutual fund and a related person, a transaction or purchase and sale of securities resulting in a related person receiving a fee, a loan between the mutual fund and a related person or a transaction to which the mutual fund and a related person of the mutual fund are joint participants.

INSTRUCTION 2

Where the transaction is categorized as a purchase or sale of securities between the mutual fund and a related person, state the issuer of the securities purchased or sold, the class or designation of the securities, the amount or number of securities and the consideration.

Where the transaction is categorized as a purchase or sale of securities resulting in a related person receiving a fee, state the name of the issuer of the securities purchased or sold, the class or designation of the securities, the amount or number of the securities, the consideration, the name of the related person receiving a fee, the name of the person that paid the fee to the related person and the amount of the fee received by the related person.

Where the transaction is categorized as a loan between the mutual fund and a related person, state the name of the lender, the name of the borrower, the amount of money loaned, the terms of the loan and the purpose of the loan.

Where the transaction is categorized as one to which the mutual fund and one or more of its related persons are joint participants, state terms of participation and the purpose of the transaction.

February 1, 1987

This is the form required under Section 139(1) of the Securities Act.

FORM 40
Securities Act
ENDORSEMENT OF WARRANT

CANADA,

PROVINCE OF

_____
(territorial division)

Pursuant to subsection _____ Securities Act and pursuant to application this day made to me, I hereby authorize the execution of this warrant within the said

_____
(territorial jurisdiction)

Dated this _____ day of _____ 19 ___ , at

_____ in the Province of British Columbia.

_____

A Justice of the Peace in
and for the Province of

_____

February 1, 1987

FORM 41

Securities Act

STATEMENT OF EXECUTIVE COMPENSATION

ITEM I   Interpretation

I.1   **Definitions**. For purposes of this Form,

"CEO" of an issuer means an individual who served as chief executive officer of the issuer or acted in a similar capacity during the most recently completed financial year;

"equity security" means securities of an issuer that carry a residual right to participate in earnings of the issuer and, upon liquidation or winding up of the issuer, its assets;

"executive officer" of an issuer for a financial year, means an individual who at any time during the year was,

(a)   the chair of the issuer, if that individual performed the functions of the office on a full- time basis,

(b)   a vice-chair of the issuer, if that individual performed the functions of the office on a full- time basis,

(c)   the president of the issuer,

(d)   a vice-president of the issuer in charge of a principal business unit, division or function such as sales, finance or production, or

(e)   an officer of the issuer or any of its subsidiaries or any other person who performed a policy-making function in respect of the issuer,

whether or not the individual was also a director of the issuer or any of its subsidiaries;

"long-term incentive plan" or "LTIP" means any plan providing compensation intended to serve as incentive for performance to occur over a period longer than one financial year, whether the performance is measured by reference to financial performance of the issuer or an affiliate of the issuer, the price for the issuer's securities, or any other measure, but does not include option or SAR plans or plans for compensation through restricted shares or restricted share units;

"Named Executive Officers" means the individuals referred to in Subitem I.3;

"normal retirement age", with respect to a pension or similar plan, means normal retirement age as defined in the plan or, if not defined in the plan, the earliest time at which a participant in the plan may retire without any benefit reduction due to age;

"options" includes all options, share purchase warrants and rights granted by the issuer or any of its subsidiaries as compensation for services rendered or otherwise in connection with office or employment (an extension of an option or replacement grant is a grant of a new option) and includes other securities if,

(a) the class or series of the securities has been created to be issued, or securities of the class or series have been or will be issued, primarily for compensation for services rendered or otherwise in connection with office or employment,

(b) the securities carry the right to purchase or otherwise acquire (e.g.,through an exchange or conversion) securities of the issuer or of any of its subsidiaries, and

(c) the securities and the terms of the purchase or acquisition of the securities in effect are similar to options;

"plan" includes, but is not limited to, any plan, contract, authorization or arrangement, whether or not set forth in any formal document and whether or not applicable to only one individual, under which cash, securities, options, SARs, phantom stock, warrants, convertible securities, restricted shares or restricted share units, performance units and performance shares, or similar instruments may be received or purchased, but does not include the Canada Pension Plan or similar government plans or any group life, health, hospitalization, medical reimbursement or relocation plan that does not discriminate in scope, terms or operation in favour of executive officers or directors of the issuer and is available generally to all salaried employees;

"public float" means the aggregate of the market value of each class of equity securities of the issuer, excluding securities that are beneficially owned, directly or indirectly, or over which control or direction is exercised by persons or companies that alone, or together with their respective associates and affiliates, beneficially own or exercise control or direction over more than 10 percent of the issued and outstanding equity securities of the issuer, but securities that would be excluded because a portfolio manager of a pension fund, mutual fund or non-redeemable investment fund exercises control or direction over them need only be excluded if the portfolio manager is an affiliate of the issuer;

"replacement grant" of an option or SAR means the grant of an option or SAR reasonably related to any prior or potential cancellation of an option or SAR, whether by,

(a) an exchange of existing options or SARs for options or SARs with new terms,

(b) the grant of new options or SARs designed to operate in tandem with previously granted options or SARs that upon exercise will operate to cancel the previously granted options or SARs,

(c) downward repricing of previously granted options or SARs, or

(d) any other means;

"repricing" of an option or SAR means the adjustment or amendment of the exercise or base price of an option or SAR previously awarded, whether through amendment, cancellation or replacement grants, or any other means, but does not include any repricing occurring through the operation of a formula or mechanism in, or applicable to, the previously awarded option or SAR that results in the periodic adjustment of the effective exercise, purchase or base price, a plan anti-dilution provision, or a recapitalization or similar transaction equally affecting all holders of the class of securities underlying the option or SAR and "repriced" has a corresponding meaning;

"small business issuer" means an issuer that:

(a) has revenues of less than $25,000,000 in the most recently completed financial year,

(b) is not a non-redeemable investment fund or mutual fund,

(c) has a public float of less than $25,000,000, and

(d) if it is a subsidiary of another issuer, that other issuer is also a small business issuer;

"stock appreciation right" ("SAR") means a right, granted by an issuer or any of its subsidiaries as compensation for services rendered or otherwise in connection with office or employment, to receive a payment of cash or an issue or transfer of securities based wholly or in part on changes in the trading price of publicly traded securities.

I.2 **Plain, Concise and Understandable Disclosure.** Information required by this Form should be provided in a plain, concise and understandable manner under the appropriate Item in the "Executive Compensation" section of the disclosure document. If any Item of this Form requires disclosure of information in tabular form, the information must be presented in the specific format set out. Any table or column of a table may be omitted if there has been no compensation that otherwise would be required to be disclosed in that table or column in any financial year covered by the table.

I.3 **Individuals Covered.** Disclosure must be provided under this Form for,

(a)   each CEO, despite the amount of compensation of that individual;

(b)   each of the issuer's four most highly compensated executive officers, other than the CEO, who were serving as executive officers at the end of the most recently completed financial year, provided that disclosure is not required under this Form for an executive officer whose total salary and bonus, as determined in accordance with Item II, does not exceed $100,000; and

(c)   any additional individuals for whom disclosure would have been provided under (b) but for the fact that the individual was not serving as an executive officer of the issuer at the end of the most recently completed financial year end.

I.4 **Determination of Most Highly Compensated Executive Officers.** The determination of which executive officers are the issuer's most highly compensated executive officers must be made on the basis of the total annual salary and bonus of each executive officer of the issuer during the most recently completed financial year calculated in accordance with Item II.

I.5 **Change in Status of a Named Executive Officer During the Financial Year.** If the CEO served in that capacity during any part of a financial year for which disclosure is required under this Form, information must be provided as to all of his or her compensation for the full financial year. If a Named Executive Officer, other than the CEO, served as an executive officer of the issuer (whether or not in the same position) during any part of a financial year for which disclosure is required under this Form, information must be provided as to all of his or her compensation for the full financial year.

I.6 **Exclusion of Executive Officer Due to Unusual Compensation or Compensation for Foreign Assignment.** It may be appropriate, in limited circumstances, for the issuer to exclude from the disclosure required by this Form an individual, other than a CEO, who is one of the issuer's most highly compensated executive officers. Among the factors that should be considered in determining to exclude an individual are,

(a)   the payment or accrual of an unusually large amount of cash compensation (such as bonus or commission) that is not part of a recurring arrangement and is unlikely to continue; and

(b)   whether the individual is one of the four most highly compensated executive officers only because of the payment of additional amounts of cash compensation intended to compensate him or her for increased living expenses that may be attributed predominately to an assignment outside of Canada.

I.7 **All Compensation Covered.** Unless otherwise specified, this Form requires disclosure of all plan and non-plan compensation awarded to, earned by, or paid to, each Named Executive Officer and each director covered by Item XI for services rendered by that individual in all capacities to the issuer or a subsidiary of the issuer or otherwise in connection with office or employment of that individual with the issuer or a subsidiary of the issuer. Except as expressly provided, no amount, benefit or right reported as compensation for a financial year need be reported as compensation for any subsequent financial year.

I.8 **Sources of Compensation.** Compensation to officers and directors from the issuer must include compensation from the issuer and its subsidiaries. In addition, if any understanding or agreement exists among any of the issuer, its subsidiaries or an officer or director of the issuer or its subsidiary and another entity, for the primary purpose of the other entity furnishing compensation to the officer or director for services rendered to, or otherwise in connection with office or employment with, the issuer or any of its subsidiaries, any compensation furnished under that understanding or agreement must be included in the appropriate category of compensation of the officer or director.

I.9 **Compensation Furnished to Associates.** If any understanding or agreement exists among any of the issuer, its subsidiaries or another entity and an officer or director of the issuer or its subsidiary for the primary purpose of the issuer, its subsidiary or the other entity furnishing compensation to the officer or director for services rendered to, or otherwise in connection with office or employment with, the issuer or any of its subsidiaries through compensation to an associate of the director or officer, any compensation to such associate under that understanding or agreement must be included in the appropriate category of compensation of the officer or director.

ITEM II   Summary Compensation Table

II.1 State the information specified in Subitem II.2 concerning the compensation of each of the Named Executive Officers for each of the issuer's three most recently completed financial years, in the tabular form under the caption set out below.

SUMMARY COMPENSATION TABLE

| | | Annual Compensation | | | Long Term Compensation | | | |
| | | | | | Awards | | Payouts | |
Name and Principal Position (a)	Year (b)	Salary ($) (c)	Bonus ($) (d)	Other Annual Compensation ($) (e)	Securities Under Options/ SARs Granted (#) (f)	Restricted Shares or Restricted Share Units ($) (g)	LTIP Payouts ($) (h)	All Other Compensation ($) (i)
CEO								
A								
B								
C								
D								

II.2 The Table required by Subitem II.1 must include:

(a)   The name and principal position of the Named Executive Officer (column (a)).

(b)   The financial year covered (column (b)).

(c)   Annual compensation (columns (c), (d), and (e)), including,

   (i) the dollar value of any cash or non-cash base salary earned by the Named Executive Officer during the financial year covered (column (c)),

(ii) the dollar value of any cash or non-cash bonus earned by the Named Executive Officer during the financial year covered (column (d)), and

(iii) the dollar value of all other annual compensation of the Named Executive Officer during the financial year covered that is not properly categorized as salary or bonus (column (e)).

(d) Long-term compensation (columns (f), (g) and (h)), including,

(i) the sum of the number of securities under option granted during the year covered (with or without tandem SARs) and, separately, the sum of the number of securities subject to freestanding SARs granted during the year covered (column (f)),

(ii) the dollar value (net of consideration paid by the Named Executive Officer) of any restricted shares or restricted share units granted during the year covered (calculated by multiplying the closing market price of the issuer's unrestricted shares on the date of grant by the number of shares or share units awarded (column (g)), and

(iii) the dollar value of all payouts under LTIPs (column (h)).

(e) All other compensation for the covered financial year that is not properly reported in any other column of the table required by this Item (column (i)).

II.3   For purposes of subparagraphs (c)(i) and (ii) of Subitem II.2 regarding salary and bonus:

(a) Amounts deferred at the election of a Named Executive Officer must be included in the salary column (column (c)) or bonus column (column (d)), as appropriate, for the financial year in which earned. If the amount of salary or bonus earned in a given financial year is not calculable, that fact must be disclosed in a footnote and that amount must be disclosed in the subsequent financial year in the appropriate column for the financial year in which earned.

(b) For securities or any other form of non-cash compensation, disclose the fair market value of the compensation at the time the compensation is awarded, earned or paid.

(c) Any amount of salary or bonus earned in a covered year that was foregone, at the election of a Named Executive Officer, under a program of the issuer under which stock, stock-based or other forms of non-cash compensation may be received in lieu of a portion of annual compensation, need not be included in the salary or bonus columns. Instead, the issuer may disclose the receipt by the Named Executive Officer during that financial year of the non-cash compensation in lieu of salary or bonus in the appropriate column of the table corresponding to that year (i.e., options or SARs (column (f)), restricted shares or restricted share units (column (g)), and all other compensation (column (i))). If the election was made under a long-term incentive plan and therefore is not reportable at the time of grant in the table required by this Item, a footnote must be added to the salary or bonus column disclosing this fact and referring to the table required by Item III for disclosure of the reward.

II.4   For purposes of subparagraph (c)(iii) of Item II.2 regarding all other annual compensation:

(a) Perquisites and other personal benefits, securities or property are to be disclosed in column (e), unless the aggregate amount of such compensation is no greater than the lesser of $50,000 and 10 percent of the total of the annual salary and bonus of the Named Executive Officer for the financial year. Each perquisite or other personal benefit exceeding 25 percent of the total perquisites and other personal benefits reported for a Named Executive Officer must be identified by type and amount in a footnote to the other annual compensation column (column (e)). Perquisites and other personal benefits must be valued on the basis of the aggregate incremental cost to the issuer and its subsidiaries.

(b)   If securities, options, SARs, loans, deferred compensation or other obligations issued to a Named Executive Officer carry a right to receive interest, dividends or other amounts that at the time of issue or reset is above-market or preferential (*i.e.*, at a rate greater than the rate ordinarily paid by the issuer or its subsidiary on securities or other obligations having the same or similar features issued to third parties), the above-market portion of all such interest, dividends or other amounts paid during the financial year or payable during that period but deferred at the election of the Named Executive Officer must be disclosed in column (e).

(c)   Earnings on long-term incentive plan compensation or dividend equivalents paid during the financial year or payable during that period but deferred at the election of the Named Executive Officer must be disclosed in column (e).

(d)   Amounts reimbursed during the financial year for the payment of taxes must be disclosed in column (e).

(e)   The dollar value of the difference between the price paid by a Named Executive officer for a security of the issuer or its subsidiaries that was purchased from the issuer or its subsidiaries (through deferral of salary or bonus or otherwise) and the fair market value of the security at the date of purchase must be disclosed in column (e), unless the discount was available generally, either to all security holders or to all salaried employees of the issuer.

(f)   The dollar value of imputed interest benefits from loans provided to, or debts incurred on behalf of, the Named Executive Officer by the issuer and its subsidiaries as computed in accordance with the *Income Tax Act* (Canada) must be disclosed in column (e).

(g)   The dollar value of amounts of loan or interest obligations of the Named Executive Officer to the issuer, its subsidiary or third parties that were serviced, settled or extinguished by the issuer or its subsidiaries without the substitution of an obligation to repay the amount to the issuer or subsidiary in its place must be disclosed in column (e).

II.5   For purposes of paragraph (d) of Subitem II.2 regarding long-term compensation:

(a)   If at any time during the most recently completed financial year the issuer has repriced downward options or freestanding SARs previously awarded to a Named Executive Officer, disclose the options or SARs so repriced as new options or SARs grants in column (f).

(b)   Awards of restricted shares or restricted share units that are subject to performance-based conditions to vesting, in addition to lapse of time or continued service with the issuer or a subsidiary, may be disclosed as LTIP awards under column (i) instead of under column (g). If this approach is selected, once the restricted share or restricted share unit vests, it must be reported as an LTIP payout in column (h).

(c)   In a footnote to the restricted shares and restricted share units column (column (g)) disclose,

      (i) the number and value of the aggregate holdings of restricted shares and restricted share units at the end of the most recently completed financial year with the value being calculated in accordance with subparagraph (d)(ii) of Subitem II.2,

      (ii) for any restricted share or restricted share unit that will vest, in whole or in part, in less than three years from the date of grant, the total number of securities awarded and the vesting schedule, and

      (iii) whether dividends or dividend equivalents will be paid on the restricted shares and restricted share units disclosed in the column.

(d)   If any specified performance target, goal or condition to payout was waived with respect to any amount included in LTIP payouts, disclose this fact in a footnote to the LTIP payout column (column (h)).

II.6 For purposes of paragraph (e) of Subitem II.2, all other compensation for the covered financial year that is not properly reported in any other column of the table required by this Item includes, but is not limited to:

(a) The amount paid, payable or accrued to a Named Executive Officer under a plan or arrangement for compensation for:

(i) the resignation, retirement or other termination of the officer's employment with the registrant or a subsidiary of the issuer, or

(ii) a change in control of the issuer or a subsidiary of the issuer or a change in the officer's responsibilities following such a change in control.

(b) If securities, options, SARs, loans, deferred compensation or other obligations issued to a Named Executive Officer carry a right to receive interest, dividends or other amounts that at the time of issue or reset is above-market or preferential (*i.e.*, at a rate greater than the rate ordinarily paid by the issuer or its subsidiary on securities or obligations having the same or similar features issued to third parties), the dollar value of the above-market portion of all such interest, dividends or other amounts earned during the financial year, or calculated with respect to that period, except that amounts that are paid during that period, or payable during that period at the election of the Named Executive Officer must be reported as other annual compensation in column (e).

(c) The dollar value of amounts earned on long-term incentive plan compensation during the financial year, or calculated with respect to that period, and dividend equivalents earned during that period except that amounts that are paid during that period, or payable during that period at the election of the Named Executive Officer must be reported as other annual compensation in column (e).

(d) Annual contributions or other allocations by the issuer or its subsidiary to vested and unvested defined contribution plans.

(e) The dollar value of any insurance premium paid by, or on behalf of, the issuer or its subsidiary during the financial year with respect to term life insurance for the benefit of a Named Executive Officer, and, if there is an arrangement or understanding, whether formal or informal, that the officer has or will receive or be allocated an interest in any cash surrender value under the insurance policy, either:

(i) the full dollar value of the remainder of the premiums paid by, or on behalf of, the issuer or its subsidiary, or

(ii) if the premiums will be refunded to the issuer or its subsidiary on termination of the policy, the dollar value of the benefit to the officer of the remainder of the premium paid by, or on behalf of, the issuer or its subsidiary during the financial year. This benefit must be determined for the period, projected on an actuarial basis, between payment of premium and the refund.

The same method of reporting under this paragraph must be used for each of the Named Executive Officers. If the issuer changes methods of reporting from one year to the next, that fact and the reason for the change must be disclosed in a footnote to the all other compensation column (column (i)).

II.7 For purposes of paragraph (e) of Subitem II.2 regarding all other compensation not otherwise properly reported in any other column:

(a) LTIP awards and amounts received on exercise of options and SARs need not be reported as all other compensation in column (i).

(b) Information on defined benefit and actuarial plans need not be reported in column (i).

II.8 If during any of the financial years covered by the table required by this Item, a Named Executive Officer was not employed by the issuer or its subsidiary for the entire financial year, disclose this fact and the number of months the officer was so employed during the year in a footnote to the table.

II.9   If during any of the financial years covered by the table required by this Item, a Named Executive Officer was compensated by a non-subsidiary affiliate of the issuer, disclose in a note to the table,

   (a)   the amount and nature of such compensation; and

   (b)   whether the compensation is included in the compensation reported in the table.

II.10   Information with respect to a financial year-end prior to the most recently completed financial year-end need not be provided if the issuer was not a reporting issuer at any time during such prior financial year.

II.11   In order to facilitate transition, the amounts reported under columns (e) and (i) of the table required by this Item need not include information for financial years ended before October 31, 1993. For small business issuers, the table required by this Item need not include amounts for financial years ended before December 31, 1993.

ITEM III   Long-term Incentive Plan Awards Table

III.1   State the information specified in Subitem III.2 concerning LTIP awards made to Named Executive Officers during the most recently completed financial year in the tabular form under the caption set out below.

LONG-TERM INCENTIVE PLANS –
AWARDS IN MOST RECENTLY COMPLETED FINANCIAL YEAR

| Name (a) | Securities Units or Other Rights (#) (b) | Performance or Other Period Until Maturation or Payout (c) | Estimated Future Payouts Under Non-Securities - Price-Based Plans | | |
			Threshold ($ or #) (d)	Target ($ or #) (e)	Maximum ($ or #) (f)
CEO					
A					
B					
C					
D					

III.2   The table required by Subitem III.1 must include for each LTIP award:

   (a)   The name of the Named Executive Officer (column (a)).

   (b)   The number of securities, units or other rights awarded under any LTIP and, if applicable, the number of securities underlying any such unit or right (column (b)).

   (c)   The performance or other time period until payout or maturation of the award (column (c)).

   (d)   For plans not based on stock price, the dollar value of the estimated payout, the number of shares to be awarded as the payout or the range of estimated payouts under the award (threshold, target and maximum amount), whether such award is denominated in stock or cash (columns (d) through (f)).

III.3   Describe in a footnote to, or a narrative that accompanies, the table required by this Item the material terms of any award, including a general description of the formula or criteria to be applied in determining the amounts payable. Issuers are not, however, required to disclose any factor, criterion or performance-related or other condition to payout or maturation of a particular award that involves confidential or business information, disclosure of which would adversely affect the issuer's competitive position.

III.4   Separate disclosure must be provided in the table required by this Item and under Subitem III.3 for each award made to a Named Executive Officer, if awards were made under more than one plan or awards under the same plan have different material terms. Identify the particular plan under which each award was made.

III.5   For purposes of this Item:

(a)   "threshold" means the minimum amount payable for a certain level of performance under the plan,

"Target" means the amount payable if the specified performance target(s) are reached, and

"Maximum" means the maximum payout possible under the plan.

(b)   A tandem grant of two instruments, only one of which is pursuant to an LTIP, need be reported only in the table applicable to the other instrument.

(c)   In column (e), the issuer must provide a representative amount based on the previous financial year's performance if the target award is not determinable.

ITEM IV   Options and SARs

IV.1   State the information specified in Subitem IV.2 concerning individual grants of options to purchase or acquire securities of the issuer or any of its subsidiaries (whether or not in tandem with SARs) and freestanding SARs made during the most recently completed financial year to each of the Named Executive Officers, in the tabular form under the caption set out below.

OPTION/SAR GRANTS DURING THE MOST RECENTLY COMPLETED FINANCIAL YEAR

Name (a)	Securities Under Options/ SARs Granted (#) (b)	% of Total Options/SARs Granted to Employees in Financial Year (c)	Exercise or Base Price ($/Security) (d)	Market Value of Securities Underlying Options/SARs on the Date of Grant ($/Security) (e)	Expiration Date (f)
CEO					
A					
B					
C					
D					

IV.2   The table required by Subitem IV.1 must include for each grant of options or SARs:

(a)   The name of the Named Executive Officer (column (a)).

(b)   The number of securities underlying the options or freestanding SARs granted (column (b)).

(c)   The percentage that the grant represents of total options and freestanding SARs granted to employees of the issuer and its subsidiaries during the financial year (column (c)).

(d)   The per-security exercise or base price of the options or freestanding SARs granted (column(d)).

(e)   The per-security market value of the underlying securities on the date of grant (column (e)).

(f)   The expiration date of the options or freestanding SARs granted (column (f)).

IV.3   For the table required by Subitems IV.1:

(a)   The information must be presented for each Named Executive Officer in groups according to each issuer and class or series of security underlying the options or SARs granted and within these groups in reverse chronological order. For each grant, disclose in a footnote the issuer and the class or series of securities underlying the options or freestanding SARs granted.

(b) If more than one grant of options or freestanding SARs was made to a Named Executive Officer during the most recently completed financial year, a separate row must be used to provide the particulars of each grant. However, more than one grant during a single financial year to a Named Executive Officer may be aggregated if each grant being aggregated was made at the same exercise or base price and has the same expiration date and the same performance vesting thresholds, if any.

(c) A single grant of options or freestanding SARs must be reported as separate grants for each tranche with a different exercise or base price, expiration date or performance vesting threshold.

(d) Each material term of the grant, including but not limited to the date of exercisability, the number of SARs, dividend equivalents, performance units or other instruments granted in tandem with options, a performance-based condition to exercisability, a re-load feature or a tax-reimbursement feature must be disclosed in a footnote to the table.

(e) Options or freestanding SARs granted in an option repricing transaction must be disclosed.

(f) If the exercise or base price is adjustable over the term of an option or freestanding SAR in accordance with a prescribed standard or formula, include in a footnote to, or a narrative accompanying, the table a description of the standard or formula.

(g) If any provision of an option or SAR (other than an anti-dilution provision) could cause the exercise or base price to be lowered, a description of the provision and its potential consequences must be included in a footnote to, or a narrative accompanying, the table.

(h) In determining the grant date market value of the securities underlying options or freestanding SARs, use either the closing market price or any other formula prescribed under the option or SAR plan. For options or SARs granted prior to the establishment of a trading market in the underlying securities, the initial offering price may be used.

IV.4 State the information specified in Subitem IV.5 concerning each exercise of options (or tandem SARS) and freestanding SARs during the most recently completed financial year by each of the Named Executive Officers and the financial year-end value of unexercised options and SARs, on an aggregated basis, in the tabular form and under the caption set out below.

AGGREGATED OPTION/SAR EXERCISES DURING THE MOST RECENTLY COMPLETED FINANCIAL YEAR AND FINANCIAL YEAR-END OPTION/SAR VALUES

Name (a)	Securities Acquired on Exercise (#) (b)	Aggregate Value Realized ($) (c)	Unexercised Options/SARs at FY-End (#) Exercisable/ Unexercisable (d)	Value of Unexercised in the-Money Options/SARs at FY-End ($) Exercisable/ Unexercisable (e)
CEO				
A				
B				
C				
D				

IV.5 The table required by Subitem IV.4 must include:

(a) The name of the Named Executive Officer (column (a)).

(b) The aggregate number of securities received on exercise or, if no securities were received, the aggregate number of securities for which options or SARs were exercised (column (b)).

(c) The aggregate dollar value realized upon exercise (column (c)).

(d) The total number of securities underlying unexercised options and SARs held at the end of the most recently completed financial year, separately identifying the exercisable and unexercisable options and SARs (column(d)).

(e) The aggregate dollar value of in-the-money, unexercised options and SARs held at the end of the financial year, separately identifying the exercisable and unexercisable options and SARs (column (e)).

IV.6 For the table required by Subitem IV.4:

(a) Options or freestanding SARs are in-the-money at financial year end if the market value of the underlying securities on that date exceeds the exercise or base price of the option or SAR.

(b) The dollar values in columns (c) and (e) are calculated by determining the difference between the market value of the securities underlying the options or SARs at exercise or financial year end, respectively, and the exercise or base price of the options or SARs.

(c) In calculating the dollar value realized on exercise (column (c)), the value of any related payment or other consideration provided (or to be provided) by the issuer or its subsidiary to, or on behalf of, a Named Executive Officer, whether in payment of the exercise or base price or related taxes, must not be included. Instead, these payments are to be disclosed in accordance with Subitem II.4.

ITEM V Option and SAR Repricings

V.1 If at any time after October 31, 1993 and during the most recently completed financial year, the issuer has repriced downward any options or freestanding SARs held by any Named Executive Officer, state the information specified in Subitem V.2 concerning all downward repricings of options or SARs held by executive officers of the issuer during the shorter of,

(a) the 10 year period ending on the date of certification of the disclosure required by this Form, and

(b) the period during which the issuer has been a reporting issuer,

in the tabular form under the caption set out below.

TABLE OF OPTION AND SAR REPRICINGS

Name (a)	Date of Repricing (b)	Securities Under Options/SARs Repriced or Amended (#) (c)	Market Price of Securities at Time of Repricing or Amendment ($/Security) (d)	Exercise Price at Time of Repricing or Amendment ($/Security) (e)	New Exercise Price ($/Security) (f)	Length of Original Option Term Remaining at Date of Repricing or Amendment (g)

V.2 The table required by Subitem V.1 must include, for each downward repricing:

(a) The name and position of the executive officer (column (a)).

(b) The date of repricing (column (b)).

(c) The number of securities underlying replacement or amended options or SARs (column (c)).

(d) The per-security market price of the underlying security at the time of repricing (column (d)).

(e) The original per-security exercise price or base price of the cancelled or amended option or SAR (column (e)).

(f) The per-security exercise price or base price of the replacement option or SAR (column (f)),

(g)   The amount of time remaining before the replaced or amended option or SAR would have expired (column (g)).

V.3   For the Table required by Subitem V.1:

(a)   Information about a replacement grant made during the financial year must be disclosed even if the corresponding original grant was cancelled in a prior year.

(b)   If the replacement grant is not made at the current market value, describe this fact and the terms of the grant in a footnote or accompanying textual narrative.

(c)   The information must be presented in groups according to issuer and class or series of security underlying options or SARs and within these groups in reverse chronological order.

V.4   In a narrative immediately before or after the table required by this Item, explain in reasonable detail the basis for all downward repricings during the most recently completed financial year of options and SARs held by any of the Named Executive Officers.

ITEM VI   Defined Benefit or Actuarial Plan Disclosure

VI.1 For defined benefit or actuarial plans under which benefits are determined primarily by final compensation (or average final compensation) and years of service, state the estimated annual benefits payable upon retirement (including amounts attributable to any defined benefit supplementary or excess pension awards plan) in specified compensation and years of service classifications separately for each plan in the tabular form under the caption set out below.

PENSION PLAN TABLE

Remuneration ($)	Years of Service				
	15	20	25	30	35
125,000					
150,000					
175,000					
200,000					
225,000					
250,000					
300,000					
400,000					
[insert additional rows as appropriate for additional increments]					

VI.2 Immediately following the table disclose:

(a)   The compensation covered by the plan(s), including the relationship of the covered compensation to the annual compensation reported in the Summary Compensation Table required by Item II and state the current compensation covered by the plan for any Named Executive Officer whose covered compensation differs substantially (by more than 10%) from that set out in the annual compensation columns of the Summary Compensation Table.

(b)   The estimated credited years of service for each of the Named Executive Officers.

(c)   A statement as to the basis upon which benefits are computed (for example, straight-life annuity amounts), and whether or not the benefits listed in the table are subject to any deduction for social security or other offset amounts.

VI.3 For purposes of Item VI.1, compensation set forth in the table must allow for reasonable increases in existing compensation levels or, alternately, the issuer may present, as the highest compensation level in the table, an amount equal to 120% of the amount of covered compensation of the most highly compensated of the Named Executive Officers.

VI.4   For defined benefit or actuarial plans under which benefits are not determined primarily by final compensation (or average final compensation) and years of service, state in narrative form:

(a)   The formula by which benefits are determined.

(b)   The estimated annual benefits payable upon retirement at normal retirement age for each of the Named Executive Officers.

ITEM VII   Termination of Employment, Change in Responsibilities and Employment Contracts

Describe the terms and conditions of each of the following contracts or arrangements:

(a)   Any employment contract between the issuer or its subsidiary and a Named Executive Officer.

(b)   Any compensatory plan or arrangement, including payments to be received from the issuer or its subsidiary, with respect to a Named Executive Officer, if such plan or arrangement results or will result from the resignation, retirement or any other termination of employment of the officer's employment with the issuer and its subsidiaries or from a change of control of the issuer or any subsidiary of the issuer or a change in the Named Executive Officer's responsibilities following a change-in-control and the amount involved, including all periodic payments or instalments, exceeds $100,000.

ITEM VIII   Compensation Committee

VIII.1   If any compensation is reported in response to Items II, III, IV, V or VI for the most recently completed financial year, under the caption "Composition of the Compensation Committee", identify each individual who served as a member of the issuer's compensation committee (or other board committee performing equivalent functions or in the absence of any such committee, the entire board of directors) during the most recently completed year, indicating each committee member who,

(a)   was, during the financial year, an officer or employee of the issuer or any of its subsidiaries,

(b)   was formerly an officer of the issuer or any of its subsidiaries,

(c)   had or has any relationship that requires disclosure by the issuer under the items captioned "Promoters", "Indebtedness of Directors, Executive Officers, and Senior Officers", "Interest of Management and Others in Material Transactions" and "Interest of Insiders in Material Transactions" in the form into which the disclosure required by this Form is being included,

(d)   was an executive officer of the issuer and also served as a member of the compensation committee (or other board committee performing equivalent functions or, in the absence of any such committee, the entire board of directors) of another issuer, one of whose executive officers served on the compensation committee (or other board committee performing equivalent functions or, in the absence of any such committee, the entire board of directors) of the issuer,

(e)   was an executive officer of the issuer and also served as a director of another issuer, one of whose executive officers served on the compensation committee (or other board committee performing equivalent functions or, in the absence of any such committee, the entire board of directors) of the issuer, and

(f)   was an executive officer of the issuer and also served as a member of the compensation committee (or other board committee performing equivalent

Forms

functions or, in the absence of any such committee, the entire board of directors) of another issuer, one of whose executive officers served as a director of the issuer.

VIII.2 Disclosure of relationships under Subitem VIII.1 need only be included for relationships that existed on or after January 1, 1994.

ITEM IX   Report on Executive Compensation

IX.1 If any compensation is reported in response to Items II, III, IV, V or VI for the most recently completed financial year, describe under the caption "Report on Executive Compensation" the policies of the compensation committee or other board committee performing equivalent functions, or in the absence of any such committee then of the entire board of directors of the issuer, during the most recently completed financial year, for determining compensation of executive officers (including the Named Executive Officers).

IX.2 In the report required by this Item, include a discussion of:

(a) The relative emphasis of the issuer on cash compensation, options, SARs, securities purchase programs, restricted shares, restricted share units and other incentive plans, annual versus long-term compensation, and whether the amount and terms of outstanding options, SARs, restricted shares and restricted share units were taken into account when determining whether and how many new option grants would be made.

(b) The specific relationship of corporate performance to executive compensation, and, in particular, if an award was made to a Named Executive Officer under a performance-based plan despite failure to meet the relevant performance criteria, disclose the waiver or adjustment of the relevant performance criteria and the bases for the decision.

IX.3 In the report required by this Item, state the following information about each CEO's compensation:

(a) The bases for the CEO's compensation for the most recently completed financial year, including the factors and criteria upon which the CEO's compensation was based and the relative weight assigned to each factor.

(b) The competitive rates, if compensation of the CEO was based on assessments of competitive rates, with whom the comparison was made, the nature of, and the basis for, selecting the group with which the comparison was made and at what level in the group the compensation was placed. Disclose if different competitive standards were used for different components of the CEO's compensation.

(c) The relationship of the issuer's performance to the CEO's compensation for the most recently completed financial year, describing each measure of issuer's performance, whether quantitative or qualitative, on which the CEO's compensation was based and the weight assigned to each measure.

IX.4 The report required under this Item must be made over the name of each member of the issuer's compensation committee (or other board committee performing equivalent functions or, in the absence of any such committee, the entire board of directors). If the board of directors modified or rejected in any material way any action or recommendation by the committee with respect to decisions in the most recently completed financial year, the report should indicate this fact, explain the reasons for the board's action and be made over the name of all members of the board.

IX.5 For purposes of this Item:

(a) Disclosure of target levels with respect to specific quantitative or qualitative performance- related factors considered by the committee (or board), or any factors or criteria involving confidential commercial or business information, the disclosure of which could have an adverse effect on the issuer, is not required.

(b) If compensation of executive officers is determined by different board committees, a joint report may be presented indicating the separate committee's responsibilities and members of each committee or alternatively separate reports may be prepared for each committee.

(c)   In the event of a dissenting committee member, a report need not be made over the name of the dissenting member; however, the report must identify the dissenting director and the reasons provided to the committee for the dissent.

IX.6   Discussion of compensation decisions made before January 1, 1994 need not be included under this Item.

IX.7   Boiler plate language should be avoided in describing factors and criteria underlying awards or payments of executive compensation.

ITEM X   *Performance Graph*

X.1   If any compensation is reported in response to Items II, III, IV, V or VI for the most recently completed financial year, immediately after the information required by Item IX provide a line graph comparing,

(a)   the yearly percentage change in the issuer's cumulative total shareholder return on each class or series of equity securities that are publicly traded, as measured in accordance with Subitem X.2, with

(b)   the cumulative total return of a broad equity market index assuming reinvestment of dividends, that includes issuers whose securities are traded on the same exchange or are of comparable market capitalization; provided, however, that if the issuer is within the TSE 300 Stock Index, the issuer must use that index.

X.2   The yearly percentage change in an issuer's cumulative total shareholder return on a class or series of securities must be measured by dividing,

(a)   the sum of,

(i)   the cumulative amount of dividends for the measurement period, assuming dividend reinvestment, and

(ii)   the difference between the price for the securities of the class or series at the end and the beginning of the measurement period, by

(b)   the price for the securities of the class or series at the beginning of the measurement period.

X.3   The issuer also may elect to include in the graph required by this Item a line charting the cumulative total return, assuming reinvestment of dividends, of,

(a)   a published industry or line-of-business index,

(b)   peer issuer(s) selected in good faith. (If the issuer does not select its peer issuer(s) on an industry or line-of-business basis, the issuer must disclose the basis for its selection.) or

(c)   issuer(s) with similar market capitalization(s), but only if the issuer does not use a published industry or line-of-business index and does not believe it can reasonably identify a peer group. (If the issuer uses this alternative, the graph must be accompanied by a statement of the reasons for this selection.)

X.4   For purposes of this Item:

(a)   "measurement period" means the period beginning at the "measurement point" established by the market close on the last trading day before the beginning of the issuer's fifth preceding financial year, through and including the end of the issuer's most recently completed financial year. If the class or series of securities has been publicly traded for a shorter period of time, the period covered by the comparison may correspond to that time period.

(b)   "published industry or line-of-business index" means any index that is prepared by a party other than the issuer or an affiliate and is accessible to the issuer's security-holders; provided, however, that an issuer may use an index prepared by it or an affiliate if such index is widely recognized and used.

X.5 Any election by an issuer to use an additional index under Subitem X.3 is considered to apply in respect of all subsequent financial years unless abandoned by the issuer in accordance with this Subitem. In order to abandon the index the issuer must have, in the information circular or annual filing for the financial year immediately preceding the most recently completed financial year,

(a) stated its intention to abandon the index,

(b) explained the reason(s) for this change, and

(c) compared the issuer's total return with that of the elected additional index.

X.6 In preparing the required graphic comparisons:

(a) Use, to the extent feasible, comparable methods of presentation and assumptions for the total return calculations required by Subitem X.2; provided, however, that if the issuer constructs its own peer group index under Subitem X.3(b), the same methodology must be used in calculating both the issuer's total return and that of the peer group index.

(b) Assume the reinvestment of dividends into additional securities of the same class or series at the frequency with which dividends are paid on the securities during the applicable financial year.

X.7 In constructing the graph:

(a) The closing price at the measurement point must be converted into a fixed investment, stated in dollars (e.g. $100), in the issuer's securities (or in the securities represented by a given index), with cumulative returns for each subsequent financial year measured as a change from that investment.

(b) Each financial year should be plotted with points showing the cumulative total return as of that point. The value of the investment as of each point plotted on a given return line is the number of securities held at that point multiplied by the then-prevailing security price.

X.8 The issuer must present information for the issuer's last five financial years, and may choose to graph a longer period but the measurement point must remain the same. A period shorter than five years may be used if the class or series of securities forming the basis for the comparison has been publicly traded for a shorter time period.

X.9 Issuers may include comparisons using performance measures in addition to total return, such as return on average common shareholders' equity, so long as the issuer's compensation committee (or other board committee performing equivalent functions or in the absence of any such committee the entire board of directors) describes the link between that measure and the level of executive compensation in the report required by Item IX of this Form.

X.10 If the issuer uses peer issuer comparisons or comparisons with issuers with similar market capitalizations, the identity of those issuers must be disclosed and the returns of each component issuer of the group must be weighted according to the respective issuer's market capitalization at the beginning of each period for which a return is indicated.

ITEM XI Compensation of Directors

XI.1 Under a separate subheading describe,

(a) any standard arrangements, stating amounts, under which directors of the issuer were compensated by the issuer and its subsidiaries during the most recently completed financial year for their services in their capacity as directors, including any additional amounts payable for committee participation or special assignments;

(b)   any other arrangements, stating the amounts paid and the name of the director, in addition to, or in lieu of, any standard arrangement, under which directors were compensated in their capacity as directors by the issuer and its subsidiaries during the most recently completed financial year;

(c)   any arrangement, stating the amounts paid and the name of the director, under which directors of the issuer were compensated by the issuer and its subsidiaries during the most recently completed financial year for services as consultants or experts.

XI.2   If information required by Subitem XI.1 is provided in response to another item of this Form, a cross-reference to where the information is provided satisfies Subitem XI.1.

ITEM XII   Unincorporated Issuers

XII.1   Unincorporated issuers must report,

(a)   the identity of and amount of fees or other compensation paid by the issuer to individuals acting as directors or trustees of the issuer for the most recently completed financial year; and

(b)   the identity of and amount of expenses reimbursed by the issuer to such individuals in respect of the fulfilment of their duties as directors or trustees during the most recently completed financial year.

XII.2   The information required by this Item may be disclosed in the issuer's annual financial statements in lieu of textual disclosure in an information circular or prospectus.

ITEM XIII   Small Business Issuers

XIII.1   Small business issuers may omit the disclosure required by Items V, VI, VIII, IX and X. Small business issuers must, in a narrative that accompanies the Table required by Subitem IV.1, disclose which grants of options or SARs result from repricing and explain in reasonable detail the basis for the repricing.

XIII.2   For purpose of determining whether an issuer is a small business issuer, the market value of each class of the issuer's equity securities must be calculated by multiplying,

(a)   the total number of equity securities of that class outstanding as at the end of the issuer's most recently completed financial year, other than the securities required to be excluded in accordance with the definition of "public float", by

(b)   the arithmetic average of the closing prices of the equity securities of that class on the stock exchange in Canada on which the securities principally trade for each of the trading days in the last calender month of the most recently completed financial year.

ITEM XIV   Issuers Reporting in the United States

XIV.1   Except as provided in Subitem XIV.2, issuers registered with the Securities Exchange Commission of the United States under the *Securities Exchange Act of 1934* (United States) may satisfy the requirements of this Form by providing the information required by Item 402 of Regulation S-K under that Act instead of the information required by this Form.

XIV.2   Subitem XIV.1 is not available to an issuer that, as a foreign private issuer, satisfies Item 402 of Regulation S-K by providing the information required by Items 11 and 12 of Form 20-F under that Act.

See NIN 93/23 "Executive Compensation".

FORM 43

Securities Act

OFFERING MEMORANDUM

ITEM 1   Non-review by Commission

Provide the following statement in bold print on the face page of the offering memorandum:

> No securities commission or similar regulatory authority has passed on the merits of the securities offered nor has it reviewed this offering memorandum and any representation to the contrary is an offence.

ITEM 2   Risk Factors

(1) If appropriate to a clear understanding by purchasers of the risk factors and speculative nature of the enterprise or the securities being offered, summarize the factors that make the purchase a risk or speculation.

(2) Without restricting the generality of subsection (1), disclose if the purchaser may become liable to make an additional contribution beyond his initial investment.

ITEM 3   Name and Incorporation of Issuer

(1) State the name, principal business address and registered address of the issuer and laws under which it was incorporated or organized. State the date of formation of the issuer.

(2) If the issuer is a limited partnership, disclose the principal clauses of the partnership agreement.

ITEM 4   Description of Securities

(1) Describe the securities to be distributed including the price of the securities and the material attributes of the securities such as redemption, retraction, conversion, restricted voting rights and similar matters.

(2) Disclose how the offering price was established, whether by negotiation, arbitrarily by the issuer or otherwise.

ITEM 5   Number and Aggregate Dollar Amount of Securities to be Distributed

(1) State the number and aggregate dollar amount of securities offered, including where applicable, both minimum and maximum figures.

(2) If a minimum amount of funds is required to be raised through the offering, disclose consequences to the purchaser of failure to raise that amount, including the return of funds to the purchaser, describing any deduction or penalty. State the name and address of any person who will hold subscription funds until the minimum amount is raised.

(3) If there are any arrangements under which any part of the net proceeds will be held in trust or will only become available to the issuer if certain conditions are fulfilled, describe those conditions and the procedure for the return of funds to the purchaser.

(4) If there is a no minimum amount that is required to be raised, then provide the following statement in bold print:

> **This offering is not subject to any minimum subscription level, and therefore any funds received from a purchaser are available to the issuer and need not be refunded to the purchaser.**

ITEM 6   Plan of Distribution

(1) Describe the means by which the securities will be distributed and the subscription procedure.

(2) State the name of any person selling the securities on behalf of the issuer, any relationship between such person and the issuer, par-

ticulars of any agency or similar agreement and the remuneration, if any, to be paid to such person for the sale of the securities.

(3) If the issuer is a limited partnership, describe the obligations and the rights of the general partner and the limited partners as well as the functions and the basis of the remuneration of the general partner.

(4) If any of the securities offered are to be offered for the account of an existing security holder, state the number or amount of securities owned by him, the number or amount to be offered for his account, and the number or amount to be owned by him after the offering. State the portion of expenses of distribution to be borne by such security holder.

ITEM 7   Exemptions From the Prospectus Requirements

Disclose the specific statutory exemption from the prospectus requirements or the discretionary exemption order, as the case may be, to be relied on in distributing the securities.

ITEM 8   Restrictions on Resale of Securities

(1) Summarize in bold print on the face page any restrictions on the resale of the securities by the purchaser.

(2) Where no market exists or will exist for the securities after the distribution, the following statement must appear in bold print on the face page:

As there is no market for these securities, it may be difficult or even impossible for the purchaser to sell them.

ITEM 9   Nature of Business of Issuer

Describe the business carried on or intended to be carried on by the issuer and by its significant subsidiaries and the general development of the business within the five preceding years. Describe the business sector in which the issuer is engaged or proposes to engage.

ITEM 10   Nature of Project to be Financed

Describe the nature of the project to be financed.

ITEM 11   Use of Proceeds by Issuer

(1) State the net proceeds that the issuer expects to obtain from the distribution, the principal uses planned for the proceeds and the funds assigned to each use.

(2) The information concerning use of the net proceeds must be meaningful. In most cases, it is not sufficient to say only that "the proceeds of the distribution will be used for general corporate purposes".

(3) If a minimum subscription level is required, the priorities for use of proceeds must be disclosed in respect of the application of both minimum and maximum proceeds from the offering. Indicate, in order of priority, the uses that will be made of the proceeds of the distribution if they are less than expected.

(4) If a particular property, project or program is to be financed only partially from proceeds of the offering, disclose the source of additional financing and particulars thereof needed to complete financing of the property, project or program.

ITEM 12   Share and Loan Capital Structure

State particulars of the share and loan capital of the issuer and each significant subsidiary whose financial statements are contained in the offering memorandum on either a consolidated or individual basis as of

(a) the date of such financial statements and

(b) a date not more than 30 days preceding the date of the certificate attached to the offering memorandum.

ITEM 13   Directors, Officers, Promoters and Principal Holders of Securities

(1) Provide the name, municipality of residence and principal occupation for the last 5 years of directors, officers, promoters and persons holding directly or indirectly more than 10% of any class of voting securities of the issuer ("principal holders"). Where a company holds more than 10% of any class of voting securities of the issuer, state the name of any individual who, directly or indirectly, owns securities representing more than 50% of the voting rights attached to that company's outstanding voting securities.

(2) Disclose all securities of the issuer, including options, held by the directors and officers as a group and by promoters and principal holders of securities at a date not more than 30 days prior to the date of the certificate attached to the offering memorandum.

(3) If the issuer is a limited partnership, provide disclosure under this Item in respect of the general partner of the limited partnership.

(4) If the promoter of the limited partnership is not the general partner, provide disclosure under this Item relating to the promoter of the limited partnership.

ITEM 14   Conflicts of Interest

Describe any existing or potential conflicts of interest among the issuer, distributor, promoter, directors, officers, principal holders and persons providing professional services to the issuer which could reasonably be expected to affect the purchaser's investment decision.

ITEM 15   Continuous Reporting Obligations to Investors

If the issuer is not a reporting issuer, describe the nature and timing of the financial and other information concerning the affairs of the issuer that will be provided to the purchaser.

ITEM 16   Financial Statements

(1) The following financial statements must be included in the offering memorandum:

(a) where the issuer has not completed one fiscal year, unaudited financial statements of the issuer as at a date not more than 60 days prior to the date of the certificate attached to the offering memorandum;

(b) where the issuer has completed one or more fiscal years:

(i) audited financial statements of the issuer for the most recent fiscal year, and

(ii) if the effective date of such statements is more than 120 days before the date of the certificate attached to the offering memorandum, unaudited financial statements for a stub period ending not more than 90 days prior to the date of the certificate attached to the offering memorandum;

(c) where the issuer is a limited partnership, the financial statements referred to in paragraph (a) or (b) must be those of the general partner.

ITEM 17   Income Tax Consequences

If income tax consequences to the purchaser are a material aspect of the offering then

(a) provide a summary disclosure of the significant income tax consequences to individuals who are residents of Canada, and

(b) provide in bold print a statement to the effect that prospective purchasers are urged to consult with their professional advisers regarding tax consequences applicable to them.

ITEM 18   Material Contracts

(1) Give particulars of every material contract entered into by the issuer or, if applicable, any of its significant subsidiaries within two years prior to the date of the certificate attached to the offering memorandum and state a time and place at which those contracts or copies thereof may be inspected during distribution of the securities being offered. If a material contract is of a confidential nature, the offering memorandum may contain a summary of such contract.

ITEM 19   Contractual Rights of Action

The offering memorandum must describe the contractual rights of action referred to in section 126 of the Securities Regulation, including any defences available to the issuer. The offering memorandum must describe the limitation periods applicable to the exercise of the contractual rights of action, and indicate that the rights are in addition to any other right or remedy available at law to the purchaser.

ITEM 20   Certification

Include a certificate in the following form:

The foregoing contains no untrue statement of a material fact and does not omit to state a material fact that is required to be stated or that is necessary to prevent a statement that is made from being false or misleading in the circumstances in which it was made.

INSTRUCTIONS:

The certificate is required to be signed by the president or chief executive officer and by the chief financial officer of the issuer. If no chief financial officer has been designated, then a director of the issuer other than the president or chief executive officer, must sign the certificate.

IT IS AN OFFENCE UNDER THE SECURITIES ACT FOR A PERSON TO MAKE A STATEMENT IN A DOCUMENT REQUIRED TO BE FILED, FURNISHED OR DELIVERED UNDER THE ACT OR THE REGULATIONS THAT, AT THE TIME AND IN THE LIGHT OF THE CIRCUMSTANCES UNDER WHICH IT IS MADE, IS A MISREPRESENTATION AS THAT TERM IS DEFINED BY THE SECURITIES ACT.

This is the form required under section 126(c) of the Securities Regulation for an offering memorandum used in connection with a distribution of securities under the Immigrant Investor Program.

FORM 43A

Securities Act

OFFERING MEMORANDUM
IMMIGRANT INVESTOR PROGRAM

The offering memorandum must be in the form, as amended from time to time, required by Employment and Immigration Canada and the Business Immigration Branch of the British Columbia Ministry of International Business and Immigration in connection with a distribution of securities under the Immigrant Investor Program.

November 1, 1989

This is the short form prospectus required under Section 95 of the regulations.

FORM 50

Securities Act

INFORMATION REQUIRED TO BE INCLUDED IN A
SHORT FORM OF PROSPECTUS OF A MUTUAL FUND

GENERAL INSTRUCTIONS:

The short form of prospectus is intended to be a concise presentation in plain language of the information required. The requirements and the instructions relating thereto should be read in light of this intention and the presentation of such information in the short form of prospectus should reflect this intention.

Item 1 - Cover Statement

Language in substantially the following form should appear on the outside cover page of the short form of prospectus:

"The information contained herein must be accompanied by the annual financial statements of the Fund for the last financial year and the auditors' report thereon, which statements and report are considered to form part of this document. As well, if subsequent financial statements have been filed with the Securities Commission a copy of the most recent of such subsequent statements must also accompany this document."

Item 2 - Introductory Statement

Language in substantially the following form should appear on the first page of the short form of prospectus:

"This short form of prospectus is a concise outline of the relevant information about the Fund which you should know before making a decision to purchase its securities. The Fund is required by law to fully disclose additional facts, related to this information, in an annual information form, financial statements and other material documents filed with securities regulatory authorities in each Province where the Fund's securities are offered, which documents collectively are known as the Fund's permanent information record.

Securities laws in Canada establish certain security holder rights which are described in this short form of prospectus. These rights are based in part on other disclosures of the Fund found in the annual information form which is incorporated into this short form of prospectus by reference, as well as upon disclosure contained in this short form of prospectus. All of these rights are available to you even though you receive only this short form of prospectus and accompanying financial statements.

The documents currently in the permanent information record may be obtained by you by writing to the Fund at:

or through a dealer."

Item 3 - Name and Formation of Issuer

State the full name of the issuer and the address of its head office. State the laws under which the issuer was formed and the manner and date of formation. If the issuer's name was changed during the past twelve months state its former name and the date on which it was changed. State the name and address of the promoter, if any.

Item 4 - Description of Business

Briefly describe the business of the issuer.

Item 5 - Risk Factors

(a)   Where appropriate to a clear understanding by investors of the risk factors and speculative nature of the enterprise or of the securities being offered, an introductory statement shall be made on the first page summarizing the factors which make the purchase a risk or speculation. The information may be given in the body of the short form of prospectus if an appropriate reference is made; on the first page to the risks and the speculative or promotional nature of the enterprise and a cross reference is made to the place in the short form of prospectus where the information is contained.

(b)   Where this is a risk that purchasers of the securities offered may become liable to make an additional contribution beyond the price of the security, disclose any information or facts that may bear on the security holder's assessment of risk associated with the investment.

Item 6 - Description of Shares or Units Offered

   (a)   State the description or the designation of the class of shares or units offered and furnish all material attributes and characteristics including, without limiting the generality of the foregoing, the following information:

        (i) dividend rights;

        (ii) voting rights;

        (iii) liquidation or distribution rights;

        (iv) pre-emptive rights;

        (v) conversion rights;

        (vi) redemption, purchase for cancellation or surrender provisions;

        (vii) liability to further calls or to assessment by the issuer; and

        (viii) provisions as to modification, amendment or variation of any such rights or provisions.

   (b)   If the rights of holders of such shares or units may be modified otherwise than in accordance with the provisions attaching to such shares or units or the provisions of the governing act relating thereto, so state and explain briefly.

INSTRUCTIONS

1.   This item requires only a brief summary of the provisions that are material from an investment standpoint. The provisions attaching to the shares or units may be entered in the permanent information record.

2.   If the rights attaching to the shares or units being offered are materially limited or qualified by those attached to any other class of securities or if another class of securities ranks ahead of or equally with the shares or units being offered, include information regarding such other securities that will enable investors to understand the rights attaching to the shares or units being offered. If any shares or units being offered are to be offered in exchange for other securities, an appropriate description of the other securities shall be given. No information need be given, however, as to any class of securities that is to be redeemed or otherwise retired, provided appropriate steps to assure redemption or retirement have been or will be taken prior to or contemporaneously with the delivery of the shares or units being offered.

Item 7 - Price of Securities on Sale or Redemption

   (a)   Describe briefly the method followed or to be followed by the issuer in determining the price at which its securities will be offered for sale and redeemed and state the frequency with which the net asset is determined and the time when the price becomes effective.

   (b)   State, where applicable, the sales charge expressed as a percentage of the total amount paid by the purchaser and as a percentage of the net amount invested in securities of the issuer. Where these charges vary on a quantity basis give particulars of the quantities and the respective sales charges applicable thereto.

   (c)   Describe briefly the procedure followed or to be followed by the purchaser for securities on sale or redemption, including any special purchase plans which may exist and any penalty for early redemption. State, where applicable, any redemption charge expressed as a percentage of the redemption price on a quantity basis, give particulars of the quantities and the respective redemption charges applicable thereto.

   (d)   Describe briefly any specific right or requirement to reinvest the proceeds of dividends or similar distributions in the issuer's securities.

   (e)   Refer the purchaser to the annual information form for a detailed statement of the information required in this item.

Item 8 - Method of Distribution

Outline briefly the method of distribution of the securities being offered. If sales are to be effected through a person (the 'contractual distributor') pursuant to an arrangement with the issuer, give brief details of any arrangements with the contractual distributor. See Item 9.

INSTRUCTIONS

1. If the securities are being offered by way of a contractual plan, give the main particulars of the contractual plan, including:

   (i)   minimum initial investment;

   (ii) subsequent minimum investment;

   (iii) sales charge deductions from such minimum investments;

   (iv) sales charges as a percentage of the amount paid by the purchaser and as a percentage of the net amount invested in securities of the issuer;

   (v)   the total amount invested contrasted to the amount paid by the purchaser.

2. As used in this item, sales charge includes all service charges including charges related to the establishment of a contractual plan and its continuing administration and maintenance.

Item 9 - Responsibility for Principal Functions

(a) Give a concise statement of the manner in which the following functions of the issuer are performed and who is responsible therefor, stating how such functions are co-ordinated and, to the extent that any such functions are not performed by bona fide employees of the issuer, the names and addresses of the persons responsible for performing such functions:

   (i)   management of the issuer other than management of the investment portfolio;

   (ii) management of the investment portfolio;

   (iii) providing investment analysis;

   (iv) providing investment recommendations;

   (v)   making investment decisions;

   (vi) purchase and sale of the investment portfolio and brokerage arrangements relating thereto;

   (vii) distribution of the securities offered.

(b) Refer the purchaser to the annual information form for greater detail regarding the purchase and sale of the investment portfolio and brokerage arrangements relating thereto.

(c) Indicate the circumstances under which the management agreement may be terminated.

(d) Indicate conflicts of interest or potential conflicts of interest between the issuer and the persons named in answer to paragraph (a).

INSTRUCTIONS

1. The address given may be the municipality of residence or a postal address, however the Superintendent may request that the home address in full be furnished to him.

2. In giving information regarding distribution of securities the name and address of only the contractual distributor need be given.

3. If one or more persons perform more than one of the functions referred to in this Item, so state, giving details of all functions so performed.

Item 10 - Management Fees

    (a)   Indicate the method of determining the amount of management fees and, distinguishing between those charged to the issuer and those charged directly to security holders, other expenses, if any, and make a cross reference to the financial statements for details as to the amount of management fees and other expenses, if any, which have been charged to the issuer.

    (b)   Set out in tabular form in the short form of prospectus or by way of note to the financial statements, a record of management expense ratio comprising the aggregate of all fees and other expenses paid or payable by the issuer during each of the last five completed financial years as a percentage of average net assets under administration during each of those financial years. Such disclosure should also include a brief description of the method of calculating the percentage and a statement that the management expense ratio may vary from one mutual fund to another.

INSTRUCTIONS

1.   Where management fees are changed or are proposed to be changed and where such change would have had an effect on the management expense ratio for the most recent financial year if the change had been in effect throughout that year, the effect of such change should be disclosed.

2.   Where the financial year is other than a full year, the management expense ratio should be annualized, the period covered specified and a statement made that the management expense ratio is annualized.

3.   For purposes of this Item, "average net assets" should be calculated to be the average of the net assets at each valuation date of the issuer and before the deduction of management fees and other expenses, and the term "other expenses" means all other expenses incurred in the course of ordinary business relating to the organization, management and operation of the issuer with the exception of the commissions and brokerage fees on the purchase and sale of portfolio securities and taxes of all kinds, other than penalties, to which the issuer is subject.

4.   Where an issuer invests in another mutual fund, the management expense ratio shall be calculated on the basis of those assets of the issuer on which a management fee is charged.

5.   The financial statements should set out in appropriate detail the amounts of the management fee and other expenses, if any, which have been charged to the issuer.

6.   The basis or rates of charges levied against security holders, rather than the issuer, for special services such as trustee fees for registered retirement savings plans, redemption fees, transfer fees between related mutual funds or any other specific charges to a class of investors, should be disclosed separately in a single table in the body of the short form of prospectus or as a note to the financial statements and should not be included as part of the management expense ratio.

Item 11 - Investment Objectives and Practices

    (a)   Precisely state the investment objectives of the issuer.

    (b)   Refer the purchaser to the annual information form for information concerning restrictions on investment practices of the issuer in pursuing its objectives.

INSTRUCTIONS

Aims such as long-term capital appreciation or current income and the types of securities in which the issuer will invest should be described.

Item 12 - Dividends or Distributions

Indicate, by way of note to the financial statements, the amount of dividends or other distributions per share or unit paid by the issuer including income allocated to security holders by way of dividend reinvestment or otherwise during the latest financial year and each of the previous four completed financial years.

INSTRUCTIONS

Dividends should be set out on a per security basis, shown separately for each class of security in respect of each of the financial years. Appropriate adjustments should be made to reflect changes in capitalization during the period.

Item 13 - Tax Status of Security Holders

State in general terms the income tax consequences to the holders of the securities offered of:

> (i) any distribution to such holders in the form of dividends or otherwise including amounts reinvested;
>
> (ii) redemption of securities;
>
> (iii) sale of securities;
>
> (iv) transfers between mutual funds.

Item 14 - Legal Proceedings

Describe briefly any legal proceedings material to the issuer, to which the issuer is a party or of which any of its property is the subject.

INSTRUCTIONS

Include the name of the court or agency, the date instituted, the principal parties thereto, the nature of the claim, the amount claimed if any, whether the proceedings are being contested, and the present status of the proceedings.

Item 15 - Other Material Facts

Give particulars of any other material facts relating to the securities proposed to be offered which are not contained in the annual information form.

Item 16 - Auditors, Transfer Agent and Registrar

(a) State the name and address of the issuer's auditor.

(b) State the name of the issuer's transfer agent and registrar and the cities in which the registers of transfer of securities of the issuer are kept.

Item 17 - Purchasers' Statutory Rights

Include the following statement in the short form of prospectus:

> " Securities legislation in certain of the provinces provides purchasers with the right to withdraw from an agreement to purchase mutual fund shares or units within two business days after receipt of a short form of prospectus or within forty-eight hours after the receipt of a confirmation of a purchase of such securities. If the agreement is to purchase such securities under a contractual plan, the time period during which withdrawal may be made may be longer. In several of the provinces and territories securities legislation further provides a purchaser with remedies for rescission or, in some jurisdictions, damages where the short form of prospectus and any amendment contains a misrepresentation or is not delivered to the purchaser but such remedies must be exercised by the purchaser within the time limit prescribed by the securities legislation of his province or territory. The purchaser should refer to any applicable provisions of the securities legislation of his province or territory for the particulars of these rights or consult with a legal adviser."

Item 18 - Identification

Each short form of prospectus shall bear encoding which identifies the date at which it becomes effective.

INSTRUCTIONS

The date need not be written in full. In fact it is preferred that it be shown as for example, 30/05/85, or included in a printer's code together with quantity printed. The purpose is to identify which version of a short form of prospectus is the subject of a specific receipt.

February 1, 1987

This is the annual information form required under Section 94 of the regulations.

FORM 51

Securities Act

INFORMATION REQUIRED TO BE INCLUDED IN THE ANNUAL INFORMATION FORM OF A MUTUAL FUND

GENERAL INSTRUCTIONS:

The Annual Information Form is used in conjunction with a short form of prospectus, financial statements, notices of material change and similar material documents required to be filed to provide disclosure of all information concerning the mutual fund and the securities it proposes to issue. Information reported in an annual information form should be complete and presented in a style similar to that used in a prospectus.

Item 1 - Name and Formation of Issuer

State the full name of the issuer and the address of its head office. State the laws under which the issuer was formed, and whether by articles of incorporation, trust indenture or otherwise and the date the issuer came into existence. If material, state whether the documents have been amended.

INSTRUCTIONS

Particulars of any such documents need be set out only if material to the securities offered by the short form of prospectus. See Form 50, Item 6.

Item 2 - Business of the Issuer

Describe the business of the issuer.

1. If the issuer has engaged in any business other than that of a mutual fund during the past five years, state the nature of the other business and give the approximate date on which the issuer commenced to operate as a mutual fund. If the issuer's name was changed during the period, state its former name and the date on which it was changed. Indicate briefly the nature and results of any bankruptcy, receivership or similar proceedings or any other material reorganization of the issuer during the period.

2. If during the past two years any affiliate of the issuer had any material interest, direct or indirect, in any transaction involving the purchase of any substantial amount of assets presently held by the issuer, describe the interest of the affiliate in such transaction and state the cost of such assets to the purchaser and to the seller.

Item 3 - Price of Securities on Sale or Redemption

Repeat disclosure from the short form of prospectus in respect of Item 7 of Form 50 and, in addition,

(a) Describe the rules used for the valuation of the issuer's assets and liabilities for the purpose of calculating net asset value and disclose all instances, within the past three years, when the discretion to deviate from these rules, if any, was exercised.

(b) Indicate briefly any difference in the sales charges imposed upon the sale of securities in connection with the conversion or exchange of securities or the reinvestment of dividends and similar distributions.

(c) In this form, "sales charge" includes all service charges including charges relating to such matters as cost of the establishment of a contractual plan and the cost of the continuing administration and maintenance of such a plan.

(d) When giving particulars of the sales charge with respect to a contractual plan indicate when during the term of the plan the sales charge will be deducted.

(e) Give particulars of the entitlement of the purchaser of a contractual plan to a refund of any sales charge incurred if the contractual plan is terminated during the term of such plan.

Item 4 - Responsibility for Principal Functions

Repeat disclosure from the short form of prospectus in respect of this Item 9 of Form 50 and, in addition;

(a) Provide the name and address in full or alternatively solely the municipality of residence or postal address of each person, or of each of the directors and officers of each of the companies, responsible for the performance of the principal functions described in the short form of prospectus and set out above.

(b) Indicate the method of determining the amount of management fees and state the total of such fees paid during each of the last five completed financial years and separately for the period from the last completed financial year to a date within thirty days of this annual information form.

(c) Indicate the circumstances under which the management agreement may be terminated.

(d) Indicate conflicts of interest or potential conflicts of interest between the issuer and the persons and companies named in answer to (a).

INSTRUCTIONS

1. Where an alternate address is listed, the Superintendent may request that the home address in full be furnished to the Commission.

2. In giving information regarding distribution of securities, the name and address of only the contractual distributor need be given. See Form 50, Item 8.

3. In giving information regarding the purchase and sale of the investment portfolio and brokerage arrangements relating thereto the name and address of only the principal broker need be given.

4. In giving information regarding the purchase and sale of the investment portfolio and brokerage arrangements relating thereto give brief details of the following matters:

   (i) the total cost, during the last completed financial year of the issuer, of securities acquired, distinguishing between,

      (a) securities of or guaranteed by the government of any country, or any political subdivision thereof;

      (b) short-term notes; and

      (c) other securities;

   (ii) the total cost of securities held at the beginning and at the end of the issuer's last completed financial year;

   (iii) the formula, method or criteria used in allocating brokerage business to persons engaged in the distribution of the securities of the issuer;

   (iv) the formula, method or criteria used in allocating brokerage business to persons furnishing statistical, research or other services to the issuer or the manager of the issuer; and

   (v) the amount of brokerage paid to the principal broker for the last three completed financial years, giving the total amount paid in each year and expressing the amount paid in each year as a percentage of the total brokerage paid by the issuer.

5. If one or more persons performs more than one of the functions referred to in this item, so state, giving details of all functions so performed.

6. As used in this Form:

    (a) "principal broker" includes,

        (i) a person through whom the investment portfolio of the issuer is purchased or sold under a contractual arrangement with the issuer or the manager of the issuer providing for an exclusive right to purchase or sell the investment portfolio of the issuer or any feature which gives or is intended to give a broker or dealer a material competitive advantage over other brokers or dealers in respect of the purchase or sale of the investment portfolio of the issuer, or

        (ii) a person together with any affiliate, by or through whom 15 percent or more of the securities transactions of the issuer were carried out; and

    (b) "brokerage arrangements" or "brokerage business" include all purchases and sales of the investment portfolio, whether effected directly or through an agent.

7. With the consent of the Superintendent, a person who would otherwise be a principal broker may, with respect to any one or more of the items of disclosure required by this Form, be treated as not coming within the definition of a principal broker.

Item 5 - Investment Policy and Restrictions

State the policy or proposed policy of the issuer with respect to each of the following types of activities describing the extent to which the issuer may engage in or is restricted from engaging in each such activity. Indicate which of the policies may not be changed without security holder approval:

(a) the issuing of securities other than those contemplated by the issuer's short form of prospectus;

(b) the borrowing of money;

(c) the firm underwriting of securities issued by other issuers;

(d) the concentration of its investments in a particular class or kind of industry;

(e) the purchase and sale of real estate;

(f) the purchase and sale of commodities or commodity futures contracts;

(g) the making of loans, whether secured or unsecured;

(h) the investment of a specific proportion of the assets of the issuer in a particular type of security (e.g. bond, preferred shares, money market instruments, etc.);

(i) the investment of more than 10% of the assets of the issuer in the securities of any one issuer;

(j) the investment in more than 10% of the securities of any one issuer;

(k) the investment in securities for the purpose of exercising control or management;

(l) the investment in securities of investment companies or other mutual funds;

(m) the purchase or sale of mortgages;

(n) the purchase of securities on margin or selling short;

(o) the investment in securities which are not fully paid;

(p) the investment in illiquid securities or securities whose resale is restricted;

(q) the investment in foreign securities;

(r) the investment in gold or gold certificates;

(s) the pledging, mortgaging or hypothecating of the issuer's assets;

(t) the sale of portfolio securities to directors, officers or trustees, of the issuer or of the manager, or the purchase of securities from those persons;

(u) the guaranteeing of the securities or the obligations of another issuer;

(v) the purchase of options, rights and warrants;

(w) the writing of covered or uncovered clearing corporation options;

(x) the investment in a security which may require the purchaser to make an additional contribution beyond the price of the security;

(y) any investment other than in securities;

(z) the lending of the issuer's portfolio securities.

INSTRUCTIONS

1. For the purpose of clause (g), the purchase of debt securities for investment purposes is not considered to be the making of a loan by the issuer.

2. For the purpose of clause (p), where the issuer invests in securities whose resale is restricted, describe how those securities are valued for the purpose of computing the net asset value of the fund.

Item 6 - Significant Holdings in Other Issuers

Furnish in substantially the tabular form indicated the following information as at a date within thirty days of the date of the annual information form with respect to each issuer, 5 percent or more of whose securities of any class are beneficially owned directly or indirectly by the mutual fund or any of its subsidiaries.

TABLE

Name and Address of company	Nature of its principal business	Percent of securities of any class owned by issuer	Percentage of value of issuer's assets invested therein

Item 7 - Tax Status of Issuer and Security Holder

(a) State in general terms the bases upon which the income and capital receipts of the issuer are taxed.

(b) Repeat disclosure from the short form of prospectus in respect of the tax status of the security holder.

Item 8 - Legal Proceedings

Describe briefly any legal proceedings material to the issuer to which the issuer is a party or of which any of its property is subject. Make a similar statement as to any such proceedings known to be contemplated.

INSTRUCTIONS

Identify the court or the agency having jurisdiction, the date on which the suit was filed, the principal parties involved, the nature of the claim and the amount claimed. State whether the proceedings are contested and indicate the present status of the proceedings.

Item 9 - Directors, Officers and Trustees

List the names and home addresses in full or, alternatively, solely the municipality of residence or postal address, of all directors, trustees and officers of the issuer and indicate all positions and offices with the issuer held by each person named, and the principal occupations, within the five preceding years, of each director, trustee and officer.

INSTRUCTIONS

1. Where the municipality of residence of postal address is listed, the Superintendent may request that the home address in full be furnished to him.

2. Where the principal occupation of a director, trustee or officer is that of an officer of a company other than the mutual fund, state the business in which such company is engaged.

3. Where a director or officer has held more than one position in the issuer, or a parent or subsidiary thereof, state only the first and last position held.

Item 10 - Remuneration of Directors, Officers and Trustees

(a) Only issuers which directly employ officers need comply fully with this Item.

(b) Other issuers, the businesses of which are managed by a management company under a contractual arrangement with the issuer, or by a corporate trustee under the terms of a trust indenture, must report in the annual financial statement of those issuers:

(i) the aggregate amount of directors' or trustees' fees paid by the issuer in respect of each of the financial years reported upon;

(ii) the aggregate amount of expenses reimbursed by the issuer to the directors or trustees in respect of the fulfillment of duties as directors or trustees.

As well, those issuers must state in the annual information form that amounts reported in the financial statements as paid or reimbursed to directors and trustees constitute the only compensation paid by the issuer to those directors and trustees.

TABLE

	From Office, Employment and Employer Contributions	Cost of Pension Benefits	Other
1. Directors (Total Number ....)	$	$	$
			Future Years - $_____
2. Five Senior Officers	$	$	$
			Future Years - $_____
3. Officers with Remuneration over $50,000 (Total Number ....)	$	$	$
			Future Years - $_____

(c) State in the form of the table shown above separately for each of the following the aggregate remuneration paid or payable by the issuer in respect of the issuer's last completed financial year to;

(i) the directors or trustees of the issuer in their capacity as directors or trustees of the issuer;

(ii) the five senior officers of the issuer in receipt of the largest amount of remuneration, in their capacity as officers or employees of the issuer; and

      (iii) the officers of the issuer including those in (ii) who received in their capacity as officers or employees of the issuer and any of its subsidiaries aggregate remuneration in excess of $50,000 in that year, provided that this disclosure shall not be required where the issuer has less than seven such officers.

  (d) State, where practicable, the estimated aggregate cost to the issuer and its subsidiaries in or in respect of the benefits proposed to be paid under any pension or retirement plan upon retirement at normal retirement age to persons to whom paragraph (c) applies, or in the alternative, the estimated aggregate amount of all such benefits proposed to be paid upon retirement at normal retirement age to those persons.

  (e) State, where practicable, the aggregate of all remuneration payments other than those of the type referred to in paragraph (c) and (d) made in or in respect of the issuer's last completed financial year and, as a separate amount, proposed to be made in the future by the issuer under an existing plan to persons to whom paragraph (c) applies.

INSTRUCTIONS

1.   For the purpose of clauses (i) and (iii) of paragraph (c), "remuneration" means amounts required to be reported as income under the Income Tax Act (Canada).

2.   For the purpose of clause (ii) of paragraph (c), "remuneration" means remuneration as defined in instruction 1 plus the value of benefits (other than those benefits provided to a broad category of employees on a basis which does not discriminate in favour of officers or directors) not included in income from an office or employment and derived from contributions made by the employer to or under a group sickness or accident insurance plan, private health service plan, supplementary unemployment benefit plan, deferred profit sharing plan or group term life insurance policy.

3.   For the purpose of paragraph (e), "plan" includes all plans, contracts, authorizations or arrangements, whether or not contained in any formal document or authorized by a resolution of the directors of the issuer but does not include the Canada Pension Plan or a similar government plan.

4.   For the purposes of paragraph (e), "remuneration payments" include payments under a deferred profit sharing plan, deferred compensation benefits, retirement benefits or other benefits, except those paid or to be paid under a pension or retirement plan of the issuer.

5.   For the purposes of paragraph (e), if it is impracticable to state the amount of proposed remuneration payments, the aggregated amount accrued to date in respect of such payments may be stated, with an explanation of the basis of future payments.

Item 11 - Indebtedness of Directors, Officers and Trustees

In regard to,

    (i) each director trustee and each senior officer of the issuer;

    (ii) each proposed nominee for election as a director or trustee of the issuer; and

    (iii) each associate or affiliate of any such director, trustee, senior officer or proposed nominee,

who is or has been indebted to the issuer or its subsidiaries at any time since the beginning of the last completed financial year of the issuer, state with respect to each such issuer or subsidiary the largest aggregate amount of indebtedness outstanding at any time during the last completed financial year, the nature of the indebtedness and of the transaction in which it was incurred, the amount thereof presently outstanding, and the rate of interest paid or charged thereon, but no disclosure need be made of routine indebtedness.

INSTRUCTIONS

1. "routine indebtedness" means indebtedness described in any of the following clauses:

    (a)   if an issuer makes loans to employees generally whether or not in the ordinary course of business then loans shall be considered to be routine indebtedness if made on terms, including those as to interest or collateral, no more favourable to the borrower than the terms on which loans are made by the issuer to employees generally, but the amount at any time remaining unpaid under such loans to any one director, senior officer or proposed nominee together with his associates or affiliates that are treated as routine indebtedness under this clause (a) shall not exceed $25,000;

    (b)   whether or not the issuer makes loans in the ordinary course of business, a loan to a director or senior officer shall be considered to be routine indebtedness if

          (i)   the borrower is a full-time employee of the issuer;

          (ii) the loan is fully secured against the residence of the borrower, and

          (iii) the amount of the loan does not exceed the annual salary of the borrower;

    (c)   where the issuer makes loans in the ordinary course of business, a loan shall be considered to be routine indebtedness if made to a person other than a full-time employee of the issuer, and if the loan

          (i)   is made on substantially the same terms, including those as to interest rate and collateral, as were available when the loan was made to other customers of the issuer with comparable credit ratings, and

          (ii) involves no more than usual risks of collectibility, and

    (d)   indebtedness arising by reason of purchases made on usual trade terms or of ordinary travel or expense advances, or for similar reasons shall be considered to be routine indebtedness if the repayment arrangements are in accord with usual commercial practice.

2. State the name and home address in full or, alternatively, solely the municipality of residence or postal address of each person whose indebtedness is described.

Item 12 - Associated Persons

Furnish the following information as to each person named in the short form of prospectus and repeated in the annual information form in answer to the request in Item 9 of Form 50.

    (a)   If a named person is associated with the issuer or is a director or senior officer of or is associated with any affiliate of the issuer or is a director or senior officer of or is associated with any company which is associated with the issuer, so state, and give particulars of the relationship.

    (b)   If the issuer is associated with a named person or is associated with any affiliate of a named company or is associated with any company which is associated with the named person or company, so state, and give particulars of the relationship.

    (c)   If any person associated with the issuer is also associated with a named person, so state, and give particulars of the relationship.

    (d)   If a named person has a contract or arrangement with the issuer, give a brief description of the contract or arrangement, including the basis for determining the remuneration of the named person and give the amount of remuneration paid or payable by the issuer and its subsidiaries to that person during the last completed financial year of the issuer.

    (e)   If a named person is associated with any other named person, so state, and give particulars of the relationship.

Forms

(f)   Where and to the extent required by the Superintendent, give the business experience of each named person and, in the case of a named company, the directors and officers thereof.

Item 13 - Promoter

If any person is or has been a promoter of the issuer within the five years immediately preceding the date of the annual information form furnish the following information;

(a)   State the names of the promoters, the nature and amount of anything of value (including money, property, contracts, options or rights of any kind) received or to be received by each promoter directly or indirectly from the issuer and the nature and amount of any assets, services or other consideration therefor received or to be received by the issuer.

(b)   As to any assets acquired within the past two years or to be acquired by the issuer from a promoter, state the amount at which acquired or to be acquired and the principle followed or to be followed in determining the amount. Identify the person making the determination and state his relationship, if any, with the issuer or any promoter. State the date that the assets were acquired by the promoter and the cost thereof to the promoter.

Item 14 - Principal Holders of Securities

Furnish the following information as of a specified date within thirty days prior to the date of the annual information form in substantially the tabular form indicated:

(a)   The number of securities in each class of voting securities of:

(i) the issuer; and

(ii) the manager of the issuer;

owned of record or beneficially directly or indirectly, by each person who owns of record, or is known by such issuer or manager to own beneficially, directly or indirectly, more than 10 percent of any class of such securities. Show in Column 5 whether the securities are owned both of record and beneficially, of record only, of beneficially only, and show in Columns 6 and 7 the respective numbers and percentages known by the issuer or manager to be owned in each such manner.

TABLE

Column 1	Column 2	Column 3	Column 4	Column 5	Column 6	Column 7
Name and address	Name of company	Issuer or relationship thereto	Designation of class	Type of ownership	Number of securities owned	Percentage of class

(b)   If any person named in answer to paragraph (a) owns of record or beneficially, directly or indirectly, more than 10 percent of,

(i) any class of voting securities of the contractual distributor or the principal broker of the issuer or any parent or subsidiary thereof, or

(ii) any proprietorship interest in the contractual distributor or the principal broker of the issuer,

give the percentage of such securities or the percentage of such proprietorship interest so owned by that person.

(c)   The percentage of securities of each class of voting securities beneficially owned, directly or indirectly by all the directors, trustees and senior officers,

(i) of the issuer in the issuer or in a parent or subsidiary thereof, and

(ii) of the manager of the issuer in such manager or in a parent or subsidiary thereof,

in the case of each company as a group, without naming them.

TABLE

Column 1	Column 2	Column 3	Column 4
Name of Company	Issuer or relationship thereto	Designation of class	Percentage of class

INSTRUCTIONS

1. Where a company is shown by the issuer as owning directly or indirectly more than 10 percent of any class of such securities, the Director may require the disclosure of such additional information as is necessary to identify any individual, who, through his direct or indirect ownership of voting securities in the company owns directly or indirectly more than 10 percent of any class of such securities. The name of such individual should be disclosed in a footnote to the table described in paragraph (a).

2. For the purposes of paragraph (a), securities owned beneficially, directly or indirectly, and of record shall be aggregated in determining whether any person or company owns more than 10 percent of the securities of any class.

3. For the purposes of clause (i) of paragraph (a), where no material change has occurred in the information required by such clause since the date of the financial statements filed for the issuer's most recently completed financial year, the information may be given as of the date of the financial statements.

4. If voting securities are being offered in connection with, or pursuant to, a plan of acquisition, amalgamation or reorganization, indicate, as far as practicable, the respective holdings of voting securities that will exist after giving effect to the plan.

5. If, to the knowledge of the issuer, more than 10 percent of any class of voting securities of the issuer or if, to the knowledge of the manager of the issuer, more than 10 percent of any class of voting securities of such manager are held or are to be held subject to any voting trust or another similar agreement, state the designation of such securities, the number held or to be held and the duration of the agreement. Give the names and addresses of the voting trustees and other powers under the agreement.

6. If, to the knowledge of the issuer, the parent of the issuer, the manager or the parent of the manager, any person or company named in answer to paragraph (a) is an associate or affiliate of any other person or company named therein, disclose, in so far as known, the material facts of such relationship including any basis for influence over the issuer enjoyed by the person or company other than the holding of voting securities of the issuer.

Item 15 - Interest of Management and Others in Material Transactions

Describe briefly, and where practicable state the approximate amount of, any material interest direct or indirect, of any of the following persons in any transaction within the three years prior to the date of the annual information form, or in any proposed transaction which has materially affected or will materially affect the issuer:

(i) the manager of the issuer;

(ii) the contractual distributor of the issuer;

(iii) the principal broker of the issuer;

    (iv) any director, senior officer or trustee of the issuer or of any company referred to in clauses (i), (ii) or (iii) hereof;

    (v) any security holder named in answer to paragraph (a) of Item 14; and

    (vi) any associate or affiliate of any of the foregoing persons or companies.

INSTRUCTIONS

1. Give a brief description of the material transaction. Include the name and address of each person whose interest in any transaction is described and the nature of the relationship by reason of which such interest is required to be described.

2. As to any transaction involving the purchase or sale of assets by or to the issuer otherwise than in the ordinary course of business, state the cost of the assets to the purchaser and the cost thereof to the seller if acquired by the seller within two years prior to the transaction.

3. This Item does not apply to any interest arising from the ownership of securities of the issuer where the security holder receives no extra special benefit or advantage not shared on an equal basis by all other holders of the same class of securities or all other holders of the same class of securities who are resident in Canada.

4. No information need be given in answer to this Item as to any transaction or any interest therein where,

    (i) the rates or charges involved in the transaction are fixed by law or determined by competitive bids;

    (ii) the interest of a specified person in the transaction is solely that of a director of another company that is a party to the transaction;

    (iii) the transaction involves services as a bank or other depository of funds, transfer agent, registrar, trustee under a trust indenture or other similar services;

    (iv) the interest of a specified person including all periodic instalments in the case of any lease or other agreement providing for periodic payments or instalments, does not exceed $50,000; or

    (v) the transaction does not directly or indirectly involve remuneration for services, and

        (A) the interest of a specified person arose from the beneficial ownership, direct or indirect, of less than 10 percent of any class of voting securities of another company that is a party to the transaction,

        (B) the transaction is in the ordinary course of business of the issuer.

5. Information shall be furnished in answer to this Item with respect to transactions not excluded above that involve remuneration directly or indirectly, to any of the specified persons or companies for services in any capacity unless the interest of the person or company arises solely from the beneficial ownership, direct or indirect, of less than 10 percent of any class of voting securities of another company furnishing the services to the issuer or its subsidiaries.

6. This Item does not require the disclosure of any interest in any transaction unless such interest and transaction are material.

Item 16 - Custodian of Portfolio Securities

    (a) State the name, principal business address and the nature of the business of each person holding portfolio securities of the issuer as custodian and the jurisdiction in which the portfolio securities are physically situated. The name of the custodian may be omitted if it is a bank to which the Bank Act (Canada) applies, or otherwise with the consent of the Director.

    (b) Give brief details of the contractual arrangement made with the custodian.

Item 17 - Material Contracts

Give particulars of every material contract entered into within the two years prior to the date of the annual information form, by the issuer and state a reasonable time and place at which any such contract or copy thereof may be inspected during distribution of the securities being offered.

INSTRUCTIONS

1. The term "material contract" for this purpose means any contract that can reasonably be regarded as presently material to the proposed investor in the securities being offered.

2. Set out a complete list of all material contracts, indicating those which are disclosed elsewhere in the annual information form or in the short form of prospectus and provide particulars with respect to those material contracts about which particulars are not given elsewhere. This item does not require disclosure of contracts entered into in the ordinary course of business of the issuer.

3. Particulars of contracts should include the dates of, parties to, consideration and general nature of the contracts succinctly described.

4. Particulars of contracts need not be disclosed, or copies of such contracts made available for inspection, if the Superintendent determines that such disclosure or making available would impair the value of the contract and would not be necessary for the protection of investors.

Item 18 - Other Material Facts

Give particulars of any other material facts relating to the securities proposed to be offered and not disclosed pursuant to the foregoing items which are not contained in the short form of prospectus.

Item 19 - Certificates

(a) Include a certificate signed by the fund's Chief Executive Officer, by the fund's Chief Financial Officer, by two directors or trustees other than the foregoing and by the fund's Manager, if any, which states:

"This annual information form, the financial statements of the fund for the financial period ended (specify) and the auditors' report thereon, with such subsequent financial statements, whether annual or semi-annual, material change reports and information circulars, or annual filings in lieu thereof, required to be filed during the currency of this annual information form together with the short form of prospectus required to be sent or delivered to a purchaser during the currency of this annual information form, which documents taken together comprise the fund's permanent information record, constitute full, true and plain disclosure of all material facts relating to the securities offered by the short form of prospectus as required by securities legislation of the various provinces in which this annual information form is filed and do not contain any misrepresentation. The short form of prospectus required to be sent or delivered to a purchaser during the currency of this annual information form, read without reference to the remainder of the permanent information record, does not contain any misrepresentation."

(b) Include a certificate signed by the fund's underwriter which states:

"To the best of our knowledge, information and belief this annual information form, the financial statements of the fund for the financial period ended (specify) and the auditors' report thereon, with such subsequent financial statements, whether annual or semi-annual, material change reports and information circulars, or annual filings in lieu thereof, required to be filed during the currency of this annual information form together with the short form of prospectus required to be sent or delivered to a purchaser during the currency of this annual information form, which documents taken together comprise the fund's permanent information record, constitute full, true and plain disclosure of all material facts relating to the securities offered by the short form of prospectus as required by securities legislation of the various provinces in which this annual information form is filed and do not contain any misrepresentation. The short form of prospectus required to be sent or delivered to a purchaser during the currency of this annual information form, read without reference to the remainder of the permanent information record, does not contain any misrepresentation."

This is the information required by Section 104(1) of the Regulations regarding the financial statements of a mutual fund.

FORM 52
Securities Act
INFORMATION REQUIRED TO BE INCLUDED IN THE FINANCIAL STATEMENTS OF A MUTUAL FUND

Item 1 - Balance Sheet

(A) A balance sheet of a mutual fund shall present fairly the financial position of the mutual fund as at the date to which it is made up and show separately, at least

  (a) cash, term deposits and, if not included in the statement of investment portfolio, short term debt instruments,

  (b) dividends and accrued interest receivable,

  (c) accounts receivable in respect of shares or units sold,

  (d) accounts receivable in respect of portfolio securities sold,

  (e) every other class of asset that is 5% or more of total assets,

  (f) other assets,

  (g) the investments at market value with a notation of their cost,

  (h) total assets,

  (i) accrued expenses,

  (j) liabilities in respect of portfolio securities purchased,

  (k) liabilities in respect of shares or units redeemed,

  (l) income tax payable,

  (m) every other class of liability that is 5% or more of total liabilities,

  (n) other liabilities,

  (o) total liabilities,

  (p) total net assets and shareholders' or unit holders' equity, and

  (q) the net asset value for each share or unit.

(B) The notes to a balance sheet of a mutual fund shall include:

  (a) where the basis of computing the cost of investments is other than average cost, a statement of the basis of computing the cost,

  (b) where a mutual fund has outstanding more than one class of shares or units ranking equally against its net assets but differing in other respects, a statement of the differences between the classes, the number of shares or units in each class and the number of shares or units in each class that have been issued and are outstanding, and

  (c) the composition of other assets and other liabilities.

(C) Where a specified class of assets or liabilities is less than 5% of the total liabilities, respectively, it may be omitted from the balance sheet as a specified item if it is included in "other assets" or "other liabilities", as the case may be, with an appropriate explanation made by note.

(D) In this item "other assets" and "other liabilities" means the sum of those classes of assets or liabilities, as the case may be, that individually do not exceed 5% of the total assets or total liabilities, respectively, of the mutual fund at the date reported on.

Item 2 - Statement of Investment Portfolio

(A) A statement of investment portfolio of a mutual fund shall present fairly as at the date to which it is made up

   (a) the name of each issuer of securities held,

   (b) the class of designation of each security held,

   (c) the number or aggregate face value of each class or designation of securities held,

   (d) the market value of each class or designation of securities held, and

   (e) the cost of each class or designation of securities held where the basis of computing cost is other than average cost, a statement of the basis of computing the cost.

(B) Subject to Item 4, paragraph (A) applies to all short term debt instruments held pending the investment of funds.

(C) Information respecting securities with an aggregate market value of less than 5% of the total net assets may be omitted from a statement of investment portfolio under paragraph (A)(d) or (e), as the case may be, if that information is included in the statement as "miscellaneous securities" and the information required by paragraph (A)(d) (and) (e) is given for the "miscellaneous securities" in the aggregate.

Item 3 - Statement of Portfolio Transactions

(A) A statement of portfolio transactions of a mutual fund shall present fairly for the period covered by the statement

   (a) the name of each issuer of every security purchased or sold,

   (b) the class or designation of every security purchased or sold,

   (c) the number of aggregate face value, by issuer, of securities of each class or designation purchased and the total cost of purchasing securities of each such class or designation, and

   (d) the number of aggregate face value, by issuer, of securities of each class or designation sold and the consideration for selling securities of each such class or designation.

(B) Subject to Item 4, paragraph (A) applies to all short term debt instruments held pending the investment of funds.

(C) A mutual fund shall, in every statement of portfolio transactions, separate debt securities from securities other than debt securities, and shall provide a total for each group.

(D) Where information on securities is omitted from a statement of investment portfolio of a mutual fund under Item 2(C), information required by this item for those securities may be omitted from the statement of portfolio transactions.

Item 4 - Modification of Items 2 and 3

(A) Where the short term debt instruments referred to in Items 2(B) and 3(B)

   (a) are issued by a bank, by a trust company approved under the *Trust Company Act* or by a loan corporation, or

   (b) have achieved an investment rating falling within the highest or next to highest categories of every service, recognized by the commission, that publishes ratings on the short term debt instruments of the issuer, the information referred to in Item 2(A) and 3(A) may be provided in the aggregate.

(B)　　Where information is omitted from a statement of investment portfolio under Item 2(C) or from a statement or portfolio transactions under Item 3(D), that information and the reason for omitting it shall be included in the next corresponding statement.

(C)　　The information required by Item 2(A) respecting mortgages may be omitted from the statement of investment portfolio if, instead, the statement presents fairly, as at the date to which it is made up

    (a)　　the total number of mortgages held,

    (b)　　the total market value of mortgages held,

    (c)　　the number and market value of

        (i)　mortgages insured under the *National Housing Act* (Canada),

        (ii) insured conventional mortgages, and

        (iii) uninsured conventional mortgages,

    (d)　　the mortgages by groups, each group representing mortgages whose contractual interest rates vary by no more than 0.25%, and

    (e)　　the number, the market value amortized cost and the outstanding principal value of mortgages in each group established under paragraph (d).

(D)　　The information required by Item 3(A) respecting mortgages may be omitted from the statement of portfolio transactions if, instead, the statement presents fairly, for the period reported on,

    (a)　　the total number of mortgages purchased and sold,

    (b)　　the total cost of mortgages purchased and the total consideration for mortgages sold,

    (c)　　the number of

        (i)　mortgages insured under the *National Housing Act* (Canada),

        (ii) insured conventional mortgages, and

        (iii) uninsured conventional mortgages, that are, in each case, purchased and sold,

    (d)　　the mortgages by groups, each group representing mortgages whose contractual interest rates vary by no more than 0.25%, and

    (e)　　the number of mortgages purchased and sold in each group established under paragraph (d).

Item 5 - Statement of Changes in Net Assets

(A)　　Subject to paragraph (B), a statement of changes in net assets of a mutual fund shall present fairly the information shown for the period covered by it and show separately, at least

    (a)　　net assets at the beginning of the period,

    (b)　　net investment income or loss,

    (c)　　aggregate proceeds on sale of portfolio securities,

    (d)　　the aggregate cost of portfolio securities owned at the beginning of the period,

    (e)　　aggregate cost of purchases of portfolio securities,

    (f)　　aggregate cost of portfolio securities owned at the end of the period,

    (g)　　aggregate cost of portfolio securities sold,

    (h)　　realized profit or loss on portfolio securities sold,

(i)   distributions, showing separately the amount out of net investment income and out of realized profits on portfolio securities sold,

(j)   proceeds from securities issued,

(k)   payments for securities redeemed,

(l)   net increase or decrease in unrealized appreciation or depreciation of portfolio securities,

(m)   net assets at the end of the period,

(n)   net asset value for each share or unit at the end of the period and at the end of each of the 4 immediately preceding periods,

(o)   distribution per share or unit out of net investment income, and

(p)   distribution per share or unit out of realized profits on portfolio securities sold.

(B)   Items of the nature described in paragraph (A)(c) to (g) and (n) to (q) may be shown by way of a note or schedule to the statement of changes in net assets.

    (a)   dividend revenue,

    (b)   interest revenue,

    (c)   every other item of revenue that is 5% or more of the total revenue,

    (d)   other revenue,

    (e)   the total management fees paid by the mutual fund for portfolio management, investment advice and other services,

    (f)   audit fees,

    (g)   directors' fees,

    (h)   custodian's fees,

    (i)   legal fees,

    (j)   salaries where the total amount of salaries is 5% or more of the total expenses,

    (k)   shareholders' or unit holders' information costs, where the total amount of those costs is 5% or more of the total expenses,

    (l)   every other item of expense that is 5% or more of the total expense,

    (m)   other expenses,

    (n)   income before taxes,

    (o)   provision for income tax,

    (p)   extraordinary gains, extraordinary losses and provision for extraordinary losses,

    (q)   net income,

    (r)   net income for each share or unit, based on the average number of shares or units outstanding during the period, and

    (s)   net income for each share or unit for the immediately preceding period, based on the average number of shares or units outstanding during that period.

(C)   The notes to an income statement of a mutual fund shall include

    (a)   the composition of other revenue referred to in paragraph (B)(d),

    (b)   the basis for calculating the management fees referred to in paragraph (B)(e), and

    (c)   the composition of other expenses referred to in paragraph (B)(m).

(D) Unless otherwise disclosed in the material of which the income statement forms a part or which it accompanies, the notes to an income statement shall also include

  (a)   a description of the services received in consideration of the management fees referred to in paragraph (B)(e),

  (b)   a description of the services provided to the mutual fund by those to whom salaries were paid,

  (c)   where the mutual fund has a "mutual fund manager" and salaries of that manager's employees are allocated to the mutual fund, the basis of and reasons for that allocation,

  (d)   the basis of the tax calculations and an explanation of the tax position of the mutual fund, and

  (e)   where an unusual change in expenses from period to period is not adequately explained by changes in total assets of the mutual fund, a description and explanation of the unusual change.

(E) Where a specified class of revenue or expense is less than 5% of the total revenue or total expenses, respectively, it may be omitted from the balance sheet as a specified item if it is included in "other revenue" or "other expenses", as the case may be, with an appropriate explanation made by note.

FORM 53
Securities Act
TRUST AGREEMENT

THIS AGREEMENT, made as of the _____ day of _____

BETWEEN _____

a company incorporated under the laws of _____

and having its head office in the _____

of _____ in the Province of British Columbia (or, as the case may be, carrying on business as a sole proprietor or in partnership) under the firm name and style of _____

in the _____ of _____

in the Province of British Columbia (hereinafter called the "Registrant")

OF THE FIRST PART

AND _____

(hereinafter called the "Trustee")

OF THE SECOND PART

WHEREAS the Superintendent of Brokers for the Province of British Columbia (hereinafter called the "Superintendent) has established certain requirements for certain classes of registrant coming under his direct supervision, for the protection of clients of such registrants;

AND WHEREAS one of such requirements is that a fund be established for the protection of certain of such clients in the event of a default of a registrant;

AND WHEREAS the Registrant is one of a number of such registrants or proposed registrants who are entering or who may hereafter enter into separate agreements with the Trustee in the form hereof in order to establish such a fund;

AND WHEREAS all necessary proceedings have been taken and conditions complied with by the Registrant to make this agreement and the execution thereof legal and valid and in accordance with the laws relating to the Registrant and with all other laws and regulations in that behalf (where applicable, i.e., corporations);

AND WHEREAS the foregoing recitals are made as representations and statements of fact by the Registrant and not by the Trustee.

NOW THEREFORE, the parties hereto do mutually covenant and agree as follows:

1. ESTABLISHMENT OF TRUST

The Registrant hereby assigns, transfers and delivers unto and in favour of the Trustee the sum of _____ dollars, receipt whereof is hereby acknowledged by the Trustee, to be held by the Trustee (together with such other sums as the Trustee may from time to time receive from the Registrant or others for the purpose and in accordance with the provisions hereof) upon the trusts hereof and in accordance with the terms and conditions of this agreement.

2. CONTINGENCY PLAN AND TRUST

The Registrant shall participate in the contingency trust plan (hereinafter called the "Plan") and the contingency trust fund (hereinafter called the "Trust Fund") established hereby and by other existing or future agreements between registrants or proposed registrants and the Trustee in the same or substantially similar form, and the instrument entitled "Terms of Contingency Trust Plan" annexed as Schedule A hereto, together with this agreement, constitute the terms and conditions of the Plan and Trust Fund and each of the Registrant and Trustee covenants and agrees with the other to be bound by and perform and observe the obligations and conditions on its part to be observed or performed hereunder.

3. SITUS OF TRUST

The situs of the trust established hereunder shall be at all times in the Province of British Columbia, and the property and interest comprising such trust shall at all times be held by the Trustee from time to time in the Province of British Columbia.

4. PROOF OF SUPERINTENDENT'S APPROVAL

The Trustee acknowledges that it has received the approval of the Superintendent to the participation of the Registrant in the Plan.

IN WITNESS WHEREOF, the parties hereto have hereunto set their hands and seals at the _____ of _____, in the Province of British Columbia, the day and year first above written.

Witness the corporate seal of

_____
per _____
per _____

Witness the corporate seal of

_____
per _____
per _____

SCHEDULE A   TERMS OF CONTINGENCY TRUST PLAN
ARTICLE I   INTERPRETATION

Section 1.01. In this agreement, unless there is something in the subject matter inconsistent therewith,

(a) "this agreement", "hereto", "herein", "hereof", "hereby", "hereunder", and similar expressions refer to this agreement and this Schedule A thereto and not to any particular article, section, or other portion hereof or thereof and include any and every instrument supplemental or ancillary hereto and thereto or in implement hereof or thereof;

(b) "Approved Securities" means:

(i) investments in which the Canadian and British Insurance Companies Act (Canada), as such Act may be amended from time to time, provides that a company registered under Part III thereof may, without availing itself for that purpose of the provisions of subsection (4) of Section 63 of the said Act, invest its funds;

(ii) guaranteed investment certificates or any other securities or participation units of securities issued or held by the Trustee and monies in any deposit or other account or investments in any fund operated by the Trustee, without regard to whether or not any securities held for or forming part of any such certificates, securities, units, account, or fund would themselves constitute Approved Securities; and

(iii) any other securities or class of securities in respect of which there has been delivered to the Trustee and Participants' Consent;

(c) "Associate", where used to indicate a relationship with any person or company means:

(i) all associates within the meaning of that term set forth in the Securities Act;

(ii) any relative or spouse of such person or of a person who is the beneficial owner directly or indirectly of more than 10 per cent of the voting rights attached to all voting shares of such company or of a partner of such person or any relative of such spouse, whether or not such relative or spouse or relative of such spouse has the same home as such person, beneficial owner, or partner; and

(iii) a related person within the meaning of that term set forth in, Section 2B [4(2)] of the Bankruptcy Act (Canada), as amended;

(d) "claim" means a claim against the capital of the Trustee Fund meeting the requirements of Section 5.01 hereof;

(e) "client", where used to indicate a relationship with a Participant, means any person or company who buys or sells securities from, to, or through such Participant or who delivers securities to or leaves securities with such Participant in anticipation of buying or as a result of selling securities from, to, or through such a Participant;

(f) "Commission" means the British Columbia Securities Commission established by the Securities Act and any consent, approval, determination, exercise of discretion, or requirement of the Commission shall mean a written letter or instrument delivered to the Trustee setting forth such consent, approval, determination, exercise of discretion, or requirement of either the superintendent of Brokers for British Columbia or of any Deputy Superintendent of Brokers;

(g) "Counsel" means any barrister or solicitor or firm of barristers and solicitors retained by the Trustee;

(h) "Default" or of by a Participant means a failure by the Participant to meet any liability or obligation to a bona fide client when due or a conversion of funds or securities of such a client while in the hands or under the control of such Participant;

(i) "insolvent" in relation to a Participant means any Participant who is an insolvent person as defined by the Bankruptcy Act (Canada);

(j) "Participant" means each person or company who is or has made or intends to make application to become a registrant, within the meaning set forth in the Securities Act who enter into an agreement with the Trustee in the form or substantially the form hereof, and every such person or company shall be a Participant from the later of the Effective Date or the date on which the Participant enters into such an agreement until his participation in the Plan is terminated in accordance with the provisions of Article VI hereof;

(k) "Participants' Consent" or "Participant' Request" means an instrument of consent or request signed in one or more counterparts by not less than 75 per cent of all Participants, exclusive of any Participant in respect of whom there is at such time any outstanding Default or any failure to perform or observe any obligation or condition hereunder on his part to be performed or observed;

(l)   "Person" means an individual, partnership, unincorporated association, unincorporated organization, unincorporated syndicate, trustee, executor, administrator, or other legal personal representative;

(m) "Plan" has the meaning provided for in Section 2.01 hereof;

(n)   "Registrant" means the particular Registrant entering into this agreement;

(o)   "security" has the meaning set forth in the Securities Act;

(p)   "Securities Act" means the Securities Act, Statutes of British Columbia, and every other statute incorporated therewith or amending the same and any statute substituted therefore and, in the case of any such substitution, the Securities Act shall mean the statute so substituted, and includes any regulation made pursuant to any thereof;

(q)   "Superintendent" means the Superintendent of Brokers or any Deputy Superintendent of Brokers or any duly authorized person performing his duties under the Securities Act;

(r)   "Trust Fund" means the trust fund described in Section 4.01 hereof, and "capital of the Trust Fund" has the meaning provided for in the said section;

(s)   "Trustee" shall include any successor trustee hereunder, provided such successor trustee is a corporation authorized to do business as a trust company in British Columbia under the provisions of the Trust Companies Act of British Columbia;

(t)   "Withdrawal Credit" of a Participant means the net amount, if any, standing to the credit of a Participant, computed in accordance with Section 6.01 hereof;

(u)   Words importing the singular number only shall include the plural and vice versa and words importing the masculine gender shall include the feminine gender and vice versa.

[Paras. (d) and (k) deleted; paras. (o) to (x) renumbered by B.C. Reg. 194/75; para. (g) deleted; paras. (h) to (v) renumbered by B.C. Reg. 704/74.]

Section 1.02. The headings of all the articles and sections hereof are inserted for convenience of reference only and shall not affect the construction or interpretation of this agreement.

Section 1.03. Whether there is a reference herein to the exercise of a discretion by either the Trustee or the Superintendent, such exercise shall be sole, absolute, and uncontrolled, and in no circumstances shall any exercise be subject to any right in respect thereof of any person for any reason whatsoever. Any consent or approval of the Superintendent may be granted or refused and any requirement may be made in his discretion as aforesaid, and any determination of the Superintendent shall constitute a binding and final exercise of his discretion.

Section 1.04. This agreement shall be governed by and construed in accordance with the laws of the Province of British Columbia.

ARTICLE II   ESTABLISHMENT OF CONTINGENCY TRUST FUND

Section 2.01. The Plan and Trust Fund hereby established shall be known and described as the Contingency Trust Plan (hereinafter referred to as the "Plan").

Section 2.02. The Plan shall be established as of the Effective Date, and this agreement shall be effective from such date in respect of Participants entering into an agreement in form the same or substantially similar to this agreement on or before such date and, in respect of Participants entering into such an agreement after such date, on the date of entering into thereof.

ARTICLE III   PAYMENTS FROM PARTICIPANTS

Section 3.01. Each Participant who becomes such prior to the Effective Date shall, subject to the provisions of Section 3.10, make an initial payment of $_____ to the Trustee in respect of the Plan, on or before the Effective Date, and each Participant who becomes such after the Effective Date shall make such initial payment before or at the time of becoming a Participant; provided that with respect to Participants who become such after the Effective Date, the Superintendent may require such additional payment or payments so that the Withdrawal Credits of all Participants are equal in amount.

Section 3.02. save as hereinafter provided, at any time when the capital of the Trust Fund is or would be reduced by reason of the payment or proposed payment by the Trustee of any claim, each Participant (except the person in respect of whose Default such claim was made) shall pay into the Trust Fund his pro rata share of such claim at the time or times and in the manner required by the Trustee. For the purposes of this section 3.02 such "pro rata share" shall be determined as follows:

the claim which is the subject of payment, together with all other claims paid in respect of any Default of the same Participant, shall be aggregated and there shall be deducted therefrom the amount of such Participant's Withdrawal Credit. The balance, if any, shall be divided by the number of Participants (except the person in respect of whose Default such claim was made), and the resulting amount, after adjustment by the Trustee as hereinafter provided, shall be the pro rata share up to the next highest even multiple of $1,000. Notwithstanding the foregoing provisions of this Section 3.02, a Participant who participates in the Plan after the Effective Date may, if the Trustee and the Superintendent jointly so determine in their discretion, be excluded from any obligation to pay all or a part of his pro rata share in respect of any claim paid by or presented to the Trustee or of which the Trustee was aware during any period prior to six months after he became such a Participant. In the event of such a determination, the pro rata shares of all other Participants required to pay pro rata shares hereunder shall be proportionately increased by the aggregate amount of the pro rata share of Participant so excluded from his obligation to pay under this Section 3.02.

Section 3.03. The Participant in respect of whose Default any claims are paid shall be liable to pay and shall pay to the Trustee the aggregate amount of all such claims paid, so that at all times the Withdrawal Credit of such Participant is equal to not less than $_____ or such other amount as may from time to time be required by the Superintendent under Section 3.10 hereof. This liability of any such Participant to the Trustee under this Section 3.03 shall not adversely affect the right of the Trustee to require any assignment of and to enforce any such claim and any security or guarantee therefor, provided that any amount so recovered shall be added to the Withdrawal Credit of such Participant and from part of the Trust Fund and shall reduce by such amount the liability, if any, of such Participant under this Section 3.03.

Section 3.04. Notwithstanding the fact that a Participant shall be in Default hereunder or shall have failed to perform or observe any obligation or condition hereof on his part to be performed or observed, such Participant shall remain liable in respect of his pro rata share under the provisions of Section 3.02 hereof.

Section 3.05. In the event one or more Participants shall fail to pay any pro rata share or other amount required to be paid to the Trustee pursuant to Section 3.02 hereof, such deficiency shall be, at the discretion of the Trustee, added on a pro rata basis among the remaining Participants required to pay such a pro rata share.

Section 3.06. Subject only to the provisions of Section 3.07 hereof, and without limiting the generality of any other provisions of this agreement, the Trustee may at any time and from time to time require an additional payment into the Trust Fund from a Participant at any time when the Withdrawal Credit of such Participant is for any reason whatsoever less than $_____ or such greater or lesser amount as the Superintendent may from time to time require under Section 3.10 hereof, provided that the Trustee need not require an additional payment otherwise required hereunder, to the extent such additional payment would result in a Withdrawal Credit for a Participant in excess of $_____ or such greater or lesser amount as aforesaid.

Section 3.07. Notwithstanding any other provision hereof, other than Section 3.10 hereof which shall not be affected by this Section 3.07, the obligation hereunder of a Participant to make additional payments into the Trust Fund shall be limited in any one period of 365 days to a maximum amount of $_____.

Section 3.08. The Trustee may at any time and from time to time retain and set off against any unpaid or unperformed liability or obligation hereunder of any Participant any any amount in its possession howsoever obtained of which the Participant would, but for this provision, be entitled to receive payment.

Section 3.09. A Participant shall not be obligated to make any payment in addition to the initial payment under Section 3.01 unless and until he shall have received a notice of the amount to be paid from the Trustee, but shall make any such payment within 60 days after receipt of such notice, and thereafter shall be liable to pay interest at the rate of 10 per cent per annum compounded annually on the amount unpaid from time to time.

Section 3.10. The Superintendent may at any time and from time to time require that the amount of the Withdrawal Credit of any Participant shall be greater than or less than $_____, in which event the Trustee shall, within such period as the Superintendent may require, demand such additional payments from Participants as may be thereby required to eliminate any Withdrawal Credit deficiency, and the Participants shall pay such amounts forthwith to the Trustee hereunder, or, as the case may be, pay such amounts to Participants as may be thereby required to eliminate any Withdrawal Credit excess.

[Secs. 3.01, 3.03, 3.06, 3.07, 3.08, 3.10 amended by B.C. Reg. 194/75.1]

Section 3.11. Wherever a Participant has failed to pay to the Trustee any amount required to be paid hereunder, as a result of which other Participants have made additional payments hereunder, and amounts are subsequently paid to or recovered by the Trustee in respect of the amounts previously not so paid by such Participant, such amounts subsequently paid shall be credited on a fair proportionate basis, having regard to all the facts among the Participants who have made such additional payments and shall reduce the amounts otherwise required to be paid by such Participant hereunder; provided further that amounts subsequently so paid shall, where amounts in respect thereof were due but not paid by other Participants, reduced the liability of such Participants on a fair proportionate basis having regard to all the facts. The Trustee shall determine what is a fair proportionate basis as aforesaid, and its decision shall be final and binding.

ARTICLE IV   TRUST FUND

Section 4.01. The Trustee shall hold all money and other property, if any, received by it from Participants or others pursuant hereto or in respect hereof and all income on any such money or from any such property, and all rights hereby conferred, in trust for the benefit of such of the holders of claims from time to time as the Trustee may from time to time in its discretion appoint, and subject thereto and hereto, for the benefit of the Participants, and all such money, property, and income thereon or therefrom shall constitute a trust fund to be dealt with and invested or distributed in accordance with the terms of this agreement. The capital of the Trust Fund shall mean all amounts held by the trustee as part of the Trust Fund other than amounts designated from time to time by the Trustee in its discretion as payable to a client, Participant, or other person hereunder.

Section 4.02. The Trustee shall maintain a record of amounts received from, on behalf of, or in respect of each Participant and shall distinguish in such record the section hereof pursuant to which each such amount was received and shall show in such record the Withdrawal Credit account from time to time of each Participant. All amounts received by the Trustee into the Trust Fund shall be credited to a Participant or Participants, and the Trustee's decision in respect of such crediting shall be final and conclusive, provided that the Trustee may in it discretion change any such crediting from time to time as it sees fit. No crediting of an amount to a Participant shall, as such, give such Participant any rights thereto, and a Participant shall only be entitled to receive any amounts from the Trust Fund in accordance with the specific provisions hereof respecting payments to a Participant.

Section 4.03. The Trustee shall keep the Trust Fund invested in Approved Securities.

Section 4.04. The Trustee shall collect and receive all income on or from the Trust Fund and shall, after deducting therefrom the fees, costs, charges, and expenses referred to in section 7.01 hereof, and subject as hereinafter provided, credit all of the income of the Trust Fund to the capital of the Trust Fund, in which event no part of such income so credited shall be paid to any of the Participants.

Section 4.05. Notwithstanding the provisions of Section 4.04, the Trustee shall from time to time, upon receipt of a Participants' Request, subject to the consent of the Superintendent, distribute the balance of the income as referred to in Section 4.04 to the Participants. From and after the receipt of such Request, income on or from the Trust Fund received during the period ended on the last day of September in each year (which date is herein referred to as the "Determination Date") shall, subject to the provisions of Section 4.06 hereof, be distributed annually on or before the last day of November in each year (which date is herein referred to as the "Distribution Date"). Each Participant having a Withdrawal Credit on the Determination Date shall, subject as hereinafter provided, receive a pro rata portion of the income distributed in respect of the period ended on such Determination Date. The Trustee shall determine in its discretion such reasonable pro rata portions of income to each Participant in respect of the distribution based on the amount of the withdrawal Credit of each Participant from time to time during such period and the portion or portions of the 12-month period covered thereby and shall forward to such Participant by first-class mail on or before the Distribution Date a cheque for the pro rata portion of income so determined. No Participant shall be entitled to a distribution of income hereunder if on the Distribution Day any claim has been made in respect of such Participant or there has been a failure by the Participant to perform or observe any obligation or condition hereunder on its part to be performed or observed. If an so long as any such claim exists and has not been paid by the Participant, or any such failure continues and has not been rectified by the Participant, such income and all other income thereafter accruing to such Participant shall be added to such Participant's Withdrawal Credit, and, where applicable, shall be treated by the Trustee in its discretion as discharging the liability to make a payment or payments under Article III hereof, in which event the amount so credited shall form part of the capital of the Trust Fund. The Trustee may pay any income tax or other tax that it honestly and in good faith believes to be payable in respect of any receipt, crediting, or payment or any such income to or in respect of a Participant, and any such payment shall constitute a discharge pro tanto of any obligation of the Trustee hereunder in respect of the payment or crediting of such income to such Participant.

Section 4.06. Notwithstanding the provisions of Section 4.05 hereof, the Trustee shall, if so required by the Superintendent or a Participants' Request, apply all or any part of the income Trust Fund to acquire such insurance payable to the Trustee having such coverage, and with such limits, deductibles, and other terms as the Trustee shall see fit, to insure against all or any part of the obligation of Participants hereunder to make payments into the Trust Fund and to apply any proceeds thereunder in discharge pro tanto of any such obligation, provided that no such application of proceeds in respect of any such obligation shall be treated as a payment by a Participant for the purpose of limiting the obligation of a Participant to make additional payments into the Trust Fund in any one period of 365 days, pursuant to section 3.07 hereof.

Section 4.07. Notwithstanding the provisions of Section 4.05, the Trustee shall from time to time, at the request of the Superintendent, credit all or any part of the income of the Trust Fund to the capital of the Trust Fund, in which event no part of such income so credited shall be paid to any of the Participants.

Section 4.08. The Trustee shall keep complete records of its administration of the Trust Fund on the basis of a fiscal year ended on the last day of _____ in each year. A copy of the financial statements of the Trust Fund, certified by the Trustee, shall be delivered to the Superintendent and the Participants within three months after the end of each fiscal year. Such statements shall include, where applicable, the following information:

(a) The amount of the Withdrawal Credit of each Participant;

(b) The amount owing hereunder by any Participant to the Trustee by reason of any provision hereof which has not been paid when due;

(c)   The amount of all receipts and the source thereof;

(d)   The amount of all payments to Participants and in respect of claims of clients of Participants;

(e)   A complete statement of all receipts and disbursements in respect of each Participant who was in Default during such fiscal year; and

(f)   A statement of all credits and debits to the capital of the Trust Fund.

In addition to the foregoing information, the Superintendent may from time to time require the Trustee to deliver such other information as he deems necessary.

Section 4.09. The Trust Fund may, at the sole discretion of the Trustee from time to time, constitute a single fund in respect of all Participants or separate funds in respect of each Participant, which separate funds may nonetheless be dealt with for the purposes of the convenient administration of the Plan as though they were a single fund.

Section 4.10. No Participant may assign any right or interest he may have in the Trust Fund to any person, nor shall any Participant, his heirs, executors, administrators, successors, or assigns assert any right at any time over and against the Trustee in respect of the Trust Fund or any Withdrawal Credit to which he might but for this section be entitled.

ARTICLE V   CLAIMS ON THE TRUST FUND

Section 5.01. The Plan is established to provide for the payment out of the capital of the Trust Fund of the amount of claims of clients of Participants, which meet the requirements hereinafter set forth, in such amounts and to such of such clients as the Trustee shall in its discretion from time to time determine and appoint:

(a)   A claim shall be limited to the direct out-of-pocket loss suffered by a person who was a bona fide client of a Participant at the time the liability, duty, or obligation was first incurred by such Participant in respect of which such loss thereafter arose, and such loss shall have arisen either due to

   (i)   the failure of such Participant to refund any payment received from a client for a security ordered by and not delivered as directed by that client, or to pay as directed by a client funds received by such Participant in connection with the sale of a security on behalf of that client; or

   (ii)   any conversion of funds or securities of such a client while in the hands of or under the control of the Participant or by or on behalf of or for the benefit of the Participant or a partner, director, or shareholder of the Participant, but only to the extent the Participant does not have a bond or insurance providing for payment in respect of any such conversion; or

   (iii)   the failure of such Participant to fulfill any contractual obligation to a client.

(b)   No claim shall be eligible for payment if the client making such claim was, at the time the liability giving rise to the loss was first incurred or at any time thereafter prior to payment,

   (i)   a Participant or a partner, director, officer, employee, agent, or shareholder of a Participant or an Associate of any of the foregoing; or

   (ii)   a person or company registered under the provisions of the Securities Act or an Associate of any thereof; or

   (iii)   a person or company described in paragraph (c) of subsection (1) of Section 21 of the Securities Act; or

   (iv)   a Promoter, as defined in the Securities Act of any person or company in respect of whose securities any loss has occurred.

(c)   No claim shall be eligible for payment to the extent that the amount of such claim is in excess of $2,500 and any amount received by the client in payment of any loss giving rise to such claim otherwise than out of the Trust Fund shall be applied to reduce the said maximum amount of $2,500. Claims by a group of persons acting together in a single transaction shall be considered to be a single claim subject to the maximum limitation and the reduction provided for in this subparagraph (c).

[Paras. (c), (d) renumbered by B.C. Reg. 194/75.]

Notwithstanding the provisions of section 5.07, if the total amount of claims made and considered payable by the Trustee is more than the total amount of the Trust Fund eligible for payment of claims, then the total amount of claims payable shall be reduced to the amount of the Trust Fund eligible for payment of claims on a pro rata basis.

If any question or doubt shall arise as to whether or not any claim meets the requirements of this Section 5.01 as to eligibility for payment out of the capital of the Trust Fund either in whole or in part, the Trustee in its discretion shall determine such eligibility, and any decision of the Trustee shall be final and conclusive for all purposes hereof and as against all persons. For greater certainty, it is hereby agreed and declared that no client of any Participant shall have any absolute or vested right to payment of any claim against the Trustee or the Trust Fund, notwithstanding such claim may qualify and be eligible for payment in every respect except only that the Trustee shall not have in its discretion appointed such client to receive such payment.

Section 5.02. A claim for payment out of the Trust Fund may only be made by a claimant giving written notice of such claim to the Trustee with full particulars thereof, including the amount thereof, any security or guarantee therefor, and any payment or recovery in respect thereof. A claim shall be deemed to have been made when written notice thereof is received by the Trustee.

Section 5.03. As a condition precedent to the authorization by the Trustee of the payment of any claim, the Trustee may, in its discretion, require that the claimant making such claim execute and deliver or arrange for the execution and delivery of such documents as the Trustee in its discretion deems necessary. The Trustee shall be entitled to seek the advice of Counsel as to the documentation necessary to support a claim and shall be entitled to rely on the opinion of Counsel as to the sufficiency of the documentation required and presented by a claimant for the purposes of paying any claim.

Section 5.04. As a condition precedent to the payment of the claim, the Trustee may in its discretion require that the client making such claim execute such documents as Counsel may advise are necessary or desirable for the purpose of transferring to the Trustee the interest of such client in the claim so as to subrogate the Trustee to the position of the client and enable the Trustee to prosecute the proceedings contemplated by Section 7.06 hereof.

Section 5.05. Notwithstanding any of the foregoing provisions of this Article V, the following limitations in respect of payments of claims shall apply:

(a) The maximum aggregate amount of claims which may be paid in respect of the Default of any one Participant shall never exceed the total amount of the Trust Fund at the time such claims are made.

(b) The Trustee may in its discretion pay claims in one or more installments, as it sees fit, in which event all claims of a Participant which the Trustee has determined and appointed for payment shall be paid on the same basis.

(c) No claims in respect of the Default of any Participant shall be paid by the Trustee until the Trustee is reasonable satisfied that all claims likely to be made in respect of Defaults of a Participant have been made or reserved against by the Trustee.

(d) The Trustee may in its discretion reserve against claims which it thinks may be validly made, and any such reservation shall be the equivalent of payment of such claim for the purposes of requiring additional payments of pro rata shares under Section 3.02 hereof.

[Para. (a) amended by B.C. Reg. 194/75.]

Section 5.06. The Trustee may in its discretion pay any claim notwithstanding that no demand for payment has been made by the client against a Participant in respect of whom a Default has occurred or that no action has been commenced or that no final judgement of a Court of competent jurisdiction has been obtained against such Participant or that no all reasonable efforts have been taken to have judgement satisfied; provided that the Trustee may require any or all of the foregoing steps to be taken by the client making the claim hereunder before paying the same or appointing such a client for payment in respect thereof. Should the Trustee pay any claim as aforesaid, then the Trustee may require the client to assign to the Trustee all the client's right, title, and interest in and to the said claim.

Section 5.07. The Trustee, on being satisfied that a claim complies with the requirements of this Article V, may in its discretion appoint the person making such claim to receive payment of all or any part thereof, in which event the Trustee shall, subject to the provisions of paragraph (b) of Section 5.05 hereof, promptly forwarded by first-class mail to the address specified by the client a cheque payable to the client in the amount of the claim or part thereof as so determined by the Trustee.

ARTICLE VI   TERMINATION OF PARTICIPATION IN PLAN

Section 6.01. The amount of the Trust Fund, if any, standing to the credit of a Participant shall constitute the Withdrawal Credit of the Participant, and such amount at any time shall be the aggregate of all payments made by or on behalf of such Participant pursuant to Article III, all income and recoveries credited to a Participant pursuant to any provision hereof, and all amounts (other than income or recoveries so credited) not distributed to a Participant pursuant to sections 4.05 and 7.06 hereof, minus the aggregate amount of:

(a)   his pro rata share of any claim subject to payment referred to in Section 3.02 (excluding any upward adjustment in such pro rata share made by the Trustee pursuant to Section 3.02); and

(b)   of any amounts charged hereunder against the Participant by the Trustee in respect of any amount paid out of the Trust Fund by the Trustee, whether to the Trustee or others.

Section 6.02.

(a)   Upon compliance with the requirements of this Section 6.02 on surrender, cancellation, or lapse of the registration of a Participant under the Securities Act or on such Participant satisfying the Trustee and the Superintendent that he has joined some other plan similar to the Plan and acceptable to the Superintendent, upon the Superintendent advising the Trustee that a Participant is no longer required to participate in the Plan as a condition of registration under the Securities Act, such Participant may apply for the withdrawal from the Plan and for the return of his withdrawal Credit, the amount of which shall be computed at the time when the Trustee determines that all such requirements are fulfilled.

(b)   A Participant wishing to so apply for withdrawal from the Plan shall give written notice of his intention to so withdraw to the Superintendent and the Trustee, but may not give any such notice at any time when such Participant has failed to perform or observe any obligation or condition on his part to be performed or observed hereunder.

(c)   The Participant so withdrawing shall file with the Superintendent and the Trustee such financial statements and other evidence as they may in their discretion require, to establish that the affairs of such Participant have been settled so as to preclude any claims on the Trust Fund arising out of such affairs which cannot be satisfied out of the Withdrawal Credit applicable to such Participant and that arrangements satisfactory to the Trustee and the Superintendent have been made to ensure that all liabilities and obligations of the Participant which could give rise to any claim have been met and discharged.

(d)   No Withdrawal Credit shall be paid to a withdrawing Participant until there are no unpaid claims which have been made against the Trust Fund and for which a payment would be required in respect of such Participant pursuant to Section 3.02 hereof if such claims were paid.

(e)   At the time provided for under paragraph (d) of this section 6.02 and provided the Participant has performed and observed all the obligations and conditions on his part to be performed or observed hereunder, the Trustee may in its discretion pay the amount of the Withdraw Credit or a Participant to the withdrawing Participant, subject only to the following:

(i) To the extent that the financial statements and other evidence referred to in this Section 6.02 disclose unsatisfied liabilities which would qualify as claims, the amount to be paid shall be reduced and such reduction shall be applied by the Trustee to the pro rata payment of such liabilities, upon receipt of such satisfactory evidence and documentation in respect of such claims as Counsel and the Trustee may require, or, if any of the events hereinafter mentioned have occurred;

(ii) the balance of any payment after reduction, if any, as provided in the preceding subsection (i) shall be paid to any receiver and manager designated by the Superintendent or appointed pursuant to the Securities Act in respect of the withdrawing Participant, or if no such receiver or receiver and manager has been so designated, to any trustee in bankruptcy or liquidator or similar person duly appointed by law to administer the estate or affairs of the withdrawing Participant.

Any such payment shall be made by the Trustee forwarding by first-class mail a cheque for the payment in the amount and to the Participant, person, or company, as the case may be, at the address specified by the withdrawing Participant or other person or company to whom the payment is to be made.

Section 6.03. Upon payment of a Withdrawal Credit to or in respect of a Participant under Section 6.02 hereof, such Participant shall cease to be a Participant, his participation in the Plan shall cease, and he shall no longer be subject to the Plan or to any further obligation under this agreement, and the Trustee may at the request and expense of the Participant give a formal release to the Participant of all his obligations hereunder in such form and subject to such conditions as Counsel may advise.

Section 6.04. For the purpose of computing a Withdrawal Credit hereunder, the Trustee may at any time and from time to time determine and use the cost or market value or the lower of cost or market value of all or any Approved securities held in the Trust Fund as the Trustee in its sole discretion shall see fit, and the Trustee shall in such event increase or decrease the Withdrawal Credit of a Participant by his proportionate share of any increase or decrease in value of Approved Securities from cost or from any previous determination hereunder, such proportionate share to be computed on such basis as the Trustee may in its sole discretion determine to be fair as among all Participants.

Section 6.05. In the event that a Participant who becomes such prior to becoming a registrant under the Securities Act does not for any reason become such a registrant, the amount paid by such Participant to the Trustee into the Trust Fund shall be returned without interest and the Trustee shall notify the Superintendent forthwith of such return. Any income earned in respect of any such amount so returned shall thereafter be held by the Trustee under the Trust Fund, but shall not be credited to the Withdrawal Credit or any Participant. Such amount shall be first applied to fees of the Trustee hereunder, and, second to any claim hereunder, and until so applied shall form part of the capital of the Trust Fund.

ARTICLE VII   THE TRUSTEE

Section 7.01. The Trustee accepts the trusts herein created upon the terms and conditions of the agreement and represents and warrants that it is a corporation authorized to do business in British Columbia as a trust company under the Trust Companies Act. The Trustee shall not be required to give any bond or other security for the faithful performance of its duties hereunder and shall not be responsible for any diminution in the funds, securities, or property of whatsoever character constituting part of the Trust Fund, or for any loss resulting from the making of any investment or from the retention in good faith for any length of time of securities or other property of whatsoever character purchased or acquired by it, notwithstanding that such securities or property may not be, or may have ceased to be, income producing, or from any mistake in judgement made in good faith, or from any loss of whatsoever character, unless resulting from its own fraud, negligence, or willful misconduct.

Section 7.02. The Trustee may rely and shall be protected in acting upon any resolution, certificate, statement, instrument, opinion, report, notice, request, consent, letter, telegram, cablegram, or other paper or document believed by it to be genuine and to have been signed, sent, or delivered by or on behalf of the proper party or parties. The Trustee may employ or retain such counsel, accountants, appraisers, or other experts or advisors as it may reasonably require for the purpose of discharging its duties hereunder; may act and shall be protected in acting in good faith on the opinion or advice of information obtained from any one of them; and shall not be responsible for any misconduct on the part of any of them.

Section 7.03. The Trustee may at any time resign as Trustee hereunder by giving 90 days' notice to the Superintendent. Either the Superintendent or the Participants by Participants' Request delivered to the Trustee may at any time require the removal of the Trustee hereunder on giving 90 days' notice to the Trustee. In the event of the resignation or removal of the Trustee or if the Trustee shall at any time be unable to act, the Superintendent shall appoint as a successor Trustee a corporation authorized to do business in British Columbia as a trust company under the Trust Companies Act of British Columbia and who, upon acceptance of such appointment, shall have vested in it without further act or formality all the rights and powers given hereunder to the Trustee, and upon written request of the superintendent the Trustee ceasing to act shall execute and deliver an instrument in writing transferring to such successor Trustee all the rights, powers, and Trust Fund assets reposing in or with the Trustee ceasing to act, and shall do all such other acts or things necessary or desirable for the vesting of the Trust Fund assets in the successor Trustee. Upon any such resignation or removal becoming effective, the Trustee ceasing to act shall render to the superintendent and to each Participant an account of its administration hereof during the period following that covered by its last annual accounting, which shall contain the information required under the provisions of Section 4.08, verified by a certificate of the Inspector of Trust Companies under the Trust Companies Act of British Columbia.

Section 7.04. Subject to section 4.03 hereof, the Trustee, in the administration of the Trust Fund, shall power and authority:

(a)   to invest and reinvest the Trust Fund in Approved Securities, and may do all acts and things and execute, acknowledge, and deliver all instruments in respect thereof;

(b)   to hold in the form of cash awaiting investment or other application hereunder any portion of the Trust Fund and without limiting the generality of the foregoing the Trustee may hold the cash in any deposit or current account operated by the Trustee;

(c)   to sell, convert, assign, exchange, transfer, or otherwise dispose of any Approved Securities at any time constituting part of the Trust Fund at public or private sale for such consideration and upon such terms and conditions as the Trustees shall see fit;

(d)   to vote in person or by proxy any Approved Security constituting part of the Trust Fund, to exercise personally or by general or limited power of attorney any right appurtenant to any Approved Securities or to any other property held by it at any time; to join in or dissent from and oppose the reorganization, redistribution, consolidation, merger, liquidation, or sale of corporations or properties; to exchange Approved Securities for other securities issued in connection with or resulting from any such reorganization.ion and retain such securities; to exercise or sell any rights issued upon or with respect to any property necessary to protect the investment of the Trust Fund in such property;

(e)   to register any Approved Security or other property held by it hereunder in its own name or in the name of a nominee with or without the addition of words indicating that such securities are held in fiduciary capacity, but the books and records of the Trustee shall at all times show that all Approved Securities and property howsoever held are part of the Trust Fund;

(f)   to compromise, adjust, or settle any claims in favour of or against the Trust Fund, and to conduct any litigation arising out of such claims.

Section 7.05. In the event that any Participant shall fail to perform or observe any obligation hereunder on its part to be performed or observed, then the Trustee may, and shall, when and to the extent requested to do so by a Participants' Request delivered to the Trustee, bring whatever legal action against such Participant which the Trustee, in its discretion deems necessary to compel such Participant to fulfill its obligations hereunder, provided that the Trustee shall only be required to take such legal action after it shall have been fully indemnified to its satisfaction by the Participants signing such Participants' Request against all actions, proceedings, claims, and demands to which it may thereby render itself liable and all fees, costs, charges, damages, and expenses whatsoever which it may have or incur by so doing. Any amount recovered as a result of any such legal action shall form part of the Trust Fund and shall be appropriately credited to the Withdrawal Credits of such Participants, with appropriate adjustments to the Withdrawal Credits of such other Participants.

Section 7.06.

(a) The Trustee may, and shall, when and to the extent requested to do so by a Participants' Request delivered to the Trustee, take all proceedings necessary to recover any monies which may be payable by any person or company to a client on account of a claim to which the Trustee has been subrogated as provided in Section 5.04 hereof or is otherwise entitled the Trustee shall only be required to take such proceedings after it shall have been fully indemnified to its satisfaction by such Participants against all actions, proceedings, claims, and demands to which it may thereby render itself liable and all fees, costs, charges, damages, and expenses which it may incur by do doing.

(b) In the event of any recovery by the Trustee of monies as a result of proceedings described in Section 7.06 hereof, all fees, costs, charges, damages, and expenses of the Trustee incurred in connection with such proceedings shall be deducted from such monies and, subject to any other provision hereof, the balance, if any, of such monies shall be distributed to Participants as provided in Section 7.06(c) hereof. In the event that any monies so recovered shall not be sufficient to defray such fees, costs, charges, and expenses, the portion of such fees, costs, charges, and expenses not so defrayed shall be added to the amounts payable to the Trustee under Section 7.07 hereof and shall be paid in the manner therein provided.

(c) Subject to the provisions of section 3.08 and of paragraph (b) of this Section 7.06, all monies recovered by the Trustee and available for distribution to Participants pursuant to this Section 7.06 shall be distributed equally among those Participants by or on behalf of whom the required payment has been made pursuant to Section 3.02 hereof on account of the claim on which such monies were received, and the Trustee shall distribute by firstclass mail to such Participants cheques representing the entitlement of such Participants pursuant to this paragraph (c) of Section 7.06.

Section 7.07. The Trustee's fees for performing its duties hereunder shall be such as may be mutually agreed upon from time to time between the Superintendent and the Trustee, and in default of such agreement shall be as fixed by a Judge of the County Court for the County of Vancouver upon application thereto by the Trustee, and the costs of such application shall be paid out of the Trust Fund, except in the case of the Trustee, in the event that the compensation so fixed is not more than the amount thereto to which the Superintendent was prepared to agree. The Trustee shall also be entitled to be reimbursed for any and all costs, charges, and expenses reasonably incurred by the Trustee in the performance of its duties pursuant to this agreement. All such fees, costs, charges, and expenses shall be deducted first from the income of the Trust Fund and, in the event of any deficiency, from the capital of the Trust Fund. Fees, costs, charges, and expenses of the Trustee accrued and unpaid shall be calculated on the last days of May and November in each year and shall be deducted from the income of the Trust Fund for the sixmonth periods ended on those dates.

Section 7.08. The Trustee shall not exercise any discretion granted to it hereunder without first notifying the Superintendent of its intention to do so and giving the Superintendent reasonable opportunity to making any views he may have known in such respect to the Trustee prior to the exercise of such discretion.

Section 7.09. The Trustee shall notify the Superintendent promptly of any

Default of any Participant, of any claim made in respect thereof, of any failure by a Participant to perform any obligation or condition on his part to be performed or observed hereunder, and shall furnish the Superintendent with all other information, records, and documents in its possession in connection with this agreement and its administration of the Trust Fund as the Superintendent may from time to time reasonably request.

ARTICLE VIII   AMENDMENT AND TERMINATION

Section 8.01. The Trustee may agree to amendments of this agreement, subject to the approval of the Participants evidenced by a Participants' Consent delivered to the Trustee and approval of the Superintendent, provided, however, that no such amendment shall be effective to prevent the payment of any claim which but for the amendment the Trustee would have determined to pay out of the Trust Fund.

Section 8.02. This Plan shall only be terminated at such time when all Participants have withdrawn from the Plan in accordance with the provisions of Article VI hereof.

ARTICLE IX   MISCELLANEOUS

Section 9.02. Notwithstanding any other provisions hereof, nothing herein contained shall be deemed to give any Participant any interest or right hereunder except the right to receive such payments out of the Trust Fund, if any, as may from time to time be determined by the Trustee in its discretion, or in default of the exercise by the Trustee of such discretion after one year following termination of the Plan, in accordance with the Withdrawal Credits of each Participant at the time of termination of the Plan.

Section 9.02. No assignment, anticipation, surrender, pledge, or encumbrance of any kind of any right of Participants or other persons to receive funds pursuant to this agreement shall be permitted or recognized under any circumstances, and any such rights shall not be subject to attachments or other legal processes for debts of such Participants or other persons.

Section 9.03. In order to protect the Trust Fund against depletion as a result of litigation, no Participant or person claiming under or against it shall bring legal or equitable action against the Trustee or the Trust Fund for any matter of cause whatsoever, except that the Participants by Participants' Request delivered to the Trustee and the Superintendent may claim against the Trustee for any loss resulting from the fraud, gross negligence, or willful misconduct of the Trustee, and in default of a satisfaction or settlement of such claim between the Participants' Consent, any Participant may commence such action or other proceeding as it may see fit against the Trustee, but in no event shall any part of the Trust Fund be attachable or otherwise made available to satisfy or settle any such claim or judgement or other Court order in respect thereof.

Section 9.04. All information, records, and documents of any kind whatsoever about any of the Participants or any officer, director or shareholder of any thereof or relating to the business relations between the Participant and any other person at any time in the possession or control of either the Trustee or the Superintendent and howsoever obtained, may be freely exchanged between the Trustee and the Superintendent; and no Participant or any such officer, director or shareholder shall have any claim of any kind whatsoever against either of the Superintendent or Trustee arising from or out of the exchange of any information by either the Superintendent or the Trustee or their use in good faith by either the Trustee or the Superintendent for any purpose hereof or of the Securities Act provided that nothing herein shall constitute an obligation of the Superintendent to furnish or disclose any information to any of the Trustee or the Participants or any other person.

Section 9.05. The Trustee or any person to whom as its representative it may in writing delegate such authority, may enter upon the premises of a Participant and examine such books, documents, and records of the Participant and make copies of such books, documents and records which, in the opinion of the Trustee or its representative, are necessary to assist in determining the validity of a claim or in the exercise of any discretion hereunder, and no person is, as against the Trustee, entitled to withhold possession of the aforesaid books, documents, and records belonging to the Participant or set up any lien thereon; all fees of and costs, charges, and expenses incurred by the Trustee in conducting such examination shall be added to the fees, costs, charges and expenses of the Trustee payable under section 7.07 hereof, and shall be paid in the manner therein provided.

Section 9.06. If at any time the Trustee is in doubt as to whether or not a person is a client of a Participant and/or whether or not such a person has a valid claim under the terms hereof, it may apply to the Supreme Court of British Columbia for a construction of the relevant sections hereof and directions as to whether or not the person is a client and/or has a valid claim under the terms hereof or the extent to which such person has a valid claim under the terms hereof; all fees of and costs, charges and expenses incurred by the Trustee in connection with any such application shall be added to the expenses of the Trustee payable under Section 7.07 hereof and shall be paid in the manner therein provided. The decision of the Supreme Court as to whether or not a person is a client of a Participant, and/or whether or not such a person or the extent to which such a person has a valid claim, shall be conclusive and binding, provided that no such decision of the Supreme Court of British Columbia shall in any way affect the discretion of the Trustee to appoint or not to appoint any part of the Trust Fund in respect of such a claim.

Section 9.07. Nothing herein shall under any circumstances whatsoever give any persons any right, demand, or claim of any kind whatsoever against or in respect of the Superintendent.

Section 9.08. Wherever an amount is recovered by the Trustee in respect of which a Participant has previously made or was liable to make but has not yet made a payment into the Trust Fund pursuant to any provision hereof, the appropriate share of the amount so recovered shall be credited to the Withdrawal Credit of such Participant; and the action by the Trustee in crediting or recrediting an appropriate share shall be final and binding on all Participants.

Section 9.09. Any notice to a Participant under the provision hereof shall be valid and effective if given by registered letter, postage prepaid, addressed to the Participant at his or its last address with the Superintendent and shall be deemed to have been received by the Participant in the ordinary course of mail.

Section 9.10. This agreement shall be binding upon and subject to the provisions of Sections 4.10, 9.01, and 9.03 hereof, shall inure to the benefit of the parties hereto and their respective heirs, executors, administrators, successors and assigns.

[Form 16 added by B.C. Reg. 116/72.]

This is the form to be used by a Natural Resource Issuer required by Section 102 of the regulations to file a report on its Mineral properties excluding Oil and Gas.

FORM 54

Securities Act

TECHNICAL REPORT ON MINERAL PROPERTIES EXCLUDING OIL AND GAS

General Instructions

1.   Reports submitted must be engineering documents. They must be factual and the recommendations must be warranted in the light of the information and data presented in the report. The author must state that, in his judgment, the venture is of sufficient merit to make the work recommended a worthwhile undertaking.

2.   The information supplied in a report should be sufficient and positive enough to warrant the recommendations made. An estimate of costs for the proposed program should be included.

3.   If the potential merit of a property is predicated entirely or in part on results obtained on neighbouring ground, the known history of the latter should also be covered.

4.   A description of mineralization encountered on the property should be given detailing the strike length, width, continuity and the basis of such measurement together with a description of the type, character and distribution of the mineralization. References as to its grade should be substantiated by assays with the dates thereof, and by assay plans and sections. In addition to giving the widths of the individual samples it should be stated whether these are the author's own samples or those of other parties. The method of sampling should be described making it clear whether assay results are based on channel samples, chip samples, grab samples, character samples or core samples.

5.   Values in precious metals should be expressed in ounces per ton or grams per metric ton and the content of other metals, etc., in percentages or pounds per ton but not in dollars or other currency.

6.   A report must be based on a personal examination of the property at a time of year when climatic conditions permit an adequate examination to be carried out.

7.   When information or data in a report is not based on his own observations, the author must provide a precise reference to the source of information used to reach his conclusions and recommendations. When such information is derived from unpublished or private reports or records, a photostatic or other authenticated copy of the original should be submitted, together with a letter of consent and a certificate of qualification respecting that author's professional qualification, except where the report is a matter of public record such as those on open file in a provincial or federal natural resources department.

8.   The author should satisfy himself that he has disclosed all relevant material of a technical nature which to the best of his knowledge might have a bearing on the viability of the project or the recommendations in his report.

9.   When an examination has been made more than a year prior to the date of the report, some assurance must be provided by the engineer that changes which have occurred during this time will not affect the conclusions or recommendations contained in the report.

Item 1 - Qualifications and General Requirements for Authors

1.1   Technical reports on mineral properties, excluding oil and gas, filed with a prospectus or statement of material facts submitted by a natural resource issuer shall be prepared by mining engineers or geologists who are members in good standing of the Association of Professional Engineers, or by geologists who are Fellows in the Geological Association of Canada, or by other qualified persons acceptable to the Superintendent.

1.2   Where a statement of material facts is involved, the author of the technical report and the report itself must also be acceptable to the Vancouver Stock Exchange.

1.3   Engineers and Officers of the Issuer are reminded that where a property is located within British Columbia, the (B.C.) ENGINEERS ACT, 1979 requires the practice of engineering to be performed by a Professional Engineer registered with the Association of Professional Engineers of the Province of British Columbia as a resident member or licenced to practice in British Columbia as a non-resident licencee.   In the case of an out-of- province or out-of-country property, the author should be a member of an acceptable professional association. For the purposes of defining "the practice of engineering", the emphasis will be placed on the structural and design aspects of engineering.

Item 2 - Conflict of Interest

2.1   Where the proceeds of the issue are being applied to the property being reported upon, the author must be free of any association with the issuer.

Forms

2.2   The report shall not be written by a director, officer or employee of the issuer or of an affiliate of the issuer or who is a partner, employer or employee or any director, officer or employee or who is an associate of any director or officer of the issuer or of an affiliate of the issuer.

2.3   The report shall not be submitted if the author or any partner or employer of or associate beneficially owns, directly or indirectly, any securities of the issuer or of a subsidiary thereof or, if the issuer is a subsidiary, any securities of the parent issuer.

2.4   This restriction in 2.3 does not apply to a person, partner, employer or associate, employer or associate is not empowered to decide whether securities of the issuer or the parent issuer, as the case may be, are to be beneficially owned, directly or indirectly, by him, or if he is not entitled to vote in respect thereof.

2.5   The author should be independent of the vendor of the property to the issuer. A qualified person, furthermore, should have no current direct, indirect or contingent interest in a property on which he is reporting.

2.6   The author should disclose any past interest, direct or indirect in the subject property or any past or present interest in any other property within a radius of ten kilometers of the subject property.

Item 3 - Form and Content of Technical Reports

The information included in a technical report shall provide full disclosure in order to assist an investor to evaluate the economic prospects of the subject property. A scholarly treatise on some technical aspect of a property having little impact on its economic prospects does not serve the needs of the investor.

Content of Reports

A complete report should include a description of the properties of the issuer and should contain all pertinent exploration data including plans and sections. The report should be presented under the following headings as applicable:

3.1   Table of Contents

3.2   Summary

3.3   Preamble or Introduction including author's terms of reference

3.4   Property, Description and Location

3.4.1   The description of the properties must include claim numbers, whether patented or unpatented and if contiguous. The percentage of interest held in the properties should be stated.

3.4.2   The author must accurately locate a *mining property* on which he is reporting by Section, Township and Range, or Latitude and Longitude and/or National Topographic Series, and by distance and direction from the nearest centre of population.

3.5   Accessibility, Climate, Local Resources

3.6   History - comprehensive, with references to all previous work for which records are available

3.7   Geology

3.8   Mineral Deposits and their state of Development - The report must clearly distinguish between mineral showings which occur on the issuer's property being reported upon and those elsewhere in the area.

3.9   Reserves and Production

3.10   Conclusions and Recommendations with Cost Estimates

3.11   In Intermediate (Development) and Senior Financing (Production) Reports, the following vital considerations must be explored:

Recoverability and amenability of the raw material

Tonnage and grade versus optimum profitability

Markets

Smelter Contracts, tolls and transportation

Taxes

Cash flow, capital and operating cost estimates

Payback of capital with interest

3.12   Recommended Work Programs

3.12.1 Where substantial drilling programs are proposed (in excess of 4,000 meters), the author in his recommendations should provide for an intermediate stage at which time an appraisal can be made to recommend continuance, substitution of some other type of exploration, or abandonment of the project.

3.12.2 Where more than one stage or phase of exploration is recommended by the author, advancing to the second stage or phase should be contingent on receiving encouraging results in the preceding stage or phase.

3.12.3 On those occasions where logistics, climatic conditions, governmental regulations or other elements suggest staging or phasing a program without regard to previous results would be advantageous, these reasons must be clearly stated by the author.

Item 4 - Maps

4.1   Reports must be well illustrated by plans and by sections to give an adequate picture of the property. All reports must be accompanied by a location or index map and a more detailed plan showing all important features described in the text. If nearby properties have an important bearing on the possibilities of the ground under consideration, their location should be known on the maps. Where the mineralized or ore-bearing structures are expected to pass from one property to the other, this should be indicated clearly on the map.

4.2   In case the potential merit of a property is predicated on geophysical or geochemical result, maps showing result of the surveys and the interpretations should be submitted.

4.3   All maps should show a scale, a North arrow, and should be signed and dated. If geological features or other data have been taken from government maps or from drawings of other engineers or geologists, this should be properly acknowledged.

4.4   Maps and sections should be provided which illustrate the pertinent geology as well as the vein or mineral pattern developed or expected to be developed and the sample and assay data.

4.5   The report should also include a map illustrating the claim outline, its size and the relative position of the samples, anomalies, outcrops, workings and mineralization and the coverage of various types of geophysical and geochemical surveys and geological mapping carried out within the claim.

4.6   Where a property has had some previous production or extensive exploration, maps and sections must be provided to illustrate why additional exploration is being proposed. If such maps are unavailable, this must be disclosed and an explanation given as to why such a proposal is being made without access to such maps. Such disclosure is essential where there is an assertion that such a property might have above average merit, since it must be demonstrated that there is some reasonable expectation that additional or higher grade ore reserves can be found and a potential continues to exist.

4.7   Where a map intended for publication is submitted in a format not suitable for commercial duplication, it should be accompanied by a copy of the map in a form adapted for duplication in the prospectus or statement of material facts.

Item 5 - Supplementary Information

5.1   Obstacles toward Exploration, Development or Production

Where an inherent obstacle toward future production is evident (e.g. serious environmental problems, shortage of water, security of title, doubtful recovery process, etc.), such obstacle should be disclosed in the report, together with the author's opinion or evaluation of the outlay and course of action required to remedy such obstacle.

5.2   Geological Environment

A report contemplating an exploration and development program should normally cover a set of claims which are in close proximity and are located within the same geological environment. If two or more properties are being reported on, a separate report should be made on each property which does not bear a close geological relationship to the other properties. However, where a report involves a program to explore a geological, geophysical or geochemical concept over an identified region prior to staking claims over anomalies, showing or mineral occurrences which may be discovered, the "close proximity" rule need not be observed.

5.3   List Related Reports

A list of all reports prepared within the past five years by the author in the area (encompassed by the subject property) including the date of each report and the name of the client for whom the report was prepared should also be included in the subject report.

5.4   Where Addendum Required

Where the date of a report predates the date of the certificate appearing on the definitive version of a prospectus or statement of material facts by more than twelve months, the author must furnish an addendum, dated within sixty days of the date of the prospectus or statement of material facts, either:

5.4.1   attesting to the continuing validity of the information contained in the report, including the recommendations and cost estimates, OR:

5.4.2   setting out any amendments to the recommendations and cost estimates prompted; by fluctuations in monetary purchasing power, by results of work carried out on the property or contiguous properties since the date of the report or for any other reason. Where there has been significant subsequent exploration on the subject property, a new report rather than an addendum is required.

5.5   Where Amendment Required

Each report published by an author on a specific property should be distinct from all reports previously published by the author on the property. Revised reports accordingly should either be noted "as revised on (current date)" or redated as at the date of revision.

Item 6 - Consent to use of Name in Prospectus

See regulation 99.

Item 7 - Certificate of the Author

The certificate must be under the professional seal or permit stamp of the individual making the report.

See regulation 103.

Item 8 - Consent Letter

7.1   The report must be accompanied by a letter from the author consenting to the inclusion of his report and/or summary thereof in the prospectus or statement of material facts.

7.2   Irrespective of the manner in which B.C. requirements are complied with, it is likely that the body of a prospectus or a statement of material facts will contain references to or excerpts from a technical report. Where such references and excerpts appear in the interest of full, true and plain disclosure rather than as the sole means of compliance with the requirement for summary, the consent of the author of the full report to such references and/or excerpts is not required.

Appendix 1

Form 54

Use of Technical Terms

Care should be taken in the use of the word "ore". The term is defined as follows:

"ore" means a natural aggregate of one or more minerals

(a)   that may be mined and sold at a profit, or

(b)   from which some part may be profitably separated,

at a specified time and place;

"proven Ore" and "measured ore" mean any material where

(a)   the tonnage of that material is computed from dimensions revealed in outcrops, trenches, underground workings or drill holes,

(b)   the grade is computed form the results of adequate sampling,

(c)   the site available for inspection, the measurement of the material and the sampling of the material are so spaced and the geological character so well defined that size, shape and mineral contents of the material are established, and

(d)   the computed tonnage and grade of the material are judged to be accurate within stated limits;

"probable ore" and "indicated ore" mean any material where

(a)   the tonnage and grade of what material are computed

   (i) partly from specific measurements,

   (ii) partly from sample data or production data, or both, and

   (iii) partly from projection for a reasonable distance on geological evidence, and

(b)   the site available for inspection, the measurement of the material and the sampling of the material are too widely or inappropriately spaced to outline the material completely or to establish its grade throughout;

"possible ore" and "inferred ore" mean any material where

(a)   quantitative estimates of that material are based largely on broad knowledge of the geological character of the deposit,

(b)   samples or measurements of deposits of that material are few, if any, and

(c)   the estimates of that material are based on

   (i) an assumed continuity or repetition of deposits of it, and

   (ii) reasonable geological indications which may be obtained by comparison with deposits of similar material, including comparison of bodies of material that are completely concealed if there is specific evidence of their presence;

Where the word "ore" may not properly be used, such terms as "mineralization", "mineralized bodies" or "concentrations", etc. should be used.

Forms

This is the form to be used by a Natural Resource Issuer required by Section 102 of the regulations to file a report on its Oil and Gas Properties.

FORM 55

Securities Act

TECHNICAL REPORT ON OIL AND GAS PROPERTIES

General Instructions

1. Reports submitted must be engineering documents. They must be factual, and any recommendations must be warranted in light of the information and data presented in the report. If the report contains recommendations, the author must state that, in his judgment, the venture is of sufficient merit to make the work recommended a worthwhile undertaking.

2. If any information and data in an engineering report are not based on the author's own observations and investigations, their source shall be clearly stated, reference shall be made to reports and records from which the information and data was obtained, and the author shall state the degree of reliance he has placed on such reports and records. When information is derived from unpublished or private reports or records, a letter of consent from, and a certificate of qualification of, the author of such reports or records shall be submitted.

3. Where a report is not based on a personal examination of a property, the author shall be availed of sufficient timely and current sub- surface data with which to make an intelligent appraisal.

4. When information or data in a report is not based on his own observations, the author must provide a precise reference to the source of information used to reach his conclusions and recommendations.

5. The author should satisfy himself that he has disclosed all relevant material of a technical nature which to the best of his knowledge might have a bearing on the viability of the project or the recommendations in his report.

6. When an examination has been made more than a year prior to the date of the report, some assurance must be provided by the author that changes which have occurred during this time will not affect the conclusions or recommendations contained in the report.

Item 1 - Qualifications and general requirements for authors

1.1 Technical reports on oil and gasas properties in Canada submitted by a natural resource issuer as material accompanying a prospectus or statement of material fact shall be prepared by a petroleum engineer who is a member in good standing of an appropriate Association of Professional Engineers, or by another qualified person acceptable to the Superintendent.

1.2 Where the report is submitted as material accompanying a statement of material fact, the author of the report and the report itself must be acceptable to the Vancouver Stock Exchange.

1.3 Engineers and Officers of the Issuer are reminded that where a property is located within British Columbia, the (B.C.) ENGINEERS ACT, 1979 requires the practice of engineering to be performed by a Professional Engineer registered with the Association of Professional Engineers of the Province of British Columbia as a non-resident licencee. In the case of an out-of-province or out-of-country property, the author should be a member of an acceptable professional association. For the purposes of defining "the practice of engineering", the emphasis will be placed on the structural and design aspects of engineering.

1.4 Where an oil and gas property is located in the United States of America, membership in the Society of Petroleum Engineers of the American Institute of Mining (S.P.E. of the A.I.M.E.) and/or membership in the American Institute of Professional Geologists is desirable for an author who is a U.S. resident, as is registration in the appropriate engineering association of the state in which the property is located. In some states, registration as a geologist and/or engineer is mandatory.

Item 2 - Conflict of Interest

2.1   Reports shall be prepared only by a registered professional engineer or a registered professional geologist who is independent of the issuer or any associate or affiliate of the issuer.

2.2   Reports shall not be written by a director, officer or employee of the issuer or any associate or affiliate of the issuer or by any person associated with such director, officer or employee.

2.3   Notwithstanding 2.2, in-house reports may be accepted at the discretion of the Superintendent, but only from large well established issuers.

2.4   Where principals in the independent consulting firm which prepared the report have or will acquire direct or indirect interests in properties or securities of the issuer or any associate or affiliate of the issuer, such interests must be clearly disclosed in the report.

2.5   The author should be independent of the vendor of property to the issuer. A qualified person, furthermore, should have no current direct, indirect or contingent interest in a property on which he is reporting.

2.6   The author should disclose any past interest, direct or indirect in the subject property or any past or present interest in any other property within a radius of ten kilometers of the subject property.

Item 3 - Form and content of Technical Reports

The information included in a technical report shall provide full disclosure in order to assist an investor to evaluate the economic prospects of the subject property. A scholarly treatise on some technical aspect of a property having little impact on its economic prospects does not serve the needs of the investor.

Content of Oil and Gas Reports

A engineering and geological report suitable as accompanying material for a prospectus or a statement of material fact shall include:

3.1   Table of Contents

3.2   Introduction

3.2.1   Author's terms of reference. State whether the report was prepared specifically for the purpose of submission to Securities Administrators or whether it will serve other purpose as well.

3.2.2   Names of principal properties. Include all major properties (including all properties to which the proceeds of issue are being applied) and identify them by the commonly referred to field or area names and disclose the jurisdiction (province, state, etc.). Briefly describe and discuss the geology of the properties. Discussion of geographic factors such as climate and accessibility need be included only in special situations such as frontier resources. A distinction should be made in the types of property being reported on, eg. - producing (with or without enhanced recovery), partly developed (being drilled), exploratory.

3.2.3   Summary of estimated net reserves and corresponding values.

3.2.3.1   Proved reserves and dollar values on a net cash-flow basis. Dollar values shall be calculated at current prices and costs, unless under contract as to price, to all future time. Additionally dollar values may be presented based on forecast prices and costs but critical assumptions in such a forecast shall be stated. Net cash-low values shall be presented at discount rates of 9%, 10%, 15% and 20%.

3.2.3.2   Probable additional reserves and dollar values on a net cash-flow basis. Dollar values shall be calculated at current prices and costs, unless under contract as to price, to all future time. Additionally, dollar values may be presented based on forecast prices and costs but critical assumptions in such a forecast shall be stated. Net cash-flow values shall be presented at discount rates of 0%, 10%, 15% and 20%. Also, probable additional reserves shall be reduced for an allowance for the risk that is associated with the probability of obtaining production form such reserves.

3.2.3.3 A statement that the values reported under 2.3.1 and 2.3.2 may not necessarily be the fair market value of the reserves.

3.2.3.4 A statement as to whether the values are before or after income tax.

3.2.3.5 The discount factor selected should relate to the discount rates currently prevailing in the monetary market. The "non-escalated" case only should be disclosed until such time as world market conditions support assumptions of escalation in price.

3.2.4 The percentage and quantity of proved producing reserves which are currently on production. (See definition 6 of appendix 1.)

3.2.5 Definitions employed shall be the same as those listed in Appendix 1 and any deviation shall be stated along with supporting reasons.

3.2.6 Discussion of methods employed. Identify the methods used to estimate reserves and production rates and to convert them to cash flows. Include any assumptions respecting the availability of markets.

3.2.7 Discussion and identification of risk factors used, particularly respecting probable additional reserves, and justification for their selection.

3.2.8 Acceptable disclaimer. State clearly any conditions respecting the responsibility of the author. For example, the author might indicate that all estimated reserve quantities were based on geological and engineering data provided by the issuer although the interpretation of the data was carried out by the author, and might state whether or not he has grounds for a judgment that the data are sound. He shall also state whether he made an on-site visit of the properties and, if not, state briefly the reasons why a visit was judged unnecessary.

3.2.9 Where proceeds of the issue are to be expended on drilling on a specified property(ies), the report shall contain recommendations, conclusions and cost estimates in respect of the proposed drilling. Where appropriate, the author shall discuss the results of prior drilling on the property and on adjoining or nearby areas.

3.2.10 Summary of undeveloped gross and net acreage and value assigned to net acreage.

3.2.11 Signature and professional seal or permit stamp of author.

Item 4 - Supporting Material

The supporting material required falls under the following general headings.

1. Listing of Properties
2. Location of Prospects
3. Maps
4. Geology
5. Tabulation detail
6. Types of Reserves
7. Status of Reserve assigned
8. Issuer's Interest
9. Quantity of Reserve assigned
10. Forecast of future net production
11. Summary table

4.1 Listings of properties shall include, jurisdictions and location therein, and names of fields and areas including an index map(s).

4.2 Where some or all properties included are prospects, the report must state the location of the prospect with respect to established producing areas, if any.

4.3   Detail maps and plats

A property map should indicate

4.3.1   the issuers interest lands and the issuer's interest in them.

4.3.2   Wells in which the issuer has an interest and wells of others together with their status.

4.3.3   Specific legal property descriptions with designations of interest if more than one interest and property are illustrated.

4.3.4   In the case of the prospect property, symbols representing data on abandoned, suspended or producing oil and gas wells as they offset or occur in the area of interest of the prospect property at the time the report is prepared.

4.3.5   Where relevant, geological plats supporting geological information by legible surface and/or subsurface geological maps, cross sections and type logs drawn at scales deemed appropriate for presentation of the data. These may include stratigraphic facies maps, structure maps, insopach maps of net pay, porosity feet or hydrocarbon pore volume and maps presenting well production statistics.

4.4   A brief descriptions of the geology of the issuer's properties.

4.4.1   The following geological information would likely be helpful:

Nature of the hydrocarbon accumulation, its relationship to known subsurface stratigraphy and/or structure; reservoir parameters which may include weighted average porosity and connate water saturation, estimated average net pay and reservoir area, any test well data pertinent to the assessment of the reservoir accumulation. Where funds are to be spent on drilling, this section would include:

(a)   Categorization of the well or wells to be drilled in terms of the degree of risk involved using the Lahee system (new field, new pool, development, etc.);

(b)   A brief description of the primary and secondary objectives (zones and anticipated depths) of the drilling program;

(c)   Influence, if any, of subsurface stratigraphic or structural considerations on a potential accumulation;

(d)   What fluids, oil or gas, can be expected;

(e)   Whatever additional data from offset wells or fields is pertinent to a proper description of the prospect, always conveying these facts in the appropriate context, pointing out the uncertainties and the possibilities of these facts not necessarily pertaining to the subject property.

4.5   Tabulations of reservoir rock and fluid parameters of each well or pool including, but not limited to, depth of each pay zone, its porosity, pay zone thickness (specify gross or net), water saturation, pressure, temperature, recovery factor, etc.

4.6   Types of reserves assigned:

4.6.1   crude oil;

4.6.2   synthetic oil, or bitumen and corresponding synthetic oil yield factor;

4.6.3   natural gas;

4.6.4   natural gas liquids;

4.6.5   sulphur.

NOTE: Reserves assigned to "tight-hole" or confidential (by-law) areas may be grouped and published as part of the listing as reserves only. Alternatively, if they are not included in the reserves listing, there shall be appropriate discussion describing the method of handling such properties.

4.7   Status of reserve assigned:

4.7.1   proved or probable additional;

4.7.2   proved producing or proved non-producing.

Methods of reserves Determination

Reserves determinations should be supported by geologic concepts and data.

Reservoir recovery mechanism (i.e. solution gas drive, water drive, gravity drainage, etc.)

An estimate of:

(a)   the original recoverable volumes of oil or gas present in the reservoir and the relation to estimated ultimate recoverable volumes;

(b)   cumulative production to date;

(c)   remaining recoverable volumes; current and optimum well spacing pattern.

4.8   Issuer's interest:

4.8.1   gross share of reserves before royalties;

4.8.2   applicable royalties and/or production payments;

4.8.3   net share of reserves after royalties;

4.9   Quantity of reserve assigned:

4.9.1   proved producing, proved non-producing, and total proved;

4.9.2   probable additional;

4.9.3   total.

4.10   Forecast of future net production, revenue, costs and net cash flow on a proved producing, proved non-producing, and total proved reserved basis and on a probable additional reserve basis, by jurisdiction (province, state, etc), and in total. Dollar values shall be calculated at current prices and costs, unless under contract as to price, to all future time. Additionally, dollar values may be presented based on forecast prices and costs but critical assumptions in such a forecast shall be stated. Net cash flow values shall be presented at discount rates of 9%, 10%, 15% and 20%. Also, probable additional reserves shall be reduced for an allowance for risk that is associated with the probability of obtaining production from such reserves.

The following may also be relevant:

(a)   For those wells which have been placed on production within the past 12 months, statistics of oil/gas production by months with watercut data if applicable;

(b)   Where production has ceased, reasons for such cessation should be disclosed together with plans (if any) for resumption of production and the estimated date on which such resumption is expected;

(c)   Where start of production has been delayed, reason for such delay should be disclosed;

(d)   Where mechanical problems have hampered production, remedial plans for putting the wells back on production, remedial plans for putting the wells back on production, plus other details should be disclosed.

4.11   A summary table itemizing the following basic assumptions, where applicable:

4.11.1 crude oil and synthetic oil price forecasts by jurisdiction;

4.11.2 natural gas price forecast by jurisdiction;

4.11.3 natural gas products price forecasts by jurisdiction;

4.11.4 capital and operating costs;

4.11.5 forecasts of inflation used respecting capital and operating costs;

4.11.6 forecasts of any other factors employed on a general basis (e.g. crown royalty scale if different from those existing as of the effective date of the study);

4.11.7 Details of undeveloped acreage (both gross and net) disclosing field or area name, jurisdiction, value assigned to each separate net acreage, and method of determining those values;

4.11.8 Where proceeds of the issue are to be expended on drilling on a specified property, the report shall contain recommendations, conclusions and cost estimates in respect of the proposed drilling. Where appropriate, the author shall discuss the results of prior drilling on the property and on adjoining or nearby areas.

It may also be relevant for the author to consider "reserves potential", i.e. would drilling the property, even if technically successful, represent an economically viable venture.

Item 5 - Consent to use of name in prospectus

See regulation 99.

Item 6 - Certificate of Author

The certificate must be under the professional seal or permit stamp of the individual making the report.

See regulation 103.

Item 7 - Consent letter

7.1 The report must be accompanied by a letter from the author consenting to the inclusion of his report and/or summary thereof in the prospectus or statement of material facts.

7.2 Irrespective of the manner in which B.C. requirements are complied with, it is likely that the body of a prospectus or a statement of material facts will contain references to or excerpts from a technical report. Where such references and excerpts appear in the interest of full, true and plain disclosure rather than as the sole means of compliance with the requirement for summary, the consent of the author of the full report to such references and/or excerpts is not required.

FORM 58

Securities Act

INFORMATION STATEMENT
REQUIRED UNDER SECTION 32(g) OF THE ACT

ITEM 1   Face Page

(1)   State in bold print on the face page of the information statement:

The issuer offering these securities is organized exclusively for educational, benevolent, fraternal, charitable, religious or recreational purposes and not for profit.

No securities commission or similar regulatory authority has passed on the merits of the securities offered nor has it reviewed this information statement and any representation to the contrary is an offence.

These securities are being offered under section 32(g) of the Securities Act, which means the issuer is not required to provide a purchaser with a prospectus. A purchaser will therefore not have any of the civil remedies available in the Securities Act.

There is no government or other insurance covering the securities.

A purchaser may lose all of his or her investment.

A purchase of the securities offered by this information statement must be considered speculative, and is not a charitable donation for income tax purposes. Refer to "RISK FACTORS" on page_____.

(2) Where no market exists or will exist for the securities after the offering, the following statement must appear in bold print on the face page:

As there is no market for these securities, it may be difficult or even impossible for the purchaser to sell them.

(3) Where applicable, the following statement must appear in bold print on the face page:

The issuer's continued viability depends on further financing, and not on profits it generates internally. Purchasing the securities offered by this information statement will not guarantee the continuation of the issuer's operations.

(4) Disclose when the offering expires.

ITEM 2   Risk Factors

(1) List the risks that could be considered material to a purchaser as follows:

    (a) risks in the issuer's activities

    (b) risks in the offering, and

    (c) any other risks.

(2) Where the issuer's annual financial statements have been prepared by the issuer's management, disclose the risk that the financial statements may not be accurate.

(3) Disclose if the purchaser may become liable to contribute more than what the purchaser invested initially.

(4) Disclose if the issuer is not in good standing under the laws in which it was organized or incorporated.

ITEM 3   Name and Organization of Issuer

(1) State the name and registered address of the issuer.

(2) If the issuer is a society, limited partnership or trust, state how the issuer was organized and the date the issuer was organized.

(3) If the issuer is a company, state the laws under which it was incorporated and the date the issuer was incorporated.

(4) Provide relevant details of the issuer's constitution and by-laws, rules, partnership agreement, trust deed or articles of incorporation.

(5) If the issuer is part of a larger group of entities, and this fact is material to the offering of securities, provide the same disclosure about these other entities that is required in sections (2), (3) and (4) of this Item and disclose the relationship of the issuer to these other entities and of the entities to each other.

ITEM 4   Description of Securities

Describe the securities being offered including their price and material attributes, such as redemption, retraction, and voting rights. If debt securities are being offered, describe how the issuer will service the debt.

ITEM 5   Outstanding shares

Provide in tabular form designation of the issuer's shares, amount authorized, amount issued as at the date of the issuer's most recent balance sheet and amount outstanding if all shares being offered under this information statement are sold.

ITEM 6   Number and Aggregate Dollar Value of Securities Being Offered

(1) State the number and aggregate dollar value of the securities being offered, including where applicable, both minimum and maximum figures.

(2) If the issuer must raise a minimum amount of funds through the offering, disclose consequences to the purchaser of failure to raise that amount, including the return of funds to the purchaser, describing any deduction or penalty. State the name and address of any person who will hold subscription funds until the minimum amount is raised.

(3) Describe any arrangements to hold any part of the net proceeds in trust and whether proceeds will become available to the issuer only if certain conditions are fulfilled. Describe the procedure for the return of funds to the purchaser.

ITEM 7   Plan of Distribution

(1) Describe how the securities will be offered and how to subscribe for the securities.

(2) State the name, address and telephone number of any person selling the securities on behalf of the issuer, and the relationship of that person to the issuer.

ITEM 8   Resale of Securities

(1) Where there are no restrictions on transfer of the securities offered under this information statement, or transfer is permitted to someone other than the existing holders or the issuer, state that a person, other than the issuer, who trades the securities must, before the trade, provide the purchaser with a copy of any information statement and financial and other information concerning the affairs of the issuer that the issuer has provided to the person trading the securities during the two years before the date of the trade of the securities to the purchaser.

(2) Each certificate representing the security must have this legend in bold print:

Before this security is traded to you, the person trading the security must provide you with any information statement and financial and other information concerning the affairs of the issuer that the issuer has provided to the person trading the security during the two years before the trade.

ITEM 9   Nature of Issuer's Not-for-Profit Activity

(1) Describe the issuer's not-for-profit activity and how that activity has developed generally within the past year.

(2) If applicable, summarize how the issuer has used proceeds from previous offerings.

ITEM 10   Nature of Project or Operations to be Financed

Describe the nature of any project or operations to be financed, including particulars of any transactions conducted on a non-arms length basis.

ITEM 11   Use of Proceeds

(1) State the net proceeds that the issuer anticipates from the offering.

(2) Provide a detailed breakdown of how the issuer anticipates it will use the net proceeds.

(3) The discussion of the net proceeds must be meaningful. In most cases, it is not sufficient to say only that "the proceeds of the offering will be used for general societal/corporate purposes".

(4) If a minimum subscription level is required, disclose the priorities for use of both minimum and maximum proceeds of the offering. Indicate, in order of priority, the uses that will be made of the proceeds of the distribution if they are less than expected.

(5) If a particular project will be financed only partially from proceeds of the offering, disclose the source and particulars of additional financing needed to complete the project.

ITEM 12   Management of Issuer

Provide the name, municipality of residence and principal occupation of:

(1) the issuer's governors where the issuer is organized as a society;

(2) the general partner where the issuer is organized as a limited partnership, or where the general partner is incorporated, the directors and officers of the general partner;

(3) the trustee and any administrators where the issuer is organized as a trust; or

(4) the directors and officers of the issuer where the issuer is incorporated.

ITEM 13   Continuous Reporting Obligations to Purchasers

Describe the nature and timing of the financial and other information concerning the affairs of the issuer that the issuer will provide to the purchaser.

ITEM 14   Financial Statements

(1) A copy of the issuer's most recent annual financial statements, audited or reviewed by an accountant if available, should form part of the information statement.

(2) Where the effective date of the most recent annual financial statements of the issuer is more than 180 days before the date of the certificate attached to the information statement, the issuer should include a section in the information statement entitled "Management Discussion of Interim Operating Activities". This section should disclose material changes in the issuer's financial affairs since the date of the financial statements.

ITEM 15   Income Tax Consequences

If income tax consequences to the purchaser are material to the offering then

(a) summarize the material income tax consequences to purchasers who are residents of Canada, and

(b) state in bold print that purchasers should consult with their professional advisers regarding tax consequences that apply to the purchasers.

ITEM 16   Material Contracts

Particularize every material contract entered into by the issuer within two years before the date of the information statement's certificate and state a time and place at which those agreements or copies of the agreements may be inspected during the offering period.

ITEM 17   Certificate

Include this certificate in bold print:

This information statement contains no untrue statement of a material fact and does not omit to state a material fact that is required to be stated or that is necessary to prevent a statement that is made from being false or misleading in the circumstances in which it was made.

The certificate must be dated and signed by:

(1) two governors of the issuer where the issuer is organized as a society;

(2) the general partner where the issuer is organized as a limited partnership, or where the general partner is incorporated, by two directors of general partner;

(3) the trustee and any administrators where the issuer is organized as a trust; or

(4) two senior officers of the issuer where the issuer is incorporated, and on behalf of the directors of the issuer, by any two directors other than the two senior officers mentioned. Where the issuer has only three directors, two of whom are senior officers, all three directors must sign the certificate.

This is the form required by Section 26 of the Securities Act Regulation.

FORM 60

Securities Act

SUBORDINATION AGREEMENT

INSTRUCTIONS:

1. All items marked * to be completed.

2. "C/S" denotes Common Seal

3. "SEAL" - The circling of the word SEAL indicates the intent of the parties to be legally bound by the Agreement. The principal's signature and circling of the word SEAL must be witnessed and the witness must sign the Agreement where noted. The attachment of a red wafer is therefore not necessary.

4. Please note in particular, item 5, page 2.

5. Please forward original to Superintendent of Brokers, 1100 - 865 Hornby Street, Vancouver, B.C., V6Z 2H4.

6. Please make copies for your own records.

AGREEMENT MADE this _____ day of _____, 199_____.*

BETWEEN:
                                     Principal's name*

                                     Address (herein called the "Principal")

AND:
                                     Firm's name*

                                     Address*
                                     (herein called the "firm")

Forms

WHEREAS:

A. The Firm desires to obtain, renew or maintain registration pursuant to the SECURITIES ACT, S.B.C. 1985, c. 83 (herein called the "Act").

B. The Firm is indebted to the Principal for the aggregate sum of _____ * Dollars ($_____)*.

C. It appears desirable that the position of the General Creditors, as hereinafter defined, be improved by the subordination of the Firm debt to the Claims of the General Creditors with the intent that all the Claims of the General Creditors will have priority to and take precedence over the Firm Debt;

D. It is a condition of registration or licensing that specified levels of working capital be maintained by the Firm; and

E. This Agreement is entered into for the purpose of fulfilling the said working capital requirements.

NOW THEREFORE THIS AGREEMENT WITNESSES that the parties hereto agree as follows:

1. In this Agreement:

    a) "General Creditors" means the persons (other than the Principal) now and from time to time having claims against the Firm; and

    b) "Claims" means all debts, liabilities and obligations which are now or may become due and owing by the Firm to any person (other than the Principal).

2.* The Firm acknowledges having borrowed from the Principal the following sums and securities:

Description of Instrument
Evidencing Debt (i.e.
shareholder loan,
promissory note, etc.)   Date of Loan   Amount

_____   _____   _____

_____   _____   _____

_____   _____   _____

(herein called the "Firm Debt")

3. The Firm Debt and all right, title and interest which the Principal now has or at any time hereafter may acquire under or by virtue of the Firm Debt in and to the undertaking, goodwill, property and assets of the Firm are hereby subordinated and postponed to and will hereafter rank subsequent to any Claims of the General Creditors so that the interest of the Principal under or by virtue of the Firm Debt will be subject to the present and future rights of the General Creditors in and to the undertaking, goodwill, property and assets of the Firm pursuant to any Claim.

4. Except as set forth in paragraph 5, the Principal will subordinate all his rights against the Firm on account of the Firm Debt to all the Claims of the General Creditors so that any and all Claims will be paid out of the assets of the Firm before any payment is made to the Principal on account of the Firm Debt.

5. The Principal will not demand or accept payment of, and the Firm will not pay, any amount in whole or partial satisfaction of the Firm Debt unless and until written permission is obtained from the Superintendent of Brokers (British Columbia).

6. The subordination and postponement herein will apply in all events and circumstances whatsoever and notwithstanding:

    a) the date or dates of creation, issuance, execution, delivery or registration of the Firm Debt and other documents evidencing Claims of the General Creditors;

b) the date or dates upon which any indebtedness under the Firm Debt or pursuant to any Claim is incurred by the Firm; and

c) the date or dates of any default by the Firm under the Firm Debt or pursuant to any documents evidencing Claims of General Creditors or the date or dates of crystallization of any floating charge respectively contained herein.

7. This Agreement will ensure to and be binding upon the heirs, executors, administrators, sucessors, and assigns of the parties hereto.

IN WITNESS WHEREOF the parties hereto have executed and sealed this Agreement on the day and year first above written.

If Principal is a Natural Person Complete this Section	SIGNED, SEALED, AND DELIVERED IN THE PRESENCE OF:	))) SEAL)

_____
Signature of Witness*)

_____
Print Name) _____
) Signature of
) Principal*

If Principal is a Corporation complete this

THE COMMON SEAL OF THE *PRINCIPAL* WAS HEREUNTO AFFIXED IN THE PRESENCE OF:

_____
Authorized Signatory*

_____
Print Name*   C/S

_____
Authorized Signatory*

_____
Print Name*

Firm to Complete this Section

THE COMMON SEAL OF THE *FIRM* WAS HEREUNTO AFFIXED IN THE PRESENCE OF:

_____
Authorized Signatory*

_____
Print Name*   C/S

_____
Authorized Signatory*

_____
Print Name*

February 1, 1987

NIN 95/19 "Form 61 - Quarterly Report" prescribes the following Form 61 as the form of Quarterly Report for all Quarterly Reports filed after July 31, 1995.

**British Columbia
Securities Commission**

QUARTERLY REPORT

FORM 61

INSTRUCTIONS

This report is to be filed by Exchange Issuers within 60 days of the end of their first, second and third fiscal quarters and within 140 days of the end of their fourth fiscal quarter. Three schedules (typed) are to be attached to this report as follows:

SCHEDULE A: FINANCIAL INFORMATION

Financial information prepared in accordance with generally accepted accounting principles for the fiscal year-to-date, with comparative information for the corresponding period of the preceding fiscal year. This financial information should consist of the following:

For the first, second and third fiscal quarters:
An interim financial report presented in accordance with Section 1750 of the C.I.C.A. Handbook. This should include a summary income statement (or a statement of deferred costs) and a statement of changes in financial position. A summary balance sheet is also to be provided.

For the fourth fiscal quarter (year end):
Annual audited financial statements.

SCHEDULE B: SUPPLEMENTARY INFORMATION

The supplementary information set out below is to be provided when not included in Schedule A.

1. *For the current fiscal year-to-date:*
   Breakdown, by major category, of those expenditures and costs which are included in the deferred costs, exploration and development expenses, cost of sales or general and administrative expenses set out in Schedule A. State the aggregate amount of expenditures made to parties not at arm's length from the issuer.

2. *For the quarter under review:*
   (a) Summary of securities issued during the period, including date of issue, type of security (common shares, convertible debentures, etc.), type of issue (private placement, public offering, exercise of warrants, etc.) number, price, total proceeds, type of consideration (cash, property, etc.) and commission paid.
   (b) Summary of options granted, including date, number, name of optionee, exercise price and expiry date.

3. *As at the end of the quarter:*
   (a) Particulars of authorized capital and summary of shares issued and outstanding.
   (b) Summary of options, warrants and convertible securities outstanding, including number or amount, exercise or conversion price and expiry date.
   (c) Total number of shares in escrow or subject to a pooling agreement.
   (d) List of directors.

SCHEDULE C: MANAGEMENT DISCUSSION

Review of operations in the quarter under review and up to the date of this report, including brief details of any significant event or transaction which occurred during the period. The following list can be used as a guide but is not exhaustive:

Acquisition or abandonment of resource properties, acquisition of fixed assets, financings and use of proceeds, management changes, material contracts, material expenditures, transactions with related parties, legal proceedings, contingent liabilities, default under debt or other contractual obligations, special resolutions passed by shareholders.

Specifically, the management discussion must include:

(a) disclosure of and reasons for any material differences in the *actual* use of proceeds from the previous disclosure by the issuer regarding its *intended* use of proceeds; and

(b) a brief summary of the investor relations activities undertaken by or on behalf of the issuer during the quarter and disclosure of the material terms of any investor relation arrangements or contracts entered into by the issuer during the quarter.

Freedom of Information and Protection of Privacy Act
The personal information requested on this form is collected under the authority of and used for the purpose of administering the *Securities Act*. Questions about the collection or use of this information can be directed to the Supervisor, Statutory Filings (604-660-4890), 1100 – 865 Hornby Street, Vancouver, British Columbia V6Z 2H4.

ISSUER DETAILS

NAME OF ISSUER		FOR QUARTER ENDED	DATE OF REPORT Y M D

ISSUER'S ADDRESS			

CITY	PROVINCE	POSTAL CODE	ISSUER FAX NO.	ISSUER TELEPHONE NO.
CONTACT PERSON		CONTACT'S POSITION		CONTACT TELEPHONE NO.

CERTIFICATE

The three schedules required to complete this Quarterly Report are attached and the disclosure contained therein has been approved by the Board of Directors. A copy of this Quarterly Report will be provided to any shareholder who requests it.

DIRECTOR'S SIGNATURE	PRINT FULL NAME	DATE SIGNED Y M D
➤		
DIRECTOR'S SIGNATURE	PRINT FULL NAME	DATE SIGNED Y M D
➤		

FIN 2061 Rev. 95 / 6 / 30

FORM 69

Securities Act

CONFLICT OF INTEREST RULES STATEMENT

GENERAL

Under certain circumstances we may deal with or for you in securities transactions where the issuer of the securities or the other party to the transaction is this firm or a party having an ownership or business relationship with us.

Since these transactions may create a conflict between our interests and yours, we are required by provincial law to disclose to you certain relevant matters relating to the transactions. This statement contains a general description of the required disclosure. A complete statement of the rules is set out in Part 13.1 of the British Columbia Securities Regulation.

IMPORTANT CONCEPTS

"Related party" - A party is related to us if, through the ownership of or direction or control over voting securities, we exercise a controlling influence over that party or that party exercises a controlling influence over us.

"Connected party" - A party is connected to us if, due to indebtedness or certain other relationships, a prospective purchaser of securities of the connected party might question our independence from that party.

"Associated party" - An associated party is either a related party or another party in a close relationship with us, such as one of our partners, salesman, directors or officers.

REQUIRED DISCLOSURE

We must make certain disclosures where we act as your broker, advise you, or exercise discretion on your behalf with respect to securities issued by us, by a related party or, in the course of an initial distribution, by a connected party. In these situations, we must disclose either our relationship with the issuer of the securities, or that we are the issuer. We must also make disclosure to you where we know or should know that, as a result of our acting as your broker or adviser, or of our exercising discretion on your behalf, securities will be purchased from or sold to us, an associated party or, in the course of an initial distribution, a connected party.

The following is a list of the time and manner in which these disclosures must be made.

-    Where we underwrite securities, the required disclosure will be contained in the prospectus or other document being used to qualify those securities.

-    Where we buy or sell securities for your account, the required disclosure will be contained in the confirmation of trade which we prepare and send to you.

-    Where we advise you with respect to the purchase or sale of securities, the disclosure must be made prior to our giving the advice.

In addition, where we exercise discretion under your authority in the purchase or sale of securities for your account, we may not exercise that discretion for the types of transactions described above unless we have obtained your prior specific and informed written consent.

LIST OF RELATED PARTIES

The following is a list as at _____ 1988 of our related parties which are reporting companies. We will provide you with a revised version of this document if the list changes.

If you have any questions, please contact

[Registrants must list all their related parties that are reporting issuers in British Columbia, or that have made a distribution of securities outside British Columbia in a manner that had they done so in British Columbia, such distribution would have made them reporting issuers in British Columbia.]

FORM 70

Securities Act

STATEMENT AND UNDERTAKING PURSUANT TO SECTION 167.3(4) OF THE SECURITIES REGULATION

TO: British Columbia Securities Commission

STATEMENT

The undersigned hereby confirms and represents that it does not engage in any activities as an adviser, dealer or underwriter (as those terms are defined in the Securities Act, S.B.C. 1985, c. 83) in respect of a security in any of the circumstances set out in sections 167.4, 167.5, 167.7, 167.8 or 167.9 of the Securities Regulation, B.C. Reg. 270/86.

UNDERTAKING

The undersigned hereby undertakes and agrees that it will not engage in any of the activities referred to in the paragraph above, except in compliance with the provisions of Part 13.1 of the Securities Regulation, B.C. Reg. 270/86.

Dated at _____ this _____ day of _____ 19 ____

_____
(Signature of Registrant)

Cheques for fees should no longer be made payable to the "Minister of Finance". They are now payable to the "British Columbia Securities Commission" pursuant to NIN 95/24 "Fee Payments under the Securities Act and the Commodity Contract Act".

**Province of
British Columbia**

BRITISH COLUMBIA SECURITIES COMMISSION

Fee Checklist
Securities Regulation

INSTRUCTIONS

1. This form **must** accompany all fee payments.
2. Cheques **must** be in Canadian funds made payable to the Minister of Finance and Corporate Relations.
3. NSF cheques will result in a $20.00 charge and all subsequent fee payments will require a certified cheque or money order.
4. The number to the left of the text below is the respective ITEM number from section 183(1) of the Securities Regulation, B.C. Reg. 270/86 (the "Regulation"). Reference should be made to the Regulation for the specific wording of each of the following items. All references to the "Act" are to the Securities Act, S.B.C. 1985, c. 83.
5. The fees set out in this fee checklist are effective April 1, 1994.

FOR COMMISSION USE ONLY

File Number

INSTRUCTION: FOR EACH FEE PAYMENT, ENTER MULTIPLYING FACTOR(S) AND AMOUNT(S).

		Amount				COMMISSION USE ONLY
1.	For registration or renewal of registration as a dealer, excluding security issuers, regardless of the number of categories to which the application relates, for a two year period					
	(a) for the dealer's chief place of business in the Province	$5,000	x		=	R1SD2
	(b) for each branch office of the dealer in the Province	$100	x		=	R1SDB2
2.	For registration or renewal of registration as a security issuer, for a one year period	$2,500	x		=	R1SI/1
3.	For registration or renewal of registration as a salesperson of a dealer in the Province other than as a salesperson of a security issuer, for a two year period	$500	x		=	R1SD/S2
	For registration or renewal of registration as a partner, of a dealer in the Province, other than as a salesperson of a security issuer, for a two year period	$500	x		=	R1SD/P2
	For registration or renewal of registration as a director of a dealer in the Province, other than as a salesperson of a security issuer, for a two year period	$500	x		=	R1SD/D2
	For registration or renewal of registration as an officer of a dealer in the Province, other than as a salesperson of a security issuer, for a two year period	$500	x		=	R1SD/O2
4.	For registration or renewal of registration as a salesperson of a security issuer, for a one year period	$500	x		=	R1SI/S1
5.	For registration or renewal of registration as an underwriter, for a two year period	$5,000	x		=	R1SU2
6.	For registration or renewal of registration as an adviser, regardless of the number of categories to which the application relates, for a two year period					
	(a) for the adviser's chief place of business in the Province	$3,000	x		=	R1SA2
	(b) for each branch office of the adviser in the Province	$100	x		=	R1SA2B
7.	For registration or renewal of registration as a partner of an adviser in the Province, for a two year period	$500	x		=	R1SA/P2
	For registration or renewal of registration as a director of an adviser in the Province, for a two year period	$500	x		=	R1SA/D2
	For registration or renewal of registration as an officer of an adviser in the Province, for a two year period	$500	x		=	R1SA/O2
8.	For reinstatement of the registration of a salesperson, partner, director or officer from one dealer to another dealer	$100	x		=	R2SD/TR
9.	For reinstatement of the registration of a partner, director or officer from one adviser to another adviser	$100	x		=	R2SA/TR

FIN 2232 (1) Rev. 94 / 6 / 1

INSTRUCTION: FOR EACH FEE PAYMENT, ENTER MULTIPLYING FACTOR(S) AND AMOUNT(S).

		COMMISSION USE ONLY
10. For notification of change under section 28 (1) or (2) of the Act	$100 x _____ = _____	S28/1/2
11. For recognition as an exempt purchaser	$2,000 x _____ = _____	SEXEMPT
12. In addition to any fees payable under item 13		
(a) for filing a preliminary prospectus or pro forma prospectus		
(i) where that preliminary prospectus or pro forma prospectus relates to only one type, class or series of security	$2,500 x _____ = _____	SPROS/1
(ii) where that preliminary prospectus or pro forma prospectus relates to more than one type, class or series of security		
(A) the fee set out in subparagraph (i) for each issuer, and		
(B) for each additional type, class or series of security for each issuer	$500 x _____ = _____	SPROS/2
(b) for filing a preliminary prospectus where no distribution is contemplated	$2500 x _____ = _____	SPROS/1
13. In addition to any fees paid under item 12, for filing a preliminary prospectus or pro forma prospectus where both an issuer and a security holder are proposing to distribute securities	$1,000 x _____ = _____	SPROSDI
14. For filing a prospectus, the amount, if any, by which		
(a) .03%, or	_____ x _____ = _____	SPROS+
(b) in the case of a money market mutual fund, .01%	_____ x _____ = _____	SPROS+M
of the proceeds realized by the issuer or security holder from the distribution under the prospectus to purchasers in the Province exceeds the aggregate of the fees paid under items 12 and 13. (Reference should also be made to section 183(3) and (4) of the Regulation.)		
15. For filing a statement of material facts	$1,500 x _____ = _____	SSMF
16. For filing an annual information form by an issuer other than a mutual fund	$1,000 x _____ = _____	SAIF
17. For filing an amendment to a preliminary prospectus, prospectus, annual information form or statement of material facts	$250 x _____ = _____	SAMEND
18. For filing a technical or engineering report with		
(a) a preliminary prospectus, pro forma prospectus, prospectus, annual information form, amendment to a preliminary prospectus or prospectus	$500 x _____ = _____	STECH
(b) an application under section 153 of the Act for revocation or variation of a decision in respect of the reactivation of a dead or dormant company	$500 x _____ = _____	STECHDD
19. For filing a notice by an issuer of its intention to offer securities under section 55(2)(7) and (13) of the Act	$500 x _____ = _____	S55/2/7
19.1 For filing a notice by a registrant of its intention to enter into a networking arrangement under section 167.10 of the Regulation	$750 x _____ = _____	NETWORK

INSTRUCTION: FOR EACH FEE PAYMENT, ENTER MULTIPLYING FACTOR(S) AND AMOUNT(S).

		COMMISSION USE ONLY
20. Subject to item 21, for filing an application to the commission or the superintendent for a decision under the Act, Regulation, another enactment or a policy statement where no other fee is prescribed. Please indicate under which section(s) of the Act or the Regulation or under which other enactment or policy statement the application is being submitted:		
Act _____ Regulation _____ Other enactment _____ Policy statement _____	$750 x [ ] = [ ]	SORDER
21. In addition to the fee paid under item 20, where the applicant requests an application filed under item 20 be expedited, or where the commission or the superintendent determines that an application filed under item 20 is complex, an additional fee	$1250 x [ ] = [ ]	SORDER+
22. For filing a report		
(a) under section 132 of the Regulation, other than for a distribution under section 55(2)(8) or (11)(i) of the Act, or pursuant to the terms of an order made under section 59 of the Act, the greater of		
(i) $100, or		
(ii) .03% of the proceeds derived by the issuer from the distribution of the securities described in the report to purchasers in the Province; or	[ ] x [ ] = [ ]	SDIST.03
(b) under section 132 of the Regulation, for a distribution under section 55(2)(8) or (11)(i) of the Act	$100 x [ ] = [ ]	SDIST
23. For filing an annual financial statement by a reporting issuer, as required under section 136 of the Regulation, where the statement is filed		
(a) by an exchange issuer		
(i) within the prescribed time period	$850 x [ ] = [ ]	SFIN/E
(ii) outside the prescribed time period	$1050 x [ ] = [ ]	SFINELAT
(iii) outside the prescribed time period and the commission or superintendent has ordered that trading in the securities of the issuer cease and the order has not been revoked	$1350 x [ ] = [ ]	SFINELCT
(b) by a reporting issuer other than an exchange issuer		
(i) within the prescribed time period	$600 x [ ] = [ ]	SFIN
(ii) outside the prescribed time period	$800 x [ ] = [ ]	SFINLAT
(iii) outside the prescribed time period and the commission or superintendent has ordered that trading in the securities of the issuer cease and the order has not been revoked	$1100 x [ ] = [ ]	SFINLCT
23.1 For filing an interim financial statement by a reporting issuer, as required under section 135 of the Regulation, where the statement is filed		
(a) within the prescribed time period, no fee is payable		
(b) outside the prescribed time period	$200 x [ ] = [ ]	SFINILAT
(c) outside the prescribed time period and the commission or superintendent has ordered that trading in the securities of the issuer cease and the order has not been revoked	$500 x [ ] = [ ]	SFINILCT
24. For filing a take over bid circular or issuer bid circular	$750 x [ ] = [ ]	SBID
25. For filing an application under section 153 of the Act for revocation or variation of a decision in respect of the reactivation of a dead or dormant company	$2,500 x [ ] = [ ]	S3/35

Forms

INSTRUCTION: FOR EACH FEE PAYMENT, ENTER MULTIPLYING FACTOR(S) AND AMOUNT(S).

					COMMISSION USE ONLY
26. For filing a prospecting syndicate agreement	$250	x	=		SPROSYN
27. Where no other fee is prescribed, for filing, under the Act or Regulation, a record other than	$25	x	=		SRECORD
(a) a press release under section 67(1)(a), 83(3)(c), 93(1)(a) or (2)(a), 94(1) or (2) of the Act or section 147 of the Regulation					
(b) a report under section 67(1)(b) of the Act					
(c) personal information under section 73.1 of the Act					
(d) an acknowledgement and undertaking under section 128, of the Regulation, or					
(e) a copy of an offering memorandum under section 131 of the Regulation					
28. For search of a file	$6	x	=		SSEARCH
29. For a copy of a record in the public file of the Securities Commission, for each page copied	$0.50	x	=		SCOPY
30. For the certification of a record					
(a) that is 10 pages or less	$10	x	=		SCERT
(b) for each additional page over 10 pages	$1	x	=		
For NSF charges	$20	x	=		SNSF
31. The fees and charges for an examination or investigation by a person appointed under section 9 or 137 of the Act are an amount equal to the amount paid by the Securities Commission for the examination or investigation, not exceeding fees of $1,000 for each day of the examination or investigation plus all charges for the costs of the examination or investigation		x	=		SEXAM
32. The fees and charges for an investigation by a person appointed under section 126 or 131 of the Act are an amount equal to the amount paid by the Securities Commission or the Minister for the investigation, not exceeding fees of $1,000 for each day of the investigation plus all charges for the costs of the investigation		x	=		SINVEST
33. The fees and charges for the costs of or related to a hearing pursuant to an order under section 154.2 of the Act		x	=		SHEAR
34. For filing an application for a certificate confirming that a reporting issuer is not in default of any requirement of the Act or the Regulation	$100	x	=		SCERTDEF
34.1 For filing a report under section 67(2) of the Act	$100	x	=		SIMC
35. For filing a report required under section 70 of the Act, where the report is filed					
(a) within the required time period, no fee is payable					
(b) outside the required time period	$50	x	=		SINSLATE
36. For an approval of a waiver of the appointment of an auditor under section 203(3)(b) of the *Company Act*	$100	x	=		SWAUD
37. For a consent to the restoration of a company or extraprovincial company to the register under section 286(4)(d) of the *Company Act*	$100	x	=		SCRES
38. For filing a listing application under Local Policy Statement 3-19	$1500	x	=		SLP3/19
39. For a waiver under Part XII of National Policy Statement No. 41	$100	x	=		SWNP41

TOTAL AMOUNT OF FEE(S) $ [   ]

SECURITIES ACT

INDEX OF LOCAL POLICY STATEMENTS

Effective June 30, 1995

Policy#	Date of Policy (mm/dd/yy)	Description	Status (mm/dd/yy)
3-01	02/01/87	Factors to be considered in arriving at a decision that a natural resource property has sufficient merit to justify an expenditure thereon of risk capital derived from public subscription	in effect see NIN#89/43
3-02	12/21/90	Prospectus filing requirements	in effect 02/04/91 see NIN#95/4
3-03	02/01/87	Requirements re filing of preliminary prospectuses and prospectuses (national issues)	in effect
3-04		Replaced	replaced by LPS#3-17
3-05	02/01/87	Rights offerings to shareholders	in effect see NIN#90/13
3-06	02/01/87	Prospectus guidelines for the mortgage investment issuer	in effect
3-07	12/21/89	Policy guidelines respecting trading shares, performance shares and other consideration	in effect 03/01/90
3-08		Rescinded	rescinded by LPS#3-07
3-09		Rescinded	rescinded by LPS#3-07
3-10		Rescinded	rescinded by LPS#3-07
3-11		Rescinded	rescinded by NIN#89/28
3-12	01/26/90	Rules for proceedings	in effect 02/01/90
3-13	02/01/87	Policy guidelines for a venture capital issuer planning to make a distribution	in effect see NIN#88/7 and NIN#89/43
3-14	09/09/93	Application for insider reporting exemptions	in effect 09/09/93
3-15	07/07/89	Exempt purchaser status	in effect 07/15/89
3-16	08/14/90	Registration for securities and insurance	in effect
3-17	01/06/95 (Interim)	Registrant due diligence	in effect see NIN#94/17
3-18		Reserved	

Local Policies

Policy#	Date of Policy (mm/dd/yy)	Description	Status (mm/dd/yy)
3-19	02/01/87	Vancouver Stock Exchange listings	in effect
3-20		Reserved	
3-21	02/01/87	Share and unit offerings of unlisted issuers and options and warrants available to registrants participating in such offerings	in effect see NIN#89/43
3-22	02/10/89 (interim)	Requirements for registration for trading in securities	in effect
	10/05/94 (draft)	Registration requirements	see NIN#94/16
3-23		Reserved	
3-24	02/01/87	Statutory exemptions and orders made under section 33 and section 59 of the Securities Act	in effect see NIN#88/5
3-25	02/01/87	Re: natural resource issuer - "best efforts" prospectus and amendments to prospectus arising from market conditions	in effect
3-26	02/01/87	Statement of material facts submitted to the Superintendent of Brokers and the Vancouver Stock Exchange for vetting	in effect
3-27		Reserved	
3-28		Reserved	
3-29		Reserved	
3-30	02/01/87	Underwriter's conflict of interest	in effect
3-31	02/01/87	Incentive options to directors and employees - unlisted issuers	in effect
3-32		Reserved	
3-33	02/01/87	R.R.S.P.'s administered by brokers on behalf of authorized trustees	in effect
3-34	02/01/87	Application for non-reporting status	in effect
3-35	10/13/89	Reactivation of dormant issuers	in effect 11/01/89
3-36		Reserved	
3-37	02/01/87	Restricted shares (uncommon equities) distributions and disclosure	in effect
3-38	02/01/87	Registration of non-residents - Securities Act	in effect
3-39	02/01/87	Guidelines for advertising issues of securities and for promotional activities during the course of a distribution	in effect
3-40		Replaced	replaced by NP47 and BOR#93/1
3-41	02/01/87	Lawyer's conflict of interest	in effect
3-42	02/01/87	Registered representatives continued fitness for registration	in effect

Policy#	Date of Policy (mm/dd/yy)	Description	Status (mm/dd/yy)
3-43	12/12/91 (interim)	Government Strip Bonds	in effect see NIN#91/23, NIN#95/9
3-44	08/01/91	Recognition of stock exchanges and jurisdictions	in effect 08/15/91
3-45	04/06/89 (draft)	Designation as a reporting issuer (extraprovincial issuers)	in effect 04/08/89 see NIN#89/17

Local Policies

LOCAL POLICY STATEMENT 3-01

FACTORS TO BE CONSIDERED IN ARRIVING AT A DECISION THAT A NATURAL RESOURCE PROPERTY HAS SUFFICIENT MERIT TO JUSTIFY AN EXPENDITURE THEREON OF RISK CAPITAL DERIVED FROM PUBLIC SUBSCRIPTION

> See NIN 87/45 "Technical Reports on Mining Properties Accompanying Prospectuses Submitted for Acceptance by the Superintendent of Brokers". This local policy statement contains inaccurate references to rescinded local policy statements. See NIN 89/43 "Local Policy Statement 3-07".

1.0 IMPLEMENTATION

    1.1   This Local Policy Statement has been revised to conform to provisions of the Securities Act S.B.C. 1985 c.83 and the Regulations thereto. The major portion of the former Local Policy Statement 3-01 can now be found in Forms 54 and 55.

    1.2   This revised Local Policy Statement incorporates the "Supplementary Notes and Comments Relating to Reports on Mining Properties", and "Supplementary Notes and Comments Relating to Oil and Gas Reports" found as a supplement Local Policy Statement 3-01 dated March 4, 1986. These notes and comments now supplement the disclosure requirements set out in Forms 54 and 55.

2.0 FACTORS TO BE CONSIDERED IN ARRIVING AT A DECISION THAT A PROPERTY HAS SUFFICIENT MERIT TO JUSTIFY AN EXPENDITURE THEREON OF RISK CAPITAL DERIVED FROM PUBLIC SUBSCRIPTION

    2.1   The merits of the following types of property are capable of identification and classification with some degree of confidence:

        2.1.1   a property in production

        2.1.2   a property which has been subjected to a feasibility study

        2.1.3   a property on which a significant mineral deposit has been developed.

    2.2   The following conditions make it difficult if not impossible to assess the merits of a property:

        2.2.1   the geology is inferred only

        2.2.2   there is no known mineralization

        2.2.3   the nearest outcrop and/or the nearest mining activity is located at some considerable distance

        2.2.4   the sole feature appears to be a weak geochemical or geophysical anomaly

        2.2.5   the geology is taken from a small scale government geology map.

Whereas in the Section 2.1 examples the risk of initiating further programs on the property has been established and reduced to some extent, in the Section 2.2 examples above, the risk is unknown. In such a case as the latter, where the risk is unknown, the founders should consider funding further exploration and development programs from private sources and deferring solicitation of public funds until the property has been sufficiently developed to merit public funding.

    2.3   Where a property reported on falls between the extremes described in Sections 2.1 and 2.2 above, the use of a checklist has been instituted by the Superintendent to profile such factors as size of property, geology, mineralization, geochemical and geophysical response, alteration, location relative to other mineral deposits and exploration activity, accessibility, successful result of previous exploration.

    2.4   Mineral deposits are diverse in their mode of occurrence and there are numerous and varied techniques which may be employed to search for and evaluate them. It would, consequently, be inappropriate to make sweeping generalizations concerning what factors are likely to contribute to a favourable profile. However, by utilizing the guidelines set out in Section 3.0, it is anticipated that consistent evaluations can be made based on the disclosure in each technical report. These guidelines should assist in determining what type of data gathering techniques are acceptable in each mineral environment and what standards apply to disclosure of the information.

2.5 Where the Superintendent elects to seek a profile from his advisors on a property described in a technical report, he will receive in addition to the profile a brief comment for each point noted and/or a brief summary statement justifying the evaluation and highlighting features of unusual merit or any serious deficiencies in the potential of the property. Such comments and/or summary statements will be released to the issuer.

3.0 GUIDELINES ON CONTENT OF FORM 54

3.1 *Geology and Metal Content*

3.1.1 Sufficient geological information must be presented to:

3.1.1.1 establish that the geological environment is favourable (or at least permissive) for the type exploration.

3.1.1.2 assist in evaluating any samples taken, or other exploration accomplished.

In the case of location ground in the vicinity of an important mineral deposit, some geological information on this important deposit should be included. If the property has not been mapped, an explanation must be provided. Where the location ground lacks a specific target, size of claim block becomes increasingly important in establishing the merits of a property.

3.1.2 Where reserves are referred to in the text, the confidence factor (proven, probably or possible) must be disclosed. Where these reserves are not shown on maps or sections, it must be clearly stated that such maps and sections cannot be provided and the reason for such unavailability given.

3.1.3 All assays must be accompanied by qualifying data indicating the significance of the results (grab sample, bulk sample, chip sample, drill core sample, selected specimen and length, width and area covered by the sample).

3.2 *Geochemistry*

3.2.1 The report should be accompanied by a plan showing the sample location for rock, silt and/or soil geochemistry, and results of significant metals, with a notation on an accompanying map or in the text stating the type of sampling (channel, grab, specimen, silt, soil), a description of the sample, the type of analytical procedure and a copy of the analytical certificates.

3.2.2 The location of the survey should be disclosed relative to the boundaries of the property.

3.3 *Geophysics*

3.3.1 The report should contain a plan and where appropriate, sections showing the relevant geophysical responses and/or anomalies or conductors.

3.3.2 If the surveyed area does not cover the entire property, the location of the survey should be disclosed relative to the boundaries of the property.

3.3.3 An acceptable geophysical survey must relate to the type of mineralization being sought. For example:

3.3.3.1 a VLF EM anomaly will be rated as acceptable only if other substantiating correlations are presented. Such substantiating correlations could include a geochemical anomaly, other definite substantiating geophysical anomalies and/or geological interpretation or projections.

        3.3.3.2   a magnetic anomaly, by itself being generally merely in-dicative of bedrock geology, should have other correlative data directly indicative of the mineralization. An exception would be the search for magnetite-rich or pyrrhotite-rich deposits.

        3.3.3.3   an airborne geophysical anomaly should have ground follow-up to locate and evaluate the correlative anomaly and this follow-up should be supported by acceptable cor-relative information and techniques.

4.0   FACTORS TO BE CONSIDERED IN ARRIVING AT A DECISION THAT AN OIL AND GAS PROPERTY HAS SUFFICIENT MERIT TO JUSTIFY EXPLORATION AND DEVELOP-MENT EXPENDITURE THEREON OF RISK CAPITAL DERIVED FROM PUBLIC SUBSCRIPTION

   4.1   The following factors are indicative of properties which may have some merit:

      4.1.1   Producing property providing some assurance of continuing yield of net revenue to issuer (i.e. the property is not near depletion and there is some prospect of enhancement of value through addition of acreage or through adoption of some form of enhanced recovery to increase the ultimate production). If a prospect of enhanced recovery is held out, examples of successful schemes carried in nearby reservoirs with similar horizons should be filed.

      4.1.2   A property offset (but not drained) by existing production appearing to have the potential to produce and contiguous to additional acreage available for exploration and development.

      4.1.3   An exploratory property of sufficient areal extent for which, on the basis of sound geological conclusions (surface/subsurface) confirmed by reliable geophysical evidence, there is an indication of the exist-ence of hydrocarbon substances in commercial quantities.

   4.2   The following conditions are indicative of a property lacking sufficient merit:

      4.2.1   The property has been depleted or nearly depleted by primary and even secondary production or the offsetting acreage has drained the tract.

      4.2.2   The reservoir is so marginal in nature that the expected life is less than that required to pay out. One or more of the following may truncate the productive life of a reservoir:

        4.2.2.1   thin pay

        4.2.2.2   insufficient reservoir energy

        4.2.2.3   lack of natural water drive

        4.2.2.4   rapid unexpected lateral changes in reservoir sediments (e.g. cementing of sands, plugging of carbonates, shaling out).

      4.2.3   The tract is small (e.g. 160 acres or less) and there is no provision for acquiring additional acreage by option or drilling commitment.

      4.2.4   The property comprises producing or non-producing wells with no prospect or provision for further development.

      4.2.5   The acreage has little or no geological attractiveness on the basis of results from subsurface drilling. Potential beds are either absent or, if present, the deposition of sediments is erratic in nature.

   4.3   The oil and gas industry has been actively engaged in researching tech-niques such as enhanced recovery. Where an issuer seeks to try out any such techniques, the costs of such experimentation should appropriately be met from private funding. Where the issuer can demonstrate that its application of some experimental technique has produced results likely to enhance the merits of a property, it may be appropriate to seek public funding for a full scale application of the technique.

5.0   GUIDELINES ON CONTENT OF FORM 55

5.1   In complying with Sections 3 and 4 of Form 55, a distinction should be made in the types of property being reported on, e.g. - producing (with or without enhanced recovery), partly developed (being drilled), exploratory.

5.2   The discount factor selected should relate to the discount rates currently prevailing in the monetary market. The "non- escalated" case only should be disclosed until such time as world market conditions support assumptions of escalation in price.

5.3   Where some or all properties included are prospects, the report must state the location of the prospect with respect to established producing areas, if any.

6.0   LAHEE CLASSIFICATION OF WELLS

AAPG and API Classification of Wells

LAHEE CLASSIFICATION OF WELLS, AS APPLIED BY CSD

DATED at Vancouver, B.C. this 1st day of February , 1987.

Jill Bodkin
Chairman
B.C. Securities Commission

LOCAL POLICY STATEMENT 3-02

PROSPECTUS FILING REQUIREMENTS

TABLE OF CONTENTS

See NIN 87/66 "Prospectus Vetting Procedures" and NIN 88/10 "Full Disclosure in Financial Statements".

1.   IMPLEMENTATION

1.1   Effective date
1.2   Defined terms

11.8   Amendments and Lapse
11.9   Application of Other Policy Statements

December 21, 1990

PART 1   IMPLEMENTATION

1.1   *Effective date* - Local Policy Statement 3 02 dated January 20, 1989 is hereby rescinded and the following substituted therefor, effective February 4, 1991.

1.2   *Defined terms* - Terms defined in the Securities Act, S.B.C. 1985, c. 83 (the "Act") and the Securities Regulation, B.C. Reg. 270/86 (the "Regulation"), and used in this local policy statement have the same meaning as in the Act and the Regulation.

PART 2   APPLICATION

2.1   *Prospectus filings in British Columbia* - This local policy statement applies to the filing of a prospectus with the Superintendent of Brokers (the "Superintendent") where:

(a)   the issuer is filing the prospectus only in British Columbia; or

(b)   the issuer is filing the prospectus under National Policy No. 1 in more than one province, including British Columbia, and falls within the filing classification contained in section 3.1.1 of Local Policy Statement 3-03 by virtue of being a junior issuer with British Columbia named as the prime jurisdiction or a junior issuer listed or planning to seek a listing on the Vancouver Stock Exchange (the "Exchange").

2.2   *Compliance with Local Policy Statement 3-03* - Filings made by issuers referred to in section 2.1(b) must comply with the requirements of section 3.2 of Local Policy Statement 3-03 in addition to the requirements of this local policy statement. However, the form of prospectus and cross-reference sheet may be those required by another jurisdiction in the case of other than B.C. prime filings.

PART 3   FILING OF PRELIMINARY MATERIAL

3.1   *Covering letter*

(a)   The filing should be addressed as follows:

Deputy Superintendent, Corporate Finance
British Columbia Securities Commission
1100-865 Hornby Street
Vancouver, B.C.
V6Z 2H4

(b)   A covering letter listing the documents being filed must accompany the preliminary material. The letter should identify the documents using the lettering system indicated in section 3.2 below. Where several documents of the same category (e.g. material contracts) are being filed, each document should be named separately and identified appropriately (e.g. N-1, N-2, etc.) in the sequence in which there is disclosure in the preliminary prospectus. Any non-applicable items should be indicated as such.

(c)   In the exceptional circumstances where required documents are not being filed, will be filed at a later date, or vary from the form or content prescribed in the Act or Regulation, the covering letter should describe the documents that have been omitted or varied, the reasons for the omission or variation and the expected date for filing any missing documents. In addition, if the proposed offering or the documents being filed do not comply with the published policies of the British Columbia Securities Commission (the "Commission"), the covering letter must provide the details of and the reasons for the non-compliance.

(d)   The issuer need not refile documents already on file with the Commission provided that they are current. The covering letter should state that the documents have previously been filed and provide relevant details of the filing.

(e)   The covering letter must state the financial year end of the issuer.

(f)   Where the issuer's securities are not listed on a stock exchange and the issuer is not planning to list its securities on the Exchange, the covering letter should indicate what steps, if any, are being taken either to list the issuer's securities on another stock exchange or to establish that liquidity will exist after completion of the distribution qualified by the prospectus. The Superintendent generally will not issue a receipt for a prospectus offering equity securities of a junior issuer that has not obtained a conditional listing on a stock exchange in Canada.

3.2   *Documents required* - The following documents must be filed in connection with the filing of a preliminary prospectus and should be marked to correspond with the disclosure in the covering letter:

A.   *Fee checklist* - a completed Fee Checklist in the required form, together with any applicable filing fees, including:

     (i)   a preliminary prospectus filing fee in the amount prescribed by items 12 and 13 of section 183(1) of the Regulation by way of a cheque made payable to the "Minister of Finance".

Where the proceeds to be derived in British Columbia from the distribution under the prospectus cannot be ascertained at the time of the filing of the preliminary prospectus, the issuer must file an undertaking to provide a report on sales in British Columbia, together with any additional fees required under item 14 of section 183(1) of the Regulation, within 10 days of the conclusion of the distribution.

     (ii)   a report filing fee in the amount prescribed by item 18 of section 183(1) of the Regulation for each report filed.

Where, within two days of filing a preliminary prospectus, the issuer requests that a preliminary receipt not be issued, the Superintendent will, upon request, refund the filing fees (less a $500 processing fee). In all other circumstances, the Superintendent will not refund any portion of the filing fees.

B.   *Preliminary prospectus* - three signed copies of the preliminary prospectus, including one fully bound copy containing

     (i)   a copy of the financial statements,

     (ii)   any future oriented financial information,

     (iii)   any technical or engineering report required under Local Policy Statement 3-01 or 3-04, or a summary thereof,

     (iv)   any valuation or appraisal report, including a valuation opinion required under Local Policy Statement 3-07, or a summary thereof, and

     (v)   any audited statement of costs required under Local Policy Statement 3-07.

Information with respect to the price of the securities and the proceeds to be received by the issuer should be included in the preliminary prospectus.

The certificates required under sections 49 and 50 of the Act must be signed by the issuer's officers, directors and promoters and by the underwriters or agents within 3 days of the date of the preliminary prospectus and the preliminary prospectus must be filed within 10 days of the date of the preliminary prospectus. All signatures must be identified by printing or typing the name of each signatory underneath the signature in accordance with section 182 of the Regulation.

C.   *Cross-reference sheet* - a cross-reference sheet keying the disclosure in the preliminary prospectus to the items set out in the applicable required form (i.e. Form 12, 13, 14 or 15).

D.   *Financial statements* - two unsigned copies, in draft form, of the audited financial statements and any unaudited financial statements, subject to a review engagement report by the issuer's public accountant. Reference should be made to paragraphs 7100.34 and 7100.35 of the Canadian Institute of Chartered Accountants ("CICA") Handbook. One copy of the financial statements must be included in the fully bound preliminary prospectus referred to in item B of this section.

Draft financial statements must be presented in accordance with sections 104 and 113 of the Regulation. In addition, where the issuer is not a reporting issuer or where the issuer is reactivating pursuant to Local Policy Statement 3-35, the draft audited statements must be dated within 120 days of the date of the receipt for the preliminary prospectus. Reference should be made to sections 4.1 and 4.3 for further guidance relating to financial statements. In addition, issuers should be aware that section 4.4 normally requires unaudited financial statements dated within 90 days of the date of the final receipt, subject to a review engagement report.

Where the issuer has completed a business combination or proposes to enter into a business combination, reference should be made to section 4.2 concerning the additional financial statements that are required to be filed. If a material change in the business or affairs of the issuer has occurred subsequent to the date of the financial statements required to be filed under this section, reference should be made to section 4.1(d).

E. *Future-oriented financial information* - where the issuer has obtained the Superintendent's prior consent under section 5.1, two unsigned copies, in draft form, of any future-oriented financial information. Reference should be made to paragraph 48 of the Auditing and Related Services Guideline of the CICA Handbook entitled "Examination of a financial forecast or projection included in a prospectus or other offering document" (the "Guideline"). One copy of the future oriented financial information must be included in the fully bound preliminary prospectus referred to in item B of this section. Reference should be made to Part 5 for further guidance relating to future oriented financial information.

F. *Audited statement of costs* - where required by Local Policy Statement 3-07, two unsigned copies, in draft form, of each audited statement of costs. One copy of each audited statement of costs must be included in the fully bound preliminary prospectus referred to in item B of this section.

G. *Auditor's comfort letters* - signed auditor's comfort letters for the audited statements filed under items D, E and F of this section, in accordance with section 114 of the Regulation and in the format specified in section 7100 of the CICA Handbook and paragraph 49 of the Guideline.

H. *Directors' resolution* - certified copy of the directors' resolution approving the preliminary prospectus and authorizing the directors and officers to sign the preliminary prospectus.

I. *Report* - two signed copies of each technical or engineering report and, if applicable, each summary report. One copy of each technical or engineering report, or a summary thereof, must be included in the fully bound preliminary prospectus referred to in item B of this section.

In lieu of signed copies, the issuer may file two unsigned copies, in draft form, of each technical or engineering report together with a comfort letter signed by the author of the report stating that he has no reason to believe that the signed report that will be filed with the final material will differ in any material respect from the draft report, except for amendments that may be made to the draft report in response to comments made by the regulatory authorities or as a result of material changes in the affairs of the issuer that occur subsequent to the date of the draft report.

If the issuer is a natural resource issuer, an engineering report should be prepared in accordance with National Policy No. 2-A or 2-B, as the case may be, Local Policy Statement 3-01 and Form 54 or 55 in respect of each major property or property on which proceeds of the offering will be expended as required by section 102 of the Regulation. The report must be accompanied by a certificate in the form prescribed by section 103 of the Regulation.

If the issuer is an industrial issuer, a technical report should be prepared in accordance with Local Policy Statement 3-04.

J.   *Valuation or appraisal report* - where required by Local Policy Statement 3-07, two signed copies of a valuation or appraisal report, containing a valuation opinion in support of the value attributed to any non-cash assets. One copy of each valuation or appraisal report, or a summary thereof, must be included in the fully bound preliminary prospectus referred to in item B of this section.

In lieu of signed copies, the issuer may file two unsigned copies, in draft form, of each valuation or appraisal report together with a comfort letter signed by the author of the report stating that he has no reason to believe that the signed report that will be filed with the final material will differ in any material respect from the draft report, except for amendments that may be made to the draft report in response to comments made by the regulatory authorities or as a result of material changes in the affairs of the issuer or the business to be acquired that occur subsequent to the date of the draft report.

K.   *Confirmation of status or good standing* - certificate respecting the status of the issuer from the British Columbia Registrar of Companies or the appropriate regulatory authority in the jurisdiction in which the issuer was incorporated, organized or continued, or a legal opinion from the filing solicitor to the same effect.

L.   *Title opinion* - legal opinion relating to the status of the issuer's interests in respect of each major property or property on which proceeds of the offering will be expended and the expiry dates of those interests. The opinion must be in a form satisfactory to the Superintendent, prepared by a person competent to express opinions on the laws of the jurisdiction in which the mineral interests are situate, and contain no material qualifications that are not described in the preliminary prospectus.

Where expenditures on oil and gas properties are proposed, the issuer will not be required to provide a title opinion if its working interest and financial commitments are not material to the issuer.

M.   *Patent and trademark opinion* - where the issuer has a registrable interest in a patent or trademark that is material to the business of the issuer and disclosed in the preliminary prospectus, a legal opinion relating to the registration of the issuer's interest in the patent or trademark and the expiry date of that interest. The opinion must be in a form satisfactory to the Superintendent, prepared by a person competent to express opinions on the laws of the jurisdiction in which the patent or trademark is registered, and contain no material qualifications that are not described in the preliminary prospectus.

N.   *Material contracts* - signed or certified true copies of all material contracts to which the issuer is a party.

O.   *Form 4B* - Form 4B for each director, officer, promoter or control person of the issuer and its existing or proposed subsidiaries. Where a promoter or control person is not an individual, a Form 4B must be filed for any individual that has direct or indirect beneficial ownership of, control or direction over, or a combination of direct or indirect beneficial ownership of and control or direction over securities carrying more than 50% (or 20%, if no individual holds more than 50%) of the voting rights attached to securities issued by the promoter or control person. This requirement must be satisfied regardless of where the promoter or control person was incorporated, organized or continued. Where a promoter or control person is a reporting issuer, no person is required to file a Form 4B with respect to that promoter or control person.

Alternatively, an individual required to file a Form 4B may make a statutory declaration that the individual has filed a Form 4B within the three year period preceding the date of the preliminary prospectus and that there has been no change in the information required to be disclosed in response to the questions dealing with change of name or business name, administrative proceedings, offences, civil proceedings, bankruptcy and settlement agreements.

The Superintendent will raise any concerns with respect to the suitability of any of the individual directors, officers, promoters or control persons of the issuer or of its existing or proposed subsidiaries during the review process.

P. *Securityholders list* - where the issuer is making its first offering under a prospectus, a list of the beneficial owners of securities of the issuer stating, for each securityholder: name, address, relationship to a specific founder or promoter of the issuer, number of securities held, date and statutory exemption under which the securities were issued and price(s) per security paid. The securityholders list must identify underwriters as defined under Local Policy Statement 3-30.

Where a securityholder is not an individual, any individual that has direct or indirect beneficial ownership of, control or direction over, or a combination of direct or indirect beneficial ownership of and control or direction over securities carrying more than 10% of the voting rights attached to securities issued by the securityholder must also be disclosed on the securityholders list, regardless of where the securityholder was incorporated, organized or continued.

The securityholders list must provide totals of all issued securities of the issuer, including pooled or escrowed securities, that accord with the figures disclosed in the preliminary prospectus.

The securityholders list must be certified by a director or officer of the issuer to the effect that, as at a date not earlier than the date of the preliminary prospectus, to the best of the director's or officer's knowledge and belief after having made due inquiries, the information contained in the list is true.

In the event that any changes in the beneficial ownership of securities of the issuer occur before a final receipt is issued, a new securityholders list must be filed.

Q. *Escrow agreements* - signed escrow agreements complying in form and content with Local Policy Statement 3-07. Where the holder of any securities subject to the terms of an escrow agreement is an issuer that is not a reporting issuer, an originally signed undertaking in the form set out as Appendix C to Local Policy Statement 3-07 must be filed.

R. *Pooling agreements* - copy of the form of any voluntary pooling agreement entered into by any securityholders, together with a list of securityholders whose securities are held in pool indicating the number of securities so held for each securityholder and the total number of securities held in pool.

S. *Insider reports* - if the issuer is not a reporting issuer on the date the preliminary prospectus is filed, the issuer must file for all insiders of the issuer holding securities of the issuer either signed insider reports or draft copies of the insider reports that will be filed within the time period prescribed in section 70(2) of the Act after the date of the final receipt.

If signed insider reports are filed with the preliminary prospectus, additional reports will not be required to be filed under section 70(2) of the Act unless changes occur in the holdings set out in the insider reports.

T. *Letter from trust company* - letter from transfer agent and escrow agent acknowledging preparedness to accept the relevant duties and responsibilities disclosed in the preliminary prospectus.

U. *Underwriting or agency agreement* - signed agreement relating to the distribution of securities under the prospectus. The issuer must be a party to an agency or underwriting agreement on the date the preliminary prospectus is filed with the Superintendent or, in the alternative, the underwriting or agency agreement may be in draft form when filed, provided that the underwriter or agent has signed the certificate in the preliminary prospectus.

V. *Underwriters' undertakings* - if applicable, undertakings of underwriters required by Local Policy Statement 3-30.

W. *Schedule of calculations* - schedule providing the background calculations to the percentages of securities quoted in the preliminary prospectus.

X. *Confirmation of name reservation* - if the securities of the issuer will be listed on a stock exchange on which they are not currently listed, written confirmation from the stock exchange that the issuer's name has been approved and reserved for use by the issuer.

Y. *Pre listing review letter* - if the securities of the issuer are not currently listed, but will be listed, on the Exchange, a letter from the Listings Department of the Exchange confirming that the Exchange has no objection to the issuer making a conditional listing application.

PART 4   FINANCIAL STATEMENTS

4.1   *General matters*

(a)   The auditor's report should be addressed to the directors of the issuer as recommended in paragraph 7100.08 of the CICA Handbook.

(b)   Comparative audited and unaudited financial statements must be presented on a period by period basis and be compiled as a single set of financial statements with supporting notes. All financial statements, including the tabular notes to the financial statements, must be presented consistently from left to right or right to left in the same chronological order.

(c)   The financial statements filed under this local policy statement, including notes thereto, must be prepared in accordance with section 3 of the Regulation. In particular, section 1500 of the CICA Handbook provides general guidance on financial statement presentation requirements.

Expenditures for exploration and development, research and development, and general and administration, whether capitalized or expensed, should be disclosed in reasonable detail either in the financial statements or in the notes or supporting schedules thereto. Reference should be made to section 104(1)(e) of the Regulation.

The notes to the financial statements should provide full disclosure concerning the matters to which they relate (for example, concerning related party transactions).

(d)   Where the financial statements filed under this local policy statement reflect little activity and the majority of the issuer's operations have taken place subsequent to the date of the financial statements, additional up-dated audited financial statements may be required by the Superintendent.

4.2   *Business combinations*

(a)   Where the issuer has completed a business combination, as described in paragraphs 1580.01 to 1580.05 of the CICA Handbook, prior to the filing of the preliminary prospectus, and the issuer's consolidated financial statements do not include the acquired business for the last 5 years, the issuer must file additional audited financial statements for the business that was acquired for the period(s) not included in the issuer's consolidated financial statements.

(b)   Where a business combination is contemplated as part of, or in conjunction with, the prospectus offering, the issuer must file separate audited financial statements for the business to be acquired dated within 120 days of the date of the receipt for the preliminary prospectus and presented in accordance with section 104 of the Regulation.

(c)   The Superintendent may permit or require the inclusion of pro forma consolidated financial statements in the preliminary prospectus in accordance with section 106 of the Regulation for the period covered by the most recent financial statements required by item D of section 3.2 and, in addition, if that period is less than 12 months, for the last completed financial year of the combined or combining businesses.

(d)   Special consideration should be given to paragraphs 1580.16 and 1580.17 of the CICA Handbook and the CICA's Emerging Issues Committee Abstract No. 10 where a reverse take over will occur or has occurred.

4.3   *Waiver of five year audit* - In accordance with section 104(6) of the Regulation, the Superintendent may, upon request by an issuer, exempt the issuer
from including the audited financial statements required by section 104 of
the Regulation provided that the issuer includes financial statements for
each of its last 5 financial years and:

   (a)   at least the last completed financial year has been audited;

   (b)   the prior periods are subject to accountant's comments or a review
         engagement report; and

   (c)   the issuer complies with all other aspects of this local policy statement
         relating to financial statements.

4.4   *Final material*

   (a)   The financial statements contained in the prospectus must consist of
         audited financial statements dated within one year of the date of the
         final receipt, or such lesser period as the Superintendent may require.
         In addition, stub period unaudited financial statements dated within
         90 days of the date of the final receipt, subject to a review engagement
         report, will normally be required.

   (b)   The Superintendent may, upon request by an issuer, waive the re-
         quirement to file unaudited stub period financial statements in cases
         where:

         (i)   the issuer was effectively dormant between the date of its last
               audited financial statements and the date of the prospectus;

         (ii) the issuer's audited financial statements are dated within 180
               days of the date of the final receipt; and

         (iii) the prospectus discloses in sufficient detail the financial ac-
               tivities of the issuer between the date of the audited financial
               statements and the date of the prospectus.

PART 5   FUTURE ORIENTED FINANCIAL INFORMATION

5.1   *Prior consent for inclusion of future oriented financial information* - Future
oriented financial information, such as financial forecasts or projections, or
information selected therefrom (e.g. revenue figures), must not be included
in a preliminary prospectus, technical or engineering report or valuation
report unless the issuer has received the prior consent of the Superintendent to do so pursuant to section 109 of the Regulation.

5.2   *Preparation and audit requirements* - Any financial forecasts or projections
must be prepared in accordance with section 4250 of the CICA Handbook
and must be audited in accordance with the Guideline, except where these
requirements have been waived by the Commission or the Superintendent.

5.3   *Documents required to obtain consent* - In order to obtain the consent
referred to in section 5.1, the issuer must submit for review the draft future
oriented financial information, the draft preliminary prospectus, historical
financial statements, the draft technical or engineering report and any
draft valuation report, together with the filing fee prescribed under item 20
of section 183(1) of the Regulation. Upon receipt of the Superintendent's
consent, the issuer may proceed with a filing under Part 3.

PART 6   INCOMPLETE SUBMISSIONS

6.1   *Return of incomplete submissions* - Section 183(2) of the Regulation
provides that where a record is filed with the Superintendent and the
record has not been completed in accordance with the Act or the Regulation, the Superintendent may return the record to the person by whom it
was filed.

6.2   *Refusal to issue receipt* - A receipt for a preliminary prospectus will not be
issued where:

   (a)   the prescribed filing fees are not remitted;

   (b)   the filing does not contain the information or documents (such as
         financial statements, technical or engineering reports, material con-

tracts or the pre listing review letter issued by the Exchange) required by this local policy statement; or

(c)   the certificates accompanying the preliminary prospectus are not in the proper form or have not been signed by all parties.

PART 7   THE REVIEW PROCESS

7.1   *Issuance of receipt* - In accordance with section 46 of the Act, the Superintendent will issue a receipt for a preliminary prospectus as soon as practicable after the preliminary prospectus has been filed. The receipt will be dated the date the Superintendent receives the preliminary prospectus and all other documents required to be filed under this local policy statement.

7.2   *Cease trade order under section 64 of the Act* - The Superintendent may issue a cease trade order under section 64 of the Act where, as a result of the review process, the Superintendent considers that the preliminary prospectus does not substantially comply with section 44(1) of the Act. The cease trade order will remain in effect until a fully executed revised preliminary prospectus satisfactory to the Superintendent has been filed together with confirmation from the agent or underwriter that the revised preliminary prospectus has been distributed to each recipient of the defective preliminary prospectus according to the distribution list required to be maintained under section 63 of the Act.

7.3   *Forwarding comment letters* - A copy of each comment letter issued by the Superintendent will be sent to the filing solicitor making the filing on behalf of the issuer, to the agents or underwriters and to the Exchange, if applicable. The filing solicitor must promptly provide a full copy of each comment letter to the issuer's public accountant and other professional persons whose consent letters will be included with the final material.

7.4   *Filing of black-lined documents* - All revised documents, including preliminary prospectuses, financial statements, future oriented financial information, engineering or technical reports, valuation or appraisal reports, audited statements of costs and material contracts, that are filed subsequent to the initial filing must be black- lined to indicate the changes made to them.

7.5   *Redating of revised preliminary prospectus* - A revised preliminary prospectus filed during the review process or under section 64 of the Act must be redated to a date within 10 days of the date of filing the revised preliminary prospectus and must include responses to comment letters, updated information relating to working capital and changes resulting from material changes in the business and affairs of the issuer. Reference should be made to Part 8, relating to amendments to a preliminary prospectus. New certificates are not required on a revised preliminary prospectus, except one filed under section 64 of the Act.

7.6   *Marking of follow-up material* - The front page of the covering letter and the envelope enclosing follow-up material should be marked "FOLLOW-UP" and be addressed to the appropriate staff member. Where the issuer has not been advised of the assignment of the filing to a specific staff member, "Manager, Corporate Finance" may be substituted for the name of the staff member. A copy of the follow-up material should also be sent concurrently to the appropriate listings officer at the Exchange, if applicable.

PART 8   AMENDMENTS TO A PRELIMINARY PROSPECTUS

8.1   *Amendment to preliminary prospectus where adverse material change* - If an adverse material change in the affairs of the issuer occurs after a receipt is issued for the preliminary prospectus but before a receipt is issued for the prospectus, section 47(1) of the Act requires the issuer to file an amendment to the preliminary prospectus no later than 10 days after the change occurs. The amendment may consist of either an amendment to the preliminary prospectus or an amended preliminary prospectus. Issuers are encouraged to file an amended preliminary prospectus where a substantial number of changes have been made to the original preliminary prospectus.

8.2   *Requirements for amendment to preliminary prospectus* -The Superintendent has not prescribed a form to be used by issuers for an amendment to a preliminary prospectus. However, in addition to providing disclosure concerning the material change, an amendment to a preliminary prospectus must:

(a) be numbered and dated (eg. "Amendment No. 1 dated * to Preliminary Prospectus dated *");

(b) contain an updated "Use of Proceeds" section which, among other things, reflects the issuer's working capital position as at the amendment date; and

(c) have the certificates required under sections 49 and 50 of the Act attached to it and dated within 3 days of the amendment date.

8.3 *Requirements for amended preliminary prospectus* - If the issuer elects to file an amended preliminary prospectus, the date of the amended preliminary prospectus should read "Dated * (date of original preliminary prospectus), as amended on *". The amended preliminary prospectus should contain an updated "Use of Proceeds" section and the certificates should refer to the preliminary prospectus "dated * as amended *" and be dated within 3 days of the amendment date.

8.4 *Directors' resolution* - A certified copy of the directors' resolution approving the amendment to the preliminary prospectus and authorizing the directors and officers to sign the amendment must be filed with the amendment.

8.5 *Delivery to each recipient of preliminary prospectus* - A copy of the amendment to the preliminary prospectus or the amended prospectus must be sent to each recipient of the preliminary prospectus as soon as it has been filed and a receipt for it has been issued by the Superintendent.

PART 9   FILING OF FINAL MATERIAL

9.1 *Timing of filing*

(a) The Superintendent will notify the filing solicitor that the Superintendent is ready to receive final material once all comments have been resolved to the satisfaction of the Superintendent and the Exchange, where applicable.

(b) A covering letter listing the documents being filed must accompany the final material. The letter should identify the documents being filed using the lettering system indicated in section 9.2 below. Any non-applicable items should be indicated as such.

9.2 *Documents required* - The documents that must be filed after satisfactory clearance of all comments consist of the following:

A. *Prospectus* - two signed copies of the prospectus, fully bound, containing

(i) signed financial statements,

(ii) any signed future oriented financial information,

(iii) signed technical or engineering report, or a summary thereof,

(iv) any signed valuation or appraisal report, or a summary thereof,

(v) any signed audited statement of costs, and

(vi) any other supporting materials to be included in the commercial copy.

Certified copies of the supporting materials may be used if signed copies have already been filed. Reference should be made to section 4.4 for further guidance on financial statement requirements.

The certificates required under sections 49 and 50 of the Act must be signed within 3 days of the date of the prospectus. The date of the prospectus must be within 10 days of the effective date of the prospectus, being the date of the final receipt for the prospectus.

B. *Auditor's consent letters* - signed consent letter, as required by section 99(2) of the Regulation, from each of the auditors who have audited the financial statements, any future oriented financial information or any audited statement of costs included in the prospectus.

C.   *Public accountant's consent letters* - signed consent letter, as required by section 99(2) of the Regulation, from each of the public accountants who have reviewed any of the unaudited financial statements included in the prospectus.

D.   *Directors' resolutions* - certified copy of the directors' resolutions approving the prospectus and the financial statements and authorizing the directors to sign the balance sheet and the directors and officers to sign the prospectus.

E.   *Report* - if the prospectus contains a summary of the technical or engineering report, two signed copies of the final version of the technical or engineering report.

F.   *Valuation or appraisal report* - if the prospectus contains a summary of a valuation or appraisal report, two signed copies of the final version of the valuation or appraisal report.

G.   *Consent of author to use of report* - signed consent letter, as required by section 99(2) of the Regulation, from the author of the technical or engineering report, or any valuation or appraisal report, to the use of the report or a summary thereof in the prospectus.

In the case of an author of a technical report, the consent must contain a statement of the author to the effect that the author has read the prospectus and, with respect to any part of the prospectus purporting to be made on the author's own authority as an expert or to be a copy of, or an extract from, the report, the author has, after reasonable investigation, reasonable grounds to believe and does believe that the relevant part of the prospectus is a fair and accurate representation of the report.

If the prospectus contains a summary of a technical or engineering report, the consent must also contain a statement of the author of the report to the effect that the summary report represents a fair and accurate summary of the report.

H.   *Consent of other professional persons* - signed consent letter from any other professional person named in the prospectus, as required by section 99(2) of the Regulation and in accordance with the policies of the Commission.

I.   *Solicitor's certificate* - if applicable, a solicitor's certificate as required by Local Policy Statement 3-41.

J.   *Underwriting or agency agreement* - signed copy of the underwriting or agency agreement, if not filed previously.

9.3 *Offering period* - The maximum offering period permitted by the Superintendent for issuers seeking a listing on the Exchange will be restricted under section 51(3) of the Act to a period ending on the earliest of

   (a)   12 months from the date of the preliminary receipt,

   (b)   180 days from the date of the final receipt, or

   (c)   120 days from the date of the issuer's next financial year end subsequent to the date of the latest audited year end financial statements contained in the prospectus.

   Where the offering period is restricted as set out in subsection (c), it may be extended under section 10.5.

9.4 *Final receipt and effective date* - The request for final material to be filed will be made when the Superintendent is satisfied that all comments have been resolved, subject, where applicable, to the Exchange confirming that it is clear to accept the conditional listing. The final material must be filed at the same time with both the Superintendent and the Exchange. A final receipt will be issued as soon as practicable after the material has been filed. The date of the final receipt will be the effective date of the prospectus. The prospectus date and the effective date must be printed on the face page of the commercial copies of the prospectus.

PART 10   AMENDMENTS TO A PROSPECTUS

10.1   *Amendment to prospectus where material change* - Section 48 of the Act requires that an issuer file an amendment to a prospectus if a material change in the affairs of the issuer occurs after a receipt is issued for the prospectus but before the completion of the distribution under the prospectus. The amendment must be filed with the Superintendent and the Exchange, if applicable, as soon as practicable and, in any event, no later than 10 days after the change occurs. Except with the written permission of the Superintendent, the distribution under the prospectus may not proceed until the Superintendent has issued a receipt for the amendment to the prospectus.

10.2   *Amendment to prospectus or amended prospectus* - The amendment may consist of either an amendment to the prospectus or an amended prospectus. Issuers are encouraged to file an amended prospectus where a substantial number of changes have been made to the original prospectus.

10.3   *Prospectus amending procedure* - The requirements set out in sections 8.2, 8.3 and 8.4 concerning the form and content of an amendment to a preliminary prospectus apply equally to an amendment to a prospectus.

10.4   *Directors' resolution* - A certified copy of the directors' resolution approving the amendment to the prospectus and authorizing the directors and officers to sign the amendment must be filed with the amendment.

10.5   *Extension of offering period*

(a)   Subject to subsection (b), the filing of an amendment to a prospectus will not extend the maximum offering period permitted or required by the Superintendent.

(b)   Where the offering period has been restricted as set out in section 9.3(c), the Superintendent is prepared to extend the offering period to the earlier of

(i) 12 months from the date of the preliminary receipt, or

(ii) 180 days from the date of the final receipt,

provided the issuer has filed and distributed to each holder of its securities, pursuant to sections 136 and 141 of the Regulation, its most recent audited year end financial statements and incorporates these financial statements into an amendment to the prospectus.

10.6   *Updated financial statements* - Unless they are available or required to be included under section 10.5(b), updated financial statements will generally not be required to be included in the amendment. However, the amendment should disclose in sufficient detail any significant changes in the financial status of the issuer between the date of the final receipt and the date of the amendment.

10.7   *Further consents* - The Superintendent may, pursuant to section 101 of the Regulation, require that further written consents be filed under section 99 of the Regulation before issuing a receipt for an amendment to a prospectus.

10.8   *Requirement for new preliminary prospectus filing* - The Superintendent considers that, for the purposes of section 48 of the Act, a complete new filing of a preliminary prospectus, rather than an amendment, will be required where one or more material changes occur that are so significant that the issuer or its business is no longer substantially the same as described in the prospectus for which a receipt was issued.

For example, a new filing will be required where a change of control of an issuer occurs after the date of the final receipt but before the conclusion of the distribution under the prospectus.

Similarly, the Superintendent will not issue a receipt for an amendment that substantially reduces the funds available to the issuer, because such a change would normally affect the entirety of the issuer's business, and therefore its prospects. While it would be inappropriate to define a "substantial reduction" of funds, as a general rule, a reduction of over 25%

of the funds that would be available to the issuer on the completion of the offering would normally require a new prospectus filing.

See BOR 95/1 "Form 12A Summary Prospectus Disclosure System" which allows issuers required to file a Form 12-A prospectus to use a summary prospectus.

PART 11   FORM 12A SUMMARY PROSPECTUS DISCLOSURE SYSTEM

11.1 *Eligibility* - A junior industrial issuer required to file a prospectus on Form 12A - Information Required in Prospectus of Junior Industrial Issuer may, in qualifying its securities for sale, use the Form 12A Summary Prospectus Disclosure System set out in this Part.

11.2 *Documents Comprising the Form 12A Summary Prospectus Disclosure System* - The documents that comprise the Form 12A Summary Prospectus Disclosure System consist of:

(a) a summary prospectus that is to be prepared in accordance with the requirements set out in the Form 12A Summary Prospectus attached as Appendix A; and

(b) a base disclosure document that is to be prepared in accordance with the requirements set out in Form 12A.

Form 12A - Summary Prospectus, which is Appendix A to Local Policy 3-02, appears in the Forms section of this book.

The document filed on Form 12A Summary Prospectus shall be referred to as the summary prospectus. The document filed on Form 12A shall be referred to as the base disclosure document. The base disclosure document shall be incorporated by reference into and deemed to form part of the summary prospectus.

11.3 *Filing Requirements* - The preliminary summary prospectus, summary prospectus, preliminary base disclosure document and base disclosure document submitted by a junior industrial issuer for filing under this Part shall be prepared and certified in accordance with the requirements of the Form 12A Summary Prospectus and the Form 12A base disclosure document, including the form of certificates, and shall be subject to acceptance for filing in accordance with the provisions of the legislation. Where an issuer elects to file a summary prospectus, the issuer shall concurrently file a base disclosure document together with the supporting documentation generally required for junior industrial issuers. The preliminary summary prospectus and the preliminary base disclosure document or the summary prospectus and the base disclosure document, as the case may be, will be reviewed together in accordance with review procedures applicable to junior industrial issuers.

11.4 *Solicitor's Certificate* - Concurrently with the filing of a summary prospectus, the junior industrial issuer shall file one extra copy of the summary prospectus together with a certificate of counsel confirming that the sections contained in the summary prospectus have been extracted verbatim from the base disclosure document and, where applicable, showing the additions, deletions, or changes that have been made to the sections that have not been extracted verbatim from the base disclosure document.

11.5 *Delivery and Undertaking* - The summary prospectus is required to be sent or delivered to a purchaser in accordance with section 66 of the Act. The summary prospectus and the base disclosure document filed under section 42(1) of the Act shall be accompanied by an undertaking of the Chief Executive Officer, the Chief Financial Officer of the issuer and, on behalf of the Board of Directors of the issuer, two directors, to the Commission, to provide to any person or company without charge, as soon as possible upon request to the issuer, one copy of the base disclosure document.

11.6 *Statutory Liability* - Where a misrepresentation is contained in a base disclosure document filed by a junior industrial issuer, the misrepresentation shall be deemed to be contained in the summary prospectus. Nothing in this Part shall be construed to provide relief from statutory civil or quasi-criminal liability arising from the provisions of the legislation.

11.7 *Consents* - Where any solicitor, auditor, accountant, engineer, appraiser, or other person or company whose profession gives authority to a statement or opinion expressed by the person is named in the summary prospectus, the base disclosure document or in a document incorporated by reference in the summary prospectus or base disclosure document, or is named as having prepared or certified a report or valuation used in the summary prospectus, base disclosure document or a document incorporated by reference into the summary prospectus or base disclosure document, the written consent of the person or company to being so named and to the use of the report, valuation, statement or opinion shall be filed not later than the time when the summary prospectus and base disclosure document are filed.

11.8 *Amendments and Lapse* - This Part does not alter the requirements of the legislation under which an amendment is required. Where, under section 48 of the Act, a change or alteration occurs to matters described in a summary prospectus or in the base disclosure document an amendment to the summary prospectus, base disclosure document, or both, as the case may be, shall be filed with the Commission. The lapse date set out in section 51 of the Act applies to the summary prospectus and base disclosure document.

11.9 *Application of Other Policy Statements* - Unless inconsistent, the applicable provisions of national and local policy statements apply to the issuance of securities by way of the Form 12A Summary Prospectus Disclosure System.

DATED at Vancouver, British Columbia, this 21st day of December 1990, as amended by NIN 95/4 on 5th January, 1995.

Douglas M. Hyndman
Chairman

LOCAL POLICY STATEMENT 3-03

REQUIREMENTS RE FILING OF
PRELIMINARY PROSPECTUSES AND PROSPECTUSES
(NATIONAL ISSUES)

1.0 IMPLEMENTATION

1.1 This Local Policy Statement has been revised solely to conform with the Securities Act S.B.C. 1985 c.83 and the Regulations thereto. Other than consequential amendments, there have been no changes of a substantive nature to this policy. It becomes effective upon proclamation of the Securities Act on February 1, 1987.

2.0 VARIATION IN FORM AND CONTENT

2.1 Section 45(2) of the Act vests in the Superintendent the discretion to accept a form of prospectus or preliminary prospectus which accords with the law of another province, provided the prospectus contains full, true and plain disclosure.

2.2 This subsection of the Act in effect makes it possible for the Superintendent to be guided by National Policy statements when dealing with "National" prospectuses filed concurrently in one or more provincial jurisdictions in addition to British Columbia. The issuer must elect to have the issue cleared under National Policy 1 if he wishes to have simultaneous clearance of his prospectus by a number of jurisdictions.

2.3 Where a receipt has been issued for a preliminary prospectus, such prospectus may be distributed by appropriate registrants as a means of soliciting an expression of interest from a prospective purchaser. Registrants distributing a preliminary prospectus shall maintain a record in British Columbia of the names and addresses of all recipients of such prospectus, and the register shall be available for inspection by the Superintendent or his designee.

2.4 Where a receipt has been issued for a preliminary prospectus, Uniform Act Policy 2-13 shall apply to any newspaper advertisement published prior to the receipting of the final prospectus.

3.0 MATERIAL TO BE FILED WITH A NATIONAL PROSPECTUS

3.1 The requirements for documents filed in support of a national prospectus vary with the nature of the filing. For purposes of convenience, the following filing classifications have been established:

3.1.1 B.C. prime junior companies, no-prime junior companies, and non-prime filings for junior companies planning to seek a listing on the Vancouver Stock Exchange;

3.1.2 B.C. prime major companies, non-B.C. prime companies other than those referred to in Section 3.1.1, and continuous offerings under National Policy 30. In order to qualify as a major company for the purpose of this classification, an issuer should generally have a history of at least 5 years of dividend payments to shareholders, or may apply to the Superintendent to be treated as a major company for other reasons acceptable to the Superintendent.

3.2 For all filings in both categories described above, the covering letter accompanying the submission should include the following information:

3.2.1 Whether the filing is being made pursuant to National Policy 1. If it is, the letter should identify the principal jurisdiction, the principal filing solicitor and the British Columbia agent filing solicitor, and should designate a recipient for prospectus receipts. In accordance with National Policy 1, communications about deficiencies will be made through the principal jurisdiction unless other arrangements satisfactory to the principal jurisdiction are made. Prior to electing British Columbia as the "principal jurisdiction" under National Policy 1, the issuer should check with the Director, Filings to insure that this jurisdiction will accept a designation as "principal".

3.2.2 If the issuer wishes to have its filing treated as a seasoned prospectus pursuant to National Policy 30, the covering letter should so state.

3.2.3 The covering letter must include a list of the accompanying documents as prescribed in Sections 3.3 and 3.4 below.

3.3 Materials Required for B.C. prime junior companies, no-prime junior companies and non-prime filings for junior companies planning to seek a listing on the Vancouver Stock Exchange.

Local Policy Statement 3-02 applies to national filings in this category except that the form of prospectus, the cross-reference sheet and the financial statements may be those required by another jurisdiction in the case of non-primes and no-primes. (Refer to Section 1, above).

Local Policy Statement 3-02 specifies requirements for covering letters in addition to those set out in Section 3.2 above as well as requirements for initial documentation, amended copy and final material. The policy also describes the procedures followed for dealing with incomplete submissions.

3.4 Materials required for B.C. prime major companies, non-B.C.-prime companies other than those referred to in Section 3.1.1 and continuous offerings under National Policy 30.

3.4.1 Initial Submission

3.4.1.1 Filing fee - greater of $1000 or .01% of the total proceeds to be realized in British Columbia. Where the total proceeds cannot be ascertained at the time of the initial filing, the issuer must submit an undertaking to provide a breakdown of sales in B.C. together with any additional fees required within 10 days of the conclusion of the subscription. Issuers making continuous offerings may file the required material with the next year's submission.

3.4.1.2 Preliminary prospectus accompanied by a dated certificate signed by the underwriters, if any, the chief executive officer, the chief financial officer, two other directors and a promoter. Note the requirement of an extra red-lined copy of the preliminary prospectus if National Policy 30 clearance is elected.

3.4.1.3 Cross reference sheet keying the prospectus disclosure to the items set out in the applicable form (i.e. Form 12, 13, 14 or 15) or the applicable form prescribed by the legislation of the principal jurisdiction.

3.4.1.4 Financial statements either in accordance with Section 104 of the Regulations or in accordance with the applicable legislation of the principal jurisdiction. Financial statements accompanying the preliminary prospectus may be submitted in draft form, accompanied by an auditor's comfort letter in the format specified in the CICA Handbook, Section 7000.10.

3.4.1.5 Although engineering reports and material contracts should not be filed initially with filings in these categories, they may be requested subsequently depending on the circumstances.

3.4.2 Final Material

The following comprises "final material" which must be submitted in acceptable form before a receipt for the final prospectus will be issued:

3.4.2.1 The final prospectus should be filed in duplicate - one copy in red-lined form to indicate changes made from the previous draft, the other copy in fully executed form. A certificate must be signed by the chief executive officer, the chief financial officer, two other directors and a promoter. A certificate must also be signed by all underwriters.

3.4.2.2 Updated cross reference sheet when major revisions to the prospectus have been made.

3.4.2.3 Financial statements.

3.4.2.4 Auditor's consent letter relating to the final prospectus and the financial statements.

3.4.2.5 Certified copy of the directors' resolution approving the definitive versions of the prospectus and the financial statements and designating the signatures for the certificate.

3.4.2.6 Underwriting or other agreement covering distribution where B.C. is the principal jurisdiction or if distribution arrangements in British Columbia vary in any respect from those of the principal jurisdiction.

3.4.2.7 Consent of other experts.

3.4.2.8 Disclosure of interest of experts.

3.4.2.9 Two commercial copies of the prospectus in the form used for delivery pursuant to Section 66 of the Act should be filed as soon as possible.

4.0 FOLLOW UP MATERIAL

The processing of all material submitted subsequent to the initial prospectus filing will be expedited if the envelope and covering letter are clearly market "Follow-up Material" and directed to the attention of the analyst responsible for vetting the filing, where the analyst's name is known to the filing solicitor. IF THE ANALYST'S NAME IS NOT KNOWN, THE MATERIAL SHOULD BE DIRECTED TO THE ATTENTION OF "SUPERVISOR, FILINGS".

DATED at Vancouver, B.C., this 1st day of February, 1987.

Jill Bodkin
Chairman
B.C. Securities Commission

LOCAL POLICY STATEMENT 3-04

Local Policy Statement 3-04 has been repealed and replaced by Local Policy Statement 3-17.

LOCAL POLICY STATEMENT 3-05

RIGHTS OFFERINGS TO SHAREHOLDERS

1.0 IMPLEMENTATION

1.1 This Local Policy Statement has been revised solely to conform with the Securities Act S.B.C. 1985 c.83 and the Regulations thereto. Other than consequential amendments, there have been no changes of a substantive nature to this policy. It becomes effective upon proclamation of the Securities Act on February 1, 1987.

2.0 TERMS OF REFERENCE

2.1 This policy statement is intended to supplement the requirements of Uniform Act Policy 2-05 and should be observed by issuers relying on exemptions under Act Sections 31(2)(8) and 55 (2)(7) and having British Columbia as the principal trading area for their securities. Issuers listed on the Vancouver Stock Exchange should also consult Part F of Vancouver Stock Exchange Rule B.3.00.

2.2 *Principal trading area outside the British Columbia jurisdiction*

Where an issuer has a principal trading area outside British Columbia, the issuer should disclose in a covering letter the jurisdiction of such principal trading area and the rights offering local policy in addition to Uniform Act Policy 2-05 with which the issuer plans to comply. Alternatively, the following information should be disclosed in the covering letter:

2.2.1 the provisions of this local policy statement with which there will not be compliance;

2.2.2 name of jurisdiction in which the greatest number of shareholders reside;

2.2.3 name of jurisdiction in which the principal trading of the issuer's securities is carried on;

2.2.4 the percentage of shares outstanding of the class which is entitled to receive rights under the proposed offering held by residents of British Columbia;

2.2.5 certificate date of the most recent prospectus (if any) of the issuer receipted in this jurisdiction.

2.3 *The "less than 5% rule"*

Where British Columbia residents hold less than 5% of the outstanding securities of the class which is entitled to receive rights under a proposed offering, the issuer may, in lieu of complying with Section 2.2, simply disclose in a covering letter that less than 5% of such securities are held by residents within British Columbia, and may disclose either that Uniform Act Policy 2-05 is being complied with or the name of the jurisdiction outside Canada whose rights offering requirements are being complied with.

2.4 *Offering by Way of Prospectus or Statement of Material Facts*

Where it appears than an issuer can raise capital expeditiously from its existing shareholder base, a rights offering serves as an appropriate vehicle for this purpose. However, where a right is transferable, someone not part of the existing shareholder base may acquire shares through the exercise of a transferred right, and a prospectus standard of disclosure may accordingly be appropriate.

Where transferability is also attended by one or more of the following circumstances, the Superintendent is likely to object to the proposed trade and to request that the rights offering be replaced by an offering by way of a prospectus or statement of material facts:

2.4.1   the proposed equity offering, if completely subscribed, would result in an increase of more than 50% in the number of shares outstanding of the class which is entitled to receive rights.

2.4.2   the offering is for the purpose of financing a major new undertaking or involves a change of control within 12 months of the completion of the issuer's first distribution of shares to the public.

2.4.3   the securities of the class which entitles shareholders to receive rights under the offering have been listed on a stock exchange but the issuer has not yet completed the programs disclosed in the use of proceeds of the prospectus whereby the issuer "went public" and/or has not yet reported on the results of such programs.

3.0   INFORMATION REQUIRED

3.1   The notice required to be given to the Superintendent under Securities Act Sections 31(2)(8) and 55(2)(7) may be provided by a covering letter referring to the disclosure in an accompanying draft rights offering memorandum directed to shareholders.

3.2   Unless the context of Uniform Act Policy 2-05 clearly indicates otherwise, the information elements stipulated by that Policy should be disclosed in the draft rights offering memorandum directed to shareholders.

3.3   The draft rights offering memorandum should include a brief description of the issuer's business activities, material asset acquisitions and disposals etc. germane to investor decisions. The following information should also be included:

3.3.1   number of rights to be issued for each share held (the minimum number of such rights being one right for each share held).

3.3.2   total number of shares or units to be offered in relation to total number of shares outstanding.

3.3.3   number of rights required to subscribe for each share or unit offered.

3.3.4   date for commencement and termination of the offering (see Section 5.2.4).

3.3.5   exercise price per share or unit offered.

3.3.6   the procedure for subscribing by exercise of rights.

3.3.7   the procedure for selling or transferring rights.

3.3.8   dollar amount of minimum subscription, if any.

3.3.9   guarantor, if any, and terms and amount of guarantee.

3.3.10   terms of pro rata over subscription. Where there is a stand-by guarantee by an insider, there must be a provision that the excess shares unsubscribed for be available on a pro rata basis (see also Section 5.3).

3.3.11   use of proceeds of offering.

3.3.12   name of the issuer's transfer agent administering the offering.

3.3.13   payments to be made to any person or company in connection with the offering.

3.3.14   warrants to be issued, if any, with shares subscribed for, exercise price and all other material terms of such warrant.

3.3.15   disclosure concerning the issuer's ongoing programs and summaries of technical reports filed with the Superintendent in compliance with Section 4.5.6 of this Local Policy Statement.

3.3.16   date of the last annual general meeting of the issuer, and particulars of any extraordinary general meeting held since the last annual general meeting.

3.3.17   any change in the directors and senior officers since the last annual general meeting.

3.3.18   particulars known to the directors of any transfer of shares which has materially affected the control of the issuer since the last meeting of shareholders or alternatively a statement that no such particulars are known.

3.4   Where the issuer is negotiating material transactions, management should consider deferring a rights offering until such negotiations have either been abrogated or sufficiently advanced to warrant a news release and disclosure in the draft rights offering. A rights offering memorandum appropriately should provide disclosure on all material transactions likely to be consummated by the conclusion of the rights offering, and the market for the issuer's securities at the onset of the offering period should be able to take such disclosure into account. Ideally there should be at the outset of an offering no undisclosed material negotiations likely to require a news release prior to the expiry date of the rights offering.

4.0   OTHER ITEMS TO BE FILED

A covering letter should accompany the draft rights offering memorandum. The letter should include:

4.1   the formal notice to the Superintendent (see Section 3.1)

4.2   request for exclusion from the provisions of this Local Policy Statement, where applicable (see Sections 2.2 and 2.3)

4.3   a list of the other jurisdictions in Canada in which the offering is being made.

4.4   where applicable, a statement that the provision of Local Policy Statement 3-35 have been complied with.

4.5   a list of the documentation prescribed under this section, identifying the documents in the numbering sequence set out below.

4.5.1   Fee $75.

4.5.2   Copy of issuer's latest annual report and annual general meeting information circular if they have not already been filed.

4.5.3   Copy of issuer's most recent financial statements if they have not already been filed.

4.5.4   Minutes of the most recent annual general meeting and any extraordinary general meeting held subsequent to the annual general meeting.

4.5.5   Where a standby guarantee is involved, the guarantor must disclose any plans for subsequent distribution of the securities so acquired and must also provide satisfactory evidence to the Superintendent of his ability to carry out the provisions of the guarantee. Such evidence may take the form of:

4.5.5.1   a statement of net worth attested to by the guarantor, or

4.5.5.2   a bank letter of credit or such other form to which the Superintendent may specifically consent.

4.5.6   Where proceeds from the rights offering memorandum are to be used to fund specific programs, appropriate technical reports conforming to the specifications of relevant policies (eg. National Policy 2A/2B, Local Policy 3-01 and Forms 54 and 55) must be filed with the Superintendent. The offering memorandum should contain summaries of any such reports unless such summaries have already been distributed to shareholders. The authors of such reports should consent to the filing of such reports and to the inclusion of summaries thereof in the rights offering memorandum.

4.5.7   Statement signed by a senior officer of the issuer to the effect that:

4.5.7.1   there have been no material changes in the circumstances of the issuer since the date of the last audited financial statement delivered to shareholders or that all such changes have been disclosed in the rights offering memorandum, and

4.5.7.2   there are no undisclosed material transactions currently under negotiation which are likely to require a news release prior to the expiry date of the rights offering. (See also Section 3.4).

4.5.8   Where the principal trading area is the British Columbia jurisdiction a facsimile of the subscription proposed to be distributed to shareholders.

5.0   STAND-BY COMMITMENTS AND WARRANTS

5.1   The Superintendent recognizes that an insider may have access to current information which may provide insights into the issuer's affairs not available to others. Any provision in a rights offering which might tend to deter non-insiders from exercising their rights or might provide an insider with an advantage in increasing his proportionate holdings would be of concern to the Superintendent.

5.2   The Superintendent, accordingly, in the absence of special circumstances which can be demonstrated to justify alternative arrangements, will object to a rights offering where:

5.2.1   the offering is priced above market; or

5.2.2   an insider has agreed to provide a stand-by commitment to take up any securities unsubscribed for by other security holders unless a second-stage right to take up any such unsubscribed securities is offered on an acceptable pro-rata basis to all security holders of the class who have exercised their initial rights in full;

5.2.3   a bonus is offered to a stand-by guarantor other than in the form of a nontransferable share purchase warrant entitling him to acquire shares of the issuer equal in number to not more than 40% of the total number of shares he has agreed to acquire on a stand-by basis, for a period not exceeding six months from the date on which such performance guarantee may be required. The exercise price of such warrant shall not be less than the exercise price of the rights; or

5.2.4   the following procedures to notify unregistered shareholders are not followed by an issuer having its principal trading area within British Columbia:

5.2.4.1   the offering shall not commence until the expiration of seven business days after the expiry of the 10 day period or the withdrawal of the objection referred to in Section 31(2)(8) and 55(2)(7) of the Act, and

5.2.4.2   forthwith after acceptance of the notice for filing, but in any event, not later than three business days after the acceptance, the issuer shall publish a notice in at least one issue of a daily newspaper published and circulating in the County of Vancouver, such notice to be addressed to the shareholders, giving the date of commencement and termination of the offering, which period shall not exceed thirty days in cases where a minimum amount has been fixed, or not more than ninety days where a minimum amount has not been fixed.

5.3   The following will be considered an acceptable pro rata basis (although other bases may be acceptable):

Each security holder who has fully exercised his initial rights may take up, at the same price per security as in the initial offering, that number of securities available through unexercised rights that is obtained by multiplying:

Local Policies

5.3.1   the number which is obtained by dividing the number of rights exercised by such security holder in the initial stage by the aggregate number of rights exercised by all security holders in that stage; times

5.3.2   the total number of securities available through all unexercised rights.

If some security holders have requested an oversubscription of less than the amount of securities equivalent to the product available to them, and some security holders have requested more than the product available to them, each such security holder requesting more may take up, at the same price per security as in the initial offering, that number of securities available through unexercised rights that is obtainable by multiplying.

5.3.3   the fraction obtained in Section 6.3.1; times

5.3.4   the remaining number of securities available through unexercised rights.

5.4   The party giving the stand-by commitment may take up all securities not taken up pursuant to the initial and second stage rights at the same price per security as in the initial and second stages.

6.0   RESPONSE BY SUPERINTENDENT TO RIGHTS OFFERING FILING

6.1   Sections 31(2)(8) and 55(2)(7) of the Act indicate that if the Superintendent objects to the rights offering, he should inform the issuer within 10 days of the giving of the notice.

6.2   An issuer should be aware that the Superintendent will find a proposed rights offering objectionable where one or more of the conditions set out in Sections 2.4 or 5.2 of this Local Policy Statement prevail.

6.3   Uniform Act Policy 2-05 lists the holding of regular annual meetings and the timely distribution to shareholders of information required under the issuer's jurisdiction of incorporation as preconditions for acceptance of a rights offering. The Superintendent accordingly will deem a rights offering objectionable where the issuer has not complied with the applicable statutory provisions for timely disclosure.

6.4   A company deemed dormant under Local Policy Statement 3-35 must first comply with the provisions of that Local Policy Statement before the Superintendent will find a rights offering acceptable.

7.0   MINIMUM SUBSCRIPTION

7.1   *Trust requirements – Unlisted Company*

Where a minimum subscription is provided for in a rights offering of an unlisted company, and the funds subscribed are placed in the hands of an independent trustee in British Columbia, there must be a provision for notifying the Superintendent of Brokers

7.1.1   that the funds have been released from trust, or

7.1.2   that the funds have been returned to the subscribers, the minimum subscription having not been attained.

7.2   *No minimum subscription*

Where no minimum subscription has been provided for a rights offering, the rights offering memorandum must disclose the risk that insufficient proceeds may be available from subscription to enable the aims and objectives of the rights offering to be carried out.

DATED at Vancouver, B.C., this 1st day of February, 1987.

Jill Bodkin
Chairman
B.C. Securities Commission

LOCAL POLICY STATEMENT 3-06

PROSPECTUS GUIDELINES FOR THE MORTGAGE INVESTMENT ISSUER

1.0 IMPLEMENTATION

    1.1   This Local Policy Statement has been revised solely to conform with the Securities Act S.B.C. 1985 c.83 and the Regulations thereto. Other than consequential amendments, there have been no changes of a substantive nature to this policy. It becomes effective upon proclamation of the Securities Act on February 1, 1987.

2.0 APPLICATION

This Local Policy Statement does not apply to:

    2.1   securities issued where the trade is exempt from registration under Section 55 of the Act

    2.2   the issuance of a "pass through" security to the public, giving each purchaser an undivided interest in the mortgage collateral

    2.3   the issuance of securities to raise funds for the purpose of developing and managing a specific real estate project such as a shopping centre or hotel.

3.0 GUIDELINES

    3.1   The owners' or shareholders' equity of the issuer shall on conclusion of any public offering be not less than $250,000, provided that if debt securities are offered to the public, the owners' or shareholders' equity shall be not less than $500,000.

    3.2   Where an issue of a mortgage-backed debt security provides for other than fixed payments of interest and principal and a stated maturity, the issuer shall satisfy the Superintendent that the variable rates and terms provided are consistent with the variable rates and terms in the mortgages held as collateral.

    3.3   Subject to paragraphs 3.4 and 3.5, the debt of the issuer shall not exceed three times the equity capital plus retained earnings and realized capital gains less deficit and capital losses whether realized or not.

    3.4   When and so long as at least 50% of the book value of the total assets of the issuer consists of:

        3.4.1   National Housing Act ("NHA") mortgages;

        3.4.2   conventional first mortgage loans whose loan to appraised value of the real estate securing the loan ratio does not exceed 75% unless the excess is insured by an insurance company registered lender the Canadian and British Insurance Company Act (Canada), the Foreign Insurance Companies Act (Canada) or the Insurance Act (B.C.); and

        3.4.3   cash, cash items and obligations of Canadian municipal, provincial and federal governments and government agencies;

    in the discretion of management the debt of the issuer may be increased so as not to exceed five times the equity capital plus retained earnings and realized capital gains less deficit and capital losses whether realized or not.

    3.5   When and so long as at least 90% of the book value of the total assets of the issuer consists of:

        3.5.1   National Housing Act ("NHA") mortgages;

        3.5.2   conventional first mortgage loans on single-family dwellings (including residential condominiums) and duplexes, whose loan to appraised value of the real estate securing the loan ratio does not exceed 75% unless the excess is insured by an insurance company registered lender the Canadian and British Insurance Company Act (Canada), the Foreign Insurance Companies Act (Canada) or the Insurance Act (B.C.); and

3.5.3   cash, cash items and obligations of Canadian municipal, provincial and federal governments and government agencies; in the discretion of management the debt of the issuer may be increased so as not to exceed ten times the equity capital plus retained earnings and realized capital gains less deficit and capital losses whether realized or not.

3.6   At least 75% of the book value of the issuers' assets must comprise mortgages secured on real property and money either on hand or on deposit with a bank, trust company or credit union.

3.7   Where there is an intention to qualify a mortgage investment company as a "Mortgage Investment Corporation" under the Income Tax Act (Canada) the effect of such qualification shall be disclosed in the prospectus. If the intention is not so to qualify, a statement to that effect shall be made in the prospectus.

3.8   Debt securities of the issuer should be issued under a trust deed or other instrument running in favour of a trustee.

4.0   PROHIBITIONS AND RESTRICTIONS

4.1   The issuer shall not participate in mining, oil or like ventures or acquire real property for development purposes (but not including development mortgage loans).

4.2   The issuer shall not invest in the securities of other real estate or mortgage investment issuers save for securities exempt from registration under Section 32(a) and (b) of the Act.

4.3   The issuer shall not invest in the securities of any other issuer either controlled, directly or indirectly by any of the directors or other insiders of the issuer or having more than 10% of its issued and outstanding voting shares controlled, directly or indirectly, by any of the directors or other insiders of the issuer.

4.4   No issuer shall invest more than 10% of the book value of its net tangible assets in an entity which is controlled, directly or indirectly, by any one person or group of persons.

5.0   DISCLOSURE ON THE CANADA DEPOSIT INSURANCE CORPORATION

5.1   Where the issuer is not a member institution of Canada Deposit Insurance Corporation and/or the debt securities offered in the prospectus are not insured through Canada Deposit Insurance Corporation, the face page of the prospectus shall contain the relevant parts of the following disclosure:

". . . . . is *not* a member institution of the Canada Deposit Insurance Corporation and the securities offered in this prospectus are *not* insured against loss through the Canada Deposit Insurance Corporation."

5.2   The issuer shall disclose in the prospectus any alternative insurance against loss which may apply to the debt securities offered.

DATED at Vancouver, B.C., this 1st day of February, 1987.

Jill Bodkin
Chairman
B.C. Securities Commission

LOCAL POLICY STATEMENT 3-07

POLICY GUIDELINES RESPECTING TRADING SHARES, PERFORMANCE SHARES AND OTHER CONSIDERATION

See NIN 92/3 "Clarification of waivers relating to Local Policy Statement 3-07". The Superintendent will not accept a waiver of the requirements in sections 134(2)(b)(i) or 134(3)(e)(iii)(A) and (B) to enter into an escrow or pooling agreement. The Superintendent confirms the waiver of the requirements to enter into a pooling or escrow agreement if a person who is not a control person holds shares in the capital of an issuer which becomes an exchange issuer.

See BOR 89/5 "Trades in Securities held Subject to Escrow or Pooling Agreement".

Re PLC Systems Inc., Logan Anderson, Harry C. Moll and Derek van Laare (1993), 1 C.C.L.S. 53 (B.C. Sec. Comm.).

Where an escrow agreement provides that the escrow shares will be released "from time to time in accordance with the general policies of the Superintendent or Exchange", the general policies to be applied by the Superintendent in deciding the appropriate application for the release of the escrow shares are the policies in effect at the time the application is made. It would be patently unreasonable for the applicants to expect the Superintendent, in deciding an escrow release application, to apply a policy inconsistent with that of the Commission. Considerable mischief will result if holders of escrow shares are able to have those shares released on a more favourable basis simply because the issuer of the shares had been delisted from the Exchange. It is in the public interest that the Commission's policy directives with respect to the release of escrow shares be consistently applied by the Superintendent and the Exchange.

Re Ingot Group Holdings Inc., [1993] 35 B.C.S.C. Weekly Summary 16 (B.C. Sec. Comm.).

An escrow agreement provided that where the property for which the escrow shares have been issued is lost or alienated, the Exchange may, at its discretion, cancel the shares as it deems advisable. The Exchange must determine on the facts whether the property has been lost or alienated prior to it exercising its discretion. In concurring reasons, Commissioner Hira stated that cancelling escrow shares is a significant alienation of property rights, particularly from the prospective of the person whose escrow shares are being cancelled.

Local Policies

TABLE OF CONTENTS

PART 1 IMPLEMENTATION

1.1 The following local policy statements are hereby rescinded and this local policy statement substituted therefor, effective March 1, 1990:

(a) Local Policy Statement 3-07, dated February 6, 1987 (the "Former Policy Statement"), and

(b) Local Policy Statements 3-08, 3-09 and 3-10, each dated February 1, 1987.

PART 2 APPLICATION

2.1 *Pre-prospectus* – This local policy statement sets out guidelines for issuance of shares and payment of consideration for assets by an issuer intending to do an initial public offering and obtain a listing on the Vancouver Stock Exchange. This local policy statement addresses

(a) the issuance of trading shares, which are common shares issued as consideration for cash or assets contributed to the issuer and, in certain cases, expenses incurred to advance the business of the issuer,

(b) the issuance of and escrow restrictions imposed on performance shares, which are common shares issued to directors, officers, promoters and other principals of the issuer to provide them with both a reasonable assurance of control during the formative stages of the issuer's development and an incentive to support the issuer, and

(c) the payment of other consideration by the issuer for assets or services.

2.2 *Reactivations and reorganizations* – This local policy statement applies, with the necessary changes, to

(a) the reactivation of an issuer by way of a prospectus, carried out in accordance with Local Policy Statement 3-35 and the policies of the Vancouver Stock Exchange, and

(b) a major reorganization of an issuer, including a reverse take over, carried out in accordance with the policies of the British Columbia Securities Commission and the Vancouver Stock Exchange.

PART 3   TRANSITION

3.1   *Agreements made under former policy statement* – Subject to section 3.2, shares issued in accordance with the Former Policy Statement will continue to be governed by any agreements made in accordance with the Former Policy Statement. Such shares, however, will be subject to the transfer restrictions and procedures set out in Part 8 and the release criteria and procedures set out in sections 9.5 through 9.10 of this local policy statement.

3.2   *Option of conforming with new policy statement* – An issuer that has issued shares in accordance with the Former Policy Statement may reorganize its capital to fully conform with this local policy statement. Before doing so, the issuer must obtain the approval of its shareholders and the written consent of the Superintendent of Brokers, if the issuer's shares are not listed on the Vancouver Stock Exchange, or the Vancouver Stock Exchange, if the issuer's shares are listed on that exchange. Both the approval and consent must be obtained by March 1, 1991.

PART 4   DEFINITIONS

4.1   *Defined terms* – In this local policy statement:

"Act" means the Securities Act, S.B.C. 1985, c. 83;

"arm's length transaction" means a transaction other than a non-arm's length transaction;

"cash flow" means net income or loss before tax, adjusted to add back the following expenses:

(a)   depreciation,

(b)   amortization of goodwill and deferred research and development costs, excluding general and administrative costs,

(c)   expensed research and development costs, excluding general and administrative costs, and

(d)   any other amounts permitted or required by the Superintendent;

"cumulative cash flow" means, at any time, the aggregate cash flow of an issuer up to that time from a date no earlier than the issuer's financial year end immediately preceding the date of its IPO, net of any negative cash flow;

> The practice of the Commission is to allow the issuer to choose either its financial year end immediately prior to or immediately subsequent to its initial public offering as the time from which the cumulative cash flow shall be calculated.

"earn-out factor" means the number obtained by squaring the performance share percentage, expressed as a decimal, and multiplying by four;

"earn-out price" means the IPO price multiplied by the earn-out factor;

"escrow agreement" means an agreement in the form attached as Appendix A to this local policy statement;

"Exchange" means the Vancouver Stock Exchange;

"industrial issuer" means an issuer other than a natural resource issuer;

"IPO" means the initial public offering of common shares of an issuer under a prospectus which has been filed with, and for which a receipt has been obtained from, the Superintendent under section 42 of the Act;

"IPO price" means the price per share paid by the public on an issuer's IPO;

"non-arm's length transaction" means a transaction between the issuer and a person that, at any time from the date of the transaction until the date of completion of the issuer's IPO, is

(a)   an insider, associate, affiliate or principal of the issuer,

    (b)   a person that

        (i)   has a control person, insider or promoter that is a control person, insider or promoter of the issuer, or

        (ii) has a control person, insider or promoter that is an associate or affiliate of a control person, insider or promoter of the issuer

        except where the person's insiders that are described in paragraphs (i) and (ii) hold in total less than 10% of the voting securities of the person, or

    (c)   determined by the Superintendent not to be at arm's length to the issuer;

"performance shares" means common shares of an issuer issued in accordance with Part 7 of this local policy statement, so long as they are held in escrow in accordance with this local policy statement;

"performance share percentage" means the percentage, determined on the date the issuer's shares are listed, posted and called for trading on the Exchange, that the issued performance shares of the issuer are of the total issued and outstanding voting securities of the issuer;

"principal" means, in relation to an issuer,

    (a)   a promoter of the issuer,

    (b)   a director of the issuer or of an operating subsidiary of the issuer,

    (c)   a full time management employee of the issuer, or of an operating subsidiary of the issuer, whose direct or indirect employment is with the issuer or the subsidiary,

    (d)   a person who has provided key services or contributed a fundamental asset to the issuer and has elected to be treated as a principal, or

    (e)   a company all the voting securities of which are owned by one or more of the persons referred to in subsections (a) through (d);

"Regulation" means the Securities Regulation, B.C. Reg. 270/86;

"Superintendent or the Exchange" means the Superintendent, if the issuer's shares are not listed on the Exchange, and the Exchange, if the issuer's shares are listed on the Exchange;

"trading shares" means shares of the class of common shares issued on an issuer's IPO, excluding performance shares issued in accordance with Part 7 of this local policy statement;

"valuation opinion" means, in respect of

    (a)   a natural resource issuer, a written opinion prepared by a qualified expert as to the fair market value of a resource property, determined either through the computation of present value or some other recognized method of valuation acceptable to the Superintendent, and

    (b)   an industrial issuer, a written opinion prepared in accordance with generally applied valuation approaches by a Chartered Business Valuator, or another expert acceptable to the Superintendent, as to the highest price available for the issuer's business, assets or shares in an open and unrestricted market between informed, prudent parties, acting at arm's length and under no compulsion to act, expressed in terms of money or money's worth.

    4.2   *Terms defined in legislation* – Subject to section 4.1, terms defined in the Act, the Regulation and the Interpretation Act, R.S.B.C. 1979, c. 206 and used in this local policy statement have the same meaning as in the Act, the Regulation and the Interpretation Act.

PART 5   GENERAL MATTERS

    5.1   *Review of opinions and reports* – The Superintendent may, with the agreement of an issuer, seek the opinion of an engineer, appraiser, business valuator, accountant or other expert to determine the acceptability of a valuation opinion or other report filed pursuant to this local policy statement and, in such circumstances, the issuer will be liable for the fees charged by such person in connection with providing the opinion.

5.2   *Requirement for valuation opinion* – The Superintendent may, at the time of reviewing an issuer's prospectus for its IPO, require a valuation opinion in support of the value attributed to any non-cash assets.

5.3   *Out of pocket costs* – Where this local policy statement provides that the value of trading shares issued or other consideration paid to a person by an issuer for a non-cash asset must be calculated on the basis of the out of pocket costs incurred by the person in respect of the non-cash asset, those out of pocket costs must

     (a)   be reasonable,

     (b)   have contributed or be reasonably expected to contribute to the future operations of the issuer,

     (c)   be supported by an audited statement of costs, and

     (d)   in respect of a resource property, be restricted to acquisition costs and such other costs as are necessary to secure a preliminary evaluation of the resource property and to lead to the identification of exploration targets.

5.4   *Confirmation of fair value* – The onus will be on an issuer, if questioned, to satisfy the Superintendent that fair value was received for costs or expenditures associated with a non-arm's length transaction.

PART 6   ISSUANCE OF TRADING SHARES

6.1   *Minimum price and maximum aggregate value* – Although in most cases trading shares will be paid for in cash, trading shares may be issued for consideration other than cash. Subject to sections 6.2 through 6.6, an issuer may issue trading shares at a minimum price of $.25 per share up to an aggregate value equal to:

     (a)   the amount of cash paid in as share capital; plus

     (b)   the fair market value of any non-cash assets contributed as share capital; plus

     (c)   the issuer's retained earnings, if any; less

     (d)   where the issuer has an accumulated deficit, that portion of the accumulated deficit that does not directly relate to the issuer's stated business purpose at the time of its IPO.

6.2   *Interest in operating subsidiary* – Where an issuer has an operating subsidiary, or is proposing to issue trading shares in order to acquire an operating subsidiary, and the value of that operating subsidiary is not supported by a current valuation opinion, the principles of this Part will apply to the operating subsidiary for the purpose of determining the number of trading shares that may be issued by the issuer in respect of its interest in the operating subsidiary.

6.3   *Value assigned to non-cash assets* – For the purpose of section 6.1(b), where non-cash assets are contributed to an issuer by a person in a non-arm's length transaction, the fair market value attributed to the non-cash assets must be either

     (a)   supported by a valuation opinion, or

     (b)   limited to an amount equal to the out of pocket costs incurred by the person in respect of the non-cash assets, determined in accordance with section 5.3.

6.4   *Purchase of interest in mineral property* – A natural resource issuer that, in an arm's length transaction, agrees to issue trading shares as consideration for a mineral property or an option on a mineral property, the value of which is not supported by a current valuation opinion, will generally be required to meet the following conditions:

(a) The consideration must consist of not more than 200,000 trading shares issuable in no fewer than four blocks, each block consisting of not more than 50,000 trading shares.

(b) One block of shares may be issued prior to the date the issuer's shares are listed, posted and called for trading on the Exchange.

(c) The remaining blocks of shares may be issued in stages upon the filing with the Exchange of engineering reports, acceptable to the Exchange, recommending further work on the mineral property.

6.5 *Accumulated deficit related to issuer's stated business purpose* – For the purpose of section 6.1(d), that portion of the issuer's accumulated deficit that directly relates to the issuer's stated business purpose at the time of its IPO includes

(a) for a natural resource issuer, expenses incurred

(i) in exploring and developing the resource properties upon which the issuer's IPO proceeds are to be spent, and

(ii) in exploring and developing other resource properties, provided that these expenses do not exceed the expenses referred to in paragraph (i), and

(b) for an industrial issuer, expenses incurred in respect of the project or business to be financed by the issuer's IPO proceeds.

6.6 *Exclusion of amounts by Superintendent* – The Superintendent may require that an amount be excluded from the determination of the number of trading shares that may be issued under this Part if in the circumstances he considers that to include any such amount would be inappropriate or unconscionable. For example, the Superintendent would question the appropriateness of issuing trading shares for non-cash assets unrelated to the issuer's stated business purpose at the time of its IPO or for excessive administrative expenses.

PART 7   ISSUANCE OF PERFORMANCE SHARES

7.1 *Issuance to principals* – Performance shares may be issued for cash to the principals of an issuer

(a) to provide the principals with a measure of control to facilitate the development of the issuer in an orderly fashion,

(b) to provide an incentive for the principals to diligently support the affairs of the issuer, and

(c) to provide an incentive for the principals to contribute management services or fundamental assets to the issuer.

7.2 *Natural resource issuer* – A natural resource issuer may issue to its principals up to a total of 750,000 performance shares, at a minimum price of $.01 per share.

7.3 *Industrial issuer* – An industrial issuer may issue performance shares to its principals, at a minimum price of $.01 per share, provided that the resulting performance share percentage does not exceed 65%.

7.4 *Escrow requirement* – Performance shares are required to be escrowed. It should be noted that the higher the performance share percentage, the more difficult it becomes to obtain a release of the performance shares from escrow. The table attached as Appendix B to this local policy statement provides some examples of the operation of the release provisions for industrial issuers set out in Part 9 of this local policy statement.

7.5 *Escrow agreement* – Prior to or at the time of acquiring performance shares, principals must execute an escrow agreement. The certificates representing the performance shares must be registered in the names of the holders of the shares and deposited with the escrow agent in accordance with the terms of the escrow agreement. Only a trust company carrying on business in British Columbia or a company approved by the Superintendent may act as an escrow agent.

7.6 *Limitations on rights of holders of performance shares* – The escrow agreement provides that the holders of performance shares waive any rights attached to those shares to receive dividends or to participate in the assets and property of the issuer on a winding up or dissolution. Holders of performance shares do retain the right to vote those shares, except on a resolution respecting their cancellation.

7.7 *Rights on ceasing to be a principal* – The escrow agreement requires that the parties to it set out in the agreement any rights or obligations of a person who ceases to be a principal, dies or becomes bankrupt to retain, transfer or surrender to the issuer for cancellation any performance shares then held by the person.

7.8 *Undertaking of holding company* – Where performance shares are to be issued to a non-reporting or closely held company, wherever situate, rather than to an individual, the company must, prior to or at the time of acquiring the performance shares, execute an undertaking in the form attached as Appendix C to this local policy statement. In the undertaking, the company agrees not to effect or permit any transfer of ownership of shares of the company nor to issue further shares of any class in the company without the consent of the Superintendent or the Exchange, so long as the company continues to hold any of the issuer's performance shares. An application for consent should be made in the same manner as an application for consent to a transfer of performance shares pursuant to Part 8 of this local policy statement.

PART 8   TRANSFER OF PERFORMANCE SHARES WITHIN ESCROW

8.1 *Permitted transferees* – Performance shares may be transferred only to

(a)   other principals, including incoming principals,

(b)   the issuer of the performance shares, or

(c)   an offeror under a formal bid (as defined in section 74 of the Act).

8.2 *Request for consent to transfer* – In order to transfer performance shares, the holder of performance shares must deliver to the Superintendent or the Exchange a written request for consent to the transfer. The request for consent to the transfer must include:

(a)   the name of the escrow agent and the reference date of the escrow agreement,

(b)   an explanation of the reason for the transfer,

(c)   a description of the consideration to be paid for the performance shares,

(d)   where the performance shares are to be transferred to a principal, confirmation that the transferee is a principal or will become a principal on or before the date of the proposed transfer, and

(e)   a description of the exemptions in the Act or the Regulation, if any, being relied upon to make the transfer.

8.3 *Documents to be filed with request for consent to transfer* – The request for consent to the transfer must be accompanied by:

(a)   a copy of the transfer agreement,

(b)   an acknowledgement and agreement to be bound in the form attached as Schedule A to the escrow agreement, executed by the transferee,

(c)   where the performance shares are to be transferred to a non-reporting or closely held company, wherever situate, rather than to an individual, an undertaking by the company in the form attached as Appendix C to this local policy statement,

(d)   where applicable, evidence that the proposed change of control has been approved by the shareholders of the issuer, and

(e)   the appropriate application fee.

8.4   *Letter of consent or objection* – Upon receiving a request for consent to a transfer and accompanying documents that comply with sections 8.2 and 8.3, the Superintendent or the Exchange will issue to the applicant a letter that either consents or objects to the transfer. A letter consenting to the transfer will be copied to the escrow agent.

8.5   *No transfer during period between prospectus receipt and listing* – The Superintendent will generally refuse to consent to a transfer of performance shares during the period between the date of the receipt for the issuer's prospectus for its IPO and the date the issuer's securities are listed, posted and called for trading on the Exchange.

PART 9   RELEASE OF PERFORMANCE SHARES FROM ESCROW

9.1   *Release of shares of natural resource issuer* – Holders of performance shares of a natural resource issuer will be entitled to the pro-rata release of those performance shares on the basis of 15% of the original number of performance shares for every $100,000 expended on exploration and development of a resource property by

(a)   the issuer, or

(b)   a person other than the issuer in order to earn an interest in the resource property, but only in respect of that proportion of the expenditure equal to the issuer's remaining proportionate interest in the resource property after the person's interest has been earned,

provided that

(c)   no more than 50% of the original number of performance shares may be released in any 12 month period, and

(d)   no expenditure on exploration and development made prior to the date of the receipt for the issuer's prospectus for its IPO may be included.

9.2   *Reduction in release for natural resource issuer* – Where administrative expenses exceed 33% of total expenditures during the period on which the calculation in section 9.1 is based,

(a)   the pro-rata release factor of 15% will be reduced to 7.5%, and

(b)   the percentage of the original number of performance shares available for release in any 12 month period will be reduced to 25%.

9.3   *Release of shares of industrial issuer* – Holders of performance shares of an industrial issuer will be entitled to the pro-rata release of a number of performance shares equal to the amount of cumulative cash flow, not previously applied towards release, divided by the earn-out price.

9.4   *Adjustment of release calculation* – On a consolidation, subdivision, amalgamation or reclassification of the issuer's shares, the release calculation must be adjusted so that the proportion of the outstanding performance shares available for release is unaffected by the consolidation, subdivision, amalgamation or reclassification.

9.5   *Requirements for release* – No performance shares may be released from escrow unless, at the time of the application for release,

(a)   the issuer is meeting its current obligations in the ordinary course of business as they generally become due, as evidenced by a statutory declaration of the president or chief financial officer of the issuer,

(b)   the issuer's shares are listed, posted and called for trading on all stock exchanges having jurisdiction over it, as evidenced by letters from those stock exchanges,

(c)   the issuer is not in default of any requirement of the Act or the Regulation, as evidenced by a certificate issued by the Commission, and

(d)   the issuer is in good standing with respect to its filing of returns with the Registrar of Companies under the Company Act or, if the issuer is incorporated, organized or continued in a jurisdiction other than British Columbia, with the registrar of companies or similar authority in that jurisdiction, as evidenced by a certificate issued by the Registrar of Companies or by that similar authority.

9.6 *Annual release based on annual audited financial statements* – Performance shares may be released only once during an issuer's financial year. The release calculation must be based on the issuer's annual audited financial statements for the year or years during which the release requirements were met in respect of the performance shares to be released.

9.7 *Request for consent to release* – In order to obtain a release of performance shares, the issuer must deliver to the Superintendent or the Exchange a written request for consent to the release. The request for consent to the release must include the name of the escrow agent and the reference date of the escrow agreement.

9.8 *Documents to be filed with request for consent to release* – The request for consent to the release must be accompanied by:

(a) written evidence of compliance with the requirements of section 9.5,

(b) annual audited financial statements of the issuer for the financial year or years during which the release requirements were met in respect of the performance shares to be released,

(c) where expenditures on a resource property were made by a person other than the issuer, an audited statement of costs,

(d) a calculation, prepared by the issuer's auditor, of the number of performance shares to be released, and

(e) the appropriate application fee.

9.9 *Letter of consent or objection* – Upon receiving a request for consent to a release and accompanying documents that comply with sections 9.7 and 9.8, the Superintendent or the Exchange will issue to the issuer a letter that either consents or objects to the release. A letter consenting to the release will be copied to the escrow agent.

9.10 *Request by holder of performance shares for consent to release* – A holder of performance shares may apply to the Superintendent or the Exchange for release where the issuer is unable or unwilling to do so. If the president or chief financial officer of the issuer refuses to provide the statutory declaration referred to in section 9.5(a), the Superintendent or the Exchange may waive that requirement.

PART 10 SURRENDER OF PERFORMANCE SHARES FOR CANCELLATION

10.1 Performance shares must be surrendered to the issuer for cancellation

(a) at the time of a major reorganization of the issuer, if required as a condition of the consent to the reorganization by the Superintendent or the Exchange,

(b) where the issuer's shares have been subject to a cease trade order issued under the Act for a period of 2 consecutive years, or

(c) 10 years from the later of the date of issue of the performance shares and the date of the receipt for the issuer's prospectus for its IPO.

PART 11 OTHER CONSIDERATION

11.1 *Natural resource issuer* – Where a natural resource issuer proposes to acquire from a person a resource property or an option on a resource property, the value of which is not supported by a valuation opinion, the following principles apply:

(a) In an arm's length transaction, the issuer may pay the person cash consideration.

(b) In an arm's length transaction, the issuer may agree to pay the person additional consideration at such time as the resource property commences commercial production. Such additional consideration may, depending on the circumstances, consist of cash consideration, reasonable payments from net profits, securities, or any combination of these.

(c)   In a non-arm's length transaction, the issuer may pay the person cash consideration up to the amount of the out of pocket costs incurred by the person in respect of the resource property, determined in accordance with section 5.3.

(d)   In a non-arms length transaction, the issuer may agree to pay the person additional consideration at such time as the resource property commences commercial production, where the person has carried out extensive exploration with results that indicate that the resource property appears to have substantial merit. The extent of the person's effort, skill and risk in developing the resource property will be taken into account by the Superintendent in determining whether additional consideration is justified. Such additional consideration may, depending on the circumstances, consist of cash consideration, reasonable payments from net profits, securities, or any combination of these. A 15% net profits interest would normally be considered reasonable.

11.2   *Industrial issuer* – Where an industrial issuer proposes to acquire from a person non-cash assets, the value of which are not supported by a valuation opinion, the following principles apply:

(a)   In an arm's length transaction, the issuer may pay the person cash consideration, a royalty or a combination of these.

(b)   In a non-arm's length transaction, the issuer may pay the person cash consideration up to the amount of the out of pocket costs incurred by the person in respect of the non-cash assets, determined in accordance with section 5.3.

DATED at Vancouver, British Columbia, this 21st day of December 1989.

Douglas M. Hyndman
Chairman

APPENDIX A TO LOCAL POLICY STATEMENT 3-07

ESCROW AGREEMENT

THIS AGREEMENT is dated for reference _____, 19__ and made

AMONG:

(the "Escrow Agent");

AND:

(the "Issuer");

AND: EACH SHAREHOLDER, as defined in this Agreement

(collectively, the "Parties").

WHEREAS the Shareholder has acquired or is about to acquire shares of the Issuer;

AND WHEREAS the Escrow Agent has agreed to act as escrow agent in respect of the shares upon the acquisition of the shares by the Shareholder;

NOW THEREFORE in consideration of the covenants contained in this agreement and other good and valuable consideration (the receipt and sufficiency of which is acknowledged), the Parties agree as follows:

1.   INTERPRETATION

In this agreement:

(a)   "Acknowledgement" means the acknowledgement and agreement to be bound in the form attached as Schedule A to this agreement;

(b)   "Act" means the Securities Act, S.B.C. 1985, c. 83;

(c)   "Exchange" means the Vancouver Stock Exchange;

(d)   "IPO" means the initial public offering of common shares of the Issuer under a prospectus which has been filed with, and for which a receipt has been obtained from, the Superintendent under section 42 of the Act;

(e) "Local Policy Statement 3-07" means the Local Policy Statement 3-07 in effect as of the date of reference of this agreement and attached as Schedule B to this agreement;

(f) "Shareholder" means a holder of shares of the Issuer who executes this agreement or an Acknowledgement;

(g) "Shares" means the shares of the Shareholder described in Schedule C to this agreement, as amended from time to time in accordance with section 9;

(h) "Superintendent" means the Superintendent of Brokers appointed under the Act; and

(i) "Superintendent or the Exchange" means the Superintendent, if the shares of the Issuer are not listed on the Exchange, or the Exchange, if the shares of the Issuer are listed on the Exchange.

2. PLACEMENT OF SHARES IN ESCROW

The Shareholder places the Shares in escrow with the Escrow Agent and shall deliver the certificates representing the Shares to the Escrow Agent as soon as practicable.

3. VOTING OF SHARES IN ESCROW

Except as provided by section 4(a), the Shareholder may exercise all voting rights attached to the Shares.

4. WAIVER OF SHAREHOLDER'S RIGHTS

The Shareholder waives the rights attached to the Shares

(a) to vote the Shares on a resolution to cancel any of the Shares,

(b) to receive dividends, and

(c) to participate in the assets and property of the Issuer on a winding up or dissolution of the Issuer.

5. ABSTENTION FROM VOTING AS A DIRECTOR

A Shareholder that is or becomes a director of the Issuer shall abstain from voting on a directors' resolution to cancel any of the Shares.

6. TRANSFER WITHIN ESCROW

(1) The Shareholder shall not transfer any of the Shares except in accordance with Local Policy Statement 3-07 and with the consent of the Superintendent or the Exchange.

(2) The Escrow Agent shall not effect a transfer of the Shares within escrow unless the Escrow Agent has received

(a) a copy of an Acknowledgement executed by the person to whom the Shares are to be transferred, and

(b) a letter from the Superintendent or the Exchange consenting to the transfer.

(3) Upon the death or bankruptcy of a Shareholder, the Escrow Agent shall hold the Shares subject to this agreement for the person that is legally entitled to become the registered owner of the Shares.

(4) [Set out in this subsection the rights and obligations of a Shareholder who ceases to be a principal, as that term is defined in Local Policy Statement 3-07, dies, or becomes bankrupt, to retain, transfer or surrender to the Issuer for cancellation any Shares held by the Shareholder.]

7. RELEASE FROM ESCROW

(1) The Shareholder irrevocably directs the Escrow Agent to retain the Shares until the Shares are released from escrow pursuant to subsection (2) or surrendered for cancellation pursuant to section 8.

(2) The Escrow Agent shall not release the Shares from escrow unless the Escrow Agent has received a letter from the Superintendent or the Exchange consenting to the release.

Local Policies

(3) The approval of the Superintendent or the Exchange to a release from escrow of any of the Shares shall terminate this agreement only in respect of the Shares so released.

8. SURRENDER FOR CANCELLATION

The Shareholder shall surrender the Shares for cancellation and the Escrow Agent shall deliver the certificates representing the Shares to the Issuer

(a) at the time of a major reorganization of the Issuer, if required as a condition of the consent to the reorganization by the Superintendent or the Exchange,

(b) where the Issuer's shares have been subject to a cease trade order issued under the Act for a period of 2 consecutive years,

(c) 10 years from the later of the date of issue of the Shares and the date of the receipt for the Issuer's prospectus on its IPO, or

(d) where required by section 6(4).

9. AMENDMENT OF AGREEMENT

(1) Subject to subsection (2), this agreement may be amended only by a written agreement among the Parties and with the written consent of the Superintendent or the Exchange.

(2) Schedule C to this agreement shall be amended upon

(a) a transfer of Shares pursuant to section 6,

(b) a release of Shares from escrow pursuant to section 7, or

(c) a surrender of Shares for cancellation pursuant to section 8,

and the Escrow Agent shall note the amendment on the Schedule C in its possession.

10. INDEMNIFICATION OF ESCROW AGENT

The Issuer and the Shareholders, jointly and severally, release, indemnify and save harmless the Escrow Agent from all costs, charges, claims, demands, damages, losses and expenses resulting from the Escrow Agent's compliance in good faith with this agreement.

11. RESIGNATION OF ESCROW AGENT

(1) If the Escrow Agent wishes to resign as escrow agent in respect of the Shares, the Escrow Agent shall give notice to the Issuer.

(2) If the Issuer wishes the Escrow Agent to resign as escrow agent in respect of the Shares, the Issuer shall give notice to the Escrow Agent.

(3) A notice referred to in subsection (1) or (2) shall be in writing and delivered to

(a) the Issuer at _____, or

(b) the Escrow Agent at _____

and the notice shall be deemed to have been received on the date of delivery. The Issuer or the Escrow Agent may change its address for notice by giving notice to the other party in accordance with this subsection.

(4) A copy of a notice referred to in subsection (1) or shall concurrently be delivered to the Superintendent or the Exchange.

(5) The resignation of the Escrow Agent shall be effective and the Escrow Agent shall cease to be bound by this agreement on the date that is 180 days after the date of receipt of the notice referred to in subsection (1) or (2) or on such other date as the Escrow Agent and the Issuer may agree upon (the "resignation date").

(6) The Issuer shall, before the resignation date and with the written consent of the Superintendent or the Exchange, appoint another escrow agent and that appointment shall be binding on the Issuer and the Shareholders.

12.   FURTHER ASSURANCES

The Parties shall execute and deliver any documents and perform any acts necessary to carry out the intent of this agreement.

13.   TIME

Time is of the essence of this agreement.

14.   GOVERNING LAWS

This agreement shall be construed in accordance with and governed by the laws of British Columbia and the laws of Canada applicable in British Columbia.

15.   COUNTERPARTS

This agreement may be executed in two or more counterparts, each of which shall be deemed to be an original and all of which shall constitute one agreement.

16.   LANGUAGE

Wherever a singular expression is used in this agreement, that expression is deemed to include the plural or the body corporate where required by the context.

17.   ENUREMENT

This Agreement enures to the benefit of and is binding on the Parties and their heirs, executors, administrators, successors and permitted assigns.

The Parties have executed and delivered this agreement as of the date of reference of this agreement.

The Corporate/Common Seal of	)	
[Escrow Agent] was affixed	)	
in the presence of:	)	
	)	
_____	)	c/s
Authorized signatory	)	
	)	
_____	)	
Authorized signatory	)	
The Corporate/Common Seal of	)	
[Issuer] was affixed	)	
in the presence of:	)	
	)	
_____	)	c/s
Authorized signatory	)	
	)	
_____	)	
Authorized signatory	)	

Where the Shareholder is an individual:

Signed, sealed and delivered by	)	
[Shareholder] in the presence of:	)	
	)	
_____	)	
Name	)	
	)	
_____	)	_____
Address	)	[Shareholder]
	)	
_____	)	
	)	
_____	)	
Occupation		

Local
Policies

Where the Shareholder is a company:

The Corporate/Common Seal of [Shareholder] was affixed in the presence of:	))))
_____ Authorized signatory	) c/s))
_____ Authorized signatory	))

SCHEDULE A TO ESCROW AGREEMENT

ACKNOWLEDGEMENT AND AGREEMENT TO BE BOUND

To: Superintendent of Brokers   or   Vancouver Stock Exchange
       #1100 - 865 Hornby Street   609 Granville Street
       Vancouver, B.C.   Vancouver, B.C.
       V6Z 2H4   V7Y 1H1

       (if the shares are not   (if the shares are listed
       listed on the Vancouver   on the Vancouver Stock
       Stock Exchange)   Exchange)

I acknowledge that

(a)   I have entered into an agreement with _____ under which _____ shares of _____ (the "Shares") will be
transferred to me upon receipt of regulatory approval, and

(b)   the Shares are held in escrow subject to an escrow agreement dated
for reference _____, 19____ (the "Escrow
Agreement"), a copy of which is attached as Schedule A to this acknowledgement.

In consideration of $1.00 and other good and valuable consideration (the receipt and
sufficiency of which is acknowledged) I agree, effective upon receipt of regulatory
approval of the transfer to me of the Shares, to be bound by the Escrow Agreement in
respect of the Shares as if I were an original signatory to the Escrow Agreement.

Dated at _____ on _____ 19____.

Where the transferee is an individual:

Signed, sealed and delivered by [transferee] in the presence of:	)))
_____ Name	)))
_____ Address	) _____) [transferee])
_____ Occupation	))

Where the transferee is a company:

The Corporate/Common Seal of [transferee] was affixed in the presence of:	)))
_____ Authorized signatory	) c/s))
_____ Authorized signatory	)

SCHEDULE C TO ESCROW AGREEMENT

NAME OF SHAREHOLDER	NUMBER OF SHARES HELD IN ESCROW

APPENDIX B TO LOCAL POLICY STATEMENT 3-07
EXAMPLES OF EARN-OUT PRICES FOR PERFORMANCE SHARES
ISSUED BY AN INDUSTRIAL ISSUER

EARN-OUT PRICE IN DOLLARS					
PERFORMANCE SHARE PERCENTAGE	5%	25%	45%	65%	
EARN-OUT FACTOR	01x	.25x	.81x	1.69x	
I					
P	$0.40	.004	.10	.34	676
O	.60	.006	.15	.486	1.014
P					
R	$0.80	.008	.20	.648	1.352
I					
C	$1.00	.010	.25	.810	1.690
E					

The earn-out price represents the amount of cash flow that must be generated to release one performance share from escrow. The following definitions are applicable to the calculation.

Earn-out Price:

> The IPO price multiplied by the earn-out factor.

IPO Price:

> The price per share paid by the public on the issuer's IPO.

Earn-out Factor:

> The number obtained by squaring the performance share percentage, expressed as a decimal, and multiplying the result by four.

Performance Share Percentage:

> The percentage, determined on the date the issuer's shares are listed, posted and called for trading on the Exchange, that the issued performance shares of the issuer are of the total issued and outstanding voting securities of the issuer.

APPENDIX C TO LOCAL POLICY STATEMENT 3-07

UNDERTAKING REQUIRED FROM NON-REPORTING

OR CLOSELY HELD COMPANY

To: Superintendent of Brokers   or   Vancouver Stock Exchange
     #1100 - 865 Hornby Street   609 Granville Street
     Vancouver, B.C.   Vancouver, B.C.
     V6Z 2H4   V7Y 1H1

     (if the Issuer's shares   (if the Issuer's shares
     are not listed on the   are listed on the
     Vancouver Stock Exchange)   Vancouver Stock Exchange)

_____ (the "Company") undertakes, for the duration of the time that the Company   is   the   registered   owner   of   escrowed   shares   of _____ (the "Issuer"),

    (a)   to effect or permit transfer of ownership in the shares of the Company, or

    (b)   to allot and issue further shares of any class of shares of the Company

only upon receipt of the written consent of the Superintendent of Brokers, if the Issuer's shares are not listed on the Vancouver Stock Exchange (the "Exchange"), or the Exchange, if the Issuer's shares are listed on the Exchange.

Dated at _____ on _____ 19____.

The Corporate/Common Seal of   )
[Company] was affixed   )
in the presence of:)
)
_____   )
Authorized signatory   )   c/s
)
_____   )
Authorized signatory   )

LOCAL POLICY STATEMENT 3-12

RULES FOR PROCEEDINGS

TABLE OF CONTENTS

PART 1   IMPLEMENTATION

1.1   *Effective date* – This local policy statement comes into effect on February 1, 1990.

1.2   *Defined terms* – Terms defined in the Securities Act, S.B.C. 1985, c.83 (the "Act"), the Securities Regulation, B.C. Reg. 270/86 (the "Regulation") and the Interpretation Act, R.S.B.C. 1979, c. 206 and used in this local policy statement have the same meaning as in the Act, the Regulation and the Interpretation Act.

PART 2   APPLICATION

2.1   *Purpose* – This local policy statement sets out the rules that apply to proceedings before the Commission or the Superintendent. These rules include those contained in the Act and the Regulation and additional rules established by the Commission in this local policy statement.

2.2   *Proceedings before the Commission or Superintendent* – This local policy statement applies to proceedings before either the Commission or the Superintendent, although the majority of the references are to the Commission only. With respect to a hearing before the Superintendent, references to the Commission should be read as applying to the Superintendent, unless the context requires otherwise.

2.3   *Opportunity to be heard* – This local policy statement does not apply where the Act or the Regulation provides that a person has an opportunity to be heard before a decision is made by the Commission or the Superintendent (sections 21(3), 22(2), 31(4), 46(3), 48(4) and 55(4) of the Act and sections 4(8)(b), 18(2), 72.3(3), 87(1), 167.2(2), 167.10(4) and 190 of the Regulation).

PART 3   TYPES OF PROCEEDINGS

3.1   *Types of proceedings* – There are two types of proceedings before the Commission:

(a)   Hearings – In a hearing, the Commission exercises original jurisdiction on matters brought forward, generally by the Superintendent.

(b)   Hearings and Reviews – In a hearing and review, the Commission reviews a decision made at a subordinate level in the regulatory system.

3.2   *Mandatory hearings* – A hearing is required prior to

(a)   the Commission or the Superintendent suspending, cancelling or restricting the registration of a registrant under section 26(1) of the Act,

(b)   the Commission or the Superintendent making an enforcement order under section 144(1) of the Act,

(c)   the Commission ordering that a person pay an administrative penalty under section 144.1 of the Act, or

(d)   the Commission determining a question referred to it by the Superintendent under section 180 of the Regulation.

Where the Commission and the Superintendent have concurrent jurisdiction, hearings are generally held before the Commission.

3.3   *Optional hearings* – Except as set out in section 3.2, a hearing is not required to be held before a decision is made under the Act or the Regulation. However, the Commission may choose to hold a hearing before making such a decision where it considers that to do so would be in the public interest or would ensure procedural fairness.

3.4   *Hearings and reviews* – The Act provides for a hearing and review by the Commission in the following circumstances:

(a)   A person directly affected by a decision made by a member of the Commission, the Superintendent, the Vancouver Stock Exchange (the "Exchange") or the Pacific District of the Investment Dealers Association of Canada (the "IDA") may request a hearing and review of the decision (sections 15, 147 and 148 of the Act).

(b)   The Superintendent may request a hearing and review of certain decisions of the Exchange and the IDA (section 148(3) of the Act).

(c)   The Commission may, on its own motion, hold a hearing and review of any decision of a member of the Commission and certain decisions of the Superintendent, the Exchange and the IDA (sections 147(2) and 148(1) of the Act).

PART 4   HEARINGS

4.1   *Notice of hearing* – The Commission or the Superintendent will send a copy of a notice of hearing to each person who is a party to the hearing and to any person considered by the Commission to be directly affected by the hearing. A notice of hearing sets out the time, place and purpose of the hearing, including particulars of the relief requested and the matters of fact and allegations to be considered by the Commission.

Where a temporary order is issued under section 26(2), 144(2) or 144(3) of the Act, a notice of hearing will accompany the temporary order.

4.2   *Publication of notice of hearing* – Notices of hearing are generally published in the British Columbia Securities Commission Weekly Summary.

PART 5   HEARINGS AND REVIEWS

5.1   *Request for a hearing and review* – A person directly affected by a decision made by a member of the Commission, the Superintendent, the Exchange or the IDA may request a hearing and review of the decision under section 15, 147(3) or 148(1) of the Act by sending a notice to the Commission within 30 days after the mailing of the notice of the decision to the person. The 30 days allowed for sending a notice requesting a hearing and review is a statutory period that cannot be extended by the Commission.

Where the request is made under section 15 of the Act, the person must also send a copy of the notice to the Superintendent and the Exchange or the IDA.

5.2   *Fees* – A notice requesting a hearing and review must be accompanied by the fee prescribed under Item 27 of section 183(1) of the Regulation. Cheques must be payable to the "Minister of Finance".

5.3   *Form of request for a hearing and review* – A notice requesting a hearing and review must identify

(a)   the decision in respect of which the hearing and review is requested,

(b)   the manner in which the person is directly affected by the decision, and

(c)   the grounds for the request.

5.4   *Parties* – The parties to a hearing and review include

(a)   the person requesting the hearing and review,

(b)   the Superintendent,

(c)   the IDA, where its decision is under review,

(d)   the Exchange, where its decision is under review, and

(e)   each person considered by the Commission to be directly affected by the decision under review.

5.5   *Stay of decision* – Section 147(5) of the Act provides that the Commission may, on application or on its own motion, grant a stay of a decision until disposition of the hearing and review.

5.6   *Record for decision under review* – The record for a decision under review includes

(a)   the decision of a member of the Commission, the Superintendent, the Exchange or the IDA,

(b)   the transcript, if any, of oral evidence considered in making the decision, and

(c)   all records considered in making the decision.

5.7   *Sending record to Commission and parties* – Upon receipt of a notice requesting a hearing and review, the person whose decision is under review must send to the Commission four copies of the record for the decision under review, excluding any transcript, and send a copy to each party to the hearing and review.

5.8   *Transcript of oral evidence* – If oral evidence was recorded and considered in making the decision under review, the person requesting the hearing and review must obtain and send to the Commission four copies of the transcript of the oral evidence and send a copy to each other party to the hearing and review.

Where the Commission considers it appropriate, it may, on application or on its own motion, order that the transcript need not be obtained and sent to the Commission or any other party to the hearing and review.

5.9   *Statements of points* – Each party to a hearing and review must send to the Commission a statement of the points to be argued, setting out the facts and law to be relied on, as follows:

(a)   If a pre-hearing conference is held pursuant to Part 6 of this local policy statement, the statements of points should be sent following that conference.

(b)   Before the Commission will fix a date for the hearing and review, the party requesting the hearing and review must send to the Commission four copies of its statement of points and send a copy to each other party to the hearing and review.

(c)   At least three business days before the date of the hearing and review, each other party to the hearing and review must send to the Commission four copies of its statement of points and send a copy to every other party.

5.10   *Notice of hearing and review* – The Commission will fix a date for a hearing and review upon receipt of

(a)   the record for the decision under review, and

(b)   the statement of points by the party requesting the hearing and review.

The secretary to the Commission will give notice of the time, place and purpose of the hearing and review to each party to the hearing and review.

5.11   *Publication of notice of hearing and review* – Notices of hearing and review are generally published in the British Columbia Securities Commission Weekly Summary.

5.12   *Form of hearing* – Hearings and reviews are generally conducted in an appellate fashion. However, where appropriate, the Commission may proceed by way of a new hearing.

5.13   *Restrictions on oral evidence* – Except where the Commission proceeds by way of a new hearing, the Commission will generally not allow oral evidence to be presented at a hearing and review unless

(a)   there was no transcript of oral evidence recorded at the prior proceeding, or

(b)   there is new and compelling evidence that was not presented at the prior proceeding.

5.14   *Scope of decision* – On a hearing and review, the Commission may confirm or vary the decision under review or make another decision it considers proper.

In hearings and reviews of decisions of the Exchange, the Commission will generally confirm the decision of the Exchange unless

(a)   the Exchange has proceeded on some incorrect principle,

(b)   the Exchange has erred in law,

(c)   the Exchange has overlooked some material evidence, or

(d)   new and compelling evidence is presented to the Commission that was not presented to the Exchange.

If one of these conditions is established, the Commission will make a decision on the merits of the case or refer the matter back to the Exchange.

PART 6   PRE-HEARING CONFERENCE

6.1   *Held by Commission* – Pre-hearing conferences are held only in respect of proceedings before the Commission.

6.2   *Purpose* – The Commission may, on application or on its own motion, direct a member of the Commission to hold a pre-hearing conference for the purpose of clarifying and simplifying issues and otherwise facilitating or expediting the proceeding.

6.3   *Directives by member* – At the pre-hearing conference, a member of the Commission may, on application or on the member's own motion, direct a party to furnish any or all of the following:

(a)   an outline of its case or defence,

(b)   the law upon which it will rely,

(c)   the identity of the witnesses who will give evidence on its behalf, and

(d)   copies of or a list of records and things that it intends to present at the proceeding.

6.4   *Matters to be considered* – The following matters will be considered at a pre-hearing conference:

(a)   admissions of facts and of authenticity and contents of records and things,

(b)   the exchange of copies of records and things intended to be presented as evidence,

(c)   settlement of the issues, and

(d)   other matters that will promote a fair and expeditious proceeding.

6.5   *Agreements and recommendations* – After a pre-hearing conference, the member of the Commission will send to each of the parties a summary of the agreements reached and any recommendations the member considers necessary or advisable arising out of the matters discussed at the pre-hearing conference.

6.6   *Disqualification of member* – The member of the Commission who conducts a pre-hearing conference will not sit on the proceeding.

PART 7   SUMMONS

7.1   *Power of Commission* – Section 154.1 of the Act empowers the Commission, in accordance with section 128 of the Act, to summon and enforce the attendance of witnesses and to compel witnesses to give evidence and to produce records and things.

7.2   *Application for summons* – On application from a party to the proceeding, the Commission may summon witnesses in accordance with section 128 of the Act.   The Commission may refuse to issue a summons where the Commission considers that

(a)   the summons sought may be unreasonable, oppressive, excessive in scope or unduly burdensome, and

(b)   the applicant has failed to show the relevance and reasonable scope of the evidence sought.

7.3   *Form of summons* – Section 170 of the Regulation requires that a summons to a witness to appear before the Commission must be in the required form. The form specified for this purpose is Form 1.

7.4   *Personal service* – Section 169(1) of the Regulation requires that a summons be served personally on the witness summoned. The party requesting a summons is responsible for service of the summons.

7.5   *Fees and allowances* – Section 169(2) of the Regulation requires that a witness summoned must be paid the fees and allowances to which a witness summoned to attend before the Supreme Court of British Columbia is entitled.   The party requesting a summons must pay the fees and allowances to the witness.

7.6   *Affidavit of service* – Section 171 of the Regulation provides that the service of a summons, the payment or tender of fees and allowances to a witness summoned and the service of a notice on a witness may be proved by an affidavit in the required form. The form specified for this purpose is Form 2.

7.7   *Contempt* – Section 128 of the Act provides that the failure or refusal of a witness to comply with a summons makes the witness, on application to the Supreme Court of British Columbia, liable to be committed for contempt as if in breach of an order or judgment of the Supreme Court of British Columbia.

Local Policies

PART 8   EVIDENCE

8.1   *On oath* – Sections 128 and 154.1 of the Act provide that a witness may be compelled to

  (a)   give evidence at a proceeding on oath or in any other manner, and

  (b)   produce records and things in the custody or possession of the witness.

8.2   *Admission of evidence* – Section 154.1 of the Act provides that the Commission must receive all relevant evidence submitted by a person to whom notice has been given and may receive relevant evidence submitted by any person. The Commission is not bound by the rules of evidence.

8.3   *Sufficient copies of records* – A party submitting records at a proceeding must ensure that sufficient copies are made available to all parties, their counsel, the presiding members and the secretary and the general counsel to the Commission.

8.4   *Admissibility in evidence of certified statements* – Section 150 of the Act provides for the admissibility of certain records certified by the Commission or its staff.

8.5   *Recording evidence* – The Commission generally directs that a court reporter take down oral evidence received at proceedings.

PART 9   GENERAL PROCEDURAL MATTERS

9.1   *Consolidation* – Proceedings involving a common question of fact or law may be joined with respect to all or any of the matters in issue in the proceedings.

9.2   *Representation by counsel* – A person attending a proceeding or submitting evidence at a proceeding may be represented by counsel.

9.3   *Notice sent by counsel* – Counsel appearing in a proceeding must send to the Commission and to each party to the proceeding a written notice identifying the party that counsel represents and stating counsel's name, address and telephone and facsimile numbers, whereupon service of any records in connection with the proceeding may be made to counsel.

9.4   *Open to the public* – A proceeding will be open to the public and all records sent to the Commission in connection with the proceeding will be available for public inspection, except where the Commission considers that

  (a)   a public proceeding would be unduly prejudicial to a party or a witness, and

  (b)   it would not be contrary to the public interest to order that the public be excluded for all or part of the proceeding.

Records may be inspected during normal business hours of the Commission at the address set out in section 9.7.

9.5   *Adjournments* – The Commission may, on application or on its own motion, order that a proceeding be adjourned. A party applying for an adjournment should attempt to obtain the consent of all parties to the proceeding.

9.6   *Fees and charges* – Under section 154.2 of the Act, the Commission may order a person whose affairs are the subject of a proceeding to pay prescribed fees or charges for the costs of or related to the proceeding that are incurred by or on behalf of the Commission or the Superintendent including, without limitation,

  (a)   costs of matters preliminary to the proceeding,

  (b)   costs for time spent by the Commission or the Superintendent or the staff of either of them,

  (c)   fees paid to an expert or witness, and

  (d)   costs of legal services.

Item 33 of section 183(2) of the Regulation sets out the prescribed fees and charges for the costs of or related to a proceeding.

9.7 *Sending records* – Section 156 of the Act and section 179 of the Regulation set out the requirements to be followed in sending records. Records required to be sent to the Commission in connection with a proceeding must be addressed as follows:

> British Columbia
> Securities Commission
> 11th Floor
> 865 Hornby Street
> Vancouver, British Columbia
> V6Z 2H4
>
> *Attention: The Secretary*

The Commission's facsimile number is (604) 660-2688 and its telephone number is (604) 660-4800.

PART 10 DECISION

10.1 *Written reasons* – Where a decision made at a proceeding adversely affects the right of a person to trade in securities and the person requests written reasons, section 177(1) of the Regulation requires the Commission to issue written reasons for the decision.

10.2 *Notice of decision* – Section 177(2) of the Regulation requires the Commission to give notice of a decision and accompanying written reasons as soon as practicable to every person to whom notice of the proceeding was given and to every person who is, in the opinion of the Commission, directly affected by the decision.

10.3 *Publication of decision* – Decisions are generally published in the British Columbia Securities Commission Weekly Summary.

10.4 *Conditions* – Section 154 of the Act provides that the Commission may impose any conditions that it considers necessary in respect of any decision made by it.

10.5 *Discretion to revoke or vary decision* – The Commission may, where it considers it would not be prejudicial to the public interest, make an order under section 153 of the Act revoking in whole or in part or varying a decision of the Commission.

DATED at Vancouver, British Columbia, this 26th day of January 1990.

> Douglas M. Hyndman
> Chairman

LOCAL POLICY STATEMENT 3-13

POLICY GUIDELINES FOR A VENTURE CAPITAL ISSUER PLANNING TO MAKE A DISTRIBUTION

> This local policy statement reflects the status of the Small Business Venture Capital Act, S.B.C. 1985, c. 56, in February 1987. Since that time, that legislation has been amended on several occasions and, as such, the Commission may be flexible with respect to providing exemptions from some of the requirements set out herein. Further, this local policy statement contains inaccurate references to rescinded local policy statements. See NIN 88/7 "Venture capital issuers" and NIN 89/43 "Local Policy Statement 3-07".

1.0 IMPLEMENTATION

1.1 This Local Policy Statement has been revised solely to conform with the Securities Act S.B.C. 1985 c. 83 and Regulations thereto. Other than consequential amendments, there have been no changes of a substantive nature to this policy. It becomes effective with proclamation of the Securities Act on February 1, 1987.

2.0 TERMS OF REFERENCE

2.1 The prospectus of an investment issuer shall be prepared in accordance with Form 60 and the prospectus of a mutual fund issuer shall be prepared in accordance with Form 15. The Regulations define an "investment issuer", and the Act defines a "mutual fund". A venture capital issuer should use Form 60 insofar as that form is relevant.

2.2 An investment issuer is essentially an incorporated entity managing a portfolio of securities characterized by the continuing investing and reinvesting in securities of other companies. A closed end investment issuer differs from an open end issuer in that it does not continuously offer its shares and it has no obligation to redeem its shares.

2.3 A mutual fund issuer is typically an open end investment issuer. Shares of a mutual fund are usually offered continuously at net asset value plus a sales load. Shareholders may redeem on due notice, at net asset value, shares held in an open end fund. A mutual fund generally offers diversification and liquidity.

2.4 A venture capital issuer is a form of investment issuer having goals and practices which differ markedly from those of the typical investment issuer. The goal of the venture capital issuer is to provide equity financing for business enterprises. Appropriately, venture capital issuers participate in distributions of securities which may not be readily marketable, so that a venture capital issuer may well be "locked" into holding a security pending its growth and development. Usually a venture capital issuer prefers to hold a minority position, leaving management in control. In start-ups and other special situations, however, a venture capital issuer may be in control of the issuer until such time as certain performance standards are met, with control reverting to management upon some agreed-on formula.

2.5 The role played by a promoter in founding and organizing an enterprise differs from the role of a venture capital issuer in providing financing for a developing enterprise. However, where the principals of a developing enterprise lack promotional expertise and experience, it may be appropriate for the venture capital issuer to assist in the promotion of such a developing enterprise. Where a venture capital issuer participates as a promoter, the number of principals' shares acquired by it as a promoter should not exceed the number of "seed capital" shares subscribed for by it, and should not exceed 33 1/3% of the total number of principals' shares issued.

2.6 This Local Policy Statement is directed towards the venture capital issuer. Certain provisions of this Local Policy Statement may be applied to other forms of investment issuers where the Superintendent deems it appropriate.

2.7 *Definitions*

2.7.1 "Seed capital shares" means shares issued for cash prior to a public offering of securities by way of a prospectus.

2.7.2 "Principals' shares" means those shares issued for cash at a minimum price of $.01 per share to principals of an issuer, as prescribed in Local Policy Statement 3-07.

3.0 CAPITAL REQUIREMENTS

3.1 An issuer must have raised at least $600,000 on completion of its first offering of which at least $100,000 must have been raised by way of seed capital distributions.

4.0 INVESTMENT RESTRICTIONS ON A VENTURE CAPITAL ISSUER

4.1 *Restrictions to be disclosed in the issuer's prospectus*

An issuer will not be permitted to:

4.1.1 invest more than 25% of its funds from share subscriptions in any one entity

The Commission will allow an issuer to invest 100% of its funds from share subscriptions into any one entity where both the venture capital corporation and the entity become reporting issuers pursuant to the filing of a joint prospectus. See NIN 88/7 "Venture Capital Issuers" for additional requirements with respect to this issue.

4.1.2 invest by way of secondary trades in securities of reporting issuers in which no shares are held as a result of a subscription either of seed capital or to some other distribution

4.1.3 engage in the purchase and sale of commodities, commodity options, commodity futures contracts or commodity futures options

4.1.4 invest in the securities of an entity where

4.1.4.1 any of the shares of such entity are held by

4.1.4.1.1 an insider of the venture capital issuer

4.1.4.1.2 an associate or an affiliate of an insider of the venture capital issuer

4.1.4.1.3 a voting trust where the trust votes shares of the venture capital issuer, or

4.1.4.2 such entity, an associate or affiliate of such entity, a shareholder of such entity or an associate or affiliate of that shareholder has provided, directly or indirectly, by means of a loan guarantee or otherwise, any financial assistance to:

4.1.4.2.1 the venture capital issuer

4.1.4.2.2 an associate or affiliate of the venture capital issuer

4.1.4.2.3 an insider of the venture capital issuer

4.1.4.2.4 an associate or affiliate of an insider of the venture capital issuer.

4.1.5 engage in the business of underwriting securities or marketing to the public the securities of any other person or issuer.

4.2 *Transactions engaged in prior to the filing of an initial public offering*

This Section applies to an entity whose memorandum or articles of incorporation or by-laws or other form of governing rules were drawn up prior to the publication of this local policy, or to an entity formed under the laws of a jurisdiction other than British Columbia.

4.2.1 An issuer which prior to filing an initial public offering has engaged in a transaction described in Section 4.1.1, will be required to demonstrate that the positions will be rectified by the conclusion of the initial public offering on the prospectus.

4.2.2 An issuer which prior to filing an initial public offering has engaged in any of the transactions described in Sections 4.1.2, 4.1.3 and 4.1.4 above must rectify the position as a condition of having the prospectus receipted.

4.3 The Superintendent may, where he deems it not to be prejudicial to the public interest, waive any of the foregoing Section 4.0 restrictions and requirements where the issuer, at the time of filing a prospectus relating to the issuer's initial public offering of shares, discloses retained earnings equal to not less than 20% of the aggregate shareholders' equity.

5.0 GENERAL CONDITIONS APPLYING TO A VENTURE CAPITAL ISSUER

5.1 An issuer must comply with the following conditions:

5.1.1 the investment restrictions as set out in Section 4.1 of this policy must be set out in the Issuer's Articles

5.1.2   The issuer must be managed by individuals with backgrounds and experience adequate to demonstrate sufficient expertise in making investment decisions

5.1.3   The issuer must maintain enough capital in the form of cash to cover one year's estimated overhead expenses.

5.1.4   The issuer cannot borrow money if after such borrowing its debt obligations will exceed an amount equal to 50% of the total assets of the issuer.

Dated at Vancouver, B.C., this 1st day of February 1987.

Jill Bodkin
Chairman
B.C. Securities Commission

LOCAL POLICY STATEMENT 3-14

APPLICATIONS FOR
INSIDER REPORTING EXEMPTIONS

TABLE OF CONTENTS

PART 1   IMPLEMENTATION AND APPLICATION OF POLICY

1.1   *Effective date* – This local policy statement comes into effect on September 9, 1993.

1.2   *Jurisdiction* – The Commission and the Superintendent are each empowered to make orders under section 152.2(b) of the Regulation. Any reference in this local policy statement to the Commission shall also be deemed to be a reference to the Superintendent.

1.3   *Terms of Reference* – Section 1(1) of the Act includes as insiders of a reporting issuer the directors and senior officers of

(a)   the reporting issuer;

(b)   subsidiaries of the reporting issuer; and

(c)   corporations that are insiders of the reporting issuer.

As a result of the combined application of section 1(4) of the Act and paragraphs (b) and (c) of the definition of insider in section 1(1) of the Act, the directors and senior officers of the following issuers are also deemed to be insiders of the reporting issuer:

(a)   affiliates of the reporting issuer; and

(b)   affiliates of a non-control insider.

1.4   *Application of policy* – This local policy statement sets out guidelines for applications under section 152.2(b) of the Regulation requesting exemptions from the requirements of section 70 of the Act to file insider reports with respect to the securities of a reporting issuer, for the directors and senior officers of

(a)   any affiliate of the reporting issuer; and

(b)   any affiliate of a non-control insider of the reporting issuer.

PART 2   DEFINITIONS

2.1   *Defined terms* – In this Policy Statement,

"Act" means the Securities Act, S.B.C. 1985, c.83;

"major affiliate" means, in relation to a reporting issuer

(a)   a subsidiary of the reporting issuer that represents, on a consolidated basis together with its own subsidiaries, 10% or more of the consolidated assets or 10% or more of the consolidated sales or operating revenues of the reporting issuer;

(b)   a non-subsidiary affiliate of the reporting issuer that supplies to the reporting issuer or any of the reporting issuer's subsidiaries materials or services, the essential nature and scale of which are such that factors affecting that supply would, or would reasonably be expected to, have a significant effect on the market price or value of the securities of the reporting issuer; or

(c)   an affiliate of the reporting issuer that, either alone or in concert with

(i)   any other affiliate of the reporting issuer,

(ii)   any non-control insider of the reporting issuer, or

(iii)   any affiliate of any non-control insider of the reporting issuer;

controls the reporting issuer;

"major insider affiliate" means an affiliate of a non-control insider of a reporting issuer that

(a)   supplies to the reporting issuer or any of the reporting issuer's subsidiaries materials or services, the essential nature and scale of which are such that factors affecting that supply would, or would reasonably be expected to, have a significant effect on the market price or value of the securities of the reporting issuer; or

(b)   either alone or in concert with

(i)   any affiliate of the reporting issuer,

(ii)   any non-control insider of the reporting issuer, or

(iii)   any affiliate of any non-control insider of the reporting issuer

controls the reporting issuer;

"major individual insider" means a director or senior officer of an affiliate of a reporting issuer or an affiliate of any non-control insider of a reporting issuer that

(a)   is a director or senior officer of the reporting issuer;

(b)   receives, in the ordinary course, knowledge of material facts or material changes with respect to the reporting issuer prior to general disclosure of these facts or changes; or

(c)   has direct or indirect beneficial ownership of, or control or direction over, or a combination of that ownership of and control or direction over, securities of the reporting issuer extending to securities carrying more than 10% of the voting rights attached to all of the reporting issuer's outstanding voting securities;

"non-control insider" means any corporate insider of the reporting issuer that is not an affiliate of the reporting issuer;

Local Policies

"non-subsidiary affiliate" means an affiliate of a reporting issuer that is not a subsidiary of the reporting issuer; and

"Regulation" means the Securities Regulation, B.C. Reg. 270/86.

2.2 *Terms defined in legislation* – Terms defined in the Act, the Regulation and the Interpretation Act, R.S.B.C., 1979, c. 206, and used in this local policy statement have the same meaning as in the Act, the Regulation and the Interpretation Act.

PART 3   APPLICATION FOR EXEMPTION

3.1 *Scope of application* – An application may be made under this local policy statement for an order exempting the directors and senior officers of

(a)   the subsidiaries of a reporting issuer, as a group;

(b)   the non-subsidiary affiliates of a reporting issuer, as a group;

(c)   the affiliates of the reporting issuer, as a group; or

(d)   the affiliates of a non-control insider of a reporting issuer, as a group.

3.2 *Scope of order* – The Commission will generally issue an order exempting the directors and senior officers of

(a)   an affiliate of a reporting issuer, other than a major affiliate, and

(b)   an affiliate of a non-control insider of the reporting issuer, other than a major insider affiliate

from the insider reporting requirements of section of section 70 of the Act. Notwithstanding the foregoing, no director or senior officer of

(a)   an affiliate of a reporting issuer, and

(b)   an affiliate of a non-control insider of the reporting issuer

shall be exempt from the insider reporting requirements of section 70 of the Act if the director or senior officer is a major individual insider.

PART 4   PROCEDURE

4.1 *Addressee* – Applications under this local policy statement should be addressed to the Deputy Superintendent, Exemptions and Orders.

4.2 *Procedure* – The application should include:

(a)   particulars relevant to the type of order requested concerning the corporate structure of the reporting issuer, its affiliates and the affiliates of any of its non-control insiders, showing the relevant percentages of voting rights controlled by or of each by way of

(i) narrative description, and

(ii) organization chart;

(b)   a list relevant to the type of order requested of

(i) each affiliate of the reporting issuer that is a major affiliate, and

(ii) each affiliate of a non-control insider of the reporting issuer that is a major insider affiliate; and

(c)   an undertaking by the applicant to the Commission that, in the event an order is issued under section 152.2(b) of the Regulation, the applicant will

(i) maintain a continuous review of the directors and senior officers exempted by the order,

(ii) file promptly with the Information and Records branch of the Commission an amended list of each major affiliate and major insider affiliate, as the case may be, whenever a change to the list occurs, and

(iii) furnish, upon the request of the Commission any information reasonably necessary to determine whether any director or senior officer is exempted by the order.

PART 5   OTHER CIRCUMSTANCES

5.1   *General* – Part 3 should enable the Commission to deal with most of the applications contemplated under this local policy statement. The Commission however, is prepared to apply the general principles of this local policy statement in other circumstances. In these circumstances, applicants should include all relevant facts and arguments in their applications.

PART 6   EFFECT OF ORDER

6.1   *Effect of order* – Any order issued under section 152.2(b) of the Regulation pursuant to this local policy statement is an exemption only from the requirement to file insider reports concerning trading by the exempted insider in securities of the reporting issuer and does not exempt the exempted insider from:

(a)   compliance with section 68 of the Act (trading or informing where undisclosed change) and section 119 of the Act (liability in special relationship where material fact or change undisclosed);

(b)   any insider reporting requirement under section 70 of the Act that arises by reason of the exempted insider having some other relationship with the reporting issuer that is not exempted by the order; and

(c)   any other applicable provision of the Act or the Regulation.

DATED at Vancouver, British Columbia, on September 9, 1993.

Douglas M. Hyndman
Chairman

LOCAL POLICY STATEMENT 3-15
EXEMPT PURCHASER STATUS
TABLE OF CONTENTS

July 7, 1989

PART 1   IMPLEMENTATION

1.1   Local Policy Statement 3-15 dated February 1, 1987 is rescinded and the following substituted therefor, effective July 15, 1989.

1.2   The terms defined in the Securities Act, S.B.C. 1985, c.83 (the "Act") and the Securities Regulation, B.C. Reg. 270/86 (the "Regulation"), and used in this local policy statement have the same meaning as in the Act and the Regulation.

PART 2   APPLICATION

2.1   This local policy statement sets out guidelines for an application to the Superintendent of Brokers (the "Superintendent") for designation as an exempt purchaser.

2.2   Sections 31(2)(4) and 55(2)(3) of the Act provide exemptions from the registration and prospectus requirements contained in sections 20 and 42 of the Act in connection with a trade in securities where a person

(a)   is purchasing as principal,

(b)   is not an individual, and

(c)   is designated as an exempt purchaser in an order of the Superintendent made for the purpose of sections 31(2)(4) and 55(2)(3).

For the purposes of the exempt purchaser exemption, a person is deemed to purchase as principal when it makes purchases either for its own account or for managed accounts over which it has absolute discretion as to purchasing and selling, and in respect of which it receives no specific instructions from any person beneficially interested in such accounts, or from any other person.

2.3   The exempt purchaser exemption is intended to enable issuers to distribute securities on an exempt basis to persons who do not fall within the categories of purchasers contained in sections 31(2)(2) and 55(2)(1) of the Act, but who are able to make investment decisions on their own behalf and do not require the information contained in and the protection provided by a prospectus.

2.4   Under the exempt purchaser exemption, the issuer is not required to provide a disclosure document to the exempt purchaser and no minimum dollar amount or number of securities are required to be purchased. However, the securities are subject to a 12 month hold period pursuant to sections 133(2) and 134(2) of the Regulation.

PART 3   CRITERIA FOR DESIGNATION AS AN EXEMPT PURCHASER

3.1   All applicants for exempt purchaser status will be required to meet the requirements of this local policy statement, both in the case of an initial application and an application for renewal.

3.2   In order for an applicant to be designated as an exempt purchaser, the Superintendent must be satisfied that the applicant is a financial institution that carries on the business of investing in securities on its own behalf or on behalf of others on a discretionary basis.

3.3   For the purposes of paragraph 3.2, a financial institution includes a bank, trust company, credit union, insurer, mutual fund, pension fund or investment fund.

3.4   In certain instances, banks, trust companies, credit unions and insurers conduct their investment activities through subsidiaries. In these situations, application for exempt purchaser status may be made by the subsidiary, provided it is wholly owned by one or more financial institutions.

3.5   In the case of a mutual fund, pension fund or investment fund, application for exempt purchaser status may be made by the fund. Exempt purchaser status will not be granted to the fund manager.

PART 4   APPLICATION PROCEDURE

4.1   The application should be addressed as follows:

> Deputy Superintendent, Exemptions and Orders
> British Columbia Securities Commission
> 1100-865 Hornby Street
> Vancouver, B.C.
> V6Z 2H4

4.2   The following documents must be filed in support of an application for exempt purchaser status or renewal of exempt purchaser status:

(a)   a completed and signed Application for Exempt Purchaser Status (Form 11), in the form attached to this local policy statement;

(b)   an annual report relating to the applicant's most recently completed fiscal year, such report to include:

(i)   audited financial statements,

(ii)   a description of the applicant's business,

(iii)   a directors' report or management report on the business of the applicant, and

(iv)   a list of the applicant's senior officers or executives, detailing their current functions,

provided that where the applicant is a subsidiary of a financial institution, the annual report of the parent of the applicant should also be filed;

(c)   the application fee prescribed in section 183 of the Regulation by way of a cheque made payable to the "Minister of Finance"; and

(d)   a completed Fee Checklist in the prescribed form.

4.3 To avoid delay, an English translation of all documents required by paragraph 4.2 should accompany any documents that are not in English.

4.4 Where any of the documents required under paragraph 4.2 are not being submitted, a covering letter should describe the documents and explain why they are not being submitted.

4.5 Designation as an exempt purchaser remains in effect for 12 months. In order to maintain continuous designation as an exempt purchaser, exempt purchasers seeking to renew their status are encouraged to submit the documents referred to in paragraph 4.2 at least six weeks before the expiry date of their current designation.

DATED at Vancouver, British Columbia, this 7th day of July 1989.

Douglas M. Hyndman
Chairman

LOCAL POLICY STATEMENT 3-16

REGISTRATION FOR SECURITIES
AND INSURANCE

See the *Lutz* decision at s. 64(1) of the Regulations with respect to an attempt to expand the scope of dual registration.

PART 1   IMPLEMENTATION

1.1 *Effective date* - Interim Local Policy Statement 3-16 dated March 7, 1990 is hereby rescinded and the following substituted therefor, effective August 14, 1990.

1.2 *Terms defined in legislation* - Terms defined in the Securities Act, S.B.C. 1985, c. 83 (the "Act"), the Securities Regulation, B.C. Reg. 270/86 (the "Regulation") and the Interpretation Act, R.S.B.C. 1979, c. 206 and used in this local policy statement have the same meaning as in the Act, the Regulation and the Interpretation Act.

PART 2   APPLICATION

2.1 *Purpose* - This local policy statement sets out the conditions under which an individual may be registered as a salesman of a registered dealer under the Act while also licensed as an insurance agent or salesperson under the Insurance Act, R.S.B.C. 1979, c. 200 (or as an insurance agent or salesperson under its successor, the Financial Institutions Act, S.B.C. 1989, c. 47) (both Acts referred to together as the "FIA").

2.2 *Scope* - Section 64 of the Regulation states that an individual who is registered under the Act as a salesman of a registered dealer must be employed full time in that capacity unless, among other things, the individual holds a licence as an insurance agent under the FIA.

This policy only sets out the requirements of the British Columbia Securities Commission. Individuals who wish to be licensed under the FIA should refer to the FIA, the regulations under the FIA and the policies of the Superintendent of Financial Institutions and the Insurance Council of British Columbia.

PART 3   CONDITIONS FOR OBTAINING REGISTRATION

3.1   *Dealer's responsibility* - A dealer has primary responsibility for deciding whether to permit its salesmen to apply to be licensed under the FIA.

3.2   *Separate entity for insurance activities* - A dealer that permits its salesmen to apply to be licensed under the FIA must ensure that insurance activities are carried on separately from securities activities, not through the dealer registered under the Act. For example, a dealer can create a subsidiary through which its insurance activities are carried on or a salesman may enter into a contract directly with an insurer, in accordance with the licensing requirements of the FIA.

3.3   *Requirements for registration as salesman* - Where an individual is licensed under the FIA, the Superintendent of Brokers (the "Superintendent") will register that individual as a salesman of a registered dealer under the Act, provided that the individual applying for registration:

(a)   is employed by a dealer registered under the Act,

(b)   advises the dealer and the Superintendent of the nature of the licence held under the FIA,

(c)   delivers to the Superintendent a letter from the registered dealer employing the individual acknowledging the individual's registration under the Act and licensing under the FIA and not objecting to the dual registration,

(d)   delivers to the Superintendent a copy of a letter notifying the Insurance Council that the individual is applying for registration under the Securities Act, and

(e)   meets all requirements for registration set out in the Act, the Regulation and Local Policy Statement 3-22.

3.4   *Superintendent's requirements for individuals applying for licensing under FIA* - Where a salesman who is registered under the Act wishes to apply to the Insurance Council for a licence under the FIA, the salesman must

(a)   first obtain the written approval of the dealer employing the salesman,

(b)   at the time of making the application for the licence, file the dealer's approval with the Superintendent, and

(c)   advise the Superintendent upon receipt of the licence.

3.5   *Superintendent may impose conditions* - In order to address the potential conflicts of interest arising from registration under the Act and licensing under the FIA, the Superintendent may impose conditions, in addition to those set out in this local policy statement, at the time of granting registration under the Act or when notified that a salesman has applied for licensing under the FIA.

PART 4   CONDITIONS FOR MAINTAINING REGISTRATION

4.1   *General conditions* - In order for an individual who is licensed under the FIA to maintain registration as a salesman under the Act

(a)   the individual must comply with the conditions of registration in section 4.2, and

(b)   the dealer employing the individual must comply with the dealer's conditions in section 4.3.

4.2　*Salesman's conditions* - In order to maintain the registration under the Act, a salesman registered under the Act and licensed under the FIA must comply with the following conditions:

(a)　All letterhead, signs, business cards and other material used by the salesman in connection with a trade in securities must state prominently the name of the dealer that employs the salesman.

(b)　The salesman must represent himself as a salesman of the dealer when acting in connection with a trade in securities.

(c)　The salesman must ensure that all securities transactions involving the salesman are handled through the dealer and not through any other person.

(d)　The salesman must notify the dealer and the Superintendent, as soon as practicable, of any disciplinary action commenced against the salesman under the FIA.

(e)　The salesman must notify the dealer and the Superintendent, as soon as practicable, of any change in the status of a licence held by the salesman under the FIA.

4.3　*Dealer's conditions* - A dealer employing a salesman registered under the Act and licensed under the FIA must:

(a)　monitor the activities of the salesman as they apply to trading in securities and ensure that all activities of the salesman are in compliance with the requirements of the Act, the Regulation, the Commission's policy statements and the rules of any self-regulatory body or stock exchange of which the dealer is a member,

(b)　pay directly to the salesman and not to any other person all commissions earned by the salesman from securities transactions, and

(c)　implement systems designed to ensure that members of the public dealing with the salesman understand

(i)　that the salesman is employed by more than one entity,

(ii)　that they will be dealing with two different entities depending on the product purchased from the salesman,

(iii)　that the remuneration earned by the salesman from the sale of different products may vary,

(iv)　the procedure for the handling of confidential client information, including the intended use of information a client has permitted to be transferred to another person, and

(v)　the identity of the entity holding the client's funds.

PART 5　NOTICE

5.1　Where notice is required to be delivered to the Superintendent under this local policy statement and where responsibility for licensing a salesman has been delegated to a self-regulatory organization or stock exchange, a reference to the Superintendent should be read as a reference to the applicable self-regulatory organization or stock exchange.

DATED at Vancouver, British Columbia, this 14th day of August 1990.

Douglas M. Hyndman
Chairman

INTERIM LOCAL POLICY STATEMENT 3-17

REGISTRANT DUE DILIGENCE

TABLE OF CONTENTS

PART 1   *IMPLEMENTATION*

    1.1   *Effective date* - This local policy statement comes into effect on January 6, 1995.

    1.2   *Defined terms* - Terms defined in the Securities Act, S.B.C. 1985, c. 83 (the **"Act"**), the Securities Regulation, B.C. Reg. 270/86 (the **"Regulation"**) and the Interpretation Act, R.S.B.C. 1979, c. 206 and used in this local policy statement have the same meaning as in the **Act**, the **Regulation** and the Interpretation Act. Other terms defined in this local policy statement are capitalized and in bold.

    1.3   *Issuers listed on the Exchange* - Where an issuer has obtained a listing of its securities on the Vancouver Stock Exchange (the **"Exchange"**), any reference in this local policy statement to the Superintendent, other than the reference in sections ? and ?, should be read as a reference to the **Exchange**.

PART 2   *APPLICATION OF POLICY*

2.1   *Distribution by junior issuers* - This local policy statement applies to distributions by prospectus or statement of material facts (**"Offering Document"**), where the issuer, whether or not listed on the **Exchange**, does not meet the initial minimum listing requirements for the senior board of the **Exchange**.

2.2   *Rationale* - An underwriter plays an important role in protecting the public interest and the integrity of the local capital market.   In view of the importance of this role, each underwriter, which signs a certificate in an **Offering Document** for a distribution to which this local policy statement applies (a **"Junior Issuer Underwriter"**), must undertake a due diligence process and prepare the due diligence report described in Part 5 (the **"Due Diligence Report"**).

2.3   *Junior Issuer Underwriter group* - Where there is more than one **Junior Issuer Underwriter**, each **Junior Issuer Underwriter** must prepare a **Due Diligence Report**.   Where required under Part 6, only one assessment and specialist's report need be obtained to support the **Due Diligence Reports**.

PART 3   *DUE DILIGENCE PROCESS*

3.1   *Due diligence* - One defence available to an underwriter against potential liability for misrepresentation in an **Offering Document** is that the underwriter has conducted reasonable investigations to provide reasonable grounds for belief that there is no misrepresentation in the **Offering Document**.   This defence is commonly known as due diligence and the reasonable investigations as the due diligence process.

3.2   *Importance of underwriter's due diligence process* - The due diligence process should provide the underwriter with a thorough understanding of the business of the issuer and the risks associated with the issuer's business.   The understanding gained from this process puts the underwriter in a better position to decide whether to proceed with a distribution and to sign the underwriter's certificate in the **Offering Document**.

3.3   *Due diligence process* - The due diligence process is not a mechanical process. It must be tailored to the particular issuer and distribution.   The nature and extent of the due diligence review performed by an underwriter will vary depending on a number of factors, including

(a)   the stage of development of the business of the issuer,

(b)   the stage of development of the issuer's product, service or technology, and

(c)   where applicable, the stated business objectives of the issuer contained in the **Offering Document**.

PART 4   *REQUIREMENT FOR DUE DILIGENCE REPORT*

4.1   *Undertaking with final Offering Document* - In accordance with section 45(1) of the **Act**, the Superintendent requires a **Junior Issuer Underwriter** to file with the final **Offering Document** an undertaking addressed to the Superintendent to file the certificate and undertaking referred to in section ? by the earlier of the offering date or 10 days after the date of the final **Offering Document**.

4.2   *Notarization of Due Diligence Report* - The **Due Diligence Report** must be notarized as at the date no earlier than the date of the certificate and undertaking referred to in section ?.

4.3   *Filing of certificate and undertaking* - Within the time period specified in section ?, the **Junior Issuer Underwriter** must file a certificate and undertaking addressed to the Superintendent.   The certificate and undertaking must state that

(a)   the **Junior Issuer Underwriter** has prepared and executed the **Due Diligence Report**,

(b)   the **Due Diligence Report** has been notarized, and

    (c)   the **Junior Issuer Underwriter** undertakes to file the notarized copy of the **Due Diligence Report** when requested by the Superintendent.

4.4   *Retention of Due Diligence Report* - The **Junior Issuer Underwriter** must retain the notarized copy of the **Due Diligence Report** and all supporting documentation for a period of six years after the distribution contemplated by the **Offering Document**.

4.5   *Superintendent's request for Due Diligence Report* - The Superintendent may require the **Junior Issuer Underwriter** to produce the notarized copy of the **Due Diligence Report** either in the context of an investigation or the renewal of an underwriter's registration as an underwriter under the **Act**.

PART 5   *CONTENT OF DUE DILIGENCE REPORT*

5.1   *Due diligence procedures* - The **Due Diligence Report** must reflect the due diligence process undertaken by the **Junior Issuer Underwriter** up to the date of the report. At a minimum, the **Due Diligence Report** must identify the individual(s) who participated in the due diligence process and describe the procedures performed to complete the process.

5.2   *Consideration of assessment and specialist's reports* - Where an assessment report is required to be obtained under Part 6, the **Due Diligence Report** must state that the **Junior Issuer Underwriter** has fully considered the findings of the consultant and, where applicable, the specialist contained in their report(s).

5.3   *Reasons to sponsor* - The **Due Diligence Report** must include a brief description of the reasons why the **Junior Issuer Underwriter** considers that it is appropriate to proceed with the distribution.

5.4   *Signature of Due Diligence Report* - The **Due Diligence Report** must be signed by a director of the **Junior Issuer Underwriter**.

PART 6   *REQUIREMENT FOR ASSESSMENT OR SPECIALISTS REPORT*

6.1   *Requirement for assessment report* - Each distribution requires a unique due diligence process. However, for certain junior issuers, the **Junior Issuer Underwriter** must retain an independent qualified consultant to carry out certain minimum review procedures and provide an assessment report to the **Junior Issuer Underwriter** in support of its **Due Diligence Report**.

An assessment report is required where an issuer making a distribution to which this policy applies, other than a natural resource issuer or an issuer subject to National Policy Statement No. 33 - "Financing of Film Productions",

    (a)   has been in business for less than three financial years,

    (b)   has been in business for three or more financial years but has not had net income after income taxes in each of its last two financial years, calculated by reference to its audited financial statements, or

    (c)   is raising funds to develop or intends to acquire, directly or indirectly, a new business, product or service that is unrelated to the issuer's existing business operations and that management anticipates will be a material part of its future business operations.

The circumstances described above are intended to serve as a general guide. The Superintendent may require any **Junior Issuer Underwriter** to obtain an assessment report, particularly where the issuer or the business it is acquiring has had insignificant cash sales or net income.

Notwithstanding paragraph (c), the **Junior Issuer Underwriter** will generally not be required to obtain an assessment report where the issuer is acquiring a business that has been in existence for three or more financial years and has had net income after income taxes in each of its last two financial years.

6.2 *Waiver of requirement to obtain an assessment report* - In exceptional circumstances, the Superintendent may waive the requirement for the **Junior Issuer Underwriter** to obtain an assessment report and file the certificates required under Part 9. For example, the Superintendent would consider granting a waiver where

(a) a **Junior Issuer Underwriter** had previously obtained an assessment report relating to the issuer's business and filed the certificates required under Part 9, or where the issuer has previously filed a technical report under prior Local Policy Statement 3-04 relating to the issuer's business, and the issuer has accomplished the business objectives contemplated by the prior assessment report or technical report, or

(b) the issuer is an investment issuer and will be complying with Local Policy Statement 3-13, "Policy Guidelines for a Venture Capital Issuer Planning to Make a Distribution".

6.3 *Information required with waiver request* - A **Junior Issuer Underwriter** requesting a waiver must provide the Superintendent with the following information and documentation prior to the filing of a preliminary **Offering Document**:

(a) reasons for the requested waiver,

(b) financial statements of the issuer and any business to be acquired

(i) for each of the last three financial years, with at least the most recent financial year being audited, and

(ii) where the last audited financial year is not within 90 days of the date of the request for the waiver, unaudited interim financial statements made up to a date that is within 90 days of the date of the request for the waiver or, where the issuer is a reporting issuer, to the date of the most recent financial statements that were required to be filed with the Superintendent,

(c) a description of the issuer's current business operations and its business objectives for the next 12 month period,

(d) where a **Junior Issuer Underwriter** had previously obtained an assessment report relating to the issuer's business and filed the certificates required under Part 9, or where the issuer has previously filed a technical report under prior Local Policy Statement 3-04 relating to the issuer's business, a description of the issuer's achievement of the business objectives that were contemplated by the prior assessment report or technical report, and

(e) a description of the proposed use of proceeds.

6.4 *Requirement for specialist's report* - The **Junior Issuer Underwriter** must retain a specialist to provide it with a report in support of its **Due Diligence Report** relating to the feasibility of the issuer's technology where

(a) the **Junior Issuer Underwriter** is required to obtain an assessment report,

(b) the issuer has an unproven or unique technology that is critical to its business, and

(c) the **Junior Issuer Underwriter** considers that its consultant or any specialist retained by its consultant does not have the necessary technical expertise.

6.5 *Filing of consultant's and specialist's certificates* - In accordance with section 45(1) of the **Act**, the Superintendent requires a **Junior Issuer Underwriter** that is required to obtain an assessment report or a specialist's report under this Part to file with the preliminary **Offering Document** the signed certificate(s) from the consultant and any specialist in the form required under Part 9.

PART 7   *ASSESSMENT REPORT*

7.1   *Content of assessment report* - Where the **Junior Issuer Underwriter** is required to obtain an assessment report, the assessment report must contain, at a minimum, the consultant's findings relating to the issuer's management, product or service or technology, operations, market, marketing plans or strategies and financial plan. Where the **Junior Issuer Underwriter** has retained a specialist to prepare a specialist's report in accordance with section 6.4, the consultant's findings may be qualified to state that the consultant has not analyzed the feasibility of the issuer's technology.

7.2   *Required review procedures* - The consultant must use professional judgment to determine what procedures are appropriate in the circumstances to be able to provide the findings contained in an assessment report to the **Junior Issuer Underwriter**. Every consultant who prepares an assessment report must perform at least the following procedures:

(a)   analyze and discuss with management the issuer's business plan relating to the issuer's principal business,

(b)   analyze the issuer's financial statements,

(c)   investigate the relevant background, including confirmation of educational credentials, of those of the directors, officers, employees and contractors of the issuer whose expertise is critical to the issuer in providing it with a reasonable opportunity to achieve its stated business objectives,

(d)   analyze the stage of development of the issuer's product, service or technology,

(e)   where the **Junior Issuer Underwriter** has not obtained a specialist's report, analyze the feasibility of any technology that is critical to the issuer's business,

(f)   inspect the issuer's material assets, whether owned or leased, including, but not limited to, property, plant, equipment and inventory used, or to be used, in connection with the issuer attempting to achieve its stated business objectives,

(g)   if applicable, analyze the issuer's production methods,

(h)   if applicable, investigate a third party's ability to supply a product, service or technology, where the third party supplies to the issuer a unique product, service or technology that is not readily available from other sources at the cost to be paid by the issuer,

(i)   investigate the issuer's relationships with its existing or proposed principal suppliers, customers and creditors to the extent appropriate in the circumstances,

(j)   analyze the business aspects of all material contracts relating to the business of the issuer,

(k)   if applicable, analyze the business aspects of all legal proceedings, including proceedings known to be contemplated, involving the issuer,

(l)   analyze the business aspects of any legislation or publicly available proposed legislation, such as industry or environmental regulations or controls on ownership or profit repatriation, or economic or political conditions that may, in the consultant's professional judgement, materially affect the issuer's operations,

(m)   investigate the industry and target markets in which the issuer's business operates or management anticipates it will operate, and

(n)   analyze the issuer's financial plan.

The consultant's review procedures can only be limited by

(i)   an arm's length third party, or

(ii)   the issuer, where the investigation will likely have a detrimental effect on the issuer's business relationship with the arm's length third party, and only with respect to the procedures in (h) or (i) above.

7.3 *Factors underlying findings* - In order for the consultant to provide their findings in the assessment report, the consultant must consider all factors relevant to the issuer's business. These factors should include at least the following:

(a) *Management* - education; business experience; expertise and experience in the issuer's industry; ability to commit sufficient time to the issuer.

(b) *Product, service or technology* - whether the issuer's product or service performs in the manner stated by management, except where the **Junior Issuer Underwriter** has obtained a specialist's report; the stage of development of the issuer's product, service or technology and of any applicable documentation; proprietary interests and licensing arrangements; governmental regulations; environmental concerns; if the issuer is required to conduct research and development in order to achieve its stated business objectives; actual or proposed research and development programs including costs, technical feasibility, economic viability, and steps required to achieve commercial production.

(c) *Operations* - if the issuer is currently marketing its product or service or will be marketing its product or service in order to achieve its stated business objectives; actual or proposed method of production; historical levels of production; dependence on subcontractors; location and condition of existing plant, property and equipment; terms and conditions of mortgages or leases; availability of skilled personnel; sources and availability of raw materials, component parts and finished products, including dependence on a limited number of suppliers or customers; existing and planned capacity; warranties and quality control; production costs; production cycles; any proposed material changes to any of the above.

(d) *Market* - market segment and specific geographical area in which the issuer is selling or is expecting to sell its product, service or technology; trends within that market segment or specific geographical area; competition within that market segment or specific geographical area, including principal competitors and their relative size and aggregate market share, principal aspects of competition and significant potential sources of competition; market share or market acceptance of the issuer's product, service or technology; likelihood of product or technological obsolescence; market controls or regulation; seasonal variations.

(e) *Marketing plans and strategies* - if the issuer is currently marketing its product or service or will be marketing its product or service in order to achieve its stated business objectives; distribution channels; actual or proposed marketing programs; pricing policy; after-sales service, maintenance or warranties.

(f) *Financial plan* - historical and anticipated costs related to research and development, production, distribution and marketing of the issuer's product, service or technology; historical and anticipated general and administrative costs, including costs required to maintain a reporting issuer in good standing with the Commission and the **Exchange**; payment terms under agreements or other arrangements with suppliers; potential revenues and payment terms under agreements or other arrangements with principal customers; costs of financing; royalty obligations; long term liabilities; working capital requirements; availability of credit and other financing alternatives.

PART 8 *QUALIFICATIONS OF CONSULTANT AND SPECIALIST*

8.1 *Qualifications of consultant* - The **Junior Issuer Underwriter** is responsible for determining that the consultant possesses the business experience and education appropriate in the circumstances to enable the consultant to sign the consultant's certificate required by section 9.1.

8.2 *Qualifications of the specialist* - The **Junior Issuer Underwriter** is responsible for determining that the specialist has the appropriate qualifications to assess the feasibility of the technology.

8.3   *Conflict of interest* - The **Junior Issuer Underwriter** must satisfy itself that the consultant and any specialist do not have a relationship with the issuer or **Junior Issuer Underwriter** that, under the circumstances, may lead a reasonable person to conclude that the consultant's or specialist's independence or objectivity could be compromised. Regardless of the conclusion reached above, the consultant and specialist must not own any direct, indirect or contingent interest in any of the securities or assets of the issuer or of any associate or affiliate of the issuer.

PART 9   *CERTIFICATES*

9.1   *Consultant's certificate* - Where the **Junior Issuer Underwriter** is required to obtain an assessment report, each individual, except as provided for in section ?, who has both prepared any part of the report and is responsible for any of the findings expressed in the report, must sign a separate certificate stating

   (a)   the individual's name, address and occupation,

   (b)   the individual's relevant educational background, including areas of principal studies,

   (c)   the individual's relevant employment history, including a description as to how it relates to the material aspects of the principal business of the issuer,

   (d)   the individual's consulting experience in the areas of corporate planning and financial analysis,

   (e)   the individual's membership in any professional organization,

   (f)   that the individual has carried out all of the review procedures required by section ? of Local Policy Statement 3-17 and considered all of the factors in section ? of Local Policy Statement 3-17 that relate to the findings that are the responsibility of the individual,

   (g)   the period during which the review procedures were carried out,

   (h)   that the individual has no conflicts of interest as the result of a relationship with the issuer or the **Junior Issuer Underwriter**, and

   (i)   that the individual does not own any direct, indirect or contingent interest in any of the securities or assets of the issuer or of any associate or affiliate of the issuer.

Where the **Junior Issuer Underwriter** has retained a specialist, the information required by item (f) of the consultant's certificate may state that the consultant has not analyzed the feasibility of the issuer's technology.

Where a consultant is not able to carry out a procedure as provided for in section ?, the information required by item (f) of the consultant's certificate may state to what extent and the reasons that the procedures were not carried out.

9.2   *Signature where consultant not an individual* - Where the consultant is not an individual, the consultant's certificate may be signed by the consultant rather than by the individual(s) identified in the certificate.

9.3   *Specialist's certificate* - Where a **Junior Issuer Underwriter** has retained a specialist, the specialist must sign a certificate that includes the information required by paragraphs (a), (b), (c), (e), (g), (h) and (i) of section 9.1 and states what procedures were conducted to arrive at the specialist's findings regarding the feasibility of the issuer's technology.

DATED at Vancouver, British Columbia, on October 5, 1994.

Douglas M. Hyndman
Chair

LOCAL POLICY STATEMENT 3-19

VANCOUVER STOCK EXCHANGE LISTINGS

1.0   IMPLEMENTATION

    1.1   This Local Policy Statement has been revised solely to conform with the Securities Act, S.B.C. 1985, c. 83 and Regulations thereto. Other than consequential amendments, there have been no changes of a substantive nature to this policy. It becomes effective with proclamation of the Securities Act on February 1, 1987.

2.0   TERMS OF REFERENCE

    2.1   This Local Policy Statement is concerned chiefly with an issuer applying for a first listing on the Vancouver Stock Exchange. Where an applicant seeks a listing subsequent to the delisting of a security, reference should be made to this Local Policy Statement and to Local Policy Statement 3-35.

    2.2   Enquiries concerning detailed requirements for listing should be directed to the Vancouver Stock Exchange.

3.0   BACKGROUND

    3.1   Financial centres outside of British Columbia, as part of their investment community, trade securities of junior issuers "over the counter". Trading in junior issues in the British Columbia jurisdiction has taken different forms in the past few years, as outlined in Section 3.2, but the thrust has been to make a "Development Company" listing on the Vancouver Stock Exchange relatively easy, and thus forestall any recurrence of a significant "over the counter" market in British Columbia. The Commission is satisfied that the best way to foster an efficient capital market which will protect the interests of the public is to ensure that all public issues of securities are traded in full view of the public with factual quotation services.

    3.2   "Over the counter" trading of equity securities of junior issuers was a prominent feature of the risk capital market in British Columbia prior to 1967. In 1967, the Interim Section of the Vancouver Stock Exchange was inaugurated to encourage "over the counter" issues to achieve listed status and thus permit the phasing out of "over the counter" markets. In 1972, the Broker-Dealers Association undertook responsibility for supervising the trading of mining and oil issues as well as the responsibility for quoting "over the counter" industrial issues, etc. After the Broker-Dealers Association ceased to function in mid-1974, "over the counter" issues were encouraged to list on a newly activated Vancouver Curb Exchange. The listing requirements of the Vancouver Curb Exchange were designed to facilitate the listing of equity securities of junior issuers. In January, 1981, the listing system of the Vancouver Stock Exchange was reorganized into three sections: Resource, Industrial and Development. All the listings on the Vancouver Curb Exchange were then transferred to the Development Section of the Vancouver Stock Exchange, with no changes being made in listing requirements. On April 29, 1985, the Vancouver Stock Exchange consolidated the three separate listing sections into one alphabetical listing of all issues. Issues formerly listed on the V.S.E. Development Section were designated "Development Company" issues, while issues formerly listed on the Industrial Section or the Resource Section were designated "Company other than a Development Company" issues. This consolidation did not alter the prevailing listing and filing requirements for the various issuers.

    3.3   Formal written consent of the Commission is no longer required by an issuer seeking to apply for a listing on the Vancouver Stock Exchange, but the Commission retains the right, pursuant to Section 14 of the Act, to prohibit any issuer from listing a security on the Exchange. All issuers seeking a listing on the Vancouver Stock Exchange must accordingly comply with the relevant conditions set out in Section 4.0 hereunder.

4.0   CONDITIONS

An issuer filing material with the Superintendent in compliance with the provisions of this Section does not require an acknowledgement from the Superintendent in order to proceed with the listing. The Superintendent will notify the

Local
Policies

issuer and the Vancouver Stock Exchange within seven working days of the receipt of the material where he considers remedial measures are required.

4.1   *Receipt Issued for a Prospectus Contemplating a Distribution Under V.S.E. Rule B.5.00*

Where the Superintendent has issued a receipt for a prospectus contemplating an offering under Rule B.5.00 (the "Initial Distribution Rule") of the Vancouver Stock Exchange, the issuer need make no additional filing with the Superintendent prior to proceeding with a listing.

4.2   *Receipt Issued for a Prospectus not Contemplating the V.S.E. Initial Distribution System*

4.2.1   Where within twelve months of the date on which a prospectus receipted by the Superintendent was certified by directors and promoters an issuer seeks a listing on the Vancouver Stock Exchange, a copy of such application for listing shall be filed with the Superintendent contemporaneously with the filing with the Vancouver Stock Exchange.

4.2.2   Where the period between the date on which a prospectus receipted by the Superintendent was certified by directors and promoters and the date of application for a V.S.E. listing exceeds twelve months, an issuer seeking a listing on the Vancouver Stock Exchange shall file the following with the Superintendent contemporaneously with the filing with the Vancouver Stock Exchange.

4.2.2.1   Copy of application for V.S.E. listing

4.2.2.2   An affirmation of the following:

4.2.2.2.1   that a Form 4 has been filed by each current or proposed director who has not already submitted such a form within a 3-year period preceding the date of application for listing

4.2.2.2.2   that Forms 36 and 37 have been filed up to date by each current or proposed director

4.2.2.2.3   that the issuer is in good standing with the Registrar of Companies in British Columbia or a similar authority in the relevant jurisdiction

4.2.2.2.4   that the issuer is up-to-date with any filings which may be required by legislation.

4.3   *Receipt for Prospectus Issued by Another Jurisdiction*

Where the applicant for a V.S.E. listing has not had a receipt issued by the Superintendent for a prospectus, the following shall be filed with the Superintendent contemporaneously with the filing with the Vancouver Stock Exchange:

4.3.1   Copy of application for V.S.E. listing

4.3.2   Copy of the most recent annual audited financial statements distributed to shareholders, and if a set of interim financial statements has subsequently been distributed, a copy of such interim financial statements as well.

4.3.3   An affirmation of the following:

4.3.3.1   that a Form 4 has been filed by each current or proposed director who has not already submitted such a form within a 3-year period preceding the date of application for listing

4.3.3.2   that Forms 36 and 37 have been filed up-to-date by each current or proposed director

4.3.3.3   that the issuer is in good standing with the Registrar of Companies in British Columbia or a similar authority in the relevant jurisdiction

4.3.4   Copy of the most recent prospectus receipted in a securities juris-diction other than British Columbia.

4.3.5   In the event the issuer has not made a distribution by way of prospectus in any securities jurisdiction, an explanation or descrip-tion of the means by which a distribution complying with V.S.E. listing rules was achieved.

5.0   PROHIBITION OF LISTING

The Superintendent will, pursuant to Section 14 of the Act, retain the right to prohibit any issuer from listing a security on the Vancouver Stock Exchange and will, without limiting the generality of the foregoing, prohibit a listing when any of the following conditions obtain:

5.1   The issuer is engaged in a distribution under a prospectus other than a distribution of outstanding brokers warrants or options.

5.2   The issuer is not in full compliance with the Company Act and the Act.

5.3   A company seeking a listing after being dead or dormant has failed to seek reinstatement in accordance with Local Policy 3-35.

5.4   The issuer does not appear to comply with the guidelines set out in the Listing Rules and Listing Policies of the Vancouver Stock Exchange.

5.5   The issuer has not made a distribution to the public by way of prospectus in any securities jurisdiction and fails to satisfy the Superintendent that:

5.5.1   the existing distribution of shares, and

5.5.2   the information on the business and affairs of the issuer available to the public

will suffice to develop an efficient market for the issuer's shares.

5.6   The issuer, subsequent to the conclusion of a distribution to the public, has incurred or initiated any of the following changes in its affairs without prior discussion with the office of the Superintendent in accordance with Uniform Policy No. 2-12:

5.6.1   Actual or proposed changes in the control of the issuer;

5.6.2   Actual or proposed acquisition or disposition of material assets;

5.6.3   Proposed take-overs, mergers, consolidations, amalgamations or re-organizations; or

5.6.4   Proposed changes in capital structure including conversions, stock consolidations, stock splits or stock dividends.

DATED at Vancouver, B.C., this 1st day of February, 1987.

Jill Bodkin
Chairman
B.C. Securities Commission

LOCAL POLICY STATEMENT 3-21

SHARE AND UNIT OFFERINGS OF UNLISTED ISSUERS AND OPTIONS AND WARRANTS AVAILABLE TO REGISTRANTS PARTICIPATING IN SUCH OFFERINGS

This local policy statement contains inaccurate references to rescinded local policy statements. See NIN 89/43 "Local Policy Statement 3-07".

1.0   IMPLEMENTATION

1.1   This Local Policy Statement has been revised solely to conform with the Securities Act S.B.C. 1985 c. 83 and Regulations thereto. Other than consequential amendments, there have been no changes of a substantive nature to this policy. It becomes effective with proclamation of the Act on February 1, 1987.

2.0 CONTENTS OF THIS POLICY

2.1 This Local Policy Statement, except where the context clearly indicates otherwise, applies to prospectus offerings of unlisted issuers (including issuers applying for a conditional listing with the Vancouver Stock Exchange under Exchange Rule B.5.01.2). For issuers already listed on a stock exchange, the rules, regulations and policies of such exchange will apply to underwritings, agency offerings, options, warrants, etc. Issuers planning rights offerings should refer to Local Policy Statement 3-05. Reference should also be made to Local Policy Statement 3-08 pronouncements on minimum prices for share issuances.

2.2 *Table of Contents*

3.0 GENERAL CONDITIONS

3.1 *Minimum price*

3.1.1 on an issuer's first prospectus offering to the public, shares shall be priced to yield not less than 30 cents net to the treasury

3.1.2 a unit comprising one share plus warrant(s) shall not be offered to the public at less than 40 cents. If a unit comprises more than one share the unit price shall not be less than the product of 40 cents times the number of shares included in the unit.

3.2 *Minimum Number of Shares or Units to be Offered*

A share or unit offering shall be for not less than 250,000 shares or units as the case may be. Any unit offering must contain not less than 300,000 warrants.

3.3 *Discounts and Commissions permitted to Underwriters and Agents*

    3.3.1 The discount to the underwriter on sales of an issuer's underwritten shares shall not exceed

        3.3.1.1 15% when the price to the public is less than or equal to $1.00 per share

        3.3.1.2 10% when the price to the public is greater than $1.00 per share

    3.3.2 The maximum commission to the agent participating in the distribution of an issuer's shares or units shall be as follows:

        3.3.2.1 15% of the gross proceeds derived from sales where the share or unit price is less than or equal to $1.00 per share or unit

        3.3.2.2 10% of the gross proceeds where the share or unit price is greater than $1.00

3.4 *Minimum Net Proceeds to Treasury from an Offering*

The minimum net proceeds to the issuer's treasury from an offering shall be the greater of:

    3.4.1 seventy-five thousand dollars ($75,000), OR

    3.4.2 one hundred seventy-five thousand dollars ($175,000) less the net cash proceeds derived from the issuance of shares for cash prior to the initial public offering

3.5 *Distribution Lists*

Distribution lists must be filed with the Superintendent upon completion of the sale of the offered or underwritten shares or units.

3.6 *Calls on Stock*

    3.6.1 When a registered dealer participating in a securities offering assumes a particular risk through a firm underwriting or a guaranteed agency offering (see Section 6.1 for a discussion on the difference between a firm underwriting and a guaranteed agency offering), consideration in addition to discounts or commissions normally allowed may be granted to the registrant by the issuer in the form of a "call on stock"

    3.6.2 A call on stock has historically been referred to as an "option" in the case of an underwriting, and a "non-transferable warrant" in the case of a guaranteed agency offering. The terms under which the call may be granted differ for the two types of offering. (See Section 4.2 for calls granted on underwritings and Sections 7.1 and 8.2 for calls granted on guaranteed agency offerings). For the sake of consistency it is preferable to refer to a call on stock as an "option" in the case of an underwriting, and a "non-transferable warrant" in the case of a guaranteed agency offering, but compliance with the terms of the call applicable for the offering rather than with nomenclature is the essential feature.

    3.6.3 The following concordance between the rules of the Superintendent and the rules of the Vancouver Stock Exchange on registrants' calls on stock may be of assistance.

Local
Policies

L.P. 3-21 Section	V.S.E. Rule
3.7	B.5.22.2
	B.5.29.2
	B.38
4.2	B.5.37
7.1	B.5.29.1
8.2	B.5.22.1

3.7   *Greenshoe Option*

3.7.1   A greenshoe option is an option which affords an underwriter or agent an option, warrant or conversion right which may be exercised at the conclusion of a distribution to provide additional units of a security to the market where the offering has been over-subscribed.

3.7.2   Where appropriate disclosure is made in the prospectus of an issuer seeking to make a first distribution to the public, a greenshoe option may be granted to the underwriter(s) or agent(s) participating in an underwriting or a fixed price agency offering, subject to the following conditions:

3.7.2.1   the option must be limited to the lesser of 15% of the number of shares involved in the public offering or the actual number of shares subscribed for by way of an over-subscription during the distribution.

3.7.2.2   a determination of the number of shares subject to greenshoe option must be made as of the date of the conclusion of the distribution, save for an initial distribution made under V.S.E. Rule B.5.00 (see also Local Policy Statement 3-19). In the case of an initial distribution the determination should be made at the conclusion of the Offering Day (as defined in V.S.E. Rule B.5.33).

3.7.2.3   the exercise price on a greenshoe option to an underwriter should be the same as the underwriting price to the underwriters, disclosed in the prospectus, while the exercise price to an agent in the case of a fixed price agency offering, should be the same price as the net price per share to the issuer's treasury disclosed on the prospectus.

3.7.2.4   the maximum exercise period for a greenshoe option should be the lesser of 30 trading days after securing a V.S.E. listing or 60 trading days after the effective date of the prospectus qualifying the offering, save for an initial distribution made under V.S.E. Rule B.5.00 in which case the maximum period should be 30 trading days commencing from the offering day.

3.8   *Qualification of Shares Acquired by a Registrant Through the Exercise of Options or Warrants*

3.8.1   Except as provided for under greenshoe option provisions, on shares acquired by a registrant through the exercise of an option or warrant may be sold unless qualified for sale pursuant to a prospectus or statement of material facts. The qualification period on the initial prospectus will be 12 months from the date of the prospectus or such lesser period as may be imposed as a condition of receipting the prospectus.

3.8.2   Notwithstanding Section 3.8.1 above, where an agent has held shares acquired through the exercise of warrants for a period of one year, he may seek a determination under Section 59 of the Act to sell all or a portion of the shares through the facilities of the Vancouver Stock Exchange, and the Superintendent may, if satisfied that appropriate notice has been furnished to the Exchange, issue a determination for such number of shares and such trading period as he shall deem fit in the circumstances.

4.0 UNDERWRITINGS

4.1 *Settlement Dates*

An underwriter shall pay the full amount of his underwriting commitment under an underwriting agreement within ten business days of the Superintendent's receipt for the prospectus.

4.2 *Options*

As an incentive for agreeing to purchase as principal an offering of and thereby assuming the full risk of an underwriting, an option to purchase additional shares may be granted to a registrant so participating in the underwriting. Such option shall be granted only when under the terms of the underwriting agreement the underwriter assumes, not later than the date of the Superintendent's receipt for the prospectus, a commitment to acquire the offering.

4.2.1 *Number of Shares Subject to Option*

The total number of shares subject to an option or options shall not be greater than the number of shares underwritten and not more than one option will be accepted for filing where the issuer is a development company as defined by Vancouver Stock Exchange and not more than two options where the issuer is other than a development company as defined by the Vancouver Stock Exchange. For an issuer not planning a listing on the Vancouver Stock Exchange not more than one option will be accepted. The number of shares subject to option at any one price shall not exceed 150,000. Where the issuer grants the underwriter two options prospectus disclosure of such options should clarify that they are issued subject to confirmation by the Vancouver Stock Exchange of the listing.

4.2.2 *Minimum Price*

The price per share of the first option shall be higher than the price initially paid by the underwriter, and the price of each subsequent option shall increase by, not less than $0.05 per share in the underwriting price range up to and including $0.50 per share, not less than $0.10 per share in the underwriting price range above $0.50 and up to an including $1.00 per share, and not less than $0.25 per share in the underwriting price range above $1.00 per share.

4.2.3 *Option Intervals*

4.2.3.1 For an issuer, other than a development issuer, that is planning a listing on the Industrial or Resource Section of the Vancouver Stock Exchange, the exercise period of options shall not collectively span a period exceeding nine months from the day on which the shares of the issuer are listed on the Vancouver Stock Exchange. The exercise period for an option at one price shall not exceed six months.

4.2.3.2 For a development company that is planning a listing on the Development Section of the Vancouver Stock Exchange, the exercise period for the one option permitted shall not exceed six months from the day on which the shares of the issuer are listed on the Vancouver Stock Exchange, and shall not in any event exceed nine months from the date of the Superintendent's receipt for the prospectus.

4.2.3.3 For an issuer not planning a listing on the Vancouver Stock Exchange, the exercise period for the one option permitted shall accord with the rules and regulations of the exchange on which the shares are listed, but shall not in any event exceed nine months from the date of the Superintendent's receipt for the prospectus. This nine months limitation shall also apply to an issuer not planning any listing whatsoever.

4.2.4   *Acceleration and Termination*

Every underwriting agreement which provides for the granting of an option shall contain the following provisions:

4.2.4.1   Where the issuer's shares trade on an Exchange in excess of the limit price for an outstanding option the underwriter must immediately exercise the entire option on which the limit price has been exceeded.

4.2.4.2   *"limit price"* means

4.2.4.2.1   200% of the option price where such option price is less than, or equal to $1.00 per share,

4.2.4.2.2   150% of the option price where such option price is greater than $1.00 per share but less than $3.00 per share,

4.2.4.2.3   140% of the option price where such option price is not less than $3.00 per share but less than $4.00 per share, and

4.2.4.2.4   130% of the option price where such option price is not less than $4.00 per share.

4.2.4.2.5   In the event than an option is not exercised in full, any subsequent option shall terminate on the expiry of the option which has not been so exercised.

4.3   *Units*

An underwriting may be in respect of units comprising a share or shares and a share purchase warrant or warrants of the issuer, in which case the relevant provisions of Section 4.2 and the provisions of Section 8.1 shall apply; ie. warrants are available to subscribers, but an option remains the appropriate incentive for the underwriter.

5.0   AGENCY OFFERINGS – BEST EFFORTS BASIS

In a "best efforts" participation, a registrant contracts with the issuer to give his best efforts to sell the issue. The registrant expects to be able to distribute the offering successfully, but does not agree to purchase the securities as principal; he therefore incurs no loss in the event of failure to distribute the full offering. The incentive offered to a registrant for such participation should appropriately be restricted to a commission from the issuer.

5.1   *Settlement Date*

Where the minimum subscription also comprises the total offering, proceeds from the sale of shares or units sold on an agency basis shall be paid to the issuer within five business days following the attainment of such offering. Where an offering continues after attaining the minimum subscription, then proceeds from the sale of shares or units comprising the minimum subscription shall be paid to the issuer within five business days following the attainment of such minimum subscription and proceeds from subsequent sales shall be paid to the issuer in accordance with the terms of the distribution agreement between issuer and agent, but in no event shall such payment be made later than five business days following the termination of the offering.

6.0   GUARANTEED AGENCY OFFERINGS

6.1   A guaranteed agency offering otherwise known as a "stand-by underwriting" differs from a firm underwriting in that the registrant only becomes obliged to purchase from the issuer those securities which at the conclusion of the offering have not been subscribed for by members of the public.

6.2   As an incentive for agreeing to purchase the unsold balance of securities on an offering, share purchase warrants as outlined in Sections 7.1 and 8.2 may be granted to a registrant.

6.3   *Settlement Date*

Proceeds shall be paid to the issuer within five business days following the conclusion of a guaranteed agency offering.

7.0   GUARANTEED AGENCY SHARE OFFERINGS

7.1   *Agents' Entitlement to Share Purchase Warrants*

7.1.1   Where an agent undertakes to purchase all the shares which may be unsubscribed for, he may be granted a non transferable share purchase warrant entitling him to subscribe for a number of shares of the issuer not exceeding 25% of the total number of shares in the offering for a period not exceeding 12 months from the date of the prospectus, but shall expire in any event 180 days from the date of listing on a Stock Exchange. Where interim warrants have been issued prior to a listing, replacement warrants must be issued disclosing the new expiry date at such time as the issuer obtains a listing.

7.1.2   *Exercise Price of Warrants*

The exercise price is subject to negotiation between the issuer and agent, provided that it is higher than the per share price at which units are sold. The share price is to be computed by dividing the number of shares in a unit into the unit price.

8.0   GUARANTEED AGENCY UNIT OFFERINGS

8.1   *Share Purchase Warrants Available to the Public — "A" Warrants*

8.1.1   *Minimum Number of Warrants*

There shall be a minimum of 300,000 warrants attached to the units sold to the public. The number of shares which may be issued pursuant to the exercise of any such warrants shall not exceed the total number of shares issued as part of the unit offering. Such warrants are usually called "A" warrants.

8.1.2   *Exercise Price of Warrants*

The exercise price is subject to negotiation between the issuer and the agent, provided that it is higher than the per share price at which the units are sold. The share price is to be computed by dividing the number of shares in a unit into the unit price. All warrants shall be exercisable at the same price.

8.1.3   *Expiry Date of Warrants*

Warrants shall be outstanding no longer than 12 months from the date of the prospectus, but shall expire in any event 180 days from the date of listing on a Stock Exchange. Where interim warrants have been issued prior to a listing, replacement warrants must be issued disclosing the new expiry date at such time as the issuer obtains a listing.

8.1.4   *Further Entitlement to Warrants*

The share purchase warrant comprising part of the unit shall not entitle the holder to acquire a further share purchase warrant upon its exercise.

8.2   *Agent's Entitlement to Share Purchase Warrants — "B" Warrants*

8.2.1   The agent shall be entitled to a non-transferable warrant entitling him to subscribe for a number of shares of the issuer not exceeding 25% of the total number of shares in the offering. Such a warrant is usually called a "B" warrant.

8.2.2   The exercise price and expiry date applicable to these warrants shall be that which applies also to share purchase warrants made available to the public.

DATED AT VANCOUVER, B.C., this 1st day of February 1987.

Jill Bodkin
Chairman
B.C. Securities Commission

INTERIM LOCAL POLICY STATEMENT 3-22

REQUIREMENTS FOR REGISTRATION FOR TRADING IN SECURITIES

The Commission has published for comment draft amended Local Policy Statement 3-22. See NIN 94/16 "Draft amended Local Policy Statement 3-22 – Registration requirements".

PART 1   IMPLEMENTATION AND APPLICATION

1.1   Local Policy Statement 3-22 dated February 1, 1987, is rescinded and the following substituted therefor, effective February 10, 1989. This revised Interim Local Policy Statement has been revised primarily as a consequence of recent amendments to the Securities Regulation, B.C. Reg.270/86.

1.2   The Commission is currently working on further and more substantive amendments resulting from reviews of the registration process and the reporting and monitoring requirements for registrants. A revised draft Local Policy Statement will be issued for public comment prior to finalization.

1.3   The Securities Act and Securities Regulation provide a legal framework for regulation of securities issued to the public and persons who trade in securities. This Local Policy Statement deals with registration provisions which apply, under Part 4 of the Act and Regulation, to persons who trade in or advise on trading in securities. Reference should be made to the Act and Regulation for information on exemptions from registration.

1.4   The legislation and this policy are intended to ensure that the investing public receives expert advice and ethical treatment from persons engaged in the securities business. Minimum required levels of competence are established for those seeking registration The Superintendent of Brokers may withdraw or withhold registration from those who demonstrate lack of competence or fail to maintain ethical standards. The Superintendent may also impose conditions or restrictions on a registrant.

PART 2   DEFINITIONS

2.1   In this Local Policy Statement:

"Canadian Investment Finance Course" means the course prepared and conducted by the Canadian Securities Institute and so designated by that Institute. Information on this course may be obtained by contacting:

The Canadian Securities Institute
1063 Bentall 3
595 Burrard Street
Vancouver, B.C. V7X 1J1
(604) 683-1338

The Canadian Investment Finance Course is now called the Canadian Investment Management Course. The address of the Canadian Securities Institute has changed to P.O. Box 49151, Bentall Centre, Suite 944 – 1055 Dunsmuir St., Vancouver, B.C., V7X 1J1.

"Canadian Investment Funds Course" means the course prepared and conducted by the Education Division of the Investment Funds Institute of

Canada and so designated by that Institute. Information on this course may be obtained by contacting:

Investment Funds Institute of Canada
Suite 400 - 70 Bond Street
Toronto, Ontario M5B IX2
(416) 363-2158

"Canadian Securities Course" means the course prepared and conducted by the Canadian Securities Institute and so designated by that Institute.

"Chartered Financial Analyst Course" means the course prepared and conducted by the Institute of Chartered Financial Analysts and so designated by that Institute. Information on this course may be obtained by contacting:

Institute of Chartered Financial
Analysts
University of Virginia
P.O. Box 3668
Charlottesville, Virginia 22903
U.S.A.

"Contingency Fund" means the British Columbia Contingency Fund as referred to in section 25 of the Regulation. Participation is required for all Securities Dealers, Mutual Fund Dealers, Scholarship Plan Dealers and Real Estate Dealers. Information may be obtained by contacting the fund's trustee:

Guaranty Trust Company of Canada
800 West Pender Street
Vancouver, B.C. V6C 2V7
(604) 681 - 0151

Local
Policies

The fund's trustee is now T.D. Trust Company at the same address as stated above.

"Investment Funds in Canada Course" means the course prepared and conducted by The Institute of Canadian Bankers. Information on this course may be obtained by contacting:

The Institute of Canadian Bankers
1981 McGill College Avenue
Montreal, Quebec H3A 2X2

"Joint Regulatory Financial Questionnaire and Report means the documents referred to in section 4(2) of the Regulation.

"National Contingency Fund" is the fund established by the Investment Dealers Association and the Canadian exchanges to protect the clients of their members. Participation is a requirement for all Brokers and Investment Dealers.

The National Contingency Fund is now called the Canadian Investor Protection Fund.

"Partners', Directors', and Senior Officers' Qualifying Examination" means the examination prepared and conducted by the Canadian Securities Institute and so designated by that Institute.

"Real Estate Security" is defined in section 13(1) of the Regulation to mean a security of an issuer whose assets that are the principal subject of its business consist of real property, a partnership interest in real property or documents evidencing an interest in real property.

"Registered Representative Examination" means the examination based on the Manual for Registered Representatives prepared and conducted by the Canadian Securities Institute and so designated by that Institute.

> The Registered Representative Examination is now called the Conduct and Practices Handbook Exam.

"Surety Bond" means a bond provided pursuant to Section 5 of the Bonding Act, which reads as follows:

"A bond provided for bonding purposes shall be provided to the obligee in a form satisfactory to him and shall be taken in the name of the obligee and his successors in office, who shall hold the bond in trust for and as representatives of claimants whose rights to recover on the bond may be established."

2.2　Terms defined in the Act and the Regulation and used in this Local Policy Statement have the same meaning as in the Act and the Regulation.

PART 3　REGISTRATION REQUIREMENTS – GENERAL

3.1　Registration under the Act is required for persons who engage in the following activities:

a)　*Dealer*

A person who engages in the trading of securities as principal or agent must be registered as a dealer. The term trade, as defined in Section 1 of the Act, encompasses a broad range of activities relating to transactions in securities. Refer to Part 4 of this Local Policy Statement for the different categories of dealer.

b)　*Underwriter*

A person who participates in distributions of securities must be registered as an underwriter. A distribution is a trade of securities either not previously issued (a primary distribution) or previously issued but subject to certain trading restrictions (a secondary distribution).

c)　*Adviser*

A person who engages in, or holds himself out as engaging in, the business of advising another with respect to investment in or the purchase or sale of securities must be registered as an adviser.

3.2　Dealers usually employ salesmen, who must also be registered under the Act. Specific registration requirements for salesmen will be found under each dealer category in Part 4 of this Local Policy Statement. The following requirements apply to all categories of salesmen registered under the Act:

a)　An individual should not hold any other class of registration concurrent with registration as a salesman. An exception, which permits dual registration of a salesman under both the Insurance Act and the Securities Act, is set out in Local Policy Statement 3-16.

b)　Unless otherwise authorized by the Superintendent, registration as a salesman shall constitute full-time employment. Reference should be made to Section 64 of the Regulation with regard to full time employment and any exemptions from this requirement.

c)　Registration as a salesman is only available to a person employed by a dealer. Termination of employment with a dealer serves to suspend the registration of a salesman.

3.3　All registrations except those for security issuers and their salesmen are issued for a 2 year anniversary period.

3.4　Educational requirements are established in Parts 4 to 6 for various categories of registrant. To ensure that persons re-entering the industry remain current, the following examinations must be rewritten after an absence of five or more years from the industry:

(1)　Registered Representatives Manual Exam
(2)　Partners/Directors/Senior Officers Qualifying Exam
(3)　Canadian Investment Funds Exam
(4)　Investment Funds in Canada Exam

The Canadian Securities Course Exam, Canadian Investment Finance Exam and Chartered Financial Analyst Exam must be rewritten after an absence of ten or more years from the industry.

> The Registered Representative Manual Exam is now called the Conduct and Practices Handbook Exam. The Canadian Investment Finance Course is now called the Canadian Investment Management Course.

3.5 As a result of recent changes in industry ownership rules, registrants are permitted to have a much broader range of affiliations than was previously allowed. However, there are several requirements that must be observed by registrants or applicants for registration.

a) Section 17 of the Regulation provides that no registrant or partner, officer or associate of a registrant shall have a direct or indirect interest in any other registrant without the approval of the Superintendent.

b) Section 72.2 of the Regulation requires a registrant to notify the Superintendent where another person is about to acquire or has acquired beneficial ownership of 10% or more of any class of the registrant's voting securities.

c) Section 72.3 of the Regulation requires that any registrant intending to carry on any other business than that of an adviser, dealer or underwriter give the Superintendent written notice at least 30 days before the registrant commences carrying on the other business.

d) Any affiliate of a bank registered under the Bank Act (Canada), of a trust company or insurance company incorporated under federal legislation, or of a foreign bank, as defined in the Bank Act, should contact the Office of the Superintendent of Financial Institutions, Canada, prior to or concurrently with making an application for registration.

3.6 Under Section 159(2) of the Act, the Commission has delegated some of its registration authority to the following organizations:

Organization	Registration of
Vancouver Stock Exchange (689-3334; Local 552) P.O. Box 10333 609 Granville Street Vancouver, B.C. V7Y 1H1	Brokers Principals Salesmen
Investment Dealers Assoc. of Canada – Pacific District (683-1338) P.O. Box 49151 #1063, Bentall Centre Three 595 Burrard Street Vancouver, B.C. V7X 1J1	Investment Dealers Principals Salesmen

Persons applying under the Broker or Investment Dealer categories must designate the relevant organization noted above as the registration organization. Enquiries and correspondence concerning registration should be directed to the registration organization. Registration fees payable to the Commission by registrants should be made out to the relevant organization as payee and sent to the organization with the application for registration or renewal.

> The address of the Investment Dealers Association of Canada – Pacific District has changed to P.O. Box 49151, Bentall Centre, Suite 944 – 1055 Dunsmuir St., Vancouver, B.C., V7X 1J1.

Local Policies

3.7　Parts 4 to 6 outline the registration requirements for each category of registrant. Registration requirements for principals are discussed first, followed by registration requirements for salesmen. The Forms referred to may be obtained from the Commission. Alternative forms as agreed to by the Vancouver Stock Exchange, the Investment Dealers Association and the Superintendent will also be accepted where registration powers and duties for a class of registrant have been delegated by the Superintendent to the self-regulatory body.

PART 4　REGISTRATION REQUIREMENTS – DEALERS

4.1　*Broker*

a)　*Principals*

Registration in this category is reserved for members of the Vancouver Stock Exchange. It permits trading in securities as agent or principal and includes registration as an underwriter. Applicants in this category should contact the Vancouver Stock Exchange before making application. The following requirements must be met in support of an application in the broker category.

i) Form 3 must be filed with the Vancouver Stock Exchange.

ii) The registration fee of $3,000 and the applicable VSE fee must be paid to the VSE.

The registration fee has increased from $3,000 to $5,000.

---

iii) Applicant must meet the requirement for minimum net free capital, computed in accordance with the Joint Regulatory Financial Questionnaire and Report.

iv) If any portion of the capital is borrowed, the application must include an unconditional subordination agreement.

v) Form 4 must be filed with the Vancouver Stock Exchange by all officers, directors, partners and beneficial owners of 10% or more of the outstanding shares of the dealer.

vi) The applicant is required to become a participant in the National Contingency Fund to comply with Section 25 of the Regulation.

vii) All employees of the registrant handling and/or responsible for receipt and delivery of cash and securities must be designated in writing by the registrant to the Superintendent and bonded for at least $5,000 each.

viii) Where the applicant is a firm or company, the application must identify a designated partner, director or officer of the applicant ("designated individual"), for whom proof must be submitted of

– passing the Canadian Securities Course, the examination based on the Registered Representatives' Manual and the Partners'/Directors'/Senior Officers' Qualifying Examination;

– at least seven continuous years experience in the securities business, two continuous years of which must have been with a member of a major stock exchange, or five years continuous experience with a member house in a sales or managerial sales capacity; and

– residence in the Province.

The examination based on the Registered Representatives' Manual is now called the Conduct and Practices Handbook Exam.

---

ix) A fee of $500 must be paid for each designated individual.

x) The applicant must obtain membership in good standing with the Vancouver Stock Exchange.

xi) The application must indicate the date of the applicant's fiscal year end.

b) *Salesmen*

   i) Form 4 to the Vancouver Stock Exchange.

   ii) Fee $500 and applicable Vancouver Stock Exchange fees.

   iii) Residence in the Province as specified in Section 21(2) of the Act.

   iv) Vancouver Stock Exchange approval.

c) *Conditions of Registration*

The following are conditions of registration for persons registered in the broker category. These are in addition to any statutory, regulatory or common law requirements.

   i) The registrant shall file with the Superintendent a copy of its annual financial statements at the same time they are filed with the Vancouver Stock Exchange.

   ii) The registrant shall comply with all local, uniform and national policies. It is the registrant's responsibility to be informed of their requirements.

4.2 *Investment Dealer*

a) *Principals*

Registration in this category is reserved for members of the Investment Dealers Association. It permits trading in securities as agent or principal and includes registration as an underwriter. Applicants in this category should contact the Investment Dealers Association before making application. The following requirements must be met in support of an application in the investment dealer category.

   i) Form 3 must be filed with the Investment Dealers Association.

   ii) The registration fee of $3,000 and the applicable Investment Dealers Association fee must be paid to the Investment Dealers Association.

> The registration fee has increased from $3,000 to $5,000.

   iii) Applicant must meet the requirement for minimum net free capital, computed in accordance with the Joint Regulatory Financial Questionnaire and Report.

   iv) If any portion of the capital is borrowed, the application must include an unconditional subordination agreement.

   v) Form 4 must be filed with the Investment Dealers Association by all officers, directors, partners and beneficial owners of 10% or more of the outstanding shares of the dealer.

   vi) The applicant is required to become a participant in the National Contingency Fund to comply with Section 25 of the Regulation.

   vii) All employees of the registrant handling and/or responsible for receipt and delivery of cash and securities must be designated in writing by the registrant to the Superintendent and bonded for at least $5,000 each.

   viii) Where the applicant is a firm or company, the application must identify a designated partner, director or officer of the applicant ("designated individual"), for whom proof must be submitted of:

     – passing the Canadian Securities Course, the examination based on the Registered Representatives' Manual and the Partners'/Directors'/Senior Officers' Qualifying Examination;

– at least seven continuous years experience in the securities business, two continuous years of which must have been with a member of a major stock exchange, or five years continuous experience with a member house in a sales or managerial sales capacity; and

– residence in the Province.

The examination based on the Registered Representatives' Manual is now called the Conduct and Practices Handbook Exam.

---

ix) A fee of $500 must be paid for each designated individual.

x) The applicant must obtain membership in good standing with the Investment Dealers Association.

xi) The application must indicate the date of the applicant's fiscal year end.

b) *Salesmen*

i) Form 4 to the Investment Dealers Association.

ii) Fee $500 and applicable Investment Dealers Association fees.

iii) Residence in the Province as specified in Section 21(2) of the Act.

iv) Investment Dealers Association approval.

c) *Conditions of Registration*

The following are conditions of registration for persons registered in the investment dealer category. These are in addition to any statutory, regulatory or common law requirements.

i) The registrant shall file with the Superintendent a copy of its annual financial statements at the same time they are filed with the Investment Dealers Association.

ii) The registrant shall comply with all local, uniform and national policies. It is the registrant's responsibility to be informed of their requirements.

4.3   *Securities Dealer*

a) *Principals*

Registration in this category authorizes the registrant to trade in all kinds of securities as an agent or principal. The registrant need not be a member of a stock exchange. The following requirements must be met in support of an application.

i) Form 3 must be filed with the Superintendent.

ii) The registration fee of $3,000, payable to the Minister of Finance, must accompany the application.

The registration fee has increased from $3,000 to $5,000.

---

iii) Minimum net free capital computed in accordance with the Joint Regulatory Financial Questionnaire and Report, but including the capital requirement or adjusted liabilities to a minimum of $50,000 instead of the minimum of $75,000 as set out in that questionnaire and report.

iv) If any portion of the capital is borrowed, the application must include an unconditional subordination agreement.

v) Form 4 must be filed with the Superintendent of Brokers by all officers, directors, partners and beneficial owners of 10% or more of the outstanding shares of the dealer.

vi) The applicant in this category is required to become a participant in the Contingency Fund, for the protection of clients, by depositing to the Fund the amount of $15,000.

vii) The applicant must obtain and maintain a surety bond in the principal amount of $25,000.

viii) All employees of the registrant handling and/or responsible for receipt and delivery of cash and securities must be designated in writing by the registrant to the Superintendent and bonded for at least $5,000 each. This bond must be filed with the Superintendent.

ix) Where the applicant is a firm or company, the application must identify a designated partner, director or officer of the applicant ("designated individual"), for whom proof must be submitted of:

– passing the Canadian Securities Course, the examination based on the Registered Representatives' Manual and the Partners'/Directors'/Senior Officers' Qualifying Examination;

– at least seven continuous years experience in the securities business, two continuous years of which must have been with a member of a major stock exchange, or five years continuous experience with a member house in a sales or managerial sales capacity; and

– residence in the Province.

The examination based on the Registered Representatives' Manual is now called the Conduct and Practices Handbook Exam.

x) A fee of $500 must be paid for each designated individual.

xi) The application must indicate the date of the applicant's fiscal year end.

xii) The application must include a copy of the direction to the applicant's auditor to conduct any audit required by the Superintendent under Section 19 of the Act and Section 72(1) of the Regulation.

b) *Salesmen*

An individual must meet the following requirements to obtain registration as a salesman of a securities dealer.

i) Form 4 must be filed with the Superintendent.

ii) Fee $500.

iii) Surety Bond for $1,000 principal amount.

iv) Three months training period and proof of passing Canadian Securities Course and the examination based on the Registered Representatives' Manual.

The examination based on the Registered Representatives' Manual is now called the Conduct and Practices Handbook Exam.

v) Residence in the Province as specified in Section 21(2) of the Act.

c) *Conditions of Registration*

The following are conditions of registration for persons registered in the securities dealer category. These are in addition to any statutory, regulatory or common law requirements.

i) Financial Assistance

The registrant shall not accept financial assistance, directly or indirectly, from any person other than a bank, trust company, insurance company or like institution, without first obtaining the Superintendent's written consent thereto.

ii) Capital Loans

Where a director, officer, partner or shareholder of the registrant advances money by way of a capital loan to the registrant, the director, officer, partner or shareholder shall forthwith execute and file with the Superintendent a Subordination Agreement in the form prescribed by the Superintendent.

iii) Local, Uniform and National Policies

The registrant shall comply with all local, uniform and national policies. It is the registrant's responsibility to be informed of all their requirements.

4.4 *Mutual Fund Dealer*

a) *Principals*

This category of registration is limited to trading exclusively in the securities of a mutual fund. The following requirements must be met to be an applicant for registration as a mutual fund dealer.

i) Form 3 must be filed with the Superintendent.

ii) The registration fee of $3,000, payable to the Minister of Finance, must accompany the application.

> The registration fee has increased from $3,000 to $5,000.

iii) The applicant must have a minimum free capital of $25,000 plus the maximum amount deductible under the applicant's surety bond (see paragraph (vi)), as evidenced by an audited financial statement made up as at a date not more than 90 days before the date of application for registration.

iv) If any portion of the capital is borrowed, the application must include an unconditional subordination agreement.

v) Form 4 must be filed with the Superintendent of Brokers by all officers, directors, partners and beneficial owners of 10% or more of the outstanding shares of the dealer.

vi) The applicant in this category is required to become a participant in the Contingency Fund, for the protection of clients, by depositing to the Fund the amount of $15,000.

vii) The applicant must obtain and maintain a surety bond in the principal amount of $15,000.

viii) The application must identify a designated partner, director or officer of the applicant ("designated individual"), for whom proof must be submitted of

– passing the Canadian Securities Course, the Canadian Investment Funds Course or Investment Funds in Canada Course;

– at least five continuous years experience in the mutual fund industry as a salesman with at least one year of that time as a sales manager.

– residence in the Province.

ix) A fee of $500 must be paid for each designated individual.

x) The application must indicate the date of the applicant's fiscal year end.

xi) The application must include a copy of the direction to the applicant's auditor to conduct any audit required by the Superintendent under Section 19 of the Act and Section 72(1) of the Regulation.

b) *Salesmen*

An individual must meet the following requirements to obtain registration as a salesman of a mutual fund dealer.

  i) Form 4 must be filed with the Superintendent.

  ii) Fee $500.

  iii) Surety Bond for $1,000 principal amount.

  iv) Proof of passing Canadian Investment Funds Course, Canadian Securities Course or Investment Funds in Canada Course.

Proof of passing the Principles of Mutual Fund Investment Course is also required.

---

  v) Residence in the Province as specified in Section 21(2) of the Act.

c) *Conditions of Registration*

The following are conditions of registration for persons registered in the mutual fund dealer category. These are in addition to any statutory, regulatory or common law requirements.

  i) Local, Uniform and National Policies

The registrant shall comply with all local, uniform and national policies. It is the registrant's responsibility to be informed of all their requirements.

4.5 *Real Estate Securities Dealer*

a) *Principals*

A registrant under this category is limited to trading in the capacity of agent or principal exclusively in real estate securities.

  i) Form 3 must be filed with the Superintendent.

  ii) The registration fee of $3,000, payable to the Minister of Finance, must accompany the application.

The registration fee has increased from $3,000 to $5,000.

---

  iii) The applicant must have a minimum free capital of $25,000 plus the maximum amount deductible under the applicant's surety bond (see paragraph vi)), as evidenced by an audited financial statement made up as at a date not more than 90 days before the date of application for registration.

  iv) If any portion of the capital is borrowed, the application must include an unconditional subordination agreement.

  v) Form 4 must be filed with the Superintendent of Brokers by all officers, directors, partners and beneficial owners of 10% or more of the outstanding shares of the dealer.

  vi) The applicant in this category is required to become a participant in the Contingency Fund, for the protection of clients, by depositing to the Fund the amount of $15,000.

  vii) The applicant must obtain and maintain a surety bond in the principal amount of $15,000.

  viii) The application must identify a designated partner, director or officer of the applicant ("designated individual"), for whom proof must be submitted of

    – passing the Canadian Securities Course, or a course approved by the Superintendent.

    – at least five continuous years experience in the securities business, two continuous years of which must have been with a broker on a major stock exchange or five continuous years experience in the real estate industry, two continuous years of which must have been as a real estate nominee.

– residence in the Province.

ix) A fee of $500 must be paid for each designated individual.

x) The application must indicate the date of the applicant's fiscal year end.

xi) The application must include a copy of the direction to the applicant's auditor to conduct any audit required by the Superintendent under Section 19 of the Act and Section 72(1) of the Regulation.

b) *Salesmen*

An individual must meet the following requirements to obtain registration as a salesman of a real estate securities dealer.

i) Form 4 must be filed with the Superintendent.

ii) Fee $500.

iii) Surety Bond for $1,000 principal amount.

iv) Proof of passing the Canadian Securities Course or a course approved by the Superintendent and proof of either passing the Real Estate Salesman Pre-licensing Course within the last two years or holding a current licence under the Real Estate Act.

v) Residence in the Province as Specified in section 21(2) of the Act.

c) *Conditions of Registration*

The following are conditions of registration for persons registered in the real estate securities dealer category. These are in addition to any statutory, regulatory or common law requirements.

i) Local, Uniform and National Policies

The registrant shall comply with all local, uniform and national policies. It is the registrant's responsibility to be informed of all their requirements.

4.6　*Scholarship Plan Dealer*

a) *Principals*

A registrant under this category is limited to trading exclusively in securities of a scholarship or educational plan or trust.

i) Form 3 must be filed with the Superintendent.

ii) The registration fee of $3,000, payable to the Minister of Finance, must accompany the application.

The registration fee has increased from $3,000 to $5,000.

---

iii) The applicant must have a minimum free capital of $25,000 plus the maximum amount deductible under the applicant's surety bond (see paragraph vi)), as evidenced by an audited financial statement made up as at a date not more than 90 days before the date of application for registration.

iv) If any portion of the capital is borrowed, the application must include an unconditional subordination agreement.

v) The applicant must obtain and maintain a surety bond in the principal amount of $15,000.

vi) Form 4 must be filed with the Superintendent of Brokers by all officers, directors, partners and beneficial owners of 10% or more of the outstanding shares of the dealer.

vii) The application must identify a designated partner, director or officer of the applicant ("designated individual")

– qualifications and experience deemed appropriate to this particular category of registration by the Superintendent.

– residence in the Province.

viii) A fee of $500 must be paid for each designated individual.

ix) The application must indicate the date of the applicant's fiscal year end.

x) The application must include a copy of the direction to the applicant's auditor to conduct any audit required by the Superintendent under Section 19 of the Act and Section 72(1) of the Regulation.

b) *Salesmen*

An individual must meet the following requirements to obtain registration as a salesman of a scholarship plan dealer.

i) Form 4 must be filed with the Superintendent.

ii) Fee $500.

iii) Surety Bond for $1,000 principal amount.

iv) Qualifications and experience deemed appropriate to this particular category of registration by the Superintendent.

v) Residence in the Province as specified in Section 21(2) of the Act.

c) *Conditions of Registration*

The following are conditions of registration for persons registered in the scholarship plan dealer category. These are in addition to any statutory, regulatory or common law requirements.

i) Local, Uniform and National Policies

The registrant shall comply with all local, uniform and national policies. It is the registrant's responsibility to be informed of all their requirements.

4.7 *Security-issuer*

a) *General Standards for Registration*

This category of registration is available to an issuer who trades in securities only for purposes of distributing securities of its own issue, exclusively for its own account. Before granting registration, the Superintendent must be satisfied that the entitlement of the public to receive expert advice and ethical treatment (see Section 1.4) is not unduly compromised in a situation where persons regularly engaged in the securities business do not participate in an offering. It will accordingly be necessary for an applicant to establish:

i) that there is strong justification for the applicant to distribute its own securities rather than using the services of registrants regularly engaged in the securities business;

ii) that the individuals designated as trading directors have sufficient experience in securities matters; and

iii) that the trading directors are sufficiently free from other commitments and from conflicts of interest to permit appropriate standards to be met in offering the issuer's securities.

b) *Principals*

The following requirements must be met by an applicant for registration in the security issuer category.

i) Where the issuer is a corporation, security issuer registration should be sought in the name of the corporation.

ii) Where a security offered is a unit of a limited partnership, the security is deemed to be a security of the member partners. Registration should be sought in the name of the general partner. Where the general partner is an individual, the partner may not take a commission. Where the general partner is a limited company, the Superintendent may designate a trading director(s) of the general partner to participate in the distribution provided no commission is taken. The general partner may also register salesmen who may take a commission. However, should the general partner as a limited company seek to take a commission for participating in a distribution then such general partner should apply for a securities dealer registration.

iii) The following documentation must be filed:

– Form 3 and supporting Forms 4 for all directors and officers.

– Registration fee of $1500. Registration is for one year.

– List of directors seeking designation by the Superintendent to trade. A trading director may participate in a distribution for one issuer only at any given time and will not be permitted to register as a salesman for that issuer. $500 fee for each trading director.

– Proof that each director seeking a trading director designation has passed the Canadian Securities Course. This requirement may be waived at the discretion of the Superintendent where a designee can demonstrate satisfactory experience in the securities industry and has not previously sought designation as a trading director of a security issuer.

– Residence in the Province as specified in Section 21(2) of the Act.

c)　*Salesmen*

i) Form 4.

ii) Fee $500. Registration is for one year.

iii) Surety Bond for $1,000 principal amount.

iv) Proof of passing the Canadian Securities Course and the examination based on the Registered Representatives Manual.

The examination based on the Registration Representatives' Manual is now called the Conduct and Practices Handbook Exam.

---

v) Residence in the Province as specified in Section 21(2) of the Act.

d)　*Conditions of Registration*

The following are conditions of registration for persons registered in the security issuer dealer category. These are in addition to any statutory, regulatory or common law requirements.

i) Local, Uniform and National Policies

The registrant shall comply with all local, uniform and national policies. It is the registrant's responsibility to be informed of all their requirements.

ii) Distribution

The registrant shall file a list of subscribers to the distribution, indicating, for each subscriber, the name, address and number of shares subscribed.

PART 5   REGISTRATION REQUIREMENTS – UNDERWRITERS

5.1   *Underwriter*

The definition of "underwriter" may be found in section 1 of the Act. Note however that registration in each of the categories of "broker", "investment dealer" and "securities dealer" entitles the registrant to act as an underwriter; therefore, separate "underwriter" registration would not be necessary.

a)   *Principals*

   i)   Form 3 must be filed with the Superintendent.

   ii)   The registration fee of $3,000, payable to the Minister of Finance, must accompany the application.

   iii)   Net free capital of $10,000 calculated in accordance with the required form (as evidenced by an audited financial statement made up as at a date not more than 90 days before the date of application for registration).

   iv)   If any portion of the capital is borrowed, the application must include an unconditional subordination agreement.

   v)   Residence in the Province as specified in Section 21(2) of the Act.

   vi)   The application must indicate the date of the applicant's fiscal year end.

   vii)   Form 4 must be filed with the Superintendent of Brokers by all officers, directors, partners and beneficial owners of 10% or more of the outstanding shares of the dealer.

b)   *Conditions of Registration*

The following are conditions of registration for persons registered in the underwriter category. These are in addition to any statutory, regulatory or common law requirements.

   i)   Trading

The registrant is prohibited from trading in securities with the public.

   ii)   Local, Uniform and National Policies

The registrant shall comply with all local, uniform and national policies. It is the registrant's responsibility to be informed of all their requirements.

PART 6   REGISTRATION REQUIREMENTS – ADVISERS

6.1   *Portfolio Manager*

A portfolio manager is a person who manages the investment portfolio of clients through discretionary authority granted by them. Persons exempted from this registration are detailed in Section 30(2) of the Act.

a)   *Application Requirements*

   i)   Form 3 must be filed with the Superintendent.

   ii)   The registration fee of $3,000, payable to the Minister of Finance, must accompany the application.

   iii)   Minimum free capital of $5,000 (as evidenced by an audited financial statement made up as at a date not more than 90 days before the date of application for registration).

   iv)   Every individual applying for registration in this category or on whose behalf application is made for designation or approval as a partner, director or officer of a portfolio manager shall file a Form 4 and shall have successfully completed the Canadian Securities Course and the Canadian Investment Finance Course and the first year of the Chartered Financial Analyst

Course and shall have been employed for at least five years performing research involving the financial analysis of investments with at least three of those years under the supervision of an adviser responsible for the management or supervision of investment portfolios having an aggregate value of at least $1,000,000.

> The Canadian Investment Finance Course is now called the Canadian Investment Management Course.

v) A fee of $500 for each individual applying for registration in this category.

vi) Form 4 must be filed with the Superintendent of Brokers by all officers, directors, partners and beneficial owners of 10% or more of the outstanding shares of the dealer.

vii) The application must indicate the date of the applicant's fiscal year end.

viii) Copies of the registrant's Managed Accounts Disclosure Document.

b) *Conditions of Registration*

The following are conditions of registration for persons registered in the portfolio manager category. These are in addition to any statutory, regulatory or common law requirements.

i) Local, Uniform and National Policies

The registrant shall comply with all local, uniform and national policies. It is the registrant's responsibility to be informed of all their requirements.

6.2 *Investment Counsel*

An investment counsel is a person who engages in or holds himself out as engaging in the business of advising others as to the investing in or buying or selling of specific securities or who is primarily engaged in giving continuous advice on the investment of funds on the basis of the particular objectives of each client. No trading as principal or agent is permitted in this category. Persons exempted from this registration are detailed in Section 30(2) of the Act.

a) *Application Requirements*

i) Form 3 must be filed with the Superintendent.

ii) The registration fee of $3,000, payable to the Minister of Finance, must accompany the application.

iii) Minimum free capital of $5,000 (as evidenced by an audited financial statement made up as at a date not more than 90 days before the date of application for registration).

iv) Every individual applying for registration in this category or on whose behalf application is made for designation or approval as a partner, director or officer of an investment counsel shall file a Form 4 and shall have successfully completed the Canadian Securities Course, the Canadian Investment Finance Course and the first year of the Chartered Financial Analyst Course and shall have been employed for at least five years performing research involving the financial analysis of investments with at least three of those years under the supervision of an adviser responsible for the management or supervision of investment portfolios having an aggregate value of at least $1,000,000.

> The Canadian Investment Finance Course is now called the Canadian Investment Management Course.

v) A fee of $500 for each individual applying for registration in this category.

vi) Form 4 must be filed with the Superintendent of Brokers by all officers, directors, partners and beneficial owners of 10% or more of the outstanding shares of the dealer.

vii) The application must indicate the date of the applicant's fiscal year end.

b) *Conditions of Registration*

The following are conditions of registration for persons registered in the investment counsel category. These are in addition to any statutory, regulatory or common law requirements.

i) Local, Uniform and National Policies

The registrant shall comply with all local, uniform and national policies. It is the registrant's responsibility to be informed of all their requirements.

6.3 *Securities Adviser*

A securities adviser is a person that engages in or holds himself out as engaging in the business of advising others either directly or through publications as to the investing in or buying or selling of specific securities, not purporting to tailor such advice to the needs of specific clients. No trading as principal or agent is permitted in this category. Persons exempted from this registration are detailed in Section 30(2) of the Act.

a) *Application Requirements*

i) Form 3 must be filed with the Superintendent.

ii) The registration fee of $3,000, payable to the Minister of Finance, must accompany the application.

iii) Minimum free capital of $5,000 (as evidenced by an audited financial statement made up as at a date not more than 90 days before the date of application for registration).

iv) Every individual applying for registration as a securities adviser or on whose behalf application is made for designation or approval as a partner, director or officer of a securities adviser shall file a Form 4 and shall have successfully completed the Canadian Securities Course and the Canadian Investment Finance Course and have performed research involving the financial analysis of investments for at least five years under the supervision of an adviser.

The Canadian Investment Finance Course is now called the Canadian Investment Management Course.

---

v) A fee of $500 for each individual applying for registration in this category.

vi) Form 4 must be filed with the Superintendent of Brokers by all officers, directors, partners and beneficial owners of 10% or more of the outstanding shares of the dealer.

vii) The application must indicate the date of the applicant's fiscal year end.

b) *Conditions of Registration*

The following are conditions of registration for persons registered in the investment counsel category. These are in addition to any statutory, regulatory or common law requirements.

i) Local, Uniform and National Policies

The registrant shall comply with all local, uniform and national policies. It is the registrant's responsibility to be informed of all their requirements.

DATED at Vancouver, British Columbia, this 10th day of February, 1989.

Douglas M. Hyndman
Chairman
B.C. Securities Commission

LOCAL POLICY STATEMENT 3-24

STATUTORY EXEMPTIONS AND ORDERS MADE UNDER SECTION 33 AND SECTION 59 OF THE SECURITIES ACT

> This policy statement is out of date and contains incorrect section references.

1.0   IMPLEMENTATION

1.1   This Local Policy Statement has been substantially revised to conform with the Securities Act, S.B.C. 1985, c.83 and Regulations thereto. It becomes effective with proclamation of the Act on February 1, 1987.

2.0   CHANGES IN EXEMPTIONS

2.1   Section 55 of the former Act permitted the Superintendent to rule that a trade or intended trade be deemed not to be a distribution to the public. Under the new Act the relevant section is Section 59.

A comparison of exemptions available under both Acts is attached for guidance as Appendix A. Some of the differences are as follows:

2.1.1   Section 59 of the new Act permits only an exemption from the prospectus requirements of the Act. Application for registration exemption must be made under Section 33 of the Act. Where both types of exemptions are sought they may be applied for in the same order. Only one fee is necessary.

2.1.2   The Act and Regulations now contain exemptions that were not previously available in British Columbia.

2.1.3   Some of the exemptions previously available have been substantially altered.

2.1.4   The Act in Section 56(1) introduces the concept of "exchange issuers". In particular, the Commission has issued a regulation entitled "Exchange Issuer First Trades Regulation". Certain applications under this regulation can be made under Section 59 of the Act.

2.1.5   Hold periods are now established by the Act and Regulations and vary according to the applicable exemption.

2.2   The net effect of all of the above is to reduce substantially the number of applications formerly made under Section 55. However, Forms 20 and 21 will have to be filed with respect to all exempt trades.

3.0   COMMISSION APPROACH

3.1   Where an application is made and it is the Superintendent's view that a statutory exemption exists the Superintendent will return the material because no order is required. The new Act has been drafted to attain a measure of uniformity with Ontario. It is the Commission's view that exemptions under Sections 33 or 59 should only be sought in exceptional or unusual circumstances when the spirit of the exemption under the Act or Regulations is met, but for technical reasons the exemption is not available. Notwithstanding the above, the Commission recognises that it may be necessary to be flexible during the transition period.

4.0 GUIDELINES

4.1 The interaction of the Statutory Exemptions from Prospectus Requirements is described below:

4.1.1 All statutory exemptions from the prospectus requirements under the Act may be used in conjunction with other statutory exemptions from the prospectus requirements except as noted in Section 4.1.3.

4.1.2 Notwithstanding Section 4.1.1, where more than one exemption is to be relied upon, it is the responsibility of the issuer, its professional advisors and its agents, if any, to ensure that one statutory exemption is compatible with another in carrying out the offering.

4.1.3 It is the Commission's position that no other exemption may be used in conjunction with the isolated trade exemption in Section 55(2)(2).

4.2 Sections 122(a) and 122(b) of the Regulations impose upper limits on the number of persons to whom securities can be sold in reliance on the so-called "seed capital" and "government incentive security" exemptions. A trade made in reliance upon an exemption other than the two just mentioned need not be counted for the purposes of the numerical limitations in Sections 122(a) or 122(b).

4.3 $97,000 Exemption Section 55(2)(4)

4.3.1 Under Section 55(2)(4) of the Act (Section 77 of the Regulations), a prospectus exemption is available in respect of a trade where the purchaser purchases as principal and the trade is in a security which has an aggregate acquisition cost to such purchaser of not less than $97,000. The $97,000 consideration may be cash and/or the assumption of liabilities having a value of $97,000 on a present value basis.

4.3.2 The intent of Section 55(2)(4) of the Act is that a transaction is exempt only if the purchaser is making a firm commitment of at least $97,000. Accordingly, a commitment not immediately satisfied by cash payment should be included only if the purchaser is certain, or virtually certain, to be called upon to make payment. This would disqualify commitments assumed under various tax oriented arrangements where the promoter or distributor has held out to the investor a hope or expectation that payment of a promissory note will be waived and would disqualify, from inclusion under this exemption, assumption of mortgages where the purchaser does not have a direct and real obligation to make payment under the mortgage. Further, to determine the amount of the commitment under a promissory note, the liability should be treated on a present value basis. The interest rate used in the calculation of present value would be the rate of interest payable on the note or the current prime rate plus one percent, whichever is higher. If the note is payable on demand, a reasonable maturity date should be assumed for the calculation, based on any representations made by the promoter or distributor as to the probable payment date.

4.3.3 The commission is of the view that "persons" in the form of syndicates, partnerships, or other forms of unincorporated organizations should not be created solely to permit purchases without a prospectus under Section 55(2)(4) of the Act by groups of individuals whose individual share of the aggregate acquisition cost is less than $97,000. The same concerns do not apply to a corporation.

This section contradicts the sister policy statement in Ontario which states that the same concerns do apply to a corporation. Notwithstanding the present wording of the policy, it is clear that an organization created solely to permit a group of individuals to purchase securities is not purchasing the securities as principal, and thus this exemption may not be relied upon.

Local Policies

4.3.4   The Commission will normally be satisfied that the vendor has exercised reasonable diligence if the vendor relies on statutory declarations from the purchasers unless the vendor had knowledge to the contrary.

4.4   The Seed Capital Exemption. Sections 122(a) and 122(b) of the Regulations.

4.4.1   The Commission notes that with respect to the "seed capital" exemption in Section 122(a) or the "government incentive securities" exemption in Section 122(b) of the Regulations, where the purchaser or prospective purchaser is a partnership, syndicate, trust or unincorporated organization, except:

4.4.1.1   Pension Plans;

4.4.1.2   Groups of pension plans under common management;

4.4.1.3   Organizations of members of a family fund formed to make investments of family funds;

4.4.1.4   Testamentary trusts and estates;

4.4.1.5   Organizations which have primary ongoing business activities other than investing in securities; i.e., law, accounting or investment firms; or

4.4.1.6   Mutual funds other than private mutual funds within the meaning of Section 1 of the Act (investment clubs);

each member of such partnership, syndicate, trust or unincorporated organization must be counted separately in calculating the numbers of prospective purchasers and purchasers.

4.4.2   It is intended that the restrictions in this Section 4.0 will affect purchasers who are non-institutional partnerships, syndicates, inter vivos trusts, and unincorporated organizations created primarily for investment purposes, including investment clubs, Vendors or their representatives who are in doubt as to the application of this Section 4.0, or who are of the view that the nature of the purchaser is such that the proposed trade should be exempted from this Section 4.0 are encouraged to consult with the Superintendent.

5.0   USE OF OFFERING MEMORANDA IN CONNECTION WITH CERTAIN STATUTORY EXEMPTIONS

5.1   The Act and Regulations provide that under certain statutory exemptions an offering memorandum must be received by a purchaser.

5.2   Offering memorandum is defined in Section 1 of the Act. Reference should also be made to Section 126 of the Regulations. Local Policy Statement 3-11 describes the contents required in an offering memorandum.

6.0   FORM 20 AND FORM 21

6.1   Form 20 must be filed with the Superintendent pursuant to Section 125(2) of the Regulations, and Section 2(2) and 2(10) of the Commission Regulation "Exchange Issuer First Trades Regulation", with respect to exempt distributions. In completing Form 20, an issuer should specify which particular statutory exemption or exemptions were relied upon in effecting the distribution of the securities.

6.2   Form 21 must be filed with the Superintendent pursuant to Section 125(3) of the Regulations, Section 2(4)(c) and 2(11)(b) of the Commission Regulation "Exchange Issuer First Trades Regulation", with respect to first trades.

7.0   DISTRIBUTION BY CONTROL PERSONS

7.1   *Definition*

7.1.1   Section 1 of the Act deals with the definition of control.

7.1.2   "Control base" is defined in Section 1 of Commission Regulation "Exchange Issuer First Trades Regulation".

7.2   *Sales from Control*

    7.2.1   Pursuant to Section 1 of the Act a trade in a previously issued security of an issuer from the holdings of a control person is a "distribution". Therefore, in order to make a trade a "control person" must either:

        7.2.1.1   Qualify a prospectus;

        7.2.1.2   Rely on a statutory exemption;

        7.2.1.3   Seek a Section 59 order; or

        7.2.1.4   Rely on Section 7.4 of this Local Policy Statement.

    7.2.2   It should be noted that Section 125 of the Regulations provides a mechanism for trades by a "control person". Please note the differences between the mechanisms for exchange issuers and non-exchange issuers. Where the "control person" purposes to trade in securities of an exchange issuer, the Commission Regulation "Exchange Issuer First Trades Regulation" should be reviewed. In all cases, Form 23 must be filed.

7.3   *Establishment of Control Base*

    7.3.1   Notwithstanding the views expressed in Section 3.0 of this Local Policy Statement it is the view of the Commission that the practice established with respect to the control base system should be continued.

    7.3.2   A control person may on a supplement to the insider report forms required to be filed with the Superintendent establish the control base in his holding of a security. The supplementary form on which the control base is to be established, is to be found as Appendix B to this Local Policy Statement.

    7.3.3   Where the computation of the control base yields a balance in the control base greater than that disclosed as the closing total on the Insider Report most recently filed, the control base balance is to be established as the amount which is equal to the said closing total.

    7.3.4   The control base balance established must be subsequently increased for all acquisitions except those of previously issued securities acquired in an ordinary market transaction through the facilities of a Stock Exchange recognized by the Commission, and may be reduced for all dispositions made from the control base.

    7.3.5   On subsequent Insider Report filings, the control person must indicate which security acquisitions and dispositions relate to the control base and which lie outside the control base. A reconciliation of the opening and closing balance in the control base should be furnished in the "additional remarks" section of the Insider Report Form.

7.4   *Sales of Securities from Outside the Control Base*

A control person who has established a control base by filing a supplement in compliance with Section 7.3.2 may proceed to trade in securities outside the "control base" pursuant to the blanket Section 59 order attached hereto as Appendix C.

8.0   GENERAL RULES

8.1   *Documentation to be Submitted*

An application for a Section 59 order should be made by letter addressed to the Superintendent of Brokers, 865 Hornby Street, Vancouver, B.C. V6Z 2H4. The letter should furnish a brief explanation of why the Section 59 order is being requested. The letter should also delineate the documentation submitted. Each application for a Section 59 order should be accompanied by:

    8.1.1   A cheque made payable to the Minister of Finance in the amount of $150.00;

8.1.2   A draft Section 59 order. Orders should be typewritten in form for signature by the Superintendent on 8 1/2" x 11" plain paper, single spaced, with room left at the top of the page for letterhead of the Superintendent. Each draft order, or set of orders, should be submitted, unfolded in a brown manila envelope marked "Section 59 Order".

8.1.3   For a listed issuer, a copy of any filing statement or statement of material facts submitted to the Exchange in support of the proposed transaction.

8.1.4   For an unlisted issuer a copy of the investment letter, purchase agreement, creditors' settlement agreement or other relevant document supporting the proposed transaction.

8.2   *Minimum Price Per Share*

The minimum price for which shares may be issued is 15 cents per share.

8.3   *Non-Resident Placees, Vendors. etc.*

Where placees, vendors, etc., are resident outside British Columbia, the issuer should keep in mind that an application may also have to be made to the jurisdiction in which the placees, vendors, etc., are resident.

8.4   *Timely Disclosure Compliance*

Before applying for an order with respect to an issue of securities:

8.4.1   The Issuer should be up-to-date in its filings with the Superintendent's Office and with the Registrar of Companies.

8.4.2   All material changes in the affairs of the issuer must have been reported to the shareholders and to the public.

8.5   Where the applicant has completed an offering through a prospectus and has not applied for listing on the Vancouver Stock Exchange, issuance of securities will not normally be given favourable consideration unless the parties involved are on an arm's-length basis.

8.6   All certificates representing shares which are subject to a "hold" period as a condition of the Section 59 order must have imprinted on the face page the following:

"This certificate is non-transferable until

_____

(Termination date of hold period)

8.7   It should be noted that the provisions of this Local Policy Statement are not intended to abrogate other specific restrictions which may exist against an applicant trading in any specific securities or any securities of a specific issuer.

DATED at Vancouver, B.C. this 1st day of February, 1987.

> Jill Bodkin
> Chairman
> B.C. Securities Commission

APPENDIX "A"

COMPARISON OF EXEMPTION UNDER THE "OLD" SECURITIES ACT VS "NEW" SECURITIES ACT

OLD ACT/POLICY	NEW ACT
1. Act, Section 20(1)/54(1) exemptions based on the nature of the trade.	1. Act, Section 31(2)/55(2) - there are more exemptions available based on the nature of the trade in the "new" Act than existed under the "old" Act.

2. Act, Section 20(2)/54(2)(a) - exemptions based on the nature of the securities issued.

3. L.P. 3-24 - Section 6.0 Private Placement Section 7.0 (Qualified Investor).

4. L.P. 3-24, Section 8.0 - Debt Settlement.

5. L.P. 3-24, Section 9.0 - Consideration for Property Rights or Services.

6. L.P. 3-24, Section 10.0

7. L.P. 3-24, Section 11.0

8. L.P. 3-24, Section 12.0 - "Exempt" takeovers.

9. Regulations, Section 58 - Director's option - listed company.

10. Regulations, Section 59 issues or transfers of securities pursuant to a previously granted right.

11. Regulations, Section 60 issue of securities involving $97,000 and by purchaser, where securities qualify "legal for life".

12. Regulations, Section 61 Dividend Stock Purchase plans.

2. Act, Section 32/58(a)

3. (a) Regulations, Section 76(a)/122(a) - "only once" to not more than 25 purchasers.

(b) Regulations, Section 76(b)/122(b) - "Government incentive security" to not more than 50 purchasers.

(c) Regulations, Section 76(c)/122(c) previous distribution

(d) Act, Section 31(2)(5)/55(2)(4) and Regulations, Section 77(1)

4. (a) Regulations, Section 76(e)/122(e)

5. (a) Act, Section 31(2)(6)/55(2)(5)

(b) Act, Section 31(2)(19)/55(2)(12)

(c) Act, Section 31(2)(21)/55(2)(18)

(d) Act, Section 55(2)(24)

6. (a) Act, Section 31(2)(10)/55(2)(9)

7. (a) Act, Section 31(2)(18)/55(2)(17) Regulations, Section 125(4) Commission Regulation, Section 2(8)(e)

8. (a) Act, Section 55(2)(25)

(b) Act, Section 55(2)(27)

(c) Act, Section 31(2)(28)

9. (a) Act, Section 31(2)(10)/55(2)(9)

10. (a) Act, Section 31(2)(12)/55(2)(11)

11. (a) Act, Section 31(2)(5)/55(2)(4) & Regulations, Section 77(1)

12. (a) Act, Section 31(2)(11)/55(2)(10)

APPENDIX "B"

SUPERINTENDENT OF BROKERS FORM SUPPLEMENT – CONTROL BASE ESTABLISHMENT

Name of Reporting Issuer of which undersigned is insider:

_____

Full Name of Insider:

_____

Closing total of form report filed for Month of

_____, 19 . _____ Shares.

COMPONENTS OF CLOSING TOTAL

A.   *Shares forming part of control base*

      1.   Principal's shares   _____

      2.   Escrowed shares unreleased   _____

      3.   Escrowed shares released   _____

      4.   Shares acquired for cash
          in pre-prospectus distribution.   _____

      5.   Shares acquired for cash in
          private placement(s)   _____

      6.   Other Control Base Shares
          (Detail how acquired)   _____

           _____   _____

           _____   _____

          Sub-total Control Base*   _____

B.   *Shares not forming part of control base*

      1.   Previously issued shares acquired in ordi-
          nary market transactions through the facili-
          ties of a stock exchange*   _____

      2.   Other previously issued shares deriving in-
          directly from ordinary market transactions
          through the facilities of a stock exchange

          (Detail how acquired)

           _____   _____

           _____   _____

          Sub-total outside Control Base**   _____

          Total (to equal closing total on
          Form as above)   _____

*   Shares acquired in a distribution effected through the facilities of stock exchange form part of the control base.

**   Where the control base sub-total exceeds the closing total of the most recent form report filed, the said closing total is to be established as the balance in the control base.

APPENDIX "C" TO LOCAL POLICY STATEMENT 3-24

IN THE MATTER OF THE SECURITIES ACT

AND

IN THE MATTER OF DISTRIBUTIONS BY A CONTROL PERSON OUTSIDE A CONTROL BASE

EXEMPTION ORDER UNDER SECTION 59

WHEREAS the Superintendent of Brokers (the "Superintendent") has considered whether an order should be made on his own motion under Section 59 of the SECURITIES ACT, S.B.C. 1985, c.83 (the "Act") that Section 42 of the Act shall not apply in respect of trades, intended trades or securities to be distributed, from outside a control base established in accordance with British Columbia Securities Commission Local Policy Statement #3-24, "Statutory Exemptions and Orders Made Under Section 33 and Section 59 of the SECURITIES ACT" as amended from time to time (the "Policy");

AND WHEREAS the Superintendent is satisfied that the following order should not be prejudicial to the public interest;

IT IS HEREBY ORDERED under Section 59 of the Act that Section 42 of the Act shall not apply in respect of trades, intended trades or securities to be distributed, from the holdings of a control person which are not part of his or its control base established in accordance with the Policy.

DATED at Vancouver, British Columbia this 3rd day of February, 1987.

Gordon D. Mulligan
Deputy Superintendent of
Brokers

LOCAL POLICY STATEMENT 3-25

RE: NATURAL RESOURCE ISSUER –
"BEST EFFORTS"
PROSPECTUS

AND

AMENDMENTS TO PROSPECTUS ARISING
FROM MARKET CONDITIONS

1.0 IMPLEMENTATION

1.1 This Local Policy Statement has been revised solely to conform with the Securities Act S.B.C. 1985 c.83 and the Regulations thereto. Other than consequential amendments, there have been no changes of a substantive nature to this policy. It becomes effective upon proclamation of the Act on February 1, 1987.

2.0 AN AMENDMENT TO A "BEST EFFORTS" PROSPECTUS OFFERING INVOLVING A CHANGE IN THE PRICE AND/OR THE NUMBER OF UNITS OF THE SECURITY OFFERED

2.1 The introduction in Part 7 of the Act of the system of filing a preliminary prospectus should drastically reduce the number of instances where an amendment is sought to a "best efforts" prospectus offering in order to change the price and/or the number of units of the security offered. Section 47 of the Act provides for an amendment to be made to a preliminary prospectus, and it is appropriate that price and volume amendments be made at the preliminary prospectus stage.

2.2 For the time being, provided management can retain a feasible plan for financing a program(s) of merit and overhead for a current period, the Superintendent will give favourable consideration to an amendment filed under Section 48 of the Act involving a change in the price and/or the number of units or the security offered.

3.0 AN AMENDMENT WHERE NO SALE HAS YET BEEN MADE FROM A "BEST EFFORTS" PROSPECTUS OFFERING

3.1 An amendment to reduce the offering price of the shares and increase the number of shares to be offered is acceptable.

3.2 An amendment to reduce the offering price of the shares, to retain the number of shares offered, and to reduce the programs set out in the use of proceeds is acceptable, provided:

3.2.1 The reduced financing is sufficient to carry out a program(s) of merit and overhead for the current period.

3.2.2 The diminished program(s) is still deemed appropriate by the issuer's independent expert and by the Commission's consultant.

3.3 An amendment to reduce the number of shares offered, whether at the original price or at a reduced price will be accepted under the same conditions as outlined in 3.2 above.

4.0 AN AMENDMENT WHERE A SALE HAS BEEN MADE FROM A "BEST EFFORTS" PROSPECTUS OFFERED

4.1 Where a sale has been made from a prospectus offering and an amendment changing the terms of the offering is found acceptable for receipting, each existing subscriber should be furnished with a copy of the amendment. The subscriber should further be afforded an appropriate form granting him 15 days from the date of acceptance of the amendment to either rescind or consent to the changed conditions of the subscription. Where such subscriber does not complete and return such a form, his subscription is to be deemed as rescinded and his subscription is to be refunded to him.

4.2   As soon as is practicable after the receipting of the amendment, the issuer or his agent shall file an affidavit with the Superintendent attesting to the following:

      4.2.1   Number of subscribers canvassed under 4.1 above.

      4.2.2   Number of subscribers rescinding and total amount refunded or credited to those rescinding.

      4.2.3   Number of subscribers consenting and total amount of subscription retained.

4.3   The following will usually be deemed acceptable proposals for an amendment:

      4.3.1   An amendment to reduce the offering price and to increase the number of units of the security offered. Under such conditions, the form sent to the existing subscriber should permit him:

          4.3.1.1.   to rescind; or

          4.3.1.2   to take down at the reduced price the number of units originally subscribed for; or

          4.3.1.3   to take down at the reduced price a greater of units than he originally subscribed for.

      4.3.2   An amendment to reduce the offering price but to retain the number of units of the security originally offered. Where such an amendment is found acceptable, the same opportunity as in 4.3.1 above should be afforded the existing subscriber.

      4.3.3   An amendment to reduce the number of units of the security offered and also to reduce the price. Where such an amendment is found acceptable, the existing subscriber should be enabled:

          4.3.3.1   to rescind; or

          4.3.3.2   to take down at the reduced price the number of units originally subscribed for.

This Local Policy Statement 3-25 does not attempt to deal with other types of amendments which may arise during the period of a distribution to the public of a security.

DATED at Vancouver, B.C. this 1st day of February, 1987.

                   Jill Bodkin
                   Chairman
                   B.C. Securities Commission

LOCAL POLICY STATEMENT 3-25
SAMPLE FORM

To:

The undersigned subscriber to _____ of _____
                          (No. of units)   (description of security)
offered on the _____ 198 __ prospectus of _____ acknowledges receipt of the 198 __ amendment to said prospectus, and hereby:

    (   )   confirms that he will take down _____ of _____ at a price of $_____ per units.

    (   ) rescinds his subscription and requests a refund or credit for the amount of the subscription rescinded.

_____ , 19 __ . _____
  (Date)   (Signature)

(Typewritten name of the Subscriber)

(Address of the Subscriber)

(City)   (Province)

(Postal Code)

LOCAL POLICY STATEMENT 3-26

STATEMENT OF MATERIAL FACTS SUBMITTED TO THE SUPERINTENDENT OF BROKERS AND THE VANCOUVER STOCK EXCHANGE FOR VETTING

See NIN 88/10 "Full Disclosure in Financial Statements".

1.0 IMPLEMENTATION

    1.1   This Local Policy Statement has been revised solely to conform with the Securities Act S.B.C. 1985 c. 83 and the Regulations thereto. Other than consequential amendments, there have been no changes of a substantive nature to this policy. It becomes effective upon proclamation of the Act on February 1, 1987.

2.0 DOCUMENTS TO BE FILED

    2.1   The documents required to be filed in support of a Statement of Material Facts have been segregated between those required by the Superintendent and those required by the Vancouver Stock Exchange. This segregation reflects a division in the vetting responsibilities between the office of the Superintendent and the Exchange.

    2.2   Covering letters directed to each of the Superintendent and the Exchange should accompany the Statement of Material Facts. Each letter should delineate the relevant documentation being submitted (see Section 2.3 for items to be submitted to the Superintendent and Section 2.4 for items to be submitted to the Exchange) and should identify the documents by the lettering systems indicated in Section 2.3 and 2.4. Where several documents of the same category (e.g. engineering reports) are being submitted, each document should be named separately and identified appropriately (e.g. (E)H-1, (E)H-2, etc.) in the sequence in which there is disclosure in the Statement of Material Facts.

    2.3   *Documents Required to be filed with the Superintendent*

The documents required to be filed are as follows:

(S)A. Filing Fee of $500.00.

(S)B. Statement of Material Facts, in duplicate, in conformity with Form 24 of the Regulations, accompanied by a certificate signed by the underwriters and at least one director and dated. The final draft of the Statement of Material Facts must be fully executed and contain the financial statements and the Engineering reports of summaries thereof.

(S)C. A statement by the issuer, signed by a director or the secretary confirming as to whether:

    (a)   the issuer has mailed to shareholders all mailings required by the Company Act, i.e. interim financial statements per Section 197 and annual financial statements and information circular or alternatively, the mailings required in the appropriate jurisdiction.

    (b)   quarterly report filings are up-to-date with the Exchange and the Superintendent.

and setting out:

   (c) The roster of the issuer's Audit Committee (Section 211, Company Act for issuers incorporated under the laws of British Columbia.) Where the issuer is not required by law to have an Audit Committee, particulars to this effect should be included in the covering letter. Where the Issuer elects to disclose the roster of the Audit Committee in the statement of material facts, a note to this effect in the covering letter will suffice.

(S)D. Form 4 unless one has been filed with the Superintendent during the 3 year period prior to the date of the certificate for all directors, senior officers and market makers other than the underwriter.

> See NIN 92/18 "Required Form of Personal Information".

(S)E. Statement signed by each director and officer confirming the following:

   (a) that he has submitted a Form 4 within a 3-year period preceding the date of the Statement of Material Facts.

   (b) That his insider reports are up-to-date.

The Statement should be dated and should identify the company for which the Statement of Material Facts has been submitted.

(S)F. Where a Section 59 order is required with respect to issuance of shares approved by the Vancouver Stock Exchange in a Statement of Material Facts, the application, the fee, and any other documentation or information required by Local Policy 3-24 should be submitted with the Statement of Material Facts, so that the Section 59 determination can be made at the same time as the acceptance of the Statement of Material Facts by the Superintendent.

Local Policy 3-24 requires the submission of ruling in form for signature by the Superintendent. Where the terms of the transaction accepted differ from those initially disclosed, it may be necessary to submit an amended ruling incorporating any changes.

(S)G. Where a transaction involving a material share issuance (i.e. an issue of treasury shares aggregating 20% or more of the issuer's current shares outstanding) is disclosed in a Statement of Material Facts, adequate documentation in the form of an evaluation and/or technical report to support the value of the property being acquired for the share consideration.

2.4 *Documents Required to be filed with the Exchange*

The documents required to be filed are as follows:

(E)A. Filing Fee.

(E)B. Statement of Material Facts, in duplicate, as in 2.3.B.

(E)C. A statement by the issuer, signed by a director or the secretary confirming as to whether:

   (a) the issuer has mailed to shareholders all mailings required by the Company Act, i.e. interim financial statements per Section 197 and annual financial statements and information circular or alternatively, the mailings required in the appropriate jurisdiction.

   (b) quarterly report filing are up-to-date with the Exchange and the Superintendent.

(E)D. Power of Attorney for any director signing the Statement of Material Facts by power of attorney.

(E)E. Financial statements approved in accordance with the Regulations, within 60 days at submission and within 120 days at the Effective Date.

(E)F. A certified copy of the directors' resolution approving the financial statements and giving two directors authority to sign must accompany all financial statements.

(E)G. Fully executed underwriting or agency agreement as well as verification prior to acceptance, that the agreement is still in effect.

(E)H. Engineering reports, filed in duplicate, prepared in accordance with National Policy 2, Local Policy 3-01 and Forms 54 and 55 on any resource property on which proceeds are to be spent. The engineer's report must be accompanied by a certificate in the form prescribed by Regulation 103. One copy of the report and the certificate must be originally signed and the original signed certificate must be signed under seal. The engineer preparing the report must be independent of the issuer and may not have an interest in the property reported on or in the securities of the issuer.

A summary of the report prepared by the engineer or by the directors and approved by the engineer may be submitted with the report and may be printed in the Statement of Material Facts instead of the full report. The Statement of Material Facts should state where the full report is available for review.

Market study or feasibility study, where applicable for an issuer other than a natural resource issuer should be included.

(E)I. The engineer's report must be accompanied by the engineer's consent to the inclusion of his report in the Statement of Material Facts, as required by National Policy 2. The consent letter must be originally signed.

In the event that a summary of the report is to be printed instead of the full report, the engineer must provide an originally signed letter consenting to the inclusion of the summary only in the Statement of Material Facts.

(E)J. A certified copy of the title opinion verifying the title to all mining properties on which it is proposed to spend any part of the net proceeds and/or all mining properties being acquired. For oil and gas properties, title opinions should be supplied only on request.

Ordinarily, the Exchange will seek assurance that a satisfactory title opinion has been obtained or will be obtained prior to drilling.

(E)K. Certified copies of all property agreements to which the Issuer is a party and not previously filed.

(E)L. Certified copies of all other material contracts not previously filed.

(E)M. Disclosure of "interest of solicitors" (Solicitor's Certificate) prescribed in Local Policy Statement 3-41.

3.0 INCOMPLETE SUBMISSIONS

3.1 Section 178(2) of the Regulations provides that, where any material is filed with the Superintendent and the material is not prepared in accordance with the Act, the Superintendent may return the material to the person by whom or by which it has been filed.

3.2 A Statement of Material Facts will be returned to the sender where the certificate has not been dated and originally executed by one director and the underwriter.

3.3 At his discretion, the Superintendent may permit vetting of the Statement of Material Facts to proceed where one or more requirements, other than those listed in the preceding paragraph, have not been met. The covering letter to the Superintendent referred to above should state clearly what documentation has not been supplied, the reason it has not been supplied, and the date it may be expected.

4. "RED-LINED" COPY AND OTHER FOLLOW-UP MATERIAL; FINAL MATERIAL

4.1 "Red-Lined" copy should be directed both to the Superintendent and the Exchange. While this Local Policy contemplates that the majority of responses to deficiencies will involve the forwarding of amended documentation to the Exchange, any amended documentation responding to a matter indicated in Section 2.3 should be forwarded to the Superintendent. The front page of a covering letter and the envelope for submission of "red-lined" copy and other follow-up material to the Superintendent should contain the entire undernoted wording:

Local Policies

"Attention: Supervisor, Operations Follow-up Material for S.M.F. Filing Filed on behalf of _____."

4.2 Unless the issuer is given specific direction to the contrary, final material for and definitive commercial copies of a statement of material facts need be directed solely to the Exchange which in turn will forward specified definitive material to the Superintendent.

5.0 AMENDMENTS TO STATEMENTS OF MATERIAL FACTS

This section applies to amendments filed under Section 118 of the Regulations.

5.1 Covering letters as described in Section 2.2 should accompany the submission of a single copy of a statement of material facts amendment to the Superintendent and of duplicate copies of the amendment to the Exchange, together with the applicable filing fees.

5.2 Where the amendment covers matters identified in Section 2.3 as of concern to the Superintendent, appropriate documentation in support of the amendment should be submitted to the Superintendent. Conversely where the amendment covers matters identified in Section 2.4, appropriate supporting documentation should be submitted to the Exchange.

DATED at Vancouver, B.C. this 1st day of February, 1987.

Jill Bodkin
Chairman
B.C. Securities Commission

LOCAL POLICY STATEMENT 3-30
UNDERWRITER'S CONFLICT OF INTEREST

1.0 IMPLEMENTATION

1.1 This Local Policy Statement has been revised solely to conform with the Securities Act S.B.C. 1985 c. 83 and the Regulations thereto. Other than consequential amendments, there have been no changes of a substantive nature to this policy. It becomes effective upon proclamation of the Act on February 1, 1987.

2.0 DEFINITION OF "UNDERWRITER"

2.1 For the purposes of this Local Policy Statement, the term "underwriter" means any registrant permitted to act as an underwriter under Section 20(1)(b) of the Act, or any person authorized to act as an underwriter in another securities jurisdiction and includes shareholders, partners, employees and associates of such registrant or such individual or entity.

2.2 Where an issuer has never had its equity securities listed on an exchange, the term "underwriter" shall mean any underwriter, not solely those underwriter(s) involved in the offering made on a specific prospectus.

2.3 Where an issuer has had its equity securities listed or currently has its equity securities listed on any exchange, the term "underwriter" shall mean any underwriter involved in the offering made by statement of material facts or prospectus.

3.0 LIMITS ON PURCHASES OF SHARES ISSUED BY A ISSUER PRIOR TO THE FILING OF A FIRST PROSPECTUS

Registrants for trading in securities should avoid conflicts of interest arising from acquisition of shares distributed by an issuer prior to making a first public offering by prospectus.

The Superintendent has accordingly imposed the following restrictions on the number of shares of such an issuer to be held by persons falling within the Section 2.0 definition of an "underwriter":

3.1 The maximum number of shares held by all underwriters prior to the first distribution to the public of an issuer shall not in the aggregate exceed the lesser of 150,000 shares or 10% of the issued shares to be outstanding after the said distribution. The same principle shall apply upon the completion of the said distribution.

3.2   The maximum number of shares held by any one person (other than a brokerage firm) on conclusion of an issuer's initial public offering shall be the lesser of 50,000 shares or 5% of the issuer's outstanding share capital on conclusion of the said distribution.

3.3   No underwriter may participate in a principals' share position or other escrow share position.

3.4   Underwriters may receive compensation in other forms when they take the initiative and an active role in reorganization of an issuer.

4.0   DISCLOSURE

4.1   *Unlisted*

When an unlisted issuer issues a prospectus, there must be a disclosure on the face page of the prospectus or in the body of the prospectus with a cross-reference on the face page of the aggregate number of shares owned, directly or indirectly, by underwriters and the prices at which such shares were purchased.

4.2   Listed

In a statement of material facts or prospectus of a listed issuer, disclosure must be made of the aggregate number of shares of the issuer owned directly or indirectly by the underwriter(s) involved in the offering, excluding the employees thereof and associates of such employees.

5.0   SALES AND UNDERTAKING BY UNDERWRITERS

5.1   Each person falling within the Section 2.0 definition of "underwriter" will be required to file an undertaking (see sample following) with the Superintendent and the Vancouver Stock Exchange to the effect that no shares acquired by him will be sold prior to the expiry of six months from the listing of the issuer's shares on the Vancouver Stock Exchange.

5.2   Where the person in Section 5.1 has acquired, directly or indirectly or together with his associates, more than 10,000 shares, the following will have to be added to the undertaking filed:

5.2.1   sales of shares in the 3-month period following the expiry of six months from the listing of the issuer's shares on the Vancouver Stock Exchange will be limited to 25% of such shares acquired,

5.2.2   sales of shares in each 3-month period thereafter will be limited to 25,000 shares,

5.2.3   no shares will be sold until at least seven (7) days after notice of the intended sale is filed with the Superintendent and the Vancouver Stock Exchange.

5.3   Where such sale or other dealing does not take place within 120 days from the date of the notice referred to in Section 5.2.3, further notice will be required.

6.0   POOLING BY UNDERWRITERS

Underwriters should also refer to Section 3.0 of Local Policy Statement 3-08 which sets out pooling requirements for shares purchased for cash prior to the first public offering of shares by prospectus.

DATED at Vancouver, B.C., this 1st day of February, 1987.

Jill Bodkin

Chairman

B.C. Securities Commission

LOCAL POLICY STATEMENT 3-30 — APPENDIX
SAMPLE UNDERTAKING FOR AN UNDERWRITER

TO: The Office of the Superintendent of Brokers

AND TO: The Vancouver Stock Exchange

RE: XYZ RESOURCES INC. (the issuer)

WHEREAS the undersigned is an underwriter within the meaning of Local Policy Statement 3-30;

AND WHEREAS the said underwriter has acquired, directly or indirectly or together with his associates, more than 10,000 shares of the issuer during the non-reporting stage of the issuer (delete this paragraph where it is not applicable);

NOW THEREFORE THIS LETTER WITNESSETH that _____ the undersigned hereby undertakes the following:

1.   No sale or other dealing in the said shares so acquired shall take place prior to the expiry of six months from the date of listing of the issuer's shares on the Vancouver Stock Exchange (delete statements 2, 3 and 4 where they are not applicable).

2.   Sales of the undersigned's holdings of the issuer's shares in the 3-month period following the expiry of six months from the date of listing of the issuer's shares on the Vancouver Stock Exchange shall be limited to 25% of such holdings.

3.   Sales of the undersigned's holdings in each 3-month period thereafter will be limited to a maximum of 25,000 shares.

4.   None of the holdings will be sold until at least seven (7) days after notice of the intended sale is filed with the Superintendent of Brokers and the Vancouver Stock Exchange. Where such sale or other dealing does not take place within 120 days from the date of notice, further notice will be given.

DATED at Vancouver, B.C. this _____ day of _____, 19_____ .

_____
Signature

_____
Name (printed)

_____
Address

LOCAL POLICY STATEMENT 3-31
INCENTIVE OPTIONS TO DIRECTORS
AND EMPLOYEES OF UNLISTED ISSUERS

1.0   IMPLEMENTATION

     1.1   This Local Policy Statement has been revised solely to conform with the Securities Act S.B.C. 1985 c. 83 and the Regulations thereto. Other than consequential amendments, there have been no changes of a substantive nature to this policy. It is becomes effective upon proclamation of the Securities Act on February 1, 1987.

2.0   TERMS OF REFERENCE

     2.1   This Local Policy Statement deals with the granting of stock options by issuers whose equity securities are not listed on a stock exchange. Incentive stock options granted to directors and employees which are outstanding at the time of filing a prospectus are the chief concern of this Local Policy Statement.

     2.2   Stock options granted to other than directors and employees which are outstanding at the time an unlisted issuer files a prospectus should be drawn up subject to approval by regulatory authority. The Superintendent anticipates that stock options granted by an issuer prior to the making of a first distribution will normally be confined to directors and employees.

2.3 For an issuer listed on a stock exchange, the rules, regulations and policies of such exchange will apply to options granted to directors and employees.

2.4 An issuer planning to seek a listing on the Vancouver Stock Exchange should insure that the terms of stock options granted will enable the optioner to comply with the terms of V.S.E. Policy Statement LD 1/82 currently in force. Sections 1(d) and 1(e) of VSE LD 1/82 should in particular be complied with.

2.5 An issuer planning to seek a listing with a stock exchange other than the Vancouver Stock Exchange should clear the terms of any outstanding stock options with the exchange concerned.

3.0 AN ISSUER CONTEMPLATING A SHARE OFFERING BY PROSPECTUS

3.1 The aggregate number of shares under option to directors and employees shall be based on the number of equity securities which would be issued and outstanding after completion of the prospectus offering, excluding shares escrowed under Local Policy 3-07, and shall be subject to the following limits:

3.1.1 5% of the above-noted base for directors of the optioner or a subsidiary thereof, and

3.1.2 An additional 5% for employees of the optionor or a subsidiary thereof. An individual employed by a issuer providing management services to the optionor may also be deemed an employee of the optionor under this section.

> The Vancouver Stock Exchange no longer specifically limits the percentage of securities that may be reserved for issuance to director or employees. There is now an overall limitation of 10% of the issuer's issued and outstanding securities and an individual limitation of 5% of the issuer's issued and outstanding securities. It is probable that the Commission would approve options that were granted pursuant to the present policies of the Vancouver Stock Exchange.

3.2 For the purpose of this policy an individual may qualify for one only of the two categories of stock option referred to in Section 3.1 above.

3.3 The minimum option price shall be the issue price to the public under the prospectus.

3.4 The term of an option granted to a director or employee shall be limited to a maximum of five years from the effective date of the prospectus (i.e. the date on which the prospectus is receipted).

3.5 The following terms must be included in all stock option agreements involving directors or employees as optionees:

3.5.1 the option is non-assignable and non-transferable.

3.5.2 the option may only be exercised while the optionee is a director or an employee or within a period of not more than 30 days after ceasing to be a director or employee.

3.5.3 the period (if any) within which the optionee's heirs or administrators may exercise any portion of the outstanding option shall not exceed one year from the optionee's death.

3.6 Where an optionee is a director, shareholder ratification of the agreement or any subsequent amendment thereto is required.

3.7 Where an optionee is an employee, the option agreement must contain a representation that the optionee is an employee of the optionor or subsidiary thereof, or that the optionee is an employee of a company under contract to provide management services to the optionor.

4.0 AN UNLISTED ISSUER IN THE POST-PROSPECTUS PHASE CONTEMPLATING THE GRANTING OF AN OPTION

4.1 The comments made in Section 2.4 apply also to an unlisted issuer contemplating the granting of a stock option subsequent to the completion of a prospectus offering but prior to seeking a listing of its shares on the Vancouver Stock Exchange. It should be noted that unless an option has been disclosed in an issuer's prospectus in accordance with this Local Policy Statement, the Vancouver Stock Exchange will not generally consider accepting an incentive option agreement until a satisfactory market in the issuer's securities has been established.

4.2 Where an unlisted issuer in the post-prospectus phase contemplates the granting of an option and also plans to seek a listing of its shares on a recognized stock exchange other than the Vancouver Stock Exchange, the terms of such option should be cleared with the exchange concerned.

4.3 An unlisted issuer in the post-prospectus phase contemplating the granting of an option but not planning to seek a listing of its shares on a stock exchange should draw up an option agreement subject to the approval of regulatory authority. The Superintendent will normally require an optionor in this situation to comply with the relevant parts of Section 3.0.

DATED at Vancouver, B.C. this 1st day of February, 1987.

Jill Bodkin
Chairman
B.C. Securities Commission

LOCAL POLICY STATEMENT 3-33

R.R.S.P.'s ADMINISTERED BY BROKERS ON BEHALF OF AUTHORIZED TRUSTEES

1.0 IMPLEMENTATION

1.1 This Local Policy Statement has been revised solely to conform with the Securities Act S.B.C. 1985 c. 83 and the Regulations thereto. Other than consequential amendments, there have been no changes of a substantive nature to this policy. It becomes effective upon proclamation of the Act on February 1, 1987.

2.0 PROCEDURES

The Vancouver Stock Exchange Service Corp. ("Service Corp.") has satisfied the Commission that it has adequate facilities to act as agents for trust companies with respect to self-directed R.R.S.P.'s. Therefore, the Service Corp. may be used as a repository for securities required for self-directed R.R.S.P.'s by brokers. Trust companies may also wish to use the facilities of the Service Corp. as a repository. The Commission will not object to arrangements between brokers and authorized trustees for the proper administration of these R.R.S.P.'s, provided that certain safekeeping disposition and segregation requirements as outlined below are adhered to.

2.1 The physical control over self-directed R.R.S.P. securities is maintained by designated employees of a broker or lodged with the Service Corp. in a "segregated" position.

2.2 The R.R.S.P. securities are kept separate from all other securities held by a broker and kept in safekeeping or lodged with the Service Corp., pursuant to a written agreement between the broker and the authorized trustee and not encumbered. Securities must be identified as being held in safekeeping for the client in the registrant's security position record, client's ledger and statement of account. Securities may only be released on an instruction from the client or authorized trustee.

2.3 The means, be it numerical code or otherwise, by which customer accounts that are self-directed R.R.S.P.'s are identified is clearly distinguishable from the manner of identifying other types of accounts and each account is itself identified as being that of the authorized trustee for the beneficial owner, each being named.

2.4 Cash received by the broker is transferred to the authorized trustee daily.

2.5 The agreement between the broker and the authorized trustee incorporates the protection afforded customers as set out in Section 2.2, and prohibits the brokers from using assets from the authorized trustee's R.R.S.P. account for the customer to pay claims the broker may have against that particular customer's non-R.R.S.P. accounts.

2.6 The broker undertakes to ensure that only qualified investments under the Income Tax Act are purchased.

2.7 Approval of the regulatory authority under which the authorized trustee operates has been obtained prior to putting the agreement in effect.

2.8 Approval of the self-regulatory organizations of which the brokers are members by audit jurisdiction, has been obtained prior to putting the agreement into effect.

2.9 The National Contingency Fund is advised in writing by the broker prior to entering into the arrangement to act as agent for a trustee.

Dated at Vancouver, B.C., this 1st day of February, 1987.

Jill Bodkin
Chairman
B.C. Securities Commission

LOCAL POLICY STATEMENT 3-34
APPLICATION FOR NON-REPORTING STATUS

1.0 IMPLEMENTATION

1.1 This Local Policy Statement has been revised solely to conform with the Securities Act S.B.C. 1985 c. 83 and the Regulations thereto. Other than consequential amendments, there have been no changes of a substantive nature to this policy. It becomes effective upon proclamation of the Act on February 1, 1987.

2.0 DEFINITION

2.1 The Company Act Section 1(1) provides that a "reporting company" may be designated by the Registrar of Companies to be not a reporting company. As well, Section 72 of the Act provides that a "reporting issuer" may be deemed by the Commission to have ceased to be a reporting issuer. Therefore, a reporting company/issuer seeking non-reporting status must apply to the Registrar of Companies if it falls within the Company Act definition of "reporting company" and/or to the Commission if it falls within the Act definition of "reporting issuer".

3.0 GENERAL REQUIREMENTS

As policy guideline, the following is the general requirement pertaining to an application by an issuer applying for the Commission's order for designation as a non-reporting issuer.

3.1 As a general rule, an order conferring non-reporting status will be granted only where close corporation concepts are demonstrated by the applicant issuer.

3.2 The following matters may be taken into consideration in determining such concepts:

3.2.1 Both debt and equity securities of the applicant issuer are held by relatively few holders.

3.2.2 The management and ownership are substantially identical or there exists a community of relationship between the members, i.e. based upon family, business, social or other common interest.

3.2.3 The securities of the issuer are not traded in any securities market.

3.2.4. The securities of the issuer are subject to restrictions on transfer.

3.2.5 The applicant issuer has either never made or, upon order being granted, would not make an offering of its securities to the public.

3.3 Even though all of the ingredients of a close corporation may exist in the applicant issuer, the overriding consideration will be the security holders' and public's "need and right to know" what is transpiring in the issuer.

3.4   Where the applicant issuer has a subsidiary which is a reporting issuer, an order will not issue unless the applicant can convince the Commission it would not be in the public interest to require the disclosure demanded by the reporting issuer provisions of the Act. Similarly, where the applicant issuer is a subsidiary of a reporting issuer, the same principle will apply.

4.0   DOCUMENTS TO BE FILED

The application should be accompanied by the undernoted documents and information duly certified by at least one director of the applicant issuer:

4.1   A copy of the last Annual Report of the issuer.

4.2   An up-to-date list of members of the issuer showing the full name, address and number of securities held by each member.

4.3   A brief summary of the current business of the issuer.

4.4   A statement as to whether the issuer's constating documents:

     4.4.1   limit the number of shareholders

     4.4.2   restrict the transfer of shares

     4.4.3   prohibit the offering of its securities to the public.

4.5   The relationship, if any, in a family business, social or other sense, existing between the directors and shareholders.

4.6   A statement respecting whether the issuer:

     4.6.1   is up-to-date in its filings under the Act and Company Act.

     4.6.2   has ever filed or issued a prospectus covering an offering of its securities in Canada, the United States of America or the United Kingdom.

4.7   A statement with respect to whether the issuer intends to seek public financing by way of an issue of securities.

4.8   A copy of the most recent financial statements.

4.9   Shareholders Resolution authorizing the application.

5.0   REGISTRAR OF COMPANIES

The Commission will forward to the Registrar of Companies, a copy of all orders issued by it.

DATED at Vancouver, B.C. this 1st day of February, 1987.

> Jill Bodkin
> Chairman
> B.C. Securities Commission

LOCAL POLICY STATEMENT 3-35

REACTIVATION OF DORMANT ISSUERS

See *Chromex* under s. 171.2 of the Regulation.

TABLE OF CONTENTS

PART 1   IMPLEMENTATION

1.1   Local Policy Statement 3-35 dated February 1, 1987 is hereby rescinded and the following substituted therefor, effective November 1, 1989.

1.2   Terms defined in the Securities Act, S.B.C. 1985, c.83 (the "Act") and the Securities Regulation, B.C. Reg. 270/86 (the "Regulation") and used in this local policy statement have the same meaning as in the Act and the Regulation.

PART 2   APPLICATION OF POLICY

2.1   This local policy statement sets out guidelines that dormant issuers must follow in order to reactivate trading in their securities. In addition, a dormant issuer will need to comply with the applicable reactivation requirements of any stock exchange on which its securities are or will be listed.

2.2   A dormant issuer is a reporting issuer whose securities have been subject to a cease trade order under section 146 of the Act for more than 90 days. An issuer that has been subject to a cease trade order for 90 days or less may reactivate trading in its securities by filing all delinquent information and records.

2.3   Once an issuer has become dormant, section 171.2 of the Regulation provides that the dormant issuer must file, concurrently with filing the record or information referred to in the cease trade order, certain additional records or information about the business and affairs of the dormant issuer that the Commission or the Superintendent considers necessary to determine whether trading in the issuer's securities is prejudicial to the public interest.

This local policy statement specifies the additional records or information that must be filed by a dormant issuer in accordance with section 171.2 of the Regulation. The filing of the additional records or information is referred to in this local policy statement as the "reactivation application".

2.4   If the additional records or information are not filed concurrently with the record referred to in the original cease trade order, a further cease trade order may be issued under section 146 of the Act which will remain in effect until satisfactory records or information have been filed by the dormant issuer.

PART 3   PROCEDURE FOR REACTIVATION

3.1   *General Requirements*

(a)   A reactivation application must be made within 2 years after the date of the original cease trade order. The Superintendent will accept a reactivation application relating to an order that has been in effect for more than 2 years only if the issuer has continuously owned its principal asset (which is the subject of its business plan) since it became dormant. An issuer seeking reactivation after more than 2 years of dormancy must file with its application a preliminary prospectus indicating that the issuer meets all applicable requirements for an initial public offering.

(b)   The information filed as part of the reactivation application must enable the Commission or the Superintendent to determine whether trading in the dormant issuer's securities is prejudicial to the public interest. If, after a review of the reactivation application, the Superintendent determines that trading in the issuer's securities is not prejudicial to the public interest, the Superintendent will issue

(i)   a letter indicating acceptance of the records or information (subject to any shareholder approval which may be required by law or by a stock exchange), and

(ii)   a certificate of good standing under section 60 of the Act which will constitute evidence that the cease trade order lapsed as of the date of the certificate.

The cease trade order will remain in effect until the Superintendent issues the letter and certificate of good standing.

(c)   An applicant must ensure that its submission is complete when filed and that it responds as quickly as possible to the Superintendent's requests for clarification or further information. The Superintendent may consider the reactivation application to be abandoned if the total number of days an issuer accumulates in responding to the Superintendent's comment letters exceeds 75 days.

3.2   *Covering Letter*

(a)   A reactivation application should be addressed as follows:

Deputy Superintendent, Registration and Statutory Filings
British Columbia Securities Commission
1100-865 Hornby Street
Vancouver, B.C.
V6Z 2H4

(b)   A covering letter listing the documents being filed must accompany the application. The letter should identify the documents using the lettering system indicated in section 3.3 below. Any non-applicable items should be indicated as such.

(c)   The issuer need not refile documents already on file with the Commission provided that they are current. The covering letter should state that the documents have previously been filed and provide relevant details of the filing.

3.3   *Documents Required to be Filed*

The following documents must be filed in connection with a reactivation application and should be marked to correspond with the disclosure in the covering letter:

A.   *Fee checklist* - a completed checklist in the required form, together with any applicable filing fees prescribed by section 183(1) of the Regulation, including:

   (i)   the reactivation application filing fee,

  (ii)   all outstanding fees payable in respect of previous filings made by the issuer and in respect of filings made as part of the reactivation application, and

(iii)   the appropriate filing fee for any prospectus or technical or engineering report filed with the application.

Cheques should be made payable to the "Minister of Finance".

B.   *Audited annual financial statements* - the issuer's audited annual financial statements for each fiscal year ending after the last year in respect of which the issuer has filed statements in accordance with the Regulation.

C.   *Interim financial statements* - the issuer's unaudited interim financial statements or, if the issuer is an exchange issuer, quarterly reports for each quarter subsequent to the end of the issuer's last fiscal year.

D.   *Confirmation of mailing* - confirmation that the financial statements referred to in paragraphs (B) and (C) have been mailed to the issuer's shareholders.

E.   *Material change reports* - unless a prospectus or statement of material facts is filed with the application, a material change report in respect of each material change in the affairs of the issuer that has not previously been reported on.

F.   *Business Plan* - unless a prospectus or statement of material facts is filed with the application, a business plan in accordance with Part 4 of this local policy statement.

G.   *Engineering or technical report* - a report will be required only if the issuer has effectively abandoned what was the principal property or business of the issuer on the date of the cease trade order, and is embarking on exploration of another property or commencing another business coincident with the reactivation application. In addition, the normal requirements for a technical or engineering report will apply if a prospectus or statement of material facts is filed with the reactivation application.

A natural resource issuer must file two signed copies of each engineering report, prepared in accordance with National Policy No. 2-A or 2-B, as the case may be, Local Policy Statement 3-01 and Form 54 or 55 in respect of each property on which the issuer intends to carry out work.

An industrial issuer must file a technical report in accordance with Local Policy Statement 3-04.

H.   *Confirmation of status or good standing* - a certificate respecting the status of the issuer from the British Columbia Registrar of Companies or the appropriate regulatory authority in the jurisdiction in which the issuer was incorporated, organized or continued, or a legal opinion from the filing solicitor to the same effect.

I.   *Title opinion* - if an engineering report is required to be filed, a legal opinion relating to the status of the issuer's interest in the new mineral resource properties that are the subject of the engineering report.

J.   *Form 4* - a list of the directors and officers holding office on the date of the reactivation application and a Form 4 for each director and officer of the issuer and its existing or proposed subsidiaries.

Alternatively, a statutory declaration may be sworn by a director or officer attesting that he has filed a Form 4 within the three year period preceding the date of the application and that there has been no change in the facts disclosed or required to be disclosed in the Form 4.

See NIN 92/18 "Required Form of Personal Information".

K.   *Insider reports* - a signed insider report for each person who is an insider of the issuer as of the date of the reactivation application.

L.   *Letter from transfer agent* - a letter from the transfer agent acknowledging that it is prepared to facilitate registration of share transfers and issuances upon reactivation of the issuer.

M.   *Confirmation of listed status* - in respect of an issuer whose securities have at any time been listed for trading on a stock exchange, written confirmation from a stock exchange in Canada that, upon reactivation, the issuer will meet all of the applicable requirements of the stock exchange and that the issuer's securities will be listed or reinstated for trading.

N.   *Directors' resolution* - a certified copy of the directors' resolution approving the making of the reactivation application.

O.   *Financing document* - a preliminary prospectus if a public offering of the issuer's securities is contemplated as part of the reactivation or if the reactivation application is made more than two years after the cease trade order. Reference should be made to Local Policy Statement 3-02 for guidance concerning the additional documents that must be filed with a preliminary prospectus.

A statement of material facts may be filed in place of a prospectus if the dormant issuer's securities are listed on the Vancouver Stock Exchange on the date of the reactivation application and the reactivation application is made less than two years after the cease trade order.

Where a private placement is proposed, a copy of the subscription agreement must be filed and the covering letter must indicate the statutory exemptions which are being relied upon. If a discretionary exemption order is being sought under sections 33 and 59 of the Act, the application for an order should be filed with the reactivation application.

3.4   *Review of Reactivation Application*

(a)   Upon filing, an initial review of the application will be carried out in order to ensure that all of the documents required under section 3.3

have been filed. If the application is incomplete or does not comply with applicable requirements of this local policy statement, it may be returned to the issuer. Where an application has been returned to the issuer, the issuer may request a partial refund of the filing fees paid in respect of the application or may apply the refundable portion of the filing fees to a refiling of the application.

(b)   A reactivation application will be assigned to an analyst for review and comment as soon as practicable after it has been filed. All further correspondence in connection with the application should be directed to that analyst. If a preliminary prospectus, statement of material facts or application for a discretionary exemption order has also been filed, it will be vetted concurrently with the application for reactivation.

(c)   After the issuer has responded satisfactorily to all requests for clarification or further information, the Superintendent will advise the issuer that the application has been accepted, subject to the issuer obtaining any shareholder approval required by law or a stock exchange, and will issue a certificate of good standing. The Superintendent will also issue, as appropriate, a receipt for a prospectus, an acceptance of a statement of material facts, or an order under sections 33 and 59 of the Act.

(d)   Throughout the application process, the issuer must file any required reports, financial statements or other information as they become due.

PART 4   BUSINESS PLAN

4.1   A reactivation application by a non-resource issuer must include a business plan prepared in accordance with the guidelines set out in Local Policy Statement 3-04. A natural resource issuer will not be required to file a business plan that complies with Local Policy Statement 3-04, but its business plan must contain the information required in section 4.2.

4.2   A business plan must include a discussion of the current financial condition of the issuer and, if applicable, the measures proposed to restore its solvency. Reactivation of a dormant issuer will not be permitted unless its business plan indicates that it will be solvent when trading of its securities resumes and will remain so in carrying out its business for at least six months thereafter.

PART 5   FINANCING AS PART OF A REACTIVATION

5.1   The business plan of the issuer may provide for certain trades in securities - for example, a public offering, the issuance of shares for debt, a private placement or a trade to effect a change in control - that must be carried out as part of the reactivation process. In most cases, these trades should not occur until the cease trade order has lapsed. To the extent that any trade must be completed before the reactivation application has been accepted, an application must be made to the Superintendent for an order under section 153 of the Act that partially revokes the cease trade order.

5.2   Where a reactivation application is accompanied by a preliminary prospectus, an application for an order under section 153 of the Act must be made if the preliminary prospectus will be distributed to any persons for the purpose of soliciting expressions of interest in the issuer's securities. No partial revocation order will be required if the preliminary prospectus is provided only to the staff of the Commission for vetting as part of the reactivation application.

DATED at Vancouver, British Columbia, this 13th day of October 1989.

Douglas M. Hyndman

Chairman

LOCAL POLICY STATEMENT 3-37
RESTRICTED SHARES (UNCOMMON EQUITIES)
DISTRIBUTIONS AND DISCLOSURE

1.0 IMPLEMENTATION

    1.1   This Local Policy Statement has been revised solely to conform with the Securities Act S.B.C. 1985 c. 83 and the Regulations thereto and to conform with Ontario Local Policy 1.3, except for paragraphs V and VI of that policy. It becomes effective upon proclamation of the Securities Act on February 1, 1987.

2.0 APPLICATIONS AND DEFINITIONS

    2.1   This Local Policy Statement applies to securities of issuers that are reporting issuers but does not apply to:

        2.1.1   shares offered by mutual funds

        2.1.2   shares that carry a right to vote subject to some limit or restriction on the number or percentage of shares that may be voted or owned by persons or companies that are not Canadian citizens or residents, or

        2.1.3   shares of financial institutions subject to statutory restrictions on the level of ownership by a person or issuer but only to the extent of such ownership restrictions.

    2.2   In this Local Policy Statement:

        2.2.1   "common shares"

        means equity securities to which are attached voting rights exercisable in all circumstances, irrespective of the number of shares owned, which voting rights are not less, on a per share basis, than the voting rights attaching to any other shares of an outstanding class of security of the issuer;

        2.2.2   "non-voting shares"

        means restricted shares that do not carry the right to vote except for a right to vote in certain limited circumstances, e.g. to elect less than 50% of the Board of Directors or to vote in circumstances where the governing corporate law provides the right to vote for shares that are otherwise non-voting;

        2.2.3   "preference shares"

        means shares to which there is attached a preference or right over any class of securities of the issuer, but does not include equity securities;

        2.2.4   "restricted share term"

        refers to the terms "non-voting shares", "subordinate voting shares", "restricted voting shares" and such other terms as the Superintendent may determine for restricted shares that are not appropriately described by the foregoing terms;

        2.2.5   "restricted shares"

        means equity securities that are not common shares;

        2.2.6   "restricted voting shares"

        means restricted shares that carry a right to vote subject to some limit or restriction on the number or percentage of shares that may be voted by a person or issuer or group of persons or issuers (except where the restriction or limit is applicable only to persons or issuers that are not Canadian citizens or residents); and

        "subordinate voting shares"

        means restricted shares that carry a right to vote where there is another class of security outstanding that carries a greater right to vote, on a per share basis.

Local
Policies

2.3   The Commission, in its discretion, may determine that, for the purposes of this Local Policy Statement, a particular class of security shall be deemed to be common, preference or restricted shares, as the case may be, notwithstanding that a literal application of the above definitions would produce a different result. The Commission may determine the restricted share term that is appropriate for a class of restricted shares. In exercising its discretion, the Commission will be guided by the principles underlying this Local Policy Statement.

2.4   As a general rule, equity securities will be considered to be restricted shares where the allocation of voting rights does not relate reasonably to the equity interests of the various classes of securities. Shares will generally be considered to be restricted shares where they have provisions that tend to nullify or restrict their voting rights or where there is another class of securities that have provisions producing similar effect. For example, shares that carry a right to vote will be considered restricted shares where:

         2.4.1   there is a class of preferred shares that carry a disproportionate vote per share, or

         2.4.2   there is a class of preferred shares that carry one vote per share but that were issued for a disproportionately low consideration per share (and hence, per vote) in relation to the other outstanding shares of the issuer, or

         2.4.3   there is another class of equity shares that carry one vote per share but that are entitled to only a fraction of a right to participate in earnings or assets to which the first class of equity securities is entitled.

2.5   In the case of issuers listed on the Vancouver Stock Exchange (the "VSE"), where that body would normally exercise its discretion as to listings, the VSE will determine whether a particular class of shares shall be deemed to be common, preference or restricted shares. The staffs of the Commission and the VSE will cooperate in making such determinations where both are involved.

3.0   DESCRIPTION OF SHARES

3.1   *Description and Legal Designation*

         3.1.1   Publicly traded shares should not be described as "common" or "preference" (or "preferred") unless such shares are common shares or preference shares, respectively. Publicly traded restricted shares should be described with the appropriate restricted share term.

         3.1.2   For all shares that are to be offered pursuant to a prospectus filed with the Commission, a receipt will not be issued therefor if the legal designation of the shares:

                 3.1.2.1   includes the word "common" and such shares are not common shares,

                 3.1.2.2   includes the word "preference" or "preferred" and such shares are not preference shares, or

                 3.1.2.3   in the case of restricted shares, does not include the appropriate restricted share term,

         in each such case, notwithstanding permissive but subject to mandatory, provisions of applicable legislation relating to the legal designation of such shares. The foregoing applies to all shares issuable upon the conversion or exchange of securities, or the exercise of rights of warrants, offered pursuant to a prospectus.

         3.1.3   Where an issuer that has not yet complied with Section 3.2 of this Local Policy Statement proposes to issue restricted shares pursuant to the rights offering exemption contained in the Act the Superintendent will require appropriate undertakings in respect of changing the legal designation of such shares at the issuer's next shareholders' meeting.

3.1.4 The VSE require similar legal designations for the listing of new classes of securities and may require listed issuers with such existing classes of securities to amend the legal designation. The Commission will require issuers of VSE listed restricted shares to comply with the foregoing VSE requirements.

3.1.5 In all reporting issuer disclosure and offering documents, each defined term used to refer to restricted shares shall include the applicable restricted share term.

3.2 *Stock Quotations*

The Commission is of the view that readers of stock quotations should be aware that certain shares are restricted shares. Therefore, in all stock quotations, such as those listed in newspapers, there should be employed a symbol to identify restricted shares. A legend should explain the meaning of the symbol.

3.3 *Dealer Confirmation*

3.3.1 Under Section 80 of the Regulations, a registered dealer who has acted in connection with a trade in a security shall promptly send or deliver to the client a written confirmation of the transaction setting forth, among other things, the description of the security. The Commission is of the view that the description of restricted shares should include the appropriate restricted share term. The Commission recognizes that compliance with this requirement could be difficult especially for securities that are not normally traded in British Columbia. The VSE publishes a daily record of trading in shares listed on the VSE which record includes, for restricted shares, a code that identifies such shares by the appropriate restricted share symbol. The obligation of registrants to comply with Section 2.3 will be limited to securities set out in the foregoing record and those identified on similar documents prepared by such other stock exchanges or self-regulatory organizations as are recognized by the Commission for the purpose of this Local Policy Statement. The Montreal Exchange, Alberta Stock Exchange, Toronto Stock Exchange, Winnipeg Stock Exchange and the Investment Dealers Association are hereby so recognized.

3.3.2 Where due to data processing restrictions the foregoing requirement cannot be satisfied, the registrant may use an abbreviation for the restricted share term provided that an explanation of the abbreviation is given on the confirmation.

3.3.3 The same disclosure of the description of the security shall be included in all statements of transactions or security positions sent to the client.

3.4 *Dealer or Advisor Literature*

In all recommendations, selling documents and other literature prepared by or for a dealer or adviser, any restricted shares referred to therein shall be described using the appropriate restricted share term. This requirement shall be limited to those shares that appear on the documents referred to in Section 3.3.1.

3.5 *Reporting Issuer Disclosure Documentation*

3.5.1 All documents that a reporting issuer sends to its shareholders pursuant to its obligations under the Act (e.g. information circulars and directors' circulars) and any annual information form, shall include a statement describing:

3.5.1.1 the restrictions on the voting rights of restricted shares, and

3.5.1.2 the rights of holders of such shares where a take-over bid is made for the securities of the reporting issuer having voting rights or superior voting rights, as the case may be provided that:

3.5.1.3   interim financial statements, annual financial statements (to which Section 3.5.3 below applies) and any accompanying discussion by management of such financial statements, need not include such a statement.

3.5.2   In press releases, material change reports and documents that the issuer sends to its shareholders otherwise than pursuant to its obligations under the Act, any reference to restricted shares shall include the appropriate restricted share term.

3.5.3   The CICA Handbook requires that in audited financial statements, there be a "brief description" of each class of securities either on the balance sheet or in the notes to the financial statements. The Commission has concluded that, other than where there is a one line reference to "capital", "shareholder's capital", "share capital", "equity capital" or like term, restricted shares shall be broken out as a separate category on the balance sheet. The Commission is of the view that where capitalization is set out in unaudited financial statements these statements should contain similar disclosure.

3.6   *Minimum Disclosure in Offering Documents and Information Circulars*

3.6.1   This section sets out the minimum disclosure that will be required in all documents describing the issue of restricted shares filed with the Commission by a reporting issuer or by an issuer that will become a reporting issuer upon the acceptance for filing of such document by the Commission, including any prospectus, short form prospectus, exchange offering prospectus, statement of material facts, rights offering circular, securities exchange take-over bid circular, offering memorandum or information circular concerning a proposed corporate reorganization or amalgamation that would have the effect of converting or subdividing, in whole or in part, existing shares into restricted shares or creating new restricted shares.

3.6.2   The minimum disclosure that is detailed below as required in a prospectus is applicable to all other documents referred to in the preceding paragraph to the extent that the form of the document permits. Offering documents other than prospectuses usually do not include summaries and may, depending on the nature of the document, not include financial statements.

3.6.2.1   Designation – The legal designation of the shares being offered or described shall be as set out in Section 3.1.2.

3.6.2.2   Face Page – The heading showing the number and class of securities offered shall include the restricted share term in the same type face as the rest of the heading. Any defined term used to refer to restricted shares shall include the applicable restricted share term.

3.6.2.3   Summary – The summary shall include:

3.6.2.3.1   a summary of the voting rights attached to the shares being offered (or a statement that there are no voting rights) and to voting rights, if any, possessed by any other class of securities of the issuer that are greater on a per share basis than those attached to the shares being offered, and

3.6.2.3.2   a summary of any significant rights in applicable corporate or securities law that are not available to the holders of the shares being offered (e.g. rights under take-over bid legislation) and the extent of any rights provided in the constating documents for the protection of holders of the shares (e.g. provisions designed to ensure that the holders have an equal opportunity to participate in a take-over bid), with a cross reference to a full explanation in the body of the prospectus.

3.6.2.4   Body – The body of the prospectus shall include full descriptions and explanations where applicable of the statements referred to in Section 3.6.2.3.1 and 3.6.2.3.2 above.

3.6.2.5   Financial Statements – The financial statements shall be in accordance with Section 3.5.

4.0   DISSEMINATION OF INFORMATION

4.1   *General*

All informational documents that are required by the governing corporate or securities law to be sent to the holders of voting securities shall also be sent at the same time to the holders of restricted shares. Such documents would include, but not be limited to, information circulars, notices or meetings and financial statements.

4.2   *Forwarding of Information by Registrants*

Section 165 of the Regulations requires a registrant or custodian, under the circumstances described in that section, to forward certain material to the beneficial owners of securities registered in its name. Registrants shall forward the information referred to in Section 4.1 to the beneficial owners of restricted shares registered in their name.

4.3   *Sending of Financial Statements*

Reporting issuers shall send financial statements to holders of Restricted Shares as required by Section 141 of the Regulations.

5.0   MEETING OF THE SHAREHOLDERS

Every reporting issuer shall give notice of shareholders' meetings to holders of restricted shares and permit the holders of such shares to attend, in person or by proxy, and to speak at all shareholders' meetings to the extent that a holder of voting securities of that issue would be entitled to attend and to speak at shareholders' meetings. For all new issues of restricted shares the constating documents must provide that the holders of such Shares shall be given notice of and be invited to attend meetings of the voting shareholders of the reporting issuer.

6.0   CONSULTATION WITH THE SUPERINTENDENT

6.1   Issuers are invited to consult with the Superintendent where there is doubt that the application of this Local Policy Statement is appropriate. Where he deems that it is not prejudicial to the public interest to do so, the Superintendent may exempt an issuer or a class of issuers from compliance with this Local Policy Statement or any requirement thereof subject to such terms and conditions as he may impose.

6.2   The Superintendent will give consideration to exempting an issuer from compliance with this Local Policy Statement where:

6.2.1   It is not a Canadian based issuer and less than 2% of any class of the issuer is held in British Columbia, or

6.2.2   The voting rights attaching to a class of shares carrying superior voting rights are not sufficient to materially affect control of the issuer.

DATED at Vancouver, B.C. this 1st day of February, 1987.

Jill Bodkin
Chairman
B.C. Securities Commission

LOCAL POLICY STATEMENT 3-38

REGISTRATION OF NON-RESIDENTS – SECURITIES ACT

1.0 IMPLEMENTATION

1.1 This Local Policy Statement has been revised solely to conform with the Securities Act S.B.C. 1985 c. 83 and the Regulations thereto. Other than consequential amendments, there have been no changes of a substantive nature to this policy. It becomes effective upon proclamation of the Act on February 1, 1987.

2.0 CONDITIONS

An applicant who wishes to be registered in British Columbia and who is not a resident of British Columbia must comply with the following conditions:

2.1 The applicant's employer must be registered in British Columbia.

2.2 The applicant and his employer must be residents of a province or territory of Canada.

2.3 The applicant and his employer must be registered and in good standing under the securities legislation of their home jurisdiction.

2.4 The applicant's employer must be a member of one of the following self-regulatory organizations: Toronto Stock Exchange, Alberta Stock Exchange, Montreal Exchange, Vancouver Stock Exchange, and the Investment Dealers Association of Canada.

2.5 The applicant must have passed the Canadian Securities Course. While no special course is being prescribed for registration of non-residents in British Columbia, applicants are put on notice that they will be held responsible for compliance with the Act of British Columbia, the Regulations thereto and any applicable Local Policy Statements. In addition, registrants will be held responsible for knowledge of Vancouver Stock Exchange By-Laws and Rules, as well as the By-Laws and Rules of the Pacific District of the Investment Dealers Association of Canada.

3.0 FORM 4

When the conditions in Section 2.0 have been complied with, the applicant may apply by completing Form 4. This office will accept a certified true copy of the most recent form, provided it is originally signed by the applicant. The applicant must also include a statement certifying that there is no change in the information on the applicable form since it was signed, dated and submitted to the regulatory authority in the home jurisdiction. An address for service in British Columbia must also be provided. This will normally be the branch office of the employer in British Columbia. Payment of the full fee will be required regardless of the number of accounts or trading the applicant intends to do.

4.0 REGISTRATION

When registration is granted, this office will notify the securities regulatory authority in the applicant's home jurisdiction, with a request that we be notified immediately if any investigation or disciplinary action is taken against the applicant. Should the registration of the applicant or his employer be suspended or cancelled in his home jurisdiction, similar action will automatically take place in British Columbia.

5.0 BREACHES

Inasmuch as this office will find it impractical to lay charges for breaches of the Act, we will be dependent upon the securities authorities within the home jurisdiction for investigation and necessary action. To the same extent, we will rely on the self-regulatory organizations to take action on other disciplinary matters.

DATED at VANCOUVER, B.C., this 1st day of February, 1987.

Jill Bodkin
Chairman
B.C. Securities Commission

LOCAL POLICY STATEMENT 3-39

GUIDELINES FOR ADVERTISING ISSUES OF SECURITIES AND FOR PROMOTIONAL ACTIVITIES DURING THE COURSE OF A DISTRIBUTION

1.0   IMPLEMENTATION

     1.1   This Local Policy Statement has been revised solely to conform with the Securities Act S.B.C. 1985 c. 83 and the Regulations thereto. Other than consequential amendments, there have been no changes of a substantive nature to this policy. It becomes effective upon proclamation of the Act on February 1, 1987.

2.0   ADVERTISERS AFFECTED BY THIS POLICY STATEMENT AND PROCEDURES TO BE FOLLOWED BY SUCH ADVERTISERS

     2.1   Registrants for trading in securities who are not members of either the Vancouver Stock Exchange or the Investment Dealers Association, (e.g. security issuer) and others authorized to distribute a security are required to file with the Superintendent a copy of all advertising material, literature, promotional information and lead getting material of any kind to be used in the course of the registrant's operations.

     2.2   Copy in the nature of institutional advertising by the dealer (i.e. copy advertising the registrant's services) and copy relating to an offer of a security need not be submitted to the Superintendent prior to publication, but must be filed at the Office of the Superintendent within five days of publication, and must be suitably red-lined and annotated (see Section 3.2 below). A tear-sheet from a newspaper display, suitably identified, red-lined and annotated, will suffice for filing purposes.

     2.3   All copy submitted under Section 2.2 above will be filed for reference in the event of inquiry, complaint, etc. and will be deemed a filing under Section 138 of the Act. All such copy should adhere to the relevant guidelines set out in Sections 3 to 5 below. A Section 2.2 filing which fails to adhere to these guidelines may prompt the Superintendent to take appropriate disciplinary measures and/or to require to be withdrawn from publication any copy which he deems to be misleading.

3.0   GUIDELINES OF GENERAL APPLICATION

     3.1   Public confidence is a significant factor in the complex process of raising capital. One of the goals of the Act is to promote such confidence in the British Columbia capital market and thus to insure continued infusion of risk capital to finance new economic activity. In furtherance of this goal, the Act prescribes full disclosure of all the pertinent facts and figures which are needed by a prospective investor making a judgement about an issuer's securities. Such full disclosure ideally should be provided by a limited amount of advertising of security offerings, the Commission is aware that full disclosure can seldom be encompassed in an advertisement, and as a result expects advertising copy to be worded so as to encourage the interested reader to consult the relevant offering circulars for the pertinent facts. Copy should be free of quotations, opinions and data which may lead the reader to make false inferences. Above all, partial disclosure of a series of facts and figures should be avoided when full disclosure of such facts and figures is required for a proper comprehension of the offering.

     3.2   Promotional assertions must be substantiated by reference to disclosure of facts in the related institutional brochure or securities offering circular. All such assertions appearing in advertising copy filed with the Superintendent must be red-lined and cross-referenced to the relevant disclosure in the brochure or circular previously filed.

     3.3   The use of words such as "preferred", "guaranteed", "liquid", and "indemnity" should be avoided. When modifiers are employed, their context must be clear, e.g. when "preferred" is used, the nature of the preference (dividends, creditor's claim) must be disclosed; when "guaranteed" is used, what it is that is guaranteed, the guarantor and the underlying security for the guarantee must be disclosed; "liquid" means "readily convertible into cash" and should be used only when such convertibility can be achieved at no loss to the investor. The onus is on the registrant or other distributor to avoid using equivocal words and phrases and to insure that copy is so worded that a reader cannot reasonably draw a false inference.

3.4   A reference to a benefit, or a comparison of outlay and benefits or returns from outlay must be free of equivocation, e.g. if a reference is made to a benefit which has specific conditions or contingencies riding on it, a reference must also be made to such conditional aspects. If matched columns of figures representing outlay and recovery or outlay and tax benefits resulting from such outlay are disclosed, the reader is entitled to infer that no conditions attach to such figures unless such conditions are clearly disclosed. Where full disclosure on such points cannot be achieved in the advertising copy, partial disclosure should be avoided.

3.5   Reference to historical financial data must be based on the results for at least three consecutive years. When the issuer has had less than three years experience, any disclosure of financial data must be accompanied by a caveat to this effect.

3.6   The foregoing guidelines should be followed, where applicable, in promotional presentations made through the medium of television or radio.

4.0   GUIDELINES FOR REGISTRANTS MAKING A DISTRIBUTION BY A PROSPECTUS

An advertisement must contain a disclaimer stating that it must not be construed as an offering and that the offering is made only by prospectus. In addition, the name and address of at least one registrant from whom more information and a copy of the prospectus may be obtained should be disclosed.

5.0   PROMOTIONAL ACTIVITIES DURING THE COURSE OF A DISTRIBUTION TO THE PUBLIC

5.1   A significant lapse of time may occur between a decision of management to seek financing by way of a prospectus offering, the preparation and filing of a preliminary prospectus, with the receipting of the final prospectus, engaging in the distribution of the securities and concluding such distribution. Any promotional activity occurring over this time should be such as to support full, true and plain disclosure provided in the prospectus.

5.2   The Act defines "trade" to include any act, advertisement, conduct or negotiation, directly or indirectly in furtherance of a trade.

5.3   Where over the time period described in Section 5.1, an issuer received coverage by way of an article in a newspaper or magazine, or by way of a broadcast to telecast, the onus is on the promoters, directors, registrants and all others having some interest in an issuer not to participate in any promotional activity which may result in the dissemination of representations about the issuer which are not supported by the prospectus disclosure.

5.4   Where in the opinion of the Superintendent material facts about an issuer as described in paragraph 5.3 have been disseminated, he may require that the prospectus contain express disclosure of such misrepresentation as a condition of receipting the prospectus or permitting a distribution to continue.

DATED at Vancouver, B.C., this 1st day of February, 1987.

Jill Bodkin
Chairman
B.C. Securities Commission

LOCAL POLICY STATEMENT 3-41

LAWYER'S CONFLICT OF INTEREST

1.0   IMPLEMENTATION

1.1   This Local Policy Statement has been revised solely to conform with the Securities Act S.B.C. 1985 c. 83 and the Regulations thereto. Other than consequential amendments, there have been no changes of a substantive nature to this policy. It becomes effective upon proclamation of the Securities Act on February 1, 1987.

2.0   TERMS OF REFERENCE

2.1   This Local Policy Statement addresses the questions of disclosure concerning lawyers' shareholding on reporting issuers for which they act as solicitors and provides legal opinions. It was developed after numerous meetings between the Superintendent and the Natural Resources and Business Law Subsection of the British Columbia branch of the Canadian Bar Association and with the assistance of special committees set up by the Law Society of British Columbia. The Law Society is considering guidelines as to the circumstances in which, as a matter of professional ethics, such a conflict would make it improper for a solicitor to act at all.

3.0   DISCLOSURE GUIDELINES

3.1   In all disclosure documents submitted for filing by or on behalf of an issuer with the Commission or the Vancouver Stock Exchange the following matters shall be disclosed:

3.1.1   the nature and extent of any material beneficial interest, direct or indirect, in any securities or property, of the issuer or any holding company or major subsidiary thereof, held by:

3.1.1.1   the responsible solicitor, or

3.1.1.2   Where known by the responsible solicitor after reasonable inquiry, any partner of the responsible solicitor's firm or any person related to the responsible solicitor or any such partner.

It is sufficient if the interests of the responsible solicitor, all partners of the responsible solicitor's firm and all persons related to the responsible solicitor or any such partner, are shown in the aggregate.

3.1.2   whether:

3.1.2.1   the responsible solicitor, or

3.1.2.2   where by the responsible solicitor after reasonable inquiry, any partner of the responsible solicitor's firm or any person related to the responsible solicitor or any such partner

is a director or senior officer in the issuer or in any holding company or major subsidiary thereof or is a promoter of the issuer.

3.2   Where the disclosure document is:

3.2.1   a takeover bid circular or a directors' circular, the disclosure required in Paragraph 3 hereof shall relate to both the offerer issuer and the offeree issuer; and

3.2.2   an information circular sent to members in connection with an amalgamation, merger or other business combination or in connection with the sale of the whole or substantially the whole of the undertaking of the issuer, the disclosure required in Paragraph 3 hereof shall relate to each of the issuers involved in such amalgamation, merger, combination or sale.

4.0   Where an opinion is provided to the Commission or the Vancouver Stock Exchange on behalf of an issuer, the solicitor signing the same shall certify in such opinion or in a separate memorandum delivered contemporaneously therewith, that neither such solicitor nor to the knowledge of such solicitor after reasonable inquiry, any partner of the solicitor's firm or any person related to such solicitor or any such partner has any material beneficial interest, direct or indirect, in any securities or in the property of the issuer or of any holding company or major subsidiary thereof.

5.0   INTERPRETATION

5.1   "materiality"

While disclosure is required pursuant to this Policy Statement of a "material" beneficial interest held by a solicitor, it is recognized that no standard of materiality can be applied with certainty. For the purposes hereof the holding of the responsible solicitor, taken together with the holdings of any partners, and any person related to such solicitor or partner of a greater than 5% interest in the issued and outstanding shares or shares under option of any class or more than 50,000 shares (including options to purchase shares) of any class shall be deemed a material interest.

5.2 "disclosure"

Disclosure means any of the following documents issued by an issuer, other than a document filed in British Columbia with the Commission and/or the Vancouver Stock Exchange and, in addition, with the Securities Commission in the province of Alberta, Saskatchewan, Manitoba, Ontario or Quebec pursuant to the laws of the said province:

5.2.1 a prospectus;

5.2.2 a statement of material facts;

5.2.3 a takeover bid circular;

5.2.4 a directors' circular;

5.2.5 an information circular sent to members in connection with an amalgamation, merger or other business combination or in connection with a sale of the whole or substantially the whole of the undertaking of the issuer; and

5.2.6 an offering memorandum or similar document distributed to investors pursuant to an order, determination or ruling under Sections 33 or 59 of the Act.

5.3 "responsible solicitor"

Responsible solicitor means the solicitor who is primarily responsible for the preparation of or for advice to the corporation or an underwriter of the corporation with respect to the contents of any disclosure document.

5.4 "person related"

Person related means, with respect to any person, a relative of such person, including his spouse, or of the spouse of such person, who in either case has the same home as such person.

5.5 "major subsidiary"

Major subsidiary means a subsidiary, either the assets or the sales and operating revenues of which, represent greater than 10% of the assets or the sales and operating revenues respectively of the holding company and the holding company's subsidiaries on a consolidated basis, according to the financial statements for its own most recently completed fiscal year.

5.6 "holding company"

A company is the holding company of a company if the last mentioned company is its subsidiary.

6.0 While the obligation to comply with this Local Policy Statement rests on the corporation concerned, and its underwriters or agents, except for Section 4 hereof, where the obligation is that of the responsible solicitor, the Commission and the Vancouver Stock Exchange will continue to rely on solicitors to exercise due diligence in the preparation of disclosure documents. If it should come to the attention of the Commission that the non-disclosure appears to have been occasioned by the failure of a solicitor to exercise such due diligence, the Commission will, in an appropriate case, refer the matter to the Law Society exercising jurisdiction over the solicitor concerned.

DATED at Vancouver, B.C., this 1st day of February, 1987.

Jill Bodkin
Chairman
B.C. Securities Commission

LOCAL POLICY STATEMENT 3-42
REGISTERED REPRESENTATIVES CONTINUED
FITNESS FOR REGISTRATION

1.0 IMPLEMENTATION

    1.1 This Local Policy Statement has been revised solely to conform with the Securities Act S.B.C. 1985 c. 83 and the Regulations thereto. Other than consequential amendments, there have been no changes of a substantive nature to this policy. It becomes effective upon proclamation of the Act on February 1, 1987.

2.0 APPLICATION

    2.1 This Local Policy Statement applies to Registered Representatives employed by non-member houses as well as by members of the Investment Dealers Association and/or the Vancouver Stock Exchange. It should be read in conjunction with National Policy 18. The chief concerns of this Local Policy Statement involve continued fitness of registered representatives who become personally insolvent or who become involved with listed and unlisted companies as property vendors, promoters, directors and/or officers or some combination thereof.

3.0 BANKRUPTCY/INSOLVENCY OF REGISTERED REPRESENTATIVES

An economic downturn may have an impact on some Registered Representatives who are facing personal financial difficulty. This poses a potential threat to the clients of the Registered Representatives, and to the individual brokerage house and any self-regulatory organization that may be guaranteeing accounts, such as the Vancouver Stock Exchange and the National Contingency Fund. It is not the intention of this office to automatically cancel or suspend licences of Registered Representatives encountering serious financial problems, such as entering into bankruptcy, as each case must be dealt with on its individual merits. Therefore, effective immediately, each Registered Representative must immediately notify his employer, the Superintendent's office, and the appropriate self-regulatory organization of the financial problem. Measures will then be taken to ensure that no threat is posed to the public. Failure to immediately disclose a serious problem may well result in immediate suspension until such time as the problem is resolved.

4.0 REGISTERED REPRESENTATIVES AS DIRECTORS, ETC., OF REPORTING COMPANIES

    4.1 Occasionally in the past, it has been found that Registered Representatives have been involved with listed and unlisted companies as property vendors, promoters, directors and/or officers or some combination thereof. The Vancouver Stock Exchange Rules presently contain provisions that preclude Registered Representatives from being directors or officers of listed companies without prior approval of the Membership Committee. Other VSE rules prevent Registered Representatives from being vendors of property or acquiring property from companies listed on the Exchange.

    4.2 This raises the question as to whether a Registered Representative who is an insider can recommend the purchase or sale of security in these issues to a client purely on the merits of the issue. The Registered Representatives may well be in possession of information respecting the affairs of the issuer, not generally known to the public, which could have an effect on the price of the security. It is therefore questionable whether such salesman, being in possession of such information, would put his client's financial well-being before that of his legal duty to the issuer. There is no question that a salesman must give paramount concern to his client and any resulting conflict must always be resolved in favour of that client.

    4.3 National Policy Statement 18 notes that every director has a fiduciary obligation not to reveal any privileged information to anyone not authorized to receive such information, and that a director's first responsibility is to the corporation. The National Policy further notes that where a Registered Representative is not a director, but is acting in an advisory capacity to an issuer and discussing confidential matters, the ground rules should be substantially the same.

Local
Policies

4.4 Both the above statements reflect fiduciary duties and the general principles of law. This need not, however, necessarily create a conflict between this Local Policy Statement and National Policy Statement 18. One rule requires a director to protect the confidentiality of information, the other requires a broker to protect his client's position.

4.5 A Registered Representative must give paramount consideration to his client, and if that obligation creates a conflict with National Policy Statement 18, by virtue of his close association with a company, then the Registered Representative's duty is to decline to act for the client in the particular transaction. Where it is found that a Registered Representative is, directly or indirectly, involved in a situation which puts him in a position of conflict of interest with his client, the mere fact of the situation will call into question his fitness for continued registration and a hearing may result.

4.6 This Local Policy Statement is meant as a warning and guide. Where a filings analyst, in the course of reviewing a prospectus submission, encounters evidence that a Registered Representative is an insider of the subject issuer, a comment to this effect will likely appear in a filing deficiency letter. It is not the responsibility of the analyst to advise as to whether or not a breach of duty is deemed to arise from the individual having placed himself in a situation of conflict of interest.

DATED at Vancouver, B.C. this 1st day of February, 1987.

Jill Bodkin
Chairman
B.C. Securities Commission

INTERIM LOCAL POLICY STATEMENT 3-43
GOVERNMENT STRIP BONDS

See NIN 91/23 "Introduction of Interim Local Policy Statement 3-43 'Government Strip Bonds' ". The interim Local Policy Statement 3-43 is more uniform with Ontario than the former policy statement. A new form of Information Statement is attached to the interim policy statement. The Commission proposes to limit the trading of government strip bonds to persons registered in an appropriate registration category under the Act. See also NIN 95/9 "Government Strip Bonds - Information Statement" which indicates the intention of the Commission to revise interim Local Policy Statement 3-43 "Government Strip Bonds" and replace BOR 91/12 "Government Strip Bonds".

TABLE OF CONTENTS

6.   TRANSITION
    6.1   Approved Information Statement During Transitional Period
    6.2   First-Time Purchasers

Appendix A   Information Statement Prepared by IDA

Appendix B   Blanket Order

December 12, 1991

PART 1   IMPLEMENTATION

    1.1   *Effective date* – Local Policy Statement 3-43 dated February 1, 1987 (the "Former Policy") is hereby rescinded and the following substituted therefor, effective December 12, 1991.

    1.2   *Defined terms* – Terms defined in the Securities Act, S.B.C. 1985, c. 83 (the "Act") and the Securities Regulation, B.C. Reg. 270/86 (the "Regulation"), and used in this local policy statement have the same meaning as in the Act and the Regulation.

PART 2   APPLICATION

    2.1   *Government Strip Bond Offerings in British Columbia* – This local policy statement applies to offerings of Government Strip Bonds as defined in section ?.

    2.2   *Meaning of Government Strip Bonds* – For purposes of this local policy statement, "Government Strip Bonds" mean:

        (a)   actual individual interest coupons and residues arising from the physical separation of bonds, debentures or other evidence of indebtedness issued or guaranteed by the Government of Canada or by a province of Canada or by a country or political division of a country recognized by the British Columbia Securities Commission (the "Commission") in an order made under section 32(a)(i.1) of the Act, and

        (b)   deposit receipts or other certificates representing an interest in certain specific instruments of the type referred to in (a), ("alter ego receipts") or an undivided interest in a pool of these instruments ("non-alter ego receipts"),

    where the purchaser's sole entitlement is to receive a fixed amount of money at a specific future date.

PART 3   INFORMATION STATEMENT

    3.1   *Attributes of Government Strip Bonds* – There are certain investment attributes of Government Strip Bonds that are unusual and may not be generally understood by the investing public. The Commission is particularly concerned about the following attributes:

        (a)   the fluctuation in the value of Government Strip Bonds resulting from fluctuations in prevailing interest rates;

        (b)   the income tax consequences of investing and trading in Government Strip Bonds;

        (c)   the anticipated secondary market environment; and

        (d)   the custodial arrangements relating to Government Strip Bonds.

    3.2   *Informing Purchasers* – Vendors and their agents must provide all first-time purchasers of Government Strip Bonds with an information statement that sets out, in a form approved by the Commission or the Superintendent of Brokers (the "Superintendent"), the investment attributes of Government Strip Bonds, including, without limitation, the investment attributes referred to in section 3.1. Persons selling Government Strip Bonds must be knowledgeable about the investment attributes of Government Strip Bonds.

    3.3   *Vendors of Government Strip Bonds* – In order to be permitted to distribute and trade Government Strip Bonds under this local policy statement persons, other than those registered under the Act, must provide an information statement approved by the Commission or the Superintendent to first-time purchasers who must acknowledge having received the statement prior to the distribution or trade. In order to distribute or trade Government Strip Bonds under this local policy statement, registrants must provide an information statement approved by the Commission or the Superintendent to first-time purchasers not later than with confirmation of the trade. In the course of discharging their obligations under the suitability rule, registrants must inform purchasers of the contents of the information statement.

PART 4   APPROVED INFORMATION STATEMENT

4.1   *Form of Information Statement prepared by IDA* – Subject to section 4.2, the Commission has approved the Information Statement prepared by the Investment Dealers Association of Canada, attached as Appendix A to this local policy statement, for the purposes of this local policy statement.

4.2   *Other Approved Form of Information Statement* – Where a vendor proposes to use an information statement that differs in any material way from the Information Statement in Appendix A, the vendor must obtain the prior written approval of the Commission or the Superintendent to use that information statement in British Columbia. Where a vendor proposes to trade or distribute Government Strip Bonds that differ in any material way from those described in the Information Statement in Appendix A ("Novel Government Strip Bonds"), the vendor must obtain the prior written approval of the Commission or the Superintendent to use in British Columbia an information statement describing the investment attributes of the Novel Government Strip Bonds including, without limitation, those referred to in section ?. Until such approval is obtained, a vendor may not trade or distribute in British Columbia Novel Government Strip Bonds. Where another securities regulatory authority in Canada has approved an information statement differing materially from the Information Statement set out in Appendix A or describing Novel Government Strip Bonds, the vendor must provide evidence of that approval to the Commission or the Superintendent.

PART 5   BLANKET ORDER

5.1   The Commission has issued a blanket order under sections 33 and 59 of the Act, attached as Appendix B, exempting from the registration and prospectus requirements of the Act, trades and distributions of Government Strip Bonds made in compliance with this local policy statement. The Commission will deny the registration exemptions contained in sections 32(a)(i) or (i.1) of the Act and the prospectus exemption contained in section 58(1)(a) of the Act in connection with any trade in Government Strip Bonds that is not made in compliance with this local policy statement.

PART 6   TRANSITION

6.1   *Approved Information Statement During Transitional Period* – Subject to section 4.2, in addition to the form of information statement attached as Appendix A, the Commission has approved the Information Statement attached as Appendix A to the Former Policy for delivery to first-time purchasers of Government Strip Bonds that are not Novel Government Strip Bonds. This approval is effective only until February 1, 1992.

6.2   *First-Time Purchasers* – A person who, prior to the effective date of this local policy statement, has purchased Government Strip Bonds that are not Novel Government Strip Bonds, and received a form of information statement approved pursuant to the Former Policy, is not a "first-time purchaser" for the purpose of purchasing Government Strip Bonds that are not Novel Government Strip Bonds pursuant to this local policy statement.

DATED at Vancouver, British Columbia, on December 12, 1991.

Douglas M. Hyndman
Chairman

APPENDIX A – LOCAL POLICY STATEMENT 3-43

Revoked. See NIN 95/9 "Government Strip Bonds - Information Statement".

APPENDIX B – LOCAL POLICY STATEMENT 3-43

IN THE MATTER OF THE SECURITIES ACT
S.B.C. 1985, c. 83

AND

IN THE MATTER OF GOVERNMENT STRIP BONDS

ORDER UNDER SECTIONS 33 AND 59

WHEREAS certain persons are distributing and trading in British Columbia

(a)   actual individual interest coupons and residues arising from the physical separation of bonds, debentures or other evidence of indebtedness issued or guaranteed by the Government of Canada or by a province of Canada or by a country or political division of a country recognized by the British Columbia Securities Commission (the "Commission") in an order made under section 32(a)(i.1) of the Act, and

(b)   deposit receipts or other certificates representing an interest in certain specific instruments of the type referred to in (a) or an undivided interest in a pool of these instruments,

where the purchaser's sole entitlement is to receive a fixed amount of money at a specific future date (together "Government Strip Bonds");

AND WHEREAS the Commission considers that to do so would not be prejudicial to the public interest;

IT IS ORDERED under sections 33 and 59 of the Act that sections 20 and 42 of the Act do not apply to a trade in Government Strip Bonds provided that an information statement approved by the Commission or the Superintendent of Brokers describing the investment attributes of Government Strip Bonds including, without limitation,

(a)   the fluctuations in the value of Government Strip Bonds resulting from fluctuations in prevailing interest rates,

(b)   the income tax consequences of investing and trading in Government Strip Bonds,

(c)   the anticipated secondary market environment, and

(d)   the custodial arrangements relating to such Government Strip bonds,

is

(e)   where the vendor is not registered under the Act, furnished to, and its receipt is acknowledged by, a first-time purchaser prior to the trade, or

(f)   where the vendor is registered under the Act, furnished to a first-time purchaser not later than with confirmation of the trade.

DATED at Vancouver, British Columbia, on December 12, 1991.

LOCAL POLICY STATEMENT 3-44

RECOGNITION OF STOCK EXCHANGES AND JURISDICTIONS

Alberta, Saskatchewan and Manitoba are now recognized for the purposes of take over and issuer bids in sections 80(1)(e) and 80(h), respectively, of the Act. Also, the Superintendent no longer allows the VSE to make exemption orders under ss. 31(2)(21) and 55(2)(18) of the Act.

PART 1   IMPLEMENTATION

1.1   *Effective date* – Local Policy Statement 3-44 dated November 1, 1989 is hereby rescinded and the following substituted therefor, effective August 15, 1991.

PART 2   APPLICATION

2.1   *Recognition of stock exchanges and jurisdictions* – This local policy statement provides for the recognition by the British Columbia Securities Commission of stock exchanges and jurisdictions for the purpose of certain sections of the Securities Act, S.B.C. 1985, c. 83 (the "Act") and the Securities Regulation, B.C. Reg. 270/86 (the "Regulation").

PART 3   RECOGNITION OF STOCK EXCHANGES

3.1   *Recognition of stock exchanges for certain purposes* – The Commission recognizes the Vancouver Stock Exchange for the purpose of

(a)   the definition of "exchange issuer" in section 1(1) of the Act,

(b)   sections 11(2) and 58(1)(b) and (c) of the Act, and

(c)   sections 13(2)(a), 74 and 143(2) of the Regulation.

3.2   *Recognition of stock exchanges for takeover bid and issuer bid purposes* – The Commission recognizes the Vancouver Stock Exchange, the Alberta Stock Exchange, The Toronto Stock Exchange and the Montreal Exchange for the purpose of sections 80(1)(a) and 81(e) of the Act.

PART 4   RECOGNITION OF JURISDICTIONS

4.1   *Recognition of jurisdictions for takeover bid and issuer bid purposes* – The Commission recognizes, for the purpose of sections 80(1)(e) and 81(h) of the Act,

(a)   Alberta, Manitoba, Ontario, Quebec, and Saskatchewan, and

(b)   the United States, where the bid complies with, and is not exempt from, the requirements of the Securities and Exchange Commission.

DATED at Vancouver, British Columbia, on August 1, 1991.

Douglas M. Hyndman
Chairman

Ref: NIN#91/15

DRAFT LOCAL POLICY STATEMENT 3-45
DESIGNATION AS A REPORTING ISSUER
(EXTRAPROVINCIAL ISSUERS)

See NIN 89/17 "Local Policy 3-45 – Designation as a Reporting Issuer and Business Investor Offerings".

PART 1   IMPLEMENTATION

1.1   Local Policy Statement 3-45 dated August 19, 1987 is rescinded and the following substituted therefor, effective *, 1989.

1.2   Terms defined in the Securities Act, S.B.C. 1985, c. 83 (the "Act") and the Securities Regulation, B.C. Reg. 270/86 (the "Regulation") and used in this local policy statement have the same meaning as in the Act and the Regulation.

PART 2   APPLICATION

2.1   This local policy statement sets out guidelines for an application to the British Columbia Securities Commission (the "Commission") for an order designating an issuer as a reporting issuer pursuant to paragraph (f) of the definition of "reporting issuer" in section 1(1) of the Act.

2.2 An order will generally be granted only to an issuer that

(a) has been a reporting issuer or held equivalent status for at least a year in another jurisdiction that has continuous disclosure requirements that are substantially the same as the requirements under the Act; and

(b) has securities listed and posted for trading on a stock exchange or quoted on a trading or quotation system.

PART 3   APPLICATION PROCEDURE

3.1 The application should be addressed as follows:

Deputy Superintendent, Exemptions and Orders
British Columbia Securities Commission
1100-865 Hornby Street
Vancouver, B.C.
V6Z 2H4

3.2 The application should state that an order designating the issuer as a reporting issuer in British Columbia is being sought under section 1(1) of the Act and should provide the following information concerning the issuer:

(a) the name of the issuer;

(b) its jurisdiction and date of incorporation, organization or continuation;

(c) its authorized and issued capital;

(d) the jurisdictions in which the issuer is a reporting issuer and the dates it became a reporting issuer in those jurisdictions;

(e) the stock exchanges or trading or quotation systems on which the issuer's securities are traded or quoted; and

(f) the reason the issuer is seeking to become a reporting issuer in British Columbia and any other relevant information concerning the issuer in support of the application.

3.3 The following documents must be filed in support of an application:

(a) a copy of the issuer's most recent prospectus, provided that if the issuer has not made a distribution under a prospectus in any jurisdiction, the application should include an explanation of the means by which the issuer's securities were distributed;

(b) a copy of all interim and annual audited financial statements and proxy solicitation materials filed by the issuer in the 12 month period preceding the date of the application;

(c) a copy of all press releases and material change reports issued or filed by the issuer in the 12 month period preceding the date of the application;

(d) a certified copy of the directors' resolution authorizing the making of the application;

(e) a certificate of good standing from the corporate regulatory authority in the issuer's jurisdiction of incorporation, organization or continuation, or a letter to the same effect from the issuer's solicitors, dated within 21 days of the date of the application;

(f) a letter confirming that the issuer is in good standing, dated within 21 days of the date of the application, from each of the stock exchanges on which the issuer's securities are listed and posted for trading;

(g) a certificate of good standing, dated within 21 days of the date of the application, from the securities regulatory authority in each jurisdiction in which the issuer is a reporting issuer;

(h) the filing fee in the amount prescribed by section 183(1) of the Regulation by way of a cheque payable to the "Minister of Finance"; and

(i) a completed Fee Checklist in the required form.

3.4   Where any of the documents required under paragraph 3.3 are not being submitted, the application should describe the documents and explain why they are not being submitted with the application.

DATED at Vancouver, British Columbia, this * of * 1989.

Douglas M. Hyndman
Chairman

LIST OF NATIONAL POLICY STATEMENTS

As at July 1, 1995

Policy	Description
1	Clearance of national issues – prospectuses or Annual Information Forms
2A	Guide for engineers, geologists, and prospectors submitting reports on mining properties to Canadian provincial securities administrators
2B	Guide for engineers and geologists submitting oil and gas reports to Canadian provincial securities administrators
3	Unacceptable auditors
4	Conditions for dealer sub-underwritings
5	Recognition of profits in real estate transactions [repealed]
6	Mutual funds: sales charges [repealed]
7	Mutual funds: management fees [repealed]
8	Mutual funds: computation of net asset value per share [repealed]
9	Mutual funds: forward pricing, sales and redemptions [repealed]
10	Mutual funds: redemption of securities [repealed]
11	Mutual funds: changes of management – change in investment policies [repealed]
12	Disclosure of "market out" clauses in underwriting agreements in prospectuses
13	Disclaimer clause on prospectus
14	Acceptability of currencies in material filed with securities regulatory authorities
15	Conditions precedent to acceptance of scholarship or educational plan prospectuses
16	Maintenance of provincial trading records
17	Violations of securities laws of other jurisdictions – conduct affecting fitness for continued registration
18	Conflict of interest – registrants acting as corporate directors
19	Mutual funds sales companies: commingling of funds and securities [repealed]
20	Trading in unqualified securities – securities in primary distribution in other jurisdictions
21	National advertising – warnings
22	Use of information and opinion re mining and oil properties by registrants and others
23	Mutual funds: "in-house" funds [repealed]
24	Mutual funds: contractual plans [repealed]
25	Registrants: advertising: disclosure of interest
26	Mutual funds: acceptance or rejection of subscriptions for fund shares or units [repealed]
27	Canadian generally accepted accounting principles
28	Mutual funds: investment restrictions – options [repealed]
29	Mutual funds investing in mortgages
30	Processing of "seasoned prospectuses"
31	Change of auditor of a reporting issuer
32	Prospectus warning re: scope of distribution

National Policies

NATIONAL POLICY No. 1
CLEARANCE OF NATIONAL ISSUES

See NIN 94/21 "Expedited Review of Short Form Prospectuses and Renewal AIFS" and NIN 94/22 "Permission Under Section 35(1)(c) of the Securities Act" with respect to the expedited review of short form prospectuses and renewal AIFS pursuant to the Memorandum of Understanding found after NIN 94/21.

To facilitate the acceptance of a prospectus, a short form prospectus, or an initial annual information form (the "AIF") in more than one Canadian jurisdiction and to provide for uniformity of administration, the securities regulatory authorities have agreed upon the procedure which may be followed by an underwriter or an issuer or a selling security holder (sometimes referred to herein as the "issuer") wishing to clear such documents in more than one jurisdiction.

1. Prospectus or Annual Information Form

    The procedure for a prospectus or an AIF is as follows:

    (a) The preliminary prospectus, pro forma prospectus or AIF, together with any supporting materials, shall be filed, as nearly as may be practicable, contemporaneously with the administrator in each of the jurisdictions in which it is proposed to qualify to distribute the issue or to become eligible to participate in the Prompt Offering Qualification System (the "POP System"), as the case may be. The preliminary or pro forma prospectuses or the AIFs filed in each jurisdiction shall be identical in form and content, including signatories and dating, except that French language documents filed in Quebec need not be filed in the other jurisdictions. (The processing of documents filed in Quebec in the French language, apart from substantive comments applying to both English and French language versions, will ordinarily be dealt with between Quebec and the issuer or its agent in Quebec directly.)

    (b) The principal jurisdiction will normally be selected by the issuer. The selected jurisdiction may or may not agree to act in such capacity. The issuer shall advise each of the jurisdictions in which the preliminary prospectus, pro forma prospectus or AIF is filed of the name of the principal jurisdiction and each of the other jurisdictions in which it is proposed to qualify to distribute the issue or to become eligible to participate in the POP System.

    (c) The principal jurisdiction will review the material and will use its best efforts to issue the first comments by letter, telex or telecopy (the "Comment Letter") within ten working days from the date of the receipt for the preliminary prospectus or the date the pro forma prospectus or AIF was received. The first Comment Letter will be transmitted by the principal jurisdiction immediately to each of the other filing jurisdictions and to the issuer or the issuer's solicitor. If applicable, the principal jurisdiction will, unless otherwise requested, advise the issuer or issuer's solicitor by telephone that the Comment Letter is available to be picked up.

    (d) The other jurisdictions will use their best efforts to advise the principal jurisdiction of any additional comments within five working days of receipt of the first Comment Letter. If any such jurisdiction has no comments it will advise the principal jurisdiction that it has no comments or, if it is not yet in a position to make its comments at the end of the five day period, it will advise the principal jurisdiction as to the date upon which its comments will be available. If the principal jurisdiction has not received a response from one of the other filing jurisdictions within the above-mentioned five-day period, the principal jurisdiction will generally contact such filing jurisdiction and enquire as to the status of the latter's response.

    (e) On the basis of the additional comments, the principal jurisdiction will then prepare and forward a second Comment Letter. Subject to the principal jurisdiction's discretion, the second Comment Letter will usually be sent after all of the other jurisdictions have advised the principal jurisdiction of their comments or that they have no comments. The second Comment Letter will identify the jurisdictions issuing the comments and will be delivered in the same manner as the first Comment Letter. The principal jurisdiction may, in its discretion, forward comments from other jurisdictions to the issuer or the issuer's solicitor prior to the receipt by it of comments or advice that jurisdictions have no comments from all of the other jurisdictions.

(f) The issuer or the issuer's solicitor will provide the principal jurisdiction with written responses to the first Comment Letter. The issuer or the issuer's solicitor will provide each non-principal jurisdiction issuing comments with written responses to the comments of the non-principal jurisdiction contained in the second and subsequent Comment Letters, with a copy to the principal jurisdiction. Each other jurisdiction will advise the principal jurisdiction whether it is satisfied with the response to its comments and is clear for the issuance of a receipt following review of a blacklined prospectus (in Quebec, the French language version) as contemplated in paragraph (h) and upon the filing of final material. If a jurisdiction advises that it is not satisfied and the principal jurisdiction concludes that the comment or comments could be most effectively dealt with by such jurisdiction, the principal jurisdiction shall so advise such jurisdiction and direct the issuer to deal directly with that jurisdiction to resolve the comment or comments. The issuer will advise the principal jurisdiction as to any changes agreed upon and the jurisdiction having issued the comment or comments will advise the principal jurisdiction when it is satisfied with the response and is clear for the issuance of a receipt upon the filing of final material.

(g) Issuers and their representatives are cautioned against dealing directly with jurisdictions other than the principal jurisdiction in an attempt to resolve comments without clearance from the principal jurisdiction, which must be kept aware at all times of such dealings and their resolution.

(h) Except in the case of short form prospectuses, it is strongly recommended that a draft prospectus or draft AIF (the French language version, in Quebec), blacklined to show changes (other than pricing information), be sent to the principal jurisdiction and to any other jurisdiction having substantive comments, as far as possible in advance of filing final material. (This blacklined version is in addition to the blacklined version of the final prospectus to be filed with final material.)

(i) When the principal jurisdiction is satisfied that all comments have been resolved and has received a signed prospectus or AIF, together with any accompanying material in acceptable form, the principal jurisdiction will issue a final receipt or a notice of acceptance for filing for the final prospectus or AIF respectively, as the case may be, and will advise the other jurisdictions immediately by telex or telecopier letter that a final receipt or notice has been issued.

(j) The signed final material shall be filed, as nearly as may be practicable, contemporaneously in each of the other jurisdictions. The other jurisdictions will issue final receipts or notices after receipt by them of acceptable final material and after receipt of the advice as to the issuance of the final receipt or notice by the principal jurisdiction.

(k) In the event that any Comment Letter or response is too lengthy for convenient transmittal to another jurisdiction by electronic means, the principal jurisdiction will, in the case of a Comment Letter, forward it by courier and, in the case of a response, request that the issuer forward such response to the other jurisdiction(s). Enclosures requested by a particular jurisdiction should always be sent directly by the issuer to such jurisdiction.

(l) A jurisdiction will not act as principal jurisdiction if it does not wish to participate actively in the process contemplated by this Policy and the principal jurisdiction will assume that any such jurisdiction will not have comments unless such comments are received by the principal jurisdiction within the five day time limit set forth in paragraph (d) above. As of the date of publication of this Policy, the securities regulatory authorities of New Brunswick, Nova Scotia, Prince Edward Island, Newfoundland, Yukon and the Northwest Territories have indicated that they wish to be included in the process contemplated by this Policy but will not participate actively in the process and accordingly will not normally respond to the principal jurisdiction.

(m) The procedure adopted by this Policy is for the convenience of the investment community. It involves no surrender of jurisdiction by any regulatory authority. Each of the administrators will retain in its entirety the statutory discretion vested in such administrator to review, accept or reject a particular prospectus or AIF.

(n) The table attached and forming part of this Policy indicates the documents that are required to be filed in the various jurisdictions in connection with any annual information form or any prospectus or amendment. The table will be amended from time to time by the Canadian Securities Administrators.

2.   Short Form Prospectus

The above-described procedures for clearing a prospectus or AIF in more than one jurisdiction apply mutatis mutandis to the clearance of a short form prospectus in more than one jurisdiction subject to the following timing and related procedural modifications:

(a) The principal jurisdiction will provide by telex or telecopy any comments on the contents of the preliminary short form prospectus (but excluding any comments on the material incorporated in the preliminary short form prospectus by reference) to the other jurisdictions involved, as well as to the issuer within three working days following the filing of the preliminary short form prospectus with the principal jurisdiction.

(b) Within two working days from the day of receipt of the comments, if any, from the principal jurisdiction, the other jurisdictions will furnish the principal jurisdiction by telex or telecopy with any additional comments they may have on the contents of the preliminary short form prospectus. If the principal jurisdiction receives no comments from any other jurisdiction within such additional two working day period, it will be assumed that such jurisdiction will accept the filing of the short form prospectus in final form.

(c) Notwithstanding the foregoing, where, in the opinion of the principal jurisdiction, the proposed offering is too complex to be reviewed adequately within the time periods prescribed herein for a short form prospectus, the time periods applicable to prospectuses and AIFs under this Policy shall apply and the principal jurisdiction shall, within one working day of the filing of such preliminary short form prospectus, so notify the issuer and the other jurisdictions.

(d) Issuers should refer to National Policy No. 47 for the procedure applicable to a renewal annual information form.

3.   The National Policy No. 1 Receipt System (the "Receipt System")

Issuers filing a short form prospectus under the Prompt Offering Qualification System may elect to receive a single National Policy No. 1 Receipt that permits securities to be distributed in all jurisdictions in which a preliminary prospectus has been filed and which have not opted out of the System during the review process. The National Policy No. 1 Receipt will bear on its face the following legend:

"This National Policy No. 1 Receipt confirms that receipts of (each of the provinces or territories of Canada [except —]) have been issued".

The National Policy No. 1 Receipt provides evidence of the approval of the issuer's prospectus by all participating jurisdictions and of the notional issue of a receipt therein. The National Policy No. 1 Receipt will be made available to the issuer by the principal jurisdiction. It is not necessary for the issuer to obtain a separate receipt document from a non-principal jurisdiction in order to commence distribution of its securities. However, each non-principal jurisdiction will subsequently provide the issuer with a receipt dated as of the same date as the National Policy No. 1 Receipt if the fee and final material filed are acceptable.

When the issuer files a preliminary short form prospectus and elects this Receipt System, it must file with each non-principal jurisdiction its undertaking to the non-principal jurisdiction to file final material together with, where appropriate,[1] the required fee, within 3 working days following the day of issue of the Receipt System receipt. Where there are comments or changes, additional filing will be required (see below). Issuers will file the usual final material with the principal jurisdiction.

Unless a non-principal jurisdiction advises the principal jurisdiction otherwise, silence as of the end of the second working day[2] next following the day on which the first comments were sent by the principal jurisdiction will constitute confirmation to the principal jurisdiction that the material reviewed complies with the requirements of the relevant securities legislation to the extent that, assuming the final material were substantially similar, a receipt would issue in that jurisdiction. The principal jurisdiction is therefore authorized to issue a receipt that provides evidence that the non-principal jurisdiction's approval has been granted, and a receipt notionally issued by that jurisdiction, subject to the terms of the undertaking to file final material described below. The principal jurisdiction must notify the non-principal jurisdiction at once that the National Policy No. 1 Receipt has been issued.

The Receipt System is primarily intended to facilitate national distributions of securities under "clean" (i.e. no comments) short form prospectuses that are not altered by the issuer. Where comments are raised, or the issuer wishes to make changes prior to filing final material, additional clearance procedures are involved, requiring additional time.

If a non-principal jurisdiction makes comments, the comments will be communicated to the issuer directly, with a copy to the principal jurisdiction, and resolved between the issuer and the non-principal jurisdiction. However, if changes are made to prospectus as a result of the comments and Quebec is a non-principal jurisdiction, blacklined facsimiles of the relevant pages of the final prospectus in both French and English must be provided to Quebec. Because Quebec has an obligation to clear a French language prospectus, it also requires a signed copy of both English and French versions of the final prospectus in all cases. In this case, as in all others, authorization must be specifically communicated by Quebec to the principal jurisdiction before the principal jurisdiction will issue a National Policy No. 1 Receipt that includes Quebec. For the other jurisdictions, silence as of the end of the later of the second working day next following the day on which the first comments were sent by the principal jurisdiction or noon on the working day next following that on which a copy of any changes was filed, will constitute approval of the prospectus including any changes that were made thereto, and authorization for the principal jurisdiction to issue a National Policy No. 1 Receipt as evidence of approval and the notional issue of a receipt in that jurisdiction.

A non-principal jurisdiction may opt out of the Receipt System at any time prior to the issue of the National Policy No. 1 Receipt. Opting out will be communicated by a telex or facsimile to that effect sent to the principal with a copy to the issuer. In this case, the National Policy No. 1 Receipt will no longer constitute evidence that the review and approval process has occurred in that non-principal jurisdiction, and therefore the issuer must deal separately with that jurisdiction in respect of a receipt. The legend on the National Policy No. 1 Receipt will specify those jurisdictions on whose behalf it is not issued.

The following chronology illustrates the integration of the Receipt System procedures into the existing POP system procedures:

Time zone of principal jurisdiction

Day 1:   Preliminary short form prospectus is filed in selected principal and non-principal jurisdictions. Covering letter indicates election of Receipt System receipt.

Issuer provides an undertaking to each non-principal to file a copy of the final material and any required additional fee within 3 working days

---

1   Although all jurisdictions require a basic fee be filed with the preliminary prospectus, Ontario and B.C. require that an additional fee be filed with final material.

2   For purposes of establishing that a working day has concluded, the time zone of the relevant jurisdiction will apply. From the point of view of the principal jurisdiction, the time zone of the principal jurisdiction will establish the end of the initial 3 day review period, and the time zone of the most westerly non-principal jurisdiction will establish the end of the subsequent 2 day review period.

following the day of issue of a National Policy No. 1 Receipt on its behalf. If no National Policy No. 1 Receipt is issued in respect of a jurisdiction, the undertaking to that jurisdiction is void.

Preliminary prospectus receipts are provided in each jurisdiction where issued.

Day 2:   POP system review by principal jurisdiction.

Day 3:   POP system review by principal jurisdiction.

Day 4:   First comment telex or facsimile sent by the principal jurisdiction to the non-principal jurisdictions, including notation "N.P. No. 1 filing per Item 3 of N.P. No. 1" or equivalent.

As part of their participation in the Receipt System, all jurisdictions have agreed that unless a non-principal jurisdiction advises the principal jurisdiction otherwise, silence as of the end of the second working day next following the day on which the first comment telex or facsimile was sent by the principal jurisdiction will constitute confirmation to the principal jurisdiction that the material reviewed complies with the requirements of the relevant provincial securities legislation to the extent that, assuming the final material were substantially similar and the comments of the principal or any other jurisdiction were addressed, a receipt would issue in that jurisdiction. The principal jurisdiction is therefore authorized to issue a receipt that provides evidence of that approval, subject to the undertaking referred to under "Day 1" for all jurisdictions except Quebec. Because Quebec has a unique obligation to clear a French language prospectus, it requires a signed copy of both English and French versions of the final prospectus. The National Policy No. 1 Receipt will not be issued by the principal until it has received a telex from Quebec specifically authorizing the issue by the principal of the N.P. No. 1 Receipt.

Responses are only required from non-principal jurisdictions that have made comments, or that wish to opt out of the Receipt System and issue a separate receipt.

Time zone of most westerly jurisdiction in which issuer has filed

Day 5:   POP system review by non-principal.

Day 6:   POP system review by non-principal jurisdictions.

           Comments and/or "opting out" telex or facsimile, if any, sent directly to issuer with a copy to the principal jurisdiction.

Day 7: (a) *if no comments by any non-principal jurisdiction*

           Silence as of end of Day 6, except for Quebec, indicates approval of material filed and authorization of the principal jurisdiction to issue a National Policy No. 1 Receipt as evidence of that approval, provided that the issuer has made no substantive changes in disclosure from the preliminary prospectus. Quebec requires a signed English and French version of the final prospectus even if identical to the preliminary and will send a telex indicating authorization to the principal to issue a National Policy No. 1 Receipt in respect of both versions.

       (b) *if comments by non-principal jurisdiction*

           Issuer and principal receive a comment telex or facsimile.

           Issuer subsequently responds to the comments by dealing directly with non-principal jurisdiction.

           When the comments are clear, the non-principal jurisdiction notifies the principal by telex or facsimile.

           Upon receipt of the clearance telex or facsimile, the principal jurisdiction is implicitly authorized, except by Quebec, to issue a National Policy No. 1 Receipt evidencing the non-principal jurisdiction's approval of the material filed as constituting a prospectus, conditional on compliance with the undertaking. Quebec will follow the same procedure as that described in case (a).

In neither case (a) nor (b) does the principal jurisdiction send a second comment telex or facsimile to the issuer summarizing comments or approvals of the other jurisdictions.

(c) *if final prospectus contains substantive changes (other than pricing) initiated by issuer*

The issuer must send in advance facsimiles of the French and English versions of the changed pages to Quebec. As in case (b) above, the principal jurisdiction will not issue a National Policy No. 1 Receipt as evidence of Quebec's approval as non-principal, until it has received a telex or facsimile from Quebec confirming the receipt and acceptance of the facsimile material.

The issuer must also provide in advance copies of the changed pages to all other jurisdictions, but silence as of noon on the working day next following that on which the changes are filed will serve as notice of approval to the principal jurisdiction; of course, a telex indicating that the non-principal is clear may be sent prior to this deadline.

Day X: Issuer files final material and fee in the principal jurisdiction.

The decision by a non-principal jurisdiction not to notify the principal jurisdiction of any objections by Day X is, in the context of the Receipt System procedures, a notional issue of a receipt within that jurisdiction immediately prior to the issue of the National Policy No. 1 Receipt.

Issuer files signed copy of both English and French versions of prospectus in Quebec, if Quebec is non-principal.

Quebec notifies principal jurisdiction that it is clear

Principal jurisdiction issues National Policy No. 1 Receipt confirming the notional issuance of a receipt by all jurisdictions in which final material has been filed and that have not opted out.

The principal jurisdiction notifies all participating non-principal jurisdictions by telex or facsimile that National Policy No. 1 Receipt has been issued.

Some jurisdictions may also provide an additional receipt on the issue of the National Policy No. 1 Receipt. Quebec will issue a receipt in all cases.

Distribution commences in all relevant jurisdictions.

Day X+3: Issuer files final material and the appropriate fee in each participating non-principal jurisdiction in compliance with its undertaking.

If the fee and final material are acceptable, and no receipt has yet been issued, some non-principal jurisdictions may issue a receipt to issuer, dated as of the date of the National Policy No. 1 Receipt.

TABLE OF DOCUMENTS TO BE FILED IN RESPECT OF THE CLEARANCE OF NATIONAL ISSUES

A table of documents required to be filed in the various jurisdictions in connection with the clearance of national issues is published immediately following, and as part of, National Policy No. 1. The Canadian Securities Administrators have agreed that compliance with the filing requirements set out in the table and the related notes shall be considered to satisfy filing requirements associated with clearing a national issue. The table will be amended from time to time by the Canadian Securities Administrators.

PRELIMINARY SHORT FORM PROSPECTUS (NP 47)

	B.C. (Note 5)	ALB. (Note 9)	SASK.	MAN.	ONT. (Note 12)	QUE.	N.B.	N.S.	P.E.I.	NFLD.	YUK	NWT.
(a) The following types and numbers of documents should be filed with a preliminary short form prospectus:												
Preliminary short form prospectus – signed	1	1	1	1	1	1 (Eng.) 1 (Fr.)	1	1	1	1	1	1
Preliminary short form prospectus – unsigned	1	4	2	2	4	2 (Eng.) 4 (Fr.)	2	–	1	–	–	–
Directors' resolution(s) – certified	1	1	1	1	1	1	1	1	1	1	1	1
Technical reports and certificates of qualification, etc. if applicable (Note 26)	– (Note 8)	–	–	–	–	1	–	–	–	–	–	–
Asset and earnings coverage calculations, if applicable	1	1	1	1	1	1	1	1	1	1	1	1
Copy or draft of all "green sheets", if any	–	–	–	–	2	1	–	–	–	–	–	–
Filing fee (Note 20)	$2,500 (Note 6)	$1,000 (Note 24)	$1,000 (Note 25)	$650 (Note 11)	$250	$500	$500 (Note 4)	$850 (Note 14)	$400	$600 (Note 16)	$150 (Note 21)	$300 (Note 21)

FINAL SHORT FORM PROSPECTUS (NP 47)

	B.C. (Note 5)	ALB. (Note 9)	SASK.	MAN.	ONT. (Note 12)	QUE.	N.B.	N.S.	P.E.I.	NFLD.	YUK	NWT.
(b) The following types and numbers of documents should be filed with a final short form prospectus:												
Final short form prospectus – signed (Note 18)	1	1	1	1	1 (Eng.) 1 (Fr.)	1 (Eng.) 1 (Fr.)	1 (Eng.) 1 (Fr.)	1	1	1	1	1
Final short form prospectus – unsigned (Note 18)	1	2	2	2	4 (Eng.) 1 (Fr.)	2 (Eng.) 2 (Fr.)	1 (Eng.) 1 (Fr.)	–	1	1	–	–
Final short form prospectus – black-lined to show changes from the preliminary short form prospectus	1	1	1	1	2	1 (Eng.) 1 (Fr.)	1	1	1	–	1	1

FINAL SHORT FORM PROSPECTUS (NP 47) (continued)

	B.C. (Note 5)	ALB. (Note 9)	SASK.	MAN.	ONT. (Note 12)	QUE.	N.B.	N.S.	P.E.I.	NFLD.	YUK.	NWT.
Directors' resolution(s) – Certified	1	1	1	1	1	1	1	1	1	1	1	1
Auditors' consent	1	1	1	1	1	1	1	1	1	1	1	1
Auditors' comfort letter on unaudited interim financial statements (if any) incorporated by reference or included in the final short form prospectus	1	1	1	1	1	1	1	–	1	1	1	1
Consents of legal counsel or other experts	1	1	1	1	1	1	1	1	1	1	1	1
Form IV	–	–	–	–	–	–	–	–	–	1	–	–
Undertaking to provide breakdown of sales and payment of additional fees, if applicable	1	–	–	–	–	–	–	–	–	1	–	–
Underwriters' certificate, if required	–	1	1	–	1	1	–	–	–	1	–	–
Filing fee (Note 20)	(Note 7)	–	–	–	0.03% of total gross max. proceeds less fee paid with preliminary short form prospectus	0.03% of 25% of total gross max. proceeds less $500 (Note 10)	–	–	–	–	–	–
Copies of underwriting or agency agreement and any other material contract requested by Commission staff												
– signed or notarized	1	1	1	1	1	1	–	1	–	–	–	–
– copies	–	–	–	–	1	–	–	–	–	–	–	–
Commercial copies – to be filed subsequently	2	2	2	2	2	5 (Eng.) 5 (Fr.)	1 (Eng.) 1 (Fr.)	2	1	1	–	–

PRELIMINARY LONG FORM PROSPECTUS

(c) The following types and numbers of documents should be filed with a preliminary long form prospectus:

	B.C. (Note 5)	ALB. (Note 9)	SASK.	MAN.	ONT. (Note 12)	QUE.	N.B.	N.S.	P.E.I.	NFLD.	YUK.	NWT.
Preliminary long form prospectus – signed	1	1	1	1	1	1 (Eng.) 1 (Fr.)	1	1	1	1	1	1
Preliminary long form prospectus – unsigned	1	4	2	2	4	2 (Eng.) 4 (Fr.)	2	–	1	1	–	–
Cross reference sheet	1	1	1	1	2	–	1	1	1	–	–	1
Directors' resolution(s) – certified	1	1	1	1	2	1	1	1	1	1	1	1
Technical reports and certificates of qualification etc., if applicable	1 (Note 8)	2	1	1	1 (signed) 1 (copy)	1	1	1	1	1	–	–
Auditors' comfort letter or consent letter, if applicable	1	1	1	1	2	1	1	1	1	1	1	1
Notice/consent forms under Freedom of Information and Protection of Privacy Act, 1987	–	–	–	–	1	–	–	–	–	–	–	–
Copy or draft of all "green sheets", if any	–	–	–	–	2	1	–	–	–	–	–	–
CUSIP/CDS number of the issuer, date of financial year and of the issuer and head office address of the issuer	–	–	–	–	1	1	–	–	–	–	–	–
Asset and earnings coverage calculations, if applicable	1	1	1	1	1	1	1	1	1	1	1	1
Dilution calculation, if applicable	1	1	1	1	1	1	1	1	1	1	1	1
Filing fee (Note 20)	$2,500 (Note 6)	$2,500 (Note 24)	$1,000 (Note 25)	$650 (Note 11)	$250	$500	$500 (Note 4)	$850 (Note 14)	$400	$600 (Note 16)	$150 (Note 21)	$300 (Note 21)

(d) The following types and numbers of documents should be filed with a pro forma prospectus (and pro forma summary statement, if applicable):

PRO FORMA PROSPECTUS

	B.C. (Note 6)	ALB.	SASK.	MAN.	ONT. (Note 12)	QUE.	N.B.	N.S.	P.E.I.	NFLD.	YUK.	NWT.
Pro forma prospectus – unsigned	–	1	1	2	2	4 (Fr.) 1 (Eng.)	1	1	1	1	1	1
Pro forma prospectus – black-lined to show changes from the prior final prospectus – certified as required by National Policy Statement No. 30	1	1	1	1	2	1 (Fr.) 1 (Eng.)	1	1	1	1	1	1
Directors' resolution(s), if applicable	–	1	–	–	1	–	–	–	–	1	1	1
Auditor's comfort letter, if applicable	1	1	1	1	1	1	1	–	1	1	1	1
Technical reports and certificates of qualifications, etc. (Note 8)	1 (Note 8)	2	1	1	2	1	1	1	1	1	–	1
Cross reference sheet	1	1	–	1	–	1	1	1	–	–	–	1
Certificate for each issuer re: proceeds from the distribution in the jurisdiction and appropriate filing fee (may be filed with final material).	1	–	–	–	1	1	–	1	–	–	–	–
Filing fee (Note 20)	$2500 (Note 6)	$1000 (Note 24)	$1000	$650	$250	$500	–	$850	$400	$600 (Note 16)	$150 (Note 21)	$300 (Note 21)

(e) The following types and numbers of documents should be filed with a final long form prospectus:

FINAL LONG FORM PROSPECTUS

	B.C. (Note 5)	ALB. (Note 9)	SASK.	MAN.	ONT. (Note 12)	QUE.	N.B.	N.S.	P.E.I.	NFLD.	YUK.	NWT.
Final long form prospectus – signed (Note 18)	1	1	1	1	1 (Eng.) 1 (Fr.)	1 (Eng.) 1 (Fr.)	1 (Eng.) 1 (Fr.)	1	1	1	1	1
Final long form prospectus – unsigned (Note 18)	1	2	2	2	4 (Eng.) 1 (Fr.)	2 (Eng.) 2 (Fr.)	1 (Eng.) 1 (Fr.)	–	1	1	–	–

FINAL LONG FORM PROSPECTUS (*continued*)

	B.C. (Note 5)	ALB. (Note 9)	SASK.	MAN.	ONT. (Note 12)	QUE.	N.B.	N.S.	P.E.I.	NFLD.	YUK.	NWT.
Final long form prospectus – blacklined to show changes from the preliminary long form prospectus	1	1	1	1	2	1 (Eng.) 1 (Fr.)	1	1	1	–	1	1
Directors' resolutions – certified	1	1	1	1	1	1	1	1	1	–	1	1
Auditors' consent	1	1	1	1	1	1	1	1	1	1	1	1
Auditors' comfort letter re: interim financial statements (if any) contained in final long from prospectus	1	1	1	1	1	1	1	1	1	1	1	1
Consents of legal counsel or other experts	1	1	1	1	1	1	1	–	1	–	1	1
Cross reference sheet	1	1	1	1	–	–	–	–	–	–	–	–
Undertaking to provide breakdown of sales and payment of additional fees, if applicable	1	–	–	–	–	–	–	–	–	–	–	–
Form IV	–	–	–	–	–	–	–	–	–	1	–	–
Underwriters' certificate, if required	–	1	1	–	1	–	1	1	1	1	–	–
Copies of the underwriting or agency agreement and any other material contract requested by commission staff												
– signed or notarized	1	1	1	1	1	1	–	1	–	–	–	–
– copies	–	–	–	–	1	–	–	–	–	–	–	–
Filing fee (Note 20)	(Note 7)	–	–	–	0.03% of total gross max. proceeds less fee paid with preliminary prospectus	0.03% of 25% of total gross max. proceeds less $500 (Note 10)	–	–				
Commercial copies – to be filed subsequently	2	2	2	2	2	5 (Eng.) 5 (Fr.)	1 (Eng.) 1 (Fr.)	2	1	–	–	–

AMENDMENTS TO PRELIMINARY PROSPECTUS AND PROSPECTUS (SHORT FORM & LONG FORM)

	B.C. (Note 5)	ALB. (Note 9)	SASK.	MAN.	ONT. (Note 12)	QUE.	N.B.	N.S.	P.E.I.	NFLD.	YUK.	NWT.
(f) The following types and numbers of documents should be filed with an amendment to a preliminary prospectus and an amendment to a prospectus:												
Amendment – signed	1	1	1	1	1	1 (Eng.) 1 (Fr.)	1 (Eng.) 1 (Fr.)	1	1	1	1	1
Amendment – unsigned	1	2	1	1	4	1 (Eng.) 1 (Fr.)	1 (Eng.) 1 (Fr.)	–	1	1	–	–
Directors' resolution(s) – certified	1	1	1	1	1	1	1	1	1	1	1	1
Auditors' consent and comfort letter – if applicable	1	1	1	1	1	1	1	1	1	1	1	1
Consent of legal counsel or other experts, if applicable	1	1	1	1	1	1	1	1	1	1	1	1
Filing fee (Note 20)	$250	$100	$100	$100	$100 plus 0.03% of total additional gross proceeds	$100 plus 0.03% of total additional gross proceeds	$100	$100	–	$100	$50 (Note 21)	$50 (Note 21)

ANNUAL INFORMATION FORM FILED UNDER THE PROMPT OFFERING QUALIFICATION SYSTEM

	B.C. (Note 5)	ALB.	SASK.	MAN.	ONT. (Note 12)	QUE. (Note 12)	N.B.	N.S.	P.E.I.	NFLD.	YUK.	NWT.
(g) The following types and numbers of documents should be filed with an annual information form (Note 23):												
Annual Information Form (Note 18)	2	2	1	1	3 (Eng.) 1 (Fr.)	1 (Eng.) 2 (Fr.) (Note 13)	1 (Eng.) 1 (Fr.)	1	1	1	1	1
Directors' resolution(s) – certified	1	1	1	1	1	1	1	1	1	1	1	1

ANNUAL INFORMATION FORM FILED UNDER THE PROMPT OFFERING QUALIFICATION SYSTEM (continued)

	B.C. (Note 5)	ALB.	SASK.	MAN.	ONT. (Note 12)	QUE.	N.B.	N.S.	P.E.I.	NFLD.	YUK.	NWT.
Eligibility Certificate of issuer	1	1	1	1	1	1	1	1	1	1	1	1
Material incorporated by reference	–	1	1	1	1	1 (Eng.) 1 (Fr.) (Note 19)	1 (Eng.) 1 (Fr.)	1	1	1	1	1
Filing fee (Note 20)	$1,000	$1,000	$600	$650	$1,000	$500	–	$1,200	$300	$1,000	$10	$300

PRELIMINARY SIMPLIFIED PROSPECTUS AND ANNUAL INFORMATION FORM (N.P. 36)

	B.C.	ALB.	SASK.	MAN.	ONT. (Note 12)	QUE. (Note 19)	N.B.	N.S.	P.E.I.	NFLD.	YUK.	NWT.
Preliminary annual information form – signed	1	1	1	1	1	1 (Eng.) 1 (Fr.)	1	1	1	1	1	1
Preliminary annual information form – unsigned	1	2	1	4	4	1 (Eng.) 1 (Fr.)	1	–	1	1	–	1
Preliminary simplified prospectus – unsigned	1	4	1	2	5	1 (Eng.) 1 (Fr.)	1	1	1	1	1	1
Notice/consent forms under Freedom of Information and Protection of Privacy Act, 1987	–	–	–	–	1	–	–	–	–	–	–	–
Audited annual financial statements referred to as accompanying the preliminary simplified prospectus												
– manually signed	1	1	1	1	1	1 (Eng.) 1 (Fr.)	1	1	1	1	1	1

(h) The following types and numbers of documents should be filed with preliminary simplified prospectus and annual information form filed pursuant to National Policy Statement No. 36:

National Policies

PRELIMINARY SIMPLIFIED PROSPECTUS AND ANNUAL INFORMATION FORM (N.P. 36) *(continued)*

	B.C.	ALB.	SASK.	MAN.	ONT. (Note 12)	QUE. (Note 19)	N.B.	N.S.	P.E.I.	NFLD.	YUK.	NWT.
– unsigned, or printed or facsimile signatures	1	1	2	1	2	1 (Eng.) 2 (Fr.)	1	–	1	1	–	–
Auditors' comfort letter or consent letter, if applicable	1	1	1	1	2	1 (signed) 1 (copy)	1	1	1	1	1	1
Directors' resolution(s) approving the preliminary annual information form, the preliminary simplified prospectus and the audited and, if applicable, unaudited financial statements referred to therein – certified	1	1	1	1	1 (signed) 1 (copy)	1	1	1	1	1	1	1
Investment restrictions and practices of the funds	1	1	1	1	1	1 (Eng.) 1 (Fr.)	1	1	1	1	1	1
Memorandum re: deviations from National Policy Statement No. 39, if applicable	1	1	1	1	1	1	1	1	1	1	1	1
Cross reference sheets												
– Annual Information Form	1	1	1	1	2	1	1	1	1	1	1	1
– Simplified Prospectus	1	1	1	1	2	1	1	1	1	1	1	1
Copy or draft of all "green sheets"	–	–	–	–	1	1	1	–	–	–	–	–
Copy or draft of all material contracts including the custodianship agreement and any sub-custodianship agreement	1	–	1	1	1	1	–	– (1 if NS is principal jurisdiction)	–	–	–	–

PRELIMINARY SIMPLIFIED PROSPECTUS AND ANNUAL INFORMATION FORM (N.P. 36) *(continued)*

	B.C.	ALB.	SASK.	MAN.	ONT. (Note 12)	QUE. (Note 19)	N.B.	N.S.	P.E.I.	NFLD.	YUK.	NWT.
Filing fee per issuer (Note 20)	Reg. 270/86 S. 183(1) – $2,500 minimum	Regs. Sch. 1 – S. 2(1), S. 2(8) S. 2(9) $1,500 minimum (Note 24)	Regs. S. 176(1) Appendix A-S.3(a) $1,000 minimum	Reg. S50 – R1 S.3(1)(h) $650 plus $600 if Manitoba is principal jurisdiction	Regs. Sch. 1 S. 4 – $250 minimum	Regs. S. 267 $500 minimum See Regs. S. 267.1, S. 267.2, S. 268(3) and S. 98	Note 21	Note 21	Note 21	Note 16	$150 Note 21	Note 21

PRO FORMA SIMPLIFIED PROSPECTUS AND ANNUAL INFORMATION FORM (N.P. 36)

	B.C.	ALB.	SASK.	MAN.	ONT. (Note 12)	QUE. (Note 19)	N.B.	N.S.	P.E.I.	NFLD.	YUK.	NWT.
(i) The following types and numbers of documents should be filed with a pro forma simplified prospectus and pro forma annual information form filed pursuant to National Policy Statement No. 36:												
Pro forma simplified prospectus	1	4	1	2	2	1 (Eng.) 1 (Fr.)	1	1	1	1	1	1
Pro forma simplified prospectus – blacklined to show changes from the prior final simplified prospectus – certified as required by National Policy Statement No. 30	1	1	1	1	2	1 (Eng.) 1 (Fr.)	1	1	1	1	–	1
Notice/consent forms under Freedom of Information and Protection of Privacy Legislation	–	–	–	–	1	–	–	–	–	–	–	–
Pro forma annual information form – unsigned	1	2	1	2	2	1 (Eng.) 1 (Fr.)	1	1	1	1	1	1
Pro forma annual information form – blacklined to show changes from the prior annual information form – certified as required by National Policy Statement No. 30	1	1	1	1	2	1 (Eng.) 1 (Fr.)	1	1	1	1	1	1

PRO FORMA SIMPLIFIED PROSPECTUS AND ANNUAL INFORMATION FORM (N.P. 36) *(continued)*

	B.C.	ALB.	SASK.	MAN.	ONT. (Note 12)	QUE. (Note 19)	N.B.	N.S.	P.E.I.	NFLD.	YUK.	NWT.
Audited annual financial statements referred to as accompanying the pro forma simplified prospectus (Note 17) – manually signed, unsigned or printed or facsimile signatures	2	2	3	2	3	2 (Eng.) 3 (Fr.)	2	1	2	1	1	1
Auditors' comfort letter	1	1	1	1	1	1 (signed) 1 (copy)	1	1	1	1	1	1
Interim financial statements referred to as accompanying the pro forma simplified prospectus, if applicable – unsigned	1	1	2	2	3	1 (Eng.) 1 (Fr.)	1	1	1	1	1	1
Auditors' comfort letter re: interim financial statements, if applicable	1	1	1	1	1 (signed)	1 (signed) 1 (copy)	1	1	1	1	1	1
Cross reference sheets												
– Annual Information Form	–	1	–	1	–	–	–	–	–	–	–	–
– Simplified Prospectus	–	1	–	1	1	–	–	–	–	–	–	–
Copy or draft of all "green sheets"	–	–	–	–	1	–	–	–	–	–	–	–
Memorandum re: deviations from National Policy Statement No. 39, if applicable	1	1	1	1	1	–	1	1	1	1	1	1
Statement of portfolio transactions, certified	1	1	1	1	1	1 (Eng.) 1 (Fr.)	1	1	1	1	1	1
Certificate for each issuer re: proceeds from the distribution in the jurisdiction and appropriate filing fee	1	–	–	–	1	1	–	–	–	–	–	–

PRO FORMA SIMPLIFIED PROSPECTUS AND ANNUAL INFORMATION FORM (N.P. 36) (*continued*)

	B.C.	ALB.	SASK.	MAN.	ONT. (Note 12)	QUE. (Note 19)	N.B.	N.S.	P.E.I.	NFLD.	YUK.	NWT.
Filing fee per issuer (Note 20)	Reg. 270/86 S. 183( ) – $2,590 minimum	Regs. Sch. 1 – S. 2(1), S. 2(8), S. 2(9) $1,500 minimum (Note 24)	Regs. S. 176(1) Appendix A-S.3(a) $1,000 minimum	Reg. $50 – R1 S. 3(1)(h) $650 plus $600 if Manitoba is principal jurisdiction	Regs. Sch. 1 S. 4 – $250 minimum	Regs. S. 267 $500 minimum See Regs. S. 267.1, S. 267.2, S. 268(3) and S. 98	Note 21	Note 21	Note 21	Note 16	$150 Note 21	Note 21

FINAL SIMPLIFIED PROSPECTUS AND ANNUAL INFORMATION FORM (N.P. 36)

	B.C.	ALB.	SASK.	MAN.	ONT. (Note 12)	QUE. (Note 19)	N.B.	N.S.	P.E.I.	NFLD.	YUK.	NWT.
(j) The following types and numbers of documents should be filed with a final simplified prospectus filed pursuant to National Policy Statement No. 36:												
Final simplified prospectus—(Note 18)		2	2	1	3 (Eng.) 1 (Fr.)	1 (Eng.) 1 (Fr.)	1 (Eng.) 1 (Fr.)	1	1	1	1	1
Final simplified prospectus – blacklined to show changes from the preliminary simplified prospectus or pro forma simplified prospectus, as the case may be	1	1	1	1	2	1 (Eng.) 1 (Fr.)	1 (Eng.) 1 (Fr.)	1	1	1	1	1
Final Annual Information Form (Note 18)												
– signed	1	1	1	1	1 (Eng.) 1 (Fr.)	–	1 (Eng.) 1 (Fr.)	1	1	1	1	1
– unsigned	1	2	1	1	3 (Eng.) 1 (Fr.)	1 (Eng.) 1 (Fr.)	1 (Eng.) 1 (Fr.)	–	1	1	–	–

National Policies

FINAL SIMPLIFIED PROSPECTUS AND ANNUAL INFORMATION FORM (N.P. 36) (continued)

	B.C.	ALB.	SASK.	MAN.	ONT. (Note 12)	QUE. (Note 19)	N.B.	N.S.	P.E.I.	NFLD.	YUK.	NWT.
Final annual information form—black-lined to show changes from the preliminary annual information form or pro forma annual information form, as the case may be	1	1	1	1	2	1 (Eng.) 1 (Fr.)	1 (Eng.) 1 (Fr.)	1	1	1	1	1
Directors' resolution(s) approving the final simplified prospectus, the final annual information form and the audited annual financial statements referred to in the final simplified prospectus – certified	1	1	1	1	1	1	1	1	1	1	1	1
Undertaking to deliver permanent information record – signed	1	1	1	1	1	1	1	1	1	1	1	1
Audited annual financial statements accompanying the final simplified prospectus if not filed in final form with the preliminary simplified prospectus or with or prior to the filing of the pro forma simplified prospectus												
– manually signed, unsigned or printed or facsimile signatures	2	2	3	2	3	2 (Eng.) 3 (Fr.)	1	1	2	1	1	1
Interim financial statements accompanying the final simplified prospectus, if applicable, and if not filed in final form with or prior to the filing of the pro forma simplified prospectus – unsigned	1	2	2	1	3	1 (Eng.) 2 (Fr.)	1	1	1	1	1	1
Statement of portfolio transactions if not filed with or prior to the pro forma simplified prospectus – certified	1	1	1	1	1	1 (Eng.) 1 (Fr.)	1	1	1	1	1	1
Compliance reports, if applicable s. 7.01(4), 11.08, and 12.04 of N.P. 39	1	1	1	1	1	1	1	1	1	1	1	1
Auditors' comfort letter re.: interim financial statements (if any) filed with the final simplified prospectus if not previously filed	1	1	1	1	1	1	1	1	1	1	1	1
Auditors' consent re.: audited annual financial statements referred to in the simplified prospectus	1	2	1	1	1	1	1	1	1	1	1	1

FINAL SIMPLIFIED PROSPECTUS AND ANNUAL INFORMATION FORM (N.P. 36) (*continued*)

	B.C.	ALB.	SASK.	MAN.	ONT. (Note 12)	QUE. (Note 19)	N.B.	N.S.	P.E.I.	NFLD.	YUK.	NWT.
Consents of legal counsel or other experts	1	2	1	1	1	1	1	1	1	1	1	1
Cross reference sheet												
– in the case of the first filing under N.P. 36	1	1	1	1	1	1	1	1	1	1	1	1
– all other filings under N.P. 36	–	1	–	1	–	–	–	–	–	–	–	–
Copies of all material contracts requested by the Commission staff												
– signed or notarized	1	1	1	1	1	1	1	1	1	1	1	1
Copy of all "green sheets"	–	–	–	–	1	1	–	–	–	–	–	–
Notarial copy of filing receipt issued by the principal jurisdiction	–	–	1	1	–	1	1	1	1	1	–	–
Form IV	–	–	–	–	–	–	–	–	1	–	–	–
Certificate for each issuer re: proceeds from the distribution in the jurisdiction and appropriate filing fee if not filed with the pro forma simplified prospectus	–	–	–	–	1	1	–	–	–	–	–	–
Commercial copies – to be filed subsequent to the issue of the receipt for the final simplified prospectus and annual information form	2	2	2	2	2 (Eng.) 1 (Fr.)	1 + 1 (Eng.) 1 + 1 (Fr.)	1 (Eng.) 1 (Fr.)	1	1	1	–	–

AMENDMENTS TO SIMPLIFIED PROSPECTUS AND ANNUAL INFORMATION FORMS (N.P. 36)

	B.C.	ALB.	SASK.	MAN.	ONT. (Note 12)	QUE. (Note 19)	N.B.	N.S.	P.E.I.	NFLD.	YUK.	NWT.
Copy(ies) of amendment – signed (annual information form)	1	1	1	1	1	1 (Eng.) 1 (Fr.)	1 (Eng.) 1 (Fr.)	1	1	1	1	1

(k) The following types and numbers of documents should be filed with an amendment to a simplified prospectus and annual information form filed pursuant to National Policy Statement No. 36:

National Policies

AMENDMENTS TO SIMPLIFIED PROSPECTUS AND ANNUAL INFORMATION FORMS (N.P. 36) (continued)

	B.C.	ALB.	SASK.	MAN.	ONT. (Note 12)	QUE. (Note 19)	N.B.	N.S.	P.E.I.	NFLD.	YUK.	NWT.
– unsigned (annual information form and simplified prospectus)	1	2	1	1	4	1 + 1 (Eng.) 1 + 1 (Fr.)	1 (Eng.) 1 (Fr.)	–	1	1	–	–
Directors' Resolution(s) approving the amendment certified	1	1	1	1	1	1	1	1	1	1	1	1
Consents of counsel and other experts, if applicable	1	1	1	1	1	1	1	1	1	1	1	1
Notarial copy of filing receipt or other proof of acceptance issued by the principal jurisdiction	–	–	1	1	–	1	1	1	1	1	–	1
Commercial copies – to be filed subsequently	2	2	2	2	2	1 + 1 (Eng.) 1 + 1 (Fr.)	1 (Eng.) 1 (Fr.)	1	1	1	–	–
Filing fee (Note 20)	$250	$100	$100	$100	$100	$100	Note 21	Note 21	Note 21	$50	$50 (Note 21)	Note 21

NOTES

1. Additional filing requirements apply to certain types of offerings eg. commodity pools. Reference should be made to the provisions of other National Policy Statements and to local policy statements of each jurisdiction to determine such requirements.

2. The information set out herein does not make reference to documents required or which may be required by the provisions of National Policy Statements Nos. 44 and 45.

3. The filing fees set out herein are the filing fees in effect as at July 1, 1991. Since that date, amendments have been made to fee schedules in various jurisdictions. In particular, amendments have been made to the filing fees referred to in the table of documents in Ontario and in Québec (both passed in May, 1992). Please refer to the securities legislation and the related regulations of each jurisdiction at the time of filing to determine the appropriate filing fee either pursuant to the amendments referred to above or pursuant to other amendments.

4. Filing fee for first class or unit where (a) principal jurisdiction is New Brunswick is $1,000; (b) principal jurisdiction is other than New Brunswick, $500; and for each additional individual class or unit an additional $100.

5. For British Columbia, the prospectus filing requirements are contained in British Columbia Local Policy Statements 3-02 and 3-03. Where the issuer is a junior company and British Columbia is the principal jurisdiction or the issuer is planning to seek a listing on the Vancouver Stock Exchange, a detailed review of British Columbia Local Policy Statements 3-02 and 3-03 should be made to determine the additional prospectus filing requirements that apply.

6. The Fee Schedule contained in Section 183 of the British Columbia regulations requires the payment of a filing fee upon the filing of a preliminary prospectus equal to the aggregate of:

    (i) $2,500, where the preliminary prospectus relates to only one type, class or series of security, or, where the preliminary prospectus or pro forma prospectus relates to more than one issuer, type, class or series of security, $2,500 for each issuer plus $500 for each additional type, class or series of security per issuer; plus

    (ii) $1,000, where security holders are proposing to distribute securities using the preliminary prospectus.

7. Where the proceeds to be derived from the distribution in British Columbia cannot be ascertained at the time of the initial filing, the issuer(s) must submit an undertaking to provide a breakdown of the sales in British Columbia together with any additional fee required within 30 days of the completion of the distribution. The additional fee is the amount by which 0.03% of the proceeds or 0.01% of the proceeds in the case of a money market fund as defined by Subsection 183(6) of the British Columbia regulations, derived from the distribution in British Columbia exceeds the fees paid with the filing of the preliminary prospectus.

8. British Columbia requires one copy of technical reports, consents and certificates of qualification, unless British Columbia is acting as the principal jurisdiction. In that case, two copies of the technical reports are required.

9. Filing requirements for Alberta are contained in ASC Local Policy 4-7.

10. In Québec, the fees will in certain circumstances be calculated on 50% of the total gross proceeds or on total gross proceeds (R. 267(2)(b)). The issuer must file upon completion of distribution a report on the securities distributed in Québec (R. 94) and the payments of an additional fee, if appropriate (R. 267.1). See note 3 for reference to an amendment to the fees payable in Quebec.

11. An additional fee of $600 is payable if Manitoba is the principal jurisdiction. If a preliminary prospectus involves more than one class of securities or more than one unit offering, each additional class of securities or unit offering shall be accompanied by an additional fee of $325.

12. Generally, applicable filing requirements for Ontario are contained in OSC Policy Statement Nos. 5.1, and 5.7. The applicable filing fees are set forth in Schedule 1 to the Regulation made under the Securities Act (Ontario). A duly

National
Policies

executed Submission to Jurisdiction and Appointment of Agent for Service of Process is required to be filed by an issuer (including a guarantor) that is incorporated or organized outside Canada and does not have an office in Canada, as well as by certain other foreign persons or companies.

13. Quebec only requires a French version of the annual information form and material incorporated by reference at the time of filing of the preliminary short form prospectus.

14. A fee of $1,250 is payable if Nova Scotia is the principal jurisdiction. If a preliminary prospectus involves more than one class of securities or more than one type of unit offering, each additional class of securities or each type of unit offering shall be accompanied by an additional fee of $300.

15. The Nova Scotia Securities Commission regards the filing of an annual information form pursuant to Notice number 3 as an application, pursuant to section 5(2) of the Regulations, to vary the prospectus requirements. The fee for such application is $350 together with a fee of $850 for the prospectus for an aggregate fee of $1,200.

16. In Newfoundland, the filing fee for a prospectus is $600 plus $600 for each additional fund or security filed under the prompt offering qualification system.

17. Where the audited annual financial statements have been previously filed with the securities authorities pursuant to the continuous disclosure requirements of applicable securities legislation, it is not necessary to file a manually signed copy of such financial statements with the pro forma material. However, a copy(ies) bearing printed or facsimile signatures should be filed with the pro forma simplified prospectus for convenience of reference.

18. With respect to all provinces other than Quebec, Ontario and New Brunswick, the French version of the final prospectus and final annual information form is required to be filed in such provinces only if the French version is to be used in such provinces.

19. With respect to the province of Quebec the number of copies shown is the number required in respect of each issuer. For example, where a combined document is used (eg. for a simplified prospectus, annual information form or financial statements) covering three issuers and the table indicates that one copy is required of the document in question, the number of copies required to be filed would be three — ie. one for each issuer included in the combined document. Also, where the table indicates that the number of copies to be filed is "1 + 1", in the case of the foregoing example, four copies of the combined document would be required to be filed — ie. one for each issuer included in the combined document plus one additional copy.

20. Filing fees should be made payable to:

British Columbia	—	Minister of Finance
Alberta	—	Provincial Treasurer of Alberta
Saskatchewan	—	Minister of Finance
Manitoba	—	Minister of Finance
Ontario	—	Treasurer of Ontario
Quebec	—	Minister of Finance
New Brunswick	—	Minister of Finance
Nova Scotia	—	Minister of Finance
Prince Edward Island	—	Provincial Secretary
Newfoundland	—	Newfoundland Exchequer Account
Northwest Territories	—	Government of the Northwest Territories
Yukon Territories	—	Government of Yukon

21. Filing fees per issuer:

Province/Territory	Prospectus		AIF	Amendments
New Brunswick	$500	or if New Brunswick is the principal jurisdiction $1,000 plus $100 for each additional class of securities	—	$100
Nova Scotia (Note 14, 15 and 22)	$850	or if Nova Scotia is the principal jurisdiction $1,250	$350	$100
Prince Edward Island	$400		$300	$100
Northwest Territories of securities	$300	per class of securities	$300	$50 per class
Yukon Territory of securities	$150	per class of securities	—	$50 per class

22. The Nova Scotia Securities Commission regards the filing of an annual information form pursuant to National Policy No. 36 as an application, pursuant to section 5(2) of the Regulations, to vary the prospectus requirements. The fee for such application is $350 which means that the total fee for filing a simplified prospectus and an annual information form is $1,200 or, if Nova Scotia is the principal jurisdiction, $1,600. Where a combined annual information form and combined simplified prospectus are filed, Nova Scotia considers that the securities of each mutual fund whose distribution is qualified pursuant to such documents are those of separate issuers.

23. The types and numbers of documents indicated apply to the filing of both an initial annual information form and a renewal annual information form.

24. In Alberta, where the proposed offering does not exceed $200,000 the filing fee is $500. Where the preliminary or pro forma prospectus or statement of material facts offers more than one class or unit of securities of an issuer, a supplementary fee of $100 is required for each additional class or unit.

25. The fee on filing of a prospectus in Saskatchewan is $1,000 per issuer. Where the prospectus offers more than one class or unit of securities of an issuer, a supplementary fee of $250 is required for each additional class or unit.

26. Unless a technical report is specifically referred to in a short form prospectus or the applicable securities regulatory authority believes that unusual circumstances warrant the exercise of discretion to require the filing of a technical report, technical reports and certificates of qualification are not required to be filed in any jurisdiction except Québec, where technical reports and certificates of qualification are required to be filed in all cases. For this purpose, a reference to the name of the independent engineer or other qualified person in the issuer's AIF does not constitute a reference to a report prepared by that person in the short form prospectus. Therefore the issuer is not require[d] to file the report but must file the consent of the person who prepared it. Where technical reports and certificates of qualification are filed in British Columbia, reference should be made to note 8 for specific filing requirements.

NATIONAL POLICY No. 2-A
GUIDE FOR ENGINEERS, GEOLOGISTS AND PROSPECTORS SUBMITTING REPORTS ON MINING PROPERTIES TO CANADIAN PROVINCIAL SECURITIES ADMINISTRATORS

General

Reports submitted must be engineering documents. They must be factual and the recommendations must be warranted in the light of the information and data presented in the report. The author must state that, in his judgment, the venture is of sufficient merit to make the work recommended a worthwhile undertaking.

Authors with professional affiliations will use their seal.

Reports will be accepted only for the purposes of a prospectus if prepared by an engineer, geologist or prospector who has gained a minimum of three years practical experience, unless the author holds exceptional qualifications and there are unusual circumstances.

Where the proceeds of the issue are being applied to the property being reported upon, the person making the report required to be filed with the administrator (Commission) must be free of any association with the issuer. Therefore, except where specifically provided for in the Regulations, the report shall not be written by a director, officer or employee of the issuer or of an affiliate of the issuer or who is a partner, employer or employee of such director, officer or employee or who is an associate of any director or officer of the issuer or of an affiliate of the issuer. The report shall not be submitted if the person making it or any partner or employer of or associate to him beneficially owns, directly or indirectly, any securities of the issuer or of a subsidiary thereof or, if the issuer is a subsidiary, any securities of the parent issuer. This latter restriction does not apply to a person, partner, employer or associate, as the case may be, if the person, partner, employer, or associate is not empowered to decide whether securities of the issuer or the parent issuer, as the case may be, are to be beneficially owned, directly or indirectly, by him, or if he is not entitled to vote in respect thereof.

Source of Information

If any of the information and data are not based on the author's own observations and investigations, their source should be clearly stated, giving exact reference to published reports and records. When such information is derived from unpublished or private reports or records, a photostatic or other authenticated copy of the original should be submitted, together with a letter of consent and a certificate of qualification respecting the author's professional qualification, except where the report is a matter of public record such as those on open file in a provincial or federal natural resources department.

Wherever reasonable and practicable, reports must be based upon the author's personal inspection of the property being reported upon.

Content of Reports

A complete report should include a description of the properties of the issuer in accordance with the requirements of the appropriate provincial legislation and regulations and should contain all pertinent exploration data including plans and sections. The report should be presented under the following headings as applicable:

Table of Contents

Summary

Preamble or Introduction including author's terms of reference

Property, Description and Location

Accessibility, Climate, Local Resources

History—comprehensive, with references to all previous work for which records are available

Geology

Mineral Deposits and their state of Development

> The report must clearly distinguish between mineral showings which occur on the issuer's property being reported upon and those elsewhere in the area.

Reserves and Production

Conclusions and Recommendations with Cost Estimates

In Intermediate (Development) and Senior Financing (Production) Reports, the following vital considerations must be explored:

> Recoverability and amenability of the raw material
>
> Tonnage and grade versus optimum profitability
>
> Markets
>
> Smelter Contracts, tolls and transportation

Taxes

Cash flow, capital and operating cost estimates

Payback of capital with interest

The description of the properties must include claim numbers, whether patented or unpatented and if contiguous. The percentage of interest held in the properties should be stated.

If the potential merit of a property is predicated entirely or in part on results obtained on neighbouring ground, the known history of the latter should also be covered.

A description of mineralization encountered on the property should be given detailing the strike length, width, continuity and the basis of such measurement together with a description of the type, character and distribution of the mineralization. References as to its grade should be substantiated by assays with the dates thereof, and by assay plans and sections. In addition to giving the widths of the individual samples it should be stated whether these are the author's own samples or those of other parties. The method of sampling should be described making it clear whether assay results are based on channel samples, chip samples, grab samples, character samples or core samples.

Values in precious metals should be expressed in ounces per ton or grams per metric ton and the content of other metals, etc., in percentages or pounds per ton, but not in dollars or other currency.

Care should be taken in the use of the word "ore". The term is defined in the most recent Ontario Regulations as follows:

(a) "Ore" means a natural aggregate of one or more minerals which, at a specified time and place, may be mined and sold at a profit, or from which some part may be profitably separated;

(b) "Proven Ore" or "measured ore" means that material for which tonnage is computed from dimensions revealed in outcrops or trenches or underground workings or drill holes and for which the grade is computed from the results of adequate sampling, and for which the sites for inspection, sampling and measurement are so spaced and the geological character so well defined that the size, shape and mineral content are established, and for which the computed tonnage and grade are judged to be accurate within limits which shall be stated and for which it shall be stated whether the tonnage and grade of proven ore or measured ore are 'in situ' or extractable, with dilution factors shown, and reasons for the use of these dilution factors clearly explained;

(c) "Probable ore" or "indicated ore" means that material for which tonnage and grade are computed partly from specific measurements, samples or production data, and partly from projection for a reasonable distance on geological evidence, and for which the sites available for inspection, measurement and sampling are too widely or otherwise inappropriately spaced to outline the material completely or to establish its grade throughout;

(d) "Possible ore" or "inferred ore" means that material for which quantitative estimates are based largely on broad knowledge of the geological character of the deposit and for which there are few, if any, samples or measurements, and for which the estimates are based on an assumed continuity or repetition for which there are reasonable geological indications, which indications may include comparison with deposits of similar type, and bodies that are completely concealed may be included if there is specific evidence of their presence, and

(i) estimates of "possible" ore or "inferred ore" shall include a statement of conditions within which the inferred material occurs, and

(ii) since the arithmetical average of any amount of sampling is not necessarily representative unless the distribution of values and number of samples are properly taken into account, a statement of how samples were taken shall be given, and where mineralization is erratic, the method of treating the erratic values shall be given in the narrative of the report.

(iii) possible or inferred reserves must not be added to other categories of reserves and their inclusion is not acceptable in any economic analysis or feasibility study of a project.

Where the word "ore" may not properly be used, such terms as "mineralization", "mineralized bodies" or "concentrations", etc. should be used.

The information supplied in the report should be sufficient and positive enough to warrant the recommendations made. An estimate of costs for the proposed programme should be included.

Maps

Reports must be well illustrated by plans and by sections to give an adequate picture of the property. All reports must be accompanied by a location or index map and a more detailed plan showing all important features described in the text. If nearby properties have an important bearing on the possibilities of the ground under consideration, their location should be shown on the maps. Where the mineralized or ore-bearing structures are expected to pass from one property to the other, this should be indicated clearly on the map.

In case the potential merit of a property is predicated on geophysical or geo-chemical results, maps showing result of the surveys and the interpretations should be submitted.

All maps should show a scale, a North arrow, and should be signed and dated. If geological features or other data have been taken from Government maps or from drawings of other engineers or geologists, this should be properly acknowledged.

Consent to Use of Name in Prospectus

Where the author of the report or valuation is named as having prepared or certified any part of a prospectus or is named as having prepared or certified a report or valuation used in connection with a prospectus, the written consent of such author to the inclusion of such report or valuation shall accompany the report or valuation when filed with the administrator. It is the responsibility of the author when giving such consent to have assured himself that it can properly be given.

Certificate of the Author

All reports must be submitted in duplicate with the author's certificate attached, both dated and signed. The certificate shall state:

(a) the name, address and occupation of the author;

(b) the qualification of such person;

(c) whether or not the report is based on personal examination;

(d) the date of any such examination;

(e) if the report is not based on personal examination, the source of the information contained in the report; and

(f) whether he has, directly or indirectly, received or expects to receive any interest, direct or indirect, in the property of the issuer or any affiliate, or beneficially owns, directly or indirectly, any securities of the issuer or any affiliate and if so give particulars.

NATIONAL POLICY No. 2-B

GUIDE FOR ENGINEERS AND GEOLOGISTS SUBMITTING OIL AND GAS REPORTS TO CANADIAN PROVINCIAL SECURITIES ADMINISTRATORS

GENERAL

1. Reports submitted must be engineering documents. They must be factual, and any recommendations must be warranted in light of the information and data presented in the report. If the report contains recommendations, the author must state that, in his judgment, the venture is of sufficient merit to make the work recommended a worthwhile undertaking.

2. If any information and data in an engineering report are not based on the author's own observations and investigations, their source shall be clearly

stated, reference shall be made to reports and records from which the information and data was obtained, and the author shall state the degree of reliance he has placed on such reports and records. When information is derived from unpublished or private reports or records, a letter of consent from, and a certificate of qualification of, the author of such reports or records shall be submitted.

3. Reports will be accepted only if prepared by a registered professional engineer or a registered professional geologist who is a member in good standing of an appropriate association of professional engineers or geologists, unless he holds exceptional qualifications and there are unusual circumstances.

4. With reference to item 4.1.5, if principals in the independent consulting firm which prepared the report have or will acquire direct or indirect interests in properties or securities of the issuer or any associate or affiliate of the issuer, such interests must be clearly disclosed in the report.

5. Although Appendix 2 lists certain material in engineering reports which shall be included in a prospectus, the issuer may include additional disclosure and staff of the Securities Commissions may require additional material or disclosure to be included in a prospectus.

6. Reports shall be prepared only by a registered professional engineer or a registered professional geologist who is independent of the issuer or any associate or affiliate of the issuer. Therefore, reports shall not be written by a director, officer or employee of the issuer or any associate or affiliate of the issuer or by any person or company associated with such director, officer or employee. Notwithstanding the foregoing, in-house reports may be accepted at the discretion of the Director of the Securities Commission, but only from large well established issuers.

CONTENT OF OIL AND GAS REPORTS

A complete engineering and geological report for submission to Canadian Provincial Securities Administrators shall include the following material:

1. TABLE OF CONTENTS

2. INTRODUCTION

2.1 Author's terms of reference. State whether the report was prepared specifically for the purpose of submission to Securities Administrators or whether it will serve other purposes as well.

2.2 Names of principal properties. Include all major properties (including all properties to which the proceeds of issue are being applied) and identify them by the commonly referred to field or area names and disclose the jurisdiction (province, state, etc.). Briefly describe and discuss the geology of the properties. Discussion of geographic factors such as climate and accessibility need be included only in special situations such as frontier resources.

2.3 Summary of estimated net reserves and corresponding values.

2.3.1 Proved reserves and dollar values on a net cash-flow basis. Dollar values shall be calculated at current prices and costs, unless under contract as to price, to all future time. Additionally dollar values may be presented based on forecast prices and costs but critical assumptions in such a forecast shall be stated. Net cash-flow values shall be presented at discount rates of 0%, 10%, 15% and 20%.

2.3.2 Probable additional reserves and dollar values on a net cash-flow basis. Dollar values shall be calculated at current prices and costs, unless under contract as to price, to all future time. Additionally, dollar values may be presented based on forecast prices and costs but critical assumptions in such a forecast shall be stated. Net cash-flow values shall be presented at discount rates of 0%, 10%, 15% and 20%. Also, probable additional reserves shall be reduced for an allowance for the risk that is associated with the probability of obtaining production from such reserves.

2.3.3 A statement that the values reported under 2.3.1 and 2.3.2 may not necessarily be the fair market value of the reserves.

2.3.4   A statement as to whether the values are before or after income tax.

2.4   The percentage and quantity of proved producing reserves which are currently on production. (See definition 6 of Appendix 1.)

2.5   Definitions employed shall be the same as those listed in Appendix 1 and any deviation shall be stated along with supporting reasons.

2.6   Discussion of methods employed. Identify the methods used to estimate reserves and production rates and to convert them to cash flows. Include any assumptions respecting the availability of markets.

2.7   Discussion and identification of risk factors used, particularly respecting probable additional reserves, and justification for their selection.

2.8   Acceptable disclaimer. State clearly any conditions respecting the responsibility of the author. For example, the author might indicate that all estimated reserve quantities were based on geological and engineering data provided by the issuer although the interpretation of the data was carried out by the author, and might state whether or not he has grounds for a judgment that the data are sound. He shall also state whether he made an on-site visit of the properties and, if not, state briefly the reasons why a visit was judged unnecessary.

2.9   Where proceeds of the issue are to be expended on drilling on a specified property(ies), the report shall contain recommendations, conclusions and cost estimates in respect of the proposed drilling. Where appropriate, the author shall discuss the results of prior drilling on the property and on adjoining or nearby areas.

2.10   Summary of undeveloped gross and net acreage and value assigned to net acreage.

2.11   Signature and professional seal or permit stamp of author.

3.   SUPPORTING MATERIAL

3.1   Listings of properties shall include, but not be limited to, the following:

3.1.1   jurisdictions and location therein, and names of fields and areas including an index map(s)

3.1.2   Detail maps showing –

3.1.2.1 the issuer's interest lands and the issuer's interest in them

3.1.2.2 wells in which the issuer has an interest and wells of others together with their status.

3.1.3   Brief descriptions of the geology of the issuer's properties.

3.1.4   Tabulations of reservoir rock and fluid parameters for each well or pool including, but not limited to, depth of each pay zone, its porosity, pay zone thickness (specify gross or net), water saturation, pressure, temperature, recovery factor, etc.

3.1.5   Types of reserves* assigned:

3.1.5.1 crude oil

3.1.5.2 synthetic oil, or bitumen and corresponding synthetic oil yield factor

3.1.5.3 natural gas

3.1.5.4 natural gas liquids

3.1.5.5 sulphur.

        *Reserves assigned to "tight-hole" or confidential (by law) areas may be grouped and published as part of the listing as reserves only. Alternatively, if they are not included in the reserves listing, there shall be appropriate discussion describing the method of handling such properties.

3.1.6   Status of reserve assigned:

3.1.6.1 proved or probable additional.

3.1.6.2 proved producing or proved non-producing.

3.1.7 Company interest:

3.1.7.1 gross share of reserves before royalties

3.1.7.2 applicable royalties and/or production payments

3.1.7.3 net share of reserves after royalties.

3.1.8 Quantity of reserve assigned:

3.1.8.1 proved producing, proved non-producing, and total proved

3.1.8.2 probable additional

3.1.8.3 total

3.1.9 Forecast of future net production, revenue, costs and net cash flow on a proved producing, proved non-producing, and total proved reserve basis and on a probable additional reserve basis, by jurisdiction (province, state, etc.), and in total. Dollar values shall be calculated at current prices and costs, unless under contract as to price, to all future time. Additionally, dollar values may be presented based on forecast prices and costs but critical assumptions in such a forecast shall be stated. Net cash flow values shall be presented at discount rates of 0%, 10%, 15% and 20%. Also, probable additional reserves shall be reduced for an allowance for risk that is associated with the probability of obtaining production from such reserves.

3.2 A summary table itemizing the following basic assumptions, where applicable:

3.2.1 crude oil and synthetic oil price forecasts by jurisdiction

3.2.2 natural gas price forecast by jurisdiction

3.2.3 natural gas products price forecasts by jurisdiction

3.2.4 capital and operating costs

3.2.5 forecasts of inflation used respecting capital and operating costs

3.2.6 forecasts of any other factors employed on a general basis (e.g. crown royalty scale if different from those existing as of the effective date of the study).

3.2.7 Details of undeveloped acreage (both gross and net) disclosing field or area name, jurisdiction, value assigned to each separate net acreage, and method of determining those values.

3.2.8 Where proceeds of the issue are to be expended on drilling on a specified property(ies), the report shall contain recommendations, conclusions and cost estimates in respect of the proposed drilling. Where appropriate, the author shall discuss the results of prior drilling on the property and on adjoining or nearby areas.

4. CERTIFICATE OF AUTHOR

4.1 All reports must be submitted in duplicate with the author's certificate attached, both dated and signed. The certificate must contain the professional seal or permit stamp of the author and shall state:

4.1.1 the name, address and occupation of the author

4.1.2 the qualifications of the author

4.1.3 any conditions respecting the responsibility of the author and whether or not an on-site visit of the properties was made. If a visit was not made, state briefly why a visit was judged unnecessary.

4.1.4 the period during which the report was prepared and the effective date of the information therein.

4.1.5 whether or not the author has or expects to receive any interest, direct or indirect, in the properties or securities of the issuer or any associate or affiliate of the issuer and, if so, the particulars of the interest or beneficial ownership.

5.   LETTER OF CONSENT

5.1   The letter shall be addressed to the Securities Commissions and shall include
        a description of the report from which the engineer or geologist is giving his
        consent for the inclusion of extracts in a prospectus or other document. It
        shall state the date of the report as well as the date of the prospectus, and
        shall contain a statement that he has read the prospectus and has no reason
        to believe that there are any misrepresentations in the information contained
        in it that is derived from his report or that is within his knowledge as a result
        of his employment.

EFFECTIVE DATE:

This policy comes into effect on 15 December 1982.

Appendix 1.

DEFINITIONS

1.   CRUDE OIL: A mixture, consisting mainly of pentanes and heavier hydrocarbons
        that may contain sulphur compounds, that is liquid at the conditions under
        which its volume is measured or estimated, but excluding such liquids obtained
        from the processing of natural gas.

2.   SYNTHETIC OIL: Oil derived from the upgrading of crude bitumen or by chemical
        modification of coal or other materials and which is largely interchangeable with
        conventional crude oil as a refinery feedstock.

3.   NATURAL GAS: The lighter hydrocarbons and associated non-hydrocarbon sub-
        stances occurring naturally in an underground reservoir, which under atmos-
        pheric conditions is essentially a gas, but which may contain liquids. The natural
        gas reserve estimates should be reported on a marketable basis, that is the gas
        which is available to a transmission line after removal of certain hydrocarbons
        and non-hydrocarbon compounds present in the raw natural gas and which
        meets specifications for use as a domestic, commercial or industrial fuel.

4.   NATURAL GAS LIQUIDS: Those hydrocarbon components recovered from raw
        natural gas as liquids by processing through extraction plants or recovered from
        field separators, scrubbers or other gathering facilities. These liquids include the
        hydrocarbon components ethane, propane, butanes and pentanes plus, or a
        combination thereof.

5.   PROVED RESERVES*: Those reserves estimated as recoverable under current
        technology and existing economic conditions, from that portion of a reservoir
        which can be reasonably evaluated as economically productive on the basis of
        analysis of drilling, geological, geophysical and engineering data, including the
        reserves to be obtained by enhanced recovery processes demonstrated to be
        economic and technically successful in the subject reservoir.

        *Where reserves are clearly known to exist in a reservoir and would be physi-
        cally recoverable but cannot be termed "proved reserves" because they are not
        commercially recoverable due to their remote location (i.e., frontier reserves),
        these reserves should be itemized separately in the report and their special
        circumstances should be fully explained.

6.   PROVED PRODUCING RESERVES: Those proved reserves that are actually on
        production or, if not producing, that could be recovered from existing wells or
        facilities and where the reasons for the current non-producing status is the
        choice of the owner rather than the lack of markets or some other reasons. An
        illustration of such a situation is where a well or zone is capable but is shut-in
        because its deliverability is not required to meet contract commitments.

7.   PROVED NON-PRODUCING RESERVES: Those proved reserves that are not cur-
        rently producing either due to lack of facilities and/or markets.

8.   PROBABLE ADDITIONAL RESERVES: Those reserves which analysis of drilling,
        geological, geophysical and engineering data does not demonstrate to be proved
        under current technology and existing economic conditions, but where such
        analysis suggests the likelihood of their existence and future recovery. Probable
        additional reserves to be obtained by the application of enhanced recovery
        processes will be the increased recovery over and above that estimated in the
        proved category which can be realistically estimated for the pool on the basis of

enhanced recovery processes which can be reasonably expected to be instituted in the future.

Appendix 2.

CERTAIN MATERIAL FROM OR RELATED TO ENGINEERING REPORTS WHICH SHALL BE INCLUDED IN A PROSPECTUS

1. A summary of the estimated net reserves of the issuer with the following detail:

1.1 Reserves by jurisdiction and category (proved, proved producing, proved non-producing, probable additional) and type (crude oil, synthetic oil, natural gas, natural gas liquids, sulphur).

1.2 The values assigned to the above reserves on a net cash-flow basis, using discount rates of 0%, 10%, 15% and 20%. Values assigned must be based on prices and costs outlined in item 3.1.9 and disclosure shall be made in the prospectus of prices and costs used.

1.2.1 Estimated total capital costs necessary to achieve the net cash flow, and the amount of such costs estimated to be incurred in each of the first two years of the cash flow estimate.

1.3 A statement in bold print that the values reported under 1.2 may not necessarily be the fair market value of the reserves.

1.4 A statement in bold print as to whether the values are before or after income tax. Disclose the values on an after tax basis, if available.

1.5 The percentage and quantity of proved producing reserves which are currently on production. (See definition 6 of Appendix 1.)

2. A statement disclosing the source of data used in the estimates, including any comments the author of the engineering report might have respecting the soundness of the data.

3. A list of definitions employed.

4. A statement regarding the degree of risk assigned to values, particularly of probable additional reserves including a statement in bold print disclosing the approximate amount, or alternatively the approximate average percentage, by which the volume of probable reserves or their values have been reduced to allow for the risk associated with obtaining production from probable reserves. Where the author has not used percentages or calculated amounts as contemplated in the preceding sentence, a statement in bold print describing the method otherwise employed to allow for such risk.

5. A summary table of the assumptions employed regarding prices, costs, inflation and other forecast factors used.

6. Names of principal properties in which the issuer has an interest, identified by the commonly referred to field or area names and by jurisdiction (province, state, etc.).

7. A summary of undeveloped gross and net acreage by jurisdiction, and value assigned to undeveloped net acreage.

8. Where proceeds of the issue are to be expended on drilling on a specified property(ies), the author's recommendations, conclusions and cost estimates in respect of the proposed drilling.

9. Identification of the complete report, effective date thereof, name of author, and address at which the complete report is available for review.

NATIONAL POLICY No. 3
UNACCEPTABLE AUDITORS

The report of an auditor will not be viewed as being acceptable under the appropriate securities legislation where:

(1) The auditor is a director, officer or employee of the company being reported upon or of an affiliate of the company or is a partner, employer or employee of any such director, officer or employee or who is an associate of any director or officer of the company or of any affiliate of the company.

(2) The auditor or any partner or employer of or associate of him beneficially owns, directly or indirectly, any securities of the company or of a subsidiary of the company or, if the company is a subsidiary, any securities of its holding corporation provided that the disqualification will not apply to the person, partner, employer or associate, as the case may be, if the person, partner, employer or associate is not empowered to decide whether securities of the company or its holding company, as the case may be, are to be beneficially owned, directly or indirectly, by him, or if he is not entitled to vote in respect thereof.

NATIONAL POLICY No. 4
CONDITIONS FOR DEALER SUB-UNDERWRITINGS

Where the plan of distribution set out in a prospectus discloses that the underwriter may sell to a dealer as principal (hereinafter called "registrant"), the registrant may in turn distribute these securities providing the following conditions are complied with:

(1) The registrant must acquire the securities for its own account as principal and distribute the securities to the public as principal in accordance with the conditions disclosed under the heading "Plan of Distribution" in the prospectus.

(2) The offering price to the public shall not be greater than that disclosed in the prospectus.

(3) Notice of intention to engage in primary distribution to the public as principals must be filed with the administrator (Commission) by the registrant.

NATIONAL POLICY No. 5
RECOGNITION OF PROFITS IN REAL ESTATE TRANSACTIONS

[Repealed]

NATIONAL POLICY No. 6
MUTUAL FUNDS: SALES CHARGES

[Repealed]

NATIONAL POLICY No. 7
MUTUAL FUNDS: MANAGEMENT FEES

[Repealed]

NATIONAL POLICY No. 8
MUTUAL FUNDS: COMPUTATION OF NET ASSET VALUE PER SHARE

[Repealed]

NATIONAL POLICY No. 9
MUTUAL FUNDS: FORWARD PRICING, SALES AND REDEMPTIONS

[Repealed]

NATIONAL POLICY No. 10
MUTUAL FUNDS: REDEMPTION OF SECURITIES

[Repealed]

NATIONAL POLICY No. 11
MUTUAL FUNDS: CHANGES OF MANAGEMENT – CHANGE IN INVESTMENT POLICIES

[Repealed]

NATIONAL POLICY No. 12
DISCLOSURE OF "MARKET OUT" CLAUSES IN
UNDERWRITING AGREEMENTS IN PROSPECTUSES

As a result of a number of situations which have developed in the past whereby Underwriters have exercised their discretion with respect to "market out" clauses contained in Underwriting Agreements which has resulted in a no offering or a cessation of an offering it was felt that prospectuses did not contain adequate disclosure with respect to the "market out" clauses contained in the Underwriting Agreement. As a result the following is required:

Cover Page:

The following wording will be required on the Cover Page of a prospectus to ensure disclosure of the conditional aspects of the Underwriting Agreement and a proper reference to the location of further details in the prospectus.

"We, as principals, conditionally offer these Debentures, subject to prior sale, if, as and when issued by the company and accepted by us in accordance with the conditions contained in the underwriting agreement referred to under Plan of Distribution on Page . . . . and subject to the approval of all legal matters on behalf of the company by Messrs. . . . . and our behalf Messrs. "

Plan of Distribution:

The following wording shall be included under this section:

"Under an agreement dated . . . . 19 . . . . between the company and . . . . as underwriter, the company has agreed to sell and the underwriter has agreed to purchase on . . . . 19 . . . . the $ . . . . principal amount of Debentures at a price of $ . . . . per $100 principal amount thereof plus accrued interest to the date of delivery, payable in cash to the company against delivery of the Debentures. The obligations of the underwriter under such agreement may be terminated at its discretion on the basis of its assessment of the state of the financial markets and may also be terminated upon the occurrence of certain stated events. The underwriter is, however, obligated to take up and pay for all the Debentures if any of the Debentures are purchased under such agreement."

The above wording represents terminology which would be considered acceptable, however, other wording would also be considered acceptable providing such wording would not alter the effectiveness of the disclosure.

NATIONAL POLICY No. 13
DISCLAIMER CLAUSE ON PROSPECTUS

The following statement shall appear on the front page of each prospectus and preliminary prospectus filed:

"NO SECURITIES COMMISSION OR SIMILAR AUTHORITY IN CANADA HAS IN ANY WAY PASSED UPON THE MERITS OF THE SECURITIES OFFERED HEREUNDER AND ANY REPRESENTATION TO THE CONTRARY IS AN OFFENCE."

NATIONAL POLICY STATEMENT NO. 14
ACCEPTABILITY OF CURRENCIES IN
MATERIAL FILED WITH SECURITIES REGULATORY AUTHORITIES

TABLE OF CONTENTS

National
Policies

4   OFFERING DOCUMENTS AND BID DOCUMENTS

    4.1   Disclosure

    4.2   Supplementary Disclosure

    4.3   Supplementary Disclosure of Hyperinflationary Effects

5   OTHER DOCUMENTS

    5.1   Supplementary Disclosure

    5.2   Supplementary Disclosure of Hyperinflationary Effects

6   COMPLIANCE

7   EFFECTIVE DATE

    7.1   Effective Date

    7.2   Policy Statement Rescinded

NATIONAL POLICY STATEMENT NO. 14

ACCEPTABILITY OF CURRENCIES IN

MATERIAL FILED WITH SECURITIES REGULATORY AUTHORITIES

PART 1   PURPOSE

This policy statement sets out the requirements of the securities regulatory authorities in each Canadian province or territory with respect to currencies used in the disclosure of financial information.

PART 2   DEFINITIONS

For purposes of this policy statement:

"Bid Documents" means all documents filed under the take-over and issuer bid requirements of the Securities Legislation and Securities Requirements and documents distributed to shareholders in connection with transactions in which a corporate reorganization is to be effected;

"Exchange Rate" means the rate used to translate a currency other than the Canadian dollar into the Canadian dollar;

"Hyperinflationary Effects" means cumulative inflationary effects, determined by reference to a broad based index such as gross domestic product, which exceed a total of 100 percent over the most recent three financial years;

"Offering Documents" means prospectuses, preliminary prospectuses, offering memoranda and rights offering circulars;

"Other Documents" means documents filed pursuant to the continuous disclosure and proxy and proxy solicitation requirements of the Securities Legislation and Securities Requirements other than those documents distributed to shareholders in connection with transactions in which a corporate reorganization is to be effected;

"Securities Legislation" means the statutes concerning the regulation of securities markets and trading in securities, and the regulations in respect of these statutes; and

"Securities Requirements" means the blanket rulings and orders made under the Securities Legislation, and the policy statements and written interpretations issued by the securities regulatory authorities.

PART 3   APPLICATION

3.1   Scope

    This policy statement applies to all financial information in Offering Documents, Bid Documents and Other Documents required to be filed or delivered under the Securities Legislation and Securities Requirements.

3.2   Currency Disclosure

    Issuers disclosing financial information in a currency that is not the unit of measure for the preparation of financial statements shall disclose the currency that is the unit of measure. Issuers may disclose financial information in any currency, however, the currency of display shall be reasonable in the circumstances (e.g. the currency of the jurisdiction in which the issuer is organized or incorporated, the currency of the issuer's primary economic environment). When financial information is disclosed in the U.S. dollar, issuers shall identify that disclosure is in the U.S. dollar.

PART 4   OFFERING DOCUMENTS AND BID DOCUMENTS

4.1   Disclosure

In each Offering Document or Bid Document filed with or delivered to the securities regulatory authorities that discloses the offering price in a currency other than either the Canadian dollar or the U.S. dollar, the issuer must disclose in bold face type on the face page of the Offering Document or Bid Document the Exchange Rate at the latest practicable date.

4.2   Supplementary Disclosure

If an issuer discloses financial information in an Offering Document or a Bid Document in a currency other than either the Canadian dollar or the U.S. dollar, the issuer shall disclose the following in the Offering Document or Bid Document:

(1)   the currency in which financial information is disclosed in bold face type;

(2)   the Exchange Rate in effect at the latest practicable date and a five year Exchange Rate history including year-end and average annual Exchange Rates;

(3)   average Exchange Rates for the periods for which income statements and statements of changes in financial position are presented and the Exchange Rate for each date at which a balance sheet is presented; and

(4)   information regarding legislation as to withholding taxes and as to foreign exchange controls.

4.3   Supplementary Disclosure of Hyperinflationary Effects

In addition to the supplementary disclosure required in section 4.2, if the currency that is the unit of measure for the preparation of the issuer's financial statements is the currency of a country that has experienced Hyperinflationary Effects, the following shall be disclosed in the Offering Document or Bid Document:

(a)   the existence of Hyperinflationary Effects;

(b)   a five year history of the average annualized rate of inflation; and

(c)   a discussion of the impact of Hyperinflationary Effects on the issuer's business.

PART 5   OTHER DOCUMENTS

5.1   Supplementary Disclosure

(1)   If an issuer discloses financial information in Other Documents in a currency other than either the Canadian dollar or the U.S. dollar, the issuer shall disclose the following in its annual audited financial statements or in documents accompanying such statements:

(a)   the currency in which financial information is disclosed;

(b)   the Exchange Rate in effect as of the latest practicable date;

(c)   average Exchange Rates for the periods for which income statements and statements of changes in financial position are presented and the Exchange Rate for each date at which a balance sheet is presented; and

(d)   information regarding legislation as to withholding taxes and as to foreign exchange controls.

(2) If a material fluctuation[1] occurs in the Exchange Rate subsequent to the filing of the issuer's annual audited financial statements, the supplementary disclosure required under subsection (1) shall be included in the issuer's interim financial statements or documents accompanying such statements required to be filed immediately following the occurrence of the material fluctuation.

5.2 *Supplementary Disclosure of Hyperinflationary Effects*

In addition to the supplementary disclosure required in section 5.1, if the currency that is the unit of measure for the preparation of the issuer's financial statements is the currency of a country that has experienced Hyperinflationary Effects, the following shall be disclosed in the issuer's annual audited financial statements or in documents accompanying such statements:

(1) the existence of Hyperinflationary Effects; and

(2) the average annualized rate of inflation for each period for which financial information is presented.

PART 6 COMPLIANCE

Where it is impracticable for an issuer to comply with the requirements of this policy statement, prior approval of the securities regulatory authorities shall be obtained.

PART 7 EFFECTIVE DATE

7.1 *Effective Date*

This policy statement is effective for preliminary prospectuses, offering memoranda, rights offering circulars and Bid Documents filed or delivered after January 1, 1993 and financial years beginning on or after January 1, 1993.

7.2 *Policy Statement Rescinded*

National Policy Statement No. 14 – Acceptability of Other Currencies in Material Filed with Provincial Securities Administrators – is rescinded and this policy statement is substituted.

NATIONAL POLICY No. 15

**CONDITIONS PRECEDENT TO ACCEPTANCE OF
SCHOLARSHIP OR EDUCATIONAL PLAN PROSPECTUSES**

The sale of contracts or plans commonly referred to as "university scholarship plans" or "scholarship agreements" must be subject to the following conditions before the prospectus will be acceptable for filing:

(1) A very clear distinction must be drawn between the "foundation" (which is described as a body without any profit motive or desire for pecuniary gain) and the distributor (the registered distribution agency who sell the plan under a commission arrangement often described as an "enrolment fee") in order that the public will not be induced into the error of believing that there are no sales charges or other commissions.

(2) The scholarship plan distributors and salesmen, of course, must hold registration under the specific provincial acts. The use of such expressions as "education counsellors", "scholarship counsellors or advisers", "enrolment counsellors" is viewed as misleading and should not be used.

(3) The funds received from the subscribers must be deposited with a Canadian chartered bank or a provincially licensed trust company or other similar financial institution whose accounts are normally insured by the Canada Deposit Insurance Corporation or La Régie de l'assurance-depôts du Québec. Where a subscriber's account is not afforded the protection of insurance by the Canada Deposit Insurance Corporation or La Régie de l'assurance-depôts du Québec, the fund administrator must ensure that

---

1 In this context, "materiality" means the financial reporting notion of materiality contained in the Handbook of the Canadian Institute of Chartered Accountants which is broader than the definition of material change in the Securities Legislation.

such subscriber's account is considered to be assets under administration in the hands of the depository.

(4) The fund administrator, which is usually the "foundation", will secure the best interest rate possible on the deposits, and the interest paid on the subscriber's capital shall be transferred to a trust fund held by the same depository which in turn will be administered for the benefit of the beneficiaries of the plans. In securing the best interest rate possible the fund administrator may, where not contrary to the scholarship agreement, cause the subscriber's deposits to be invested in mortgages provided that such mortgages are:

(a) first mortgages on residential properties of 8 units or less located in Canada and having a maturity not exceeding 5 years, provided that first mortgages may be on residential properties of more than 8 units when the following conditions are met:

(i) the scholarship plans under administration have total net assets of at least $50,000,000;

(ii) the mortgages are insured under the National Housing Act (Canada) or any similar provincial statute or are insured by an insurance company registered or licensed under the Canadian and British Insurance Companies Act (Canada), the Foreign Insurance Companies Act (Canada), or any similar statute of a Canadian province or territory; and

(iii) not more than 20 percent of the funds from sources described in 4(h)(i) and 4(h)(ii) below are invested in such mortgages on residential properties of more than 8 units;

(b) an amount which is not more than 75% of the fair market value of the property securing the mortgage, except when:

(i) such a mortgage is insured under the National Housing Act (Canada) or any similar act of a province; or

(ii) the excess over 75% is insured by an insurance company registered or licensed under the Canadian and British Insurance Companies Act (Canada), the Foreign Insurance Companies Act (Canada) or insurance acts or similar acts of a Canadian province or territory;

(c) acquired from a lending institution with which the fund, the administrator of the fund, the trustee(s) and the distributor of the fund are dealing at arm's length;

(d) purchased and sold at fair market value, i.e. that principal amount which produces at least the yield prevailing for the sale of comparable fully serviced mortgages as established by major mortgage lenders under similar conditions;

(e) fully funded, serviced and not in arrears at the date of acquisition;

(f) not on a property in which:

(i) the administrator, the trustee or the distributor of the fund or any senior officer or director thereof, or

(ii) any person or company who is a substantial security-holder of the administrator, a trustee or the distributor of the fund, or

(iii) any associate or affiliate of persons or institutions mentioned in subparagraphs (i) and (ii),

has an interest as mortgagor or as an associate of a mortgagor;

(g) limited in amount, in respect of any one mortgage, to $75,000 for funds having less than $5,000,000 in net assets; and to the lesser of $500,000 or 2.5 per cent of its net assets where they exceed $5,000,000 but are less than $50,000,000; and to the amount not exceeding 1.0 percent of its net assets for funds having $50,000,000 or more in net assets, and for the purpose of this paragraph, a series of mortgages on one condominium development shall be considered as one mortgage;

National
Policies

(h) restricted in total to an amount not greater than 75% of

  (i) funds arising from new contracts sold to subscribers pursuant to a prospectus which contains disclosure of the arrangements in respect of mortgage investment and which has been accepted for filing by the Administrator; and

  (ii) funds held on behalf of subscribers who, after receipt of an information circular which has first been filed with and accepted by the Administrator, have agreed in writing to permit their plan contracts to be included in the mortgage investment arrangement;

(i) on properties appraised by a qualified appraiser such as a bank, trust company, loan company or insurance company, or other person or company which makes appraisals and whose opinions are relied upon in connection with lending or servicing activities, and who in the judgment of the management company or trustee of the specific fund is properly qualified to make such a determination;

(j) not on raw land or undeveloped land.

(5) The depository must maintain an accounting system which will permit it to determine the total amount of deposits made by each subscriber, all deductions from such deposits and the amount of interest produced by the deposits of each subscriber.

(6) The trust funds shall be administered pursuant to a trust indenture or deed in accordance with the terms detailed in the prospectus, and must contain a provision under which a licensed trust company agrees to act in the place of the foundation in the event that the foundation refuses to or is unable to act.

(7) The fees charged, including the commissions of the distributor and its salesmen, must not exceed $200 per plan. The first $100 paid under the plan may be applied against this fee and the balance may be deducted at a maximum rate of 50% of each of the further contributions.

(8) From these fees sufficient funds must be set aside in trust to pay the future costs of administering the trusts established under 6. These funds shall not be used directly or indirectly for any other purpose. The costs of distribution must be borne fully by the distribution company. Any additional sums rebated or otherwise paid by the depository to assist in the payment of the charges for administration of the funds shall be held in trust by the foundation solely for this purpose and shall not be paid directly or indirectly for any other purpose.

(9) The plan must grant the subscriber the right to withdraw from the plan without any cost to the subscriber within 60 days from the execution of the contract.

(10) Where the subscriber wishes to withdraw from a plan after 60 days from the date of the execution of the contract, the subscriber shall not be obliged to pay any fees in addition to those already paid, but may lose the total amount of fees paid to that point.

(11) It is considered contrary to the public interest to accept for filing a scholarship plan which calls for the complete forfeiture of the capital and accumulated interest in cases where the plan is abandoned before its maturity. The same shall apply to so-called "special" plans which consist of the simple deposit by the subscriber of an amount equivalent to the interest, without any right to reimbursement.

(12) The schedule of instalment payments must be equitable for all children enrolled. In the setting of the schedules, accounts must be kept of the age of the children and the number of instalments foreseen so that there is an actuarial equivalent between the instalments foreseen for each age and each plan. Accordingly the so-called "family plans" are not acceptable.

(13) All beneficiaries must participate equally in the advantages of the plan. The foundation or trustee must make provision in the trust indenture for the payment of equivalent scholarships for each of the eligible participants.

(14) Scholarship plan agreements must be filed with the preliminary prospectus (or prospectus as the case may be) as part of the supporting material together with a copy of the trust agreement.

(15) The prospectus shall clearly indicate on its front page the speculative nature of the scholarship plans and the real cost of participation in the plan to the subscriber.

NATIONAL POLICY No. 16
MAINTENANCE OF PROVINCIAL TRADING RECORDS

In order that complete details concerning trades in a specific province should be readily available to the administrator (Commission) in that province and its staff it shall be a condition attaching to all registrations, excepting salesmen and under-writers, whose head office records are maintained other than in the specific province, that there shall be maintained in that province and readily available for examination by the administrator's (Commission's) staff such ledgers, books of account, correspondence and other documents and records as are necessary to provide complete details of each transaction from or within that province.

NATIONAL POLICY No. 17
VIOLATIONS OF SECURITIES LAWS OF OTHER JURISDICTIONS – CONDUCT AFFECTING FITNESS FOR CONTINUED REGISTRATION

Notice is hereby given to all securities registrants that violations of the securities laws of any jurisdiction and violations of the rules of a recognized self-regulatory organization that are adopted for the protection of investors are considered in principle to be prejudicial to the public interest and may affect their fitness for continued registration.

NATIONAL POLICY No. 18
CONFLICT OF INTEREST – REGISTRANTS ACTING AS CORPORATE DIRECTORS

The position of a representative of a registrant acting as a director of a public company is one that is fraught with the possibility of a conflict of interest. This arises more particularly in regard to questions of insider information and trading and timely disclosure.

The administrators (Commission) emphasize that all registrants should be most conscious of their responsibilities in such situations and weigh the burden of dealing in an ethical manner with the conflict of interest problems against the advantages of acting as a director of a public company, many shareholders of which may be clients of the registrant. In this regard, the statement on conflict of duty arising out of the position of registrants acting as directors of public corporations issued by The Toronto Stock Exchange on December 5, 1978, is called to the attention of all registrants, whether members of The Toronto Stock Exchange or not, since it defines acceptable conduct in this area.

"Every director has a fiduciary obligation not to reveal any privileged information to anyone not authorized to receive it. Not until there is full public disclosure of such data, particularly when the information might have a bearing on the market price of the securities, is a director released from the necessity of keeping information of this character to himself. Any director of a corporation who is a partner, officer or employee of a member organization should recognize that his first responsibility in this area is to the corporation on whose board he serves. Thus, a member firm director must meticulously avoid any disclosure of inside information to his partners and employees of the firm, his customers or his research or trading departments.

Where a representative of a member organization is not a director but is acting in an advisory capacity to a company and discussing confidential matters, the ground rules should be substantially the same as those that apply to a director. Should the matter require consultation with other personnel of the organization adequate measures should be taken to guard the confidential nature of the information to prevent its misuse within or outside the member organization."

Whenever questions arise regarding the fitness for registration of individuals, the administrator (Commission) will consider the conduct of such individuals in relation to the manner in which they have complied with the standards set out above.

NATIONAL POLICY No. 19
MUTUAL FUNDS SALES COMPANIES: COMMINGLING OF FUNDS AND SECURITIES
[Repealed]

NATIONAL POLICY No. 20
TRADING IN UNQUALIFIED SECURITIES – SECURITIES IN PRIMARY DISTRIBUTION IN OTHER JURISDICTIONS

Registrants executing orders on behalf of residents of the province in which they are registered must ensure that the securities being purchased are qualified for sale in that province. The receipt of an order by a registrant, even though it is transmitted to and executed on an exchange outside the province, is still an act in furtherance of trading within the province. If the security is in primary distribution, a prospectus duly accepted for filing by the administrator (Commission) must be delivered to or received on behalf of the client in all cases.

The securities of open-end investment companies or common law trusts ordinarily referred to as "mutual funds" are always in primary distribution. It is particularly important for registrants to take care when orders are placed with them for American funds. Some of these funds are qualified for sale in the provinces but many are not. Similar situation applies when orders are received for securities in primary distribution in other jurisdictions. It is the responsibility of the registrant to ensure that the orders which he is executing are for securities that are duly qualified in this province.

NATIONAL POLICY No. 21
NATIONAL ADVERTISING – WARNINGS

All advertisements placed in national publications and which name registrants or their affiliates and which concern issues that are in primary distribution, should contain a warning in the following words or to like effect:

"This advertisement is not to be construed as a public offering in any province in Canada unless a prospectus relating thereto has been accepted for filing by a securities commission or similar authority in such province. The offering is made by the prospectus only and copies thereof may be obtained from such of the undersigned and other dealers as may lawfully offer these securities in such province."

If an offering is qualified in all provinces, the language above should be changed to suit such a situation.

Advertisements "of record" which name registrants or their affiliates may appear in such national publications when the issue has been completely sold and is no longer in primary distribution without the above warning. In such cases, a statement to the effect that the issue has been so sold should be included.

NATIONAL POLICY No. 22
USE OF INFORMATION AND OPINION RE MINING AND OIL PROPERTIES BY REGISTRANTS AND OTHERS

For the guidance of registrants and companies who wish to make use of information or opinion concerning mining or oil properties in reports, letters or other publications which may be used directly or indirectly to further the sale of the securities of the company owning or having an interest in particular properties being reported or commented upon and, to ensure a uniform minimum standard in the use of such facts or opinion either orally or through publication, the following standards of disclosure and definition shall be complied with:

(1) In general the standards shall be those found in the "Guide for Mining Engineers, Geologists and Prospectors" (National Policy No. 2 [now 2-A and 2-B]) under the headings "General" and "Sources of Information". The manner of description and the definitions used shall conform to those set out in the "Guide" under the heading "Contents".

(2)   Sources of information and opinion shall be named specifically either by reference to a named person or an official publication.

(3)   Where technical data are quoted or opinions based on technical information are expressed, the source of such facts or opinions must be in writing and made by a person who, in the opinion of the administrator (Commission), is a qualified Mining Engineer, Geologist or Prospector.

(4)   Where the person making a report or offering opinions has any interest, direct or indirect, in the company whose shares are being distributed whether by way of shareholdings or other financial interest or, where such person is an officer, director or employee of that company, the interest or position must clearly be disclosed.

(5)   Such facts or opinions must be quoted verbatim and not out of context. The omission of unfavourable or negative facts or comment will be viewed as misleading.

(6)   Where the results obtained fairly warrant either an upgrading or downgrading of the engineering reports already submitted and accepted for filing by the administrator (Commission), this is a material change and must be the subject of an amendment to the prospectus.

Failure to comply with these minimum standards will be viewed as affecting the fitness for registration of the registrant in whose name or on whose behalf such material is published or used.

NATIONAL POLICY No. 23
MUTUAL FUNDS: "IN-HOUSE" FUNDS

[Repealed]

NATIONAL POLICY No. 24
MUTUAL FUNDS: CONTRACTUAL PLANS

[Repealed]

NATIONAL POLICY No. 25
REGISTRANTS: ADVERTISING: DISCLOSURE OF INTEREST

Under the *Uniform Securities Act* registered advisers are required to disclose in a conspicuous position on every circular, pamphlet, advertisement, letter, telegram and other publication issued, published or sent by him a full and complete statement of any financial or other interest that he may have either directly or indirectly in any of the securities referred to in those publications or in the sale or purchase thereof including any commissions, financial arrangements or other remuneration he may expect to receive if his recommendation is followed. The provincial securities administrators are of the view that the standard of conduct outlined above ought to be followed by all classes of registrant when they recommend the purchase or sale of a security in which they have a material interest.

This arises most frequently when a registrant endorses or recommends the acceptance of a takeover bid, a share exchange offer, or the purchase of an issue being offered through a rights offering, through warrants, or by way of conversion. Where such endorsements or recommendations are made orally or in writing by registrants they should include a clear statement of interest in the following circumstances:

(1)   where the registrant acts as an agent for the offeror;

(2)   where the registrant will receive a fee for shares tendered, exchanged or taken up through him;

(3)   where the named officers or directors of the registrant are also officers or directors of the offeror; or

(4)   where the registrant has any other material financial interest, direct or indirect, in the offer.

Failure to comply with the spirit of this policy will be considered by the administrators as being contrary to the public interest – affecting the registrant's fitness for continued registration.

EFFECTIVE DATE: DECEMBER 6th, 1971.

NATIONAL POLICY No. 26
MUTUAL FUNDS: ACCEPTANCE OR REJECTION OF
SUBSCRIPTIONS FOR FUND SHARES OR UNITS

[Repealed]

NATIONAL POLICY STATEMENT NO. 27
CANADIAN GENERALLY ACCEPTED ACCOUNTING PRINCIPLES

TABLE OF CONTENTS

NATIONAL POLICY STATEMENT NO. 27
CANADIAN GENERALLY ACCEPTED ACCOUNTING PRINCIPLES

PART 1   PURPOSE

This policy statement sets out the position of the securities regulatory authorities with respect to the accounting principles to be applied to, and the disclosure to be included in, the financial statements of an issuer, a registrant or other person (collectively an "Issuer") required to file financial statements with a securities regulatory authority in any province or territory in Canada in accordance with the requirements of:

    (i) the statutes concerning the regulation of securities markets and trading in securities in a jurisdiction, and the regulations in respect of these statutes ("Securities Legislation"), or

    (ii) the blanket rulings and orders made under the Securities Legislation of a jurisdiction, and the policy statements and written interpretations issued by the securities regulatory authority of that jurisdiction ("Securities Requirements").

PART 2   APPLICATION

This policy statement applies to all financial statements that are required to be filed by an Issuer under the Securities Legislation of any jurisdiction, unless otherwise specified in, or exempted by, the Securities Legislation of that jurisdiction, and that are required to be prepared in accordance with, or reconciled to, generally accepted accounting principles in Canada ("Canadian GAAP"). Where an Issuer is required to file other financial information, such as selected financial data or management's discussion and analysis of financial condition and results of operations, with the securities regulatory authorities of a jurisdiction, that information must be prepared on a basis that is consistent with the principles applied in the financial statements.

PART 3   DEFINITION OF CANADIAN GAAP

3.1   Financial statements to be prepared in accordance with Canadian GAAP – The Securities Legislation of certain jurisdictions requires, subject to certain exceptions, that financial statements be prepared in accordance with Canadian GAAP and any applicable provisions of the Securities Legislation. Where the Securities Legislation of a jurisdiction is silent on the issue of compliance with generally accepted accounting principles, the securities regulatory authorities nonetheless require that Issuers prepare their financial statements in accordance with Canadian GAAP.

3.2 *Interpretation of Canadian GAAP* – When used in Securities Legislation, "generally accepted accounting principles" has the meaning ascribed to this term in the Handbook of the Canadian Institute of Chartered Accountants (the "CICA Handbook"). Issuers and their advisors should refer to section 1000 of the CICA Handbook for a full discussion of financial statement concepts and other sources of Canadian GAAP.[1]

3.3 *Pre-filing conferences* – In those rare circumstances where following a CICA Handbook recommendation would result in the preparation of misleading financial statements, the Issuer together with its auditor should discuss the situation with the appropriate representative of the securities regulatory authority (the "Applicable Regulator"). In addition, in those circumstances when Canadian GAAP is unclear, or where there are no established accounting principles, because of the new or unique nature of the transaction or activity, the Issuer together with its auditor is encouraged to discuss the situation with the Applicable Regulator. Failure to consult with the Applicable Regulator on a pre-filing basis may result in delays in the processing of regulatory filings.

3.4 *Additional requirements* – The Securities Legislation and Securities Requirements of certain jurisdictions may impose accounting and disclosure requirements in addition to those set out under Canadian GAAP. Issuers are reminded that they must review the Securities Legislation and Securities Requirements of each jurisdiction in which they are required to file to ensure that their financial statements comply with all applicable requirements.

PART 4 DISCRETION AVAILABLE TO APPLICABLE REGULATOR

Where the accounting principles or practices that the Issuer intends to apply in preparing its financial statements will result in a departure from Canadian GAAP, the Issuer together with its auditor should discuss the situation with the Applicable Regulator. The Applicable Regulator may, if it has the necessary authority under the Securities Legislation of that jurisdiction and it considers it to be in the public interest,

(1) at the request of the Issuer, and

(2) upon receipt in writing from the Issuer and its auditor, sufficiently in advance of the filing deadline applicable to the financial statements that give rise to the departure from Canadian GAAP, of all relevant information including the basis of accounting or disclosure that is not in accordance with Canadian GAAP and that has been selected by the Issuer,

exercise its discretion to accept financial statements that are not prepared in accordance with Canadian GAAP when the financial statements are filed. In certain jurisdictions the Applicable Regulator may require the holding of a public hearing as part of its consideration of the Issuer's request. Reference should be made to National Policy Statement No. 50 for further information on the securities regulatory authorities' position where financial statements are accompanied by an auditor's report containing a reservation of opinion.

PART 5 EFFECTIVE DATE

5.1 Effective date – This policy statement is effective December 31, 1992.

5.2 Policy statement repealed – National Policy Statement No. 27 dated December 7, 1972 and its subsequent revisions dated July 26, 1977, October 21, 1977 and November 2, 1979 are repealed upon the coming into effect of this policy statement. The notice issued in relation to National Policy No. 27 entitled "Recommendations of the Canadian Institute of Chartered Accountants –

---

1 Regulated Issuers – The Securities Legislation of certain jurisdictions may exempt certain regulated Issuers from preparing their financial statements in accordance with Canadian GAAP and the applicable provisions of the Securities Legislation where Canadian GAAP has not been established. In these circumstances, where the regulator establishes the accounting principles to be followed or where the regulator clarifies Canadian GAAP to be applied by the regulated Issuer in the preparation of its financial statements, the financial statements prepared in accordance with the regulatory requirements will be acceptable for purposes of Securities Legislation as long as there are no departures from Canadian GAAP.

3470.13 Tax Allocation Accounting Practices" dated March 28, 1974 is also repealed upon the coming into effect of this policy statement as the principles enunciated in that notice are contained in the CICA Handbook.

NATIONAL POLICY No. 28
MUTUAL FUNDS: INVESTMENT RESTRICTIONS – OPTIONS

[Repealed]

NATIONAL POLICY No. 29
MUTUAL FUNDS INVESTING IN MORTGAGES

SECTION I
APPLICABILITY

I.(1) This policy applies to any mutual fund having 10% or more of its portfolio invested in mortgages or hypothecs, except that sub-section III(1) applies only to a mutual fund having 50% or more of its portfolio invested in mortgages or hypothecs.

(2) Except where in conflict with this policy, all relevant mutual fund policies apply.

SECTION II
DEFINITIONS

II. For the purpose of this policy:

(1) "qualified appraiser" means a bank, trust company, loan company or insurance company, or other person or company which makes appraisals and whose opinions are relied upon in connection with lending or servicing activities, and who in the judgment of the management company or trustee of the specific fund is properly qualified to make such a determination;

(2) "substantial security holder" means any person, company or combination of persons or companies that beneficially owns directly or indirectly more than 10% of the voting rights attached to all outstanding equity shares;

(3) "liquid assets" means cash or deposits with a Canadian chartered bank or with any trust company registered under the laws of any province of Canada which are cashable or saleable prior to maturity, debt securities valued at market issued or guaranteed by the governments of Canada or any of the Canadian provinces, and money market instruments maturing prior to one year from the date of issue.

SECTION III
INVESTMENT POLICY

III. (1) Liquidity:

(a) The prospectus of a mutual fund investing in mortgages shall include a provision that the fund will not invest in mortgages if such acquisition would have the effect of reducing the fund's liquid assets to an amount less than the amount established by the following formula:

Net assets of the fund
(market value)

$ 1,000,00 or less	$ 100,000
$ 1,000,000	$ 100,000 + 10% on next $ 1,000,000
$ 2,000,000	$ 200,000 + 9% on next $ 3,000,000
$ 5,000,000	$ 470,000 + 8% on next $ 5,000,000
$10,000,000	$ 870,000 + 7% on next $10,000,000
$20,000,000	$1,570,000 + 6% on next $10,000,000
$30,000,000 or over	$2,170,000 + 5% on excess

(b) To provide liquidity for redemption purposes only, a fund may borrow an amount not exceeding 10% of its net assets.

(2) Restrictions:

(2.1) A fund may not invest in mortgages:

    (a) more than 10% of its net assets until its net assets have reached and continue to be maintained at a minimum of $350,000;

    (b) on raw land or undeveloped land;

    (c) other than first mortgages on properties located in Canada;

    (d) on residential properties of more than 8 units and on commercial and industrial properties, until the fund has net assets of at least $15,000,000. In any event, the total amount of such mortgages must never exceed 40% of the net assets of the fund provided that those mortgages constituting the excess of 20% of the net assets of the fund that are invested in such mortgages must be insured either by an agency of the Government of Canada or of a Province of Canada;

    (e) unless the property securing the mortgage has been appraised by a qualified appraiser;

    (f) an amount which is more than 75% of the fair market value of the property securing the mortgage, except when:

        (i) such mortgage is insured under the National Housing Act (Canada) or any similar act of a province, or

        (ii) the excess over 75% is insured by an insurance company registered or licensed under the Canadian and British Insurance Companies Act (Canada), the Foreign Insurance Companies Act (Canada) or insurance acts or similar acts of a Canadian province or territory;

    (g) with a maturity exceeding 10 years for mortgages on the types of properties referred to in subsection 2.1(d) and 5 years in all other cases except that up to 10% of the net assets of the fund may be invested in residential mortgages with a maturity not exceeding 10 years; the amortization period of each mortgage must not exceed 30 years, except for mortgages insured under the National Housing Act (Canada) or any similar act of a province;

    (h) an amount exceeding $75,000 for funds having less than $1,500,000 in net assets; and the lesser of $1,000,000 or 5% of its net assets when they exceed $1,500,000, but are less than $50,000,000; and an amount exceeding 2% of its net assets for funds having $50,000,000 or more in net assets, for any one mortgage, and for the purpose of this paragraph, a series of mortgages on one condominium development shall be considered as one mortgage;

    (i) on a property in which:

        (i) any senior officer, director or trustee of the mutual fund, its management company or distribution or

        (ii) any person or company who is a substantial security holder of the mutual fund, its management company or its distribution company, or

        (iii) any associate or affiliate of persons or institutions mentioned in subparagraphs (i) or (ii), except in the case of a mortgage on a family dwelling for less than $75,000,

    has an interest as mortgagor.

(2.2) Neither the fund nor the management company on behalf of the fund shall enter into forward commitments binding on the fund with regard to mortgages to be acquired by it if, at the time moneys are to be disbursed by the fund as a result of such commitments, the liquidity requirements established under sub-section III.(1)(a) would be violated by such a disbursement.

ARM'S LENGTH TRANSACTIONS
INVESTOR'S YIELD

(2.3) Where a fund acquires mortgages from a lending institution with which the fund, its management company and/or the insiders of either of them are dealing at arm's length, such mortgages shall be acquired at that principal amount which produces at least the yield prevailing for the sale of comparable unserviced mortgages by major mortgage lenders under similar conditions.

NOT AT ARM'S LENGTH TRANSACTIONS

(2.4) In all cases not covered by sub-section (2.3), mortgages shall be acquired by the fund according to only one of the following three methods:

LENDER'S RATE

(a) at that principal amount which will produce a yield to the fund equal to the interest rate at which the lending institution is making commitments to loan on the security of comparable mortgages at the time of purchase by the fund;

FORWARD COMMITMENT RATE

(b) at that principal amount which will produce the same yield to the fund as the interest rate charged by the lending institution to the mortgagor on the date of commitment provided that the date of commitment is not more than 120 days prior to the date of acquisition of the mortgage by the fund, and the interest rate is equal to the rate at which the lending institution made commitments to loan mortgages on the date of commitment; or

MODIFIED LENDER'S RATE

(c) at that principal amount which will produce a yield to the fund of not more than a quarter of one per cent less than the interest rate at which the lending institution is making commitments, at the time of purchase, to loan on the security of comparable mortgages provided that the lending institution which sells mortgages to the fund has entered into an agreement to repurchase the mortgages from the fund in circumstances benefiting the fund and that such an agreement is considered by the administrators to justify the difference in yield to the fund.

(2.5) For the purpose of determining the net asset value of mortgages in the portfolio:

(a) the value of conventional mortgages shall be calculated on a consistent basis, to produce a principal amount which will produce a yield,

(i) equal to the yield prevailing for the sale of comparable conventional mortgages by major lending if ascertainable on the date of valuation; or

(ii) equal to or not less than one quarter of one per cent below the interest rate at which major lending institutions are making commitments on the date of valuation.

(b) in the case of mortgages guaranteed under the National Housing Act such mortgages shall be valued at market value.

(2.6) Any change by a fund from one of the methods of acquisition described in subsection (2.4) to another of these methods, or in the method of valuation of mortgages included in its portfolio, shall be subject to the prior approval of the Administrators.

SECTION IV
DISCLOSURE

IV.   The prospectus of the fund shall include:

(a)   (i) A statement of the various methods used by mutual funds generally for determining the price at which mortgages are acquired in the terms of subsection III(2.3) and (2.4), and a brief comparison of the effects these methods may have on the yield to the fund under the assumptions of increasing, decreasing and stable interest rates;

(ii) A designation of which of the methods outlined in paragraph IV(a)(i) is used by the fund;

(iii) The method used for determining the price at which mortgages have been sold by the fund during the preceding financial year, if any;

(b) A description of the methods used to value all portfolio holdings (including mortgages in arrears) in determining the net asset value of the fund;

(c) A statement of the benefits or advantages derived by the management company or an affiliate or associate of the management company, from managing the fund and the sale or purchase of mortgages to or from the fund;

(d)   (i) The origin of the mortgages acquired by the fund during the preceding financial year;

(ii) The distribution of mortgages between mortgages insured under the National Housing Act (Canada) insured and uninsured conventional mortgages;

(iii) The fund's policy concerning the origin and distribution of mortgages to be acquired by the fund in the future;

(e) A table showing the distribution of the mortgage portfolio according to the type of property securing the mortgage (single family dwelling, condominium, multi-unit dwelling of up to 8 units, multi-unit dwelling of more than 8 units, commercial, industrial);

(f) A table showing the contractual interest rate in groups of not more than one quarter per cent for the mortgages in the portfolio;

(g) A table showing, with one year intervals, the date at which mortgages included in the portfolio reach maturity;

(h) A table showing the geographical distribution of the mortgage portfolio;

(i) A table showing the status of mortgages having instalments 90 days or more in arrears;

(j) In each of the tables required under this Section, the number of mortgages and market value shall be shown. Furthermore, in the case of the tables required under subsections IV(e) and (f) the amortized cost and outstanding principal value shall be shown.

Effective September 1, 1977

Revised October 28, 1987

NATIONAL POLICY No. 30
PROCESSING OF "SEASONED PROSPECTUSES"

The Administrators wish, in the interests of all concerned with the prospectus filing process, to endeavour to accelerate the review procedure where feasible. A number of issuers file prospectuses on a repetitive basis, or have prospectuses continuously in effect. The Administrators believe that processing of these prospectuses is one area in which the review procedure may be accelerated, particularly where the prospectuses are prepared in accordance with the high standard of care that is necessary to ensure compliance with statutory requirements.

For this purpose, a preliminary prospectus is a "seasoned prospectus" if it qualifies securities of:

(a) a mutual fund refiling an already current prospectus;

(b) any other issuer, apart from junior mining and oil exploration companies and other issuers of a speculative nature, which has filed a prospectus, the final receipt for which was dated not more than two years prior to the date of the preliminary receipt for the current issue.

To assist in the effort to accelerate processing of these prospectuses, when a preliminary prospectus that is a seasoned prospectus is filed, it should be accompanied by an extra copy thereof marked to show which sections did not appear in the preceding prospectus of the same issuer and, as to the other sections, to show where additions, deletions, or changes have been made. The prospectus should be accompanied by a certificate or certificates of lawyers, accountants, or other responsible persons. These certificates should, alone or together, refer to the entire prospectus and confirm that the markings accurately indicate the information they purport to indicate as to the relationship between the content of the newly filed prospectus and the previous prospectus of the same issuer.

The Administrators recognize that preparation of the extra marked copy and the accompanying certificate will involve some inconvenience for those responsible for filings, but the Administrators anticipate that resultant improvement in prospectus review procedures will compensate for this inconvenience.

This policy is applicable to filings made on or after December 5, 1978.

MEMORANDUM

From: The Ontario Securities Commission

To: The Director and Staff of the Commission

Re: "SEASONED PROSPECTUSES"

During the October meeting of the Canadian Securities Administrators, National Policy No. 30 was adopted, providing certain special procedures for the filing of "seasoned prospectuses". The policy requests that such prospectuses be accompanied, when filed, by copies showing where additions, changes or deletions have been made from the most recently filed prospectuses of the same issuer. The purpose of this memorandum is to outline the procedure that the Commission considers to be appropriate for the processing of seasoned prospectuses by our staff.

Section 61 of the Securities Act sets out certain situations in which the Director is under an obligation to refuse issuance of a final prospectus receipt. By definition, no prospectus will be a seasoned prospectus unless a final receipt for an earlier prospectus of the same issuer has been issued within the two preceding years. In the view of the Commission, experience indicates that situations are rare in which a seasoned prospectus contains a deficiency that is sufficiently serious to require that the Director reject the prospectus pursuant to section 61. These few situations ordinarily involve a matter that is quickly apparent from the newly-filed prospectus.

In view of the foregoing, the Commission suggests that upon receipt of a preliminary prospectus that is a seasoned prospectus and is accompanied by the material referred to in National Policy No. 30, the material be assigned to a qualified analyst who would conduct an examination sufficient to indicate whether any apparent change has developed since the prior filing which is of a nature to indicate that a problem may arise under section 61. The examination should, for example, include:

–   changes in disclosure from the prior prospectus;

–   attributes of the new issue of securities if different in a material respect from those qualified under the prior prospectus;

–   significance of any material changes in financial position or of interest and asset coverage;

–   any material reorganization or non-arm's length transaction since the preceding final receipt; and

–   any other relevant matters that expeditiously become apparent.

If any significant concern arises from this examination, then a full prospectus review should be conducted.

The Commission anticipates, and recognizes, that the examination outlined above will be comparatively limited, involving less detailed comments on at least some seasoned prospectuses than would be the case under current practice. In the Commission's judgment, this procedure will satisfy the responsibilities arising under the Act and will recognize that principal responsibility rests on those responsible for the preparation and filing of the prospectus. Further, the Commission anticipates that adoption of the procedure will contribute to a more effective use of our resources.

Copies of this memorandum are being supplied to the other securities administrators in Canada, with whom it has already been discussed. Where Ontario is designated as the principal jurisdiction for a seasoned prospectus being filed under National Policy No. 1, Ontario's comments thereon should be prefaced with a specific statement that the prospectus is a "seasoned prospectus", when these comments are transmitted to other jurisdictions. They will then assume that the prospectus has received only the limited review contemplated by this memorandum, unless the contrary is specifically stated.

NATIONAL POLICY No. 31
CHANGE OF AUDITOR OF A REPORTING ISSUER

PART 1   *INTRODUCTION AND PURPOSE*

1.1. The purpose of this Policy Statement is to specify certain reporting requirements that apply when the auditor of a reporting issuer changes. These requirements will help to ensure that the public interest is served and that relevant information is disclosed to shareholders, regulators and other members of the public.

1.2 This Policy Statement replaces National Policy Statement No. 31 which was issued by the Canadian Securities Administrators in June 1990.

PART 2   *APPLICATION*

2.1 This Policy Statement does not in any way affect the rights or obligations of a reporting issuer under the laws in which it is incorporated or organized.

2.2 This Policy Statement does not apply to a change of auditor when such a change is required by statute.

2.3 This Policy Statement requires a reporting issuer to prepare a notice of change of auditor, as described in paragraph 4.6. whenever:

(a) the reporting issuer receives notification from its auditor of the auditor's resignation or refusal to stand re-appointment (a "Resignation"); or

(b) the reporting issuer decides to propose to its shareholders that the auditor be removed from office during the auditor's term of office, or there is a proposal or intention not to reappoint the auditor on the expiry of the auditor's term of office (a "Termination").

2.4 This Policy Statement requires the auditor referred to in paragraph 2.3(a) and 2.3(b) (the "former auditor") to prepare the letter referred to in paragraphs 4.7 and 4.8 and the proposed successor auditor (the "successor auditor") to prepare the letter referred to in paragraph 4.9.

2.5 A reporting issuer that is a registrant with the U.S. Securities and Exchange Commission (the "SEC") may satisfy the requirements of this Policy Statement by complying with SEC Regulation S-K, item 304, provided that the information filed with the SEC is, at the same time, filed, delivered and published as required by this Policy Statement.

2.6 This Policy Statement is effective for Terminations or Resignations occurring after May 31, 1991.

PART 3   *REPORTABLE EVENTS*

3.1 The reporting obligations set out in this Policy Statement require disclosure by the reporting issuer of any reportable event which has occurred prior to a Resignation or Termination. A reportable event is an occurrence in the relationship between the reporting issuer and the former or successor auditor which may have been a contributing factor to the Resignation or Termination.

3.2   Reportable events are those that occurred in connection with:

   (a) the audits of the reporting issuer's two most recently completed fiscal years; or

   (b) any period subsequent to the most recently completed period for which an audit report was issued and preceding the date of the Resignation or Termination.

3.3   There are three types of reportable events: disagreements, unresolved issues and consultations.

Disagreements

3.4   Disagreements refer to any matter of audit scope, accounting principles or policies or financial statement disclosure that, if not resolved to the satisfaction of the former auditor, would have resulted in a reservation in the auditor's report.

3.5   Disagreements include both those resolved to the former auditor's satisfaction and those not resolved to the former auditor's satisfaction. Disagreements should have occurred at the decision making level, i.e., between personnel of the reporting issuer responsible for the finalization of its financial statements and personnel of the auditing firm responsible for authorizing the issuance of audit reports with respect to the reporting issuer.

3.6   The term disagreement is to be interpreted broadly. It is not necessary for there to have been an argument to have had a disagreement, merely a difference of opinion. The term disagreement does not include initial differences of opinion, based on incomplete facts or preliminary information, that were later resolved to the former auditor's satisfaction, provided that the reporting issuer and the former auditor do not continue to have a difference of opinion upon obtaining additional facts or information.

Unresolved Issues

3.7   Unresolved issues refer to matters which came to the former auditor's attention and which, in the former auditor's opinion, materially impact on the financial statements or audit reports (or which could have a material impact on them), where the former auditor has advised the reporting issuer about the matter and:

   (a) the former auditor has been unable to fully explore the matter and reach a conclusion as to its implications to a Resignation or Termination;

   (b) the matter was not resolved to the former auditor's satisfaction prior to a Resignation or Termination; or

   (c) the former auditor is no longer willing to be associated with the financial statements prepared by management of the reporting issuer.

Consultations

3.8   Consultations refer to situations where the reporting issuer (or someone acting on its behalf) consulted the successor auditor regarding:

   (a) the application of accounting principles to a specified transaction (either proposed or completed);

   (b) the type of audit opinion that might be rendered on the reporting issuer's financial statements; or

   (c) a disagreement as defined in paragraphs 3.4 to 3.6 of this Policy Statement;

and a written report or seriously considered oral advice was provided by the successor auditor to the reporting issuer.

PART 4 *REPORTING OBLIGATIONS*

4.1 When a Resignation or Termination occurs the reporting issuer must:

  (a) prepare a notice of change of auditor (a "Notice") (see paragraph 4.6);

  (b) obtain

    (i) a letter from the former auditor (see paragraphs 4.7 and 4.8) and

    (ii) a letter from the successor auditor (see paragraph 4.9); and,

  (c) obtain written confirmation that the Notice and letters referred to in subparagraphs (a) and (b) have been reviewed by the audit committee or board of directors of the reporting issuer.

4.2 The documents mentioned in paragraph 4.1 are referred to as the Reporting Package. The reporting issuer must include a copy of the Reporting Package in the information circular accompanying the notice of any meeting of shareholders at which action is to be taken concerning a change of auditor. If such a meeting is not held because the laws in which the reporting issuer is incorporated or organized do not require a meeting of shareholders be held in connection with a change of auditor, a copy of the Reporting Package must be included in the information circular for the first meeting of shareholders held subsequent to the change of auditor.

4.3 The reporting issuer must deliver the Reporting Package to:

  (a) the securities administrators in each province or territory in which it is a reporting issuer (the "relevant securities administrators");

  (b) the former auditor; and

  (c) the successor auditor

within the time period imposed by paragraph 4.12.

4.4 If there are any reportable events, the information contained in the Reporting Package must be described in a press release which is to be issued to appropriate media and filed with the relevant securities administrators.

4.5 If the former auditor or the successor auditor becomes aware that the required disclosures under this Policy Statement have not been made by the reporting issuer (as may happen when an auditor has not been asked to furnish the required letter), the auditor must promptly advise the reporting issuer in writing and deliver a copy of the letter to the relevant securities administrators.

Notice of Change of Auditor

4.6 The Notice must include a statement as to whether:

  (a) the former auditor resigned, was asked to resign, declined to stand for reappointment or was not to be proposed for re-appointment and the date of it thereof;

  (b) there were any reservations in the auditor's reports for the periods specified in paragraph 3.2 of this Policy Statement, and if there were, a description of each such reservation;

  (c) the Termination or the Resignation and the recommendation to appoint the successor auditor was considered or approved by the audit committee or the board of directors of the reporting issuer;

  (d) there were any reportable events and, if there were, a description of each reportable event that includes the following information:

    (i) for disagreements and unresolved issues:

      (a) a description of each reportable event;

      (b) a statement as to whether the audit committee or board of directors discussed the subject matter of each reportable event with the former auditor; and

      (c) a statement as to whether the reporting issuer authorized the former auditor to respond fully to the inquiries of the successor auditor concerning the subject matter of each reportable event and, if not, a description of the nature of any limitation and the reason for it;

(ii) for consultations:

(a) identification of the issues that were the subjects of consultation;

(b) a brief description of the views of the successor auditor as expressed orally or in writing to the reporting issuer on each issue; and

(c) a statement as to whether the former auditor was consulted by the reporting issuer and, if so, provide a summary of his views; and

If, in the opinion of the reporting issuer, there were no reportable events, a statement to that effect.

Letter from the Former Auditor

4.7 When a copy of the Notice is delivered to the former auditor in accordance with paragraph 4.10, the reporting issuer must request that the former auditor respond by letter. In this letter, addressed to the relevant securities administrators, the former auditor must state whether or not they agree with the information contained in the Notice, based on the former auditor's knowledge of the information at the time. If the former auditor does not agree with the information in the Notice, the former auditor must give reasons in the letter.

4.8 If the reporting issuer is not in a position to provide the reasons for a Resignation in the Notice, the reporting issuer must request that the former auditor describe the reasons in the letter from the former auditor.

Letter from the Successor Auditor

4.9 When a copy of the Notice is delivered to the successor auditor in accordance with paragraph 4.10, the reporting issuer must request that the successor auditor respond by letter. In this letter, addressed to the relevant securities administrators, the successor auditor must state whether or not they agree with the information contained in the Notice, based on the successor auditor's knowledge of the information at the time. If the successor auditor does not agree with the information in the notice, the successor auditor must give reasons in the letter.

Timing

4.10 Within ten calendar days of the date of the Resignation or Termination (the "Notification Date"), the reporting issuer must prepare the Notice and deliver it to the former and successor auditors.

4.11 Within twenty calendar days of the Notification Date, the former auditor must prepare the letter from the former auditor and the successor auditor must prepare the letter from the successor auditor and each deliver them to the reporting issuer and the other auditor.

4.12 Within thirty calendar days of the Notification Date, the reporting issuer must deliver the Reporting Package and issue and file the press release as required in paragraphs 4.3 and 4.4.

PART 5 *RESOLVING QUESTIONS*

5.1 Where a reporting issuer has reporting obligations in more than one jurisdiction and the reporting issuer, the former auditor or the successor auditor need to resolve a question as to the application of this Policy Statement, the questions must be addressed to the jurisdiction which would be selected by the reporting issuer for clearing documents in accordance with National Policy Statement No. 1. Other securities administrators normally will accept the principal jurisdiction's decisions but this procedure implies no surrender of jurisdiction by any securities regulatory authority.

NATIONAL POLICY No. 32
PROSPECTUS WARNING RE: SCOPE OF DISTRIBUTION

Background

The Canadian Securities Administrators at their meeting on October 30, 1980, concluded that it would be useful to adopt the widespread practice of noting through a legend at the top of preliminary and final prospectuses through which it is intended to effect distributions in more than one jurisdiction that those securities may lawfully only be sold in those jurisdictions in which a prospectus has been accepted for filing. In addition, it was thought that the warning should also note that the securities could only be distributed in that jurisdiction by persons registered in the jurisdiction.

Policy

Where it is proposed to distribute securities through a prospectus in more than one Canadian jurisdiction the following legend shall appear at the top of the front page of the preliminary prospectus and prospectus:

"This prospectus constitutes a public offering of these securities only in those jurisdictions where they may be lawfully offered for sale and therein only by persons permitted to sell such securities."

NATIONAL POLICY No. 33
FINANCING OF FILM PRODUCTIONS

PART I

General Provisions

1. The requirements under this policy statement apply to the distribution of securities in a limited partnership for film productions or videos ("film productions") that are subject to the prospectus or offering memorandum requirements ("disclosure document") of any securities legislation in force in a province or territory of Canada where the disclosure document is filed. Distributions of securities subject to the offering memorandum requirements are those distributions where the offering memorandum is prepared and filed pursuant to the seed capital exemption or the government incentive securities exemption available in certain provinces and territories or pursuant to the $25 000 exemption in British Columbia.

    They also apply, mutatis mutandis, to the distribution of:

    1. units in any other partnership for film productions;

    2. securities of a corporation formed for film productions and;

    3. undivided interests in a film production.

    The Canadian Securities Administrators ("administrators") may apply these requirements to other transactions when they are a distribution of securities representing an interest in a film production.

2. Although not specifically directed at other types of productions of a creative nature such as theatre and recordings, this policy statement may have relevance to them.

3. All major contracts with respect to the production and distribution of publicly financed film productions shall be drafted so as not to conflict with the requirements of this policy statement.

4. The administrators will only issue a prospectus receipt or grant or permit the use of a prospectus exemption if the proceeds of the distribution are to be used for one or more identified film productions and if the terms and conditions for the complete financing of the film productions are established by the time the disclosure document is filed and are described therein.

5. In this policy,

    "above-the-line costs" refer to costs incurred for the acquisition of literary rights, the writing of the screenplay, the hiring of the director, the producer and any other person performing the producer's role, and the principal actors, as well as costs incurred in relation to the development of the screenplay.

"below-the-line costs" refer to all production-related costs, including post-production costs which are not included in the above-the-line costs. The salaries of all production personnel and all non-principal actors, as well as the costs of all materials bought in relation to the production of the film production are to be included.

"completion guarantee" refers to an agreement under which a person or a company agrees to guarantee the completion and delivery of the film production by a predetermined date and to assume any production cost, necessary to the completion of the film production, in excess of the original production cost estimates.

"financial partner" refers to investors in the film production, other than the purchasers of the securities pursuant to the disclosure document, identified at the time of filing such document.

"indirect costs" refer to costs that are not attributable to the creation of actual on-screen images, such as financing, legal, overhead and office expenses.

"person having vested interest in the film production" refers to a person or company who provides services of a material nature to the film production, and in particular, shall include the production company, the director and the co-producer.

"producer's gross revenue" means all sums generated by the exploitation of the film production, including interest revenues, after deduction, in the case of an international co-production, of those sums attributable to the foreign co-producer for his interest in the film production, as stipulated by contract, and of those amounts paid to the exhibitors of the film production, the various taxes paid to governmental authorities, and permitted fees and expenses of the distributor and sub-distributor.

"promoter" means the person or company acting independently or in concert with one or more persons or companies and which takes the initiative in the production or financing of a film production, in particular, the producer and any person or company that has the responsibility for arranging the financing.

"tax expert" refers to either a public accountant or lawyer experienced in the field of taxation.

Unless otherwise indicated, all other technical or trade terms used in this policy statement should be interpreted according to current industry usage.

6. Funds provided by the sale of securities shall be deposited in trust with a Canadian financial institution and only withdrawn, at the date of closing, if all of the conditions of closing are met, according to the use of proceeds as described in the disclosure document. The trustee shall undertake to return the funds to the subscribers if any of the conditions of closing are not met.

7. For a period of at least five years, all producer's gross revenue shall be deposited in a trust account with a Canadian financial institution which shall allocate such funds in accordance with section 14 and as described in the disclosure document. This provision shall not apply to a distribution which includes a put option which has been exercised if, following such exercise, there remains no securityholders, except for the promoter, persons having a vested interest in the film production and persons with whom they are associated.

8. On an annual basis for the period of at least five years specified in section 7, a senior officer of the issuer or of the general partner of the issuer shall obtain from the producer a report signed by a senior officer of the producer, addressed to the appropriate administrators and in the format provided in Schedule A. Such report shall confirm compliance with the applicable requirements of sections 7 and 14 for the last completed financial year of the issuer and shall be filed by the issuer with the appropriate administrators within 120 days of the applicable financial year end of the issuer.

A copy of this compliance report shall accompany the annual financial statements sent to the securityholders.

9. Where the financing initially contemplated for the film production was through other sources of financing, the administrators may examine the reasons for abandoning this source of financing and may investigate any increase in the budget originally presented to prospective investors.

PART II

Structuring of the Offering

10.   The position of producer shall be filled pursuant to a written agreement at the time of filing the disclosure document. The director and the principal actors shall be identified at the time of filing the disclosure document. Written agreements with the director and principal actors shall be signed by the date of closing of the offering. Written notice from the person's agent confirming the terms of the engagement will be deemed acceptable evidence of a written agreement.

     The producer shall have at least three years continuous experience in either feature length film productions, short productions, television series or documentaries if the proceeds will be used for any of the foregoing or in videos if the proceeds will be used for the production of videos. If the producer does not have the required experience, the services of a co-producer who has the required experience shall be retained.

11.   In the case of a feature length film production, if the film production is not completed prior to the date of filing the disclosure document, a completion guarantee from a recognized independent guarantor shall be obtained in accordance with the current industry practice. The guarantor shall agree to complete the said film prior to a determined date without compromising the film's eligibility for certification.

     In the case of other film productions, the promoter shall obtain a guarantee providing for all costs in excess of those originally budgeted and which are necessary for the completion of the film production.

12.   If distribution agreements for major markets are not concluded by the date of filing the disclosure document, there must be procedures initiated for the marketing of the film production. The promoter, a person having a vested interest in the film production, or a person with whom they are associated may negotiate distribution agreements provided the promoter or such person has the relevant experience and ability; the fees paid to this person shall be in accordance with current industry practice for similar functions.

13.   When the distribution includes a put option offered to the securityholders, adequate arrangements prior to the offering must be made to ensure that the required funds are available at the exercise date to effect payment in full for all securities acquired pursuant to the exercise of the option.

14.   The revenue derived from the film production cannot be allocated in a manner that would be less advantageous to the securityholder than the following:

     1°   First the producer's gross revenue shall flow to the issuer and the financial partners, pro rata, according to their investment in the film production, until such time as the full amount of their investment has been recouped.

     2°   Thereafter, advances made by a completion guarantor may be recovered, with interest.

     3°   Next, the producer's gross revenue shall be divided among the issuer, the financial partners and the producer. The issuer and the financial partners shall receive at least 50% of the producer's gross revenue to be distributed pro rata according to their investment in the film production.

     4°   The amounts payable to principal actors, the other creative personnel, interim lenders and other lenders shall be deducted directly from that portion of the producer's gross revenue flowing to the producer.

     The revenue allocations shall be described in the disclosure document.

15.   All offerings must provide for payment to the producer of a percentage of revenue sufficient to guarantee a continued interest in the successful operation of the project.

16.   Loans advanced by the interim lender shall be repaid at the date of closing in either, or both, of the following manners:

     1°   payment to the interim lender of amounts due out of the proceeds of the offering;

2°   issuance to the interim lender of securities remaining unsold after completion of the distribution in satisfaction of the debt owing. In such instances, there can be no preference given interim lenders over the other investors except that the interim lenders may invest in the securities without paying selling commissions. Such interim lender shall not be treated any differently, as investor, than any other investor in terms of the revenue allocation contemplated in section 14.

17.   After the date of closing, no person, other than a foreign co-producer, shall have a security interest in the film production or in the revenues therefrom.

18.   Deferred fees to be paid from revenues are permitted if the fees are deferred to reduce the financed portion of the film production. For purposes of section 14, those persons receiving deferred fees will be considered as financial partners.

PART III

Conflicts of Interest

19.   The promoter, a person having a vested interest in the film production, or a person with whom they are associated may not subscribe in total for more than 25% of the securities distributed unless the securities are subscribed for in satisfaction of amounts due pursuant to section 16 or if, at the date of filing the disclosure document, there is a firm commitment to subscribe for a specified amount of securities. The face page of the disclosure document shall disclose the amount of securities subscribed for by the promoter, a person having a vested interest in the film production or a person with whom they are associated.

20.   Production services and equipment including, for example, laboratory services, studios, equipment rental and editing facilities provided by the promoter, by a person having a vested interest in the film production, or by a person with whom they are associated shall be provided at a price no higher than current industry practice.

21.   Financing charges payable to the promoter, to a person having a vested interest in the film production, or to a person with whom they are associated, shall not exceed the rate that would be charged by an arm's length financial institution in similar conditions.

PART IV

Rights and Obligations

22.   A list of securityholders' names and addresses shall be maintained and given to any securityholder or creditor upon request in accordance with National Policy Statement No. 34, where the issuer is an unincorporated issuer, and to any person upon request in accordance with the issuer's incorporating legislation, where the issuer is a corporation.

23.   Where the issuer is a limited partnership or other unincorporated entity, the limited partnership agreement or other agreement establishing the rights of the securityholders shall be attached to the disclosure document. The material terms of this agreement shall be disclosed in the disclosure document. The agreement shall specify the procedures for securityholders' meetings, including those matters to be raised at the meeting and the majority required. The matters that must be submitted to securityholders shall include, in particular, the dissolution of the partnership or other unincorporated entity, amendments to the agreement, dismissal of the securityholders' agent or of the general partner, if applicable, the sale of one or more film productions and approval of any capital calls whether or not otherwise provided for in the agreement.

Where the issuer is a corporation, its articles or bylaws must require that securityholder approval be obtained for the sale of one or more film productions and, in addition to any approval required under its incorporating legislation, the articles or bylaws must require the additional approval specified in the following paragraph for dissolution of the corporation, amendments to the articles or bylaws of the corporation and the sale of one or more film productions.

The securityholders' meeting shall vote on the issues stipulated in the two preceding paragraphs by way of a resolution adopted by a majority representing at least two thirds of the securities issued, excluding those held by the promoter, by persons having a vested interest in the film production, or by persons with whom they are associated.

Stricter rules for approval of a resolution by securityholders may be provided for in the limited partnership agreement, any other agreement establishing the rights of securityholders or in the articles or bylaws of a corporate issuer.

24. Where the issuer is a limited partnership or other unincorporated entity, the securities of the securityholder who defaults on a call for additional contributions may not be seized. The general partner or the securityholders' agent may only reduce the interest of that securityholder in the issuer. These provisions shall be disclosed under the heading "Risk Factors".

The preceding paragraph does not apply to a call related to the initial subscription or pursuant to the provisions of the statute under which the issuer is established.

25. In the case where unitholders were offered a put option, the compulsory acquisition of units held by unitholders who have not exercised the said option shall be permitted provided that holders of at least 75% of the securities distributed, excluding those held by the promoter, by persons having a vested interest in the film production or by persons with whom they are associated, have exercised the option. The takeover bid provisions of any applicable securities legislation and any applicable policy statements of the administrators shall apply to the put option.

PART V

Disclosure Document

26. *General*

26.01 In addition to information normally required in a prospectus or offering memorandum by any securities legislation in force in each province or territory of Canada where the disclosure document is filed, the disclosure document shall also include the information prescribed in this part.

26.02 The disclosure document should include a glossary of those terms specific to the film industry contained in the document. However, the term "certified production" shall not be used in the disclosure document unless its meaning corresponds to the relevant definition in the regulations to the Income Tax Act.

27. *Film Property*

27.01 The disclosure document shall clearly state that the issuer owns or will own at the date of closing a clear title to an original master negative that is completed or will be completed and to all other commercial rights arising from each film production. If any rights are to be excluded in whole or in part, they are to be specified as exclusions showing beneficial ownership. The face page shall clearly state whether the offering is for 100% of the film production or some lesser interest.

27.02 The disclosure document shall clearly describe all of the media, territorial and ancillary rights of a material nature which may be commercially exploited. The disclosure document shall also indicate and describe those media, territorial or ancillary rights of a material nature which have been retained by a third party, or by the promoter, a person having a vested interest in the film production, or a person with whom they are associated.

In the case of a foreign co-production, disclosure shall be made on the face page of the excluded aspects of the film production.

28. *Scenario and Story Outline*

The disclosure document shall indicate the persons from whom the film property and other rights were acquired, the amount paid for such rights and, if they have been acquired from the promoter, a person having a vested interest in the film production or a person with whom they are associated, the cost to such person for acquiring the said rights. The name of the principal writers and the total amount paid for producing the script shall be identified in the disclosure document. The story outline or the major elements of the plot, except perhaps for its ending, should be sufficiently detailed to enable a well advised investor to make a prudent assessment as to the commercial attractiveness of the film production.

29. *Principal Actors*

The names of the principal actors shall be specified in the disclosure document. Statements, quotation or extracts from critical reviews shall not be permitted in the disclosure document.

30. *Producer and Director*

30.01 The disclosure document shall describe the usual functions of a producer, and director. It shall identify by name the persons in those positions and clearly summarize the function to be performed with respect to the film production. The amounts payable to the producer, or any person performing the producer's role, and the director shall be clearly stated in the budget.

30.02 The disclosure document shall contain a detailed description of both the producer's and the director's experience in the film industry and related areas over the previous five years.

If the producer has already produced a film production financed through the sale of securities by way of prospectus or offering memorandum, disclosure shall be made, in tabular form, of the title of the film production, the year of release, the budgeted production costs as presented in the disclosure document for that film production, the final production costs, the subscription price and the amount of reimbursements to securityholders to date on a per security basis. For those offerings which include a put option, disclosure shall also be made of the stipulated exercise price of the option as stated in the disclosure document for that film production, whether the option has been exercised and the actual exercise price.

If the producer or director has not previously produced or directed a film production, this must be stated.

30.03 The disclosure document shall describe the normal sequence of events involved in film production, being development, pre-production, principal photography and post-production. To the extent practicable, amounts allocated to each stage should be identified in the budget.

30.04 If the principal photography has not commenced by the date of filing the disclosure document, the date at which this stage is scheduled to start and end shall be given. However, if principal photography is in progress, disclosure shall be made as to whether production is on schedule and on budget, or, if not, to what extent the production is ahead or behind of schedule and to what extent expenses have gone over or under original budget estimates.

The disclosure document shall indicate the stage of completion of the film production, the costs incurred as of the date of filing, the anticipated completion date and the anticipated costs for the completion of the film production.

30.05 If interim financing has been obtained to provide funds for the production, sufficient details shall be given of amounts committed and the cost of such financing as well as the sources of financing. If the interim lender is the promoter, a person having a vested interest in the film production or a person with whom they are associated, the name of the lender, the amounts advanced, and the terms of the loan shall be described.

30.06 The disclosure document shall also contain a summary of insurance coverage regarding various hazards, including maximum coverable amount and deductibles and the extent to which time delays are covered.

30.07 The disclosure document shall state that the promotion will indemnify and hold the unitholders harmless in the case of any claims for damages being brought for libel, slander, or violation of the rights of a person or a group, to the extent that such claims are not covered by an insurance policy. The consequences of a default by the promoter shall be described in the disclosure document under the heading "Risk Factors".

This provision also applies to the securityholders in a partnership and to the holders of undivided interests.

31. *Budget*

    31.01 The disclosure document shall include a detailed budget, in accordance with film industry practice, stating the major above-the-line costs, below-the-line costs and indirect costs, indicating the percentage of total budget each item represents and each subtotal represents.

    31.02 The disclosure document shall state that any amount remaining unspent on completion of the film production will be spent for the marketing of the film production or returned to the securityholders.

32. *Completion Guarantee*

All material terms of any guarantee shall be described in the disclosure document. The name of the guarantor shall be given as well as the fees payable. If the guarantor has a vested interest in the film production, this fact shall be disclosed. The non financial role of the third party guarantor shall be described, including budget analysis and review, monitoring of the production and the right to intervene and assume control of the project. The disclosure document shall also state that the guarantor guarantees the technical quality of the film production, but not its aesthetic quality. Any right to a rebate of a portion of the fee shall be disclosed in the disclosure document as should the identity of the recipients of the rebate. Finally, if there is no completion guarantee, or if the completion guarantee is not given by an independent guarantor, it shall be stipulated in the disclosure document what services the production has not had and will not have access to as a result of there being no such guarantee.

33. *Commercial Exploitation*

    33.01 The disclosure document shall describe the sources of revenues generated by the commercial exploitation of the film production: movie theatres, television, television series, pay-television, videocassettes, in-flight movies and other ancillary rights. The commercial impact of any media, territorial or ancillary rights which are excluded shall be specified.

    33.02 The disclosure document shall describe in detail the usual provisions of the distribution agreements, gross and net receipts, variations in foreign territories and flow of revenues generated in each case from box-office receipts to the producer's gross. The normal range of fees paid to exhibitors and distributors shall also be set out, as well as typical sales and promotional expenses, and the names of those persons who bear these expenses.

    With regard to television exploitation of a film production, the requirements set out in the previous paragraph shall also cover U.S. network and syndicated television.

    33.03 The disclosure document shall identify the person responsible for compliance with respect to certification of the film production for tax purposes and for maintaining the records relating to the tax position of the securityholders.

34. *Distribution*

    34.01 If distribution agreements are in place, the material terms of the agreements shall be disclosed including those concerning the territories and media to which they apply, fees and expenses to be charged, minimum amounts required for sales and promotion or the absence of such an amount, audit rights, powers of securityholders or their agent to veto sub-distribution agreements, and the distributor's right to refuse delivery of the film production.

    34.02 If negotiations of distribution agreements are in progress at the time of filing of the disclosure document, the status of these negotiations for each of the major markets shall be disclosed.

    34.03 If distribution agreements for the major markets have not been concluded, this specific risk shall be mentioned on the face page of the disclosure document.

    34.04 All fees associated with negotiations of distribution agreements shall be described. If the promoter, a person having a vested interest in the film production or a person with whom they are associated is appointed as distribution agent, disclosure shall be made of this fact as well as such person's remuneration.

35. *Risk Factors*

All the risk factors pertaining to the nature of the issuer, the securities being offered or any other relevant consideration shall be fully disclosed. The face page of the disclosure document shall include a bold face reference to the risk factors section in the body of the disclosure document.

36. *Financial Disclosure*

36.01 Financial statements required to be sent to the securityholders pursuant to continuous disclosure requirements of any securities legislation in force in a province or territory in Canada where the disclosure document is filed shall disclose the various sources of the producer's gross revenue, as well as the distribution of such revenue, by group of beneficiaries. In all financial statements, amounts pertaining to securities offered in the disclosure document shall be presented on a per security basis as well as on an aggregate basis.

36.02 The name of the person responsible for providing continuous disclosure information shall be included in the disclosure document.

36.03 When the promoter, a person having a vested interest in the film production or a person with whom they are associated provides any guarantees with respect to the completion or distribution of the film production, such guarantor's audited financial statements shall be filed with the administrators at the time of filing the disclosure document. The administrators may require that these audited financial statements be included in the disclosure document.

36.04 Where the distribution includes a put option, the disclosure document shall state the exercise price of the put option and the arrangements made to ensure that the required funds will be available to effect full payment of the acquired securities. If revenue guarantees are not obtained for the full amount of the predetermined maximum exercise price, disclosure shall be made of the fact that there is no assurance that the securityholder will receive the full amount of the predetermined maximum exercise price.

Tables showing tax savings and rate of return shall be calculated based on the amount of revenue guarantees obtained at the date of filing the disclosure document.

The disclosure document may also include tables showing tax savings and rate of return based on the predetermined maximum exercise price; for a film production that has not obtained any revenue guarantees, tables showing the effect of a median exercise price shall also be included. However, disclosure shall be made in bold face type that there is no assurance that the actual exercise price of the put option will equal the predetermined maximum exercise price, and that consequently, the securityholder may not realize the stipulated tax savings and rate of return.

36.05 Where deferred fees are not covered by a revenue guarantee given by an independent party, the tables showing tax savings and rate of return shall exclude the amount of deferred fees. The disclosure document may also provide tables of tax savings and rate of return which include the amount of deferred fees provided that disclosure is made that there is no assurance that the amount of deferred fees will be considered by tax authorities as a capital cost of the film production.

37. *Tax Considerations*

The disclosure document shall include the opinion or comments of a tax expert as to the availability to the securityholder of the tax deductions described in the disclosure document. Notwithstanding any such opinion or comments, the administrators reserve the right to request a ruling from the Minister of Communications (Canada) and from the provincial counterpart as to whether the film production meets the conditions required for issuing the appropriate production certificate.

The disclosure document shall stipulate that as a condition of closing, evidence will be provided of the issuance of a provisional certificate from the Minister of Communications (Canada) and provincial counterparts, if applicable.

The tax expert shall be named and such tax expert's consent shall be filed with the disclosure document.

38. *Conflicts of Interest*

The disclosure document shall disclose all amounts payable to the promoter, to a person having a vested interest in the film production, or to a person with whom they are associated arising from the film production offering, in particular, deferred expenses, amounts contained in any budgeted item (including any fees payable to such person), fees for acting as completion guarantor, fees and interest earned on interim financing, fees charged for acting as general partner or as agent for the securityholders, if applicable, and that share of the producer's gross revenue to which such general person or agent is entitled following recoupment. This information shall be disclosed separately for each particular person. Any conflicts of interest resulting from a plurality of functions shall be clearly stated.

39. *Return on Investment*

The rate of return on investment contained in the disclosure document shall be calculated according to the formula prescribed in Schedule B. The rate of return may be included in the disclosure document only for those offerings which include a put option. No other method of calculation shall be used without the prior approval of the administrator of the jurisdiction in which the offering is contemplated.

The disclosure document shall indicate that the rate of return is a hypothetical number based on tax assumptions (which shall be fully disclosed) and does or does not consider the time value of money.

SCHEDULE A

Producer's Compliance Report

TO: The appropriate securities regulatory authorities

FROM: Name of producer

RE: Compliance Report on National Policy Statement No. 33

For the year ended _____, 19XX

FOR: Name of the issuer

Dear Sirs:

We, (name of producer), hereby confirm the following:

1– the year ended _____, 19XX, producer's gross revenue, as defined in section 5 of National Policy Statement No. 33, amounted to $_____, and this amount has been deposited in a trust account with a Canadian financial institution in accordance with section 7 of National Policy Statement No. 33; and

2– all producer's gross revenue has been allocated by such Canadian financial institution in accordance with section 14 of National Policy Statement No. 33 and as described in the disclosure document dated _____.

Signed on behalf of the producer

_____
Signature

_____
Name and office of the person executing this report

_____
Date

SCHEDULE B

Calculation of the rate of return

The rate of return shall be disclosed for each twelve-month period or, if it is anticipated that a put option will be exercised within a period of less than twelve months, the rate of return shall be disclosed for the number of months remaining until the anticipated date for the exercise of said option. In the latter case, there shall be no extrapolation of the rate of return to cover a twelve-month period. If the put option may be exercised within a period that exceeds twelve months, the rate of return shall consider the time value of money. The disclosure document may also include the rate of return for the entire exercise period of the put option, if that period exceeds twelve months.

Moreover, the rate of return shall be provided based on the hypotheses that an investor will benefit from a capital gains exemption, has exhausted his capital gains exemption or has not completely exhausted his capital gains exemption. If the cumulative net investments loss account can affect the capital gains exemption available on disposition of other investments, the rate of return shall take into account this additional tax liability.

The rate of return shall be calculated as follows:

$$\frac{\text{maximum} \atop \text{rate} \atop \text{of} \atop \text{return}} = \frac{\text{tax saving} + \text{exercise price of the put option} - \text{tax on disposal of unit} - \text{other expenses}}{\text{total unit price}}$$

NATIONAL POLICY No. 34
UNINCORPORATED ISSUERS
REQUIREMENT TO MAINTAIN A REGISTER OF
SECURITY HOLDERS

1. This policy applies to all issuers not required by legislation to maintain a register of their security holders wishing to make a distribution pursuant to the Securities Act, whether under a prospectus, exempting order or otherwise.

2. The issuer shall maintain, or cause to be maintained, an up to date register of:

   (a) the names, alphabetically arranged, and the latest known address of each person who is a security holder;

   (b) the number of securities held by each security holder; and

   (c) the date and particulars of the issue and transfer of each security.

3. The party maintaining the register shall be acceptable to the administrator in whose jurisdiction the principal office of the issuer is located or, if the issuer's principal office is outside Canada, then by the administrator in the jurisdiction which the issuer selects, under or analogous to National Policy No. 1, as its "principal jurisdiction".

4. The information contained in the register shall be made available for inspection at reasonable time and place by security holders and creditors or their duly authorized representatives free of charge.

5. Provisions shall be made for security holders and creditors to obtain a copy of the information contained in the register by mail on written request, within a reasonable period of time from the date of receipt of such request, subject to the security holder or creditor:

   (a) agreeing, in writing, that the information contained in the register will not be used by the person obtaining the information except in connection with:

      (i) an effort to influence the voting of security holders of the issuer;

      (ii) an offer to acquire securities of the issuer; or

      (iii) any other matter relating to the affairs of the issuer; and

   (b) paying, if requested, a fee in an amount not exceeding the reasonable costs to the issuer of providing the information.

NATIONAL POLICY No. 35
PURCHASER'S STATUTORY RIGHTS

With the adoption of the prompt offering prospectus system, the Canadian Securities Administrators adopted a short statement of withdrawal and rescission rights to be included in the short form, or simplified, prospectus. The Administrators have now agreed to extend the use of the short statement to any other form of prospectus. The following text should appear in each prospectus filed with more than one Administrator after July 1st, 1983.

"Securities legislation in several of the provinces provides purchasers with the right to withdraw from an agreement to purchase securities within two business days after receipt or deemed receipt of a prospectus and any amendment. In several of the provinces and territories securities legislation further provides a purchaser with remedies for rescission or, in some jurisdictions, damages where the prospectus and any amendment contains a misrepresentation or is not delivered to the purchaser, provided that such remedies for rescission or damages are exercised by the purchaser within the time limit prescribed by the securities legislation of his Province or Territory. The purchaser should refer to any applicable provisions of the securities legislation of his Province or Territory for the particulars of these rights or consult with a legal advisor."

NATIONAL POLICY No. 36
MUTUAL FUNDS: SIMPLIFIED PROSPECTUS
QUALIFICATION SYSTEM

SECTION 1
APPLICATION

Section 1.1 A mutual fund may in qualifying its securities for sale use the simplified prospectus disclosure system set out in this policy unless otherwise expressly provided herein or in another policy statement or by an order of any of the Canadian securities authorities.

Section 1.2 The following types of mutual funds may not use the simplified prospectus system set out in this policy:

    (a) a mutual fund which invests in real property;

    (b) a mutual fund which constitutes a commodity pool programme.

Section 1.3 All terms which are defined in National Policy No. 39 are used in this policy with the same meaning as ascribed to such terms in National Policy No. 39.

SECTION 2
DOCUMENTS COMPRISING THE SIMPLIFIED
PROSPECTUS DISCLOSURE SYSTEM

Section 2.1 The documents which comprise the simplified prospectus disclosure system consist of:

    (a) a simplified prospectus which is to be prepared in accordance with the requirements set out in Schedule A;

    (b) an annual information form which is to be prepared and certified in accordance with the requirements set out in Schedule B;

    (c) such other information as is required to be filed by the mutual fund in any province or territory in which the simplified prospectus is filed pursuant to the securities legislation of such province or territory, including the most recent annual financial statements together with the auditor's report thereon, such subsequent annual audited financial statements or interim unaudited financial statements, material change reports and information circulars or the annual filing made in lieu thereof, which are required to be filed during the currency of the annual information form referred to in clause (b) above.

The documents referred to in clauses (a), (b) and (c) of Section 2.1 constitute the mutual fund's permanent information record.

Section 2.2 Where two or more mutual funds have a common manager and their affairs are conducted in a similar manner, the mutual funds may file one annual information form and one simplified prospectus to qualify the mutual fund securities of such mutual funds for distribution, provided that in any jurisdiction the appropriate representative of the Canadian securities authorities in such jurisdiction (the "Regulator") may exercise his discretion to refuse to accept an annual information form or to issue a receipt for a simplified prospectus on the basis that the disclosure contained therein is unduly complex or unclear.

SECTION 3
ANNUAL INFORMATION FORM

Section 3.1 Each annual information form submitted by a mutual fund for filing under this policy statement shall be prepared and certified in accordance with the requirements of Schedule B and shall be subject to acceptance for filing in accordance with the provisions of the securities legislation in force in each province or territory of Canada where it is filed, with such amendments or additions thereto, if any, as the Regulator in each such province or territory considers necessary in order to comply with the requirements set out in Schedule B and notification of such acceptance shall be provided annually to the mutual fund in writing.

Section 3.2 The annual information form which accompanies a preliminary simplified prospectus may be described as a preliminary annual information form. The annual information form which accompanies a pro-forma simplified prospectus may be described as a pro-forma annual information form. Where pursuant to the provisions of Section 2.2, one annual information form and one simplified prospectus are used to qualify the mutual fund securities of more than one mutual fund for distribution and it is desired at the time of filing the pro-forma annual information form relating to the continued offering of the mutual fund securities of such mutual funds to include the securities of a mutual fund which has not been previously qualified for distribution, it is permissible to include the securities of such mutual fund in a pro-forma annual information form relating to the continued offering of the mutual fund securities of the mutual funds in question, provided that such pro-forma annual information form is identified as being a preliminary annual information form in respect of the mutual fund securities of the new mutual fund and as a pro-forma annual information form in respect of the mutual fund securities of the mutual funds in respect of which it is a pro-forma annual information form. Where a preliminary annual information form is combined with a pro-forma annual information form, such document shall not be used in connection with the solicitation of expressions of interest.

Section 3.3 The annual information form shall be accompanied by an undertaking of the manager of the mutual fund or, if the mutual fund has no manager, by an undertaking of the mutual fund, to the Canadian securities authorities with which the annual information form is filed, to provide to any person or company without charge, upon request to the mutual fund or its manager, one copy of the permanent information record of the mutual fund.

Section 3.4 Where any solicitor, auditor, accountant, engineer, appraiser, or other person or company whose profession gives authority to a statement or opinion expressed by him is named in the annual information form and/or the simplified prospectus or in a document incorporated therein by reference, or is named as having prepared or certified a report or valuation used in a document incorporated by reference into or deemed to form part of an annual information form and/or simplified prospectus, the written consent of the person or company to being so named and to the use of the report, valuation, statement or opinion shall be filed not later than the time when the annual information and simplified prospectus are filed.

Section 3.5 Where a misrepresentation is contained in an annual information form filed by a mutual fund, the misrepresentation shall be deemed to be contained in the mutual fund's simplified prospectus. As used in this policy, a misrepresentation means an untrue statement of a material fact or the omission to state a material fact required to be stated or that is necessary to make a statement not misleading in light of the circumstances in which it was made.

SECTION 4
SIMPLIFIED PROSPECTUS

Section 4.1 A mutual fund which files an annual information form shall file concurrently therewith a simplified prospectus which is to be prepared in accordance with the requirements set out in Schedule A. Prior to the filing of a simplified prospectus, the mutual fund shall file either a preliminary simplified prospectus in the case of the initial offering of mutual fund securities or a pro-forma simplified prospectus in the case of continuing the offering of such mutual fund securities. Where pursuant to the provisions of Section 2.2, one annual information form and one simplified prospectus are used to qualify the mutual fund securities of more than one mutual fund for distribution and it is desired at the time of filing the pro-forma simplified prospectus relating to the continued offering of the mutual fund securities of such mutual funds to include the securities of a mutual fund which has not been previously qualified for distribution, it is permissible to include the securities of such mutual fund in a pro-forma simplified prospectus relating to the continued offering of the mutual fund securities of the mutual funds in question, provided that such pro-forma simplified prospectus is identified in the manner provided in Section 4.2 as being a preliminary simplified prospectus in respect of the mutual fund securities of the new mutual fund and as a pro-forma simplified prospectus in respect of the mutual fund securities of the mutual funds in respect of which it is a pro-forma simplified prospectus. Where a preliminary simplified prospectus is combined with a pro-forma simplified prospectus, such document shall not be used to solicit expressions of interest.

Section 4.2 Every preliminary (but not pro-forma) simplified prospectus shall have printed in red ink on the outside front cover page the following statement or such variation thereof as the Regulator may permit:

"This is a preliminary simplified prospectus relating to these securities, a copy of which has been filed with the securities authorities in [insert names of provinces and territories in which the preliminary simplified prospectus has been filed] but which has not yet become final for the purpose of a distribution to the public. Information contained herein is subject to completion or amendment. These securities may not be sold to, nor may offers to buy be accepted from, residents of such jurisdictions prior to the time a receipt for the final simplified prospectus is obtained from the appropriate securities commission or other regulatory authority."

Section 4.3 Where it is proposed to distribute securities in more than one Canadian jurisdiction, the following legend shall appear at the top of the outside cover page of the preliminary or pro-forma simplified prospectus and of the simplified prospectus:

"This simplified prospectus constitutes a public offering of these securities only in those jurisdictions where they may be lawfully offered for sale and therein only by persons permitted to sell such securities."

Section 4.4 The simplified prospectus filed by a mutual fund is a prospectus within the meaning of the securities legislation of the various provinces and territories of Canada in which it is filed. Consequently a preliminary or pro-forma simplified prospectus and a simplified prospectus must be filed within the time periods prescribed by such legislation.

Section 4.5 The simplified prospectus submitted by a mutual fund for filing under this policy shall be subject to acceptance for filing in accordance with the provisions of the securities legislation in force in each province or territory of Canada where it is filed with such amendments or additions thereto, if any, as is considered necessary by the Regulator in each such province or territory in order to comply with the requirements set out in Schedule A or as may be necessary to ensure that it is not contrary to the public interest or to the provisions of applicable securities legislation to issue a receipt for such simplified prospectus and a receipt for such simplified prospectus shall be provided to the mutual fund concurrently with the notification prescribed in Section 3.1 of this policy.

Section 4.6 It is the intention of the Canadian securities authorities that a simplified prospectus need not be revised annually but only so often as is necessary to reflect therein a change in the affairs of the mutual fund which is required to be disclosed therein and the Canadian securities authorities anticipate that the pro-forma simplified prospectus and simplified prospectus, although filed annually, frequently will not be required to be revised annually.

Section 4.7 Where a material change occurs in the affairs of the mutual fund relating to matters described in a simplified prospectus and thereby requiring an amendment to a simplified prospectus for which a receipt has been issued, an amendment to the simplified prospectus and annual information form or an amended simplified prospectus and annual information form shall be filed with the appropriate Canadian securities authorities and a receipt obtained therefor within the time required pursuant to applicable securities legislation.

SECTION 5
FINANCIAL STATEMENTS

Section 5.1 Every annual information form and simplified prospectus filed under this policy shall be accompanied by a copy of:

    (a) a balance sheet,

    (b) a statement of income,

    (c) a statement of investment portfolio,

    (d) a statement of portfolio transactions, and

    (e) a statement of changes in net assets,

of the mutual fund, each such statement being for or as at the end of, as appropriate, its last completed financial year with comparative figures (except for the statements referred to in clauses (c) and (d)) for or as at the end of its preceding completed financial year, or for any other period or periods permitted or required pursuant to applicable securities legislation, together with an auditors' report thereon. It should be noted that the copy of the abovementioned material which accompanies the annual information form and simplified prospectus filed under this policy is in addition to the copy(ies) required to be filed under the continuous disclosure provisions of the applicable securities legislation and that the signatures on the balance sheet included in such material evidencing the approval of such material and the signature of the auditors on the auditors' report included in such material may be either manual or printed or facsimile signatures or photocopies thereof of the persons signing such documents.

In addition, where the annual information form and simplified prospectus filed under this policy are filed after the earlier of (i) the date that is 60 days after the end of the six month period that commenced immediately following the end of the mutual fund's last completed financial year, and (ii) the date on which the interim financial statements of the mutual fund hereinafter referred to are first sent to securityholders, the annual information form and simplified prospectus filed under this policy shall be accompanied, unless the same have been previously filed, by a copy of the interim financial statements of the mutual fund for the six month period of the current financial year of the mutual fund that commenced immediately following the end of the mutual fund's last completed financial year consisting of:

    (i) a statement of income,

    (ii) a statement of investment portfolio,

    (iii) a statement of portfolio transactions, and

    (iv) a statement of changes in net assets,

prepared for and as at the end of the period as applicable, which interim financial statements shall present the financial information for the current financial year to the date to which the financial statements are prepared and, except in the case of the financial statements referred to in clauses (ii) and (iii), the comparative financial information for the corresponding six month period in the preceding financial year of the mutual fund, which interim financial statements may but need not include an auditor's report.

Where the interim financial statements do not include an auditor's report, there shall be filed with any annual information form and simplified prospectus which are filed under this policy after the end of the above mentioned six month period, such advice from the auditor as is suggested by the Handbook of The Canadian Institute of Chartered Accountants for circumstances where financial statements which are not reported on by the auditor are filed in conjunction with an offering of securities under a prospectus or such other advice as may reasonably be required by the Regulator in the respective provinces or territories, the purpose of which shall be to assist the Canadian securities authorities in discharging their responsibilities and the advice may include a statement to that effect.

Section 5.2 Each simplified prospectus required to be sent or delivered to a purchaser under the provisions of the securities legislation of any province or territory of Canada in which the simplified prospectus is filed shall be accompanied by:

(a) a copy of the annual financial statements referred to in Section 5.1; and

(b) following the filing of the interim financial statements required to be filed with the Canadian securities authorities pursuant to applicable securities legislation for periods subsequent to those referred to in Section 5.1 in respect of the annual financial statements, a copy of the interim financial statements that were filed most recently before the day the simplified prospectus is sent or delivered.

Section 5.3 Notwithstanding Section 5.1, a statement of portfolio transactions need not be reported on by an auditor and need not be sent or delivered to a purchaser if the statement of portfolio transactions:

(a) contains a certificate signed by the chief executive officer and chief financial officer of the mutual fund, or the person or persons temporarily carrying out the responsibilities of either of them or such other persons as the Canadian securities authorities may permit, that the statement of portfolio transactions presents fairly the required information; and

(b) the statement of portfolio transactions forms part of the mutual fund's permanent information record and is forwarded to a person or company who requests a copy of the permanent information record.

Section 5.4 A statement of investment portfolio included in the annual or interim financial statements of a mutual fund shall disclose with respect to clearing corporation options in an "open" position at least the following:

(1) For options purchased:

(i) the number, the underlying security, the exercise price, the expiration month, the cost and the market value;

(2) For options written:

(i) the underlying security shall be identified by an asterisk or other notation as being the subject of an option written;

(ii) particulars of the deferred credit account indicating the number of options, the underlying security, the exercise price, the expiration month, the premium received and the market value.

Section 5.5 The net asset value per security as at the end of the last completed financial year of the mutual fund and as at the end of each of the four preceding financial years (or such shorter period as the mutual fund has been in existence) shall be stated either in the simplified prospectus or in the annual financial statements of the mutual fund.

SECTION 6
REVIEW PROCEDURE

Section 6.1 The preliminary or pro-forma annual information form, the preliminary or pro-forma simplified prospectus, the annual financial statements and, if applicable, the interim financial statements will be reviewed together, annually, in accordance with normal review procedures applicable to mutual funds. Where copies of the annual financial statements and, if applicable, copies of the interim financial statements have been previously filed with the Canadian securities authorities pursuant to applicable securities legislation, additional copies of such financial statements (which may be commercially printed copies and need not bear manual signatures) are to be filed with the preliminary or pro-forma annual information form and the preliminary or pro-forma simplified prospectus in order to assist in the review procedure.

Section 6.2 The preliminary or pro-forma annual information form and the preliminary or pro-forma simplified prospectus may be filed pursuant to National Policy No. 1, whereupon the prospectus clearance procedures referred to therein will apply to both documents.

National Policies

Section 6.3 National Policy No. 30 respecting the processing of seasoned prospectuses applies mutatis mutandis to a pro-forma annual information form and a pro-forma simplified prospectus.

SCHEDULE A
INFORMATION REQUIRED TO BE
INCLUDED IN A SIMPLIFIED PROSPECTUS

GENERAL INSTRUCTION

The simplified prospectus is intended to be a concise presentation in plain language of the information required. The requirements and the instructions relating thereto should be read in light of this intention and the presentation of such information in the simplified prospectus should reflect this intention.

Item 1.   Cover Statement

Language in substantially the following form should appear on the outside cover page of the simplified prospectus:

"This simplified prospectus incorporates by reference and is accompanied by the audited annual financial statements of the Fund for its last completed financial year. Following the filing thereof with securities regulatory authorities, a copy of the Fund's most recent interim financial statements for its current financial year will also accompany this simplified prospectus."

Item 2.   Introductory Statement

Language in substantially the following form should appear on the first page of the simplified prospectus:

"This simplified prospectus is a concise outline of the relevant information about the Fund which you should know before making a decision to purchase its securities. The Fund is required by law to make full disclosure of additional facts related to this information in an annual information form, financial statements and other documents which are required to be filed with securities regulatory authorities in each province or territory of Canada where the Fund's securities are offered, which documents, when filed, are collectively known as the Fund's permanent information record.

Securities laws in Canada provide certain rights for security holders which are described in this simplified prospectus. These rights are based in part on the disclosure made in the annual information form which is incorporated into this simplified prospectus by reference, as well as upon disclosure contained in this simplified prospectus. All of these rights are available to you even though you may only receive this simplified prospectus and the financial statements which are required to accompany it.

The documents currently in the permanent information record may be obtained by you by writing to the Fund at:

(Address of Fund)

or (if applicable) through a dealer."

Item 3.   Name and Formation of Issuer

State the full name of the issuer and the address of its head or registered office. State the laws under which the issuer was formed and the manner and date of formation. If the issuer's name was changed during the past twelve months state its former name. State the name and address of the promoter, if any.

Item 4.   Description of Business

Briefly describe the business of the issuer.

Item 5.   Risk Factors

(a) Where appropriate to a clear understanding by investors of the risk factors and speculative nature of the issuer's activities or of the securities being offered, make an introductory statement on the first page summarizing the factors which make the purchase a risk or speculation. The information may be given in the body of the simplified prospectus if an appropriate reference is made on the first page to the risks and the speculative nature of the issuer's activities and a cross reference is made to the place in the simplified prospectus where the information is contained.

(b) Where there is a risk that purchasers of the securities offered may become liable to make an additional contribution beyond the price of the security, disclose any information or facts that may bear on the securityholder's assessment of risk associated with the investment.

Item 6.　Description of Securities Offered

(a) State the description or the designation of the class of securities offered by the simplified prospectus and describe all material attributes and characteristics including, without limiting the generality of the foregoing, the following:

　(1)　dividend rights;

　(2)　voting rights;

　(3)　liquidation or distribution rights;

　(4)　pre-emptive rights;

　(5)　conversion rights;

　(6)　redemption or purchase for cancellation or surrender rights;

　(7)　liability to further calls or to assessment by the issuer; and

　(8)　provisions as to modification, amendment or variation of any such rights or provisions.

(b) If the rights of securityholders may be modified otherwise than in accordance with the provisions attaching to such securities or the provisions of the governing act relating thereto, so state and explain briefly.

Instructions

1.　This item requires only a brief summary of the provisions that are material from an investment standpoint. If desired, the provisions attaching to the securities may be filed with the respective Canadian securities authorities as part of the issuer's permanent information record.

2.　If the rights attaching to the securities being offered are materially limited or qualified by those attached to any other class of securities or if another class of securities ranks ahead of or equally with the securities being offered, include information regarding such other securities that will enable investors to understand the rights attaching to the securities being offered. If any securities being offered are to be offered in exchange for other securities, include an appropriate description of the other securities. No information need be given, however, as to any class of securities that is to be redeemed or otherwise retired, provided appropriate steps to assure redemption or retirement have been or will be taken prior to or contemporaneously with the delivery of the securities being offered.

Item 7.　Price of Securities on Sale or Redemption

(a) Describe briefly the method followed or to be followed by the issuer in determining the price at which its securities will be offered for sale and redeemed and state the frequency with which the issue price is determined and the time when the price becomes effective and how long it remains in effect.

(b) State, where applicable, the sales charge expressed as a percentage of the total amount paid by the purchaser and expressed as a percentage of the net amount invested in securities of the issuer. Where these charges vary on a quantity basis give particulars of the quantities and the respective sale charges applicable thereto.

(c) Describe briefly the procedure followed or to be followed by investors who desire to purchase securities or to redeem securities, including particulars relating to special arrangements which may exist and any penalty for early redemption. State, where applicable, any redemption charge expressed as a percentage of the redemption price. Where redemption charges vary on any basis, give particulars of the same.

(d) Where applicable, disclose the obligation of:

    (i) the issuer to cancel a purchase order placed by an investor who, after placing the purchase order, fails to make payment of the issue price by causing the securities allotted pursuant to such purchase order to be redeemed, and

    (ii) the investor to pay any difference if the redemption price is less than the issue price of such securities.

(e) Where applicable, disclose the obligation of:

    (i) the issuer to cancel a redemption order placed by an investor who, after requesting redemption, fails to deliver all documentation required to complete the redemption and to repurchase an equal number of the mutual fund securities that were redeemed, and

    (ii) the investor to pay any difference if the repurchase price exceeds the redemption price.

(f) Describe briefly any right or requirement to reinvest the proceeds of dividends or other distributions in the issuer's securities.

(g) Include a statement referring the purchaser to the annual information form for a more detailed statement of the information required by this item.

Instructions

1.   As used in this item and in Items 8 and 10, the term "special arrangement" includes a periodic accumulation plan, an open account plan, a contractual plan, a withdrawal plan, a registered retirement savings plan, a registered retirement income fund, a registered education savings plan, an exchange or transfer privilege and any other type of arrangement respecting the acquisition or disposition of securities of the issuer.

Item 8.   Method of Distribution

Outline briefly the method of distribution of the securities being offered. If sales are to be effected through a principal distributor, give brief details of any arrangements with the principal distributor.

Instructions

1.   If the securities are being offered by way of a special arrangement, give the main particulars of the special arrangement, including, where applicable, particulars of:

    (1)   any minimum initial investment;

    (2)   any subsequent minimum investment;

    (3)   any sales charge deductions from the initial and from the subsequent minimum investments;

    (4)   the sales charges expressed as a percentage of the amount paid by the purchaser and expressed as a percentage of the net amount invested in securities of the issuer, provided that in making this calculation, insurance premiums and the fees payable to a trustee of a registered retirement savings plan or of a registered retirement income fund or of a registered education savings plan may be excluded in determining the amount of the sales charge;

    (5)   the total amount invested contrasted to the total amount paid by the purchaser.

2.   As used in this Item, the term sales charge includes all sales commissions or sales charges plus all other charges related to the establishment of the special arrangement and its continuing administration and maintenance.

3.   Where there are any special withdrawal rights that are applicable to a special arrangement, include a statement referring the purchaser to the annual information form for particulars thereof.

4.   The term "special arrangement" as used in this Item has the same meaning as ascribed to such term in Item 7.

Item 9. Responsibility for Principal Functions

(a) Give a concise statement of the manner in which the following functions of the issuer are performed and who is responsible therefor, stating how such functions are co-ordinated and, to the extent that any such functions are not performed by bona fide employees of the issuer, the names and addresses of the persons or companies responsible for performing such functions:

    (1) the management of the issuer other than the management of the investment portfolio;

    (2) the management of the investment portfolio;

    (3) providing investment analysis;

    (4) providing investment recommendations;

    (5) making investment decisions;

    (6) purchasing and selling the investment portfolio and making the brokerage arrangement relating thereto;

    (7) the distribution of the securities offered.

(b) Include a statement referring the purchaser to the annual information form for greater detail regarding the purchase and sale of the investment portfolio and the brokerage arrangements relating thereto.

(c) Indicate the circumstances under which the management agreement may be terminated.

(d) Indicate conflicts of interest or potential conflicts of interest between the issuer and the persons or companies named in answer to paragraph (a).

Instructions

1. The address given may be the municipality of residence or a postal address, provided that upon request, the full residential address shall be furnished to the Canadian securities authorities requesting the same.

2. In giving information regarding the distribution of securities the name and address of only the principal distributor need be given.

3. If one or more persons or companies performs more than one of the functions referred to in this Item, so state, giving details of all functions so performed.

Item 10. Management Fees and Other Expenses

(a) Indicate:

    (i) what fees and other charges and expenses are charged to the issuer and the basis for the calculation of the same,

    (ii) what fees and other charges and expenses are borne by the manager of the issuer;

    (iii) what fees and other charges and expenses, if any, are charged directly to all securityholders generally. or to any securityholder who participates in a special arrangement, and the basis of the calculation of the same.

(b) All fees and other charges and expenses which are charged directly to securityholders shall be summarized in tabular form under the heading "Summary of Fees, Charges and Expenses Payable by the Securityholder" or such variation thereof as is acceptable to the Regulator. The table shall be substantially in the form of the table set out in Appendix 1 to Schedule A or such variation thereof as is acceptable to the Regulator. Reference to this table shall be made on the outside cover page or on the first facing page of the simplified prospectus.

(c) Make a cross reference to the financial statements for details as to the amount of management fees and other expenses, if any, which have been charged to the issuer.

(d) Set out in tabular form in the simplified prospectus or by way of note to the financial statements, a record of the management expense ratio for each of the last five completed financial years of the issuer with a brief description of the method of calculating the management expense ratio.

Instructions

1. Where the basis of the calculation of the management fees or of the other fees or expenses that are charged to the issuer is changed or is proposed to be changed and where such change would have had an effect on the management expense ratio for the last completed financial year of the mutual fund if the change had been in effect throughout that year, the effect of such change should be disclosed.

2. Where any financial period referred to in Item 10(d) is less than 12 months, the management expense ratio should be shown on an annualized basis, with reference to the period covered and to the fact that the management expense ratio for the period has been annualized.

3. The management expense ratio of an issuer for any financial year shall be calculated by dividing (i) the aggregate of all fees and other expenses paid or payable by the issuer during or in respect of the financial year in question, by (ii) the amount of the average net asset value of the issuer for the financial year in question and multiplying the quotient by 100; for the purpose of making this calculation:

    (a) the expression "the average net asset value of the issuer for a financial year" shall mean and be the result obtained by:

        (i) adding together the amounts determined to be the net asset value of the issuer as at the close of business of the issuer on each day during the financial year in question on which the net asset value of the issuer has been determined in the manner from time to time prescribed in the constating documents of the issuer;

        (ii) dividing the amount resulting from the addition provided for in clause (i) by the number of days during the financial year in question on which the net asset value of the issuer has been determined;

    (b) the expression "all fees and other expenses" means all fees and other expenses paid or payable by the issuer with the exception of commissions and brokerage fees on the purchase and sale of portfolio securities, interest charges (if any) and taxes of all kinds to which the issuer is subject.

4. Where an issuer invests in another mutual fund, the management expense ratio shall be calculated on the basis of those assets of the issuer on which a management fee is charged.

5. The financial statements should set out in appropriate detail the amounts of the management fee and of all other fees and expenses, if any, which have been charged to the issuer, during the period covered by the financial statements.

6. The fees and other charges and expenses, if any, that are charged directly to all security-holders generally or to any securityholder who participates in a special arangement and the basis of calculation of the same are to be excluded in determining the management expense ratio of the issuer.

7. The term "special arrangement" as used in this Item has the same meaning as ascribed to such term in Item 7.

Item 11.   Investment Objectives and Practices

    (a) State the fundamental investment objectives of the issuer and, where relevant, any fundamental investment policies and practices.

    (b) Briefly indicate the nature of any securityholder or other approval that may be required in order to change any of the fundamental investment objectives and any of the fundamental investment policies and practices of the issuer.

    (c) Refer the purchaser to the annual information form for information concerning restrictions on investments and on investment policies and practices of the issuer in pursuing its objectives.

    (d) If the issuer has adopted the standard investment restrictions and practices contained in National Policy No. 39, include a statement to the effect that (i) the issuer has adopted such standard investment restrictions and practices, and (ii) a copy of the standard investment restrictions and practices will be provided by or on behalf of the issuer or by or on behalf of the principal distributor of the issuer to any person requesting the same.

Instructions

1. Aims such as long-term capital appreciation or current income and the types of securities in which the issuer proposes to invest should be described.

2. Where the issuer intends to:

   (i) invest a specific portion of its assets in Canadian securities or in foreign securities;

   (ii) invest in foreign securities;

   (iii) invest a specific portion of its assets in a particular type of security (e.g. bonds, common shares, preferred shares, money market instruments);

   (iv) concentrate its investments in a particular class or kind of industry;

   (v) invest in property other than securities;

3. Where the securities of the issuer are or will be a qualified investment within the meaning of the Income Tax Act (Canada) for retirement savings plans, deferred profit sharing plans or other savings plans registered under the Income Tax Act (Canada) and where the issuer is or will be recognized as a registered investment within the meaning of such Act, the relevant information and the effect of such qualification must be stated together with a statement as to the limitations, if any, imposed by such Act on the portion of such plans which may be invested in the securities of the issuer without subjecting such plans to taxes or penalties under such Act. A statement as to whether the securities of the issuer will or will not be qualified investments for such plans is to be included.

Item 12.   Dividends or Distributions

Include a statement making reference to the issuer's financial statements for information as to the amount of dividends or other distributions per security paid by the issuer including income allocated to securityholders by way of dividend reinvestment or otherwise during the last completed financial year of the issuer and each of the previous four completed financial years and include such information by way of note to the issuer's financial statements.

Instructions

1. Dividends should be set out on a per security basis, shown separately for each class of securities in respect of each of the financial years. Appropriate adjustments should be made to reflect changes in capitalization during the period.

2. Where dividends or other distributions have been paid by way of capitalizing the same (i.e. increasing the value of the securities held by securityholders of record), the amount per security of the dividends or other distributions so capitalized shall be referred to by way of note to the issuer's financial statements. As well, any statement in the issuer's simplified prospectus, annual information form or financial statements as to the amount of the net asset value per security as at any date shall be presented in such a manner so as to indicate clearly the portion of the net asset value per security that is represented by dividends or other distributions that were capitalized during the year or period in question and the portion of the net asset value per security that is represented by the changes that occurred in the market value of the assets and liabilities of the issuer during the year or period in question. The intention of this provision is to avoid any misunderstanding or double counting that may otherwise occur in evaluating the performance of the issuer during the year or period in question.

Item 13.   Tax Status of Securityholders

State in general terms the income tax consequences to the holders of the securities offered of:

   (a) any distribution to such holders in the form of dividends or otherwise, including amounts reinvested;

   (b) the redemption of securities;

    (c) the sale of securities;

    (d) any transfers between mutual funds.

Item 14. *Legal Proceedings*

Describe briefly any legal proceedings material to the issuer, to which the issuer is a party or any of its property is subject.

Instructions

1.   Identify the name of the court or agency having jurisdiction, the date on which the suit was instituted, the principal parties thereto, the nature of the claim and the amount claimed, if any. State whether the proceedings are being contested and the present status of the proceedings.

Item 15. *Other Material Facts*

Give particulars of any other material facts relating to the securities proposed to be offered which are not contained in the annual information form.

Item 16. *Auditors, Transfer Agent and Registrar*

    (a) State the name and address of the issuer's auditor.

    (b) State the name of the issuer's transfer agent and registrar and the cities in which the registers of transfer of securities of the issuer are kept.

Item 17. *Purchasers' Statutory Rights*

Include the following statement in the simplified prospectus.

"Securities legislation in certain of the provinces provides purchasers with the right to withdraw from an agreement to purchase mutual fund securities within two business days after receipt of a simplified prospectus or within forty-eight hours after the receipt of a confirmation of a purchase of such securities. If the agreement is to purchase such securities under a contractual plan, the time period during which withdrawal may be made may be longer. In several of the provinces and territories securities legislation further provides a purchaser with remedies for rescission or, in some jurisdictions, damages where the simplified prospectus and any amendment contains a misrepresentation or is not delivered to the purchaser but such remedies must be exercised by the purchaser within the time limit prescribed by the securities legislation of his province or territory. The purchaser should refer to any applicable provisions of the securities legislation of his province or territory for the particulars of these rights or consult with a legal adviser".

Item 18. *Identification*

Each simplified prospectus shall bear encoding which identifies the date at which it becomes effective.

Instructions

1.   The date need not be written in full. In fact it is preferred that it be shown as for example, "30/05/89" or included in a printer's code together with the quantity printed. The purpose is to identify which version of a simplified prospectus is the subject of a specific receipt.

APPENDIX 1 TO SCHEDULE A

Summary of Fees, Charges and Expenses Payable by the Securityholder

The following table contains a summary of the fees, charges and expenses payable directly by securityholders:

Type of Charge	Description including amount/rate

Capital Transactions

Amounts payable on

(a) acquisition of securities

(b) exchange/transfer of securities to a related fund

(c) redemption of securities

Registered Plan[1]

Amounts payable in connection with

(a) retirement savings plan

(b) retirement income fund

(c) education savings plan

Services

Amounts payable with respect to

(a) management fees paid directly by securityholder

(b) obtaining certificates

(c) purchase plans

(d) withdrawal plans

(e) other (insert descriptions)
    – eg. dividend reinvestment charges, courier or wire order charges for special services, charges for dishonoured cheques, etc.

SCHEDULE B
INFORMATION REQUIRED TO BE
INCLUDED IN THE ANNUAL INFORMATION FORM

GENERAL INSTRUCTIONS

The Annual Information Form is to be used in conjunction with the simplified prospectus, financial statements, notices of material change and similar documents which are required to be filed to provide disclosure of all information concerning the mutual fund and the securities it proposes to issue. Information contained in an annual information form should be complete and presented in a style similar to that used in a prospectus.

Item 1.   Name and Formation of Issuer

State the full name of the issuer and the address of its head or registered office. State the laws under which the issuer was formed and the manner and date of its formation. If material, state whether the issuer's constating documents have been amended. If the issuer's name was changed during the past twelve months, state the issuer's former name.

Item 2.   Business of the Issuer

Describe the business of the issuer.

Instructions

1. If the issuer has engaged in any business other than that of a mutual fund during the past five years, state the nature of the other business and give the approximate date on which the issuer commenced to operate as a mutual fund. If the issuer's name was changed during the period, state its former name and the date on which it was changed. Indicate briefly the nature and results of any bankruptcy, receivership or similar proceedings or any other material reorganization of the issuer during the period.

2. If during the past two years any affiliate of the issuer has had any material interest, direct or indirect, in any transaction involving the purchase of any substantial amount of assets presently held by the issuer, describe the interest of the affiliate in such transaction and state the cost of such assets to the purchaser and to the seller.

---

1   Only registered plans which are sponsored by the Fund(s) and which are described in this prospectus are included.

Item 3.   Price of Securities on Sale or Redemption

Repeat the disclosure required to be contained in the simplified prospectus in respect of this Item and, in addition:

(a) Describe the basis for valuing the issuer's assets and liabilities for the purpose of calculating net asset value and, if there is discretion to deviate from these rules, disclose all instances within the past three years where the discretion to deviate from these rules was exercised.

(b) Indicate briefly any difference in the sales charges imposed upon the sale of securities in connection with the conversion or exchange of securities or the reinvestment of dividends or distributions.

(c) Give particulars of the entitlement of the purchaser of a contractual plan to a refund of any sales charge incurred if the contractual plan is terminated during the term of such plan.

Item 4.   Method of Distribution

Repeat the disclosure required to be contained in the simplified prospectus in respect of this Item and, in addition:

(a) Disclose when during the term of a special arrangement the sales charge will be deducted.

(b) Give particulars of any special withdrawal rights that are applicable to a special arrangement.

(c) Give particulars of any entitlement in respect of a special arrangement to a refund of any sales charge if the special arrangement is terminated during the term thereof.

Instruction

1.   The term "special arrangement" as used in this Item has the same meaning as ascribed to such term in Item 7 of Schedule A.

Item 5.   Responsibility for Principal Functions

Repeat the disclosure from the simplified prospectus in respect of this Item and in addition:

(a) Provide the names and addresses in full or, alternatively, solely the municipality of residence or postal address of each person or company referred to in the simplified prospectus who is responsible for the performance of the principal functions described in this Item. In addition, where a company is named as being responsible for the performance of any such functions, provide the names in full and addresses as aforesaid in respect of each of the directors and officers of the company.

(b) Indicate the method of determining the amount of management fees and state the total of such fees paid during each of the last five completed financial years and during the period from the end of the last completed financial year to a date within thirty days of the date of the annual information form.

Instructions

1.   Where an alternate address is listed, the Regulator may request that the home address in full be furnished to him.

2.   In giving information regarding the distribution of securities the name and address of only the principal distributor need be given. See Schedule A, Item 9.

3.   In giving information regarding the purchase and sale of the investment portfolio and brokerage arrangements relating thereto the name and address of only the principal broker need be given.

4.   In giving information regarding the purchase and sale of the investment portfolio and brokerage arrangements, state:

(i) the total cost, during the last completed financial year of the issuer, of securities acquired, distinguishing between:

(a) securities of or guaranteed by the government of any country, or any political subdivision thereof,

(b) short-term notes, and

(c) other securities;

(ii) the total cost of securities held at the beginning and at the end of the issuer's last completed financial year;

(iii) the formula, method or criteria used in allocating brokerage business to persons or companies engaged in the distribution of the securities of the issuer;

(iv) the formula, method or criteria used in allocating brokerage business to persons or companies furnishing statistical, research or other services to the issuer or the manager of the issuer; and

(v) the amount of brokerage paid to the principal broker for the last three completed financial years, giving the total amount paid in each year and expressing the amount paid in each year as a percentage of the total brokerage paid in such year by the issuer.

5.   As used herein:

(i) "principal broker" includes,

(a) a person or company through whom the investment portfolio of the issuer is purchased or sold pursuant to a contractual arrangement with the issuer or the manager of the issuer providing for an exclusive right to purchase or sell the investment portfolio of the issuer or any feature which gives or is intended to give a broker or dealer a material competitive advantage over other brokers or dealers in respect of the purchase or sale of the investment portfolio of the Issuer, or

(b) a person or company, together with any affiliate, by or through whom 15 per cent or more of the securities transactions of the issuer were carried out; and

(ii) "brokerage arrangements" or "brokerage business" include all purchases and sales of the investment portfolio, whether effected directly or through an agent.

6.   With the consent of the Regulator, a person or company who would otherwise be a principal broker may, with respect to any one or more of the items of disclosure required herein, be treated as not coming within the definition of a principal broker.

Item 6.   Investment Objectives and Practices

Repeat the disclosure from the simplified prospectus in respect of this Item and in addition:

(a) Subject to the provisions contained in Instruction 3, state any restrictions on investments and on investment policies and practices of the issuer in pursuing its objectives, with particular reference to the following types of activities:

(i) the issuing of securities other than those contemplated by the issuer's simplified prospectus;

(ii) the borrowing of money;

(iii) the firm underwriting of securities issued by other issuers;

(iv) the purchase and sale of real estate;

(v) the purchase and sale of commodities or commodity futures contracts;

(vi) the making of loans, whether secured or unsecured;

(vii) the investment of more than 10% of the assets of the issuer in the securities of any one issuer;

(viii) the investment in more than 10% of the securities of any one issuer;

(ix) the investment in securities for the purpose of exercising control or management;

(x) the investment in securities of investment companies or other mutual funds;

(xi) the purchase or sale of mortgages;

(xii) the purchase of securities on margin or selling short;

(xiii) the investment in securities which are not fully paid;

(xiv) the investment in illiquid securities or securities whose resale is restricted;

(xv) the investment in gold or gold certificates;

(xvi) the pledging, mortgaging or hypothecating of the issuer's assets;

(xvii) the sale of portfolio securities to directors, officers or trustees of the issuer or of the manager or the purchase of portfolio securities from such persons;

(xviii) the guaranteeing of the securities or the obligations of another issuer;

(xix) the purchase of options, rights and warrants;

(xx) the writing of covered or uncovered clearing corporation options;

(xxi) the investment in a security which may require the purchaser to make an additional contribution beyond the price of the security;

(xxii) the lending of the issuer's portfolio securities.

(b) Briefly indicate the nature of any securityholder or other approval that may be required in order to change any of the restrictions referred to in clauses (a).

Instructions

1. For the purpose of clause (vi), the purchase of debt securities for investment purposes is not considered to be the making of a loan by the issuer.

2. For the purpose of clause (xiv), where the issuer invests in securities whose resale is restricted, describe how those securities are valued for the purpose of computing the net asset value of the issuer.

3. Reference should be made to National Policy No. 39 for a statement as to the standard investment restrictions and practices that a mutual fund is required to adopt unless the prior approval of the securities authorities has been obtained to permit any variation. If the issuer has adopted the standard investment restrictions and practices contained in National Policy No. 39, it is not necessary to state these in the annual information form provided that:

(i) the annual information form includes a statement to the effect that (i) the issuer has adopted the standard investment restrictions and practices; (ii) the standard investment restrictions and practices are deemed to be incorporated in the annual information form; and (iii) a copy of the standard investment restrictions and practices will be provided by or on behalf of the issuer or by or on behalf of the principal distributor of the issuer to any person requesting the same; and

(ii) any investment restrictions or investment practices in addition to the standard investment restrictions and practices that have been adopted by the issuer (including any variations from the standard investment restrictions and practices that have been approved by the securities authorities) are set forth in the annual information form.

Item 7.   Significant Holdings in Other Issuers

Furnish in substantially the tabular form indicated the following information as at a date within thirty days of the date of the annual information form with respect to each issuer, 5 per cent or more of whose securities of any class are beneficially owned directly or indirectly by the mutual fund or any of its subsidiaries.

TABLE

Name and Address of Issuer	Nature of its Principal Business	Percentage of Securities of any Class Owned by Issuer	Percentage of Value of Issuer's Assets Invested Therein
—	—	—	—

Item 8. Tax Status of Issuer and Security Holder

    (a) State in general terms the bases upon which the income and capital receipts of the issuer are taxed.

    (b) Repeat disclosure from the simplified prospectus in respect of the tax status of the securityholder.

Item 9. Legal Proceedings

Repeat the disclosure from the simplified prospectus in respect of this Item and in addition make a similar statement as to any such proceedings known to be contemplated.

Item 10. Directors, Officers and Trustees

List the names and home addresses in full or, alternatively, solely the municipality of residence or postal address, of all directors, officers or trustees of the issuer and indicate all positions and offices with the issuer held by each person named, and the principal occupations, within the five preceding years, of each director, officer or trustee.

Instructions

1.   Where the municipality of residence or postal address is listed, the director may request that the home address in full be furnished to the Regulator.

2.   Where the principal occupation of a director, trustee or officer is that of an officer of a company other than the issuer, state the business in which such company is engaged.

3.   Where a director or officer has held more than one position in the issuer, or a parent or subsidiary thereof, state only the first and last position held.

Item 11. Remuneration of Directors, Officers and Trustees

    (a) Only issuers which directly employ officers need comply fully with this Item.

    (b) Other issuers, the businesses of which are managed by a management company pursuant to a contractual arrangement with the issuer, or by a corporate trustee pursuant to the terms of a trust indenture, must report in the annual financial statement of such issuers:

        (i) the aggregate amount of directors' or trustees' fees paid by the issuer in respect of each of the financial years reported upon;

        (ii) the aggregate amount of expenses reimbursed by the issuer to the directors or trustees in respect of the fulfillment of duties as directors or trustees.

As well, such issuers must confirm in the annual information form that the amounts reported in the financial statements as paid or reimbursed to directors and trustees constitute the only compensation paid by the issuer to such directors and trustees.

Where any compensation is in non-cash form, the value of the benefit conferred should be stated or, if it is not possible to state the value, the benefit conferred should be described.

    (c) State the information respecting executive compensation that is required to be disclosed pursuant to the Statement of Executive Compensation annexed hereto as Appendix 1.

Item 12.   Indebtedness of Directors, Officers and Trustees

In regard to,

    (i) each director, trustee and each senior officer of the issuer;

   (ii) each proposed nominee for election as a director or trustee of the issuer; and

  (iii) each associate or affiliate of any such director, trustee, senior officer or proposed nominee,

who is or has been indebted to the issuer or its subsidiaries at any time since the beginning of the last completed financial year of the issuer, state with respect to each such issuer or subsidiary the largest aggregate amount of indebtedness outstanding at any time during the last completed financial year, the nature of the indebtedness and of the transaction in which it was incurred, the amount thereof presently outstanding, and the rate of interest paid or charged thereon, but no disclosure need be made of routine indebtedness.

    1.   "routine indebtedness" means indebtedness described in any of the following clauses:

        (a) if an issuer makes loans to employees generally whether or not in the ordinary course of business then loans shall be considered to be routine indebtedness if made on terms, including those as to interest or collateral, no more favourable to the borrower than the terms on which loans are made by the issuer to employees generally, but the amount at any time remaining unpaid under such loans to any one director, senior officer or proposed nominee together with his associates or affiliates that are treated as routine indebtedness under this clause (a) shall not exceed $25,000;

        (b) Whether or not the issuer makes loans in the ordinary course of business, a loan to a director or senior officer shall be considered to be routine indebtedness if:

           (i) the borrower is a full-time employee of the issuer;

          (ii) the loan is fully secured against the residence of the borrower; and

         (iii) the amount of the loan does not exceed the annual salary of the borrower;

        (c) where the issuer makes loans in the ordinary course of business, a loan shall be considered to be routine indebtedness if made to a person or company other than a full-time employee of the issuer, and if the loan:

           (i) is made on substantially the same terms, including those as to interest rate and collateral, as were available when the loan was made to other customers of the issuer with comparable credit ratings; and

          (ii) involves no more than usual risks of collectability; and

        (d) indebtedness arising by reason of purchases made on usual trade terms or of ordinary travel or expense advances, or for similar reasons shall be considered to be routine indebtedness if the repayment arrangements are in accord with usual commercial practice.

    2.   State the name and home address in full or, alternatively, solely the municipality of residence or postal address of each person or company whose indebtedness is described.

Item 13.   Associated Persons

Furnish the following information as to each person or company named in the simplified prospectus and repeated in the annual information form in respect of the information given pursuant to Item 9 of Schedule A:

(a) If a named person or company is associated with the issuer or is a director or senior officer of or is associated with any affiliate of the issuer or is a director or senior officer of or is associated with any company which is associated with the issuer, so state, and give particulars of the relationship.

(b) If the issuer is associated with a named person or company or is associated with any affiliate of a named company or is associated with any company which is associated with the named person or company, so state, and give particulars of the relationship.

(c) If any person or company associated with the issuer is also associated with a named person or company, so state, and give particulars of the relationship.

(d) If a named person or company has a contract or arrangement with the issuer, give a brief description of the contract or arrangements, including the basis for determining the remuneration of the named person or company and give the amount of remuneration paid or payable by the issuer and its subsidiaries to such person or company during the last completed financial year of the issuer.

(e) If a named person or company is associated with any other named person or company, so state, and give particulars of the relationship.

(f) Where and to the extent required by the Regulator, give the business experience of each named person or company and, in the case of a named company, the directors and officers thereof.

Item 14. Promoter

If any person or company is or has been a promoter of the issuer within the five years immediately preceding the date of the annual information form furnish the following information:

(a) State the names of the promoters, the nature and amount of anything of value (including money, property, contracts, options or rights of any kind) received or to be received by each promoter directly or indirectly from the issuer and the nature and amount of any assets, services or other consideration therefor received or to be received by the issuer.

(b) As to any assets acquired within the past two years or to be acquired by the issuer from a promoter, state the amount at which they were acquired or are to be acquired and the principle followed or to be followed in determining the amount. Identify the person making the determination and state his relationship, if any, with the issuer or any promoter. State the date that the assets were acquired by the promoter and the cost thereof to the promoter.

Item 15. Principal Holders of Securities

Furnish the following information as of a specified date within thirty days prior to the date of the annual information form in substantially the tabular form indicated:

(a) The number of securities of each class of voting securities of:

(i) the issuer; and

(ii) the manager of the issuer;

owned of record or beneficially, directly or indirectly, by each person or company who owns of record, or is known by such issuer or manager to own beneficially, directly or indirectly, more than 10 per cent of any class of such securities. Show in Column 5 whether the securities are owned both of record and beneficially, of record only, or beneficially only, and show in Columns 6 and 7 the respective numbers and percentages known by the issuer or manager to be owned in each such manner.

TABLE

Name of Company	Relationship Thereto	Issuer or nation of Class	Desig- Type of Ownership	Securities Owned	Number of Percentage of Class	Name and Address
—	—	—	—	—	—	—

(b) If any person or company named in answer to paragraph (a) owns of record or beneficially, directly or indirectly, more than 10 per cent of:

(i) any class of voting securities of the principal distributor or the principal broker of the issuer or any parent or subsidiary thereof, or

(ii) any proprietorship interest in the principal distributor or the principal broker of the issuer,

give the percentage of such securities or the percentage of such proprietorship interest so owned by such person or company.

(c) The percentage of securities of each class of voting securities beneficially owned, directly or indirectly, by all the directors, trustees and senior officers:

(i) of the issuer in the issuer or in a parent or subsidiary thereof, and

(ii) of the manager of the issuer in such manager or in a parent or subsidiary thereof,

in the case of each company as a group, without naming them.

TABLE

Designation of Class	Issuer or Percentage of Class	Name of Company	Relationship Thereto
—	—	—	—

Instructions

1. Where a company is shown by the issuer as owning directly or indirectly more than 10 per cent of any class of such securities, the Regulator may require the disclosure of such additional information as is necessary to identify any individual who, through his direct or indirect ownership of voting securities in the company owns directly or indirectly more than 10 per cent of any class of such securities. The name of such an individual should be disclosed in a footnote to the table described in paragraph (a).

2. For the purposes of paragraph (a), securities owned beneficially, directly or indirectly, and of record are to be aggregated in determining whether any person or company owns more than 10 per cent of the securities of any class.

3. For the purposes of clause (i) of paragraph (a), where no material change has occurred in the information required by such clause since the date of the financial statements filed for the issuer's most recently completed financial year, the information may be given as of the date of the financial statements.

4. If voting securities are being offered in connection with, or pursuant to, a plan of acquisition, amalgamation or reorganization, indicate, as far as practicable, the respective holdings of voting securities that will exist after giving effect to the plan.

5. If, to the knowledge of the issuer, more than 10 per cent of any class of voting securities of the issuer or if, to the knowledge of the manager of the issuer, more than 10 per cent of any class of voting securities of such manager are held or are to be held subject to any voting trust or other similar agreement, state the designation of such securities, the number held or to be held and the duration of the agreement. Give the names and addresses of the voting trustees and outline briefly their voting rights and other powers under the agreement.

6. If, to the knowledge of the issuer, the parent of the issuer, the manager or the parent of the manager, any person or company named in answer to paragraph (a) is an associate or affiliate of any other person or company named therein, disclose, insofar as known, the material facts of such relationship, including any basis for influence over the issuer enjoyed by the person or company other than the holding of voting securities of the issuer.

Item 16.   Interest of Management and Others in Material Transactions

Describe briefly, and where practicable state, the approximate amount of any material interest, direct or indirect, of any of the following persons or companies in any transaction within the three years prior to the date of the annual information form, or in any proposed transaction which has materially affected or will materially affect the issuer:

    (i) the manager of the issuer;

    (ii) the principal distributor of the issuer;

    (iii) the principal broker of the issuer;

    (iv) any directors, senior officers or trustees of the issuer or of any company referred to in clauses (i), (ii) or (iii) hereof;

    (v) any securityholder named in answer to paragraph (a) of Item 14; and

    (vi) any associate or affiliate of any of the foregoing persons or companies.

Instructions

1.   Give a brief description of the material transaction. Include the name and address of each person or company whose interest in any transaction is described and the nature of the relationship by reason of which such interest is required to be described.

2.   As to any transaction involving the purchase or sale of assets by or to the issuer otherwise than in the ordinary course of business, state the cost of the assets to the purchaser and the cost thereof to the seller if acquired by the seller within two years prior to the transaction.

3.   This Item does not apply to any interest arising from the ownership of securities of the issuer where the securityholder receives no extra or special benefit or advantage not shared on an equal basis by all other holders of the same class of securities or all other holders of the same class of securities who are resident in Canada.

4.   No information need be given in answer to this Item as to any transaction or any interest therein, where:

    (i) the rates or charges involved in the transaction are fixed by law or determined by competitive bids;

    (ii) the interest of a specified person or company in the transaction is solely that of a director of another company that is a party to the transaction;

    (iii) the transaction involves services as a bank or other depository of funds, transfer agent, registrar, trustee under a trust indenture or other similar services;

    (iv) the interest of a specified person or company, including all periodic instalments in the case of any lease or other agreement providing for periodic payments or instalments, does not exceed $50,000; or

    (v) the transaction does not directly or indirectly, involve remuneration for services, and

        (a) the interest of a specified person or company arose from the beneficial ownership, direct or indirect, of less than 10 per cent of any class of voting securities of another company that is a party to the transaction,

        (b) the transaction is in the ordinary course of business of the issuer.

5.   Information shall be furnished in answer to this Item with respect to transactions not excluded above that involve remuneration, directly or indirectly, to any of the specified persons or companies for services in any capacity unless the interest of the person or company arises solely from the beneficial ownership, direct or indirect, of less than 10 per cent of any class of voting securities of another company furnishing the services to the issuer or its subsidiaries.

National
Policies

6. This Item does not require the disclosure of any interest in any transaction unless such interest and transaction are material.

Item 17.   Custodian of Portfolio Securities

(a) State the name, principal business address and the nature of the business of the person or company holding portfolio securities of the issuer as custodian. The name of the custodian may be omitted if it is a bank to which the Bank Act (Canada) applies, or otherwise with the consent of the Regulator.

(b) Give brief details of the contractual arrangement made with the custodian.

Item 18.   Material Contracts

Give particulars of every material contract entered into within the two years prior to the date of the annual information form, by the issuer and state a reasonable time and place at which any such contract or copy thereof may be inspected during the distribution of the securities being offered. Indicate that in addition to any such contracts, the declaration of trust establishing the mutual fund as well as any management agreement, principal distributorship agreement or copies thereof are available for inspection at such time and place.

Instructions

1. The term "material contract" for this purpose means any contract that can reasonably be regarded as presently material to the proposed investor in the securities being offered. This Item does not require disclosure of contracts entered into in the ordinary course of business of the issuer.

2. Set out a complete list of all material contracts, indicating those which are disclosed elsewhere in the annual information form or in the simplified prospectus and provide particulars with respect to those material contracts about which particulars are not given elsewhere.

3. Particulars of contracts should include the date of, parties to, consideration and general nature of the contracts, succinctly described.

4. Particulars of contracts need not be disclosed or copies of such contracts made available for inspection if the Regulator determines that such disclosure or making available would impair the value of the contract and would not be necessary for the protection of investors.

Item 19.   Other Material Facts

Give particulars of any other material facts relating to the securities proposed to be offered and not disclosed pursuant to the foregoing items which are not contained in the simplified prospectus.

Item 20.   Certificates

(a) Include a certificate signed by the chief executive officer and the chief financial officer of the issuer and by two directors of the issuer other than the foregoing and by the manager of the issuer, if any, which states:

"This annual information form, the financial statements of the fund (specify) for the financial period ended (specify) and the auditors' report thereon, together with the simplified prospectus required to be sent or delivered to a purchaser during the currency of this annual information form constitute full, true and plain disclosure of all material facts relating to the securities offered by the simplified prospectus and do not contain any misrepresentation."

(b) Include a certificate signed by the principal distributor of the issuer which states:

"To the best of our knowledge, information and belief this annual information form, the financial statements of the fund (specify) for the financial period ended (specify) and the auditors' report thereon, together with the simplified prospectus required to be sent or delivered to a purchaser during the currency of this annual information form constitute full, true and plain disclosure of all material facts relating to the securities offered by the simplified prospectus and do not contain any misrepresentation."

Instructions

1. The certificate required to be signed by the manager of the issuer shall be signed in the manner prescribed by National Policy No. 39.

2. The certificate required to be signed by an issuer that has been established as a trust shall be signed in the manner prescribed by National Policy No. 39.

3. Where National Policy No. 39 requires evidence of the authority to sign to be provided, such evidence shall be filed with the filing of the annual information form.

APPENDIX 1 TO SCHEDULE B
STATEMENT OF EXECUTIVE COMPENSATION

Item I.   *General*

I.1 For the purposes of this form "executive officer" of an issuer means the chairman and any vice-chairman of the board of directors of the issuer, where that person performs the functions of such office on a full-time basis, the president, any vice-president in charge of a principal business unit such as sales, finance or production and any officer of the issuer or of a subsidiary who performs a policy-making function in respect of the issuer, whether or not such officer is also a director of the issuer or the subsidiary.

I.2 An unincorporated issuer, including a mutual fund, that does not itself directly employ officers and the business of which is managed by a manager pursuant to a management contract with the issuer or by a trustee pursuant to a trust indenture, need comply only with items VI and VII, to the extent those items are applicable.

Item II.   *Cash*

II.1 State the number of executive officers of the issuer.

II.2 State the aggregate cash compensation paid to the issuer's executive officers by the issuer and its subsidiaries for services rendered during the most recently completed financial year.

II.3 For the purposes of subitem II.2.

(a) cash compensation includes salaries, fees (including directors' fees), commissions and bonuses and, in addition to amounts actually paid during and for the most recently completed financial year, cash compensation includes:

(i) bonuses to be paid for services rendered during the most recently completed financial year unless such amounts have not been allocated,

(ii) bonuses paid during the most recently completed financial year for services rendered in a previous financial year, and

(iii) any compensation other than bonuses earned during the most recently completed financial year, the payment of which is deferred;

(b) compensation for a period during which an individual was not then an executive officer shall not be included in a determination of cash remuneration of executive officers; and

(c) compensation paid during the most recently completed financial year that was disclosed in a filing of a document complying with the requirements of this form or a predecessor thereof in respect of a financial year other than the most recently completed financial year shall not be included.

II.4 At the option of the issuer, the cash compensation figure set out pursuant to subitem II.2 may be broken down into categories such as salaries, fees, commissions and bonuses.

Item III. Plans

III. Plans

*III.1 Describe briefly any plan pursuant to which cash or non-cash compensation was paid or distributed to executive officers during the most recently completed financial year or is proposed to be paid or distributed in a subsequent year and include in the description,

(a) a summary of how the plan operates;

(b) the criteria used to determine amounts payable;

(c) the time periods over which the measurement of benefits will be determined;

(d) payment schedules;

(e) any recent material amendments to the plan;

(f) amounts paid or distributed during the most recently completed financial year, and

(g) amounts accrued for the group during the most recently completed financial year, inasmuch as the distribution or unconditional vesting of same is not subject to future events.

[Practice Notes:

The phrase in the first sentence in subitem III.1 "in a subsequent year" means in any future year or years.

Clauses III.1(f) and (g) of Form 41 do not apply to defined benefit plans.

A defined benefit plan is one which determines employees' entitlements to pension benefits as a function of the years of employee service and/or earnings. It specifies certain pension benefits to be received after retirement and usually sets up a funding medium designed to provide the benefits.]

*III.2 With respect to options to purchase securities granted to executive officers during the most recently completed financial year set out,

(a) a summary of how the plan operates;

(b) the criteria used to determine the number of securities under option;

(c) the time periods over which the measurement of benefits will be determined;

(d) payment schedules;

(e) all recent material amendments to the plan;

(f) the number of securities optioned during the most recently completed financial year;

(g) the designation and aggregate number of securities under option;

(h) the average per security exercise price (when options with differing terms are granted, the information should be given for each class or type of option) and when such price is less than the market value of the security underlying the option on the date the option is granted, provide the market price on such date.

III.3 With respect to options exercised during the issuer's most recently completed financial year, provide, with respect to each class or type of option, in addition to the information prescribed by clauses III.2(a) to (f), the aggregate net value (market value less exercise price at the date of the exercise) of the securities under option.

---

* *Subitems III.1 and 111.2; Item IV; Item V; and Subitem VI.1 – Subsidiaries*

Practice Note: References in the above items and subitems to the payment or distribution of compensation to executive officers or directors or receipt of such compensation by executive officers, the granting of options to executive officers and the incurrence of cost by the issuer include such payments, distributions, grants and incurrences by and such receipts from the issuer or any subsidiaries of the issuer.

III.4　For the purpose of this item,

　　(a)　compensation pursuant to a plan need be taken into account only to the extent that the plan discriminates in scope, terms or operation in favour of executive officers and is not available to all full time employees other than those covered by a collective agreement;

　　(b)　where disclosure of an amount paid or distributed pursuant to a plan is made under clause III.1(f), that amount shall not be included in the cash compensation under item II;

[Practice Note: Where disclosure of an amount paid or distributed pursuant to a plan is made under cash compensation in item II, that amount shall not be included under clause III.1(f), provided that a statement to that effect is made under item III.]

　　(c)　amounts paid or distributed that are disclosed under clause III.1(f) shall not include amounts paid or distributed that have been disclosed in a previous filing of a document, other than a prospectus, complying with the requirements of this form under clause III.1(g) as accruing to the group in respect of a financial year other than the most recently completed financial year;

　　(d)　"options" includes all options, share purchase warrants or rights other than those issued to all securityholders of the same class or to all securityholders of the same class resident in Canada on a pro rata basis and an extension of an option shall be deemed to be a granting of an option;

　　(e)　"plan" includes any plan, contract, authorization or arrangement, whether or not set forth in any formal document and may be applicable to only one person, but does not include the Canada Pension Plan or a similar government plan.

Item IV.　Other

IV.1　Describe all other compensation not referred to in item II or III paid during the most recently completed financial year, including personal benefits and securities or property paid or distributed other than pursuant to a plan referred to in item III, which compensation is not offered on the same terms to all full time employees other than those covered by a collective agreement.

IV.2　For the purposes of describing other compensation under subitem IV.1, the value to be given for such compensation shall be the issuer's and subsidiaries' aggregate incremental cost.

IV.3　For the purposes of subitem IV.2, "incremental cost" is the cost to the issuer or subsidiary of conferring a benefit upon an individual where such cost would not be otherwise incurred by the issuer if the benefit were not so conferred.

IV.4　When the aggregate value of the compensation disclosed under subitem IV.1 does not exceed the lesser of $10,000 times the number of persons in the group or 10 per cent of the compensation stated under item II, it is necessary to declare that fact only and in the discretion of the Director, the $10,000 threshold may be increased to $25,000.

Item V.　Termination of Employment or Change of Control

V.1　Describe any plan or arrangement in respect of compensation received or that may be received by executive officers in the issuer's most recently completed or current financial year in view of compensating such officers in the event of the termination of employment (resignation, retirement,

---

*　*Subitems III.1 and 111.2; Item IV; Item V; and Subitem VI.1 – Subsidiaries*

Practice Note: References in the above items and subitems to the payment or distribution of compensation to executive officers or directors or receipt of such compensation by executive officers, the granting of options to executive officers and the incurrence of cost by the issuer include such payments, distributions, grants and incurrences by and such receipts from the issuer or any subsidiaries of the issuer.

change of control) or in the event of a change in responsibilities following a change in control, where in respect of an executive officer the value of such compensation exceeds $60,000.

Item VI. *Compensation of Directors*

VI.1 Describe,

(a) any standard arrangements, stating amounts, pursuant to which directors are compensated by the issuer for their services in their capacity as directors, including any additional amounts payable for committee participation or special assignments; and

(b) any other arrangements, stating amounts, in addition or in lieu of any standard arrangement, pursuant to which directors were compensated by the issuer in their capacity as directors during the most recently completed financial year.

VI.2 Where compensation is in non-cash form, state the value of the benefit conferred, or it if is not possible to state the value, describe the benefit conferred.

Mutual Fund Documents	Alberta	British Columbia	Manitoba	Ontario	Quebec Note 3	Saskatchewan	New Brunswick Newfoundland Nova Scotia Prince Edward Island	Yukon Territory	Northwest Territories
The following types and numbers of documents should be filed with a Preliminary Simplified Prospectus or a Pro Forma Simplified Prospectus filed pursuant to National Policy No. 36:									
• Preliminary or Pro Forma Simplified Prospectus – unsigned	4	1	2	5(Preliminary) 2(Pro Forma)	1 (French) 1 (English)	1	1	1	1
• Pro Forma Simplified Prospectus – black lined to show changes from the prior final simplified prospectus – certified as required by National Policy No. 30	1	1	1	2	1 (French) 1 (English)	1	1	–	1
• Preliminary Annual Information Form – signed	1	1	1	1	1 (French) 1 (English)	1	1	1	1
– unsigned	2	–	1	4	1 (French) 1 (English)	1	1	–	–
• Notice/Consent Forms under Freedom of Legislation/Protection of Privacy Legislation	–	–	–	1	–	–	–	–	–
• Notarial copy of filing receipt issued by principal jurisdiction or telex confirmation of issue	–	–	–	–	–	–	–	–	–
• Pro Forma Annual Information Form – signed	–	–	–	–	–	–	–	–	–
– unsigned	2	1	2	2	1 (French) 1 (English)	1	1	1	1
• Pro Forma Annual Information Form – black-lined to show changes from the prior Annual Information Form – certified as required by National Policy No. 30	1	1	1	2	1 (French) 1 (English)	1	1	1	1

National
Policies

Mutual Fund Documents	Alberta	British Columbia	Manitoba	Ontario	Quebec Note 3	Saskatchewan	New Brunswick Newfoundland Nova Scotia Prince Edward Island	Yukon Territory	Northwest Territories
• Audited Annual Financial Statements referred to as accompanying the Preliminary or Pro Forma Simplified Prospectus (Note 1)									
– manually signed	1	1	1	1	1 (French) 1 (English)	1	1	1	1
– unsigned or printed or facsimile signatures	1	1	1	2	2 (French) 1 (English)	2	1	–	–
• Auditors' Comfort Letter if auditors' report is unsigned	1	1	1	1 (signed) 1 (copy)	1	1	1	1	1
• Interim Financial Statements referred to as accompanying the Pro Forma Simplified Prospectus if applicable – unsigned	1	1	2	3	2 (French) 1 (English)	2	1	1	1
• Auditors' Comfort Letter re interim financial statements if applicable	1	1	1	1 (signed) 1 (copy)	–	1	1	1	1
• Directors' Resolution approving the Preliminary Annual Information Form, the Preliminary Simplified Prospectus and the audited financial statements referred to – therein – certified	1	1	1	1 (signed) 1 (copy)	1	1	1	1	1
• Cross Reference Sheet									
– in the case of the first filing under National Policy No. 36	1	1	1	2	1	1	1	1	1
– in the case of all subsequent filings under National Policy No. 36	1	–	1	–	–	–	–	–	–

Mutual Fund Documents	Alberta	British Columbia	Manitoba	Ontario	Quebec Note 3	Saskatchewan	New Brunswick Newfoundland Nova Scotia Prince Edward Island	Yukon Territory	Northwest Territories
• Copy or draft of all material contracts including the Custodianship Agreement and any Sub-Custodianship Agreement	–	1	1	1	1	1	– (1 in N.S. if N.S. is the principal jurisdiction)	–	1
• Copy or draft of all "green sheets"	–	–	–	1	1	–	–	–	–
• Certificate for each issuer re proceeds from the distribution in the jurisdiction and appropriate filing fee	–	1	–	1	1	–	–	–	–
• Filing fee per issuer (Note 4)	Regs. Sch. 1– S.2(1) S.2(8) S.2(9) $1,500 minimum prospectus; $500– AIF	Reg. 270/86 S.183(1)– $2,500 minimum	Reg. S50– R1 S.3(1)(h) $650 plus $600 if Manitoba is principal jurisdiction	Regs. Sch. 1 S.4–$250 minimum	Regs. S.267 $500 minimum See Regs. S.267.1, S.267.2, S.268(3) and S.98	Regs. S.176(1) Appendix A–S.3(a) Initial Filing $1,000 Reflings $1,000	Note 5	Note 5	Note 5
The following types and numbers of documents should be filed with a final simplified prospectus filed pursuant to National Policy No. 36:									
• Final Simplified Prospectus-unsigned	2	1	1	3 (English) 1 (French)	1 (French) 1 (English)	2	1(N.S., P.E.I., Nfld.) 1 English (N.B.) 1 French (N.B.)	1	1
• Final Simplified Prospectus – black lined to show changes from the Preliminary Simplified Prospectus or Pro Forma Simplified Prospectus as the case may be	1	1	1	2	1 (French) 1 (English)	1	1	1	1
• Final Annual Information Form									

Mutual Fund Documents	Alberta	British Columbia	Manitoba	Ontario	Quebec Note 3	Saskatchewan	New Brunswick Newfoundland Nova Scotia Prince Edward Island	Yukon Territory	Northwest Territories
– signed	1	1	1	1 (English) 1(French)	1 (French) 1 (English)	1	1(N.S., P.E.I., Nfld.) 1 English (N.B.) 1 French (N.B.)	1	1
– unsigned	2	1	1	3 (English) 1 (French)	1 (French) 1 (English)	1	1 (N.S., P.E.I., Nfld.) 1 English (N.B.) 1 French (N.B.)	–	–
• Final Annual Information Form – black-lined to show changes from the Preliminary Annual Information Form or Pro Forma Annual Information Form as the case may be	1	1	1	2	1 (French) 1 (English)	1	1	1	1
• Directors' Resolution(s) approving the Final Simplified Prospectus, the Final Annual Information Form and the audited annual financial statements referred to in the Final Simplified Prospectus – certified	1	1	1	1	1	1	1	1	1
• Undertaking to deliver permanent information record – signed	1	1	1	1	1	1	1	1	1
• Audited Annual Financial Statements accompanying the Final Simplified Prospectus if not filed in final form with the Preliminary Simplified Prospectus or with or prior to the filing of the Pro Forma Simplified Prospectus									
– manually signed	1	1	1	1	1 (French) 1 (English)	1	1	1	1
– printed or facsimile signatures	1	1	–	2	2 (French) 1 (English)	1	1	–	–
• Interim Financial Statements accompanying the Final Simplified Prospectus if applicable and if not filed in final form with or prior to the filing of the Pro Forma Simplified Prospectus – unsigned	2	1	1	3	2 (French) 1 (English)	2	1	1	1

Mutual Fund Documents	Alberta	British Columbia	Manitoba	Ontario	Quebec Note 3	Saskatchewan	New Brunswick Newfoundland Nova Scotia Prince Edward Island	Yukon Territory	Northwest Territories
• Statement of Portfolio Transactions if not filed with or prior to the Pro Forma Simplified Prospectus – Certified	–	1	1	1	1 (French) 1 (English)	1	1	1	1
• Report on Sub-Custodians – s. 7.01(4) of N.P. 39	1	1	1	1	1	1	1	1	1
• Auditors' Comfort Letter re Interim Financial Statements (if any) filed with the Final Simplified Prospectus if not previously filed	1	1	1	1	1	1	1	1	1
• Auditors' Consent re Audited Annual Financial Statements referred to in the Simplified Prospectus	2	1	1	1	1	1	1	1	1
• Consents of legal counsel or other tax expert re tax status disclosure	2	1	1	1	1	1	1	1	1
• Cross Reference Sheet									
– in the case of the first filing under National Policy No. 36	1	1	1	1	1	1	1	1	1
– all other filings under National Policy No. 36	1	–	1	–	–	–	–	–	–
• Copies of material contracts requested by Commission staff									
– signed or notarized	1	1	1	1	1	1	1	1	1
– copies of signed or notarized material contracts	–	–	–	–	–	–	–	–	–
• Copy of all "green sheets"	–	–	–	1	1	–	–	–	–
• Notarial copy of filing receipt issued by the principal jurisdiction	–	–	1	–	1	1	1	1	1
• Commercial copies – to be filed subsequent to the issue of the receipt for the Final Simplified Prospectus and Annual Information Form	2	2	2	2 (English) 1 (French)	1+1 (French) 1+1 (English)	2	1 (English) N.B.) 1 (French) (N.B.) 1 (N.S., P.E.I., Nfld.)	1	1

National Policies

Mutual Fund Documents	Alberta	British Columbia	Manitoba	Ontario	Quebec Note 3	Saskatchewan	New Brunswick Newfoundland Nova Scotia Prince Edward Island	Yukon Territory	Northwest Territories
The following types and numbers of documents should be filed with an amendment to the Simplified Prospectus and Annual Information Form filed pursuant to National Policy No. 36:									
• Copy(ies) of amendment									
– signed	1	1	1	1	1 (French) 1 (English)	1	1	1	1
– unsigned	2	1	1	3	1+1 (French) (1+1) (English)	1	1	–	–
• Directors' Resolution approving the Amendment – certified	1	1	1	1	1	1	1	1	1
• Consents of Counsel and other experts if applicable	1	1	1	1	1	1	1	1	1
• Filing Fee (Note 4)	$100	$250	$100	$100	$100	$100	Note 5	Note 5	Note 5
• Notarial copy of filing recipt or other proof of acceptance issued by the principal jurisiction	–	–	1	–	1	1	1	1	1
• Commercial copies – to be filed subsequently	2	2	2	2	1+1 (French) 1 (English)	2	1	1	1

NOTES

1. Where the audited annual financial statements have been previously filed with the securities authorities pursuant to the continuous disclosure requirements of applicable securities legislation, it is not necessary to file a manually signed copy of such financial statements with the pro forma material. However, a copy(ies) bearing printed or facsimile signatures should be filed with the pro forma simplified prospectus for convenience of reference.

2. With respect to all provinces other than Quebec, Ontario and New Brunswick, the French version of the Final Simplified Prospectus and Final Annual Information Form is required to be filed in such Provinces only if the French version is to be used in the Province.

3. With respect to the Province of Quebec the number of copies shown is the number required in respect of each issuer. For example, where a combined document is used (e.g. for a simplified prospectus, annual information form or financial statements) covering three issuers and the table indicates that one copy is required of the document in question, the number of copies required to be filed would be three – i.e. one for each issuer included in the combined document. Also, where the table indicates that the number of copies to be filed is "1 + 1", in the case of the foregoing example, four copies of the combined document would be required to be filed – i.e. one for each issuer included in the combined document plus one additional copy.

4. Filing fees should be made payable to:

British Columbia	—	Minister of Finance
Alberta	—	Provincial Treasurer of Alberta
Saskatchewan	—	Minister of Finance
Manitoba	—	Minister of Finance
Ontario	—	Treasurer of Ontario
Quebec	—	Minister of Finance
New Brunswick	—	Minister of Finance
Nova Scotia	—	Minister of Finance
Prince Edward Island	—	Provincial Secretary
Newfoundland	—	Registrar of Companies
Northwest Territories	—	Government of the Northwest Territories
Yukon Territory	—	Deputy Head, Department of Finance

The filing fees set forth in this table reflect the filing fees in effect at March 1, 1990. Securities legislation in each jurisdiction should be checked at the time of each filing to ascertain whether there have been changes in the filing fees shown in this table.

National Policies

5. Filing Fees per issuer:

Province	Prospectus	AIF	Amendments
New Brunswick	$500 or if New Brunswick is the Principal Jurisdiction $1,000 plus $100 for each additional class of securities	—	$100
Nova Scotia (Note 5A)	$600 or if Nova Scotia is the Principal Jurisdiction $1,000	$250	$100
Prince Edward Island	$400	$300	$100
Newfoundland	$500 plus $200 for each additional Fund/Security	—	$100
Northwest Territories	$200	—	$ 50 (prospectus); $10 AIF
Yukon Territory	$150	—	$50

Note 5A:

The Nova Scotia Securities Commission regards the filing of an Annual Information Form pursuant to National Policy No. 36 as an application, pursuant to s. 5(2) of the Regulations, to vary the prospectus requirements. The fee for such application is $250 which means that the total fee for filing a simplified prospectus and an annual information form is $850 or, if Nova Scotia is the principal jurisdiction, $1,250. Where a combined Annual Information Form and a combined Simplified Prospectus are filed, Nova Scotia considers that each mutual fund which is qualified for sale pursuant to such documents is a separate issuer.

GS1a-8/8a

NATIONAL POLICY NO. 37
TAKE-OVER BIDS: RECIPROCAL CEASE TRADING ORDERS

INTRODUCTION

This policy addresses the policy concerns that arise from take-over bids that are made to all shareholders resident in one or more provinces but are not made to holders resident in one or more other provinces in Canada.

Each of the securities acts in Canada which govern take-over bids embodies the principle of equal treatment of shareholders of a target company. The Canadian securities administrators are concerned that the failure to make a bid in one or more provinces which is made generally in other provinces is prejudicial to the interests of shareholders whose address on the books of the target company is in the excluded province(s). This practice is disruptive of the existing framework of securities regulation in Canada, which aims to ensure that all holders of securities of the target company are treated equally, regardless of the province in which they are resident. In addition, the administrators are concerned that by not technically making an offer in a province offerors may effectively be able to evade the securities requirements of that province while still acquiring the shares held by shareholders in that province. Where a take-over bid is not made in a province shares are simply moved to a jurisdiction in which the bid is made.

The Administrators are of the view that by adopting this National Policy they are furthering the interests of shareholders in their own province and of a national capital market.

POLICY:

1. Where a take-over bid is made in some provinces, but is not made in one or more other provinces, the administrators in the provinces in which the bid is made may issue cease trading orders in respect of the bid. The administrators will generally not issue a cease trading order without providing the offeror an opportunity to address whether the offer offends the principles of this policy.

2. This policy will not be invoked to compel compliance with laws other than securities laws of a province in which the offeror did not make the bid.

3. Where there is a minimal number of security holders in a province, an offeror may apply for an exemption from the take-over-bid requirements of that province, on the basis that the bid will be made to such security holders in accordance with requirements of another jurisdiction whose requirements are acceptable to the administrator in the province to whom the application is made.

    Generally, there will be considered to be a minimal number of security holders in a province where the number of registered holders of securities of the class subject to the bid and of securities convertible into that class is fewer than 50 and the securities held by such security holders constitute less than 2 per cent of the outstanding securities of that class.

4. In appropriate circumstances, and where paragraph 3 is not applicable, an offeror may apply for an exemption from this policy from the administrator(s) in the province(s) in which it is proposing not to make the bid, and, where the administrators in the provinces where the bid will be made receive confirmation that exemptions have been granted in all provinces where the bid will not be made, cease trading orders will not issue.

This policy will come into effect immediately.

NATIONAL POLICY NO. 38
TAKE-OVER BIDS — DEFENSIVE TACTICS

1. The Canadian securities administrators recognize that take-over bids play an important role in the economy by acting as a discipline on corporate management and as a means of reallocating economic resources to their best uses. In considering the merits of a take-over bid, there is a possibility that the interests of management of the target company will differ from those of its shareholders. Management may take one or more of the following actions in response to a bid that it opposes:

    (i) attempt to persuade the shareholders to reject the offer;

    (ii) take action to maximize the return to shareholders including soliciting a higher offer from a third party; or

    (iii) take other defensive measures to defeat the bid.

2. The primary objective of take-over bid legislation is the protection of the bona fide interests of the shareholders of the target company. A secondary objective is to provide a regulatory framework within which take-over bids may proceed in an open and even-handed environment. The rules should favour neither the offeror nor the management of the target company, but should leave the shareholders of the offeree company free to make a fully informed decision. The administrators are concerned that certain defensive measures taken by management may have the effect of denying to shareholders the ability to make such a decision and of frustrating an open take-over bid process.

3. The administrators have determined that it is inappropriate at this time to specify a code of conduct for directors of a target company, in addition to the fiduciary standard required by corporate law. Any fixed code of conduct runs the risk of containing rules that might be insufficient in some cases and excessive in others. However, the administrators wish to advise participants in the capital markets that they are prepared to examine target company tactics in specific cases to determine whether they are abusive of shareholder rights. Prior shareholder approval of corporate action would, in appropriate cases, allay such concerns.

4. Without limiting the foregoing, defensive tactics that may come under scrutiny if undertaken during the course of a bid, or immediately prior to a bid if the board of directors has reason to believe that an offer might be imminent, include:

    (i) the issuance, or the granting of an option on, or the purchase of, securities representing a significant percentage of the outstanding securities of the target company;

    (ii) the sale or acquisition, or granting of an option on, or agreeing to sell or acquire, assets of a material amount; and

    (iii) entering into a contract other than in the normal course of business or taking corporate action other than in the normal course of business.

5. The administrators consider that unrestricted auctions produce the most desirable results in take-over bids and is reluctant to intervene in contested bids. However, the administrators will take appropriate action where they become aware of defensive tactics that will likely result in shareholders being deprived of the ability to respond to a take-over bid or to a competing bid.

6. The administrators appreciate that defensive tactics, including those that may consist of some of the actions listed in paragraph 4, may be taken by a board of directors in genuine search of a better offer. It is only those tactics that are likely to deny or severely limit the ability of the shareholders to respond to a take-over bid or a competing bid, that may result in action by the administrators.

7. As a general rule, the administrators or their staffs will not advise parties as to the propriety of proposed action in a particular case except in the context of a meeting or proceeding of which interested parties have been given notice.

This policy will come into effect immediately.

NATIONAL POLICY No. 39
MUTUAL FUNDS

See Canadian Securities Administrators' Notice 95/2 "Mutual Fund Sales Incentives Point-of-Sale Disclosure Statement" in which the CSA announced that, pending the completion of the overall review of the regulation of investment funds, which was announced by the Chairman of the Ontario Securities Commission in February 1994, the CSA do not expect industry participants to provide a point-of-sale disclosure statement as originally contemplated in Canadian Securities Administrators' Notice 93/1 "Mutual Fund Sales Incentives".

INDEX

PREAMBLE

Unless otherwise expressly provided herein or in another policy statement this policy applies to all mutual funds that offer securities pursuant to a prospectus filed under any securities legislation in force in each Province or Territory of Canada. The requirements of this policy are in addition to the requirements of the securities legislation in force in each Province or Territory of Canada where the prospectus of a mutual fund is filed. For example, in the case of a mutual fund which invests more than 10% of its assets in mortgages or which invests in mortgages other than "permitted mortgages" as defined in Section 1.01 of this policy, National Policy 29 will also apply to such mutual fund.

SECTION 1
INTERPRETATION

SECTION 1.01 – DEFINITIONS

As used in this policy, unless the subject matter or context otherwise requires, the following expressions have the following meanings:

(1) "approved credit rating" means a credit rating which is equal to or higher than the levels indicated in Schedule I attached to this policy and any other credit rating that may be designated in writing by the securities authorities;

(2) "Canadian securities" means all securities that are not foreign securities;

(3) "cash" means

(a) cash on deposit at the mutual fund's custodian, or

(b) treasury bills or other evidences of indebtedness issued, or fully guaranteed as to principal and interest, by:

(i) any of the Federal, Provincial or Territorial Governments of Canada; or

(ii) the Government of the United States or any political subdivision thereof, the Government of any sovereign state or any supranational agency, provided that such treasury bills or other evidences of indebtedness have an approved credit rating;

all maturing in less than one year;

(c) an evidence of deposit, maturing in less than one year, issued, or fully guaranteed as to principal and interest, by:

(i) a bank to which the Bank Act (Canada) applies; or

(ii) a loan corporation or trust company registered under applicable federal or provincial legislation; or

(iii) a foreign financial institution

provided that the short term debt instruments of such institution have an approved credit rating.

(4) "cash cover" means cash held by a mutual fund, in addition to any cash required to be held for other purposes, such as redemptions and other positions in permitted derivatives;

(5) "clearing corporation option" means an option issued by a permitted clearing corporation but does not include an option on futures;

(6) "commodity", means, whether in the original or a processed state, any agricultural product, forest product, product of the sea, mineral, metal or hydrocarbon fuel product or precious stone or other gem but does not include cash;

(7) "contractual plan" means any contract or other arrangement for the purchase of securities of a mutual fund by payments over a specified period or by a specified number of payments where the amount deducted for any one of the payments as sales charges is larger than the amount that would have been deducted from such payment for sales charges if deductions had been made from each payment at a constant rate for the duration of the plan;

(8) "conventional convertible securities", refers to securities of an issuer that are convertible into, or exchangeable for, other securities of the issuer, or an affiliate thereof, provided that the conversion or exchange thereunder cannot be settled or satisfied by a cash payment in lieu thereof;

(9) "conventional warrants or rights", refers to listed securities of an issuer (other than a clearing corporation) which give the holder the right to purchase additional securities of the issuer, or of an affiliate of the issuer, and none of the obligations of the issuer or its affiliate thereunder can be settled or satisfied by a cash payment in lieu thereof;

(10) "dealer manager" means:

(a) any dealer who acts as a portfolio adviser;

(b) any portfolio adviser in which any dealer or any partner, director, officer, salesman or principal shareholder of a dealer directly or indirectly has in the aggregate a more than 10% interest; and

(c) any partner, director or officer of any portfolio adviser referred to in clause (b);

and the expression "dealer" as used in this definition of dealer-manager means a dealer other than a dealer whose activities as a dealer are restricted to acting solely in respect of mutual fund securities;

(11) "dealer managed mutual fund" means a mutual fund whose portfolio adviser is a dealer manager;

(12) "debt-like security" means a security (other than a conventional convertible security or a conventional floating rate debt instrument) which evidences an indebtedness of the issuer where (i) the amount of interest and/or principal to be paid to the holder is linked in whole or in part by formula to

the appreciation or depreciation in the market price, value or level of one or more underlying interests on a predetermined date or dates, or (ii) where the security provides the holder with a right to convert or exchange the security for the underlying interest or to purchase the underlying interest; provided, however, that for the purposes of this policy, if on the date of initial issue the value of the component which is linked to an underlying interest accounts for less than 20% of the total market value of the security, the security shall not be considered to be a debt-like security but instead shall be considered to be debt;

(13) "derivatives" means instruments, agreements or securities the value of which is based upon the market price, value or level of an index, or the market price or value of a security, commodity, economic indicator or financial instrument other than:

   (a) conventional convertible securities;

   (b) asset backed securities;

   (c) securities of a mutual fund;

   (d) index participation units;

   (e) securities of a non-redeemable fund;

   (f) government or corporate strip bonds;

   (g) listed equity dividend shares of subdivided equity or fixed income securities;

(14) "equivalent debt" shall mean any debt which ranks equally with, or, if there is no such debt, is subordinate to, the claim for payment which may arise under an over-the-counter option, forward contract or debt-like security;

(15) "foreign securities" means securities issued by an issuer that is constituted under the laws of a jurisdiction other than Canada or a Province or Territory of Canada and carries on a substantial portion of its activities outside of Canada;

(16) "forward contract" means a contract to:

   (a) make or take delivery of the specified interest underlying the contract; or

   (b) settle in cash in lieu of delivery;

at a designated future date at a price agreed upon when the contract is entered into, where the contract is neither traded on a permitted futures exchange nor issued by a permitted clearing corporation;

(17) "futures contract" means a contract traded on a permitted futures exchange to:

   (a) make or take delivery of the underlying interest of the contract at a future date; or

   (b) settle the difference between the future value of a specified quantity of the underlying interest at the time that the contract was entered into and its value at the expiration date;

pursuant to standardized terms and conditions as set out in the by-laws, rules or regulations of the futures exchange upon which the contract is entered into, where trades in such contracts are cleared by a clearing corporation;

(18) "government securities" means bonds, debentures or other evidences of indebtedness (other than debt-like securities), having a term of one year or more, issued or fully guaranteed as to principal and interest by any of the Federal, Provincial or Territorial Governments of Canada, or the Government of the United States of America, or the bonds, debentures or other evidences of indebtedness (other than debt-like securities) having an approved credit rating and a term of one year or more, issued or guaranteed by the government of any sovereign state or any supranational agency;

(19) "hedging" or to "hedge" means to enter into a transaction, or a series of

transactions, the intended effect of which, or the intended cumulative effect of which, is the offset or reduction of the risk associated with all or a portion of an existing investment or group of investments. A transaction which offsets or reduces the risk associated with all or a portion of an existing investment, or group of investments, is a transaction, or a series of transactions, of equivalent underlying market exposure that is opposite to the position, or the portion of the position, being hedged. For the transaction to offset or reduce the risk associated with an investment, or group of investments, there must be a high degree of correlation between changes in the market value of the investment, or group of investments, being hedged and the instrument or instruments with which the position is hedged. There need not be complete congruence between the hedging instrument, or instruments, and the position being hedged provided that it is reasonable to regard the one as a hedging instrument for the other, taking into account the closeness of the relationship between fluctuations in the price of the two. It is essential that changes in the price of the hedging instrument do not more than offset the effect of price changes in the investment, or group of investments, being hedged. The term "hedging" shall also include the hedging of all or a portion of the currency exposure of an existing investment or group of investments either directly or by currency cross hedging. The term "hedge" shall mean the investment or position resulting from the activity of hedging.

(20) "illiquid investments" means the investments which are referred to in Section 2.06;

(21) "listed" means listed on a stock exchange, options exchange, permitted futures exchange or quoted on the National Association of Securities Dealers Automated Quotation System;

(22) "listed warrants", means listed securities of an issuer (other than a clearing corporation) which are put or call options, the capital shares of subdivided equity securities, or warrants or rights (including conventional warrants or rights and index and commodity warrants);

(23) "long position", with respect to:

    (a) clearing corporation options, over-the-counter options and listed warrants, refers to a mutual fund holding a position which entitles the mutual fund to purchase, sell, receive or deliver the underlying interest (or pay or receive cash in lieu thereof);

    (b) futures and forward contracts, refers to a mutual fund holding a position which obliges the mutual fund to accept delivery of the underlying interest (or pay or receive cash in lieu thereof);

    (c) call options on futures, refers to a mutual fund holding a position which entitles the mutual fund to elect to assume a long position in futures; and

    (d) put options on futures, refers to a mutual fund holding a position which entitles the mutual fund to elect to assume a short position in futures.

(24) "manager" means a person or company who has the power or responsibility to direct the affairs of the mutual fund but does not include a person or company who is not associated or affiliated with the promoter or trustee of the mutual fund and whose duties are limited to managing the investment portfolio of the mutual fund and the provision of investment advice in connection therewith;

(25) "option on futures" means an option cleared by a clearing corporation and traded on a permitted futures exchange to assume a long or short position in a futures contract;

(26) "over-the-counter option" refers to an option which is neither listed nor cleared by a permitted clearing corporation;

(27) "permitted clearing corporation" means any of the clearing corporations identified in Schedule II hereto, or any other clearing corporation that may be recognized by the securities authorities;

(28) "permitted derivatives" means clearing corporation options, futures con- tracts, options on futures, over-the-counter options, forward contracts, debt- like securities and listed warrants;

(29) "permitted futures exchange" means any of the futures exchanges iden- tified in Schedule III hereto or any other futures exchange designated in writing by the securities authorities;

(30) "permitted mortgages" means mortgages guaranteed or insured by the Government of Canada or by the Government of any Province of Canada or by any agency of any such Government and includes mortgages insured under the National Housing Act (Canada) or similar provincial statutes;

(31) "portfolio adviser" means a person or company that provides investment advice pursuant to a contractual arrangement with the mutual fund or its trustees or other legal representative or with the manager of the mutual fund under which the mutual fund is provided with investment advice, alone or together with administrative or management services, for valuable consideration;

(32) "portfolio securities" includes all cash, gold, permitted derivatives, mort- gages and securities owned by the mutual fund;

(33) "principal distributor" means a person or company through whom securities of a mutual fund are distributed pursuant to a contractual arrangement with the mutual fund or its trustees or other legal representative or with the manager of the mutual fund providing for an exclusive right to dis- tribute the securities of the mutual fund in a particular area or any feature which gives or is intended to give such person or company a material competitive advantage over others in respect of the distribution of the securities of the mutual fund;

(34) "prospectus" means a conventional prospectus or a simplified prospectus, together with the related annual information form, and all amendments thereto;

(35) "restricted securities" means securities, the resale of which is restricted or limited by means of a representation, undertaking or agreement by the mutual fund or by the mutual fund's predecessor in title or by law, but "restricted securities" do not include permitted derivatives;

(36) "short position", with respect to:

(a) clearing corporation options, over-the-counter options and listed war- rants refers to a mutual fund having a position which, at the election of another, obliges the mutual fund to purchase, sell, receive or deliver the underlying interest (or pay or receive cash in lieu thereof);

(b) futures and forward contracts refers to a mutual fund holding a position which obliges the mutual fund to deliver the underlying interest (or pay or receive cash in lieu thereof);

(c) call options on futures, refers to a mutual fund holding a position which, at the election of another, obliges the mutual fund to assume a short position in futures; and

(d) put options on futures, refers to a mutual fund holding a position which, at the election of another, obliges the mutual fund to assume a long position in futures.

(37) "standard investment restrictions and practices" means the investment restrictions and investment practices set out in Sections 2.04 and 2.05;

(38) "underlying market exposure" with respect to a position in:

(a) an option, refers, at any time, to the quantity of the underlying interest of the option position multiplied by the current market value of one unit of such underlying interest, multiplied, in turn, by the option's delta, where delta is a positive or negative number that measures the sensitivity of an option's market value to changes in the value of the underlying interest of the option; or

(b) a futures or forward contract, refers, at any time, to the quantity of the underlying interest in respect of such position multiplied by the current market value of one unit of such underlying interest.

SECTION 1.02 – APPROVAL OF SECURITIES AUTHORITIES

Where this policy contemplates that action may not be taken without the approval of the securities authorities, the approval of the securities authorities to any such action being taken, unless otherwise expressly provided, shall be considered to be given if the action is disclosed in a prospectus and a receipt is issued for the prospectus by the respective securities authorities with which the prospectus is filed, provided that at or prior to the time of filing the prospectus all such matters requiring the approval of the securities authorities are expressly brought to the attention of the securities authorities by means of a separate letter or memorandum addressed to the securities authorities specifying the matters which require the approval of the securities authorities and indicating the reasons why consideration should be given by the securities authorities to granting such approval.

SECTION 2
INVESTMENTS

SECTION 2.01 – INVESTMENT POLICY STATEMENTS

Where a mutual fund intends to:

(1)   invest a specific portion of its assets in Canadian securities or in foreign securities;

(2)   invest in foreign securities;

(3)   invest a specific portion of its assets in a particular type of security (e.g. bonds, common shares, preferred shares, money market instruments);

(4)   concentrate its investments in a particular class or kind of industry;

(5)   invest in property other than securities;

(6)   invest in or use permitted derivatives;

the policy shall be stated in the prospectus of the mutual fund.

SECTION 2.02 – QUALIFICATION FOR PLANS REGISTERED UNDER THE INCOME TAX ACT (CANADA)

Where the securities of the mutual fund are or will be a qualified investment within the meaning of the Income Tax Act (Canada) for retirement savings plans, deferred profit sharing plans or other savings plans registered under the Income Tax Act (Canada) and where the mutual fund is or will be recognized as a registered investment within the meaning of such Act, the relevant information and the effect of such qualification shall be disclosed in the prospectus of the mutual fund, together with a statement as to the limitations, if any, imposed by such Act on the portion of such plans which may be invested in the securities of the mutual fund without subjecting such plans to taxes or penalties under such Act.

If the securities of the mutual fund are not or will not be qualified investments for such plans, a statement to that effect shall be made in the prospectus.

SECTION 2.03 – "LEGAL FOR LIFE" STATEMENTS

A prospectus may not contain reference to an opinion that the securities issued by the mutual fund are eligible investments for pension funds, insurance companies, trust companies or loan companies governed by specified statutes unless the mutual fund satisfies the securities authorities that the reference to the eligibility opinion is not misleading in the context having regard to the fact that the securities of the mutual fund are being offered for sale on a continuous basis rather than being sold on the fixed date as at which the eligibility opinion is given as well as to any other relevant facts.

SECTION 2.04 – INVESTMENT RESTRICTIONS

(1)   A mutual fund shall not without the prior approval of the securities authorities:

(a)   purchase securities of any issuer, (other than the securities issued or guaranteed by the Government of Canada or an agency thereof or by the Government of any Province of Canada or any agency thereof or by the Government of the United States of America or an agency thereof) if, after giving effect thereto, more than 10% of the net assets of the mutual fund, taken at market value at the time of such purchase, would be invested in the securities of such issuer;

(b) purchase securities of any issuer, (other than the securities issued or guaranteed by the Government of Canada or an agency thereof or by the Government of any Province of Canada or any agency thereof or by the Government of the United States of America or an agency thereof) if, after giving effect thereto, the mutual fund would hold more than 10% of any class or series of a class of securities of such issuer, provided that for the purpose of making this determination, all debt obligations of an issuer maturing in less than one year and all unlisted permitted derivatives of an issuer, shall be regarded as a single series of a class of securities;

(c) purchase real estate;

(d) purchase mortgages other than permitted mortgages;

(e) purchase permitted mortgages if following such purchase more than 10% of the total assets of the mutual fund (taken at market value at the time of such purchase) would consist of permitted mortgages;

(f) purchase restricted securities if following such purchase more than 10% of the total assets of the mutual fund (taken at market value at the time of purchase) would consist of illiquid investments;

(g) purchase securities for the purpose of exercising control or management of the issuer of such securities;

(h) purchase gold or gold certificates if following such purchase more than 10% of the total assets of the mutual fund (taken at market value at the time of such purchase) would consist of gold and gold certificates, provided that any purchase of gold certificates shall be restricted to gold certificates issued by an issuer approved by the securities authorities;

(i) purchase or sell derivatives except for permitted derivatives, and except as specifically permitted by this policy;

(j) purchase or sell commodities, provided that the restriction herein contained will not restrict the mutual fund from purchasing or selling gold or gold certificates to the extent that such purchase or sale is not otherwise restricted pursuant to Section 2.04(1)(h);

(k) invest in securities of any other mutual fund, provided that nothing herein contained will prevent a mutual fund from investing in:

(i) securities of any other mutual fund where:

(A) adequate provisions are made to address any conflicts which result in the mutual funds by reason of such investment and such provisions are described in the prospectus of the mutual fund; and

(B) the arrangement between or in respect of the mutual funds is such so as to avoid the duplication of management fees and sales charges and such arrangement is described in the prospectus of the mutual fund; and

(C) either such other mutual fund is qualified for sale pursuant to a prospectus which has been filed and accepted in the Provinces or Territories of Canada where the securities of the mutual fund are qualified for sale pursuant to a prospectus which has been filed and accepted in such Provinces or Territories of Canada; or

(D) the only way that the mutual fund may invest in a foreign country is through a mutual fund established with the approval of the Government of such foreign country and there is disclosure in the prospectus of the mutual fund of the risk factors which may be associated with the investment in foreign countries such as the imposition of foreign investment and exchange control laws and the fact that financial and other reporting and auditing standards and practices and disclosure may be less extensive than comparable requirements in Canada and the United States; or

(ii) Toronto 35 Index Participation Units which are listed or are qualified for sale pursuant to a prospectus which has been filed and accepted in the Provinces and Territories of Canada;

(2) A mutual fund may purchase, sell or otherwise take a position in a permitted derivative for non-hedging purposes, provided that, for the purpose of complying with Section 2.04(1), the mutual fund must determine its exposure to the investment that forms the underlying interest of the permitted derivative by adding:

(i) the underlying market exposure that the position in the permitted derivative provides to such investment;

to:

(ii) the underlying market exposure to such investment provided by other permitted derivatives, if any, held by the mutual fund for non-hedging purposes; and

(iii) the exposure represented by the direct holding of such investment, if any, held by the mutual fund,

provided that, with respect to a permitted derivative which has underlying market exposure to a stock or bond index that includes the investment as a component, the market exposure that such investment represents in such index shall not be included in the foregoing calculation where the investment represents less than 10% of the stock or bond index.

(3) The provisions of Section 2.04(1)(d) and (1)(e) do not apply to a mutual fund that is subject to and complies with the provisions of National Policy No. 29.

(4) With respect to the provisions of Section 2.04(1)(k)(i):

(a) The securities authorities recommend that representatives of a mutual fund which proposes to invest in another mutual fund approach the securities authorities prior to filing any material to review the adequacy of the provisions proposed to be made to address any conflicts which result in the mutual funds by reason of such investment.

(b) The prior approval of the securities authorities is required to be obtained before a mutual fund may:

(i) invest more than 10% of its net assets (taken at market value at the time of such investment) in another mutual fund, or

(ii) hold more than 10% of any class or series of a class of securities of another mutual fund.

In determining whether or not such approvals will be granted a number of factors will be considered by the securities authorities including what provisions have been or will be made to address concerns such as the compatibility of the fundamental investment objectives of the mutual funds, any conflicts which result in the mutual funds by reason of such investment, the right of securityholders of the mutual fund to receive notice of and to vote upon fundamental changes occurring in the other mutual fund, the arrangements for continuous disclosure materials of the other mutual fund to be provided to the securityholders of the mutual fund, whether or not there are redemption fees or other charges if securityholders of the mutual fund should redeem the securities of the mutual fund which they own in response to a fundamental change occurring in the other mutual fund. Accordingly, the securities authorities recommend that, if a mutual fund is contemplating an investment in another mutual fund which will exceed the limits referred to in clauses (i) or (ii) of this paragraph, representatives of the mutual fund should approach the securities authorities prior to filing any material to determine whether such an investment would be permitted and if so what conditions will be applicable to such an investment.

National Policies

SECTION 2.05 – INVESTMENT PRACTICES

A mutual fund shall not without the prior approval of the securities authorities:

(1) pledge any of its assets (except as may be required for posting margin to effect the transactions described in Section 2.07) or mortgage any of its assets or borrow money except as a temporary measure for the purpose of accommodating requests for the redemption of securities issued by the mutual fund while effecting an orderly liquidation of portfolio securities, and then only if provided that after giving effect to such borrowing the outstanding amount of all such borrowings does not exceed 5% of the net assets of the mutual fund taken at market value at the time of such borrowing;

(2) invest more than 10% of its net assets (taken at market value at the time of investment) in illiquid investments;

(3) purchase securities on margin, and, for greater certainty, margin pledged on account for positions in permitted derivatives as described in Section 2.07 shall not be deemed to be the purchase of securities on margin for the purpose of this Section 2.05(3);

(4) sell securities short, other than as specifically permitted by Section 2.07;

(5) purchase any security which may by its terms require the mutual fund to make a contribution in addition to the payment of the purchase price, other than a permitted derivative pursuant to a transaction described in Section 2.07 and provided that this restriction shall not apply to the purchase of securities which are paid for on an instalment basis where the total purchase price and the amount of all such instalments is fixed at the time the first instalment is paid;

(6) engage in the business of underwriting securities or marketing to the public securities of any other issuer;

(7) lend money, provided that this restriction shall not apply so as to prevent the purchase of debt obligations;

(8) lend portfolio securities;

(9) guarantee the securities or obligations of any other person or corporation;

(10) purchase securities other than through normal market facilities unless the purchase price approximates the prevailing market price or is negotiated on an arm's length basis;

(11) contract with the manager or the portfolio adviser or the trustee of the mutual fund or with any director or officer of the mutual fund or of the manager or of the portfolio adviser or of the trustee of the mutual fund or with any of their respective associates or affiliates or with any entity having fewer than 100 participants of record of which any director or officer of the mutual fund may be a director, officer or participant as principals in making purchases or sales of portfolio securities.

SECTION 2.06 – ILLIQUID INVESTMENTS

The expression "illiquid investments" as used in this policy means investments which may not be readily disposed of, in a marketplace where such investments are normally purchased and sold and public quotations in common use in respect thereof are available, at an amount at least equal to the amount at which such investments are valued for the purpose of determining the net asset value of the mutual fund. Where in the case of any investment there is no marketplace where such investment may normally be purchased and sold and public quotations in common use in respect thereof are available, such investment will be considered to be an illiquid investment notwithstanding the fact that the manager or the portfolio adviser of a mutual fund or a director or officer of the manager or portfolio adviser of a mutual fund or any of their respective associates or affiliates has agreed to purchase the investment. Examples of illiquid investments include but are not limited to: limited partnership interests that are not listed and securities of a private company. Over-the-counter options entered into for non-hedging purposes are deemed to be illiquid investments. Over-the-counter options entered into for hedging purposes in accordance with this policy are not deemed to be illiquid investments.

SECTION 2.07 – PERMITTED TRANSACTIONS IN DERIVATIVES

(1) Where consistent with its expressed investment objectives and not contrary to its investment restrictions and subject to the conditions as herein provided, a mutual fund may:

(a) for hedging purposes only;

    (i) use permitted derivatives;

(b) with respect to options, options on futures, listed warrants and debt-like securities which have an options component:

    (i) purchase clearing corporation options, over-the-counter options, options on futures, listed warrants and debt-like securities which have an options component, provided that not more than 10% of the net assets of the mutual fund, taken at market value at the time of such purchase, would consist of such instruments;

    (ii) write clearing corporation call options or over-the-counter call options, provided that, as long as the position remains open, the mutual fund holds, and continues to hold:

        (A) an equivalent quantity of the underlying interest of such options; or

        (B) a right or obligation to acquire an equivalent quantity of the underlying interest of the options and cash cover in an amount which together with margin on account in respect of such position is not less than the amount, if any, by which the strike price of the right or obligation to acquire the underlying interest exceeds the strike price of the written options; or

        (C) any combination thereof, from time to time;

    (iii) write clearing corporation put options or over-the-counter put options, provided that, as long as the position remains open, the mutual fund holds, and continues to hold:

        (A) a right or obligation to sell an equivalent quantity of the underlying interest of the options and cash cover in an amount which together with margin on account in respect of such positions is not less than the amount, if any, by which the strike price of the written options exceeds the strike price of the right or obligation to sell the underlying interest; or

        (B) cash cover in an amount which, together with margin on account in respect of the options position, is not less than the strike price of the options; or

        (C) any combination thereof, from time to time.

(c) with respect to futures, forwards and debt-like securities which have a component which is a long position in a forward contract:

    (i) open and continue to maintain long positions in futures contracts, forward contracts or debt-like securities which have a component which is a long position in a forward contract, provided that the mutual fund holds, and continues to hold, cash cover in an amount which, together with margin on account in respect of the permitted derivative and the market value of the permitted derivative, is not less than, on a daily marked-to-market basis, the underlying market exposure of the permitted derivative;

    (ii) open and continue to maintain short positions in futures contracts or forward contracts, provided that the mutual fund holds and continues to hold:

        (A) an equivalent quantity of the underlying interest of such contracts; or

        (B) a right or obligation to acquire an equivalent quantity of the underlying interest of the contracts and cash cover together with margin on account in respect of such position in an amount which is not less than the amount, if any, by which the strike price of the right or obligation to acquire the underlying interest exceeds the forward price of such contracts; or

(C) any combination thereof, from time to time;

(iii) assume the position in the futures contracts underlying options on futures upon the exercise of the option, provided that the mutual fund complies with the other provisions of this paragraph (c).

(2) In addition to the provisions of Section 2.07(1):

(a) a mutual fund that has written a clearing corporation call option or an over-the-counter call option, and, in accordance with sub-paragraph 2.07(1)(b)(ii)(B), holds the right or obligation to acquire an equivalent quantity of the underlying interest, must ensure that the expiry date of the right or obligation to acquire the underlying interest occurs on or after the expiry date of the written call option;

(b) a mutual fund that has written a clearing corporation put option or an over-the-counter put option, and, in accordance with sub-paragraph 2.07(1)(b)(iii)(A), holds the right or obligation to sell an equivalent quantity of the underlying interest, must ensure that the expiry date of the right or obligation to sell the underlying interest occurs on or after the expiry date of the written put option;

(c) a mutual fund may not purchase an over-the-counter option or enter into a forward contract unless:

(i) the over-the-counter option or forward contract has a term not exceeding three years, and, at the time of the transaction, the over-the-counter option or forward contract, or equivalent debt of the issuer of such option or contract, has an approved credit rating; or

(ii) the over-the-counter option or forward contract has a term exceeding three years but not exceeding five years and, at the time of the transaction:

(A) the over-the-counter option or forward contract provides the mutual fund with a right, at its election, to eliminate its exposure to the issuer of the over-the-counter option or forward contract after 3 years; and

(B) the over-the-counter option or forward contract, or equivalent debt of the other party thereto has, at the time of the transaction, an approved credit rating.

In the event that the credit rating in respect of an over-the-counter option or forward contract, or the credit rating of the equivalent debt of the issuer thereof, falls below the level of approved credit rating during the term thereof, the mutual fund must take such steps as are reasonably required to close out its position in an orderly fashion with respect thereto.

(3) Notwithstanding anything else provided for in this policy statement, a mutual fund may enter into trades to close out positions in permitted derivatives and the cash cover held to cover the underlying market exposure may be released to the extent a position is closed out.

(4) In addition to purchases of derivatives permitted under sub-paragraphs 2.07(1)(a) and (b), nothing herein contained will prevent:

(a) the acquisition of securities that have attached thereto conventional warrants or rights;

(b) the acquisition of securities that are offered in units consisting in part of conventional warrants or rights; or

(c) the acquisition of conventional warrants or rights that are issued to the mutual fund as a holder of any security.

(5) (a) A mutual fund may only invest in or use clearing corporation options and over-the-counter options if the portfolio adviser advising with respect to such investments or uses is registered as an adviser and

meets the proficiency requirements for advising with respect to options in the principal jurisdiction in Canada in which the portfolio adviser carries on its business.

(b) A mutual fund may only invest in or use futures and options on futures if the portfolio adviser advising with respect to such investments or uses is registered as an adviser in a jurisdiction within Canada where such registration is required and meets the proficiency requirements for advising with respect to futures and options on futures in such jurisdiction.

(c) Notwithstanding subsections 2.07(5)(a) and (b), a mutual fund may invest in or use clearing corporation options, over-the-counter options, futures and options on futures, as the case may be, provided that:

    (i) a portfolio adviser of the mutual fund, qualified as provided in paragraphs (a) or (b), as the case may be, receives advice in respect of such investment or use from a portfolio adviser whose principal place of business is located outside of Canada ("non-resident adviser") so long as:

        (A) the obligations and duties of the non-resident adviser are set out in a written agreement with the portfolio adviser; and

        (B) the portfolio adviser agrees, in a document providing rights to the mutual fund, to be responsible for the advice received from the non-resident adviser; or

    (ii) if the mutual fund is advised directly by a non-resident adviser, the mutual fund receives the prior approval of the securities authorities to the use of such non-resident adviser. In applying for such approval the mutual fund must provide the following information:

        (A) the name of the non-resident adviser;

        (B) the address of the principal place of business of the non-resident adviser;

        (C) the assets under the administration of the non-resident adviser;

        (D) the jurisdictions in which the non-resident adviser is registered, if any;

        (E) the registration requirements to which the non-resident adviser is subject; and

        (F) such other information as the securities authorities may require.

In considering whether to grant such approval the securities authorities may require the registration of the non-resident adviser where the non-resident adviser is not registered in a comparable jurisdiction or does not meet proficiency requirements comparable to the requirements in the jurisdictions within Canada that impose a registration requirement and in making such determination the securities authorities may consider whether the non-resident adviser has the equivalent educational qualifications or experience.

(6) A mutual fund whose constating documents do not prohibit it from using a permitted derivative and which intends to use such a permitted derivative must in its annual information form or prospectus:

    (a) explain how the permitted derivative will be used in conjunction with other securities to achieve the mutual fund's investment and risk objectives; and

    (b) describe the limits of and risks involved in the mutual fund's intended use of the permitted derivative; and provide an abbreviated version of such information in its simplified prospectus.

(7)   A mutual fund using permitted derivatives in accordance with this policy is not required to comply with the rules and policies applicable to a commodity pool and shall not describe itself as a commodity pool or as a vehicle for investors to participate in the speculative trading of, or leveraged investment in, derivatives.

(8)   Writing over-the-counter options and selling forward transactions constitutes distributions of securities for which a prospectus may be required or for which specific or blanket exemptive relief may be necessary under the applicable securities legislation. The mutual fund, as the writer of the over-the-counter option or seller of the forward contract may be, in effect, an issuer distributing securities. Accordingly a mutual fund and its advisers, before writing over-the-counter options or selling forward contracts should ensure that such distribution of derivatives is in compliance with the applicable securities legislation.

SECTION 2.08 – DISCLOSURE IN PROSPECTUS OF ADHERENCE TO STANDARD INVESTMENT RESTRICTIONS AND PRACTICES

It shall not be necessary to state the standard investment restrictions and practices in a prospectus provided that:

(1)   the prospectus includes a statement to the effect that

(i) the mutual fund has adopted the standard investment restrictions and practices;

(ii) the standard investment restrictions and practices are deemed to be incorporated in the prospectus; and

(iii) a copy of the standard investment restrictions and practices will be provided by or on behalf of the mutual fund to any person requesting the same;

(2)   any investment restrictions or investment practices in addition to the standard investment restrictions and practices that have been adopted by the mutual fund (including any variations from the standard investment restrictions and practices that have been approved by the securities authorities) are set forth in the prospectus.

SECTION 3
NEW MUTUAL FUNDS

SECTION 3.01 – INITIAL INVESTMENT IN A NEW MUTUAL FUND

The initial investment in a new mutual fund shall be at least $150,000, which investment shall be provided by the manager of the mutual fund or by the portfolio adviser or promoter or sponsor of the mutual fund or by the directors, officers or shareholders of the manager of the mutual fund or of the portfolio adviser or promoter or sponsor of the mutual fund. The securities issued upon such investment shall not be redeemed until an additional $500,000 has been received from other investors. Where such initial investment has not been provided, the minimum amount which must be subscribed through a "best efforts offering" is $500,000. If a mutual fund consists of sections or parts, each section or part is considered to be a separate mutual fund.

SECTION 3.02 – PROHIBITION AGAINST REIMBURSEMENT OF ORGANIZATION COSTS

The costs of incorporation or formation and of the initial organization of the mutual fund (including, without limitation, the costs of the preparation and filing of the initial prospectus and the preliminary prospectus filed in connection therewith) shall be borne by either the promoter or the sponsor or the manager of the mutual fund and the mutual fund shall not reimburse any of them for these expenses or assume any of such expenses.

SECTION 3.03 – DESIGNATION OF SECURITIES

Securities issued by an unincorporated mutual fund shall be described by a term other than "shares".

SECTION 4
DEALER MANAGED MUTUAL FUNDS

SECTION 4.01 – QUALIFICATIONS OF DEALER MANAGER

Any registered dealer may act as a dealer manager provided that:

(1) the securities authorities are satisfied that the dealer manager has one or more individuals who are directly responsible for the portfolio management of the mutual fund who would qualify, if separately registered, for registration as an investment counsel and portfolio manager; and

(2) the dealer manager complies with the laws and policies from time to time promulgated and applicable to portfolio managers.

SECTION 4.02 – PROHIBITED INVESTMENTS

A dealer managed mutual fund shall not knowingly make an investment in any class of securities of any issuer,[1] other than those issued or guaranteed by the Government of Canada or by an agency thereof or by the Government of a Province of Canada or by an agency thereof,

(a) for which any person or company who is a dealer manager of such mutual fund or who is an associate or affiliate of such dealer manager has acted as an underwriter in the distribution of such class of securities of the issuer (except as a member of the selling group distributing 5% or less of the securities underwritten) for a period of at least 60 days following the conclusion of the distribution of the underwritten securities to the public; or

(b) of which any partner, director, officer or employee of a person or company who is a dealer manager of such mutual fund or any partner, director, officer or employee of any affiliate or associate of such dealer manager is an officer or director, provided that this prohibition shall not apply where any such partner, director, officer or employee does not:

(i) participate in the formulation of investment decisions made on behalf of the dealer managed mutual fund,

(ii) have access prior to implementation to investment decisions made on behalf of the dealer managed mutual fund, and

(iii) influence (other than through research, statistical and other reports generally available to clients) the investment decisions made on behalf of the dealer managed mutual fund.

It shall not be necessary to state the foregoing provisions in a prospectus if the constating documents of the mutual fund or the laws applicable to the mutual fund contain substantially similar provisions to those set out in this Section 4.02.

SECTION 4.03 – DEALER MANAGER ACTING AS PRINCIPAL

Notwithstanding the provisions of Section 2.05(11), the dealer manager of a dealer managed mutual fund or an affiliate or associate of the dealer manager may contract with the dealer managed mutual fund as principal in making purchases or sales of portfolio securities, provided that the price payable for the portfolio securities, in the case of a purchase of portfolio securities, is not more than the ask price of such portfolio securities as reported by any public quotations in common use which may be available and, in the case of a sale of portfolio securities, is not less than the bid price of such portfolio securities as reported by any public quotations in common use which may be available.

SECTION 5
CERTIFICATES

SECTION 5.01 – MANAGER TO SIGN PROSPECTUS

In addition to any other certificates that may be required to be signed by any person or body corporate under applicable law, the manager of a mutual fund shall sign the same certificate in a prospectus that is required to be signed by the mutual

---

1 including certain permitted derivatives

fund, which certificate shall be signed by the chief executive officer of the manager, by the chief financial officer of the manager, and on behalf of the board of directors of the manager; by any two directors of the manager, other than the foregoing, duly authorized to sign.

Where the manager has only three directors, the certificate shall be signed by all of the directors of the manager.

Where the securities authorities are satisfied upon evidence satisfactory to them that either or both of the chief executive officer or chief financial officer of the manager is for adequate cause not available to sign the certificate, the securities authorities may permit the certificate to be signed by any other responsible officer or officers of the manager in lieu of either or both of the chief executive officer or chief financial officer.

Where the manager of the mutual fund is a body corporate, evidence of the authority of the officers and directors of the manager who sign the certificate on behalf of the manager must be filed with the prospectus.

SECTION 5.02 – TRUSTEED MUTUAL FUNDS

Where a mutual fund is established as a trust, the certificate required to be signed by the mutual fund shall be signed as follows:

> (i) where any trustee of the mutual fund is an individual, by each individual who is a trustee or by a duly authorized attorney of such individual, with evidence of such attorney's authority to sign the certificate being filed with the prospectus;
>
> (ii) where any trustee of the mutual fund is a body corporate, by the duly authorized signing officer(s) of such body corporate, with evidence of the authority of such signing officer(s) to sign the certificate being filed with the prospectus;

provided that, where the declaration of trust establishing the mutual fund delegates the authority to do so, the certificate required to be signed by the mutual fund may be signed by the person to whom such authority is delegated with evidence of the authority of the person signing the certificate to be filed with the prospectus and, where such signing authority has been delegated to a body corporate, with evidence of the authority of the person signing the prospectus on behalf of the body corporate, also to be filed with the prospectus.

Notwithstanding the foregoing, where any trustee of the mutual fund is also the manager of the mutual fund, the certificate required to be signed by the mutual fund shall, in addition to any other requirements that there may be under applicable law, be signed in the same manner as is prescribed in Section 5.01.

SECTION 6
APPROVAL OF SECURITYHOLDERS FOR CERTAIN CHANGES

SECTION 6.01 – MATTERS REQUIRING SECURITYHOLDER APPROVAL

A meeting of the securityholders of the mutual fund shall be convened to consider and approve:

> (a) a change (other than a change referred to in Section 6.03) in any contract or the entering into of any new contract as a result of which the basis of the calculation of the fees or of other expenses that are charged to a mutual fund could result in an increase in charges to the mutual fund;
>
> (b) a change of the manager of the mutual fund (other than to an affiliate of the present manager);
>
> (c) any change in the fundamental investment objectives of the mutual fund;
>
> (d) any change of auditors;
>
> (e) any decrease in the frequency of calculating net asset value;
>
> (f) subject to Section 6.03(3), the commencement of the use by the mutual fund of permitted derivatives.
>
> (g) any other matter which is required by the constating documents of the mutual fund or by the laws applicable to the mutual fund or by any

agreement to be submitted to a vote of the securityholders of the mutual fund.

It shall not be necessary to state the foregoing requirements in a prospectus if the constating documents of the mutual fund or the laws applicable to the mutual fund confer substantially similar rights of approval on securityholders of the mutual fund;

SECTION 6.02 – APPROVAL OF SECURITYHOLDERS

Unless a greater majority is required by the constating documents of the mutual fund or by the laws applicable to the mutual fund or by any applicable agreement, the approval of the securityholders of the mutual fund shall be deemed to be given if expressed by a resolution passed at a meeting or meetings of the securityholders of the mutual fund duly called and held for the purpose of considering the same by at least a majority of the votes cast.

SECTION 6.03 – CIRCUMSTANCES IN WHICH APPROVAL OF SECURITY-
HOLDERS NOT REQUIRED

The approval of securityholders is not required to be obtained for a change referred to in Section 6.01(a) where:

(1) the mutual fund contracts at arm's length and with parties other than the manager of the mutual fund or an associate or affiliate of the manager of the mutual fund, for all or part of the services it requires to carry on its operations and the prospectus makes reference to the fact that, although the approval of securityholders will not be obtained before making the changes, securityholders will be given at least 60 days notice before the effective date of any change which is to be made which could result in an increase in charges to the mutual fund and such notice is actually given; or

(2) the mutual fund has neither a sales charge nor a redemption fee (other than a redemption fee applicable only to redemptions effected within 90 days of the purchase of the securities of the mutual fund) if the prospectus of the mutual fund indicates that securityholders will be given at least 60 days notice before the effective date of any change which is to be made which could result in an increase in charges to the mutual fund and such notice is actually given.

The approval of security holders is not required to be obtained for a change referred to in Section 6.01(f) where:

(3) a change is made to permit the mutual fund to use permitted derivatives in accordance with this policy, the change would not otherwise require securityholder approval pursuant to Section 6.01, securityholders will be given at least 60 days notice of the change before the effective date of any such change, the notice includes the disclosure required by Section 2.07(6) of this policy and such notice is actually given.

SECTION 6.04 – FORMALITIES WITH RESPECT TO MEETINGS OF
SECURITYHOLDERS

A meeting of securityholders of a mutual fund called to consider any matter referred to in Section 6.01 shall be called on at least 21 days notice and the provisions of National Policy No. 41, to the extent that they are applicable to such meeting, shall be complied with in respect thereof. The notice calling the meeting shall contain or be accompanied by a statement which includes:

(1) a description of the change proposed and, where the matter is one referred to in Section 6.01(a), the effect that it would have had on the management expense ratio of the mutual fund had the change been in force throughout the mutual fund's last completed financial year;

(2) the date of the proposed implementation; and

(3) all other information and documents necessary to comply with the applicable proxy solicitation requirements in respect of such meeting.

SECTION 7
CUSTODIANSHIP OF PORTFOLIO SECURITIES

SECTION 7.01 – CUSTODIANSHIP OF PORTFOLIO SECURITIES

(1) Except as provided in Section 7.01(12), all portfolio securities of the mutual fund must be held under the custodianship of a Canadian custodian that meets the guidelines prescribed in Section 7.02, which custodian is hereinafter referred to as the "Custodian".

(2) Except as provided in Sections 7.01(3), 7.01(9) and in Section 7.01(12), all portfolio securities of a mutual fund shall be held by the Custodian in Canada.

(3) Where it is desirable for the purpose of more expeditiously effecting portfolio transactions outside of Canada, the Custodian may hold the relevant portfolio securities of the mutual fund outside of Canada or may appoint sub-custodians to hold such portfolio securities outside of Canada and enter into sub-custodianship agreements with such sub-custodians to provide for the safekeeping of portfolio securities of the mutual fund on terms and conditions similar to the terms and conditions contained in the custodianship agreement between the mutual fund and the Custodian, provided that adequate provision is made in the sub-custodianship agreements for the mutual fund, acting through the Custodian, to enforce its rights in respect thereof and provide further that any sub-custodianship agreement may not permit any further delegation of custodial authority unless the prior written consent of the Custodian and the mutual fund has been given to the specific custodial appointments which are to be made by the sub-custodian. Where any further delegation of custodial authority is made, adequate provision must also be made for the mutual fund, acting through the Custodian and the sub-custodian or sub-custodians, to enforce its rights in respect thereof. The term "sub-custodian" as used in this Section 7 includes any sub-custodian, whether appointed by the Custodian or appointed by a sub-custodian under the authority of the Custodian. Any sub-custodian appointed by or under the authority of the Custodian shall be a sub-custodian which meets the guidelines prescribed in Section 7.03.

All custodianship agreements shall provide that the Custodian shall be required to review on a periodic basis, not less frequently than annually, all custodial arrangements with the sub-custodians appointed by or under the authority of the Custodian to ensure that all custodial arrangements are in compliance with the provisions of this Section 7 and that all sub-custodians so appointed comply with the guidelines prescribed in Section 7.03 for sub-custodians and the Custodian shall make or cause to be made any changes that may be necessary to ensure that all sub-custodians appointed by or under the authority of the Custodian comply with the guidelines prescribed in Section 7.03 for sub-custodians.

(4) All custodianship agreements shall provide that the Custodian shall, within 60 days following the end of each financial year of the mutual fund, advise the mutual fund in writing of the names and addresses of all sub-custodians appointed by or under the authority of the Custodian and whether to the best of the knowledge and belief of the Custodian after making reasonable enquiry, the sub-custodians comply with the guidelines prescribed in Section 7.03 for sub-custodians and whether the custodial arrangements are in compliance with the provisions of Section 7. A copy of such report shall be filed with the respective securities authorities in the jurisdictions where the securities of the mutual fund are qualified for sale pursuant to a prospectus filed with and accepted by such securities authorities at the time of the annual refiling thereof.

(5) All custodianship agreements shall provide that, where the portfolio securities are not registered in the name of the mutual fund, they shall be registered in the name of the Custodian or of a sub-custodian or their respective nominees with an account number or other designation in the records of the Custodian or sub-custodian or their respective nominees sufficient to establish that the beneficial ownership of the portfolio securities is vested in the mutual fund. Where the portfolio securities are issued in bearer form, the custodianship agreement shall provide that such portfolio securities shall be designated or segregated by the Custodian or sub-custodian or their respective nominees so as to establish that the beneficial ownership of such property is vested in the mutual fund. Comparable provisions shall be included in any sub-custodianship agreements entered into by or under the authority of the Custodian.

(6) All custodianship agreements shall provide, as a minimum standard of care, that the Custodian in carrying out its duties in respect of the safekeeping of the portfolio securities of the mutual fund or in dealing with the portfolio securities of the

mutual fund under the instructions of the mutual fund shall exercise at least the same degree of care which the Custodian gives to its own property of a similar kind being kept by the Custodian and must provide that the Custodian shall assume the entire responsibility for loss occasioned by reason of the negligence of or wrongful act of the Custodian's employees, directors or officers. Comparable provisions shall be included in any sub-custodian agreements entered into by or under the authority of the Custodian.

(7) No custodianship agreement or sub-custodianship agreement may provide for the creation of any mortgage, pledge, hypothec, charge, lien, security interest or other encumbrance of any nature or kind on the portfolio securities except in respect of a claim for payment of the fees and expenses of the Custodian or sub-custodian as the case may be in connection with acting as Custodian or sub-custodian as the case may be.

(8) No custodianship agreement or sub-custodianship agreement may contain a provision that would require the payment of any fee to the Custodian or sub-custodian in respect of the transfer of the beneficial ownership of portfolio securities of the mutual fund other than the fees and expenses of the Custodian or sub-custodian as the case may be for safekeeping and administrative services in connection with acting as Custodian or sub-custodian as the case may be.

(9) Where it is desired to permit portfolio securities to be held in a book-based system, the custodianship agreement may provide that the Custodian may arrange for the deposit and delivery of eligible portfolio securities with The Canadian Depository For Securities Limited or the Depository Trust Company or with any other domestic or foreign depository or clearing agency which is incorporated or organized under the laws of a country or a jurisdiction within a country and is duly authorized to operate a book-based system in that country or is duly authorized to operate a transnational book-based system. Any book-based system in which the Custodian arranges for the deposit and delivery of eligible portfolio securities shall not for the purposes of this policy statement be considered to be a Custodian or a sub-custodian of the mutual fund. As used herein, the expression "book-based system" means a system for the central handling of securities or equivalent book-based entries pursuant to which system all securities of any particular class or series of any issuer deposited within the system are treated as fungible and may be transferred or pledged by bookkeeping entry without physical delivery of such securities.

(10) A custodianship agreement and sub-custodianship agreement shall contain such additional provisions as the mutual fund deems necessary or desirable to provide for the safekeeping of the portfolio securities of the mutual fund.

(11) Upon request, a copy of the Custodianship Agreement and of any sub-custodian agreements entered into by or under the authority of the Custodian shall be delivered to the securities authorities requesting the same.

(12)   (a) Where a mutual fund trades in clearing corporation options, options on futures or futures in accordance with this policy, the mutual fund may deposit portfolio securities or cash as margin in respect of such transactions with a dealer that is a member of a self-regulatory organization that is a participating member of the Canadian Investor Protection Fund, provided that the amount of initial margin so deposited does not, when aggregated with the amount of margin held by the dealer, exceed 10% of the net assets of the mutual fund.

     (b) Where it is desirable for the purpose of more expeditiously effecting trades in clearing corporation options, options on futures or futures outside Canada, the mutual fund may deposit portfolio securities or cash as margin outside Canada in respect of such trades provided that;

         (i) in the case of futures and options on futures, the dealer is a member of a permitted futures exchange or, in the case of clearing corporation options, is a member of a stock exchange, and, as a result, is subject to a regulatory audit;

         (ii) the dealer through which such trades have been effected and through which margin has been deposited holds such margin in segregated safekeeping such that it would not be available to satisfy the claims of any creditor of such dealer;

    (iii) the dealer has a net worth, determined from its latest published audited financial statements, in excess of $50 million; and

    (iv) the amount of initial margin so deposited does not, when aggregated with the amount of margin held by the dealer, exceed 10% of the net assets of the mutual fund.

(c) Where a mutual fund trades in over-the-counter options or forward contracts in accordance with this policy, the mutual fund may deposit portfolio securities or cash as margin with the other party to the transaction.

SECTION 7.02 – PRESCRIBED GUIDELINES FOR ACTING AS CUSTODIAN

The following institutions may act as a Custodian of portfolio securities of a mutual fund:

(a) a Canadian chartered bank;

(b) a trust company incorporated and licensed under the laws of Canada or a Province of Canada having Shareholders' Equity as reported in its audited financial statements for its last completed financial year of not less than $10,000,000;

(c) a wholly owned subsidiary of a Canadian chartered bank or of a trust company referred to in clauses (a) and (b) provided that such subsidiary has Shareholders' Equity as reported in its audited financial statements for its last financial year of not less than $10,000,000 or all of the obligations of such subsidiary are unconditionally guaranteed by such bank or trust company.

SECTION 7.03 – PRESCRIBED GUIDELINES FOR ACTING AS SUB-CUSTODIAN

The following institutions may act as a sub-custodian of portfolio securities of a mutual fund:

(a) any institution referred to in section 7.02;

(b) a banking institution or trust company incorporated or organized under the laws of a country other than Canada that is regulated as such by that country's government or an agency thereof and that has Shareholders' Equity as reported in its audited financial statements for its last completed financial year of not less than the equivalent in Canadian funds of $100,000,000;

(c) a wholly owned subsidiary of a banking institution or trust company referred to in clause (b) provided that such subsidiary has Shareholders' Equity as reported in its audited financial statements for its last completed financial year of not less than the equivalent in Canadian funds of $100,000,000 or all of the obligations of such subsidiary are unconditionally guaranteed by such bank or trust company.

SECTION 8
MANAGEMENT FEES

SECTION 8.01 – DISCLOSURE OF FEES AND EXPENSES

The prospectus of a mutual fund shall clearly disclose:

(1) what fees and other charges and expenses are charged to the mutual fund and the basis for the calculation of the same;

(2) what fees and other charges and expenses are borne by the manager of the mutual fund;

(3) what fees and other charges and expenses, if any, are charged directly to all securityholders generally, or to any securityholder who participates in a special arrangement such as a contractual plan, a periodic accumulation plan, an open account plan, a withdrawal plan, a registered retirement savings plan, a registered retirement income plan, or exercises an exchange or transfer privilege, and the basis of the calculation of the same.

Any fees and other charges and expenses which are charged directly to securityholders shall be summarized in tabular form in a separate section of the prospectus under the heading "Summary of Fees, Charges and Expenses Payable by the Securityholder" or such variation thereof as is acceptable to the securities authorities. Reference to this table shall be made on the cover page or on the first facing page of the prospectus.

SECTION 8.02 – INCENTIVE FEES

A mutual fund may not be charged an incentive fee without the prior approval of the securities authorities.

Where an incentive fee is proposed to be charged, it will be necessary to establish an appropriate benchmark or relevant index, satisfactory to the securities authorities, against which performance is to be measured and to provide that if the performance of the mutual fund in any period should not be equal to or exceed such benchmark or index that no incentive fee may be paid in any subsequent period unless and until the performance of the mutual fund on a cumulative basis has equalled or exceeded such benchmark or index.

SECTION 8.03 – MANAGEMENT EXPENSE RATIO

(1) The prospectus or the financial statements shall set out in tabular form the management expense ratio for each of the last five completed financial years of the mutual fund, together with a brief description of the method of calculating the management expense ratio.

(2) Where the basis of the calculation of fees and of other expenses that are charged to a mutual fund are changed or proposed to be changed and where such change would have an effect on the management expense ratio for the last completed financial year of the mutual fund if such change had been in effect for such year, the prospectus shall disclose the effect of such change.

(3) Where any financial period referred to in Section 8.03(1) is less than 12 months, the management expense ratio shall be shown on an annualized basis with reference to the period covered and to the fact that the management expense ratio for the period has been annualized.

(4) The management expense ratio of a mutual fund for any financial year shall be obtained by dividing (i) the aggregate of all fees and other expenses paid or payable by the mutual fund during or in respect of the financial year in question, by (ii) the amount of the average net asset value of the mutual fund for the financial year in question and multiplying the quotient by 100; for the purpose of making this calculation:

(a) the expression "the average net asset value of the mutual fund for a financial year" shall mean and be the result obtained by:

(i) adding together the amounts determined to be the net asset value of the mutual fund as at the close of business of the mutual fund on each day during the financial year in question on which the net asset value of the mutual fund has been determined in the manner from time to time prescribed in the constating documents of the mutual fund;

(ii) dividing the amount resulting from the addition provided for in clause (i) by the number of days during the financial year in question on which the net asset value of the mutual fund has been determined;

(b) the expression "all fees and other expenses" means all fees and expenses paid or payable by the mutual fund with the exception of commissions and brokerage fees on the purchase and sale of portfolio securities, interest charges (if any) and taxes of all kinds to which the mutual fund is subject.

(5) The financial statements of the mutual fund shall set out in appropriate detail the amounts of all fees and other expenses, if any, which have been charged to the mutual fund during the period covered by the financial statements.

SECTION 9
APPROVAL OF SECURITIES AUTHORITIES FOR CERTAIN CHANGES

SECTION 9.01 – PRIOR APPROVAL REQUIRED FOR CERTAIN CHANGES

The prior approval of the securities authorities is required before:

(1)   a change of the manager of a mutual fund (other than to an affiliate of the present manager) may be made;

(2)   a change in the control of the manager of a mutual fund may be made;

(3)   a change of the custodian of the assets of a mutual fund may be made where there has been in connection therewith or is to be:

(i)   a change of the manager of the mutual fund (other than to an affiliate of the present manager); or

(ii)   a change in the control of the manager of the mutual fund.

SECTION 9.02 – APPLICATIONS FOR PRIOR APPROVAL

Applications for the approval referred to in Section 9.01, as well as for any other approvals referred to in this policy or any exemptions therefrom, may be made to the securities authority in the Province or Territory of Canada where the mutual fund is managed (the "principal jurisdiction") provided that a copy of such application is sent at the same time to the securities authorities in the other Provinces or Territories where the securities of the mutual fund are offered for sale. The principal jurisdiction will, on behalf of the applicant, contact the securities authorities in the other Provinces or Territories of Canada where the securities of the mutual fund are offered for sale for their comments. The principal jurisdiction may then be authorized to grant approval or to approve exemptions from this policy on behalf of the Provinces or Territories concerned.

An application for the approval referred to in Section 9.01 must contain or be accompanied by sufficient information to establish:

(1)   the reputation, honesty and competence of the management group including the controlling shareholders;

(2)   where custodial arrangements are proposed to be changed, that the proposed custodial arrangements will be in compliance with the requirements of Section 7;

(3)   where the change is one that requires the approval of securityholders, that such approval has been obtained or will be obtained before the change is implemented;

and the application shall be accompanied by a draft amendment to the prospectus of the mutual fund.

SECTION 10
CONTRACTUAL PLANS

SECTION 10.01 – CONTRACTUAL PLANS

Where it is proposed to deduct an amount from any periodic payment under a contractual plan by way of Sales Charges which amount exceeds the maximum sales charge from time to time prevailing for a single payment or lump sum purchase, the contractual plan must comply with the following requirements:

(1)   the payments under the plan must be scheduled to be made in equal amounts on a weekly, monthly, quarterly, half-yearly or yearly basis, provided that a double or a triple instalment may be required as the first payment;

(2)   the Sales Charges levied against any payment scheduled to be made during the first 12 months of the contractual plan shall in no case exceed 50% of the individual payments under the contractual plan, provided that:

(i)   the Sales Charges levied against the remaining payments made under the contractual plan shall to the extent reasonably practicable be levied at an equal rate or percentage, the size of the payment for or on account of Sales Charges varying only with the size of the amount of the individual payment selected by the planholder with the total Sales Charges levied during the term of the contractual plan in no case to exceed 12% of the face amount of the contractual plan;

    (ii) where the contractual plan calls for an initial payment to be retained by the plan sponsor or distributor such initial payment shall not exceed three times the scheduled monthly payments under the contractual plan and the Sales Charges levied against the remaining payments made under the contractual plan shall comply with the provisions of Section 10.01(2)(i); and

    (iii) the contractual plan provides that there will be added to each monthly payment scheduled to be made and made under the contractual plan for investment a pro-rata portion of the initial payment, such pro-rata portion being based on the term of the contractual plan.

(3) Where the Sales Charges levied against the payments scheduled to be made in the first 12 months of the contractual plan are less than 50% of the individual payments under the contractual plan (thereby making a larger sum available for investment) the contractual plan may provide in respect of the second 12 payments to be made under the contractual plan for a Sales Charge which, when combined with the Sales Charges levied against the first 12 payments under the contractual plan, does not exceed 50% of the total payments scheduled to be made during the first 12 months of the contractual plan, provided that the percentage deducted from any payment for Sales Charges shall not exceed the percentage deducted from any previous payment and provided further that the Sales Charges levied against the remaining payments made under the contractual plan comply with the provisions of Section 10.01(2)(i).

SECTION 10.02 – EXTENDED MEANING OF SALES CHARGES

As used in Sections 10.01, 10.03 and 10.04, the expression "Sales Charges" means all sales commissions or sales charges plus all other charges made in respect of the contractual plan with the exception of insurance premiums and any fees paid to the trustee of a registered retirement savings plan or to the trustee of a registered retirement income fund for acting as trustee.

SECTION 10.03 – WITHDRAWAL RIGHTS UNDER CONTRACTUAL PLANS

A planholder under a contractual plan shall have a right to withdraw from the contractual plan, which right of withdrawal shall, as a minimum, entitle the planholder to rescind his obligations under the contractual plan:

(a) within 60 days after receipt of the confirmation for the initial payment under the contractual plan (the "plan date") and to receive a refund equal to the amount of all Sales Charges paid in respect of the contractual plan plus an amount equal to:

    (i) all payments scheduled to be made and made during the first 60 days of the contractual plan, and

    (ii) in the case of prepayments of additional payments made under the contractual plan within the said 60 day period, the net asset value of the securities purchased for the planholder under the contractual plan with such prepayments, such net asset value to be the net asset value of such securities next determined after the time the right of withdrawal is exercised, provided that the amount to be refunded pursuant to this clause (ii) may be limited to the total amount of the prepayments made under the contractual plan within the said 60 day period; and

(b) at any time during the period from the date that is 60 days after the plan date up to and including 365 days after the plan date and to receive a refund equal to that portion of the Sales Charges which exceeds 30% of the payments scheduled to be made and made under the contractual plan during the period commencing with the plan date and ending 365 days after the plan date, plus the net asset value of the securities purchased for the planholder under the contractual plan during such last-mentioned period, such net asset value to be the net asset value of such securities next determined after the time the right of withdrawal is exercised. (Note: This means that prepayments of instalments normally falling due during the second and subsequent years of the contractual plan will not be taken into account in arriving at the 30% penalty.)

The withdrawal rights referred to above shall be described in the prospectus of the mutual fund and a document setting out the withdrawal rights shall accompany or form part of the copy of the contractual plan supplied to the planholder or shall be contained in the confirmations delivered in respect of the purchase of securities of the mutual fund made under a contractual plan during the first 60 days of the contractual plan.

SECTION 10.04 – RECORDS RELATING TO WITHDRAWAL RIGHTS

Plan sponsors and distributors shall maintain adequate records of contractual plan cancellations to show on a month-to-month basis such cancellations and the amounts paid to planholders in respect of the refund of payments and Sales Charges in respect thereof.

SECTION 11
SALE AND REDEMPTION OF SECURITIES OF A MUTUAL FUND

SECTION 11.01 – OBJECTIVES

The provisions of Sections 11 and 12 of this policy are aimed at:

(1)   ensuring that an investor's funds which are to be invested in a mutual fund are received by the mutual fund promptly and preferably concurrently with the investor's order being accepted by the mutual fund;

(2)   eliminating or at least reducing the opportunity for loss of an investor's funds during the period from the delivery of such funds by the investor in respect of the investor's purchase of securities of the mutual fund to the time of receipt of such funds by the mutual fund;

(3)   ensuring that interest earned on an investor's funds during the period from the delivery of such funds by the investor in respect of the investor's purchase of securities of the mutual fund to the time of receipt of such funds by the mutual fund, accrues to the benefit of either the mutual fund or the investor;

(4)   ensuring that interest earned on an investor's funds during the period from the acceptance by the mutual fund of the investor's order for redemption of securities of the mutual fund to the time of receipt of such funds by the investor, accrues to the benefit of the mutual fund, regardless of whether the redemption monies are paid directly by the mutual fund or by an agent of the mutual fund.

The provisions of Sections 11 and 12 are to be interpreted with these objectives in mind and all arrangements between or among a mutual fund, its principal distributor, its manager, any dealer participating in the distribution of securities of the mutual fund or anyone else should be made or brought into line to give effect to these objectives and their intent. In particular, and without limitation, in making arrangements for services to or in respect of the mutual fund, it should be ensured that an investor's funds which are required by Section 12 of this policy to be held as trust funds retain their character as trust funds in the hands of respective parties providing services and provision should be made for the mutual fund, its manager and its principal distributor, through their designated representatives, to examine the books and records of the respective parties providing services to or in respect of the mutual fund for the purpose of monitoring compliance with the requirements of the agreements and of this policy.

In order to implement these objectives, it is essential that all persons participating in the distribution of securities of a mutual fund be adequately organized to do so and have adequate facilities and procedures in place to do so. In addition, in order to shorten the period between the placing of an order for the purchase of securities of a mutual fund and the time that the funds in respect of that order are actually received by the mutual fund, a dealer receiving an order for the purchase of securities of a mutual fund must at the time of receipt of the investor's order obtain from the investor all relevant documentation, information and registration instructions so that the same is available at the time the order is transmitted to the mutual fund or its principal distributor for transmittal in conjunction with the acceptance of the order by or on behalf of the mutual fund. Similarly, in order to shorten the period between the placing of an order for the redemption of securities of a mutual fund and the payment to the investor of the redemption proceeds, a dealer receiving an order for redemption must at the time of receipt of the investor's order obtain from the investor all relevant documentation required by the mutual fund in respect of the redemption including, without limitation, any written request for redemption that may be required by the mutual fund, duly completed and executed, and any certificates representing the mutual fund securities to be redeemed so that all required documentation is available at the time the redemption order is transmitted to the mutual fund or its principal distributor for transmittal in conjunction with the acceptance of the order by or on behalf of the mutual fund.

In all arrangements that are made with respect to the distribution of securities of a mutual fund, a dealer transmitting an order for the purchase of securities of a mutual fund shall be responsible for ensuring that payment of the issue price of such securities is made when due. Accordingly, dealers participating in the sale of mutual fund securities should ensure that their arrangements with their clients are adequate to cover such obligations as any loss which arises due to a failure of an investor to deliver funds or to a cheque being dishonoured on presentation for payment or for any other reason shall be borne as between the mutual fund, its principal distributor and the dealer in question by the dealer or principal distributor and not by the mutual fund. Similarly, on the redemption of securities of a mutual fund, any loss resulting from the failure to verify the identity of the person requesting the redemption of securities of a mutual fund shall be borne as between the mutual fund and anyone participating in the distribution or redemption of securities of the mutual fund by such other participants and not by the mutual fund.

SECTION 11.02 – TRANSMITTAL OF ORDERS FOR THE PURCHASE OR REDEMPTION OF SECURITIES

(1) Subject to Section 11.02(2), where an order for the purchase or the redemption of securities of a mutual fund is received by a sales representative of the principal distributor of the mutual fund, the order shall be transmitted to the principal office of the principal distributor of the mutual fund or to such other office as the principal distributor may designate on the same day that the order is received by such sales representative.

(2) Where it is the policy of the principal distributor of a mutual fund to maintain a sales servicing office for the purpose of reviewing applications for contractual plan purchases before having the applications forwarded to its principal office or other designated office, the sales representative shall transmit such application together with the initial payments to be made under the plan to the appropriate sales servicing office on the same day that the application is received. The sales servicing office shall review the application and shall transmit all applications thought to be acceptable to the principal distributor together with the initial payments to be made under the plan to the principal office of the principal distributor or to such other office as the principal distributor may designate no later than the next business day following the day that the application is received in the sales servicing office.

(3) Where an order for the purchase or redemption of securities of a mutual fund is received by a sales representative of a dealer other than the principal distributor of the mutual fund, the order shall be transmitted to the dealer in question on the same day that the order is received whereupon such dealer shall transmit the same to the principal office of the principal distributor of the mutual fund or to such other office as may be designated for the purpose on the same day that the order is received by the dealer.

(4) Notwithstanding the foregoing provisions of this Section 11.02, where an order for the purchase or redemption of securities of a mutual fund is received after normal business hours on any business day or on a day that is not a business day, the order may be transmitted to the respective offices referred to above on the next business day if it is not practical to transmit the same on the day of actual receipt.

(5) All orders for the purchase or redemption of securities of a mutual fund shall be transmitted to the respective offices referred to above without charge to the investor and shall be transmitted wherever practical by courier or priority post or telecommunications facility so as to reduce to the shortest possible time the period between the transmittal of the order and its receipt by or on behalf of the mutual fund.

SECTION 11.03 – ACCEPTANCE OF ORDERS TO PURCHASE SECURITIES

A mutual fund may reserve the right to accept or reject an order to purchase securities of the mutual fund provided that:

(1)   the decision to accept or reject the order is made promptly and in any event within two days of receipt of the order;

(2)   in the event that an order is to be rejected all monies received with the order are refunded immediately; and

(3)   the prospectus clearly states that the right to accept or reject orders for the purchase of securities is reserved and discloses the provisions of clauses (1) and (2) hereof.

SECTION 11.04 – FORWARD PRICING – SALES AND REDEMPTIONS

(1) All orders for the purchase or redemption of securities of a mutual fund shall be implemented at a price equal to the net asset value of the securities of the mutual fund next determined after the receipt by the mutual fund of the order, provided that a mutual fund may provide that orders received after a specified time on any business day or on any day which is not a business day will for the purposes of the foregoing be deemed to be received by the mutual fund on the next business day following the day of actual receipt thereof.

(2) A mutual fund shall be deemed to receive an order for the purchase or redemption of securities of the mutual fund when the order is in fact received by the mutual fund at its principal office or at the principal office of the principal distributor of the mutual fund or at such other office as may be designated for the purpose.

(3) The implementation of sales or redemptions at a price equal to the net asset value determined as at a time earlier than the time of the receipt of the relevant orders as aforesaid (i.e. "backward pricing") is unacceptable.

SECTION 11.05 – FREQUENCY OF DETERMINING NET ASSET VALUE

(1) The net asset value of a mutual fund for the purpose of the issue or redemption of securities of the mutual fund shall be calculated no less frequently than once in each week, provided that with the approval of the securityholders of the mutual fund, the net asset value of the mutual fund for the purpose of the issue or redemption of securities of the mutual fund may be calculated no less frequently than once in each month.

(2) If at January 1, 1988, the net asset value of a mutual fund is being calculated only once in each month, no approval of the securityholders of the mutual fund is required to be obtained in order for the mutual fund to continue to calculate the net asset value of the mutual fund only once in each month.

(3) Notwithstanding section 11.05, if a mutual fund invests in, uses or holds permitted derivatives, then the net asset value of the mutual fund must be calculated no less frequently than once every business day.

SECTION 11.06 – DISCLOSURE OF SALES CHARGES

The rates of sales charges or commissions in respect of the sale of securities of a mutual fund shall be expressed as a percentage of the amount paid by the purchaser as well as being expressed as a percentage of the net amount invested wherever reference is made in a prospectus or in any sales communication to such sales charges or commissions.

SECTION 11.07 – MAXIMUM PERIOD OF TIME FOR PAYMENT OF THE ISSUE PRICE OF SECURITIES

(1) The maximum period of time from but not including the date as of which the issue price of the securities of a mutual fund is determined in respect of any order for the purchase of such securities (which date is hereinafter referred to as the "Trade Date") to and including the date on which the mutual fund or its principal distributor receives payment for such securities shall be kept to the shortest possible time and in any event shall not exceed five business days (which date is hereinafter referred to as the "Settlement Date").

(2) Payment of the issue price of the securities of a mutual fund referred to in any order for the purchase of securities of a mutual fund shall be satisfied by a cash payment to the mutual fund, provided, however, in the case of a mutual fund that has

received the approval of the securities authorities to do so, the purchase price may be satisfied by making good delivery to the mutual fund of securities that meet the mutual fund's investment criteria and that are acceptable to the portfolio adviser, with such securities being valued on the same basis that the mutual fund would use in determining the value of such securities if such securities were owned by the mutual fund and the value of such securities so delivered to the mutual fund shall be at least equal to the issue price of the securities being issued by the mutual fund.

(3) If payment of the issue price of the securities of a mutual fund referred to in any order has not been received by the mutual fund on or before the Settlement Date, the mutual fund shall be deemed to have received and accepted on the first business day following the Settlement Date an order for the redemption of such securities and the amount of the redemption proceeds derived therefrom shall be applied to reduce the amount owing to the mutual fund in respect of the purchase of such securities. If the amount of the redemption proceeds exceeds the issue price of the securities, the excess shall belong to the mutual fund. If the amount of the redemption proceeds is less than the issue price of the securities:

(a) the principal distributor shall be required to pay forthwith to the mutual fund the amount of the deficiency and shall be entitled to collect such amount together with its costs, charges and expenses in so doing and interest thereon from the dealer (or, if no other dealer is involved, from the investor who has failed to settle the order in question), and

(b) if the mutual fund does not have a principal distributor, the dealer placing the order shall be required to pay forthwith to the mutual fund the amount of the deficiency and shall be entitled to collect such amount together with its costs, charges and expenses in so doing and interest thereon from the investor who has failed to settle the order in question, and

(c) if the mutual fund does not have a principal distributor and no dealer is involved, the mutual fund shall be entitled to collect the amount of the deficiency together with its costs, charges and expenses in so doing and interest thereon from the investor who has failed to settle the order in question.

SECTION 11.08 – COMPLIANCE REPORT

The principal distributor of a mutual fund or, if there is no principal distributor of the mutual fund, the mutual fund shall complete and file with the securities authorities a report with respect to compliance, during the last completed financial year of the principal distributor of the mutual fund or of the mutual fund, as the case may be, with the applicable requirements of Section 11, such compliance report to be filed within 120 days of the applicable fiscal year end and to be accompanied by a letter from the auditors of the principal distributor of the mutual fund or of the mutual fund, as the case may be, advising whether the auditors are in agreement with the information given in the report as to compliance with the applicable requirements of Section 11.

SECTION 12
COMMINGLING OF MONEY

SECTION 12.01 – PRINCIPAL DISTRIBUTORS – COMMINGLING OF MONEY

Subject to Section 12.02, a principal distributor of a mutual fund shall comply with the following requirements:

(1) all monies received by a principal distributor:

(a) for investment in securities of the mutual fund; or

(b) upon the redemption of securities of the mutual fund;

shall be separately accounted for and shall be deposited in an interest-bearing trust account or trust accounts, but may not otherwise be commingled with the assets of the principal distributor and may not be commingled with money received by the principal distributor with respect to the sale or redemption of securities other than mutual fund securities or with respect to the sale or redemption of investment contracts;

(2) the principal distributor shall not use any of the monies referred to in clause (1) to finance its own or any other operations in any way;

(3) the principal distributor may withdraw monies from the trust account or trust accounts referred to in clause (1) for the purpose of

    (i) remitting the net amount to be invested in the securities of the mutual fund to the mutual fund;

    (ii) paying redemption proceeds to the investors entitled thereto; or

    (iii) paying sales charges, service fees and any other similar amounts to which the principal distributor may be entitled;

(4) unless the interest is paid to the investors pro rata, all interest earned on the trust account or trust accounts referred to in clause (1) less any bank charges applicable thereto shall be paid to the mutual fund no less frequently than monthly and where the monies in the trust account or trust accounts are held for more than one mutual fund, the amount payable on account of interest shall be prorated among the mutual funds based on cash flow; the participating dealer shall not be entitled under any circumstances to any interest earned on the trust account or trust accounts referred to in clause (1);

(5) all monies received by the principal distributor for the purchase of securities of the mutual fund shall be paid to the mutual fund forthwith and in any event no later than the second business day following the date of receipt;

(6) the principal distributor shall not transfer, lend, pledge, encumber or otherwise deal in any way with securities of a mutual fund held for investors in safekeeping or under plans or otherwise except to the extent expressly provided for in any written agreement between the principal distributor and the investor setting out the terms on which the securities of the mutual fund are held and may be dealt with.

SECTION 12.02 – DEEMED COMPLIANCE

Where the principal distributor commingles in one trust account the monies referred to in Section 12.01(1)(a) and (b), the principal distributor may net the proceeds from sales against the proceeds from redemptions and make one cash settlement.

SECTION 12.03 – SUB-DISTRIBUTORS – COMMINGLING OF MONEY

Where any dealer participates with a mutual fund or with the principal distributor of the mutual fund (the "participating dealer") in the distribution of securities of the mutual fund, such participating dealer shall comply with the following requirements:

(1) all monies received by the participating dealer for investment in securities of the mutual fund shall be separately accounted for and shall be deposited in an interest-bearing trust account or trust accounts, but may not otherwise be commingled with the assets of the participating dealer and may not be commingled with money received by the participating dealer with respect to the sale or redemption of securities other than mutual fund securities or with respect to the sale or redemption of investment contracts;

(2) the participating dealer shall not use any of the monies referred to in clause (1) to finance its operations in any way;

(3) the participating dealer shall be entitled to withdraw monies from the trust account or trust accounts referred to in clause (1) only for the purpose of

    (i) remitting the net amount to be invested in the securities of the mutual fund to the mutual fund or the principal distributor of the mutual fund; or

    (ii) for the purpose of paying sales charges, service fees and any other similar amounts to which the participating dealer or the principal distributor may be entitled;

(4) unless the interest is paid to the investors pro rata, all interest earned on the trust account or trust accounts referred to in clause (1) less any bank charges applicable thereto shall be paid to the mutual fund no less frequently than monthly and where the monies in the trust account or trust accounts are held for more than one mutual fund, the amount payable on

account of interest shall be prorated among the mutual funds based on cash flow; the participating dealer shall not be entitled under any circumstances to any interest earned on the trust account or trust accounts referred to in clause (1);

(5) all monies received by the participating dealer for the purchase of securities of the mutual fund shall be paid to the mutual fund or its principal distributor as soon as practicable and in any event no later than the Settlement Date;

(6) the mutual fund or the principal distributor, as the case may be, shall be entitled through their respective auditors or other designated representatives to examine the books and records of the participating dealer for the purpose of verifying the participating dealer's compliance with the foregoing.

SECTION 12.04 – COMPLIANCE REPORT

The principal distributor of a mutual fund and each of the participating dealers referred to in Section 12.03 shall complete and file with the securities authorities a report with respect to its compliance during the last completed financial year with the applicable requirements of Section 12, such compliance report to be filed within 120 days of the applicable fiscal year end and to be accompanied by a letter from the auditors of the principal distributor of the mutual fund or the participating dealer, as the case may be, advising whether the auditors are in agreement with the information given in the report as to compliance with the applicable requirements of Section 12.

SECTION 12.05 – EXEMPTION

The provisions of Section 12 of this policy, with the exception of Sections 12.01(5), 12.03(5), 12.03(6) and 12.04, do not apply to members of The Investment Dealers Association of Canada.

SECTION 13
REDEMPTION OF SECURITIES

SECTION 13.01 – DISCLOSURE OF REDEMPTION PROCEDURES

Securityholders of a mutual fund shall be provided at least annually with a statement outlining the procedures to be followed by a securityholder who desires to redeem securities of the mutual fund and specifying the documents to be furnished by such securityholder in connection with a request for redemption. This statement may be contained in the mutual fund's annual financial statements or annual report.

SECTION 13.02 – PAYMENT OF REDEMPTION PROCEEDS

(1) Subject to Section 13.02(2) and to Section 13.03 a mutual fund shall make payment in Canadian currency for the securities which are redeemed, which payment shall be made within five business days from the date of the determination of the net asset value for the purpose of effecting such redemption, provided that a mutual fund may permit securityholders to request that such payment be made in United States currency, with the amount of such payment being based upon the rate of conversion used by the mutual fund in determining the net asset value for the purpose of effecting such redemption of mutual fund securities. Payment of the redemption proceeds shall be made to or to the order of the registered holder of the securities which are being redeemed.

(2) No payment of redemption proceeds may be made prior to the receipt by the mutual fund of a written request for redemption of the mutual fund securities to be redeemed, duly completed and delivered, properly executed, together with any certificates representing such securities, provided that nothing herein contained shall prevent a mutual fund which has established procedures for investors who desire to do so to make arrangements for the acceptance of telephone or other telecommunication requests for redemption, from paying the redemption proceeds to an investor who has made such prior arrangements where the redemption order is processed in accordance with such arrangements.

(3) If all of the requirements of the mutual fund that must be complied with prior to the payment by the mutual fund of the redemption proceeds payable on the redemption of the mutual fund securities which have been redeemed have not been complied with on or before the tenth business day from the date of the determination of

the net asset value for the purpose of effecting such redemption, the mutual fund shall be deemed to have received and accepted on the next business day an order for the purchase of the equivalent number of the mutual fund securities which have been redeemed and shall apply the amount of the redemption proceeds to the payment of the issue price of such securities. If the amount of the issue price of such securities is less than the redemption proceeds, the excess shall belong to the mutual fund. If the amount of the issue price of such securities exceeds the redemption proceeds:

(a) the principal distributor shall be required to pay forthwith to the mutual fund the amount of the deficiency and shall be entitled to collect such amount together with its costs, charges and expenses in so doing and interest thereon from the dealer (or if no other dealer is involved, from the investor who has failed to settle the order in question);

(b) if the mutual fund does not have a principal distributor, the dealer placing the order shall be required to pay forthwith to the mutual fund the amount of the deficiency and shall be entitled to collect such amount together with its costs, charges and expenses in so doing and interest thereon from the investor who has failed to settle the order in question; and

(c) if the mutual fund does not have a principal distributor and no dealer is involved, the mutual fund shall be entitled to collect the amount of the deficiency together with its costs, charges and expenses in so doing and interest thereon from the investor who has failed to settle the order in question.

(4) The redemption procedures established by a mutual fund should contain the necessary provisions to make the provisions contained in Section 13.02(3) binding upon investors.

SECTION 13.03 – PAYMENT OF REDEMPTION PROCEEDS IN SPECIE

With the prior written consent of the securityholder, payment of the amount payable to the securityholder on account of the redemption of securities of the mutual fund may be satisfied by making good delivery to the securityholder of portfolio securities, provided that such portfolio securities are valued at an amount equal to the amount at which such portfolio securities were valued for the purpose of determining the net asset value of the mutual fund for the purpose of determining the redemption price.

A report setting forth the details of any payment of the redemption proceeds in specie, including a list of the portfolio securities delivered to the securityholder and the value assigned to such portfolio securities shall be filed with the securities authorities. Any such report will be placed on the public files.

SECTION 13.04 – SUSPENSION OF REDEMPTIONS

A mutual fund may suspend the right to tender its securities for redemption or may postpone the date of payment upon redemption:

(1) for any period when normal trading is suspended on any stock exchange, options exchange or futures exchange within or outside Canada on which securities are listed and traded, or on which permitted derivatives are traded, which represent more than 50% by value or underlying market exposure of the total assets of the mutual fund without allowance for liabilities;

(2) where the head office or registered office of the mutual fund is in Canada, with the consent of the securities authority in the Province or Territory of Canada in which such office is situate; or

(3) where the head office or registered office of the mutual fund is in the United States of America, with the consent of the Securities and Exchange Commission.

A mutual fund shall not accept any subscription for the purchase of securities of the mutual fund during any period when the right to tender its securities for redemption is suspended.

SECTION 14
COMPUTATION OF NET ASSET VALUE

SECTION 14.01 – PORTFOLIO TRANSACTIONS

Each transaction of purchase or sale of portfolio securities effected by a mutual fund shall be reflected in the computation of the net asset value of the mutual fund not later than the first computation of such net asset value made after the date on which the transaction becomes binding.

SECTION 14.02 – CAPITAL TRANSACTIONS

The issue or redemption of securities of a mutual fund shall be reflected in the computation of the net asset value of the mutual fund no later than the next computation of such net asset value made after the time as at which the net asset value per security is determined for the purpose of the issue or redemption of the securities of the mutual fund.

SECTION 14.03 – VALUATION OF PORTFOLIO SECURITIES

The basis used for valuing the mutual fund's assets and liabilities for the purpose of calculating net asset value shall be described in the prospectus. The basis used by the mutual fund for valuing any type of its portfolio securities must comply with the requirements of this policy where this policy prescribes the basis for valuing such type of portfolio securities.

SECTION 14.04 – VALUATION OF RESTRICTED SECURITIES

Restricted securities shall be valued at the less of:

(1) the value thereof based on reported quotations in common use; and

(2) that percentage of the market value of securities of the same class, the trading of which is not restricted or limited by reason of any representation, undertaking or agreement or by law, equal to the percentage that the mutual fund's acquisition cost was of the market value of such securities at the time of acquisition, provided that a gradual taking into account of the actual value of the securities may be made where the date on which the restrictions will be lifted is known.

SECTION 14.05 – VALUATION OF PERMITTED DERIVATIVES

Long positions in clearing corporation options, options on futures, over-the-counter options, debt-like securities and listed warrants shall be valued at the current market value thereof.

Where a covered clearing corporation option, option on futures or over-the-counter option is written, the premium received by the mutual fund shall be reflected as a deferred credit which shall be valued at an amount equal to the current market value of the clearing corporation option, option on futures or over-the-counter option that would have the effect of closing the position. Any difference resulting from revaluation shall be treated as an unrealized gain or loss on investment. The deferred credit shall be deducted in arriving at the net asset value of the mutual fund. The securities, if any, which are the subject of a written clearing corporation option or over-the-counter option shall be valued at their current market value.

The value of a futures contract, or a forward contract, shall be the gain or loss with respect thereto that would be realized if, on the valuation date, the position in the futures contract, or the forward contract, as the case may be, were to be closed out unless "daily limits" are in effect, in which case fair value shall be based on the current market value of the underlying interest.

Margin paid or deposited in respect of futures contracts and forward contracts shall be reflected as an account receivable and margin consisting of assets other than cash shall be noted as held as margin.

SECTION 14.06 – INFORMATION ABOUT PERMITTED DERIVATIVES

A mutual fund shall disclose the following information with respect to each of the following permitted derivatives in either the Statement of Investment Portfolio included in the financial statements of the mutual fund or in the notes thereto:

(1) (a) for long positions in clearing corporation options disclose the number of options, the underlying interest, the strike price, the expiration month and year, the cost and the market value;

(b) for long positions in options on futures disclose the number of options on futures, the futures contract that forms the underlying interest, the strike price, the expiration month and year of the option on futures, the delivery month and year of the futures contract that forms the underlying interest of the option on futures, the cost and the market value;

(c) for written clearing corporation options disclose the particulars of the deferred credit account indicating the number of options, the underlying interest, the strike price, the expiration month and year, the premium received and the value as determined under Section 14.05;

(d) for purchased over-the-counter options disclose the number of options, the credit rating of the issuer of the options, whether such rating has fallen below the approved credit rating, the underlying interest, the principal amount or quantity of the underlying interest, the strike price, the expiration date, the cost and the market value;

(e) for written over-the-counter options disclose the particulars of the deferred credit account indicating the number of options, the underlying interest, the principal amount or quantity of the underlying interest, the exercise price, the expiration date, the premium received and the value as determined under Section 14.05;

(f) for positions in futures contracts disclose the number of futures contracts, the underlying interest, the price at which the contract was entered into, the delivery month and year and the value as determined under Section 14.05;

(g) for positions in forward contracts disclose the number of forward contracts, the credit rating of the counterparty, whether such rating has fallen below the approved credit rating level, the underlying interest, the quantity of the underlying interest, the price at which the contract was entered into, the settlement date and the value as determined under Section 14.05; and

(h) for debt-like securities, disclose the principal amount of the debt, the interest rate, the payment dates, the underlying interest, the principal amount or quantity of the underlying interest, the strike price, the cost, the market value and a description of whether the derivative component is an option or a forward contract with respect to the underlying interest.

(2) If applicable, identify by an asterisk or other notation the underlying interest which is being hedged by each position in a permitted derivative.

SECTION 14.07 – NET ASSET VALUE TO BE STATED

The net asset value per security as at the end of the last completed financial year of the mutual fund as at the end of each of the four preceding financial years (or such shorter period as the mutual fund has been in existence) shall be stated either in the prospectus or in the annual financial statements of the mutual fund.

SECTION 15
DISTRIBUTIONS

SECTION 15.01 – RECORD DATE

The record date for determining the right of securityholders of a mutual fund to receive payment of any dividend or other distribution payable by a mutual fund or to receive any right issued by a mutual fund shall not be fixed at a date that is earlier than the date on which the net asset value per security is determined for the purpose of the issue or redemption of securities of the mutual fund next preceding the payment date of such dividend or other distribution or the issue date of such right.

SECTION 16
ADVERTISING

> See Canadian Securities Administrators Notice 93/5 "National Policy Statement No. 39 – Mutual Funds Section 16 – Sales Commissions".

SECTION 16.01 – DEFINITIONS

(a) For the purposes of this Section 16, the following terms have the following meanings:

(i) "advertisement" means a sales communication that is published or designed for use on a telephone or tape recording, videotape, display, sign or billboard, motion picture or other public media or, if paid for, in a newspaper, magazine or other periodical, radio or television;

(ii) "cash equivalents" means cash or an evidence of deposit issued or fully guaranteed by a bank to which the Bank Act (Canada) applies or by a loan corporation or trust company registered under applicable federal or provincial legislation, provided that the short-term debt instruments of such institution have one of the ratings specified in Section 16.01(a)(iv)(D);

(iii) "fees and charges" means all sales charges, distribution fees, management fees, administrative fees, account set-up or closing charges, redemption fees, transfer fees or any other fees, charges or expenses whether or not contingent or deferred which are or may be payable in connection with the purchase, holding or redemption of securities of a mutual fund;

(iv) "money market fund" means a mutual fund the securities of which are qualified for distribution under a prospectus and which has and intends to continue to have:

A. all of its assets invested in cash equivalents or debt obligations maturing in 13 months (25 months for government obligations) or less or in floating rate debt obligations where the principal amount of such obligations had a market value of approximately par at the time of each change in the rate to be paid to the holders of such obligations;

B. a portfolio with a dollar-weighted average term to maturity not exceeding 180 days;

C. not less than 95 percent of its assets invested in cash equivalents or securities, which assets are denominated in the same currency as the units of the mutual fund; and

D. not less than 95 percent of its assets invested in cash equivalents or debt obligations of issuers having an approved credit rating for commercial paper as set out in Schedule 1 attached to this policy.

For purposes of calculating the dollar-weighted average term to maturity of the money market fund's portfolio, the term of a floating rate obligation shall be the period remaining to the date of the next rate setting;

(v) "performance data" means any rating,[1] ranking, quotation, discussion or analysis regarding rate of return, yield, volatility or other measurement or description of the investment performance of a mutual fund;

(vi) "report to securityholders" means any report that includes annual or interim financial statements that is delivered to securityholders of a mutual fund;

(vii) "sales communication" means:

A. any oral communication or written communication (which written communication may consist of one or more components provided they are delivered as a package at the same time) used to induce the

---

[1] For greater certainty, ratings prepared by independent organizations which reflect the credit quality of a mutual fund's portfolio are not ratings within the meaning of Section 16.01(a)(v).

purchase of securities issued by a mutual fund whether such communication is made by the mutual fund, the promoter, manager, principal distributor or portfolio adviser of the mutual fund or by any other person or corporation; and

B. a report to securityholders;

but does not include:

A. a communication solely between a mutual fund or its promoter, manager, principal distributor or portfolio adviser and a registered dealer or between a registered dealer and its registered salespersons that is indicated to be internal or confidential and which is not designed to be passed on by the registered dealer or registered salespersons to any investor or potential investor;[2] and

B. a preliminary prospectus or prospectus;

(viii) "standard performance data" means:

A. in the case of a money market fund, current yield or current yield and effective yield calculated in accordance with the provisions of Sections 16.05(a) and (b) provided that any statement of effective yield is no more prominent than the statement of current yield; and

B. in the case of any mutual fund other than a money market fund, total return calculated in accordance with the provisions of Sections 16.05(a) and (c); and

(ix) "underlying fund" means a mutual fund in which an asset allocation service recommends investment.

(b) Any written or oral communication used to induce the purchase of an asset allocation service that is described in a mutual fund's prospectus is deemed to be a sales communication and such an asset allocation service is deemed to be a mutual fund for the purposes of Section 16.

SECTION 16.02 – GENERAL REQUIREMENTS

(a) Notwithstanding any other provision of Section 16, no sales communication shall:

(i) include an untrue or misleading statement of a fact or omit to state a fact necessary to prevent such sales communication from being misleading;

(ii) include a statement that conflicts with information that is contained in the preliminary prospectus or prospectus of such mutual fund;[3]

(iii) present information in a manner that distorts information contained in the preliminary prospectus or prospectus of such mutual fund either as a result of selective presentation or otherwise; or

(iv) include a visual image such as a photograph, sketch, drawing, logo or graph which provides a misleading impression.

(b) Whether or not a particular description, representation, illustration or other statement is misleading depends upon an evaluation of the context in which it is made. The following list sets forth some of the reasons why a sales communication will be considered to be misleading and has been included for the assistance of mutual funds and their advisers. No attempt has been made to enumerate all such reasons since each sales communication must be assessed individually.

(i) A statement will be misleading if it lacks explanations, qualifications, limitations or other statements necessary or appropriate to make such statement not misleading.

---

2   Where such a communication is passed on by the registered dealer or registered salesperson, such a communication will be a sales communication made by the party passing on the communication.

3   For greater certainty, where the mutual fund is an asset allocation service, references to preliminary prospectus and prospectus in Sections 16.02(a)(ii) and (iii) are deemed to be references to the preliminary prospectus or prospectus of an underlying fund.

(ii) Representations about past or future investment performance will be misleading if they are:

    A. portrayals of past income, gain, or growth of assets that convey an impression of the net investment results achieved by an actual or hypothetical investment that is not justified under the circumstances;

    B. representations about security of capital or expenses associated with an investment that are not justified under the circumstances or representations about possible future gains or income; and

    C. representations that or presentations of past investment performance that imply that future gains or income may be inferred from or predicted based on past investment performance or portrayals of past performance.

(iii) A statement about the characteristics or attributes of a mutual fund will be misleading if:

    A. it concerns possible benefits connected with or resulting from services to be provided or methods of operation and does not give equal prominence to discussion of any risks or associated limitations;

    B. it makes exaggerated or unsubstantiated claims about management skill or techniques, characteristics of the mutual fund or an investment in securities issued by such fund, services offered by the fund or its manager, or effects of government supervision; or

    C. it makes unwarranted or incompletely explained comparisons to other investment vehicles or indexes.

(c) A sales communication that compares the performance of one or more mutual funds with a consumer price index, any stock, bond or other index, average, or any guaranteed investment certificate or other certificate of deposit, real estate or any other investment of any kind or nature, including another mutual fund, must:

    (i) include all facts that, if disclosed, would be likely to materially alter the conclusions reasonably drawn or implied by the comparison;

    (ii) present data for each subject of the comparison for the same period or periods;

    (iii) where differing types of investments are compared, explain clearly any relevant differences in guarantees, fluctuation of principal, income or total return, insurance, tax features and any other factors necessary to make the comparison fair and not misleading; and

    (iv) where the performance of an index or average is compared, if appropriate in view of the nature of the comparison, describe the index or average, point out if there are material differences between the composition of or calculation of the performance of the index or average and the investment portfolio of the mutual fund and state any other factors necessary to make the comparison fair and not misleading.

(d) A written sales communication must bear the name of the person or entity which prepared the sales communication, may bear the name of the registrant distributing the sales communication and, except in the case of an advertisement, must indicate the date of first publication of the sales communication.

(e) All text of a written sales communication must be at least as large as 8-point type and in the case of sales communications broadcast on television, the warnings prescribed in Sections 16.06(a) and (b) must, if not given orally, be clearly displayed and visible for a reasonable period of time.

(f) Whenever a written sales communication includes a rate of return or a mathematical table illustrating the potential effect of a compound rate of return, such sales communication must contain a statement to the effect that such rate of return or mathematical table is used only for the purpose of illustrating the effects of the compound growth rate and is not intended to reflect future values of the mutual fund or returns on investment in the mutual fund.

(g) No sales communication may refer to a mutual fund as a money fund, cash fund or money market fund or imply that a mutual fund is a money market fund unless at the time the sales communication is used and for each period for which money market fund standard performance data is provided the fund satisfies the definition of money market fund and it intends to continue to satisfy such definition.

(h) A sales communication shall not imply that a registered retirement savings plan, registered retirement income fund or registered education savings plan in itself, rather than the mutual fund to which the sales communication relates, is an investment.

SECTION 16. 03 – DISCLOSURE REGARDING FEES AND CHARGES

(a) A mutual fund may not be described in a sales communication as a "no-load fund" where any fee or charge (whether or not contingent) is payable by an investor in respect of a trade in the mutual fund's securities to the fund manager or any registrant named in the sales communication in connection with the purchase or redemption of securities of the mutual fund, other than:

    (i) optional fees and charges related to specific services (e.g. transfer fees and fees and charges for registered education savings plans, registered retirement savings plans, registered retirement income funds, pre-authorized chequing plans, systematic withdrawal plans and contractual plans);

    (ii) redemption fees in respect of the redemption of securities of any mutual fund that is not a money market fund which are redeemed within 90 days of the purchase of such mutual fund securities provided the existence of such fees is disclosed in the sales communication; or

    (iii) one-time account set-up costs which reflect the administrative costs of establishing a securityholder's account provided the existence of such costs is disclosed in the sales communication.

If a mutual fund is described in a sales communication as "no-load", the sales communication must indicate a registrant through which an investor may purchase the mutual fund on a "no-load" basis.

(b) If a sales communication contains any reference, other than a reference to "no-load" or to the disclosure required by Sections 16.04(a)(v), (vi) or (vii), to the existence or absence of fees or charges, the sales communication must provide a summary of the types of fees and charges and must not give undue prominence to the existence or absence of any particular fee or charge.

SECTION 16.04 – PERFORMANCE DATA

(a) No sales communication may contain performance data unless it complies with the following guidelines:

    (i) it contains standard performance data for each mutual fund for which it contains performance data and where it is a written sales communication the standard performance data is presented in type which is at least as prominent as that used to present the other performance data;

    (ii) any performance data reflects or includes references to all elements of return;

    (iii) the sales communication does not contain any performance data relating to a mutual fund for any period or part thereof that is prior to the time when the mutual fund first commenced distributing its securities to the public under a prospectus, or where the mutual fund is an asset allocation service, prior to the time when the asset allocation service was first offered to the public and described in a prospectus of an underlying fund;

    (iv) where the sales communication is an advertisement, the performance data relates only to a mutual fund or to mutual funds which are under common management, or to the comparison of a mutual fund with another fund or other funds with similar investment objectives or with an index or average;[4]

---

4   For greater certainty, where the mutual fund is an asset allocation service, mutual funds with similar investment objectives are other asset allocation services and mutual funds which are based upon a tactical asset allocation model.

(v) where the standard performance data relates to a money market fund, the sales communication:

  (A) includes a description of the specific application of the general assumptions provided in Section 16.05(a) upon which the standard performance data is calculated or includes disclosure in the following words or to like effect:

   [standard performance data] assumes [assume] reinvestment of distributions only and does [do] not take into account sales, redemption, distribution or optional charges payable by any securityholder which would have reduced returns; and

  (B) includes a statement in the following words or to like effect:

   Annualized historical yield[s] is [are] for the seven day period ended on [insert a specific date] [, annualized in the case of effective yield by compounding the seven day return];

  provided that in written sales communications such statement is made in close proximity to the standard performance data;

(vi) where the standard performance data relates to a mutual fund other than a money market fund the sales communication includes a description of the specific application of the general assumptions provided in Section 16.05(a) upon which the standard performance data is calculated or includes disclosure in the following words or to like effect:

   The indicated rate[s] of return is [are] the historical annual compounded total return[s] including changes in [insert share or unit] value and reinvestment of all [insert dividends or distributions] and does [do] not take into account sales, redemption, distribution or optional charges payable by any securityholder which would have reduced returns;

(vii) where the standard performance data relates to an asset allocation service, the sales communication includes a description for both the asset allocation service and the underlying funds of the specific application of the general assumptions provided in Section 16.05(a) upon which the standard performance data is calculated or includes disclosure in the following words or like effect:

   The indicated rate[s] of return is [are] the historical annual compounded total return[s] assuming the investment strategy recommended by the asset allocation service is used and after deduction of the fees and charges in respect of the service. These returns are based on the performance of the underlying funds including changes in [insert share or unit] value and reinvestment of all [insert dividends or distributions] and does [do] not take into account sales, redemption, distribution or optional charges payable by any securityholder in respect of an underlying fund which would have reduced returns;

(viii) if there have been any changes during the performance measurement period in the mutual fund's management, fundamental investment objectives, characterization as a money market fund, or in any portfolio adviser or in the ownership of the manager of the mutual fund or in fees or charges, including the waiving or absorbing of fees or charges, that would or could have materially affected the mutual fund's performance, the sales communication contains:

  (A) summary disclosure of the change or a statement to the effect that the mutual fund has undergone changes during or subsequent to the performance measurement period which would or could have [insert as appropriate: affected/increased/decreased] the mutual fund's performance had those changes been in effect throughout the period; and

  (B) for a money market fund which during the performance measurement period did not pay or accrue the full amount of any fees and charges of the type described under Sections 16.05(a)(i) and (iii), disclosure of the difference between such full amounts and the amounts actually charged, expressed as an annualized percentage on a basis comparable to current yield as described in Section 16.05(b);

National Policies

   (ix) where the sales communication is not a report to securityholders and relates to a money market fund, the standard performance data which is given has been calculated for the most recent 7 day period for which it is practicable to calculate the standard performance data taking into account publication deadlines, provided that this 7 day period is not more than 45 days prior to the date of the appearance or use of the advertisement in which it is included and not more than 45 days prior to the date of first publication of any other sales communication in which it is used;[5]

   (x) where the sales communication is not a report to securityholders and relates to a mutual fund other than a money market fund, the standard performance data which is given has been calculated for the 1, 3, 5 and 10 year periods ending on a calendar month end that is not more than 45 days prior to the date of the appearance or use of the advertisement in which it is included and that is not more than 3 months prior to the date of first publication of any other sales communication in which it is included, in each case ending on the same calendar month end;

   (xi) where the sales communication is a report to securityholders, the standard performance data that is given has been calculated for the applicable standard performance data period or periods ended on the last day of the most recent period for which financial statements are provided in the report to securityholders;

   (xii) the sales communication clearly identifies the periods for which the performance data is calculated and indicates, if appropriate, how more up to date standard performance data may be obtained;

   (xiii) the sales communication includes a statement that all performance data represents past performance and is not necessarily indicative of future performance;

   (xiv) where the sales communication refers to a mutual fund performance rating or ranking, the rating or ranking must be prepared by an independent organization and standard performance data must be provided for any mutual fund whose rating or ranking is quoted; and

   (xv) where a sales communication refers to a credit rating which reflects the credit quality of a mutual fund's portfolio, the rating must be prepared by an independent rating organization, only the most current rating of that rating organization may be quoted and the lowest such rating of any independent rating organization must be quoted if the mutual fund is rated by more than one such organization.

 (b) Advertisements broadcast on radio or television may not contain performance data.

SECTION 16.05 – CALCULATION OF STANDARD PERFORMANCE DATA

 (a) The following are general assumptions for the calculation of standard performance data:[6]

   (i) any fees and charges payable by the mutual fund are accrued or paid;

   (ii) any dividends or distributions by the mutual fund are reinvested in the

---

5 Under certain market conditions, standard performance data for a money market fund which is calculated for a 7 day period ended not more than 45 days prior to the date of the appearance or use of the sales communication in which it is included may be misleading. For example, where interest rates have declined significantly from the levels they were at during a 7 day period, performance information which does not reflect this decline may be misleading and consequently more current information may be necessary. Similarly, standard performance data for a non-money market mutual fund which is calculated for a 1, 3 or 5 year period ending on a calendar month end that is not more than 45 days prior to the date of the appearance or use of the advertisement in which it is included or that is not more than 3 months prior to the date of first publication of any other sales communication in which it is included may be misleading.

6 Where the mutual fund is an asset allocation service, these assumptions are to be used for both the asset allocation service and the underlying funds, where applicable.

fund at the net asset value per security of the mutual fund on the reinvestment dates during the performance measurement period;

(iii) any recurring fees and charges that are payable by all securityholders and any fees and charges that are payable by subscribers in connection with an asset allocation service are accrued or paid in proportion to the length of the performance measurement period. (For any such fees and charges which would result in the performance information being dependent upon the size of the account, assume the greater of a $10,000 account size or the minimum amount that may be invested; provided that, in the case of fees and charges which are fully negotiable, assume the average amount actually paid by an account of the same size);

(iv) there are no non-recurring fees and charges that are payable by some or all securityholders (e.g. front-end sales commissions and contingent deferred redemption charges) and no recurring fees and charges that are payable by some but not all securityholders (e.g. distribution fees);

(v) there are no optional fees and charges related to specific services (e.g. transfer fees[7] and fees and charges for registered retirement savings plans, registered retirement income funds, registered education savings plans, pre-authorized chequing plans, systematic withdrawal plans and contractual plans);

(vi) a complete redemption occurs at the end of the performance measurement period so that the ending redeemable value includes elements of return such as income that has been accrued but not yet paid to securityholders;

(vii) the calculation of standard performance data is based on actual historical performance and the fees and charges payable by the mutual fund and by securityholders in effect during the performance measurement period;

(viii) in the case of an asset allocation service, the calculation of standard performance data is based on the assumption that the investment strategy recommended by the asset allocation service is utilized for the performance measurement period; and

(ix) in the case of an asset allocation service, transfer fees are assumed to be accrued or paid. (For any such fees and charges which would result in the performance information being dependent upon the size of the account, assume the greater of a $10,000 account size or the minimum amount that may be invested; provided that, in the case of fees and charges which are fully negotiable, assume the average amount actually paid by an account of the same size).

(b) For purposes of this Section 16.05(b), the following terms have the following meanings:

(i) "current yield" means the current yield of a money market fund expressed as a percentage and determined by applying the following formula:

current yield = [seven day return x 365/7] x 100;

(ii) "effective yield" means the effective yield of a money market fund expressed as a percentage and determined by applying the following formula:

effective yield = [(seven day return + 1)$^{(365/7)}$-1] x 100; and

(iii) "seven day return" means the income yield (i.e. excluding realized or unrealized net capital gains) of a securityholder's account in a money market fund which is calculated by:

(A) determining the net change, exclusive of new subscriptions (other than from the reinvestment of distributions) or redemption of units of the money market fund, in the value of a securityholder's account;

(B) subtracting all fees and charges of the type described in Section 16.05(a)(iii) at the end of the seven day period; and

---

7   Where the mutual fund is an asset allocation service, transfer fees are not optional fees or charges related to specific services.

(C) dividing the result by the value of the account at the beginning of the seven day period.

Money market fund standard performance data must be calculated to the nearest one hundredth of one percent.

(c) For purposes of this Section 16.05(c), "total return" has the following meaning:

"total return" means the annual compounded rate of return for a mutual fund for a period that would equate the initial value to the redeemable value at the end of the period, expressed as a percentage, and determined by applying the following formula:

total return = [(redeemable value/initial value)$^{(1/N)}$ - 1] x 100

Where N = the length of the performance measurement period in years, with a minimum value of 1;

If there are fees and charges of the type described in Section 16.05(a)(iii), "redeemable value" and "initial value" will have to be determined by applying assumptions to a hypothetical securityholder account.

If there are no fees and charges of the type described in Section 16.05(a)(iii), the calculation of total return using the above formula for a mutual fund which is not an asset allocation service may be simplified by assuming a hypothetical investment of one unit or share of the mutual fund as follows:

(i) "initial value" means the net asset value of one unit or share of a mutual fund at the beginning of the performance measurement period; and

(ii) "redeemable value" =

$$R \times (1 + D_1/P_1) \times (1 + D_2/P_2) \times (1 + D_3/P_3)...\times (1 + D_n/P_n)$$

Where		
R =	the redemption value of one unit or share of the mutual fund at the end of the performance measurement period
D =	dividend or distribution amount per unit or share of the mutual fund at the time of each distribution
P =	dividend or distribution reinvestment price per unit or share of the mutual fund at the time of each distribution
n =	number of dividends or distributions during the performance measurement period.

Standard performance data for a mutual fund other than a money market fund must be calculated to the nearest one tenth of one per cent.

SECTION 16.06 – WARNINGS

(a) Subject to this section, all sales communications, other than reports to securityholders, must contain a warning in the following words or to like effect:

Important information about this mutual fund is contained in its simplified prospectus. Obtain a copy from [insert name and address or telephone number of registrant, or in the case of a financial institution, indicate branches as appropriate] and read it carefully before investing. [For money market funds disclose: yield will fluctuate and there is no assurance the fund can maintain a fixed net asset value]. [For other funds disclose: unit/share value, [insert yield for income funds only] and investment return will fluctuate].

(b) Every sales communication distributed after the time a receipt for the preliminary prospectus of the mutual fund described in the sales communication is issued but prior to the time a receipt for its prospectus is issued must, in place of the warning language required by Section 16.06(a), contain a warning in the following words or to like effect:

A preliminary simplified prospectus relating to these securities has been filed with the securities commissions or similar authorities in certain provinces or territories of Canada but has not yet become final for the purpose of offering these securities. There may be no sale of these securities prior to the issuance of a receipt for the simplified prospectus by the applicable securities regulatory authorities in the jurisdiction where the sale or offer is made. Important information concerning this offering will be contained in the issuer's simplified prospectus. Obtain a copy from [insert name and address or telephone number of registrant, or in the case of a financial institution, indicate branches as appropriate] and read the simplified prospectus before investing. [For money market funds disclose: yield will fluctuate and there is no assurance that the fund can maintain a fixed net asset value]. [For other funds disclose: unit/share value, [insert yield for income funds only] and investment return will fluctuate].

(c) Where a mutual fund has not filed pursuant to National Policy Statement No. 36, these warnings should be amended to refer to its long form prospectus.

(d) Where the mutual fund is an asset allocation service, the warnings in Sections 16.06(a) and 16.06(b) should be modified to refer to the prospectuses and performance of the underlying funds.

(e) Where a sales communication is broadcast on radio the warnings in Sections 16.06(a) and 16.06(b) must be communicated orally and where the sales communication is broadcast on television, the warnings may be communicated orally or visually.

(f) A sales communication need not contain the warning required by Section 16.06(a) if:

    (i) the sales communication does not contain any performance data; and

    (ii) the warning, if it was included, would constitute more than 50% of the sales communication.

SECTION 16.07 – SALES COMMUNICATIONS DURING THE WAITING PERIOD

Where a sales communication is used after the time a receipt for the preliminary prospectus of the mutual fund described in the sales communication is issued but prior to the time a receipt for its prospectus is issued, the sales communication may only identify the security by indicating:

(1) whether the security represents a share in a company or an interest in a non-corporate entity (e.g. a trust);

(2) the issuer of the security and its manager;

(3) briefly the investment objectives of the issuer (e.g. whether the mutual fund is a money market fund, whether the mutual fund invests in Canadian equities or bonds or is a balanced fund, etc.);

(4) without giving details, whether the security is or will be a qualified investment for a registered retirement savings plan, registered retirement income fund or registered education savings plan or qualifies or will qualify the holder for special tax treatment; and

(5) any additional information permitted by applicable securities legislation.

SECTION 16.08 – APPLICATION OF OTHER POLICIES

The Principles of Regulation regarding the distribution of mutual funds by financial institutions apply to sales communications.

The provisions of National Policy Statements Nos. 21 and 25, Interim National Policy Statement No. 42 and Uniform Act Policy No. 2-13 do not apply to sales communications.

SECTION 16.09 – EFFECTIVE DATE AND TRANSITION PERIOD

(a) The effective date of Section 16 is August 1, 1992.

(b) For the purposes of this section, a mutual fund that:

    (i) at any time during the month of June, 1992 described itself as a money fund, cash fund or money market fund; or

    (ii) published its current yield or current and effective yields in accordance with the CSA Notice - Rates of Return on Money Market Funds (which took effect on November 12, 1990);

may, if it so elects, be deemed to satisfy the definition of money market fund in Section 16.01(a)(iv) and the requirements of Section 16.02(g) for the period up to and including December 31, 1992.

(c) Existing supplies of written sales communications (other than advertisements and reports to securityholders) that do not comply with Section 16 may be utilized until December 31, 1992. There is no restriction on the continued use of reports to securityholders that were initially published prior to the effective date of Section 16.

SCHEDULE I
APPROVED CREDIT RATING

(1) The approved credit rating for purposes of Subsections 1.01(1), (3) and (18) and the approved credit rating with respect to the over-the-counter options and forward contracts, or the equivalent debt of the other party thereto, required by paragraph 2.07(2)(c), is a credit rating that is equal to or higher than the level indicated in the table below:

Approved Rating Agency	Commercial Paper	Debt
Canadian Bond Rating Service Inc.	A-1	A
Dominion Bond Rating Service Limited	R-1-L	A
IBCA Limited	A-1	A
Moody's Investors Service, Inc.	P-1	A
Standard & Poor's Corporation	A-1	A

provided that

(i) there has been no announcement that the rating may be down-graded to a level below the level so indicated; and

(ii) no other Approved Rating Agency, as noted above, has rated the over-the-counter option or forward contract, or equivalent debt of the other party to the transaction, below the level so indicated unless the over-the-counter option or forward contract is issued or guaranteed by the Federal, Provincial or Territorial Governments of Canada or is issued or guaranteed by the Government of the United States of America.

SCHEDULE II
PERMITTED CLEARING CORPORATIONS

Trans Canada Options Inc.

The Options Clearing Corporation

International Options Clearing Corporation

The Intermarket Clearing Corporation

SCHEDULE III
LIST OF PERMITTED FUTURES EXCHANGES

The securities authorities, at the request of The Investment Funds Institute of Canada, are publishing with National Policy Statement No. 39, a list of permitted futures exchanges. By including the permitted futures exchanges set out in this Schedule the securities authorities make no representation as to the suitability of trading on such exchanges and have not examined the trading practices, clearing arrangements, by laws, rules or regulations under which such exchanges operate nor the regulatory regimes to which they are subject.

Australia

Sydney Futures Exchange Limited
Australian Financial Futures Market

Austria

Österreichische Termin-und Option börse (OTOB - The Austrian Options and Futures Exchange)

Belgium

Belfox CV (Belgium Futures and Options Exchange)

Brazil

Bolsa Brasileira de Futuros
Bolsa de Mercadorias & Futuros
Bolsa de Valores de Rio de Janeiro

Canada

The Winnipeg Commodity Exchange
The Toronto Futures Exchange
The Montreal Exchange

Denmark

Kobenhavus Fondsbørs (Copenhagen Stock Exchange)
Garenti fonden for Dankse Optioner og Futures (Guarantee Fund for Danish Options and Futures)
Futop (Copenhagen Stock Exchange)

Finland

Suomen Optionmeklarit Oy (Finnish Options Market)
Oy Suomen Optiopörssi (Finnish Options Exchange)

France

Marché à terme international de France S.A. (MATIF S.A.)

Germany

DTB Deutsche Terminbörse GmbH

Hong Kong

Hong Kong Futures Exchange Limited

Ireland

Irish Futures and Options Exchange

Japan

Osaka Shoken Torihikisho (Osaka Securities Exchange)
The Tokyo Commodity Exchange for Industry
The Tokyo International Financial Futures Exchange
Tokyo Stock Exchange

Netherlands

EOE-Optiebeurs (European Options Exchange)
Financiele Termijnmarkt Amsterdam N.V.

New Zealand

New Zealand Futures and Options Exchange

Philippines

Manila International Futures Exchange

Singapore

Singapore International Monetary Exchange Limited (SIMEX)

Spain

Meff Renta Fija
Meff Renta Variable

Sweden

OM Stockholm Fondkommission AB

Switzerland

Swiss Options and Financial Futures Exchange (SOFFEX)

National
Policies

United Kingdom

London International Financial Futures and Options Exchange (LIFFE)

OM London

United States

Chicago Board of Trade (CBOT)
Chicago Mercantile Exchange (CME)
Commodity Exchange, Inc. (COMEX)
Financial Instrument Exchange (Finex) a division of the New York Cotton Exchange
Board of Trade of Kansas City, Missouri, Inc.
MidAmerica Commodity Exchange
New York Futures Exchange, Inc. (NYFE)
Pacific Stock Exchange
Philadelphia Board of Trade (PBOT)
Twin Cities Board of Trade

NATIONAL POLICY No. 40
TIMELY DISCLOSURE

A. INTRODUCTION

This policy statement applies to all issuers whose securities are publicly traded in Canada, including reporting issuers or the equivalent in any Canadian jurisdiction. It replaces Uniform Act Policy 2-12, and is effective as of December 1, 1987.

Where the requirements of the Policy go beyond the technical requirements of existing legislation, the securities administrators and stock exchanges request that issuers, their counsel, and market professionals regard such requirements as guidelines to follow in order to assist in the operation in Canada of an open and fair marketplace which merits the trust and confidence of the investing public.

Issuers are reminded that this policy statement does not replace the disclosure requirements set out in the provincial securities statutes and compliance with this Policy must be supplementary to compliance with the relevant provincial statutes. Moreover, if securities of an issuer are listed on one or more stock exchanges in Canada, the issuer must also comply with the rules of the relevant exchange(s) concerning timely disclosure.

Further, nothing in this Policy Statement abrogates from the discretion of a securities administrator to request information from an issuer or to issue cease trading orders or apply other sanctions within its jurisdiction where, in the view of the administrator, there is inadequate public disclosure as to the affairs of an issuer whose securities are publicly traded.

B. BASIC PRINCIPLE – DISCLOSURE OF MATERIAL INFORMATION

It is a cornerstone principle of securities regulation that all persons investing in securities have equal access to information that may affect their investment decisions. Public confidence in the integrity of the securities markets requires that all investors be on an equal footing through timely disclosure of material information concerning the business and affairs of reporting issuers and of companies whose securities trade in secondary markets. Therefore, immediate disclosure of all material information through the news media is required.

C. DETERMINING THE RELEVANT REGULATORY AUTHORITY FOR CONSULTATION, DISCLOSURE AND FILING OF MATERIAL INFORMATION

The following sections discuss the meaning of "material information" and how such information is to be disclosed. This section discusses the general rules for determining which securities administrator and/or stock exchange is to be consulted for requirements relating to, and the disclosure and filing of, material information. Any references to "the relevant securities regulator" in the following commentary should refer to this part of the policy statement.

It is intended that the number of regulatory authorities that must be consulted in a particular matter be kept to a minimum. There are six general principles in determining the relevant securities regulator for consultation on, disclosure, and filing of material information. The particular rules that apply depend on the jurisdiction, whether the security is listed and, if so, the particular exchange on which the security is listed. These rules are as follows:

1. In the case of unlisted securities, the relevant securities regulator is the administrator in the jurisdiction having the principal market for the unlisted security.

2. In the case of securities listed on The Toronto Stock Exchange ("TSE"), the Montreal Exchange ("ME"), or the Vancouver Stock Exchange ("VSE") the stock exchange is the relevant securities regulator, although the issuer may consult with the securities administrator of the particular jurisdiction.

3. In the case of securities listed on any other Canadian stock exchange, both the stock exchange and the securities administrator in the jurisdiction having the principal market for the listed security are considered to be the relevant securities regulators.

4. In the case of securities listed on two or more Canadian stock exchanges, each stock exchange is a relevant securities regulator, and must be dealt with. The issuer may also consult with the securities administrator in the jurisdiction having the principal market for the listed security.

5. Material change reports and media releases must be filed in accordance with the requirements of legislation in jurisdictions having such legislation. See Part D.

6. The rules of all stock exchanges upon which securities are listed must be observed.

These rules for determining the relevant securities regulator for consultation, disclosure, and filing of material information are fundamental to the commentary that follows. For example, where a news release is required these rules will determine the relevant securities regulator(s) for disclosure and the jurisdiction(s) in which the news release must be filed.

D. MATERIAL INFORMATION

The requirement to disclose material information supplements the provisions of the Securities Acts of Alberta, British Columbia, Ontario, Quebec and Nova Scotia which require disclosure of any "material change" by issuing a press release, and filing with the securities administrator the press release in the case of Quebec, and the press release and a material change report in the case of Alberta, British Columbia, Ontario and Nova Scotia.

Definition

Material information is any information relating to the business and affairs of an issuer that results in or would reasonably be expected to result in a significant change in the market price or value of any of the issuer's securities.

Material information consists of both material facts and material changes relating to the business and affairs of an issuer. The market price or value of an issuer's securities is sometimes affected by, in addition to material information, the existence of rumours and speculation. Where this is the case, the issuer may be required to make an announcement as to whether such rumours and speculation are factual or not.

It is the responsibility of each issuer to determine what information is material according to the above definition in the context of the issuer's own affairs. The materiality of information varies from one issuer to another according to the size of its profits, assets and capitalization, the nature of its operations and many other factors. An event that is "significant" or "major" in the context of a smaller issuer's business and affairs is often not material to a larger issuer. The issuer itself is in the best position to apply the definition of material information to its own unique circumstances.

Consultation with Regulatory Authorities

Decisions on disclosure require careful subjective judgments and issuers are encouraged to consult on a confidential basis the relevant regulatory authority and, where applicable, the relevant exchange when in doubt as to whether disclosure should be made.

Immediate Disclosure

An issuer is required to disclose material information concerning its business and affairs forthwith upon the information becoming known to management, or in the case of information previously known, forthwith upon it becoming apparent that the information is material. Issuers are required to provide the relevant regulatory authority with a copy of any news release concurrently upon dissemination to the public.

Immediate release of information is necessary to ensure that it is promptly available to all investors and to reduce the risk that persons with access to that information will act upon undisclosed information. Unusual trading marked by significant changes in the price or trading volumes of any of an issuer's securities prior to the announcement of material information is embarrassing to management and damaging to the reputation of the securities market since the investing public may assume that certain persons benefited from access to material information which was not generally disclosed.

In restricted circumstances disclosure of material information may be delayed for reasons of corporate confidentiality. See Part G.

Developments to be Disclosed

Issuers are not generally required to interpret the impact of external political, economic and social developments on their affairs. However, if an external development will have or has had a direct effect on the business and affairs of an issuer that is both material (in a sense outlined above) and uncharacteristic of the effect generally experienced by other issuers engaged in the same business or industry, the issuer is urged to explain, where practical, the particular impact on them. For example, a change in government policy that affects most issuers in a particular industry does not require an announcement, but if it affects only one or a few issuers in a material way, such issuers should make an announcement.

The market price or value of an issuer's securities may be affected by factors relating directly to the securities themselves as well as by information concerning the issuer's business and affairs. For example, changes in an issuer's issued capital, stock splits, redemptions and dividend decisions may all impact upon the market price of a security.

Actual or proposed developments that are likely to give rise to material information and thus to require prompt disclosure include, but are not limited to, the following:

1. Changes in share ownership that may affect control of the issuer.

2. Changes in corporate structure, such as reorganizations, amalgamations etc.

3. Take-over bids or issuer bids.

4. Major corporate acquisitions or dispositions.

5. Changes in capital structure.

6. Borrowing of a significant amount of funds.

7. Public or private sale of additional securities.

8. Development of new products and developments affecting the issuer's resources, technology, products or market.

9. Significant discoveries by resource companies.

10. Entering into or loss of significant contracts.

11. Firm evidence of significant increases or decreases in near-term earnings prospects.

12. Changes in capital investment plans or corporate objectives.

13. Significant changes in management.

14. Significant litigation.

15. Major labour disputes or disputes with major contractors or suppliers.

16. Events of default under financing or other agreements.

17. Any other developments relating to the business and affairs of the issuer that would reasonably be expected to significantly affect the market price or value of any of the issuer's securities or that would reasonably be expected to have a significant influence on a reasonable investor's investment decision.

Disclosure is only required where a development is material according to the definition of material information. Announcements of an intention to proceed with a transaction or activity should be made when a decision has been made to proceed with it by the issuer's board of directors, or by senior management with the expectation of concurrence from the board of directors. However, a corporate development in respect of which no firm decision has yet been made but that is reflected in the market place may require prompt disclosure. See "Rumours" under Part E and Part G "Confidentiality".

Forecasts of earnings and other financial forecasts need not be disclosed, but where a significant increase or decrease in earnings is indicated in the near future, such as in the next fiscal quarter, this fact must be disclosed. Forecasts should not be provided on a selective basis to certain investors not involved in the management of the affairs of the issuer. If disclosed, they should be generally disclosed. Reference should be made to National Policy Statement No. 48, "Future-Oriented Financial Information".

E. DISCLOSURE

Decisions as to the dissemination of information and the temporary halting of trading are, in the case of listed securities, usually made by the relevant stock exchange, with or without consultation with the securities administrator of the jurisdiction. However, in certain circumstances, trading in a listed security may be halted as a result of a cease trading order issued by a securities administrator. Decisions relating to unlisted securities are made by securities administrators.

Timing of Announcements

The general principle is that significant announcements are required to be released immediately. This rule is subject to exception in certain situations for issuers whose securities are listed for trading on a stock exchange or other organized market (at this time only CDN in Ontario). Subject to the approval of the relevant securities regulator, release of certain announcements may be delayed until the close of trading, provided the material information is not reflected in the price of the stock. Issuer officials are encouraged to seek assistance and direction from the relevant securities regulator as to when an announcement should be released and whether trading in the issuer's securities should be halted for dissemination of an announcement.

Pre-Notification

The policy of immediate disclosure frequently requires that media releases be issued during trading hours, especially when an important corporate development has occurred. Where this is so, it is essential that issuer officials notify the relevant securities regulator by telephone prior to issuance of a media release. The relevant securities regulator will then be able to determine whether trading in any of the issuer's securities should be temporarily halted.

Where a media release is to be issued during trading hours, securities administrators of provinces in which there is a market for the securities and stock exchanges or where securities are listed should be supplied with a copy forthwith upon its release.

Trading Halts

If an announcement is to be made during trading hours, trading in the stock may be halted until the announcement is made public and disseminated. The relevant securities regulator will determine the amount of time necessary for dissemination in any particular case, which determination will be dependent upon the significance and complexity of the announcement. Issuers should understand that a trading halt does not reflect upon the reputation of an issuer's management nor upon the quality of its securities, but is simply for the purpose of providing for adequate dissemination of the relevant information.

In order to determine whether a trading halt is justified, the relevant securities regulator will consider the impact which the announcement is expected to have on the market for the issuer's securities. Any trading halts that are imposed are normally for less than a two hour duration. Where an issuer's securities are listed or traded elsewhere, those exchanges or other markets will coordinate trading halts. There is a convention among exchanges, NASDAQ and CDN that trading in a security traded or listed in more than one market shall be halted and resumed at the same time in each market.

Rumours

Unusual market activity is often caused by the presence of rumours. If the issuer makes a public statement about a rumoured activity, the disclosure must be accurate and not misleading. It is impractical to expect management to be aware of, and comment on, all rumours, but when market activity indicates that trading is being unduly influenced by rumour the relevant securities administrator will request that the issuer make a clarifying statement. A trading halt may be imposed pending a "no corporate developments" statement from the issuer. If a rumour is correct in whole or in part, the issuer, in response to the request, must make immediate disclosure of the relevant material information and a trading halt may be imposed pending release and dissemination of that information.

F. DISSEMINATION

Transmission to Media

A media release should be transmitted to the media by the quickest possible method and in a manner which provides for wide dissemination. Media releases should be made to news services that disseminate financial news nationally, to the financial press and to daily newspapers that provide regular coverage of financial news.

Content of Announcements

Announcements of material information should be factual and balanced, neither over-emphasizing favourable news nor under-emphasizing unfavourable news. Unfavourable news must be disclosed just as promptly and completely as favourable news. While it is clear that news releases may not be able to contain all the details that would be included in a prospectus or similar document, news releases should contain sufficient detail to enable media personnel and investors to appreciate the true substance and importance of the information so that investors may make informed investment decisions. The guiding principle should be to communicate clearly and accurately the nature of the information, without including unnecessary details, exaggerated reports or editorial commentary designed to colour perception of the announcement. The issuer should be prepared to supply further information when appropriate; the name and telephone number of the company official available for comment should be provided in the release.

Misleading Announcements

While all material information must be released immediately, the timing of an announcement of material information must be handled carefully, since either premature or late disclosure may damage the reputation of the securities market. Misleading disclosure activity designed to influence the price of a security is improper. Misleading news releases send signals to the investment community which are not justified by an objective examination of the facts, and may detract from the issuer's credibility. Announcements of an intention to proceed with a transaction or activity should not be made unless the issuer has the ability to carry out the intent (although proceeding may be subject to contingencies) and a decision has been made to proceed with the transaction or activity by the issuer's board of directors, or by senior management with the expectation of concurrence from the board of directors.

G. CONFIDENTIALITY

When Information May be Kept Confidential

In certain circumstances disclosure of material information concerning an issuer's business and affairs may be delayed and kept confidential temporarily where immediate release of the information would be unduly detrimental to the issuer's interests. In such a situation, issuers are required under the law of certain provinces to disclose to the securities administrator on a confidential basis, information that is not being disclosed immediately to the public. Issuers are reminded of subsection 75(4) of the *Securities Act* (Ontario), subsection 67(3) of the *Securities Act* (British Columbia), subsection 118(3) of the *Securities Act* (Alberta), subsection 84(3) of the *Securities Act, 1988* (Saskatchewan), subsection 81(4) of the *Securities Act* (Nova Scotia), and subsection 76(4) of the *Securities Act* (Newfoundland) which stipulate that a reporting issuer that wishes to keep information confidential must renew that request every 10 days. Subsection 118(4) of the *Securities Act* (Alberta) also provides, however, that a reporting issuer must file and issue a news release and file a material change report not later than 180 days from the day such changes became known to the issuer. Section 74 of the *Securities Act* (Quebec) provides that a reporting issuer need not prepare a press release where senior management has reasonable grounds to believe not only that disclosure would be seriously prejudicial to the issuer, but also that no transaction in the issuer's securities has been or will be carried out on the basis of the information not generally known. The issuer must issue and file a press release only once the circumstances justifying non-disclosure have ceased to exist.

Examples of instances in which disclosures might be unduly detrimental to an issuer's interests are where:

(1) Release of the information would prejudice the issuer's ability to pursue specific and limited objectives or to complete a transaction or series of transactions that are under way. For example, premature disclosure of the fact that an issuer intends to purchase a significant asset may increase the cost of the acquisition.

(2) Disclosure of the information would provide competitors with confidential corporate information that would significantly benefit them. Such information may be kept confidential if the issuer is of the opinion that the detriment to it resulting from disclosure would outweigh the detriment to the market in not having access to the information. A decision to release a new product, or details on the features of a new product, may be withheld for competitive reasons, but such information should not be withheld if it is available to competitors from other sources.

(3) Disclosure of information concerning the status of ongoing negotiations would prejudice the successful completion of those negotiations. It is unnecessary to make a series of announcements concerning the status of negotiations with another party concerning a particular transaction. If it seems that the situation is going to stabilize within a short period, public disclosure may be delayed until a definitive announcement can be made. Disclosure should be made once "concrete information" is available, such as a final decision to proceed with the transaction or, at a later point in time, finalization of the terms of the transaction.

Withholding of material information on the basis that disclosure would be unduly detrimental to the issuer's interests can only be justified where the potential harm to the issuer or to investors caused by immediate disclosure may reasonably be considered to outweigh the undesirable consequences of delaying disclosure. While recognizing that there must be a trade-off between an issuer's legitimate interest in maintaining secrecy and the investing public's right to disclosure of corporate information, securities administrators and stock exchanges discourage delaying disclosure for a lengthy period of time since it is unlikely that confidentiality can be maintained beyond the short term.

Maintaining Confidentiality

Where disclosure of material information is delayed, the issuer must maintain complete confidentiality. In the event that such confidential information, or rumours respecting the same, is divulged in any manner (other that in the necessary course of business), the issuer is required to make an immediate announcement on the matter. The relevant securities regulator must be notified of the announcement, in advance, in the usual manner. During the period before material information is disclosed, market activity in the issuer's securities should be closely monitored by the issuer. Any unusual market activity probably means that news of the matter is being disclosed and that certain persons are taking advantage of it. In such case, the relevant securities regulator should be advised immediately and a halt in trading will be imposed until the issuer has made disclosure on the matter.

At any time when material information is being withheld from the public, the issuer is under a duty to take precautions to keep such information completely confidential. Such information should not be disclosed to any of the issuer's officers, employees or advisers, except in the necessary course of business. The directors, officers and employees of an issuer should be reminded on a regular basis that confidential information obtained in the course of their duties must not be disclosed.

H. INSIDER TRADING

Issuers should make insiders and others who have access to material information about the issuer before it is generally disclosed aware that trading in securities of the issuer while in possession of undisclosed material information or tipping such information is an offence under the securities laws of a number of jurisdictions, and may give rise to civil liability.

In any situation where material information is being kept confidential because disclosure would be unduly detrimental to the issuer's best interests, management is under a duty to take every possible precaution to ensure that no trading whatsoever takes place by any insiders or persons in a "special relationship" with the issuer in which use is made of such information before it is generally disclosed to the public.

In the event that a stock exchange or securities administrator is of the opinion that insider or improper trading may have occurred before material information has been disclosed and disseminated, that stock exchange or securities administrator may require that an immediate announcement be made disclosing such material information.

I. RECIPIENTS OF COMMUNICATIONS

Material change reports and media releases should be delivered to the Market Surveillance Branch or the equivalent in all jurisdictions where there is a legal requirement to file such reports and media releases.

Confidential communications should be made as follows:

British Columbia Securities Commission –
> Deputy Superintendent, Registration & Statutory Filings or, if unavailable, Deputy Superintendent, Compliance & Enforcement, or Superintendent of Brokers

Alberta Securities Commission –
> Director, Market Standards

Saskatchewan Securities Commission –
> Registrar or, if unavailable, Chairman

Manitoba Securities Commission –
> Director or, if unavailable, Chairman or Senior Counsel

Ontario Securities Commission –
> Office of the General Counsel

Commission des valeurs mobilières du Québec –
> Directeur du contentieux, or, if unavailable Vice-President or President

Government of New Brunswick –
> Administrator of the Securities Act

Nova Scotia Securities Commission–
> Director, Securities

Government of Newfoundland and Labrador –
> Director of Securities

Government of Prince Edward Island –
> Registrar

Office of the Registrar of Securities for the Northwest Territories –
> Registrar

Office of the Registrar of Securities for Yukon Territory –
> Registrar of Securities or, if unavailable, Deputy Registrar of Securities

It is suggested that confidential written communications be made in sealed envelopes within outer envelopes.

NATIONAL POLICY STATEMENT No. 41
SHAREHOLDER COMMUNICATION

PART I – INTRODUCTION

Holders of securities whose securities are held in the names of clearing agencies, or securities dealers, banks or trust companies ("non-registered holders"), often:

–   do not receive the information from issuers that securities and corporate legislation requires to be delivered to registered shareholders of the same class; and

–   where the securities carry voting rights, are effectively disenfranchised.

Obligations under corporate and securities legislation to send information to and to accept votes from shareholders are cast as obligations in respect of registered security holders. However, market efficiency exerts strong pressure for the registration of securities in the names of either clearing agencies or financial intermediaries (or their nominees).

The number of security holders that are affected is significant, and will increase. Presently, almost 100 billion dollars in value of securities are held in the book-based system of Canadian clearing agencies; that is, The Canadian Depository for Securities Limited ("CDS") or the Vancouver Stock Exchange Service Corp. ("VSESC"). An estimated 30-35% of the public float of issuers is registered in the name of clearing agencies, and in the case of new issues, more than 90% may be so registered. Those percentages do not include securities registered in the names of securities dealers, banks or trust companies.

The Canadian Securities Administrators recognize the right of non-registered holders to receive the materials and voting rights that reporting issuers are currently required by corporate and securities legislation to provide to registered shareholders. This Policy Statement provides a framework to ensure that certain materials, i.e. those materials relating to meetings of security holders, including proxies and audited annual financial statements, will be provided to those non-registered holders of securities of reporting issuers.

The Canadian Securities Administrators also recognize the need for implementation of any system of shareholder communication on a national basis and the issuance of this National Policy Statement underlines the recognition of the need for uniformity in this area.

This Policy Statement essentially embodies the recommendations of the Joint Regulatory Task Force on Shareholder Communication contained in its Report to the Canadian Securities Administrators dated July, 1987.

The goals of the Task Force, and of this National Policy Statement are:

1. To ensure that non-registered holders have the same access to corporate information and voting rights as registered holders;

2. To ensure that the obligations of each participant in the communication chain are equitable and clearly defined; and

3. To ensure that regulation and procedure is uniform nationwide.

PART II – DEFINITIONS

"clearing agency" means a person or company that acts as an intermediary in paying funds or delivering securities or both in connection with trades in securities, and that provides centralized facilities for the clearing of trades in securities, or that provides centralized facilities as a depository in connection with the clearing of trades in securities;

"intermediary" means

(i) a registrant;

(ii) a financial institution (bank or trust company);

(iii) a participant;

(iv) a trustee or administrator of a self-administered retirement savings plan, retirement income fund, education savings plan, or other similar self-administered savings or investment plan registered under the Income Tax Act (Canada); or

(v) a nominee of any of the foregoing;

that holds a security on behalf of another person or company who is not the registered holder of the security, but does not include a person or company that holds a security, or a trustee pursuant to a will, court order, inter vivos trust, or trust for a pension plan, deferred profit sharing plan, retirement savings plan (other than as described in subparagraph (iv) of this definition) or other similar capital accumulation plan, with discretionary voting powers;

"non-registered holder" of a security of an issuer means a person or company, other than a registered holder or another intermediary, on whose behalf an intermediary holds the security;

"participant" in respect to a clearing agency means a securities dealer, trust company, bank or other person or company, including another clearing agency, on whose behalf the clearing agency or its nominee holds securities of an issuer;

"proxy-related materials" in respect of a meeting of security holders of an issuer means the notice of meeting, information circular, and all other material relating to the meeting of security holders that the issuer is required by law to deliver to its registered holders of a class of its securities, including a form of proxy and envelope for return of the proxy where the holders of the class of securities are entitled to vote, and includes for annual meetings its annual report or audited annual financial statements;

"record date" means the date fixed by the issuer for the determination of the registered holders of securities of the issuer who are entitled to receive notice of a meeting of security holders;

"registered holder" in respect of an issuer means a holder of securities of the issuer as shown on the books or records of the issuer; and

"service company" means a person or company, including a transfer agent, stock exchange, or a clearing agency, that carries on the business of facilitating the communication from issuers or other persons or companies required by law to communicate with security holders.

PART III – EFFECTIVE APPLICATION OF POLICY STATEMENT

This Policy Statement applies to meetings of security holders occurring on or after March 1, 1988. Blanket rulings will be issued by securities administrators, where permitted by law, exempting issuers from delivering interim financial statements to registered security holders. The exemption will commence for each issuer for the interim financial statements relating to the first fiscal period ending after the first annual meeting of the issuer taking place on or after March 1, 1988.

Intermediaries and clearing agencies will be required to have their systems in place by December 31, 1987. Intermediaries are required to use reasonable efforts to obtain the instructions from their existing clients who are non-registered holders of securities as to voting and the receipt of proxy-related materials by that date.

The National Policy Statement applies, subject to the exemptions in Part XI, to issuers who are reporting issuers or who have a comparable status in any provincial jurisdiction, to securities dealers, banks and trust companies, to CDS and to VSESC.

The Policy Statement applies to intermediaries who carry on business in Canada or who hold securities on behalf of clients whose addresses are in Canada.

PART IV – ISSUERS' OBLIGATIONS

1.   *Establishment of Record Date*

A reporting issuer shall fix a record date for the determination of those security holders entitled to receive notice of a meeting of security holders to be a date no fewer than 35 or more than 60 days prior to the date of the meeting.

Notice of the meeting and record date must be filed with securities administrators of jurisdictions wherein the issuer's registered shareholders have their addresses, and given to stock exchanges upon which securities of the issuer are listed, and clearing agencies, at least 25 days before the record date.

Notice of the meeting and record date will be published in an index available to the financial press and widely available to the public, no later than 7 days before the record date, pursuant to arrangements made by the security administrators with CDS and VSESC. Issuers may also place individual advertisements if desired.

2.   *Early Search*

At least 25 days before the record date, a reporting issuer shall deliver a notice to each of CDS and VSESC requesting the names and addresses of their participants holding securities of a class the holders of which are entitled to receive notice of the meeting, and their respective holdings.

3.   *Intermediaries and Registered Nominees*

At least 25 days before the record date, the issuer shall obtain the names of intermediaries and their registered nominees and their addresses from a current register maintained by CDS or VSESC, or other designated agent of the securities administrators. This requirement shall be satisfied where the issuer's transfer agent obtains and keeps a list of intermediaries and registered nominees on file and updates the list monthly.

4.   *Search Card*

At least 20 days prior to the record date, a reporting issuer shall deliver a search card,

    (a) to each participant whose name is given to the issuer in response to the request in paragraph 2, and

    (b) to each intermediary and registered nominee on the register of intermediaries and registered nominees whose name appears on the issuer's security holders' list as a registered holder of securities of a class the holders of which are entitled to receive notice of the meeting.

Only one search card need be sent where there is duplication of the names of participants and intermediaries or registered nominees in (a) and (b). Where more than one search card is sent to a particular intermediary, care must be taken by both issuer and intermediary to avoid duplicate responses.

5.   *Contents of Search Card*

A search card shall contain the following information:

    (i) the name of the issuer;

    (ii) the CUSIP number of the issuer;

    (iii) the date of the meeting;

    (iv) the record date for the meeting;

    (v) the class or classes of securities whose holders are entitled to receive notice of the meeting;

    (vi) the class or classes of securities whose holders are entitled to vote at the meeting;

    (vii) if the issuer is willing to deliver the material to non-registered holders itself, a statement to that effect;

    (viii) the items of proxy related material that are to be delivered; and

    (ix) an undertaking to pay the fee established by this Policy Statement for delivery of material to non-registered holders.

6.   *Bulk Delivery of Proxy-Related Materials*

The issuer shall deliver the number of sets of proxy-related materials specified by each intermediary in the intermediary's response to a search card (see Part V, section IV, clause 1) not later than 33 days before the meeting date. The 33 day period is to permit the bulk delivery to and preparation for mailing of the proxy-related material by intermediaries, in order that the intermediaries may mail the material no later than 25 days before the meeting date.

7.   *Payment of Costs of Intermediary*

An issuer shall pay the fees and costs of an intermediary for its services in transmitting proxy-related material in accordance with Schedule 1 to this Policy Statement.

8.   *Exemption from Delivering Interim Financial Statements*

Issuers that deliver proxy-related materials to their non-registered holders and establish and maintain a Supplemental Mailing List will be exempted from delivering their interim financial statements to their registered holders by blanket rulings of security administrators of Quebec, Ontario, Manitoba, Alberta and British Columbia, provided that the issuer files such statements in each jurisdiction where filing is required and with stock exchanges upon which securities are listed, and releases such statements to the financial media.

Companies incorporated under the Company Act (British Columbia) cannot by law be so exempted.

The laws of Saskatchewan require applications for such exemptions to be made by individual issuers. Saskatchewan will grant such exemptions where the majority of the shareholders reside outside Saskatchewan.

Nova Scotia will provide such a blanket exemption, which will not, however, apply to issuers that have a significant percentage of security holders resident in Nova Scotia, or that have issued shares under the Nova Scotia Stock Savings Plan.

9. *Supplemental Mailing List*

An issuer shall deliver its interim financial statements, to any person or company who delivers to the issuer a request in writing for such material, including a statement signed by the person or company that the person or company is the owner of securities (other than debt instruments) of the issuer, and the issuer shall maintain a supplemental mailing list for this purpose.

Issuers shall include with the proxy-related materials delivered in respect of their first annual meeting occurring on or after March 1, 1988, and each annual meeting thereafter, a return card permitting the security holder to request that the security holder be placed on the issuer's supplemental mailing list. Issuers may update their supplemental mailing lists annually in accordance with responses received.

Where an issuer, such as an unincorporated mutual fund, is not required by law to hold annual meetings and does not in fact hold annual meetings, the issuer must deliver return cards annually to registered unitholders, and to unitholders who have requested the receipt of audited annual financial statements, before the exemption from delivering interim financial statements in paragraph 8 above is available.

10. *Audited Annual Financial Statements or Annual Report*

An issuer shall deliver its audited annual financial statements, or, in the case of non-registered holders resident in Quebec, its annual report, to non-registered holders in accordance with the communication system in this Policy Statement.

11. *Use of System for Non Proxy-Related Materials*

An issuer may request intermediaries to deliver to clients who are non-registered holders interim financial statements or any other material the issuer is required by law or wishes to deliver to registered security holders, other than proxy-related materials. Issuers are encouraged to use the communication system for rights offerings, dividend reinvestment plans, and issuer bids where practicable.

12. *Sending of Materials Notwithstanding Waiver*

An issuer may request that an intermediary deliver, in accordance with this Policy Statement, proxy-related materials to non-registered holders who have waived the right to receive such material, and the intermediary shall so comply.

PART V – INTERMEDIARIES' OBLIGATIONS

I. Register of Intermediaries and Registered Nominees

Every intermediary shall furnish in writing its name and full mailing address and those of each of its nominees in whose names securities are held on behalf of such non-registered holders to CDS and VSESC, or other designated agent of the securities administrators. Intermediaries are encouraged to restrict the number of nominees in whose name securities are registered on the books of issuers.

II. Instructions as to Voting and Receipt of Proxy-Related Material

1. *Information to Clients – Form B*

An intermediary shall, upon the opening of an account for a client on whose behalf the intermediary will hold securities, and as soon as possible after the effective date of this Policy Statement with respect to a client on whose behalf the intermediary currently holds securities ("existing clients"), advise the client of the rights of a non-registered holder under this Policy Statement by delivering the Shareholder Communication Information Form in Form B.

2.   *Written Instructions from Clients – Form C*

An intermediary shall deliver to its clients, together with the Shareholder Communication Information Form in Form B, Form C – Shareholder Communication Instructions, providing for written instructions from the client as to the receipt of proxy-related materials, disclosure of the name, address and security holdings of the client to issuers and other senders of material, and the voting of securities held by the client.

3.   *Failure to Return Instructions*

Where a client fails to return instructions in Form C to the intermediary, the client shall be deemed to have given instructions to the effect that the client shall not receive either proxy-related material pertaining to annual meetings of security holders or audited financial statements. The intermediary shall, however, forward proxy-related materials pertaining to special meetings of security holders to the client.

Where instructions in Form C are not returned, the client shall be deemed to have consented to the disclosure of the client's name, address and holdings to issuers or other senders of material for the purposes of this Policy Statement, unless the intermediary has other written instructions to the contrary.

4.   *Exception – Prior Written Authorization*

Where an intermediary currently has legally valid written authorization regarding the exercise of voting rights and the forwarding of materials to a client, the intermediary advises the clients of the rights of a non-registered holder by the delivery of Form B, and the client fails to deliver instructions in Form C, the client shall be deemed to have given instructions in accordance with the authorization held by the intermediary.

5.   *Separate Accounts*

The instructions in Form C shall be applicable to all securities held by the client in an account. Clients who wish to receive proxy-related material and to vote in respect of some securities but not others should be encouraged to hold the securities in separate accounts.

6.   *Reasonable Efforts to Obtain Instructions*

Intermediaries shall use reasonable efforts to achieve the return of the instructions in Form C from their existing clients, including the provision of postage-paid return envelopes, and must obtain a completed Form C from new clients.

7.   *Annual Renewal of Information*

Intermediaries shall advise their clients annually in writing of their current instructions regarding the exercise of voting rights and the forwarding of material, and advise their clients that their instructions can be varied by providing written notice to the intermediary. Alternatively, intermediaries may mail Forms B and C to their clients annually.

III. Voting

1.   *Specific Voting Instructions*

An intermediary shall vote a security of which it is not the owner in accordance with specific written voting instructions received from a non-registered holder upon whose behalf it holds the security.

2.   *Intermediary May Not Exercise Voting Rights*

Except as provided in this Policy Statement, or in the case of an intermediary as provided in a legally valid written agreement, a clearing agency or an intermediary shall not exercise any voting rights in respect of a security of which it is not the owner.

3.   *Revocation of Instructions*

A non-registered holder may revoke instructions or a waiver of the right to receive materials and to vote given to an intermediary at any time by written notice to the intermediary and the intermediary shall use its best efforts to carry out the instructions. The intermediary is not required to act on a revocation of voting instructions in respect of a meeting that is not received by the intermediary at least 7 days before the meeting.

IV. Events in Respect of a Specific Meeting

1. *Response to Search Card*

Within 3 business days of receipt of a search card from an issuer the intermediary shall deliver to the issuer a response to the search card that sets out,

(i) the identity of the intermediary;

(ii) the approximate number of sets of proxy-related materials that the intermediary requires to distribute to the non-registered holders on its books and records who are entitled to receive the materials pursuant to instructions given or deemed to be given under this Policy Statement; and

(iii) where the intermediary intends to use a service company for the delivery of materials, the name and mailing address of the service company.

An intermediary that holds, as of the record date, securities of a class entitled to receive notice of a meeting of shareholders, that does not receive a search card from the issuer, but which learns of the meeting, shall advise the issuer and use reasonable efforts to comply with the requirements of this Policy Statement.

2. *Delivery of Proxy-Related Material*

An intermediary shall deliver proxy-related materials to each non-registered holder of securities of a class whose holders are entitled to receive notice of a meeting of security holders, and in the case of voting securities, to vote such securities, as shown on its books or records as of the record date, within 3 business days after receipt of the materials, provided that,

(a) the intermediary has received notice of the meeting and the record date;

(b) the intermediary receives reasonable assurance of payment for the delivery of such materials; and

(c) the non-registered holder has not waived the right to receive proxy-related material and to vote by executing instructions in Form C or by other written authorization in accordance with this Policy Statement.

Where an intermediary receives insufficient proxy-related materials, they should be sent out to the extent possible and the issuer advised as to the shortfall.

Where the intermediary receives materials that are unlikely to reach non-registered holders to allow sufficient time for non-registered holders to vote, the issuer should be contacted for instructions.

3. *Bearer Proxy or Voting Instructions*

(a) The form of proxy that is delivered to the non-registered holder by the intermediary shall be signed by the intermediary as proxy holder or registered security holder as the case may be, restricted in accordance with the security holdings of the non-registered holder, and undirected as to voting. Where a clearing agency is the registered holder, the proxy shall so indicate.

(b) In lieu of delivering a form of proxy, an intermediary may deliver a request for voting instructions to a client with the proxy-related materials, and the intermediary shall deliver a proxy, directed in accordance with the voting instructions received, to be received by the issuer not later than 2 days before the meeting date.

4. *Certificate of Mailing*

The intermediary shall deliver to the issuer a certificate of mailing certifying as to the number of sets of materials mailed, the date of mailing and the postage incurred.

PART VI – CLEARING AGENCIES' OBLIGATIONS

1. *Response to Early Search*

Upon receipt of a request and a statutory declaration addressed to the issuer as set out in paragraph 2 following, by any person or company, CDS or VSESC shall deliver in writing, within two business days of the receipt of the request, a list of its participants who hold securities of a class or classes of equity securities of an issuer, their addresses, and their holdings of securities of the class or classes.

An issuer or its transfer agent making such a request is not required to deliver a statutory declaration.

2. *Contents of Statutory Declaration*

The statutory declaration shall state:

(a) the name and address, including street and number, of the applicant;

(b) the name and address for service of the applicant, if the applicant is not an individual;

(c) that the information will not be used except in connection with,

(i) an effort to influence the voting of shareholders of the corporation;

(ii) an offer to acquire shares of the corporation; or

(iii) any other matter relating to the affairs of the corporation.

CDS or VSESC shall furnish the issuer with the statutory declaration and a copy of the request received from an applicant forthwith upon receipt.

3. *Participants as of Record Date*

Within 2 business days after the record date specified in the search card, both CDS and VSESC shall deliver to the issuer:

(a) a list of its participants holding securities of the class or classes specified in the search card with their addresses and holdings of securities of that class or classes, as of the record date; and

(b) an omnibus proxy in Form A appointing the participants described above as proxy holders in respect of their respective holdings of securities of the class.

CDS or VSESC shall forthwith notify each of its participants referred to above as to the information and omnibus proxy given in respect of the participant to the issuer.

4.

Register of Intermediaries and Registered Nominees

CDS, VSESC or other designated agent for the Canadian Securities Administrators shall maintain a current register of intermediaries and registered nominees, and shall communicate the names and addresses of the intermediaries and registered nominees to any person or company upon request and upon payment of a reasonable fee.

5. *Index of Meeting and Record Dates*

CDS and VSESC as designated agents of the Canadian Securities Administrators have agreed to maintain an index of meeting dates and record dates and make them available to the financial press. This is intended to meet the requirement in corporate legislation for the issuer to advertise record dates. An issuer may place individual advertisements of meeting and record dates if desired.

PART VII – GENERAL

1. *Unauthorized Use of Names*

No person or company shall use the names of non-registered holders, intermediaries, registered nominees, or participants furnished in compliance with this Policy Statement, except,

(a) in the case of the issuer, in connection with the dissemination of information as to the affairs of the issuer, and

(b) in the case of any person or company, including the issuer, in connection with,

(i) an effort to influence the voting of shareholders of the corporation;

(ii) an offer to acquire share of the corporation; or

(iii) any other matters relating to the affairs of the corporation.

2. *Trafficking in Names Prohibited*

No person shall offer for sale or purchase or otherwise traffic in a list of non-registered holders, intermediaries or participants furnished in compliance with this Policy Statement.

3. *Use of Third Party Service Company*

When an issuer or intermediary advises the other in writing that it will use a service company for the purpose of distributing material to non-registered holders in compliance with this Policy Statement, notice to or by or delivery to or by the service company shall be deemed to be notice to or by or delivery to or by the issuer or intermediary, as the case may be.

4. *Disclosure by Service Company*

No service company shall disclose, except to another service company or transfer agent for the purpose of proxy tabulation, or except with the consent of the intermediary, the identity of an intermediary that supplied the name of a non-registered holder.

5. *Application to Special Meetings*

The time limits in this Policy Statement reflect the time frames that permit material for annual meetings of security holders to be prepared and delivered to non-registered holders without undue timing pressure or undue delay by any party in the communication chain. The Canadian Securities Administrators recognize that the urgency of special meetings does not necessarily allow for a 60 day lead time. It is however necessary to mail the material to non-registered holders 25 days before the meeting date in order for them to receive the material, review it and return proxies or voting instructions, given current mail delivery times. In order that the material be in the hands of intermediaries and prepared for mailing by them, a record date of 35 days before the meeting date will normally be required.

If the issuer or other sender of material can arrange to complete the preliminary steps in less than the time limits prescribed in this Policy Statement, administrators will be prepared to grant exemptions from the time limits.

6. *Default of Party in Communication Chain*

Where any party in the communication chain delays or fails to deliver information or materials as required under this Policy Statement, the parties whose response or action is dependent thereon shall use reasonable efforts to obtain the required information or materials from the party in default, and to comply with the spirit of the Policy Statement.

7. *Corporate Law*

The Policy Statement has been developed so that it can co-exist with provincial and federal corporate statutes. Issuers and their advisers should, however, satisfy themselves in this respect.

PART VIII – MEANS OF DELIVERY

The Securities Administrators are of the view that the most efficient means of delivery of notices or material should be employed by all parties in the communication chain.

1. *Delivery to Non-registered Holders*

Delivery to non-registered holders shall be by postage-paid first class mail or by personal delivery.

2. *Electronic Communication*

Generally, notices among issuers or their transfer agents, clearing agencies, intermediaries and service companies should be given by electronic means, if possible, including telephone where timing is critical, provided that original hard copies are retained on the files of the sender. In the case of telephoned notices, and in the case of omnibus proxies, or proxies given by intermediaries based upon voting instructions given by non-registered holders, original hard copies must be delivered to the issuer or its transfer agent following information transmitted by any other means than pre-paid first class mail or hand delivery.

3.   *Provisions of Postage*

Issuers should (but are not obliged to) provide postage paid envelopes for return of proxies or voting instructions by non-registered holders since the failure to do so will generally severely impact on the level of voting. Similarly issuers are encouraged to provide postage paid cards to shareholders for requests to be placed on or remain on the supplemental mailing list.

4.   *Materials in Bulk*

Materials in bulk in respect to a mailing delivered to intermediaries or service companies should as far as possible arrive together. If the materials come from different printers, at least all the required quantities of a particular item should arrive at one time. Failure to ensure bulk delivery of sufficient materials that can be processed by intermediaries or service companies conveniently will result in unnecessary delays. The Canadian Securities Administrators are also of the view that intermediaries are entitled to charge additional fees to cover their costs if late delivery of bulk materials results in special over-time work by their staffs.

5.   *Mail to and from the U.S.*

It has been brought to the attention of the Canadian Securities Administrators that mail between Canada and the United States may often take an excessive amount of time. It is advisable for issuers, transfer agents and intermediaries to take this time period into account and make suitable arrangements in respect to delivery of materials. This will be particularly important for U.S. reporting issuers who are required to mail to Canadian shareholders.

PART IX – APPLICATION TO MATERIAL OTHER THAN PROXY-RELATED MATERIALS

The use of the Shareholder Communication system set forth in this Policy Statement is not mandated for materials other than proxy-related materials delivered on behalf of issuers.

However,

(i)   Issuers and other senders of material that is required by law to be delivered to registered holders, including shareholders soliciting proxies, are entitled to and encouraged to use the communication system set forth in this Policy Statement;

(ii) Intermediaries are required to advise their clients who are non-registered holders of the commencement of take-over bids, issuer bids, rights offerings and other events notice of which is required to be delivered to registered holders, and to advise how materials may be obtained.

PART X – FEES AND CHARGES

The fee schedule is based upon the following principles:

1.   The issuer should bear the basic cost of communicating with its shareholders;

2.   The intermediary should bear the cost of protection of the client-intermediary relationship or confidentiality;

3.   All participants in the communication chain should bear their own start-up costs; and

4.   The fee schedule should encourage computerization and centralization of records of intermediaries.

There is a basic fee, payable by the issuer to the intermediary, of $1.00 per name of non-registered holder to whom the intermediary delivers proxy-related materials, with minimum fee of $15.00 per intermediary whose search discloses at least one non-registered holder entitled to receive the materials. The issuer also pays the actual cost of postage incurred by the intermediary in delivering the material upon receipt of a certificate of mailing. See Schedule 1 to this Policy Statement.

The $15.00 fee is payable to an intermediary, and not to each registered nominee of that intermediary and it is not expected to cover the actual cost of a search. Intermediaries, on the basis of cost efficiency, are encouraged to computerize and centralize their records and reduce the number of their registered nominees.

The fees are intended to cover the intermediary's costs for a basic service of searching records for non-registered holders and delivering material to non-registered holders, and contemplates the delivery from the issuer (or supplier) of various items of proxy-related material on a timely basis. The fees are not intended to cover the cost of preparation of bearer proxies or requests for voting instructions.

The issuer has the alternative of offering to deliver the material itself or through its transfer agent or service company if it can do so on a less costly basis. The issuer is free to make arrangements with intermediaries that will encourage them to use this option.

All participants in the communication chain will bear their own start-up costs. The start-up costs will include, for intermediaries, the cost of obtaining instructions from their clients as to voting and the receipt of materials.

Fees and charges by intermediaries other than in respect of proxy-related material should be dealt with by issuers or other senders of material on a negotiated basis. The Canadian Securities Administrators are prepared to regulate this area on consultation with issuers and intermediaries, if experience proves regulation to be necessary.

PART XI – EXEMPTIONS

An issuer may apply for an exemption or waiver from any of the requirements of this Policy to the securities commission or similar securities administrator in a province in which it is a reporting issuer or has comparable status.

It is the intention, at least in certain provinces, to grant exemptions or waivers where the cost of compliance with this Policy Statement would be disproportionate, having regard for the size of the shareholder body, or, alternatively, on the basis of no corporate activity. It would not be appropriate for issuers to request exemptions on the basis of cash flow. To raise money from the public carries responsibilities, and the effective right to vote is a minimum right of shareholders of an issuer as is the right to receive a status report on the issuer at least annually through an information circular and financial statements.

Exemptions will not generally be granted in respect of notice of meetings to CDS and VSESC, so that non-registered shareholders may receive notice of meetings through a published index of meetings. Notwithstanding the granting of an exemption from this Policy Statement, issuers are required to send proxy-related material to non-registered holders who request such material through their intermediaries and intermediaries are required to do what is necessary to enable such non-registered holders to vote their securities.

The British Columbia and Alberta Securities Commissions exempt from the operation of this Policy on an interim basis respectively all exchange issuers which are listed only on the Vancouver Stock Exchange, and all issuers listed only on the Alberta Stock Exchange, or that are listed only on these two exchanges, owing to the existing systems capability of the VSESC. These blanket exemptions do not apply to issuers that are reporting issuers in other jurisdictions.

PART XII – NATIONAL CLEARANCE OF APPLICATION FOR WAIVERS OR EXEMPTIONS

1. *Waivers Not Required*

If an issuer arranges to have carried out all of the requirements of the Policy within time limitations shorter than those time limitations established by the Policy, leaving a minimum of 25 days between the time of mailing materials by intermediaries to the non-registered shareholders and the date of the meeting in question, no application for a waiver from the Policy will be required.

Intermediaries must be placed in a position to actually mail the material at least 25 days before the meeting date. Intermediaries are entitled to 3 business days to prepare the material for mailing after their receipt of the material in bulk.

Issuers are cautioned that the costs to intermediaries of complying with the Policy within a shorter time frame may be increased, and the intermediaries are entitled to recover costs attributable to the shorter time frame (e.g. courier, long-distance telephone calls) that would not otherwise have been incurred by the intermediary. Moreover, intermediaries may not be in a position to respond to searches more quickly than the Policy requires.

2.   *Waivers – National Clearance*

If an issuer requires a waiver of some of the requirements of the Policy to take account of a particular situation or difficulty and the intent of the Policy and its basic procedures will be followed, but the proposal provides for fewer than 25 days to transpire between the time of sending materials by intermediaries to the non-registered shareholders and the date of the meeting, an issuer will be required to make application for a waiver from such requirements of the Policy. The issuer should set out its proposal in reasonable detail in a letter (the "letter of application") and send it to a jurisdiction of its choice among the following jurisdictions that are prepared to act as principal jurisdictions in respect of National Policy Statement No. 41: British Columbia, Alberta, Ontario, Quebec.

If the proposals are satisfactory to the principal jurisdiction, it will so confirm in writing indicating that the Commission of that jurisdiction will waive non-compliance with the strict terms of the Policy (the "waiver"). The issuer then will deliver copies of both the letter of application and waiver to all jurisdictions in which it is a reporting issuer or has the equivalent status. If a jurisdiction does not advise the issuer to the contrary within 3 business days after receipt of the letter of application and the waiver of the principal jurisdiction, it will be deemed to have agreed with the position of the principal jurisdiction. A written waiver must, in each instance, be obtained from Alberta.

Issuers are encouraged to work out satisfactory arrangements with the staff of the principal jurisdiction prior to writing a letter requesting waiver to facilitate this process. Again, issuers are cautioned that arrangements involving a shortening of the time limitations set out in the Policy may involve renegotiation with the inter-mediaries of the fees set out in Schedule 1 to the Policy, particularly if delivery of meeting materials is to be made by courier.

3.   *Exemptions – National Clearance*

If the request is for an exemption from the Policy, that is, from the basic requirement to deliver proxy-related material and audited financial statements to non-registered holders, or where the time periods proposed are so short as to make receipt and return of proxies unlikely, a formal application must be made to each jurisdiction wherein the issuer is a reporting issuer or the equivalent. The application should set forth all the jurisdictions in which the application is made and should again designate British Columbia, Alberta, Ontario or Quebec as principal jurisdiction.

Every application, with a draft exempting order and supporting material, shall be faxed (originals to follow by mail) or delivered by courier to each applicable jurisdiction so that the applications will be received as nearly as may be on the same date.

Staff of the non-principal jurisdictions will transmit their comments to the principal jurisdiction within 3 business days of receipt of the application.

The Commission of the principal jurisdiction will make its determination having regard to comments received and will communicate its order to the other jurisdictions named in the application. Each concerned Commission will issue its own order in its own discretion, but will have the benefit of the decision of the principal jurisdiction.

4.   *Authority to Grant Waivers*

In order to facilitate the operation of the procedure described in paragraph 2 above, the authority to grant waivers (but not exemptions except in Nova Scotia) under National Policy Statement No. 41 has been delegated by the respective Commissions as follows:

Alberta	– Director or Deputy Director
British Columbia	– Manager, Exemptions and Orders
Nova Scotia	– Registrar
Ontario	– Legal Adviser or Manager, Financial Disclosure
Quebec	– Chef du Service de l'information continue

5.   *General*

All applications, whether for waivers or exemptions, should clearly indicate that they are made pursuant to this Part XII of the Policy, should indicate the principal jurisdiction in which the application is made, and should indicate where relevant the time in which the appropriate response is required under the Policy.

If the issuer is not a reporting issuer in British Columbia, Alberta, Ontario or Quebec, it should deal with the securities administrator in its home jurisdiction as principal jurisdiction.

Issuers are advised that if the effect of an exemption from under this Policy is that the issuer does not deliver proxy-related material, including audited annual financial statements, to its non-registered holders, or does not establish and maintain a Supplemental Mailing List in accordance with the Policy, the issuer will not have the benefit of the exempting orders given by the various Commissions in respect of the delivery of interim financial statements to registered shareholders.

PART XIII – APPLICATION OF POLICY TO ISSUERS HAVING NO NON-REGISTERED HOLDERS OR NO UNIDENTIFIED NON-REGISTERED HOLDERS

A number of issuers, for example mutual funds whose shares or units are distributed through their own distribution arms, or limited partnerships, either have no shares or units registered in the name of clearing agencies or intermediaries and so have no non-registered holders, or know the name and address and holdings of all their non-registered holders.

Such issuers are not required to follow the search procedures in the Policy that are obviously irrelevant. However, such issuers are required to set a record date for their meetings of security holders and advise CDS and VSESC in accordance with the Policy, so that the meetings are included in the comprehensive national index of meeting and record dates of reporting issuers. They should also check their shareholder list against the registered nominee list that is maintained by CDS, and if there are intermediaries or their nominees thereon, send search cards in accordance with the Policy.

It is strongly recommended that proxy-related material be mailed by such issuers to security holders no later than 25 days before a meeting of security holders.

Such issuers are reminded that they must comply with the requirements in the Policy relating to establishing and maintaining a Supplemental Mailing List, if they wish to avail themselves of the exempting order of the various Commissions in respect of the delivery of interim financial statements to registered security holders.

Shareholder Communication
Schedule I – Fees and Charges

1.(i) $1.00 per name of non-registered holder to whom the intermediary delivers proxy-related material, with a $15.00 minimum fee where there is at least one non-registered holder.

(ii) The actual cost of postage incurred by the intermediary in delivering the proxy-related materials to the underlying owners.

FORM A
OMNIBUS PROXY

The undersigned, being a registered security holder or proxy holder of _____ (the issuer), hereby appoints each of the persons or companies identified in the attached schedule, with power of substitution in each, to attend, vote and otherwise act for and on behalf of the undersigned, to the extent of the number of securities specified, in respect of all matters that may come before the meeting of security holders described below, and at any adjournment thereof.

This instrument supersedes and revokes any prior appointment of proxy made by the undersigned with respect to the voting of the securities specified below at said meeting.

_____
Issuer

_____
Title of Security (and CUSIP Number)

_____   _____
Record Date of Meeting   Date of Meeting

_____
Place of Meeting

_____   _____
Date   Registered Security Holder or Proxy Holder

                                                              _____
                                                              Signing Officer

FORM B

Letterhead of Intermediary

SHAREHOLDER COMMUNICATION INFORMATION FORM

As a non-registered security holder of a corporation or other issuer, you have the same right as a registered security holder to vote at annual and special meetings of that issuer. Most common shares carry this privilege, as do preferred shares in certain circumstances. This voting right is provided to registered security holders in securities and corporate legislation and carries with it the right to receive such material as notices of meetings, information circulars, and proxies from the issuer of the securities. As your securities are held in safe custody by [named intermediary] and not registered in your name, we may provide material directly to you or may, unless you object, provide the issuer with your name, address and extent of security ownership so that the issuer can provide material directly to you. You are also entitled to receive the audited financial statements of the issuer.

You may indicate your desire to receive notice of meetings of security holders, including audited annual financial statements, and proxies entitling you to vote by initialling Option 1 on the enclosed Form C – Shareholder Communication Instructions.

If you do not wish to receive such material, please initial Option 2 on the enclosed Form C.

Please indicate whether or not you consent to have your name, address and security holdings disclosed to issuers or other senders of material that is required by law to be delivered to security holders by initialling YES or NO on the enclosed Form C.

Form C – Shareholder Communication Instructions – covers all securities held in your accounts with [named intermediary]. Should you have different instructions for a particular security, it should be placed in another account and another Form C in respect of that account completed.

Additional material from the issuer, such as quarterly reports, may be obtained by completing and returning the card enclosed with the notice of annual meeting of the issuer, or by writing directly to the issuer requesting

that your name and address be added to the issuer's supplemental mailing list. We will assist you to do this upon your request.

You may change your instructions at any time by writing to us.

Please mail or deliver the enclosed Form C in the enclosed postage-paid envelope promptly to [named intermediary].

If you fail to return Form C:

1. You will not receive proxy-related material in respect of annual meetings of security holders or audited annual financial statements from the issuers of securities held in your account(s) with us unless they are registered in your name.

2. [Named intermediary] may at its option disclose your name, address and security holdings to issuer of securities held by you and other senders of material required by law to be delivered to security holders.

FORM C

Letterhead of Intermediary

SHAREHOLDER COMMUNICATION INSTRUCTIONS
CLIENT NAME _____ ACCOUNT NUMBER(s)

TO:　[Named Intermediary]

I have been provided with and have read the Shareholder Communication Information Form (Form B) and, as my securities held with you are registered in your name or the name of your agent, I request the following arrangements be made as indicated. I understand that these elections apply to all securities held in my accounts with you that are not registered in my name, unless I have given other instructions regarding securities in another account.

Please indicate your choice by initialling appropriate selection(s) below.

1. _____ Send all material relating to annual or special meetings of security holders, including proxies, and annual audited financial statements, to me.

2. _____ I do not wish to receive material relating to annual or special meetings of security holders, or audited financial statements of the issuers whose securities I hold.

3. You may disclose my name and security holdings to the issuer of the security or other sender of material required by law to be sent to securities holders in order that, at your option, material may be forwarded to me directly from the issuer or other sender of material.

    Yes _____ No _____

I understand that an issuer is entitled to deliver material to me notwithstanding my instructions in paragraph 2; but is not required to do so.

I understand that these instructions may be changed at any time in writing and that you will use reasonable efforts to act upon changes in instructions where advice is received between record date and meeting date.

_____　　_____
　　　　Signature　　　　　　　　　　　　　　Date

INTERIM NATIONAL POLICY STATEMENT No. 42
ADVERTISING OF SECURITIES ON RADIO OR TELEVISION

Part I – Background

Until September 1986, the regulations established by the Canadian Radio and Television Commission (the "C.R.T.C.") prohibited the advertising of securities on radio or television, except for certain exempt securities. These restrictions were removed by the C.R.T.C. for radio as of September 19, 1986, and for television as of September 1, 1988.

In its public notice dated September 19, 1986, announcing amendments to regulations respecting radio broadcasting the C.R.T.C. stated:

"The Commission has also eliminated provisions dealing with the advertising of bonds, shares and other securities as it considers that those matters do not fall within its mandate under the Broadcasting Act."

In response to the repeal of the restrictions on advertising of securities by the C.R.T.C., the Canadian Securities Administrators issued a Draft Policy Statement No. 42 in April of 1988, and invited public comment. The effect of the Draft Policy was essentially to replace the C.R.T.C. restrictions with similar restrictions. The Draft Policy was intended to be an interim measure while a thorough study of the issues involved in the advertising of securities generally was undertaken.

Such a study involves the consideration of, among other matters, the report of the private sector committee given to the Ontario Securities Commission in October 1987, the registration requirements under securities legislation, and recent decisions of the courts, and will involve consultation with the broadcast industry.

In the meantime, in view of the September 1, 1988, repeal of the C.R.T.C. regulations in respect of the advertising of securities on television, the Canadian Securities Administrators are of the view that an Interim Policy should be finalized to restrict advertising before problems occur and economic interests arise that might be prejudiced by future restrictions.

Part II – Purpose of the Interim Policy

Provincial securities regulation serves to protect investors within the province by regulating the conduct of persons involved in the sale of securities, and by regulating disclosure in respect of both new issues and securities traded on the secondary market.

It is appropriate that securities regulation restrict the advertising of securities on the basis of investor protection, so long as the restrictions are reasonable and not unduly restrictive in the light of their objective.

The Canadian Securities Administrators are of the view that the most effective way of ensuring that advertising of securities is not false, misleading or deceptive is to restrict such advertising to the period of a distribution by way of prospectus, and to require that the advertising be placed either by registrants, who have a direct responsibility to both their clients and the securities administrators, or by the issuers that are making the distribution.

A brief advertisement of securities may have a high impact but nonetheless be misleading, although it may not be intentionally false or deceptive, as it cannot by its nature give appropriate cautions or address the issue of suitability. Accordingly, only very basic information specifically as set out in the Policy Statement may be included in advertisements of securities other than exempted securities.

Securities exempted from the Policy are those in respect to which investors have historically been viewed as not requiring registration and prospectus protections under securities legislation.

Part III – Statement of Policy

No person or company shall promote, by radio or television broadcast, investment in specific securities other than those exempted securities listed in Part IV below, except in accordance with this Policy Statement.

Advertisements of specific securities, other than exempted securities, the contents of which are restricted in accordance with Part V below, may be placed on radio or television only during a distribution of the securities pursuant to a prospectus or preliminary prospectus for which a receipt has been issued by the securities administrator in the jurisdiction in which the advertisement is placed. Advertising of such securities may be placed only by a person or company who is registered as a dealer in the jurisdiction in which the advertisement is placed and who is authorized to sell such securities, or by the issuer of the securities.

Issuers placing advertisements directly rather than through a registrant are reminded that the advertising of specific securities is considered under provincial securities legislation to be trading in securities and, accordingly, registration as a securities issuer or an exemption from registration must be obtained from the jurisdiction in which the advertisement is placed.

Where any person contravenes this Policy Statement, it may, in the discretion of the securities administrator having jurisdiction, result in the issuance of a cease trade order in respect of the security in question, the suspension or revocation of the registration of any registrant involved, or such other action as is warranted in the circumstances.

This Policy Statement is not intended to affect advertisements by issuers in respect to publicity campaigns that are aimed at either selling products or raising public awareness in respect to the issuer, provided that they are not accompanied by an advertisement for the sale of securities. In this context, a reference to a listing on an exchange is not appropriate. Further, nothing in this Policy Statement prohibits corporate or generally informative advertising by registrants.

Part IV – Exempted Securities

The following securities are exempted from this Policy Statement:

1.　Bonds, debentures or other evidences of indebtedness,

　　(a) of or guaranteed by the Government of Canada or any province of Canada;

　　(b) of any municipal corporation in Canada, including debentures issued for public, separate, secondary or vocational school purposes, or guaranteed by any municipal corporation in Canada, or secured by or payable out of rates or taxes levied under the law of any province of Canada on property in such province and collectable by or through the municipality in which such property is situated; or

　　(c) of or guaranteed by a bank to which the Bank Act (Canada) applies, or by a trust company or loan corporation licensed or registered under provincial or federal regulatory statutes.

2.　Certificates or receipts issued by a loan or trust company registered under a provincial or federal regulatory statute for moneys received for guaranteed investment.

Part V – Permitted Advertisements

Advertising of specific securities as permitted in Part III, other than exempted securities, is restricted to giving the following information:

　　(a) the name of the issuer of the securities;

　　(b) a concise statement of the nature of the business of the issuer;

　　(c) the specific type of securities offered (e.g., common shares, subordinated shares, bonds, etc.), the number offered for subscription and their price;

　　(d) a concise statement of whether the securities are qualified for special tax treatment;

　　(e) the name of the registrant, if any, placing the advertisement; and

　　(f) instructions for obtaining a copy of the prospectus or preliminary prospectus.

Notwithstanding section 15.02 of National Policy Statement No. 39, advertising of specific mutual funds is permitted on the same restricted basis.

Part VI – Duration of Policy

This Policy will expire on the date a comprehensive National Policy on the advertisement of securities in all media is adopted in final form.

NATIONAL POLICY NO. 44

RULES FOR SHELF PROSPECTUS OFFERINGS AND FOR PRICING OFFERINGS AFTER THE FINAL PROSPECTUS IS RECEIPTED

CONTENTS

1.　INTRODUCTION AND PURPOSE

1.1　This Policy Statement provides for:

(a) the creation of a Canadian shelf prospectus system; and

(b) rules for the pricing of offerings after the prospectus is receipted.

The shelf system is available only for prospectuses filed under the prompt offering qualification ("POP") system. The rules for the pricing of offerings after the prospectus is receipted are available for offerings under the POP system, offerings of securities of issuers which have equity securities outstanding that are listed on a Recognized Stock Exchange and offerings of non-convertible Approved Rating debt or preferred shares of other issuers. The shelf system and the rules for the pricing of offerings after the prospectus is receipted are available for offerings of derivative securities only with prior regulatory approval. The shelf system and rules for pricing of offerings after the prospectus is receipted are not available for rights offerings.

1.2 The rules for shelf prospectus offerings and for pricing of offerings after the prospectus is receipted are intended to provide more flexibility and reduce the burdens, costs and time pressures for issuers seeking to raise capital under changing market conditions while maintaining investor protections.

2. GENERAL PROVISIONS

2.1 *Definitions*

As used in this Policy Statement, unless the subject matter or context otherwise requires, the following terms shall have the following meanings:

(a) "AIF" means the annual information form required to be filed by POP Issuers under the POP System;

(b) "Approved Rating", where used to describe debt or preferred shares means that such securities have received at the time the receipt for the prospectus is issued a provisional rating by an Approved Rating Organization in one of the generic categories applicable to debt or preferred shares, as the case may be, that is set out opposite the Approved Rating Organization's name:

Approved Rating Organization	Debt	Preferred Shares
Canadian Bond Rating Service Inc.	A++, A+, A or B++	P-1+, P-1, P-2 or P-3
Dominion Bond Rating Service Limited	AAA, AA, A or BBB	Pfd-1, Pfd-2 or Pfd-3
Moody's Investors Service, Inc.	Aaa, Aa, A or Baa	"aaa", "aa", "a" or "baa"
Standard & Poor's Corporation	AAA, AA, A or BBB	AAA, AA, A or BBB

(c) "Approved Rating Organization" means each of Canadian Bond Rating Service Inc., Dominion Bond Rating Service Limited, Moody's Investors Service, Inc. and Standard & Poor's Corporation;

(d) "at-the-market", where used to describe an offering of equity securities, means that the securities are being offered for sale into an existing trading market for outstanding securities of the same class at other than a fixed price on or through the facilities of a stock exchange or to or through a market maker otherwise than on an exchange;

(e) "equity securities" means securities of an issuer that carry a residual right to participate in earnings of the issuer and, upon liquidation or winding up of the issuer, in its assets;

(f) "lapse date" means the date which is 24 months after the date of the issuance by a securities regulatory authority of a province or territory of a receipt for the prospectus for an offering under the Shelf Procedures;

(g) "Method 1" means the first of the two alternative methods of providing prospectus certificates under the Shelf Procedures as described in Section 3.9 of this Policy Statement;

(h) "Method 2" means the second of the two alternative methods of providing prospectus certificates under the Shelf Procedures as described in Section 3.9 of this Policy Statement;

(i) "MTN Program" means a continuous offering of debt securities in which the specific variable terms of the individual debt securities and the offering thereof are determined at the time of sale;

(j) "MTN Terms" means the specific variable terms of the individual debt securities and the offering thereof under an MTN Program;

(k) "non-convertible", where used to describe debt or preferred shares, means that the rights and attributes attaching to such securities do not include any right or option to purchase, convert or exchange or otherwise acquire any equity securities of the issuer or of any other issuer, or any other security which itself has a right to purchase, convert or exchange or otherwise acquire any equity securities of the issuer or any other issuer;

(l) "POP Issuers" means the issuers using the POP System in the applicable jurisdiction;

(m) "POP System" means the prompt offering qualification system for the distribution of securities of certain issuers established pursuant to the securities laws or policies of a province or territory;

(n) "PREP Changes" means the changes that are permitted or required to be made to a prospectus filed under the PREP Procedures as defined in Section 4.3(b) of this Policy Statement;

(o) "PREP Information" means the information which may be omitted from a prospectus filed under the PREP Procedures as defined in Section 4.3(a) of this Policy Statement;

(p) "PREP Procedures" means the rules and procedures established pursuant to this Policy Statement for the pricing of securities in certain prospectus offerings after a receipt has been obtained for the prospectus;

(q) "Pricing Supplement" means the special form of prospectus supplement which may be used in MTN Programs as defined in Section 3.4(f) of this Policy Statement;

(r) "Recognized Stock Exchange" means a stock exchange recognized by the Canadian Securities Administrators for the purpose of this Policy Statement, all such stock exchanges being listed in Appendix "A" of this Policy Statement;

(s) "Shelf Information" means the information that may be omitted from a prospectus filed under the Shelf Procedures as defined in Section 3.3(c) of this Policy Statement;

(t) "Shelf Procedures" means the rules and procedures established pursuant to this Policy Statement for the distribution of securities of POP Issuers on a continuous or delayed basis; and

(u) "Supplemented PREP Prospectus" means a supplemented prospectus used under the PREP Procedures as defined in Section 4.3(b) of this Policy Statement.

2.2 *Election to Use the Shelf Procedures and/or PREP Procedures*

(a) Where an issuer satisfies the criteria set forth in Sections 3.1 and 3.2 of this Policy Statement, the issuer may elect to use the Shelf Procedures for an offering of its securities. Where an issuer satisfies the criteria set forth in Sections 4.1 and 4.2, the issuer may elect to use the PREP Procedures for an offering of its securities. All such elections shall be communicated to the applicable securities regulatory authorities at the time of filing the preliminary prospectus.

(b) An issuer that has elected to use the Shelf Procedures or PREP Procedures may change its election, upon notice to the applicable securities regulatory authorities, prior to filing the prospectus. An issuer which elects no longer to use the Shelf Procedures must file and distribute an amended preliminary prospectus.

2.3 *Form of Prospectus and Disclosure Requirements*

(a) The short form prospectus prescribed under the POP System shall be used for all offerings under the Shelf Procedures and for all offerings under the POP System where the PREP Procedures are being used.

Where the PREP Procedures are being used in connection with an offering that is not under the POP System, the form of prospectus prescribed by applicable securities laws shall be used. Unless otherwise expressly provided in this Policy Statement, the prospectus disclosure requirements applicable to any such offering of securities are unaltered.

(b) Each prospectus from which Shelf Information or PREP Information is omitted shall have printed in red ink on the outside front cover page the following statement:

"This prospectus has been filed under procedures in [insert names of the provinces and territories where qualified] which permit certain information with respect to these securities to be determined after the prospectus has become final and permit the omission from this prospectus of such information. Such procedures require the delivery to purchasers of a prospectus or a prospectus supplement containing this omitted information within a specified period of time after agreeing to purchase any of these securities."

2.4 *Incorporation by Reference*

(a) Issuers using the Shelf Procedures and/or the PREP Procedures for an offering under the POP System shall incorporate by reference into the short form prospectus for each offering the documents required to be incorporated into a short form prospectus under the POP System,[1] which include:

    (1) the issuer's latest AIF;

    (2) the following continuous disclosure documents that at the date of the prospectus have been filed by the issuer since the commencement of the issuer's financial year in which its latest AIF was filed:

        i. material change reports (excluding confidential reports)[2];

        ii. interim financial statements;

        iii. comparative financial statements for the issuer's last completed financial year, together with the auditor's report thereof; and

        iv. the portion of the issuer's information circulars incorporated by reference into the issuer's latest AIF.[2]

(b) There shall be deemed to be incorporated into the short form prospectus of an issuer using the Shelf Procedures and/or the PREP Procedures for an offering under the POP System any documents of the type referred to in Sections 2.4(a)(1) and 2.4(a)(2) of this Policy Statement that are filed by the issuer subsequent to the date of the prospectus and prior to the completion or withdrawal of the offering. A statement to that effect shall be contained in the short form prospectus.

(c) Issuers also shall be deemed to have incorporated by reference into the prospectus for an offering under the Shelf Procedures, the documents deemed to be incorporated therein pursuant to Section 3.4(c) of this Policy Statement.

---

1   Where applicable securities laws permit, issuers which are registrants with the Securities and Exchange Commission of the United States may satisfy certain of their continuous disclosure and incorporation by reference obligations through the use of disclosure documents that have been prepared in accordance with the securities laws of the United States.

2   An issuer is not entitled to file a confidential material change report or to maintain an already filed material change report as confidential during the period of distribution of securities pursuant to a final prospectus unless distribution is suspended until the material change is generally disclosed or the decision to implement such material change has been rejected.

(d) Issuers also shall be deemed to have incorporated by reference into the prospectus for an offering under the PREP Procedures, the information deemed to be incorporated therein pursuant to Section 4.3(c) of this Policy Statement.

(e) Any statement contained in a document incorporated or deemed to be incorporated by reference into a prospectus or contained in the prospectus itself shall be deemed to be modified or superseded, for purposes of the prospectus, to the extent that a statement contained in the prospectus or any other subsequently filed document which also is or is deemed to be incorporated by reference into the prospectus modifies or replaces such statement. The modifying or superseding statement need not state that it has modified or superseded a prior statement or include any other information set forth in the document which it modifies or supersedes. The making of such a modifying or superseding statement shall not be deemed an admission for any purposes that the modified or superseded statement, when made, constituted a misrepresentation, an untrue statement of a material fact or an omission to state a material fact that is required to be stated or that is necessary to make a statement not misleading in light of the circumstances in which it was made. Any statement so modified or superseded shall not be deemed in its unmodified or superseded form to constitute part of the prospectus.

(f) Upon a new AIF and the related annual financial statements being filed by an issuer with, and where required, accepted by, the applicable securities regulatory authorities during the currency of a prospectus, the previous AIF, the previous annual financial statements, all interim financial statements, material change reports and information circulars filed prior to the commencement of the issuer's financial year in which the new AIF was filed shall be deemed no longer to be incorporated into the prospectus for purposes of future offers and sales of securities thereunder.

2.5 *Prospectus Amendments*

Except as expressly provided in Section 3.8 of this Policy Statement, the requirements of applicable securities laws, which apply to preliminary prospectuses (including preliminary short form prospectuses) and prospectuses (including final short form prospectuses):

(a) to amend a preliminary prospectus where a material adverse change occurs after the receipt is obtained;

(b) to amend a prospectus where a material change occurs after the receipt is obtained;

(c) to amend a prospectus if the issuer increases the amount of securities being offered;

(d) to file prospectus amendments, together with supporting documentation, with the securities regulatory authorities; and

(e) to deliver prospectus amendments to purchasers, are unaltered.

2.6 *Civil Liability*

(a) Nothing in this Policy Statement shall be construed to provide relief from statutory civil or quasi-criminal liability arising under the provisions of the securities laws of each province or territory in which a prospectus for an offering pursuant hereto is filed.

(b) An issuer's prospectus certificate contained in an amendment to a prospectus filed under the Shelf Procedures supersedes and replaces the issuer's certificate contained in the prospectus. Accordingly, an officer who signed the later dated certificate and the directors at the time such certificate was filed would be subject to statutory civil liability for subsequent purchases of securities under the prospectus.

(c) An issuer's prospectus certificate contained in a prospectus supplement filed under the Shelf Procedures supersedes and replaces the issuer's certificate contained in the prospectus for purposes of the distribution of securities under that supplement. Accordingly, an officer who signed the later dated certificate and the directors at the time such certificate was filed would be subject to statutory civil liability to purchasers of securities under such supplement.

2.7 Other Regulatory Matters

(a) The procedures for review and filing of prospectuses under the POP System apply to offerings under the POP System where the Shelf Procedures and/or the PREP Procedures are being used. The procedures for review and filing of prospectuses under National Policy Statement No. 1 are available for offerings not being made under the POP System for which the PREP Procedures are being used.

(b) Certain securities legislation provides that the prospectus for the distribution of securities underwritten on a firm commitment basis, other than securities to be distributed continuously, shall indicate that the securities are to be taken up by the underwriter, if at all, on or before a date not later than a specified number of days after the date of the final receipt. This requirement is waived for offerings filed under the Shelf Procedures or PREP Procedures, provided that:

(1) for distributions under the Shelf Procedures, each prospectus supplement for the distribution of securities underwritten on a firm commitment basis, other than securities to be distributed continuously, indicates that the securities offered thereby are to be taken up by the underwriter, if at all, on or before a date not later than a specified number of days after the date of the prospectus supplement; and

(2) for distributions under the PREP Procedures of securities underwritten on a firm commitment basis, the Supplemented PREP Prospectus or the amendment to the prospectus providing the PREP Information indicates that the securities offered thereby are to be taken up by the underwriter, if at all, on or before a date not later than that same specified number of days after the date of the supplemented PREP Prospectus or amendment, as the case may be.

(c) Certain securities legislation provides that, where a minimum amount of funds are required by an issuer, the prospectus for the distribution of securities on a best efforts basis, other than securities to be distributed continuously, shall indicate that the offering may not continue for more than a specified number of days where such minimum amount of funds are not subscribed within the specified period without regulatory consent and the consent of those persons or companies who subscribed within such period. This requirement is waived for offerings filed under the Shelf Procedures or PREP Procedures, provided that:

(1) for distributions under the Shelf Procedures, each prospectus supplement for the distribution of securities underwritten on a best efforts basis where a minimum amount of funds are required indicates that the offering may not continue for more than that same specified number of days from the date of the prospectus supplement where such minimum amount of funds are not subscribed within such period without regulatory consent and the consent of those persons or companies who subscribed within such period; and

(2) for distributions under the PREP Procedures of securities underwritten on a best efforts basis where a minimum amount of funds are required, the Supplemented PREP Prospectus or the amendment to the prospectus providing the PREP Information indicates that the offering may not continue for more than that same specified number of days from the date of the Supplemented PREP Prospectus or amendment providing the PREP Information, as the case may be, where such minimum amount of funds are not subscribed within such period without regulatory consent and the consent of those persons or companies who subscribed within such period.

3. SHELF PROCEDURES

  3.1 Eligibility Criteria

  (a) To be eligible to use the Shelf Procedures for the distribution in a province or territory by or on behalf of an issuer or a selling security holder of securities of an issuer, the issuer must:

  (1) satisfy the eligibility criteria to use the POP System for the distribution of such securities in such province or territory (including, if relevant, the alternative eligibility criteria relating to issues of non-convertible Approved Rating debt or preferred shares and to issuers which subsist after a business reorganization); or

  (2) have obtained a ruling or order from the securities regulatory authority for such province or territory that permits it to use the POP System for the distribution of such securities and be in compliance with the terms of such ruling or order.

  (b) If after the filing of a prospectus for an offering of securities under the Shelf Procedures the issuer ceases to satisfy the foregoing criteria, further distribution of such securities under such prospectus shall not be made in the applicable province or territory.[3] An issuer that has filed a prospectus under the Shelf Procedures shall, however, have sixty business days after the end of its most recently completed financial year in which to determine whether it has ceased to satisfy any such eligibility criteria (applicable either under the POP System or pursuant to a ruling or order of the type referred to in Section 3.1(a)(2) of this Policy Statement) that requires it to have an aggregate market value of certain securities held by certain persons of not less than a specified amount during the last calendar month of its most recently completed financial year. Where it has ceased to satisfy such criteria, it shall cease further distribution under the prospectus no later than sixty business days after the end of its most recently completed financial year.[3]

  3.2 Types of Permissible Shelf Offerings

  (a) Subject to Sections 3.2(b) and (c) of this Policy Statement, issuers which meet the eligibility criteria set forth in Section 3.1 of this Policy Statement may use the Shelf Procedures to offer securities of one basic type (i.e., debt, preferred shares or common shares) for cash on a continuous or delayed basis. The Shelf Procedures may also be used for such offerings by selling security holders.

  (b) The Shelf Procedures may not be used for rights offerings.[4]

---

3 For example, if an issuer is relying on the alternative POP System eligibility criteria to make a shelf offering of non-convertible Approved Rating debt securities or preferred shares and the securities being offered are downgraded after the prospectus is filed to have a rating that does not qualify as an Approved Rating, further distribution of such securities under the prospectus shall not be made.

4 Right offerings include:

  i. the distribution by an issuer to holders of its securities of a right to purchase additional securities of its own issue and the distribution of securities pursuant to the exercise of that right; and

  ii. the distribution by an issuer to holders of its securities of a right to purchase additional securities of an issuer held by it and the distribution of securities pursuant to the exercise of that right.

(c) Special considerations apply to offerings of derivative securities[5] as such offerings may involve novel or complex issues, particularly with respect to the terms of the securities, that require case-by-case analysis. It may or may not be appropriate in such an offering for the Shelf Procedures to be used. Accordingly, the Shelf Procedures may be used for an offering of derivative securities only with prior approval of the appropriate securities regulatory authorities. As a condition of granting such approval, among other things, the securities regulatory authorities may require that prospectus supplements for the distribution of derivative securities be pre-cleared with them and that the issuer undertake in writing at the time of filing the prospectus that it will distribute derivative securities under the prospectus only pursuant to prospectus supplements pre-cleared with, and accepted by, the appropriate securities regulatory authorities.

(d) A prospectus filed under the Shelf Procedures shall cover no more than the amount of securities the issuer or selling security holder reasonably expects to offer and sell within two years from the date of filing the prospectus. Reasonable expectation shall be measured at the time the prospectus is filed. Securities remaining unsold at the expiration of the two-year period shall not thereafter be offered for sale under the prospectus, but may be offered under the next prospectus that is filed upon the expiry of the prospectus.

(e) Provided that the requirements set forth in Section 3.5 of this Policy Statement are complied with, non-fixed price offerings of non-convertible Approved Rating debt or preferred shares and at-the-market equity offerings may be made under the Shelf Procedures.

(f) Offerings of securities on a delayed basis may only be made by eligible POP issuers in accordance with the Shelf Procedures.

3.3 Disclosure in Shelf Offering Prospectuses

(a) The prospectus shall set forth the aggregate amount of securities offered and shall contain all other non-variable information with respect to such securities and the offering thereof. It shall, if applicable, contain disclosure of asset and earnings coverage ratios and dilution in accordance with Sections 3.6 and 3.7, respectively, of this Policy Statement.

(b) The prospectus may set forth a description of two or more alternative methods of distribution (such as underwriting on a firm commitment or agency basis or direct sales) provided that the description is not so complex as to reduce substantially the effectiveness of the disclosure.

(c) Subject to Section 3.2(c) of this Policy Statement, there may be omitted from the prospectus, to the extent only that such information is not known at the date the prospectus is filed:

(1) the variable terms of the securities, including:

i. the amount of each tranche of securities that will be offered and sold under the prospectus; and

---

5   Derivative securities generally include securities the value of or return from which is based upon the market price, value or return of one or more underlying securities or commodities or upon the level of one or more financial benchmarks such as interest rates, foreign exchange rates or stock market indices. For purposes of this Policy Statement, derivative securities do not include securities issued by mutual funds or non-redeemable investment funds or warrants or other securities exchangeable for, or convertible into, securities issued by the issuer of the derivative securities or an affiliate or affiliated company thereof. Accordingly, issuers do not require prior regulatory approval to use the procedures established under this Policy Statement for offerings of such warrants or exchangeable or convertible securities.

Issuers which are uncertain as to whether securities which they propose to issue are derivative securities should consult with the applicable securities regulatory authorities.

ii. the other specific terms of each such tranche of securities, including, as applicable, the designation of such tranche, maturities, denominations, interest or dividend provisions, purchase or redemption provisions, retraction provisions, conversion or exchange provisions, the terms for extension or early repayment, the currencies in which the securities are issued or payable, sinking fund provisions and any special covenants or other terms applicable to the securities of such tranche;

(2) the variable terms of the plan of distribution of the securities, including:

i. if the prospectus sets forth alternative methods of distribution, which method will be applicable to each tranche of securities offered and sold under the prospectus; and

ii. for each such tranche, the specific terms not included in the description of the applicable method of distribution in the prospectus, including, as applicable, the names of any underwriters, the distribution spread and underwriting fees, discounts and commissions;

(3) for any underwriter that is not named in the prospectus, disclosure of any conflicts of interest and prospectus certificates of such underwriter; and

(4) other specific transaction information, including the public offering price, delivery dates, legal opinions regarding the eligibility for investment of the securities and tax matters, statements regarding listing of the securities, actual amount of proceeds and, if applicable, more specific information about the use of proceeds.

The information that may be omitted from the prospectus pursuant to this Section 3.3(c) is referred to in this Policy Statement as the "Shelf Information".

(d) The prospectus shall indicate that all Shelf Information will be set forth in one or more prospectus supplements that will be delivered to purchasers together with the prospectus.

3.4   *Supplement Procedure*

(a) If securities are being offered and sold under a prospectus from which Shelf Information is omitted, a prospectus supplement containing:

(1) all such omitted Shelf Information with respect to the tranche of securities being offered;

(2) if applicable, prospectus certificates pursuant to Section 3.9 of this Policy Statement;

(3) if applicable, disclosure of asset and earnings coverage ratios pursuant to Section 3.6 of this Policy Statement;

(4) if applicable, disclosure of dilution pursuant to Section 3.7 of this Policy Statement;

(5) if applicable, in the case of the financing of the acquisition of a business, financial statements pursuant to Section 3.10 of this Policy Statement;

(6) if applicable, in the case of a natural resource issuer, disclosure relating to a particular resource property pursuant to Section 3.11(b) of this Policy Statement; and

(7) a list identifying and briefly describing each document then incorporated by reference into the prospectus (other than prospectus supplements and documents already listed in the prospectus or any other prospectus supplement to be delivered together with such prospectus supplement),

shall be filed with the securities regulatory authority of the principal jurisdiction no later than the second business day following the date of determination of the offering price of such securities. Such supplement shall be filed, as nearly as practicable, contemporaneously with the securities regulatory authority for each other jurisdiction in which securities are being offered pursuant to such supplement. The supplement shall state on the cover page thereof the name of the issuer and the date of the prospectus and/or the supplement(s) to which it relates. The prospectus supplement may also contain such additional information as the issuer may elect to include therein provided that such information does not describe a material change that has not already been the subject of a material change report or prospectus amendment.

(b) In addition to prospectus supplements required by Section 3.4(a) of this Policy Statement, a supplement to the prospectus may be used:

(1) to establish an MTN Program in accordance with Section 3.4(f) of this Policy Statement;

(2) as a Pricing Supplement in an MTN Program in accordance with Section 3.4(f) of this Policy Statement;

(3) to provide updated disclosure of asset and earnings coverage ratios as provided in Section 3.6 of this Policy statement;

(4) to provide revised disclosure of dilution as provided in Section 3.7 of this Policy Statement;

(5) as a preliminary form of the supplement to be used to describe a tranche of securities in accordance with Section 3.4(g) of this Policy Statement; and

(6) to supply any additional or updated information as the issuer may elect to include provided that such information does not describe a material change that has not already been the subject of a material change report or prospectus amendment.

Each such supplement, other than Pricing Supplements, shall be filed with the securities regulatory authority of the principal jurisdiction within two business days of its first use and, as nearly as practicable, contemporaneously with:

(7) in the case of supplements referred to in Section 3.4(b)(1), (3) and (4), the securities regulatory authority for each other jurisdiction in which securities are being distributed under the MTN Program or the continuous offering, as the case may be;

(8) in the case of supplements referred to in Section 3.4(b)(5), the securities regulatory authority for each other jurisdiction in which securities covered by that supplement are proposed to be distributed; and

(9) in the case of supplements referred to in Section 3.4(b)(6), the securities regulatory authority for each other jurisdiction where the prospectus was filed.

Each Pricing Supplement shall be filed with the securities regulatory authority for each jurisdiction in which securities have been offered pursuant to such Pricing Supplement within five business days of the end of the month in which such Pricing Supplement was first used.

(c) Each prospectus supplement shall be deemed to be incorporated by reference into the prospectus as of the date of such supplement. A prospectus supplement will not be considered to be an amendment within the meaning of applicable securities laws. To avoid affecting subsequent offerings, unless otherwise expressly provided herein or by the issuer, a prospectus supplement will be deemed to be incorporated into the prospectus only for purposes of the offering of the securities covered by that prospectus supplement.

(d) The prospectus supplement generally will take the form of a "sticker", a "wrap-around" or a one or more page supplement to the prospectus. All prospectus supplements applicable to any securities being sold, except for any preliminary form of the supplement to be used to describe a tranche of securities in accordance with Section 3.4(g) of this Policy Statement, must be attached to, or included with, the prospectus that is delivered to purchasers of such securities in accordance with applicable securities laws.

(e) Prospectus supplements will not be subject to prior review by the securities regulatory authorities, but each such authority reserves the right to require an issuer to provide a prospectus amendment to purchasers in circumstances where it considers:

    (1) the issuer to have failed to comply with the supplement procedure prescribed by this Policy Statement; or

    (2) the use of a prospectus supplement in the circumstances not to be in the public interest.

(f) MTN Programs may be established by a prospectus or under a prospectus by a prospectus supplement. In MTN Programs, the MTN Terms are determined at the time of sale. The MTN Terms for each security sold may be set forth in a special form of prospectus supplement (a "Pricing Supplement") provided that:

    (1) the prospectus or prospectus supplement establishing the MTN Program sets forth a complete description of the options and parameters for the MTN Terms (e.g., the range of maturities of the securities being offered, any interest rate options and any currency options)[6];

    (2) such prospectus or prospectus supplement sets forth a complete description of the applicable method of distribution that includes the name of any underwriter through which the securities are being sold and the amount of any underwriting fees, discounts or commissions (or a narrow range thereof); and

    (3) such prospectus or prospectus supplement contains all required prospectus certificates in accordance with Method 1.

Pricing Supplements shall contain:

    (4) the MTN Terms for the securities covered thereby; and

    (5) a list identifying and briefly describing each document then incorporated by reference into the prospectus (other than prospectus supplements and documents already listed in the prospectus or any prospectus supplement to be delivered together with such Pricing Supplement).

Pricing Supplements need not contain prospectus certificates or disclosure of asset and earnings coverage ratios.

Prospectus supplements used to establish an MTN Program shall contain:

    (6) to the extent known, all Shelf Information as to the offering covered thereby;

    (7) the issuer's certificate in accordance with Method 1 as required by Section 3.9 of this Policy Statement;

    (8) where there is an underwriter, the underwriter's prospectus certificate in accordance with Method 1 as required by Section 3.9 of this Policy Statement; and

    (9) a list identifying and briefly describing each document then incorporated by reference into the prospectus (other than

---

6   Specific variable terms of individual debt securities and the offering thereof that are not within the options and parameters set forth in the prospectus or supplement establishing the MTN Program may be set forth in a Pricing Supplement, provided the issuer has reserved the ability so to do.

prospectus supplements and documents already listed in the prospectus or any other prospectus supplement to be delivered together with such prospectus supplement).

(g) An issuer may prepare a preliminary form of the prospectus supplement to be used to describe a tranche of securities for use in marketing such securities before the public offering price is determined or to pre-clear a prospectus supplement for the distribution of derivative securities. This preliminary form of prospectus supplement may omit, at the issuer's election, any one or more of the items required by Sections 3.4(a)(1), (3) or (4) of this Policy Statement and, if Method 1 of providing prospectus certificates has been complied with, the certificates required by Section 3.4(a)(2) of this Policy Statement.

(h) The prospectus supplement procedures set forth in Section 3.4 of this Policy Statement are not intended to prevent the filing of prospectus amendments to supply some or all of the information that is permitted to be included in a prospectus supplement.

3.5 Non-fixed Price Offerings

(a) Disclosure of the following additional information shall be made on the cover page of the prospectus or a prospectus supplement for the offering of securities on a non-fixed price basis:

  (1) the discount allowed to the underwriters or the commission payable to the underwriters and any other compensation payable to the underwriters, including, if applicable, a reference to the fact that the underwriters' compensation will be increased or decreased by the amount by which the aggregate price paid for the securities by the purchasers exceeds or is less than the gross proceeds paid by the underwriters to the issuer[7];

  (2) the proceeds or, where applicable, in the case of an offering to be made on a best efforts basis, the minimum amount of proceeds to be received by the issuer;

  (3) how the price at which the securities will be offered and sold will be determined, specifically that the securities will be offered either at prices determined by reference to the prevailing price of a specified security in a specified market, at market prices prevailing at the time of sale, or at prices to be negotiated with purchasers;

  (4) that the price at which the securities will be offered and sold may vary as between purchasers and during the distribution period;

  (5) where the price of the securities is to be determined by reference to prevailing prices of a specified security in a specified market, the price of the specified security in the specified market at the latest practicable date; and

  (6) where the price of the securities will be the market price prevailing at the time of sale, the market price of the security at the latest practicable date.

(b) In addition, for at-the-market offerings of equity securities:

  (1) the amount of equity securities offered on an at-the-market basis must not exceed 10% of the aggregate market value of the issuer's outstanding equity securities of that class held by security holders of the issuer none of whom (together with its respective associates, affiliates and affiliated companies) beneficially own, directly or indirectly, or exercise control or direction

---

7   For non-fixed price offerings that are being made on a best efforts basis, the disclosure of the discount allowed to the underwriters or the commission or other compensation payable to the underwriters may be set forth as a percentage or a range of percentages and the distribution spread need not be set forth in tabular form.

over, more than 10% of the issued and outstanding equity securities of the issuer (calculated as of a date within 60 days prior to the date of filing of the prospectus);

(2) the securities must be sold through an underwriter acting as principal or agent;

(3) such underwriter must be named in, and must sign a prospectus certificate for, the prospectus or an amendment thereto; and

(4) it shall be disclosed in the prospectus or prospectus supplement establishing the at-the-market offering that none of the underwriters and dealers involved in the distribution or any affiliates of any of them, or any person or company acting jointly or in concert with any of the foregoing have or will in connection with the offering over-allot the securities or effect any other transactions which are intended to stabilize or maintain the market price of the securities.

3.6   Disclosure of Asset and Earnings Coverage Ratios

(a) Subject to Section 3.6(b) of this Policy Statement, issuers using the Shelf Procedures to offer debt or preferred shares having a term to maturity of more than one year shall:

(1)   i. disclose in the prospectus, historical asset and earnings coverage ratios based on the twelve month period ended on the date of the most recently completed period for which audited annual financial statements of the issuer have been, or are required to have been, filed with any securities regulatory authority; and

ii. disclose in the prospectus, historical asset and earnings coverage ratios based on the twelve month period ended on the date of the most recently completed period for which interim financial statements of the issuer have been, or are required to have been, filed with any securities regulatory authority, provided that such period is subsequent to the date of the most recently completed period for which audited annual financial statements of the issuer have been, or are required to have been, filed with any securities regulatory authority;

(2) disclose in each prospectus supplement filed to describe a particular tranche of securities offered under the prospectus:

i. asset and earnings coverage ratios that are based on the twelve month period ended on the date of the most recently completed period for which audited annual financial statements of the issuer have been, or are required to have been, filed with any securities regulatory authority;

ii asset and earnings coverage ratios that are based on the twelve month period ended on the date of the most recently completed period for which interim financial statements of the issuer have been, or are required to have been, filed with any securities regulatory authority, provided that such period is subsequent to the date of the most recently completed period for which audited annual financial statements of the issuer have been, or are required to have been, filed with any securities regulatory authority; and

iii. the ratios in Sections 3.6(a)(2) i. and ii. shall be adjusted to reflect:

A. the issuance of all long term debt and, in addition in the case of an issue of preferred shares, all preferred shares issued since the date of such annual or interim financial statements;

B. the issuance of the specific tranche which is the subject of the prospectus supplement; and

C. the repayment or redemption of all long term debt since the date of such annual or interim financial statements, all long-term debt to be repaid or redeemed from the proceeds realized from the sale of securities under the prospectus supplement and, in addition in the case of an issue of preferred shares, all preferred shares repaid or redeemed since the date of such annual or interim financial statements and all preferred shares to be repaid or redeemed from the proceeds realized from the sale of securities under the prospectus supplement.

(b) Disclosure of the type required by Section 3.6(a)(2) of this Policy Statement shall not be required for MTN Programs or other continuous offerings. Instead, an issuer making such an offering shall, concurrently with filing its interim and audited annual financial statements, provide, either as an exhibit to such financial statements or in a prospectus supplement filed with the applicable securities regulatory authorities updated historical asset and earnings coverage ratios, based on the twelve month period ended on the date of such financial statements. Such exhibit need not be audited. If such coverage ratios are provided in a prospectus supplement, such supplement shall, until such time as more recently updated coverage ratios are available to purchasers pursuant to this Section 3.6(b):

(1) be deemed to be incorporated into the prospectus for purposes of the offering of securities thereunder; and

(2) be attached to, or delivered with, the prospectus delivered to purchasers.

3.7 *Disclosure of Dilution*

(a) Issuers using the Shelf Procedures to offer equity securities shall disclose in each prospectus supplement filed to describe a particular tranche of securities offered and sold under the prospectus the dilution which would result from the issuance of the securities offered in such tranche. The calculation of dilution shall be based upon the financial statements of the issuer for the most recently completed period for which audited annual financial statements have been, or are required to have been, filed with any securities regulatory authority.

(b) For at-the-market offerings of equity securities, dilution shall be set forth in the prospectus or the prospectus supplement establishing the at-the-market offering. Such disclosure shall be based upon a reasonable range of the selling terms. Where appropriate, the dilution may also be set forth as a range. If during the distribution of the securities the dilution differs from that disclosed in the prospectus or prospectus supplement, a prospectus supplement to revise the range of selling terms and dilution shall be filed with the applicable securities regulatory authorities and delivered to purchasers. Any such revision shall be based upon the financial statements of the issuer for the most recently completed period for which audited annual financial statements have been, or are required to have been, filed with any securities regulatory authority.

3.8 *Amendments*

(a) Changes in the Plan of Distribution

An amendment to a prospectus shall be filed and cleared with the applicable securities regulatory authorities to reflect any new material information relating to, or any material change in, the plan of distribution described in the prospectus before further distributions under the prospectus may proceed. For example, a prospectus amendment would be required to include information regarding a new method of distribution not previously described in the prospectus. Where a method of distribution is described in the prospectus, the variable terms of the distribution of a specific tranche of securities under such method (i.e., the information referred to in Section 3.3(c)(2) of this Policy Statement) may be set forth in the prospectus supplement relating to such securities.

(b) Other Amendments

(1) Amendments to a prospectus of the type referred to in Section 2.5(b) of this Policy Statement are required in respect of material changes only if such changes occur during a period when actual offers and sales of securities pursuant thereto are being made. Thus, an issuer using the Shelf Procedures to make a series of discrete, delayed offerings is not required to file amendments in respect of material changes which occur during the periods between offerings when securities are not being offered and sold.[8]

(2) An amendment to a prospectus required to describe a material change which occurred during a period when actual offers and sales are being made, may take the form of a material change report with prospectus certificates in the form set out in Section 3.9 of this Policy Statement added thereto.

(3) Offers and sales of securities of an issuer may not be made as part of a continuous shelf offering or during a delayed offering if the issuer has filed a report of a material change on a confidential basis unless such material change has been generally disclosed or the decision to implement such material change has been rejected.

3.9 Prospectus Certificates

Except as set forth herein, issuers, promoters and underwriters may choose between two alternative methods of providing prospectus certificates in shelf offerings. Either method can be substituted for the other until the filing of the prospectus. The method chosen for the provision of an issuer's, promoter's and underwriter's prospectus certificates need not be the same.

Method 1 allows the use of prospectus supplements that do not contain prospectus certificates, provided a "forward-looking" prospectus certificate has been included in the prospectus. For an MTN Program established by a prospectus supplement, Method 1 allows the use of Pricing Supplements that do not contain prospectus certificates, provided a "forward-looking" prospectus certificate has been included in the prospectus supplement establishing such program. Method 2 requires the inclusion of prospectus certificates in each prospectus supplement filed under the Shelf Procedures.

The forms of prospectus certificates under Method 1 and Method 2 are set forth in Appendix "B" hereto. All such prospectus certificates shall be signed in accordance with applicable securities law.

3.10 Acquisitions

(a) Where the proceeds of securities offered pursuant to the Shelf Procedures are to be applied in whole or in part, directly or indirectly, to finance the acquisition of a business, by a purchase of assets or

---

8   Such an issuer would not, however, be relieved of its obligation under applicable securities laws to issue and file forthwith a press release and report describing such material change, to publish where required such press release and to incorporate by reference any such report into the prospectus for the purposes of future offers and sales.

shares, and such acquisition is material[9] to the issuer, the prospectus for the offering of such securities or an amendment or supplement thereto shall include:

(1) a balance sheet of the acquired business:

    i. as at the date of the last financial year end of the acquired business and as at the corresponding date of the immediately preceding financial year; and

    ii. if such last financial year end date is more than 120 days prior to the date of the prospectus supplement or amendment setting the terms of the securities, as at a date that is not more than 120 days prior to the date of such supplement or amendment;

(2) an income statement, a statement of retained earnings and a statement of changes in financial position (or where the acquired business is primarily engaged in the business of investing, a statement of changes in net assets) of the acquired business:

    i. for each of the last three financial years of the acquired business; and

    ii. for any part of a subsequent financial year of the acquired business to the date at which the balance sheet required by Section 3.10(a)(1)ii. is made up and for the comparative period in the immediately preceding financial year;

(3) a pro forma balance sheet combining the assets and liabilities of the issuer with the assets and liabilities of the acquired business as shown by their respective balance sheets each as at the date of their respective last financial year ends; and

(4) pro forma financial statements combining, in respect of the last financial year of each of the acquired business and the issuer:

    i. the income or losses of the issuer with the income or losses of the acquired business; and

    ii. the changes in financial position of the issuer with the changes in financial position of the acquired business.

(b) Each financial statement required pursuant hereto, other than a financial statement that relates to any part of a financial year subsequent to the last audited financial year, shall be accompanied by an auditor's report. An auditor's report prepared in connection with any pro forma financial statements required pursuant hereto may be solely a compilation report.

(c) Consent and comfort letters with respect to the financial statements required pursuant hereto shall be provided in accordance with Sections 3.11(c) and (d) of this Policy Statement.

---

9   Investors, analysts and other users of financial information are interested in information that may affect their decision making. Materiality should be determined in the context of the overall financial position of the issuer, both prior to and after such acquisition, taking into account both quantitative and qualitative factors. Materiality is a matter of judgement in the particular circumstances and should generally be determined in relation to the significance of the acquisition to investors, analysts and other users of financial statement information. The acquisition of a business is considered material to an issuer if it is probable that its omission from the financial statement information would influence or change a decision.

Measures of materiality would generally include gross revenues, expenses, net income, shareholders' equity and total assets of the acquired business relative to those of the issuer.

While this concept of materiality is broader than the definition of "material change" contained in securities legislation of various provinces and territories, it is consistent with the financial reporting notion of materiality contained in the Canadian Institute of Chartered Accountants' Handbook.

3.11 Filing Packages and Commercial Copies

All documents required to be filed with a preliminary short form prospectus, a short form prospectus and a prospectus amendment under the POP System shall be filed in connection with preliminary prospectuses, prospectuses and prospectus amendments filed under the Shelf Procedures, subject to the following:

(a) Directors' Resolutions

The directors' resolution filed with the prospectus also shall authorize the filing and, if Method 2 is being used, the signing of prospectus supplements or a separate directors' resolution shall be filed with each prospectus supplement.

(b) Natural Resource Issuers

The provisions of the securities laws of certain provinces and territories which require the filing of an engineering report and the inclusion of prescribed disclosure in a short form prospectus where a significant portion of the proceeds of the offering are to be expended on a particular resource property shall be satisfied for each tranche of securities offered under the prospectus by:

(1) filing such report with the applicable securities regulatory authorities at the time of filing the prospectus supplement describing the securities in the related tranche; and

(2) including in such supplement the prescribed disclosure.

(c) Consent Letters

(1) If an expertised statement appears in the preliminary prospectus, prospectus or a document which is incorporated by reference into the prospectus and was filed prior to the filing of such prospectus, the related consent letter shall be filed at the time of filing the prospectus.

(2) If an expertised statement appears in an AIF, a prospectus supplement or other disclosure document which is incorporated by reference into a prospectus and is filed after the filing of such prospectus, the related consent shall be filed:

i. where the offering is being made on a continuous basis, at the time of filing such disclosure document; and

ii. where the offering is not being made on a continuous basis, at the time of the filing of the prospectus supplement or amendment to disclose the terms of securities in the first tranche to be offered pursuant to the prospectus after the filing of such disclosure document.

(3) If an expertised statement appears in a prospectus amendment, the related consent shall be filed at the time of filing such amendment.

(d) Comfort Letters

Comfort letters shall be required in connection with offerings under the Shelf Procedures in jurisdictions where comfort letters are required to be filed under the POP System. In such jurisdictions the following procedures apply:

(1) If unaudited financial statements appear in the prospectus or are incorporated by reference into such prospectus and were filed prior to the filing of such prospectus, any required auditor's comfort letter shall be filed at the time of filing the prospectus.

(2) If unaudited financial statements appear in a prospectus supplement or amendment, any required auditor's comfort letter shall be filed at the time of filing such prospectus supplement or amendment, as the case may be.

(3) If unaudited financial statements are otherwise incorporated by reference into a prospectus after the filing of such prospectus, any required auditor's comfort letter in respect thereof shall be filed:

  i. where the offering is being made on a continuous basis, at the time of filing such unaudited financial statements; and

  ii. where the offering is not being made on a continuous basis, at the time of the filing of the prospectus supplement or amendment to disclose the terms of securities in the first tranche of securities to be offered pursuant to the prospectus after the filing of such unaudited financial statements and such comfort letter need only address the most recent unaudited financial statements in or incorporated by reference into the prospectus.

(e) Material Contracts

The underwriting or agency agreement and any other material contract required to be filed that cannot be completed until a specific tranche of securities is offered shall be filed in final form, signed or notarized, together with the prospectus supplement containing the Shelf Information.

(f) Certificate Regarding the Portion of a Distribution Underwritten by Each Underwriter

The provisions of the securities laws of certain provinces and territories require the filing of a certificate which sets forth certain information about the amount of a distribution underwritten by each underwriter. The certificate shall be filed for each tranche of a delayed offering under the Shelf Procedures together with the prospectus supplement containing the Shelf Information.

(g) Commercial Copies

Commercial copies of the prospectus and prospectus supplements and amendments shall be filed only if they are used in connection with offers or sales. Once a commercial copy of a prospectus, prospectus supplement or amendment has been filed, it need not be refiled when it is used, without change, in offers or sales of additional tranches of securities.

(h) Green Sheets

The green sheets and other marketing material required to be filed with certain securities regulatory authorities shall be filed for each tranche of a delayed offering under the Shelf Procedures together with the prospectus supplement containing the Shelf Information.

3.12 Other Matters

(a) Refiling of Shelf Prospectuses

In order to maintain the uninterrupted ability to offer securities under the Shelf Procedures in a province or territory the following procedures for the refiling of a shelf prospectus with the securities regulatory authority in such province or territory may be followed. The issuer must:

  (1) file with such securities regulatory authority for such province or territory not less than twenty business days prior to the lapse date a preliminary prospectus prepared in accordance with this Policy Statement;

  (2) file with such securities regulatory authority not later than five business days prior to the lapse date a prospectus prepared in accordance with this Policy Statement; and

  (3) have obtained a receipt from such securities regulatory authority on or before the lapse date.

(b) Underwriters' Conflicts of Interest

The provisions of the securities laws of certain provinces and territories regarding relationships between an underwriter or selling group member and the issuer must be satisfied for delayed offerings under the Shelf Procedures for each tranche and required disclosure, if any, to the extent not previously provided in the prospectus, shall be included in the prospectus supplement for such tranche. Such provisions may be satisfied for continuous offerings under the Shelf Procedures on the basis of the total amount of securities covered by the prospectus.

(c) Transition Rules for Existing MTN Programs

The distribution of a security pursuant to a prospectus for an MTN Program, for which a receipt has been issued prior to the effectiveness of this Policy Statement, may continue until such prospectus is required to be refiled pursuant to applicable securities law. In order to continue distribution of such security after such date, a prospectus must be filed in accordance with this Policy Statement.

3.13 Shelf Fees

Fees shall be paid upon filing a preliminary prospectus, prospectus, amendment or prospectus supplement in a province or territory under the Shelf Procedures in accordance with the requirements of such jurisdiction. Appendix "C" hereto sets forth a description of the fees currently payable in the various provinces and territories for filings under such procedures.

4. PREP PROCEDURES

4.1 Eligibility for the PREP Procedures

Subject to Section 4.2(a) of this Policy Statement, to be eligible to use the PREP Procedures for the distribution of securities by or on behalf of an issuer or a selling security holder of securities of an issuer, the issuer must:

(a) satisfy the eligibility criteria to use the POP System for the distribution of such securities in such province or territory (including, if relevant, the alternative eligibility criteria relating to issues of nonconvertible Approved Rating debt or preferred shares and to issuers which subsist after a business reorganization);

(b) have obtained a ruling or order from the securities regulatory authority for such province or territory that permits it to use the POP system for the distribution of such securities and be in compliance with the terms of such ruling or order; or

(c) have equity securities outstanding which are listed and posted for trading on a Recognized Stock Exchange.

4.2 Types of Permissible PREP Offerings

(a) Subject to Sections 4.2(c) and 4.2(d), issuers which meet the eligibility criteria set forth in Section 4.1 of this Policy Statement may use the PREP Procedures to offer securities for cash and issuers which do not satisfy such eligibility criteria may use the PREP Procedures to offer non-convertible Approved Rating debt or preferred shares for cash. The PREP Procedures may also be used for such offerings by selling security holders.

(b) Provided that the requirements of Section 4.3(1) are complied with, non-fixed price offerings of non-convertible Approved Rating debt or preferred shares may be made under the PREP Procedures.

(c) The PREP Procedures may not be used for rights offerings.[10]

(d) Special considerations apply to offerings of derivative securities[11] as such offerings may involve novel or complex issues, particularly with

---

10 *Supra*, note 4.

11 *Supra*, note 5.

respect to the terms of the securities, that require case-by-case analysis. It may or may not be appropriate in such an offering to allow some or all of the PREP Information to be omitted from the prospectus and therefore not subject to prior regulatory review. Accordingly, the PREP Procedures may be used for an offering of derivative securities only with prior approval of the appropriate securities regulatory authorities. As a condition of granting such approval, among other things, the securities regulatory authorities may restrict the information that may be omitted from the prospectus.

4.3 PREP Prospectus Disclosure

(a) The following information (the "PREP" Information") may be omitted from the prospectus:

(1) public offering price;

(2) dividend or interest rate;

(3) cash underwriting fees, discounts and commissions;

(4) actual amount of proceeds;

(5) redemption, purchase for cancellation, conversion and exchange prices;

(6) dividend or interest payment dates, record dates and the dates from which dividends or interest accrue;

(7) redemption, purchase for cancellation, conversion and exchange dates;

(8) delivery dates; and

(9) other terms of the securities dependent upon the offering date or offering price.

(b) The PREP Information omitted from the prospectus shall be set forth in a supplemented prospectus (the "Supplemented PREP Prospectus") and shall be filed with the securities regulatory authority of the principal jurisdiction no later than the second business day following the date of the determination of the information omitted from the prospectus and, as nearly as practicable, contemporaneously with each other applicable securities regulatory authority. The Supplemented PREP Prospectus shall take the form of the prospectus modified:

(1) to include the PREP Information that was omitted from the prospectus;

(2) to include disclosure of asset and earnings coverage ratios and/or dilution in accordance with Section 4.3(g) of this Policy Statement;

(3) to be dated the date that the public offering price of the securities was determined;

(4) to delete the legend required by Section 2.3(b) of this Policy Statement;

(5) to delete the prospectus certificate required under Section 4.3(i) and to include an issuer's prospectus certificate and, where there is a promoter, a promoter's prospectus certificate in the following form:

"The foregoing [insert, in the case of POP System offerings – ", together with the documents incorporated herein by reference,"] constitutes full, true and plain disclosure of all material facts relating to the securities offered by this [insert, in the case of POP System offerings – "short form"] prospectus as required by [insert applicable references] [insert if offering made in Quebec – "and does not contain any misrepresentation likely to affect the value or the market price of the securities to be distributed"]."

(6) to delete any prospectus certificate required under Section 4.3(j) and to include an underwriter's prospectus certificate in the following form:

> "To the best of our knowledge, information and belief, the foregoing [insert, in the case of POP System offerings – ", together with the documents incorporated herein by reference,"] constitutes full, true and plain disclosure of all material facts relating to the securities offered by this [insert, in the case of POP System offerings – "short form"] prospectus as required by [insert applicable references] [insert if offering made in Quebec – "and does not contain any misrepresentation likely to affect the value or the market price of the securities to be distributed"]."

(7) to add a list identifying and briefly describing each document which has been incorporated by reference into the prospectus since the issuance of the receipt; and

(8) to include any other information specifically permitted to be included in the Supplemented PREP Prospectus by the applicable securities regulatory authorities.

The changes made to a prospectus in accordance with this Section 4.3(b) are referred to as the "PREP Changes".

(c) The PREP Changes contained in the Supplemented PREP Prospectus shall be deemed to be incorporated by reference into the prospectus as of the date of the Supplemented PREP Prospectus. A statement to that effect shall be contained in the prospectus. The Supplemented PREP Prospectus will not be considered to be a prospectus amendment within the meaning of applicable securities laws.

(d) It is expected that offerings under the PREP Procedures will be priced shortly after the prospectus is filed and a receipt obtained. Accordingly, subject to Section 4.3(f) of this Policy Statement, if the PREP Information is not provided in a Supplemented PREP Prospectus that is filed with the applicable securities regulatory authorities within five business days after the date of the receipt for the prospectus and it is desired that the offering proceed:

(1) such information shall be provided in an amendment to the prospectus that is filed with the applicable securities regulatory authorities; or

(2) an amended prospectus shall be filed as a prospectus amendment to commence a new five business day period for filing a Supplemented PREP Prospectus.

Any such amendment or amended prospectus shall update the disclosure contained in the prospectus.

(e) When updating the disclosure contained in a prospectus pursuant to Section 4.3(d) of this Policy Statement, the issuer shall, among other things amend the disclosure contained in the prospectus so that all disclosure requirements are complied with as if the prospectus had been filed on the date of the filing of such amendment or amended prospectus. Where disclosure is to be provided with reference to the date of the receipt for the preliminary prospectus, the date of the preliminary prospectus, the date of the receipt for the prospectus or the date of the prospectus, such disclosure shall be updated to be provided as if the reference was to the date of the amendment or amended prospectus, as the case may be.

(f) If the PREP Information omitted from the prospectus has not been provided in a Supplemented PREP Prospectus or an amended prospectus that is filed within 75 days of the date of the receipt for the prospectus, no distribution of a security under the prospectus may be made.

(g) Asset and earnings coverage ratios and dilution, where required, shall be set forth in the prospectus based on a reasonable estimate of the

PREP Information. The estimated PREP Information, asset and earnings coverage ratios and dilution may be set forth as ranges which are disclosed in the prospectus. Where the actual coverage ratios or dilution differ from the estimates contained in the prospectus, the actual coverage ratios or dilution, as the case may be, shall be included in the Supplemented PREP Prospectus, unless such difference constitutes a material change, in which case a prospectus amendment must be filed.

(h) The procedures set forth in Section 4.3 of this Policy Statement for a Supplemented PREP Prospectus are not intended to prevent the filing of prospectus amendments to make some or all of the changes to the prospectus that are permitted to be made by a Supplemented PREP Prospectus.

(i) (1) Each preliminary prospectus and prospectus filed under the PREP Procedures;

(2) each amendment to a preliminary prospectus filed under the PREP Procedures;

(3) each amended prospectus filed under the PREP Procedures of the type referred to in Section 4.3(d)(2); and

(4) each amendment to a prospectus filed under the PREP Procedures before the PREP Information has been filed in either a Supplemented PREP Prospectus or an amendment;

shall contain an issuer's prospectus certificate and, where there is a promoter, a promoter's certificate in the following form:

"The foregoing, together with the documents incorporated herein by reference and the information deemed to be incorporated herein by reference, as of the date of the supplemented prospectus providing the information permitted to be omitted from this prospectus, will constitute full, true and plain disclosure of all material facts relating to the securities offered by this prospectus as required by [insert applicable references] [*if offering made in Quebec* – "and will not contain any misrepresentation likely to affect the value or the market price of the securities to be distributed"]."

(j) Where there is an underwriter,

(1) each preliminary prospectus and prospectus filed under the PREP Procedures;

(2) each amendment to a preliminary prospectus filed under the PREP Procedures;

(3) each amended prospectus filed under the PREP Procedures of the type referred to in Section 4.3(d)(2); and

(4) each amendment to a prospectus filed under the PREP Procedures before the PREP Information has been filed in either a Supplemented PREP Prospectus or an amendment;

shall contain a certificate in the following form signed by the underwriter or underwriters who, with respect to the securities offered by the prospectus, are in a contractual relationship with the issuer:

"To the best of our knowledge, information and belief, the foregoing, together with the documents incorporated herein by reference and the information deemed to be incorporated herein by reference, as of the date of the supplemented prospectus providing the information permitted to be omitted from this prospectus, will constitute full, true and plain disclosure of all material facts relating to the securities offered by this prospectus as required by [insert applicable references] [*if offering made in Quebec* – "and will not contain any misrepresentation likely to affect the value or the market price of the securities to be distributed"]."

(k) Each amendment to a prospectus filed under the PREP Procedures after the PREP Information has been filed in either a Supplemented PREP Prospectus or an amended prospectus shall contain prospectus certificates in the form set forth in Sections 4.3(b)(5) and (6).

(l) Disclosure of the following additional information shall be made on the cover page of the prospectus or Supplemented PREP Prospectus for the offering of non-convertible Approved Rating debt or preferred shares on a non-fixed price basis:

(1) the discount allowed to the underwriters or the commission payable to the underwriters and any other compensation payable to the underwriters, including, if applicable, a reference to the fact that the underwriters' compensation will be increased or decreased by the amount by which the aggregate price paid for the securities by the purchasers exceeds or is less than the gross proceeds paid by the underwriters to the issuer[12];

(2) the proceeds or, where applicable, in the case of an offering to be made on a best efforts basis, the minimum amount of proceeds to be received by the issuer;

(3) how the price at which the securities will be offered and sold will be determined, specifically that the securities will be offered either at prices determined by reference to the prevailing price of a specified security in a specified market, at market prices prevailing at the time of sale, or at prices to be negotiated with purchasers;

(4) that the price at which the securities will be offered and sold may vary as between purchasers and during the distribution period;

(5) where the price of the securities is to be determined by reference to prevailing prices of a specified security in a specified market, the price of the specified security in the specified market at the latest practicable date; and

(6) where the price of the securities will be the market price prevailing at the time of sale, the market price of the security at the latest practicable date.

4.4 Filing Packages and Commercial Copies

All documents required to be filed with a preliminary short form prospectus, a short form prospectus and a prospectus amendment under the POP System shall be filed in connection with preliminary short form prospectuses, short form prospectuses and prospectus amendments filed in respect of offerings under the POP System for which the PREP Procedures are being used. All documents required to be filed with a preliminary prospectus, prospectus and prospectus amendment under applicable securities requirements shall be filed in connection with preliminary prospectuses, prospectuses and prospectus amendments filed in respect of offerings not under the POP System for which the PREP Procedures are being used. In either case, the above-described requirements are subject to the following:

(a) Directors' Resolutions

The directors' resolution filed with the prospectus and any amended prospectus of the type referred to in Section 4.3(d)(2) shall authorize the filing and the signing of the Supplemented PREP Prospectus or a separate directors' resolution shall be filed with the Supplemented PREP Prospectus.

(b) Consent Letters

(1) If an expertised statement appears in the preliminary prospectus, prospectus or a document which is incorporated by reference into the prospectus and was filed prior to the filing of the

---

12 *Supra*, note 7.

prospectus, the related consent letter shall be filed at the time of filing the prospectus.

(2) If an expertised statement appears in an AIF, the Supplemented PREP Prospectus or other disclosure document which is incorporated by reference into a prospectus and is filed after the filing of such prospectus, the related consent shall be filed at the time of filing the Supplemented PREP Prospectus or prospectus amendment to disclose the PREP Information.

(3) If an expertised statement appears in an amendment to a prospectus, the related consent shall be filed at the time of filing such amendment.

(c) Comfort Letters

Comfort letters shall be required in connection with offerings made under the PREP Procedures in jurisdictions where comfort letters are required to be filed under applicable securities requirements. In such jurisdictions the following procedures apply:

(1) If unaudited financial statements appear in the prospectus or are incorporated by reference into such prospectus and were filed prior to the filing of such prospectus, any related auditor's comfort letter shall be filed at the time of filing the prospectus.

(2) If unaudited financial statements are incorporated by reference into a prospectus after the filing of such prospectus, any related auditor's comfort letter shall be filed at the time of filing the Supplemented PREP Prospectus or prospectus amendment to disclose the PREP Information or, if such Supplemented PREP Prospectus or prospectus amendment has already been filed, at the time of filing such unaudited financial statements.

(d) Material Contracts

The underwriting or agency agreement and any other material contract required to be filed that cannot be completed until the offering is priced shall be filed with the prospectus in draft form and may omit PREP Information. Any such document filed with the prospectus in draft form shall be refiled in final form, signed or notarized, together with the Supplemented PREP Prospectus or prospectus amendment containing the PREP Information and a black-lined copy of such agreement.

(e) Commercial Copies

Commercial copies of the Supplemented PREP Prospectus shall be filed.

4.5 *Delivery Obligations*

The Supplemented PREP Prospectus shall be delivered to purchasers, in lieu of the prospectus, in accordance with applicable securities laws. Statutory rights of rescission or withdrawal thus shall commence from the time of the purchaser's receipt of such Supplemented PREP Prospectus.

4.6 *Where PREP Offering is Part of a Larger Shelf Offering*

Where an issuer proposes to offer any securities for sale, on other than a continuous basis, within two business days of filing the prospectus for a shelf offering, the Shelf Procedures will not be available for such initial offering and instead a combination of the PREP Procedures and Shelf Procedures must be used. The unavailability of the Shelf Procedures in such circumstances is intended to prevent issuers from filing non-delayed, discrete offerings as shelf offerings under the Shelf Procedures. Such initial offering may, however, be made under the PREP Procedures by filing and clearing with the applicable securities regulatory authorities, contemporaneously with the prospectus filed under the Shelf Procedures, a prospectus supplement for the purpose of describing the terms of the securities being initially offered. When taken together, the prospectus and such supplement shall not omit any information with respect to the offering of such securities other than the PREP Information. The PREP Information shall be contained in a final form of such supplement that is filed with the securities regulatory authorities and delivered to purchasers in accordance with Section 4.3 of this Policy Statement. The prospectus certificates for such an initial offering shall be provided in accordance with the Shelf Procedures.

If, having taken steps to effect part of a shelf offering under the PREP Procedures, such offering is in fact not made immediately after filing the prospectus, it is not necessary for the issuer to file a prospectus amendment or an amended prospectus. Instead, all securities to be offered pursuant to such prospectus, including the securities that were to be offered under the PREP Procedures, may be offered in compliance with the Shelf Procedures.

4.7   PREP Fees

Fees shall be paid upon filing a preliminary prospectus, prospectus, amendment or Supplemented PREP Prospectus in a province or territory under the PREP Procedures in accordance with the requirements of such jurisdiction. Appendix "D" hereto sets forth a description of the fees currently payable in the various provinces and territories for filings under such procedures.

APPENDIX "A" TO NATIONAL POLICY STATEMENT No. 44
RECOGNIZED STOCK EXCHANGES

The following stock exchanges are recognized for the purposes of National Policy Statement No. 44:

1.   the "Exempt Companies" designation of the Alberta Stock Exchange;

2.   the American Stock Exchange;

3.   the International Stock Exchange of the United Kingdom and the Republic of Ireland Limited;

4.   the Montreal Exchange;

5.   the National Market System of the National Association of Securities Dealers Automated Quotation System;

6.   the New York Stock Exchange;

7.   The Toronto Stock Exchange; and

8.   the "Senior Board" of the Vancouver Stock Exchange.

APPENDIX "B" TO NATIONAL POLICY STATEMENT No. 44
FORMS OF PROSPECTUS CERTIFICATES

1.   *Method 1: Supplements Without Prospectus Certificates*

   1.1   Issuer's Certificates

   (a) To use Method 1, the prospectus filed under the Shelf Procedures must contain an issuer's certificate and, where there is a promoter, a promoters certificate in the following form:

   "The foregoing, together with the documents incorporated herein by reference, as of the date of each supplement hereto, will constitute full, true and plain disclosure of all material facts relating to the securities offered by this prospectus and such supplement as required by [insert applicable references] [*insert if offering made in Quebec* – "and will not contain any misrepresentation likely to affect the value or the market price of the securities to be distributed"]."

   The preliminary prospectus shall contain the same certificate if Method 1 has been elected at the time the preliminary prospectus is filed.

   (b) To use Method 1 for an MTN Program established under a

prospectus by a prospectus supplement, where a prospectus certificate of the issuer of the type referred to in Paragraph 1.1(a) of this Appendix was not included in the prospectus, the supplement establishing such program must contain an issuer's certificate and, where there is a promoter, a promoter's certificate in the following form:

"The prospectus dated ***, [insert if applicable – "as amended,"] together with the documents incorporated therein by reference, as supplemented by the foregoing, as of the date of each supplement hereto, will constitute full, true and plain disclosure of all material facts relating to the securities offered hereby and by such supplement as required by [insert applicable references] [insert if offering made in Quebec – "and will not contain any misrepresentation likely to affect the value or the market price of the securities to be distributed"]."

(c) To use Method 1, each amendment to a prospectus filed under the Shelf Procedures, where the prospectus contained a certificate of the type referred to in Paragraph 1.1(a) of this Appendix, must contain an issuer's certificate and, where there is a promoter, a promoter's certificate in the following form:

"The prospectus dated ***, as amended, together with the documents incorporated therein by reference, as of the date of each supplement thereto, will constitute full, true and plain disclosure of all material facts relating to the securities offered by such prospectus and supplement as required by [insert applicable references] [insert if offering made in Quebec – "and will not contain any misrepresentation likely to affect the value or the market price of the securities to be distributed"]."

1.2 Underwriters' Certificates

(a) To use Method 1, each underwriter who, at the time of filing a prospectus under the Shelf Procedures, is, or who it is known will be, in a contractual relationship with the issuer with respect to the securities to be offered thereby must sign a certificate in such prospectus in the following form:

"To the best of our knowledge, information and belief, the foregoing, together with the documents incorporated herein by reference, as of the date of each supplement hereto, will constitute full, true and plain disclosure of all material facts relating to the securities offered by this prospectus and such supplement as required by [insert applicable references] [insert if offering made in Quebec – "and will not contain any misrepresentation likely to affect the value or the market price of the securities to be distributed"]."

The preliminary prospectus shall contain the same certificate if Method 1 has been elected at the time the preliminary prospectus is filed.

(b) To use Method 1 for an MTN Program established under a prospectus by a prospectus supplement, where a prospectus certificate of the type referred to in Paragraph 1.2(a) of this Appendix of an underwriter who, with respect to the securities being offered pursuant to such supplement, is, or will be, in a contractual relationship with the issuer was not included in the prospectus, the supplement establishing such program must contain a certificate in the following form signed by such underwriter:

"To the best of our knowledge, information and belief, the prospectus dated ***, [insert if applicable – "amended,"] together with the documents incorporated therein by reference, as supplemented by the foregoing, as of the date of each supplement hereto, will constitute full, true and plain disclosure of all material facts relating to the securities offered hereby and by such supplement as required by [insert applicable references] [*insert if offering made in Quebec* – "and will not contain any misrepresentation likely to affect the value or the market price of the securities to be distributed"]."

(c) To use Method 1, each amendment to a prospectus filed under the Shelf Procedures, where the prospectus contained a certificate of an underwriter of the type referred to in Paragraph 1.2(a) of this Appendix, shall contain a certificate in the following form signed by such underwriter:

"To the best of our knowledge, information and belief, the prospectus dated ***, as amended, together with the documents incorporated therein by reference, as of the date of each supplement thereto, will constitute full, true and plain disclosure of all material facts relating to the securities offered by such prospectus and supplement as required by [insert applicable references] [*insert if offering made in Quebec* – "and will not contain any misrepresentation likely to affect the value or the market price of the securities to be distributed"]."

2. *Method 2: Prospectus Certificates in Each Supplement*

2.1 Issuer's Certificates

(a) To use Method 2, the prospectus filed under the Shelf Procedures must contain an issuer's certificate and, where there is a promoter, a promoter's certificate in the following form:

"The foregoing, together with the documents incorporated herein by reference, constitutes full, true and plain disclosure of all material facts relating to such securities as required by the securities laws of [insert applicable references] [*insert if offering made in Quebec* – "and does not contain any misrepresentation likely to affect the value or the market price of the securities to be distributed"]."

The preliminary prospectus shall contain the same certificate if Method 2 has been elected at the time the preliminary prospectus is filed.

(b) To use Method 2, each prospectus supplement filed under the Shelf Procedures must contain an issuer's certificate and, where there is a promoter, a promoter's certificate in the following form:

"The prospectus dated ***, [*insert if applicable* – "as amended,"] together with the documents incorporated therein by reference, as supplemented by the foregoing, constitutes full, true and plain disclosure of all material facts relating to the securities offered by such prospectus and this supplement as required by [insert applicable references] [*insert if offering made in Quebec* – "and does not contain any misrepresentation likely to affect the value or the market price of the securities to be distributed"]."

(c) To use Method 2, each amendment to a prospectus filed under the Shelf Procedures must contain an issuer's certificate and, where there is a promoter, a promoter's certificate in the following form:

"The prospectus dated ***, as amended, together with the documents incorporated therein by reference, constitutes full, true and plain disclosure of all material facts relating to the securities offered thereby as required by [insert applicable references] [*insert if offering made in Quebec* – "and does not contain any misrepresentation likely to affect the value or the market price of the securities to be distributed"]."

2.2 Underwriters' Certificates

(a) To use Method 2, each underwriter who, at the time of filing a prospectus under the Shelf Procedures, is, or who it is known will be, in a contractual relationship with the issuer with respect to the securities to be offered thereby must sign a certificate in such prospectus in the following form:

"To the best of our knowledge, information and belief, the foregoing, together with the documents incorporated herein by reference, constitutes full, true and plain disclosure of all material facts relating to such securities as required by [insert applicable references] [*insert if offering made in Quebec* – "and does not contain any misrepresentation likely to affect the value or the market price of the securities to be distributed"]."

The preliminary prospectus shall contain the same certificate if Method 2 has been elected at the time the preliminary prospectus is filed.

(b) To use Method 2, each prospectus supplement filed under the Shelf Procedures shall contain a certificate in the following form signed by the underwriter(s) who, with respect to the securities being offered thereby, are in a contractual relationship with the issuer:

"To the best of our knowledge, information and belief, the prospectus dated ***, [*insert if applicable* – "s amended,"] together with the documents incorporated therein by reference, as supplemented by the foregoing, constitutes full, true and plain disclosure of all material facts relating to the securities offered by such prospectus and this supplement as required by [insert applicable references] [*insert if offering made in Quebec* – "and does not contain any misrepresentation likely to affect the value or the market price of the securities to be distributed"]."

(c) To use Method 2, each amendment to a prospectus filed under the Shelf Procedures, where the prospectus contained a certificate of an underwriter of the type referred to in Paragraph 2.2(a) of this Appendix, shall contain a certificate in the following form signed by such underwriter:

"To the best of our knowledge, information and belief, the prospectus dated ***, as amended, together with the documents incorporated therein by reference, constitutes full, true and plain disclosure of all material facts relating to the securities offered thereby as required by [insert applicable references] [*insert if offering made in Quebec* – "and does not contain any misrepresentation likely to affect the value or the market price of the securities to be distributed"]."

(d) If:

(1) Method 2 is being used;

(2) an amendment to a prospectus is filed with respect to a material change that occurred during a period when offers and sales of securities are being made by an underwriter; and

(3) such prospectus did not contain a certificate of such underwriter of the type referred to in Paragraph 2.2(a) of this Appendix,

such underwriter shall sign, as of the date of the amendment, a certificate in the form that it previously provided pursuant to Paragraph 2.2(b) of this Appendix in the prospectus supplement describing the securities being so offered (except that such certificate shall refer to the amendment). This certificate shall be separately filed with the securities regulatory authorities concurrently with the amendment.

APPENDIX "C" TO NATIONAL POLICY STATEMENT NO. 44
SHELF PROCEDURES FILING FEES

1. *British Columbia*

The fee payable in British Columbia upon the filing of a preliminary prospectus under the Shelf Procedures shall be the same as the fee then payable upon the filing of a preliminary prospectus qualifying one class of securities which, at the date of this Policy Statement, is $2,500.

An additional fee is payable in British Columbia based upon the proceeds realized in British Columbia. At the date of this Policy Statement, such additional fee is equal to the amount, if any, by which 0.03 per cent of the proceeds realized in British Columbia exceeds the $2,500 fee paid upon the filing of the preliminary prospectus.

For continuous offerings under the Shelf Procedures, other than MTN Programs, any additional fee shall be paid within five business days after the end of each month with respect to the securities sold during that month. For MTN Programs, any additional fee shall be paid together with the monthly filing of Pricing Supplements, with respect to the sale of securities covered by such Pricing Supplements. For delayed offerings under the Shelf Procedures, any additional fee shall be paid within 30 days after the completion of the offering of securities for each tranche. A written notice stating the relevant proceeds realized in British Columbia shall be filed with each payment of an additional fee and within 30 days after the earlier of (i) the completion of the offering of securities under the prospectus, and (ii) the second anniversary of the filing of the prospectus.

At the time an issuer files a prospectus under the Shelf Procedures, the issuer must also file an undertaking that such additional fees will be paid in accordance with this Policy Statement.

2. *Ontario*

2.1   The fee payable in Ontario upon the filing of a preliminary prospectus under the Shelf Procedures shall be $250.

2.2   No fee shall be payable in Ontario upon the filing of a prospectus under the Shelf Procedures.

2.3   Subject to Sections 2.4 and 2.5 of this Appendix, each prospectus supplement filed under the Shelf Procedures to describe the terms of securities distributed or to be distributed in Ontario shall be accompanied by a fee equal to the amount calculated using the formula,

$$A - B$$

where,

"A" is 0.03 per cent of the aggregate gross proceeds realized, or the maximum aggregate gross proceeds to be realized, from the distribution of securities under the prospectus supplement, and

"B" is the amount of any fee paid under Section 2.1 of this Appendix with respect to the related preliminary prospectus, to the extent that such fee previously has not been applied toward the payment of fees under this Section or Section 2.4, 2.5 or 2.6 of this Appendix,

provided that, where the issuer and any selling security holder certify the aggregate gross proceeds realized from the distribution in Ontario of securities under the prospectus supplement, "A" may be 0.03 per cent of the aggregate gross proceeds realized in Ontario from such distribution.

2.4   Where an MTN Program has been established under the Shelf
      Procedures, each monthly filing of Pricing Supplements describing the
      terms of securities distributed or to be distributed in Ontario shall be
      accompanied by a fee equal to the amount calculated using the for-
      mula,

$$A - B$$

where,

"A" is 0.03 per cent of the aggregate gross proceeds realized, or
the maximum aggregate gross proceeds to be realized, from the
distribution of securities under such Pricing Supplements, and

"B" is the amount of any fee paid under Section 2.1 of this
Appendix with respect to the related preliminary prospectus, to
the extent such fee previously has not been applied toward the
payment of fees under this Section or Section 2.3, 2.5 or 2.6 of
this Appendix,

provided that, where the issuer and any selling security holder certify
the aggregate gross proceeds realized from the distribution in Ontario
of securities under such Pricing Supplements, "A" may be 0.03 per
cent of the aggregate gross proceeds realized in Ontario from such
distribution.

2.5   Except as set forth in Section 2.4 of this Appendix, where pursuant to
      a prospectus filed under the Shelf Procedures securities are dis-
      tributed on a continuous basis in Ontario, there shall be paid by the
      issuer or the selling security holder, as applicable, within five busi-
      ness days of the end of each month a fee equal to the amount
      calculated using the formula,

$$A - B$$

where,

"A" is 0.03 per cent of the aggregate gross proceeds realized, or
the maximum aggregate gross proceeds to be realized, from the
distribution of securities under such continuous offering
program during such month, and

"B" is the amount of any fee paid under Section 2.1 of this
Appendix with respect to the related preliminary prospectus, to
the extent that such fee previously has not been applied toward
the payment of fees under this Section or Section 2.3, 2.4 or 2.6
of this Appendix,

provided that, where the issuer and any selling security holder certify
the amount of the aggregate gross proceeds realized from the distribution in Ontario during the month under such continuous offering
program, "A" may be 0.03 per cent of the aggregate gross proceeds
realized in Ontario from such distribution.

2.6   An amendment to a prospectus filed under the Shelf Procedures shall
      be accompanied by a fee equal to the greater of:

      (a) $250; and

      (b) where the amendment is used instead of a supplement to
          describe the terms of a tranche of securities to be distributed in
          Ontario, the amount calculated using the formula,

$$X - Y$$

where,

"X" is 0.03 per cent of the maximum aggregate gross proceeds to
be realized from the distribution of securities in the tranche
described by the amendment, and

"Y" is the amount of any fee paid under Section 2.1 of this
Appendix with respect to the related preliminary prospectus, to
the extent that such fee previously has not been applied to-

wards the payment of fees under this Section or Section 2.3, 2.4, or 2.5 of this Appendix.

2.7   An issuer that has filed a prospectus under the Shelf Procedures and any selling security holder shall file within ninety days after the earlier of:

   (a) the completion of the distribution of securities under the prospectus; and

   (b) the date that is 24 months after the date of the receipt for the prospectus,

a written notice stating the aggregate gross proceeds realized in Ontario from the distribution of securities under the prospectus.

2.8   Subject to Section 2.9 of this Appendix, if the written notice filed under Section 2.7 of this Appendix discloses that the aggregate of the fees paid under Sections 2.3, 2.4, 2.5 and 2.6 of this Appendix exceeds the fees that would have been paid had the payments been based upon the aggregate gross proceeds realized in Ontario from the distribution of securities under the prospectus, the Director shall authorize the payment of a refund equal to the amount calculated using the formula,

$$A + B - C$$

where,

   "A" is the aggregate of the fees paid under Sections 2.3, 2.4 and 2.5 of this Appendix with respect to the related prospectus,

   "B" is the aggregate of each fee paid under Section 2.6 of this Appendix in respect of an amendment used instead of a prospectus to describe the terms of a tranche of securities; and

   "C" is the amount calculated using the formula,

$$X - Y$$

where,

   "X" is 0.03 per cent of the aggregate gross proceeds realized in Ontario from the distribution of securities under the prospectus, and

   "Y" is the amount of any fee paid under Section 2.1 of this Appendix with respect to the related prospectus.

2.9   Upon request, any refund payable under Section 2.8 of this Appendix may be credited towards the fee payable in respect of a prospectus subsequently filed under the Shelf Procedures.

2.10 If the written notice filed under Section 2.7 of this Appendix discloses that the aggregate of the fees paid under Sections 2.3, 2.4, 2.5 and 2.6 of this Appendix is less than the fees that should have been paid, the written notice shall be accompanied by a fee equal to the amount calculated using the formula,

$$A - B - C$$

where,

   "A" is the amount calculated using the formula,

$$X - Y$$

where,

   "X" is 0.03 per cent of the aggregate gross proceeds realized in Ontario from the distribution of securities under the prospectus, and

   "Y" is the amount of any fee paid under Section 2.1 of this Appendix with respect to the related prospectus,

   "B" is the aggregate of the fees paid under Sections 2.3, 2.4 and 2.5 of this Appendix with respect to the related prospectus, and

"C" is the aggregate of each fee paid under Section 2.6 of this Appendix in respect of an amendment used instead of a prospectus supplement to describe the terms of a tranche of securities.

3.   *Quebec*

The fee payable in Quebec upon the filing of a preliminary prospectus under the Shelf Procedures shall be the same as the fee then ordinarily payable upon the filing of a preliminary prospectus, which is $500 at the date of this Policy Statement.

The fee payable in Quebec upon the filing of a prospectus under the Shelf Procedures shall be the fee then ordinarily payable upon the filing of a prospectus and shall be paid based on a bona fide estimate of the maximum offering price for the securities being offered. For a distribution made in Quebec and elsewhere by an issuer with its head office outside of Quebec and not qualified for the Quebec Share Saving Plan, such fee is equal to the amount, if any, by which 0.03 per cent of 25 per cent of the estimated total gross proceeds exceeds the $500 fee paid upon the filing of the preliminary prospectus. For a distribution made in Quebec and elsewhere by an issuer with its head office in Quebec and not qualified for the Quebec Share Savings Plan such fee is equal to the amount, if any, by which 0.03 per cent of 50 per cent of the estimated total gross proceeds exceeds the $500 fee paid upon the filing of the preliminary prospectus. For a distribution made in Quebec and elsewhere and qualified for the Quebec Share Savings Plan such fee is equal to the amount by which 0.03 per cent of the estimated total gross proceeds exceeds the $500 fee paid upon the filing of the preliminary prospectus.

A written notice stating the total gross proceeds realized in Quebec from the distribution under the Shelf prospectus shall be filed within 15 business days after the earlier of (i) the completion of the offering of securities under the prospectus and (ii) the second anniversary of the filing of the prospectus. The fee for a distribution of securities is set at the excess over $500 of 0.03 per cent of the total gross proceeds of the issue, including any overallotment, realized in Quebec. The balance payable or the refund requested is equal to the difference between that figure and the total fee paid upon the filing of the preliminary prospectus and the prospectus. Where that figure is less than $500 the issuer is only entitled to a refund of the amount paid upon filing of the prospectus.

4.   *Provinces Which Do Not Assess Fees Based on Proceeds*

The fee payable upon the filing of a preliminary prospectus under the Shelf Procedures in any province or territory which does not assess fees based on the proceeds of the distribution (which at the date of this Policy Statement are all of the provinces and territories other than British Columbia, Ontario and Quebec) shall be the same as the fee then ordinarily payable upon the filing of a preliminary prospectus. No fee shall be payable upon the filing of a prospectus. The fee payable upon the filing of a prospectus supplement (other than a Pricing Supplement) shall be the same as the fee then ordinarily payable upon the filing of a preliminary prospectus. No fee shall be payable upon the filing of a Pricing Supplement.

APPENDIX "D" TO NATIONAL POLICY STATEMENT NO. 44
PREP PROCEDURES FILING FEES

1.   *British Columbia*

The fee payable in British Columbia upon the filing of a preliminary prospectus under the PREP Procedures shall be the same as the fee then ordinarily payable upon the filing of a preliminary prospectus, which at the date of this Policy Statement is $2,500 for each class of securities.

An additional fee may be payable in British Columbia based upon the proceeds realized in British Columbia. At the date of this Policy Statement, such additional fee is equal to the amount, if any, by which 0.03 per cent of the proceeds realized in British Columbia exceeds the $2,500 fee paid upon the filing of the preliminary prospectus.

Upon filing of a prospectus under the PREP Procedures, an undertaking that such additional fees will be paid must be filed with the British Columbia Securities Commission.

Not more than 30 days after the completion of the distribution under the PREP Prospectus, a written notice stating the relevant proceeds realized in British Columbia, together with the additional fees, must be filed with the British Columbia Securities Commission.

2.   *Ontario*

2.1   The fee payable in Ontario upon the filing of a preliminary prospectus under the PREP Procedures shall be $250.

2.2   Each prospectus filed under the PREP Procedures shall be accompanied by a fee equal to the amount calculated using the formula,

$$A - B$$

where,

"A" is 0.03 per cent of the maximum aggregate gross proceeds to be realized from the distribution of securities under the prospectus, based on a bona fide estimate of the maximum offering price for the securities being distributed, and

"B" is the fee paid under Section 2.1 of this Appendix with respect to the related preliminary prospectus.

2.3   An amendment to a prospectus for a distribution of securities where the securities are to be priced after a receipt for the final prospectus has been issued shall be accompanied by a fee equal to the greater of:

(a) $250; and

(b) 0.03 per cent of the maximum aggregate gross proceeds to be realized from the distribution of additional securities under the prospectus as a result of the amendment, based on a bona fide estimate of the maximum offering price for the additional securities being distributed.

2.4   An issuer that has filed a prospectus under the PREP Procedures and any selling security holder shall file a written notice stating the aggregate gross proceeds realized in Ontario from the distribution of securities under the prospectus within twelve months after the date of the receipt for the prospectus.

2.5   If the written notice filed under Section 2.4 of this Appendix discloses that the aggregate gross proceeds realized in Ontario were less than the maximum aggregate gross proceeds to be realized from the distribution of securities under the prospectus, the Director shall authorize the payment of a refund equal to the amount calculated using the formula,

$$A + B - C$$

where,

"A" is the fee paid under Section 2.2 of this Appendix with respect to the related prospectus,

"B" is the aggregate of each fee paid under Section 2.3 of this Appendix in respect of an amendment for the purpose of distributing securities in addition to the securities previously disclosed in the prospectus or an amendment to the prospectus, and

"C" is the fee that would have been payable had the aggregate gross proceeds realized in Ontario from the distribution of securities under the prospectus been used in making the calculation in Section 2.2 of this Appendix.

2.6   If the written notice filed under Section 2.4 of this Appendix discloses that the aggregate gross proceeds realized in Ontario exceeded the maximum aggregate gross proceeds to be realized from the distribu-

National Policies

tion of securities under the prospectus, the written notice shall be accompanied by a fee equal to the amount calculated using the formula,

$$A - B - C$$

where,

"A" is the fee that would have been payable had the aggregate gross proceeds realized in Ontario from the distribution of securities under the prospectus been used in making the calculation under Section 2.2 of this Appendix,

"B" is the fee paid under Section 2.2 of this Appendix with respect to the related prospectus, and

"C" is the aggregate of each fee paid under Section 2.3 of this Appendix in respect of an amendment for the purpose of distributing securities in addition to the securities previously disclosed in the prospectus or an amendment to the prospectus.

3.   *Quebec*

The fee payable in Quebec upon the filing of a preliminary prospectus under the PREP Procedures shall be the same as the fee then ordinarily payable upon the filing of a preliminary prospectus, which is $500 at the date of this Policy Statement.

The fee payable in Quebec upon the filing of a prospectus under the PREP Procedures shall be the fee then ordinarily payable upon the filing of a prospectus and shall be paid based on a bona fide estimate of the maximum offering price for the securities being offered. For a distribution made in Quebec and elsewhere by an issuer with its head office outside of Quebec and not qualified for the Quebec Share Saving Plan, such fee is equal to the amount, if any, by which 0.03 per cent of 25 per cent of the estimated total gross proceeds exceeds the $500 fee paid upon the filing of the preliminary prospectus. For a distribution made in Quebec and elsewhere by an issuer with its head office in Quebec and not qualified for the Quebec Share Savings Plan such fee is equal to the amount, if any, by which 0.03 per cent of 50 per cent of the estimated total gross proceeds exceeds the $500 fee paid upon the filing of the preliminary prospectus. For a distribution made in Quebec and elsewhere and qualified for the Quebec Share Savings Plan such fee is equal to the amount by which 0.03 per cent of the estimated total gross proceeds exceeds the $500 fee paid upon the filing of the preliminary prospectus.

A written notice stating the total gross proceeds realized in Quebec from the distribution under the PREP prospectus shall be filed within 15 business days after the completion of the offering under the prospectus. The fee for a distribution of securities is set at the excess over $500 of 0.03 per cent of the total gross proceeds of the issue, including any overallotment, realized in Quebec. The balance payable or the refund requested is equal to the difference between that figure and the total fee paid upon the filing of the preliminary prospectus and the prospectus. Where that figure is less than $500 the issuer is only entitled to a refund of the amount paid upon filing of the prospectus.

4.   *Provinces Which Do Not Assess Fees Based on Proceeds*

The fee payable upon the filing of a preliminary prospectus under the PREP Procedures in any province or territory which does not assess fees based on the proceeds of the distribution (which at the date of this Policy Statement are all of the provinces and territories other than British Columbia, Ontario and Quebec) shall be the same as the fee then ordinarily payable upon the filing of a preliminary prospectus. No fee shall be payable upon the filing of a prospectus or a Supplemented PREP Prospectus.

NATIONAL POLICY STATEMENT No. 45
MULTIJURISDICTIONAL DISCLOSURE SYSTEM

CONTENTS

1. INTRODUCTION

The multijurisdictional disclosure system is a joint initiative by the Canadian Securities Administrators and the Securities and Exchange Commission of the United States (the "SEC") to reduce duplicative regulation in cross-border offerings, issuer bids, take-over bids, business combinations and continuous disclosure and other filings.

The multijurisdictional disclosure system implemented in Canada pursuant to this Policy Statement (the "MJDS") is intended to remove unnecessary obstacles to certain offerings of securities of U.S. issuers in Canada and to facilitate take-over and issuer bids and business combinations involving securities of U.S. issuers having less than a specified percentage of Canadian security holders, while ensuring that Canadian investors remain adequately protected.

The MJDS permits public offerings of securities of U.S. issuers that meet specified eligibility requirements to be made in Canada on the basis of disclosure documents prepared in accordance with the laws of the United States (with certain additional Canadian disclosure). A public offering of securities of a U.S. issuer may be made under the MJDS both in Canada and the United States or in Canada only.

The MJDS also reduces disincentives to the extension to Canadian security holders of rights offerings by U.S. issuers by permitting such rights offerings to be made in Canada on the basis of U.S. disclosure documents. Similarly, it facilitates the extension to Canadian security holders of U.S. issuers of take-over bids, issuer bids and business combinations in the circumstances contemplated by this Policy Statement. The MJDS permits such transactions to be made in Canada generally in the same manner as in the United States and on the basis of U.S. disclosure documents.

Regulatory review of disclosure documents used under the MJDS for offerings made by a U.S. issuer both in Canada and the United States will be that customary in the United States, with the SEC being responsible for carrying out the review. Canadian securities regulatory authorities will monitor materials filed under the MJDS in order to check compliance with the specific disclosure and filing requirements of this Policy Statement. In addition, the substance of the disclosure documents will be reviewed in the unusual case where, through monitoring of the materials or otherwise, the Canadian securities regulatory authorities have reason to believe that there may be a problem with a transaction or the related disclosure or other special circumstances exist.

The MJDS does not change the liability provisions of the securities laws of any province or territory or the discretionary authority of a Canadian securities regulatory authority to halt a distribution, remove an exemption, cease trade the related securities, or refuse to issue a receipt for a preliminary prospectus or prospectus. The Canadian securities regulatory authorities also will continue to exercise their public interest jurisdiction in specific cases where they determine that it is necessary to do so in order to preserve the integrity of the Canadian capital markets.

Use of the MJDS is based on compliance with U.S. law. Thus, any person or company doing a transaction or filing a document in Canada under the MJDS must comply in full with all applicable U.S. requirements. However, violation of a U.S. requirement will not automatically disqualify a person or company from using the MJDS with respect to a transaction or document. Instead, a person or company that violates a U.S. requirement may, depending upon the circumstances, be considered to have violated an equivalent requirement of a Canadian jurisdiction with respect to the transaction or document.

Concurrently with the adoption of this Policy Statement, the SEC is adopting rules, forms and schedules for the implementation of a similar multijurisdictional disclosure system in the United States. The U.S. system removes unnecessary impediments to certain offerings of securities of Canadian issuers in the United States and facilitates the extension to U.S. security holders of Canadian issuers of take-over bids, issuer bids and business combinations in the circumstances contemplated by the U.S. system.

The procedures to be followed in Canada when the U.S. system is used for a U.S.-only offering of securities of a Canadian issuer are set out in Section 7.

2.   DEFINITIONS

As used in this Policy Statement, unless the subject matter or context otherwise requires, the following terms shall have the following meanings:

    (1)   "affiliate", with respect to an issuer, means a person or company that directly, or indirectly through one or more intermediaries, controls or is controlled by, or is under common control with, the issuer;

    (2)   "applicable Canadian securities legislation" means the securities legislation of each Canadian province and territory in which securities are offered, or a bid is made, under this Policy Statement;

    (3)   "applicable securities regulatory authority" means the securities regulatory authority in each Canadian province and territory in which securities are offered, or a bid is made, under this Policy Statement;

    (4)   "Approved Rating", with respect to debt or preferred shares, means a provisional rating by an Approved Rating Organization in one of the categories applicable thereto, as set out below opposite the Approved Rating Organization's name:

APPROVED RATING ORGANIZATION	DEBT	PREFERRED SHARES
C.B.R.S. Inc.	A++, A+, A or B++	P-1+, P-1, P-2 or P-3
Dominion Bond Rating Service Limited	AAA, AA, A or BBB	Pfd-1, Pfd-2 or Pfd-3
Moody's Investors Service, Inc.	Aaa, Aa, A or Baa	"aaa", "aa", "a" or "baa"
Standard & Poor's Corporation	AAA, AA, A or BBB	AAA, AA, A or BBB

    An Approved Rating for an Approved Rating Organization that is not listed above shall be a rating by such organization in one of its generic rating categories that signifies investment grade. Typically, the four highest rating categories (within which there may be subcategories or gradations indicating relative standing) signify investment grade by an Approved Rating Organization;

    (5)   "Approved Rating Organization" means each of C.B.R.S. Inc., Dominion Bond Rating Service Limited, Moody's Investors Service, Inc., Standard & Poor's Corporation and any entity recognized by the SEC as a nationally recognized statistical rating organization as that term is used in relation to Rule 15c3-1(c)(2)(vi)(F) under the 1934 Act;

    (6)   "bid" means a take-over bid or an issuer bid;

    (7)   "bid circular", in respect of the application of this Policy Statement in a province or territory, means a take-over bid circular or an issuer bid circular as those terms are used in the securities legislation of such province or territory, consisting, for purposes of this Policy Statement, of the tender offer materials used in the United States, as modified pursuant to Section 4.5;

(8) "business combination" means a statutory merger or consolidation or similar plan or acquisition requiring the vote or consent of security holders of a company or person, in which securities of such company or person or another company or person held by such security holders will become or be exchanged for securities of any other company or person;

(9) "Canadian GAAP" means the accounting principles generally accepted in Canada, and, where a principle is recommended in the Handbook of the Canadian Institute of Chartered Accountants which is applicable in the circumstances, means such principle;

(10) "commodity pool issuer" means an issuer formed and operated for the purpose of investing in commodity futures contracts, commodity futures and/or related products;

(11) "company", in respect of the application of this Policy Statement in a province or territory, has the meaning assigned thereto in the securities legislation of such province or territory;

(12) "Conflicts Rules" has the meaning assigned thereto in Section 3.12;

(13) "connected issuer" or "connected party", in respect of the application of this Policy Statement in a province or territory, has the meaning assigned thereto in the Conflicts Rules of such province or territory;

(14) "control", with respect to an issuer, means the possession, direct or indirect, of the power to direct or cause the direction of the management and policies of the issuer, whether through the ownership of voting securities, by contract or otherwise, and "under common control with" shall be construed accordingly;

(15) "convertible", with respect to debt or preferred shares, means that the rights and attributes attaching to such securities include a right or option to purchase, convert or exchange or otherwise acquire any equity shares of the issuer or of any other issuer (or any debt or preferred shares not having an Approved Rating in the case of debt or preferred shares having an Approved Rating), or any other security which itself has a right to purchase, convert or exchange or otherwise acquire any equity shares of the issuer or any other issuer (or any debt or preferred shares not having an Approved Rating in the case of debt or preferred shares having an Approved Rating), "convert" shall be construed accordingly, and "non-convertible" means securities that are not convertible;

(16) "equity shares", with respect to an issuer, means common shares, non-voting equity shares and subordinate or restricted voting equity shares of the issuer, but excludes preferred shares;

(17) "foreign issuer" means an issuer that is not incorporated or organized under the laws of Canada or a province or territory of Canada, except where:

(a) voting securities carrying more than 50% of the votes for the election of directors are held by persons or companies whose last address as shown on the books of the issuer is in Canada; and

(b) either:

(i) the majority of the senior officers or directors of the issuer are citizens or residents of Canada;

(ii) more than 50% of the assets of the issuer are located in Canada; or

(iii) the business of the issuer is administered principally in Canada;

(18) "independent underwriter", in respect of the application of this Policy Statement in a province or territory, means a dealer that is not the issuer and in respect of which the issuer is not a related party or related issuer or connected party or connected issuer or, where the dealer is not a registrant in such province or territory, would not be a connected party or connected issuer if the dealer were a registrant;

(19) "insider bid", in respect of the application of this Policy Statement in a province or territory, has the meaning assigned thereto in the securities legislation of such province or territory;

(20) "International Accounting Standards" means the accounting principles issued by the International Accounting Standards Committee;

(21) "issuer", in respect of the application of this Policy Statement in a province or territory, has the meaning assigned thereto in the securities legislation of such province or territory;

(22) "issuer bid", in respect of the application of this Policy Statement in a province or territory, has the meaning assigned thereto in the securities legislation of such province or territory;

(23) "majority-owned subsidiary" means a person or company of which voting securities carrying more than 50% of the votes for the election of directors are held by (i) another person or company and (ii) the other majority-owned subsidiaries of that other person or company;

(24) "Method 1" means the first of the two alternative methods of providing prospectus certificates for Rule 415 Offerings made under the MJDS described in Section 3.11(2);

(25) "Method 2" means the second of the two alternative methods of providing prospectus certificates for Rule 415 Offerings made under the MJDS described in Section 3.11(2);

(26) "MJDS" means the multijurisdictional disclosure system rules and procedures set forth in Sections 1-6 of this Policy Statement;

(27) "MTN Program" means a continuous Rule 415 Offering of debt in which the specific variable terms of the individual securities and the offering thereof are determined at the time of sale;

(28) "Nasdaq" means The Nasdaq Stock Market;

(29) "NNM" means the Nasdaq National Market;

(30) "offeree issuer" means an issuer whose securities are the subject of a bid;

(31) "offeror", in respect of the application of this Policy Statement in a province or territory, has the meaning assigned thereto in the securities legislation of such province or territory;

(32) "parent", with respect to a majority-owned subsidiary, means a person or company that, together with the parent's other majority-owned subsidiaries, holds voting securities of the majority-owned subsidiary carrying more than 50% of the votes for the election of directors;

(33) "person", in respect of the application of this Policy Statement in a province or territory, has the meaning assigned thereto in the securities legislation of such province or territory;

(34) "principal market", with respect to a class of securities, means the single securities market with the largest aggregate trading volume for the class of securities in the preceding 12 calendar month period;

(35) "principal jurisdiction" means the principal jurisdiction selected in accordance with Section 3.8(2);

(36) "public float", with respect to a class of securities, means the aggregate market value of such securities held by persons or companies that are not affiliates of the issuer of such securities, calculated by using the price at which such securities were last sold in the principal market for such securities on the date specified in the applicable provision of this Policy Statement, or the average of the bid and asked prices of such securities in such market on such date if there were no sales on such date, and where there is no market for such class of securities, it means the book value of such securities held by persons or companies that are not affiliates of the issuer of such securities computed on such date, provided that if the issuer of such class of securities is in bankruptcy or receivership or has an accumulated capital deficit, it means one-third of the principal amount, par value or stated value of such securities held by persons or companies that are not affiliates of the issuer of such securities;

(37) "related issuer" or "related party", in respect of the application of this Policy Statement in a province or territory, has the meaning assigned thereto in the Conflicts Rules of such province or territory;

(38) "review jurisdiction" means the review jurisdiction selected in accordance with Section 7;

(39) "Rule 415 Offering" means an offering under Rule 415 under the 1933 Act that is made in Canada pursuant to Section 3.7;

(40) "Rule 430A Offering" means an offering under Rule 430A under the 1933 Act that is made in Canada pursuant to Section 3.7;

(41) "Rule 430A Pricing Prospectus" means a prospectus prepared in connection with a Rule 430A Offering that contains the information omitted from the related registration statement as permitted by Rule 430A under the 1933 Act;

(42) "SEC" means the Securities and Exchange Commission of the United States;

(43) "securities exchange bid" means a bid for which the consideration for the securities of the offeree issuer consists, in whole or in part, of securities of an offeror or other issuer;

(44) "securities legislation" in respect of the application of this Policy Statement in a province or territory, means the statutes concerning the regulation of securities markets and trading in securities of such province or territory, the regulations and blanket rulings and orders thereunder, and the policy statements and written interpretations issued by the securities regulatory authority of such province or territory;

(45) "take-over bid", in respect of the application of this Policy Statement in a province or territory, has the meaning assigned thereto in the securities legislation of such province or territory;

(46) "U.S. issuer" means a foreign issuer that is incorporated or organized under the laws of the United States or any state or territory of the United States or the District of Columbia;

(47) "voting securities" means securities the holders of which have a present entitlement to vote for the election of directors;

(48) "1933 Act" means the Securities Act of 1933 of the United States;

(49) "1934 Act" means the Securities Exchange Act of 1934 of the United States; and

(50) "1940 Act" means the Investment Company Act of 1940 of the United States.

3.		PROSPECTUS OFFERINGS BY U.S. ISSUERS

3.1	*General*

The MJDS permits the following types of securities of a U.S. issuer to be distributed by prospectus in Canada, either by the issuer or by a selling security holder, on the basis of documentation prepared in accordance with U.S. requirements (with certain additional Canadian disclosure):

(1)	non-convertible debt and non-convertible preferred shares that have an Approved Rating;

(2)	debt and preferred shares that have an Approved Rating and may not be converted for at least one year after issuance, if the issuer meets a substantiality requirement;

(3)	other securities, if the issuer meets a greater substantiality requirement; and

(4)	certain rights to acquire securities of the issuer.

The availability of the MJDS for rights offerings is discussed in Section 3.4(1), for securities exchange bids in Section 4.1 and for business combinations in Section 5.1.

The purpose of the "substantiality" requirement is to single out issuers whose size is such that (i) information about them is publicly disseminated and (ii) they have a significant market following. As a result, the marketplace can be expected to set efficiently a price for the securities of these issuers based on publicly available information.

Non-convertible debt and preferred shares that have an Approved Rating are particularly appropriate for the MJDS because these securities trade primarily on the basis of their yield and an assessment of creditworthiness by an independent rating organization. The lack of a "substantiality" requirement for offerings of these securities reflects this and allows the MJDS to be used by issuers of securities having an Approved Rating, such as finance subsidiaries, that access that market frequently, but do not meet the public float requirements. Debt and preferred shares that have an Approved Rating and are not convertible into other securities for at least one year after issuance can be expected to trade primarily on the basis of their yield and independent rating, but are also priced to some extent on the basis of the anticipated value of the security into which they are convertible. Thus, the MJDS is available for these securities on the basis of their Approved Rating, coupled with a "substantiality" requirement.

In the case of offerings of common shares or other securities other than non-convertible debt and preferred shares that have an Approved Rating, the MJDS is available upon satisfaction of a "substantiality" requirement.

The MJDS may not be used for offerings of derivative securities, except warrants, options, rights or convertible securities where the issuer of the underlying securities to which the warrants, options, rights or convertible securities relate is eligible under this Policy Statement to distribute the underlying securities. Therefore, offerings of derivative securities such as stock index warrants, currency warrants and debt the interest on which is based upon the performance of a stock index may not be made under the MJDS.

All prospectus offerings remain subject to the fundamental principle that transactions must not be prejudicial to the public interest. The applicable securities regulatory authorities will continue to exercise their public interest jurisdiction in specific cases where they determine that it is necessary to do so in order to preserve the integrity of the Canadian capital markets.

3.2 *Offerings of Debt or Preferred Shares Having an Approved Rating*

The MJDS may be used for the distribution in Canada of debt that has an Approved Rating or preferred shares that have an Approved Rating or rights that, upon issuance, are immediately exercisable for any such securities, provided that:

(1) the issuer is a U.S. issuer;

(2) the issuer (i) has a class of securities registered pursuant to section 12(b) or 12(g) of the 1934 Act; or (ii) is required to file reports pursuant to section 15(d) of the 1934 Act;

(3) the issuer has filed with the SEC all the material required to be filed pursuant to sections 13, 14 and 15(d) of the 1934 Act for a period of 12 calendar months immediately preceding the filing of the preliminary prospectus with the principal jurisdiction;

(4) the issuer is not registered or required to be registered as an investment company under the 1940 Act;

(5) the issuer is not a commodity pool issuer; and

(6) the securities being offered or issuable upon the exercise of the rights either:

(a) are not convertible; or

(b) if convertible, may not be converted for at least one year after issuance, and the equity shares of the issuer of the securities into which the offered securities are convertible have a public float of not less than U.S. $75,000,000, determined as of a date that is within 60 days prior to the filing of the preliminary prospectus with the principal jurisdiction.

For purposes of this Section 3, whether debt or preferred shares have an Approved Rating shall be determined as of the time the preliminary prospectus is filed in the principal jurisdiction.

3.3 *Offerings of Other Securities*

The MJDS may be used for the distribution in Canada of any securities of an issuer, provided that:

(1) the issuer meets the eligibility requirements specified in Sections 3.2(1)-(5); and

(2) the equity shares of the issuer have a public float of not less than U.S. $75,000,000, determined as of a date that is within 60 days prior to the filing of the preliminary prospectus with the principal jurisdiction.

Offerings of debt and preferred shares that are not eligible to be made pursuant to Section 3.2, rights offerings that are not eligible to be made pursuant to Section 3.4, securities exchange bids that are not eligible to be made pursuant to Section 4.2 and business combinations that are not eligible to be made pursuant to Section 5.2 may be made pursuant to this Section 3.3, provided that (1) and (2) above are satisfied.

3.4 *Rights Offerings*

(1) General

Subject to certain limitations, the MJDS permits U.S. issuers to make rights offerings by prospectus to existing security holders in Canada on the basis of documentation prepared in accordance with U.S. requirements (with certain additional Canadian disclosure). There is no market value or public float requirement for rights offerings since existing security holders can reasonably be expected to be familiar with the issuer and follow publicly available information concerning it.

(2) Issuer Eligibility Requirements

The MJDS may be used for the distribution by an issuer of rights to purchase additional securities of its own issue to its existing security holders in Canada, provided that the issuer:

(a) meets the eligibility requirements specified in Sections 3.2(1), (2), (4) and (5);

(b) the issuer has filed with the SEC all the material required to be filed pursuant to sections 13, 14 and 15(d) of the 1934 Act for a period of 36 calendar months immediately preceding the filing of the preliminary prospectus with the principal jurisdiction; and

(c) has had a class of its securities listed on the New York Stock Exchange or the American Stock Exchange or quoted on the NNM for a period of at least 12 calendar months immediately preceding the filing of the preliminary prospectus with the principal jurisdiction and is in compliance with the obligations arising from such listing or quotation.

(3) Limitations on Rights Offerings

Rights offerings by issuers relying on the eligibility requirements of Section 3.4(2) shall be subject to the following limitations:

(a) the rights must be exercisable immediately upon issuance;

(b) subject to (c) below, the rights issued to residents of Canada have the same terms and conditions as the rights issued to residents of the United States; and

(c) beneficial ownership of rights issued to a resident of Canada may not be transferable to a resident of Canada (other than residents to whom rights of the same issue were granted), provided that (i) the securities issuable upon exercise of the rights may be so transferable, and (ii) this limitation shall not restrict the transfer of rights on a securities exchange or inter-dealer quotation system outside of Canada.

(4)   Dealer Registration Requirements

Registration as a dealer is not required by an issuer in respect of a rights offering made under Section 3.4. A standby underwriter or dealer manager for a rights offering made under Section 3.4 is not required to register as a dealer if it does not engage in soliciting activity in Canada or resell in Canada any securities acquired under the standby underwriting arrangement.

3.5   *Successor Issuers*

A successor issuer subsisting after a business combination shall be deemed to meet the respective eligibility requirements set forth in Sections 3.2(3), 3.4(2)(c), 4.4(3) and 5.2(3) if:

(1)   since the business combination the successor issuer has filed all the material required to be filed pursuant to sections 13, 14 and 15(d) of the 1934 Act and, if applicable, has had a class of its securities listed on the New York Stock Exchange or the American Stock Exchange or quoted on NNM;

(2)   if applicable, the successor issuer is in compliance with the obligations arising from such listing or quotation; and

(3)   the filing, listing or quotation requirement to be satisfied for a period of 12 or 36 months is satisfied in respect of each predecessor by separately adding the period during which the successor issuer satisfied the requirement to the immediately preceding period during which the predecessor satisfied the requirement, provided that the 12 or 36 month requirement need not be satisfied with respect to any predecessors whose assets and gross revenues in aggregate con-tributed less than 20% of the total assets and gross revenues from continuing operations of the successor issuer, based on a pro forma combination of each predecessor's financial position and results of operations for its most recently completed fiscal year ended prior to the business combination for which financial statements have been filed.

3.6   *Alternative Eligibility Requirements for Certain Guaranteed Issues*

An issuer that does not meet the eligibility requirements set forth in Section 3.2 or 3.3 may use the MJDS to offer the securities respectively specified in such Sections, subject to the following requirements and limita-tions:

(1)   the securities being offered are:

(a)   non-convertible debt having an Approved Rating or non-convertible preferred shares having an Approved Rating of a majority-owned subsidiary whose parent meets the eligibility requirements set forth in Sections 3.2(1)-(5);

(b)   debt having an Approved Rating or preferred shares having an Approved Rating of a majority-owned subsidiary that may not be converted for at least one year after issuance and are con-vertible only into securities of a parent that meets the eligibility requirements set forth in Sections 3.2(1)-(5) and (6)(b);

(c)   non-convertible debt or non-convertible preferred shares of a majority-owned subsidiary whose parent meets the eligibility requirements set forth in Section 3.3; or

(d)   debt or preferred shares of a majority-owned subsidiary that are convertible only into securities of a parent that meets the eligibility requirements set forth in Section 3.3;

(2)   the issuer meets the eligibility requirements set forth in Sections 3.2(1), (4) and (5); and

(3)   the parent fully and unconditionally guarantees payment in respect of the securities being offered as to principal and interest if such securities are debt and as to liquidation preference, redemption and dividends if such securities are preferred shares.

3.7   *Rule 415 Offerings and Rule 430A Offerings*

The procedure permitted by Rule 415 and Rule 430A under the 1933 Act may be used for offerings of securities under the MJDS. The shelf procedures and post-receipt pricing rules set forth in National Policy Statement No. 44 do not apply to such offerings. A prospectus supplement filed in accordance with the procedures permitted by Rule 415 or Rule 430A shall not be subject to the review procedures set out in Section 3.8(3) or the receipt procedures set out in Section 3.8(4).

3.8   *Mechanics of Making an Offering*

(1)   General

In order to use the MJDS to distribute securities in Canada, an issuer that meets the relevant eligibility requirements set forth in this Policy Statement shall prepare a registration statement for the offering for filing with the SEC, the related preliminary prospectus and prospectus for use in Canada and any amendments and supplements thereto in accordance with U.S. disclosure requirements as interpreted and applied by the SEC. The preliminary prospectus and prospectus used in Canada shall contain the additional information, legends and certificates required by this Policy Statement, shall provide full, true and plain disclosure of all material facts relating to the securities proposed to be distributed, and shall contain no untrue statement of a material fact or omit to state a material fact that is required to be stated or that is necessary to make a statement not misleading in light of the circumstances in which it was made. The issuer may use either a separate Canadian prospectus or a wrap-around prospectus that includes the prospectus filed with the SEC. The issuer is required to prepare a preliminary prospectus for use in Canada even if the issuer does not prepare a preliminary prospectus for use in the United States.

Notwithstanding the foregoing, a preliminary prospectus, prospectus or amendment or supplement thereto used in Canada need not contain any disclosure relevant solely to U.S. offerees or purchasers, including, without limitation: (i) any "red herring" legend required by U.S. law; (ii) any legend regarding approval or disapproval by the SEC; (iii) any discussion of U.S. tax considerations other than those material to Canadian purchasers; and (iv) the names of any U.S. underwriters not acting as underwriters in Canada or a description of the U.S. plan of distribution (except to the extent necessary to describe facts material to the Canadian offering). Except as specifically provided in this Policy Statement, such documents are not required to comply with the form and content requirements set forth in applicable Canadian securities legislation.

If the offering is also being made in the United States, one unsigned copy of the registration statement and all amendments and exhibits thereto and one signed and two unsigned copies of the preliminary prospectus, prospectus and each amendment and supplement thereto used in Canada (together with one copy of all documents incorporated by reference in the prospectus and the supporting documentation required by this Policy Statement) shall be filed in the manner set forth in this Policy Statement with the securities regulatory authority in the principal jurisdiction as nearly as practicable contemporaneously with the filing of the registration statement with the SEC. One signed and one unsigned copy of the preliminary prospectus, prospectus and each amendment and supplement thereto used in Canada (together with one copy of all documents incorporated by reference in the prospectus and the supporting documentation required by this Policy Statement) shall be filed with the other applicable securities regulatory authorities. Such filings shall be made as nearly as practicable contemporaneously with the filing in the principal jurisdiction.

For filings made in Quebec, both English and French language versions of the preliminary prospectus, prospectus and each amendment and supplement thereto shall be filed in the requisite numbers. French language versions of the documents incorporated by reference into any of those documents shall be filed in Quebec not later than the time the incorporating document is filed. Thus, French language versions of continuous disclosure documents need not be filed until incorporated by reference. In addition, information contained in a Form 10-K or Form 10-Q prescribed under the 1934 Act that is not required to be disclosed under Quebec requirements applicable to offerings not made under the MJDS need not be included in the French language versions of those documents. Notwithstanding the foregoing, French language versions of the disclosure documents are not required to be filed for rights offerings made pursuant to Section 3.4, unless (i) the issuer is a reporting issuer in Quebec other than solely as a result of rights offerings made pursuant to Section 3.4, or (ii) 20% or more of the class of securities in respect of which the rights are issued is held by persons or companies whose last address as shown on the books of the issuer is in Canada.

If the offering is being made solely in Canada, the preliminary prospectus, prospectus and each amendment and supplement thereto shall be prepared as if the offering were also being made in the United States. The issuer need not prepare or file the cover page of the U.S. registration statement and other information required in the U.S. registration statement, but not required in the U.S. prospectus.

Representations that securities offered under the MJDS will be listed on a stock exchange or that application has been or will be made to list such securities upon a stock exchange may be made in connection with offerings made under the MJDS.

The provisions of applicable Canadian securities legislation relating to the advertising of securities or the making of representations or undertakings in respect of offerings of securities, including, without limitation, the distribution of material to potential investors and the provision of information to the press prior to the issuance of a receipt for the prospectus, shall apply to offerings made under the MJDS. Solicitations of expressions of interest with respect to an issue of securities to be qualified for distribution under the MJDS may be made prior to the filing of a preliminary prospectus under the following conditions:

(a) the issuer has entered into an enforceable agreement with an underwriter whereby the underwriter has agreed to purchase the securities and which agreement has fixed the terms of the issue and requires the issuer to file with the principal jurisdiction, and obtain a receipt from it for, the preliminary prospectus within two business days from the date that the agreement is entered into by the parties thereto and to file with the other applicable securities regulatory authorities, and obtain a receipt from them for, the preliminary prospectus within three business days from the date that the agreement is entered into by the parties thereto;

(b) once a receipt for the preliminary prospectus has been obtained, a copy of the preliminary prospectus is forthwith forwarded to any person who has expressed an interest in acquiring the securities;

(c) no contract of purchase and sale with respect to the securities is entered into until such time as the prospectus with respect to such securities has been filed and a receipt obtained for it; and

(d) neither the underwriter nor the issuer has been advised in writing by an applicable securities regulatory authority that such issuer or underwriter is not entitled to rely on this sentence.

(2)　Selection of Principal Jurisdiction

At the time of filing a preliminary prospectus under the MJDS, the issuer shall select a principal jurisdiction in Canada and advise the applicable securities regulatory authorities and, unless the offering is being made in Canada only, the SEC of its selection and that the offering is being made under the MJDS. The jurisdiction so selected may or may not agree to act, the issuer shall select another jurisdiction as principal jurisdiction. As of the date of this Policy Statement, the securities regulatory authorities of New Brunswick, Prince Edward Island, Newfoundland, Yukon Territory and the Northwest Territories have indicated that they will not agree to act as principal jurisdiction in connection with offerings made under the MJDS.

(3)　Review Procedure

Disclosure documents filed for an MJDS offering will be subject to SEC review procedures if the offering is being made both in Canada and the United States. Whether the offering is made both in Canada and the United States or solely in Canada, the applicable securities regulatory authorities will monitor materials filed under the MJDS in order to check compliance with the specific disclosure and filing requirements of this Policy Statement. In addition, the substance of the disclosure documents will be reviewed in the unusual case where, through monitoring of the materials or otherwise, the applicable securities regulatory authorities have reason to believe that there may be a problem with a transaction or the related disclosure or other special circumstances exist.

If the SEC notifies an issuer that a filing made under the MJDS has been selected for review, the issuer shall so notify the principal jurisdiction.

(4)　Receipt Procedures

The receipt for a preliminary prospectus filed under the MJDS will be issued by each applicable securities regulatory authority when the preliminary prospectus and all required supporting documentation have been filed with it in the manner required by this Policy Statement.

Where the offering also is being made in the United States, the receipt for a prospectus filed under the MJDS will be issued by each applicable securities regulatory authority, unless it has reason to believe that there may be a problem with the transaction or the related disclosure or other special circumstances exist, upon the following conditions having been satisfied:

(a) in the case of the principal jurisdiction, the related registration statement has been declared effective by the SEC, as certified by the issuer in writing (which may be in facsimile form);

(b) in the case of the other Canadian provinces and territories, the principal jurisdiction has notified such securities regulatory authority that the principal jurisdiction has issued a receipt for the prospectus; and

(c) the prospectus, all documents incorporated therein by reference and all supporting documentation required by this Policy Statement have been filed with such securities regulatory authority in the manner required by this Policy Statement.

Where the offering is being made solely in Canada, the receipt for a prospectus filed under the MJDS will be issued by each applicable securities regulatory authority upon the conditions set out in (b) and (c) above having been satisfied, unless it has reason to believe that there may be a problem with the transaction or the related disclosure or other special circumstances exist.

Issuers filing a prospectus under the MJDS may elect to use the National Policy No. 1 Receipt System. Reference should be made to National Policy Statement No. 1 for the procedures, requirements and benefits of that system.

(5)   Amendment, Supplement and Incorporation by Reference Procedures

The provisions of applicable Canadian securities legislation that prescribe the circumstances under which a preliminary prospectus or prospectus is required to be amended and the form and content of an amendment shall not apply to offerings made under the MJDS. Instead, disclosure documents filed under the MJDS shall be amended and supplemented in accordance with U.S. securities law, but shall contain the legends, where applicable, and certificates required by this Policy Statement.

Where a registration statement is amended in a manner that modifies the related U.S. prospectus, two copies of the documents containing the modification shall be filed with each applicable securities regulatory authority as nearly as practicable contemporaneously with the filing of the amendment with the SEC. If the receipt for the prospectus has not been issued and the filing has been made as a result of the occurrence of a material adverse change since the last filing, such documents are required to be filed as an amendment to the preliminary prospectus. The issuer shall specify, upon filing, that such documents have been filed as such under applicable Canadian securities legislation. Otherwise such documents will not be considered to be amendments to the preliminary prospectus within the meaning of applicable Canadian securities legislation. Any modifications made to a prospectus by filing a post-effective amendment to the registration statement with the SEC must be made by filing an amendment to the prospectus with the applicable securities regulatory authorities.

An amendment is required to be filed with the applicable securities regulatory authorities in the event of a material adverse change in the additional disclosure contained only in the preliminary prospectus used in Canada or a material change in the additional disclosure contained only in the prospectus used in Canada.

A prospectus supplement used in connection with a Rule 415 Offering to modify a U.S. prospectus is required to be filed with the applicable securities regulatory authorities, as set forth below, as nearly as practicable contemporaneously with the filing thereof with the SEC and shall be deemed to be incorporated into the prospectus as of the date thereof, but only for the purpose of the offering of securities covered by the supplement. Such a prospectus supplement will not be considered to be a prospectus amendment within the meaning of applicable Canadian securities legislation.

Notwithstanding the preceding paragraph, a prospectus supplement is not required to be filed in a province or territory other than the principal jurisdiction if:

(a) (i) the prospectus supplement is used to describe the terms of a tranche of securities distributed under the prospectus (or is a preliminary form of such supplement for use in marketing), and (ii) the securities covered by the supplement will not be distributed in such province or territory; or

(b) (i) the prospectus supplement is used to establish an MTN Program or other continuous offering program or to update disclosure for such program, and (ii) securities will not be distributed under such program in such province or territory.

Where (i) a revised prospectus, filed with the SEC other than as an amendment to the related registration statement pursuant to Rule 424(b) under the 1933 Act or otherwise, or (ii) a prospectus supplement is used to modify a prospectus other than a prospectus for a Rule 415 Offering or a Rule 430A Offering, such revised prospectus or prospectus supplement shall be filed with each applicable securities regulatory authority as nearly as practicable contemporaneously with the filing of the revised prospectus or prospectus supplement with the SEC and shall be deemed to be incorporated into the prospectus as of the date thereof. Such revised prospectus or prospectus supplement will not be considered to be a prospectus amendment within the meaning of applicable Canadian securities legislation.

A Rule 430A Pricing Prospectus shall be filed with the applicable securities regulatory authorities as nearly as practicable contemporaneously with the filing of the Rule 430A Pricing Prospectus with the SEC. The information contained in a Rule 430A Pricing Prospectus that was omitted from the prospectus in accordance with Rule 430A under the 1933 Act and any other additional information which the issuer has elected to include therein shall be deemed to be incorporated by reference into the prospectus as of the date of the Rule 430A Pricing Prospectus. A Rule 430A Pricing Prospectus will not be considered to be a prospectus amendment within the meaning of applicable Canadian securities legislation.

Except as otherwise provided in this Policy Statement, documents shall be, and shall be deemed to be, incorporated by reference into each preliminary prospectus or prospectus filed under the MJDS in accordance with U.S. securities law. All documents that are incorporated by reference into a prospectus after issuance of the receipt therefor shall be filed with the applicable securities regulatory authorities as nearly as practicable contemporaneously with the filing thereof with the SEC.

Any statement contained in a document incorporated by reference into a prospectus shall be deemed to be modified or superseded, for the purposes of the prospectus, to the extent that a statement contained in the prospectus or in any other subsequently filed document that is incorporated by reference into the prospectus modifies or supersedes such statement. The making of such a modifying or superseding statement shall not be deemed an admission for any purposes that the modified or superseded statement, when made, constituted a misrepresentation, an untrue statement of material fact or an omission to state a material fact that is required to be stated or that is necessary to make a statement not misleading in light of the circumstances in which it was made. Any statement so modified or superseded shall not be deemed in its unmodified or superseded form to constitute part of the prospectus.

(6)　Delivery Requirements

Preliminary prospectuses, prospectuses and amendments and supplements thereto filed under the MJDS shall be delivered to offerees and purchasers in accordance with applicable Canadian securities legislation. All prospectus supplements applicable to the securities being purchased shall be attached to, or included with, the prospectus that is delivered to offerees and purchasers of such securities in accordance with applicable Canadian securities legislation. A Rule 430A Pricing Prospectus shall be delivered to offerees and purchasers, in lieu of the related prospectus, in accordance with applicable Canadian securities legislation.

Documents that are incorporated by reference into a preliminary prospectus or a prospectus filed under the MJDS, other than prospectus supplements and Rule 430A Pricing Prospectuses, are not required to be delivered to offerees or purchasers unless they are required to be so delivered under the securities laws of the United States. Such documents, in addition to being filed with applicable securities regulatory authorities as required by this Policy Statement, shall be provided by the issuer without charge to any person upon request.

3.9　*Additional Legends and Disclosure*

The following are the texts of certain additional legends and disclosure required to be included in a preliminary prospectus and/or prospectus used in Canada under the MJDS.

(1)　There shall be printed in red ink on the outside front cover page (or on a sticker thereto) of each preliminary prospectus the following statement:

"This is a preliminary prospectus relating to these securities, a copy of which has been filed with the securities commission or similar authority in [insert the names of the provinces and territories where filed], but which has not yet become final for the purpose of a distribution to the public. Information contained herein is subject to completion or amendment. These securities may not be sold to, nor may offers to buy be accepted from, residents of such jurisdictions prior to the time a receipt is obtained for the final prospectus from the appropriate securities regulatory authority."

(2) There shall be printed on the outside or inside front cover page (or on a sticker thereto) of each preliminary prospectus and prospectus the following statement:

(a) "This offering is being made by a U.S. issuer pursuant to disclosure documents prepared in accordance with U.S. securities laws. Purchasers should be aware that these requirements may differ from those of [insert the names of the provinces and territories where qualified]. The financial statements included or incorporated by reference in this prospectus have not been prepared in accordance with Canadian generally accepted accounting principles and thus may not be comparable to financial statements of Canadian issuers."

(b) "[All of] [Certain of] the directors and officers of the issuer and [all of] [certain of] the experts named herein reside outside of Canada. [[Substantially] all of the assets of these persons and of the issuer may be located outside of Canada.] The issuer has appointed [name and address of agent for service] as its agent for service of process in Canada, but it may not be possible for investors to effect service of process within Canada upon the directors, officers and experts referred to above. It may also not be possible to enforce against the issuer, its directors and officers and [certain of] the experts named herein judgments obtained in Canadian courts predicated upon the civil liability provisions of applicable securities laws in Canada."

(c) "This prospectus constitutes a public offering of these securities only in those jurisdictions where they may be lawfully offered for sale and therein only by persons permitted to sell such securities. No securities commission or similar authority in Canada or the United States has in any way passed upon the merits of the securities offered hereunder and any representation to the contrary is an offence."

(3) If documents are incorporated by reference in a preliminary prospectus or prospectus, the portion of the preliminary prospectus or prospectus which provides information about incorporation by reference shall include a statement that such documents have been filed with securities commissions or similar authorities in each jurisdiction in Canada in which the offering is being made and shall provide the name, address and telephone number of an officer of the issuer from whom copies of such documents may be obtained on request without charge.

(4) The following shall be included in each preliminary prospectus and prospectus:

"Securities legislation in certain of the provinces and territories of Canada provides purchasers with the right to withdraw from an agreement to purchase securities within two business days after receipt or deemed receipt of a prospectus or any amendment. In several provinces and territories of Canada, securities legislation further provides a purchaser with rights of rescission or, in some jurisdictions, damages where the prospectus or any amendment contains a misrepresentation or is not delivered to the purchaser, provided that such remedies for rescission or damages are exercised by the purchaser within the time limit

National Policies

prescribed by the securities legislation of the province or territory. Purchasers should refer to the applicable provisions of the securities legislation of their province or territory for particulars of these rights or consult with a lawyer. Rights and remedies also may be available to purchasers under U.S. law; purchasers may wish to consult with a U.S. lawyer for particulars of these rights."

(5) An underwriter of the Canadian offering named in the preliminary prospectus or prospectus remains subject to any obligation under applicable Canadian securities legislation to disclose the names of persons or companies having an interest in its capital.

3.10 *Reconciliation of Financial Statements*

An issuer offering securities pursuant to Section 3.3 shall provide a reconciliation to Canadian GAAP or to International Accounting Standards of the financial statements contained in or incorporated by reference in the preliminary prospectus or prospectus in the notes to such financial statements or as a supplement included or incorporated by reference in the preliminary prospectus and prospectus. The reconciliation shall explain and quantify as a separate reconciling item any significant differences between the principles applied in the financial statements (including note disclosure) and Canadian GAAP or International Accounting Standards, as the case may be, and, in the case of the annual financial statements, shall be covered by an auditor's report.

Reconciliation of financial statements to Canadian GAAP or International Accounting Standards is not required for other offerings made under the MJDS.

3.11 *Certificates*

(1) General

Except as otherwise provided for Rule 415 Offerings and Rule 430A Offerings, each preliminary prospectus and prospectus used for an offering under the MJDS shall contain the following issuer's certificate:

> "The foregoing, together with the documents incorporated herein by reference, constitutes full, true and plain disclosure of all material facts relating to the securities offered by this prospectus as required by [insert applicable references] [insert if offering made in Quebec – "and does not contain any misrepresentation likely to affect the value or the market price of the securities to be distributed"]."

Where there is an underwriter, except as otherwise provided for Rule 415 Offerings and Rule 430A Offerings, each preliminary prospectus and prospectus used for an offering under the MJDS shall contain the following underwriters' certificate signed by the underwriter or underwriters who, with respect to the securities offered by the prospectus, are in a contractual relationship with the issuer or a selling security holder:

> "To the best of our knowledge, information and belief, the foregoing, together with the documents incorporated herein by reference, constitutes full, true and plain disclosure of all material facts relating to the securities offered by this prospectus as required by [insert applicable references] [insert if offering made in Quebec – "and does not contain any misrepresentation likely to affect the value or the market price of the securities to be distributed"]".

(2) Rule 415 Offerings

In Rule 415 Offerings, issuers and underwriters may choose between two alternative methods of providing certificates. Either method can be substituted for the other until the filing of the prospectus. The method chosen for the provision of the issuer's and underwriters' certificates need not be the same.

Method 1 allows the use of prospectus supplements and in the case of MTN Programs, pricing supplements (i.e., supplements setting the price and certain variable terms of the securities rather than establishing the program) that do not contain certificates, provided that a "forward-looking" certificate has been included in the prospectus or in the supplement establishing the program.

Method 2 requires the inclusion of certificates in each prospectus supplement and pricing supplement filed under the MJDS, provided that no certificate is required to be included in a prospectus supplement filed with the securities regulatory authority in the principal jurisdiction if the securities covered by such prospectus supplement are not offered in Canada.

The text of the certificates for Rule 415 Offerings is set forth in Appendix "A".

(3)   Rule 430A Offerings

(a) Issuer's Certificate

Each (i) preliminary prospectus and prospectus filed with the applicable securities regulatory authorities for a Rule 430A Offering, (ii) each amendment to a preliminary prospectus filed with the applicable securities regulatory authorities for a Rule 430A Offering, (iii) each amended prospectus filed with the applicable securities regulatory authorities to commence a new period for filing a Rule 430A Pricing Prospectus, and (iv) each amendment to a prospectus filed with the applicable securities regulatory authorities for a Rule 430A Offering before the information omitted from the prospectus has been filed in either a Rule 430A Pricing Prospectus or an amendment shall contain the following issuer's certificate:

"The foregoing, together with the documents incorporated herein by reference and the information deemed to be incorporated herein by reference, as of the date of the prospectus providing the information permitted to be omitted from this prospectus, will constitute full, true and plain disclosure of all material facts relating to the securities offered by this prospectus as required by [insert applicable references] [insert if offering made in Quebec – "and will not contain any misrepresentation likely to affect the value or the market price of the securities to be distributed"]".

(b) Underwriters' Certificate

Where there is an underwriter, each (i) preliminary prospectus and prospectus filed with the applicable securities regulatory authorities for a Rule 430A Offering, (ii) each amendment to a preliminary prospectus filed with the applicable securities regulatory authorities for a Rule 430A Offering, (iii) each amended prospectus filed with the applicable securities regulatory authorities to commence a new period for filing a Rule 430A Pricing Prospectus, and (iv) each amendment to a prospectus filed with the applicable securities regulatory authorities for a Rule 430A Offering before the information omitted from the prospectus has been filed in either a Rule 430A Pricing Prospectus or an amendment shall contain the following underwriters' certificate signed by the underwriter or underwriters who, with respect to the securities offered by the prospectus, are in a contractual relationship with the issuer or a selling security holder:

"To the best of our knowledge, information and belief, the foregoing, together with the documents incorporated herein by reference and the information deemed to be incorporated herein by reference, as of the date of the prospectus providing the information permitted to be omitted from this prospectus, will constitute full, true and plain disclosure of all material facts relating to the securities offered by this prospectus as required by [insert if offering made in Quebec – "and will not contain any misrepresentation likely to affect the value or the market price of the securities to be distributed"]".

(c) Issuer's Certificate for Rule 430A Pricing Prospectus

Each Rule 430A Pricing Prospectus shall contain, in place of the certificate referred to in (a) above, the following issuer's certificate:

"The foregoing [insert, if applicable – ", together with the documents incorporated herein by reference,"] constitutes full, true and plain disclosure of all material facts relating to the securities offered by this prospectus as required by [insert applicable references] [insert if offering made in Quebec – "and will not contain any misrepresentation likely to affect the value or the market price of the securities to be distributed"]".

(d) Underwriters' Certificate for Rule 430A Pricing Prospectus

Where there is an underwriter, each Rule 430A Pricing Prospectus shall contain, in place of the certificate referred to in (b) above, the following underwriters' certificate signed by the underwriter or underwriters who, with respect to the securities offered by the prospectus, are in a contractual relationship with the issuer or a selling security holder:

"To the best of our knowledge, information and belief, the foregoing [insert, if applicable – ", together with the documents incorporated herein by reference,"] constitutes full, true and plain disclosure of all material facts relating to the securities offered by this prospectus as required by [insert applicable references] [insert if offering made in Quebec – "and will not contain any misrepresentation likely to affect the value or the market price of the securities to be distributed"]".

(4) Rights Offerings

A rights offering prospectus used under Section 3.4 need not contain an underwriters' certificate, provided that there is no soliciting activity in Canada other than the dissemination by the issuer of the rights and the prospectus and any securities acquired under a standby underwriting arrangement are not resold in Canada.

(5) Signing of Certificates

Certificates contained in a preliminary prospectus, prospectus, amendment to a preliminary prospectus or prospectus, prospectus supplement or Rule 430A Pricing Prospectus shall be signed in accordance with applicable Canadian securities legislation. However, the chief executive officer, chief financial officer and two directors, on behalf of the board of directors, of the issuer, and the underwriters may each sign such certificates for an offering made under the MJDS by an agent duly authorized in writing.

3.12 *Conflicts of Interest*

(1) General

Any provisions of applicable Canadian securities legislation which regulate conflicts of interest in connection with the distribution of securities of a registered dealer or a related party or related issuer or connected party or connected issuer of a registered dealer (the "Conflicts Rules") apply to offerings under the MJDS as follows:

(a) the Conflicts Rules shall not apply so as to require any specified disclosure in the preliminary prospectus or prospectus; and

    (b) the Conflicts Rules shall apply so as to require the participation of an independent underwriter to the extent provided in Sections 3.12(2) and (3).

(2) Participation of Independent Underwriter

    (a) Canada-U.S. Offerings

In an offering made under the MJDS in both Canada and the United States, any requirement in the Conflicts Rules for the underwriting of a portion of a distribution by an independent underwriter shall be satisfied if the aggregate of the portions of the distribution in Canada and the United States underwritten by at least one independent underwriter and its affiliates is not less than the aggregate of the portions of the distribution in Canada and the United States underwritten by dealers in respect of which the issuer is a related issuer, related party, connected issuer or connected party or, where a dealer is not a registrant, would be a connected party or connected issuer if the dealer were a registrant.

    (b) Canada-Only Offerings

In an offering made under the MJDS solely in Canada, any requirement in the Conflicts Rules for the underwriting of a portion of a distribution by an independent underwriter shall be satisfied if the aggregate of the portions of the distribution underwritten by at least one independent underwriter and its affiliates is not less than the aggregate of the portions of the distribution underwritten by dealers in respect of which the issuer is a related issuer, related party, connected issuer or connected party.

(3) Rule 415 Offerings

The Conflicts Rules must be satisfied for a delayed Rule 415 Offering for each tranche. The Conflicts Rules may be satisfied for a continuous Rule 415 Offering on the basis of the total amount of securities proposed to be distributed on a continuous basis.

3.13 *Trust Indenture Requirements*

Any requirement of a Canadian province or territory, applicable to trust indentures, in respect of any debt outstanding or guaranteed thereunder (including without limitation, any requirement that a person or company appointed as a trustee under a trust indenture be resident or authorized to do business in the province or territory) shall not apply to offerings made under the MJDS, provided that:

(1) the trust indenture under which the obligations are issued or guaranteed is subject to and complies with the Trust Indenture Act of 1939 of the United States; and

(2) at least one person or company appointed as trustee under a trust indenture (i) is resident in such province or territory, (ii) is authorized to do business in such province or territory, or (iii) has filed with the applicable securities regulatory authority in such province or territory duly executed Submission to Jurisdiction and Appointment of Agent for Service of Process in the form set forth in Part C of Appendix "B".

3.14 *Filing Packages and Commercial Copies*

The supporting documentation specified below shall be filed with the applicable securities regulatory authorities in connection with offerings made under the MJDS in the manner specified. In addition, any exhibit to a registration statement shall be provided to an applicable securities regulatory authority upon request.

(1) Certificate Confirming Satisfaction of Eligibility Requirements

A certificate of the issuer, signed on its behalf by a senior officer, confirming that it satisfies the applicable eligibility criteria shall be filed with each applicable securities regulatory authority at the time of filing the preliminary prospectus for each offering made under the MJDS.

(2) Consents

The written consent of a solicitor, auditor, accountant, engineer, appraiser or any other person or company who is named as having prepared or certified any part of a disclosure document for an offering made under the MJDS or a document that is incorporated by reference therein, or who is named as having prepared or certified a report used in or in connection with such disclosure document or any document incorporated by reference therein (such part or report being referred to herein as an "expertised statement"), shall be prepared in accordance with the requirements of applicable Canadian securities legislation and shall be filed with each applicable securities regulatory authority in accordance with applicable Canadian securities legislation as follows:

(a) If the expertised statement appears in the preliminary prospectus, an amendment thereto, the prospectus or a document incorporated by reference into the prospectus that was filed prior to the filing of the prospectus, the related consent shall be filed at the time of filing the prospectus.

(b) If the expertised statement appears in an amendment to the prospectus, a prospectus supplement, a Rule 430A Pricing Prospectus, or a document incorporated by reference into a prospectus that was filed after the filing of the prospectus, the related consent shall be filed at the time of filing such amendment, prospectus supplement, Rule 430A Pricing Prospectus or document.

A further consent may be required to be filed with an amendment to a prospectus pursuant to the requirements of applicable Canadian securities legislation as a result of a material change to an expertised statement.

(3) Reports on Property

A report on the property of a natural resource company is not required to be filed for offerings made under the MJDS, unless such report is also required to be filed with the SEC.

(4) Appointment of Agent for Service

At the time of filing a prospectus under the MJDS, the issuer shall file a duly executed Submission to Jurisdiction and Appointment of Agent for Service of Process in the form set forth in Part A of Appendix "B" with each applicable securities regulatory authority.

(5) Powers of Attorney

If a person or company signs a certificate by an agent pursuant to Section 3.11(5), a duly executed copy of the document authorizing the agent to sign the certificate shall be filed with each applicable securities regulatory authority not later than the time of filing the document in which the certificate is included.

(6) Fees

The provisions of Canadian securities legislation regarding fees shall apply to an offering made under the MJDS in the same manner as though the offering had not been made under the MJDS.

Fees shall be payable for a Rule 415 Offering or Rule 430A Offering in the manner prescribed for offerings made under the shelf procedures and post-receipt pricing rules set forth in National Policy Statement No. 44, respectively.

(7) Commercial Copies

Commercial copies of any prospectus, prospectus supplement, preliminary prospectus used in connection with solicitations of expressions of interest, Rule 430A Pricing Prospectus or prospectus amendment used in an MJDS offering in connection with offers or sales of securities shall be filed with the applicable securities regulatory authorities. Once so filed, the commercial copy need not be refiled if it is used, without change, in offers or sales of additional tranches of securities.

4.   BIDS FOR SECURITIES OF U.S. ISSUERS

   4.1 *General*

Subject to the provisions of this Section 4, the MJDS permits eligible take-over bids and issuer bids for securities of a U.S. issuer to be made in accordance with U.S. requirements to Canadian residents where Canadian residents hold less than 40% of the securities. The MJDS enables offerors generally to comply with applicable U.S. disclosure requirements and requirements governing the conduct of the bid in lieu of complying with Canadian requirements.

The MJDS is extended to take-over bids and issuer bids primarily to encourage fair treatment of Canadian investors. Security holders in a particular jurisdiction who are excluded from an offer may be relegated to choosing, without the disclosure and procedural safeguards available under either the Canadian or the U.S. regulatory scheme, whether to sell into the secondary market at less than the full bid price and incur additional transactional costs or to remain minority security holders subject to the possibility of being forced out of their equity position in a subsequent merger. The application of the MJDS to bids is intended to facilitate bids by reducing duplicative regulation and avoiding conflict between the two regulatory schemes. Because the substantive protections and disclosure obligations applicable to bids are, as a whole, comparable to those prescribed by applicable Canadian securities legislation, Canadian resident holders of securities of U.S. issuers should remain adequately protected by the application of U.S. rather than Canadian rules in the circumstances contemplated by this Policy Statement.

Particularly when relatively few securities are held by Canadian residents, there may be a disincentive to extend a bid to them if doing so would require compliance with additional Canadian regulatory requirements. The availability of the MJDS for bids for securities of U.S. issuers is intended to alter the offeror's cost-benefit analysis in favour of extending those bids to Canadian residents.

There are no offeror eligibility requirements except in the case of securities exchange bids. For securities exchange bids, compliance with U.S. disclosure requirements satisfies Canadian disclosure requirements with respect to the offeror and the offered securities only if the offeror meets certain reporting history, listing and other eligibility requirements and, in the case of securities exchange take-over bids, a substantiality or Approved Rating requirement. In take-over bids, unlike issuer bids and rights offerings, the investor has not already made an investment decision with respect to the issuer of the securities that are being offered in the exchange.

Bids made under the MJDS must be extended to all holders of the class of securities subject to the bid in Canada and the United States. Further, bids must be made on the same terms and conditions to all security holders.

Provision is made in the securities legislation of some Canadian provinces for exemption from take-over bid and issuer bid requirements if the bid is for the securities of a non-Canadian issuer, the bid is made in compliance with the laws of a recognized jurisdiction and there are relatively few holders in the province holding a relatively small percentage of the class of securities subject to the bid. An offeror is permitted to make a bid under the MJDS in certain provinces and territories and pursuant to such an exemption in others.

   4.2 *Eligibility Requirements for a Bid*

The MJDS may be used for a bid made to security holders in Canada if:

(1)   the offeree issuer is a U.S. issuer;

(2)   the offeree issuer is not registered or required to be registered as an investment company under the 1940 Act;

(3)   the offeree issuer is not a commodity pool issuer;

(4)   the bid is subject to section 14(d) of the 1934 Act in the case of a take-over bid or section 13(e) of the 1934 Act in the case of an issuer bid and is not exempt therefrom;

(5)   the bid is made to all holders of the class of securities in Canada and the United States;

(6)   the bid is made to residents of Canada on the same terms and conditions as it is made to residents of the United States; and

(7)   less than 40% of each class of securities that is the subject of the bid is held by persons or companies whose last address as shown on the books of the issuer is in Canada.

The calculation of the percentage of securities held by persons and companies having an address in Canada in this Section 4 shall be made as of the end of the offeree issuer's last quarter preceding the date of filing the Tender Offer Statement or Issuer Tender Offer Statement with the SEC or, if such quarter terminated within 60 days of such filing date, as of the end of the offeree issuer's preceding quarter. If another bid for securities of the same class of the offeree issuer is in progress at the date of such filing, the foregoing calculation for the subsequent bid shall be made as of the same date as for the first bid already in progress.

Where (i) a take-over bid is made without the prior knowledge of the directors of the offeree issuer who are not insiders of the offeror or acting jointly or in concert with the offeror, or (ii) upon informing such directors of the proposed bid the offeror has a reasonable basis for concluding that the bid is being regarded as a hostile bid by a majority of such directors, and in either such case the offeror lacks access to the relevant list of security holders of the offeree issuer, it will be conclusively presumed that (7) above is satisfied and clause (a) in the definition of "foreign issuer" is not satisfied, unless (i) the aggregate published trading volume of the class on the Toronto, Montreal, Vancouver and Alberta stock exchanges and the Canadian Dealing Network Inc. exceeded the aggregate published trading volume of the class on national securities exchanges in the United States and Nasdaq for the 12 calendar month period prior to commencement of the bid (or, if another bid for securities of the same class is in progress, the 12 calendar month period prior to commencement of the first bid already in progress); (ii) disclosure that (7) above was not satisfied or such clause (a) was satisfied had been made by the issuer in its Form 10-K prescribed under the 1934 Act most recently filed with the SEC; or (iii) the offeror has actual knowledge that (7) above is not satisfied or such clause (a) is satisfied.

4.3   *Effect of Making a Bid*

Subject to the provisions of this Section 4.3 and of Section 4.4, any bid made under the MJDS shall be exempt from compliance with the provisions of applicable Canadian securities legislation governing the conduct of bids, except any requirement to file with the applicable securities regulatory authorities and deliver a bid circular, a directors' circular or an individual officer's or director's circular and any notice of change or notice of variation to holders of the securities subject to the bid. Except as specifically provided in this Policy Statement, such documents are not required to comply with the form and content requirements set forth in applicable Canadian securities legislation. Such documents shall contain the information required to be disseminated to security holders in accordance with U.S. requirements and the additional information, legends and certificates required by this Policy Statement. They shall contain no untrue statement of material fact or omit to state a material fact that is required to be stated or that is necessary to make a statement not misleading in light of the circumstances in which it was made, but need not contain any disclosure relevant solely to U.S. security holders.

Provisions of applicable Canadian securities legislation that require disclosure of acquisitions reaching a certain threshold or restrict acquisitions of securities once such a threshold has been reached continue to apply.

Bids made under the MJDS must comply with the relevant requirements of applicable Canadian securities legislation relating to going private transactions, other than the requirement to provide a valuation at the time of a take- over bid where it is anticipated by the offeror that a going private transaction will follow the bid.

Where 20% or more of any class of securities that is the subject of a bid made under the MJDS is held by persons or companies whose last address as shown on the books of the issuer is in Canada, such bid must comply with the requirements of applicable Canadian securities legislation respecting integration of pre-bid transactions with the bid.

Where 20% or more of any class of securities that is the subject of an issuer bid or insider bid made under the MJDS is held by persons or companies whose last address as shown on the books of the issuer is in Canada, such bid must comply with the valuation requirements of applicable Canadian securities legislation.

All bids remain subject to the fundamental principle that transactions must not be prejudicial to the public interest. The applicable securities regulatory authorities also will continue to exercise their public interest jurisdiction in specific cases where they determine that it is necessary to do so in order to preserve the integrity of the Canadian capital markets.

The offeror shall comply with sections 14(d) and 14(e) of the 1934 Act and Regulations 14D and 14E thereunder in connection with any take-over bid made under the MJDS. The offeror shall comply with sections 13(e) and 14(e) of the 1934 Act and Regulations 13E and 14E thereunder in connection with any issuer bid made under the MJDS. The offeree issuer and its officers and directors shall comply either with the requirements of applicable Canadian securities legislation or with sections 14(d) and 14(e) of the 1934 Act and Regulations 14D and 14E thereunder in connection with any bid made under the MJDS.

4.4 *Securities Exchange Bids*

In the case of a securities exchange bid, the provisions of applicable Canadian securities legislation applicable as a result of the consideration for the of the offeree issuer being at least in part securities of the offeror or other issuer shall be satisfied by compliance with U.S. requirements only if:

(1) the offeree issuer and the bid satisfy the eligibility requirements set forth in Section 4.2;

(2) the offeror or, if the securities are of another issuer, such other issuer, meets the eligibility requirements set forth in Sections 3.2(1), 3.2(2), 3.2(4), 3.2(5) and 3.4(2)(b), except that the reference in Section 3.4(2)(b) to the filing of a preliminary prospectus with the principal jurisdiction shall be replaced by the filing of the registration statement with the SEC;

(3) the offeror or, if the securities being offered are of another issuer, such other issuer, has had a class of its securities listed on the New York Stock Exchange or the American Stock Exchange or quoted on NNM for a period of at least 12 calendar months immediately preceding the filing of the registration statement with the SEC and is in compliance with the obligations arising from such listing or quotation; and

(4) any of the following are satisfied:

(a) the equity shares of such offeror or if the securities being offered are of another issuer, such other issuer, have a public float of not less than U.S. $75,000,000, determined as of a date within 60 days prior to the filing of the registration statement with the SEC;

(b) the securities being offered are non- convertible debt having an Approved Rating or non-convertible preferred shares having an Approved Rating; or

(c) the bid is an issuer bid made under the MJDS with securities of the issuer being offered as consideration.

4.5 *Mechanics of Making a Bid*

(1) Filing Requirements

In order to use the MJDS to make a bid in Canada or to any security holder whose last address as shown on the books of the offeree issuer is in Canada, an offeror shall prepare a Tender Offer Statement or Issuer Tender Offer Statement, any exhibits and amendments thereto and any information required to be disseminated to security holders in accordance with U.S. requirements as interpreted and applied by the SEC. The bid circular shall consist of the tender offer materials disseminated to security holders resident on the date of commencement of the bid in the United States as modified pursuant to this Policy Statement. French language versions of these documents are not required to be filed for bids made under the MJDS, unless (i) the offeree issuer is a reporting issuer in Quebec, or (ii) 20% or more of any class of securities that is the subject of the bid is held by persons or companies whose last address as shown on the books of the issuer is in Canada.

As nearly as practicable contemporaneously with the filing with the SEC, the offeror shall file one unsigned copy of the Tender Offer Statement or Issuer Tender Offer Statement and all exhibits and amendments thereto, and one signed and two unsigned copies of the bid circular, together with the following supporting documentation, with each applicable securities regulatory authority:

(a) a certificate of the offeror, signed on its behalf by a senior officer, confirming that the eligibility criteria set forth in Section 4.2 and, if applicable, Section 4.4 are satisfied;

(b) the written consent of a solicitor, auditor, accountant, engineer, appraiser or any other person or company who is named as having prepared or certified any part of such materials or any document filed pursuant to Section 4.5(5) or incorporated by reference therein, or who is named as having prepared or certified a report used in or in connection with such materials or document;

(c) a duly executed Submission to Jurisdiction and Appointment of Agent for Service of Process in the form set forth in Part B of Appendix "B"; and

(d) if a person or company signs a certificate by an agent pursuant to Section 4.8, a duly executed copy of the document authorizing the agent to sign the certificate.

An offeror filing a bid circular under the MJDS must so notify the offeree issuer at its principal office not later than the business day following the day the bid circular is filed with any applicable securities regulatory authority.

(2) Directors' and Individual Officer's and Director's Circulars

If a bid is made under the MJDS, the offeree issuer and its officers and directors shall comply with the requirements of applicable Canadian securities legislation or with U.S. requirements in respect of the bid. In the case of compliance by the directors or by individual officers or directors with Canadian requirements, the requirements set out in this Policy Statement regarding directors' circulars or individual officer's or director's circulars, as the case may be, shall not apply. Otherwise, a Tender Offer Solicitation/Recommendation Statement, if applicable, and any exhibits and amendments thereto shall be prepared in accordance with U.S. requirements as interpreted and applied by the SEC. The directors' circular or an individual officer's or director's circular and any notice of change shall consist of the materials disseminated by the offeree issuer or its board of directors, an individual officer or officers, and an individual director or directors, respectively, to security holders resident in the United States and containing the certificates prescribed by Section 4.8. As nearly as practicable contemporaneously with the filing with the SEC, one unsigned copy of the Tender Offer Solicitation/Recommendation Statement and all exhibits and amendments thereto and one signed and two unsigned copies of the directors' circular or an individual officer's or directors' circular or an individual officer's or director's circular, together with the following supporting documentation, shall be filed with each applicable securities regulatory authority:

(a) a statement that the circular has been prepared in accordance with U.S. requirements;

(b) the written consent of a solicitor, auditor, accountant, engineer, appraiser or any other person or company who is named as having prepared or certified any part of such materials or any document incorporated by reference therein, or who is named as having prepared or certified a report used in connection with such materials; and

(c) if a person or company signs a certificate by an agent pursuant to Section 4.8, a duly executed copy of the document authorizing the agent to sign the certificate.

Notwithstanding that a bid was eligible to be made under the MJDS, the offeree issuer and its officers and directors may not use the MJDS in respect of the bid if the offeror did not make the bid under the MJDS.

(3) Notices of Variation and Notices of Change

The provisions of applicable Canadian securities legislation that prescribe the circumstances under which a bid circular, directors' circular, or individual officer's or director's circular is required to be changed or varied and the form and content of the applicable disclosure documents shall not apply to bids made under the MJDS, unless, in respect of the directors' circular or individual officer's or director's circular, the directors or individual officer or director have elected to comply with the requirements of applicable Canadian securities legislation. Instead, disclosure documents filed under the MJDS shall be changed or varied in accordance with U.S. requirements as additional tender offer materials, but shall contain the legends, where applicable, and certificates required by this Policy Statement.

Any additional tender offer materials that vary the terms of the bid shall be filed, as modified, with the applicable securities regulatory authorities as a notice of variation and identified as such. Any additional tender offer materials that contain a change in the information from that contained in the tender offer materials or previous additional tender offer materials, other than information in respect of a variation in the terms of the bid, shall be filed, as modified, with the applicable securities regulatory authorities as a notice of change and identified as such. Any additional tender offer materials required to be identified as a notice of variation and a notice of change shall be identified as both. Any additional materials prepared by the directors or an individual officer or director shall be filed, as modified, with the applicable securities regulatory authorities as a notice of change and identified as such.

Any notice of variation or notice of change shall be filed in the requisite numbers referred to in Section 4.5(1) as nearly as practicable contemporaneously with the filing with the SEC. The filing package shall contain, if applicable, a duly executed copy of a document authorizing an agent to sign a certificate, and, in the event of a material change in the relevant part of the materials or document referred to in Section 4.5(1)(b), a further consent.

(4)   Dissemination Requirements

Bid circulars, notices of change thereto and notices of variation thereto filed under the MJDS shall be mailed be prepaid first class mail or delivered by personal delivery to security holders whose last address as shown on the books of the offeree issuer is in a province or territory in which the bid is made under the MJDS (and, in respect of notices of change and variation, whose securities were not taken up at the date of the occurrence of the change or variation), whether those materials are published, sent or given to security holders resident in the United States by the use of stockholder lists and security position listings, by long-form publication or by summary publication. Any such documents generally sent or given to security holders resident in the United States shall be mailed or delivered to security holders whose last address as shown on the books of the offeree issuer is in Canada at the same time as they are sent or given to security holders resident in the United States. Any such documents published by long-form publication or by summary publication in the United States shall be mailed or delivered to security holders whose last address as shown on the books of the offeree issuer is in Canada as soon as practicable following such publication.

Directors' circulars and individual officer's and director's circulars and notices of change thereto shall be mailed by first class mail or delivered by personal delivery to every person or company to whom a take-over bid circular was required to be delivered under the preceding paragraph. Any such document generally sent or given to security holders resident in the United States shall be mailed or delivered to security holders whose last address as shown on the books of the offeree issuer in Canada at the same time as such document is sent or given to security holders resident in the United States. Any such document published in the United States shall be mailed or delivered to security holders whose last address as shown on the books of the offeree is in Canada as soon as practicable following such publication.

(5)   Securities Exchange Bids

In the case of securities exchange bids made under the MJDS for which a registration statement is filed with the SEC, one signed copy of the registration statement and all exhibits and amendments thereto (together with all documents incorporated therein by reference) shall be filed with each applicable securities regulatory authority as nearly as practicable contemporaneously with the filing with the SEC. The prospectus forming part of the registration statement shall be included in or incorporated by reference into the bid circular.

(6)   Incorporation by Reference Procedures

Except as otherwise provided in this Policy Statement, documents shall be, and shall be deemed to be, incorporated by reference into materials filed under this Section 4.5 in accordance with U.S. securities law. Any statement contained in a document so incorporated by reference shall be deemed to be modified or superseded to the extent that a statement contained in such materials or in any other subsequently filed document which is incorporated by reference into such materials modifies or supersedes such statement. The making of such a modifying or superseding statement shall not be deemed an admission for any purposes that the modified or superseded statement, when made, constituted a misrepresentation, an untrue statement of material fact or an omission to state a material fact that is required to be stated or that is necessary to make a statement not misleading in light of the circumstances in which it was made. Any statement so modified or superseded shall not be deemed in its unmodified or superseded form to constitute part of such materials.

Documents that are incorporated by reference into materials filed under this Section 4.5 are not required to be delivered to security holders unless they are required to be delivered to security holders under U.S. securities law; such documents, in addition to being filed with the applicable securities regulatory authorities, shall be provided without charge to any person upon request.

4.6   *Additional Legends*

The following are the texts of the additional legends and other disclosure required to be included in bid circulars used for a bid made under the MJDS. The legend contained in paragraph (1)(b) shall not be required if the offeror is incorporated or organized under the laws of Canada or a province or territory of Canada.

(1)   The following shall be printed on the outside front cover page (or on a sticker thereto) of each bid circular used in Canada under the MJDS:

    (a)   "This bid is made in Canada [for applicable securities exchange bids – "by a U.S. issuer"] for securities of a U.S. issuer in accordance with U.S. securities laws. Security holders should be aware that the U.S. requirements applicable to the bid may differ from those of [insert the names of the provinces and territories where bid is made]. [For securities exchange bids, also insert the following – "The financial statements included or incorporated by reference herein have not been prepared in accordance with Canadian generally accepted accounting principles and thus may not be comparable to financial statements of Canadian issuers."]

    (b)   "[All of] [Certain of] the directors and officers of the offeror and [all of] [certain of] the experts named herein reside outside of Canada. [[Substantially] all of the assets of these persons and of the offeror may be located outside of Canada.] The offeror has appointed [name and address of agent for service] as its agent for service of process in Canada, but it may not be possible for security holders to effect service of process within Canada upon the directors, officers and experts referred to above. It may also not be possible to enforce against the offeror, its directors and officers and [certain of] the experts named herein judgments obtained in Canadian courts predicated upon the civil liability provisions of applicable securities laws in Canada."

(2)   If documents are incorporated by reference into the bid circular, include in the section which provides information about incorporation by reference a statement that information has been incorporated by reference from documents filed with securities commissions or similar authorities in each jurisdiction in Canada in which the documents have been filed and provide the name, address and telephone number of a person in Canada or the United States from whom copies of the documents so incorporated by reference may be obtained on request without charge.

(3)   The following shall be included in bid circulars used in Canada under the MJDS:

        "Securities legislation in certain of the provinces [and territories] of Canada provides security holders of the offeree issuer with, in addition to any other rights they may have at law, rights of rescission or to damages, or both, if there is a misrepresentation in a circular or notice that is required to be delivered to such security holders. However, such rights must be exercised within the prescribed time limits. Security holders should refer to the applicable provisions of the securities legislation of their province [or territory] for particulars of those rights or consult with a lawyer. Rights and remedies also may be available to security holders under U.S. law; security holders may wish to consult with a U.S. lawyer for particulars of these rights."

4.7 *Reconciliation of Financial Statements*

Reconciliation of financial statements to Canadian GAAP or International Accounting Standards is not required for securities exchange bids made under the MJDS that satisfy the eligibility requirements of Section 4.4.

4.8 *Certificates*

The text of the certificate for bid circulars and directors' and individual officer's and director's circulars used under the MJDS is as follows:

> "The foregoing contains no untrue statement of a material fact and does not omit to state a material fact that is required to be stated or that is necessary to make a statement not misleading in the light of the circumstances in which it was made."

The text of the certificate for notices of variation and notices of change shall be in the form required in the preceding paragraph, amended to refer to the initial circular and all notices of variation or change thereto.

The certificate shall be signed in accordance with applicable Canadian securities legislation. However, the chief executive officer, the chief financial officer, and two directors, on behalf of the board of directors, of the offeror or the offeree issuer, may each sign the certificate by an agent duly authorized in writing.

4.9 *Fees*

The provisions of Canadian securities legislation regarding fees shall apply to a bid made under the MJDS in the same manner as though the bid had not been made under the MJDS.

5.   BUSINESS COMBINATIONS

5.1 *General*

The MJDS permits securities of a U.S. issuer to be distributed by prospectus in Canada on the basis of documentation prepared in accordance with U.S. requirements (with certain additional Canadian disclosure) in connection with a business combination where less than 40% of the securities to be distributed by the successor issuer would be held by Canadian residents. As in the case of take-over bids, the MJDS is available for business combinations primarily to encourage fair treatment of Canadian investors.

Securities legislation of most of the Canadian provinces and territories provides for an exemption from prospectus requirements for certain distributions of securities issued in connection with a statutory amalgamation, merger or arrangement. As a result, an issuer may elect not to use the MJDS, but to distribute securities issued in a business combination pursuant to a prospectus exemption. A consequence of using a prospectus exemption instead of the MJDS may be resale restrictions on the distributed securities. However, under blanket rulings issued in certain provinces, the resale of securities acquired under such an exemption is not a distribution in respect of which a prospectus is required if the issuer meets certain eligibility and reporting requirements and the resale is executed through the facilities of a stock exchange outside of Canada or on Nasdaq.

A business combination done under the MJDS must comply with the relevant requirements of applicable Canadian securities legislation relating to going private transactions and, if it constitutes a related party transaction, the relevant requirements of applicable Canadian securities legislation relating to minority approvals and valuations. All business combinations remain subject to the fundamental principle that transactions must not be prejudicial to the public interest. The applicable securities regulatory authorities also will continue to exercise their public interest jurisdiction in specific cases where they determine that it is necessary to do so in order to preserve the integrity of the Canadian capital markets.

5.2 *Eligibility Requirements*

The MJDS may be used for the distribution of securities to security holders in Canada in connection with a business combination by a successor issuer subsisting after the business combination if:

(1)   each person or company participating in the business combination meets the eligibility requirements specified in Sections 3.2(1), 3.2(2), 3.2(4), 3.2(5), and 3.4(2)(b), provided that the eligibility requirements specified in Sections 3.2(2) and 3.4(2)(b) shall not be required to be met in respect of participating persons or companies whose assets and gross revenues in aggregate would contribute less than 20% of the total assets and gross revenues from continuing operations of the successor issuer, based on a pro forma combination of each participating person's and company's financial position and results of operations for its most recently completed fiscal year ended prior to the business combination for which financial statements have been filed;

(2)   the equity shares of each person or company participating in the business combination have a public float of not less than U.S. $75,000,000, determined as of a date within 60 days prior to the filing of the preliminary prospectus with the principal jurisdiction, provided that this requirement shall not apply in respect of participating persons or companies whose assets and gross revenues in aggregate would contribute less than 20% of the total assets and gross revenues from continuing operations of the successor issuer, based on a pro forma combination of each participating person's and company's financial position and results of operations for its most recently completed fiscal year ended prior to the business combination for which financial statements have been filed, and provided further that such requirement may be satisfied in respect of a participating person or company whose securities were the subject of a bid made under or eligible to have been made under the MJDS that terminated within the preceding 12 months if such requirement would have been satisfied immediately prior to commencement of the bid;

(3)   each person or company participating in the business combination has had a class of its securities listed on the New York Stock Exchange or the American Stock Exchange or quoted on NNM for a period of at least 12 calendar months immediately preceding the filing of the preliminary prospectus with the principal jurisdiction and is in compliance with the obligations arising from such listing or quotation, provided that this requirement shall not apply in respect of participating persons or companies whose assets and gross revenues in aggregate would contribute less than 20% of the total assets and gross revenues from continuing operations of the successor issuer, based on a pro forma combination of each participating person's and company's financial position and results of operations for its most recently completed fiscal year ended prior to the business combination for which financial statements have been filed;

(4)   the issue or exchange of securities in connection with the business combination is made to residents of Canada on the same terms and conditions as it is made to residents of the United States; and

(5)   less than 40% of the class of securities to be distributed in the business combination by the successor issuer would be distributed to persons or companies whose last address as shown on the books of the participating person or company is in Canada.

The calculation of the percentage of securities held by persons or companies having an address in Canada shall be made with respect to each participating person or company as of the end of such participating person's or company's last quarter preceding the date of filing the preliminary prospectus with the principal jurisdiction or, if such quarter terminated within 60 days of such filing date, as of the end of the participating person's or company's preceding quarter. Such calculation shall be made on the basis of the assumption that all persons or companies who have an option in respect of the consideration to be received pursuant to the business combination elect the option that would result in the issuance of the greatest number of securities.

5.3   *Mechanics*

If the eligibility requirements set forth in Section 5.2 are met, securities may be distributed in Canada under the MJDS in connection with a business combination by complying with the procedures set forth in Sections 3.8, 3.9, 3.11(1), 3.11(5) and 3.14. The disclosure documents would be required to be filed both as a prospectus and as an information circular. Reconciliation of financial statements to Canadian GAAP or International Accounting Standards is not required for business combinations done under the MJDS.

6.   CONTINUOUS DISCLOSURE, PROXIES AND PROXY SOLICITATION, SHAREHOLDER COMMUNICATIONS AND INSIDER REPORTING

An issuer that files a prospectus or a bid circular for a securities exchange take-over bid in certain provinces of Canada becomes a reporting issuer in those provinces, subject, among other things, to certain continuous disclosure, proxy and proxy solicitation, and shareholder communication requirements, with its insiders being subject to certain insider reporting requirements.

Compliance with U.S. requirements relating to (i) current reports, (ii) annual reports, and (iii) proxy statements, proxies and proxy solicitation by a U.S. issuer that has a class of securities registered pursuant to section 12 of the 1934 Act (or, in the case of current reports and annual reports, is required to file reports pursuant to section 15(d) of the 1934 Act) will satisfy the requirements of the Canadian provinces and territories relating to (i) reports of material change, (ii) annual information forms, annual reports and management's discussion and analysis of financial condition and results of operations, and (iii) information circulars, proxies and proxy solicitation, respectively, provided that (a) two copies of any material filed with the SEC are filed with the applicable securities regulatory authorities that require the filing of material of that nature (i) in the case of current reports, forthwith after the earlier of the date the report is filed with the SEC and the date it is required to be filed with the SEC, and (ii) in the case of other documents, within 24 hours after they are filed with the SEC, and (b) such documents are provided to security holders whose last address as shown on the books of the issuer is in Canada in the manner and at the time required by applicable U.S. law.

Compliance by any other person or company with U.S. requirements relating to proxies and proxy solicitation with respect to a U.S. issuer that has a class of securities registered pursuant to section 12 of the 1934 Act will satisfy the requirements of the Canadian provinces and territories relating to proxies and proxy solicitation, provided that (i) two copies of any material relating to a meeting of security holders filed with the SEC are filed with the applicable securities regulatory authorities that require the filing of material of that nature within 24 hours after they are filed with the SEC, and (ii) such documents are provided to security holders whose last address as shown on the books of the issuer is in Canada in the manner and at the time required by applicable U.S. law.

Compliance with U.S. requirements relating to quarterly reports and annual reports by a U.S. issuer that has a class of securities registered pursuant to section 12 of the 1934 Act or is required to file reports pursuant to section 15(d) of the 1934 Act will satisfy the requirements of the Canadian provinces and territories relating to interim financial statements and annual financial statements, respectively, provided that:

(1)   two copies of any material filed with the SEC are filed with the applicable securities regulatory authorities that require the filing of financial statements within 24 hours after they are filed with the SEC; and

(2)   (a) if:

(i)   the issuer is a reporting issuer in the Canadian provinces and territories solely as the result of offerings, bids and business combinations made under the MJDS;

(ii)   the issuer meets the eligibility requirements specified in Sections 3.3(1) and (2); or

(iii)   the issuer meets the eligibility requirements specified in Sections 3.2(1)-(5) and the issuer is a reporting issuer in the Canadian provinces and territories solely as the result of the distribution of securities that have an Approved Rating and meet the eligibility requirements of Section 3.2(6);

then such documents are provided to security holders whose last address as shown on the books of the issuer is in Canada in the manner and at the time required by applicable U.S. law; or

(b) otherwise such documents are provided to security holders whose last address as shown on the books of the issuer is in Canada in the manner and at the time required by applicable Canadian securities legislation.

A U.S. issuer that has a class of its securities listed on the New York Stock Exchange or the American Stock Exchange or quoted on Nasdaq may satisfy any obligation under Canadian securities legislation to issue and file a press release by (i) complying with the requirements of either such exchange or Nasdaq in respect of making public disclosure of material information on a timely basis, and (ii) forthwith issuing in Canada, and filing with the applicable securities regulatory authorities that require the filing of press releases, any press release that discloses a material change in its affairs.

A U.S. issuer shall not be required to comply with the requirements of National Policy Statement No. 41 (Shareholder Communication) so long as it complies with the requirements of Rule 14a-13 under the 1934 Act with respect to any Canadian clearing agency (i.e., The Canadian Depository for Securities Limited and West Canada Depository Trust Company) and any intermediary whose last address as shown on the books of the issuer is in Canada. Any such clearing agency or intermediary shall be required to comply only with the requirements of National Policy Statement No. 41 with respect to any such issuer, including, without limitation, responding to search cards and delivering proxy-related materials within the time periods specified in National Policy Statement No. 41. Any such intermediary shall be entitled to receive the fees and charges set out in National Policy Statement No. 41. For purposes of this paragraph, an intermediary means a registered dealer or adviser, a financial institution (bank or trust company), a participant in a clearing agency, a trustee or administrator of a self-administered retirement savings plan, retirement income fund, education savings plan, or other similar self-administered savings or investment plan registered under the Income Tax Act (Canada), or a nominee of any of the foregoing, that holds a security on behalf of another person or company who is not the registered holder of the security, unless excluded from the definition of "intermediary" by National Policy Statement No. 41.

An insider of a U.S. issuer that has a class of securities registered pursuant to section 12 of the 1934 Act shall not be required to file with any securities regulatory authority in Canada insider reports with respect to holdings of securities of such issuer so long as such insider files with the SEC on a timely basis all reports required to be filed with the SEC pursuant to section 16(a) of the 1934 Act and the rules and regulations thereunder.

7.   U.S.-ONLY OFFERINGS BY CANADIAN ISSUERS

Where a Canadian issuer uses Form F-9 or F-10 prescribed under the 1933 Act to make an offering solely in the United States under the multijurisdictional disclosure system adopted by the SEC, the issuer shall select a review jurisdiction in Canada no later than the time of filing the registration statement with the SEC and shall advise the SEC of its selection. The jurisdiction selected may or may not agree to act in such capacity. If a jurisdiction does not agree to act, the issuer shall select another jurisdiction. As of the date of this Policy Statement, the securities regulatory authorities of New Brunswick, Prince Edward Island, Newfoundland, Yukon Territory and the Northwest Territories have indicated that they will not agree to act as the review jurisdiction in connection with offerings made under the MJDS. The issuer shall file with the review jurisdiction the documents that it files with the SEC no later than the time such documents are filed with the SEC, provided that the preliminary prospectus and prospectus filed with the review jurisdiction need not contain a certificate signed by the underwriters.

If the review jurisdiction selects a U.S.-only offering for review, it will so notify the issuer and the SEC within three business days of the date of filing of the preliminary prospectus. The review jurisdiction will give its comments, if any, to the issuer. Once all the comments have been resolved, the review jurisdiction will notify the issuer and the SEC of the receipt of the prospectus.

The issuer shall pay a fee of $2,500 to the review jurisdiction at the time of filing the preliminary prospectus.

The selection of a review jurisdiction does not affect any obligation the issuer otherwise may have to file a prospectus with a securities regulatory authority in Canada, whether as a result of the likelihood that the securities will not come to rest outside of Canada, as a result of a distribution being made from a province or territory, or otherwise.

APPENDIX "A" TO NATIONAL POLICY STATEMENT NO. 45
FORMS OF CERTIFICATES FOR RULE 415 OFFERINGS

1.   METHOD 1: SUPPLEMENTS WITHOUT CERTIFICATES

   (a) *Issuer's Certificate*

      (i) To use Method 1, the preliminary prospectus and prospectus used for a Rule 415 Offering must contain the following issuer's certificate:

         "The foregoing, together with the documents incorporated herein by reference, as of the date of each supplement hereto, will constitute full, true and plain disclosure of all material facts relating to the securities offered by this prospectus and such supplement as required by [insert applicable references] [insert if offering made in Quebec – "and will not contain any misrepresentation likely to affect the value or the market price of the securities to be distributed"]".

      (ii) To use Method 1 for an MTN Program established under a prospectus for a Rule 415 Offering by a prospectus supplement, where a certificate of the issuer of the type referred to in Paragraph 1(a)(i) of this Appendix was not included in the prospectus, the supplement establishing such program in Canada must contain the following issuer's certificate:

         "The prospectus dated *** [insert if applicable – "as amended,"] together with the documents incorporated therein by reference, as supplemented by the foregoing, as of the date of each supplement hereto, will constitute full, true and plain disclosure of all material facts relating to the securities offered hereby and by such supplement as required by [insert applicable references] [insert if offering made in Quebec – "and will not contain any misrepresentation likely to affect the value or the market price of the securities to be distributed"]".

      (iii) To use Method 1, each amendment to a prospectus used for a Rule 415 Offering, where the prospectus contained a certificate of the type referred to in Paragraph 1(a)(i) of this Appendix, must contain the following issuer's certificate:

         "The prospectus dated ***, as amended, together with the documents incorporated therein by reference, as of the date of each supplement thereto, will constitute full, true and plain disclosure of all material facts relating to the securities offered by such prospectus and supplement as required by [insert applicable references] [insert if offering made in Quebec – "and will not contain any misrepresentation likely to affect the value or the market price of the securities to be distributed"]".

   (b) *Underwriters' Certificate*

      (i) Where there is an underwriter, to use Method 1 each preliminary prospectus and prospectus for a Rule 415 Offering shall contain the following underwriters' certificate signed by the underwriter or underwriters who, with respect to the securities offered by the prospectus supplement, are, or it is known will be, in a contractual relationship with the issuer or a selling security holder:

> "To the best of our knowledge, information and belief, the foregoing, together with the documents incorporated herein by reference, as of the date of each supplement hereto, will constitute full, true and plain disclosure of all material facts relating to the securities offered by this prospectus and such supplement as required by [insert applicable references] [insert if offering made in Quebec – "and will not contain any misrepresentation likely to affect the value or the market price of the securities to be distributed"]".

(ii) To use Method 1 for an MTN Program established by a prospectus supplement, where the prospectus did not contain a certificate of an underwriter of the type referred to in Paragraph 1(b)(i) of this Appendix of an underwriter, such supplement shall contain the following underwriters' certificate signed by the underwriter or underwriters who, with respect to the securities offered by such supplement, are, or will be, in a contractual relationship with the issuer or a selling security holder:

> "To the best of our knowledge, information and belief, the prospectus dated ***, [insert if applicable – "as amended,"] together with the documents incorporated therein by reference, as supplemented by the foregoing, as of the date of each supplement hereto, will constitute full, true and plain disclosure of all material facts relating to the securities offered hereby and by such supplement as required by [insert applicable references] [insert if offering made in Quebec – "and will not contain any misrepresentation likely to affect the value or the market price of the securities to be distributed"]".

(iii) To use Method 1, each amendment to a prospectus used for a Rule 415 Offering, where the prospectus contained a certificate of an underwriter of the type referred to in Paragraph 1(b)(i) of this Appendix, shall contain the following underwriters' certificate signed by the underwriter or underwriters who, with respect to the securities offered by the prospectus are, or it is known will be, in a contractual relationship with the issuer or a selling security holder:

> "To the best of our knowledge, information and belief, the prospectus dated ***, as amended, together with the documents incorporated therein by reference, as of the date of each supplement thereto, will constitute full, true and plain disclosure of all material facts relating to the securities offered hereby and by such supplement as required by [insert applicable references] [insert if offering made in Quebec – "and will not contain any misrepresentation likely to affect the value or the market price of the securities to be distributed"]".

2. METHOD 2: CERTIFICATES IN EACH SUPPLEMENT

(a) *Issuer's Certificate*

(i) To use Method 2, the preliminary prospectus and prospectus used for a Rule 415 Offering must contain the following issuer's certificate:

> "The foregoing, together with the documents incorporated herein by reference, constitutes full, true and plain disclosure of all material facts relating to such securities as required by [insert applicable references] [insert if offering made in Quebec – "and will not contain any misrepresentation likely to affect the value or the market price of the securities to be distributed"]".

(ii) To use Method 2, each prospectus supplement used for a Rule 415 Offering must contain the following issuer's certificate:

"The prospectus dated ***, [insert if applicable – "as amended,"] together with the documents incorporated therein by reference, as supplemented by the foregoing, constitutes full, true and plain disclosure of all material facts relating to the securities offered by such prospectus and supplement as required by [insert applicable references] [insert if offering made in Quebec – "and will not contain any misrepresentation likely to affect the value or the market price of the securities to be distributed"]".

(iii) To use Method 2, each amendment to a prospectus used in Canada for a Rule 415 Offering must contain the following issuer's certificate:

"The prospectus dated ***, as amended, together with the documents incorporated therein by reference, constitutes full, true and plain disclosure of all material facts relating to the securities offered thereby as required by [insert applicable references] [insert if offering made in Quebec – "and will not contain any misrepresentation likely to affect the value or the market price of the securities to be distributed"]".

(b) *Underwriters' Certificate*

(i) Where there is an underwriter, to use Method 2, each preliminary prospectus and prospectus for a Rule 415 Offering shall contain the following underwriters' certificate signed by the underwriter or underwriters who, with respect to the securities offered by the prospectus, are, or it is known will be, in a contractual relationship with the issuer or a selling security holder:

"To the best of our knowledge, information and belief, the foregoing, together with the documents incorporated herein by reference, constitutes full, true and plain disclosure of all material facts relating to such securities as required by [insert applicable references] [insert if offering made in Quebec – "and will not contain any misrepresentation likely to affect the value or the market price of the securities to be distributed"]".

(ii) Where there is an underwriter, to use Method 2, each prospectus supplement used for a Rule 415 Offering shall contain the following underwriters' certificate signed by the underwriter or underwriters who, with respect to the securities offered by the prospectus supplement, are in a contractual relationship with the issuer or a selling security holder:

"To the best of our knowledge, information and belief, the prospectus dated ***, [insert if applicable – "as amended,"] together with the documents incorporated therein by reference, as supplemented by the foregoing, constitutes full, true and plain disclosure of all material facts relating to the securities offered hereby and by such supplement as required by [insert applicable references] [insert if offering made in Quebec – "and will not contain any misrepresentation likely to affect the value or the market price of the securities to be distributed"]".

(iii) To use Method 2, each amendment to a prospectus used for a Rule 415 Offering, where the prospectus contained a certificate of an underwriter of the type referred to in Paragraph 2(b)(i) of this Appendix, shall contain the following underwriters' certificate signed by the underwriter or underwriters who, with respect to the securities offered by the prospectus are, or it is known will be, in a contractual relationship with the issuer or a selling security holder:

"To the best of our knowledge, information and belief, the prospectus dated ***, as amended, together with the documents incorporated therein by reference, constitutes full, true and plain disclosure of all material facts relating to the securities offered thereby as required by [insert applicable references] [insert if offering made in Quebec – "and will not contain any misrepresentation likely to affect the value or the market price of the securities to be distributed"]".

(iv) If:

    A. Method 2 is being used;

    B. an amendment to a prospectus for a Rule 415 Offering is filed with respect to a material change that occurred during a period when offers and sales of securities are being made by an underwriter in Canada; and

    C. such prospectus did not contain a certificate of such underwriter of the type referred to in Paragraph 2(b)(i) of this Appendix,

such underwriter shall resign the certificate that it previously provided pursuant to Paragraph 2(b)(ii) of this Appendix in the prospectus supplement describing the securities being so offered. This resigned underwriters' certificate shall be filed with the applicable securities regulatory authorities concurrently with the amendment.

APPENDIX "B" TO NATIONAL POLICY STATEMENT NO. 45
FORMS OF SUBMISSION TO JURISDICTION AND APPOINTMENT OF AGENT FOR SERVICE OF PROCESS

A.   PROSPECTUS OFFERING OF SECURITIES

1.   Name of issuer (the "Issuer"): _____ .

2.   Jurisdiction of incorporation of Issuer: _____ .

3.   Address of principal place of business of Issuer: _____ .

4.   Description of securities (the "Securities"): _____ .

5.   Date of prospectus (the "Prospectus") pursuant to which the Securities are offered: _____ .

6.   Name of agent (the "Agent"): _____ .

7.   Address for service of process of Agent in Canada: _____ .

8.   The Issuer designates and appoints the Agent at the address of the Agent stated above as its agent upon whom may be served any notice, pleading, subpoena, summons or other process in any action, investigation or administrative, criminal, quasi-criminal, penal or other proceeding (the "Proceeding") arising out of or relating to or concerning the distribution of the Securities made or purported to be made pursuant to the Prospectus or the obligations of the Issuer as a reporting issuer, and irrevocably waives any right to raise as a defence in any such Proceeding any alleged lack of jurisdiction to bring such Proceeding.

9.   The Issuer irrevocably and unconditionally submits to the non-exclusive jurisdiction of:

    (a) the judicial, quasi-judicial and administrative tribunals of each of the provinces [and territories] of Canada in which the Securities are distributed pursuant to the Prospectus; and

    (b) any administrative proceeding in any such province [or territory],

in any Proceeding arising out of or related to or concerning the distribution of the Securities made or purported to be made pursuant to the Prospectus.

10.   Until six years after it has ceased to be a reporting issuer in any Canadian province or territory, the Issuer shall file a new Submission to Jurisdiction and Appointment of Agent for Service of Process in the form hereof at least 30 days prior to termination of this Submission to Jurisdiction and Appointment of Agent for Service of Process for any reason whatsoever.

11.   Until six years after it has ceased to be a reporting issuer in any Canadian province or territory, the Issuer shall file an amended Submission to Jurisdiction and Appointment of Agent for Service of Process at least 30 days prior to any change in the name or above address of the Agent.

12. This Submission to Jurisdiction and Appointment of Agent for Service of Process shall be governed by and construed in accordance with the laws of _____ [province of above address of Agent].

Dated: _____

_____ [Issuer]

By: _____
[Name and title]

The undersigned accepts the appointment as agent for service of process of _____ [Issuer] pursuant to the terms and conditions of the foregoing Appointment of Agent for Service of Process.

Dated: _____

_____ [Agent]

By: _____
[Name and title]

B.   TAKE-OVER OR ISSUER BID

1.   Name of offeror (the "Offeror"): _____ .

2.   Jurisdiction of incorporation of Offeror: _____ .

3.   Address of principal place of business of Offeror: _____ .

4.   Description of securities (the "Securities"): _____ .

5.   Date of bid (the "Bid") for the Securities: _____ .

6.   Name of agent (the "Agent"): _____ .

7.   Address for service of process of Agent in Canada: _____ .

8.   The Offeror designates and appoints the Agent at the address of the Agent stated above as its agent upon whom may be served any notice, pleading, subpoena, summons or other process in any action, investigation or administrative, criminal, quasi-criminal, penal or other proceeding (the "Proceeding") arising out of or relating to or concerning the Bid [insert for securities exchange bids – "or the obligations of the Offeror as a reporting issuer"], and irrevocably waives any right to raise as a defence in any such Proceeding any alleged lack of jurisdiction to bring such Proceeding.

9.   The Offeror irrevocably and unconditionally submits to the non-exclusive jurisdiction of:

(a) the judicial, quasi-judicial and administrative tribunals of each of the provinces [and territories] of Canada in which the Bid is made; and

(b) any administrative proceeding in any such province [or territory],

in any Proceeding arising out of or related to or concerning the Bid.

10. Until six years from the date of the Bid, the Offeror shall file a new Submission to Jurisdiction and Appointment of Agent for Service of Process in the form hereof at least 30 days prior to termination of this Submission to Jurisdiction and Appointment of Agent for Service of Process for any reason whatsoever.

11. Until six years from the date of the Bid, the Offeror shall file an amended Submission to Jurisdiction and Appointment of Agent for Service of Process at least 30 days prior to any change in the name or above address of the Agent.

12. This Submission to Jurisdiction and Appointment of Agent for Service of Process shall be governed by and construed in accordance with the laws of _____ [province of above address of Agent].

Dated: _____

_____ [Offeror]

By: _____
[Name and title]

The undersigned accepts the appointment as agent for service of process of _____ [Offeror] pursuant to the terms and conditions of the foregoing Appointment of Agent for Service of Process.

Dated: _____

_____ [Agent]

By: _____
[Name and title]

C. TRUST INDENTURE

1. Name of trustee (the "Trustee"): _____ .

2. Jurisdiction of incorporation of Trustee: _____ .

3. Address of principal place of business of Trustee: _____ .

4. Description of securities (the "Securities"): _____ .

5. Date of trust indenture (the "Indenture") pursuant to which the Securities are issued: _____ .

6. Name of agent (the "Agent"): _____ .

7. Address for service of process of Agent in Canada: _____ .

8. The Trustee designates and appoints the Agent at the address of the Agent stated above as its agent upon whom may be served any notice, pleading, subpoena, summons or other process in any action, investigation or administrative, criminal, quasi- criminal, penal or other proceeding (the "Proceeding") arising out of or relating to or concerning the Indenture, and irrevocably waives any right to raise as a defence in any such Proceeding any alleged lack of jurisdiction to bring such Proceeding.

9. The Trustee irrevocably and unconditionally submits to the non-exclusive jurisdiction of:

   (a) the judicial, quasi-judicial and administrative tribunals of each of the provinces [and territories] of Canada in which the Securities are issued; and

   (b) any administrative proceeding in any such province [or territory],

   in any Proceeding arising out of or related to or concerning the Indenture.

10. Until six years from the termination of the Indenture, the Trustee shall file a new Submission to Jurisdiction and Appointment of Agent for Service of Process in the form hereof at least 30 days prior to termination of this Submission to Jurisdiction and Appointment of Agent for Service of Process for any reason whatsoever.

11. Until six years from the termination of the Indenture, the Trustee shall file an amended Submission to Jurisdiction and Appointment of Agent for Service of Process at least 30 days prior to any change in the name or above address of the Agent.

12. This Submission to Jurisdiction and Appointment of Agent for Service of Process shall be governed by and construed in accordance with the laws of _____ [province of above address of Agent].

Dated: _____

_____ [Trustee]

By: _____
    [Name and title]

The undersigned accepts the appointment as agent for service of process of _____ [Issuer] pursuant to the terms and conditions of the foregoing Appointment of Agent for Service of Process.

Dated: _____

_____ [Agent]

By: _____
    [Name and title]

Schedule "A"

NATIONAL POLICY STATEMENT NO. 47
PROMPT OFFERING QUALIFICATION SYSTEM

See NIN 94/21 "Expedited Review of Short Form Prospectuses and Renewal AIFs" and NIN 94/22 "Permission Under Section 35(1)(c) of the Securities Act" with respect to the expedited review of short form prospectuses and renewal AIFS pursuant to the Memorandum of Understanding found after NIN 94/21.

TABLE OF CONTENTS

9   GENERAL PROVISIONS

9.1   Effective date
9.2   Transition
9.3   Application of other policy statements

APPENDIX A   AIF

Guidelines

Instructions

Contents of AIF

Schedule 1 to Appendix A – Industry segments

Schedule 2 to Appendix A – MD&A

APPENDIX B   SHORT FORM PROSPECTUS

Contents of short form prospectus

APPENDIX C   APPLICABLE REGULATOR

NATIONAL POLICY STATEMENT NO. 47
PROMPT OFFERING QUALIFICATION SYSTEM

PART 1   PURPOSE

The prompt offering qualification system for the distribution of securities of eligible issuers was first introduced in 1982. It was designed to shorten the time period and to streamline the procedures by which these issuers and their selling security holders could have access to the Canadian capital markets through a prospectus offering. The Canadian Securities Administrators are satisfied that the prompt offering qualification system in its present form has achieved its objectives without reducing the existing benefits of investor protection or the degree and quality of disclosure to the public. The Canadian Securities Administrators, however, believe that by adopting a national policy statement on the prompt offering qualification system, further efficiencies in the timing and procedures for access to the Canadian capital markets will be gained by eligible issuers and their selling security holders.

PART 2   APPLICATION

The Commission des valeurs mobilières du Québec agrees with the purpose and intent of this Policy Statement, but is not a participant in the Policy Statement, as its Act, Regulation and policy statements have, since 1982, provided for accessibility to a simplified prospectus procedure by any issuer that has been a reporting issuer for 12 months and has filed a permanent information record. Issuers are reminded to refer specifically to the Québec legislation when considering a distribution of securities in the Province of Québec and concurrently in other jurisdictions under this Policy Statement.

PART 3   INTERPRETATION

In this Policy Statement and its appendices, unless the context otherwise requires:

"AIF"[1] means an annual information form prepared in accordance with the provisions of Appendix A;

"Applicable Regulator" means the appropriate representative of the relevant Securities Regulatory Authority in each Jurisdiction as set out in Appendix C;

"Approved Rating" means any one of the following generic rating categories applicable to debt or preferred shares, as the case may be, set opposite each Approved Rating Organization's name:

---

1   See part 9 for transitional provisions and provisions relating to the coming into effect of this Policy Statement.

Approved Rating Organization	Debt	Preferred Shares
C.B.R.S. Inc.	A++, A+, A or B++	P-1+, P-1, P-2 or P-3
Dominion Bond Rating Service Limited	AAA, AA, A or BBB	Pfd-1, Pfd-2 or Pfd-3
Moody's Investors Service, Inc.	Aaa, Aa, A or Baa	"aaa", "aa", "a" or "baa"
Standard & Poor's Corporation	AAA, AA, A or BBB	AAA, AA, A or BBB;

"Approved Rating Organization" means each of C.B.R.S. Inc., Dominion Bond Rating Service Limited, Moody's Investors Service, Inc. and Standard & Poor's Corporation[2];

"Associate" means, for purposes of section 4.1(2)(a), where used to indicate a relationship with any Person,

(a)   a partner, other than a limited partner, of that Person,

(b)   a trust or estate in which that Person has a substantial beneficial interest or for which that Person serves as trustee or in a similar capacity,

(c)   an issuer in respect of which that Person beneficially owns or controls, directly or indirectly, voting securities carrying more than 10% of the voting rights attached to all outstanding voting securities of the issuer,

(d)   a relative of that Person who has the same home as that Person,

(e)   any individual who has the same home as that Person and who is either married to that Person or is living with that Person as husband or wife, or

(f)   any relative of the individual mentioned in paragraph (e) who has the same home as that Person, and

for all other purposes, "associate" as defined in the Securities Legislation of a Jurisdiction;

"Canadian GAAP" refers to the generally accepted accounting principles described in National Policy Statement No. 27;

"Capital Resources" means indebtedness, share capital and any other financial arrangement, whether reflected on the balance sheet or not, that can reasonably be considered to provide resources to an issuer (e.g., leases and put options);

"CICA" means the Canadian Institute of Chartered Accountants;

"CICA Handbook" means the Handbook of the CICA;

"Connected Party" in respect of the application of this Policy Statement in a Jurisdiction, has the meaning assigned to "connected party" or "connected issuer" or "related party" or "related issuer" in the provisions of the Securities Legislation or Securities Requirements of that Jurisdiction regulating conflicts of interest in connection with the distribution of securities of a registrant or of a "related party" or "related issuer" or "connected party" or "connected issuer" of a registrant;

"Convertible", where used to describe debt or preferred shares, means that the rights and attributes attaching to those securities include the right or option to purchase, convert or exchange or otherwise acquire any Equity Securities of any issuer, or any other security that itself includes the right or option to purchase, convert or exchange or otherwise acquire any Equity Securities of any issuer;

"Current AIF"[3] means

(a)   during the period of 140 days following an issuer's most recently completed financial year

---

2   Canadian issuers contemplating making a cross border offering using Form F-9 of the multijurisdictional disclosure system adopted by the SEC should refer to section 8 of National Policy Statement No. 45, as amended.

3   See part 9 for transitional provisions and provisions relating to the coming into effect of this Policy Statement.

(i) if an issuer's AIF for its most recently completed financial year has been accepted for filing in accordance with section 5.1 or 5.2(1), the AIF of the issuer for that financial year, or

(ii) if an issuer's AIF for its most recently completed financial year has not been accepted for filing in accordance with section 5.1 or 5.2(1), the AIF of the issuer for its immediately preceding financial year provided that AIF has previously been accepted for filing in accordance with section 5.1 or 5.2(1) or (2), and

(b) at any other time, the AIF of the issuer for its most recently completed financial year provided it has been accepted for filing under section 5.1 or 5.2(1) or (2);

"Designated Countries" means countries designated from time to time by the Office of the Superintendent of Financial Institutions Canada as requiring provisions against general country risk;

"Equity Securities" means securities of an issuer that carry a residual right to participate in earnings of the issuer and, upon liquidation or winding up of the issuer, in its assets;

"Failure Date" means

(a) where preferred shares are to be distributed, the date on which the issuer of the preferred shares is expected to pay any amount referred to in section 4.3(1)(b)(i)(A) but fails to do so, or

(b) where debt is to be distributed, the date on which the issuer of the debt is required to pay any amount referred to in section 4.3(1)(b)(i)(B) but fails to do so;

"Implementation Order" means the blanket order or ruling issued by the Securities Regulatory Authority of a Jurisdiction giving effect to this Policy Statement;

"Initial AIF"[4] means the AIF filed by an issuer under this Policy Statement in order to participate in the POP System in a Jurisdiction

(a) for the first time, or

(b) upon the issuer again becoming eligible to participate in the Pop System in that Jurisdiction after having ceased to be eligible to participate in the POP System in that Jurisdiction;

"Investee" means a company, partnership, joint venture or other arrangement in which the issuer holds an equity interest and that is not a subsidiary of, controlled by, or a temporary investment of, the issuer;

"Jurisdiction" means a province or territory of Canada;

"MD&A" means management's discussion and analysis of financial condition and results of operations of an issuer required to be disclosed in the AIF under item 5 in Appendix A;

"NPS 1" means National Policy Statement No. 1;

"NPS 44" means National Policy Statement No. 44;

"Non-Convertible", where used to describe debt or preferred shares, means securities that are not Convertible;

"Participants" means all the issuers that, directly or indirectly, are parties to a Reorganization; for greater certainty, "Participants" includes any issuer that issues securities pursuant to a Reorganization to holders of securities of any party to the Reorganization;

"Person" means "company" or "person" as defined in the Securities Legislation of a Jurisdiction;

"POP System" means the prompt offering qualification system for the distribution by or on behalf of an issuer or a Selling Security Holder of securities of an issuer by means of a short form prospectus as contemplated in this Policy Statement;

---

4 See part 9 for transitional provisions and provisions relating to the coming into effect of this Policy Statement.

"Principal Jurisdiction" means the Jurisdiction selected by an issuer pursuant to NPS 1; where an issuer must select a Principal Jurisdiction under this Policy Statement in circumstances that are not discussed in NPS 1, the issuer shall be guided by the principles set out in NPS 1 in selecting its Principal Jurisdiction; where only one Jurisdiction is involved, the "Principal Jurisdiction" shall be the relevant Jurisdiction;

"Renewal AIF"[5] means any AIF that is not an Initial AIF;

"Reorganization" means

(a)   an amalgamation, other than an amalgamation of an issuer and one or more of its wholly-owned subsidiaries where the issuer's audited consolidated financial statements for its last three financial years include the results of the subsidiary or subsidiaries that are a party to the amalgamation,

(b)   a merger,

(c)   an arrangement, or

(d)   any other similar transaction;

"Revised AIF" means, as appropriate, the final version of

(a)   any Initial AIF, Renewal AIF or Current AIF, if revisions are necessary as a result of the review undertaken under section 5.1; and

(b)   any Renewal AIF, if revisions are necessary as a result of the selective review undertaken under section 5.2(6);

"SEC" means the Securities and Exchange Commission of the United States of America;

"Securities Legislation" means the statutes concerning the regulation of securities markets and trading in securities in a Jurisdiction, and the regulations in respect of these statutes;

"Securities Regulatory Authority" means the securities commission or similar regulatory authority in existence from time to time in a Jurisdiction;

"Securities Requirements" means the blanket rulings and orders made under the Securities Legislation of a Jurisdiction, and the policy statements and written interpretations issued by the Securities Regulatory Authority of that Jurisdiction;

"Selling Security Holder" means a holder of the securities of an issuer, provided the issuer satisfies the applicable eligibility criteria of part 4;

"Successor Issuer" means any issuer existing as an issuer after a Reorganization[6]; and

"1934 Act" means the Securities Exchange Act of 1934 of the United States of America.

PART 4   ELIGIBILITY CRITERIA

4.1   Basic eligibility criteria

    (1)   An issuer is eligible to participate in the POP System in a Jurisdiction if:

        (a) the issuer meets the following reporting issuer requirements:

            (i) the issuer has been a reporting issuer under the Securities Legislation of the Jurisdiction for the 12 calendar months immediately preceding the date of filing of its AIF in the Jurisdiction, or

            (ii) the issuer has been a reporting issuer under the Securities Legislation of another Jurisdiction for the 12 calendar months immediately preceding the date of filing of its AIF in the Jurisdiction, provided

---

5   See part 9 for transitional provisions and provisions relating to the coming into effect of this Policy Statement.

6   Where there is a spin-off of a part of the business of an issuer, the resulting issuer is not a Successor Issuer as defined above. However, the Securities Regulatory Authorities will consider applications requesting that the resulting issuer be permitted to use the POP System.

(A) the issuer files with its AIF, or has previously filed, all continuous disclosure documents that it was required to file under the Securities Legislation and Securities Requirements of each Jurisdiction in which it was a reporting issuer for the 12 calendar months immediately preceding the date of filing of its AIF, and

(B) if the issuer is not a reporting issuer in the Jurisdiction or is not deemed to be, or designated as, a reporting issuer under the Implementation Order issued by the Jurisdiction,

    (aa) the issuer files with its AIF, or has previously filed, an application to be deemed to be, or designated as, a reporting issuer in accordance with the Securities Legislation and the Securities Requirements of the Jurisdiction and the Jurisdiction issues an order deeming the issuer to be, or designating the issuer as, a reporting issuer in that Jurisdiction, or

    (bb) if the Jurisdiction is unable to deem an issuer to be, or designate an issuer as, a reporting issuer[7], the issuer files with its AIF an undertaking to file all continuous disclosure documents that it would be required to file under the Securities Legislation and the Securities Requirements of that Jurisdiction if it were a reporting issuer in that Jurisdiction from the time of the filings required under section 4.1(1)(a)(ii)(A) until the issuer becomes a reporting issuer in that Jurisdiction;

(b) at the time its AIF is filed, the issuer is not in default of any requirement of the Securities Legislation of the Jurisdiction; and

(c) the aggregate market value of the issuer's Equity Securities, listed and posted for trading on a stock exchange in Canada, is $75,000,000 or more.

(2) For purposes of section 4.1(1)(c), the market value of each class of Equity Securities[8] of the issuer shall be calculated by multiplying:

(a) the total number of Equity Securities of that class, outstanding as at the end of the applicable period referred to in (b) below, excluding those Equity Securities of the class that are beneficially owned, directly or indirectly, or over which control or direction is exercised by Persons that alone or together with their respective affiliates and Associates, beneficially own or exercise control or direction over more than 10% of the issued and outstanding Equity Securities of the issuer (provided that Equity Securities that would be excluded because a portfolio manager of a pension fund, mutual fund or non-redeemable investment fund exercises control or direction over those securities

---

7   For example, the Securities Legislation in Ontario does not permit an issuer to be deemed to be, or designated as, a reporting issuer.

8   Where an issuer wishes to include the market value of instalment receipts representing its Equity Securities in the calculation of the market value of its Equity Securities, the issuer shall use the total number of instalment receipts, held by security holders that meet the requirements of section 4.1(2)(a), and the arithmetic average of the closing prices of the instalment receipts determined under section 4.1(2)(b).

need not be excluded unless the portfolio manager is an affiliate of the issuer)[8a]; by

(b) the arithmetic average of the closing prices of the Equity Securities of that class, on the Canadian stock exchange on which that class of Equity Securities is principally traded, for each of the trading days during

   (i) if the calculation is made for the filing of an Initial AIF, the last calendar month of the financial year in respect of which that Initial AIF is filed, and

   (ii) if the calculation is made for the filing of a Renewal AIF[9], at the option of the issuer

      (A) the last calendar month of the financial year in respect of which that Renewal AIF is filed, or

      (B) the last calendar month before the date of filing of that Renewal AIF.[10, 11]

The aggregate market value of the Equity Securities of the issuer shall be the aggregate of the market value of each class of its Equity Securities as calculated above.

(3) An issuer or Selling Security Holder may make a distribution under the POP System in a Jurisdiction if:

   (a) the issuer has a Current AIF; and

   (b) at the time of the filing of a preliminary short form prospectus and the issuance of the receipt for a short form prospectus, the issuer is not in default of any requirement of the Securities Legislation of the Jurisdiction.

[8a] The following examples are provided to assist issuers and their advisers in the calculation of the market value of the issuer.

Example (1): A portfolio manager manages a pension fund. The pension fund holds 11% of the Equity Securities of the issuer. *Result*: These Equity Securities must be excluded in calculating the market value of the issuer's Equity Securities.

Example (2): A portfolio manager (not an affiliate of the issuer) manages three mutual funds each of which holds 3% of the Equity Securities of the issuer. An affiliate of the portfolio manager (not an affiliate of the issuer) manages two mutual funds each of which holds 3% of the Equity Securities of the issuer (15% in the aggregate). *Result*: The aggregated Equity Securities do not have to be excluded in calculating the market value of the issuer's Equity Securities.

Example (3): Facts are the same as in Example (2) above except that, in this example, assume that the portfolio manager and the affiliate of the portfolio manager are affiliates of the issuer. *Result*: The aggregated Equity Securities must be excluded in calculating the market value of the issuer's Equity Securities.

Example (4): A portfolio manager (not an affiliate of the issuer) manages three non-redeemable funds ("A, B and C"). A holds 12% of the Equity Securities of the issuer. B and C each hold 6% of the Equity Securities of the issuer. *Result*: The Equity Securities of the issuer held by A must be excluded in calculating the market value of the issuer's Equity Securities but the Equity Securities held by B and C (12% in the aggregate) need not be excluded in calculating the market value of the issuer's Equity Securities.

[9] An issuer that has previously filed an Initial AIF or a Renewal AIF because it was eligible to distribute its Non-Convertible debt or Non-Convertible preferred shares under section 4.3(1)(a) is entitled, at its option, to rely on either of the time periods provided for the calculation of the market value of an issuer's Equity Securities in respect of the filing of a Renewal AIF pursuant to section 4.1(2)(b)(ii) provided it has Non-Convertible debt or Non-Convertible preferred shares with an Approved Rating outstanding at the time of the filing of its Renewal AIF.

[10] Issuers should note that the Québec Securities Legislation does not permit calculation on the basis of the last calendar month before the date of filing of the AIF but that an issuer may apply for an exemption from the Commission des valeurs mobilières du Québec.

[11] An issuer that does not satisfy either of the market value requirements in section 4.1(2)(b)(ii) for its Renewal AIF should refer to section 5.2(2) and footnote (17) for further guidance.

(4) For purposes of section 4.1(1)(a)(ii)(A), an issuer that has filed with a Jurisdiction some or all of the continuous disclosure documents contemplated in that section is not required to file those documents again in that Jurisdiction. However, an issuer that has filed only some of the continuous disclosure documents contemplated in section 4.1(1)(a)(ii)(A) in a Jurisdiction is required to file the balance of those documents in that Jurisdiction.

4.2 *Alternative eligibility criteria for certain substantial Canadian issuers*

(1) The POP System may be used to distribute in a Jurisdiction securities of an issuer that meets all the eligibility criteria of section 4.1, except for the reporting issuer requirements of section 4.1(1)(a) provided:

(a) the issuer meets the following alternative reporting issuer requirements:

(i) the issuer is a reporting issuer under the Securities Legislation of the Jurisdiction, or

(ii) the issuer is a reporting issuer under the Securities Legislation of another Jurisdiction and

(A) the issuer files with its AIF, or has previously filed[12], all continuous disclosure documents that it was required to file under the Securities Legislation and Securities Requirements of each Jurisdiction in which it is a reporting issuer, and

(B) if the issuer is not deemed to be, or designated as, a reporting issuer under the Implementation Order issued by the Jurisdiction, the issuer complies with section 4.1(1)(a)(ii)(B)(aa) or (bb); and

(b) the issuer is incorporated, continued or organized under the laws of Canada or a province or territory of Canada and the aggregate market value of its Equity Securities, listed and posted for trading on a stock exchange in Canada, is $300,000,000 or more.

(2) For purposes of section 4.2(1)(b), the aggregate market value of the Equity Securities of the issuer shall be calculated in accordance with section 4.1(2), except that the issuer may, at its option if the calculation is made for the filing of an Initial AIF, use the relevant closing prices during the last calendar month before the date of filing of its Initial AIF.

4.3 *Alternative eligibility criteria for certain issues of debt and preferred shares*

(1) The POP System may be used to distribute in a Jurisdiction Non-Convertible debt or Non-Convertible preferred shares of an issuer that

(a) meets all the eligibility criteria of section 4.1, except for the market value requirement of section 4.1(1)(c), provided the issuer meets the following alternative market value requirements:

(i) at the time of the filing of its AIF, the issuer

(A) reasonably believes that any Non-Convertible debt or Non-Convertible preferred shares that it may issue will receive an Approved Rating, on a provisional basis, from at least one Approved Rating Organization, and

(B) reasonably believes that any Non-Convertible debt or Non-Convertible preferred shares that it may issue will not receive a rating lower than an Approved Rating from any Approved Rating Organization, and

(ii) at the time of the filing of the preliminary short form prospectus, the securities to be issued

---

12 An issuer may rely on section 4.1(4) in determining its continuous disclosure document filing requirement under this section.

   (A) have received an Approved Rating, on a provisional basis, from at least one Approved Rating Organization, and

   (B) have not received a provisional or final rating lower than an Approved Rating from any Approved Rating Organization, except where the distribution is made under NPS 44 in which case the requirements of that policy statement apply; or

  (b) does not meet the eligibility criteria of section 4.1 provided:

   (i) an issuer that meets the eligibility criteria of section 4.1(1)(a) and (b) and 4.1(3)(a), section 4.2, or section 4.3(1)(a) fully and unconditionally guarantees[13] payment

    (A) where preferred shares are to be distributed, of

     (aa) any dividend, whether declared or not, that is expected to be paid at fixed intervals and in a fixed amount or in an amount to be determined by formula, or

     (bb) a fixed amount in relation to any capital amount expected by the terms of the securities to be repaid in the event of redemption or liquidation, dissolution or winding up, or

    (B) where debt is to be distributed, of the principal of or premium, if any, or interest on the securities being distributed, together with any other amounts that may be due under

     (aa) any provisions of the trust agreement or other agreement relating to the securities to be distributed, or

     (bb) the provisions of the securities to be distributed;

    within 15 days from any Failure Date,

   (ii) at the time of the filing of the preliminary short form prospectus, the guarantor

    (A) is not in default of any requirement of the Securities Legislation of the Jurisdiction, and

    (B) has issued and outstanding Non-Convertible debt or Non-Convertible preferred shares that

     (aa) have received an Approved Rating from at least one Approved Rating Organization, and

     (bb) have not received a rating lower than an Approved Rating from any Approved Rating Organization, and

   (iii) at the time of the filing of the preliminary short form prospectus, the securities to be issued

    (A) have received an Approved Rating, on a provisional basis, from at least one Approved Rating Organization, and

    (B) have not received a provisional or final rating lower than an Approved Rating from any Approved Rating Organization,

    except where the distribution is made under NPS 44 in which case the requirements of that policy statement apply;

---

13 In this context, the Securities Regulatory Authorities take the position that an issuer that fully and unconditionally guarantees payment of securities is not, simply by providing that guarantee, issuing a security.

(2) The POP System may also be used to distribute in a Jurisdiction Convertible debt or Convertible preferred shares of an issuer that does not meet the eligibility criteria of section 4.1 provided:

    (a) the debt or the preferred shares are Convertible into securities that could be issued under section 4.1 or 4.2 concurrently with the Convertible debt or Convertible preferred shares;

    (b) the issuer of the underlying securities described in (a) above fully and unconditionally guarantees payment of the Convertible debt or Convertible preferred shares in accordance with section 4.3(1)(b)(i); and

    (c) at the time of the filing of the preliminary short form prospectus, the conditions set out in section 4.3(1)(b)(ii) and (iii) are met.

4.4 *Eligibility criteria for Reorganizations* – A Successor Issuer may distribute securities in a Jurisdiction under the POP System if the Successor Issuer meets all the eligibility requirements of section 4.1 in that Jurisdiction. The Successor Issuer shall be considered to have met the following eligibility requirements of section 4.1 in a Jurisdiction if:

(1) in the case of the reporting issuer requirements of section 4.1(1)(a),

    (a) prior to the Reorganization, at least one of the Participants that satisfied the reporting issuer requirements in section 4.1(1)(a) also satisfied the market value requirements in section 4.1(1)(c), and

    (b) at the time of the Reorganization, none of the Participants was in default of any requirement of the Securities Legislation of that Jurisdiction;

(2) in the case of the market value requirement of section 4.1(1)(c), the calculation is made on the basis of the relevant closing prices for each of the 10 trading days prior to the filing of the AIF referred to in paragraph (3) below; and

(3) in the case of the requirement to have a Current AIF pursuant to section 4.1(3)(a), the Successor Issuer files an AIF in the Jurisdiction promptly after the Reorganization; this AIF shall be subject to the review procedures referred to in section 5.1.[14]

4.5 *Waiver procedure* – The procedure to obtain a waiver of any provision of this part in more than one Jurisdiction is as follows:

(1) the applicant shall file an application in writing simultaneously[15] in all Jurisdictions where it requires a waiver;

(2) the application shall set out in detail the reasons for the application, the precedents[16] relied upon and the relief sought and shall indicate the name of the Principal Jurisdiction selected by the applicant and of each other Jurisdiction where the application is being filed;

(3) the Applicable Regulator of the Principal Jurisdiction may grant a waiver upon the terms and conditions that are deemed appropriate in the circumstances having regard for any comments raised by the other Jurisdictions;

---

14 In the past, a number of issuers were granted waivers from the requirements of section 4.4(3) in certain circumstances. The Securities Regulatory Authorities do not expect that waivers will be required under this Policy Statement because the definition of Reorganization now excludes the circumstances that gave rise to waivers in the past.

15 The Securities Regulatory Authorities will apply strictly the procedure set out in section 4.5. Where an issuer does not file its application simultaneously in all Jurisdictions in which it requires a waiver or where the issuer has pre-filing discussions with one Jurisdiction before filing its application in all Jurisdiction, all of the Securities Regulatory Authorities may not be able to issue a waiver on a timely basis.

16 Issuers should not expect to be able to rely on orders or rulings granted under the provisions governing the prompt offering qualification system in a Jurisdiction prior to the date of publication of this Policy Statement as precedents in determining whether discretionary relief will be granted from the provisions of this Policy Statement in their particular circumstances.

a document to that effect shall be issued by the Principal Jurisdiction and sent to the applicant with a copy to the Applicable Regulator in each of the other Jurisdictions where the application was filed; and

(4) each of the other Jurisdictions may grant a waiver upon the terms and conditions that it deems appropriate in the circumstances having the benefit of the decision of the Principal Jurisdiction.

PART 5 AIF

See NIN 94/2 "Filing Requirements for Annual Information Forms".

5.1 *Initial AIF review procedures* – An issuer may at any time file an Initial AIF in one or more Jurisdictions in which it satisfies the applicable eligibility criteria of part 4. An Initial AIF and supporting documents filed in more than one Jurisdiction shall be subject to the AIF review procedures contained in part 1 of NPS 1. An Initial AIF filed in only one Jurisdiction shall be subject to the provisions of the AIF review procedures applicable to the Principal Jurisdiction contained in part 1 of NPS 1. An Initial AIF shall be subject to acceptance for filing in each Jurisdiction in which it is filed with such alterations or additions, if any, as may be necessary to comply with the requirements of this Policy Statement. If revisions to an issuer's Initial AIF are necessary as a result of this review, the issuer shall file a Revised AIF, identified as such, in all Jurisdictions in which the Initial AIF has been filed. The Applicable Regulator of each relevant Jurisdiction shall forward to the issuer a written notice of acceptance of its Initial AIF or Revised AIF, as the case may be.

5.2 *Renewal AIF review procedures*

(1) To comply with the requirements of section 4.1(3)(a), an issuer that has filed an Initial AIF that has been accepted for filing pursuant to section 5.1 or a Renewal AIF must thereafter, within 140 days from the end of each financial year, file a Renewal AIF and supporting documents in each Jurisdiction in which it wishes to remain eligible to participate in the POP System. The Applicable Regulator in each relevant Jurisdiction shall immediately accept for filing a Renewal AIF filed in accordance with this section and shall forward to the issuer a written notice of acceptance for filing of its Renewal AIF. The Applicable Regulator of any Jurisdiction may delegate the authority to accept a Renewal AIF to a member of the staff of that Applicable Regulator.

(2) Where an issuer does not satisfy the relevant market value requirement during either of the calendar months contemplated in section 4.1(2)(b)(ii), the issuer may remain eligible to participate in the POP System if it

(a) files its Renewal AIF and all supporting documents, except for the certificate of eligibility described in section 5.3(2), within the 140 day period referred to in section 5.2(1),

(b) satisfies the relevant market value requirement during any calendar month before the end of the financial year in which its Renewal AIF is filed, and

(c) files the eligibility certificate referred to in (a) above promptly upon satisfying the market value requirement described in (b) above.

In these circumstances, a Renewal AIF shall be subject to the review procedures referred to in section 5.1; however, it will not be accepted for filing in accordance with that section until the eligibility certificate referred to in (c) above is filed.[17]

---

[17] Issuers are cautioned that the Securities Regulatory Authorities will not issue a receipt for a preliminary short form prospectus or short form prospectus before all the conditions set out in section 5.2(2) are satisfied. Furthermore, where an issuer does not satisfy either of the conditions set out in section 5.2(2)(b) or (c), the Securities Regulatory Authorities will consider that the issuer has ceased to participate in the POP System; thereafter, the issuer will only become eligible to participate in the POP System again if it satisfies the applicable eligibility criteria of part 4 and files an Initial AIF under section 5.1.

(3) Where a Renewal AIF and supporting documents are filed

    (a) after the the 140 day period referred to in section 5.2(1) or (2) and before the end of the financial year in which that 140 day period expires, or

    (b) in respect of a financial year in which an offeror made a take-over bid that was material[18] to the offeror[19],

the Renewal AIF shall be subject to the review procedures referred to in section 5.1.[20]

(4) An issuer wishing to participate in the POP System in one or more additional Jurisdictions other than the one or ones in which it has already filed an Initial AIF that has been accepted for filing, under this Policy Statement may file its Renewal AIF, concurrently, or its Current AIF, at any time, together with supporting documents in each of those additional Jurisdictions provided the issuer satisfies the applicable eligibility criteria of part 4 and notifies all the Jurisdictions in which it has already filed its Initial AIF. A Renewal AIF or Current AIF filed in additional Jurisdictions shall be subject to the review procedures referred to in section 5.1.

(5) When filing its Renewal AIF, the issuer shall advise each of the Jurisdictions in which the Renewal AIF is filed of the name of each other Jurisdiction in which its Renewal AIF is being filed.

(6) Subject to sections 5.2(7) and 5.2(8), an issuer's Renewal AIF is subject to selective review by the Securities Regulatory Authority of any Jurisdiction in which it is filed at any time after it is selected for review and before a receipt is issued for a short form prospectus incorporating by reference the Renewal AIF; where an issuer's Renewal AIF is selected for review by a Jurisdiction, the following procedure shall apply:

    (a) the Applicable Regulator of any Jurisdiction reviewing the issuer's Renewal AIF shall forward, within 10 days of the date of filing of the Renewal AIF in that Jurisdiction, by facsimile, a notice to the issuer and to the Applicable Regulator in the other Jurisdictions in which the Renewal AIF was filed stating that the issuer's Renewal AIF will be reviewed;

    (b) the Applicable Regulator of any other Jurisdiction wishing to conduct its own review of the issuer's Renewal AIF shall, within 5 days of receipt of the notice referred to in (a) above, forward by facsimile a similar notice to the issuer and to the Applicable Regulator of the other Jurisdictions in which the issuer's Renewal AIF was filed;

    (c) during any review period, all copies of the Renewal AIF provided to any Person by the issuer shall have in bold face type[21] on the outside front cover page the following statement or any variation that the Applicable Regulator of the issuer's Principal Jurisdiction may permit:

---

18 The discussion of the concept of materiality set out in paragraph (2) of item 13 of Appendix B applies with necessary changes in this context.

19 For greater certainty, where an issuer files a renewal AIF under section 5.2(3)(b), the issuer should indicate in its covering letter that a take-over bid that was material to the issuer has occurred.

20 Issuers are cautioned that the Securities Regulatory Authorities will not issue a receipt for a preliminary short form prospectus or short form prospectus until the Renewal AIF referred to in section 5.2(3) has been accepted for filing in their Jurisdiction. Furthermore, where an issuer does not file an AIF before the end of the financial year referred to in section 5.2(3)(a), the Securities Regulatory Authorities will consider that the issuer has ceased to participate in the POP System; thereafter, the issuer will only become eligible to participate in the POP System again if it satisfies the applicable eligibility criteria of part 4 and files an Initial AIF under section 5.1.

21 The statement required to be in bold face type on the outside front cover page of an issuer's Renewal AIF during a review period may be added by way of a stamp, sticker or other method that will ensure that the statement may not be deleted or removed from the issuer's Renewal AIF.

This annual information form has been accepted for filing in [insert name of each Jurisdiction in which Renewal AIF has been filed] but is currently subject to review by the securities regulatory authorities of one or more provinces or territories of Canada. Information contained herein is subject to change.;

(d) any Jurisdiction reviewing the issuer's Renewal AIF shall forward, by facsimile, its comments to the issuer with a copy to all other Jurisdictions reviewing the Issuer's Renewal AIF;

(e) the issuer shall provide any Jurisdiction reviewing the issuer's Renewal AIF with a written response to its comments and shall send a copy of its response to all the other Jurisdictions reviewing the issuer's Renewal AIF;

(f) as soon as practicable after completion of any review, or upon the issuer filing a Revised AIF, if necessary, the Applicable Regulator of a Jurisdiction reviewing the issuer's Renewal AIF shall issue a document stating that the review is completed and that either the Renewal AIF as filed or the Revised AIF, if any, is satisfactory to the Applicable Regulator of that Jurisdiction; this document shall be sent to the issuer with a copy to the Applicable Regulator in each of the other Jurisdictions in which the Renewal AIF was filed;

(g) upon receipt of the document referred to in (f) above from all Jurisdictions reviewing the issuer's Renewal AIF, the issuer shall promptly

(i) if revisions were necessary, file the Revised AIF with the other Jurisdictions in which the Renewal AIF was filed and forward a copy of the Revised AIF to any Person who received a legended Renewal AIF pursuant to (c) above, and

(ii) if revisions were not necessary, forward a notice that the review of the Renewal AIF is completed and that no revisions were necessary to any Person who received a legended Renewal AIF pursuant to (c) above;

(h) if a Revised AIF is filed, it shall be identified as such; and

(i) an issuer shall not be entitled to a receipt for a final prospectus under the POP system until the issuer notifies each Jurisdiction in which its Renewal AIF was filed that a Revised AIF, if any, has been filed with all the Jurisdictions in which its Renewal AIF was filed.

(7) If, after the Applicable Regulator of a Jurisdiction notifies an issuer that its Renewal AIF will be reviewed under section 5.2(6)(a) or (b) and before the document referred to in section 5.2(6)(f) is issued, the issuer files a preliminary short form prospectus, both the issuer's preliminary short form prospectus and its Renewal AIF shall be reviewed at the same time in accordance with the time limits applicable to the review of a short form prospectus contained in part 2 or 3 of NPS 1; in that case, comments arising in the course of the review of the Renewal AIF will be taken into account during the review of the preliminary short form prospectus and the document referred to in section 5.2(6)(f) must be issued prior to, or concurrently with, the issuance of the receipt for the short form prospectus. This procedure is also available for a renewal AIF filed under section 5.2(3)(b).

(8) If an issuer intends to file a preliminary short form prospectus in one or more Jurisdictions within the time period available for the Applicable Regulator of a Jurisdiction to notify the issuer that it intends to review the issuer's Renewal AIF under section 5.2(6)(a) or (b), the issuer shall, at the time of filing its Renewal AIF if its decision to file a preliminary short form prospectus has already been made or, if not, immediately upon making that decision, notify the Applicable Regulator in each Jurisdiction in which it is filing or has filed its Renewal AIF of its intention to file a preliminary short form prospectus; each Applicable Regulator who receives this notices shall as soon as practicable notify, by facsimile, the issuer and the Applicable Regulator in all the other Jurisdictions if it intends to review the issuer's Renewal AIF; in this case, the issuer's preliminary short form prospectus and its Renewal AIF shall be reviewed within the time limits referred to in section 5.2(7) and the issuance of the receipt for the short form prospectus

shall be subject to the same condition as set out in that section.[22] This procedure is also available for a renewal AIF filed under section 5.2(3)(b).

5.3   *Supporting documents*

(1)   Each AIF filed under this Policy Statement or under the Securities Legislation and Securities Requirements of the Province of Québec shall be submitted in the number of copies specified for each Jurisdiction in the "Table of Documents to be filed in respect of the Clearance of National Issues" forming part of NPS 1 and shall be accompanied by the supporting documents in the number of copies indicated in that table. Where an annual report on Form 10-K or 20-F is filed under Section 5.4 in lieu of an AIF, an issuer shall be deemed to have met the requirement to file a certified copy of the resolution(s) of the directors of the issuer approving the AIF if an original or a certified copy of a document evidencing approval of the Form 10-K or 20-F, in a form acceptable to the Applicable Regulator of the issuer's Principal Jurisdiction, is filed.

(2)   The certificate of eligibility filed with an AIF shall be executed on behalf of the issuer by one of its senior officers and shall state that the issuer satisfies:

(a)   the requirements in section 4.1(1)(a) and (b) and the requirements in section 4.1(1)(c) or section 4.3(1)(a)(i), or

(b)   the requirements in sections 4.1(1)(b) and 4.2(1)(a) and (b).

(3)   No solicitor's, auditor's[23], accountant's, engineer's, appraiser's or other consent is required when an AIF is filed pursuant to this Policy Statement. They will be required with a short form prospectus in accordance with section 6.3(3).

5.4   *Alternative form of AIF* – An issuer that has securities registered with the SEC may satisfy the requirement for filing an AIF by filing a current annual report on Form 10-K or on Form 20-F filed with the SEC pursuant to the 1934 Act provided, in the case of a Canadian issuer filing a current annual report on Form 20-F, where a disclosure requirement of the Form 20-F refers to a requirement of the issuer's home country, Canadian disclosure requirements shall apply. Issuers filing Forms 10-K or 20-F shall also file a document cross-referencing the Form 10-K or 20-F disclosure to the items of the Contents of AIF in Appendix A. Canadian issuers filing Forms 10-K or 20-F shall file the relevant form within the earlier of the time periods required by this policy statement and by the 1934 Act. Foreign issuers filing Forms 10-K or Forms 20-F shall file the relevant form within the time period required by the 1934 Act.[24]

---

22   The accelerated review procedure contemplated by this paragraph will not be extended to issuers if the Securities Regulatory Authorities consider that an issuer is abusing the provision. For example, the Securities Regulatory Authorities will consider it abusive if an issuer, on more than one occasion, requests expedited review and no short form prospectus is filed.

23   There is no regulatory requirement for auditor involvement with respect to the preparation of an AIF. However, reporting issuers may choose to involve their auditors. The auditing profession's standards may require limited auditor involvement in certain circumstances. In addition, in order to be able to provide the necessary consent letter on a short form prospectus, an auditor will be required to comply with the requirements of the CICA Handbook and the Securities Legislation of the Jurisdictions in which the AIF is filed.

24   Foreign issuers should refer to the Securities Legislation of each Jurisdiction for the provisions relating to the reconciliation of financial statements to Canadian GAAP in a prospectus. These provisions apply to a preliminary short form prospectus and a short form prospectus whether or not the foreign issuer is satisfying the requirement for filing an AIF by filing a current annual report on Form 10-K or on Form 20-F filed with the SEC pursuant to the 1934 Act. The issuer may include the reconciliation of its financial statements to Canadian GAAP in the notes to its financial statements or in its short form prospectus. Where an issuer does not include this information in the notes to its financial statements, the issuer shall provide the information or discussion required in footnotes (36) and (37) in its short form prospectus.

PART 6   SHORT FORM PROSPECTUS

6.1   Form of prospectus and disclosure requirements

(1)   In any Jurisdiction in which it satisfies the applicable eligibility criteria of part 4, an issuer may, at its option, qualify its securities for distribution on its own behalf or on behalf of a Selling Security Holder by filing with the Securities Regulatory Authority of that Jurisdiction a short form prospectus prepared and certified in accordance with Appendix B.

(2)   Any statement contained in a document incorporated or deemed to be incorporated by reference into a short form prospectus shall be deemed to be modified or superseded, for purposes of the short form prospectus, to the extent that a statement contained in the short form prospectus or in any other subsequently filed document that also is or is deemed to be incorporated by reference into the short form prospectus modifies or replaces that statement. The modifying or superseding statement need not state that it has modified or superseded a prior statement or include any other information set forth in the document that it modifies or supersedes. The making of a modifying or superseding statement shall not be deemed an admission for any purposes that the modified or superseded statement, when made, constituted a misrepresentation, an untrue statement of a material fact or an omission to state a material fact that is required to be stated or that is necessary to make a statement not misleading in light of the circumstances in which it was made. Any statement so modified or superseded shall not be deemed in its unmodified or superseded form to constitute part of the short form prospectus.

(3)   Except to the extent provided in section 6.1(2), nothing in this Policy Statement shall be construed to provide relief from liability arising under the provisions of the Securities Legislation of any Jurisdiction in which the short form prospectus is filed where the short form prospectus contains an untrue statement of a material fact or omits to state a material fact that is required to be stated therein or that is necessary to make a statement not misleading in light of the circumstances in which it was made.

(4)   This Policy Statement does not alter the requirements of the Securities Legislation of any Jurisdiction in which a distribution of securities is effected under the POP System to:

(a)   amend a prospectus if the issuer increases the amount of securities being offered or alters the terms and conditions of the securities being offered; and

(b)   file a new preliminary prospectus and prospectus where necessary.

(5)   Notwithstanding the provisions of item 16 of Appendix B regarding documents incorporated by reference, an amendment to a preliminary short form prospectus must be filed where a material adverse change occurs after a receipt for the preliminary short form prospectus has been issued and before the receipt for the short form prospectus is issued, and an amendment to a short form prospectus must be filed where a material change occurs after a receipt for the short form prospectus has been issued but prior to completion of the distribution under the short form prospectus. Where an amendment to a preliminary short form prospectus or short form prospectus is required to be filed, the issuer shall file a prospectus amendment, together with supporting documents, with the applicable Securities Regulatory Authorities and deliver the prospectus amendment in accordance with the applicable Securities Legislation.

(6)   An issuer is not entitled to file a confidential material change report or to maintain an already filed material change report as confidential during the distribution period of securities pursuant to a short form prospectus unless all activities related to the distribution cease until

(a)   the material change is generally disclosed; or

(b)   the decision to implement the material change has been rejected and the issuer has so notified the Applicable Regulator of each Jurisdiction where the confidential material change report was filed.

(7)   Subject to section 6.1(9), Non-Convertible debt or Non-Convertible preferred shares may be offered for cash at non-fixed prices provided, at the time of the filing of the preliminary short form prospectus, the securities

   (a) have received an Approved Rating, on a provisional basis, from at least one Approved Rating Organization; and

   (b) have not received a provisional or final rating lower than an Approved Rating from any Approved Rating Organization.

(8)   Subject to section 6.1(9), where securities are offered for cash under a short form prospectus, the price at which these securities may be distributed may be decreased from the initial public offering price fixed in the short form prospectus and thereafter changed, from time to time, to an amount not greater than the initial public offering price, without the filing of an amendment to the short form prospectus to reflect the change, provided

   (a) the securities to be distributed under the short form prospectus are distributed through an underwriter or underwriters that have agreed to underwrite the distribution of the securities on a firm commitment basis;

   (b) the proceeds to be received by the issuer and/or any Selling Security Holder are fixed in the short form prospectus; and

   (c) the underwriters have made a bona fide effort to sell all of the securities distributed under the short form prospectus at the initial public offering price fixed in the short form prospectus.

(9)   The methods of distribution referred to in sections 6.1(7) and 6.1(8) may not be used for rights offerings.

6.2   *Use of short form prospectus disclosure in securities exchange take-over bid circulars*

(1)   Where a take-over bid provides that the consideration for the securities of the offeree issuer is to be, in whole or in part, securities of an issuer (which issuer may or may not be the offeror) that is eligible to participate in or use the POP System pursuant to sections 4.1, 4.2 or 4.3(1)(a), the offeror may comply with the take-over bid circular requirement of the Securities Legislation of a Jurisdiction to include information prescribed by the form of prospectus appropriate for the issuer whose securities are being offered in exchange for the securities of the offeree issuer, by including the information to be included in a short form prospectus under this Policy Statement in the take-over bid circular to be sent to security holders and filed in that Jurisdiction. For the purpose of this provision, any eligibility criteria that are required to be satisfied at the time of filing the preliminary short form prospectus shall be satisfied if they are met at the time of filing the take-over bid circular.

(2)   Where a securities exchange take-over bid contemplated in (1) above is material[25] to the offeror, include in the take-over bid circular

   (a) the pro forma financial statements required under paragraph (1)(c) and (d) of item 13 of Appendix B to which shall be attached the report referred to in paragraph (4) of that item, and

   (b) the additional information required under paragraph (1)(e) and (f) of item 13 of Appendix B,

   as if the references in those paragraphs to the issuer and the acquired business were references to the offeror and the offeree, respectively.

(3)   The provisions of item 13 of Appendix B apply with necessary changes to a securities exchange take-over bid contemplated in (1) above where the securities exchange take-over bid would result in the offeror making the

---

25 The discussion of the concept of materiality set out in paragraph (2) of item 13 of Appendix B applies with necessary changes in this context. Issuers should note that the Québec Securities Legislation does not limit the requirement for pro forma financial statements to those situations where the take-over bid is material to the offeror.

acquisition of a business and that acquisition is material[26] to the offeror.

(4)   The provisions of (1) above apply with necessary changes to an issuer bid circular in respect of an issuer bid by an issuer for securities of that issuer, where the consideration for those securities is to be, in whole or in part, securities of an issuer that is eligible to participate in or use the POP System pursuant to sections 4.1, 4.2 or 4.3(1)(a).

6.3   *Filing procedures for short form prospectus*

(1)   A preliminary short form prospectus and short form prospectus and supporting documents filed in

(a) only one Jurisdiction, shall be subject to the relevant provisions of the short form prospectus review procedures contained in part 2 of NPS 1, or

(b) more than one Jurisdiction, shall be subject to the short form prospectus review procedures contained in part 2 or 3 of NPS 1,

except in the circumstances described in section 9.3(2).[27]

(2)   Each preliminary short form prospectus and short form prospectus filed under this Policy Statement or under the Securities Legislation and Securities Requirements of the Province of Québec shall be submitted in the number of copies specified for each Jurisdiction in the "Table of Documents to be filed in respect of the Clearance of National Issues" forming part of NPS 1 and shall be accompanied by the supporting documents in the number of copies indicated in that table.

(3)   Where any solicitor, auditor, accountant, engineer, appraiser or any other Person whose profession gives authority to a statement made by that Person is named

(a) in a short form prospectus or a document specifically incorporated by reference in a short form prospectus as having prepared or certified any part of that document, or

(b) as having prepared or certified a report or valuation used in a short form prospectus or in a document specifically incorporated by reference into a short form prospectus,

the written consent of the Person to being so named and to that use of the report or valuation shall be filed no later than the time the short form prospectus is filed. In the Jurisdictions where specific provisions as to consent exist in the Securities Legislation, those provisions shall apply with necessary changes to the consent as if it were required to be filed pursuant to those specific provisions.[28]

(4)   Where financial statements included or incorporated by reference in a short form prospectus relate to any part of an issuer's financial year subsequent to the ending date of its last audited financial year, the issuer shall file an auditors' comfort letter in accordance with the requirements of the Securities Legislation of the Jurisdiction in which the short form prospectus is being filed.

(5)   Where a preliminary short form prospectus is filed in respect of a proposed distribution of preferred shares or debt having a term to maturity in excess of one year, the issuer, on its own behalf or on behalf of a Selling Security

---

26 See paragraph (2) of item 13 of Appendix B for a discussion of the concept of materiality in the context of a business acquisition.

27 Where the Securities Legislation of a Jurisdiction requires that there be a specified period of time between the issuance of a receipt for a preliminary short form prospectus and the issuance of a receipt for a short form prospectus, the Implementation Order provides an exemption from that requirement.

28 Although the disclosure in a preliminary short form prospectus or short form prospectus of a rating in compliance with paragraph (5) of item 10 of Appendix B is expertized information, each Jurisdiction has taken steps, where necessary, to waive the requirement for an Approved Rating Organization to file a consent in connection with this disclosure requirement.

Holder, shall file with the preliminary short form prospectus an explanation of the manner by which the asset and earnings coverage ratios are calculated.

(6) If an issuer files a preliminary short form prospectus or a short form prospectus subsequent to its directors having approved the comparative audited annual financial statements for its last completed financial year but prior to these comparative audited annual financial statements having been filed by the issuer pursuant to the continuous disclosure requirements of the Securities Legislation in the Jurisdictions in which the preliminary short form prospectus or short form prospectus is filed, the issuer will be required to:

(a) issue and file a press release summarizing or setting out the comparative audited annual financial statements,

(b) file the comparative audited annual financial statements[29] pursuant to the continuous disclosure requirements regarding annual financial statements of the Securities Legislation in the Jurisdictions in which the preliminary short form prospectus or short form prospectus is filed, and

(c) incorporate by reference in the preliminary short form prospectus and short form prospectus the comparative audited annual financial statements,

before a receipt will be issued for its preliminary short form prospectus to short form prospectus.[30]

(7) If an issuer files a short form prospectus prior to its directors having approved the comparative audited annual financial statements for its last completed financial year, the issuer may rely upon the interim financial statements for the third quarter of that financial year provided the issuer is in compliance with the continuous disclosure requirements of the Securities Legislation in each of the Jurisdictions in which the short form prospectus is filed.[31]

(8) The receipt for a short form prospectus relating to securities underwritten on a firm commitment basis, other than securities to be distributed continuously, will not be issued unless the short form prospectus indicates that the securities are to be taken up by the underwriter, if at all, on or before a date not later than six weeks after the date of the final receipt.[32]

(9) Where a minimum amount of funds are required by an issuer, the receipt for a short form prospectus relating to securities proposed to be distributed on a best efforts basis, other than securities to be distributed continuously,

29 An issuer required to file its comparative audited annual financial statements under this paragraph is not required to comply with the requirements of the Securities Legislation of a Jurisdiction to send these statements concurrently to holders of its securities and, in British Columbia, to file written confirmation of having sent these statements, provided the financial statements are sent within the time periods and in accordance with all the other provisions otherwise contemplated by the continuous disclosure requirements of the Securities Legislation of each Jurisdiction for the filing and sending of an issuer's comparative audited annual financial statements and the filing of the written confirmation of sending in British Columbia.

30 Issuers are reminded of their obligation to disclose all material facts relating to the securities to be distributed. For example, where there have been significant variations in an issuer's financial results, the issuer is expected to discuss the variations in its prospectus.

31 Issuers are reminded of their obligation to disclose all material facts relating to the securities to be distributed.

32 Where the Securities Legislation of a Jurisdiction requires that a prospectus indicate that the securities must be taken up by the underwriter within a period that is different than the period provided under this Policy Statement, each Jurisdiction has taken appropriate steps to implement the requirement of the Policy Statement.

will not be issued unless the short form prospectus indicates that the offering will cease if the minimum amount of funds is not subscribed within ninety days.[33]

PART 7 DISCRETIONARY POWERS

7.1 *AIF* – Notwithstanding that an issuer may satisfy the applicable eligibility criteria of part 4, the Applicable Regulator in any Jurisdiction where the issuer satisfies those criteria may, after the issuer has filed its initial AIF, advise the issuer and all other Jurisdictions that it will not accept the Initial AIF for filing pursuant to this Policy Statement. In this case, the Applicable Regulator will provide reasons for its decision and an opportunity for the issuer to be heard.

7.2 *Short form prospectus* – Notwithstanding that an issuer has received notice that its AIF was accepted for filing as contemplated in section 5.1 or 5.2(1) or (2), the Applicable Regulator in any Jurisdiction where the AIF has been so accepted may advise the issuer and all other Jurisdictions that it will not issue a receipt for a short form prospectus that subsequently may be filed by the issuer, on its own behalf or on behalf of a Selling Security Holder, pursuant to this Policy Statement.[34] This notification shall include the reasons that appear to the Applicable Regulator to constitute a basis under the Securities Legislation of its Jurisdiction for a refusal to issue a receipt for a short form prospectus and shall provide, in accordance with the applicable provisions of the Securities Legislation or otherwise, an opportunity for the issuer to be heard.

7.3 *Relief without filing a formal application* – Where an issuer anticipates not being in a position to comply with one or more of the provisions of this Policy Statement, other than the provisions of part 4 in respect of which a formal application must be made and a waiver issued pursuant to section 4.5, the issuer shall at or prior to the time of filing a preliminary short form prospectus so notify in writing the Applicable Regulator in each Jurisdiction in which the preliminary short form prospectus is to be filed[35] providing the reasons why the applicable Securities Regulatory Authority should grant relief. Relief shall be deemed to have been granted if a receipt in respect of the short form prospectus is issued.

PART 8 INFORMATION CIRCULAR

Any information circular required to be delivered to security holders with respect to an issuer that has a Current AIF filed with the Securities Regulatory Authorities pursuant to this Policy Statement must contain a statement describing the availability of the documents referred to in paragraph (1)(b) of item 8 in Appendix A.

PART 9 GENERAL PROVISIONS

9.1 *Effective date* – Compliance with this Policy Statement will be required for

(a) Renewal AIFs filed for financial years ended on or after December 31, 1992;

(b) Initial AIFs filed on or after March 1, 1993; and

(c) preliminary short form prospectuses filed on or after March 1, 1993.

Issuers may elect to file the documents referred to in paragraphs (a), (b) or (c) earlier than for the periods or on the dates specified in those paragraphs.

---

33 Where the Securities Legislation in a Jurisdiction requires that an offering may not continue for more than a specified period if the minimum amount of funds are not subscribed within that period and the specified period is different than the period provided under this Policy Statement, each Jurisdiction has taken appropriate steps to implement the requirement of the Policy Statement.

34 This provision does not in any way restrict the ability of the Applicable Regulator, under the provisions of the Securities Legislation of a Jurisdiction, to exercise its discretion not to issue a receipt in respect of a prospectus that has been filed with the Securities Regulatory Authority of that Jurisdiction.

35 The Securities Legislation and Securities Requirements of the Province of Québec require that a formal application for exemption be filed in all cases where an issuer does not anticipate complying with the requirements of the Securities Legislation and Securities Requirements of that Jurisdiction relating to the simplified prospectus procedure.

9.2 Transition

(1) For purposes of section 9.1(a), an issuer's first AIF filed in a Jurisdiction under this Policy Statement is a Renewal AIF, where the issuer has filed an annual information form that has been accepted for filing under the prompt offering qualification system of that Jurisdiction in respect of the financial year immediately preceding the financial year in respect of which the first AIF is filed under this Policy Statement.

(2) Prior to filing its first AIF under section 9.1(a), an issuer shall be entitled to use as its Current AIF in a Jurisdiction the annual information form that has been accepted for filing under the prompt offering qualification system of that Jurisdiction for the financial year immediately preceding the financial year applicable to it under section 9.1(a).

(3) An issuer that, prior to the time compliance with this Policy Statement is required or prior to the issuer voluntarily complying with this Policy Statement, was eligible to participate in the prompt offering qualification system in a Jurisdiction pursuant to an exemption, ruling, order, decision or other action of the Applicable Regulator of the Jurisdiction is eligible to use the POP System in that Jurisdiction in reliance on that waiver after compliance with this Policy Statement is required or voluntarily undertaken, unless otherwise stated in the exemption, ruling, order, decision or other action of the Applicable Regulator.

9.3 Application of other policy statements

(1) Unless inconsistent, the applicable provisions of national and local policy statements in a Jurisdiction apply to the issuance of securities by way of a short form prospectus in that Jurisdiction. In addition, certain provisions of the Securities Legislation or Securities Requirements in effect in one or more Jurisdictions may be repeated in this Policy Statement because they are not found in the provisions of the Securities Legislation or Securities Requirements of one or more other Jurisdictions.

(2) A distribution of derivative securities by an issuer under a short form prospectus shall be subject to the review procedures contained in part 1 of NPS 1 until specific review procedures for the distribution of derivative securities are included in other Securities Requirements. Issuers who are uncertain as to whether securities that they propose to issue are derivative securities should consult with the Applicable Regulator in each Jurisdiction in which they propose to issue those securities.

NATIONAL POLICY STATEMENT NO. 47
APPENDIX A
AIF

GUIDELINES

(1) The AIF is intended to provide relevant background material essential to a proper understanding of the nature of the issuer, its operations, and prospects for the future.

(2) The focus of the AIF disclosure shall be on the issuer. There is no requirement to provide extensive discussion of factors external to the issuer.

(3) Issuers are required to disclose information that is material. Materiality is a matter of judgement in particular circumstances, and should generally be determined in relation to an item's significance to investors, analysts and other users of the information. An item of information, or an aggregate of items, is considered material if it is probable that its omission or misstatement would influence or change a decision with respect to the issuer. In determining whether information is material, an issuer shall take into account both quantitative and qualitative factors. While this concept of materiality is broader than the definition of "material change" contained in the Securities Legislation of any Jurisdiction, it is consistent with the financial reporting notion of materiality contained in the CICA Handbook.

(4) Issuers are required to discuss certain forward-looking information. A disclosure duty exists where a trend, commitment, event or uncertainty is both presently

known to management and reasonably expected to have a material impact on the issuer's business, financial condition or results of operations. A discussion of forward-looking information based on the issuer's expectations as of the date of the AIF is required.

(5)   Issuers are encouraged, but not required, to supply other forward-looking information. Optional forward-looking disclosure involves anticipating a future trend or event or anticipating a less predictable impact of a known event, trend or uncertainty. This other forward-looking information is to be distinguished from presently known information that is reasonably expected to have a material impact on future operating results, such as known future increases in costs of labour or materials, which information is required to be disclosed.

(6)   Although information provided in the AIF may involve some discussion or disclosure of forward looking information, these provisions do not call for a forecast or projection as defined in the CICA Handbook. In the event that an issuer chooses to provide a forecast or projection, National Policy Statement No. 48 must be complied with.

INSTRUCTIONS

(1)   Any information required in the AIF may be incorporated by reference in the AIF. Where information is incorporated by reference in an AIF, the referenced document shall be clearly identified and the information incorporated by reference shall be identified by page, caption, paragraph or otherwise.

(2)   The AIF shall be dated no earlier than the date of the auditor's report on the annual financial year covered by the AIF and all disclosures in, or incorporated by reference in, the AIF shall be no later than that date. The date of the AIF shall appear on the cover page of the document.

(3)   Unless otherwise specified, information in an Initial AIF shall be presented

   (a) as at the end of the issuer's most recently completed financial year, provided the issuer met the market value requirement described in section 4.1(2)(b)(i) during the last calendar month of that year;

   (b) in the case of an issuer referred to in section 4.2, as at the end of the most recently completed financial year of the issuer whether or not the issuer met the market value requirement during the last calendar month of that year; or

   (c) in the case of an issuer referred to in section 4.3(1)(a), as at the end of the most recently completed financial year of the issuer even though the issuer is not required to meet any market value requirement under this Policy Statement.

   Unless otherwise specified, information in a Renewal AIF shall be presented as at the end of the most recently completed financial year of the issuer. Where material events or conditions arise prior to the date of the AIF this information shall be included in the AIF.

(4)   The segmented information required in item 3 of this Appendix goes beyond the requirements of the CICA Handbook. However, the required information is predicated on the CICA disclosure framework.

(5)   All references to the issuer in items 2 to 5 of this Appendix shall be to the issuer, its subsidiaries and Investees.

CONTENTS OF AIF

Item 1:   Incorporation

(1)   State the full corporate name of the issuer and the statute under which the issuer is incorporated, continued or organized. State whether the articles or other constating documents of the issuer have been amended and describe the substance of the amendments.

(2)   Provide a list of each subsidiary of the issuer as of the most recent financial year end, indicating the place of incorporation, continuance, or organization and stating separately the percentage of voting securities beneficially owned or over which control or direction is exercised, by the issuer. Also disclose the percentage of each class of non-voting securities owned. The list of subsidiaries may exclude

any subsidiary of an issuer whose total assets do not constitute more than 10% of the consolidated assets of the issuer at the most recent financial year end and whose total revenues do not constitute more than 10% of the consolidated revenues of the issuer for the most recently completed financial year, provided the excluded subsidiaries, in the aggregate, represent less than 30% of total consolidated assets and total consolidated revenues of the issuer.

Item 2: General Development of the Business

Briefly describe the business of the issuer. This description shall encompass the general development of the business of the issuer over the last five years. This discussion shall include only major events or conditions that have influenced the general development of the business. Changes in the business that are expected shall also be discussed.

Item 3: Narrative Description of the Business

(1) Describe the business with reference to the dominant industry segment of the issuer or each reportable industry segment of the issuer. The description shall focus upon reportable industry segments as defined in the CICA Handbook and the issuer's business in general. The disclosure for each industry segment of the issuer shall include the following information:

(a) with respect to principal products or services:

(i) a description of the principal products or services, the methods of distribution of these products or services, and their principal markets; and

(ii) for each of the last two completed financial years, the revenues for each category of principal products or services which accounts for 15% or more of total consolidated revenues for all segments for the applicable financial year, as dollar amounts or as percentages, derived from:

(A) sales to customers outside the consolidated entity, and

(B) sales or transfers to Investees

(see Schedule 1 to this Appendix for suggested format for presenting this segmented information);

(b) when sales made to or income received from one customer (by one or more segments) amount, in the aggregate, to 10% or more of consolidated revenues in either of the last two completed financial years, the number of such customers and the aggregate percentage of sales to or income from those customers; where it is known that a group of customers is under common control, the group shall be considered one customer;

(c) where more than 40% of an industry segment's sales are made to a geographic segment in either of the last two completed financial years, the geographic segment and the percentage of the industry segment's sales made to that geographic segment;

(d) when there has been a public announcement of the introduction of a new product or industry segment, the status of the product or segment;

(e) the sources and availability of raw materials;

(f) a description, including the importance, duration and effect on the segment, of identifiable intangible properties such as brand names, circulation, copyrights, franchises, licences, patents, software, subscription lists, and trademarks;

(g) the extent to which the business of the industry segment is seasonal;

(h) a description of any aspect of the issuer's business that may be affected in the current financial year by renegotiation or termination of contracts or sub-contracts;

(i) with respect to the natural resource operations of an issuer, other than oil and gas operations:

(i) the location, size and net interest in important properties and the nature of the right to hold or operate the properties as at the most recent financial year end,

(ii) reserves by deposit, identified as either in situ or mineable, and by category reporting proven, probable and possible reserves as at the most recent financial year end,

(iii) a reconciliation of reserves by category as at the financial year end immediately preceding the most recently completed financial year to the information furnished under (ii) above, including the effects of production, acquisition, discoveries, etc., and

(iv) the dollar amounts expended on exploration and development in the last two completed financial years;

(j) with respect to the oil and gas operations of an issuer:

(i) the number of wells the issuer has drilled or participated in, the number of these wells completed as oil wells and gas wells capable of production, and the number of dry holes expressed in each case as gross and net wells, during each of the last two financial years of the issuer,

(ii) important oil and gas properties, plants, facilities and installations owned, leased or held under option as at the most recent financial year end,

(iii) the location by province or state if in Canada or the United States and by country otherwise, of important producing wells and non-unitized wells capable of producing in which the issuer has an interest as at the most recent financial year end, with the interest expressed in terms of net wells, separately for oil wells and gas wells,

(iv) with respect to interests in properties on which there are no current reserves, the gross acreage in which the issuer has an interest as at the most recent financial year end and the issuer's net interest in the acreage and the geographical location of that acreage,

(v) the quantity and type of the estimated proved and developed reserves, and proved and undeveloped reserves on both a gross and net basis of crude oil, natural gas and natural gas liquids as at the most recent financial year end; where royalty rates are subject to noticeable variation, provide a brief discussion of these variations,

(vi) a reconciliation of the reserves as at the financial year end immediately preceding the most recent financial year to the reserve information furnished under (v) above, including the effects of production, acquisitions, discoveries, etc., and

(vii) the dollar amounts expended on exploration, including drilling, and on development for the last two financial years of the issuer;

(k) if estimates of reserves are represented as being based on estimates prepared or reviewed by an independent engineer or other qualified Person, identify the independent engineer or other qualified Person; the Applicable Regulator may request that a copy of the report of that engineer or other qualified Person be furnished as supplemental information and not as material filed as part of these requirements;

(l) with respect to bank operations of an issuer's business, the following:

(loan terminology referred to in this paragraph shall have the meaning attributed to those terms in the Guidelines for Canadian Chartered Banks, published by the Office of the Superintendent of Financial Institutions Canada, or its predecessor)

(i) non-performing loans

(A) dollar amount of non-accrual consumer loans by personal plan and credit card category as at the most recent financial year end,

(B) dollar amount of non-accrual loans by Canadian residents – residents elsewhere as at the most recent financial year end,

(C) in aggregate, for sovereign risk and private sector loans to banks and other entities, dollar amount of non-personal renegotiated reduced rate loans by Canadian residents – residents elsewhere as at the most recent financial year end in excess of the greater of:

(aa) 1/10 of 1% of the aggregate paid-in capital, contributed surplus and retained earnings of the bank at that time, and

(bb) $500,000,

(ii) other past due loans

dollar amount of loans 90-179 days past due and 180 days or more past due, separately, for loans by Canadian residents – residents elsewhere as at the most recent financial year end,

(iii) interest income

separately, interest income as reported for the most recently completed financial year for domestic and international non-accrual loans, renegotiated reduced rate loans, and other past due loans,

(iv) loans with provisions for doubtful credits

for sovereign risk and private sector loans to banks and other entities, dollar amount of loans with provision for doubtful credits other than general country risk provisions as at the most recent financial year end,

(v) restructured loans

(A) dollar amount of loans classified as restructured loans in the most recently completed financial year for loans by Canadian residents – residents elsewhere,

(B) dollar amount of loans classified as restructured loans in the most recently completed financial year listed by country for sovereign risk and private sector loans to banks and other entities,

(vi) foreign loans

(A) for Designated Countries, total claims for sovereign risk and private sector loans to banks and other entities by country as at the most recent financial year end,

(B) total sovereign risk claims by country for any other countries towards which provisions against claims have been established as at the most recent financial year end, and

(vii) allowance for credit losses

(A) dollar amount of specific provisions as at the most recent financial year end,

(B) dollar amount of provisions for doubtful credits as at the most recent financial year end,

(C) dollar amount of general country risk provisions for Designated Countries by country or countries, if the general provision is established on a basket of countries, as at the most recent financial year end;

(m) for trust, mortgage loan and credit union (caisse d'épargne et de crédit) operations of the issuer's business:

(i) interest income

separately, interest income for consumer, commercial, and residential mortgage loans as reported for the most recently completed financial year,

(ii) non-accrual loans

  (A) dollar amount of non-accrual consumer loans and residential mortgages as at the most recent financial year end,

  (B) dollar amount of other non-accrual loans as at the most recent financial year end, and

  (C) dollar amount of total non-accrual loans as at the most recent financial year end,

(iii) other past due loans

dollar amount of other past due loans as at the most recent financial year end,

(iv) provisions

dollar amount of provisions with respect to total non-accrual loans and total loans as at the most recent financial year end, and

(v) definition

the definition on non-accrual loans; and

(n) with respect to the principal properties of the issuer including, but not limited to, manufacturing plants, warehouses, service and retail outlets, offices and investment properties:

  (i) the location of each principal property

except that where issuers have numerous locations, such as retailers, the information may be presented on a regional basis by reporting the total number and capacity of properties for each region,

  (ii) the capacity in terms of floor space, output or other measures suitable for the respective industry,

  (iii) the general character including the purpose or principal use of properties and the state of the properties,

  (iv) the segment using the property and

  (v) how the property is held (e.g., owned freehold or otherwise, leased, or held subject to any major encumbrances) including a brief description of any major encumbrances against the property.

(2) With respect to the issuer's business in general, discuss the following matters and identify the industry segments affected:

(a) the competitive conditions in the principal markets in which the issuer operates, including an assessment of the issuer's competitive position if possible;

(b) the dollar amount spent by the issuer on research and development activities for the most recently completed financial year;

(c) the financial or operational effect of environmental protection requirements on the capital expenditures, earnings and competitive position of the issuer for the current financial year and any expected impact on future years;

(d) the number of employees, as at the most recent financial year end or as an average for the year, whichever is more relevant; and

(e) any risks associated with the foreign operations of the issuer and any dependence of one or more of the issuer's industry segments upon such foreign operations.

Item 4: Selected Consolidated Financial Information[36]

(1) Provide the following financial data for the issuer for the last five completed financial years, in summary form, accompanied by a discussion of those factors affecting the comparability of the data including discontinued operations,

---

36 Where an issuer is required to reconcile its financial statements to Canadian GAAP, the issuer may present the selected consolidated financial information on the basis of the accounting principles used in its primary financial statements. In that case, the issuer shall provide in accordance with Canadian GAAP any of the information required under this item that is reconciled to Canadian GAAP in its financial statements.

changes in accounting policies, significant acquisitions or disposals and major changes in the direction of the business:

(a) net sales or total revenues;

(b) income or loss before discontinued operations and extraordinary items, in total and on a per share and fully diluted per share basis calculated in accordance with the CICA Handbook;

(c) net income or loss, in total and on a per share and fully diluted per share basis calculated in accordance with the CICA Handbook;

(d) total assets;

(e) total long-term debt, retractable preferred shares and redeemable preferred shares (where the redemption privilege is required or expected to be exercised) from which there shall be deducted the amounts required or expected to be repaid, retracted or redeemed in the financial year immediately following the relevant financial year;

(f) cash dividends declared per share for each class of share; and

(g) such other information that the issuer believes would enhance an understanding of and would highlight other trends in financial condition and results of operations.

(2) For each of the last eight quarters ending with the most recently completed financial year, provide the information required in paragraph (1)(a), (b) and (c). If the issuer is only required to file six month interim financial statements, for each of the last four completed six month periods ending with the most recently completed financial year, provide the information required in paragraph (1)(a), (b) and (c).

(3) Describe any restriction that could prevent the issuer from paying dividends. Disclose the issuer's dividend policy and where there is an authorized intention to change the dividend policy in the near future, disclose the intended change in dividend policy.

Item 5: Management's Discussion and Analysis[37]

Incorporate by reference or reproduce the disclosure required by Schedule 2 to this Appendix. An issuer that has securities registered under the 1934 Act may satisfy the MD&A disclosure requirements of Schedule 2 to this Appendix by complying with the analogous requirements applicable to it under the 1934 Act.

Item 6: Market for Securities

Identify the exchange(s) or quotation system(s) on which the issuer's securities are listed and posted for trading or quoted.

Item 7: Directors and Officers

(1) List the names and municipality of residence for all the directors and officers of the issuer and indicate their respective principal occupations within the five preceding years.

(2) State the period or periods during which each director has served as a director and state when the term of office of each director will expire.

(3) State the percentage of securities of each class of voting securities of the issuer or any of its subsidiaries beneficially owned, directly or indirectly, or over which control or direction is exercised by all directors and senior officers of the issuer as a group.

(4) State whether the issuer has an executive committee or is required to have an audit committee, and, if so, identify those directors who are members of each of those committees.

---

37 Where an issuer is required to reconcile its financial statements to Canadian GAAP, the discussion in the issuer's MD&A shall focus on its primary financial statements. The issuer shall include in its MD&A a reference to the reconciliation and a discussion of any aspects of the difference between the foreign accounting principles applied and Canadian GAAP not discussed in the financial statement reconciliation that the issuer believes is necessary for an understanding of the financial statements as a whole.

Item 8: Additional Information

(1) Include a statement, or if the issuer is filing an annual report on Form 10-K or 20-F pursuant to section 5.4 of this Policy Statement then file an undertaking with the Applicable Regulator of the relevant Jurisdiction, to the effect that the issuer shall provide to any Person, upon request to the secretary of the issuer:

(a) when the securities of the issuer are in the course of a distribution pursuant to a short form prospectus or a preliminary short form prospectus has been filed in respect of a distribution of its securities,

(i) one copy of the AIF of the issuer, together with one copy of any document, or the pertinent pages of any document, incorporated by reference in the AIF,

(ii) one copy of the comparative financial statements of the issuer for its most recently completed financial year together with the accompanying report of the auditor and one copy of any interim financial statements of the issuer subsequent to the financial statements for its most recently completed financial year,

(iii) one copy of the information circular of the issuer in respect of its most recent annual meeting of shareholders that involved the election of directors or one copy of any annual filing prepared in lieu of that information circular, as appropriate, and

(iv) one copy of any other documents that are incorporated by reference into the preliminary short form prospectus or the short form prospectus and are not required to be provided under (i) to (iii) above; or

(b) at any other time, one copy of any other documents referred to in (1)(a)(i), (ii) and (iii) above, provided the issuer may require the payment of a reasonable charge if the request is made by a Person who is not a security holder of the issuer.

(2) Include a statement to the effect that additional information including directors' and officers' remuneration and indebtedness, principal holders of the issuer's securities, options to purchase securities and interests of insiders in material transactions, where applicable, is contained in the issuer's information circular for its most recent annual meeting of shareholders that involved the election of directors, and that additional financial information is provided in the issuer's comparative financial statements for its most recently completed financial year.

NATIONAL POLICY STATEMENT NO. 47
SCHEDULE 1
TO APPENDIX A
INDUSTRY SEGMENTS

The table set forth below is illustrative of the format that might be used for presenting the segment information required by item 3(1)(a) regarding industry segments and classes of similar products or services.

Revenue by Industry Segments and
Classes of Products or Services

Year	XXX2		XXX1	
	Third party customers	Investees	Third party customers	Investees
Industry segment A:				
Class of product 1				
Class of product 2				
Segment subtotal				

Industry segment B:
Class of product 1   _____ _____   _____ _____
Class of product 2   _____ _____   _____ _____
Segment subtotal   _____ _____   _____ _____

Other revenues   _____ _____   _____ _____

Totals by customer type _____ _____   _____ _____
                         ↳   ↳

Sales from third party
customers as above   _____   _____

Total consolidated
revenues   _____   _____

NATIONAL POLICY STATEMENT NO. 47
SCHEDULE 2 TO
APPENDIX A
MD&A

INSTRUCTIONS

(1)   MD&A is supplemental analysis and explanation that accompanies but does not form part of the financial statements. MD&A provides management with the opportunity to explain in narrative form its current financial situation and future prospects. MD&A is intended to give the investor the ability to look at the issuer through the eyes of management by providing both a historical and prospective analysis of the business of the issuer. MD&A requirements ask management to discuss the dynamics of the business and to analyze the financial statements. Coupled with the financial statements this information should allow investors to assess an issuer's performance and future prospects.

(2)   Known material trends, commitments, events or uncertainties that are reasonably expected to have a material impact on the issuer's business, financial condition or results of operations are to be disclosed. The focus of MD&A is on information about the financial condition of an issuer as well as its operations with particular emphasis on liquidity and Capital Resources. Sufficient information on risks and uncertainties should be provided given the rapidly changing economic environment within which most issuers operate.

(3)   To allow issuers to discuss their business in the manner most appropriate to their individual circumstances, to encourage flexibility and to avoid boilerplate, the MD&A form is intentionally general and contains a minimum of specific instructions.

CONTENTS OF MD&A

Item 1:   General

(1)   Discuss and compare the issuer's financial condition, changes in financial condition and results of operations for the last two completed financial years. Provide any information necessary to understand this discussion and comparison. Where a discussion of information related to a segment or other division of the business would be appropriate or necessary to an understanding of such business, focus the discussion on each relevant, reportable segment or other division of the business and on the issuer as a whole. In making this determination consideration should be given to whether any segment or other division of the business has a disproportionate effect on revenues, profitability or cash needs; or whether there are legal or other restrictions upon the free flow of funds from one segment, subsidiary or division of the issuer to others; or whether known trends, demands, commitments, events or uncertainties within a segment are reasonably likely to have an effect on the business as a whole. The discussion should include internal factors as well as relevant economic and industry factors affecting the issuer.

(2)   The discussion and analysis shall focus on the financial statements and on financial, operational and other data that the issuer believes will enhance a reader's understanding of the issuer's financial condition, changes in financial condition and results of operations.

(3) Issuers need only include information in their discussion and analysis that is available to the issuer without undue effort or expense and that does not clearly appear in the issuer's financial statements. The discussion and analysis should principally explain why changes have or have not occurred in the financial condition and results of operations of the issuer. This should include a discussion of the effect of discontinued operations, extraordinary items and changes in accounting policies where these items have had or are expected to have an effect on the financial condition and results of operations of the issuer. Numerical data included in or readily calculable from the financial statements and reports need not be repeated in the discussion. For example, where it is clear from the comparative financial statements what the amount of increase or decrease in revenues or the respective percentage change would be from the prior year, it is not necessary to include this information in the discussion since it is readily calculable.

(4) Describe the causes for changes in the financial statements from year to year to the extent necessary to understand the business as a whole. An overall analysis of causes affecting more than one item will be sufficient.

(5) Disclose information on risks and uncertainties facing the issuer necessary for an understanding of the issuer's financial condition, changes in financial condition and results of operations. The emphasis should be on disclosing risks and uncertainties likely to be factors within the next two financial years.

(6) Discuss and analyze risks, events and uncertainties that would cause reported financial information not necessarily to be indicative of future operating results or of future financial condition. This would include descriptions and amounts of

(a) matters that would have an impact on future operations and have not had an impact in the past;

(b) matters that have had an impact on reported operations and are not expected to have an impact upon future operations.

(7) Describe any changes in the accounting policies of the issuer adopted subsequent to its most recent financial year end or any changes in its accounting policies that are known to the issuer but that the issuer has not yet implemented, including those resulting from a change in an accounting standard, or the issuance of a new accounting standard, that does not require adoption until some future date. Disclose, if known, the estimated effect on the financial statements of the implementation of any changes in the accounting policies described. Where the estimated effect is not known, provide a statement to that effect.

(8) Provide information about the nature and magnitude of financial instruments and their effect on the issuer's liquidity, Capital Resources and results of operations. At the present time there is no widely accepted definition of financial instruments. Accounting standard setting bodies in several countries are working on projects that will define financial instruments and recommend appropriate accounting and disclosure requirements in this area. Information about financial instruments may be important to gaining an understanding of the issuer's liquidity, Capital Resources and results of operations. Financial instruments include financing instruments (debt and equity instruments), asset backed securities (e.g. mortgage backed securities, repurchase agreements) and hedging instruments (e.g. future contracts, options and swaps). These categories and examples are not exhaustive and judgement must be used to identify other financial instruments.

(9) When an issuer intends to proceed with a business acquisition or disposition or asset acquisition or disposition not in the normal course of operations that will have a material effect on its future financial condition or results of operations, the transaction and its effect should be discussed as part of MD&A. Disclosure must be made when a decision to proceed with the transaction has been made by the issuer's board of directors or by senior management with the expectation of concurrence from the board of directors. If this disclosure is considered unduly detrimental to the issuer, confidentiality may be requested in conjunction with a confidential filing pursuant to specific provisions of the Securities Legislation in each Jurisdiction in which the AIF is to be filed.

Item 2: Liquidity and Capital Resources

(1)   Discussions of liquidity and Capital Resources may be combined whenever this facilitates the discussion. The discussion of liquidity shall be on both a historical and prospective basis in the context of the issuer's business (e.g., a discussion of working capital may be appropriate for certain manufacturing, industrial or related operations but might be inappropriate for a financial institution or public utility) and shall focus on the ability of the issuer to generate adequate amounts of cash and cash equivalents when needed. The discussion of liquidity and Capital Resources should focus on both short term and long term needs. Generally, short-term liquidity and short-term Capital Resources relate to cash needs for the next 12 months. This discussion should encompass matters such as the issuer's need to settle obligations as they mature and to maintain capacity to provide for planned growth.

(2)   With respect to the issuer's liquidity,

(a) identify any known trends or expected fluctuations in the issuer's liquidity, taking into account known demands, commitments, events or uncertainties; if a deficiency is identified indicate the course of action that has been taken or is proposed to be taken to remedy the deficiency;

(b) describe those balance sheet conditions or income or cash flow items that the issuer believes may be indicators of its liquidity condition;

(c) disclose the requirements relating to working capital items (e.g., where significant quantities of inventory are required to be carried to meet rapid delivery requirements of customers or where extended payment terms have been provided to customers);

(d) disclose the nature and extent of legal or practical restrictions on the ability of subsidiaries to transfer funds to the issuer; disclose the impact these restrictions have had and are expected to have on the ability of the issuer to meet its obligations; and

(e) if the issuer is in arrears on the payment of dividends, interest, or principal payment on borrowings, disclose this fact and provide details; if the issuer is in default on any debt covenants at the present time or was in default during the most recently completed financial year, disclose information concerning the default and the method or anticipated method of curing the default.

(3)   With respect to the issuer's Capital Resources,

(a) describe and quantify commitments for capital expenditures as of the end of the most recently completed financial year, and indicate the general purpose of these commitments and the anticipated source of funds needed to fulfil these commitments; also quantify expenditures that are necessary but not yet committed to meet plans discussed under MD&A or elsewhere in the AIF; and

(b) describe any known trends, favourable or unfavourable, in the issuer's Capital Resources; indicate any expected changes in the mix and relative cost of these resources; briefly discuss other sources of financing that have been arranged but not yet utilized.

Item 3: Results of Operations

(1)   Describe any unusual or infrequent events or transactions or any significant economic changes that materially affect income or loss from continuing operations and the extent to which income or loss from continuing operations was affected. Also disclose any other significant components of revenue or expense necessary to understand the results of operations.

(2)   Describe any known trends or uncertainties that have had or that the issuer reasonably expects will have a favourable or unfavourable impact on net sales or revenues or income or loss from continuing operations. If the issuer knows of events that are expected to cause a change in the relationship between costs and revenues (such as known future changes in costs of labour or materials or price changes or inventory adjustments), the change in the relationship shall be disclosed.

(3)   Provide a narrative discussion of the extent to which any changes in net sales or revenues are attributable to changes in selling prices or to changes in the volume or quantity of goods or services being sold or the introduction of new products or services.

(4)   Discuss briefly any impact of inflation and specific price changes on the issuer's net sales and revenues and on income or loss from continuing operations. For purposes of the discussion, no specific numerical financial data need be presented.

NATIONAL POLICY STATEMENT NO. 47
APPENDIX B
SHORT FORM PROSPECTUS

CONTENTS OF SHORT FROM PROSPECTUS

Item 1:   Legends

(1)   Every preliminary short form prospectus shall have printed in red ink on the outside front cover page the following legend or any variation as the Applicable Regulator in the issuer's Principal Jurisdiction may permit:

> This is a preliminary short form prospectus relating to these securities, a copy of which has been filed with [insert name of each Jurisdiction in which the preliminary short form prospectus has been filed] but which has not yet become final for the purpose of a distribution or a distribution to the public. Information contained herein is subject to completion or amendment. These securities may not be sold to, nor may offers to buy be accepted from, residents of such jurisdictions prior to the time a receipt for the final short form prospectus is obtained from the appropriate securities commission or other regulatory authority.

(2)   Every preliminary short form prospectus and short form prospectus shall contain the following legends on the cover page:

> This short form prospectus constitutes a public offering of these securities only in those jurisdictions where they may be lawfully offered for sale and therein only by persons permitted to sell such securities. No securities commission or similar authority in Canada has in any way passed upon the merits of the securities offered hereunder and any representation to the contrary is an offence.

> Information has been incorporated by reference in this prospectus from documents filed with securities commissions or similar authorities in Canada. Copies of the documents incorporated herein by reference may be obtained on request without charge from the secretary of the issuer at [insert complete address and telephone No.]. [insert if the offering is made in Québec – "For the purpose of the Province of Québec, this simplified prospectus contains information to be completed by consulting the permanent information record A copy of the permanent information record may be obtained from the secretary of the issuer at the above-mentioned address and telephone no."].

Item 2:   Distribution Spread

(1)   The information called for by the following table shall be given, in substantially the tabular form indicated, on the cover page of the short form prospectus as to all securities being offered for cash (estimate amounts, if necessary). For non-fixed price offerings that are being made on a best efforts basis, disclosure of the information called for by the table may be set forth as a percentage or a range of percentages and need not be set forth in tabular form.

	Price to public	Underwriting discounts or commissions	Proceeds to issuer or selling security holders*
Per Unit			
Total			

* Before deducting expenses of issue estimated at $

(2)　In the case of a non-fixed price offering of Non-Convertible debt or Non-Convertible preferred shares permitted by this Policy Statement, disclose on the cover page of the short form prospectus:

　　(a)　the information required in paragraph (4) of item 7 of this Appendix; and

　　(b)　the net proceeds or, where applicable, in the case of an offering to be made on a best efforts basis, the minimum amount of net proceeds to be received by the issuer or Selling Security Holder.

(3)　Where an issuer, underwriter or Selling Security Holder wishes to be able to decrease the price at which securities are offered for cash from the initial public offering price fixed in the short form prospectus and thereafter change, from time to time, the price at which securities are distributed under the short form prospectus in accordance with the procedures permitted by this Policy Statement, disclose on the cover page of the short form prospectus the information required in paragraph (4) of item 10 of this Appendix.

Item 3:　Name of Issuer

State the full corporate name of the issuer and the address of its head office and principal place of business.

Item 4:　Summary Description of Business

Provide a brief summary of the business carried on and intended to be carried on by the issuer and its subsidiaries.

Item 5:　Share and Loan Capital Structure

Describe any material change in, and the effect thereof on, the share and loan capital of the issuer, on a consolidated basis, since the date of the comparative financial statements for the issuer's most recently completed financial year filed with the Securities Regulatory Authorities.

Item 6:　Use of Proceeds

(1)　State the estimated net proceeds to be received by the issuer, or in the case of a non-fixed price offering to be made on a best efforts basis, the minimum amount of net proceeds to be received by the issuer, from the sale of the securities to be offered, the principal purposes for which the net proceeds, or minimum amount of net proceeds, as the case may be, are intended to be used and the approximate amount intended to be used for each purpose.

(2)　Where disclosure is required pursuant to item 15 of this Appendix, provide the disclosure relating to use of proceeds required by the applicable form for a long form prospectus under the Securities Legislation of each Jurisdiction in which the short form prospectus is filed.

Item 7:　Plan of Distribution

(1)　If the securities being offered are to be sold through underwriters, give the names of the underwriters, state briefly the nature of the underwriters' obligation, including the particulars of any "market out" clause, to take up and pay for the securities and indicate the date by which the underwriters are to purchase the securities.

(2)　Outline briefly the plan of distribution of any securities being offered other than through underwriters. Where there is a "best efforts" offering, indicate, where practicable, on the cover page the minimum amount, if any, required to be raised, and also indicate, where practicable, the maximum amount that could be raised and the latest date that the offering is to remain open.

(3)　If the issuer or Selling Security Holder or any of the underwriters knows or has reason to believe that there is an intention to over-allot or that the price of any security may be stabilized to facilitate the offering of the securities to be distributed, the issuer, Selling Security Holder or underwriter shall disclose their intention in accordance with the restrictions on trading rules of the Securities Legislation or Securities Requirements of the Jurisdiction in which the short form prospectus is being filed.

(4)　Where Non-Convertible debt or Non-Convertible preferred shares are to be offered at non-fixed prices as permitted by this Policy Statement, disclose:

(a) the discount allowed to the underwriters or the commission payable to the underwriters;

(b) any other compensation payable to the underwriters and, if applicable, reference to the fact that the underwriters' compensation will be increased or decreased by the amount by which the aggregate price paid for the securities by the purchasers exceeds or is less than the gross proceeds paid by the underwriters to the issuer or Selling Security Holders;

(c) that the securities will be offered either at prices determined by reference to the prevailing price of a specified security in a specified market, at market prices prevailing at the time of sale or at prices to be negotiated with purchasers, which prices may vary as between purchasers and during the period of distribution of the securities;

(d) where the price of the securities is to be determined by reference to the prevailing price of a specified security in a specified market, the price of the specified security in the specified market at the latest practicable date; and

(e) where the price of the securities will be the market price prevailing at the time of sale, the market price at the latest practicable date.

(5) Where an issuer, underwriter or Selling Security Holder wishes to be able to decrease the price at which securities are offered for cash from the initial public offering price fixed in the short form prospectus and thereafter change, from time to time, the price at which securities are distributed under the short form prospectus in accordance with the procedures permitted by this Policy Statement, disclose that the compensation realized by the underwriters will be decreased by the amount that the aggregate price paid by purchasers for the securities is less than the gross proceeds paid by the underwriters to the issuer or Selling Security Holder.

Item 8: Market for Securities

Identify on the cover page of the short form prospectus the exchange(s) upon which the issuer's securities to be distributed are traded, if any.

Item 9: Asset and Earnings Coverage Ratios

In connection with an offering of debt having a term to maturity in excess of one year or an offering of preferred shares, provide:

(a) asset and earnings coverage ratios that are based on the twelve month period ended on the last day of the most recently completed period for which audited annual financial statements of the issuer have been, or are required to have been, filed with any Securities Regulatory Authority, and

(b) asset and earnings coverage ratios that are based on the twelve month period ended on the last day of the most recently completed period for which interim financial statements of the issuer have been, or are required to have been, filed with any Securities Regulatory Authority, provided this period is subsequent to the last day of the most recently completed period for which audited annual financial statements of the issuer have been, or are required to have been, filed with any Securities Regulatory Authority,

adjusted in each case to reflect

(c) the issuance of all long term debt and, in addition in the case of an issuance of preferred shares, all preferred shares issued, since the date of these annual or interim financial statements;

(d) the issuance of the securities that are to be offered pursuant to the short form prospectus, based on a reasonable estimate of the price at which these securities will be distributed;

(e) the repayment or redemption of all long term debt since the date of these annual or interim financial statements, all long term debt to be repaid or redeemed from the proceeds to be realized from the sale of securities under the short form prospectus and, in addition, in the case of an issuance of preferred shares, all preferred shares repaid or redeemed since the date of the annual or interim financial statements and all preferred shares to be repaid or redeemed from the proceeds to be realized from the sale of securities under the short form prospectus; and

(f) in the case of earnings coverage ratios, the servicing costs that were incurred, or will be incurred, in relation to the adjustments in (c), (d) and (e) above.

Item 10: Details of the Distribution

(1) If shares are being distributed, provide the designation of the class of shares offered and furnish information concerning all material attributes and characteristics including, without limiting the generality of the foregoing, dividend rights, voting rights, liquidation or distribution rights, pre-emptive rights, conversion rights, redemption, purchase or cancellation or surrender provisions, sinking or purchase fund provisions, liability to further calls or to assessment, and provisions as to modification, amendment or variation of any such rights or provisions. If the rights of holders of such shares may be modified otherwise than in accordance with the provisions attaching to the shares or to the provisions of the governing statute relating thereto, so state and briefly explain.

(2) If debt obligations are being distributed, give a brief summary of the material attributes and characteristics of the indebtedness and the security therefor, if any, including without limiting the generality of the foregoing, provisions with respect to interest rate, maturity, redemption, other retirement, sinking fund and conversion rights, the nature and priority of any security for the debt obligations with a brief identification of the principal properties subject to lien or charge, provisions permitting or restricting the issuance of additional securities, the incurring of additional indebtedness and other material negative covenants (including restrictions against payment of dividends, restrictions against giving security on the assets of the issuer or its subsidiaries) and provisions as to the release or substitution of assets securing the debt obligations, the modification of the terms of the security and similar provisions. Also provide the name of the trustee under any indenture relating to the debt obligations and briefly describe the nature of any material relationship between the trustee and the issuer or any of its affiliates, and any financial arrangements between the issuer and any of its affiliates or among its affiliates that could affect the security for the indebtedness.

(3) If securities other than shares or debt obligations are being distributed, describe fully the material attributes and characteristics of those securities.

(4) Where an issuer, underwriter or Selling Security Holder wishes to be able to decrease the price at which securities are offered for cash from the initial public offering price fixed in the short form prospectus and thereafter change, from time to time, the price at which securities are distributed under the short form prospectus in accordance with the procedures permitted by this Policy Statement, disclose that after the underwriters have made a bona fide effort to sell all of the securities at the initial public offering price fixed in the short form prospectus, the public offering price may be decreased and thereafter further changed, from time to time, to an amount not greater than the initial public offering price fixed in the short form prospectus.

(5) Where one or more ratings, including provisional ratings, have been received from one or more Approved Rating Organizations in respect of the securities to be distributed, whether as a result of a requirement of this Policy Statement or not, disclose the following information in each preliminary short form prospectus and short form prospectus, other than a preliminary short form prospectus filed in accordance with NPS 44:

(a) each security rating, including a provisional rating, received from an Approved Rating Organization, whether or not it is an Approved Rating;

(b) the name of each Approved Rating Organization that has assigned a rating in respect of the securities to be distributed;

(c) a definition or description of the category in which each Approved Rating Organization rated the securities to be distributed and the relative rank of each rating within the organization's overall classification system;

(d) a statement that a security rating is not a recommendation to buy, sell or hold securities and that it may be subject to revision or withdrawal at any time by the rating organization; and

(e) any announcement made by an Approved Rating Organization that the organization intends to revise or withdraw a rating previously assigned and required to be disclosed pursuant to this paragraph.

Item 11: Selling Security Holder

If any of the securities being distributed are to be distributed for the account of a Selling Security Holder, name the Selling Security Holder and state the number or amount of the securities owned by the Selling Security Holder, the number or amount to be distributed for the account of the Selling Security Holder, and the number or amount to be owned by the Selling Security Holder after the distribution.

Item 12: Resource Property

Where a significant portion of the proceeds of a distribution is to be expended on a particular resource property and where the Current AIF does not contain the disclosure required by paragraph (1)(i) or (j) of item 3 in Appendix A, as appropriate, with respect to the property or that disclosure is inadequate due to recent changes, disclose the required information.[38]

Item 13: Business Acquisitions

(1) Where the proceeds of the securities offered are to be applied, in whole or in part, directly or indirectly, to finance the acquisition of a business by a purchase of assets or shares and that acquisition is material[39] to the issuer, the short form prospectus relating to the securities being offered shall include:

(a) a balance sheet of the acquired business

　　(i) as at the date of the last financial year end of the acquired business and as at the corresponding date of the immediately preceding financial year, and

　　(ii) if that last financial year end date is more than 120 days prior to the date of the preliminary short form prospectus, as at a date that is not more than 120 days prior to the date of the preliminary short form prospectus;

(b) an income statement, a statement of retained earnings and a statement of changes in financial position (or where the acquired business is primarily engaged in the business of investing, a statement of changes in net assets) of the acquired business

　　(i) for each of its last three financial years, and

　　(ii) for any part of its subsequent financial year to the date at which the balance sheet required by (a)(ii) above is made up and for the comparative period in the immediately preceding financial year;

(c) a pro forma balance sheet that combines the assets and liabilities of the issuer and the acquired business as shown by their respective balance sheets, each as at the date of their respective last financial year ends, giving effect to the underlying assumptions and events described in (f) below;

(d) pro forma financial statements that combine, in respect of the last financial year of each of the acquired business and the issuer,

　　(i) the income or losses of the issuer with the income or losses of the acquired business, and

　　(ii) the changes in financial position of the issuer with the changes in financial position of the acquired business,

　　in each case, giving effect to the underlying assumptions and events described in (f) below;

---

38 See note 26 to the "Table of Documents to be Filed in respect of the Clearance of National Issues" in NPS 1.

39 See paragraph 2 of this item for a discussion of materiality in this context. Issuers should note that the Québec Securities Legislation does not limit the requirements for pro forma financial statements to those situations when the business acquisition is material to the issuer.

(e) the pro forma basic and pro forma fully diluted earnings per share based on the pro forma combined financial statements and calculated in accordance with the CICA Handbook; and

(f) a description of the underlying assumptions and the events on which the pro forma combined financial statements are predicated.

(2)   In this item, materiality should be determined in the context of the issuer's overall financial position prior to and after the acquisition taking into account both quantitative and qualitative factors. Materiality is a matter of judgement in the particular circumstances and should generally be determined in relation to the significance of the acquisition to investors, analysts and other users of financial statement information. Measures of materiality would generally include gross revenues, expenses, net income, shareholder's equity and total assets of the acquired business relative to those of the issuer. While this concept of materiality is broader than the definition of "material change" contained in the Securities Legislation of any Jurisdiction, it is consistent with the financial reporting notion of materiality contained in the CICA Handbook.

(3)   Subject to paragraph (4) below, each financial statement required pursuant to this item, other than a financial statement that relates to any part of a financial year subsequent to the last audited financial year and the comparative period in the immediately preceding financial year, shall be accompanied by an auditor's report.

(4)   Any pro forma financial statement required pursuant to this item shall have attached a report, prepared by the auditor of the issuer, that may be solely a compilation report.

Item 14:   Issues of Guaranteed Securities

(1)   Where a distribution of securities is guaranteed[40] by another issuer, provide the following information with respect to the issuer of the securities:

(a) where the issuer is a wholly owned subsidiary of the guarantor, has no operations or minimal operations that are independent of the guarantor and is an entity that functions essentially as a special purpose division of the guarantor, a brief reference to the issuer's business, a statement that the financial results of the issuer are included in the consolidated financial results of the guarantor and a cross-reference to the description of the issuer's business contained in the AIF of the guarantor;

(b) where the issuer is a wholly owned subsidiary of the guarantor but has more than minimal operations that are independent of the guarantor, a summary of the narrative description of the business of the issuer and, in a note to the audited financial statements of the guarantor for its most recently completed financial year, a summary of financial information relating to the issuer's operations[41]; or

(c) where the issuer is not a wholly owned subsidiary of the guarantor, a full narrative description of the business of the issuer and separate audited fin-

---

40 See footnote (13) above.

41 If the issuer is a reporting issuer and has filed an annual information form for its most recently completed financial year as required under the provisions of the Securities Legislation or Securities Requirements of a Jurisdiction, the requirement for a summary narrative description of the business of the issuer may be satisfied by incorporating by reference into the issuer's preliminary short form prospectus and short form prospectus that annual information form, provided the issuer's annual information form is distributed to purchasers together with its preliminary short form prospectus and short form prospectus.

ancial statements of the issuer for its most recently completed financial year.[42]

(2)   Only for purposes of paragraph (1) above, an issuer shall be deemed to be a wholly owned subsidiary of the guarantor, if the guarantor owns 96% or more of the outstanding voting securities of the issuer.

(3)   Where a distribution of securities is guaranteed by another issuer, provide information with respect to the guarantor by complying with the requirements of paragraph (5) of item 16 of this Appendix.

Item 15:   Relationship between Issuer and Underwriter

Provide the disclosure required by the applicable form for a long form prospectus under the Securities Legislation of each Jurisdiction in which the short form prospectus is filed relating to conflicts of interest in connection with a distribution of securities of a registrant or a Connected Party of a registrant.

Item 16:   Documents Incorporated by Reference

(1)   The documents set forth below shall be specifically incorporated by reference in the short form prospectus by means of a statement to that effect in the short form prospectus listing all those documents:

    (a) the issuer's Current AIF; and

    (b) material change reports (except confidential material change reports), comparative interim financial statements, comparative financial statements for the issuer's most recently completed financial year, together with the accompanying report of the auditor, and information circulars or annual filings where information circulars are not required[42a], filed by the Issuer pursuant to the requirements of the Securities Legislation of any Jurisdiction in which a distribution of securities is made pursuant to the short form prospectus, since the commencement of the issuer's financial year in which the issuer's Current AIF was filed.

(2)   The short form prospectus shall also state that documents referred to above filed by the issuer pursuant to the requirements of the Securities Legislation or Securities Requirements of any Jurisdiction in which a distribution of securities is made pursuant to the short form prospectus, after the date of the short form prospectus and prior to the termination of the distribution, shall be deemed to be incorporated by reference into the short form prospectus.

---

42   If the issuer is a reporting issuer and has filed an annual information form for its most recently completed financial year as required by the Securities Legislation or Securities Requirements of a Jurisdiction, the requirement for a full narrative description of the business of the issuer may be satisfied by incorporating certain documents by reference. The issuer may incorporate by reference into its preliminary short form prospectus and short form prospectus the annual information form referred to above and all other documents required to be incorporated by reference in a preliminary short form prospectus and short form prospectus, other than material change reports filed after the date of the annual information form. Any material change occurring after the date of the annual information form must be disclosed by providing a narrative description of the material change in the preliminary short form prospectus and short form prospectus. Any document incorporated by reference as provided in this footnote must be distributed to purchasers together with the issuer's preliminary short form prospectus and short form prospectus.

42a   In Ontario and British Columbia, an information circular or an annual filing where an information circular is not required must include a Statement of Executive Compensation in accordance with Form 40 under the regulations to the Securities Act (Ontario) or Form 41 specified by the Superintendent of Brokers in British Columbia. The items of disclosure in these forms which are required to be included in an information circular or an annual filing include, without limitation, Item V – Option and SAR Repricings, Item VIII – Compensation Committee, Item IX – Report on Executive Compensation and Item X – Performance Graph. The disclosure required by Items V, VIII, IX and X of these forms need not be incorporated by reference into the short form prospectus. Where similar changes are made to the executive compensation disclosure rules in other Jurisdictions, the disclosure required by the equivalent of Items V, VIII, IX and X of these forms need not be incorporated by reference into the short form prospectus.

(3) List the material change reports filed by the issuer since the filing of the issuer's Current AIF. In each case, provide the date of filing and a brief description of the material change.

(4) The short form prospectus shall contain a statement in bold face type substantially to the effect of section 6.1(2) of this Policy Statement.

(5) Where an issuer is doing a distribution contemplated by item 14 of this Appendix, the provisions of paragraphs (1), (2) and (3) of this item apply with necessary changes to the guarantor.

Item 17: Interest of Experts

(1) Where any solicitor, auditor, accountant, engineer, appraiser or other Person whose profession gives authority to a statement made by that Person is named in a short form prospectus or a document specifically incorporated by reference in a short form prospectus as having prepared or certified any part of that document or is named as having prepared or certified a report or valuation used in a short form prospectus or in a document specifically incorporated by reference into a short form prospectus and

    (a) has received or expects to receive any interest, whether direct or indirect in the property of the issuer or any Associate or affiliate of the issuer, or

    (b) beneficially owns, directly or indirectly, any securities of the issuer or any Associate or affiliate of the issuer,

disclose that interest or ownership.

(2) Where any Person referred to in paragraph (1) above is or is expected to be elected, appointed or employed as a director, officer or employee of the issuer or any Associate or affiliate of the issuer, disclose the fact or expectation.

Item 18: Other Material Facts

Give particulars of any material facts relating to the securities proposed to be offered and not disclosed pursuant to the foregoing items or in the documents referred to in item 16 of this Appendix incorporated by reference into the short form prospectus.

Item 19: Statutory Rights of Withdrawal and Rescission

The short form prospectus shall contain a statement of withdrawal and rescission rights in the following form:

> Securities legislation in several of the provinces provides purchasers with the right to withdraw from an agreement to purchase securities within two business days after receipt or deemed receipt of a prospectus and any amendment. In several of the provinces and territories securities legislation further provides a purchaser with remedies for rescission or, in some jurisdictions, damages where the prospectus and any amendment contains a misrepresentation or is not delivered to the purchaser, provided that such remedies for rescission or damages are exercised by the purchaser within the time limit prescribed by the securities legislation of the purchaser's Province or Territory. The purchaser should refer to any applicable provisions of the securities legislation of the purchaser's Province or Territory for the particulars of these rights or consult with a legal adviser.

Item 20: Certificates

(1) The preliminary short form prospectus and short form prospectus shall contain a certificate in the following form signed by the chief executive officer, the chief financial officer, and, on behalf of the board of directors of the issuer, any two directors of the issuer, other than the foregoing, duly authorized to sign and any person who is a promoter of the issuer:

> The foregoing, together with the documents incorporated herein by reference, constitutes full, true and plain disclosure of all material facts relating to the securities offered by this prospectus as required by the securities laws of [insert name of each Jurisdiction in which qualified] [insert if offering made in Québec – "For the purpose of the Province of Québec, this simplified prospectus, as supplemented by the permanent information record, contains no misrepresentation that is likely to affect the value or the market price of the securities to be distributed."].

(2) Where there is an underwriter, the preliminary short form prospectus and the short form prospectus shall contain a certificate in the following form signed by the underwriter or underwriters who, with respect to the securities offered by the prospectus, are in a contractual relationship with the issuer or Selling Security Holders:

> To the best of our knowledge, information and belief, the foregoing, together with the documents incorporated herein by reference, constitutes full, true and plain disclosure of all material facts relating to the securities offered by this prospectus as required by the securities laws of [insert name of each Jurisdiction in which qualified] [insert if offering made in Québec – "For the purpose of the Province of Québec, to our knowledge, this simplified prospectus, as supplemented by the permanent information record, contains no misrepresentation that is likely to affect the value or the market price of the securities to be distributed."].

(3) Where the disclosure in item 14 of this Appendix is required to be included, the preliminary short form prospectus and short form prospectus shall contain a certificate of the guarantor and a certificate of the issuer, in each case, in the form required in paragraph (1) above.[43, 44]

NATIONAL POLICY STATEMENT NO. 47
APPENDIX C
APPLICABLE REGULATOR

Jurisdiction	Representative
Alberta	Director, Securities Analysis
British Columbia[46]	Deputy Superintendent, Corporate Finance
Manitoba	Deputy Director, Corporate Finance
New Brunswick	Administrator of Securities
Newfoundland	Director of Securities
Northwest Territories	Deputy Registrar of Securities
Nova Scotia	Director of Securities
Ontario	Director, Corporate Finance
Prince Edward Island	Registrar of Securities
Québec[45]	
Saskatchewan[47]	Director
Yukon Territory	Registrar of Securities

---

43 Reference should be made to the provisions of the Securities Legislation of a Jurisdiction that provide for a right of action against every person who signs a prospectus or an amendment to a prospectus.

44 The Securities Regulatory Authorities recognize that, in certain circumstances, a guarantor may consider that its knowledge of the affairs of the issuer is not such that it considers it appropriate to sign a certificate in the form specified under this paragraph. In these circumstances, provided the guarantor is not a promoter of the issuer or a Selling Security Holder, the Securities Regulatory Authorities may agree to allow the guarantor to sign a different form of certificate. Guarantors who wish to request such permission should make their request in accordance with section 7.3.

45 Issuers considering a distribution of securities in the Province of Québec and concurrently in other Jurisdictions under the POP System should contact the "Directeur des Opérations financières et de l'Information continue" in circumstances where they would contact the Applicable Regulator in other Jurisdictions.

46 For purposes of applications pursuant to section 4.5 of this Policy Statement, the Applicable Regulator is the Deputy Superintendent, Exemptions and Orders.

47 For purposes of applications pursuant to section 4.5 of this Policy Statement, the Applicable Regulator is the Saskatchewan Securities Commission.

NATIONAL POLICY STATEMENT NO. 48
FUTURE-ORIENTED FINANCIAL INFORMATION

TABLE OF CONTENTS

NATIONAL POLICY STATEMENT NO. 48
FUTURE-ORIENTED FINANCIAL INFORMATION

PART 1   PURPOSE

The purpose of this policy statement is to specify the manner in which FOFI in General Purpose Documents shall be prepared, disclosed, dated, subsequently compared with actual results and updated where applicable, and to specify the involvement of independent public accountants, referred to as auditors in this policy statement, with all such documents.

The decision whether to publish FOFI and the responsibility for published FOFI rests with the issuer. Issuers who choose to publish FOFI shall comply with this policy statement. Factors to be considered in making their decision include the issuer's history of operations and experience in preparing such information, including the degree of variance between previously prepared FOFI and the actual results that were attained before the forecasted periods. However, the securities regulatory authorities recognize that such history and experience may not always be available. Section 4.1 sets out the requirements that apply in such a circumstance.

PART 2   DEFINITIONS

"CICA Handbook" means the Handbook of the Canadian Institute of Chartered Accountants;

"FOFI" means future-oriented financial information which is information about prospective results of operations, financial position or changes in financial position, based on assumptions about future economic conditions and courses of action. Future-oriented financial information is presented as either a forecast or a projection;

"Forecast" means FOFI prepared using assumptions all of which reflect the entity's planned courses of action for the period covered given management's judgement as to the most probable set of economic conditions;

"General Purpose Documents" means prospectuses, preliminary prospectuses, certain offering memoranda as set out in Appendix A, rights offering circulars, documents delivered or filed with the securities regulatory authorities under or with the continuous disclosure, proxy and proxy solicitation, take-over bid and issuer bid requirements of Securities Legislation and Securities Requirements and documents incorporated by reference into, or that amend the foregoing;

"Hypotheses" means assumptions that assume a set of economic conditions or courses of action that are consistent with the issuer's intended course of action and represent plausible circumstances;

"Projection" means FOFI prepared using assumptions that reflect the entity's planned courses of action for the period covered given management's judgement as to the most probable set of economic conditions, together with one or more Hypotheses;

"Securities Legislation" means the statutes concerning the regulation of securities markets and trading in securities, and the regulations in respect of these statutes; and

"Securities Requirements" means the blanket rulings and orders made under the Securities Legislation and the policy statements and written interpretations issued by the securities regulatory authorities.

PART 3   APPLICATION

3.1   Scope

    (1)   Inclusion of FOFI for offerings where the proceeds are to be used to acquire as yet undetermined or unidentified assets is not permitted.

    (2)   This policy statement does not apply to discounted future cash flow data provided by resource issuers to the extent such data complies with the requirements of National Policy Statements No. 2-A and No. 2-B where the data is extracted from an engineering or geologist's report and specific reference is made to such report. This policy statement also does not apply to financial information pertaining to the future provided in management's discussion and analysis disclosure that is required under the Securities Legislation and Securities Requirements – that information does not take the form of a Forecast or Projection as those terms are used in this policy statement.

    (3)   Offerings for which the minimum acquisition cost as defined in the Securities Legislation and Securities Requirements is at least $500,000 are exempt from the requirements of this policy statement.

3.2   Preparation

    (1)   FOFI shall be prepared in accordance with the recommendations of the CICA Handbook and the additional requirements of this policy statement.

    (2)   When FOFI is included for an issuer that is proposed to be acquired, it shall be prepared by the issuer to be acquired.

    (3)   In the case of real estate or oil and gas filings, it may be appropriate to include cash flow information in FOFI in addition to the minimum disclosures otherwise required by the CICA Handbook for FOFI.

3.3   Materiality

For purposes of the application of this policy statement, materiality should be determined in the context of the overall financial position of the issuer taking into account both quantitative and qualitative factors. Materiality is a matter of judgement in the particular circumstances and should generally be determined in relation to the significance of an item to investors, analysts and other users of financial information. An item is considered material to an issuer if it is probable that its omission from the financial information would influence or change a decision. Measures of materiality would generally include gross revenues, expenses, net income, shareholders' equity and total assets. While this concept of materiality is broader than the definition of "material change" contained in the Securities Legislation and Securities Requirements, it is consistent with the financial reporting notion of materiality contained in the CICA Handbook.

PART 4   REQUIREMENTS OF GENERAL APPLICATION[1]

4.1   Forecasts and Projections

(1)   FOFI included in General Purpose Documents shall be in the form of a Forecast, subject to subsection (2).

(2)   Notwithstanding subsection (1), Projections may be included in General Purpose Documents for issuers engaged in a business with less than 24 months of relevant operating history. In certain limited circumstances, issuers engaged in a business with more than two years of operating history may be permitted to provide FOFI in the form of a Projection.

For example, the issuer and its auditors may not have access to the prior operating history because the property to be acquired is privately owned prior to acquisition and the records are not available to the new owners. In such circumstances, it is acceptable to the securities regulatory authorities to treat a business as start up although it may have an operating history of more than two years. Another example is where there is a substantial change in the use of the property such as an upgrade from an economy hotel to a luxury hotel. In such cases the operating history may not be relevant to the new usage.

(3)   A Forecast or Projection may be included but not both.

4.2   Period to be Covered by FOFI

The period covered by FOFI shall not extend beyond the point in time for which such information can be reasonably estimated (normally the end of the next financial year i.e., a maximum of 24 months). In certain circumstances the period covered by FOFI may extend beyond the following financial year when there is reasonable assurance as to the operations in the FOFI period. The guidelines in this policy statement for determining an extended FOFI period apply equally to Forecasts and Projections.

Examples of issuers in a position to prepare extended FOFI include existing real estate projects for which FOFI could be prepared up to the date of the mortgage renewal and issuers engaged in long term contracts for which FOFI could be prepared up to the expiry date of such contracts, provided that all revenues and expenses can be reasonably estimated during the extended FOFI period.

4.3   Restrictions

(1)   FOFI is information about future operating results of the enterprise. As such it is not expected that FOFI can be provided with respect to capital appreciation or sale of a real estate property in the future. However, information can be included which shows the potential impact of capital appreciation or sale of a real estate property in the future provided that it is presented in the format of a sensitivity analysis which reflects the effects of an equal range of capital appreciation and depreciation percentages. For example, in the case of a real estate property, a range of projected percentages from an appreciation of 6% to a depreciation of 6% could be provided. However, due to the significant uncertainties involved, the maximum projected increase presented should be no greater than the historically experienced appreciation rate for a period of time comparable to the length of time of the sensitivity analysis. The maximum increase presented

---

1   Issuers are advised to review the Securities Legislation and Securities Requirements in each jurisdiction in order to determine the requirements for pre-filing of FOFI. For example, Quebec requires pre-filing for non-reporting issuers and reporting issuers distributing securities by prospectus for the first time.

should be lower if the historic rate showed significant volatility or if there is reason to believe the historic rate may not be sustainable in the future.

(2) The effective date of the underlying assumptions shall not precede by more than 120 days the date of filing or delivery of the document in which FOFI is included. In the case of prospectuses, this requirement applies to both the preliminary and the final documents.

(3) Where FOFI includes actual results of the issuer for part of the FOFI period, these results should be separately disclosed.

4.4 Distribution and Delivery

(1) Issuers and distributing firms are reminded that during the course of a distribution of securities to which this policy statement applies, any FOFI disseminated must only be that which is set out in the prospectus or offering memoranda set out in Appendix A. In those rare circumstances where an extract of FOFI is disseminated, the extract or summary must be reasonable and balanced and shall have a cautionary note in bold face stating that the FOFI presented is not complete and that complete FOFI is included in the General Purpose Document.

(2) Where FOFI is incorporated by reference in General Purpose Documents, a copy of FOFI shall be provided with the General Purpose Document. This requirement also applies to updated FOFI.

PART 5   ADDITIONAL REQUIREMENTS APPLICABLE TO PROJECTIONS

5.1 Disclosure

(1) The purpose of the Projection is to be disclosed.

(2) A cautionary note shall appear in bold face in the lead paragraph under Projections stating that the Projection is based on Hypotheses and that there is a significant risk that actual results will vary, perhaps materially, from the results projected.

5.2 Hypotheses

(1) Hypotheses used in preparing Projections shall be consistent with the purpose of the Projection. When many Hypotheses are used a Projection becomes less reliable and therefore is more likely to be challenged by the securities regulatory authorities. However, the use of multiple Projections (i.e., using different assumptions) is permitted provided that it results in an unbiased presentation and provided that no one Projection is significantly more likely to occur than any other.

(2) The notes accompanying the Projections must disclose that the Hypotheses assume a set of economic conditions or courses of action that are consistent with the issuer's intended course of action and represent plausible circumstances. These requirements apply to each set of Hypotheses used in preparing multiple Projections.

PART 6   COMPARISON WITH ACTUAL RESULTS

6.1 Review and Comparison

(1) FOFI and updated FOFI included in a General Purpose Document shall be reviewed each time the issuer is required to file historical financial statements with the securities regulatory authorities under the continuous disclosure requirements of the Securities Legislation and Securities Requirements to identify material changes resulting from events that have occurred since it was issued. FOFI covering an annual period shall be compared with actual annual audited results for the same period and FOFI covering an interim period shall be compared with actual interim results for the same period. FOFI included in offering memoranda set out in Appendix A is not required to be reviewed and compared with actual results, however, issuers are encouraged to do so.[2]

---

2   Issuers should note that the securities regulatory authorities in Québec require that FOFI included in an offering memorandum be compared with actual results.

(2) The comparison shall address each material individual item, including assumptions, which were included in the FOFI or updated FOFI. If the results of the comparison identify material difference between actual results and FOFI or updated FOFI, such material differences shall be disclosed. For example, where the actual dollar amount of sales approximates the amount forecasted but the sales mix or sales volume differs from what was expected, it is necessary to explain this fact.

If there are no material differences, issuers shall disclose that a comparison has been made and no material differences were identified.

6.2   Disclosure

The results of the comparison in section 6.1 shall accompany the annual or interim financial statements required to be filed under the continuous disclosure requirements of the Securities Legislation and Securities Requirements immediately following the end of the FOFI period and does not necessarily form part of the financial statements. For purposes of this policy statement, FOFI period means each financial year or part thereof for which FOFI is prepared.

PART 7   UPDATING FOFI

7.1   Reporting

(1) When a change occurs in the events or in the assumptions used to prepare FOFI that has a material effect on such FOFI, such a change shall be reported in a manner identical to that followed when a material change occurs as defined under the Securities Legislation and Securities Requirements.

(2) If there are no changes in the events or in the assumptions used to prepare FOFI that have a material effect on FOFI, this fact shall be disclosed in documents accompanying the issuer's annual or interim financial statements required to be filed under the continuous disclosure requirements of the Securities Legislation and Securities Requirements immediately following the end of the FOFI period.

7.2   When to Update

FOFI shall be updated when a change occurs in the events or in the assumptions used to prepare FOFI that has a material effect on such FOFI. When FOFI is required to be updated, previously issued FOFI shall be withdrawn.

7.3   Disclosure

(1) If updated FOFI is required to be provided, it shall be accompanied by explanations of changes, disclosure of the dates of FOFI and of updated FOFI, and disclosure of the fact that changes have occurred which require FOFI to be updated.

(2) Updated FOFI shall accompany the issuer's annual or interim financial statements required to be filed under the continuous disclosure requirements of the Securities Legislation and Securities Requirements immediately following the occurrence of the change in the events or assumptions used to prepare FOFI that has a material effect on FOFI, and does not necessarily form part of the financial statements.

PART 8   WITHDRAWAL OF FOFI

8.1   Approval

The securities regulatory authorities must approve withdrawals of FOFI when the withdrawn FOFI is not replaced by updated FOFI. Approval will only be granted in those situations where the occurrence of an event makes it impossible for the issuer to prepare reliable updated FOFI.

8.2   Disclosure

When FOFI is withdrawn, the reasons for the withdrawal shall be clearly disclosed in the manner set out in subsection 7.1(1).

PART 9 AUDITORS' INVOLVEMENT

9.1 Auditors' Report

FOFI included in a preliminary prospectus, prospectus, rights offering circular, offering memorandum set out in Appendix A, information memorandum, takeover bid circular, directors' circular or issuer bid circular or other materials disseminated in connection with a take-over bid or an issuer bid shall be accompanied by the auditors' report thereon, which shall not contain any reservations of opinion. The update required under Part 7 needs not be accompanied by the auditors' report thereon, however, issuers are encouraged to obtain auditors' reports that shall accompany such a document.

9.2 Engagement Standards

The standards for such an engagement are found in the CICA Auditing Guideline entitled "Examination of a Financial Forecast or Projection Included in a Prospectus or Other Public Offering Document".

9.3 Comfort and Consent Letters

(1) Where the auditors' report on FOFI included in a preliminary prospectus is not signed there shall be filed, at the time the preliminary prospectus is filed, a letter addressed to the securities regulatory authorities and signed by the auditors in which such statement shall be made with respect to the examination of FOFI as may be appropriate in the circumstances and acceptable to the securities regulatory authorities.

(2) Auditors' consent letters shall also contain specific reference to FOFI included in the final prospectus. This may be done by adding a statement to the effect that the auditors also consent to the inclusion of their audit report dated _____ on the (Forecast) (Projection) of (issuer), dated _____ consisting of (briefly describe FOFI _____ being presented). No other amendment to the usual form of consent is required.

PART 10 TAKE-OVER BID

Where in the context of a take-over bid it is not practicable to provide an auditors' report on FOFI, the securities regulatory authorities will consent instead to the inclusion of a statement signed by the chief financial officer of the company to which it relates that FOFI was prepared in accordance with the recommendations of the CICA Handbook and the requirements of this policy statement.

PART 11 EFFECTIVE DATE

11.1 Effective Date

This policy statement is effective for FOFI filed or delivered on or after January 1, 1993.

NATIONAL POLICY STATEMENT NO. 48

APPENDIX A

OFFERING MEMORANDA SUBJECT TO FOFI

Offering memoranda subject to this policy statement are those provided in connection with a distribution of a security under the legislative provisions noted below:

Jurisdiction	Securities Legislation Reference
ALBERTA	Subclauses 107(1)(d), 107(1)(p) or 107(1)(q) of the Alberta Securities Act, S.A. 1981, c. S-6.1, as amended.
BRITISH COLUMBIA	Section 55(2)(4) of the Securities Act, S.B.C. 1985, c. 83, as amended (where a person advertises in connection with the distribution), or sections 117(a), 117(b) or 117(i) of the Securities Regulation, B.C. Reg. 270/86.
MANITOBA	Clause 91(b) of the Securities Regulation, M.R. 491/88R.

NEWFOUNDLAND

Subclauses 73(1)(d), 73(1)(p) or 54(3)(p) of *The Securities Act*, S. Nfld. 1990, c. 48.

NOVA SCOTIA

Subclauses 77(1)(d), 77(1)(p), 77(1)(w) or 77(1)(ag) of the *Securities Act*, R.S.N.S. 1989, c. 418, as amended, or clause 127(p) of the Securities Regulations.

ONTARIO

Subclauses 72(1)(d) or 72(1)(p) of the *Securities Act*, R.S.O. 1990, c. S-5 (the "Act") or clause 14(g) of the Regulation made under the Act, R.R.O. 1980, Reg. 910, as amended.

QUEBEC

Sections 47, 48 or 52 of the Quebec *Securities Act*, R.S.Q., c. V-1.1, as amended.

NATIONAL POLICY STATEMENT NO. 49
SELF-REGULATORY ORGANIZATION MEMBERSHIP

PART 1   PURPOSE AND BACKGROUND

This Policy Statement applies to dealers that are not members of a self-regulatory organization (an "SRO"), as defined in this Policy Statement, but that are affiliated with an SRO member provided that those affiliated dealers carry on business in more than one jurisdiction and that otherwise fall within the definition of "national dealer". This Policy Statement responds to the concern of the securities regulatory authorities that those dealers should be members of a self-regulatory organization and contribute to the Canadian Investor Protection Fund ("CIPF"), the national contingency trust fund for clients of SRO member firms.

In May, 1989 the Canadian Securities Administrators (the "CSA") created the National Regulatory Working Group, which tabled its Final Report on "Capital, Financial Reporting and Audit Requirements for the Securities Industry" in December, 1989. Among the recommendations contained in that report is one which would require certain dealers to become members of an SRO.

SRO membership has been voluntary to date. SRO members participate in CIPF. CIPF is the primary insurance fund for investor protection with respect to failed securities firms in Canada and it covers losses of securities and cash balances, within prescribed limits, suffered by clients of a participating firm in the event of that firm's insolvency. Participation in CIPF carries with it the responsibility of financing CIPF through regular levies assessed on participating firms. These levies are based on the firm's level of activity in the capital markets, i.e. gross revenues.

There are substantial benefits involved in an SRO system of regulation. An SRO system helps to ensure compliance with regulatory requirements and also helps to provide consistent application and interpretation of the rules, to the extent that they are harmonized. The CSA remain concerned that dealers that are SRO members not carry on any of their securities or securities-related business through affiliated entities that are not SRO members and that do not contribute to CIPF.

PART 2   INTERPRETATION

In this Policy Statement:

"adviser", "affiliate", "company", "financial intermediary dealer", "limited market dealer", "mutual fund dealer", "real estate securities dealer", "securities", "securities issuer", "scholarship plan dealer", and "trade", in respect of the application of this Policy Statement in a jurisdiction, have the meaning, if any, assigned to those terms in the securities legislation of that jurisdiction.

"dealer" means a person or company who trades in securities in the capacity of principal or agent and who is, or is required to be, registered pursuant to the securities legislation of a jurisdiction to carry on its trading activities. For the purposes of this Policy Statement, an adviser who holds client funds, securities or other assets will be considered a dealer.

"national dealer" means a dealer, other than a restricted dealer, that is an affiliate of an SRO member where:

1. the dealer carries on business in more than one jurisdiction;

2. the affiliated SRO member carries on business in more than one jurisdiction; or

3. the dealer carries on business in one jurisdiction and the affiliated SRO member carries on business in another jurisdiction.

"jurisdiction" means a province or territory of Canada.

"restricted dealer" means a dealer that is registered with restrictions as to the classes or categories of securities in which it may trade or that is registered as a financial intermediary dealer, limited market dealer, mutual fund dealer, scholarship plan dealer, real estate securities dealer or a securities issuer.

"self-regulatory organization" or "SRO" means, for the purposes of this Policy Statement, any of the following:

1. the Investment Dealers Association of Canada;

2. a District Council of The Investment Dealers Association of Canada which has been recognized by a securities regulatory authority in Canada;

3. The Toronto Stock Exchange;

4. the Montreal Exchange;

5. the Vancouver Stock Exchange; or

6. the Alberta Stock Exchange.

PART 3   SELF-REGULATORY ORGANIZATION MEMBERSHIP

3.1   *Implementation*

The securities regulatory authorities have concluded that it is in the public interest that, absent unusual circumstances, national dealers be members of a self-regulatory organization and contribute to CIPF. Commencing June 30, 1993 the securities regulatory authorities, in determining whether to register or permit the registration of a national dealer, will consider whether that national dealer is a member of a self-regulatory organization and contributes to CIPF.

3.2   *Transition*

After June 30, 1994, the securities regulatory authorities, in determining whether to renew the registration of any national dealer which was a national dealer on June 30, 1993, will consider whether that national dealer is a member of a self-regulatory organization and contributes to CIPF.

In Quebec, with respect to each dealer which is a national dealer on June 30, 1993, the Commission des valeurs mobilieres du Quebec will consider, after June 30, 1994, whether that national dealer is a member of a self-regulatory organization and contributes to CIPF.

NATIONAL POLICY STATEMENT NO. 50
RESERVATIONS IN AN AUDITOR'S REPORT

TABLE OF CONTENTS

PART 1   PURPOSE

This policy statement sets out the position of the securities regulatory authorities with respect to the acceptability of the financial statements of an issuer, a registrant or other person (collectively an "Issuer") required to file financial statements with a securities regulatory authority in any province or territory in Canada in accordance with the requirements of the statutes concerning the regulation of securities markets and trading in securities in a jurisdiction, and the regulations in respect of these statutes ("Securities Legislation"), where the financial statements are accompanied by an auditor's report containing a reservation of opinion.

PART 2   APPLICATION

This policy statement applies to all financial statements filed by an Issuer, that are required to be audited, under the requirements of the Securities Legislation of any jurisdiction, unless otherwise specified in, or exempted by, the specific provisions of the Securities Legislation of that jurisdiction. The application of this policy statement to the financial statements that are required to be audited of an Issuer incorporated or organized in a jurisdiction other than Canada or a province of Canada (a "Non-Canadian Issuer") is set out in part 6.

PART 3   FINANCIAL STATEMENTS TO BE PREPARED IN ACCORDANCE WITH CANADIAN GAAP

The Securities Legislation of certain jurisdictions requires, subject to certain exceptions, that financial statements be prepared in accordance with generally accepted accounting principles in Canada ("Canadian GAAP") and with any applicable provisions of the Securities Legislation. Where the Securities Legislation of a jurisdiction is silent on the issue of compliance with generally accepted accounting principles, the securities regulatory authorities nonetheless require that Issuers prepare their financial statements in accordance with Canadian GAAP. See National Policy Statement No. 27 for a discussion of the meaning of "Canadian GAAP" and information on the additional accounting and disclosure requirements that may be imposed by certain jurisdictions.

PART 4   AUDITS TO BE PERFORMED IN ACCORDANCE WITH CANADIAN GAAS

Where an Issuer is required to file audited financial statements, the Securities Legislation of certain jurisdictions requires that the auditor make the necessary audit to be able to prepare an auditor's report in accordance with generally accepted auditing standards as set out in the Handbook of the Canadian Institute of Chartered Accountants ("Canadian GAAS") and with any applicable provisions of the Securities Legislation. In these jurisdictions, as well as in jurisdictions where the Securities Legislation is silent on the issue of compliance with generally accepted auditing standards, the securities regulatory authorities expect that the auditor will complete the audit, and prepare the auditor's report, in accordance with Canadian GAAS. For a full discussion of the meaning of "Canadian GAAS", see section 5100 of the Handbook of the Canadian Institute of Chartered Accountants.

PART 5   RESERVATIONS IN AN AUDITOR'S REPORT

5.1   *Acceptability of financial statements accompanied by an auditor's report containing a reservation of opinion* – Where financial statements accompanied by an auditor's report containing a reservation of opinion are filed with the securities regulatory authorities, the securities regulatory authorities will generally take the position that the Issuer has not filed financial statements that are in compliance with the requirements of the Securities Legislation.

5.2 *Meaning of reservation of opinion–* The expression "reservation of opinion" is used when an auditor

(1) forms a positive opinion on the financial statements as a whole, but qualifies that opinion with respect to a departure from generally accepted accounting principles or a limitation in the scope of the audit (a "Qualified Opinion");

(2) forms an opinion that the financial statements are not presented fairly in accordance with generally accepted accounting principles (an "Adverse Opinion"); or

(3) is unable to form an opinion on the financial statements as a whole because of a limitation in the scope of the audit (a "Denial of Opinion").

See section 5510 of the Handbook of the Canadian Institute of Chartered Accountants for a discussion of the circumstances when the auditor is unable to express an opinion without reservation on financial statements.

5.3 *Financial statements accompanied by a reservation of opinion acceptable in limited circumstances* – The securities regulatory authorities recognize that, in certain limited circumstances, it may be in the public interest to accept, for the purpose for which they are filed, financial statements on which the auditor is not able to express an opinion without reservation. Subject to part 7, where the Securities Legislation gives the appropriate representative of the securities regulatory authority (the "Applicable Regulator") the discretion to accept financial statements accompanied by an auditor's report in which the auditor is not able to express an opinion without reservation, these financial statements will generally be accepted except where the reservation is:

(1) due to a departure from Canadian GAAP; or

(2) due to a limitation in the scope of the auditor's examination that

(a) results in a Denial of Opinion,

(b) is imposed or could reasonably be eliminated by management, or

(c) could reasonably be expected to be recurring.

5.4 *Example of application of section 5.3* – Financial statements will generally be accepted where the reservation of opinion is due to a limitation in the scope of the auditor's examination resulting from an event that clearly limits the availability of accounting records that substantiate a specific financial statement balance to such an extent that the Issuer is unable to provide its auditor with sufficient appropriate audit evidence to afford a reasonable basis for the auditor to express an opinion without reservation on the financial statements as a whole. In such a circumstance, for the financial statements to be considered for acceptance the auditor must have performed all of the other procedures necessary and reasonable under the circumstances and as required by Canadian GAAS on the financial statements except those that cannot be performed because of the limiting event.

5.5 *Action by securities regulatory authorities where financial statements accompanied by a reservation of opinion* – Subject to part 7, where financial statements accompanied by an auditor's report containing a reservation of opinion are filed with the securities regulatory authorities in circumstances other than those acceptable to the securities regulatory authorities, the securities regulatory authorities may:

(1) require the Issuer to revise its financial statements or provide its auditor with the necessary information, as is appropriate in the circumstances, such that the financial statements are prepared in accordance with Canadian GAAP and the audit is completed, and auditor's report is prepared, in accordance with Canadian GAAS,

(2) issue a cease trading order, if the financial statements are filed as part of an Issuer's continuous disclosure obligations under the Securities Legislation,

(3) suspend, cancel or restrict the registration of an Issuer, if the financial statements are filed as part of the Issuer's obligation to file financial statements under the Securities Legislation,

(4)   refuse to issue a receipt for a preliminary or final prospectus, if the financial statements form part of, or are incorporated by reference into, that prospectus, or

(5)   use the remedies available under the Securities Legislation, if the financial statements form part of, or are incorporated by reference into, an offering memorandum or a take-over bid circular.

PART 6   FINANCIAL STATEMENTS OF NON-CANADIAN ISSUERS

6.1   *Financial statements of Non-Canadian Issuers accompanied by an auditor's report containing a reservation of opinion* – Where the financial statements of a Non-Canadian Issuer are accompanied by an auditor's report that contains a reservation of opinion due to either

(1)   a departure from the applicable non-Canadian generally accepted accounting principles ("Non-Canadian GAAP"), or

(2)   a limitation in the scope or application of the audit under the applicable non-Canadian generally accepted auditing standards ("Non-Canadian GAAS"),

the principles set out in part 5 will apply. The principles set out in part 5 will also apply where Non-Canadian GAAS does not require the expression of a reservation of opinion in situations where Canadian GAAS would require a reservation to be included.

6.2   *Financial statements of Non-Canadian Issuers where reservation not required by Canadian GAAS* – Where Non-Canadian GAAS requires the expression of a reservation of opinion in situations where Canadian GAAS would not require such a reservation, and in all other respects the financial statements and auditor's report comply with all of the requirements of the applicable Securities Legislation, the securities regulatory authorities will generally take the position that the Non-Canadian Issuer has filed financial statements that are acceptable for the purpose for which they were filed. This position will also be taken when the auditor's report that accompanies a Non-Canadian Issuer's financial statements includes additional emphasis paragraphs in situations that do not represent or require a reservation of opinion under Canadian GAAS.

6.3   *Example of application of section 6.2* – A report prepared in accordance with generally accepted auditing standards in the United States may include an additional emphasis paragraph where there is uncertainty as to an issuer's ability to continue to operate as a going concern. As Canadian GAAS does not permit this reference when there is adequate disclosure in the financial statements, the securities regulatory authorities will generally take the position that the Non-Canadian Issuer has filed financial statements that are acceptable for the purpose for which they were filed, if, in all other respects,

(1)   the financial statements are prepared in accordance with generally accepted accounting principles in the United States,

(2)   the audit has been performed in accordance with generally accepted auditing standards in the United States, and

(3)   there is adequate disclosure of the uncertainty in the financial statements.

PART 7   DISCRETION AVAILABLE TO APPLICABLE REGULATOR

Where an Issuer, including a Non-Canadian Issuer, or the Issuer's auditor believes that the auditor's report on the Issuer's financial statements will contain a reservation of opinion that is not, or may not be, otherwise acceptable to the securities regulatory authorities, the Issuer together with its auditor should discuss the situation with the Applicable Regulator. The Applicable Regulator may, if it has the necessary authority under the Securities Legislation of that jurisdiction and it considers it to be in the public interest,

(1)   at the request of the Issuer, and

(2)   upon receipt in writing from the

(a)   Issuer of all relevant information, and

(b)   Issuer's auditor of the impact of the relevant information on the preparation of the financial statements in accordance with Canadian GAAP or the auditor's ability to complete the audit in accordance with Canadian GAAS or Non-Canadian GAAS, as applicable, together with the anticipated form of the auditor's report,

sufficiently in advance of the filing deadline applicable to the financial statements that will be accompanied by an auditor's report containing a reservation of opinion, exercise its discretion to accept financial statements that are accompanied by an auditor's report containing a reservation of opinion when the financial statements are filed. In certain jurisdictions the Applicable Regulator may require the holding of a public hearing as part of its consideration of the Issuer's request.

PART 8   EFFECTIVE DATE

This policy statement is effective December 31, 1992.

NATIONAL POLICY STATEMENT No. 51
CHANGES IN THE ENDING DATE OF A FINANCIAL YEAR AND IN REPORTING STATUS

TABLE OF CONTENTS

NATIONAL POLICY STATEMENT NO. 51
CHANGES IN THE ENDING DATE OF A FINANCIAL YEAR
AND IN REPORTING STATUS

PART 1 INTERPRETATION

In this policy statement:

"AIF" means an annual information form required under the Securities Legislation or Securities Requirements of a Jurisdiction;

"Current AIF" has the meaning ascribed to this term in NPS 47;

"Filing Issuer" means an issuer required to file financial statements under the Securities Legislation of a Jurisdiction;

"Jurisdiction" means a province or territory of Canada;

"MD&A" means management's discussion and analysis of financial condition and results of operations required under the Securities Legislation or Securities Requirements of a Jurisdiction;

"NPS 47" means National Policy Statement No. 47 and the comparable provisions in the Securities Legislation and Securities Requirements of the Province of Québec;

"New Financial Year" means the financial year of a Filing Issuer that immediately follows its Transition Year;

"Old Financial Year" means the financial year of a Filing Issuer that immediately precedes its Transition Year;

"Part 4 Notice" means a notice that complies with the provisions of part 4 and that is filed pursuant to the requirements of part 4 or part 8;

"Reverse Take-over" means a reverse take-over as defined in section 1580 of the Handbook of the Canadian Institute of Chartered Accountants and supplemented in Abstract No. 10 issued by the Emerging Issues Committee of the Canadian Institute of Chartered Accountants;

"SEC" means the Securities and Exchange Commission of the United States of America;

"Securities Legislation" means the statutes concerning the regulation of securities markets and trading in securities in a Jurisdiction, and the regulations in respect of these statutes;

"Securities Requirements" means the blanket rulings and orders made under the Securities Legislation of a Jurisdiction, and the policy statements and written interpretations issued by the securities regulatory authority of that Jurisdiction;

"Transition Year" means the financial year of a Filing Issuer in which a change in the ending date of its financial year occurs; and

"U.S. Issuer" has the meaning ascribed to this term in National Policy Statement No. 45.

PART 2   PURPOSE

2.1   *Change in ending date of financial year* – This policy statement sets out the position of the securities regulatory authorities with respect to

     (1)   the periods required to be presented in, and the filing deadlines applicable to, financial statements that are required to be filed under the continuous disclosure requirements of the Securities Legislation of a Jurisdiction,

     (2)   the filing deadlines applicable to an AIF, and the disclosure required in the MD&A, filed with the securities regulatory authority of a Jurisdiction, and

     (3)   the disclosure required in, and the additional requirements applicable in the event of the filing of a prospectus or a short form prospectus with a securities regulatory authority during certain time periods,

as a result of a change in the ending date of a Filing Issuer's financial year.

2.2   *Change in reporting status* – This policy statement also sets out the position of the securities regulatory authorities with respect to the financial statements required to be filed under the Securities Legislation of a Jurisdiction by

     (1)   an entity that becomes a Filing Issuer, or

     (2)   in certain circumstances, a Filing Issuer that ceases to be a Filing Issuer.

PART 3   APPLICATION

3.1   *General application* – This policy statement applies to

     (1)   all financial statements required to be filed under the continuous disclosure requirements of the Securities Legislation of a Jurisdiction as a result of a change in

         (a)   the ending date of the financial year of a Filing Issuer, or

         (b)   reporting status,

     (2)   any AIF filed with a securities regulatory authority in a Jurisdiction in respect of a Filing Issuer's Transition Year,

     (3)   any MD&A disclosure that includes a discussion of the results of the Filing Issuer for its Transition Year, and

     (4)   any prospectus or short form prospectus that includes, or incorporates by reference, financial statements in respect of a Transition Year and that is filed in a Jurisdiction during certain time periods by a Filing Issuer,

unless otherwise specified in, or exempted by, the Securities Legislation of that Jurisdiction.

3.2   *Application to Filing Issuer registered with SEC* – The application of this policy statement to a Filing Issuer registered with the SEC is set out in part 11.

3.3   *Application to a registrant* – Although this policy statement applies only to Filing Issuers, the securities regulatory authorities take the position that registrants should review and consider the principles set out in this policy statement in the event they decide to change the ending date of their financial year to ensure their financial reporting periods are reasonable in the circumstances.

3.4   *No application where change to or from a 52-53 week financial year* – A change in the ending date of a financial year from

(1)   the last day of a 12 month financial year to the last day of a 52-53 week financial year, or

(2)   from the last day of a 52-53 week financial year to the last day of a 12 month financial year,

does not constitute a change in the ending date of a financial year for purposes of this policy statement or a change in the ending date of a financial year for purposes of the Securities Legislation of a Jurisdiction. In the circumstances referred to above, either of the financial years affected by the change can be as short as 359 days, or as long as 371 days (372 days in a leap year).

3.5   *Sending of financial statements* – Where a Filing Issuer changes the ending date of its financial year and the Filing Issuer

(a)   is not a U.S. Issuer, the Filing Issuer is required to send its financial statements to its security holders for

(i) each interim period in its Transition Year, and

(ii) its Transition Year

concurrently with the filing of these statements under this policy statement; or

(b)   is a U.S. Issuer, the Filing Issuer is required to send its financial statements to its security holders for

(i) each interim period in its Transition Year, and

(ii) its Transition Year

in accordance with the requirements of National Policy Statement No. 45.

3.6   *Examples* – Examples of the application of this policy statement have been made available for general information purposes and are set out in Appendix A. These examples are provided for illustrative purposes only and in the event of any inconsistency between the examples and the provisions of this policy statement, the provisions of the policy statement shall prevail.

PART 4   NOTICE OF CHANGE IN THE ENDING DATE OF A FINANCIAL YEAR

4.1   *Notice required* – Where a Filing Issuer elects to change the ending date of its financial year, the Filing Issuer must prepare a notice containing the information set out in section 4.3.[1]

4.2   *Filing deadline for Part 4 Notice* – All approvals required by applicable laws together with any applicable governmental or regulatory approvals must be obtained by a Filing Issuer prior to making the change in the ending date of its financial year. A Filing Issuer must file the notice required by section 4.1 forthwith upon receipt of the necessary approvals but, in any event, no later than the earlier of:

(1)   the new ending date selected for its financial year, and

(2)   360 days from the end of its latest financial year that is required to have been reported on by an auditor.

If a change in the ending date of the financial year is approved by the board of directors of the Filing Issuer before the earlier of the two dates contemplated above but any additional approvals required to effect the change are not obtained before that date, the Filing Issuer must file the notice by the earlier of the two dates contemplated above. Upon receipt of the additional required approvals, the Filing Issuer must file a supplement to the notice indicating that all remaining approvals have been received and the date of their receipt.

---

1   The British Columbia Securities Commission and the Ontario Securities Commission require that a Filing Issuer issue and file a press release when it elects to change the ending date of its financial year.

4.3   Information in Part 4 Notice – The notice must indicate

(1)   the intention of the Filing Issuer to change the ending date of its financial year;

(2)   the reasons for the change;

(3)   the approvals required to effect the change and whether each approval has been received by the Filing Issuer and, where the Filing Issuer has not received all the required approvals, the approvals that it has received, those that are still outstanding and, if known, the anticipated date of their receipt;

(4)   the date or dates of:

    (a)   the last day of the Filing Issuer's Old Financial Year,

    (b)   the last day of the Filing Issuer's Transition Year, and

    (c)   the periods, including the comparative reporting periods, to be covered in the interim and annual financial statements to be filed for the Filing Issuer's Transition Year and its New Financial Year; reference should be made to section 6.3 for the specific provisions applicable to the information to be contained in the notice where a Filing Issuer intends to file, during its Transition Year, its interim financial statements based on the interim reporting periods in its New Financial Year; and

(5)   where, due to the provisions of section 6.2, the filing deadline for the Filing Issuer's interim financial statements is 10 days after the date on which the Old Financial Year's audited financial statements are required to be filed, the due date of the interim financial statements.

PART 5   LENGTH OF TRANSITION YEAR

5.1   Maximum length – Provided a Filing Issuer has filed a Part 4 Notice stating its intention to change the ending date of its financial year by the date indicated in section 4.2, the Filing Issuer may have a Transition Year as long as, but no longer than,

(1)   15 months, or

(2)   if the Filing Issuer has a Current AIF, 18 months.

5.2   Minimum length – Provided a Filing Issuer has filed a Part 4 Notice stating its intention to change the ending date of its financial year by the date indicated in section 4.2, the Filing Issuer may have a Transition Year of less than 12 months. Reference should be made to section 7.2 for the specific provisions applicable to a Transition Year that is shorter than nine months where the Transition Year's financial statements are filed as comparatives to those for the New Financial Year.

PART 6   FINANCIAL STATEMENT FILING REQUIREMENTS DURING TRANSITION YEAR

6.1   Audited financial statements filing deadline – Where a Filing Issuer changes the ending date of its financial year so that its Transition Year is longer than 12 months, the Filing Issuer must file its Transition Year audited financial statements on or before the date which is the later of

(1)   90 days after the end of its Transition Year, and

(2)   140 days after the first anniversary of the ending date of its Old Financial Year.

Where a Filing Issuer changes the ending date of its financial year so that its Transition Year is less than 12 months, the filing deadline for its Transition Year audited financial statements is 140 days after the ending date of its Transition Year.

6.2   Interim financial statements filing deadline – Where a Filing Issuer changes the ending date of its financial year, the Filing Issuer must file its Transition Year interim financial statements within 60 days of the date to which they are made up unless this date is prior to the date on which the Old Financial Year's audited financial statements are required to be filed. In this case the filing deadline for the interim financial statements shall be 10 days after the date on which the Old Financial Year's audited financial statements are required to be filed.

6.3   *Interim reporting periods during Transition Year* – A Filing Issuer must, during its Transition Year, file interim financial statements based on the interim reporting periods in its Old Financial Year unless it clearly states in its Part 4 Notice that it will file interim financial statements based on the interim reporting periods in its New Financial Year. In the latter case, the Filing Issuer may file interim financial statements during its Transition Year based on the interim reporting periods in its New Financial Year for any interim period that ends after the filing of the Filing Issuer's Part 4 Notice with the securities regulatory authorities. Where a Filing Issuer chooses to file its interim financial statements based on the interim reporting periods in its New Financial Year, the interim reporting period that serves as the transition period between the interim reporting periods in the Old Financial Year and those in the New Financial Year cannot exceed four months in length; in addition, the periods presented due to the change in interim reporting periods must be consecutive.

6.4   *Interim reporting where interim period ends within 32 days of year end* – Provided it filed a Part 4 Notice within the time frame contemplated in section 4.2, a Filing Issuer will not be required to file interim financial statements for any interim period in its Transition Year that ends up to 32 days

   (1)   after the end of its Old Financial Year, or

   (2)   prior to the commencement of its New Financial Year.

6.5   *Interim reporting where the Transition Year is longer than 13 months* – Where a Filing Issuer changes the ending date of its financial year so that its Transition Year exceeds 13 months, the Filing Issuer must, subject to section 6.4, also file interim financial statements for the period from the commencement of the Transition Year to the end of each three month period that ends after the third interim reporting period of its Transition Year and before the end of its Transition Year. This provision applies whether the Filing Issuer prepares its interim financial statements on the basis of the interim reporting periods in its Old Financial Year or its New Financial Year.

PART 7   COMPARATIVE FINANCIAL STATEMENT REQUIREMENTS FOR TRANSITION YEAR AND NEW FINANCIAL YEAR

7.1   *Comparative audited financial statements to the Transition Year* – Where a Filing Issuer changes the ending date of its financial year, the Filing Issuer must include the audited annual financial statements for its Old Financial Year as comparatives to those for its Transition Year.

7.2   *Comparative audited financial statements to the New Financial Year* – Where a Filing Issuer changes the ending date of its financial year and the change results in a Transition Year of

   (1)   less than nine months, the Filing Issuer must include audited statements of income, retained earnings and changes in financial position for both its Transition Year and its Old Financial Year as comparatives to those for its New Financial Year; or

   (2)   nine months or more, the Filing Issuer need only include the audited statements of income, retained earnings and changes in financial position for its Transition Year as comparatives to those for its New Financial Year.

In each case, the Filing Issuer need only include as a comparative the audited balance sheet as at the ending date of its Transition Year.

7.3   *Comparative Interim financial statements where no change in interim reporting periods in Transition Year* – Where, during its Transition Year, a Filing Issuer continues to file its interim financial statements based on the interim reporting periods in its Old Financial Year, the Filing Issuer must include

   (1)   as comparative interim financial statements to its Transition Year's

      (a)   three, six and nine month interim financial statements, the interim financial statements for the corresponding periods in its Old Financial Year, as appropriate; and

    (b)   12 or 15 month interim financial statements, where the Filing Issuer is required to file interim financial statements for a 12 or 15 month interim period pursuant to section 6.5, the 12 month reporting period that constitutes its Old Financial Year; and

  (2)   as comparative interim financial statements to its New Financial Year's interim financial statements, the interim financial statements from its Transition Year or Old Financial Year, or both, as appropriate, that:

    (a)   cover the same number of months as the New Financial Year's Interim financial statements; and

    (b)   cover a period which ends 11, 12 or 13 months prior to the ending date of the New Financial Year's interim reporting period.

7.4   *Comparative Interim financial statements where change in Interim reporting periods in Transition Year* – Where, during its Transition Year, a Filing Issuer files its interim financial statements based on the interim reporting periods in its New Financial Year, the Filing Issuer must include

  (1)   as comparative interim financial statements to its Transition Year's

    (a)   interim financial statements for its first, second and third interim reporting period, the interim financial statements for its first, second or third interim reporting periods in its Old Financial Year, as appropriate; and

    (b)   interim financial statements for any interim reporting period of 11 months or more, where the Filing Issuer is required to file interim financial statements for a period of 11 months or more pursuant to section 6.5, interim financial statements that cover the 12 month reporting period that constitutes its Old Financial Year; and

  (2)   as comparative interim financial statements to its New Financial Year's interim financial statements, the interim financial statements from its Transition Year or Old Financial Year, or both, as appropriate, that

    (a)   where section 6.4 does not apply to the comparative period,

        (i)   cover the same number of months, plus or minus one month, as the New Financial Year's interim financial statements, and

       (ii)   cover a period that ends 12 months prior to the ending date of the New Financial Year's interim reporting period; or

    (b)   where section 6.4 applies to the comparative period,

        (i)   cover the same number of months as the New Financial Year's Interim financial statement; and

       (ii)   cover a period which ends 11, 12 or 13 months prior to the ending date of the New Financial Year's interim reporting period.

PART 8   FILING REQUIREMENTS AFTER A REVERSE TAKE-OVER OR STATUTORY AMALGAMATION

8.1   *Notification of transaction* – Upon the effective date of a Reverse Take-over or a statutory amalgamation involving one or more Filing Issuers, the continuing Filing Issuer shall forthwith provide the securities regulatory authorities with a notice indicating

  (1)   the names of the parties to the transaction;

  (2)   the effective date of the transaction;

  (3)   the approvals required to effect the transaction and the date or dates on which each approval was received by the parties to the transaction;

  (4)   for each party to the transaction that was a Filing Issuer immediately prior to the effective date of the transaction, the date of its last financial year end prior to the effective date of the transaction;

  (5)   the method of accounting for the transaction and, where appropriate, the entity that is identified as being the acquirer for accounting purposes; and,

(6)　with respect to the continuing Filing Issuer

　　(a)　the date of its first financial year end subsequent to the transaction; and

　　(b)　the periods, including the comparative reporting periods, if any, to be covered in the interim and annual financial statements to be filed for the continuing Filing Issuer's first financial year subsequent to the transaction.

8.2　*Where change in ending date of financial year end deemed to occur* – Where the continuing Filing Issuer's financial year end is the same as the financial year end of one of the Filing Issuer's involved in the Reverse Take-Over or statutory amalgamation, the continuing Filing Issuer shall not be deemed to be changing the ending date of its financial year. Where the continuing Filing Issuer's financial year end is different than the financial year end of any of the Filing Issuer's involved in the relevant transaction, the continuing Filing Issuer shall be deemed to be changing the ending date of its financial year and must ensure that the notice filed under this part also includes all of the information set out in part 4 as being required in a Part 4 Notice and that the year end date selected complies with the requirements of this policy statement relating to a change in the ending date of a financial year.

PART 9　AIF AND MD&A REQUIREMENTS

9.1　*Filing deadline for AIF* – Where a Filing Issuer changes the ending date of its financial year, the Filing Issuer must file an AIF in respect of its Transition Year no later than the last day it is required to file its Transition Year audited financial statements under section 6.1 in order, as applicable, to

(1)　continue to have a Current AIF and be eligible to make a distribution of securities under NPS 47; and

(2)　satisfy any AIF filing requirement that may apply to a Filing Issuer other than a Filing Issuer filing a Current AIF under NPS 47.

9.2　*Required disclosure in MD&A* – Where a Filing Issuer has changed the ending date of its financial year, the Filing Issuer must, in addition to any other information required to be included in its MD&A, discuss the periods covered in its audited financial statements regardless of the length of its Transition Year. The MD&A must also include a discussion of any quarterly, seasonal, operational or other factors as are deemed appropriate in the circumstances to provide the reader with a clear understanding of the impact of the length of the Transition Year on the reported results.

PART 10　EFFECT OF CHANGE IN ENDING DATE OF FINANCIAL YEAR ON PROSPECTUS REQUIREMENTS

The requirements of the Securities Legislation of a Jurisdiction that the prospectus of an issuer contain a balance sheet as at a date not more that a specified number of days before the date of the receipt for the preliminary prospectus shall apply to a Filing Issuer that changes the ending date of its financial year. However, where a Filing Issuer must, pursuant to section 6.1, file its Transition Year audited financial statements within 90 days after the end of its Transition Year, any preliminary prospectus filed after the due date or filing date of the annual audited financial statements of the Filing Issuer must include, or incorporate by reference, its Transition Year audited financial statements in the preliminary prospectus.[2]

2　The requirements for financial statements in a preliminary short form prospectus or a short form prospectus that is filed prior to the most recent financial year's comparative financial statements having been filed pursuant to the continuous disclosure requirements of the Securities Legislation in the Jurisdiction in which the preliminary short form prospectus or short form prospectus is filed are set out in NPS 47. Those requirements also apply when the preliminary short form prospectus or short form prospectus is filed prior to the filing deadline for the Transition Year's financial statements that is set out in this part.

PART 11   FILING ISSUERS REGISTERED WITH THE SEC

A Filing Issuer registered with the SEC may satisfy the requirements of parts 4 to 7, inclusive, of this policy statement by filing a Part 4 Notice and by filing with the securities regulatory authorities the financial statements, reports and other documents required by the SEC's Financial Reporting Release No. 35.

PART 12   CHANGE IN REPORTING STATUS

12.1   *Commencement of reporting status* – An entity that becomes subject to the continuous disclosure requirements under the Securities Legislation of a Jurisdiction is required to file

(1)   interim financial statements for its first interim reporting period, and

(2)   annual audited financial statements for its first financial year,

that ends after it becomes subject to those requirements. There are no requirements to include comparative interim financial statements to a Filing Issuer's interim financial statements for any interim period that ends within the first 12 months subsequent to the Filing Issuer becoming subject to continuous disclosure requirements.

12.2   *Termination of reporting status in event of acquisition* – Where a Filing Issuer ceases to be subject to the continuous disclosure requirements of the Securities Legislation of a Jurisdiction because it is acquired by another Filing Issuer, the Filing Issuer that has been acquired must file the financial statements otherwise required by Securities Legislation for entities that are subject to continuous disclosure requirements in the Jurisdiction, for all financial statement reporting periods, or parts thereof, up to and including the day immediately preceding the date on which it was acquired. This may result in a shorter or longer continuous disclosure reporting period in the financial statements than is normally required under Securities Legislation if the acquisition date is not the day after a usual ending date of a financial reporting period of the Filing Issuer that has been acquired. In this case, the general principles of this policy statement apply with respect to acceptable variations in the length of financial statement reporting periods.

12.3   *Termination of reporting status for mutual fund* – Where a mutual fund ceases to be subject to the continuous disclosure requirements of the Securities Legislation of a Jurisdiction, the mutual fund must file the financial statements otherwise required by securities legislation for mutual funds that are subject to continuous disclosure requirements in the Jurisdiction, for all financial statement reporting periods, or parts thereof, up to and including the day immediately preceding the date on which the mutual fund ceases to be subject to those requirements. This may result in a shorter or longer continuous disclosure reporting period than is normally required under Securities Legislation if the day the mutual fund ceases to be subject to continuous disclosure requirements is not the day after a usual ending date of a financial reporting period of the mutual fund. In this case, the general principles of this policy statement apply with respect to acceptable variations in the length of financial statement reporting periods.

PART 13   EXCEPTIONS

Where a Filing Issuer anticipates that it will not be in a position to comply with the requirements of this policy statement or believes that an alternate approach is more appropriate in the circumstances, the Filing Issuer is encouraged to discuss the situation with the securities regulatory authority of each Jurisdiction in which it is required to file its financial statements. For this purpose, the securities regulatory authorities will require the Filing Issuer to submit all relevant information in writing sufficiently in advance of the time by which compliance with this policy statement would otherwise be required.

PART 14   EFFECTIVE DATE

This Policy Statement is effective for financial years ending on or after August 31, 1993.

NATIONAL POLICY STATEMENT NO. 51
APPENDIX A

EXAMPLES OF FILING REQUIREMENTS FOR CHANGES IN
THE ENDING DATE OF A FINANCIAL YEAR AND IN REPORTING STATUS

The following examples demonstrate the principles set out in the policy statement. The first four examples assume that a Filing Issuer that has had a December 31 financial year end elects to change the ending date of its financial year and files the Part 4 Notice in accordance with the policy statement on January 30, 1993. In addition, these examples assume that the last set of audited annual financial statements filed under continuous disclosure requirements with the securities regulatory authorities prior to the change in the ending date of the financial year were for the year ended December 31, 1992. Note that if the Part 4 Notice was filed after January 30, 1993 the interim reporting periods, and the comparative interim reporting periods, during the Transition Year and the New Financial Year, could be different from those set out in the examples. Readers should note that section 6.3 of this policy statement requires that a Filing Issuer file a Part 4 Notice prior to changing its interim reporting periods during the Transition Year.

Included in the examples are bracketed references to the specific sections of the policy statement that are being exemplified. This reference is in the form "[#]" where the "#" is the section reference.

In the examples, defined terms have the same meaning as in the policy statement.

National
Policies

NATIONAL POLICY STATEMENT NO. 51　APPENDIX A　EXAMPLES OF FILING REQUIREMENTS FOR CHANGES IN THE ENDING OF A FINANCIAL YEAR

Year End Changed By [5.1]	Transition Year [5.1]	Comparative Annual Financial Statements To Transition Year [7.1]	Filing Deadline Transition Year (# of days after year end) [6.1]	New Financial Year	Comparative Annual Financial Statements To New Financial Year [7.2]	Interim Periods For Transition Year [6.3 to 6.5]	Comparative Interim Periods To Transition Year [7.3 and 7.4]	Filing Deadline Transition Year Interim Report [6.2]	Interim Periods For New Financial Year	Comparative Interim Periods To New Financial Year [7.3 and 7.4]
1. up to 3 months	a) 2 months ended February 28, 1993	12 months ended December 31, 1992	140 days	12 months ended February 28, 1994	2 months ended February 28, 1993 and 12 months ended December 31, 1992***	not applicable	not applicable	not applicable	3 months ended May 31, 1993; 6 months ended August 31, 1993; 9 months ended November 30, 1993	3 months ended June 30, 1992; 6 months ended September 30, 1992; 9 months ended December 31, 1992
	or									
	b) 14 months ended February 28, 1994	12 months ended December 31, 1992	90 days	12 months ended February 28, 1995	14 months ended February 28, 1994	a) 3 months ended March 31, 1993; 6 months ended June 30, 1993; 9 months ended September 30, 1993; 12 months ended December 31, 1993 or if indicated in Part 4 Notice	3 months ended March 31, 1992; 6 months ended June 30, 1992; 9 months ended September 30, 1992; 12 months ended December 31, 1992	*	3 months ended May 31, 1994; 6 months ended August 31, 1994; 9 months ended November 30, 1994	3 months ended June 30, 1993; 6 months ended September 30, 1993; 9 months ended December 31, 1993

* Interim financial statements must be filed within 60 days of the end of the Interim period.

*** Balance sheet required at transition year end date only.

NATIONAL POLICY STATEMENT NO. 51   APPENDIX A   EXAMPLES OF FILING REQUIREMENTS FOR CHANGES IN THE ENDING OF A FINANCIAL YEAR

Year End Changed By	Transition Year [5.1]	Comparative Annual Financial Statements To Transition Year [7.1]	Filing Deadline Transition Year (# of days after year end) [6.1]	New Financial Year	Comparative Annual Financial Statements To New Financial Year [7.2]	Interim Periods For Transition Year [6.3 to 6.5]	Comparative Interim Periods To Transition Year [7.3 and 7.4]	Filing Deadline Transition Year Interim Report [6.2]	Interim Periods For New Financial Year	Comparative Interim Periods To New Financial Year [7.3 and 7.4]
2) 4 to 6 months	a) 6 months ended June 30, 1993	12 months ended December 31, 1992	140 days	12 months ended June 30, 1994	6 months ended June 30, 1993 and 12 months ended December 31, 1992***	b) 2 months ended February 28, 1993	3 months ended March 31, 1992	**	3 months ended May 31, 1994	3 months ended May 31, 1993
						5 months ended May 31, 1993	6 months ended June 30, 1992	*	6 months ended August 31, 1994	6 months ended August 31, 1993
						8 months ended August 31, 1993	9 months ended September 30, 1992	*	9 months ended November 30, 1994	9 months ended November 30, 1993
						11 months ended November 30, 1993	12 months ended December 31, 1992	*		
						3 months ended March 31, 1993	3 months ended March 31, 1992	*	3 months ended September 30, 1993	3 months ended September 30, 1992
									6 months ended December 31, 1993	6 months ended December 31, 1992
									9 months ended March 31, 1994	9 months ended March 31, 1993

* Interim financial statements must be filed within 60 days of the end of the Interim period.

** Interim financial statements must be filed within 10 days of the due date of the annual financial statements for the Old Financial Year.

*** Balance sheet required at transition year end date only.

National Policies

NATIONAL POLICY STATEMENT NO. 51   APPENDIX A   EXAMPLES OF FILING REQUIREMENTS FOR CHANGES IN THE ENDING OF A FINANCIAL YEAR

Year End Changed By	Transition Year [5.1]	Comparative Annual Financial Statements To Transition Year [7.1]	Filing Deadline Transition Year (# of days after year end) [6.1]	New Financial Year	Comparative Annual Financial Statements To New Financial Year [7.2]	Interim Periods For Transition Year [6.3 to 6.5]	Comparative Interim Periods To Transition Year [7.3 and 7.4]	Filing Deadline Transition Year Interim Report [6.2]	Interim Periods For New Financial Year	Comparative Interim Periods To New Financial Year [7.3 and 7.4]
	or, if Filing Issuer has a Current AIF and so chooses									
b) 18 months ended June 30, 1994	12 months ended December 31, 1992	90 days	12 months ended June 30, 1995	18 months ended June 30, 1994	3 months ended March 31, 1993	3 months ended March 31, 1992	*	3 months ended September 30, 1994	3 months ended September 30, 1993
						6 months ended June 30, 1993	6 months ended June 30, 1992	*	6 months ended December 31, 1994	6 months ended December 31, 1993
						9 months ended September 30, 1993	9 months ended September 30, 1992	*	9 months ended March 31, 1995	9 months ended March 31, 1994
						12 months ended December 31, 1993	12 months ended December 31, 1992	*		
						15 months ended March 31, 1994	12 months ended December 31, 1992	*		

* Interim financial statements must be filed within 60 days of the end of the Interim period.

NATIONAL POLICY STATEMENT NO. 51   APPENDIX A   EXAMPLES OF FILING REQUIREMENTS FOR CHANGES IN THE ENDING OF A FINANCIAL YEAR

Year End Changed By	Transition Year [5.1]	Comparative Annual Financial Statements To Transition Year [7.1]	Filing Deadline Transition Year (# of days after year end) [6.1]	New Financial Year	Comparative Annual Financial Statements To New Financial Year [7.2]	Interim Periods For Transition Year [6.3 to 6.5]	Comparative Interim Periods To Transition Year [7.3 and 7.4]	Filing Deadline Transition Year Interim Report [6.2]	Interim Periods For New Financial Year	Comparative Interim Periods To New Financial Year [7.3 and 7.4]
3) 7 or 8 months	7 months ended July 31, 1993	12 months ended December 31, 1992	140 days	12 months ended July 31, 1994	7 months ended July 31, 1993 and 12 months ended December 31, 1992***	a) 3 months ended March 31, 1993 or, if indicated in Part 4 Notice b) 4 months ended April 30, 1993	3 months ended March 31, 1992 3 months ended March 31, 1992	*	3 months ended October 31, 1993 6 months ended January 31, 1994 9 months ended April 30, 1994 3 months ended October 31, 1993 6 months ended January 31, 1994 9 months ended April 30, 1994	3 months ended September 30, 1992 6 months ended December 31, 1992 9 months ended March 31, 1993 5 months ended September 30, 1992 6 months ended December 31, 1992 10 months ended April 30, 1993

* Interim financial statements must be filed within 60 days of the end of the Interim period.

*** Balance sheet required at transition year end date only.

National Policies

NATIONAL POLICY STATEMENT NO. 51   APPENDIX A   EXAMPLES OF FILING REQUIREMENTS FOR CHANGES IN THE ENDING OF A FINANCIAL YEAR

Year End Changed By	Transition Year [5.1]	Comparative Annual Financial Statements To Transition Year [7.1]	Filing Deadline Transition Year (# of days after year end) [6.1]	New Financial Year	Comparative Annual Financial Statements To New Financial Year [7.2]	Interim Periods For Transition Year [6.3 to 6.5]	Comparative Interim Periods To Transition Year [7.3 and 7.4]	Filing Deadline Transition Year Interim Report [6.2]	Interim Periods For New Financial Year	Comparative Interim Periods To New Financial Year [7.3 and 7.4]
4) 9 to 11 months	10 months ended October 31, 1993	12 months ended December 31, 1992	140 days	12 months ended October 31, 1994	10 months ended October 31, 1993	a) 3 months ended March 31, 1993 6 months ended June 30, 1993 or if indicated in Part 4 Notice	3 months ended March 31, 1992 6 months ended June 30, 1992	*	3 months ended January 31, 1994 6 months ended April 30, 1994 9 months ended July 31, 1994	3 months ended December 31, 1992 6 months ended March 31, 1993 9 months ended June 30, 1993
						b) 4 months ended April 30, 1993 7 months ended July 31, 1993	3 months ended March 31, 1992 6 months ended June 30, 1992	*	3 months ended January 31, 1994 6 months ended April 30, 1994 9 months ended July 31, 1994	3 months ended December 31, 1992 7 months ended April 30, 1993 10 months ended July 31, 1993

* Interim financial statements must be filed within 60 days of the end of the Interim period.

5.   **Change to a 52-53 week year** – The Filing Issuer proposes to change the ending date of its financial year from December 31, 1992 to the last day of a 52 or 53 week period. So long as the 52 or 53 week period commences with January 1, 1993, this will not be deemed to be a change in the ending date of a financial year for purposes of this policy statement and no Part 4 Notice is required to be filed. [3.4]

6.   **Change of year end after a Reverse Take-over** – Filing Issuer "A" enters into a transaction with Filing Issuer "B" that is accounted for as a Reverse Take-over with "A" being deemed to be the acquirer for accounting purposes. The financial year end of the (legal) continuing issuer ("B") can be any date so long as the year end selected complies with the maximum length of year provisions in section 5.1 relative to the most recently completed financial year of "A" and "B". The continuing issuer must file the notification required by part 8 of the policy statement. [8.1] If "B" proposes to use a year end other than that of one of the predecessor Filing Issuers, the information in this notification shall be included in a Part 4 Notice. [8.2]

7.   **Filings made under prompt offering qualification system** – A Filing Issuer with a Current AIF changes its financial year end to May 31 commencing in 1994 (i.e., its Transition Year is for a period of 17 months from January 1, 1993 to May 31, 1994). [5.1]

     The Filing Issuer is required to file an AIF and audited financial statements for the Transition Year within 90 days of May 31, 1994. [6.1 and 9.1] The comparative financial statements to those for the Transition Year ended May 31, 1994 will be for the Old Financial Year (i.e., the year ended December 31, 1992). [7.1]

     The MD&A included with the AIF for the Transition Year shall cover the 17 month period reported on in the Transition Year's audited financial statements. The MD&A shall include a discussion of any quarterly, seasonality, operational and other factors as are deemed appropriate in the circumstances to provide the reader with a clear understanding of the impact of the length of the financial year on the reported results. [9.2]

     The Filing Issuer's interim reporting periods, including comparative reporting periods, during the Transition Year and the New Financial Year are set out in parts 6 and 7 of this policy statement, and are illustrated elsewhere in this Appendix.

8.   **Commencement of reporting status** – An entity with a year end of December 31 files an initial public offering and becomes subject to continuous disclosure requirements on May 15, 1992. At that date the entity becomes a Filing Issuer. The Filing Issuer will commence filing interim financial statements for the six month period ended June 30, 1992 and its first annual audited financial statement will be for the year ended December 31, 1992. No comparative financial statements are required to be filed to the Filing Issuer's interim financial statements for the periods ending June 30 and September 30, 1992 and March 31, 1993. [12.1]

9.   **Termination of reporting status** – Filing Issuer "C" has a December 31, 1992 financial year end. On March 15, 1993 Filing Issuer "D" acquires 100% of the issued and outstanding shares of "C". On March 16, 1993, "C" ceases to be subject to continuous disclosure requirements under Securities Legislation. Notwithstanding that the termination date of reporting status for "C" is prior to the due date of the December 31, 1992 financial statements, "C" is required to file audited financial statements for its year ended December 31, 1992 and interim financial statements for the period from January 1, 1993 to March 15, 1993 to comply with the requirements of this policy statement and Securities Legislation.

UNIFORM ACT POLICIES

ALBERTA, BRITISH COLUMBIA, MANITOBA, SASKATCHEWAN AND ONTARIO

LIST OF UNIFORM ACT POLICIES

As at July 1, 1995

UNIFORM ACT POLICY No. 2-01

"UNDERTAKINGS" – EXTRA-PROVINCIAL COMPANIES

The Commission has directed the Director to refuse to issue a receipt for a prospectus until such time as the company proposing to distribute the equity shares to be offered by the prospectus has delivered undertakings satisfying the requirements of section 106 in Part X, section 117 in Part XI and section 132 in Part XII of the Securities Act, 1966, and the regulations made thereunder relating to proxies and proxy solicitation, insider trading reports and financial disclosure.

UNIFORM ACT POLICY No. 2-02

PROSPECTUSES – ANNUAL RE-FILINGS

Section 56 of the Securities Act, 1966, states:

"Where primary distribution to the public of the security is in progress twelve months from,

(a) the date of the issuance of the receipt for the preliminary prospectus relating to such security; or

(b) the date of the last prospectus relating to such security filed under this section,

as the case may be, a new prospectus that complies with this Part shall be filed with the Commission and a receipt therefor obtained from the Director within twenty days from the expiration of the applicable twelve-month period or, subject to such terms and conditions as the Commission may require, within such greater number of days as it may permit".

If primary distribution is to continue more than twelve months from the relevant date it is first necessary that a new prospectus complying with the Act is not only submitted but a receipt issued for it within twenty days of the expiration of the applicable twelve-month period. To minimize the possibility of a break in primary distribution, the following procedure may be followed,

(1) Material in the form of a preliminary prospectus under section 35 may be signed and submitted at least 30 days prior to the anniversary date of the prospectus. This will enable the Commission staff to review it and point up any deficiencies well before the anniversary date.

(2) The signed annual re-filing should be received by the Commission, dated not later than the anniversary date.

(3) In order to facilitate the processing of annual filings any changes in the narrative portion of the material filed under (1) should be underlined or otherwise clearly marked to indicate changes from the last prospectus filed. The cross-index sheet should offer an explanation for the reason for such changes.

UNIFORM ACT POLICY No. 2-03

PROSPECTUSES AND AMENDMENTS – CERTIFICATION (SECTION 52) SUPPORTING DOCUMENTATION

For clarification it is essential that the supporting documents (which are re-quired) include a certified copy of the resolution authorizing the two signing Directors to sign a final prospectus on behalf of the Board of Directors.

UNIFORM ACT POLICY No. 2-04

CONSENT OF SOLICITORS – DISCLOSURE OF INTEREST

The names of lawyers or legal firms frequently appear on the face page of prospectuses in two connections. Firstly, the underwriter and/or the company will name the lawyer upon whose advice he or it is relying. Secondly, the opinion of counsel that the securities may be purchased by insurance companies under the Canadian and British Insurance Companies Act or the Foreign Insurance Companies Act will be expressed.

In the first case the Commission is of the opinion that the solicitor, in the language of subsection (1) of section 50, is not named as having prepared or certified any part of the prospectus or is not named as having prepared or certified a report of valuation used in or in connection with a prospectus. This being so the written consent of the solicitor and the disclosure of interest required by subsections (1) and (4) would not be required.

In the second case, the opinion or similar reports are clearly prepared for the purpose of inclusion in the prospectus, section 50 applies and the consent and dis-closure of interest is required.

UNIFORM ACT POLICY No. 2-05

APPLICATIONS UNDER SECTIONS 34(1)14 and 71(1)(h) OF THE SECURITIES ACT, R.S.O. 1980, c. 466 BY A COMPANY WISHING TO SELL ADDITIONAL SECURITIES TO ITS SECURITY HOLDERS

Under the above sections of the Securities Act, a company wishing to sell additional securities of its own issue to holders of its securities is required to give notice to the Commission of its intention. The Commission, in turn, is required within 10 days of receipt of the notice to notify the company if it objects to the sale. To assist the Commission in determining whether it should object to the sale, the Commission wishes to be assured that the shareholders have been supplied with current infor-mation concerning the affairs of the company. Accordingly, the notice should be accompanied by the following information which, if it has not already been provided to the shareholders, must accompany the offer to them;

(1)   Notice of the last annual meeting.

(2)   A copy of its last annual report.

(3)   The latest audited financial statement.

(4)   In addition to the information concerning the date, amount, nature and conditions of the proposed sale, including the approximate net proceeds to be derived by the company on the basis of such additional securities being fully taken up and paid for, required to be provided by section 71(1)(h), there should be a brief statement of the purposes for which the additional funds are required and, if a minimum amount is required to carry out that purpose, the directors should state what in their opinion is the minimum amount required for that purpose. Where the offer is being made in another jurisdiction through a prospectus, a copy of the prospectus submitted for acceptance in that jurisdiction.

(5)   Any change in the directors and officers of the company since the last annual meeting.

(6)   Particulars known to the directors of any transfer of shares which has materially affected the control of the company since the last meeting of shareholders, or alternatively a statement that no such particulars are known.

(7)   The length of time during which the offer will be open should be clearly specified together with the details of any payments to be made to any person or company in connection with the offering.

(8)   If a minimum amount has been specified as being necessary under (4) and the offering is being made on a "best efforts" basis, the subscriptions shall be held in trust until that minimum amount is received. In the event that the minimum amount is not reached during the time specified in the offer, the subscriptions shall be returned to the subscribers in full. An independent trustee should be named to administer these funds.

(9)   If the minimum amount is to be provided through a stand-by underwriting, the name and address of the underwriter must be specified. (The Commission must be furnished with evidence of the financial ability of the underwriter to meet this commitment.) Where the underwriting agreement contains a "market-out" clause, or similar provision, this must be disclosed together with the arrangements made to assure that the subscriptions are returned to the subscribers in full in the event that the minimum amount required is not obtained. This would require the establishment of a Trust, as in (8) above.

(10) Where there is an agreement to compensate dealers for obtaining exercise of rights, there shall be no provision for payment of a higher fee for the exercise of rights by new security holders than is payable for the exercise of rights by existing security holders. Such an agreement indicates an intent to distribute to the public requiring a prospectus.

The following information must be submitted to the Commission with the notice but need not be forwarded to the shareholders unless otherwise directed by the Commission:

(1)   Copy of the minutes of the last annual meeting.

(2)   A statement signed by a senior officer of the company that there have been no material changes in the circumstances of the company since the date of the last audited financial statement delivered to the shareholders.

OTHER CONSIDERATIONS

While each situation will be dealt with on its own facts, generally speaking if the information stipulated above is furnished, the Commission will not object to a sale by a company of additional securities of its own issue to the holders of its securities, providing the company has been holding regular annual meetings, distributing the information required by the Act incorporating it to its shareholders, and there has been no change in the management elected by the shareholders at the last annual meeting or change in effective control of a company.

In considering the length of time in which it is proposed to leave the offer open the Commission will consider whether the purpose of the offer requires a minimum amount to be raised or whether the funds are being sought for the general purpose of the company. Where this is a minimum amount required the Commission will not consider unreasonable any offer left open for not more than 30 days. In the other cases the Commission will not consider as unreasonable any offer left open for not more than 90 days.

Where there is a stand-by underwriting, in reviewing its financial ability the fact that the underwriter is a registrant and subject to minimum capital requirements will be given favourable consideration.

The purpose of this policy is not to hamper offerings through this exemption. It will permit the Commission to ascertain whether the company has supplied adequate information to its shareholders and to ascertain whether the terms and conditions of the offer are clearly stipulated.

It is not the Commission's intention that this material be reviewed in the same stringent fashion as filings made under the prospectus requirements of the Act.

UNIFORM ACT POLICY No. 2-06

USE OF SHAREHOLDERS' LISTS BY REGISTRANTS

Sections 156, 157 and 158 of the Business Corporations Act restrict the use of a list of all of or any of the shareholders of a corporation only for purposes connected with the corporation of which they are shareholders. The purposes connected with the corporation are defined and the use of a list of all or any of the shareholders for other purposes is constituted an offence punishable on summary conviction. The buying or selling or otherwise trafficking in such a list is also constituted an offence punishable on summary conviction. While similar conduct is not prohibited by the Canada Corporations Act, notwithstanding the Commission feels the same restrictions should apply in so far as the use of shareholders' lists by registrants is concerned.

Accordingly, the Commission hereby gives notice to all registrants that the use by a registrant of all or any part of a list of shareholders of any corporation for any purpose other than a purpose similar to that authorized in the Business Corporations Act, and the buying and selling of or trafficking in such a list by a registrant will be considered by the Commission to be conduct contrary to the public interest and affecting his fitness for continued registration.

Although the corporation legislation of each jurisdiction varies in the Provinces of Alberta, British Columbia, Manitoba and Saskatchewan concur in the principle expressed.

UNIFORM ACT POLICY No. 2-07

SURRENDER OF REGISTRATION – OTHER THAN SALESMAN

Upon receipt of a notification that a registrant, other than a salesman, wishes to terminate its or his registration by surrender, the Commission normally will suspend the registration as a matter of routine procedure pending receipt of satisfactory evidence that all obligations to its or his clients have been discharged. Upon receipt of such evidence the suspension may be removed and the registration shall thereupon be regarded as having been voluntarily terminated.

UNIFORM ACT POLICY No. 2-08

DECLARATION AS TO SHORT POSITION –
LISTED AND UNLISTED SECURITIES

Registrants and the public are reminded of the provisions of section 78 of the Securities Act, 1966, which are as follows:

"Any person or company who places an order for the sale of a security through an agent acting for him that is registered for trading in securities and,

(a) at the time of placing the order, does not own the security; or

(b) if acting as agent, knows his principal does not own the security, shall at the time of placing the order to sell, declare to his agent that he or his principal, as the case may be, does not own the security".

The declaration by the client that he (or his principal) does not then own the security (a short sale) must be made at the time the order to sell is given. This requirement applies equally to unlisted and listed securities. Where the client has not declared a "short sale", failure by him to make delivery of the securities within the normal time for delivery and in the absence of any reasonable explanation is prima facie an indication of a violation by the client of section 78. Contraventions of provisions of the Act are an offence and punishable on summary conviction under section 136.

Registrants are requested to record and maintain for inspection a list of declared short sales of securities (listed or unlisted). Where the client fails to make delivery of the security sold within a reasonable time and offers no explanation for that failure, the facts should be forthwith reported to the Commission.

UNIFORM ACT POLICY No. 2-09

INSIDER TRADING REPORTS – LOAN AND TRUST COMPANIES

Notice is hereby given to insiders of Loan and Trust Companies that guaranteed deposit receipts or certificates of Trust Companies and deposit or savings accounts which are evidenced by a pass book, are not considered by the Commission to be capital securities for the purposes of insider trading reports.

UNIFORM ACT POLICY No. 2-10

INSIDER TRADING REPORTS – PERSONS REQUIRED TO REPORT IN MORE THAN ONE CAPACITY

Where an individual is an insider by virtue of being a director or senior officer of a principal company, and is also an insider by virtue of being a director or senior officer of a company that is itself an insider of that principal company he need only file one insider trading report. It is sufficient if he describes in the report the two or more capacities under which he is required to report.

UNIFORM ACT POLICY No. 2-11

POLICY STATEMENT IN CONNECTION WITH APPLICATIONS TO THE COMMISSION FOR AN ORDER UNDER SECTION 121(3) OF THE SECURITIES ACT, 1966 (ONTARIO) (now Section 79(a) of the new Act or section 173(3) of the Business Corporations Act, 1970 (Ontario))

Any applicant corporation applying under the Securities Act, for an order permitting sales or gross operating revenue results to be omitted from the statement of profit and loss or the interim financial statement, as the case may be, should make such application prior to the end of the fiscal period for which such statement is to be drawn up unless the said applicant can show substantial reasons why application was not made as herein provided.

The purpose of this new policy is to ensure final disposition of the application prior to the date the company is required by the legislation to file the financial statements with the Commission.

UNIFORM ACT POLICY No. 2-12

TIMELY DISCLOSURE

[Repealed]

UNIFORM ACT POLICY No. 2-13

ADVERTISING DURING WAITING PERIOD BETWEEN PRELIMINARY AND FINAL PROSPECTUSES

Under section 64(2) of the Securities Act and the equivalent provisions in the securities legislation of other Uniform Act provinces, it is permissible during the waiting period between the issuance of the receipt for the preliminary prospectus and the receipt for the final prospectus to advertise specific matters concerning the securities proposed to be offered. Newspaper advertisements can:

- "identify" the security;

- state the price of such security, if then determined;

- state the name and address of a person or company from whom purchases of securities may be made; and

- solicit expressions of interest in the securities.

The administrators are of the view that the "identification" of the security does not permit an issuer or dealer to include in the advertisement a summary of the commercial features of the issue. These details are set out in the preliminary prospectus which is intended as the main disclosure vehicle pending the issuance of the final receipt. The purpose of the advertisements permitted by the legislation during the waiting period is essentially to alert the public to the availability of the preliminary prospectus.

For the purpose of identifying a security, the administrators consider that the advertisement may only:

- indicate whether a security represents debt or a share in a company or an interest in a non-corporate entity (e.g. a unit of undivided ownership in a film property) or a partnership interest;

- name the issuer if the issuer is a reporting issuer; or

- name and describe briefly the business of the issuer if the issuer is not already a reporting issuer. The description of the business should be cast in general terms and should not attempt to summarize the proposed use of proceeds;

- indicate, without giving details, whether the security qualifies the holder for special tax treatment; and;

- indicate how many securities will be made available.

Every advertisement should include in bold face type as large as that used in the body of the text words to the effect of the following legend:

A preliminary prospectus relating to these securities has been filed with securities commissions or similar authorities in certain provinces of Canada but has not yet become final for the purpose of a distribution to the public. This advertisement shall not constitute an offer to sell or the solicitation of an offer to buy, nor shall there be any sale or any acceptance of an offer to buy these securities in any province of Canada prior to the time a receipt for the final prospectus or other authorization is obtained from the securities commission or similar authority in such province.

SECURITIES ACT

INDEX OF BLANKET ORDERS AND RULINGS

Effective June 30, 1995

BOR#	Date of BOR (mm/dd/yy)	Description	Status (mm/dd/yy)
87/18	03/23/87	Certain certificates for government securities and zero coupon strip bonds	revoked effective 07/04/95 (see NIN#95/25)
87/29	06/11/87	A policy of the Toronto Stock Exchange on small shareholder selling and purchase arrangements	in effect
87/30	06/11/87	A policy of the Montreal Exchange on small shareholder selling and purchase arrangements	in effect 05/26/87
88/2	08/12/88	The definition of "exchange issuer"	in effect 09/01/88
88/3	08/12/88	Transitional rules respecting securities traded prior to September 1, 1988 under a exemption from section 42 of the Securities Act	in effect 09/01/88
88/5	08/12/88	Legending of certificates	in effect 09/01/88
88/6	08/12/88	Filing of insider reports by control persons	in effect 09/01/88
88/11	11/28/88	Conflict of interest rules statement - confirmation and reporting of transactions by registrants	in effect
89/1	01/26/89	Registration of persons trading in IOCC options	in effect
89/2	03/17/89	Requirement to send interim financial statements to shareholders of a reporting issuer	in effect 03/01/88
89/5	10/05/89	Trades in securities held subject to an escrow or pooling agreement	in effect
89/8	10/13/89	Reporting companies under the British Columbia Company Act and the definition of "reporting issuer"	in effect 11/01/89
89/10	10/31/89	Required form of offering memorandum	in effect 11/01/89
90/1	01/29/90	Trades of government warrants	in effect
90/2	02/27/90	Trades in shares issued in accordance with the Employee Investment Act	in effect
90/4	10/11/90	Trades in deposit-type or self-directed registered educational savings plans	in effect
91/2	05/03/91	Rules for shelf prospectus offerings and for pricing offerings after the prospectus is receipted	in effect 05/10/91
91/4	06/06/91	Trades of securities of private issuers	in effect 07/01/91
91/5	06/06/91	Resale of rights acquired under a rights offering	in effect 07/01/91

Blanket Orders

BOR#	Date of BOR (mm/dd/yy)	Description	Status (mm/dd/yy)
91/6	06/06/91	Recognition of certain countries and political divisions of countries issuing bonds, debentures or other evidence of indebtedness	in effect 07/01/91
91/7	06/25/91	Multijurisdictional Disclosure System	in effect 07/01/91 (see NIN#93/12)
91/8	08/01/91	Registration of Persons Trading in TCO Commodity Options	in effect 05/17/91
91/10	08/08/91	First Renewal Prospectuses Filed by Mutual Funds under National Policy Statement No. 36	in effect
91/12	12/12/91	Government Strip Bonds	in effect (see NIN#95/9)
92/1	04/23/92	Fees payable by members of the press for a subscription to the Weekly Summary and for search of a file	in effect
92/2	08/06/92	Limitations on a registrant underwriting securities of a related party or connected party of the registrant	in effect
92/3	11/18/92	Revocation of BOR#91/11 [AND] recognized options traded through recognized clearing agencies (recognized options rationalization order)	in effect 08/11/92
93/1	02/17/93	Prompt Offering Qualification System - Exemption Orders under Section 59 of the Act and Sections 99(2), 115(6) and 143(1)(b)(iii) of the Regulation	in effect 02/19/93 (see NIN#93/12)
93/3	06/16/93	The multijurisdictional disclosure system - Exemption order under Section 97(2) of the Company Act	in effect
93/4	12/22/93	Networking Arrangements Governed by the Principle of Regulations	in effect
94/1	11/23/94	Prompt Offering Qualification System - Memorandum of Understanding for expedited review of short form prospectuses and renewal AIFs	in effect 11/23/94 (see NIN#94/22)
95/1	01/05/95	Form 12A summary prospectus disclosure system - Order under Section 59 of the Act	in effect (see NIN#95/4)
95/2	06/22/95	Revocation of BOR#87/18	in effect 07/04/95 (see NIN#95/25)

IN THE MATTER OF THE SECURITIES ACT
AND
IN THE MATTER OF A POLICY OF THE TORONTO STOCK EXCHANGE
ON SMALL SHAREHOLDER SELLING AND PURCHASE ARRANGEMENTS

EXEMPTION ORDER UNDER SECTION 33

UPON the Superintendent considering whether an order should be made on his own motion under Section 33 of the Securities Act, S.B.C. 1985 c. 83 ("Act") with respect to trades made under small shareholder selling arrangements ("Selling Arrangements") and/or small shareholder purchase arrangements ("Purchase Arrangements") (collectively, the "Arrangements") by companies ("Listed Companies") listed on The Toronto Stock Exchange (the "Exchange") which participate in such Arrangements;

AND UPON it being represented to the Superintendent that:

1. Part XXXI of the Exchange Policy Statements entitled "Policy Statement on Small Shareholder Selling and Purchase Arrangements" was originally passed and enacted by the Board of Governors of the Exchange on April 15, 1986 with effect from such date (the "Original Policy");

2. Under the Original Policy, a Listed Company participating in the Arrangements agreed to pay a fee per odd lot account to firms which were members of the Exchange ("Member Firms") in order to facilitate both the sale of shares on behalf of odd lot holders and the purchase of a sufficient number of shares on behalf of odd lot holders to constitute a board lot;

3. On November 25, 1986, the board of Governors of the Exchange adopted an amended Policy (the "Revised Policy") which became effective on November 25, 1986 and a copy of which is attached hereto as Schedule "A";

4. Pursuant to the Revised Policy, Listed Companies and directed to request odd lot holders wishing to participate in Selling Arrangements and/or Purchase Arrangements to either:

    (i)   place orders under the Arrangements with any Member Firm; or

    (ii) transmit orders under the Arrangements directly to the Listed Company or an agent (such as a Member Firm or transfer agent) designated by it;

5. Only persons who are holders of less than one board lot as defined in the General By-law of the Exchange are eligible to participate in the Arrangements;

6. the procedure described in the Revised Policy constitutes the exclusive method by which a Listed Company may seek the assistance of a Member Firm either to solicit odd lots for sale, or to acquire additional shares to make up a board lot, through the facilities of the Exchange; and

7. The revised Policy enables Listed Companies to reduce the number of holders of odd lots through participation in the Arrangements described in the said Revised Policy and reduces the commission rates otherwise payable by odd lot holders on the purchase or sale of odd lots;

AND UPON it appearing to the Superintendent that the solicitation by Listed Companies of odd lot holders with respect to participation in the aforesaid Arrangements and all acts, negotiations or conduct engaged in by the Listed Companies or their transfer agents in furtherance of odd lot holder participation in the Arrangements and in accordance with the provisions of the Revised Policy including, but not restricted to, the receipt by Listed Companies or their transfer agents of orders to buy or sell securities on behalf of odd lot holders, constitute trades within the meaning of the Act;

AND UPON the Superintendent being satisfied that to do so would not be prejudicial to the public interest;

IT IS RULED pursuant to Section 33 of the Act that the solicitation by Listed Companies of odd lot holders with respect to participation in the aforesaid Arrangements and all acts, negotiations or conduct engaged in by Listed Companies or their

Blanket Orders

transfer agents in furtherance of odd lot holder participation in the Arrangements and in accordance with the provisions of the Revised Policy including, but not restricted to, the receipt by Listed Companies or their transfer agents of orders to buy or sell securities on behalf of odd lot holders, are not subject to Section 20 of the Act;

DATED at Vancouver, British Columbia, this 11th day of June, 1987.

Neil de Gelder
Superintendent of Brokers

BOR#87/30

IN THE MATTER OF THE SECURITIES ACT
AND
IN THE MATTER OF A POLICY OF THE MONTREAL EXCHANGE
ON SMALL SHAREHOLDER SELLING AND PURCHASE ARRANGEMENTS

EXEMPTION ORDER UNDER SECTION 33

UPON the application of the Montreal Exchange (the "Exchange") to the Superintendent for an order pursuant to Section 33 of the Securities Act, S.B.C. 1985 c. 83 (the "Act") with respect to trades made under small shareholder selling arrangements ("Selling Arrangements") and/or small shareholder purchase arrangements ("Purchase Arrangements") (collectively, the "Arrangements") by companies listed on the Exchange ("Listed Companies") which participate in such Arrangements.

AND UPON it being represented to the Superintendent that:

1. The Exchange adopted on May 26, 1987 Policy 1-9 in respect of "Small Shareholder Selling and Purchase Arrangements" (the "Policy"), a copy of which is attached hereto as Schedule "A";

2. Pursuant to the Policy, Listed Companies are directed to request odd lot holders wishing to participate in Selling Arrangements and/or Purchase Arrangements to either:

   (i) place orders under the Arrangements with any member firm; or

   (ii) transmit orders under the Arrangements directly to the Listed Company or an agent (such as a member firm or transfer agent) designated by it;

3. Only persons who are holders of less than one board lot as defined in the General By-law of the Exchange are eligible to participate in the Arrangements;

4. The procedure described in the Policy constitutes the exclusive method by which a Listed Company may seek the assistance of a member firm either to solicit odd lots for sale, or to acquire additional shares to make up a board lot, through the facilities of the Exchange; and

5. The Policy enables Listed Companies to reduce the number of holders of odd lots through participation in the Arrangements described in the said Policy and reduces the commission rates otherwise payable by odd lot holders on the purchase or sale of good lots;

AND UPON it appearing to the Superintendent that the solicitation by Listed Companies of odd lot holders with respect to participation in the aforesaid Arrangements and all acts, negotiations or conduct engaged in by the Listed Companies or their transfer agents in furtherance of odd lot holder participation in the Arrangements and in accordance with the provisions of the Policy including, but not restricted to, the receipt by Listed Companies or their transfer agents of orders to buy or sell securities on behalf of odd lot holders, constitute trades within the meaning of the Act;

AND UPON the Commission being satisfied that to do so would not be prejudicial to the public interest;

IT IS RULED pursuant to Section 33 of the Act that the solicitation by Listed Companies of odd lot holders with respect to participation in the aforesaid Arrangements and all acts, negotiations or conduct engaged in by Listed Companies or their transfer agents in furtherance of odd lot holder participation in the Arrangements and in accordance with the provisions of the Policy including, but not restricted to, the receipt by Listed Companies or their transfer agents of orders to buy or sell securities on behalf of odd lot holders, are not subject to Section 20 of the Act;

AND IT IS FURTHER RULED that this ruling shall be effective as and from the 26th day of May, 1987.

DATED at Vancouver, British Columbia, this 11th day of June, 1987.

> Neil de Gelder
> Superintendent of Brokers

BOR#88/2

IN THE MATTER OF THE SECURITIES ACT
S.B.C. 1985, c. 83
AND
IN THE MATTER OF THE
DEFINITION OF "EXCHANGE ISSUER"

ORDER UNDER SECTION 1(1)

WHEREAS effective September 1, 1988, the definition of "exchange issuer" in section 1 of the Securities Act, S.B.C. 1985, c. 83 (the "Act"), provides for the recognition of stock exchanges for the purpose of the definition;

AND WHEREAS effective September 1, 1988, Local Policy Statement 3-44 dated August 12, 1988 provides that the British Columbia Securities Commission (the "Commission") recognizes the Vancouver Stock Exchange for the purpose of the definition of "exchange issuer";

AND WHEREAS effective September 1, 1988, under the definition of "exchange issuer" in section 1 of the Act the Commission may make an order excluding an issuer or a class of issuers for the purpose of the definition;

AND WHEREAS the Commission intends that those issuers whose securities are listed on the Vancouver Stock Exchange, but are not listed or quoted on any other stock exchange or trading or quotation system in Canada, should be "exchange issuers";

IT IS ORDERED effective September 1, 1988, that all issuers whose securities are listed on the Vancouver Stock Exchange and are listed or quoted on any other stock exchange or trading or quotation system in Canada are not included in the definition of "exchange issuer" in section 1(1) of the Act.

DATED at Vancouver, British Columbia, this 12th day of August, 1988.

> Doug Hyndman
> Chairman
> British Columbia Securities Commission

REF: Local Policy Statement 3-44

BOR#88/3

IN THE MATTER OF THE SECURITIES ACT
S.B.C. 1985, c. 83
AND
IN THE MATTER OF TRANSITIONAL RULES RESPECTING SECURITIES TRADED PRIOR TO SEPTEMBER 1, 1988 UNDER AN EXEMPTION FROM SECTION 42 OF THE SECURITIES ACT

ORDER UNDER SECTION 181.1 OF THE SECURITIES REGULATION AND VARIATION ORDER UNDER SECTION 153 OF THE SECURITIES ACT

WHEREAS effective September 1, 1988

a) the Exchange Issuer First Trades Regulation, B.C. Reg. 285/86 (the "EIFTR"), is repealed,

b) Part 8 (the "Old Part 8") of the Securities Regulation, B.C. Reg. 270/86 (the "Regulation"), is repealed, and

c) a new Part 8 (the "New Part 8") of the Regulation is substituted for the EIFTR and the Old Part 8;

AND WHEREAS the rules contained in the EIFTR and Old Part 8 (the "Old Resale Rules") respecting the resale of a security acquired under an exemption from section 42 of the Securities Act, S.B.C. 1985 c. 83 (the "Act"), are different from the resale rules contained in the New Part 8 (the "New Resale Rules");

AND WHEREAS it is desirable to have transitional rules respecting the resale of securities traded prior to September 1, 1988 under an exemption from section 42 of the Act;

IT IS ORDERED by the British Columbia Securities Commission under section 181.1 of the Regulation that, effective September 1, 1988:

1.   where a trade of a security was completed prior to September 1, 1988 under section 55 or 58 of the Act, the security shall be subject, at the option of the purchaser, to either:

      (a)   the Old Resale Rules that would have been applicable to that security had the EIFTR and Old Part 8 not been repealed, except as those rules may be varied by paragraph 4 of this order; or

      (b)   the New Resale Rules applicable to that security;

2.   where a trade of a security was completed prior to September 1, 1988 under section 122(a) to (d) of Old Part 8, the security shall be subject to the Old Resale Rules that would have been applicable to that security had the EIFTR and the Old Part 8 not been repealed, except as those rules may be varied by paragraph 4 of this order;

3.   where a trade of a security was completed prior to September 1, 1988 under section 122(e) of the Old Part 8, the security shall be subject to the New Resale Rules applicable to a security traded under section 117(f) of the New Part 8; and

4.   where the Old Resale Rules impose a hold period that is longer than 12 months, that hold period shall be reduced to 12 months.

IT IS ORDERED by the Superintendent of Brokers (the "Superintendent") under section 153 of the Act that, effective September 1, 1988:

1.   where a trade of a security was completed prior to September 1, 1988 under a blanket order issued by the Superintendent under section 59 of the Act and revoked effective September 1, 1988 (a "BOR"), the security shall be subject to the resale rules set out in the BOR that would have been applicable to that security had the BOR not been revoked, except as those rules may be varied by paragraph 3 of this order;

2.   where a security was traded under an order issued under section 59 of the Act in respect of an application received by the Superintendent prior to September 1, 1988 (a "Section 59 Order"), the security shall be subject to the resale rules set out in the Section 59 Order, except as those rules may be varied by paragraph 3 of this order; and

3.   where a BOR or a Section 59 Order imposes a hold period that is longer than 12 months, that hold period shall be reduced to 12 months.

DATED at Vancouver, British Columbia, this 12th day of August, 1988.

Doug Hyndman   Neil de Gelder
Chairman   Superintendent of Brokers
British Columbia Securities Commission

REF: BOR#88/4

BOR#88/5

IN THE MATTER OF THE SECURITIES ACT
S.B.C. 1985, c. 83
AND
IN THE MATTER OF THE LEGENDING OF CERTIFICATES

ORDER UNDER SECTION 120(3) OF THE SECURITIES REGULATION

WHEREAS effective September 1, 1988, section 120(2) of the Securities Regulation, B.C. Reg. 270/86 (the "Regulation"), requires that where a security, at the date of its issue, is subject to a hold period as defined in section 120(1) of the Regulation (the "Hold Period"), the issuer shall endorse the certificate representing the security with a statement respecting the Hold Period;

AND WHEREAS effective September 1, 1988, section 120(3) of the Regulation provides that the Commission on its own motion may order that section 120(2) of the Regulation does not apply to a particular issuer or class of issuers;

IT IS ORDERED under section 120(3) of the Regulation, effective September 1, 1988, that section 120(2) of the Regulation does not apply to an issuer that is not an "exchange issuer" as defined in section 1 of the Securities Act, S.B.C. 1985, c. 83, on the condition that, prior to the completion of the distribution, the issuer gives notice in writing to each purchaser of a security subject to a Hold Period that

(a)   the purchaser must file

    (i) a report in the attached form (the "Initial Trade Report"), or

    (ii) the report required under the laws of the jurisdiction in which the issuer carries on business or in which the issuer is incorporated, organized or continued, provided that the report requires substantially the same information as is required in the Initial Trade Report (the "Purchaser's Report"),

within 10 days of the initial trade of the security by the purchaser; and

(b)   where the purchaser has filed an Initial Trade Report or the Purchaser's Report with respect to a security, the purchaser is not required to file a further report in respect of additional trades of securities acquired on the same date and under the same exemption as the security which is the subject of the Initial Trade Report or the Purchaser's Report.

DATED at Vancouver, British Columbia, this 12th day of August, 1988.

Doug Hyndman
Chairman
British Columbia Securities Commission

Attachment

BOR#88/6

IN THE MATTER OF THE SECURITIES ACT
S.B.C. 1985, c. 83
AND
IN THE MATTER OF THE FILING OF INSIDER REPORTS
BY CONTROL PERSONS

EXEMPTION ORDER UNDER SECTION 152.2
OF THE SECURITIES REGULATION

WHEREAS effective September 1, 1988, section 130 of the Securities Regulation, B.C. Reg. 270/86 (the "Regulation"), provides that a person who distributes a security under section 117(c) or (d) of the Regulation shall file a report in the required form not later than 3 days after the distribution;

AND WHEREAS section 70(4) of the Securities Act, S.B.C. 1985, c. 83 (the "Act"), requires that an insider report in the required form be filed within 10 days after the end of the month in which a change takes place in the direct or indirect beneficial ownership of, or control or direction over, securities of a reporting issuer from that shown or required to be shown in the latest report filed by a person who has filed or is required to file an insider report in the required form under section 70(2) of the Act;

AND WHEREAS in NIN#88/24, the Superintendent of Brokers prescribes Form 37 as the report required to be filed under section 130 of the Regulation and Form 37 is the insider report required to be filed under section 70(4) of the Act;

AND WHEREAS it is not necessary for the same report to be filed twice where the facts required to be reported under section 130 of the Regulation are identical to those required to be reported under section 70(4) of the Act;

AND WHEREAS section 152.2 of the Regulation provides that the Commission may on its own motion make an order exempting, in whole or in part, a class of persons from the filing requirements of section 70 of the Act;

AND WHEREAS the Commission is satisfied in the circumstances of the particular case that there is adequate justification for so doing and to so order would not be prejudicial to the public interest;

IT IS ORDERED under section 152.2 of the Regulation that, effective September 1, 1988, a person who files a report under section 130 of the Regulation is exempt from the filing requirements of section 70 of the Act where the facts required to be reported under section 70 are identical to those reported under section 130 of the Regulation.

DATED at Vancouver, British Columbia, this 12th day of August, 1988.

Doug Hyndman
Chairman
British Columbia Securities Commission

REF: NIN#88/24

BOR#88/11

IN THE MATTER OF THE SECURITIES ACT
S.B.C. 1985, c. 83
AND
IN THE MATTER OF THE CONFLICT OF INTEREST RULES STATEMENT
AND
IN THE MATTER OF THE CONFIRMATION AND REPORTING
OF TRANSACTIONS BY REGISTRANTS

EXEMPTION ORDER UNDER SECTION 167.12
OF THE SECURITIES REGULATION
AND
REVOCATION ORDER UNDER SECTION 153
OF THE SECURITIES ACT

WHEREAS section 167.3 of the Securities Regulation, B.C. Reg. 270/86 (the "Regulation") and BOR#88/9 require that a registrant prepare, file and provide to each of its clients a copy of its current Conflict of Interest Rules Statement (the "CIRS") (Form 69) or, alternatively, prepare and file with the British Columbia Securities Commission a Statement and Undertaking (Form 70), by December 15, 1988;

AND WHEREAS section 167.5(1)(c) of the Regulation and BOR#88/9 require that a registrant trading in or purchasing a security after December 15, 1988 in circumstances set out in section 167.5(1)(a) or (b) must, before entering into an agreement of purchase and sale respecting the security, deliver its current CIRS to the client or inform him orally or by some other means of substantially all the information required to be included in the CIRS;

AND WHEREAS section 167.6 of the Regulation and BOR#88/10 require that certain information be disclosed by a registrant in any written confirmation or other report sent or delivered after December 31, 1988 by the registrant to a client respecting a trade or purchase of a security made by the registrant with, from or on behalf of the client;

AND WHEREAS representations have been made to the Superintendent of Brokers (the "Superintendent") by members of the brokerage industry concerning both the time limits within which a registrant must deliver the CIRS to its clients in compliance with sections 167.3 and 167.5(1)(c) of the Regulation and the disclosure required to be made in written confirmations or other reports sent to clients in compliance with section 167.6 of the Regulation;

AND WHEREAS under section 167.12 of the Regulation the Superintendent may exempt a registrant from any provision of Part 13.1 of the Regulation where he considers that it would not be prejudicial to the public interest to do so;

AND WHEREAS the Superintendent considers that it would not be prejudicial to the public interest to do so;

IT IS ORDERED under section 167.12 of the Regulation that:

1.   all registrants are exempt from section 167.3(1), (3) and (4) of the Regulation for a period of time expiring on February 28, 1989;

2.   all registrants are exempt from section 167.3(2) of the Regulation on the condition that the registrant provide free of charge a copy of its current CIRS to each of its clients at the time he becomes a client of the registrant or by February 28, 1989, whichever is later;

3.   all registrants are exempt from section 167.5(1)(c) of the Regulation for a period of time expiring on February 28, 1989;

4. all registrants are exempt from section 167.6(1) of the Regulation for a period of time expiring on February 28, 1989; and

5. all registrants are exempt from section 167.6(2) of the Regulation.

IT IS ORDERED under section 153 of the Securities Act, S.B.C. 1985, c. 83 that BOR#88/9 and BOR#88/10 be revoked.

DATED at Vancouver, British Columbia this 28th day of November, 1988.

Neil de Gelder
Superintendent of Brokers

BOR#89/1

IN THE MATTER OF THE COMMODITY CONTRACT ACT
R.S.B.C. 1979, c. 56
AND
IN THE MATTER OF THE REGISTRATION
OF PERSONS TRADING IN IOCC OPTIONS

EXEMPTION ORDER UNDER SECTION 29(1)

WHEREAS commodity options issued by the International Options Clearing Corporation (the "IOCC") are commodity contracts within the meaning of section 1 of the Commodity Contract Act, R.S.B.C. 1979, c.56 (the "Act");

AND WHEREAS the Vancouver Stock Exchange (the "VSE") is a recognized commodity exchange under the Act pursuant to CCA BOR#89/1, an order issued by the British Columbia Securities Commission under section 24(2) of the Act on January 26, 1986;

AND WHEREAS the form of gold option, silver option, Canadian dollar option and platinum option issued by the IOCC (the "IOCC Options") were accepted for trading on the VSE pursuant to CCA BOR#89/5 issued by the Superintendent of Brokers (the "Superintendent") under section 24(3) of the Act on January 26, 1989;

AND WHEREAS section 13(1) of the Act prohibits any person from trading in a commodity contract unless the person is registered as a commodity contracts dealer, as a commodity contracts salesman or as a floor trader, or is registered as a partner or as an officer of a registered commodity contracts dealer and is acting on behalf of that commodity contracts dealer;

AND WHEREAS representations have been made to the Superintendent that persons who trade in IOCC Options, and no other commodity contracts, should be exempt from registration under the Act if they are registered under the Securities Act, S.B.C. 1985, c. 83, and satisfy certain additional requirements;

AND WHEREAS pursuant to section 29(1) of the Act, the Superintendent may, on his own initiative, order that a class of persons is not subject to Section 13 of the Act;

AND WHEREAS the Superintendent is satisfied that to do so would not be prejudicial to the public interest;

IT IS ORDERED under section 29(1) of the Act that a person who trades in IOCC Options, and no other commodity contracts, is exempt from section 13(1)(a) of the Act provided that:

1. if the person is not an individual, the person is registered as a broker or investment dealer (a "Dealer") under the Securities Act; or

2. if the person is an individual, the person:

   (a) is employed by a Dealer as a floor trader and is recognized as an options attorney under Rule I.1.73 of the VSE; or

   (b) is registered under the Securities Act as a salesman, partner, director or officer of a Dealer and has successfully completed the Canadian Options Course prepared and conducted by the Canadian Securities Institute.

DATED at Vancouver, British Columbia, this 26th day of January, 1989.

Neil de Gelder
Superintendent of Brokers

IN THE MATTER OF THE SECURITIES ACT
S.B.C. 1985, c. 83
AND
IN THE MATTER OF THE REQUIREMENT TO SEND INTERIM
FINANCIAL STATEMENTS TO SHAREHOLDERS OF A REPORTING ISSUER

EXEMPTION ORDER UNDER SECTION 143(1)(b) OF THE REGULATION

WHEREAS under section 141 of the Securities Regulation, B.C. Reg. 270/86 (the "Regulation"), a reporting issuer who is required to file an interim financial statement under section 135 of the Regulation is required to concurrently send it to each holder of its securities, other than holders of debt instruments, whose latest address as shown on the books of the reporting issuer is in British Columbia;

AND WHEREAS the British Columbia Securities Commission (the "Commission") has adopted National Policy Statement No. 41 (the "Policy") which requires a reporting issuer to send its interim financial statements to each non-registered holder of its securities who requests them;

AND WHEREAS the Policy contemplates that, where an exemption from section 141 of the Regulation is provided, a reporting issuer may elect to send its interim financial statements only to those registered holders of its securities who request them;

AND WHEREAS under section 143(1)(b) of the Regulation the Commission may on its own motion make an order exempting a class of reporting issuers from a specific requirement of Part 10 of the Regulation;

AND WHEREAS the Commission considers it is not harmful to the public interest and is satisfied that, in the circumstances, there is adequate justification to do so;

IT IS ORDERED under section 143(1)(b) of the Regulation, effective March 1, 1988, that a reporting issuer is exempt from section 141 of the Regulation in respect of an interim financial statement filed under section 135 of the Regulation on the condition that:

(a) the reporting issuer complies with all the requirements of the Policy respecting interim financial statements, provided that:

  (i) if the reporting issuer has not sent its annual financial statements to each registered holder of its securities since becoming subject to the Policy, the reporting issuer has sent a return card to each registered holder of its securities and, in accordance with the search and bulk delivery procedures set out in the Policy, to each non-registered holder of its securities; or

  (ii) if the reporting issuer does not hold an annual meeting, the reporting issuer has sent a return card to each registered holder of its securities with its most recent annual financial statements prepared in accordance with section 136 of the Regulation; and

(b) the reporting issuer concurrently files written confirmation that it has sent the interim financial statement to each registered and non-registered holder of its securities on the supplemental mailing list maintained in accordance with the Policy.

DATED at Vancouver, British Columbia, this 17th day of March, 1989.

Douglas M. Hyndman
Chairman

IN THE MATTER OF THE SECURITIES ACT
S.B.C. 1985, c. 83
AND
IN THE MATTER OF TRADES IN SECURITIES
HELD SUBJECT TO AN ESCROW OR POOLING AGREEMENT

EXEMPTION ORDER UNDER SECTION 33

WHEREAS a person who beneficially owns securities that are subject to the terms of an escrow or pooling agreement in the form required by the British Columbia Securities Commission ("Escrowed Securities") may not trade in the Escrowed

Securities unless the person (a "Transferor") complies with, or is otherwise exempt from section 20 of the Securities Act, S.B.C. 1985, c. 83 (the "Act");

AND WHEREAS the required form of escrow or pooling agreement provides that a Transferor may not trade in Escrowed Securities without the prior consent of the Superintendent of Brokers (the "Superintendent") or the Vancouver Stock Exchange (the "VSE");

AND WHEREAS the Superintendent has considered whether an order should be made on his own motion under section 33 of the Act that section 20 of the Act does not apply to a Transferor in respect of a trade in Escrowed Securities by the Transferor;

AND WHEREAS the Superintendent considers that it would not be prejudicial to the public interest to do so;

IT IS ORDERED under section 33 of the Act that section 20 of the Act does not apply to a Transferor in respect of a trade in Escrowed Securities by the Transferor provided that

(a) the Superintendent, if the Escrowed Securities are not listed on the VSE, or

(b) the VSE, if the Escrowed Securities are listed on the VSE,

has consented in writing to the trade by the Transferor.

DATED at Vancouver, British Columbia, this 5th day of October, 1989.

Neil de Gelder
Superintendent of Brokers

BOR#89/8

IN THE MATTER OF THE SECURITIES ACT
S.B.C. 1985, c. 83
AND
IN THE MATTER OF REPORTING COMPANIES UNDER THE BRITISH COLUMBIA COMPANY ACT AND THE DEFINITION OF "REPORTING ISSUER"

DESIGNATION ORDER UNDER SECTION 1(1)

WHEREAS effective November 1, 1989, the Securities Amendment Act, 1989, S.B.C. 1989, c. 78 amends the definition of "reporting issuer" in section 1 of the Securities Act, S.B.C. 1985, c. 83 (the "Act") to provide that "reporting issuer" no longer includes an issuer that is a reporting company under the British Columbia Company Act;

AND WHEREAS it is expedient to provide that each issuer that is, as of October 31, 1989, a reporting issuer under the Act by virtue only of being a reporting company under the Company Act will continue to be a reporting issuer under the Act;

AND WHEREAS under section 1(1) of the Act, the British Columbia Securities Commission may make an order designating an issuer as a reporting issuer for the purpose of the definition of reporting issuer;

IT IS ORDERED under section 1(1) of the Act that, effective November 1, 1989, each issuer that is, as of October 31, 1989, a reporting issuer under the Act by virtue only of being a reporting company under the Company Act is designated as a reporting issuer under the Act.

DATED at Vancouver, British Columbia, this 13th day of October 1989.

Douglas M. Hyndman
Chairman

Blanket Orders

BOR#89/10

IN THE MATTER OF THE SECURITIES ACT
S.B.C. 1985, c. 83
AND
IN THE MATTER OF THE REQUIRED
FORM OF OFFERING MEMORANDUM

EXEMPTION ORDER UNDER SECTIONS 33 AND 59

WHEREAS effective November 1, 1989, section 126 of the Securities Regulation, B.C. Reg 270/86 (the "Regulation") was amended by the addition of paragraph (c) which provides that an offering memorandum required to be used in connection with a distribution of securities under the exemptions in section 55(2)(4) of the Securities Act, S.B.C. 1985, c. 83, (the "Act") and section 117(a), (b) and (i) of the Regulation (the "Specified Exemptions") must be in the required form;

AND WHEREAS by NIN#89/31 the Superintendent of Brokers specified Form 43 as the required form of offering memorandum for the purpose of section 126(c);

AND WHEREAS for transitional purposes, it is expedient to allow, for a limited period of time, a person distributing a security under a Specified Exemption to use an offering memorandum that does not conform with Form 43 and to provide resale restrictions with respect to securities so distributed;

AND WHEREAS the Superintendent considers that it would not be prejudicial to the public interest to do so;

IT IS ORDERED

1. under sections 33 and 59 of the Act that, effective November 1, 1989, sections 20 and 42 of the Act do not apply to a distribution which meets all of the conditions for the use of one of the Specified Exemptions (the "Statutory Exemption"), except for compliance with section 126(c), provided that:

    (a) prior to November 1, 1989, an offering memorandum complying with the requirements of the Act and Regulation in effect on October 31, 1989 has been prepared with an attached certificate in substantially the form specified by NIN#88/42 and signed by the principals involved in the offering;

    (b) all securities to be distributed are issued prior to January 1, 1990; and

    (c) the issuer complies with the requirements of sections 120, 128, 131 and 132 of the Regulation, that would have been applicable had the distribution been made under the Statutory Exemption; and

2. under Section 59 of the Act that a trade in a security acquired under this order is deemed to be a distribution unless the resale restrictions set out in sections 133 and 134 of the Regulation that would have been applicable to the trade had the security been acquired under the Statutory Exemption have been complied with.

DATED at Vancouver, British Columbia, this 31st day of October 1989.

Neil de Gelder
Superintendent of Brokers

REF: NIN#89/31

BOR#90/1

IN THE MATTER OF THE SECURITIES ACT
S.B.C. 1985, c. 83
AND
IN THE MATTER OF TRADES OF GOVERNMENT WARRANTS

EXEMPTION ORDER UNDER SECTIONS 33 AND 59

WHEREAS an issuer may issue bonds, debentures or other evidence of indebtedness of or guaranteed by the government of Canada or a province ("Government Bonds") under sections 32(a)(i) and 58(1)(a) of the Securities Act, S.B.C. 1985, c. 83 (the "Act");

AND WHEREAS an issuer is unable to rely on the exemptions from sections 20 and 42 contained in sections 32(a)(i) and 58(1)(a) of the Act to distribute securities ("Government Warrants") entitling the holder to acquire Government Bonds;

AND WHEREAS the Commission considers that it would not be prejudicial to the public interest to do so;

IT IS ORDERED under Sections 33 and 59 of the Act that sections 20 and 42 of the Act do not apply to a trade of Government Warrants issued by an issuer of Government Bonds.

DATED at Vancouver, British Columbia, this 29th day of January 1990.

Douglas M. Hyndman
Chairman

BOR#90/2

**IN THE MATTER OF THE SECURITIES ACT
S.B.C. 1985, c. 83
AND
IN THE MATTER OF TRADES IN SHARES ISSUED
IN ACCORDANCE WITH THE EMPLOYEE INVESTMENT ACT**

EXEMPTION ORDER UNDER SECTIONS 33 AND 59

WHEREAS the Employee Investment Act, S.B.C. 1989, c. 24 (the "EI Act") encourages employees resident in the Province to invest in their employers, either

(a) indirectly, through employee venture capital corporations formed for that purpose, or

(b) directly, through employee share ownership plans;

AND WHEREAS for the purpose of this order

"Act" means the Securities Act, S.B.C. 1989, c. 83,

"Affiliate" means an affiliate as defined in the EI Act,

"Constitution" means a constitution as defined in the EI Act,

"Eligible Business" means,

(a) when used in relation to an ESOP, the issuer that has registered the ESOP under the EI Act, and

(b) when used in relation to an EVCC, the issuer in whose shares the Constitution of the EVCC permits the EVCC to invest;

"Employee" means, when used in relation to an Eligible Business, an employee of the Eligible Business or of an Affiliate of the Eligible Business;

"Employee Venture Capital Plan" means an employee venture capital plan registered under the EI Act;

"ESOP" means an employee share ownership plan registered under the EI Act by an Eligible Business;

"EVCC" means an employee venture capital corporation registered under the EI Act, the Constitution of which

(a) restricts the EVCC to investing in shares of a particular Eligible Business and in investments permitted by section 22(1)(b), (d), (e) and (f) of the EI Act, and

(b) prohibits the EVCC from issuing shares to any person other than a Permitted Purchaser;

"Permitted Purchaser" means, when used in relation to an EVCC, an Employee of the Eligible Business in whose shares the Constitution of the EVCC permits the EVCC to invest;

"Regulation" means the Securities Regulation, B.C. Reg. 270/86;

AND WHEREAS an EVCC may not distribute its shares to Permitted Purchasers in reliance on sections 31(2)(10) and 55(2)(9) of the Act unless the Eligible Business in whose shares the Constitution of the EVCC permits it to invest is a subsidiary of the EVCC;

AND WHEREAS although an Eligible Business may distribute its shares to Employees under an ESOP in reliance on sections 31(2)(10) and 55(2)(9) of the Act, the resale of those shares will be restricted for an indefinite period of time unless the Eligible Business is or becomes a reporting issuer;

AND WHEREAS the Commission considers that it would not be prejudicial to the public interest to do so;

IT IS ORDERED

1.   under sections 33 and 59 of the Act that sections 20 and 42 of the Act do not apply to an EVCC in respect of a trade in a share of its own issue to a Permitted Purchaser provided that

    (a)   the EVCC has not distributed any of its shares to persons other than Permitted Purchasers, except for shares distributed to the first sub-scriber or subscribers pursuant to section 5(1) of the Company Act, R.S.B.C. 1979, c. 59,

    (b)   the trade is made pursuant to the Employee Venture Capital Plan of the EVCC,

    (c)   the certificate representing the share contains a legend stating that the share may be transferred only in compliance with the provisions of the Act, the Regulation and this order, and

    (d)   prior to the trade, the EVCC notifies the Permitted Purchaser in writ-ing of the resale restrictions imposed by this order;

2.   under section 59 of the Act that a trade

    (a)   in a share that was issued by an EVCC in reliance on

        (i) paragraph 1 of this order, or

        (ii) section 55(2)(9) of the Act, or

    (b)   in a share that was issued by an Eligible Business under an ESOP in reliance on section 55(2)(9) of the Act

is deemed to be a distribution unless the share was acquired in a trade made in reliance on paragraph 4(a)(iv) or (b)(ii) of this order;

3.   under section 33 of the Act that section 20 of the Act does not apply to

    (a)   a Permitted Purchaser in respect of a trade in a share that was issued by an EVCC in reliance on

        (i) paragraph 1 of this order, or

        (ii) section 55(2)(9) of the Act

    provided that the trade is to a Permitted Purchaser, or

    (b)   an Employee in respect of a trade in a share that was issued by an Eligible Business under an ESOP in reliance on section 55(2)(9) of the Act provided that the trade is to an Employee; and

4.   under section 59 of the Act that section 42 of the Act does not apply to

    (a)   a Permitted Purchaser in respect of a trade in a share that was issued by an EVCC in reliance on

        (i) paragraph 1 of this order, or

        (ii) section 55(2)(9) of the Act

    provided that the trade is

        (iii) to a Permitted Purchaser, or

        (iv) made in compliance with the resale restrictions set out in sections 133 and 134 of the Regulation that would have been applicable to the trade had the share been acquired under section 55(2)(9) of the Act, or

(b) an Employee in respect of a trade in a share that was issued by an Eligible Business under an ESOP in reliance on section 55(2)(9) of the Act provided that the trade is

(i) to an Employee, or

(ii) made in compliance with the resale restrictions set out in sections 133 and 134 of the Regulation that would have been applicable to the trade had the share been acquired under section 55(2)(9) of the Act.

DATED at Vancouver, British Columbia, this 27th day of February 1990.

Douglas M. Hyndman
Chairman

BOR#90/4

IN THE MATTER OF THE SECURITIES ACT
S.B.C. 1985, c. 83
AND
IN THE MATTER OF TRADES IN DEPOSIT-TYPE OR SELF-DIRECTED REGISTERED EDUCATIONAL SAVINGS PLANS

EXEMPTION ORDER UNDER SECTIONS 33 AND 59

WHEREAS section 1(1) of the Securities Act, S.B.C. 1989, c. 83 (the "Act") defines a security to include "a document evidencing an interest in a scholarship or educational plan or trust";

AND WHEREAS an educational savings plan registered under the Income Tax Act (Canada) (the "ITA") (a "RESP") issues a document evidencing an interest in the RESP to a person who subscribes for an interest in the RESP (the "subscriber");

AND WHEREAS contributions by a subscriber to a deposit-type or self-directed RESP are not pooled with the funds of other subscribers but are either deposited directly in an account in the subscriber's name or used, at the subscriber's sole discretion, to purchase other investments as may be permitted under applicable law;

AND WHEREAS the subscriber maintains control and direction over the subscriber's RESP, directing the manner in which the assets of the subscriber's RESP are to be held, invested or reinvested;

AND WHEREAS the subscriber's control and direction over the subscriber's RESP parallels the control and direction exercised by a person subscribing to a self-directed registered retirement savings plan ("RRSP"), which RRSP is not subject to the registration and prospectus requirements of the Act;

AND WHEREAS prior to February 20, 1990, the ITA required a RESP to file a prospectus with a securities regulatory authority in Canada;

AND WHEREAS the most recent federal budget has proposed that, effective February 20, 1990, a RESP not be required to file a prospectus with a securities regulatory authority in Canada in order to be registered under the ITA where the RESP is not required to file a prospectus under applicable securities law;

AND WHEREAS the Commission considers that it would not be prejudicial to the public interest to do so;

IT IS ORDERED under sections 33 and 59 of the Act that sections 20 and 42 of the Act do not apply to a trade in a RESP to a subscriber, provided that the contributions by the subscriber are not pooled with the funds of other subscribers but are either deposited directly in an account in the subscriber's name or used, at the subscriber's sole discretion, to purchase other investments as may be permitted under applicable law.

DATED at Vancouver, British Columbia, this 11th day of October 1990.

Douglas M. Hyndman
Chairman

IN THE MATTER OF THE SECURITIES ACT
S.B.C. 1985, c. 83
AND
IN THE MATTER OF RULES FOR SHELF PROSPECTUS OFFERINGS AND FOR PRICING OFFERINGS AFTER THE PROSPECTUS IS RECEIPTED

EXEMPTION ORDER UNDER SECTION 59

WHEREAS the British Columbia Securities Commission (the "Commission") has issued National Policy Statement No. 44 – Rules for Shelf Prospectus Offerings and For Pricing Offerings After the Prospectus Is Receipted (the "Policy");

AND WHEREAS the Policy is structured on the basis that issuers of securities in compliance with the Policy will be exempted from certain requirements of the Securities Act, S.B.C. 1985, c. 83 (the "Act");

AND WHEREAS the Commission considers that providing such an exemption will increase flexibility and reduce costs and time pressures for issuers making public offerings without reducing investor protection;

AND WHEREAS the Commission considers that to do so would not be prejudicial to the public interest;

IT IS ORDERED, effective May 10, 1991, under section 59 of the Act that section 42 of the Act does not apply to a trade in a security by an issuer in compliance with the Policy provided that the trade is made in compliance with section 42 of the Act, except for the requirements contained in

1. section 42 of the Act, as to the form and content of a preliminary prospectus and a prospectus,

2. sections 47 and 48 of the Act,

3. sections 49 and 50 of the Act, as to the form of certificates of the issuer, promoter and underwriter, and

4. section 51 of the Act, as to the date by which the distribution of securities pursuant to a prospectus must cease;

provided that either a preliminary short form prospectus and short form prospectus or a preliminary prospectus and prospectus

1. are filed under section 42 of the Act pursuant to, and in accordance with, the requirements and procedures of the Policy, and

2. are supplemented and amended pursuant to, and in accordance with, the requirements and procedures of the Policy, including the requirement with respect to the filing of amendments, where required by the Policy, in compliance with sections 47 and 48 of the Act.

DATED at Vancouver, British Columbia, on May 3, 1991.

Douglas M. Hyndman
Chairman

IN THE MATTER OF THE SECURITIES ACT
S.B.C. 1985, c. 83
AND
IN THE MATTER OF TRADES OF SECURITIES OF PRIVATE ISSUERS

ORDER UNDER SECTIONS 33 AND 59

WHEREAS it is expedient to provide limited exemptions for trades by holders of securities of issuers that are not reporting issuers and have fewer than 50 holders, excluding employees and former employees, of securities ("Designated Securities") that are voting securities, or are securities that are not debt securities and that carry a residual right to participate in the earnings of the issuer or, upon the liquidation or winding up of the issuer, in its assets;

AND WHEREAS the Commission considers that to do so would not be prejudicial to the public interest;

IT IS ORDERED, effective July 1, 1991

1. under sections 33 and 59 of the Securities Act, S.B.C. 1985, C. 83 (the "Act") that sections 20 and 42 of the Act do not apply to a trade in a security of an issuer by a person other than the issuer provided that

   (a) the security is not offered for sale to the public, and

   (b) immediately upon the completion of the trade

      (i) the issuer is not a reporting issuer or a mutual fund,

      (ii) all of the issuer's Designated Securities are beneficially owned, directly or indirectly, by not more than 50 persons, counting any 2 or more joint registered owners as one beneficial owner, exclusive of persons

         (A) that are employed by the issuer or an affiliate of it, or

         (B) that beneficially owned, directly or indirectly, Designated Securities of the issuer while employed by it or by an affiliate of it and, at all times since ceasing to be so employed, have continued to beneficially own, directly or indirectly, at least one Designated Security of the issuer;

2. under section 59 of the Act that a trade in a security acquired under this order or BOR#89/11 is deemed to be a distribution unless the trade is made in compliance with the resale restrictions set out in sections 133 and 134 of the Securities Regulation, B.C. Reg. 270/86 that would have applied had the security been acquired under section 58(1)(a) of the Act where at the time the security was acquired it was described in section 32(j) of the Act.

DATED at Vancouver, British Columbia, on June 6, 1991.

Douglas M. Hyndman
Chairman

REF: NIN#89/41
NIN#91/8
BOR#89/11

BOR#91/5

IN THE MATTER OF THE SECURITIES ACT
S.B.C. 1985, c. 83
AND
IN THE MATTER OF THE RESALE OF
RIGHTS ACQUIRED UNDER A RIGHTS OFFERING

EXEMPTION ORDER UNDER SECTION 59

WHEREAS it is expedient to provide an exemption from section 42 of the Securities Act, S.B.C. 1985, c. 83 (the "Act") to enable a seller to trade in a right acquired by the seller, whether or not the issuer has been a reporting issuer in the Province for the 12 months preceeding the trade;

AND WHEREAS the Commission considers that to do so would not be prejudicial to the public interest;

IT IS ORDERED, effective July 1, 1991, under section 59 of the Act that section 42 of the Act does not apply to a trade in a right acquired by a seller under section 55(2)(7) of the Act or BOR#90/3 provided that

1. if the seller is an insider of the issuer, the issuer is not in default of any requirement of the Act or the Securities Regulation, B.C. Reg. 270/86,

2. the trade is not a distribution from the holdings of a control person,

3. no unusual effort is made to prepare the market or create a demand for the security, and

4.   no extraordinary commission or other consideration is paid in respect of the trade.

DATED at Vancouver, British Columbia, on June 6, 1991.

Douglas M. Hyndman
Chairman

REF: NIN#91/8
           BOR#90/3

BOR#91/6

IN THE MATTER OF THE SECURITIES ACT
S.B.C. 1985, c. 83
AND
IN THE MATTER OF THE RECOGNITION OF CERTAIN COUNTRIES AND POLITICAL DIVISIONS OF COUNTRIES ISSUING BONDS, DEBENTURES OR OTHER EVIDENCE OF INDEBTEDNESS

RECOGNITION ORDER UNDER SECTION 32(a)(i.1)

WHEREAS effective July 1, 1991, the British Columbia Securities Act, S.B.C. 1985, c. 83 (the "Act") provides an exemption for a trade in bonds, debentures or other evidence of indebtedness of or guaranteed by a country, or a political division of a country, recognized by the Commission for the purpose of section 32(a)(i.1) of the Act;

AND WHEREAS it is expedient for the Commission to recognize, for the purpose of section 32(a)(i.1) of the Act, those countries and political divisions of countries that are currently referred to in section 32(a)(i) of the Act;

AND WHEREAS the Commission considers that to do so would not be prejudicial to the public interest;

IT IS ORDERED, effective July 1, 1991, under section 32(a)(i.1) of the Act that the following countries and political divisions of countries be recognized:

1.   the United States of America;

2.   a state of the United States of America;

3.   the District of Columbia in the United States of America;

4.   the territories of Puerto Rico and the Virgin Islands of the United States of America; and

5.   the United Kingdom.

DATED at Vancouver, British Columbia, on June 6, 1991.

Douglas M. Hyndman
Chairman

REF: NIN#91/8

BOR#91/7

IN THE MATTER OF THE SECURITIES ACT
S.B.C. 1985, c. 83
AND
IN THE MATTER OF THE MULTIJURISDICTIONAL DISCLOSURE SYSTEM

EXEMPTION ORDERS UNDER SECTIONS 33, 59, 96 AND 103 OF THE ACT AND SECTIONS 143, 152.2 AND 167.12 OF THE REGULATION

WHEREAS the Commission has issued National Policy Statement No. 45 – Multijurisdictional Disclosure System (the "Policy");

AND WHEREAS the Policy is structured on the basis that exemptions will be provided, on the condition that the requirements of the Policy are met, from certain requirements of the Securities Act, S.B.C. 1985, c. 83 (the "Act") and the Securities Regulation, B.C. Reg. 270/86 (the "Regulation") relating to

(a) certain prospectus offerings (including rights offerings) of securities of a U.S. issuer, as defined in the Policy (a "U.S. Issuer"),

(b) bids for securities of certain U.S. Issuers made to Canadian security holders,

(c) continuous disclosure and shareholder communication requirements that otherwise must be met by U.S. Issuers that have a class of securities registered under section 12 of the Securities Exchange Act of 1934 of the United States (the "1934 Act"),

(d) financial reporting requirements that otherwise must be met by U.S. Issuers that are required to file reports pursuant to section 15(d) of the 1934 Act, and

(e) insider reporting requirements that otherwise must be met by insiders of U.S. Issuers that have a class of securities registered under section 12 of the 1934 Act;

AND WHEREAS the Securities and Exchange Commission of the United States (the "SEC") has applied to the Commission for an order under section 103(2) of the Act that Part 12 of the Act does not apply to U.S. Issuers in respect of the solicitation of proxies in compliance with the Policy;

AND WHEREAS the Commission and the Superintendent consider that providing the exemptions will facilitate certain cross-border securities transactions;

AND WHEREAS "MJDS" means the requirements of the Policy, as they have been waived or varied by the Commission or the Superintendent;

AND WHEREAS the Commission considers that there is adequate justification for doing so and that to do so would not be prejudicial to the public interest;

Effective July 1, 1991, THE COMMISSION ORDERS

Trade by issuer in right granted to holders of its securities

1. under section 33 of the Act that section 20 of the Act does not apply to a trade by a U.S. Issuer in

   (a) a right granted by the issuer to holders of its securities to purchase additional securities of its own issue, or

   (b) a security of its own issue that is transferred or issued through the exercise of a right of the holder to purchase, convert or exchange or otherwise acquire in accordance with the terms and conditions of a security distributed under subparagraph (a),

   provided that the trade is made in compliance with the MJDS;

Trade in security issued in connection with an issuer bid

2. under sections 33 and 59 of the Act that sections 20 and 42 of the Act do not apply to a trade in a security of a U.S. Issuer that is exchanged by or for the account of the issuer with the security holders of the issuer under an issuer bid made in compliance with the MJDS;

Prospectus offerings

3. under section 59 of the Act that section 42 of the Act does not apply to a distribution of a security by a U.S. Issuer made in compliance with the MJDS provided that the distribution is made in compliance with section 42 of the Act, except for the requirements contained in

   (a) section 42 of the Act, as to the form and content of a preliminary prospectus and a prospectus,

   (b) sections 47 to 50 of the Act,

   (c) section 51 of the Act, as to the date by which the distribution of securities pursuant to a prospectus must cease, with respect to a distribution of a security made in compliance with Rule 415 of the Securities Act of 1933 of the United States, and

   (d) division 2 of Part 7 of the Regulation,

   provided that a preliminary prospectus and prospectus complying with the MJDS

(e)   are filed under section 42 of the Act in accordance with the require-ments and procedures set out in the MJDS,

(f)   are supplemented and amended in accordance with the requirements and procedures set out in the MJDS, and, with respect to the filing of amendments, in compliance with sections 47 and 48 of the Act, and

(g)   contain the certificates of the issuer and the underwriter required under sections 49 and 50 of the Act, in the form set out in, and signed in compliance with, the MJDS;

Solicitations of expressions of interest

4.   under section 59 of the Act that section 42 of the Act does not apply to the solicitation of expressions of interest with respect to a distribution of a security to be made in compliance with the MJDS, prior to the filing of a preliminary prospectus with respect to the security, provided that

(a)   the issuer of the security has entered into an enforceable agreement with an underwriter that

   (i)   requires the underwriter to purchase the security,

   (ii)   requires the issuer to file, and obtain a receipt for, the preliminary prospectus from the securities regulatory authority of

      (A)   the jurisdiction selected as the principal jurisdiction within two business days, and

      (B)   all other jurisdictions in Canada in which the distribution is to be made within three business days

      from the date that the issuer and the underwriter entered into the agreement, and

   (iii)   fixes the terms of issue of the security,

(b)   as soon as a receipt for the preliminary prospectus has been obtained, a copy of the preliminary prospectus is forwarded to any person who has expressed an interest in acquiring the security,

(c)   no contract of purchase and sale with respect to the security is entered into until the prospectus has been filed and a receipt obtained for it from the Superintendent, and

(d)   the Superintendent has not advised the underwriter or the issuer in writing that it cannot rely on the exemption set out in this paragraph;

See NIN 93/12 "Restriction Applicable to the Solicitation of Expressions of Interest under BOR #91/7 and BOR #93/1".

Offerors making a take over bid or issuer bid

5.   under section 96(2)(c) of the Act that an offeror making a take over bid or issuer bid in compliance with the MJDS is exempt from the requirements contained in

(a)   sections 83, 84, 86, 88 and 89 of the Act and sections 160(1) and (2), 161 and 163.5 of the Regulation,

(b)   section 85 of the Act, except subsection (1) where security holders of the offeree issuer whose last address as shown on the books of the issuer is in Canada, as determined in accordance with the Policy, hold 20% or more of any class of securities that is subject to the bid,

(c)   section 87 of the Act, except the requirement in paragraph (a) to deliver the bid to all holders in the Province of securities of the class of securities that is subject to the bid,

(d)   section 90 of the Act, except

   (i)   the requirement in subsection (1) to deliver a take over bid cir-cular or issuer bid circular,

   (ii)   the requirement in subsection (2) to deliver a notice of change to every person to whom the take over bid circular or issuer bid circular was required to be delivered and whose securities were not taken up at the date of the occurrence of the change,

(iii) the requirement in subsection (4) to deliver a notice of variation to every person or company to whom the take over bid circular or issuer bid circular was required to be delivered and whose securities were not taken up at the date of the variation,

(iv) the requirement in Form 32, prescribed under subsection (7), applicable where the offeror anticipates that a going private transaction will follow the take over bid,

(v) where the bid is a securities exchange take over bid and the eligibility requirements specified in section 4.4 of the Policy are not met, the requirement in Form 32, prescribed under subsection (7), applicable where the take over bid provides that the consideration for the securities of the offeree issuer is to be, in whole or in part, securities of the offeror or other issuer, and

(vi) where the bid is a securities exchange issuer bid and the eligibility requirements specified in section 4.4 of the Policy are not met, the requirement in Form 33, prescribed under subsection (7), applicable where an issuer bid provides that the consideration for the securities of the offeree issuer is to be, in whole or in part, securities of the issuer,

(e)   section 92 of the Act, except the requirement in subsection (1) to file any notice of change or notice of variation,

(f)   section 153 of the Regulation, except with respect to a take over bid circular in respect of an insider bid, or an issuer bid circular, where security holders of the offeree issuer whose last address as shown on the books of the issuer is in Canada, as determined in accordance with the Policy, hold 20% or more of any class of securities that is subject to the bid, and

(g)   section 163.7 of the Regulation, except that a circular or notice must be filed within the time set out in the MJDS,

provided that any delivery or filing by the offeror of any take over bid circular, issuer bid circular, notice of change or notice of variation under the Act is made in compliance with the MJDS;

Directors and officers of offeree issuer

6.   under section 96(2)(c) of the Act that the directors and an individual director or officer of an offeree issuer whose securities are the subject of a take over bid or issuer bid made in compliance with the MJDS are exempt from the requirements contained in

(a)   section 91 of the Act, except

(i) the requirement in subsection (1) to deliver a directors' circular to every person to whom a take over bid must be delivered under section 87(a),

(ii) the requirement in subsection (6)(a) to deliver a notice of change to every person to whom the directors' circular was required to be delivered, and

(iii) the requirement in subsection (7) to deliver an individual director's or officer's circular or notice of change to every person to whom a take over bid must be delivered under section 87(a),

(b)   section 92 of the Act, except the requirement in subsection (2) to file every directors' circular and every individual director's or officer's circular and any notice of change, and

(c)   sections 160(3), 163.5 and 163.7 of the Regulation,

provided that

(d)   the directors or the individual director or officer of the offeree issuer, as the case may be, comply with the MJDS, and

(e)   any delivery or filing by the directors of the offeree issuer of any directors' circular, individual director's or officer's circular or notice of change under the Act, is made in compliance with the MJDS;

Proxy solicitation

7.   under section 103(2)(b) of the Act that a person soliciting proxies from holders of voting securities of a U.S. Issuer that has a class of securities registered pursuant to section 12 of the 1934 Act is exempt from the requirements of Part 12 of the Act, except for the requirements contained in section 101(1) and (2) of the Act to send a form of proxy and information circular to each holder in the Province of the voting securities of the issuer whose proxy is solicited, provided that

(a)   the form of proxy and information circular may be in a form complying with U.S. requirements, and

(b)   the person complies with the MJDS;

Financial Statements

8.   under section 143(1)(b)(iii) of the Regulation that a U.S. Issuer that has a class of securities registered pursuant to section 12 of the 1934 Act or that is required to file reports pursuant to section 15(d) of the 1934 Act is exempt from the requirements contained in

(a)   sections 135, 136, and 142 of the Regulation, provided that the issuer files financial statements under sections 135(1) and 136(1) of the Regulation in accordance with the requirements and procedures set out in the MJDS, and

(b)   sections 141(b), 145, and 182 of the Regulation,

provided that the issuer complies with the MJDS;

9.   under section 143(1)(b)(iii) of the Regulation that a U.S. Issuer that has a class of securities registered pursuant to section 12 of the 1934 Act or that is required to file reports pursuant to section 15(d) of the 1934 Act is exempt from the requirement contained in section 141(a) of the Regulation, provided that

(a)   the issuer

(i)   is a reporting issuer in the Province solely as a result of distributions of securities made in compliance with the MJDS,

(ii)   meets the eligibility requirements specified in sections 3.3(1) and (2) of the Policy, or

(iii)   meets the eligibility requirements specified in sections 3.2(1) to (5) of the Policy and the issuer is a reporting issuer in the Province solely as a result of distributions of securities that have an Approved Rating, as defined in the Policy, and meet the eligibility requirements of section 3.2(6) of the Policy, and

(b)   the issuer complies with the MJDS; and

Insider reports

10.   under section 152.2 of the Regulation that an insider of a U.S. Issuer that has a class of securities registered pursuant to section 12 of the 1934 Act is exempt from section 70 of the Act, provided that the insider files with the SEC on a timely basis all reports required to be filed with the SEC pursuant to section 16(a) of the 1934 Act and the rules and regulations thereunder;

AND WHEREAS the Superintendent considers that to do so would not be prejudicial to the public interest;

Effective July 1, 1991, THE SUPERINTENDENT

Representation of listing on stock exchange

1. PERMITS, under section 35(1)(c) of the Act, a U.S. Issuer making a distribution of a security in compliance with the MJDS to make a representation that the security will be listed and posted for trading on a stock exchange or that application has been made or will be made to list and post the security for trading on a stock exchange;

Conflict of interest

2. ORDERS, under section 167.12 of the Regulation, that a distribution of a security issued by a registrant or issued by or held by a related party or connected party of a registrant is exempt from the requirements of section 167.4(2)(a) and (d) of the Regulation, provided that the distribution is made in compliance with the MJDS; and

3. ORDERS, under section 167.12 of the Regulation, that a distribution of a security issued by a registrant or issued by or held by a related party or connected party of a registrant is exempt from the requirements of section 167.4(2)(b) and (c) of the Regulation, provided that

    (a)   if the distribution is made in both Canada and the United States, the aggregate of the portions of the distribution in Canada and the United States underwritten by at least one independent underwriter, as defined in the Policy, and its affiliates, as defined in the Policy, is not less than the aggregate of the portions of the distribution in Canada and the United States underwritten by dealers in respect of which the issuer is a related party or connected party or, where a dealer is not a registrant, would be a connected party if the dealer were a registrant, or

    (b)   if the distribution is made in Canada only, the aggregate of the portions of the distribution underwritten by at least one independent underwriter, as defined in the Policy, and its affiliates, as defined in the Policy, is not less than the aggregate of the portions of the distribution underwritten by dealers in respect of which the issuer is a related party or connected party or, where a dealer is not a registrant, would be a connected party if the dealer were a registrant, and

    the distribution is made in compliance with the MJDS.

DATED at Vancouver, British Columbia, on June 25, 1991.

Douglas M. Hyndman   Wade D. Nesmith
Chairman   Superintendent of Brokers

BOR#91/8

CCA BOR#91/2

IN THE MATTER OF THE COMMODITY CONTRACT ACT
R.S.B.C. 1979, c. 56
AND
IN THE MATTER OF THE SECURITIES ACT
S.B.C. 1985, c. 83
AND
IN THE MATTER OF THE REGISTRATION
OF PERSONS TRADING IN TCO COMMODITY OPTIONS

EXEMPTION ORDER UNDER SECTION 29(1)

WHEREAS a commodity option issued by Trans Canada Options Inc. ("TCO") is a commodity contract within the meaning of section 1 of the Commodity Contract Act, R.S.B.C. 1979, c. 56 ("Act");

AND WHEREAS the Vancouver Stock Exchange ("VSE") is a recognized commodity exchange under the Act pursuant to CCA BOR#89/1, an order issued by the British Columbia Securities Commission under section 24(2) of the Act on January 26, 1989;

AND WHEREAS the form of 10 Ounce Gold option issued by TCO ("TCO Option") was accepted for trading on the VSE, effective May 17, 1991, by the Superintendent of Brokers ("Superintendent") under section 24(3) of the Act on August 1, 1991 pursuant to CCA BOR#91/1;

AND WHEREAS section 13(1) of the Act prohibits any person from trading in a commodity contract unless the person is registered as a commodity contracts dealer, a commodity contracts salesman or as a floor trader, or is registered as a partner or as an officer of a registered commodity contracts dealer and is acting on behalf of that commodity contracts dealer;

AND WHEREAS representations have been made to the Superintendent that persons who trade in the TCO Option should be exempt from registration under the Act if they are registered under the Securities Act, S.B.C. 1985, c. 83, and satisfy certain additional requirements;

AND WHEREAS pursuant to section 29(1) of the Act the Superintendent may, on the Superintendent's own initiative, order that a class of persons is not subject to section 13 of the Act;

AND WHEREAS the Superintendent is satisfied that to do so would not be prejudicial to the public interest;

IT IS ORDERED under section 29(1) of the Act, effective May 17, 1991, that a person who trades in the TCO Option is exempt from section 13(1)(a) of the Act provided that

1. if the person is not an individual, the person is registered as a broker or as an investment dealer (a "Dealer") under the Securities Act; or

2. if the person is an individual, the person:

    (a) is employed by a Dealer as a floor trader and is recognized as an options attorney under Rule I.1.73 of the VSE; or

    (b) is registered under the Securities Act as a salesman, partner, director or officer of a Dealer and has successfully completed the Canadian Options Course prepared and conducted by the Canadian Securities Institute.

DATED at Vancouver, British Columbia, on August 1, 1991.

Wayne Redwick, CGA
Deputy Superintendent of Brokers

REF: BOR#89/1
         CCA BOR#89/6
         CCA BOR#91/1

BOR#91/10

IN THE MATTER OF THE SECURITIES ACT
S.B.C. 1985, c. 83
AND
IN THE MATTER OF FIRST RENEWAL PROSPECTUSES FILED BY MUTUAL FUNDS UNDER NATIONAL POLICY STATEMENT NO. 36

EXEMPTION ORDER UNDER SECTION 59

WHEREAS the lapse date for a prospectus (the "First Prospectus") filed by a mutual fund under section 42 of the Securities Act, S.B.C. 1985, c. 83 (the "Act") is calculated by reference to the date of the receipt for the preliminary prospectus, in accordance with section 51(2)(a) of the Act (the "Earlier Lapse Date");

AND WHEREAS the documents that comprise the simplified prospectus disclosure system set out in National Policy Statement No. 36 ("NPS 36") include the most recent annual audited financial statements and any subsequent financial statements that are required to be filed during the currency of the annual information form by a mutual fund using the simplified prospectus disclosure system in NPS 36 (a "NPS 36 Mutual Fund");

AND WHEREAS copies of the most recent annual audited financial statements and any subsequent financial statements of a NPS 36 Mutual Fund that have been filed with any securities regulatory authority in Canada must accompany, and form part of, the prospectus of the NPS 36 Mutual Fund;

AND WHEREAS, because current financial statements form part of the prospectus of a NPS 36 Mutual Fund, the Commission considers that it is appropriate for the lapse date of the First Prospectus of a NPS 36 Mutual Fund to be calculated by reference to the date of the First Prospectus;

AND WHEREAS the Commission considers that to do so would not be prejudicial to the public interest;

IT IS ORDERED under section 59 of the Act that section 42 of the Act does not apply to a trade in a security by a NPS 36 Mutual Fund after the Earlier Lapse Date, provided that the trade is made in compliance with section 42 of the Act, except for the requirement contained in section 51(2) of the Act, and provided that

(a) for the purposes of section 51(4) and (5) of the Act, "lapse date" means the date 12 months from the date of the First Prospectus (the "Later Lapse Date"), and

(b) the NPS 36 Mutual Fund does not distribute a security under the First Prospectus after the Later Lapse Date, except in compliance with section 51(4) of the Act.

DATED at Vancouver, British Columbia, on August 8, 1991.

Douglas M. Hyndman
Chairman

See NIN 95/9 "Government Strip Bonds - Information Statement" which indicates the intention of the Commission to revise interim Local Policy Statement 3-43 "Government Strip Bonds" and replace BOR 91/12 "Government Strip Bonds".

BOR#91/12

IN THE MATTER OF THE SECURITIES ACT
S.B.C. 1985, C. 83
AND
IN THE MATTER OF GOVERNMENT STRIP BONDS

ORDER UNDER SECTIONS 33 AND 59

WHEREAS certain persons are distributing and trading in British Columbia

(a) actual individual interest coupons and residues arising from the physical separation of bonds, debentures or other evidence of indebtedness issued or guaranteed by the Government of Canada or by a province of Canada or by a country or political division of a country recognized by the British Columbia Securities Commission (the "Commission") in an order made under section 32(a)(i.1) of the Act, and

(b) deposit receipts or other certificates representing an interest in certain specific instruments of the type referred to in (a) or an undivided interest in a pool of these instruments,

where the purchaser's sole entitlement is to receive a fixed amount of money at a specific future date (together "Government Strip Bonds");

AND WHEREAS the Commission considers that to do so would not be prejudicial to the public interest;

IT IS ORDERED under sections 33 and 59 of the Act that sections 20 and 42 of the Act do not apply to a trade in Government Strip Bonds provided that an information statement approved by the Commission or the Superintendent of Brokers describing the investment attributes of Government Strip Bonds including, without limitation,

(a) the fluctuations in the value of Government Strip Bonds resulting from fluctuations in prevailing interest rates,

(b) the income tax consequences of investing and trading in Government Strip Bonds,

(c) the anticipated secondary market environment, and

(d) the custodial arrangements relating to such Government Strip Bonds,

is

(e) where the vendor is not registered under the Act, furnished to, and its receipt is acknowledged by, a first-time purchaser prior to the trade, or

(f) where the vendor is registered under the Act, furnished to a first-time purchaser not later than with confirmation of the trade.

DATED at Vancouver, British Columbia, on December 12, 1991.

Douglas M. Hyndman
Chairman

BOR#92/1

IN THE MATTER OF THE SECURITIES ACT
S.B.C. 1985, C. 83
AND
IN THE MATTER OF FEES PAYABLE BY MEMBERS OF THE PRESS
FOR A SUBSCRIPTION TO THE WEEKLY SUMMARY
AND FOR SEARCH OF A FILE

VARIATION ORDER AND WAIVER
UNDER SECTION 183(1.1) OF THE REGULATION

WHEREAS items 28 and 36 of section 183(1) of the Securities Regulation, B.C. Reg. 270/86 (the "Regulation") prescribe the fees payable for search of a file and for an annual subscription to the periodical referred to in section 152 of the Regulation (the "Weekly Summary");

AND WHEREAS section 183(1.1) of the Regulation authorizes the Commission to order that items 28 and 36 of section 183(1) of the Regulation be varied, by reducing the fee payable, or do not apply in respect of a person who is a representative of the media or any class of persons who are representatives of the media;

AND WHEREAS, for the purpose of this order, a member of the press includes

(a) a newspaper, magazine, radio or television station, or other bona fide medium of mass communication, or

(b) a news service, network or other affiliation of newspapers, magazines, radio or television stations, or other bona fide media of mass communication,

but does not include a newspaper, magazine, newsletter, pamphlet or other record published or sponsored by an issuer, registrant, promoter, public relations or investor relations firm, law firm, accounting firm, geological or engineering firm, consulting firm, or other person whose principal business is not publishing;

AND WHEREAS the Commission considers that to do so would be in the public interest;

IT IS ORDERED under section 183(1.1) of the Regulation that:

1. the fee prescribed under item 36 of section 183(1) of the Regulation be varied by reducing it to $100 per year in respect of a member of the press; and

2. the fee prescribed under item 28 of section 183(1) of the Regulation does not apply in respect of a member of the press who subscribes to the Weekly Summary for the reduced fee of $100 per year.

DATED at Vancouver, British Columbia, on April 23, 1992.

Douglas M. Hyndman
Chairman

REF: NIN#92/6

IN THE MATTER OF THE SECURITIES ACT
S.B.C. 1985, c. 83
AND
IN THE MATTER OF THE LIMITATIONS ON A REGISTRANT UNDERWRITING SECURITIES OF A RELATED PARTY OR CONNECTED PARTY OF THE REGISTRANT

ORDER UNDER SECTION 167.12 OF THE REGULATION

WHEREAS section 167.4 of the Securities Regulation, B.C. Reg. 270/86 (the "Regulation") imposes limitations on a registrant acting as an underwriter or special selling group member in connection with an initial distribution of securities issued by the registrant or issued by or held by a related party or connected party of the registrant;

AND WHEREAS, except in the circumstances described in section 167.4(2)(c), (4) or (5) of the Regulation, section 167.4(2)(b) of the Regulation requires that in the case of an initial distribution made under a prospectus or under a statement of material facts, the portion of the initial distribution underwritten by at least one independent underwriter is not less than the aggregate of the portions of the initial distribution underwritten by or, in the capacity of special selling group member, sold by the registrant and each other registrant in respect of which the issuer is a related party or a connected party;

AND WHEREAS the Superintendent of Brokers (the "Superintendent") has concluded that the requirement in section 167.4(2)(b) of the Regulation is not necessary to protect investors and, if the requirement were enforced, it would unduly disrupt industry practice and issuer's needs;

AND WHEREAS the Superintendent considers that it would not be prejudicial to the public interest to do so;

IT IS ORDERED under section 167.12 of the Regulation that section 167.4(2)(b) does not apply to a registrant acting as an underwriter or special selling group member in connection with an initial distribution, made under a prospectus or under a statement of material facts, of securities issued by or held by a related party or connected party of the registrant provided that

1. the aggregate of the portions of the initial distribution underwritten by the independent underwriters is not less than the aggregate of the portions of the initial distribution underwritten by or, in the capacity of special selling group member, sold by the registrant and each other registrant in respect of which the issuer is a related party or a connected party,

2. the portion of the initial distribution underwritten by at least one of the independent underwriters is not less than the largest portion of the initial distribution underwritten by or, in the capacity of special selling group member, sold by a registrant in respect of which the issuer is a related party or a connected party, and

3. each independent underwriter signs the prospectus certificate or the statement of material facts certificate required by section 50 of the Securities Act, S.B.C. 1985, c. 83 and section 122 of the Regulation, respectively.

DATED at Vancouver, British Columbia, on August 6, 1992.

Wade D. Nesmith
Superintendent of Brokers

Blanket
Orders

IN THE MATTER OF THE SECURITIES ACT
S.B.C. 1985, c. 83
AND
IN THE MATTER OF THE COMMODITY CONTRACT ACT
R.S.B.C. 1979, c. 56
AND
IN THE MATTER OF THE REVOCATION OF BOR#91/11
AND
IN THE MATTER OF RECOGNIZED OPTIONS TRADED
THROUGH RECOGNIZED CLEARING AGENCIES
(RECOGNIZED OPTIONS RATIONALIZATION ORDER)

REVOCATION ORDER UNDER SECTION 153
OF THE SECURITIES ACT
AND EXEMPTION ORDERS UNDER
SECTIONS 33 AND 59 OF THE SECURITIES ACT
AND SECTION 29 OF THE COMMODITY CONTRACT ACT

WHEREAS on December 2, 1991 the Superintendent issued an Order (the "Order"), effective September 27, 1991, under sections 33, 59 and 153 of the Securities Act, S.B.C. 1985, c. 83 (the "Act") and under section 29 of the Commodity Contract Act, R.S.B.C. 1979, c. 56 that, among other things, a trade in a Recognized Option by a dealer registered under the Act or a Recognized Dealer registered under the Commodity Contract Act is not subject to section 42 of the Act, provided the conditions contained in the Order are satisfied;

AND WHEREAS capped index options, capped stock index options and capped international index options (collectively, "CIOs") are similar to other Recognized Options because,

1. like current European-style options, a holder of a CIO has the right to exercise the option during a specified period immediately prior to the expiration of the option, and

2. other specifications of CIOs, including contract size, exercise price, expiration date, cap price, and time of day at which the option settlement price is determined, are fixed by the markets on which the CIOs trade;

AND WHEREAS, unlike other Recognized Options, a CIO is automatically exercised if, as determined by the exchange on which the option is traded, the exercise settlement value for the CIO on any trading day equals or exceeds (in the case of a call) or equals or is less than (in the case of a put) the cap price for the option;

AND WHEREAS CIOs are fully described in the supplemental disclosure document for CIOs (the "CIO Disclosure Document") prepared by **The Options Clearing Corporation** and which, pursuant to this order, dealers registered under the Act and Recognized Dealers registered under the Commodity Contract Act will mail or deliver to clients prior to trading on their behalf in CIOs;

AND WHEREAS the Superintendent wishes to include CIOs in the list of Recognized Options set out in paragraph (b) of the definition of "Recognized Option" in the Order;

AND WHEREAS it is expedient to revoke the Order and to issue a comprehensive order in this regard;

AND WHEREAS for the purposes of this order

"Recognized Advisor" means

    (a) an investment counsel or portfolio manager registered under the Act, or

    (b) a partner, officer or director or an investment counsel or portfolio manager registered under the Act, where the registrant has successfully completed The Canadian Options Course administered by the Canadian Securities Institute;

"Recognized Clearing Agency" means

    (a) Trans Canada Options Inc. ("TCO"),

    (b) The Options Clearing Corporation ("OCC"), or

(c) The Intermarket Clearing Corporation ("ICC");

"Recognized Dealer" means

(a) a dealer registered under the Act that is a member of a self regulatory body recognized by the Commission under the Act,

(b) a dealer registered under the Commodity Contract Act that is a member of a self regulatory body recognized by the Commission under the Commodity Contract Act, or

(c) a salesman, partner, officer or director of a dealer registered under the Act or the Commodity Contract Act, where the registrant has successfully completed the Canadian Options Course administered by the Canadian Securities Institute;

"Recognized Option" means

(a) an equity, debt, currency, index, precious metal or participation unit option traded on one or more of The Toronto Stock Exchange, Toronto Futures Exchange, Montreal Exchange or Vancouver Stock Exchange (the "Canadian Exchanges"), and cleared through TCO, or

(b) an equity, capped index, capped stock index, capped international index, debt, currency, index or precious metal option traded on one or more of the American Stock Exchange, Chicago Board Options Exchange, New York Stock Exchange, Pacific Stock Exchange, Amex Commodities Corporation, Philadelphia Stock Exchange, Philadelphia Board of Trade or the automated quotation system of the National Association of Securities Dealers, and cleared through OCC or ICC;

AND WHEREAS the Superintendent considers that to do so would not be prejudicial to the public interest;

IT IS ORDERED, effective August 11, 1992,

1. under section 153 of the Act that the Order is revoked;

2. under section 33 of the Act that section 20 of the Act does not apply to a trade in a Recognized Option on an underlying asset that is a security, effected through a Recognized Dealer registered under the Commodity Contract Act;

3. under section 29 of the Commodity Contract Act that section 13 of the Commodity Contract Act does not apply to

(a) a trade in a Recognized Option on an underlying asset that is not a security, effected through a Recognized Dealer registered under the Act, or

(b) a Recognized Advisor acting as an advisor with respect to a Recognized Option on an underlying asset that is not a security; and

4. under section 59 of the Act that section 42 of the Act does not apply to a trade in a Recognized Option by a dealer registered under the Act or a Recognized Dealer registered under the Commodity Contract Act provided that, prior to the trade, the registered dealer or Recognized Dealer sends by prepaid mail or delivers to the client

(a) a copy of the Disclosure Statement for Recognized Market Options in the form attached as Schedule "A" to this order, and

(b) where the trade is in a CIO, a copy of the CIO Disclosure Document, in the form of attached as Schedule "B" to this order.

DATED at Vancouver, British Columbia, on November 18, 1992.

Wade D. Nesmith
Superintendent of Brokers

REF: BOR#91/11

**IN THE MATTER OF THE SECURITIES ACT
S.B.C. 1985, c. 83
AND
IN THE MATTER OF THE
PROMPT OFFERING QUALIFICATION SYSTEM**

*EXEMPTION ORDERS UNDER SECTION 59 OF
THE ACT AND SECTIONS 99(2), 115(6) AND
143(1)(B)(III) OF THE REGULATION*

WHEREAS the Commission has issued National Policy Statement No. 47 - Prompt Offering Qualification System (the "Policy");

AND WHEREAS the Policy is structured on the basis that issuers of securities in compliance with the Policy will be exempted from certain of the requirements of the Securities Act, S.B.C. 1985, c.83 (the "Act") and the Securities Regulation, B.C. Reg. 270/86 (the "Regulation");

AND WHEREAS the Commission and the Superintendent consider that Local Policy Statement No. 3-40 ("LPS 3-40") shortened the time periods and streamlined the procedures by which issuers that qualified under LPS 3-40 had access to the capital markets through a prospectus offering without reducing the existing benefits of investor protection or the degree and quality of disclosure to the public;

AND WHEREAS the Commission and the Superintendent consider that replacing LPS 3-40 with the Policy is desirable in order to provide a national policy statement for the prompt offering qualification system;

AND WHEREAS the "POP System" means the requirements of the Policy, as they have been waived or varied by the Commission or the Superintendent;

AND WHEREAS the Commission considers that to do so would not be prejudicial or harmful to the public interest and there is adequate justification to do so;

Effective February 19, 1993, THE COMMISSION ORDERS

Prospectus offerings

1.   under section 59 of the Act that section 42 of the Act does not apply to a distribution of a security by an issuer made in compliance with the POP System provided the distribution is made in compliance with section 42 of the Act, except for the requirements contained in

    (a) section 42(2) of the Act, as to the form and content of a preliminary prospectus and a prospectus, and

    (b) sections 49(1) and 50(1) of the Act, as to the form of certificates of the issuer, promoter and underwriter,

  provided a preliminary short form prospectus and short form prospectus

    (c) are filed under section 42(2) of the Act in accordance with the requirements and procedures set out in the POP System, and

    (d) contain the certificates of the issuer, promoter and underwriter required under sections 49(1) and 50(1) of the Act, in the form set out in the POP System;

Solicitations of expressions of interest

2.   under section 59 of the Act that section 42 of the Act does not apply to the solicitation of expressions of interest with respect to a distribution of a security to be made in compliance with the POP System, prior to the filing of a preliminary short form prospectus with respect to the security, provided

    (a) the issuer of the security has entered into an enforceable agreement with an underwriter that

        (i) requires the underwriter to purchase the security,

        (ii) requires the issuer to file, and obtain a receipt for, the preliminary short form prospectus from the securities regulatory authority of

(A) the jurisdiction selected as the principal jurisdiction within two business days, and

(B) all other jurisdictions in Canada in which the distribution is to be made within three business days from the date that the issuer and the underwriter entered into the agreement, and

(iii) fixes the terms of issue of the security,

(b) as soon as a receipt for the preliminary short form prospectus has been obtained, a copy of the preliminary short form prospectus is forwarded to any person who has expressed an interest in acquiring the security,

(c) no contract of purchase and sale with respect to the security is entered into until the short form prospectus has been filed and a receipt obtained for it from the Superintendent, and

(d) the Superintendent has not advised the underwriter or the issuer in writing that it cannot rely on the exemption set out in this paragraph; and

---

See NIN 93/12 "Restriction Applicable to the Solicitation of Expressions of Interest under BOR #91/7 and BOR #93/1".

Financial Statements

3. under section 143(1)(b)(iii) of the Regulation that section 141 of the Regulation does not apply where an issuer is required to file its comparative audited annual financial statements with the Commission in order for a receipt to be issued for its preliminary short form prospectus or short form prospectus under the POP System provided the relevant financial statements are sent, and the written confirmation of sending is filed, within the time period contemplated by the continuous disclosure requirements of the Regulation for the filing and sending of an issuer's comparative audited annual financial statements;

AND WHEREAS the Superintendent considers that obtaining a consent is impracticable where any security rating received from one or more Approved Rating Organizations, as defined in the Policy, is required to be disclosed in a preliminary short form prospectus and short form prospectus;

AND WHEREAS the Superintendent is satisfied that there is sufficient justification to do so;

Effective February 19, 1993, THE SUPERINTENDENT WAIVES

Consent

1. under section 99(2) of the Regulation, the requirement set out in that section to file a consent in respect of any security rating disclosed in a preliminary short form prospectus or a short form prospectus in accordance with the POP System; and

Securities underwritten on a firm commitment basis

2. under section 115(6) of the Regulation, the requirement of section 115(3)(d) of the Regulation, provided the short form prospectus indicates that the securities are to be taken up by the underwriter, if at all, on or before a date not later than six weeks from the date on which the final receipt is issued.

DATED at Vancouver, British Columbia, on February 17, 1993.

Douglas M. Hyndman   Dean E. Holley
Chair   Superintendent of Brokers

IN THE MATTER OF THE COMPANY ACT
R.S.B.C. 1979, c. 59
AND
IN THE MATTER OF
THE MULTIJURISDICTIONAL DISCLOSURE SYSTEM

EXEMPTION ORDER UNDER SECTION 97(2) OF THE COMPANY ACT

WHEREAS on July 1, 1991 the British Columbia Securities Commission (the "Commission") published National Policy Statement No. 45, entitled "Multijurisdictional Disclosure System" (the "Policy");

AND WHEREAS the Policy implements the multijurisdictional disclosure system, which permits substantial Canadian issuers to distribute securities in the United States using Canadian disclosure documents and substantial U.S. issuers to distribute securities in Canada using U.S. disclosure documents;

AND WHEREAS "MJDS" means the requirements of the Policy, as they have been waived or varied by the Commission or the Superintendent of Brokers (the "Superintendent");

AND WHEREAS the trust indenture provisions in sections 96 to 107 of the Company Act, R.S.B.C. 1979, c. 59 (the "Company Act") apply to a trust indenture under which any corporation, including a U.S. issuer as defined in the Policy (a "U.S. issuer"), issues or guarantees debentures;

AND WHEREAS, on June 5, 1992, the Company Act was amended to authorize the Superintendent to exempt a trust indenture or class of trust indentures from one or more of the provisions of sections 96 to 107 of the Company Act;

AND WHEREAS, in order for the Securities and Exchange Commission of the United States to exempt B.C. issuers distributing debt securities in the United States pursuant to the multijurisdictional disclosure system from certain requirements of the Trust Indenture Act of the United States, the Superintendent must exempt trust indentures of U.S. issuers distributing debentures in British Columbia in compliance with the MJDS from sections 96 to 107 of the Company Act;

AND WHEREAS the Superintendent considers that providing this exemption will facilitate cross-border securities transactions under the multijurisdictional disclosure system;

AND WHEREAS the Superintendent considers that to do so would not be prejudicial to the public interest;

IT IS ORDERED, under section 97(2) of the Company Act, that a trust indenture under which a U.S. issuer issues or guarantees a debenture distributed under a prospectus, an issuer bid circular or a take over bid circular filed under the Securities Act, S.B.C. 1985, c.83 in compliance with the MJDS is exempted from sections 96 to 107 of the Company Act.

DATED at Vancouver, British Columbia, on June 16, 1993.

Dean E. Holley
Superintendent of Brokers

IN THE MATTER OF THE SECURITIES ACT
S.B.C. 1985, c. 83
AND
IN THE MATTER OF NETWORKING ARRANGEMENTS
GOVERNED BY THE PRINCIPLES OF REGULATION

ORDER UNDER SECTION 167.12 OF THE REGULATION

WHEREAS section 167.10(2) of the Securities Regulation, B.C. Reg. 270/86 (the "Regulation") requires a registrant that intends to enter into a networking arrangement, as defined in section 167.10(1) of the Regulation, at least 30 days before entering into the networking arrangement, to give written notice of its intention to the Superintendent of Brokers (the "Superintendent") providing all relevant facts relating to the networking arrangement;

AND WHEREAS the Canadian Securities Administrators has published guidelines respecting a registrant related to a financial institution and the financial institution, namely "Distribution of Mutual Funds By Financial Institutions" dated November 9, 1988 (the "First Principles"), "Full Service and Discount Brokerage Activities of Securities Dealers In Branches of Related Institutions" dated November 25, 1988 (the "Second Principles") and "Activities of Registrants Related To Financial Institutions" undated but effective July 1, 1990 (the "Third Principles") (collectively, the "Principles of Regulation");

AND WHEREAS the British Columbia Securities Commission has adopted the First Principles, Second Principles and Third Principles by, respectively, NIN#88/40 dated November 9, 1988, NIN#88/48 dated December 20, 1988 (as modified by NIN#90/7 dated March 7, 1990) and NIN#90/16 dated May 10, 1990;

AND WHEREAS the Superintendent has concluded that the requirement to file a notice of a networking arrangement under section 167.10(2) of the Regulation is not necessary to protect investors where a registrant related to a financial institution complies with the guidelines set out in the Principles of Regulation;

AND WHEREAS the Superintendent considers that it would not be prejudicial to the public interest to do so;

IT IS ORDERED under section 167.12 of the Regulation that section 167.10(2) of the Regulation does not apply to a registrant that is related to a financial institution provided that the registrant complies with the guidelines set out in the Principles of Regulation.

DATED at Vancouver, British Columbia, on December 22, 1993.

Dean E. Holley
Superintendent of Brokers

BOR#94/1

IN THE MATTER OF THE SECURITIES ACT
S.B.C. 1985, c. 83
AND
IN THE MATTER OF THE
PROMPT OFFERING QUALIFICATION SYSTEM
AND
IN THE MATTER OF THE
MEMORANDUM OF UNDERSTANDING
FOR EXPEDITED REVIEW OF
SHORT FORM PROSPECTUSES AND RENEWAL AIFS

EXEMPTION ORDER UNDER SECTION 59 OF THE ACT

WHEREAS the Commission issued National Policy Statement No. 47 on the Prompt Offering Qualification System (the "Policy") and blanket order BOR#93/1, which gave effect to the Policy, on February 17, 1993;

AND WHEREAS the "POP System" means the requirements of the Policy, as they have been waived or varied by the Commission or the Superintendent of Brokers (the "Superintendent");

AND WHEREAS eligible issuers under the POP System may use a preliminary short form prospectus and a short form prospectus in connection with the distribution of securities;

AND WHEREAS the Commission has entered into a Memorandum of Understanding for Expedited Review of Short Form Prospectuses and Renewal AIFs (the "MOU") with certain Canadian securities regulatory authorities (the "Participating Jurisdictions");

AND WHEREAS the MOU sets out, among other things, the procedure to be followed to expedite the review and receipt of preliminary short form prospectuses and short form prospectuses filed in more than one jurisdiction under the POP System ("Expedited Review");

AND WHEREAS the MOU provides that

1. the preliminary expedited review receipt document issued by the designated jurisdiction, as defined in the MOU, ("Designated Jurisdiction") of the issuer, as

defined in the MOU, (the "Issuer") will confirm that each Participating Jurisdiction in which an Issuer has filed a preliminary short form prospectus under the
MOU has issued a preliminary receipt; and

2.   the expedited review receipt document issued by the Issuer's Designated Jurisdiction will confirm that each Participating Jurisdiction in which the Issuer has
filed a preliminary short form prospectus under the MOU, other than a Participating Jurisdiction that has opted out of Expedited Review, has issued a final receipt;

AND WHEREAS the MOU further provides that certain Participating Jurisdictions will in fact be issuing a local preliminary receipt and a local final receipt and
that, in those jurisdictions, a filing under Expedited Review will be treated as a
request to hold the local preliminary receipt and local final receipt on behalf of the
Issuer unless the Issuer requests physical possession of the preliminary receipt or final
receipt from those jurisdictions;

AND WHEREAS section 42 of the Act provides that a person shall not distribute a
security unless a preliminary prospectus and a prospectus respecting that security
have been filed with the Superintendent and receipts have been obtained for them
from the Superintendent;

AND WHEREAS in cases where British Columbia is not an Issuer's Designated
Jurisdiction under the MOU and the Issuer's Designated Jurisdiction issues a preliminary expedited review receipt document for the Issuer's preliminary short form
prospectus and an expedited review receipt document for the Issuer's short form
prospectus in accordance with the MOU, the Superintendent will issue and hold in the
Issuer's file a receipt for the Issuer's preliminary short form prospectus and a receipt
for the Issuer's short form prospectus filed under the MOU;

AND WHEREAS the Commission considers that to do so would not be prejudicial
to the public interest;

IT IS ORDERED under section 59 of the Act that, effective November 23, 1994, a
person making a distribution of securities using the procedure set out in the MOU,
where that person is an Issuer whose Designated Jurisdiction is not British Columbia,
is exempt from the requirement contained in section 42(1)(b) of the Act to obtain a
receipt for a preliminary prospectus and a receipt for a prospectus from the Superintendent provided

(a)   the Issuer obtains from the Issuer's Designated Jurisdiction an expedited preliminary review receipt document confirming the issuance of a receipt in British
Columbia for the Issuer's preliminary short form prospectus; and

(b)   the Issuer obtains from the Issuer's Designated Jurisdiction an expedited review
receipt document confirming the issuance of a receipt in British Columbia for the
Issuer's short form prospectus.

DATED at Vancouver, British Columbia, on November 23, 1994.

Douglas M. Hyndman
Chair

BOR#95/1

IN THE MATTER OF THE SECURITIES ACT
S.B.C. 1985, c. 83
AND
IN THE MATTER OF THE
FORM 12A SUMMARY PROSPECTUS DISCLOSURE SYSTEM

ORDER UNDER SECTION 59 OF THE ACT

WHEREAS Part 11 of Local Policy Statement 3-02 - Prospectus Filing Requirements ("LPS 3-02") sets out the rules for the use of a Form 12A summary prospectus
and base disclosure document (the "Form 12A Summary Prospectus Disclosure
System");

AND WHEREAS the Form 12A Summary Prospectus Disclosure System has been
structured on the basis that issuers of securities in compliance with the Form 12A
Summary Prospectus Disclosure System will be exempted from certain requirements of
the Securities Act, S.B.C. 1985, c. 83, as amended (the "Act");

AND WHEREAS the Commission considers that providing such an exemption will reduce costs for issuers making public offerings and will provide investors with a shorter, user friendly document without reducing the existing benefits of investor protection or the degree and quality of disclosure to the public;

AND WHEREAS the Commission considers that it would not be prejudicial to the public interest to do so;

EFFECTIVE JANUARY 6, 1995, IT IS ORDERED under section 59 of the Act that sections 42(2), 49(1) and 50(1) of the Act, do not apply to a distribution of securities by a junior industrial issuer required to file a prospectus on Form 12A – Information Required in Prospectus of Junior Industrial Issuer, provided that a preliminary Form 12A summary prospectus, preliminary base disclosure document, Form 12A summary prospectus and base disclosure document (including the required certificates) are filed under section 42(1) of the Act in accordance with the requirements and procedures of the Form 12A Summary Prospectus Disclosure System set out in Part 11 of LPS 3-02.

DATED at Vancouver, British Columbia, on January 5, 1995.

Douglas M. Hyndman
Chair

References: LPS 3-02
Form 12A

BOR#95/2

IN THE MATTER OF THE SECURITIES ACT
S.B.C. 1985, c. 83
AND
IN THE MATTER OF THE REVOCATION OF BOR#87/18

REVOCATION ORDER UNDER SECTION 153

WHEREAS a Deputy Superintendent of Brokers issued BOR#87/18, dated March 23, 1987 (the "Order"), to provide registration and prospectus exemptions respecting the distribution and trading of Certificates as defined in the Order;

AND WHEREAS the Superintendent has received a number of enquiries about the Order from persons who propose to rely upon the Order in circumstances in which the Superintendent considers such reliance would not be in the public interest;

AND WHEREAS the Superintendent considers that to do so would not be prejudicial to the public interest;

IT IS ORDERED, effective July 4, 1995, under section 153 of the Act, that the Order is revoked for distributions of Certificates on or after July 4, 1995.

DATED at Vancouver, British Columbia, on June 22, 1995.

Dean E. Holley
Superintendent of Brokers

Ref: BOR#87/18

Blanket
Orders

Only NINs that are presently effective or have recently lapsed are set out in the index. Only NINs that are presently effective are set out in the text. Appendices to NINs have only been included where the information set forth therein remains pertinent and is not otherwise available.

SECURITIES ACT

INDEX OF NOTICES AND INTERPRETATION NOTES

Effective June 30, 1995

NIN#	Date of NIN (mm/dd/yy)	Description	Status (mm/dd/yy)
87/45	06/11/87	Technical reports on mining properties accompanying prospectuses submitted for acceptance by the Superintendent of Brokers	in effect
87/52	07/24/87	Flow-through shares	in effect
87/66	10/09/87	Prospectus vetting procedures	in effect
87/67	10/09/87	Leveraged mutual fund purchases	in effect
88/5	03/31/88	Guidelines for applications to the Securities Commission or the Superintendent of Brokers for decisions or orders	in effect
88/7	06/01/88	Venture capital issuers	in effect
88/10	06/02/88	"Full disclosure" in financial statements	in effect
88/11	06/06/88	The effect of criminal and civil litigation on trading rights and registration	in effect
88/40	11/09/88	Sale of mutual funds by financial institutions - principles of regulation	in effect
88/43	11/18/88	Form 20A - clarification of requirements	in effect
88/45	12/01/88	National Policy Statement No. 41 - shareholder communication - removal of exemption	in effect
88/48	12/20/88	Full service and discount brokerage activities by financial institutions - principles of regulation	in effect
89/2	01/17/89	Execution of memorandum of understanding	lapsed 04/01/89 MOU still in effect
89/3	01/20/89	Conflict of interest rules statement - clarification of filing requirements	in effect
89/5	01/27/89	Introduction of revised quarterly report	lapsed 04/20/95
89/13	03/02/89	Statutory filings	in effect
89/17	04/06/89	Local Policy Statement 3-45 - designation as a reporting issuer and business investor offerings	in effect
89/21	07/21/89	Orders pursuant to section 145 of the Securities Act - removal of trading exemptions	in effect
89/29	10/13/89	Interpretation note - meaning of "the public"	in effect

NIN#	Date of NIN (mm/dd/yy)	Description	Status (mm/dd/yy)
89/30	10/13/89	Qualifications of auditors filing reports	in effect
89/32	10/31/89	Required form of offering memorandum	in effect
89/34	11/17/89	Settlements with the British Columbia Securities Commission	in effect
89/35	11/24/89	Disclosure of promotional or investor relations arrangements	in effect
89/36	11/15/89	Disclosure of experience of directors, officers, promoters and control persons	in effect
89/43	12/21/89	Local Policy Statement 3-07	in effect
90/4	02/09/90	National Policy No. 39 - mutual funds distributor's report and auditor's letter	in effect
90/7	03/07/90	Dual employment of individuals employed by financial institutions and securities registrants	in effect
90/13	04/05/90	Rights offerings	in effect
90/16	05/10/90	Principles of regulation re: activities of registrants related to financial institutions	in effect
90/20	06/07/90	Availability of weekly summary and material published under the Securities Act	in effect
90/22	06/14/90	Filing of specified forms	in effect
90/29	08/30/90	Proposals for securities firms	in effect
91/12	07/11/91	Ontario Securities Commission Policy Statement 9.1 - disclosure, valuation, review and approval requirements and recommendations for insider bids, issuer bids, going private transactions and related party transactions	in effect
91/17	09/25/91	Section 203(3)(b) of the Company Act - consent by the Superintendent of Brokers to the waiver of the appointment of an auditor for a subsidiary corporation	in effect
91/18	10/02/91	Auditor's report on comparative financial statements	in effect
91/19	10/10/91	New computer system for insider reports	in effect
91/20	10/31/91	Comparative interim financial statements	in effect
91/21	11/01/91	Accounting for business combinations and corporate reorganizations	in effect
91/22	11/13/91	Guide for use of the multijurisdictional disclosure system by Canadian issuers in the U.S. Market	in effect
91/23	12/12/91	Introduction of Interim Local Policy Statement 3-43 - government strip bonds	in effect
92/2	02/06/92	Communication with the Securities Commission	in effect
92/3	02/12/92	Waivers consequential to Local Policy Statement 3-07	in effect
92/4	03/05/92	Draft National Policy Statement No. 46 - index and commodity warrants and other derivative securities	in effect
92/8	05/07/92	Ontario Securities Commission Policy No. 4.8 - non-resident advisers	in effect

NIN#	Date of NIN (mm/dd/yy)	Description	Status (mm/dd/yy)
92/15	06/25/92	Securities Amendment Act, 1992	in effect
92/18	07/10/92	Required form of personal information	in effect
92/19	07/16/92	Revised Draft Local Policy Statement 3-04 - filing of assessment reports	in effect
92/20	07/16/92	Draft Form 12A, Prospectus for a junior industrial issuer, and related disclosure initiatives	lapsed 01/06/95
92/21	07/16/92	Proposed junior POP system - request for comment	in effect
92/22	07/16/92	Fiscal agency agreements - request for comment	in effect
92/24	07/24/92	Amendments to the Securities Act	in effect
92/29	11/06/92	Accounting for performance shares	in effect
92/30	11/26/92	National Policy Statement No. 39 - mutual funds - draft section 2.09 - certain related parties acting as principals in purchases or sales of portfolio debt securities and proposed revocation of section 4.03 - dealer manager acting as principal	in effect
93/2	01/07/93	Specification of required forms under the Securities Act and Securities Regulation	in effect
93/3	01/07/93	Decisions of the British Columbia Securities Commission	lapsed 05/11/95
93/5	02/17/93	Section 115(3)(f) of the Securities Regulation - time limit for raising a minimum subscription	in effect
93/8	04/01/93	Money laundering: new federal regulations	in effect
93/12	06/10/93	Restriction applicable to the solicitation of expressions of interest under BOR#91/7 and BOR#93/1	in effect
93/16	08/19/93	Draft National Policy Statement No. 53 - Foreign issuer prospectus and continuous disclosure system	in effect
93/18	09/09/93	Fiscal agency agreement - Restrictions on exemption orders	in effect
93/19	09/09/93	New form of certificate under section 60(3) of the Securities Act	lapsed 11/23/94
93/21	11/25/93	Fiscal agency agreements - Application for discretionary exemption orders	in effect
93/23	12/16/93	Executive compensation	in effect
93/24	12/22/93	Exemption for filing notice of networking arrangements governed by the principles of regulation	in effect
94/2	01/06/94	Filing requirements for annual information forms	in effect
94/3	03/03/94	Amendments to the Fee Schedule under the Securities Regulation	lapsed 01/06/95
94/4	05/17/94	Decision of the Court of Appeal for British Columbia in the matter of Hamelin v. Seven Mile High Group Inc.	in effect

Notices

NIN#	Date of NIN (mm/dd/yy)	Description	Status (mm/dd/yy)
94/5	06/08/94	National Policy Statement No. 39 - Definition of debt-like securities	in effect
94/6	06/08/94	Proposed Interpretation Note on sections 31(2)(21) and 55(2)(18) of the Securities Act - Request for comment	in effect
94/7	06/07/94	Task Force on Operational Efficiencies in the Administration of Securities Regulation - request for comments	lapsed 01/06/95
94/8	06/30/94	Revised indices of notices and interpretation notes, blanket orders and rulings, local policy statements and forms under the Securities Act and Securities Regulation	lapsed 01/06/95
94/9	07/26/94	Amendments to sections 154.3 and 154.4 of the Securities Act	in effect
94/10	08/05/94	Proposal for expedited review of short form prospectus and renewal AIFs	lapsed 01/06/95
94/11	09/14/94	Course announcement - The Securities Program	lapsed 06/30/95
94/12	09/21/94	Joint release of IOSCO/BIS derivatives papers	in effect
94/13	10/05/94	Summary of legislative and policy initiatives	in effect
94/14	10/05/94	Proposed amendments to the Securities Act	in effect
94/15	10/05/94	Proposed amendments to Securities Regulation	in effect
94/16	10/05/94	Draft amended Local Policy Statement 3-22 - Registration requirements	in effect
94/17	10/05/94	Form 12A - Prospectus for a junior industrial issuer, interim Local Policy Statement 3-17 - Registrant due diligence and related disclosure initiatives	in effect
94/18	10/05/94	Form 12A - Prospectus for a junior industrial issuer	in effect
94/19	10/12/94	Draft Amended National Policy Statement No. 41 - Security holder communication	in effect
94/20	10/14/94	Draft National Policy Statement No. 43 - Advertisements of securities and related sales practices	in effect
94/21	11/03/94	Expedited review of short form prospectus and renewal AIFs	in effect
94/22	11/01/94	Permission under section 35(1)(c) of the Securities Act	in effect
94/23	11/03/94	XIXth annual conference of IOSCO, Tokyo, October 16 to 21, 1994	lapsed 01/06/95
94/24	11/09/94	Part XIII of the Regulation to the Securities Act (Ontario) - Conflict of interest: related and connected issuers	in effect
94/25	11/23/94	Amendments to the Securities Act	in effect
94/26	11/23/94	Required form under section 32(g) of the Securities Act	in effect

NIN#	Date of NIN (mm/dd/yy)	Description	Status (mm/dd/yy)
94/27	11/23/94	New form of certificate under section 60(3) of the Securities Act	in effect
94/28	11/23/94	Proposed amendments to the Securities Act	in effect
94/29	12/22/94	Transitional relief - Interim Local Policy Statement No. 3-17 - Registrant due diligence	in effect
95/1	01/05/95	Revised indices of notices and interpretation notes, blanket orders and rulings, local policy statements and forms under the Securities Act and Securities Regulation	lapsed 06/30/95
95/2	01/05/95	Proposed revocation of Blanket Order #87/18	lapsed 06/22/95
95/3	01/05/95	Draft Form 14A - Information required in prospectus of junior natural resource issuer	lapsed 04/20/95
95/4	01/05/95	Amendments to Local Policy Statement 3-02, Blanket Order #95/1 and Form 12A Summary Prospectus Disclosure System	in effect
95/5	01/04/95	Principles of fair trading	in effect
95/6	01/12/95	Draft amendments to Form 30 and additional draft amendments to Section 146 of the Securities Regulation	in effect
95/7	01/12/95	Duties of registrants in the supervision of accounts operating under Powers of Attorney or Trading authorities	in effect
95/8	01/26/95	Task force in operational efficiencies in the administration of Securities Regulation - Interim report	in effect
95/9	02/08/95	Government strip bonds - information statement - Local Policy Statement 3-43 - Blanket Order #91/12	in effect
95/10	02/09/95	Proposed amendments to the *Securities Act*, Securities Regulation and *Vancouver Stock Exchange Act*	in effect
95/11	02/16/95	Proposed amendments to the Securities Act concerning Related Party Transactions Involving Mutual Funds	in effect
95/12	03/01/95	Executive Compensation and Indebtedness Disclosure - Ontario Staff Report	in effect
95/13	03/16/95	Amendments to the Securities Regulation Relating to Filing Requirements and Fees Applicable to Certain Mutual Funds	in effect
95/14	03/23/95	Amendments to the Insider Report Form (Form 36)	in effect
95/15	03/23/95	Interpretation Note - Disclosure of Securities under "Control or Direction"	in effect
95/16	04/20/95	Amendments to Form 30 (Information Circular)	in effect
95/17	04/20/95	Form 14A - Information Required in Prospectus of a Natural Resource Issuer	in effect
95/18	04/20/95	Draft National Policy Statement No. 54 - Expedited Registration System for Advisers	in effect
95/19	04/20/95	Form 61 - Quarterly Report	in effect

Notices

NIN#	Date of NIN (mm/dd/yy)	Description	Status (mm/dd/yy)
95/20	04/26/95	Draft Forms 12B and 14B - Information Required in Exchange Offering Prospectus of an Industrial Issuer and Information Required in Exchange Offering Prospectus of a Natural Resource Issuer	in effect
95/21	05/11/95	Decisions of the B.C. Securities Commission	in effect
95/22	06/01/95	Release of IOSCO/BIS Joint Report on the Framework for Supervisory Information About the Derivatives Activities of Banks and Securities Firms	in effect
95/23	06/14/95	Securities Amendment Act (No. 1), 1995	in effect
95/24	06/22/95	Fee payments under the Securities Act and the Commodity Contract Act	in effect
95/25	06/22/95	Revocation of Blanket Order #87/18	in effect
95/26	06/28/95	Report of Committee on Underwriting Conflicts of Interest - Request for Comment	in effect
95/27	06/29/95	Revised indices of notices and interpretation notes, blanket orders and rulings, local policy statements and forms under the Securities Act and Securities Regulation	in effect

NOTICE

TECHNICAL REPORTS ON MINING PROPERTIES ACCOMPANYING PROSPECTUSES SUBMITTED FOR ACCEPTANCE BY THE SUPERINTENDENT OF BROKERS

The following are the current reference materials which have been published to provide guidance on technical reports on mining properties accompanying prospectuses submitted for acceptance by the Superintendent of Brokers:

1. National Policy #2A.

2. Form 54 of the B.C. Securities Act.

3. Local Policy Statement # 3-01.

Engineers and other qualified persons may also obtain from the B.C. and Yukon Chamber of Mines, 840 West Hastings Street, Vancouver, B.C. V6C 1C8 (Tel.: 681-5328), for a manual service fee, a copy of a GEOSCIENCE RATING SYSTEM prepared by J.R. Woodcock, P.Eng. This rating system establishes a framework on which to list and value, in a logical and consistent manner, the characteristics of a property that warrant consideration when assessing its merit. It is used in making a recommendation to the Superintendent as to whether a property is sufficiently developed to warrant public funding for further exploration and development, and should accordingly be of assistance to experts in the field.

Notwithstanding the availability of the above reference materials, we continue to encounter deficiencies in reports submitted, and the remedying of such deficiencies contributes significantly to delays encountered in processing and receipting prospectus submissions.

While we hesitate to add to the volume of literature already published on technical reports, we have decided in the interest of expediting the prospectus review process to:

(A) Publish the undernoted compilation of deficiencies encountered in reports which contributed to processing delays in 1986;

(B) Publish a checklist for authors of technical reports pertaining to mining properties.

(A) LIST OF TYPICAL DEFICIENCIES IN TECHNICAL REPORTS

1. Failure on the part of the Issuer to provide full, true and plain disclosure as required under both National and Local Policy.

2. Too many inconsistencies or a lack of distinction in the technical report between what the writer himself actually observed and what he is merely reporting as the observance of others who may not be credible. Similarly, a writer may fail to distinguish between data personally accumulated by others and data supplied by others or obtained from totally anonymous sources. Data from an anonymous source may well rate as heresay and should not form part of a report unless properly qualified.

3. Not enough attention to the proper documentation and description of the mineralization or of sample assays. This information should be the most important and significant part of a property description, but rather than being presented in a precise fashion it is very frequently handled casually so that it is difficult to know what the assays represent. Sampling information should include: who took the sample, the location of the sample, the type of sample, what type of material was sampled, the portion of the vein or structure sampled, the length or size of sample, etc. The writer should either attest to the veracity of the samples or otherwise qualify the authenticity of the sample. The name of the laboratory used and their assay procedures and certificate should be provided.

It is a common failure of report writers to not understand, or to misrepresent the "grab sample." All too often the term "grab sample" is used to describe what is actually a selected sample, or even worse, a carefully selected specimen. A proper grab sample is just what the name implies, i.e. a sample of material grabbed or taken at random that is consequently roughly representative of that portion of the medium sampled. This would be equivalent, say, to filling a sample bag from a rock pile with your eyes closed and without bias. Values obtained from a grab sample should therefore be reasonably reproducible by others taking a similar type of sample of the same material.

4. The source of samples not being clearly reported or depicted on maps as to which of the samples have been collected from within the claim boundaries and which from outside.

5. Samples and assay values often inadequately described and documented. Type of sample (grab, channel, character) and the sample length should be clearly stated.

6. The generally poor quality of many of the maps and sections and the manner in which the data are depicted thereon in technical reports. We encourage the liberal use of properly drafted maps and sections as information can be more clearly shown in this manner than in pages of description.

   In many instances, the maps are hastily drawn, they are reduced in size with a copy machine making figures illegible, sometimes resulting in improper scales, they lack the actual geochemical values, or they contain uncontoured geochemical and geophysical values where such contouring is applicable.

7. Tendency to overstate the significance of:

   (a) Airborne VLF-EM conductors or ground VLF-EM conductors where there is little or no correlation with other geophysical, geochemical, or geological support.

   (b) Geochemical anomalies based on indiscriminate use of means and standard deviations.

   (c) Single sample geochemical anomalies.

8. Failure by writers of technical reports often to state clearly and precisely the positive features of a property such as:

   (a) favorable host rocks

   (b) soil and lithochemical anomalies

   (c) geophysical anomalies

   (d) alteration zones

   (e) mineral occurrences

   Furthermore, the relative location of the above features is often unclear. It is important to know whether some of these positive features are coincident as this will enhance the merits of the property.

9. Failure by authors to state the date of revision when a report has been revised.

10. With location ground, often a failure to show clearly the extent, if any, to which mineral-bearing features trend onto the property.

(B) CHECKLIST FOR AUTHORS OF TECHNICAL REPORTS PERTAINING TO MINING PROPERTIES

The general form of the report is suggested below although sections may be re-arranged, the suggested sections may be further subdivided, and additional sections may be added in order to provide full disclosure of information and convincing reasons to do the proposed work. The scope of each proposed work program should be reasonable, relative to the available information and the perceived potential of the property.

I *TITLE PAGE*

Goal: sufficient information to identify the report and the proposed work program.

1. Type of report identified (e.g. Geological, Progress, Summary, Valuation).

2. Name of property and general location (e.g. county, mining division, township).

3. Specific location (e.g. latitude and longitude, NTS number, township and range).

4. Disclosure of issuer for which report is filed.

5. Disclosure of author and company with whom the author is associated.

6. Title page should readily distinguish the report from all other reports on the property. (If a report is revised, then the date of revision should be added to

the title page and to the signature page. Reports written after completion of a stage of work may be entitled "Progress Report No. 1 dated _____ ").

II   *TABLE OF CONTENTS AND APPENDICES*

III *SUMMARY*

1.   Salient points listed, with particular emphasis on the potential for economic success.

2.   Other properties cited clearly distinguished from the subject property.

IV   *INTRODUCTION*

1.   Author's terms of reference.

2.   Acknowledgement of outside sources of data.

3.   Statement that the reports are based on personal examination of the property or other adequate personal familiarity with the region including the dates of examination and comments on any climatic conditions (e.g. snow) that may have inhibited the examination.

V   *PROPERTY*

1.   Form of tenure stated.

2.   Disclosure of number of claims (or size of the property) and whether the claims are contiguous.

3.   Existing claims listed with expiry dates, record number, owner and percentage interest held by the issuer.

4.   Disclosure of obvious problems with title known to writer.

5.   Placer claims distinguished from the lode claims.

VI   *LOCATION AND ACCESS*

1.   Latitude and longitude; NTS.

2.   Location relative to land surveys (e.g. township, range and section, county, mining division).

3.   Location relative to nearest town or other geographic unit.

4.   Means of access to and on the property in the context of exploration phase as well as for future commercial production.

5.   Climate, elevation, topography, infrastructure, power sources.

6.   Potential impediments to commercial exploration; metallurgy, environment, topography, transportation, water, infrastructure, lack of power, etc.

VII *HISTORY OF PROPERTY*

1.   Sufficiently comprehensive and detailed to enable the reader to understand how present status came about.

2.   Disclosure of concepts tested by previous work that are proposed for testing in present work.

3.   Explanation of why an exploration concept remains.

VIII *GEOLOGY*

1.   Divided into subsections such as "Regional Geology" and "Local Geology".

2.   Lithology, alteration, structure, etc.

3.   Clear distinction between mineralization on the subject property and mineralization on adjacent properties or on properties in a similar geological or structural setting.

IX   *MINERALIZATION*

1.   Sample descriptions should be of sufficient detail to enable a newcomer to the property to visualize length, width, grade, vertical potential, frequency.

2.   Rock samples should have description of samples taken, rock type and source (e.g. surface, trench, underground).

3.   The type of sample - channel, chip, character, bulk, grab, diamond drill core, diamond drill cuttings, or percussion or rotary cuttings - should be disclosed.

4.   Length (width) or diameter of sample along with its orientation relative to the orientation of the body being sampled should be disclosed.

5.   Names of person(s) who took the samples should be available.

6.   Where historical values are in currency an estimation of metals price then obtaining should be provided.

7.   Results of metallurgical tests should be provided.

X   GEOPHYSICAL & GEOCHEMISTRY

1.   Subdivided into sections on geochemistry, geophysics, results of last exploration program.

2.   Where geophysical or geochemical anomalies, or geological characteristics are cited as support of a program, they should be consistent with the characteristics of the anticipated mineralization.

XI   CONCLUSIONS

1.   A concise, clear, logical and convincing series of statements, based on the previously described work, which established a potential for economic mineralization, it should say where the mineralization may be located and how that potential should be tested.

XII   RECOMMENDATIONS

1.   Should flow logically from the Conclusions and be feasible under the conditions that prevail on the property.

2.   Drilling programs for more than 4,000 meters should be divided into success-contingent stages.

3.   Where successive stages or work are proposed, each stage should be constructed so that it reaches a decision point.

4.   Advancing to a subsequent stage should be contingent on successful results in the previous phase.

5.   Where climate, logistics or environmental regulations require advancement to a subsequent stage an appropriate explanation should be given.

6.   Where the examination was made more than one year prior to the date of the report, the author should provide assurance that any intervening work will not invalidate his conclusions, recommendations and cost estimate.

XIII COST ESTIMATE

1.   Should be consistent with the Conclusions and Recommendations. Where drilling is recommended, the type of drilling must be stated, and cost per foot/metre provided.

XIV CERTIFICATE

The author's certificate (or statement of qualification, etc.) should state:

1.   His general qualifications and his professional qualification.

2.   Whether the report is based on personal observations, and the date thereof.

3.   If the report is not based on personal observations, the source of the information.

4.   That he is independent of the applicant and vendor, or if he is not independent, there is an additional certificate (and supporting statement) from an expert who is independent of the applicant and vendor, verifying the Report and its Recommendations.

5.   That the author consents to the use of his report and his name by the issuer and of his name in the prospectus (consent may be in a separate letter).

XV *MAPS*

Maps should provide:

1. Location showing an overview of where the property is located.

2. The property boundary, reference information, and if reasonable, the internal claim boundaries.

3. Key map. If any of the survey maps cover less than the full property, then there must be a key map showing the outline of the areas covered by each map (or survey) relative to the property boundaries. The claim map may sometimes be used as a key map by adding the appropriate information.

4. Survey map (such as geochemistry or geophysics) with sufficient detail and data for the reader to check the interpretation.

5. Geology map in a format that can be read, and at an appropriate scale.

6. The locations of the rock samples drill holes guidelines.

7. If the value of the property or the justification for the proposed work depends in whole or in part, upon features of an adjacent property such features along with their relationship to the subject property should be shown.

8. Scale (preferably a bar scale), a north arrow, a date, and an acknowledgement of the source of the detail if it is from outside sources.

9. Format that is suitably legible for reproduction in a prospectus.

10. Signature as required for all maps by National Policy No.2-A.

DATED at Vancouver, British Columbia, this 11th day of June, 1987.

Neil de Gelder
Superintendent of Brokers

NIN#87/52

NOTICE

FLOW-THROUGH SHARES

With the introduction of the "closed system" under the new Securities Act S.B.C. 1985, c. 83 the Commission has received numerous inquiries as to the treatment of flow-through shares. The questions asked most frequently are:

1. What is the route through the "closed system" followed by shares acquired by a limited partnership and ultimately either distributed to the limited partners or "rolled over" into a mutual fund or similar entity.

2. When does the hold period commence for flow-though shares.

3. When, and how many times, should a Form 20 be filed by an issuer of flow-through shares.

4. What is the Commission's position with respect to issuers of flow-through shares who are not reporting issuers under the Securities Act.

1. *Limited Partnerships*

It is accepted that in most every case limited partnerships acquire flow-through shares from issuers pursuant to the "$97,000 exemption" section contained in Section 55(2)(4) of the Act. With respect to securities acquired from non- exchange issuers these flow-through shares may then be transferred to a mutual fund, again pursuant to the exemption under Section 55(2)(4) of the Act, thus avoiding the resale restrictions otherwise applicable under Section 125(3) of the Securities Regulation, including the 12 month hold period.

However, in respect of securities acquired from exchange issuers, it is proposed to amend the Securities Regulation to require purchasers to sign an undertaking agreeing to hold securities acquired pursuant to the "private placement" exemptions, including Section 55(2)(4) of the Act, unconditionally for 12 months. The Commission takes the position that it is appropriate in these circumstances for the limited partnership to undertake to hold the securities for the period up to the date of transfer to the mutual fund or other similar entity, as disclosed in the limited partnership's offering material, and for the mutual fund to undertake to hold the securities for the remainder of the twelve month hold period. This will enable the transfer to take place without the limited partnership requiring an order or waiver of its undertaking.

In either case, whether the securities are those of an exchange issuer or a non-exchange issuer, they may then be traded by the mutual fund at the end of the applicable hold period in accordance with the appropriate resale rules.

On the other side of the transaction, the securities of the mutual fund which are exchanged for the flow-through shares are issued to the limited partnership pursuant to the "shares for assets" exemption contained in Section 55(2)(5) of the Act. These shares may then be distributed to the limited partners pursuant to the "winding up" exemption contained in Section 55(2)(11)(ii) of the Act.

Similarly, this last exemption may be used where there is no mutual fund or similar entity involved. In such cases, the limited partnership simply dissolves and distributes the flow- through shares directly to its limited partners.

2.   *The Hold Period*

For the purpose of dealing with flow-through shares only, the Commission, like several other securities commission across Canada, is treating the agreement to subscribe for flow- through shares as a security. This agreement is considered to be a right entitling the holder to acquire flow-through securities as the qualifying resource expenditures are incurred. Accordingly, the single hold period for these flow- through securities commences from the date the funds for same are irrevocably committed. When this occurs is a question of fact. A commitment letter would not be sufficient to trigger commencement of the hold period, but an agreement in writing committing the purchaser to pay for flow-through shares subject to regulatory approval of the agreement would suffice. In situations where the agreement is subject to the ability of a limited partnership to raise public money in an amount sufficient to fully fund its commitment, the closing of the partnership's public offering would normally be required in order to trigger the commencement of hold periods in respect of flow-through shares subscribed for under agreements entered into prior to the partnership having funds available. In the event that this interpretation conflicts with that of other jurisdictions in cases of national limited partnership offerings, the Commission will entertain submissions as to the appropriate date for the commencement of the hold period.

As discussed in NIN#87/21 dated March 13, 1987 proposed amendments to the Securities Regulation and the Exchange Issuer First Trades Regulation will clarify matters by setting out that the resale restrictions attaching to securities acquired upon the exercise of a right will be identical to those imposed upon the right itself. Further the amendments will provide that hold periods applicable to these "converted securities" will run from the date the right was acquired. Thus it is intended that there be only one hold period in respect of flow-through shares, regardless of when the shares are actually issued.

In the interim, should concerns arise on the issue of hold periods as a result of the above position and the effect of Section 124(3) and (4) of the Securities Regulation, which deal with the first trade of "converted" securities, discretionary orders pursuant to Section 59 of the Act may be granted where appropriate.

3.   *Form 20*

As set out above, the Commission will treat the agreement to subscribe for flow-through shares as a security. It is in respect of this security that the Form 20 must be filed pursuant to Section 55(2)(4) of the Act. The form should be filed within 10 days of the occurrence of the event which triggered the hold period, as discussed in the previous section. Further, in completing the form the "amount or number of securities purchased" should be an "up to" number indicating the maximum number of securities which could be acquired from the issuer pursuant to the subscription agreement.

In some instances, the price at which flow-through shares are issued is not a fixed amount but is determined by reference to a formula. In those cases, the formula should be appended and the appropriate reference to this fact made in that part of Form 20 which refers to the issue price of the security.

4. *Non-Reporting Issuers*

Another issue which has arisen in dealing with flow-through shares is the problem of the first trade of securities acquired by a person in British Columbia from an issuer which is not a reporting issuer in British Columbia. This problem is not unique to the flow-through share situation and the position set out herein is of general application.

Where an issuer is a reporting issuer in another jurisdiction and has its securities listed and posted for trading on an exchange outside of British Columbia, an order may issue pursuant to Section 59 allowing the first trade of those securities. This order would required that the securities be traded on the appropriate exchange and that the shareholders resident in British Columbia be provided with all information provided to shareholders in the jurisdiction where the issuer is report-ing. In exercising his discretion in this regard the Superintendent will need to be satisfied that it is not appropriate to require the issuer to become a reporting issuer in British Columbia. In reaching this conclusion the Superintendent will consider the nature of the transaction, particularly whether this is an isolated issuance of securities in British Columbia or is, or can reasonably expected to become, an ongoing practice of the issuer.

The above sets out the position of the Commission on the most frequently raised concerns respecting flow-through shares. It is accepted that other concerns may exist and that schemes involving flow-through shares may not fit exactly into the trans-actions described in above. In these circumstances it is requested that questions be directed in writing to the Superintendent setting out the nature of the transaction, the perceived problems and the recommendation as to how the matter can be properly dealt with, both in the specific instance and as a matter of general application.

As a result of this notice it is anticipated that most transactions involving flow-through shares will be covered by exemptions available under the Securities Act. As indicated above, where appropriate the Superintendent will issue orders pursuant to Sections 33 and/or 59 of the Act. These orders will only be given where necessary and will not be given solely to provide comfort to the issuer. It is therefore suggested that prior to making application to the Superintendent, the applicant be satisfied that no applicable exemption exists.

DATED at Vancouver, British Columbia, this 24th day of July, 1987.

                    Neil de Gelder
                    Superintendent of Brokers

REF: NIN#87/21

NIN#87/66

NOTICE

PROSPECTUS VETTING PROCEDURES

This office is currently implementing a new system for the vetting of prospectuses. The goal in adopting this system is to significantly reduce, as quickly as possible, the turn-around time for the issuance of initial deficiency letters, thereby eliminating a persistent impediment to the efficient operation of the local securities market. The system is also intended to enable the Securities Commission to operate within the time limits for national offerings which are set out in National Policy No. 1. The system will not and cannot reduce the amount of time which an offering spends in the hands of counsel or the underwriters after the issuance of deficiencies, which often represents a significant component of the total time required to bring a public offering to comple-tion.

There are many reasons for the increased turn-around time, including a record number of prospectus submissions, the increasing diversity and complexity of public offerings, and staffing difficulties at the Securities Commission. The latter is a problem which is currently being addressed by the addition of a significant number of analysts in the Corporate Finance department, but this step will not solve a problem which consumes a disproportionate amount of analysts' time - poorly prepared submissions.

An analyst may spend five times as long vetting a poorly prepared submission as a properly prepared one. This has created a bottleneck in the vetting system, resulting in delays for all issuers, including those whose offering documents are well prepared. For

Notices

poorly prepared submissions, the delay in getting out initial deficiencies is only the first step in the long and frustrating process of clearing the deficiencies, for example by revision of technical reports, financial information, prospectus disclosure or business aspects of the offering.

The number of inadequate submissions and the extent of their problems has also led analysts to ask many of the questions which should be part of every due diligence procedure. The due diligence process is the responsibility of issuers, underwriters and their professional advisers. The Superintendent acknowledges that the apparent involvement by analysts in this process is inappropriate. Unfortunately, in some instances it has been the only way in which full, true and plain disclosure of all material facts, as well as compliance with applicable regulations and policies, could be achieved.

In order to address this problem, a "three-track" system is being adopted to ensure that well prepared submissions are not backed-up behind poorly prepared ones. Under this system, all incoming prospectuses will be checked for completeness of the required filing materials, and then immediately assigned to a supervisor who will review the prospectus in sufficient detail to decide which of three "tracks" the prospectus will be on:

1. The fast track, which means that the prospectus is in compliance with applicable law and policies, and appears to contain full, true and plain disclosure of all material facts, although there may be a small number of disclosure deficiencies or other questions, as is normally the case.

2. The center track, which means that the required due diligence appears to have been done, but the submission requires a more in-depth analysis because of a particular area of concern. Examples of such concerns would include a novel or unusually complex type of security or issuer, or a departure from applicable policies for reasons peculiar to the particular offering.

3. The third, or "circular track", so named because the prospectus will be returned to the issuer for failure to meet the minimum standards required to initiate the formal vetting process. The return of submissions on this track means that, in this office's view, the required amount of due diligence has not been done before the preliminary prospectus and related documents were submitted to this office. An analyst will no longer raise matters which should have been raised in the exercise of due diligence, nor will he or she spend an inordinate amount of time detailing all the shortcomings or meeting with the issuer or its advisers in an attempt to "clarify" the terms of the offering. The documents must stand alone and it should not be necessary to qualify them with significant supplementary written or oral information.

In order to avoid the third track it is important to keep two things in mind:

1. Under section 44(2) of the Securities Act, a preliminary prospectus should represent the final form of the offering, subject to necessary amendments arising out of comments from this office or from developments between the time of filing the preliminary prospectus and the final prospectus; and

2. Under section 120 of the Securities Regulation, the Superintendent is required to refuse a receipt for a prospectus where, among other things:

   "(a)　The prospectus or any record required to be filed with it

   　　(i) does not comply substantially with the appropriate requirements of the Act and this regulation, or

   　　(ii) contains a misrepresentation or a statement, promise, estimate or forecast that is misleading, false or deceptive,

   (b)　an unconscionable consideration has been paid or given or is intended to be paid or given for any services or promotional purposes or for the acquisition of property,

   (c)　the aggregate of

   　　(i) the proceeds from the sale of the securities under the prospectus that are to be paid into the treasury of the issuer, and

   　　(ii) the other resources of the issuer is insufficient to accomplish the purpose of the issue stated in the prospectus,

(d)   the issuer cannot reasonably be expected to be financially responsible in the conduct of its business because of the financial condition of the issuer or that of its officers, directors, promoters or control persons,

(e)   because of the past conduct of the issuer or that of its officers, directors, promoters or control persons, the business of the issuer will not be conducted with integrity and in the best interests of the security holders of the issuer, ..."

In order to minimize the number of prospectuses on the third track, the following guidelines have been developed to assist issuers, underwriters and their advisers. These guidelines are not intended to be a due diligence checklist; they are to be used by analysts as indicators to determine whether the minimum amount of due diligence has been done. The presence in a submission of only one of the following features by itself will not necessarily, except in extreme circumstances, put a submission on the third track. However, a combination of those features will result in a brief letter from this office referring to the guidelines which have not been satisfied, and indicating that except as to item 1 below, a formal appeal of the decision may be requested.

The key indications of lack of due diligence, in no particular order of importance or frequency of occurrence, are as follows:

1.   *Incomplete submissions*

The Securities Act, the regulations thereunder and Local Policy Statement #3-02 (in the case of local issuers) or Local Policy Statement #3-03 (in the case of national issuers) set out the filing requirements for preliminary and final prospectuses. Many submissions contain prospectuses or financial statements which are not properly executed or omit items such as consents, fees, Form 4's, auditor's comfort letters, financial statements for operating subsidiaries and the like. The omitted items then dribble in one by one, making a proper and timely vetting task virtually impossible. In these situations, a letter will be sent to the filing solicitor describing documents which are required and stating that a receipt for the preliminary prospectus will not be issued until the submission is complete. If all the required material is not received within 5 days, the entire submission will be returned pursuant to section 183(2) of the Securities Regulation.

2.   *Lack of Merit*

Section 120(2) of the Securities Regulation clearly empowers and requires the Superintendent to consider the merits of a proposed offering. The extent of enquiry into merit is perhaps the most subjective and controversial aspect of the vetting process. It is clear that this office has neither the mandate nor the experience to second-guess business judgments or make predictions about markets or the viability of products, business plans or operations. It is equally clear that it is not in the public interest to permit companies without any realistic foundation for carrying on business to solicit funds from the public. For this reason, the Mining Evaluation Committee was established some time ago to review technical reports on resource properties to screen out companies which were promoting properties which clearly had no merit. The technical report process for non-resource companies is intended, in part, to accomplish the same purpose. In rare situations, this office will reject submissions by issuers where it is apparent that the property, business plan, product, or past operations of the issuer do not constitute a basis for carrying on the business in which the public is being asked to invest. This step will generally not be taken unless a confirming, independent assessment by a qualified person has been obtained by the Superintendent.

3.   *Noncompliance with Legislation or Policies*

Offering documents which indicate that the Securities Act or regulations, or applicable local, uniform or national policies have not been complied with, immediately attract further inquiry by analysts, who are generally left to guess at the reasons for the departure from accepted rules. Where this departure is a result of oversight or a deliberate attempt to circumvent the rules, the vetting process inevitably slows down. In order to avoid this, the parties involved in the offering should carefully review all applicable legislation and policies to ensure the offering

Notices

complies. If there are valid, exceptional reasons for non-compliance, it is important that they be set out in detail in the filing solicitor's letter, and be accompanied by submissions from underwriters, auditors, or engineers where it may be helpful to the analyst.

4. *Confusing or Incomprehensible Submissions*

   This too is a subjective matter. Occasionally, a prospectus or technical report simply does not make sense. The analyst comes away from the document without any clear picture of the offering, the issuer or its business. This goes beyond the disclosure simply not being "plain", as required by the Securities Act; it extends to an inability to answer the question "what does this mean?" in connection with entire portions of a document. If an experienced analyst cannot make sense of a document, it is unlikely that other readers will be able to do so, and disclosure which is so seriously flawed usually means that the necessary care and attention has not been given to the document or, worse, to the offering as a whole.

5. *Serious or Extensive Inconsistencies*

   This is a common problem which should not occur if documents are properly reviewed prior to being submitted. The inconsistencies may be internal to the prospectus, or prospectus information may conflict, without explanation, with that in a technical report, material contract or financial statement. This not only makes the submission confusing; it raises the question as to what the true state of affairs is and whether the required due diligence has been done.

6. *Failure to Deal with Obvious Regulatory Concerns*

   If an offering involves features which could possibly result in refusal of a receipt under section 120 of the Securities Regulation, this should be dealt with right from the start either in the prospectus or in a letter from appropriate person at the time of the submission. The most commonly neglected area is the track record or financial condition of officers, directors, promoters or control persons of the issuer, or the acceptability of persons who have expressed professional opinions in the prospectus. A proper due diligence review should identify these areas of concern. Where such problems are found, the participants or the structure of the offering should be changed before the submission is filed or, where appropriate, there should be disclosure in the prospectus.

7. *Hyperbole*

   A prospectus must be a balanced disclosure document, not promotional literature. Too many prospectuses contain claims which cannot be substantiated or are exaggerated, and may in addition fail to give a balanced summary of the risk factors to which the issuer and its business are subject. A due diligence review should challenge every claim, expose unsupportable assumptions and recognize risks which may not be readily apparent. When an analyst is required to raise these issues, it means the required due diligence has not been done.

All of the above situations are avoidable by the exercise of due diligence prior to filing the preliminary prospectuses. In the coming months, the Securities Commission will be working closely with issuers, underwriters and their professional advisors to reach an understanding as to the appropriate standards of due diligence, particularly in the case of offerings by junior issuers.

As a final matter, on local prospectus filings, this office will now send copies of deficiency letters to the underwriter or agent, auditor, and technical report writer involved in the offering, as well as to the filing solicitor and the issuer. Where more than one underwriter or agent is involved, the filing solicitor's letter should indicate the name of a person who will at as a "lead" agent or underwriter for the purpose of receiving the deficiencies, and that person will then be responsible for keeping the other agents or underwriters advised of the progress of the filing. It is anticipated that this procedure will reduce delays in responding to deficiencies, and disseminate more widely the concerns and standards of this office.

DATED at Vancouver, British Columbia, this 9th day of October, 1987.

Neil de Gelder
Superintendent of Brokers

NOTICE

LEVERAGED MUTUAL FUND PURCHASES

The B.C. Securities Commission has a strong concern that the practice of leveraging mutual fund purchases is increasing and that excessive leveraging is contrary to the interests of the investors and potentially destabilizing for the mutual fund industry.

In an effort to bring to investors' attention the risks of excessive leveraging, all mutual fund dealers will now be required to deliver a disclosure document to prospective purchasers of mutual funds.

The form of disclosure document is attached to this Notice.

DATED at Vancouver, British Columbia, this 9th day of October, 1987.

> Doug Hyndman
> Chairman
> B.C. Securities Commission

BRITISH COLUMBIA SECURITIES COMMISSION
DISCLOSURE DOCUMENT
BORROWING MONEY TO BUY INVESTMENT FUNDS (LEVERAGING)

The B.C. Securities Commission requires the delivery of this document to investors who are considering buying mutual funds (investment funds).

Mutual funds may be purchased using available cash, or a combination of cash and borrowed money. If cash is used to pay for the mutual fund purchase in full, the percentage gain or loss will equal the percentage increase or decrease in the value of the fund shares. The purchase of mutual funds using borrowed money magnifies the gain or loss on the cash invested. This effect is called leveraging. For example, if $100,000 of fund shares are purchased and paid for with $25,000 from available cash and $75,000 from borrowings, and the value of the funds shares declines by 10% to $90,000, your equity interest (the difference between the value of the fund shares and the amount borrowed) has declined by 40%, i.e. from $25,000 to $15,000.

It is important that an investor proposing to borrow for the purchase of mutual funds be aware that a leveraged purchase involves greater risk than a purchase using cash resources only.

To what extent a leveraged purchase involves undue risk is a determination to be made by each purchaser and will vary depending on the circumstances of the purchaser and the mutual fund purchased.

It is also important that the investor be aware of the terms of a loan secured by mutual fund shares. The lender may require that the amount outstanding on the loan not rise above an agreed percentage of the market value of the shares. Should this occur, the borrower must pay down the loan or sell the shares so as to return the loan to the agreed percentage relationship. In our example above, the lender may require that the loan not exceed 75% of the market value of the shares. On a decline of value of the shares to $90,000 the borrower must reduce the loan to $67,500 (75% of $90,000). If the borrower does not have cash available, the borrower must sell shares at a loss to provide money to reduce the loan.

Money is, of course, also required to pay interest on the loan. Under these circumstances, investors who leverage their investment are advised to have adequate financial resources available both to pay interest and also to reduce the loan if the borrowing arrangements require such a payment.

NOTICE

GUIDELINES FOR APPLICATIONS TO THE SECURITIES COMMISSION
OR THE SUPERINTENDENT OF BROKERS FOR DECISIONS OR ORDERS

This notice is intended to serve as a guideline, in conjunction with Local Policy Statement 3-24 (which is currently under review), for applications to the British Columbia Securities Commission (the "Commission") and the Superintendent of

Brokers (the "Superintendent) for decisions or orders granting relief from certain requirements of the Securities Act, S.B.C. 1985, c.83 (the "Act"), the Securities Regulation, B.C. Reg. 270/86 (the "Regulation") and the Company Act, R.S.B.C. 1979, c.59 (the "Company Act") (collectively, the "Legislation").

This notice sets out the procedure for submitting applications made under the sections of the Legislation set out below, as well as the required form and content of application letters and draft orders. The verification described in Section 3(e) of this notice is a new requirement and must be included with all applications made after May 1, 1988.

1. TYPES OF APPLICATIONS

    1.1 The procedures described in this notice apply to all applications made to the Commission or the Superintendent under the following sections of the Legislation:

Section of the Act	Section of the Regulation
33(1)	4(8)(b)
51(7)	104(6)
59(1)	119
72	142(5)
97	143
103(2)	149
107	152.2
108(b)	153
113	
153*	

Section of the Company Act
179
286(4)

*Where an application made under Section 153 of the Act relates to a decision following a hearing, the procedure set out in NIN#87/33 should be followed.

    1.2 In addition, other sections of the Legislation and some of the Local Policy Statements provide for decisions to be made by the Commission or the Superintendent that do not require the formal application contemplated herein. Applicants will, however, be subject to the requirements of the applicable sections of the Legislation or the Local Policy Statements.

    1.3 If a statutory exemption exists and can be relied upon for any part of a proposed transaction, an exemption order for that part of the transaction should not be sought.

    1.4 The sections of the Legislation referred to in Section 1.1 of this notice empower either the Commission or the Superintendent to grant orders or to make decisions. Careful attention should be paid to whether an application is required to be made to the Commission or to the Superintendent. Applications to the Commission and the Superintendent can be made in the same submission but the orders must be kept separate.

2. SUBMISSION OF APPLICATIONS

    2.1 All applications must be addressed to:

                    Manager, Exemptions and Orders
                    British Columbia Securities Commission
                    1100 - 865 Hornby Street
                    Vancouver, B.C.
                    V6Z 2H4

    2.2 An application should be submitted well in advance of the proposed transaction for which an order or decision is sought. The Commission and the Superintendent will generally not issue orders which have a retroactive effect.

    2.3 In order for applications to be processed by the Commission staff, they must be complete when submitted. Each application should consist of:

          (a) an application letter setting out the information described in Section 3 of this notice, either originally signed by the applicant or, if submitted by the applicant's agent, accompanied by a verification described in Section 3(e) of this notice;

(b) one copy of all supporting material;

(c) two copies of the draft order in the form described in Section 4 of this notice; and

(d) the applicable filing fee as referred to in Section 5 of this notice.

2.4 Additional material filed in respect of an application should be addressed to the staff member handling the application and the envelope and the covering letter should be marked "Follow- up Material".

2.5 Any revised draft order submitted as follow-up material should be accompanied by a black-lined copy indicating the amendments made by the applicant to the order previously submitted.

3. *REQUIRED ELEMENTS OF THE APPLICATION*

Each application should be divided into sections and include the information, where relevant, indicated below:

(a) *Summary*

    (i) the name of the issuer

    (ii) the name of the applicant (if different from the issuer);

    (iii) the section of the Legislation pursuant to which the application is made; and

    (iv) the nature of the relief sought.

(b) *The Issuer*

    (i) the name of the issuer;

    (ii) jurisdiction and date of incorporation, organization or continuation;

    (iii) capital structure - authorized and issued capital and debt obligations (where not otherwise dealt with in an exhibit such as financial statements or an annual report);

    (iv) whether the issuer is a reporting issuer;

    (v) whether the issuer is an exchange issuer;

    (vi) listing status - whether listed on the Vancouver Stock Exchange or any other stock exchange or trading over-the-counter and recent price and volume trading data; and

    (vii) a statement that the issuer, if it is a reporting issuer, is not in default of any requirement of the Act or the Regulation.

(c) *The Applicant*

If the applicant is a person other than the issuer, include those items in clause (b) which are relevant to the applicant and explain the applicant's relationship to the issuer.

(d) *Order or Decision Sought*

The application should clearly set out all relevant information and argument in support of the request for the granting of the order. The submission should clearly show that the applicant falls within the spirit of the Legislation. The information and argument should include:

    (i) the facts on which the application is based;

    (ii) the reasons for making the application;

    (iii) relevant considerations including case law, prior decisions of the Commission or the Superintendent, parallels between statutory exemptions which may not be relied upon by the applicant in the particular circumstances for some technical reason and policies and argument regarding the foregoing;

    (iv) other relevant circumstances including regulatory decisions of other jurisdictions or regulatory bodies or similar applications pending in other jurisdictions; and

Notices

(v) supporting documents - such documents may be included as schedules or exhibits to the application and references in the application may be made to such supporting documents.

(e) *Verification*

Each application must be signed by the party submitting the application and must contain a statement certifying the truth of the facts contained therein. If the Application is not signed by the applicant and is made by an agent for the applicant, such statement may be omitted if the application is accompanied by a separate written statement signed by the applicant authorizing the agent to prepare and file the application and confirming the truth of the facts contained in the application. Sample language might include:

"We authorize the making and filing of the attached application by _____ and confirm the truth of the facts contained herein.

DATED at _____ this _____ day of _____, 19 ___

                                                    _____
                                                    Authorized Officer

4. *CONVENTIONS FOR DRAFTING ORDERS*

4.1 *Headings*

(a) Every draft order should have a heading which refers to the Act or the Company Act and sets out the name of the issuer and any other party seeking the order.

(b) Every draft order should also have a sub-heading which refers to the section of the Legislation under which the request for the order is being made. If the application is being made under the Act, no reference to the Act need be made in the sub-heading.

(c) Applicants are encouraged to refer to Chapter 3 of the Weekly Summary published by the Commission for examples of orders previously granted by the Commission and the Superintendent.

4.2 *Recitals*

(a) The first recital should start with the word "WHEREAS" and all subsequent recitals should start with the words "AND WHEREAS".

(b) The first recital should state the name of the applicant, whether the application is being made to the Commission or the Superintendent, the section of the Legislation under which the order is requested and the specific requirements from which the applicant is seeking relief.

(c) The basis on which the order is being sought should be clear from the facts set out in the recitals. Accordingly, representations should be included in a recital which give all necessary background information and show why the order should be granted. The representations should show that the applicant falls within the spirit of the Legislation and that the granting of the order would not be prejudicial to the public interest.

(d) The last recital should confirm that the specific requirements of the section of the Legislation under which the request for the order is being made have been satisfied. For example, the last recital for orders under Section 59(1) of the Act should read:

"AND WHEREAS the Superintendent considers that to so order would not be prejudicial to the public interest;"

4.3 *Operative Part of the Order*

(a) The operative part should commence with the words "IT IS ORDERED" or "IT IS DECIDED", as the case may be, rather than "IT IS RULED".

(b) The wording should reflect the discretionary power granted to the Commission or the Superintendent under the application section of the Legislation. For example, Section 59 of the Act gives the Superintendent the power to exempt a person or class of persons from Section 42 of the Act, not to exempt a trade.

(c) Any conditions, such as filing requirements and resale restrictions, that would have applied had the applicant been able to rely upon a statutory exemption, which for technical reasons could not be relied upon by the applicant, should be included in the order. If the applicant feels that certain conditions are not appropriate in the particular circumstances of the case, reasons should be given in the application.

4.4 *General Drafting Rules*

(a) The "Act" may be used as a defined term for the Securities Act, S.B.C. 1985, c.83 provided that it is defined in the first recital in the following way:

"... has made application to the ... for an order under Section _____ of the Securities Act, S.B.C. 1985, c.83 (the "Act") ..."

(b) The "Regulation" may be used as a defined term for the Securities Regulation, B.C. Reg. 270/86, provided that it is defined as follows:

"...the Securities Regulation, B.C. Reg. 270/86 (the "Regulation") ..."

(c) The full term "Superintendent of Brokers" should be used in the order unless it has been defined as the "Superintendent". Similarly, reference should be made to the "British Columbia Securities Commission" unless it is defined as the "Commission".

4.5 *Form of Orders*

(a) Proofreading of draft orders is essential as orders in an acceptable form are copied directly onto the letterhead of the Commission or the Superintendent, as the case may be.

(b) Orders should be typewritten on 8-1/2" x 11" plain paper, single spaced, with room left at the top of the page for the appropriate letterhead and at the bottom of the page for the appropriate signature.

(c) Each draft order should be submitted unfolded.

(d) In an effort to speed up the processing of applications, all corrections and redrafting will be done by the applicant or his agent.

5. *FILING FEES*

5.1 Each application must be accompanied by the applicable filing fee as prescribed in the Regulation. Applications submitted without the prescribed filing fee will not be processed until the fee is received by the Commission.

5.2 An additional fee is prescribed in the Regulation for expedited or complex applications. Satisfactory evidence of circumstances requiring immediate attention must be provided if an application is to be processed on an expedited basis; otherwise it will be dealt with as promptly as possible. The additional fee for complex orders will normally be requested by the Commission when the time required to assess and process an application is significantly longer than usual.

5.3 Fees should be paid by cheque made payable to the "Minister of Finance".

Cheques for fees should no longer be made payable to the "Minister of Finance". They are now payable to the "British Columbia Securities Commission" pursuant to NIN 95/24 "Fee Payments under the Securities Act and the Commodity Contract Act".

6. *PROCEDURE FOR PROCESSING APPLICATIONS*

6.1   Upon receipt of a complete application, a member of the Commission staff
       will be assigned to review the application and recommend disposition.

6.2   The staff member may contact the applicant if further information or
       clarification is required. Where such information or clarification is not
       provided by the applicant within a reasonable period of time, the Commis-
       sion or the Superintendent, on its or his own motion or on the recommen-
       dation of the staff member, may decide that the application should be
       treated as abandoned. No application will be treated as abandoned simply
       because a staff member has not had an opportunity to review it.

DATED at Vancouver, British Columbia, this 31st day of March, 1988.

Neil de Gelder
Superintendent of Brokers

NIN#88/7

NOTICE

VENTURE CAPITAL ISSUERS

A concern has been expressed that the restriction is Local Policy Statement 3-13
"Policy Guidelines for a Venture Capital Issuer Planning to Make a Distribution"
prohibiting a venture capital issuer (a "VCI") from investing more than 25% of its
funds in any one entity has been an impediment to the Small Business Venture
Capital Program (the "SBVC Program") under the Small Business Venture Capital Act
(British Columbia).

The Superintendent has determined that the investment restriction in section 4.1.1 of
Local Policy Statement 3-13 will not apply to prohibit a VCI from investing more than
25% of its funds from share subscriptions in any one entity, provided that:

1.   the VCI is registered and in good standing under the SBVC Program;

2.   the specific entities in which the VCI proposes to invest are disclosed in the VCI's
     prospectus;

3.   the VCI's prospectus has appended to it an advanced ruling of the Administrator
     of the SBVC Program for each proposed investment;

4.   all contracts relating to each investment of the VCI are disclosed in its prospectus
     as material contracts and are made available to prospective investors; and

5.   each entity in which the VCI proposes to invest is a reporting issuer.

This notice should be considered as an exercise of discretion by the Superintendent and
not as an amendment of Local Policy Statement 3-13.

DATED at Vancouver, British Columbia, this 1st day of June, 1988.

Neil de Gelder
Superintendent of Brokers

NIN#88/10

NOTICE

"FULL DISCLOSURE" IN FINANCIAL STATEMENTS

Section 44(1) of the Securities Act and Section 116 of the Regulation (the
"Regulations") thereunder call for "full" disclosure of all material facts relating to
distributions of securities under prospectuses and statements of material facts, which
includes financial information contained in those documents. The principle of full
disclosure can also be applied to financial statements filed pursuant to Division (1) of
Part 10 of the Regulations.

Financial statements are integral to investment decisions. They enable an investor to
review how an issuer has managed its financial resources in the past which may be
helpful in assessing future performance. Consequently, the information contained in
the financial statements, when combined with the disclosure made in the body of an

offering document, should enable an investor to make an informed investment decision.

Section 1500.01 of the Handbook of the Canadian Institute of Chartered Accountants states that:

"Financial reporting is essentially *a process of communication* of information. While the success of this communication depends upon the appropriateness of the accounting principles followed and ultimately upon the degree of understanding by the readers of the financial statements, it also depends upon the *extent of disclosure* in the financial statements." (emphasis added)

A fundamental objective of this office is to ensure that prospective investors, as well as existing shareholders, are provided with "full" disclosure. Balanced against this need is recognition of the fact that if there is too much data, material items may become lost in a sea of immaterial detail.

Our Corporate Finance department has noted a recurring tendency to present information in financial statements as aggregate accumulations of data without providing a specific analysis of same.

For example, an issuer may provide an income statement showing "general, administrative and selling expenses" as a one-line item with no further elaboration. Consequently, neither we nor the public are given any useful information with respect to the magnitude of items such as rent, salaries and wages, travel, promotion, and advertising. Similarly, "deferred research and development" and "deferred exploration and development" costs frequently appear as one-line entries on balance sheets with no supporting detailed analysis found in either the financial statement notes or as separate schedules. Finally, "Note" disclosure often appears to suffer from a lack of adequate detail, for example, in the provision of information pertaining to related party transactions.

The use of certain aggregation may be appropriate for well established companies, with proven track records, where annual changes in the level of revenue/expenditures are, comparatively speaking, stable. Investors in such companies are primarily concerned with gross revenues/profit, net income and earnings/loss per share information. In contrast, such presentation does not usually constitute sufficient or adequate disclosure for the majority of issuers approaching the British Columbia venture capital market for public funds.

Local reporting companies filing pursuant to Local Policy 3-02, Local Policy 3-26 or Division (1) of the Part 10 of the Regulations are encouraged to provide sufficiently detailed disclosure in their financial statements, either in the body of the statements themselves or in the notes and schedules attached thereto, to provide the extent of disclosure necessary to facilitate informed investment decisions.

DATED at Vancouver, British Columbia this 2nd day of June, 1988.

Neil de Gelder
Superintendent of Brokers
British Columbia Securities Commission

NIN#88/11

NOTICE

THE EFFECT OF CRIMINAL AND CIVIL LITIGATION ON TRADING RIGHTS AND REGISTRATION

Over the past several months the Securities Commission's staff have been reviewing the position of this office concerning situations where criminal charges are laid that relate, in some way, to trading in securities. While each case will be dealt with on an individual basis after a complete assessment of all available information, the following represents the general position of this office regarding such circumstances:

1. Where a registrant is charged with a criminal offence that points to an abuse of that individual's registration, an order pursuant to Section 26(2) of the British Columbia Securities Act (the "Act") will be issued suspending that registration until the holding of a hearing at which time the registrants continued registration will be determined. In addition, in most circumstances, an order will be issued pursuant to 145(2) of the Act removing trading rights. The order will remain

outstanding pending the completion of a hearing pursuant to Section 145(1) of the Act.

2.   Where an individual, other than a registrant, is charged with a criminal offence that relates in some way to trading in securities, in most circumstances an order will be issued pursuant to Section 145(2) of the Act removing trading rights. The order will remain outstanding until a hearing is held pursuant to Section 145(1) of the Act.

3.   Where a registrant or individual is named as a defendant in a civil action alleging serious improprieties in relation to trading in securities, an investigation may be expected and, if judgment is granted in favour of the plaintiff, orders pursuant to Section 26(2) and Section 145(2) of the Act, as the case may be, will usually be issued. The orders will remain outstanding pending hearings pursuant to Section 26(1) and Section 145(1) of the Act.

The above policy represents an attempt to balance the rights of individuals who are the subject of criminal or civil litigation with the public interest of residents of this Province and persons and companies active on the Vancouver Stock Exchange.

DATED at Vancouver, British Columbia, this 6th day of June, 1988.

Neil de Gelder
Superintendent of Brokers

NIN#88/40

NOTICE

SALE OF MUTUAL FUNDS BY FINANCIAL INSTITUTIONS –
PRINCIPLES OF REGULATION

The Canadian Securities Administrators have jointly released a notice entitled "Distribution of Mutual Funds by Financial Institutions - Principles of Regulation" (the "Notice"), which sets out the principles of regulation to be applied to the distribution of mutual fund securities through branches of financial institutions. The Notice is attached hereto as Appendix "A".

In the next few weeks a second notice will be released which will set out the principles of regulation applicable to full service and discount brokerage activities being carried out by securities dealers in branches of their related financial institutions.

DATED at Vancouver, British Columbia, this 9th day of November, 1988.

Douglas Hyndman, Chairman
British Columbia Securities Commission

Appendix "A"   November 9, 1988

NOTICE

Canadian Securities Administrators

Distribution of Mutual Funds
by Financial Institutions

Principles of Regulation

Preamble

Prior to 1988 financial institutions ("FIs") were able to distribute certain mutual fund securities through their branch networks on a largely unregulated basis. In some cases the FIs were exempt from both registration and prospectus requirements while in other cases prospectus requirements were applied and registration requirements were minimal. Regulatory changes initiated in 1987 had the effect of subjecting the branch distribution of mutual fund securities by FIs to the full scope of securities regulation. When these changes were first implemented in 1988 it was apparent that the provincial and territorial securities regulators were implementing rules which were not consistent on a national basis. It was also apparent that this lack of regulatory consistency would, if continued, have a negative impact on the efficient delivery of financial products and services to the public.

In May of 1988 the Canadian Securities Administrators ("CSA") formed a subcommittee ("Subcommittee") to review the approaches being followed in the provinces and territories regarding the regulation of mutual fund distribution by FIs. The Subcommittee has met on three occasions and its members have discussed this issue with representatives of the Canadian Bankers' Association ("CBA"), The Trust Companies Association of Canada ("TCA"), the Investment Funds Institute of Canada ("IFIC"), self regulatory organizations and officials of FIs.

The Subcommittee's objective has been to develop a basic regulatory approach which will be consistently applied in all provinces and territories. This objective has, for the most part, been realized. This notice sets out those areas where, unless otherwise noted, the provincial and territorial securities commissions ("Commissions") were able to arrive at a consensus. Any registration requirements not expressly dealt with in this notice have been left to be dealt with as prescribed by existing provincial or territorial regulation.

The Subcommittee considered whether these Principles of Regulation should be implemented as a National Policy Statement. In order to ensure timely implementation of the rules contained in this notice it was decided that each provincial or territorial securities commission would adopt the Principles of Regulation in its own fashion (eg. through the exercise of regulatory discretion). The CSA also decided that the Subcommittee should continue its work with a view to developing the Principles of Regulation into a National Policy statement as soon as possible.

In the course of the Subcommittee's deliberations it became apparent that the new rules allowing FIs to participate more actively in the securities industry raise a number of regulatory concerns and issues for which no clear answers or guidelines exist. Accordingly, in areas of uncertainty the Commissions have adopted a cautious approach with a view to revisiting these issues as experience dictates. While any particular issue could be reviewed in a shorter time frame, the Commissions are of the view that the approached set out in the National Policy statement which is developed from the Principles of Regulation should be reviewed in no later than three years time to assess whether they adequately serve legitimate regulatory and business concerns.

The procedures described below apply only to the distribution of mutual fund securities through the premises of the branch network of a FI where such activity is otherwise permitted by the legislation to which the FI is subject. The Dealer (as defined in paragraph 1) may sell mutual fund securities from locations other than the branches of the FI provided that all conditions of registration applicable to the proposed activity have been satisfied. For the purposes of this notice a FI means any financial institution carrying on business through a branch office network including banks, trust companies, loan companies, insurance companies, treasury branches, credit unions and caisse populaires. In Quebec, the Confederation des caisses populaires et d'economie Desjardins du Quebec will be considered to be a financial institution and each individual caisse populaire will be considered to be a branch of the Confederation.

The province of Manitoba participated in some of the Subcommittee's discussions but has refrained from adopting the Principles of Regulation at this time. The present interim position in Manitoba is that the distribution of FI sponsored mutual funds through the FI's branch system is either a statutorily exempt activity or is subject to a regulatory scheme which may or may not require the licensing of individual salespersons, depending on the institution and the circumstances of each case. Interested parties should contact the Manitoba Commission directly to ascertain what requirements might apply.

Regulation

1. *Control of registrant.* A FI may distribute mutual fund securities in its branches only through a corporation ("Dealer") which it controls directly or indirectly or with which it is affiliated. The Dealer must be registered as a dealer in each province or territory where the mutual fund securities are distributed and must satisfy normal registration requirements except where modified by this notice.

2. *Registration of employees.* Individuals involved in the sale of mutual fund securities must be registered as salespersons and must satisfy normal registration requirements except where modified by this notice.

3. *Dual employment.* Employees of a FI who are engaged in financial services activities may also become registered as salespersons of the Dealer for the purpose of selling mutual fund securities provided that such dual employment is permitted by the legislation to which the FI is subject.

Notices

4. *Conflicts of Interest.* The Subcommittee gave close attention to the question of the conflicts of interest that can arise as a result of dual employment and the sale of mutual fund securities in a branch of a FI. For example, a FI employee who receives compensation based directly on the sale of mutual fund securities but not on the sale of other products may be inclined to sell mutual fund securities even if that is not the best alternative for a particular client. This situation would be exacerbated if the FI employee was also able to make a loan to the client to finance the purchase of the securities. Even when the dually employed person is paid on a salary-only basis a conflict of interest concern may arise if the dually employed person can both sell mutual fund securities to a client and lend that client the funds to pay for that purchase. In these situations the potential exists for excessive lending to encourage mutual fund sales.

These concerns could have been dealt with by restricting the ability of the Dealer to compensate its salespersons in any manner based directly on sales. Similarly, other concerns could have been dealt with by restricting the ability of the dually employed person to make loans to mutual fund clients in respect of their purchases. The Commissions concluded that such an approach, if applied in all circumstances, would be overly restrictive in view of the business and lending controls followed by most FIs.

To address these concerns the Dealer must adopt and implement supervisory rules to prevent conflicts of interest arising due to the dual employment of a registered salesperson. These procedures must address potential conflicts and must be filed with and approved by the relevant provincial securities administrators unless such procedures provide that, inter alia:

    (a)   dually employed salespersons are paid on a salary-only basis (any form of compensation linked directly to the activity of selling mutual funds, including bonus payments, would require conflict procedures to be filed with and approved by the relevant Commissions); and either

    (b)   any loan made by a dually employed salesperson for the purpose of financing the purchase of mutual fund securities sold by that salesperson is approved by a senior lending officer of the FI; or

    (c)   the dually-employed salesperson is not permitted to make loans to finance the purchase of mutual fund securities sold by that salesperson.

5. *In-house funds.* The registration requirements contained in this notice are based on the presumption that the Dealer will only be distributing, through branches of the FI, mutual fund securities which are issued by a mutual fund which is sponsored by the FI or a corporation controlled by or affiliated with the FI. Mutual funds which are sponsored by a third party and managed by the FI would not satisfy this requirement. If a FI wants to sell through its branches mutual fund securities sponsored by a third party it should discuss its proposal with the securities regulator in the relevant jurisdiction to determine what amendments, if any, to the regulation of the sale of such securities are necessary.

6. *Proficiency.* Officers, directors and salespersons of the Dealer shall satisfy normal proficiency requirements. Some Commissions have approved courses offered by the Institute of Canadian Bankers ("ICB") and the Trust Companies Institute ("TCI") to employees of their respective members as equivalent to the IFIC mutual fund course. The relevant securities commission should be contacted to determine whether the ICB and TCI courses have been approved in that province or territory. The Commissions will also consider applications from other national industry groups, or similar organizations, to treat training courses developed by them as equivalent to the IFIC mutual fund course.

7. *Premises and Disclosure.* The Dealer shall carry on business in such a way as to make it clear to its clients that there is a distinction between the mutual fund business of the Dealer and the activities of the FI. This may be achieved through a combination of physical separation and signage, (separate premises within the branch are not required), and shall include adequate disclosure to customers of the FI.

This disclosure shall advise clients that the Dealer is a separate corporate entity from the FI and that an investment in mutual fund securities is not insured by the Canada Deposit Insurance Corporation, the Regie d'assurance depots du Quebec or any other government deposit insurer, as may be appropriate in the circumstances, is not guaranteed in whole or in part by the FI and is subject to fluctuations in market value. The specific wording of this disclosure will not be mandated by the Commission. It should, however be prepared by each Dealer in a form which will be the same in all jurisdictions. The disclosure shall be printed in bold face type and shall appear on the following documents within the specified time frames:

(a) *prospectus*: the disclosure should currently be contained in the body of the prospectus. On renewal of the prospectus the disclosure shall appear on the face page of that document;

(b) *subscription or order forms*: if these forms are used (eg. order forms may not be required to process transactions initiated by telephone) the disclosure shall appear on them as soon as possible and no later than December 31, 1988. If the Dealer has existing stocks of these forms which do not contain the disclosure they may be used for no more than one year from the date of this notice provided that such existing stocks of forms are replaced as soon as possible with forms which contain the disclosure and, in the interim, the required disclosure is provided in writing to the purchaser at the time the order is made. (This may be accomplished in a number of ways eg. handing out a separate document, stamping existing documents with the disclosure or using add-on stickers containing the disclosure);

(c) *confirmation slips*: the disclosure shall appear on these forms as soon as possible and no later than December 31, 1988. If the Dealer has existing stocks of these forms which do not contain the disclosure they may be used for no more than one year from the date of this notice provided that such existing stocks of forms are replaced as soon as possible with forms which contain the disclosure and, in the interim, the required disclosure is provided in writing to the purchaser at the time of delivery of the confirmation slip. (This may be accomplished in a number of ways eg. handing out a separate document, stamping existing documents with the disclosure or using add-on stickers containing the disclosure);

(d) *statements of account*: the disclosure is not required on these forms;

(e) *promotional material*: the disclosure shall appear on all promotional material appearing or handed out in any branch of the FI (eg. newspaper advertisements are not required to contain the disclosure). If a Dealer has existing promotional material which does not contain the disclosure it may be used for no more than one year from the date of this notice provided that all of the Dealer's existing supplies of promotional material are replaced as soon as possible with material which contains the disclosure.

If the FI which is related to the Dealer lends money to a client for the purpose of purchasing mutual fund securities sold by the Dealer, the Dealer shall disclose or arrange to have disclosed to the client that the full amount of the loan must be repaid even if there is a decline in the market value of the mutual fund securities purchased with the loan proceeds. The Nova Scotia Commission may require more specifics with respect to this disclosure. Inquiries on this point should be made directly to the Nova Scotia Commission.

8. *Administration Officer.* The Dealer shall appoint an administration officer in each of its branches where mutual fund securities are being distributed to ensure that the conflicts of interest policy described in paragraph 4 is adhered to, the disclosure required in paragraph 7 is being provided, only registered salespersons of the Dealer are involved in the sale of mutual fund securities, and the restrictions on certain activities as set out in paragraph 11 are adhered to. The administration officer may be an employee of the FI who is not registered to sell mutual fund securities. Unless a Commission requests the names of the administration officers it will not be necessary to provide the Commissions with the names of such officers.

9. *Branch manager requirements.* Some jurisdictions impose specific requirements on a manager of a branch of a securities or mutual fund dealer and look to that person to supervise business practices and monitor compliance with securities regulatory requirements. Such branch manager requirements are additional to the requirement that every Dealer devote adequate resources and employ appropriate systems to ensure that securities regulatory requirements are being complied with (this requirement is described in paragraph 12). The Commissions have concluded that it is not necessary to impose specific branch manager requirements on Dealers provided that:

(a) in accordance with paragraph 8, each Dealer appoints an administration officer in each branch of the FI which distributes mutual fund securities;

(b)   FIs adequately supervise business practices in their branches through normal operating procedures;

(c)   the mutual fund securities sold by each Dealer are limited to funds sponsored by the FI or one of its affiliates;

(d)   a sufficient number of qualified, registered persons are employed to monitor regulatory compliance from one or more centralized locations, (this requirement is described in paragraph 12); and

(e)   monitoring compliance with securities regulation at the FI branch level becomes a component of each FI's internal inspection process.

10. *Non-registered employees.* There is a statutory requirement in each province and territory that only registered salespersons of a Dealer are allowed to be involved in the sale of mutual fund securities. This requirement would preclude non-registered employees of a FI from assisting in the sale of mutual fund securities. There are, however, some activities involved in the marketing of mutual fund securities in branches of a FI that do not raise any regulatory concerns (to the extent that any of these activities constitute trading in securities each Commission will consider issuing a blanket ruling to permit them to be carried out without the need to obtain registration). Based on this analysis the Commissions have concluded that:

(a)   in any branch of a FI where there is no registered salesperson of the Dealer, prospectuses and order forms may not be distributed. These documents are essential to the sale of any security and handing them out clearly constitutes a selling activity;

(b)   in any branch of a FI where there are one or more registered salespersons of the Dealer, prospectuses and order forms may be distributed. These documents may be made available to clients from a self-serve supply located in the area where the registered salesperson sells mutual fund securities;

(c)   a non-registered employee of a FI may not distribute or assist a client with the completion of an order form for mutual fund securities;

(d)   a client who requires assistance in completing an order form shall be directed to a registered salesperson or requested to contact a registered salesperson through the Dealer's toll-free telephone line;

(e)   a redemption request or completed order form may be given to any employee of any branch of a FI for the purpose of processing the redemption or forwarding the order form to a registered salesperson for processing;

(f)   any branch of a FI will be permitted to advertise the availability of the mutual fund securities through the use of posters, brochures and other informational materials and may refer clients to a toll-free telephone line or the nearest branch which employs a registered salesperson; the content of any such posters, brochures or other informational material should only briefly describe the products and services offered by the Dealer. Lengthy explanations of the products would not be appropriate; and

(g)   any branch of a FI will be permitted to hand out account opening application forms (if the account opening application form also contains an order form, paragraphs 10(a) and (b) will apply) provided that:

    (i)   in branches of a FI where there are one or more registered persons of the Dealer, assistance to a client in completing the form is only given by a registered person of the Dealer;

    (ii)   in branches of a FI where there is no registered person of the Dealer, such assistance is only given by the manager, assistant manager or credit officer in the branch who possesses a high degree of knowledge about the client's financial affairs; and

    (iii)   before the Dealer conducts any trades on behalf of a client the completed form is approved by a registered person with the Dealer who is responsible for approving the opening of new accounts and ensuring that the know-your-client and suitability obligations under applicable securities legislation have been satisfied.

11. *Toll-free lines.* In British Columbia, Alberta and Ontario calls made on the toll-free line during normal business hours must be handled by an individual properly regis-

tered and resident in the province from which the call originates while calls made after normal business hours may be handled by an individual who is properly registered but not resident in the province from which the call originates.

In Saskatchewan and Quebec all calls made on the toll-free line must be handled by an individual properly registered and resident in the province from which the call originates.

In New Brunswick, Nova Scotia, Prince Edward Island, Newfoundland and the Yukon and Northwest Territories calls made on the toll-free line may be handled by an individual properly registered but not resident in the province or territory from which the call originates provided that the Dealer also employs registered salespersons who are resident in the province.

12. *Central Office and Compliance Officer.* The securities registered in each province and territory requires every dealer to establish written procedures for dealing with its clients and conducting its business in accordance with prudent business practice and all regulatory requirements. It is also necessary to designate a senior official of the registrant who is registered with the local securities commission and is responsible for ensuring compliance with those procedures and all other securities regulatory requirements. These are often referred to as the "central office" and "compliance officer" requirements. It is not necessary for a Dealer to obtain separate premises from which these responsibilities will be discharged. Any office or branch of the Dealer may be designated as its central location in a province. Similarly the compliance "officer" need not be an officer of the FI. It will be sufficient for the compliance officer to be a senior manager of the Dealer and the FI so that the relevant securities commission can be satisfied that the compliance function is being handled by an individual who is senior enough in the organization to ensure compliance with the rules. The proficiency or experience requirements for a compliance officer will be those currently established in each province or territory. As noted in paragraph 9, it is the responsibility of each Dealer to ensure that all regulatory requirements are being complied with. Among other things this requires each Dealer to employ an adequate number of registered, qualified compliance personnel to properly handle the Dealer's volume of business. These compliance employees will be in addition to the Dealer's designated compliance officer. The Alberta Commission has concluded that, as a minimum, the obligation to devote adequate resources to the compliance function will require each Dealer to have in the province at least one registrant who has successfully completed the Partners', Directors' and Senior Officers' Qualifying Examination and at least one other registrant who has successfully completed the Branch Managers' Examination. The Alberta Commission will consider variations from this requirement in exceptional circumstances. Any questions on this matter should be directed to the Alberta Commission.

13. *Electronic Sales.* Sales of mutual fund securities through electronic means (eg. automated teller machines) will not be permitted. As technology advances the Commissions will be prepared to review this restriction at the request of one or more Dealers of FIs. This limitation will not be interpreted to restrict sales activity conducted by telephone or other means through which a registered salesperson may communicate directly with a customer. Electronic means may be used to effect redemptions or payments for prior purchases of mutual fund securities.

14. *Completion of Form 4A/3A.* It is a requirement of provincial and territorial securities legislation that every applicant for registration as a salesman of a registered dealer complete Form 4 or, in Quebec, Form 3, in the form prescribed by securities legislation. The Commissions recognize that not all of the content of this form may be relevant to the activities of salespersons of Dealers carrying out the trading activities contemplated by this notice or to the activities of other registrants carrying out directly competing activities. Accordingly, the CSA has authorized the Subcommittee to institute a review of this form to determine if it can be shortened and simplified for the benefit of all applicants for registration. Although this process will commence in the near future it will not be concluded for some time. The Commissions concluded that it would not be sensible to require every salesperson of all FI related Dealers to complete a Form 4/3 at a time when the content of that document is under review. As an interim measure while Form 4/3 is being reviewed salespersons of Dealers will not be required to complete and file Form 4/3 provided that:

(a)   each salesperson of a Dealer complete an abbreviated registration application (ie. Form 4A/3A) substantially in the form attached as Schedule "A" hereto, and

(b)   each Dealer and its related FI undertake in writing to each securities commission that it shall grant to such commission the right to immediate access upon request to the personnel records maintained by the Dealer and the FI with respect to each registered salesperson of the Dealer. It will be acceptable to limit such access to information which a registrant is normally obliged to make available to the securities commission.

By following this process the FI will be presumed to be acting as a character reference for each salesperson being registered by its related Dealer. In most provinces and the territories salespersons will be registered upon receipt by the relevant Commission of a properly completed Form 4A/3A on the condition that a salesperson's registration may be revoked if the Commission does not receive a satisfactory response to police record inquiries. In Saskatchewan salespersons of the Dealer will not be registered until the Saskatchewan Commission receives a preliminary favourable response to its police record inquiries.

15. *Record-keeping.* Securities legislation in each province and territory requires every registered dealer to maintain prescribed books and records. The Subcommittee has been asked to permit this activity to be performed by the related FI on behalf of the Dealer. It is essential that each registrant be in control of its books and records to enable it to discharge regulatory requirements and to allow the Commissions to have access to necessary information as may be required from time to time. Accordingly, FIs will be permitted to maintain the books and records of a related Dealer provided that the Commissions receive written assurance that the Dealer's books and records can be produced separately at any time and that each Commission will be given immediate access to such books and records (including copies of all supporting documents) on request. Such books and records may be electronically stored in a central location provided that such books and records as are required to carry on the Dealer's business in the province are maintained in that province or territory and each commission receives written assurance that such centrally stored information will be available to each commission upon request.

16. *Reporting.* Securities legislation in each province and territory requires that certain reports (eg. confirmation of trades, statements of account) be sent to clients of a dealer on a periodic basis. In some cases compliance by a Dealer with these requirements could result in a duplication of reporting (eg. a mutual fund security purchased for a RRSP account) which would be both costly and potentially confusing to the client. Accordingly, the reporting requirement will be waived if it would result in a duplication of reports and information. Each Dealer must satisfy itself that the report of the FI is truly duplicative, both in terms of content (eg. see requirement for confirmation slip disclosure in paragraph 7(c)) and frequency (eg. reports must be sent in respect of each purchase of mutual fund securities and each subsequent transaction within a client's account), of the requirements of securities legislation.

17. *Other requirements.* Each Dealer shall comply with all applicable provisions of National Policy 39 and also must satisfy all of the normal registration requirement of each jurisdiction to the extent that such requirements are not addressed in this notice. These requirements include completion of Form 3 or, in Quebec, Form 2, obtaining appropriate bonding and insurance coverage (the Dealer may be covered by an extension of appropriate coverage already carried by the related FI), complying with capital requirements, participation in the applicable contingency fund (if any) and providing reports to the securities commissions.

Reference: B.C. – Andrew Walker (604) 660-4800
Alberta – Walter Kunicki (403) 427-5201
Sask. – Barbara Shourounis (306) 787-5842
Manitoba – Tom Tapley (204) 945-2548
Ontario – Jamie Scarlett (416) 593-8211
               Joan Smart (416) 593-3666
Quebec – Pierre Lize (514) 873-5326
N.S. – Nick Pittas (902) 424-7768
N.B. – Donne Smith (506) 658-2504
P.E.I. – Merrill Wigginton (902) 368-4563
Nfld. – George Kennedy (709) 576-3316
Yukon – Malcolm Florence (403) 667-5225
N.W.T. – Gerald Stang (403) 873-7490

NOTICE

FORM 20A - CLARIFICATION OF REQUIREMENTS

Form 20A was specified under NIN#88/24 as the form of acknowledgment and under-taking required to be filed under section 128 of the Securities Regulation, B.C. Reg. 270/86 (the "Regulation").

Part 7 of the Form requires that an undertaking be given if the purchaser is a company. The requirement that all corporate purchasers give the undertaking is broader than intended. The undertaking need be given only if the purchaser is a company described in section 117(a)(ii)(C) or 117(i)(iv)(B) of the Regulation.

DATED at Vancouver, British Columbia, this 18th day of November, 1988.

Neil de Gelder
Superintendent of Brokers

NOTICE

NATIONAL POLICY STATEMENT NO. 41 –
SHAREHOLDER COMMUNICATION - REMOVAL OF EXEMPTION

All reporting issuers listed only on the Vancouver Stock Exchange, or The Alberta Stock Exchange, or both Exchanges, holding meetings of security holders on and after March 1, 1989 will be required to comply with National Policy Statement No. 41 on shareholder communication. Under Part IX of the Policy, these reporting issuers have been exempted from the Policy on an interim basis. The removal of the interim exemption was approved by the Canadian Securities Administrators in October 1988.

The Policy imposes obligations on reporting issuers, on intermediaries who hold securities beneficially owned by others (called non-registered holders), and on depositories used by those intermediaries. These obligations require reporting issuers

(a)   to set meeting dates earlier than in the past,

(b)   to set record dates where the issuer may not have set a record date in the past,

(c)   to give the depositories notice of meeting dates and record dates,

(d)   by sending search cards to depositories and intermediaries, to determine those non-registered holders who wish to receive proxy related materials for the meeting, and

(e)   to send proxy related materials to intermediaries, who must in turn mail them to non-registered holders at least 25 days before the meeting date.

All intermediaries, including brokers and transfer agents, and depositories have been complying with the Policy for the past year. Reporting issuers required to comply with the Policy for the first time should discuss their obligations with their transfer agents.

DATED at Vancouver, British Columbia this 1st day of December, 1988.

Doug Hyndman
Chairman
B.C. Securities Commission

NOTICE

FULL SERVICE AND DISCOUNT BROKERAGE ACTIVITIES
BY FINANCIAL INSTITUTIONS – PRINCIPLES OF REGULATION

The Canadian Securities Administrators have jointly released a notice entitled "Full Service and Discount Brokerage Activities of Securities Dealers in Branches of Related Financial Institutions - Principles of Regulation" (the "Principles of Regulation"), which sets out regulatory guidelines for trading by registered securities dealers located within branches of related financial institutions ("FIs"). The Principles of Regulation are attached as Appendix A.

Notices

Securities dealers who are related to FIs and intend to carry on full service or discount brokerage activities in branches of their related FIs, must comply with all relevant securities legislation and policies as well as with the Principles of Regulation. Section 167.10 of the Securities Regulation, B.C. Reg 270/86 (the "Regulation") requires that FI-related securities dealers give written notice (the "Notice") to the Superintendent of Brokers (the "Superintendent") of their intention to carry on full service or discount brokerage activities in branches of related FIs at least 30 days prior to their entering into such arrangements.

The Notice must describe the nature of the arrangement between the securities dealer and its related FI in detail sufficient to enable the Superintendent to decide under section 167.10 of the Regulation whether to allow the parties to enter into the arrangement. The Notice must adhere to the guidelines set out in the Principles of Regulation and must include specifically:

   (i) a description of the manner in which the premises and activities of the securities dealer will be separated from the premises and activities of its related FI;

  (ii) a set of plans for the FI's premises which are to be occupied by the securities dealer; and

 (iii) a copy of the disclosure document to be delivered to clients by the securities dealer, prior to the commencement of trading for the client's account.

DATED at Vancouver, British Columbia, this 20th day of December, 1988.

Douglas M. Hyndman
Chairman

APPENDIX A   November 25, 1988

NOTICE

CANADIAN SECURITIES ADMINISTRATORS

Full Service and Discount Brokerage Activities of Securities Dealers in Branches of Related Financial Institutions

PRINCIPLES OF REGULATION

PREAMBLE

As a result of legislation recently enacted by several provinces and the federal government, a number of financial institutions ("FIs") have, in the past year, invested in existing securities dealers or have incorporated securities dealer subsidiaries. Some of the securities dealers who are related to FIs ("FI related dealers") have indicated an interest in setting up securities dealer branches within branches of their related FIs.

The Canadian Securities Administrators ("CSA") have certain regulatory concerns about a FI related dealer trading securities within branches of its related FI. In an effort to address those regulatory concerns and achieve as much uniformity as possible in dealing with those concerns, a subcommittee of the CSA, consisting of representatives from the securities commissions of British Columbia, Alberta, Saskatchewan, Manitoba, Ontario, Quebec, Nova Scotia and New Brunswick, considered the issues regarding full service and discount brokerage securities activities of FI related dealers within branches of their related FIs. Members of the subcommittee have also discussed these issues with representatives of several FIs, several FI related dealers, self-regulatory organizations ("SROs"), the Canadian Bankers' Association, the Trust Companies Association of Canada and the Office of the Superintendent of Financial Institutions. The subcommittee has reported to the CSA as a whole, which confirmed the positions taken by the subcommittee.

This notice regarding Principles of Regulation outlines those areas where a consensus has been reached on the subject issues by all of the provinces and territories, unless otherwise indicated. At this time, the principles outlined will be implemented by the securities commission of each province and territory by such means as might be appropriate. The CSA subcommittee will continue its work on the subject issues with a view to eventually turning the Principles of Regulation into a National Policy Statement.

The Principles of Regulation apply only to FI related dealers who conduct full service or discount brokerage securities activities in dealer branches situated within branches of their related FIs. For the purposes of the Principles of Regulation, a FI means any financial institution, including a bank, trust company, loan company, insurance company, treasury branch, credit union and caisse populaire that carries on business through a branch office network. In Quebec, the Confederation des caisses populaires et d'economie Desjardins du Quebec will be considered to be a financial institution and each individual caisse populaire will be considered to be a branch of the Confederation. Also, for the purposes of the Principles of Regulation, a dealer is related to a FI if it is a subsidiary or affiliate of the FI or if the dealer would otherwise fall within the definition of a "related party" (as defined in Section 167.1 of the Regulation made under the British Columbia Securities Act S.B.C. 1985, c. 83) in respect of the dealer.

In the case of Manitoba, pending development of a policy regarding other FIs, the Principles of Regulation will only apply to dealers related to banks or trust companies who have dealer branches situated within branches of their related banks or trust companies.

FI related dealers will be registrants under the Securities Acts in the provinces or territories in which they operate and will be subject to the relevant legislation and National, Uniform and Local Policies. In many cases FI related dealers will be members of an SRO and subject to SRO rules. Accordingly, the Principles of Regulation assume such SRO membership. The securities legislation and SRO rules address certain kinds of self-dealing and conflicts of interest which might arise as a result of the relationship between the FI related dealer and its related FI. The Principles of Regulation set out additional rules which are necessary as a result of FI related dealers conducting securities activities within branches of their related FIs. Many of the rules are designed to address concerns about public confusion and possible result-ing financial losses that might occur when risk oriented securities are traded in branches of FIs where the public is generally accustomed to making deposits or investing in products guaranteed by the FI or insured by the Canada Deposit In-surance Corporation ("CDIC") or some other government deposit insurer. Several of the rules are designed to address certain conflicts of interest that may arise. In those provinces and territories which allow a registered person of the FI related dealer to also be employed by the related FI, certain specific restrictions are imposed to deal with potential conflicts of interest. For example, a conflict might arise if such a dually employed salesperson is paid on a commission basis in that he would have an incentive to sell securities over other products of the related FI when the other products might be more appropriate for the client. Such a conflict might also arise if a dually employed registered salesperson was permitted to authorized a loan on behalf of the FI so that a client could buy securities from the salesperson acting on behalf of the FI related dealer.

Although not specifically addressed in the Principles of Regulation, the CSA has concerns about public confusion and conflicts of interest that may arise as a result of FI related dealers trading the following securities in branches of their related FIs:

(i) securities issued by their related FIs;

(ii) securities owned by their related FIs; and

(iii) securities which may also be sold by their related FIs.

The CSA has instructed its subcommittee to further consider these issues and consult with appropriate industry groups before deciding on principles of regulation which are necessary to deal with those concerns.

In the course of the subcommittee's deliberations it became apparent that allowing dealers to conduct full service or discount brokerage securities activities in dealer branches located in branches of their related FIs raises a number of regulatory concerns for which no clear answers exist. Accordingly, in areas of uncertainty, the CSA has adopted a generally cautious approach, with a view to revisiting these issues in the future after the public, FIs, FI related dealers and regulators have had more experience regarding full service and discount brokerage securities activities conducted in branches of FIs. While any particular issue could be reviewed in a shorter time frame, the CSA is of the view that the Principles of Regulation and any resulting National Policy Statement should be reviewed in no later than three years' time to assess whether they adequately serve legitimate regulatory and business concerns.

Notices

The Principles of Regulation are designed to address issues raised by specific networking applications made by several FI related dealers to conduct full service and discount brokerage securities activities within branches of their related FIs. Other FI related dealers who enter into similar arrangements with their related FIs will, in the first instance, be required to comply with the Principles of Regulation. The CSA recognizes that variations may have to be made to the Principles of Regulation to address issues raised by other FI related dealers who may wish to conduct securities activities within branches of their related FIs.

PRINCIPLES OF REGULATION

1.   General

FI related dealers will be permitted to conduct full service or discount brokerage securities activities in dealer branches situated within branches of their related FIs, subject to complying with all relevant FI legislation, securities legislation and policies, SRO by-laws and rules, and the Principles of Regulation set out herein.

A FI related dealer planning to conduct full service or discount brokerage securities activities in dealer branches situated within branches of its related FI shall provide notice of its plans to the securities commission in each province or territory where such activities will be carried on and obtain the consent of the relevant securities commission or commissions before proceeding to commence such activities.

2.   Separation of Premises and Activities

The FI related dealer shall have identifiably separate premises, under the name of the FI related dealer, within the branch of the related FI so that it is clear to the public that the operations of the FI related dealer are separate and distinct from the operations of the related FI.

If a branch of a FI where the FI related dealer has established separate premises, the FI related dealer must not conduct any of its securities activities on the premises of the related FI, other than the activities referred to in paragraph 6(a) or (b), (the other activities referred to in paragraph 6 may only be conducted on the premises of the FI related dealer in that branch of the FI). The related FI must not conduct any of its FI activities on the premises of the FI related dealer. These restrictions must be adhered to in all provinces and territories, including those which permit registered persons of the FI related dealer to also be employed by the related FI (see paragraph 5). For example, a dually employed salesperson of the FI related dealer must not, while standing at one of the counters of the FI, take orders from clients to buy securities through the FI related dealer. Similarly, a dually employed salesperson of the FI related dealer must not, in his capacity as an employee of the FI, open a FI savings account for a client while on the premises of the FI related dealer.

The FI related dealer must have a telephone number which is different from and is listed separately from that of the related FI.

3.   Disclosure

The FI related dealer shall make disclosure to the following effect to each client by way of a separate document which shall be delivered to each client before any trading is done for the account of the client:

(a)   the FI related dealer is a separate corporate entity from the related FI;

(b)   monies held by the FI related dealer in securities accounts are not insured by CDIC or by any other government deposit insurer; and

(c)   unless, with respect to a particular security, the FI related dealer informs the client to the contrary,

(i)   securities sold by the FI related dealer are not insured by CDIC or by any other government deposit insurer;

(ii)   securities sold by the FI related dealer are not guaranteed by the related FI; and

(iii)   values of securities sold by the FI related dealer are subject to market fluctuations.

The FI related dealer must make such further disclosure of the foregoing matters as is necessary so that its clients continue to be aware of those matters. This might include sending regular disclosure statements to all clients and the use of a sign disclosing these matters prominently displayed on the premises of the FI related dealer.

4. *Solicitation of Clients*

Registered persons and other employees of the FI related dealer must not actively solicit business from customers of the related FI who enter the FI for the purpose of conducting business with the FI. For example, such persons should not solicit customers who are waiting in the teller line to buy securities from the FI related dealer. This does not prevent a FI related dealer from advertising its services and products, as permitted by these Principles of Regulation, within branches of the related FI.

5. *Dual or Sole Employment*

(a) *Saskatchewan, Manitoba, Ontario, Quebec, the Yukon and the Northwest Territories*

A registered person of the FI related dealer may also be employed by the related FI and conduct FI activities on the premises of the related FI, provided that such dual employment is permitted by the legislation governing the FI. However, in that case, the FI related dealer must comply with the following:

(i) a dually employed registered person shall be paid on a salary only basis (this would preclude any form of compensation, including bonus payments, linked to the volume of sales of securities services or products);

(ii) a dually employed registered person shall not act on behalf of the related FI in lending money to a client for the purpose of purchasing securities services or products from the same such person acting on behalf of the FI related dealer; and

(iii) the FI related dealer shall adopt and implement rules and supervisory procedures to prevent other conflicts of interest from arising due to dual employment.

If a FI related dealer wants to implement a form of performance-based compensation for dually employed registered persons, it should raise the matter with the relevant securities commissions to determine if the conflict of interest concerns, such as those referred to in the Preamble, can be satisfied in some other manner.

A registered person of a FI related dealer who does not conduct any FI activities on behalf of the related FI may be paid on a commission basis.

(b) *British Columbia, Alberta, New Brunswick, Nova Scotia, Prince Edward Island, and Newfoundland*

Registered persons of a FI related dealer will not be allowed to also conduct FI activities on behalf of the related FI. Such persons may be paid on a commission basis.

The Securities Commission of Nova Scotia is giving further consideration to this issue and will release a separate notice at a later date if it decides to alter its position.

6. *Securities Activities in Non-Registered Branches*

In accordance with securities legislation of the provinces and territories, non-registered FI personnel are not permitted to engage in activities which constitute trading in securities, other than those with respect to which an exemption from registration exists under the relevant Securities Acts, Regulations and rulings.

The FI related dealer will be permitted to conduct the following activities through branches of the related FI in which there are no registered persons of the FI related dealer:

(a) advertise the services and products of the FI related dealer, subject to (b) below, through such means as posters, brochures and other informational materials;

(b) advertise the fact that specific securities are available for sale through the FI related dealer, provided that the advertising only refers to matters such as the identity of the security, the price of the security and the name and address of the dealer from whom the security may be purchased, and does not elaborate on the merits or substance of the security;

Notices

(c)   deliver or receive securities to or from clients;

(d)   distribute securities account opening application forms, provided that

 (i) if assistance is given to a client in completing the form, it is given by a registered person of the FI related dealer or by the manager, assistant manager or credit officer in the branch of the related FI who possesses a high degree of knowledge about the client's financial affairs, (in branches where there are registered persons of the FI related dealer, assistance in completing the form should only be given by one of those registered persons), and

 (ii) before the FI related dealer conducts any trades on behalf of a client, the completed form is approved by an appropriate registered person of the FI related dealer who is responsible for approving the opening of new accounts and ensuring that the know-your-client and suitability obligations under the applicable securities legislation have been satisfied;

(e)   receive completed account opening application forms to forward to an appropriate registered person of the FI related dealer for approval; and

(f)   install a toll-free line to the FI related dealer, provided that

 (i) in British Columbia, Alberta, Manitoba and Ontario, calls made on the toll-free line during normal business hours are handled by an individual registered and resident in the province from which the call originates. Calls made after normal business hours may be handled by an individual who is registered but not necessarily resident in the province from which the call originates;

 (ii) in Saskatchewan and Quebec, all calls made on the toll-free line are handled by an individual registered and resident in the province from which the call originates; and

 (iii) in New Brunswick, Nova Scotia, Prince Edward Island, Newfoundland, the Yukon and the Northwest Territories, calls made on the toll-free line may be handled by an individual registered but not necessarily resident in the province or territory from which the call originates provided that the FI related dealer also employs registered persons who are resident in the province or territory.

The FI related dealer will not be permitted to conduct any of its other activities through branches of the related FI in which there are no registered persons of the FI related dealer, including:

(a)   distributing prospectuses; and

(b)   distributing or assisting clients in completing order forms for securities.

Nothing in paragraph 6 is intended to restrict

(a)   a related FI from trading in securities which the FI is permitted to trade in itself; or

(b)   a FI related dealer from trading in securities which the FI related dealer would be permitted to trade in without being subject to registration under the relevant Securities Acts, Regulations and rulings.

Reference: B.C. – Andrew Walker (604) 660-4800
                                  Alberta – Walter Kunicki (403) 427-5201
                                  Sask. – Barbara Shourounis (306) 787-5842
                                  Manitoba – Tom Tapley (204) 945-2548
                                  Ontario – Jamie Scarlett (416) 593-8211
                                       Joan Smart (416) 593-3666
                                  Quebec – Pierre Lize (514) 873-5326
                                  N.S. – Nick Pittas (902) 424-7768
                                  N.B. – Donne Smith (506) 658-2504
                                  P.E.I. – Merrill Wigginton (902) 368-4563
                                  Nfld. – George Kennedy (709) 576-3316
                                  Yukon – Malcolm Florence (403) 667-5225
                                  N.W.T. – Gerald Stang (403) 873-7490

NOTICE

EXECUTION OF MEMORANDUM OF UNDERSTANDING

> The following Memorandum of Understanding was published under this notice, which has since lapsed. The memorandum is still included, as it is not published elsewhere.

MEMORANDUM OF UNDERSTANDING

The Office of the Superintendent of Financial Institutions Canada ("OSFI") and the British Columbia Securities Commission (the "BCSC") have reached the following understanding.

1. *Definitions*

    1.01 In this Memorandum of Understanding:

    (a) "capital adequacy rules" means sections 18 and 19 of the Securities Act, and sections 20 to 26, inclusive of the Regulation, including the minimum free capital, bonding, insurance, contingency trust fund and audit requirements provided by those sections, and the corresponding provisions of the by-laws of the self-regulatory organizations;

    (b) "federal financial institution (FFI)" means a body corporate to which the Bank Act (S.C. 1980-81-82-83, c. 40) other than a foreign bank within the meaning of that Act, the Trust Companies Act (R.S.C. 1970, c. T-16), the Loan Companies Act (R.S.C. 1970, c. L-12), the Canadian and British Insurance Companies Act (R.S.C. 1970, c. I-15), the Foreign Insurance Companies Act (R.S.C. 1970, c. I-16), or the Cooperative Credit Associations Act (R.S.C. 1970, c. C-29) or any statute replacing one of the above mentioned Acts applies, which has sought or is seeking approval to have an interest in the capital of an FFI-related dealer;

    (c) "FFI-related dealer" means a dealer in securities or an advisor with respect to securities that is or will be a registrant under the Securities Act and in which an FFI has sought or is seeking approval to have an interest, the purchase or acquisition of which requires the prior approval of the Minister of Finance for Canada;

    (d) "Securities Act" means the British Columbia Securities Act S.B.C. 1985 c. 83 and the Regulation thereunder; and

    (e) "self-regulatory organization" means the Vancouver Stock Exchange, the Pacific District of the Investment Dealers Association of Canada or any other comparable organization recognized from time to time by the BCSC for purposes of the self-regulation of dealers or advisors under the Securities Act.

2. *General Principles*

    2.01 This Memorandum of Understanding sets forth a statement of intent of OSFI and the BCSC with respect to the coordination of certain policies for the regulation of FF-related dealers by the BCSC, and of FFIs by OSFI.

3. *SRO Membership and Capital Adequacy Rules*

    3.01 The BCSC acknowledges that OSFI, in recommending that Ministerial approval be given to the acquisition by FFIs of interests in FFI-related dealers, is relying on the system of regulation currently applicable under the Securities Act and the by-laws of the self-regulatory organizations and, in particular, the capital adequacy rules.

    3.02 The BCSC will require that an FFI-related dealer be registered in an appropriate category of registrant under the Securities Act, and be a member of a self-regulatory organization, if appropriate. Prior to any granting of the necessary approval of the Minister of Finance to the purchase of an interest by an FFI in an FFI-related dealer, the BCSC will inform OSFI of the category in which the FFI-related dealer is or will be registered, its conditions of registration, the self-regulatory organization, if any, that is or will be responsible for its audit, and any other relevant details with respect to its regulation.

3.03 The BCSC will not, without the prior written consent of OSFI, allow an FFI-related dealer to cease to be a member of a self-regulatory organization or to change its category of registration unless:

(a) the BCSC requires the FFI-related dealer to be registered in an appropriate category of registration under the Securities Act having capital adequacy rules that are substantially equivalent to the capital adequacy rules of its former category of registration; or

(b) in the case of ceasing to be a member of a self-regulatory organization, the FFI-related dealer continues to be a member of another self-regulatory organization having capital adequacy rules that are substantially equivalent to the capital adequacy rules of the former self-regulatory organization.

3.04 Before making, approving or determining not to object to any material change to the capital adequacy rules, the BCSC will consult with OSFI and give it a reasonable opportunity to review and to comment upon the proposed change. If OSFI considers that the proposed change would materially weaken the capital adequacy rules, the BCSC and OSFI will use their best efforts to reach agreement on an appropriate change, if any. If, within a reasonable period of time, no agreement is reached, the BCSC will not permit the proposed change to be implemented earlier than 180 days thereafter.

4. *Activities of FFI-Related Dealers*

4.01 The BCSC acknowledges that OSFI has legitimate policy concerns as to the scope of the business carried on by FFI-related dealers, including the concern that an FFI not make use of an FFI-related dealer to carry on a business that the FFI is not itself permitted to carry on.

4.02 The BCSC will not permit an FFI-related dealer to carry on directly or indirectly the business of a bank, trust company, loan corporation or insurance company if the related FFI is not then permitted to carry on that business.

5. *Sharing of Information*

5.01 Each of OSFI and the BCSC acknowledges that the other, in the ordinary course of carrying out its regulatory responsibilities, has the right to obtain certain information about, or access to the books and records of FFI-related dealers or FFIs, respectively.

Notwithstanding any legal right to do so, neither OSFI nor the BCSC will seek information about, or access to the books and records of an FFI-related dealer or an FFI, respectively, from the FFI-related dealer or the FFI, or cause or seek to cause the related FFI or FFI-related dealer, respectively, to provide such information or access to the books and records without first making a request in accordance with this paragraph.

Subject to applicable law, each of OSFI and the BCSC will cooperate with all reasonable requests of the other for such information or access.

5.02 Each of OSFI and the BCSC will use its best efforts to provide the other with information it has that an FFI-related dealer or an FFI, respectively, has or appears to have breached, or is expected to breach, in any material way the Securities Act or the by-laws of a self regulatory organization of which the FFI-related dealer is a member, or the governing legislation of the FFI, respectively.

5.03 If OSFI or the BCSC receives a request made in accordance with paragraph 5.01, and the information or books and records requested are not in its possession or subject to its control and direction, it will use its best efforts to obtain the information or books and records.

5.04 All requests made under paragraph 5.01 shall be made in writing and addressed to the contact officer listed in Annex "A". Each request shall specify:

(a) a general description of the information or books and records being sought;

(b) a general description of the regulatory concern that forms the basis for the request, and the purpose for which the request is made; and

(c) the desired time period for reply.

In the case of an urgent matter, a request may be made orally, provided that the request is subsequently confirmed in writing.

Where certain information of a routine nature is requested to be provided from time to time, one specific request pursuant to paragraph 5.01 will suffice for the information to be provided on the basis set forth in the request.

5.05 OSFI and the BCSC will use any information or books and records furnished in response to a request made in accordance with paragraph 5.01 solely for the purpose stated in connection with the making of the request.

5.06 Each of OSFI and the BCSC will keep confidential any request made to it in accordance with paragraph 5.01, and any information or books and records furnished to it in accordance with this Memorandum of Understanding.

6. *Ongoing Regulation*

OSFI will regulate FFIs and the BCSC will regulate FFI-related dealers in accordance with the terms and underlying principles of this Memorandum of Understanding. Without limiting the generality of the foregoing, OSFI will not:

(a) require or request any undertaking from any FFI that is inconsistent with this Memorandum of Understanding;

(b) require or request any undertaking from any FFI in respect of an FFI-related dealer, other than in the form agreed upon and attached hereto as Annex B, or publish or establish any guideline, policy or rule, or recommend any regulation that prescribes the manner in which FFI-related dealers are to carry on business or that is otherwise directed specifically at FFI-related dealers, without first giving the BCSC a reasonable opportunity to review and to comment upon it. If, within a reasonable period of time not to exceed 180 days after the date upon which the guideline, policy or rule was first released for review, no agreement is reached, the guideline, policy or rule will not be implemented earlier than 180 days thereafter.

For greater certainty, nothing in this Memorandum of Understanding restricts in any fashion OSFI's ability to set capital rules for FFIs.

6.02 Promptly after the BCSC receives notice of any change of control of any FFI-related dealer, the BCSC will give notice of the change to OSFI and will permit OSFI to review and to comment upon the change during the period which the BCSC has to review it.

7. *Effective Date and Termination*

7.01 This Memorandum of Understanding will be effective from the date of its execution by OSFI and the BCSC.

7.02 This Memorandum of Understanding may be terminated by OSFI or the BCSC by giving 180 days notice to the other. Neither OSFI nor the BCSC will give notice of termination on the basis of a dispute between them without first using its best efforts to resolve the dispute.

DATED this 15th day of December, 1988.

Office of the Superintendent of Financial Institutions	British Columbia Securities Commission
by _____	by _____
Michael A. Mackenzie Superintendent	Douglas M. Hyndman Chairman

ANNEX A
CONTACT OFFICERS

Office of the Superintendent
  of Financial Institutions
255 Albert Street, 13th Floor
Kent Square Building
Ottawa, Ontario
K1A 0H2

Telephone: (613)
Telecopy: (613) 952-8219

Attention: Director, Rulings

British Columbia Securities
  Commission
11th Floor, 865 Hornby Street
Vancouver, British Columbia
V6Z 2H4

Telephone: (604) 660-4800
Telecopy: (604) 660-2688
Telex: 04-54599

Attention: The Chairman

ANNEX B

INDIRECT INVESTMENT BY BANK IN A SECURITIES DEALER CORPORATION

APPLICATION FOR MINISTERIAL APPROVAL UNDER PARAGRAPH 193(6.1)(b) OF THE BANK ACT BY . . . . ("BANK") TO PURCHASE AN INTEREST IN . . . . ("HOLDCO"), WHICH HOLDS AN INTEREST IN . . . ("DEALER")

WHEREAS BANK has sought the prior approval of the Minister of Finance (the "Minister") to own more than ten per cent (10%) of the shares of a class of shares of HOLDCO pursuant to paragraph 193(6.1)(b) of the Bank Act;

NOW THEREFORE, in consideration of the granting of the said approval by Minister, BANK hereby agrees with Her Majesty the Queen in right of Canada as follows:

1.   This Undertaking shall come into effect when, and shall remain in effect so long as, BANK owns more than ten per cent (10%) of the shares of any class of shares of HOLDCO and HOLDCO holds, directly or indirectly, any share of DEALER.

2.   In this Undertaking,

    (a)   "subsidiary" shall mean an existing and/or future subsidiary (as defined in the Bank Act, as amended from time to time) that is (except for the purposes of paragraph 3 hereof) a Canadian corporation (as so defined), or a foreign corporation (as so defined) referred to in subsection 193(3) of the Bank Act, as amended from time to time;

    (b)   "dealing in securities", or any derivative thereof, includes portfolio management and investment counselling; and

    (c)   "Superintendent" means the Superintendent of Financial Institutions.

3.   BANK represents that each of HOLDCO and DEALER owns, directly or indirectly, 100% of the issued and outstanding shares of each of its subsidiaries in existence as of the date hereof, and that the following is a complete list of all such subsidiaries:

Name of Subsidiary	Activity of Subsidiary
a) HOLDCO:	
b) DEALER:	

4. BANK shall cause HOLDCO to refrain from carrying on any activity other than holding the shares or subordinated debt of DEALER, unless the Superintendent provides his approval of such activity.

5. BANK represents that DEALER, and each of its subsidiaries that carries on in Canada the activity of dealing in securities, are registered, where required, under the applicable securities laws in those provinces in which they carry on that activity, and that bank shall cause DEALER and each of its subsidiaries that carries on in Canada the activity of dealing in securities, to register, where required, under the applicable securities laws in those provinces in which they hereafter carry on that activity.

6. BANK represents that DEALER, and each of its subsidiaries that carries on in Canada the activity of dealing in securities, are members in good standing of the following self-regulatory organizations and/or are registered in the following category of registrant:

Name of Securities Dealer	Self-Regulatory Organization	Category of Registrant

7. Should BANK cease to exercise direct control of HOLDCO or indirect control of DEALER, either in law or in fact, BANK shall forthwith notify the Superintendent, and, where the decreased holding raises prudential concerns with respect to BANK, the Minister may require that BANK dispose of any or all of its holdings in HOLDCO in excess of ten per cent (10%) of the shares of each class of shares of HOLDCO within the period of time specified by the Minister, and BANK agrees to comply with that requirement.

8. BANK agrees that all loans (which for this purpose shall include all forms of indebtedness, other than subordinated loans which are treated as capital of HOLDCO or DEALER or any of their subsidiaries by any or all of the self-regulatory organizations of which HOLDCO or DEALER or any of their subsidiaries is a member) and guarantees made or extended by it to or on behalf of HOLDCO or DEALER or any of their subsidiaries, shall be on terms and conditions consistent with, and shall be secured to the extent that the granting of security is in accordance with, usual banking practices respecting loans and guarantees made or extended to or on behalf of corporations or partnerships dealing in securities, and in accordance with applicable guidelines respecting loans and guarantees that the Office of the Superintendent of Financial Institutions may from time to time hereinafter issue.

    In the event of a conflict between usual banking practices and the guidelines, the guidelines shall, in each case, prevail.

9. Notwithstanding anything to the contrary herein contained, BANK shall cause DEALER, and each of its subsidiaries, to refrain from engaging, directly or indirectly, in any transaction in which BANK, at the time of the transaction, would be prohibited from engaging pursuant to paragraphs 174(2)(f) and (g) of the Bank Act, as amended from time to time, provided that the prohibitions and limitations set out in the said paragraphs 174(2)(f) and (g) of the Bank Act, as amended from time to time, shall not be deemed to apply to transactions between DEALER and any of its subsidiaries, and any officer, employee or director of DEALER or any of its subsidiaries, who is not an officer, employee or director of BANK.

    This paragraph shall not be deemed to impose any obligation on BANK with respect to any investment made prior to the date upon which BANK acquires its indirect interest in DEALER until 90 days after BANK has acquired its interest in HOLDCO.

10. BANK shall forward to the Superintendent, within ninety (90) days next following the end of each financial year, a copy of the audited financial statements of HOLDCO and DEALER.

11. BANK shall provide the Superintendent with details of any change with respect to any matter herein represented.

12. If any representation of or by BANK contained in this Undertaking is not true and correct, or if BANK is, at any time, in default under this Undertaking, and such default is not remedied within ninety (90) days from the date on which written

notice of such default is provided to BANK by the Superintendent, the Minister may require that BANK dispose of any or all of its holdings in HOLDCO in excess of ten percent (10%) of the shares of each class of shares of HOLDCO, within the period of time specified by the Minister, and BANK agrees to comply with that requirement.

13. It is agreed that, should legislation be enacted or should regulations be issued pursuant to the Bank Act, as amended from time to time, that relate to the matters governed by this Undertaking, that legislation or those regulations, whether more or less restrictive than the provisions of this Undertaking, apply to those matters in lieu of these provisions. To the extent that such legislation or regulations do not govern those matters, the provisions of this Undertaking shall remain effective and enforceable.

IN WITNESS WHEREOF BANK has executed this Undertaking and affixed its corporate seal under the hands of its proper signing officers duly authorized in that behalf.

DATED at   , this   day of   .

BANK

Per:

_____

_____

NIN#89/3

NOTICE

CONFLICT OF INTEREST RULES STATEMENT – CLARIFICATION OF FILING REQUIREMENTS

Section 167.3(1) of the Securities Regulation, B.C. Reg. 270/86 (the "Regulation"), requires every registrant to prepare and file a conflict of interest rules statement in the required form. Section 167.3(4) provides an exemption from this requirement if the registrant does not engage in activities as an adviser, dealer or underwriter in the circumstances set out in sections 167.4, 167.5, 167.7, 167.8 or 167.9 of the Regulation and files a statement and undertaking in the required form.

For greater certainty, registrants that engage only in activities that fall within the exceptions contained in sections 167.4(3), (4) or (5), 167.5(2), 167.7(2), (3) or (4), 167.8(2) or 167.9(3) of the Regulation are able to rely on the exemption contained in section 167.3(4) provided they file a statement and undertaking in the required form.

DATED at Vancouver, British Columbia, this 20th day of January, 1989.

Neil de Gelder
Superintendent of Brokers

NIN#89/13

NOTICE

STATUTORY FILINGS

The British Columbia Securities Commission hereby gives notice that it will be stepping up its review and enforcement procedures on all statutory filings. These filings - which include financial statements, quarterly reports, insider reports, acquisition reports and notices of exempt distributions - are the cornerstone of continuous public disclosure upon which a well-regulated public market for securities is based. In an effort to ensure that all persons comply with the reporting requirements of the Securities Act and the Regulation, the Securities Commission will act promptly to cease trade those persons and issuers that do not comply.

In order to allow insider reports to be brought up to date, the Securities Commission will accept, without further action or requirement for explanation, all properly completed insider reports filed before the close of business on April 28, 1989, even if such reports disclose trading which ought to have been reported earlier. After this date, failure to file a properly completed insider report as required by the Securities Act may result in a cease trade order being issued against the insider, without further notice, pursuant to Section 146 of the Regulation. In addition, the Superintendent of Brokers may issue notices of hearing to persons who repeatedly file insider reports late. The purpose of the hearings before the Commission will be to determine whether the insiders' trading rights should be withdrawn.

The statutory filing requirements of Part 10 of the Regulation, which relate to continuous disclosure by reporting issuers, will also be subject to greater regulatory review. Reference is made to NIN#88/27 issued August 25, 1988, dealing with this subject, and to NIN#89/5 issued January 27, 1989, which now requires all exchange issuers to file certain financial information on a quarterly basis as part of their quarterly report. These reports will be reviewed by the statutory filings department on a random basis. Exchange issuers that do not file within the required time, or file material which is not in compliance with the requirements will be placed on the Defaulting Reporting Issuers List (the "Default List").

The Securities Commission will be more vigilant in the issuance of cease trade orders against reporting issuers on the Default List. A reporting issuer can no longer expect to stay on the Default List for several months without action being taken. Once a reporting issuer appears on the Default List it may be cease traded at any time without further notice.

Finally, the Securities Commission will be monitoring, on a random basis, the filing of Form 20's and of the reports of acquisitions of securities required by sections 93, 95 and 96 of the Securities Act. As no forms have been prescribed for the acquisition reports, the Securities Commission will accept a letter containing the required information or the form of report prescribed by the laws of another province for comparable reporting requirements.

As with the filing of insider reports, no action will be taken with respect to any Form 20's or acquisition reports filed on or before April 28, 1989. Persons found to have not filed a Form 20 or acquisition report as required after that date may be subject to a cease trade order or a hearing regarding their trading rights.

In addition to the exercise of powers available to the Securities Commission, in appropriate circumstances evidence of breaches of the statutory filings requirements of the Securities Act or Regulation will be turned over to the Criminal Justice Branch of the Ministry of Attorney General for consideration for prosecution.

DATED at Vancouver, British Columbia, this 2nd day of March, 1989.

Neil de Gelder
Superintendent of Brokers

NIN#89/17

NOTICE

LOCAL POLICY STATEMENT 3-45
DESIGNATION AS A REPORTING ISSUER
AND BUSINESS INVESTOR OFFERINGS

In an agreement with the Securities Commission, the Ministry of International Business and Immigration (the "Ministry") recently assumed primary responsibility in British Columbia for the review of all offering memoranda prepared in connection with the Immigrant Investor Program (the "Program") established under the Immigration Act (Canada). As a result of this change in the administration of the Program, it is no longer necessary to require that issuers wishing to qualify under the Program become reporting issuers under the Securities Act.

Accordingly, Local Policy Statement 3-45 dated August 19, 1987 is revoked effective April 7, 1989. A revised form of Local Policy Statement 3-45 has been published for comment in Chapter 6 of the Weekly Summary of today's date. Reference should be made to the discussion below concerning the application of the draft policy.

Immigrant Investor Offerings

On March 23, 1989, the Ministry issued detailed guidelines known as "Instructions for Applicants" that must be satisfied by issuers wishing to qualify under the Program. These guidelines are in addition to the rules issued by Employment and Immigration Canada. The requirements that must be satisfied by issuers include a minimum investment to be made by each investor and a high level of disclosure to be made in the offering memorandum delivered to investors.

Interested persons should contact the Business Immigration Branch of the Ministry at 660-3998 (Vancouver) or 387-0296 (Victoria) for further information.

Although issuers that qualify under the Program will no longer be required to become reporting issuers, they will continue to be subject to and must comply with all applicable provisions of the Securities Act, some of which include:

(a)   ensuring that they qualify for registration and prospectus exemptions contained in Parts 5 and 8 of the Act in connection with any distribution of securities;

(b)   filing a copy of any offering memorandum delivered to investors in accordance with sections 127 and 131 of the Securities Regulation; and

(c)   filing a Form 20 in accordance with section 132 of the Securities Regulation.

All files currently under review at the Securities Commission will be transferred to the Ministry and the filing solicitors will be notified of the transfer.

While a number of issuers that previously became reporting issuers will be required by the Commission to maintain that status, and certain other issuers may consider it expedient to do so, some issuers may wish to discontinue their reporting issuer status. Any issuer wishing to become a non-reporting issuer may apply for an order under section 72 of the Securities Act in the normal manner.

Applicants for such an order should be up to date with all statutory filings, state the number of their shareholders in the application and provide a certified copy of the appropriate shareholders' resolution. As a condition of the order, issuers will be required to send a copy of the order to each of their shareholders.

Draft Local Policy Statement 3-45

All references to the Program have been deleted from the draft policy. In addition, the guidelines relating to applications for reporting issuer status by extraprovincial issuers have been updated and expanded.

Written comments concerning the draft policy should be directed to Adrienne Wanstall, Deputy Superintendent, Policy and Legislation, prior to May 5, 1989.

Until publication of the final policy, all applications for reporting issuer status made after April 7, 1989 must comply with the guidelines set out in the draft policy.

DATED at Vancouver, British Columbia, this 6th day of April, 1989.

Douglas M. Hyndman
Chairman

NIN#89/21

NOTICE

ORDERS PURSUANT TO SECTION 145
OF THE SECURITIES ACT
REMOVAL OF TRADING EXEMPTIONS

The British Columbia Securities Act contains, in Section 145, the power of the British Columbia Securities Commission or Superintendent of Brokers to remove trading exemptions from any person.

Over the past eighteen months orders have been issued pursuant to Section 145 against approximately 70 individuals. A number of inquiries have been received regarding potential relief from these orders, both by persons named in the orders and by registrants trading on their behalf.

The purpose of this notice is to provide guidance regarding the effect of these orders and to outline procedures to be followed for applications for relief.

An order issued under Section 145 of the Act usually removes all of the exemptions described in Sections 30 to 32, 55, 58, 81 and 82 of the Act, effectively making it an offence for a person subject to an order to trade securities in the province. The definition of trade encompasses a number of activities including:

"(a)   a disposition of a security for valuable consideration whether the terms of payment be on margin, instalment or otherwise . . .

(c)   the receipt by a registrant of an order to buy or sell a security . . .

(e)   any act, advertisement, solicitation, conduct or negotiation directly or indirectly in furtherance of any of the activities specified in paragraphs (a) to (d);".

The staff of the Commission takes the position that given the broad scope of this definition, a person subject to an order pursuant to Section 145 cannot escape the effect of that order by trading indirectly through nominees or intermediaries, such as a company or an account controlled by him. In addition, the order applies to any trade conducted by a person who, at the time of the trade, is in British Columbia, even though the trade might be executed on a stock exchange outside British Columbia and the order placed through a registrant in another jurisdiction.

There is a further implication for registrants who hold accounts for persons subject to such orders. Due to the broad definition of "trade", registrants who wish to sell securities of a person subject to an order under Section 145 so as to cover a debit in the account require an order of the Commission varying the original order.

The following guidelines are provided to assist individuals and registrants who wish to obtain relief from such orders.

1.   In a hearing pursuant to Section 145, the Commission will entertain submissions from counsel and from the Superintendent as to whether the respondent should be permitted to dispose of any of his securities in an orderly and timely fashion through a registrant if an order is issued under Section 145.

2.   Where registrants hold securities of a person subject to an order and wish to trade the securities in order to cover debts owed to the registrant, the following guidelines will apply:

(a)   If the securities were acquired by the registrant on behalf of the client subsequent to the issuance of a notice of hearing, relief from the order will be provided only in extraordinary circumstances.

(b)   If the securities were acquired on behalf of the client prior to the issuance of the notice of hearing, the Commission will normally entertain applications for relief by the registrant, provided the registrant has notified its client of the application.

(c)   The application should be directed to the Secretary of the Commission under Section 153 of the Act and accompanied by the required filing fee of $350 and all appropriate documentation relating to the application.

All notices of hearing and orders issued by the Commission pursuant to Section 145 are public. They are widely distributed at the time of issuance and are published in the Weekly Summary. It is the intention of the Commission to publish in the Weekly Summary, on a regular basis, a list of all outstanding notices of hearing and outstanding orders issued under Sections 144, 145 and 145.1. Registrants should refer to this list when deciding whether to conduct trades on behalf of their clients.

DATED at Vancouver, British Columbia, this 21st day of July, 1989.

Neil de Gelder
Superintendent of Brokers

NIN#89/29

Notices

INTERPRETATION NOTE

MEANING OF "THE PUBLIC"

Effective November 1, 1989, the Securities Amendment Act, 1989, amends the definition of "private issuer" in section 1(1) of the Securities Act (the "Act") to provide that an issuer will be a private issuer if, among other things, it has not distributed any of its securities to the public.

This Interpretation Note sets out the position taken by the Commission with respect to the meaning of "the public" for the purposes of the definition of private issuer in section 1(1) of the Act and the exemption in section 32(j) of the Act.

The Commission recognizes that the common law interpretation of the public is very broad and that whether or not a person is a member of the public is a factual matter to be determined by an issuer and its legal advisors in each particular situation.

Without limiting the circumstances in which a person would not be a member of the public, the Commission takes the position that a trade by an issuer or by a person holding securities of an issuer to any of the following persons is not a trade to the public:

(a) a person holding the issuer's securities on the date of the trade,

(b) a spouse, parent, brother, sister or child of the person making the trade,

(c) a director, officer or employee of the issuer,

(d) a spouse, parent, brother, sister or child of a director or officer of the issuer, or

(e) a company, all of the voting securities of which are beneficially owned by any combination of the persons referred to in (a),(b),(c) or (d) above.

Further, the Commission takes the position that a distribution of securities by a private issuer in the context of an amalgamation or merger of two or more private issuers to holders of securities of those private issuers is not a distribution to the public.

DATED at Vancouver, British Columbia, this 13th day of October 1989.

Douglas M. Hyndman
Chairman

NIN#89/30

NOTICE

QUALIFICATIONS OF AUDITORS FILING REPORTS

The Securities Regulation has been amended, effective November 1, 1989, to clarify who is qualified to prepare an auditor's report in respect of financial statements required to be filed with the Securities Commission.

Prior to the amendment, the Securities Act and the Securities Regulation did not address this issue.

WHO MAY PREPARE AN AUDITOR'S REPORT

Section 4(4) and (4.1) of the Securities Regulation provide that a person is qualified to make an auditor's report only if:

(a) the person is a member, or is a partnership whose partners are members, in good standing of, and is authorized to carry on the practice of public accounting by, the institute of chartered accountants of a province of Canada,

(b) the person is a member, or is a partnership whose partners are members, in good standing of, and is authorized to carry on the practice of public accounting by, the Certified General Accountants' Association of British Columbia,

(c) the person is certified as an auditor by the Auditor Certification Board established under section 205 of the British Columbia Company Act, or

(d) the person

(i) has qualifications as an auditor in a jurisdiction other than a province of Canada that the Superintendent considers are similar to the qualifications for membership in the Institute of Chartered Accountants of British Columbia, and

(ii) is authorized to carry on the practice of public accounting by the appropriate authority in that jurisdiction.

AUDITORS IN CANADA

Auditors carrying on the practice of public accounting in Canada must qualify under one of paragraphs (a), (b) or (c) set out above.

The requirement in paragraphs (a) and (b) that, in addition to being a member of a professional association, the person must be authorized to practice public accounting ensures that the person will be subject to requirements of the association relating to liability insurance, professional development and practice review.

AUDITORS OUTSIDE OF CANADA

Auditors carrying on the practice of public accounting outside of Canada must qualify under paragraph (d) set out above.

In addition to being authorized to carry on the practice of public accounting by the appropriate authority, the person must also have qualifications that the Superintendent considers are similar to the qualifications required for membership in the Institute of Chartered Accountants of British Columbia.

The Superintendent considers that an auditor carrying on the practice of public accounting in the United States who is

(a)   a certified public accountant, and

(b)   in good standing and authorized to carry on the practice of public accounting under the laws of the state in which he has his residence or principal office

is qualified to file an auditor's report under section 4 of the Securities Regulation.

Questions as to whether the qualifications of an auditor in another country will be acceptable to the Superintendent should be directed to the Deputy Superintendent, Registration and Statutory Filings.

RESPONSIBILITY OF REPORTING ISSUERS

It is the responsibility of each reporting issuer to ensure that it has engaged an auditor qualified to file an auditor's report on the issuer's audited financial statements.

Where an issuer files financial statements that have been reported on by an auditor with qualifications that do not satisfy the requirements under the Securities Regulation, the financial statements will not be acceptable to the Superintendent and the issuer will be delinquent in its continuous disclosure filings.

DATED at Vancouver, British Columbia, this 13th day of October 1989.

Neil de Gelder
Superintendent of Brokers

NIN#89/32

NOTICE

REQUIRED FORM OF OFFERING MEMORANDUM

B.C. Reg. 316/89 amends section 126 of the Securities Regulation (the "Regulation") by adding paragraph (c) which provides for the use of a required form of offering memorandum.

By NIN#89/31, Form 43 was specified as the required form of offering memorandum for the purpose of section 126(c) of the Regulation.

In order to allow for an orderly transition , BOR#89/11 provides that, for a limited period of time, Form 43 need not be used by persons complying with the terms of the order.

The Superintendent will also consider applications for individual orders exempting issuers from using Form 43 if the exemption provided for in BOR#89/11 does not adequately address their particular transitional problems.

The Canadian Securities Administrators are in the process of finalizing a national form of offering memorandum . Until the national form is available, the disclosure required in Items 1, 5 and 8 and the form of certificate in Item 20 may be reworded to comply with the requirements of one or more of the uniform act provinces where the offering memorandum will be delivered to purchasers in those provinces. The substance of the disclosure and the certificate, however, must continue to meet the Form 43 standard.

DATED at Vancouver, British Columbia, this 31st day of October 1989.

Neil de Gelder
Superintendent of Brokers

REF: NIN#89/31
          BOR#89/11

Notices

NIN#89/34

NOTICE

SETTLEMENTS WITH THE BRITISH COLUMBIA SECURITIES COMMISSION

INTRODUCTION

The settlement process is a relatively new one for the British Columbia Securities Commission. The current adminstration's first settlement agreement was announced in April of 1988; since that time, approximately 30 settlements have been reached on a wide variety of issues. This notice summarizes some of the lessons learned and directions taken by the Securities Commission as a result of our experience with this developing process.

In this notice, our securities regulatory body as a whole is referred as the "Securities Commission", and individual Commissioners or panels of Commissioners are referred to as the "Commission proper". When discussing the policies or actions of staff of the Securities Commission with the intention of excluding reference to the Commission proper, the reference will be to the "staff" or to its chief administrative officer, the "Superintendent". All parties with whom the Securities Commission deals on settlement matters will be referred to as "respondents", without in any way adopting the legal implications of that word. Finally, all section references are to the Securities Act, unless otherwise stated.

1. WHY SETTLE?

This question needs to be asked in each instance by both sides. From the Securities Commission's perspective, a settlement can be faster, more cost efficient, and more flexible than a full hearing, while still retaining the desired regulatory end, which includes the creation of a body of precedents. The financial burden to the Securities Commission of a full hearing, which once played a significant role in deciding whether to proceed (particularly since the Securities Commission is now essentially a self-financing entity), has become less pronounced since the Commission proper was granted the power under section 154.2 to order payment of costs after a hearing. (The schedule of hearing costs is set out in item 33 of section 138(1) of the Regulation). Consequently, the emphasis in deciding whether or not to settle can now more easily be determined on the broader basis of regulatory initiatives and the public interest.

Generally speaking, the settlement option is always open. Only in circumstances where the staff considers it essential that guidance be given by the Commission proper in a particular area, or where the Commission proper expresses a desire to deal with a particular type of issue at a full hearing, will settlement discussions not be entertained, and the respondents will be told that at an early stage. Whether a settlement can be reached depends, of course, on a variety of factors, some of which are discussed below.

From a respondent's perspective, there are a number of reasons why a settlement may be preferred to a full hearing:

   (1)   the settlement process is almost always less expensive, particularly in respect of legal fees and possible hearing costs;

   (2)   settlements are by their nature more predictable than hearings, - the respondent can to a limited extent 'control' the issues dealt with and their resolution;

   (3)   hearings generally tend to attract more media attention than settlements, in part because hearings involve day by day disclosures through testimony instead of a single voluntary written statement;

   (4)   the settlement process can be less intrusive and gruelling - the respondent is not, for example, subjected to cross examination in full public view; and

   (5)   the sanctions resulting from the settlement process are usually lighter than those which the Superintendent would ask for at a full hearing, and there is a greater range of alternative solutions available in the context of a negotiated settlement than is available to the Commission proper in the context of a hearing.

Despite these apparent advantages, there are situations where the respondent perceives it to be in his best interest to have his case dealt with in a full public hearing. This usually occurs when the respondent feels his conduct will withstand or benefit from a review or thinks the settlement terms are too onerous, or where for one reason or another he wishes to avoid voluntary contact with the Securities Commission, which often means he will also not appear at a hearing.

2.   WITH WHOM DO YOU SETTLE?

All settlement agreements to date have been entered into between the respondent and the Superintendent, without the involvement of the Commissioners. The Securities Commission has developed an internal policy whereby the Superintendent is responsible for directing the investigation, "prosecution", and settlement of cases, while the Commission proper conducts impartial hearings of cases that are not settled.

This arrangement is facilitated because, under the British Columbia Securities Act, many of the powers of the Commission proper are also exercisable by the Superintendent. For example, the Superintendent can issue temporary or permanent cease-trade orders, remove a director or officer of an issuer, remove statutory exemptions from any person, or suspend or cancel a registration. Therefore, the involvement of the Commission proper is not legally required to issue the orders that typically accompany a settlement nor, as a matter of policy, is the consent of the Commission proper required in order for the Superintendent to enter into a settlement agreement.

A settlement with the Superintendent may not end matters, since the issues raised by the fact of concurrent jurisdictions can complicate the settlement process or involve several different settlements. The jurisdictional overlap arises most often between the Securities Commission and a securities commission of another province or country (notably the United States), a self regulatory organization (an "SRO", which in Canada means a stock exchange or the Investment Dealers Association) or a civil or criminal court in British Columbia or elsewhere. It is readily apparent that complex issues may arise out of these situations.

Without attempting to deal with the myriad circumstances which may require consideration by respondent's counsel, it is possible to set out a few guiding principles that the staff will apply in its settlement deliberations.

(1)   We will generally be amenable to entering into the same settlement agreement as a securities commission in another province if the conduct at issue in each jurisdiction is the same and the settlement is reasonably consistent with what we would normally expect.

(2)   We will generally defer to the jurisdiction of an SRO in matters clearly within its mandate, for example 'churning' of an account or a breach of the SRO's rules, even if the Securities Commission participated in the investigation. If the conduct also has a larger aspect relating to the public interest, such as market manipulation (in the criminal context or otherwise), we would become involved and might enter into settlement negotiations, even if the respondent was also being disciplined by the SRO. In many cases, the sanctions imposed by the Securities Commission in these instances would be in addition to, and could go beyond, the sanctions imposed by the SRO, particularly with respect to the exercise of regulatory powers (such as removal of trading rights) that an SRO does not have. The guiding principle in this context is the protection of the public interest, which requires the Securities Commission to consider a person's fitness to participate in the securities markets, and not just his status as a member of an SRO. Accordingly, a registrant's conduct will not be immune from review by the Securities Commission solely because he is a member of an SRO that has disciplinary powers which may also be brought to bear against him.

(3)   The Securities Commission would normally proceed with a hearing or settlement even if criminal or civil proceedings are underway or contemplated in connection with the conduct at issue. Reference is made to Securities Commission Notice 88/11 which sets out the staff response that a respondent might expect in those circumstances. The Securities Commission takes the view that its regulatory function in protecting the public interest generally requires it to take action in those circumstances, and that it cannot stand by or expect other processes, criminal or civil, to deal with the Securities Commission's concerns or areas of responsibility.

3.　WHEN DO YOU SETTLE?

There are three distinct stages of Securities Commission involvement in a matter during which settlement may be reached.

The first is after an investigation has commenced, but before the proceedings have been initiated through a formal notice of hearing. Because these settlement agreements are based only on information known to the investigators at the time of signing, they often reserve to the Securities Commission the right to take further action if that is warranted by further facts that come to light. Occasionally the settlement will involve an understanding on the part of the Superintendent to cease investigations, but that kind of arrangement is usually based on a fairly clear indication that further investigation will not be fruitful. At this first stage for settlement, the staff is inclined to be the most flexible, and the sanctions sought will normally never be less than at this stage.

The second stage for settlement is after a notice of hearing has been issued, with or without accompanying temporary orders. At this stage, the investigation is relatively advanced, the Attorney General's office - which provides legal services to the Securities Commission - has become involved, hearing dates have been booked and a panel of Commissioners has been established. The allegations and issues which must be dealt with in any settlement will usually have been set out in the notice of hearing. Any temporary orders issued will normally be kept in place pending the hearing settlement. The sanctions sough at this stage will still be less than those the Superintendent feels are likely to be imposed by the Commission proper after a hearing.

The third stage of settlement is after the hearing has commenced but before a decision is rendered. These are the most difficult settlements, particularly in hearings with multiple respondents. the reason is that such settlements may involve factual matters which it is the purpose of the hearing to determine, and may be perceived as in some way tying the hands of the Commissioners on the issue of sanctions for remaining respondents before the Commissioners have reached a conclusion on the entire matter. To date, a small number of settlements have been entered into under these circumstances with no apparent ill effects, but it is not a practice which is recommended or encouraged. Different, possibly less difficult, considerations would arise if the sole respondent or all respondents in a hearing were to propose settlement during a hearing, but to date this has not occurred.

4.　HOW DO YOU SETTLE?

Very little needs to be said about his, as the procedures are not in any way unusual, and in fact will be familiar for most respondents' counsel. Several observations may be of assistance in obtaining the most favourable arrangement for a respondent.

(1)　The respondent should have counsel conduct the negotiations for all the usual reasons, but particularly because admissions or evidence must be properly dealt with so that the respondent is not prejudiced by incorrect procedures should the matter go to a hearing.

(2)　Settlement discussions prior to a notice of hearing being issued should normally be held with the enforcement person handling the matter; that person will involve his or her superior or counsel, depending on the circumstances and the significance of the matter under investigation. After a notice of hearing is issued, settlement discussions should be held with the Superintendent's counsel.

(3)　Avoid unrealistic opening offers. While staff are prepared to do a certain amount of 'horse-trading' to finalize matters, their time is properly spent preparing the evidence and arguments for a hearing, not pursuing settlements which are a long way from the staff's intended goal. Stick to the main issues, deal with the key evidence, and review past settlement agreements and decisions of the Commission proper. Be prepared to listen to the staff's regulatory objective and place the respondent's position into that context.

(4)　Expect the staff's position to be negotiable if new evidence or the respondent's particular circumstances warrant it, but do not mistake an initial suggestion for sanctions as an early 'high-ball' offer. We have had uniformly unsatisfactory experiences with such approaches, and are now much more inclined to give a very realistic first estimate as to where we wish to end up.

(5) Notwithstanding the Securities Commission's regulatory role, it too must allocate limited resources and select cases out of competing priorities. From a purely practical perspective, we will be less inclined to pursue minor matters if evidence of more serious wrongdoing is available or made available.

(6) Be prepared to include a provision for costs in any settlement. While the amount is negotiable, the principle generally is not, particularly after a notice of hearing has been issued. These funds will be required to be paid at the time of signing the settlement; deferral of the obligation is unlikely.

5. WHAT FORM DOES A SETTLEMENT TAKE?

A settlement is finalized by way of an agreement between the respondent and the Superintendent. It involves an agreed statement of facts, and a payment of any settlement amount or contribution to investigative costs. If the settlement involves non-financial sanctions, it will be accompanied by an order (usually from the Superintendent although occasionally from the Commission proper if it involves an exercise of powers exclusive to it) or by an undertaking from the respondent if there is no provision in the Securities Act for an order relating to the conduct undertaken or restrained.

Undertakings usually are given in respect of remedies such as restitution, disgorgement of profits, fees, or other improperly obtained benefits, obtaining certain training or experience, or improving internal organization or procedures.

The Securities Commission will not entertain settlements of the 'neither admit nor deny' variety. These types of settlements, popular in the United States as "consent injunctions", are in our view of insufficient value to warrant forgoing full proceedings. While we are sensitive to the complications that admissions in a settlement may create in cases where further criminal or civil actions are pending or prospective, the hearing process poses similar problems for the respondent. As indicated previously, a settlement may be the best method for dealing flexibly with these issues.

All settlement agreements are published in the Securities Commission's bulletin (the "Weekly Summary") and in some cases, particularly after a notice of hearing has been issued, are sent to interested members of the media, usually with a summary to ensure accuracy in the case of complex issues or proceedings. No public comments, 'clarifications' or elaborations are given by the Superintendent or the staff, as the settlement agreement should speak for itself.

As a final note, settlement agreements always contain a waiver of any right the respondent may have to a hearing or appeal, and may indicate the course of action which the Superintendent is forgoing as a consequence of the settlement.

6. ENFORCEMENT OF SETTLEMENTS

To date, the enforcement of settlement agreements has not proven to be a major issue. In situations where an undertaking is breached or an order is not complied with, it is likely that an application would be made to the Supreme Court under section 140 of the Securities Act for an order directing the respondent to comply with or cease violating the order or the Securities Act. This method would make available all the contempt powers of the Supreme Court. Alternatively, the Securities Commission would, in appropriate circumstances, turn the matter over to the Attorney General's office for prosecution under section 138 of the Securities Act.

SUMMARY

Settlements are an effective way of dealing with a wide variety of situations that warrant regulatory attention but not necessarily a formal hearing. Experience may modify some of the procedures or approaches described above, but the Securities Commission will continue to encourage the voluntary and more informal resolution of issues through the settlement process. Suggestions as to how this process may be improved are always welcome.

Dated at Vancouver, British Columbia, this 17th day of November, 1989.

Neil de Gelder
Superintendent of Brokers

NIN#89/35

NOTICE

DISCLOSURE OF PROMOTIONAL OR
INVESTOR RELATIONS ARRANGEMENTS

The attached draft notice is being published for industry and public comment. Although it is not the Securities Commission's normal procedure to publish exposure drafts of notices (as opposed to policy statements), we are of the view that given the subject matter of the notice, a comment period would be beneficial.

Comments on the proposed notice should be submitted in writing to the Securities Commission, attention of Adrienne Wanstall, Deputy Superintendent, Policy and Legislation on or before January 31, 1990.

DATED at Vancouver, British Columbia, this 24th day of November, 1989.

Neil de Gelder
Superintendent of Brokers

EXPOSURE DRAFT

NOTICE

DISCLOSURE OF PROMOTIONAL OR
INVESTOR RELATIONS ARRANGEMENTS

One of the most pertinent items of information about an exchange issuer is the arrangements that it or its principals may have made to ensure continued interest in the issuer's securities. Unfortunately, this information is often not made available to investors, either because it is not specifically called for in the prescribed forms for a prospectus or statement of material facts, or because the information is for some reason not considered by management of an exchange issuer to be a material fact or material change triggering disclosure obligations.

The Securities Act requires disclosure of any arrangements or activities designed to enhance after-market support of, or liquidity in, an issuer's securities if the result of such arrangements or activities could reasonably be expected to significantly affect the market price or value of the issuer's securities. If the arrangements are in place at the time of a public offering, they must be disclosed as a material fact in the issuer's prospectus or statement of material facts. If the arrangements are made subsequent to a public offering, or if the arrangements disclosed in a prospectus or statement of material facts change, this would generally be a material change in which case the issuer must file a press release and material change report in accordance with section 67 of the Securities Act.

Given the variety of market support arrangements which may be entered into, it would be unnecessarily restrictive for the Securities Commission to set out a checklist for the type and breadth of disclosure required. Notwithstanding this, some general principles can be stated, particularly in the context of junior issuers listed on the Vancouver Stock Exchange for which these types of arrangements are often significant.

1. Disclosure should be made of any arrangements – written, oral or implicit – that the issuer has with any individual or company to act as a promoter, as an investor relations representative or consultant, or as a market maker for the issuer or its securities. The term 'promoter' is used here in its colloquial sense, and is not restricted to the definition in the Securities Act. The principle set out in this paragraph is not intended to extend to brokers or investment dealers in the province that, at their discretion and with their own funds, make a market in an issuer's securities from time to time, provided that there is no arrangement with the issuer, as contemplated by this notice, pursuant to which such activities are required to be performed.

2. Disclosure should be made of arrangements made by

    (i)   an issuer with any third party, including any director, officer, or employee or other insider of the issuer,

    (ii) a director, promoter or other insider of the issuer, on behalf of or with the concurrence of the issuer, with any third party, or

(iii) a director, promoter or other insider of the issuer on his or its own initiative where the issuer, after having made reasonable enquiries, knows that such arrangements have been made.

3. Disclosure should include a brief description of the background, business and place of business of the person providing the services. It should indicate whether that person has any interest, directly or indirectly, in the issuer or its securities, or whether the person has any right to acquire such an interest, either as full or partial compensation for his services or otherwise.

4. Full particulars of the arrangements for all remuneration, direct or indirect, should be made, including whether any payments will be made in advance of services being provided. If the issuer does not have sufficient funds to pay for the services, it should indicate the anticipated source of funds to meet its obligations in this regard.

5. The nature of the services to be provided should be summarized, including the means by which and the period during which the services will be provided, whether the person providing the services will commit his or its funds to the purchase of the issuer's securities, or whether the person will act as agent for any other persons who will do so.

It is the issuer's responsibility to ensure that any arrangements are consistent in scope with the operations and financial resources of the issuer, and comply with applicable companies and securities legislation and applicable stock exchange policies. It is also the issuer's responsibility to ensure that the arrangements do not create or result in a misleading appearance of trading activity in, or artificial price for, the issuer's securities, for example by requiring or providing incentives for the maintenance of a price or volume for the issuer's securities at a certain level by a certain date, or for a specified period of time. Finally, the issuer should be satisfied that persons with whom arrangements are made are qualified to provide their services. This could include registration under any securities legislation that may be applicable.

DATED at Vancouver, British Columbia, this * day of * , 1990.

Superintendent of Brokers

NIN#89/36

NOTICE

DISCLOSURE OF EXPERIENCE OF DIRECTORS, OFFICERS, PROMOTERS AND CONTROL PERSONS

The experience of the directors, officers, promoters and control persons of an exchange issuer in managing or promoting start-up companies would normally be expected to be an important factor in an investor's decision to purchase the issuer's securities. Furthermore, section 115(2) of the Securities Regulation requires the Superintendent to refuse to issue a receipt for a prospectus or accept a statement of material facts if he considers that because of the past conduct of such persons, the business of the issuer will not be conducted with integrity and in the best interests of the security holders of the issuer.

Most local prospectuses provide little or no information with respect to the track records of the issuer's directors, officers, promoters and control persons in forming and managing the affairs of exchange issuers although the current form or a statement of material facts requires limited disclosure of this information.

In the interests of improved and uniform disclosure in offering documents of important matters relating to the experience of individuals involved in the formation and management of exchange issuers, the Securities Commission will require exchange issuers to disclose the following information in prospectuses, statements of material facts and rights offering documents filed after the date of this notice.

1. If any director, officer or promoter of the issuer is, or within the past five years has been, a director, officer or promoter of any other reporting issuer, the offering document must state the names of such issuers and the periods during which the individual so acted. If the individual has been a director, officer or promoter of more than 12 other reporting issuers during that period, the prospectus must disclose the names of at least 12 of the reporting issuers, starting with current

associations and working back through the most recent associations, and the total list of such associations must be made available at the issuer's records office for inspection upon request.

2. If any director, officer or promoter of the issuer is, or within the past five years has been, a director, officer or promoter of any other reporting issuer that, while he was acting in that capacity,

    (i) was struck off the register of companies by the British Columbia Registrar of Companies or other similar authority, or

    (ii) was the subject of a cease trade or suspension order for a period of more than 30 consecutive days,

the offering document must describe the reasons for the striking from the register or the cease trade or suspension order, and the outcome thereof. For example, the offering document must disclose whether the reporting issuer was dissolved, abandoned, reorganized, sold or restored to good standing and trading status, and must briefly describe the individual's role therein.

3. The offering document must disclose whether any director, officer or promoter of the issuer has, within the last ten years, been the subject of any penalties or sanctions by a court or securities regulatory authority relating to trading in securities, the promotion, formation or management of a publicly traded company or involving theft or fraud. The disclosure should include convictions, cease-trade orders, removal of statutory exemptions, settlement agreements, injunctions, or suspensions of any other applicable rights, privileges or registrations.

4. If the control person of the issuer is not a director, officer or promoter of the issuer, the disclosure required by items 1 through 3 must be provided for the control person. If the control person is a corporation, the disclosure must extend to control persons of the corporation.

DATED at Vancouver, British Columbia, this 15th day of November, 1989.

Neil de Gelder
Superintendent of Brokers

NIN#89/43

NOTICE

LOCAL POLICY STATEMENT 3-07

Local Policy Statement 3-07 entitled "Policy Guidelines Respecting Trading Shares, Performance Shares and Other Consideration" (the "Policy") has been issued today by the Securities Commission, to become effective on March 1, 1990.

A draft of the Policy was published for comment late last year. As a result of the comment letters received in response to that draft, as well as further analysis and discussions with representatives of the securities industry, trust companies, the Vancouver Stock Exchange and with a number of lawyers and accountants, a considerable number of changes have been made to the draft. The most significant change eliminates the proposed separate class of performance shares in favour of a prescribed escrow arrangement.

Once the Policy becomes effective, the existing Local Policy Statements 3-07 to 3-10 will be rescinded. The salient features of these policy statements that the Securities Commission wishes to retain are incorporated into the Policy.

As a result, several other local policy statements (specifically, Local Policy Statements 3-01, 3-02, 3-04, 3-13 and 3-21) now contain inaccurate references to the rescinded local policy statements. As it is anticipated that all of these local policy statements will be revised or rewritten over the course of the coming year, they are not being amended at this time to note the changes that are solely consequential to the implementation of the Policy. Until the updated local policy statements are published, they should be read to refer, with the necessary changes, to the Policy.

Consequential to the implementation of the Policy, the Superintendent of Brokers, by NIN#89/44, is making two changes to waiver provisions in respect of escrow or pooling arrangements. First, the waiver in respect of shares issued for assets under section 55(2)(5) will be rescinded effective March 1, 1990. As a result, the normal twelve month hold period will apply to all shares issued under section 55(2)(5). Second, a blanket waiver will be granted in respect of all trading shares issued under Part 6 of the Policy. As a result, all shares issued before an issuer's initial public offering, other than performance shares, and held by a person other than a control person will become free trading after the issuer becomes an exchange issuer.

During the period before the Policy comes into effect, the Vancouver Stock Exchange will be developing policies, in conjunction with the Securities Commission, for the application of the Policy to major reorganizations, particularly reverse take overs, of VSE-listed issuers.

Once a sound working familiarity with the Policy has developed, the Securities Commission will be requesting comments as to whether, among other things, the performance share provisions applicable to industrial issuers can or should be extended to natural resource issuers.

DATED at Vancouver, British Columbia, this 21st day of December 1989.

Douglas M. Hyndman
Chairman

NIN#90/4

NOTICE

NATIONAL POLICY NO. 39 – MUTUAL FUNDS
DISTRIBUTOR'S REPORT AND AUDITOR'S LETTER

National Policy No. 39, sections 11.08 and 12.04 require the preparation of a compliance report by a mutual fund, or a principal distributor of the mutual fund or a participating dealer of the mutual fund, as the case may be (the "Distributor") and the preparation of a letter from the auditor advising whether the auditor is in agreement with the information given in the compliance report. Questions have arisen as to the form of reporting which will be acceptable to the Canadian Securities Administrators ("CSA") under these requirements.

Attached is a distributor's report and an auditor's letter which will be acceptable to the CSA. Mutual fund distributors and their auditors should particularly note that the distributor's report does not recite all the individual requirements of sections 11 and 12 but rather requires reporting only of exceptions to those sections. When drafting the distributor's report, the CSA considered requiring a long-form report which would have required a specific comment on each requirement in the sections. For the time being, this is not being required; however, the CSA will be monitoring adherence to this policy and may subsequently require the filing of a long-form report.

When preparing the distributor's report and auditor's letter, particular attention should be paid to section 11.01 – Objectives since these objectives relate to requirements in all of sections 11 and 12. The completed report and letter should be sent to the Corporate Finance Department of the British Columbia Securities Commission.

The CSA have agreed that where a mutual fund distributor has reporting obligations to more than one jurisdiction and either the distributor's report has an exception or the auditor's letter is qualified, the mutual fund distributor must bring this matter to the attention of the principal jurisdiction (as would normally be selected when clearing documents as called for by National Policy No. 1). In such circumstances the distributor's report and the auditor's letter should have an additional paragraph specifying the prime jurisdiction selected. Normally, the other jurisdictions will accept the principal jurisdiction's resolution of the matter, although this procedure involves no surrender of jurisdiction by any regulatory authority.

DATED in Vancouver, British Columbia this 9th day of February 1990.

Douglas M. Hyndman
Chairman

Auditor's Letter

Date

To the appropriate securities regulatory authority(ies)

We have examined (name of Distributor)'s report on compliance with the applicable requirements of sections 11 and 12 of National Policy No. 39 during the year ended *, 19*. Our examination was designed in accordance with generally accepted auditing standards to seek reasonable assurance that the report of (name of Distributor) fairly presents its compliance with the applicable requirements of sections 11 and 12 of National Policy No. 39 and, accordingly, included such tests and other procedures as we considered necessary in the circumstances. Absolute assurance is not attainable because of such factors as the need for judgment, the use of testing, the inherent limitations of internal control, and because much of the evidence available to us is persuasive rather than conclusive in nature.

In our opinion, (name of Distributor)'s report on compliance with the applicable requirements of sections 11 and 12 of National Policy No. 39 during the year ended *, 19* is fairly presented in all material respects.

This letter is provided solely for the purpose of assisting the securities regulatory authority(ies) to which it is addressed in discharging its responsibilities and should not be relied upon for any other purpose.

Yours truly,

Chartered Accountants

Distributor's Report

To:　　The appropriate securities regulatory authority(ies)

From:　Name of mutual fund or principal distributor of the mutual fund or participating dealer of the mutual fund, as the case may be (the "Distributor")

Re:　　Compliance Report on National Policy No. 39
　　　　　For the year ended *, 19*

For:　　Name(s) of the mutual funds (the "Funds")

Dear Sirs:

We, (name of Distributor) hereby confirm that we have complied with respect to the applicable requirements of sections 11 and 12 of National Policy No. 39 for the Funds for the year ended *, 19* (except as follows; list exceptions).

Signed on behalf of the Distributor

_____

Signature

_____

Name and office of the person executing this report

_____

Date

NIN#90/7

NOTICE

DUAL EMPLOYMENT OF INDIVIDUALS EMPLOYED BY
FINANCIAL INSTITUTIONS AND SECURITIES REGISTRANTS

By NIN#88/48, the Commission published "Principles of Regulation - Full Service and Discount Brokerage Activities of Securities Dealers in Branches of Related Financial

Institutions" (the "Principles"). The Principles were jointly released by the Canadian Securities Administrators. The Principles state that in certain provinces including British Columbia, a registered individual employed by a dealer related to a financial institution is not permitted to be employed concurrently by the financial institution or to conduct activities on behalf of the financial institution. The Commission has reconsidered the issue and is now prepared to permit dual employment in these circumstances, provided that dually employed individuals meet the requirements for registration under the Securities Act set out in Interim Local Policy Statement 3-22 and provided that dealers related to financial institutions and their dually employed salesmen comply with the requirements of the Principles.

Dated at Vancouver, British Columbia, this 7th day of March 1990.

Douglas M. Hyndman
Chairman

NIN#90/13

NOTICE

RIGHTS OFFERINGS

Recent experience has shown that there are a number of inconsistencies in the legislation, policies and procedures relating to rights offerings being carried out in British Columbia. This Notice:

(a) discusses the rationale underlying the blanket order, BOR#90/3, issued today by the Commission,

(b) outlines a change in the application of Local Policy Statement 3-05 with respect to the use of statements of material facts, and

(c) summarizes some other issues related to rights offerings currently being reviewed by the Commission.

Blanket order - rights offering exemption

The rights offering exemption is contained in sections 31(2)(8) and 55(2)(7) of the Securities Act (the "Act"). It is the registration and prospectus exemption relied upon by an issuer to grant a right to each holder in the Province of a class of its securities to purchase additional securities of its own issue.

The rights offering exemption is limited in scope in that it enables an issuer to distribute rights only to "holders in the Province" of a class of its securities, meaning registered shareholders with a British Columbia address.

BOR#90/3 provides a broader exemption from sections 20 and 42 of the Act that parallels the rights offering exemption but enables an issuer to distribute rights to all holders of a class of its securities. The laws of the jurisdictions in which an issuer's security holders reside will also apply to the distribution of rights in those jurisdictions.

The blanket order establishes resale rules that apply to any trade of rights issued in reliance on the order. Where rights are exercised, an issuer may rely upon sections 31(2)(12)(iii) and 55(2)(11)(iii) of the Act to issue the underlying securities. Sections 133 and 134 of the Securities Regulation establish resale rules that apply to securities issued on the exercise of the rights.

Policy changes - statements of material facts

There is some confusion as to whether the rights offering exemption or the statement of material facts exemption (section 58(1)(c) of the Act) is being relied upon by issuers that file a statement of material facts in connection with the issuance of rights under a rights offering. The rights offering exemption is the only exemption that may be relied upon by those issuers because the distribution of rights is not made "on or through the facilities" of the Vancouver Stock Exchange. As a result, section 58(1)(c) of the Act can not be relied upon by issuers to distribute rights to their shareholders. A statement of material facts filed in connection with a rights offering under section 55(2)(7) of the Act serves only as the disclosure document required under Local Policy Statement 3-05.

Section 2.4 of Local Policy Statement 3-05 requires issuers to carry out a rights offering under a prospectus or statement of material facts in certain circumstances. Effective immediately, the Superintendent will not accept a statement of material facts that qualifies the issuance of rights in the circumstances described in section 2.4 of that Policy. In those circumstances, an issuer will not be permitted to rely on the rights offering exemption and must file a prospectus under section 42 of the Act that complies with applicable policies of the Commission. The Superintendent will not issue a receipt for a prospectus where the issuer does not have an ongoing business or a specific project to be funded by the proceeds.

The Superintendent will no longer permit a statement of material facts to be used as the disclosure document for both the distribution of rights and the resale of shares that are issued to a guarantor under the terms of a guarantee or on the exercise of a bonus warrant. A prospectus can be used to qualify both distributions; otherwise the issuer must file

(a)   a disclosure document in accordance with Local Policy Statement 3-05 to qualify the distribution of the rights, and

(b)   a separate statement of material facts to qualify the sale of the guarantor's securities.

Issues under review

There are a number of issues relating to rights offerings currently under review by the Commission. Areas of concern include:

(a)   whether it is appropriate to permit issuers to place restrictions on which holders of rights may exercise the rights and, if not, what steps need to be taken to provide a framework to enable all shareholders to participate in rights offerings,

(b)   whether it is appropriate to permit the payment of a bonus to a related party of an issuer that guarantees a rights offering,

(c)   whether it is appropriate to require that all beneficial shareholders receive the rights offering disclosure document before making an investment decision,

(d)   whether it is appropriate to require an issuer to employ a registered dealer where it makes a distribution of rights under a prospectus,

(e)   whether the shareholder notification requirements under Local Policy Statement 3-05 are adequate, and

(f)   whether the thresholds set out in section 2.4 of Local Policy Statement 3-05 are appropriate.

CSA paper

A paper concerning rights offerings and the need for a national policy will be presented at the Canadian Securities Administrators meeting to be held in Montreal on May 7-9, 1990.

Interested persons are encouraged to provide written comments concerning any of the matters discussed in this Notice to Adrienne Wanstall, Deputy Superintendent, Policy and Legislation. Comments received by the end of April will be considered in the preparation of the CSA paper.

DATED at Vancouver, British Columbia, this 5th day of April 1990.

Douglas M. Hyndman
Chairman

REF: BOR#90/3

NIN#90/16

NOTICE

PRINCIPLES OF REGULATION RE:
ACTIVITIES OF REGISTRANTS RELATED
TO FINANCIAL INSTITUTIONS

The Canadian Securities Administrators are releasing a third set of Principles of Regulation entitled "Principles of Regulation Re: Activities of Registrants Related to Financial Institutions" (the "Related Issues Principles"). The Related Issues Principles are attached as Appendix "A".

The effective date of the Related Issues Principles is July 1, 1990.

The Related Issues Principles deal with several issues which arise because of ownership by financial institutions of securities registrants, namely selling arrangements between a registrant and its related financial institution, transfer of confidential client information by a registrant to a related financial institution, and settling of securities transactions through a client's account at a related financial institution.

The Related Issues Principles also establish a national clearing system for review of:

(a) networking notices required under the Securities Regulation,

(b) notices required by the Related Issues Principles, and

(c) notices required by two previous Principles of Regulation, one Re: Distribution of Mutual Funds by Financial Institutions dated November 4, 1988 and the second Re: Full Service and Discount Brokerage Activities of Securities Dealers in Branches of Related Financial Institutions dated November 17, 1988.

DATED at Vancouver, British Columbia, this 10th day of May 1990.

Joyce C. Maykut Q.C.
Vice Chairman

APPENDIX A

PRINCIPLES OF REGULATION

*RE: ACTIVITIES OF REGISTRANTS RELATED
TO FINANCIAL INSTITUTIONS*

PREAMBLE

As a result of legislation enacted by several provinces and the federal government, a number of financial institutions ("FIs") have, in the past three years, invested in existing securities dealers or incorporated subsidiary securities dealers or advisers ("FI related registrants").

To deal with certain issues arising from ownership by FIs of FI related registrants, the Canadian Securities Administrators (the "CSA") previously published Principles of Regulation Re: Distribution of Mutual Funds by Financial Institutions dated November 4, 1988 (the "Mutual Fund Principles") and Principles of Regulation Re: Full Service Discount Brokerage Activities of Securities Dealers in Branches of Related Financial Institutions dated November 17, 1988 (the "Full Service Principles"). The CSA has regulatory concerns about some situations which may arise because of the relationship between FI related registrants and their related FIs, which concerns were not addressed in the previous Principles of Regulation. These Principles of Regulation entitled "Activities of Registrants Related to Financial Institutions" ("these Related Issues Principles") are intended to address the outstanding concerns.

The CSA Capital Markets Subcommittee (consisting of representatives from British Columbia, Alberta, Saskatchewan, Manitoba, Ontario, Quebec, New Brunswick and Nova Scotia) has considered the outstanding concerns and worked toward developing appropriate responses which are as uniform as possible. Members of the subcommittee also discussed the issues with representatives of several FIs and FI related registrants, self-regulatory organizations ("SROs"), The Canadian Bankers' Association, The Trust Companies Association of Canada, the Canadian Life and Health Insurance Association Inc., the Canadian Co-Operative Credit Society, provincial FI regulators and the federal Office of the Superintendent of Financial Institutions. The CSA has approved these Related Issues Principles developed by the subcommittee.

These Related Issues Principles outline those areas where a consensus has been reached on the subject issues by the securities administrators of all the provinces and territories (the "Commissions"), unless otherwise indicated. The principles outlined will be implemented by the Commission of each province and territory by such means as might be appropriate.

These Related Issues Principles address the following areas of concern:

Section 1   selling arrangements between FI related registrants and their related FIs;

Section 2   transfer of confidential client information by FI related registrants to their related FIs;

Section 3   settling of transactions through clients' accounts at related FIs; and

Section 4   national clearing system for the review of:

> (a)   networking notices under the Regulations of Nova Scotia, Quebec, Ontario and British Columbia, and Policy 7.1 in Alberta, and
>
> (b)   notices required by the Mutual Fund Principles, the Full Service Principles and these Related Issues Principles to be filed with each Commission.

For the purposes of these Related Issues Principles, a FI means a bank, trust company, loan company, insurance company, treasury branch, credit union or caisse populaire. In the case of Manitoba, these Related Issues Principles will only apply to registrants related to banks and trust companies, pending development of a policy in Manitoba regarding registrants related to other FIs.

For the purposes of these Related Issues Principles, a registrant is related to a FI if it is an affiliate of the FI or if the FI is otherwise a "related party" of the registrant. The FI will be a "related party" of the registrant if:

(a)   the FI influences the registrant;

(b)   the FI is influenced by the registrant;

(c)   both the FI and the registrant influence the same third person or company; or

(d)   both the FI and the registrant are influenced by the same third person or company.

For the purposes of the definition of "related party", influence means, in respect of a person or company, having the power, directly or indirectly, to exercise a controlling influence over the management and policies of the person or company, other than an individual, or the activities of an individual, whether alone or in combination with one or more other persons or companies and whether through the beneficial ownership of voting securities, through one or more other persons or companies or otherwise. For the purposes of the definition of influence in respect of a company or person, other than an individual, any other person or company that, directly or indirectly and whether alone or in combination with one or more other persons or companies, beneficially owns or exercises control or direction over more than 20 per cent of any class or series of voting securities of the company or person, other than an individual, in the absence of evidence to the contrary, shall be deemed to influence the company or person.

FI related registrants will be subject to certain duties and obligations in dealings with their clients. Also, FI related registrants will be registered under the Securities Acts in the provinces or territories in which they operate and will be subject to relevant securities legislation and National, Uniform and Local Policies. In some cases FI related registrants will be members of an SRO and subject to SRO rules. The securities legislation and SRO rules address certain kinds of self-dealing and conflicts of interest which might arise as a result of the relationship between a FI related registrant and its related FI. These Related Issues Principles are not intended to lessen a FI related registrant's obligations under securities legislation or otherwise.

In the course of the subcommittee's deliberations it became apparent that no clear answers exist to some of the regulatory concerns arising from arrangements between FI related registrants and their related FIs which are dealt with in these Related Issues Principles. Accordingly, in areas of uncertainty, the CSA has adopted a generally cautious approach, with a view to revisiting these issues in the future after the public, FIs, FI related registrants and regulators have had more experience regarding these issues. While any particular issue could be reviewed in a shorter time frame, the CSA is of the view that these Related Issues Principles should be reviewed at the end of one year to assess whether they adequately serve legitimate regulatory and business concerns.

The CSA has addressed the regulatory concerns which arise out of the relationship between FI related registrants and their related FIs solely from the perspective of securities regulators. These Related Issues Principles only apply to activities within the jurisdiction of securities regulators. Federal and provincial regulators of FIs may impose requirements on FIs which are related to securities registrants.

These Related Issues Principles will be effective on July 1, 1990.

PRINCIPLES OF REGULATION

1. Selling Arrangements

For the purposes of these Related Issues Principles, a selling arrangement is an arrangement between a FI related registrant and its related FI under which the registrant induces clients or requires clients as a condition of dealing with or purchasing products or services from the registrant to deal with or purchase products or services from the related FI.

The CSA has a concern that in some cases a selling arrangement between a FI related registrant and its related FI may be contrary to the interests of investors. A selling arrangement between a FI related registrant and its related FI will constitute a networking arrangement pursuant to the Regulations under the Securities Acts (the "Regulations") of Nova Scotia, Quebec, Ontario and British Columbia and Policy 7.1 in Alberta, with respect to which the registrant must give prior written notice to the Commission in each of those provinces in which the registrant intends to operate under the arrangement. While Newfoundland, New Brunswick, Prince Edward Island, Manitoba, Saskatchewan, the Yukon and the Northwest Territories do not have the same statutory or policy requirements described above, the Commissions of those provinces and territories will also require that a FI related registrant that intends to operate under a selling arrangement with its related FI must give 30 days prior written notice to the Commission in each of those provinces or territories in which the registrant intends to operate under the arrangement. Each Commission requiring notice will review the selling arrangement to determine whether to object to it. This section of these Related Issues Principles is intended to provide some guidance on the approach that the Commissions will take toward selling arrangements.

The Commissions expect that in responding to the required notices of networking arrangements they will distinguish between selling arrangements which involve inducements and those which impose conditions on clients. The Commissions recognize that a selling arrangement may include both the offering of inducements and the imposition of conditions. Accordingly, the Commissions, in reviewing the arrangement, will look at the substance of the arrangement and how it will operate in practice.

Generally, the Commissions do not expect that they will object to a selling arrangement in which clients of a FI related registrant are offered inducements to deal with or purchase products or services from the related FI. An example would be where a FI related registrant and its related FI agree that if a client purchases securities through the registrant he will be offered reduced rate financing from the related FI.

The CSA is concerned about they type of selling arrangement in which a FI related registrant makes it a condition that a client who wishes to trade a security or purchase a product or service from the registrant must acquire another product or service from its related FI. This is of particular concern in circumstances where competitive products and services are not readily available to the public from other sources or where an investor's freedom of choice is unduly inhibited. An example might be where a client wishes to purchase a particular security in a distribution from a FI related registrant who is the sole underwriter of the security, but as a condition of dealing with the registrant the client must have an account with its related FI. The Commissions will not necessarily object to all selling arrangements in which FI related registrants impose requirements on clients to deal with their related FIs as some such arrangements may not be contrary to the public interest. However, in Quebec, the Commission will object to all selling arrangements in which FI related registrants impose obligations on clients to buy products from their related FIs.

In addressing selling arrangements between FI related registrants and their related FIs, the Commissions will consider similar issues to those they would consider in respect of other networking arrangements. Generally, where the Commissions do not object to a selling arrangement, they will require that the FI related registrant disclose the particulars of the arrangement to clients who are purchasing a product or service under the arrangement, including the relationship between the parties to the arrangement and the benefits which will accrue to each party.

Registrants are reminded that selling arrangements may also be subject to review under the Competition Act (Canada).

2. *Transfer of Confidential Client Information*

For the purposes of these Related Issues Principles, confidential client information includes all facts relating to a client, and any analysis or opinions based thereon, that the FI related registrant is aware of because of its relationship with the client. This includes, but is not limited to, the client's name, address, phone number, income, assets, debts, investment objectives and financing plans.

The CSA has a concern that FI related registrants and their related FIs may enter into arrangements under which confidential client information is passed from registrants to their related FIs in circumstances and for purposes that may be contrary to the interests of investors. In some cases the arrangement will constitute a networking arrangement pursuant to the Regulations of Nova Scotia, Quebec, Ontario and British Columbia and Policy 7.1 in Alberta, with respect to which the FI related registrant must give prior written notice to the Commission in each of those provinces in which the registrant intends to operate under the arrangement. Irrespective of whether the arrangement constitutes a networking arrangement, this section of these Related Issues Principles sets out the procedure all Commissions will require a FI related registrant to follow prior to transferring confidential client information to its related FI. In cases where the arrangement constitutes a networking arrangement, the Commissions in those provinces which require prior notice of the arrangement may impose additional requirements depending on the terms of the arrangement.

Subject to the following paragraph, all Commissions will require that, if a FI related registrant intends to disclose confidential client information to its related FI, the registrant must first obtain the client's informed written consent to do so. The consent form must either be separate document or, in appropriate cases, the consent form may be part of the disclosure document required by section 3 of the Full Service Principles. In obtaining the consent, the FI related registrant must advise the client of:

(a) the fact that the registrant will pass confidential client information to its related FI;

(b) the relationship between the registrant and its related FI;

(c) the nature of the information that will be passed to the related FI;

(d) the use which will be made of the information by the related FI, including whether the related FI will pass the information on to others; and

(e) the effect, if any, that a revocation of consent in the future may have on the client's ability to continue to deal with the registrant.

The Commissions will not require compliance with the rule outlined in the preceding paragraph in certain circumstances and under certain conditions as follows:

(a) The first exception is available where an FI related registrant wants to disclose to its related FI confidential client information relating to an existing client (i.e. a client on the effective date of these Related Issues Principles) where:

    (i) the client has purchased from the FI related registrant securities of a mutual fund sponsored by the related FI or by a corporation controlled by or affiliated with the related FI, and

    (ii) such purchase was made within a branch of the related FI in which the FI related registrant employs persons who are at the same time employees of the related FI.

In these circumstances, if it would be unduly difficult to obtain written consent in accordance with the preceding paragraph, the FI related registrant must give the client written notice within thirty days of the effective date of these Related Issues Principles that confidential client information has been and will be disclosed to the related FI. In giving the client such notice, the FI related registrant must advise the client of the matters referred to in (a) to (d) of the preceding paragraph, as well as the fact that the client may object to the transfer of confidential client information to the related FI and the effect that such an objection will have.

(b) The second exception is where a FI related registrant engaged in full service or discount brokerage activities (the "full service dealer") wants to disclose the name, address and phone number of a client to a specific individual at the related FI so that individual can contact the client to discuss a specific product or service offered by the related FI. For example, a salesman employed by a full service dealer may ask a client whether the client would be interest in discussing a specific product or service offered by the related FI with a specific individual at the related FI and, if so, whether the client would object to his name, address and phone number being given to the individual at the related FI. In these circumstances, if it would be unduly difficult to obtain written consent in accordance with the preceding paragraph, the full service dealer must obtain the client's oral consent and record in writing that consent was obtained. In obtaining the oral consent of the client, the full service dealer must advise the client of the matters referred to in (a) to (d) of the preceding paragraph.

(c) The third exception is where a FI related registrant trades money market instruments on behalf of its related FI and wants to disclose to its related FI confidential client information concerning purchases by an institutional client of money market instruments from the registrant (i.e. the name of the client and the amount purchased) where such information is important to the related FI in respect of its funding operations. In this case, if it would be unduly difficult to obtain written consent in accordance with the preceding paragraph, the registrant must give the client prior written notice of the intention to disclose such confidential client information to its related FI.

(d) The fourth exception is where a FI related registrant wants to disclose confidential client information to its related FI for purely internal audit, statistical or record keeping purposes and such information will not be used by the related FI for any other purpose. In this case, the FI related registrant will not be required to obtain client consent to do so. For example, where under the Mutual Fund Principles a related FI is maintaining the books and records on behalf of its FI related registrant, information may be transferred for that purpose from the FI related registrant to its related FI without the clients' consent.

Subject to the exception hereinafter referred to in this paragraph, a FI related registrant must not make it a condition of a client dealing with the registrant that the client initially consent to the registrant transferring confidential client information to its related FI. A FI related registrant may require that the client initially consent to the FI related registrant transferring confidential client information to the related FI as a condition of dealing with the registrant where the FI related registrant employs persons who are at the same time employees of the related FI.

When confidential client information is being held by the FI related registrant in a central computer or other system to which its related FI might have access, safeguards must be put in place to prevent access by the related FI where the required client consent to transfer information to the related FI has not been obtained.

3. *Settling Securities Transactions Through Client's Account at Related FI*

The CSA has a concern that in some cases an arrangement that a FI related registrant may enter into with its related FI and clients under which the registrant may debit client accounts at its related FI to settle securities transactions may be contrary to the interests of investors. In some cases the arrangement will constitute a networking arrangement pursuant to the Regulations of Nova Scotia, Quebec, Ontario and British Columbia and Policy 7.1 in Alberta, with respect to which the FI related registrant must give prior written notice to the Commission in each of those provinces in which the registrant intends to operate under the arrangement. Irrespective of whether the arrangement constitutes a networking arrangement, this section of these Related Issues Principles sets out the procedure all Commissions will require a FI related registrant to follow prior to debiting a client's account at its related FI. In cases where the arrangement constitutes a networking arrangement, the Commissions in those provinces which require prior notice of the arrangement may impose additional conditions depending on the terms of the arrangement.

If a FI related registrant wishes to settle securities transactions through a client's account at a related FI, the registrant must first obtain the client's informed written authorization to do so. Such prior informed written authorization may be obtained either at the time the client opens a securities account with the FI related registrant or subsequently, provided that:

(a) the client lists the specific account or accounts at the related FI to which the authorization relates;

(b) the FI related registrant ensures that the client is aware of the fact that he is authorizing the registrant to debit certain of his accounts at the related FI to settle securities transactions and the effect of such authorization; and

(c) the FI related registrant does not make it a condition of the client having a securities account with the registrant that the client give authorization to debit more than one of his accounts at the related FI to settle securities transactions.

A FI related registrant that settles clients' securities transactions through client accounts at its related FI must continue to comply with all relevant legislation and SRO By-laws, Regulations and Rules regarding cash accounts and margin accounts.

4. *National Clearing System for Notices of Networking Arrangements and for Other Matters Arising from Principles of Regulation*

Under the Regulations of Nova Scotia, Quebec, Ontario and British Columbia and Policy 7.1 in Alberta, a registrant that intends to enter into a networking arrangement with a FI must give prior written notice to the Commission in each of those provinces in which it intends to operate under the networking arrangement and each such Commission will consider whether or not to object to the arrangement. Under these Related Issues Principles as well as under the Mutual Fund Principles and the Full Service Principles (together the "Three Sets of Principles"), a FI related registrant that intends to carry on specified activities in specified ways must notify the Commission in each jurisdiction in which the registrant proposes to carry on the activities and such Commission will consider whether the activity should be permitted.

In order to facilitate the clearing in more than one Canadian jurisdiction of notices of networking arrangements and other matters arising from the Three Sets of Principles and to provide for more uniformity in approach to such notices, the CSA has agreed upon a procedure which may be followed by a registrant wishing to obtain the non-objection or permission, as the case may be, from the Commissions in more than one jurisdiction.

The procedure is as follows:

(a) The registrant shall file a written notice of networking arrangement or notice of a proposed activity ("Notice") contemporaneously with the Commission in each jurisdiction in which it proposes to operate under the networking arrangement or carry on the subject activity, where such jurisdiction requires the filing of a Notice.

(b) The registrant shall select the principal jurisdiction and shall indicate in the Notice which jurisdiction will be the principal jurisdiction and in which other jurisdictions the networking arrangement or other activity will be carried on (the "other jurisdictions"). It is intended that the principal jurisdiction will be either the one in which the registrant has its principal place of business or the main one in which the registrant will carry on the networking arrangement or other activity. A jurisdiction may decline to act as principal jurisdiction.

(c) The principal jurisdiction will review the Notice and will use its best efforts to provide its comments on the Notice to the other jurisdictions by way of letter, telex, telecopy or telephone within 15 days from receipt of the Notice. If the principal jurisdiction will not be able to provide its comments within the 15 day period it will inform the other jurisdictions of that fact.

(d) The other jurisdictions will review the Notice and will use their best efforts to inform the principal jurisdiction of any additional comments they may have by way of letter, telex, telecopy or telephone within 7 days from the receipt of comments from the principal jurisdiction. If one of the other jurisdictions has no comments on the Notice it will inform the principal jurisdiction of that fact or if one of the other jurisdictions requires more time to consider the Notice it will inform the principal jurisdiction of that fact.

(e) If more information is required from the registrant in order for the Commission to properly assess the Notice, the principal jurisdiction will request such information and the registrant will forward the additional information to the principal jurisdiction and the other jurisdictions.

(f) If the principal jurisdiction and the other jurisdictions all concur on their responses to the Notice, the principal jurisdiction will inform the registrant of that fact by letter and will provide each of the other jurisdictions with a copy of the letter.

(g) If some of the jurisdictions object to the Notice and others do not object, the principal jurisdiction will inform the registrant of that fact by letter, will provide each of the other jurisdictions with a copy of the letter and will advise the registrant to deal directly with the jurisdictions which object in order to resolve the matter with those jurisdictions. The registrant will inform the principal jurisdiction and the other jurisdictions if it intends to make any changes to the networking arrangement or the proposed activity described in the Notice in order to satisfy a jurisdiction which objected to the Notice.

This procedure is for the convenience of registrants. It involves no surrender of jurisdiction by any Commission. Each Commission will retain its discretion in formulating its response to a Notice.

Reference:			
	B.C.	–	Brenda Benham (604) 660-4853
	Alberta	–	Joan MacBeth (403) 422-1083
	Sask.	–	Barbara Shourounis (306) 787-5842
	Manitoba	–	Tom Tapley (204) 945-2548
	Ontario	–	Joan Smart (416) 593-3666
	Quebec	–	Pierre Lize (514) 873-5326
	N.S.	–	Nick Pittas (902) 424-7768
	N.B.	–	Donne Smith (506) 658-3060
	P.E.I.	–	Merrill Wigginton (902) 368-4563
	Nfld.	–	George Kennedy (709) 576-3316
	Yukon	–	Malcolm Florence (403) 667-5225
	N.W.T.	–	Douglas McNiven (403) 873-7490

NIN#90/20

NOTICE

AVAILABILITY OF WEEKLY SUMMARY AND
MATERIAL PUBLISHED UNDER THE SECURITIES ACT

This Notice sets out where copies of the Weekly Summary, Securities Act (the "Act"), Securities Regulation (the "Regulation") and material published under the Act can be obtained.

Weekly Summary

The British Columbia Securities Commission Weekly Summary is a weekly publication containing new and amended notices and interpretation notes ("NINs"); blanket orders ("BORs"); local, uniform act and national policy statements; and legislation and regulations. The Weekly Summary also contains a list of current proceedings before the Commission; notices of hearing; Commission decisions and settlements; orders; the defaulting reporting issuers list; cease trade orders; particulars of new issues and secondary financings; particulars of registrations; particulars of exempt financings; and insider and other acquisition reports. The Weekly Summary is used by issuers and their professional advisors and by the securities industry to stay up to date on current developments in securities regulation. Subscriptions to the Weekly Summary are available from the Information and Records Branch of the Commission. Individual copies can be purchased from the Commission's receptionist on the 11th floor, 865 Hornby Street of the Vancouver Stock Exchange Visitors Centre, 609 Granville Street.

Act, Regulation and Material Published Under the Act

Copies of the Act and Regulation can be obtained from:

Crown Publications	or	Worldwide Books and Maps
546 Yates Street		736A Granville Street
Victoria, B.C.		Vancouver, B.C.
V8W 1K8		V6Z 1G3
(604) 386-4636		(604) 687-3320
Fax: (604) 386-0221		Fax: (604) 687-5925

Complete sets or single copies of NINs; BORs; local, uniform act and national policy statements; and forms (mock-up format only) can be obtained from:

Superior Repro
#200-1112 West Pender Street
Vancouver, B.C.
V6E 2S1
(604) 683-2181
Fax: (604) 683-2539

When ordering single copies, quote the number of the policy, NIN, BOR or form.

Preprinted, type-set registration forms, insider report forms, quarterly report forms and fee checklists are available from the Commission's receptionist on the 11th Floor, 865 Hornby Street.

Complete sets of all material noted above are available in loose-leaf form on a subscription basis from:

Continuing Legal	CCH Canadian Limited
Education Society	Canadian Securities
of British Columbia	Law Reporter
#200-1148 Hornby Street	#2674-1055 Dunsmuir Street
Vancouver, B.C.	Vancouver, B.C.
V6Z 2C3	V7X 1K8
Toll free 1-800-663-0437	
(604) 669-3544	(604) 688-7510
Fax: (604) 669-9260	Fax: (604) 688-0451

DATED at Vancouver, British Columbia, this 7th day of June 1990.

Wade D. Nesmith
Superintendent of Brokers

NIN#90/22

NOTICE

FILING OF SPECIFIED FORMS

Section 158(1) of the Securities Act (the "Act") authorizes the Superintendent of Brokers to specify the form, content and other particulars of a record required to be filed in a required form (the "Required Form") under the Act and the Securities Regulation (the "Regulation").

Certain types of Required Forms (such as Forms 12 to 15, 24, 27, 28, 30 to 35, 41, 43, 50 and 51) provide an outline of their contents. Information may be added to this type of form whether or not such information is specifically referred to in the outline. Where the section of the Regulation respecting such a form or the Required Form itself specifically indicates that inapplicable sections may be deleted, a person completing the Required Form may modify or delete sections of the Required Form. For example, section 90(2) of the Regulation permits a person using a Required Form of prospectus to delete inapplicable items or items answered in the negative. Similarly, Form 30, the Required Form of information circular, indicates that no statement need be made in response to any item that is inapplicable and negative answers to any item may be omitted.

Except as permitted by this notice, other types of Required Forms (such as Forms 4, 5, 7, 11, 20, 20A, 23 and 37) must be completed and filed without additions, deletions or modifications. Where this type of Required Form contains inapplicable sections, lines may be drawn through the inapplicable sections or "N/A" may be inserted next to or beneath the inapplicable sections. Where deletions are made for reasons other than to cross out inapplicable alternatives set out in the Required Form, the reasons for such deletions must be set out in a letter accompanying the Required Form. For example, section 2 of Form 20A, which states that the purchaser is the beneficial owner of the securities, may be deleted where the purchaser is a portfolio manager purchasing for fully managed accounts and this fact is set out in a letter accompanying the Required Form. Information that is not submitted in the Required Form will not be considered to be "filed" under the Act.

DATED at Vancouver, British Columbia, this 14th day of June 1990.

Wade D. Nesmith
Superintendent of Brokers

REF:	NIN#87/10	NIN#89/20
	NIN#88/24	NIN#89/31
	NIN#89/5	NIN#89/45
	NIN#89/6	NIN#90/15

NOTICE

PROPOSALS FOR SECURITIES FIRMS

The Canadian Securities Administrators ("CSA") are seeking comments on a number of proposals respecting the capital, financial reporting and audit requirements to be met by firms registered to operate in the securities industry in Canada ("registrants").

Over the past several years, the Canadian securities industry has undergone significant structural changes and has faced uncertain market conditions. These circumstances have given rise to concerns as to whether the existing capital, audit and financial reporting requirements for registrants are adequate in today's industry and market environment. Client funds have become major sources of financing and trading. Also, firms are able to use client margined securities in their business to the extent necessary to finance the customer receivables arising from buying the securities on margin. Protection of these client funds and securities is paramount.

A review of the existing capital, audit and financial reporting requirements is being conducted by the Regulatory Working Group, which is composed of staff members of the Ontario, Quebec, Alberta and British Columbia Securities Commissions. To date, this review has largely concentrated on those registrants that are members of self-regulatory organizations ("SROs") and has included consideration of changes to the CSA's oversight of the self-regulatory process. A final report ("Capital Report") concerning these issues, which contained 36 recommendations for change, was tabled with the CSA at their Fall 1989 meeting (See NIN#90/05).

In order to consider the issues related to capital adequacy (8 of the 36 recommendations), a joint industry/regulatory task force ("Task Force") has been formed. The Task Force is comprised of the members of the Regulatory Working Group, senior representatives of the securities industry and staff representatives from the SROs and the Canadian Investor Protection Fund ("CIPF"). The Regulatory Working Group is consulting the Task Force in developing specific proposals in the area of capital adequacy and segregation. Prior to amending the existing capital adequacy rules, the specific proposals affecting the public interest will be published for comment.

22 of the 36 recommendations in the Capital Report deal with oversight of the self-regulatory process. The CSA is dealing directly with the SROs and CIPF on these matters and will be drafting legislative provisions to implement these changes.

The regulatory working group is now beginning its review of the capital, audit and financial reporting requirements in respect of non-SRO member registrants, many of which conduct restricted activities in the securities business (e.g. provide advice only). It is anticipated that a discussion document on these issues will be tabled with the CSA this Fall. If this review generates proposals affecting the public interest, these proposals will then be published by the Commissions for public comment once they have been endorsed by the CSA.

The attached paper presents for public comment recommendations in the Capital Report (other than those pertaining to capital adequacy and the oversight of the self-regulatory process) together with the background discussion of the reasons for change. The comments received will be taken into consideration in drafting the specific legislative provisions.

Comments should be forwarded to the CSA on or before September 30, 1990 and addressed to:

> Dan Iggers
> Secretary to the
> Ontario Securities Commission
> Suite 1800, Box 55
> 20 Queen Street West
> Toronto, Ontario

DATED at Vancouver, British Columbia, this 30th day of August 1990.

> Douglas M. Hyndman
> Chairman

Notices

NIN#91/12

NOTICE

ONTARIO SECURITIES COMMISSION POLICY STATEMENT 9.1
DISCLOSURE, VALUATION, REVIEW AND APPROVAL REQUIREMENTS
AND RECOMMENDATIONS FOR INSIDER BIDS, ISSUER BIDS, GOING
PRIVATE TRANSACTIONS AND RELATED PARTY TRANSACTIONS

The Ontario Securities Commission published for comment in the OSC Bulletin of May 25, 1990 a draft Policy Statement 9.1. The British Columbia Securities Commission published with NIN#90/18 dated May 24, 1990, [1990] 20 B.C.S.C. Weekly Summary ch.1, a copy of the draft OSC Policy 9.1, noting that the Commission intends to develop a similar policy and requesting comment on the draft OSC Policy 9.1.

After reviewing the comments received, the OSC has developed the final version of OSC Policy 9.1, which was published in the OSC Bulletin of July 5, 1991.

OSC Policy 9.1 was developed to help ensure that all security holders of an issuer receive complete and accurate information and fair treatment in respect of transactions between the issuer and persons that are related to the issuer. The Policy sets out specific requirements and recommended procedures for insider bids, issuer bids, going private transactions and related party transactions. While the Policy does not suggest that these types of transactions are inherently unfair, the nature of the transactions and the relationships between the parties involved do present opportunities for unequal treatment of minority shareholders. This is the concern addressed by the Policy.

As indicated in our earlier notice, this concern is shared by the Commission. The Commission will not be adopting a policy identical to OSC Policy 9.1, because of concerns as to the appropriateness and effectiveness of that policy in relation to junior issuers. However, the Commission will be developing its own local policy statement with respect to this matter, which should be published for comment by the end of this year.

Until a new local policy statement is in place, Commission staff will continue to deal with related party transactions in accordance with the fundamental principles of fairness underlying OSC Policy 9.1.

DATED at Vancouver, British Columbia, on July 11, 1991.

Douglas M. Hyndman
Chairman

REF: NIN#90/18

NIN#91/17

NOTICE

SECTION 203(3)(B) OF THE COMPANY ACT
CONSENT BY THE SUPERINTENDENT OF BROKERS TO THE WAIVER
OF THE APPOINTMENT OF AN AUDITOR FOR A SUBSIDIARY CORPORATION

Section 203(3)(b) of the Company Act, R.S.B.C. 1979, c. 59 (the "Company Act") authorizes the Superintendent of Brokers (the "Superintendent") to approve in writing the waiver of the appointment of an auditor for a "subsidiary", as defined in section 1(3) of the Company Act.

The Superintendent will generally approve a waiver of the appointment of an auditor for a subsidiary only where the following criteria are met:

1. the subsidiary is not a "reporting issuer", as defined in section 1(1) of the Securities Act, S.B.C. 1985 , c. 83 (the "Act");

2. the subsidiary is wholly-owned by its parent or "holding company", as defined in section 1(5) of the Company Act; and

3. if the parent or holding company is a reporting issuer, it is not in default of any requirement of the Act or the Securities Regulation, B.C. Reg. 270/86.

The waiver will be for a period of one year. If the waiver is not approved by the Superintendent, the subsidary and its parent or holding company may refer to section 203(3)(a) of the Company Act for an alternate form of relief.

No fee will be charged for an application to the Superintendent under section 203(3)(b) of the Company Act.

DATED at Vancouver, British Columbia, on September 25, 1991.

Wade D. Nesmith
Superintendent of Brokers

NIN#91/18

NOTICE

AUDITOR'S REPORT ON
COMPARATIVE FINANCIAL STATEMENTS

This Notice is intended to clarify the requirements of the British Columbia Securities Commission (the "Commission") respecting auditor's reports filed with comparative financial statements, including requirements where there has been a change in auditor during the periods presented in the financial statements.

The Securities Act, S.B.C. 1985, c. 83 (the "Act") and Securities Regulation, B.C. Reg. 270/86 (the "Regulation") impose certain requirements for the filing of financial disclosure purposes. Section 4(4) of the Regulation requires, with certain exceptions, that all financial statements filed under the Act or Regulation include an auditor's report.

Audited Financial Statements Filed in Offering Documents or Under Continuous Disclosure Requirements

The Commission will require that each auditor's report dated after October 31, 1991 - whether included in or incorporated by reference into an offering document or filed pursuant to continuous disclosure requirements - specifically identify all audited financial periods presented that have been reported on by the auditor.

Change in Auditor

Where audited comparative financial statements are to be included in or incorporated by reference into an offering document, and there has been a change in auditor during the periods presented in the financial statements, a separate auditor's report from each auditor must be filed with the financial statements.

Where audited comparative financial statements are filed with the Commission under continuous disclosure requirements, and there has been a change in auditor during the periods presented in the financial statements, the auditor's report on the most recent financial statements should refer to the former auditor's report on the prior, comparative periods. The former auditor's report is not, in this circumstance, required to be refiled with the financial statements.

CICA Handbook

This Notice is intended to be compatible with Ontario Securities Commission "Staff Accounting Communique No. 3" and the October 1990 auditing and related services guideline entitled "Auditor's Report on Comparative Financial Statements" in the Handbook of the Canadian Institute of Chartered Accountants (the "Handbook"). Issuers and their auditors should refer to the Handbook for additional guidance on the appropriate form of the auditor's report.

DATED at Vancouver, British Columbia, on October 2, 1991.

Wade D. Nesmith
Superintendent of Brokers

NIN#91/19

NOTICE

NEW COMPUTER SYSTEM FOR INSIDER REPORTS

The British Columbia Securities Commission recently began using a new computer system to facilitate record keeping and publication in the Weekly Summary of information summarized from insider reports. It is critical for the successful operation of this new system that insiders follow the instructions on the back of the insider report in Form 36 as well as the following guidelines:

1. On each transaction line, insiders must keep a running balance in column D of their securities held.

2. On each transaction line, insiders must include in the sixth column of section C the unit price.

3. Insiders must report their holdings and changes in their holdings of securities first, by class of security and second, by type of ownership (direct or indirect). Within each class of security and type of ownership, insiders must report transactions in chronological order. In particular, insiders must report indirect ownership in chronological order regardless of who is the registered (direct) holder.

To assist insiders in the completion of Forms 36, attached to this Notice is an example of a Form 36 completed in accordance with the guidelines discussed in this Notice.

The failure of insiders to properly complete Forms 36 increases the cost of regulation. Where an insider files a Form 36 that has been improperly completed, the Superintendent of Brokers will return the form to the insider for correction and refiling.

DATED at Vancouver, British Columbia, on October 10, 1991.

Wade D. Nesmith
Superintendent of Brokers

NIN#91/20

NOTICE

COMPARATIVE INTERIM FINANCIAL STATEMENTS

Comparative Figures Required

Section 135(1)(b) of the Securities Regulation, B.C. Reg. 270/86 (the "Regulation") requires that a reporting issuer other than a mutual fund file comparative interim financial statements,

"where the reporting issuer has completed its first financial year, for the periods commencing after the end of its last completed financial year and ending 3, 6 and 9 months after that date and a comparative financial statement to the end of the corresponding periods in the last financial year."

It has been noted in certain circumstances that reporting issuers are failing to prepare their interim financial statements on a comparative basis. In particular, this is occurring in two situations. The first is in the twelve months following a reverse take-over (a "RTO"), as defined under generally accepted accounting principles in Canada, where the acquirer for accounting purposes was not previously a reporting issuer required to file or otherwise prepare interim financial statements. The second is after a change in the ending date of a financial year.

The purpose of this Notice is to clarify, subject to the comments set out below, that interim financial statements required under section 135(1)(b) of the Regulation must be prepared on a comparative basis and that the comparative period must correspond to the interim reporting period in the current financial year.

While this Notice specifically discusses requirements for continuous disclosure filings, the principles set out provide guidance in other circumstances, such as those involving offering documents.

Reporting Issuer Status Continues After RTO

The RTO of a reporting issuer does not change its status or obligations under the Securities Act, S.B.C. 1985, c. 83 and Regulation. Accordingly, regardless of whether the acquirer for accounting purposes was required to prepare interim financial statements prior to the RTO, the reporting issuer continues to be required to prepare and file its post-RTO interim financial statements on a comparative basis. These financial statements must be prepared in accordance with generally accepted accounting principles. As the financial statements for the comparative periods will be those of the acquirer for accounting purposes, this may require that pre-RTO interim financial statements of the acquirer for accounting purposes be prepared.

Acceptable Comparative Periods After RTO or Change in Year End

Section 135(1)(b) of the Regulation requires that comparative interim financial statements be prepared to the end of the corresponding periods in the last financial year. Subsequent to a RTO or change of financial year end, the Commission will accept comparative financial statements from the previous financial year that:

(a)   cover the same number of months as the current financial year's interim financial statements, and

(b)   cover a period that ends eleven, twelve or thirteen months prior to the ending date of the current financial year's interim reporting period.

Exceptions

Exceptions from these requirements will be considered only in connection with an application for an exemption under section 143 of the Regulation.

DATED at Vancouver, British Columbia, on October 31, 1991.

Wade D. Nesmith
Superintendent of Brokers

NIN#91/21

NOTICE

*ACCOUNTING FOR BUSINESS COMBINATIONS AND
CORPORATE REORGANIZATIONS*

I.   *INTRODUCTION*

The Canadian Institute of Chartered Accountants (the "CICA") provides guidance on accounting for business combinations as described in section 1580 of the CICA Handbook (the "Handbook"). The alternatives are the purchase method and the pooling of interests method. These are defined in paragraphs 1580.06 to .09 of the Handbook. The fundamental distinction between the two methods lies in the ability to identify an economic (as opposed to a legal) acquirer. The purchase method is used for all business combinations where an acquirer can be identified, and the pooling of interests method where an acquirer cannot be identified.

A lack of consistency has been noted in the manner in which issuers have been accounting for business combinations, particularly in situations where a reverse takeover (a "RTO") has occurred.

Although it describes a RTO, section 1580 of the Handbook does not offer specific guidance on the accounting for this form of business combination. On January 17, 1990 the CICA's Emerging Issues Committee, after reviewing the problems relating to RTO accounting, issued an abstract (the "Abstract") which addressed a number of RTO accounting issues. Issuers and their advisors should refer to the Abstract for further guidance.

On occasion issuers have accounted for a transfer of net assets or exchange of shares between companies under common control as a business combination. As indicated in paragraph 1580.05 of the Handbook, this type of transaction is excluded from the definition of a business combination for the purpose of section 1580. In such cases, the change is largely one of form and not substance.

This Notice has been drafted after consultation with professional accountants and market participants. It is intended to assist issuers in the preparation of financial statements to be filed with the British Columbia Securities Commission (the "Commission") where a business combination has been or will be accomplished by a RTO, to distinguish the accounting treatment of corporate reorganizations from business combinations, to set out the circumstances where an issuer will be required to revise its financial statements, and to address other related issues.

While this Notice does not specifically address business combinations involving one or more unincorporated businesses, the principles set out provide guidance in such situations.

Notices

II. *RTO ACCOUNTING*

Paragraphs 1580.02 and .03 of the Handbook set out certain types of transactions that are representative of business combinations. Frequently, situations arise where the shareholders of a private business entity will go public by exchanging their shares, or a group of assets that constitute a business, for a controlling interest in the shares of a reporting issuer. This transaction represents a RTO, and is viewed as an alternative to an initial public offering (an "IPO") as a method for a business entity to obtain a listing on a stock exchange.

The Abstract sets out definitive rules on the accounting for RTOs. In essence, the purchase method of accounting is applied, but from the perspective of the legal subsidiary, as this term is defined in the Abstract, being the acquirer.

In a RTO, the fair value (the "F/V") of the shares issued by the legal subsidiary is conceptually the best determinant of the cost of the purchase. In most RTOs, however, this method is neither practical nor reliable since there is no existing market for the legal subsidiary's shares. Accordingly, the cost of the purchase should be determined by reference to the F/V of the shares acquired from the legal parent, as this term is defined in the Abstract, or, failing that, the F/V of the net assets acquired from the legal parent. This approach is recommended on page 10.4 of the Abstract where it states:

> "In some cases, the legal parent will be a dormant company or there will be a thin or inactive market for its shares. In these instances, the fair value of the net assets of the legal parent should be used to determine the cost of the purchase if the quoted market price of the shares of the legal parent (as adjusted, where appropriate) is not indicative of the fair value of the shares of the legal parent. CICA 1580.28 provides some guidance on this calculation".

This Notice expands on the Abstract in order to address:

(a)   the determination of the cost of acquiring the legal parent when the F/V of the shares of the legal subsidiary cannot be determined and the F/V of the legal parent's shares or net assets cannot be readily determined, and

(b)   the accounting for the transaction when the legal parent has a net asset deficiency.

1. *Determining the Acquisition Cost – F/V of Legal Parent Not Determinable*

In situations where the F/V of the legal parent's shares or net assets cannot be determined in an expeditious and economical manner, the net book value (the "NBV") of the legal parent, after any necessary adjustments (for example, to put the accounting practices previously followed by the legal parent on a common basis with those of the legal subsidiary), will be acceptable as the most appropriate measure of the F/V of the legal parent's net assets acquired.

2. *Accounting for a Net Asset Deficiency in Legal Parent – Capital Transaction*

There may be situations where the F/V of the legal parent's liabilities exceeds its assets. This deficiency effectively represents the cost of obtaining a listing on a stock exchange. The deficiency has frequently been capitalized in the consolidated financial statements as goodwill. Where an inactive listed company with negative NBV is party to a RTO, it would be misleading to create an asset for accounting purposes. Therefore, any purchase price deficiency associated with a RTO must be recorded as a capital transaction concurrently with the completion of the business combination. See section 3610 of the Handbook for further guidance.

3. *Prior Operations – Supplemental Information*

Where financial statements are filed as part of a public offering of securities, supplemental information regarding the legal parent's prior financial operations must be incorporated into the notes of the issuer's financial statements that form part of, or are incorporated by reference into, the offering document. The supplemental information must cover the legal parent's most recently completed financial year and any subsequent period to the date of the RTO.

Where the financial statements are filed pursuant to continuous disclosure requirements, supplemental information regarding the legal parent's prior financial operations must be incorporated into the notes of the issuer's next annual audited consolidated financial statements that are filed with the Commission and delivered to the issuer's security holders. The supplemental information must cover the period from the legal parent's most recently completed financial year end to the date of the RTO.

Whether filed with a public offering of securities or as part of the annual financial statements, the supplemental information must form part of the audited financial statements.

An exchange issuer will also be required to incorporate this supplemental information into the Quarterly Reports (Form 61) filed with the Commission subsequent to the transaction but prior to the issuer's next financial year end. When filed with a Quarterly Report that includes interim financial statements, the supplemental information is not required to be audited.

For exchange issuers, the supplemental information regarding the legal parent's prior financial operations must include a statement of income or deficit, a schedule of deferred costs, if any, and a statement of changes in financial position. As an alternative, an exchange issuer may file with the Commission a separate set of audited financial statements of the legal parent for the period from the date of the most recent audited financial statements filed with the Commission to the date of the RTO.

III. *CORPORATE REORGANIZATION DISTINGUISHED FROM BUSINESS COMBINATION*

Issuers should recognize that an exchange of shares or assets between issuers under common control is a form of corporate reorganization rather than a business combination. Reorganizations are specifically excluded from the Handbook section relating to business combinations. See paragraph 1580.05 of the Handbook.

While the Handbook is silent on how to account for such reorganizations, where a corporate reorganization has occurred principles similar to the pooling of interests method should be applied to the transaction. Specifically, net assets of both entities should be combined at their previously recorded values. No appraisal increases or goodwill are to be recognized as a result of the reorganization.

IV. *REVISED FINANCIAL STATEMENTS – CONTINUOUS DISCLOSURE*

Part 1 of the Securities Regulation, B.C. Reg. 270/86 (the "Regulation") requires that financial statements be prepared in accordance with generally accepted accounting principles.

Part 10 of the Regulation imposes continuous disclosure requirements on a reporting issuer, including a requirement to file interim and annual financial statements with the Commission and to deliver them to its security holders.

It is essential that financial statements filed with the Commission fairly present an issuer's financial position, results of operations and changes in financial position. Where an issuer's previously issued financial statements have not accounted for a business combination or a corporate reorganization in accordance with the Handbook, the Abstract and this Notice, and the difference is material, the issuer must correct this error in its next interim or annual financial statements filed with the Commission and delivered to its security holders.

Where an error in accounting treatment materially affects its financial position, an issuer should consider whether its previously issued financial statements complied with generally accepted accounting principles at the time the statements were prepared. If they did not, the issuer should consider the need to, and it may be required to, retract them with appropriate amendments. See paragraphs 1506.26 to 30 and 5405.12 to 18 of the Handbook for guidance in situations where there has been a subsequent discovery of an error.

Where corrections to financial statements constitute a material change in the affairs of the issuer, the issuer must file a material change report and issue a news release under section 67 of the Securities Act, S.B.C. 1985, c. 83 detailing the corrections, including their financial impact.

V. *OTHER RELATED ISSUES*

1. *Valuing Consideration – Business Combination Other Than RTO*

The purchase method is appropriate for all business combinations where an acquirer can be identified. Accordingly, there may be situations, other than a RTO when the purchase method of accounting is applied, and where:

Notices

(a)　　the F/V of the consideration given by the acquirer cannot be determined, for example, because the shares are escrowed shares or thinly traded, and

(b)　　the F/V of the net assets acquired cannot be determined, for example, where the acquiree is an issuer other than a reporting issuer in the start-up stage of its development.

In these situations, the acquiree's NBV, after any necessary adjustments, will be acceptable as the most appropriate measure of the F/V of the net assets acquired. A cost of the purchase that is greater than the NBV of the net assets acquired will be acceptable only where an acceptable valuation opinion, as defined in Local Policy Statement 3-07, has been prepared.

Issuers should recognize that the deemed price per share permitted by regulators in connection with the approval of a transaction is not necessarily an appropriate measure of F/V for accounting purposes.

2.　*Changes in Year-End*

Where a reporting issuer is party to a business combination or a corporate reorganization, continuous disclosure requirements remain unchanged. Pursuant to section 136(3) of the Regulation, where a change in the ending date of a financial year is anticipated, issuers must provide the Superintendent of Brokers with a notice of the change, and the reasons for the change, on or before the earlier of:

(a)　　the new date elected for the financial year end, or

(b)　　360 days from the end of the latest financial year in respect of which the issuer was required to file annual audited financial statements.

This notice should be addressed to the Deputy Superintendent, Registration and Statutory Filings, and should indicate the date of:

(a)　　the last year end prior to the change in year end,

(b)　　the first new year end subsequent to the change of year end, and

(c)　　the issuer's anticipated interim and annual financial reporting periods, including comparative reporting periods, to be included in filings made in accordance with sections 135 and 136 of the Regulation for the two calendar years subsequent to the change.

3.　*Note Disclosure*

It has been noted, in a number of cases, that the disclosure contained in the notes to financial statements subsequent to a business combination or corporate reorganization is inadequate. In particular, the notes do not contain the disclosure required by paragraphs 1580.79 and 1580.81 of the Handbook.

In addition to complying with the Handbook's disclosure requirements, in financial statements prepared in connection with an IPO or by an exchange issuer the issuer will be required to provide a breakdown of net assets acquired by major category.

VI.　*EXCEPTIONS*

There may be situations where issuers consider the requirements set out in this Notice to be inappropriate. In these cases an issuer should discuss the proposed accounting treatment with staff at the Commission prior to the financial statements being finalized.

DATED at Vancouver, British Columbia, on November 1, 1991.

Wade D. Nesmith
Superintendent of Brokers

NIN#91/22

NOTICE

*GUIDE FOR USE OF THE MULTIJURISDICTIONAL
DISCLOSURE SYSTEM BY CANADIAN ISSUERS IN THE U.S. MARKET*

The British Columbia Securities Commission is today publishing a guide entitled "Use of the Multijurisdictional Disclosure System by Canadian Issuers in the U.S. Market" (the "Guide"). The Guide provides an overall summary of the use of the U.S.

multijurisdictional disclosure system by Canadian issuers and discusses the requirements of state securities laws.

By NIN#91/11 (the "Notice"), which introduced National Policy Statement No. 45 - Multijurisdictional Disclosure System, the Commission gave notice that it would publish this Guide once the Canadian Securities Administrators made it available.

As set out in the Notice, the provisions of the Release relating to continuous disclosure documents, proxy solicitation and insider reporting requirements apply to all Canadian foreign private issuers, including those listed on the Vancouver Stock Exchange, whether or not those issuers are otherwise entitled to use the MJDS. The provisions of the Release relating to rights offerings and securities exchange take over bids apply to issuers listed on The Toronto Stock Exchange, the Montreal Exchange and the senior board of the Vancouver Stock Exchange. The Commission believes that the Guide will assist issuers in determining how the MJDS will be of greatest benefit to them.

DATED at Vancouver, British Columbia, on November 13, 1991.

Douglas M. Hyndman
Chairman

NIN#91/23

NOTICE

INTRODUCTION OF INTERIM LOCAL POLICY
STATEMENT 3-43 – GOVERNMENT STRIP BONDS

The British Columbia Securities Commission has revoked, effective immediately, Local Policy Statement 3-43 dated February 1, 1987 (the "Former Policy") and Blanket Order #87/17 (the "Former Order"). The Commission is releasing, with this Notice, Interim Local Policy Statement 3-43 (the "Interim Policy") and Blanket Order #91/12 (the "Current Order"), which are effective immediately.

The Commission has adopted the Interim Policy to reflect current legislative and policy requirements in British Columbia. Several changes have been made to make the Interim Policy more uniform than the Former Policy with Ontario Securities Commission Policy No. 1.6 - Strip Bonds. The new form of Information Statement, prepared by the Investment Dealers Association of Canada (the "IDA") and attached as Appendix A to the Interim Policy, is an approved form of information statement for the purposes of the Interim Policy, where the government strip bonds being distributed or traded do not differ in any material way from those described in the Information Statement in Appendix A. The Interim Policy contains certain transitional provisions.

The Current Order, like the Former Order, contains registration and prospectus exemptions for trading and distribution of Government Strip Bonds. The Commission proposes to remove the registration exemption and thereby limit the trading of government bonds to persons registered in an appropriate registration category under the Securities Act. While the Commission does not know who is using the registration exemption available for the sale of government strip bonds, the Commission is of the view that government strip bonds, like other strip bonds, are sufficiently complex that only persons who are subject to the educational, suitability and other requirements imposed on registrants should be permitted to trade government strip bonds. Because this proposal would change the current practice, the Commission will not make this change before March 1, 1992.

Interested persons are encouraged to direct written comments to the Commission, attention Adrienne Wanstall, Executive Director, Policy and Legislation, on or before March 1, 1992.

DATED at Vancouver, British Columbia, on December 12, 1991.

REF: LPS#3-43
       BOR#87/17
       BOR#91/12
       BOR#91/13

Douglas M. Hyndman
Chairman

Notices

NIN#92/2

NOTICE

COMMUNICATION WITH THE SECURITIES COMMISSION

This Notice describes the functions of the British Columbia Securities Commission and suggests how to ensure that your filings with and enquiries to the Commission are handled promptly. This Notice replaces NIN#89/11.

ORGANIZATION

The Commission is responsible for the regulation of trading in securities and commodity contracts (also known as "exchange contracts") in British Columbia. As a result of a recent review and reclassification of staff positions, there have been several changes in positions and titles of Commission staff. An organization chart is attached.

Commission

The Commission consists of up to nine members, including the Chairman and Vice Chairman. The Chairman is the chief executive officer. The members of the Commission are responsible for the administration of the Securities Act and the Commodity Contract Act and the regulations made under these Acts.

The purpose of the legislation is to regulate trading in securities and exchange contracts. The members are responsible for establishing policy within the framework of the legislation and making decisions under specific legislative provisions. The basic test governing the members in the exercise of their discretion is the public interest. Decisions made by the members include granting exemptions from compliance with the legislation and making orders intended to enforce the legislation. The members may delegate the power to make decisions to individual members or, in some cases, to Commission staff. Panels of members participate in quasi-judicial hearings on matters, usually related to enforcement, brought forward by Commission staff. The members also conduct hearings and reviews, on the application of persons directly affected, of decisions made by individual members, by Commission staff, by the Vancouver Stock Exchange and by the Pacific District of the Investment Dealers Association of Canada.

The Secretary and the General Counsel provide support for the members of the Commission. The Secretary is responsible for administrative matters relating to the members fulfilling their responsibilities, including attending hearings and meetings of members. The General Counsel provides legal advice to the members and provides advice to the Policy and Legislation and Exemptions and Orders Divisions.

Commission Staff

The Superintendent of Brokers is the chief administrative officer of the Commission and is responsible for the day to day administration of the securities and exchange contract legislation. The Commission staff, headed by the Superintendent, consists of six divisions.

Compliance and Enforcement

The Compliance and Enforcement Division monitors industry and market activity to ensure compliance with the securities and exchange contract legislation and policy, conducts investigations regarding perceived or alleged contraventions of the legislation and policy, prepares matters for hearings before the Commission, and cooperates with Crown counsel in the prosecution of matters in Provincial Court and with regulators in other jurisdictions in mutual enforcement efforts.

Corporate Finance

The Corporate Finance Division processes prospectuses, rights offering circulars, statements of material facts, applications for reactivation of dead and dormant issuers and applications to extend lapse dates of prospectuses. The Division also conducts post-offering reviews of the activities of issuers.

Corporate Planning and Management Services

The Corporate Planning and Management Services Division is responsible for the internal operations of the Commission, including financial management, personnel services, computer systems and administrative services.

The Public Information and Records Branch of the Division maintains files and ensures public access to appropriate records. This Branch is responsible for preparing and publishing the Commission Weekly Summary, which is the document of record under the legislation. The Weekly Summary is used to disseminate policy statements, notices, interpretation notes, legislation, orders, decisions, and statistical reports.

Exemptions and Orders

The Exemptions and Orders Division analyses certain applications and exercises delegated powers to grant or deny exemptions from certain requirements of the securities and exchange contracts legislation and from certain provisions of the Company Act. It also processes Forms 20 respecting exempt distributions of securities.

Policy and Legislation

The Policy and Legislation Division develops and recommends amendments to securities and exchange contract legislation and develops policy statements, blanket orders, notices and interpretation notes to assist market participants in complying with the legislation.

Registration and Statutory Filings

The Registration and Statutory Filings Division is divided into three branches: Registration, Statutory Filings and Insider Reporting. The Registration Branch processes applications for registration under the securities and exchange contract legislation, and monitors compliance of registrants with the requirements of the legislation and policy. The Statutory Filings Branch processes all statutory filings of reporting issuers, issues cease trade orders under section 146 of the Securities Act and issues certificates that an issuer is a reporting issuer and not in default of any requirements of the Securities Act or Securities Regulation as provided in section 60 of the Securities Act. The Insider Reporting Branch processes all insider trading reports.

TELEPHONE ENQUIRIES

The Commission receives between 200 and 400 telephone enquiries each day to the main switchboard number alone. To ensure prompt service, you should direct telephone calls to the appropriate Commission staff. The description of responsibilities contained in this Notice, together with the attached organization chart and the telephone directory published in the Weekly Summary, should assist you in identifying the appropriate person. General inquiries may be directed to the Information Distribution Officer, who will attempt to answer your question or identify the appropriate Commission staff member to do so.

CORRESPONDENCE

The Commission receives an average of 700 pieces of mail each day. You should send all deliveries and mail to the Commission on the 11th floor, 865 Hornby Street, Vancouver, British Columbia, V6Z 2H4.

You should accompany all documents that are filed with the Commission to comply with specific filing requirements under the securities and exchange contract legislation with a covering letter identifying the Division, Branch and/or individual intended to receive the documents, fully describing the purpose of the filing, and identifying the section of the legislation under which it is filed.

"Follow-up material" are documents sent to the Commission on a specific matter concerning which there has been previous communication with the Commission. You will cause delays in processing correspondence if you use the follow-up procedure for originating communication or filings.

When you send follow-up material to the Commission, you should put the following wording on the envelope and first page of the covering letter:

FOLLOW UP MATERIAL

ATTENTION: _____
            (name of staff member)

FILED ON BEHALF OF: _____
                     (name of issuer, dealer, etc)

If you intend that the Chairman or Superintendent personally review correspondence, you should indicate this on the envelope and letter.

If you provide documents to the Commission for information only, you should clearly indicate on the face of the letter and all attachments that the copy is being filed for information purposes only and not pursuant to a statutory filing requirement. The Commission recommends the use of a stamp, such as: "FILED FOR INFORMATION PURPOSES ONLY". Staff will automatically place documents filed in this manner in the public file unless you have made an application for confidentiality.

CONFIDENTIALITY

Section 151 of the Securities Act provides that material filed with the Commission under the Act may be held in confidence only if, in the opinion of the Commission, the material discloses intimate financial, personal or other information, and the desirability of avoiding disclosure of the information outweighs the desirability of adhering to the principle of public disclosure. Therefore, if you wish information that you have filed with the Commission to be held in confidence, you must apply to the Division that reviews the information and give reasons why you are seeking confidentiality.

In addition to the general provision regarding confidentiality found in section 151 of the Securities Act, section 67(2) and (3) of the Securities Act provides for circumstances where a material change report may be kept confidential. Material change reports that are filed under section 67(2) of the Securities Act should be marked "confidential". Confidential material change reports and follow-up material should be addressed to the Secretary and enclosed in an envelope marked "Confidential - section 67 of the Act".

As a matter of practice, certain sensitive documents or information including certain registration information, are not made public. However, all Commission and Superintendent's orders, except those relating to investigations or frozen assets, are published in the Weekly Summary.

Under the Commodity Contract Act, the Commission will keep material filed with the Commission confidential unless disclosure would be required in the public interest. An exception to this practice is made with respect to certain orders concerning registration matters.

EXEMPTION APPLICATIONS

For information on how to prepare an application for an exemption order, you should refer to the Commission's published guidelines.

NOTICES OF REVIEW

The Commission has jurisdiction under securities and exchange contract legislation to review decisions made under the legislation by individual members of the Commission, Commission staff, the Vancouver Stock Exchange and the Pacific District of the Investment Dealers Association of Canada.

You may commence a proceeding before the Commission by filing a Notice of Review. The Notice should be sent to the Secretary of the Commission. For information on how to prepare a Notice of Review, you should refer to the Commission's published guidelines.

FEE CHECKLIST

Please use a fee checklist when filing documents with the Commission for which a fee is prescribed. The checklists, one for each of the Securities Act and the Commodity Contract Act, set out the fees prescribed in the regulations and assist in calculating the fees required.

REQUESTS FOR FORMS

Requests for Forms under the securities and exchange contracts legislation and the fee checklists, are handled through the Commission's receptionist on the 11th Floor.

DATED at Vancouver, British Columbia, on February 6, 1992.

Douglas M. Hyndman
Chairman

NOTICE

WAIVERS CONSEQUENTIAL TO LOCAL POLICY STATEMENT 3-07

Local Policy Statement 3-07, entitled "Policy Guidelines Respecting Trading Shares, Performance Shares and Other Consideration" (the "Policy"), came into effect on March 1, 1990.

NIN#89/44, entitled "Waivers Consequential to Local Policy Statement 3-07", was issued on December 21, 1989 and dealt with two issues concerning waivers which arose from the implementation of the Policy. This Notice, which replaces NIN#89/44, clarifies the position of the Superintendent with respect to those issues.

The Superintendent confirms the rescission, effective March 1, 1990, of NIN#88/23, entitled "Waiver of Requirement to Enter into an Escrow Agreement or Pooling Agreement in Respect of Securities Issued by an Exchange Issuer under Section 55(2)(5) of the Securities Act". As a result of the rescission of NIN#88/23, and the Superintendent's decision not to specify a form of escrow agreement or pooling agreement in respect of a distribution under section 55(2)(5) of the Securities Act, S.B.C. 1985, c. 83 (the "Act"), securities issued by an exchange issuer under section 55(2)(5) are subject to a 12 month hold period, pursuant to section 134(2)(b)(i) and (3)(e)(iii) of the Securities Regulation, B.C. Reg. 270/86 (the "Regulation").

The Superintendent also confirms the waiver, effective March 1, 1990, of the requirement under section 134(6)(b)(i) of the Regulation to enter into an escrow agreement or pooling agreement in respect of trading shares issued in accordance with Part 6 of the Policy. As a result of this waiver, trading shares that are issued pursuant to Part 6 of the Policy by an issuer that subsequently becomes an exchange issuer and that are held by a person that is not a control person satisfy the resale rules in section 134(6)(b)(i) of the Regulation and therefore become free trading on the date the issuer becomes an exchange issuer.

While the wording of NIN#89/44 may have been ambiguous on this point, the March 1, 1990 waiver does not, and was never intended to, waive the requirement under section 134(2)(b)(i) or (3)(e)(iii) of the Regulation to enter into an escrow agreement or pooling agreement in the required form in respect of securities issued by an exchange issuer under section 55(2)(5) of the Act after the issuer became an exchange issuer.

DATED at Vancouver, British Columbia, on February 12, 1992.

Wade D. Nesmith
Superintendent of Brokers

NOTICE

DRAFT NATIONAL POLICY STATEMENT NO. 46
INDEX AND COMMODITY WARRANTS AND OTHER DERIVATIVE SECURITIES

The Canadian Securities Administrators (the "CSA") are releasing for comment Draft National Policy Statement No. 46 – Index and Commodity Warrants (the "Draft Policy").

Each jurisdiction will issue whatever blanket rulings or orders are necessary to give effect to the final form of this policy.

The CSA recognize that the introduction of derivative securities, including Warrants (as defined), to the Canadian retail marketplace has provided investors with opportunities that were not previously available to satisfy certain investment and hedging objectives. However, many prospectus, continuous disclosure, trading and sales requirements of securities legislation in Canada do not adequately address the novel regulatory issues raised by public offerings of Warrants.

To address these deficiencies, the Draft Policy prescribes prospectus, continuous disclosure, trading and sales requirements that are based on the unique attributes of Warrants and speculative investment nature of certain Warrants. The Draft Policy also provides that (i) the issuer of Warrants must meet or exceed net asset and working capital thresholds and satisfy hedging requirements; (ii) novel underlying interests must satisfy certain criteria and (iii) certain calculations, valuations and determinations relating to Warrants must be made by an independent and qualified entity.

Notices

Scope of the Draft Policy

The provisions of the Draft Policy apply to distributions of Warrants by prospectus and, in the case of Warrants offered by the government of Canada or a province or territory of Canada, distributions by offering circular.

In the Draft Policy, Warrants are defined as: (i) certain put or call options the value of which is based upon the market price, value or level of one of more underlying interest and (ii) debt-like securities (as defined), which include as a substantial component either an obligation to pay to the holder a contingent amount based on the market price, value or level of one or more underlying interests or a right to convert or exchange the security for the underlying interest or to purchase the underlying interest.

The Draft Policy does not apply to: (i) rights, warrants, options or other securities exercisable or exchangeable for, or convertible into, securities issued by the issuer of the Warrant or by its affiliates or (ii) options issued by a clearing corporation.

Issuer

The issuance of Warrants may create a theoretically unlimited contingent liability for the issuer. Even where an issuer is hedged, the hedge may not be effective for credit or other reasons and/or hedge proceeds may not be for the sole benefit of Warrant-holders. Under these unique circumstances, the CSA does not believe it is in the public interest for issuers without significant liquid capital to issue Warrants. Accordingly, the Draft Policy requires that an issuer or, if applicable, guarantor of Warrants has minimum net assets of $10 million, maintains minimum working capital of $10 million and hedges the Warrant offering to the extent necessary to be able to satisfy its obligations. The net asset and working capital thresholds are not intended to ensure that an issuer will be able to satisfy all of its obligations under the Warrants but simply to ensure that the issuer is of substance having regard to the nature of Warrant offerings.

Underlying Interest

When exchanges propose to list a new clearing corporation future or option, they are required to obtain approval of the underlying interest from the securities regulatory authorities. This is to ensure that the underlying interest is visible and liquid, and that market price is easily and objectively determinable. In the view of the CSA, the underlying interest of Warrants should meet similar criteria. Accordingly, the Draft Policy establishes criteria for underlying interests.

Terms, Conditions and Mechanics

The Draft Policy sets out a number of requirements pertaining to the terms, conditions and mechanics of Warrants, including requirements regarding adjustments to underlying interests, physical settlement, minimum exercise, delay between exercise and valuation, early termination, automatic exercise at maturity and the required form of Warrants.

Liquidity

The Draft Policy requires that Warrants be listed unless pre-approved alternative arrangements have been made to ensure sufficient market liquidity.

Trading and Sales Requirements

Because Warrants closely resemble clearing corporation options, the Draft Policy adopts many of the requirements applicable to clearing corporation options, including

(a)   all retail purchases of Warrants must have an account to trade in Recognized Market Options;

(b)   persons trading in and/or rendering advice with respect to Warrants must have successfully completed the Canadian Options Course or an alternative education program acceptable to the CSA; and

(c)   Warrants, other than debt-like securities, may not be purchased on margin.

Prospectus Disclosure

The Standard Prospectus Form (as defined) is not appropriate for Warrant offerings as it does not provide any guidance with respect to disclosure relating to underlying interests or the terms, conditions and mechanics of Warrants. Accordingly, for offerings of Warrants, other than debt-like securities, the Standard Prospectus Form is being replaced by the Appendix to the Draft Policy which sets out prospectus disclosure requirements for Warrant offerings. For offerings of Warrants that are debt-like securities, the Appendix to the Draft Policy applies to the component linked to the underlying interest and the Standard Prospectus Form is applicable to the debt-like component of the Warrant.

Expedited and Confidential Review Procedures and Post Receipt Pricing Procedures

The Draft Policy establishes expedited prospectus review procedures for offerings that meet certain eligibility requirements. It is the intention of the CSA that the greater consistency in preliminary prospectus disclosure that should result from issuers complying with the Appendix to the policy, together with expedited prospectus review procedures under certain circumstances, will shorten the prospectus review process and thereby address the market timing sensitivity of Warrant offerings.

As well, in recognition of the unique characteristics and the proprietary nature of Warrants, the Draft Policy establishes confidential prospectus review procedures under which the prospectus remains confidential until the comments of the securities regulatory authorities are resolved.

Procedures are also set out for pricing offerings after the issuance of a prospectus receipt.

Continuous Disclosure

The Draft Policy changes certain continuous disclosure requirements for issuers and guarantors of Warrants. The Draft Policy also provides for continuous disclosure of changes relating to the underlying interest or to the Warrants.

Other Derivatives

Subdivided equity securities, corporate strip bonds and certain other debt-like securities ("Other Derivatives") are similar to Warrants in certain respects. The CSA believe it would be helpful to set out fundamental principles applicable to offerings of Other Derivatives because securities legislation in Canada does not adequately address certain regulatory issues raised by these offerings. The CSA are in the process of completing draft policy provisions applicable to offerings of Other Derivatives and expect to publish these provisions for comment in the near future.

Request for Comments

The CSA are requesting comments on the Draft Policy and, in particular: (i) the appropriate length of a transition period to allow those registrants trading in, or rendering advice with respect to, Warrants time to meet the proficiency requirements set out in the Draft Policy; (ii) the Extraordinary Event provisions pertaining to permitted Extraordinary Events, confirmation of the occurrence of Extraordinary Events and the amount to be paid to Warrantholders on termination; (iii) the utility to issuers and underwriters of the confidential review procedure and whether any party's rights could be adversely affected by these procedures; and (iv) the disclosure requirements that must or may be made where the issuer of a Warrant has not had an opportunity to independently verify the accuracy and completeness of the information pertaining to the issuer of the underlying interest.

The Draft Policy does not specifically provide that if the obligations of the issuer are guaranteed, the prospectus contain financial statements of the guarantor as if it were the issuer. However, it is the present intention of the CSA to include this specific requirement in the final form of the policy. If the guarantor is eligible to use the POP System, it is intended that this requirement may be satisfied by incorporating by reference into the prospectus the appropriate documents. Concerns have been advanced that this requirement has the effect of unduly restricting the ability of an issuer to obtain a guarantee. Persons who share this concern should comment on why this requirement is particularly inappropriate for offerings of Warrants.

Written comments on the Draft Policy are invited. Seven copies of the comments should be delivered to the CSA on or before May 29, 1992 at the following address:

Canadian Securities Administrators
Corporate Finance Committee
c/o Secretary, Ontario Securities Commission
8th Floor
20 Queen Street West
Toronto, Ontario
M5H 3S8

Notices

Comment letters submitted in response to Requests for Comments are placed in the public file and form part of the public record in certain jurisdictions unless confidentiality is requested. Comment letters will be circulated among securities regulatory authorities for purposes of finalizing the Draft Policy whether or not confidentiality is requested. Accordingly, although comment letters requesting confidentiality will not be placed in the public file, freedom of information legislation may require the securities regulatory authorities in certain jurisdictions to make comment letters available. Persons submitting comment letters should therefore be aware that the press and members of the public may be able to obtain access to any comment letter.

DATED at Vancouver, British Columbia, on March 5, 1992.

> Douglas M. Hyndman
> Chairman

NIN#92/8

NOTICE

ONTARIO SECURITIES COMMISSION POLICY NO. 4.8
NON-RESIDENT ADVISERS

The Ontario Securities Commission (the "OSC") is publishing OSC Policy No. 4.8 in the OSC Bulletin of May 8, 1992. OSC Policy No. 4.8 sets out the circumstances under which a "non-resident adviser", whether an "international adviser" or an "extraprovincial adviser", will be permitted to act as an adviser in Ontario. The policy assumes broad jurisdictional scope on the part of the OSC in respect of advisory activities.

Under OSC Policy No. 4.8, a non-resident adviser is an adviser that does not have a place of business in Ontario with partners or officers resident in Ontario who are acting as advisers on its behalf in Ontario. An international adviser is an adviser that does not have a place of business in Canada with partners or officers resident in Canada who are acting as advisers on its behalf in Canada. An extra-provincial adviser is a non-resident adviser that is not an international adviser.

OSC Policy No. 4.8 permits a non-resident adviser to act as an adviser in Ontario either as a registrant, with terms and conditions that include restrictions as to type of client, or in reliance upon limited exemptions set out in the policy and effected by blanket order.

The British Columbia Securities Commission shares the concerns of the OSC with respect to the activities of non-resident advisers. However, the Commission will not be adopting a policy identical to OSC Policy No. 4.8, because of concerns as to the appropriateness of providing blanket registration exemptions to non-resident advisers. The Commission is in the process of amending its Local Policy Statement 3-38, Registration of Non-Residents - Securities Act ("LPS 3-38"). The amended LPS 3-38 should be published for comment later this year.

Until the amended LPS 3-38 is in place, non-resident advisers will be dealt with on a case-by-case basis. Enquiries should be directed to the Deputy Superintendent, Registration and Statutory Filings.

DATED at Vancouver, British Columbia, on May 7, 1992.

> Douglas M. Hyndman
> Chairman

NIN#92/15

NOTICE

SECURITIES AMENDMENT ACT, 1992

The Securities Amendment Act, 1992, S.B.C. 1992, c. 52 (the "Amendment Act") received royal assent on June 23, 1992.

AMENDMENTS

The Amendment Act makes several substantive and a number of miscellaneous and technical amendments to the Securities Act (the "Act") and consequential amendments to the Securities Amendment Act, 1990 and the Company Act. A copy of the Amendment Act is attached to this Notice.

1. *Major Amendments*

Section 5(a) of the Amendment Act amends section 32(g) of the Act by requiring that a specified form of information statement be delivered to purchasers and filed with the Commission not later than 10 days after the trade. Prior to bringing this amendment into force, the Commission must develop a form of information statement for use in these circumstances. A draft of the proposed form will be published for comment.

Section 7 of the Amendment Act amends section 51 of the Act by permitting many substantive, and particularly timing, requirements relating to the lapse date of a prospectus and to the continuation of a distribution under a new prospectus to be prescribed in the Securities Regulation (the "Regulation"). Section 51 has been substantially restructured into two new sections, 50.1 and 51. The new section will not be brought into force until the corresponding regulations are ready to be introduced. The Corporate Finance Committee of the Canadian Securities Administrators has recommended that all jurisdictions move substantive and timing requirements relating to continuous distributions into their regulations. The Committee also recommended that the procedure for continuous distributions be streamlined. However, because most continuous distributions are done on a national basis and because jurisdictions are not able to coordinate changes to their legislation, this streamlining can only be done once all Canadian jurisdictions have moved the substantive procedures into their regulations and after consultation with the Investment Funds Institute of Canada and other interested parties. Therefore, although the Act and Regulation are being restructured at this time, there will be no change in the actual procedure for continuous distributions until such time as the other jurisdictions are ready to proceed.

Section 9 of the Amendment Act repeals the statement of material facts ("SMF") exemption in section 58 of the Act. The Commission recommended this amendment due to the technical problems with the use of the exemption, particularly when the exemption is used to qualify shares acquired on a private placement for resale. The SMF exemption will be replaced by administrative arrangements that will permit a distribution under section 42 by means of an exchange offering prospectus ("EOP"). The repeal of the SMF exemption will not be brought into force until the new form of EOP and the circumstances in which it may be used have been finalized. Criteria for use of an EOP, such as the length of time an issuer must have had its securities listed on the Vancouver Stock Exchange (the "Exchange") and the maximum size of the offering, will be determined in consultation with the Exchange and published for comment prior to implementation. As is currently the case with an SMF, the primary review of an EOP would be conducted by the Exchange.

Section 11 of the Amendment Act narrows the wording of the certificate under section 60 of the Act to refer to not being in default of filing financial statements and fees. This amendment will not be brought into force until consequential changes have been made to certain sections of the Regulation requiring that the issuer not be in default of any requirement of the Act or Regulation, such as sections 133 and 134 of the Regulation.

Section 14 of the Amendment Act facilitates the implementation of the Multijurisdictional Disclosure System (the "MJDS") by providing the Commission with the power to exempt an issuer from Part 10 of the Act and Part 10 of the Regulation dealing with continuous disclosure. The Superintendent and Commission currently have the power to exempt issuers from some of the continuous disclosure requirements. A more comprehensive exempting power was required.

Section 29 of the Amendment Act provides the Commission with the power to apply to the British Columbia Supreme Court to get the assistance of a court outside of British Columbia to compel a person in that jurisdiction to give evidence for use in an enforcement proceeding before the Commission. The Amendment Act also provides that a court outside of British Columbia can seek the assistance of the British Columbia Supreme Court in examining witnesses in a securities enforcement proceeding started in another jurisdiction. It is anticipated that other Canadian securities regulators will propose similar amendments to the securities legislation in their provinces and territories.

Sections 30 and 32 of the Amendment Act provide issuers with cost savings in respect of the sending of material to security holders. An issuer is required by various sections of the Act and Regulation, including section 101 of the Act and section 141 of the Regulation, to continue to send records to security holders even when those records have been repeatedly returned to the issuer because the security holder no longer lives at the last address shown on the records of the issuer. The Amendment Act relieves an issuer from this obligation by providing that the issuer is no longer required to send records to security holders where the records have been returned to the issuer on three separate occasions. A similar amendment is made to the Company Act.

Section 31(c) of the Amendment Act permits the establishment of fees for activities carried out by the Commission or Superintendent under policy statements or legislation other than the Act. Currently, the Commission and Superintendent are required to make decisions on applications under policy statements, such as National Policy Statements No. 33, 39 and 41, and other legislation, such as the Company Act, but do not recover the costs of these activities. Fees for these applications will be set by regulation.

2. *Miscellaneous Amendments*

The Amendment Act also makes miscellaneous amendments to:

1. clarify the delegation and exercise of powers by the Commission and Superintendent: see sections 1, 2, 27(a) and 28;

2. expand the Commission's and an investigator's power to compel production of classes of records and things: see sections 3 and 22(a);

3. clarify the circumstances in which trades in securities on an amalgamation or other reorganization, under a dividend reinvestment plan or on a share exchange issuer bid are exempt from the registration and prospectus requirements of the Act: see sections 4 and 8;

4. clarify that the exemption in section 32(n) of the Act for securities of a cooperative corporation is available whether a disclosure statement or prospectus is filed under the Real Estate Act: see section 5(b);

5. harmonize the wording of discretionary exempting powers, establish consistent thresholds for granting exemptions and allow the Commission and the Superintendent to specify the individual requirements of the Act or the Regulation that should be waived in particular circumstances: see sections 6, 10, 14, 15, 16(b), 18 and 26(a).

6. correct drafting or technical errors: see sections 12, 13, 17, 21, 22(b), 23 and 26;

7. clarify how the proxy requirements of the Act may be satisfied: see section 16;

8. provide a right of action for a misrepresentation in, and for failure to deliver, a notice of change or notice of variation in a take over bid or issuer bid: see sections 19 and 20;

9. improve administrative efficiency in respect of the issuance of cease trade orders for failure to file records completed in accordance with the Act or Regulation: see section 25; and

10. remove a requirement that is redundant in light of the Court of Appeal Rules: see section 27(b).

PROCLAMATION

The Amendment Act is not yet in effect, but the Commission anticipates that the majority of the amendments will be proclaimed in force within the next few months. Certain of the amendments, discussed above, will require the preparation of supporting material such as Regulation amendments or forms, and will not be proclaimed until that material has been completed. The Commission will issue a notice advising of these proclamations.

ADDITIONAL COPIES

Additional copies of the Amendment Act are available at a cost of $3.58 per copy (including G.S.T.) from

Crown Publications
546 Yates Street
Victoria, B.C.
V8W 1K8

tel: (604) 386-4636

fax: (604) 386-0221

DATED at Vancouver, British Columbia, on June 25, 1992.

Douglas M. Hyndman
Chairman

NIN#92/18

NOTICE

REQUIRED FORM OF PERSONAL INFORMATION

Section 73.1 of the Securities Act (the "Act") provides that the Superintendent of Brokers may require the directors, officers, promoters and control persons (the "Principals") of an issuer or of a class of issuers to file personal information in the required form. To date, the form specified by the Superintendent has been Form 4.

The Form 4, however, was designed for and is used by individuals seeking registration from a Canadian securities commission or self-regulatory body or both, or seeking registration as a partner, director or officer of an adviser. As a result, the disclosure required by the Form 4 is not always appropriate for Principals of issuers. For example, the sections of Form 4 dealing with the type of registration or approval requested, to which self-regulatory body or commission the application is being made, and the certificate and agreement of the applicant and sponsoring firm, are all irrelevant in respect of Principals and have caused confusion. For these reasons, the Superintendent has developed a more appropriate form of personal information for Principals.

Effective September 1, 1992, the Superintendent specifies, in accordance with section 158 of the Act, Form 4B, attached to this Notice, as the required form of personal information for the purpose of section 73.1 of the Act. Local Policy Statement 3-02 has already been amended to require the Principals of issuers filing a prospectus subject to Local Policy Statement 3-02 to file a Form 4B in lieu of a Form 4 (see NIN#90/33). References to Form 4 in Local Policy Statements 3-26 and 3-35 are replaced effective September 1, 1992 with references to Form 4B.

Effective September 1, 1992, the Superintendent requires that a Form 4B be filed in the following circumstances:

1. Persons who become directors or officers of an exchange issuer or of an issuer that is a reporting issuer in British Columbia but in no other Canadian jurisdiction (an "Issuer") must file a Form 4B, or statutory declaration in lieu (see below), within 30 days of assuming the position.

2. Principals of an Issuer must file a Form 4B, or statutory declaration in lieu (see below), at the time the Issuer files a reactivation application under Local Policy Statement 3-35 or an offering document, such as a prospectus, a statement of material facts or a rights offering circular.

However, where the reactivation application or offering document is filed within three years of the Principal's latest filing of a Form 4B, the Principal may file the following in lieu of a Form 4B:

1. a statutory declaration that there has been no significant change, as defined below, in the contents of the Principal's latest Form 4B; or

2. a statutory declaration that there has been a significant change, as defined below, in the contents of the Principal's latest Form 4B and that discloses the nature of the change.

A "significant change" in the contents of a Form 4B refers to a change in the information disclosed in response to the questions dealing with change of name or business name, administrative proceedings, offences, civil proceedings, bankruptcy and settlement agreements.

Notices

Prior to September 1, 1992, the Superintendent will accept a Form 4B from Principals who would otherwise be required to file a Form 4.

Directors and officers of Issuers should advise the Superintendent by letter, or by filing a copy of the Form 10 or Form 11 filed under the British Columbia *Company Act*, when there is a change in the capacity in which they are acting, when they cease to act in that capacity in respect of an Issuer or when they become a director or officer of an issuer that they did not refer to in question 7 of their latest Form 4B.

The Commission will not charge a fee under section 189 of the Securities Regulation ("Regulation") for the filing of a Form 4B. An amendment will be made to item 27 of section 183(1) of the Regulation to exclude Form 4B from the $25 filing fee for documents for which no other fee is prescribed. It is expected that this amendment will become effective prior to September 1, 1992. A Notice will be published at that time, advising of the amendment.

Pre-printed copies of Form 4B are available, free of charge, from the Commission's 11th floor reception desk.

DATED at Vancouver, British Columbia, on July 9, 1992.

Douglas M. Hyndman   Wade D. Nesmith
Chairman   Superintendent of Brokers

REF: NIN#90/33
        LPS 3-02
        LPS 3-26
        LPS 3-35

NIN#92/19

NOTICE

REVISED DRAFT LOCAL POLICY STATEMENT 3-04
FILING OF ASSESSMENT REPORTS

BACKGROUND

In May of 1990, the British Columbia Securities Commission released for comment Draft Local Policy Statement 3-04 (the "Draft Policy"), which will, when finalized, replace Local Policy Statement 3-04 dated February 1, 1987 (the "Existing Policy"). In NIN#90/14, which accompanied the Draft Policy, the Commission indicated that, in order to assist issuers in meeting disclosure requirements, Form 12 would be revised to set out in detail the disclosure that must be contained in the prospectus of an issuer required to file an assessment report under the Draft Policy.

A revised draft of Local Policy Statement 3-04 (the "Revised Draft Policy") is published for comment with this notice. The Commission has decided to publish another draft of the policy because there are a number of specific issues on which the Commission requires further input from interested persons and because the Commission is concurrently publishing for comment Form 12A with NIN#92/20. Interested persons are encouraged to review the Form 12A and NIN#92/20 in conjunction with their review of the Revised Draft Policy.

The Revised Draft Policy takes into account many of the comments received concerning the Draft Policy and input the Commission has received from a committee consisting of accountants, consultants, lawyers, brokers and representatives of the Vancouver Stock Exchange (the "Exchange").

Purpose of an assessment report

The Revised Draft Policy, like the Draft Policy, is intended to streamline the review process and improve the quality of business assessments provided to investors by consultants engaged by junior industrial issuers. An assessment report is required to be filed by a junior industrial issuer in order to

- assist the issuer in considering the various factors that will impact on its ability to achieve its stated business objectives,

- provide for a review of the issuer's business by a qualified independent consultant,

- assist issuers in identifying risk factors associated with the issuer's business, and

- provide prospective investors and analysts with additional information to assist them in making informed investment decisions and recommendations.

DISCUSSION OF ISSUES

Some of the major changes to the Draft Policy and issues on which comments are specifically being sought are discussed below. The Revised Draft Policy includes other changes to the Existing Policy and the Draft Policy. The Commission encourages comments on any aspect of the Revised Draft Policy that raises concern.

Qualifications Of Consultant

The Draft Policy required the consultant to have at least five years of management experience and two years of consulting experience. The Commission received a number of comments indicating that this requirement would exclude qualified individuals from preparing assessment reports. The Revised Draft Policy requires five years of recent consulting experience in the area of corporate planning and financial analysis together with either specific post secondary education or 10 years of direct industry experience. The Revised Draft Policy also authorizes the Superintendent to permit an individual who does not meet these requirements to prepare an assessment report.

Are the required qualifications appropriate?

Opinion of Specialist

The Revised Draft Policy requires a consultant to retain a specialist where the consultant lacks the technical expertise to assess a technology that is critical to the issuer's business. It does not, however, provide specific examples of situations where the Commission expects the consultant will engage a specialist to enable the consultant to provide the required opinions in the assessment report.

The Commission invites comments on whether

- **there are situations where a consultant will always require the assistance of a specialist in preparing an assessment report, and**

- **it is appropriate for the Revised Draft Policy to require the use of a specialist where the issuer is engaged in certain industries or business activities (for example, where the issuer is engaged in activities involving the application of biomedical or other unique technologies).**

Conflicts of interest

The Draft Policy required that the consultant be paid in full for any services rendered prior to filing the preliminary prospectus. In response to a number of comments, the Revised Draft Policy no longer contains this requirement.

The Revised Draft Policy identifies two new circumstances in which the consultant would not be considered to be independent of the issuer. These are where the consultant is a close relative of a director, officer or employee of the issuer or of an associate or affiliate of the issuer, and where a public distribution of securities is contemplated and the consultant is the underwriter, or an associate or affiliate of the underwriter.

The Committee invites comments on whether

- **the circumstances set out in section 4.3 of the Revised Draft Policy indicate a lack of independence between the consultant and the issuer, and,**

- **there are other circumstances that should be added to the list.**

Issuer's stated business objectives

The Draft Policy was silent on whether the consultant is permitted to disclose future oriented financial information ("FOFI") in describing the issuer's business objectives. The Revised Draft Policy prohibits the disclosure of specific prospective financial information, such as sales expressed in terms of dollars or units. For example, a consultant is not permitted to state that the issuer expects to generate X dollars in sales during the 12 month period following the completion of the offering.

The Commission notes that junior issuers with limited operating histories have rarely achieved their publicly disclosed estimates of expected sales or net income. In addition, prior to the Canadian Institute of Chartered Accountants ("CICA") introducing an audit requirement for FOFI, studies had indicated that FOFI published by more senior companies frequently and materially overestimated future sales and earnings.

Therefore, in the Commission's view, an issuer required to file an assessment report is generally unable to provide FOFI or other specific prospective financial information that would be credible, reliable and not misleading. However, where achievement of sales is a stated business objective of the issuer, the Revised Draft Policy proposes that it must be stated in general terms in the assessment report. In addition, under Local Policy Statement 3-02, the Superintendent may consent to the inclusion of FOFI in a prospectus. Where this occurs and the issuer includes specific financial information extracted from the FOFI in its stated business objectives, the consultant's summary of the issuer's stated business objectives can include this specific financial information.

The Commission invites comments on whether

- **the consultant can provide a meaningful assessment of business objectives that include prospective financial information stated in general terms,**

- **there is a specific stage of the issuer's development at which a consultant is able to provide a meaningful assessment of business objectives that include prospective financial information stated in general terms,**

- **the consultant can provide a more meaningful assessment of business objectives that include prospective financial information stated in specific terms (e.g., sales by number of units or dollars), and**

- **prospective financial information stated in specific terms should be supported by FOFI prepared and audited in accordance with the CICA Handbook and Draft National Policy Statement No. 48.**

Form of assessment report and opinions

The Commission received a number of comments on the Draft Policy indicating concern over the extent of reliance that may be placed on the opinions contained in the assessment report. The concern expressed was that this may lead investors to not consider other information contained in the prospectus. Comment letters also indicated that it was unrealistic to expect a consultant to be able to provide the opinions required in the assessment report.

The Revised Draft Policy has substituted "review procedures" for "investigations". In addition, the precise forms of the required opinions are no longer specified. The Revised Draft Policy requires that the consultant's opinions be formulated by responding to certain questions. The Commission anticipates that the opinions to be provided will contain fewer qualifications because the questions incorporate a reasonableness test relative to the issuer's business objectives. The Revised Draft Policy continues to require the consultant to include any other opinions considered relevant to an assessment of the issuer's business.

A number of the comment letters indicated that the form of assessment report did not place sufficient emphasis on the risks associated with the issuer's business. The Revised Draft Policy clarifies that any qualifications or limitations to the opinion would generally be considered risks that must be disclosed in the prospectus. The conclusion section of the assessment report also provides the consultant with the opportunity to address other risks that have not been identified elsewhere in the assessment report.

The Commission invites comments on whether

- **the form of assessment report that is set out in the Revised Draft Policy will provide information that assists investors in making an informed investment decision,**

- **the structure of the opinions, being responses to specific questions, is appropriate,**

- the questions included in Appendix A to the Revised Draft Policy provide sufficient guidance to the consultant in preparing the opinions,

- there are additional questions that should be added to Appendix A to the Revised Draft Policy in order to provide a more comprehensive and useful assessment report,

- the required review procedures in Part 5 and the factors identified in Part 7 of the Revised Draft Policy provide sufficient guidance to the consultant in preparing the opinions, and

- the consultant's conclusions in the assessment report should include a summary of all of the business risks associated with the various material components of the issuer's operations.

OTHER ISSUES

Issuers required to file

The Draft Policy would have required an issuer to file an assessment report where it has been in business for more than three years but has not been profitable in each of its last two fiscal years. The Commission received comments that the term "profitable" should be defined. Notwithstanding any uncertainty as to the meaning of the term "profitable", the Commission prefers not to set out an arbitrary figure, but rather to consider the matter on a case by case basis. The Revised Draft Policy has not changed the criteria for filing an assessment report except to indicate that an assessment report may also be required where cash sales or net income are not material.

Is further clarification of the term "profitability" required and, if so, how it should be defined?

Waiver of filing requirement

The Draft Policy stated that the Superintendent may waive the requirement to file an assessment report in exceptional circumstances. Comment was received that the Draft Policy gave no indication under what circumstances the Superintendent might consider a waiver. The Revised Draft Policy identifies situations where a waiver would be considered and how to make an application for a waiver. One example is where an issuer has previously filed an assessment report under the Revised Draft Policy or a technical report under the Existing Policy and the issuer has accomplished the business objectives stated in the report.

Are there any other common situations where the Superintendent should consider a waiver?

TRANSITION

In order to assist the Commission in ensuring that the final policy resulting from the Revised Draft Policy will be an improved policy and result in the assessment report providing prospective investors with a useful assessment of the issuer's business, issuers and their advisors are encouraged to apply to the Superintendent for permission to file an assessment report in accordance with the Revised Draft Policy prior to the policy being finalized. The Superintendent will provide expedited review of documents filed by these issuers. Where a consultant wishes to prepare the assessment report in accordance with the Revised Draft Policy, the issuer must prepare its prospectus in accordance with Form 12A.

Applications should be addressed to the Deputy Superintendent, Corporate Finance and should include a brief description of the issuer's business and business objectives, the identity of the consultant and a copy of the issuer's most recent financial statements in draft form.

REQUESTS FOR COMMENT

The Commission is requesting written comments on the Revised Draft Policy, particularly on the issues raised in this notice. Comment letters should be submitted by September 30, 1992 to

Adrienne Wanstall
Executive Director, Policy & Legislation
British Columbia Securities Commission
1100 - 865 Hornby Street
Vancouver, B.C. V6Z 2H4

In order to provide the maximum benefit to the Commission, the comments should identify the specific issue being addressed and, where applicable, fully explain any problems with the proposed provision and provide an alternative solution.

Comment letters submitted in response to Requests for Comment are placed in the public file and form part of the public record, unless confidentiality is requested. Although comment letters requesting confidentiality will not be placed in the public file, freedom of information legislation in future may require the Commission to make comment letters available. Persons submitting comment letters should therefore be aware that the press and members of the public may be able to obtain access to any comment letter.

DATED at Vancouver, British Columbia, on July 16, 1992.

> Douglas M. Hyndman
> Chairman

NIN#92/21

NOTICE

PROPOSED JUNIOR POP SYSTEM
REQUEST FOR COMMENT

INTRODUCTION

The British Columbia Securities Commission proposes to develop a system for junior issuers (the "Junior POP System") similar to the prompt offering qualification system (the "POP System") currently available to certain senior issuers on a national basis. Draft National Policy Statement No. 47 with respect to the POP System was published for comment in the Weekly Summary of December 20, 1991 under NIN#91/24.

The Commission recognizes that the current process for raising funds from the public is both expensive and time consuming. This is a particular problem for the junior issuers that comprise most of the listings on the Vancouver Stock Exchange (the "Exchange"). The Junior POP System addresses this problem by establishing a procedure that would allow issuers using the system quick access to the public capital markets.

BRIEF DESCRIPTION OF THE JUNIOR POP SYSTEM

As currently proposed, the Junior POP System is optional and available only for securities of issuers listed on the Exchange. In order for its securities to be distributed under the Junior POP System, the issuer must

- have been a reporting issuer for at least 18 months,

- have been in the same business for the last 18 months and met the business objectives of its most recent public offering,

- not have been cease traded or on the list of delinquent reporting issuers for failure to file required records at any time during the last 18 months,

- not have met the criteria to be considered inactive as set out in the Exchange's Listing Policy Statement No. 17 at any time during the last 18 months,

- have filed audited financial statements with respect to its current business covering a period of at least 12 months, and

- be in compliance with all filing and disclosure requirements of the Securities Act, the Securities Regulation and national and local policy statements, including requirements to file material change reports, news releases, quarterly reports and financial statements ("Continuous Disclosure").

The issuer would file an annual information form for junior issuers (the "Junior AIF"), on a yearly basis, and a short form exchange offering prospectus ("Short Form EOP") at such times as the issuer or a selling security holder wished to distribute its securities to the public. The Short Form EOP would be considerably shorter, and would be reviewed more quickly, than a long form prospectus or exchange offering prospectus. While the Commission anticipates that, at least initially, filings under the Junior POP System cannot be used for distributions in other Canadian jurisdictions, issuers may be able to use the Junior POP System to distribute securities in certain countries outside of Canada.

The Junior AIF would be based on the new forms of local prospectus currently being developed. The first of these is Draft Form 12A, the proposed form of prospectus for junior industrial issuers, which is published concurrently with this notice under cover of NIN#92/20. While the Junior AIF would be modelled on the new prospectus forms, the exact nature of the information to be included in the Junior AIF is still under review. See "Information in the Junior AIF" below. The chief executive officer, chief financial officer and two directors of the issuer would be required to sign a certificate attached to the Junior AIF stating

"The foregoing, together with any documents incorporated by reference, constitutes full, true and plain disclosure of all material facts required to be disclosed in this Junior Annual Information Form."

Whether the Junior AIF would be subject to a due diligence review conducted by an independent person is still under review. See "Independent Due Diligence at the time of the Junior AIF" below. As currently proposed, both initial and subsequent Junior AIFs would be subject to review by the Superintendent of Brokers.

An issuer proposing to make a public offering using the Junior POP System would file a Short Form EOP simultaneously with the Superintendent and the Exchange. The Exchange would carry out the primary review of a Short Form EOP by issuers entitled to use an EOP and would be required to provide comments within ten business days of the date of filing. The nature of the information that should be included in the Short Form EOP is under consideration. See "Information in the Short Form EOP" below. The Short Form EOP would include a certificate signed by the chief executive officer, chief financial officer and two directors of the issuer stating:

"The foregoing, together with the documents incorporated by reference, constitutes full, true and plain disclosure of all material facts relating to the securities offered by this short form exchange offering prospectus as required by the securities laws of British Columbia."

The Short Form EOP would also include a certificate signed by a registered dealer that is a member of the Exchange stating:

"To the best of our knowledge, information and belief, the foregoing, together with the documents incorporated by reference, constitutes full, true and plain disclosure of all material facts relating to the securities offered by this short form exchange offering prospectus as required by the securities laws of British Columbia."

ISSUES ON WHICH THE COMMISSION IS SEEKING COMMENT

The specific issues on which the Commission is seeking comment are discussed below. However, the Commission encourages comments on any aspect of the Junior POP System.

Eligibility criteria for Junior POP System

As currently proposed, the Junior POP System would be available to issuers listed on the Exchange that have been in the same business for at least 18 months, have not been cease traded or on the list of defaulting reporting issuers for at least 18 months, have not met the criteria to be considered inactive for at least 18 months, have filed the required audited financial statements and are in compliance with their obligation to file Continuous Disclosure.

The first requirement for use of the system is that the issuer must be listed on the Exchange. Permitting listed issuers that are also listed on other exchanges to use the Junior POP System raises questions regarding legislative and regulatory requirements in other jurisdictions that may limit the ability of these issuers to use the system.

Two of the additional limitations are that the issuer must have been a reporting issuer for at least 18 months and in the same business for at least 18 months. The purpose of these limitations is to ensure that Continuous Disclosure relating to the issuer's current business has been available to the market for a minimum period of time.

The Commission invites comments on

- **the proposed eligibility criteria for the Junior POP System,**

- **whether other eligibility criteria (e.g. issuers listed on the senior board of the Exchange) would be more appropriate, and**

- **whether interlisted issuers would utilize the Junior POP System.**

Reliance on Continuous Disclosure System

It is crucial to the effectiveness of the Junior POP System that issuers using the system be in compliance with their obligation to file Continuous Disclosure, namely that all filings have been made in accordance with both the timing and content requirements of the Act, the Regulation and national and local policy statements. The Superintendent will not accept a Junior AIF nor issue a receipt for a Short Form EOP where the Superintendent considers that the issuer has not complied with the obligation to file Continuous Disclosure.

What steps can be taken to ensure that issuers using the Junior POP System are providing adequate Continuous Disclosure?

Independent Due Diligence at the time of the Junior AIF

The question has been raised whether independent due diligence at the time of preparation of the Junior AIF is necessary to ensure that this basic disclosure document contains full, true and plain disclosure of all material facts. In addition, a concern has been raised that, if the registered dealer that will ultimately conduct the offering under the Short Form EOP is not involved at the time of filing the Junior AIF, the time for an issuer to obtain a receipt for the Short Form EOP, including the time required for a registered dealer to carry out its due diligence, may significantly reduce the benefits of the Junior POP System.

The Commission invites comment on

- **whether independent due diligence at the time of the Junior AIF should be required,**

- **whether the Commission should specify who should perform any independent due diligence on the Junior AIF (registered dealers or other qualified persons),**

- **what evidence of due diligence should be required at the time the Junior AIF is filed (e.g. certificate, comfort letter or other evidence), and**

- **whether the Junior POP System will still be of benefit to issuers, if the registered dealer conducting the offering has not carried out a due diligence review at the time of the Junior AIF.**

Cost of using Junior POP System

There are certain costs associated with the use of the Junior POP System. The major costs identified by the Commission are the annual fee for the filing of the Junior AIF and the professional fees for the preparation of this comprehensive disclosure document. Issuers may encounter cash flow problems because these expenses will be incurred at a time when no financing is in process.

For an issuer whose securities are registered with the Securities and Exchange Commission of the United States ("SEC"), many of these costs are already incurred and the cash flow problems already dealt with because the issuer is required to file an annual report on Form 20-F or Form 10-K with the SEC. The Commission anticipates that the issuer could prepare its AIF using its annual report on Form 20-F or Form 10-K as a basis.

The Commission invites comments on whether

- **there are other expenses that would increase the cost of using the Junior POP System, and**

- **the costs and cash flow problems of using the Junior POP System would be offset by the ability to access the market quickly and to provide purchasers with free trading shares.**

Delivery of documents to purchasers

Under the POP System, issuers are required to deliver only the prospectus to purchasers. The AIF and other continuous disclosure material must be made available to purchasers at their request and without charge. The rationale for permitting this under the POP System is that issuers entitled to use it have a sufficiently large public float that material changes in their affairs will be reported in the financial press and promptly assessed by the investment community.

Issuers entitled to use the Junior POP System are unlikely to receive the same level of coverage on a regular basis. The Commission's view is that purchasers should receive both the Short Form EOP and the Junior AIF.

The Commission invites comments on whether

- **prospective purchasers need to receive the Junior AIF or whether it would be sufficient to make the Junior AIF available on request, and**

- **requiring delivery of the Junior AIF, in addition to the Short Form EOP, when considered with the other costs of using the Junior POP System, would cause issuers to be unwilling to use the system.**

Information in the Junior AIF

The Junior AIF would be a "snapshot" of the issuer and its business at a particular time each year. The Junior AIF would include the issuer's most recent annual audited financial statements but would not include information relating to the offering of any particular securities.

The new Form 12A for junior industrial issuers would be used as the basis for development of the Junior AIF for those issuers. A new form of prospectus for junior natural resource issuers is being developed that will likely mirror Form 12A, except that Item 9 of current Form 14 (to be redrafted) will replace Item 5 of Form 12A. This new natural resource prospectus for junior issuers would form the basis for development of a Junior AIF for use by natural resource issuers.

The Commission invites comments on

- **whether certain information required in the Form 12A (such as prior sales) should not be required in the Junior AIF of an industrial issuer,**

- **whether information that is not required in the Form 12A should be required in the Junior AIF of an industrial issuer, and**

- **what changes would be needed in the Junior AIF of a natural resource issuer, assuming the new form of natural resource prospectus is based on Form 12A.**

Information in the Short Form EOP

The Short Form EOP should include a description of the offering, including distribution spread, use of proceeds, plan of distribution and details of the offering. As well, there should be a brief description of the issuer's business, the risk factors associated with the business, interim financial statements since the date of the Junior AIF and a discussion of any material changes since that time.

The Commission invites comment on whether the proposed information to be included in the Short Form EOP is appropriate and whether other information should also be provided.

REQUEST FOR COMMENT

The Commission is requesting written comments on the proposed Junior POP System, particularly on the issues raised in this notice. Comment letters should be submitted by September 30, 1992 to

> Adrienne Wanstall
> Executive Director, Policy & Legislation
> British Columbia Securities Commission
> 1100 - 865 Hornby Street
> Vancouver, B.C. V6Z 2H4

In order to provide the maximum benefit to the Commission, comments should identify the specific issue being addressed and, where applicable, fully explain any problems with the proposed provision and provide an alternative solution.

Comment letters submitted in response to Requests for Comment are placed in a public file and form part of the public record, unless confidentiality is requested. Although comment letters requesting confidentiality will not be placed in the public file, freedom of information legislation in future may require the Commission to make comment letters available. Persons submitting comment letters should therefore be aware that the press and members of the public may be able to obtain access to any comment letter.

DATED at Vancouver, British Columbia, on July 16, 1992.

Wade D. Nesmith
Superintendent of Brokers

NIN#92/22

NOTICE

*FISCAL AGENCY AGREEMENTS
REQUEST FOR COMMENT*

INTRODUCTION

In the past two years, approximately 80 issuers listed on the Vancouver Stock Exchange (the "Exchange") have entered into fiscal agency agreements, most of them with Exchange member firms. Under the typical agreement, the agent undertakes to provide certain fiscal services in exchange for compensation, generally in the form of securities issued under an order exempting the distribution from the registration and prospectus requirements of the Securities Act.

A number of issues have arisen with respect to fiscal agency agreements as a result of the experience of market participants and regulators with these agreements. In order that all of these issues can be addressed in a uniform and effective fashion, the British Columbia Securities Commission is soliciting comment on certain questions relating to fiscal agency agreements, the answers to which will form the basis for the development of consistent Commission and Exchange policies in this area.

ISSUES ON WHICH THE COMMISSION IS SEEKING COMMENT

This request for comment sets out certain key issues of concern to the Commission and the Exchange that have arisen over the past two years. Market participants and their advisers are requested to provide comments on these issues and any other related issues that they consider relevant.

The Purpose of Fiscal Agency Agreements

In recent years, the regulators have encouraged member firms to maintain a continuing interest and involvement in the affairs of issuers on whose behalf they have completed distributions. In addition, market conditions have caused member firms to seek additional sources of revenue. Fiscal agency agreements have developed in response to these two factors.

From a regulatory perspective, the involvement of member firms in the ongoing monitoring of issuers assists the Commission and the Exchange, both of whose regulatory resources are limited. As well, member firms have an interest in ensuring that issuers on the Exchange carry out their activities properly.

Many member firms have argued that this increased monitoring creates additional expense for them. Fiscal agency agreements have been viewed as one way of compensating them for that increased expense. These agreements have also been seen as an additional source of revenue in times when other sources of revenue have been scarce.

Some issuers have argued that few, if any, additional services are provided under fiscal agency agreements. They suggest that these agreements merely provide a basis for the imposition of additional fees for services that were previously provided in connection with individual transactions, for which member firms receive commissions and broker's warrants.

Do fiscal agency agreements serve a necessary or useful purpose in the Vancouver market?

The Relationship between Member Firms and Issuers

Many issuers have expressed the concern that the relationship between member firms and issuers is fundamentally unequal and that member firms have the upper hand in the negotiation process. Some have gone further and suggested that issuers are "coerced" by member firms to enter into fiscal agency agreements.

Is the bargaining relationship between issuers and member firms sufficiently balanced so that fiscal agency agreements can be negotiated in an equitable manner, free of inappropriate pressures?

Who Can Act as a Fiscal Agent

To date, the Commission has not generally been prepared to issue orders in respect of fiscal agency agreements involving persons who are not registrants in British Columbia. This reflects the relatively cautious approach by the Commission to this recent development. However, interest in fiscal agency agreements has been expressed by U.S. registrants, B.C. registrants who are not members of either the Investment Dealers Association (the "IDA") or the Exchange and persons who are registered in neither Canada nor the United States.

Should fiscal agency agreements be permitted only where the agent is an IDA or Exchange member? If compensation is by way of cash as opposed to securities, does this affect the response?

Investor Relations Agreements

The standard fiscal agency agreement provides that the agent will provide some or all of the following services:

- locating additional financing;

- providing market and business plan consultation;

- providing advice regarding the review of potential joint ventures, acquisitions, projects, mergers, take overs or other corporate reorganizations;

- introducing the issuer to institutional investors, public and investor relations firms, business consultants and other potential strategic partners; and

- assessing the impact on the market for the issuer's shares of proposed market acquisitions, investments or reorganizations.

The Commission has noted that these services are substantially the same as those provided under many investor relations agreements.

In the Vancouver market, do the services provided under investor relations agreements differ in substance from those provided under fiscal agency agreements? If not, should issuers be permitted to enter into investor relations agreements only with those persons with whom they can enter into fiscal agency agreements?

Compensation

Many of the concerns identified by the Commission with respect to fiscal agency agreements have involved the terms of compensation. As a rule, agreements involving cash consideration do not require orders. Therefore, the Commission generally sees only those fiscal agency agreements providing for consideration in the form of securities.

There are difficulties associated with the issuance of shares as compensation as a result of the requirements of the Company Act. Specifically, section 43 of the Company Act provides that shares cannot be issued until they are fully paid. If the consideration for the shares is services, those services must be services that were actually performed for the issuer. The value of those services must be established by a resolution of the directors and must not exceed fair market value.

Many of the agreements submitted to the Commission in respect of applications for orders have involved the issuance of a pre-determined block of shares in equal monthly tranches over the term of the agreement. Such agreements fly squarely in the face of the Company Act provisions and the Commission has required these agreements to be amended before issuing the requested orders.

What compensation models should be used in fiscal agency agreements involving the issuance of shares to ensure that the shares are issued in compliance with the Company Act?

Recently, the Commission has seen a number of fiscal agency agreements providing for compensation in the form of warrants. Warrants are attractive to issuers because the issuers receive some cash at the time the shares are issued. Generally, the warrants are issued at no cost at the time the agreement is entered into and are exercisable at the market price at that time.

Notices

Should warrants issued pursuant to a fiscal agency agreement be exercisable immediately or in tranches as services are provided over the term of the agreement?

Where a fiscal agency agreement provides for compensation in the form of warrants, the consideration paid for the services provided under the agreement is determined by the difference between the exercise price and the market price of the shares at the time of exercise.

Does this form of compensation, which is solely dependent on an increase in the price of the issuer's shares, create an inappropriate incentive or detract from the perceived fairness of the market?

The current practice of the Exchange is to limit the compensation provided under a fiscal agency agreement to 2% of the issuer's issued capital, in the case of shares, and 4% of the issuer's issued capital, in the case of warrants.

Should these limits on compensation be maintained, changed or removed?

Prior to the development of fiscal agency agreements, many of the services covered by these agreements were provided by registrants, with compensation in the form of commissions on particular transactions. The Commission understands that the current practice is to continue to require commissions on specific transactions in addition to the compensation under the fiscal agency agreement.

Does this practice result in a double payment for services?

Conflict of Interest Issues

A fiscal agency agreement creates a conflict of interest for a registrant between its duties to its clients and its obligations to the issuer under the agreement. Specifically, where a fiscal agency agreement is in place between an issuer and a registrant, the issuer is a "connected party" of the registrant as that term is defined in Part 13.1 of the Securities Regulation. Part 13.1 sets out certain disclosure and procedural requirements for a registrant in respect of a distribution of securities by a connected party of the registrant.

Should similar requirements be imposed on registrants with respect to secondary trading in securities of an issuer with whom the registrant has a fiscal agency agreement?

Part 13.1 also sets out disclosure requirements for a registrant making recommendations with respect to securities of an issuer to whom the registrant has provided financial advice for consideration during the past year.

Are there additional circumstances in which the registrant should be required to make this disclosure?

Special Relationship Issues

Where a fiscal agency agreement is in place between an issuer and a registrant, the registrant is in a "special relationship" with the issuer as that term is defined in the Act. In the course of discharging its duties under the agreement, the registrant is likely to come into possession of undisclosed material information. This relationship and this information must be managed in such a way as to avoid breaches of the insider trading and tipping prohibitions in the Act.

It has been the Commission's experience that fiscal agency agreements are generally negotiated by a salesperson and that the services to be provided are performed by a salesperson. This means that the undisclosed material information revealed in connection with an agreement will generally be in the hands of a salesperson, thus exacerbating the concern about possible insider trading and tipping.

The Commission invites comments on whether

- **it is appropriate that salespeople be involved in negotiating and providing services under fiscal agency agreements, given the risks associated with the receipt of undisclosed material information,**

- **the ability to enter into fiscal agency agreements should be restricted to registrants that have corporate finance departments with established rules for protection of undisclosed material information, that is, so-called "Chinese walls", and**

- **a registrant should be restricted in its ability to trade the shares of issuers with whom the registrant has a fiscal agency agreement.**

REQUEST FOR COMMENT

The Commission is requesting written comments on fiscal agency agreements, particularly on the issues raised in this notice. Comment letters should be submitted by September 30, 1992 to

Adrienne Wanstall
Executive Director, Policy & Legislation
British Columbia Securities Commission
1100-865 Hornby Street
Vancouver, B.C. V6Z 2H4

Comment letters submitted in response to Requests for Comment are placed in a public file and form part of the public record, unless confidentiality is requested. Although comment letters requesting confidentiality will not be placed in the public file, freedom of information legislation in future may require the Commission to make comment letters available. Persons submitting comment letters should therefore be aware that the press and members of the public may be able to obtain access to any comment letter.

DATED at Vancouver, British Columbia, on July 16, 1992.

Wade D. Nesmith
Superintendent of Brokers

NIN#92/24

NOTICE

AMENDMENTS TO THE SECURITIES ACT

A number of amendments to the Securities Act were brought into force on July 24, 1992.

The Securities Amendment Act, 1992, S.B.C. 1992, c. 52 (the "Amendment Act") received royal assent on June 23, 1992. Certain sections of the Amendment Act were brought into force, effective July 24 1992, by B.C. Reg. 289/92. A copy of the Amendment Act was attached to NIN#92/15 and a copy of B.C. Reg. 289/92 is attached to this Notice. The amendments

1. clarify the delegation and exercise of powers by the British Columbia Securities Commission and the Superintendent of Brokers: see sections 1, 2, 27(a) and 28,

2. expand the Commission's and an investigator's power to compel production of classes of records and things: see sections 3 and 22(a),

3. clarify the circumstances in which trades in securities on an amalgamation or other reorganization, under a dividend reinvestment plan or on a share exchange issuer bid are exempt from the registration and prospectus requirements of the Act: see sections 4 and 8,

4. clarify that the exemption in section 32(n) for securities of a cooperative corporation is available whether a disclosure statement or prospectus is filed under the Real Estate Act: see section 5(b),

5. harmonize the wording of discretionary exempting powers, establish consistent thresholds for granting exemptions and allow the Commission and the Superintendent to specify the individual requirements of the Act or the Securities Regulation that should be waived in particular circumstances: see sections 15, 16(b) and 18,

6. correct drafting or technical errors: see sections 12, 13, 21, 22(b), 23 and 26(b),

7. clarify how the proxy requirements of the Act may be satisfied: see sections 16(a) and 17,

8. provide a right of action for a misrepresentation in, and for failure to deliver, a notice of change or notice of variation in a take over bid or issuer bid: see sections 19 and 20,

Notices

10. remove a requirement that is redundant in light of the Court of Appeal Rules: see section 27(b),

11. provide the Commission with the power to apply to the British Columbia Supreme Court to get the assistance of a court outside of British Columbia to compel a person in that jurisdiction to give evidence for use in an enforcement proceeding before the Commission; the Amendment Act also provides that a court outside of British Columbia can seek the assistance of the British Columbia Supreme Court in examining witnesses in a securities enforcement proceeding started in another jurisdiction: see section 29,

12. provide that an issuer is no longer required to send records to security holders where the records have been returned to the issuer on three separate occasions; a similar amendment is made to the Company Act: see sections 30 and 32,

13. permit substantive, and particularly timing, requirements relating to the lapse date of a prospectus and continuation of a distribution under a new prospectus to be prescribed: see section 31(b),

14. permit the establishment of fees for activities carried out by the Commission or Superintendent under policy statements or legislation other than the Act: see section 31(c),

15. repeal provisions of the Securities Amendment Act, 1990 that are no longer required: see section 33.

The remaining amendments contained in the Amendment Act will require the preparation of supporting material, such as amendments to the Regulation or forms, and will not be proclaimed until that material has been completed. The Commission will issue a notice to advise of the proclamation of these amendments.

Additional Copies

Additional copies of the Amendment Act are available at a cost of $3.58 per copy (including G.S.T.) from

> Crown Publications
> 546 Yates Street
> Victoria, B.C.
> V8W 1K8
>
> tel: (604) 386-4636
> fax: (604) 386-0221

DATED at Vancouver, British Columbia, on July 24, 1992.

> Douglas M. Hyndman
> Chairman

REF: NIN#92/15

NIN#92/29

NOTICE

ACCOUNTING FOR PERFORMANCE SHARES

Local Policy Statement 3-07 of the British Columbia Securities Commission (the "Commission") and Listings Policy Statement 18 of the Vancouver Stock Exchange (the "Exchange") provide for the issuance of performance shares to principals of an issuer in specified situations. Reference should be made to these Policy Statements for information on performance shares, including the basis of the calculation of the number of shares available to be issued and the means by which these shares can be released from escrow.

A lack of consistency has been noted in the manner in which issuers have been accounting for the issuance and subsequent release from escrow of performance shares. This Notice is being issued, after consultation with professional accountants and market participants, to assist issuers and their advisors in the preparation of financial statements to be filed with the Commission or the Exchange where the issuer has or had performance shares outstanding.

Accounting for Performance Shares On Issue

Performance shares are issued for nominal consideration (generally $0.01 per share), are required to be held in escrow pending the satisfaction of certain predetermined tests and do not represent contingent consideration as contemplated in section 1580 of the Handbook of the Canadian Institute of Chartered Accountants ("CICA Handbook"). At the time of issue, performance shares should be recorded at the fair value of the consideration received. In substantially all situations, this will be the $0.01 per share cash issuance price that is set out in Local Policy Statement 3- 07.

Where the performance shares have been issued for non- cash consideration, the performance shares should be recorded at a nominal value unless a valuation opinion acceptable to the Commission has been prepared that indicates that the fair value of the non-cash consideration is other than a nominal value.

The ascribing of a nominal value to performance shares reflects the uncertainty associated with the ultimate release of these shares from escrow.

Accounting for Performance Shares On Release

The value ascribed to performance shares at the time of their issuance should not be adjusted when the shares are released or become releasable from escrow.

Revised Financial Statements

It is essential that financial statements filed with the Commission or the Exchange fairly present an issuer's financial position, results of operations and changes in financial position. Where an issuer's previously issued financial statements do not reflect the issuance or release of performance shares in accordance with generally accepted accounting principles and this Notice, and the difference is material, the issuer must amend its next interim or annual financial statements, that are filed with the Commission or the Exchange and delivered to its security holders, on a retroactive basis.

Where the required change in accounting practice materially affects its financial position, an issuer should consider whether its previously issued financial statements complied with generally accepted accounting principles at the time the statements were prepared. If they did not, the issuer should consider the need to, and the Commission may require it to, retract the previously released financial statements and reissue them with appropriate amendments. See sections 1506 and 5405 of the CICA Handbook for guidance in situations where financial statements must be restated or retracted.

Where corrections to financial statements constitute a material change in the affairs of the issuer, the issuer must file a material change report and issue a news release under section 67 of the Securities Act, S.B.C. 1985, c.83 detailing the corrections and noting their financial impact on the issuer.

DATED at Vancouver, British Columbia, on November 6, 1992.

Wade D. Nesmith
Superintendent of Brokers

NIN#92/30

NOTICE

NATIONAL POLICY STATEMENT No. 39 – MUTUAL FUNDS
DRAFT SECTION 2.09 – CERTAIN RELATED PARTIES
ACTING AS PRINCIPALS IN PURCHASES OR SALES
OF PORTFOLIO DEBT SECURITIES
AND
PROPOSED REVOCATION OF SECTION 4.03 –
DEALER MANAGER ACTING AS PRINCIPAL

1. *Introduction*

The Canadian Securities Administrators ("CSA") today release for comment proposed amendments ("Proposed Amendments") to National Policy Statement No. 39 ("NPS 39"). It is proposed that a new section 2.09 be added to NPS 39 which would permit principal trading between a mutual fund to which NPS 39 applies and the portfolio manager, portfolio adviser or other related parties in certain circumstances. It is also proposed that section 4.03 - Dealer Manager Acting As Principal of NPS 39 be revoked.

2.   Current Requirements

NPS 39 and the securities legislation in certain jurisdictions in Canada, among other things, prohibit a mutual fund from:

(a)   purchasing or selling portfolio securities (regardless of the type of security or the identity of the issuer of the security) from or to its manager, portfolio adviser, and certain other related parties;

(b)   investing in the securities of certain related parties;

(c)   lending money to certain related parties; and

(d)   where the mutual fund is "dealer managed", investing in securities (other than government securities) underwritten by the dealer manager or by an affiliate or associate of the dealer manager for a period commencing with the distribution of the securities and ending 60 days following completion of such distribution.

3.   Proposed Relief in Section 2.09 of NPS 39

The CSA determined that it is appropriate to grant some relief to mutual funds in respect of the restrictions described in paragraph 2(a) above by amending NPS 39.

Provided that investor protection safeguards are in place to appropriately address potential conflicts that may arise between the interests of the holders of the securities of a mutual fund and the interests of the manager or the portfolio adviser of the mutual fund or other related parties, the CSA believe that certain principal trading transactions between the mutual fund and related parties may be in the best interests of the mutual fund, on the basis that such trading may:

(a)   increase the market available to the mutual fund for its purchases or sales of portfolio securities; and

(b)   facilitate access to trading strategies formulated by related parties that may enhance the performance of the mutual fund.

The CSA have determined that the proscribed activities referred to in paragraphs 2(b) through 2(d), above, raise conflict of interest concerns that have not yet been adequately canvassed.

The proposed relief would remove the absolute prohibition on mutual funds purchasing and selling from and to related parties government debt and government guaranteed debt securities and certain other debt securities that have received a rating in one of the specified categories from specified rating agencies.

The credit worthiness of these securities should serve to minimize downside risk to the mutual fund and allow the mutual fund to more easily satisfy the purchase price requirements in subparagraph (ii) of section 2.09(1) because of the narrower spread between prices quoted for such instruments.

A purchase or sale that meets section 2.09 requirements would also have to comply with all other applicable securities laws and the investment restrictions and practices of the mutual fund. Further, the purchase or sale must be consistent with the fundamental investment objectives of the mutual fund and be in the best interests of the mutual fund.

4.   Revocation of section 4.03 of NPS 39

The CSA request comment on the revocation of section 4.03 of NPS 39. The relief provided for in section 4.03 was never implemented in Ontario, Alberta or Quebec.

Section 4.03 would have provided relief from section 2.05(11) of NPS 39 for trading in securities by dealer managed mutual funds with the dealer manager or an associate or affiliate of the dealer manager, acting as principal, subject to compliance with a term relating to the publicly quoted bid or ask price for the securities.

Insofar as section 2.09 contemplates trading in securities referred to in section 4.03, section 2.09 would replace section 4.03. There is no replacement provision for relief from the prohibition against principal trading in section 2.05(11) of NPS 39 for other securities, including equity securities, not referred to in section 2.09.

5. *Request for Comments*

The CSA are requesting comments on the Proposed Amendments. Comments are specifically requested on:

(a) whether the relief proposed in section 2.09 from the prohibitions in section 2.05(11) should be made available to all of the parties referred to in section 2.05(11);

(b) the adequacy or appropriateness of the requirements in subparagraph (ii) of the proposed section 2.09(1), particularly the efficacy of the requirements for obtaining an independent quote; and

(c) the revocation of section 4.03.

The CSA is presently working with the stock exchanges and the Investment Dealers Association to consider corresponding changes to their by-laws and regulations that may be appropriate.

Comment letters submitted in response to Requests for Comments are placed in the public file in certain jurisdictions and form part of the public record, unless confidentiality is requested. Comment letters will be circulated among the securities regulatory authorities for purposes of finalizing the amendments to NPS 39 whether or not confidentiality is requested. Accordingly, although comment letters requesting confidentiality will not be placed in the public file, freedom of information legislation may require the securities regulatory authorities in certain jurisdictions to make comment letters available. Persons submitting comment letters should therefore be aware that the press and members of the public may be able to obtain access to any comment letter.

Twelve copies of each comment letter should be delivered by January 15, 1993 to:

Canadian Securities Administrators
c/o The Secretary
Ontario Securities Commission
8th Floor, 20 Queen Street West
Toronto, Ontario
M5H 3S8

For further information please contact any of the following:

Wayne Redwick
Deputy Superintendent
Corporate Finance
British Columbia
Securities Commission
(604) 660 4800

Ron Sczinski
Director
Securities Analysis
Alberta Securities
Commission
(403) 427 5201

Robert Bouchard
Deputy Director
Corporate Finance
Manitoba Securities
Commission
(204) 945 2548

Johanne Duchesne
Deputy Director
Corporate Finance
Commission des Valeurs
Mobilieres du Quebec
(514) 873 5326

Robert F. Kohl
Solicitor, Capital Markets
Ontario Securities
Commission
(416) 593 8233

Susan McCallum
Director,
Corporate Finance
Ontario Securities
Commission
(416) 593 8248

Bernadette Dietrich
Solicitor, Capital Markets
Ontario Securities Commission
(416) 593 8121

Arnold Hochman
Deputy Director,
Corporate Finance
Ontario Securities
Commission
(416) 593 8247

DATED at Vancouver, British Columbia, on November 26, 1992.

Douglas M. Hyndman
Chairman

Notices

NIN#93/2

NOTICE

SPECIFICATION OF REQUIRED FORMS UNDER THE SECURITIES ACT AND SECURITIES REGULATION

For convenience, effective January 7, 1993, the Superintendent is specifying, in accordance with section 158 of the Securities Act, the Forms referred to in the index of Forms attached to this Notice. In addition, the index lists those sections of the Act or Regulation which refer to a required Form but for which no Form has been specified.

DATED at Vancouver, British Columbia, on January 7, 1993.

Dean E. Holley
Superintendent of Brokers

Attachment

NIN#93/5

NOTICE

SECTION 115(3)(f) OF THE SECURITIES REGULATION TIME LIMIT FOR RAISING A MINIMUM SUBSCRIPTION

NIN#88/22, entitled "Section 115(3)(f) of the Securities Regulation - Time limit for raising a minimum subscription", was issued on August 12, 1988. This Notice, which replaces NIN#88/22, distinguishes between the number of days permitted by the Superintendent of Brokers for best efforts distributions in the case of distributions under National Policy Statement No. 47 ("NPS 47") and other distributions.

The number of days permitted by the Superintendent under section 115(3)(f) is

(a)   90 days from the date of issue of the final receipt for the short form prospectus, for distributions under NPS 47; and

(b)   180 days from the date of issue of the final receipt for the prospectus, for all other distributions.

Issuers doing a distribution other than under NPS 47 should refer to item 2 of Forms 12, 13 and 14 for further information.

DATED at Vancouver, British Columbia, on February 17, 1993.

Dean E. Holley
Superintendent of Brokers

NIN#93/8

NOTICE

MONEY LAUNDERING: NEW FEDERAL REGULATIONS

The federal Proceeds of Crime (Money Laundering) Act (the "Proceeds of Crime Act") and regulations under that act (the "Regulations") came into force on March 26, 1993. A copy of that legislation is attached to this notice.

As part of a coordinated international effort to control money laundering and to help enforce various Canadian laws, the Proceeds of Crime Act imposes record keeping and related requirements on financial institutions, foreign exchange dealers, **securities dealers**, life insurers and others. This notice is intended to help registered dealers and advisers ("registrants") comply with the Proceeds of Crime Act and Regulations.

1.   What is money laundering?

Money laundering is the conversion of the proceeds of economic crime into seemingly legitimate funds using complex transactions through the financial institution deposit and withdrawal system. Money laundering begins when the proceeds of crime are deposited into the financial system. Complex transactions are then used to obscure the audit trail of the funds so they appear to be legitimate when eventually withdrawn. The three typical stages of money laundering are *placement, layering* and *integration*.

2. Money laundering through the securities industry.

Because securities transactions are generally not settled in cash the securities industry is less at risk than mainstream banking from the initial *placement* of proceeds of crime. Most securities transactions are settled by cheque drawn on another financial institution at which the funds have already been deposited. Nevertheless, payment for securities in cash is not uncommon and the risk of registrants being used at the placement stage of a money laundering scheme cannot be ignored.

Registrants are probably more at risk of being used in the second stage of money laundering, *layering*, the use of multiple transactions and institutions to obscure the original source and the final destination of funds. Securities markets are attractive to the money launderer for several reasons. Markets offer a wide variety of available investment options, liquidity, portability and ease of transfer. Securities markets also have the capacity to absorb huge amounts of capital, lawful or illicit, without attracting extensive regulatory review. Unlike mainstream banking, securities transactions allow the money launderer to change the form of funds, not just from cash in-hand to cash on-deposit, but from cash to a secure and liquid asset in an entirely different form. Instruments that are cash equivalents, such as bearer bonds and other "street form" negotiable securities, may be particularly attractive as vehicles for money laundering.

For these reasons, securities markets can offer the sophisticated money launderer an ideal route for effective *integration* of the proceeds of crime into the legitimate economy.

3. Purpose and consequences of the Proceeds of Crime Act.

The Proceeds of Crime Act and Regulations establish the minimum records that registrants and other financial businesses must create and retain. These records will facilitate detection, investigation and prosecution of money laundering offences under the Criminal Code, the Food and Drugs Act and the Narcotic Control Act. The Proceeds of Crime Act also requires that registrants verify the identity of their clients and those who have authority over client accounts.

Anyone contravening or failing to comply with the Proceeds of Crime Act is guilty of an offence and liable to fine or imprisonment. Registrants should review the Proceeds of Crime Act and Regulations carefully and discuss the requirements of the legislation with their professional advisers and staff to ensure that violations do not occur.

The staff of the Commission will consider compliance with this legislation in assessing a registrant's ongoing suitability for registration in this jurisdiction.

4. What records must registrants keep?

Many of the records required to be kept under the Proceeds of Crime Act are already required under section 29 of the Securities Regulation, B.C. Reg. 270/86. Others, such as the large cash transaction records described later in this notice, are new.

The new legislation requires that registrants keep the following records:

(a) *Signature of Authorized Individuals*

Registrants must obtain and keep on file the signature of each individual authorized to give instructions for an account. The signature can be on a signature card, account agreement or new account application form.

(b) *Account Number of a Bank, Trust Company, Credit Union or Caisse Populaire*

To develop an audit trail for client funds, registrants must record and keep on file the chequing or savings account number of the deposit taking institution used by the authorized individuals.

(c) *Client Documentation and Monthly Statements*

Registrants must keep, for each client, a file containing the account application forms, trade confirmations, account agreements, correspondence with the client, and copies of all monthly account statements.

(d)   *Large Cash Transaction Records*

Registrants must keep records of all cash transactions greater than $10,000 for any account.

5.   Who must the registrant identify?

A registrant must verify the identity of all individuals authorized to give instructions for a client's account. **This requirement is effective for all new accounts opened after March 26, 1993.** However, if the account is owned or operated by a Canadian financial institution (such as a chartered bank, co-operative, insurance company, or trust and loan company), or another Canadian registrant, then the registrant need not verify the authorized individual. In these circumstances the registrant may rely on the financial institution, dealer or adviser who is operating the account to verify the identity of the client.

6.   How should a Registrant verify the identity of an authorized individual?

The Proceeds of Crime Act provides three ways for registrants to verify the identity of the individuals authorized to give instructions for accounts.

a.   *Physical Verification*

The registrant can compare the signature of an authorized individual to the signature on a driver's licence, passport, or similar document. The registrant can verify the signature in the initial meeting with the client when the client completes the new account application form.

b.   *Cheque Verification*

The registrant can ensure that a cheque from the authorized individual is properly cleared through the Canadian financial institution on which it was drawn.

c.   *Bank Reference Check*

Registrants can confirm that the authorized individual holds the bank, trust or credit union account disclosed on the new account application form by checking directly with the financial institution.

Regardless of how the identity is verified, a registrant must do so within six months of opening an account.

Practically speaking, in many cases the client's signature can be obtained at the time of account opening. The Commission expects that registrants opening accounts by telephone should generally ensure that the client's signature is on file within three weeks, which is a reasonable length of time to mail the application form or signature card to the client and have it signed and returned.

7.   What are large cash transactions?

Large cash transactions are defined as cash transactions greater than $10,000 in any one day, by or on behalf of one person. Multiple transactions on the same day must be treated as a single transaction for the purpose of the reporting requirement. Under the Proceeds of Crime Act registrants must record significant information relating to every large cash transaction, including:

- the name of person from whom the cash is received

- the person's address, occupation and nature of business

- the date and nature of the transaction

- the number and identity of the accounts which are affected by the transaction

- amount of cash received and the currency

Registrants may wish to use the attached "Declaration of Funds" form for this purpose.

8.   How long must registrants keep client records?

The Proceeds of Crime Act requires that registrants must keep the required client records for five years. This is the same period of retention specified by the Securities Regulation.

9.   Can registrants keep automated records?

Registrants meet the record retention requirement by keeping, on file, computer coded or microfiche records of client documents, monthly statements, and large cash transactions. Registrants must be able to provide printed copies of these records if requested.

10.   Designated director or other officer.

Registrants must designate a director or other officer to be responsible for compliance by the registrant and its employees and agents with the Proceeds of Crime Act.

Registrants should formulate and adopt a clear policy statement on money laundering based on the current federal statutory requirements. This statement should be provided in writing to all management and staff involved in investment operations and the registrant should review the statement on a regular basis.

11.   How does a registrant recognize suspicious transactions?

Money launderers use an almost unlimited array of types of transactions, and therefore it is difficult to define a suspicious transaction. However, a suspicious transaction will often be one which is inconsistent with an investor's known legitimate business or personal activities or with the normal business of that type of investor. The key to recognizing a suspicious transaction is knowing enough about the investor's business or investment objectives to recognize when a transaction, or series of transactions, is unusual.

To prevent the investment industry from being used for money laundering, registrants should consider the following questions before entering into a transaction:

- Does the registrant know the investor personally?

- Is the transaction in question in keeping with the investor's investment objectives?

- Is the transaction in keeping with normal practice in the market to which it relates, i.e., with reference to market size and frequency?

- Is the role of any intermediary involved in this transaction unusual?

- Is the transaction to be settled normally?

- Are there other transactions linked to the transaction in question that could be designed to disguise money and divert it into other destinations and beneficiaries?

Some situations are more prone to money laundering activities. Registrants may need to make additional enquiries in situations in which:

- payment is offered in cash

- payment is by way of third party cheque without any apparent connection to the prospective investor

- payment is by cheque where there is a variation between the account holder, the signatory, and the prospective investor

- settlement either by registration or delivery of securities will be made to an unverified third party

- settlement will be made by way of bearer securities from outside a recognized clearing system

Registrants should introduce appropriate procedures to generate a level of awareness and vigilance to enable a report to be made to the designated director or officer responsible for compliance with the Act if suspicious transactions are encountered. The designated director or officer should be able to provide direction on suspicious transactions both internally and to law enforcement agencies.

At present there is no Canadian federal or provincial legislation requiring registrants to report suspicious transactions. However section 462.47 of the Criminal Code provides immunity from civil and criminal prosecution for individuals providing information relating to transactions suspected of being the proceeds of crime. The designated director or officer responsible for compliance

Notices

with the Proceeds of Crime Act should report suspicious transactions to the proper law enforcement agencies.

If you have further questions about the contents of this notice, please contact Langley E. Evans, Deputy Superintendent Registration and Statutory Filings.

DATED at Vancouver, British Columbia, on April 1, 1993.

Dean E. Holley
Superintendent of Brokers

NIN#93/12

NOTICE

RESTRICTION APPLICABLE TO
THE SOLICITATION OF EXPRESSIONS
OF INTEREST
UNDER BOR#91/7 AND BOR#93/1

The British Columbia Securities Commission is publishing, concurrently with this Notice, Canadian Securities Administrators' Notice #93/3 on Pre-marketing Activities in the Context of Bought Deals (the "CSA Notice"). The CSA Notice summarizes the conclusions of staff of each of the Canadian Securities Administrators on the legality of "pre-marketing" activities in the context of bought deals. Reference should be made to the CSA Notice for a full discussion of this matter.

The CSA Notice states, among other things, that "pre- marketing" activities may not be undertaken from the commencement of distribution (as defined in the CSA Notice) until the earliest of:

– the issuance of a receipt for a preliminary prospectus in respect of the distribution,

– the time at which a press release that announces the entering into of an enforceable agreement in respect of a bought deal is issued and filed in accordance with any blanket ruling or order, or notice made pursuant to an existing blanket ruling or order, of a securities regulatory authority of a province or territory of Canada, and provided that all of the conditions set forth in such blanket ruling or order or such notice and its related blanket ruling or order are met, and

– the time at which the dealer determines not to pursue the distribution.

The Ontario Securities Commission (the "OSC") is publishing together with the CSA Notice, a blanket order and ruling (the "OSC Ruling") requiring, among other things, as an additional condition to the availability of the exemption in respect of the solicitation of expressions of interest in that jurisdiction, that forthwith, upon the entering into of an enforceable underwriting agreement, a press release that announces the entering into of that agreement be issued by the issuer and filed with the OSC.

The Commission does not propose, at this time, to revoke BOR#91/7 on the Multijurisdictional Disclosure System (the "MJDS BOR") and BOR#93/1 on the Prompt Offering Qualification System (the "POP BOR"), each of which contains an exemption dealing with the solicitation of expressions of interest, and replace them with new blanket orders for the sole purpose of introducing as an additional condition for the availability of the exemption the requirement to issue and file the press release referred to above. The Commission wishes, however, to make it clear that issuers and underwriters will be required to comply with the press release requirement in order to rely on the exemption.

The Superintendent, therefore, advises issuers and underwriters pursuant to paragraph 4(d) of the MJDS BOR and paragraph 2(d) of the POP BOR that they may not rely on the exemption set out in paragraph 4 of the MJDS BOR and paragraph 2 of POP BOR unless, without delay after the issuer enters into an enforceable underwriting agreement, the issuer

– issues a press release that announces that the issuer has entered into that underwriting agreement, and

– files that press release with the Commission.

The OSC Ruling makes other changes to the original conditions for the availability of the exemption dealing with the solicitation of expressions of interest in that jurisdiction. These further changes are not discussed in the Pre-marketing Notice. The Commission is not adopting any of the other changes introduced in the OSC Ruling. Issuers and underwriters are therefore advised that the conditions for the availability of the exemption dealing with the solicitation of expressions of interest in British Columbia are different from the conditions of the same exemption in Ontario.

DATED at Vancouver, British Columbia, on June 10, 1993.

Dean E. Holley
Superintendent of Brokers

NIN#93/16

NOTICE

DRAFT NATIONAL POLICY STATEMENT NO. 53
FOREIGN ISSUER PROSPECTUS AND
CONTINUOUS DISCLOSURE SYSTEM

INTRODUCTION

The Canadian Securities Administrators (the "CSA") are releasing for comment draft National Policy Statement No. 53 (the "Draft Policy"). The Draft Policy sets out the CSA view that it is in the public interest to implement a national policy to facilitate world-class foreign issuers offering securities in Canada as part of an international offering.

The Draft Policy is intended to reduce barriers to entry to the Canadian capital markets for world-class foreign issuers and to provide increased opportunity for investment by Canadian investors in the securities of such issuers while maintaining an appropriate level of investor protection.

BACKGROUND

The CSA has been advised that the Canadian market for foreign securities is inhibited by the restricted access of Canadian investors to primary distributions. Primary distributions are generally sold at a discount to current market prices and are sold without commissions. To the extent that Canadian investors are excluded from the primary distribution market, they cannot benefit from such pricing. In addition, primary offerings provide for the dissemination of an offering document containing information that might not otherwise be readily available in secondary market transactions alone.

Primary offerings of foreign securities have grown dramatically in recent years and continued expansion is expected given the increasing globalization of investment, trend towards reduced government ownership of major enterprises, liberalization of world economic markets and increasing size and placement capability of major dealers.

It has also been suggested that increased participation by Canadian investors at a retail level may encourage Canadian stock exchange listings which, in turn, may provide increased domestic liquidity for foreign securities.

In global terms, Canada is a relatively small capital market. Historically, the Canadian investor participation in most foreign offerings has represented less than 5% to 10% of the global offering (8% to 13% of the international tranche) when the issue was offered publicly in Canada.

The CSA believe it is important to implement a policy to facilitate world-class foreign issuers offering securities in Canada as part of an international offering.

The Draft Policy is restricted to equity security offerings and is not available for offerings of convertible securities, debt securities or derivative products.

When the Draft Policy is finalized the Canadian securities regulatory authorities will issue blanket rulings and orders to provide the necessary relief.

THEORY

One of the basic premises of the Draft Policy is that the securities of the world's most senior issuers have or will have substantial liquidity and market following in the world's most sophisticated capital markets. The Draft Policy defines the world's most

Notices

sophisticated capital markets as being the markets in Japan, United States, United Kingdom, Germany, Canada, France and Italy (the current G-7 countries). In the aggregate, the stock markets of these countries represent approximately 90% of global market capitalization.

In order to be considered world-class, the Draft Policy requires that the issuer have a market capitalization of Cdn $3 billion and a public float of Cdn $1 billion, both after giving effect to the offering.

The second premise of the Draft Policy is that the document used in Canada must be receipted as a prospectus and will therefore comply with the requirement of full, true and plain disclosure of all material facts. The civil liability provisions of applicable Canadian legislation will apply.

The Draft Policy also preserves the requirements applicable to the exercise of discretion under applicable securities legislation to grant or refuse a receipt for a prospectus. In addition, the securities regulators must be satisfied the continuous disclosure regime which the issuer proposes to use meets certain fundamental requirements.

Under the Draft Policy the Canadian tranche will be limited to 10% of the offering and the issuer must have less than 10% of its equity securities held by Canadian residents. Both of these requirements ensure that Canada is not one of the principal markets for the offering or likely secondary trading.

REQUEST FOR COMMENTS

The Draft Policy requires that the issuer have less than 10% of its equity securities held by Canadian residents. The CSA invite specific comment on whether this provision is necessary or desirable and, if so, on the methods provided in the Draft Policy for foreign issuers to determine that percentage, particularly where shares are held in bearer form. In the event that commentators find that the tests included in the Draft Policy are not appropriate, they are invited to provide alternatives.

The Draft Policy does not contain a provision requiring that transfer facilities for the issuer be maintained in Canada. The CSA invite specific comment on whether such a provision is necessary or desirable and, if so, how such a provision should be implemented.

The Draft Policy requires that all experts provide the necessary consents. The CSA invite specific comment on whether this provision is necessary or desirable for foreign experts.

Written comment responding to these specific requests for comment, as well as any other aspect of the Draft Policy are invited.

Seven copies of any comment letters should be submitted by September 17, 1993 to:

Canadian Securities Administrators
Corporate Finance Committee
c/o Secretary, Ontario Securities Commission
8th Floor
20 Queen Street West
Toronto, Ontario
M5H 3S8

Comment letters submitted in response to Requests for Comments are placed in the public file in certain jurisdictions and form part of the public record unless confidentiality is requested. Comment letters will be circulated among the securities regulatory authorities for purposes of finalizing the Draft Policy whether or not confidentiality is requested. Accordingly, although comment letters for which confidentiality is requested will not be placed in the public file, freedom of information legislation may require the securities regulatory authorities in certain jurisdictions to make the comment letters available. Persons submitting comment letters should be aware that the press and members of the public may be able to obtain access to any comment letter.

For further information, please contact any of the following:

Susan I. McCallum
Director, Corporate Finance
Ontario Securities
Commission
(416) 593-8248

Robert Garneau
Directeur des Opérations
financières et de
l'Information continue
Commission des valeurs
mobilières du Québec
(514) 873-5326

Catherine E. Wade
Deputy Director,
  Corporate Finance
Ontario Securities
Commission
(416) 593-8211

Rosetta Gagliardi
Policy Coordinator
Commission des valeurs
  mobilières du Québec
(514) 873-5326

Ava Yaskiel
Special Assistant,
Legal & Policy
  to the Executive Director
Ontario Securities
Commission
(416) 593-8225

Brenda Benham
Acting Executive Director
British Columbia
  Securities Commission
(604) 660-4800

Ron Sczinski
Director of Securities
Analysis
Alberta Securities
Commission
(403) 427-5201

Louyse Gauvin
Policy Advisor
British Columbia
  Securities Commission
(604) 660-4800

DATED at Vancouver, British Columbia, on August 19, 1993.

Douglas M. Hyndman
Chair

NIN#93/18

NOTICE

FISCAL AGENCY AGREEMENTS
RESTRICTIONS ON EXEMPTION ORDERS

BACKGROUND

In July 1992, the Superintendent of Brokers issued a notice (NIN#92/22) requesting comment on a number of issues relating to fiscal agency agreements. The Superintendent has considered the comments received, and has also considered the practical experience gained by staff in the past year in reviewing applications for exemption orders concerning fiscal agency agreements. Several of the fiscal agency issues warrant further review and will be considered in greater detail by staff over the coming months. However, some concerns have been identified respecting compensation arrangements that require more immediate attention.

The Superintendent has concluded that significant concerns arise from the manner in which compensation is paid under some forms of fiscal agency agreements. The Superintendent's view is that compensation for fiscal agency services should be based on the value of the services provided, whether the actual compensation takes the form of cash or securities. If fiscal agent compensation takes the form of share purchase warrants, the remuneration to the agent is dependant on an increase in share price rather than on the value of the services provided. Therefore, the Superintendent will no longer issue orders authorizing the issuance of warrants as compensation under fiscal agency agreements.

RESTRICTIONS

Pending further assessment of the issues and the comments received, the Superintendent will favourably consider applications for orders under sections 33 and 59 of the Securities Act permitting the issuance of securities under a fiscal agency agreement only if the agreement:

Notices

(a) provides that the securities to be issued are shares, not warrants;

(b) details the services to be provided and specifies the value (price per hour) to be paid by the issuer for those services;

(c) requires the fiscal agent to submit to the issuer a detailed invoice, on a pre-determined monthly or quarterly basis, specifying the services provided and the fees earned during that period;

(d) provides that the shares are to be issued at the market price on the date of the invoice, and

(e) provides, where the issuer is not an exchange issuer, that the total number of shares issued pursuant to the agreement will not exceed 2% of the issuer's issued share capital and that the shares will be subject to a 12 month hold period from the date of issue.

Further review of the issues surrounding fiscal agency agreements will be conducted over the next few months. Additional public and industry comment may be sought during that process. The conclusions reached by staff as a result of the review will be publicized in future notices.

DATED at Vancouver, British Columbia, on September 9, 1993.

Dean E. Holley
Superintendent of Brokers

REF: NIN#92/22

NIN#93/21

NOTICE

FISCAL AGENCY AGREEMENTS –
APPLICATIONS FOR DISRETIONARY EXEMPTION ORDERS

On September 9, 1993, the Superintendent of Brokers issued NIN#93/18 entitled "Fiscal Agency Agreements – Restrictions on Exemption Orders". The notice set out staff concerns relating to the form of compensation paid under fiscal agency agreements for which discretionary relief under sections 33 and 59 of the Securities Act was required. The notice also set out several conditions that would be required in the future for fiscal agency agreements requiring discretionary relief under the Act. The notice was published in the Weekly Summary of September 10, 1993, which was publicly distributed on or about September 15, 1993.

The notice did not provide for a transition period in the application of the new requirements. Several applicants affected by the notice have requested that their application be "grandfathered". These requests have been carefully considered, with regard for the interests of the applicants as well as the public interest.

The decision has been made that grandfathering will only be provided for those applications where

1. the application was filed no later than September 15, 1993,

2. the Fiscal Agency Agreement is dated prior to September 15, 1993, and

3. written stock exchange acceptance of the Fiscal Agency Agreement was received (if required) prior to September 15, 1993.

All subsequent applications will be expected to comply with the terms and restrictions set out in NIN#93/18.

The very limited transitional provisions in this instance are unusual and reflect the serious nature of the concerns that arose during the review of fiscal agency procedures.

DATED at Vancouver, British Columbia, on November 25, 1993.

Dean E. Holley
Superintendent of Brokers

NOTICE

EXECUTIVE COMPENSATION

The British Columbia Securities Commission is publishing new executive compensation disclosure rules applicable to reporting issuers in the Province (the "New Rules").

The New Rules are the same as the executive compensation disclosure rules recently adopted in Ontario although drafting changes have been made to clarify the disclosure required in a few areas (see items II.2(d), III.2(d), VI.2(a) and X.4(b) in Form 41). These changes are not intended to result in different disclosure in British Columbia than in Ontario.

The Superintendent is specifying, in accordance with section 158 of the Securities Act (the "Act"), amendments to certain required forms under the Act (the "Required Forms") to implement the New Rules (the "Amendments"). The Amendments are attached to this Notice and relate to the following Required Forms:

- items 22 and 23 of Form 12,
- items 26 and 27 of Form 13,
- items 22 and 23 of Form 14,
- items 19 and 20 of Form 15,
- item 7 of Form 28,
- item 7 of Form 30, and
- Form 41, in its entirety.

IMPLEMENTATION OF AMENDMENTS

The Amendments come into effect at different times depending on whether the issuer is a small business issuer and on the type of document filed.

A "small business issuer" is an issuer that has revenues of less than $25,000,000 in the most recently completed financial year, is not a non-redeemable investment fund or mutual fund, has a public float of less than $25,000,000 and if it is a subsidiary of another issuer, that other issuer is also a small business issuer.

The rules dealing with the implementation of the Amendments (the "Implementation Rules") provide that, in certain circumstances, issuers may comply with the Required Forms as they existed before the Amendments (the "Old Rules").

Except as discussed below, the Implementation Rules are consistent with the effective date and the transitional provisions contained in Ontario Regulation 638/93, which implemented the new executive compensation disclosure rules in Ontario, and the additional transitional provisions contained in a blanket order under subsection 88(2) of the Ontario Securities Act and in a blanket permission under section 81 of the Regulation under the Ontario Securities Act, each dated December 1, 1993 (collectively referred to as "the Ontario Transitional Rules").

The Implementation Rules are not consistent with the Ontario Transitional Rules where a non-reporting issuer that does an initial public offering becomes a small business issuer upon completion of its initial public offering. Under the Implementation Rules, the issuer is allowed to file a prospectus prepared in accordance with the Old Rules until May 1, 1994 whereas under the Ontario Transitional Rules the issuer is required to file a prospectus prepared in accordance with the new Ontario executive compensation disclosure rules on or after January 1, 1994. For greater certainty, a prospectus prepared in accordance with the new Ontario executive compensation disclosure rules will be deemed to satisfy the applicable requirements in British Columbia.

In addition, the Implementation Rules are not consistent with the Ontario Transitional Rules as to the latest date by which an issuer must comply with the New Rules when filing a prospectus or an information circular for a meeting, other than one at which directors are to be elected or an executive officer or director compensation plan is to be approved (a "general meeting"). In Ontario, the latest date is November 1, 1994 for all issuers. In British Columbia, the latest date is February 15, 1995 for issuers, other than small business issuers, and June 15, 1995 for small business issuers.

Small business issuers that are exchange issuers are subject to the additional rules discussed under "Exchange Issuers" below.

Implementation Rules for a small business issuer

(1)　A small business issuer, or a non-reporting issuer that will become a small business issuer upon completion of its initial public offering, may before May 1, 1994 file a prospectus, an annual report in lieu of an information circular (an "annual filing") or an information circular prepared in accordance with the Old Rules.

(2)　A non-reporting issuer that will become a small business issuer upon completion of its initial public offering, must on or after May 1, 1994 file a prospectus prepared in accordance with the New Rules.

(3)　Subject to paragraph (6), a small business issuer must on or after May 1, 1994 file a prospectus prepared in accordance with the New Rules.

(4)　A small business issuer filing, on or after May 1, 1994, an information circular for a general meeting or an annual filing must comply with the New Rules.

(5)　A small business issuer, other than a small business issuer that has completed its initial public offering on or after May 1, 1994, may file an information circular for a meeting, other than a general meeting, prepared in accordance with the Old Rules until the issuer mails or is required to mail its first information circular for a general meeting under the New Rules or until the issuer files or is required to file its first annual filing under the New Rules. The issuer is not entitled to this relief after June 15, 1995.

(6)　A small business issuer, other than a small business issuer that has completed its initial public offering on or after May 1, 1994, may file a prospectus prepared in accordance with the Old Rules until the issuer mails or is required to mail its first information circular for a general meeting under the New Rules or until the issuer files or is required to file its first annual filing under the New Rules. The issuer is not entitled to this relief after June 15, 1995.

Implementation Rules for an issuer other than a small business issuer

(1)　A non-reporting issuer that will not become a small business issuer upon completion of its initial public offering, may before January 1, 1994 file a prospectus prepared in accordance with the Old Rules.

(2)　A non-reporting issuer that will not become a small business issuer upon completion of its initial public offering, must on or after January 1, 1994 file a prospectus prepared in accordance with the New Rules.

(3)　Subject to paragraph (8), an issuer other than a small business issuer must on or after January 1, 1994 file a prospectus prepared in accordance with the New Rules.

(4)　Where the most recently completed financial year of an issuer, other than a small business issuer, ended before October 31, 1993, the issuer may before January 1, 1994 file an information circular or an annual filing prepared in accordance with the Old Rules.

(5)　Where the most recently completed financial year of an issuer, other than a small business issuer, ended before October 31, 1993, the issuer must on or after January 1, 1994 file an information circular for a general meeting or an annual filing prepared in accordance with the New Rules.

(6)　Where the most recently completed financial year of an issuer, other than a small business issuer, ended on or after October 31, 1993, the issuer must file an information circular for a general meeting or an annual filing prepared in accordance with the New Rules.

(7)　An issuer, other than an issuer that has completed its initial public offering on or after January 1, 1994, may file an information circular for a meeting, other than a general meeting, prepared in accordance with the Old Rules until the issuer mails or is required to mail its first information circular for a general meeting under the New Rules or until the issuer files or is required to file its first annual filing under the New Rules. The issuer is not entitled to this relief after February 15, 1995.

(8) An issuer, other than an issuer that has completed its initial public offering on or after January 1, 1994, may file a prospectus prepared in accordance with the Old Rules until the issuer mails or is required to mail its first information circular for a general meeting under the New Rules or until the issuer files or is required to file its first annual filing under the New Rules. The issuer is not entitled to this relief after February 15, 1995.

SUMMARY OF THE NEW RULES

The New Rules require that reporting issuers in the Province provide details of salaries, bonuses, stock options and other compensation paid to the chief executive officer and each of the four highest-paid executive officers. The disclosure must appear in prospectuses, information circulars and annual filings.

The New Rules also require issuers to provide:

- compensation information for any executive officer who left during the fiscal year but would otherwise have been in the highest-paid group;

- a five-year performance chart, comparing the total return of the issuer's shares to that of a broad market index (the issuer may also show a peer-group comparison);

- information on benefits that add significantly to compensation;

- details of non-routine loans made or guaranteed by an issuer to executive officers, directors, or senior officers;

- information on any contract that would result in an executive officer getting more than $100,000 as a result of being dismissed or having to change duties;

- details on directors' compensation;

- a report from the issuer's compensation committee, explaining how committee members decided on compensation, and indications of members' independence.

In order to make it easier to understand, much of the information must be given in tables with accompanying text providing details.

There are some exemptions. Small business issuers will not have to provide a stock performance chart, pension plan table or compensation committee report, because of the costs. Executive officers apart from chief executive officers who earn less than $100,000 a year in salary and bonus are exempt from disclosure. Issuers that comply with the U.S. executive compensation disclosure rules are exempt from the new requirements. Other foreign issuers may seek exemptions on a case-by-case basis.

EXCHANGE ISSUERS

Where an exchange issuer, or an issuer that would be an exchange issuer after completion of its initial public offering, has filed a prospectus with the Commission, staff has generally required disclosure in the prospectus of the information called for under sections 9.1 and 9.3 of Draft Form 12A published in July 1992. Staff will continue to require the disclosure of that information until such time as the New Rules are reviewed to determine whether any changes should be made for small business issuers. The Commission understands that exchange issuers filing a Statement of Material Facts with the Vancouver Stock Exchange provide the same information when material.

Sections 9.1 and 9.3 of Draft Form 12A refer to disclosure required under Form 41. When preparing the disclosure, reference should be made to the requirements of Form 41 under the Old Rules until compliance with the New Rules is required as set out under "Implementation of Amendments".

$100,000 RULE

Staff is reviewing the adequacy of the provision of the New Rules that exempts from disclosure the amounts paid in salary and bonuses to executive officers, other than chief executive officers, who earn less than $100,000. This provision could result in the disclosure of information relating only to the chief executive officer of an issuer.

Staff is considering whether this result is appropriate and, if not, whether different rules should apply. Staff may propose changes to the New Rules once it has completed its review.

DATED at Vancouver, British Columbia, on December 16, 1993.

Douglas M. Hyndman
Chair

Dean E. Holley
Superintendent of Brokers

Attachment

NIN#93/24

NOTICE

EXEMPTION FOR FILING NOTICE OF NETWORKING ARRANGEMENTS GOVERNED BY THE PRINCIPLES OF REGULATION

There are several provisions in the Securities Regulation and in other documents published by the British Columbia Securities Commission that deal with relationships between a registrant that is related to a financial institution and the financial institution. Section 167.10(2) of the Securities Regulation requires a registrant that intends to enter into a networking arrangement, as defined in section 167.10(1) of the Regulation, to give the Superintendent of Brokers written notice of its intention (a "Networking Notice").

Three sets of Principles of Regulation published by the Canadian Securities Administrators provide guidelines respecting these relationships: "Distribution of Mutual Funds By Financial Institutions" dated November 9, 1988 (the "First Principles"), "Full Service and Discount Brokerage Activities of Securities Dealers In Branches of Related Institutions" dated November 25, 1988 (the "Second Principles") and "Activities of Registrants Related To Financial Institutions" undated but effective July 1, 1990 (the "Third Principles") (collectively, the "Principles of Regulation"). The Third Principles also establishes a national clearing system for review of notices of networking arrangements that are filed in various jurisdictions, including those required to be filed under section 167.10(2) of the Regulation.

In order to increase the efficiency of the regulatory process, the Superintendent is today issuing a blanket order, BOR#93/4 (the "Blanket Order"). The Blanket Order exempts a registrant that complies with the Principles of Regulation from filing a Networking Notice.

The Ontario Securities Commission (the "OSC") has published a notice and ruling in the OSC Bulletin of December 17, 1993 providing similar relief. The OSC notice also exempts registrants involved in networking arrangements from the requirement to file, or continue to file, promotional material for review and non-objection by the OSC – including marketing information, documents, brochures and publications. The Blanket Order does not provide equivalent relief in British Columbia because the Superintendent has rarely imposed a requirement, as a condition of non-objection to a networking arrangement, that a registrant file promotional material.

The OSC notice also discusses a chequing feature or privilege attached to a money market or treasury bill mutual fund that permits a unitholder to write cheques against the unitholder's mutual fund holdings. The OSC notice concludes that no notice of a networking arrangement need be filed, provided that full disclosure of the chequing feature, its related fees and charges and the relationship, if any, between the mutual fund's manager and the financial institution has been made in the fund's simplified prospectus and annual information form. The Commission has arrived at a similar conclusion, based on the fact that a mutual fund manager is not a registrant and, hence, not caught by the definition of networking arrangement set out in section 167.10(1) of the Regulation.

The Superintendent reminds registrants that section 125.1 of the Securities Act authorizes the Superintendent to require a registrant to provide any information or produce any records the Superintendent requires, including information relating to networking arrangements that comply with the guidelines set out in the Principles of Regulation.

DATED at Vancouver, British Columbia, on December 22, 1993.

Dean E. Holley
Superintendent of Brokers

NIN#94/2

NOTICE

FILING REQUIREMENTS FOR ANNUAL INFORMATION FORMS

NIN#90/10, issued on March 23, 1990, clarified the annual filing requirement for a reporting issuer in British Columbia following changes in annual filing requirements by the Ontario Securities Commission ("OSC") and the Commission des Valeurs Mobilieres du Quebec ("CVMQ"). Since that Notice, the British Columbia Securities Commission has published National Policy Statement No. 47 ("NP47") under NIN#93/4 replacing Local Policy Statement 3-40. This Notice restates those parts of NIN#90/10 which continue to apply and are not incorporated in NP47.

Although the British Columbia Securities Commission does not impose management's discussion and analysis disclosure requirements and annual information form ("AIF") filing requirements comparable to those set out in the OSC Policy Statement No. 5-10 and the CVMQ Policy No. Q-24 (together, the "MD&A Policies"), a reporting issuer in British Columbia subject to one or both of the MD&A Policies as a result of being a reporting issuer in Ontario or Quebec is required to send its shareholders in British Columbia the same documents that are sent to its shareholders in Ontario or Quebec and is required to file in British Columbia all documents that it files with the OSC or the CVMQ in accordance with the MD&A Policies.

A reporting issuer that files an AIF in British Columbia must clearly indicate in a covering letter or on the face page of the AIF whether the AIF is being filed to enable the issuer to rely on the prompt offering qualification system (the "POP system") set out in NP47 or, if the issuer is not in the POP system, whether the AIF is being filed for information purposes only.

Where an AIF is filed to enable the issuer to rely on the POP system in accordance with NP 47, the issuer must pay:

(a) the fee prescribed in item 16 of section 183(1) of the Securities Regulation where the AIF is not accompanied by the issuer's annual financial statements, or

(b) the fees prescribed in items 16 and 23 of section 183(1) of the Securities Regulation where the AIF is accompanied by the issuer's annual financial statements.

Where an AIF is filed for information purposes, the issuer is not required to pay a filing fee unless the AIF is accompanied by the issuer's annual financial statements, in which case the issuer must pay the filing fee prescribed in item 23 of section 183(1) of the Securities Regulation.

DATED at Vancouver, British Columbia, on January 6, 1994.

Douglas M. Hyndman
Chair

NIN#94/4

NOTICE

DECISION OF THE COURT OF APPEAL FOR BRITISH COLUMBIA IN THE MATTER OF HAMELIN V. SEVEN MILE HIGH GROUP INC.

Because of its potential relevance to participants in the local securities market, particularly to reporting issuers listed on the Vancouver Stock Exchange, the attached decision of the Court of Appeal for British Columbia has been included in the Weekly Summary.

DATED at Vancouver, British Columbia, on May 17, 1994.

Dean E. Holley
Superintendent of Brokers

Attachment

NOTICE

NATIONAL POLICY STATEMENT NO. 39
DEFINITION OF DEBT-LIKE SECURITIES

The Ontario Securities Commission (the "OSC") published a notice regarding the definition of "debt-like securities" in National Policy Statement No. 39 ("NP 39") in the OSC Bulletin dated April 15, 1994. The OSC notice identifies concerns with the improper classification of a debt-like security as debt. As this concern is shared by the British Columbia Securities Commission (the "Commission"), the Commission is issuing a similar notice.

The definition of debt-like securities contained in NP 39 encompasses instruments commonly referred to as "structured" or "commodity-linked" notes. This definition permits securities to be categorized as debt securities rather than debt-like securities if on the date of initial issue the value of the component that is linked to the underlying interest accounts for less than 20% of the total market value of the security. NP 39 does not prescribe any method of valuation for determining whether the component that is linked to the underlying interest accounts for less than 20% of the total market value of the security.

It has been brought to the attention of the Commission that there are several different methods of valuation that might be used for determining the value of the component that is linked to the underlying interest. Depending on the method of valuation used, a security that should more properly be classified as a debt-like security, having regard to the underlying policy concerns addressed by NP 39, might be classified as a debt security. An improper classification could result in the mutual fund exceeding the investment restrictions relating to debt-like securities in NP 39.

The Canadian Securities Administrators' Mutual Fund Committee is currently reviewing the definition of debt-like security contained in NP 39. Interested persons are invited to comment on:

(1) the appropriateness of the current definition of debt-like security;

(2) the appropriateness of changing the current definition to reflect that an instrument should be categorized as a debt-like security if the amount to be paid at maturity (because of the performance of the component that is linked to the underlying interest) could be less than 80% of the original "principal" amount; and

(3) if the definition requires the component that is linked to the underlying interest to be valued, what valuation method should be specified in NP 39.

Seven copies of any comment letter should be submitted by June 30, 1994 to:

Canadian Securities Administrators
c/o Office of the Secretary
Ontario Securities Commission
Suite 800, Box 55
20 Queen Street West
Toronto, Ontario
M5H 3S8

Comment letters submitted in response to Requests for Comments are placed on the public file in certain jurisdictions and form part of the public record unless confidentiality is requested. Comment letters will be circulated among the securities regulatory authorities. Accordingly, although comment letters requesting confidentiality will not be placed in the public file, freedom of information legislation may require the securities regulatory authorities in certain jurisdictions to make the comment letters available. Persons submitting comment letters should accordingly be aware that the press and members of the public may be able to obtain access to any comment letter.

It is expected that proposals for comment will be published in the summer of 1994. Pending a determination of these issues, the Commission has instructed staff to take the view that an instrument should be regarded as a debt-like security if the amount to be paid at maturity (because of the performance of the component of the instrument that is linked to the underlying interest) could be less than 80% of the original principal amount. Mutual funds and their advisers should discuss with staff the classification of potential investments as debt or debt-like securities.

DATED at Vancouver, British Columbia, on June 8, 1994.

Douglas M. Hyndman
Chair

NIN#94/6

NOTICE

PROPOSED INTERPRETATION NOTE ON
SECTIONS 31(2)(21) AND 55(2)(18)
OF THE SECURITIES ACT
REQUEST FOR COMMENT

Staff intends to recommend that the Commission issue an Interpretation Note to clarify its position on the availability of the exemptions in sections 31(2)(21) and 55(2)(18) of the Securities Act, S.B.C. 1985, c. 83 (the "Act") (the "exemptions") for the indirect acquisition of properties or interests in them. Comment is being sought on staff's preliminary views set out below.

BACKGROUND

The exemptions provide relief from registration and prospectus requirements where a trade is made

"by an issuer in a security of its own issue as consideration for the acquisition of mining, petroleum or natural gas properties or any interest in them so long as the seller of those properties enters into an escrow or pooling agreement in the required form when ordered by

(i) the superintendent, or

(ii) a stock exchange in the Province authorized to so order by the superintendent".

Staff have received a number of queries about whether it is appropriate for an issuer to rely on the exemptions where the issuer of the securities does not directly acquire the mining, petroleum or natural gas properties (the "properties") or any interest in them. The queries raise concerns about how to interpret the term "interest" and whether the exemptions are available for the indirect acquisition of properties or interests in them.

For example, questions have been raised about whether or not an issuer can rely on the exemptions:

(a) to distribute its securities in consideration for the acquisition *by its wholly-owned subsidiary* of a resource property or property interest;

(b) to distribute securities *of its parent* in consideration for a resource property or property interest; or

(c) to distribute its securities in consideration for the acquisition of *some or all of the securities of another issuer* that owns a resource property or property interest.

The exemptions permit an issuer to acquire properties or property interests using the issuer's securities as consideration, thus encouraging and facilitating natural resource exploration. Prospectus filing and registration are not required for several reasons, among them the nature and knowledge of the parties generally involved and the balanced position of the parties with respect to the valuation of the assets exchanged. In the past, shares issued under the exemptions have not generally been subject to escrow or pooling requirements and are not subject to statutory hold periods.

The term "interest" recognizes that transactions dealing with the exploration of natural resources do not generally involve the transfer of 100% of the property to one person. Rather, transactions may often involve the acquisition of a joint venture interest, a leasehold interest or an interest in profits derived from properties, such as a net profit interest or a net smelter interest.

STAFF'S PRELIMINARY VIEW OF THE AVAILABILITY OF THE EXEMPTIONS FOR INDIRECT ACQUISITIONS

Given the nature and extent of the relief provided by the exemptions, staff believe that the exemptions warrant narrow interpretation. The exemptions are clearly available where the properties or property interests, as described above, are acquired directly by the issuer of the securities. It is staff's view, however, that the exemptions do not apply to other forms of transaction that result in "indirect" acquisitions. Specifically, staff believes that the exemptions are not available in circumstances where:

(a) an issuer distributes its securities in consideration for the acquisition of a property or property interest by its wholly-owned subsidiary;

(b) an issuer distributes securities of its parent in consideration for the acquisition of a property or property interest by the issuer; and

(c) an issuer distributes its securities in consideration for the acquisition of some or all of the securities of another issuer that holds a property or property interest (either as its sole asset or with other assets).

Provided there are no other exemptions available, the Superintendent is prepared to consider applications for relief in circumstances where the properties or property interests are acquired by the issuer's wholly-owned subsidiary or, in limited circumstances, where the issuer of the securities acquires all of the outstanding securities of a private issuer that holds a property or property interest as its sole asset. An application will, however, be necessary and staff will assess applications on a case by case basis.

REQUEST FOR COMMENT

Staff are seeking public and industry comment on the views set out above regarding the availability of the exemptions, on the policy rationale that does or should support the exemptions, and on the issues that should be most important to staff in considering applications for discretionary relief. Comment would also be appreciated on whether there are any common forms of indirect property acquisition that, in light of the Legislature's policy and investor protection objectives, warrant consideration for blanket relief or statutory amendment.

Staff expect to recommend to the Commission that an Interpretation Note be issued after consideration of the comments received.

Comment letters should be submitted by July 22, 1994 to:

Susan Adams
A/Director, Policy & Legislation
British Columbia Securities Commission
1100 - 865 Hornby Street
Vancouver, B.C.
V6Z 2H4

Comment letters submitted in response to Requests for Comment are placed in the public file and form part of the public record, unless confidentiality is requested. Although comment letters requesting confidentiality will not be placed on the public file, freedom of information legislation may require the Commission to make comment letters available. Persons submitting comment letters should therefore be aware that the press and members of the public may be able to obtain access to any comment letter.

DATED at Vancouver, British Columbia, on June 8, 1994.

Dean E. Holley
Superintendent of Brokers

NOTICE

AMENDMENTS TO
SECTIONS 154.3 AND 154.4 OF THE SECURITIES ACT

Sections 154.3 and 154.4 of the Securities Act have been amended effective July 8, 1994. These amendments are contained in sections 10 and 11 of the Miscellaneous Statutes Amendment Act (No. 3), 1994, S.B.C. 1994, c. 51, which received royal assent on July 8, 1994.

Section 154.3 provides a mechanism for the British Columbia Securities Commission to obtain evidence from a person outside the province. The Commission may apply to the British Columbia Supreme Court for a letter requesting a court outside of British Columbia to compel a person in that jurisdiction to give evidence for use in an investigation or a hearing before the Commission.

Section 154.4 provides a mechanism for a regulator outside British Columbia to obtain evidence from a person in the province. It permits the Supreme Court to respond to a request for assistance from a court outside of British Columbia, made on behalf of the securities regulator in the court's jurisdiction, in obtaining evidence for use in an investigation or a hearing in the other jurisdiction.

These sections were enacted in 1992. In March 1994, the Court of Appeal for British Columbia ruled that section 154.3, as then worded, could be used to obtain evidence for an investigation but not a hearing. The amendments make clear that evidence can be obtained under this mechanism for either an investigation or a hearing, as was originally intended.

An excerpt from the Miscellaneous Statutes Amendment Act (No. 3), 1994, is attached to this Notice.

DATED at Vancouver, British Columbia, on July 26, 1994.

Douglas M. Hyndman
Chair

Attachment

REF: NIN#92/15
NIN#92/24

NIN#94/12

NOTICE

JOINT RELEASE OF IOSCO / BIS DERIVATIVES PAPERS

The British Columbia Securities Commission is publishing two papers, one issued by the Technical Committee of the International Organization of Securities Commissions ("IOSCO") and the other issued by the Basle Committee on Banking Supervision ("BIS"). These papers provide guidance to securities regulators and bank supervisors on sound risk management of derivative activities. The papers set out the views shared by both IOSCO and BIS on the importance of sound risk management for prudential operation of banks and securities firms as well as for promoting stability in the financial system generally. The Commission encourages industry participants to review and consider the guidelines set out in the attached papers.

DATED at Vancouver, British Columbia, on September 21, 1994.

Douglas M. Hyndman
Chair

Attachments

Notices

NOTICE

SUMMARY OF LEGISLATIVE AND POLICY INITIATIVES

The Commission is publishing a series of legislative and policy initiatives to implement part of the Government's response to the Matkin Report as announced by The Honourable Elizabeth Cull, Minister of Finance and Corporate Relations as well as other initiatives that are intended to address regulatory issues not raised in the Matkin Report. These initiatives are intended to strengthen and update British Columbia's securities regulatory system and improve its efficiency and effectiveness.

CURRENT INITIATIVES

Proposed amendments to the *Securities Act*, Securities Regulation and Local Policy Statement 3-22, and new Local Policy Statement 3-17, Form 12A and Form 12A Summary Prospectus are being published in a special supplement to the Weekly Summary.

Proposed Amendments to the Act

The Commission is publishing for comment a significant package of proposed amendments to the Act for introduction in the Spring 1995 legislative session. Certain of the proposed amendments implement part of the Government's response to the Matkin Report. These proposed amendments strengthen the regulation of underwriting and promotional activity and authorize the Commission to conduct compliance reviews of self regulatory bodies. See NIN#94/14.

Proposed Amendments to the Regulation

The Commission is also publishing for comment a significant package of proposed amendments to the Regulation. Certain of these proposed amendments implement part of the Government's policy to strengthen the regulation of underwriting and promotional activity in response to the Matkin Report. In particular, the dealer and underwriter registration categories are separated to facilitate the imposition of specific requirements on underwriters. The Commission is publishing a draft amended policy regarding registration requirements and an interim policy regarding registrant due diligence that reflect these amendments. Other amendments being proposed by the Commission are consequential to the *Securities Amendment Act, 1990* and *Securities Amendment Act, 1992*; address abuses and inequities in the market; simplify the regulatory regime through reorganizing some provisions and repealing others; codify existing practices; and incorporate plain language. The amendments focus on exchange contracts (which are currently regulated under the *Commodity Contract Act*), financial reporting, registration requirements, prospectus renewals, exempt market transactions, electronic filing of records, and other miscellaneous amendments. See NIN#94/15, NIN#94/16 and NIN#94/17.

Draft Amended Local Policy Statement 3-22 - Registration Requirements

The Commission is publishing for comment draft amended Local Policy Statement 3-22, which sets out, in plain language and convenient form, the principal educational and experience requirements for registration in British Columbia as a dealer, underwriter or adviser and for registration as an individual acting on behalf of a dealer or adviser. The requirements for underwriters have been significantly revised. LPS#3-22 also sets out the requirements for a new category of registrant, an "exchange contracts dealer" who, together with mutual fund dealers, security issuers, real estate securities dealers and scholarship plan dealers, are grouped under the new general category "limited dealer". See NIN#94/16.

Interim Local Policy Statement 3-17 - Registrant Due Diligence

Interim Local Policy Statement 3-17 provides guidelines and reporting requirements for due diligence conducted by registrants that underwrite public offerings by junior issuers. This Policy will replace Local Policy Statement 3-04 effective January 6, 1995. Interim LPS#3-17 continues the requirement that an independent qualified consultant investigate and review the junior industrial issuer's business, including the risks associated with the business, as well as the management of the issuer. However, Interim LPS#3-17 requires the underwriter, not the issuer, to retain the independent consultant to prepare the assessment report. The assessment report is intended to assist the underwriter in determining whether to proceed with the distribution and in assessing the proposed disclosure in the preliminary prospectus. See NIN#94/17.

Form 12A - Prospectus for a Junior Industrial Issuer

Form 12A is introduced effective January 6, 1995, as the required form of prospectus for a junior industrial issuer. It is expected to reduce the time and expense to issuers for staff's review of prospectuses by providing a comprehensive guide to the disclosure requirements. The new form incorporates in the prospectus more complete disclosure about the issuer's business, replacing disclosure previously contained in technical reports, and provides guidance on deficiencies in disclosure that staff routinely raise. See NIN#94/17 and NIN#94/18.

Form 12A Summary Prospectus

The Form 12A Summary Prospectus Disclosure System, is being introduced to make available to junior issuers certain features of the proposed Junior POP System. Effective January 6, 1995, the System provides investors with a shorter, easy-to-read prospectus and aims to make investors more informed about an issuer and its securities. The Form 12A Summary Prospectus is a verbatim extract of a limited number of sections from the base disclosure document that contain the essential information necessary to make an investment decision. The System will be brought into force by an amendment to Local Policy Statement 3-02 and a blanket order. See NIN#94/17.

FUTURE INITIATIVES

Over the next six to nine months, the Commission will be publishing further policy initiatives related to the current initiatives as announced by the Government and the Commission.

Policy Statements

LPS#3-02 - Prospectus Filing Requirements

An amendment is required to implement the Form 12A Summary Prospectus Disclosure System.

LPS#3-24 - Statutory and Discretionary Exemptions

LPS#3-24 will be substantially amended and updated to provide guidance to market participants about the use of statutory exemptions from the registration and prospectus requirements of the legislation that staff believes require interpretation. It will also set out how to apply for discretionary orders from the Superintendent and the Commission.

National Policy Statements

The Commission anticipates issuing for comment several national policies over the next few months relating to security holder communication, advertising, and expedited registration of advisers. The Commission also anticipates publishing in final form a procedure for expedited review of short form prospectuses and renewal annual information forms.

Orders

Blanket order - Form 12A Summary Prospectus Disclosure System

A blanket order will be issued to implement the Form 12A Summary Prospectus Disclosure System.

Forms

Form 14A - Prospectus for a Natural Resource Issuer

Form 14A will be based on Form 12A and modified to recognize the different business of a natural resource issuer.

Form 30 - Information Circular

Amendments will be made to ensure that prospectus-level disclosure is provided for certain transactions requiring security holder approval, including amalgamations, mergers, arrangements, reorganisations and reverse take-overs. Consideration will be given to whether amendments are necessary to other policies and forms to ensure that prospectus level disclosure will be required for all reverse take-overs.

Form 61 - Quarterly Report

Amendments will be made to require an ongoing reconciliation of corporate operations to the issuer's stated business objectives and proposed use of proceeds, and to require the Management Discussion and Analysis section of the report to provide enhanced discussion of investor relations activities.

Exchange Offering Prospectus and Delegation Agreement

The *Securities Amendment Act, 1992* repeals the exemption for a statement of material facts contained in section 58(1)(c). This amendment will be brought into force once a form of exchange offering prospectus and a related policy, which will replace LPS#3-26, are finalized for junior issuers. The delegation to the Exchange of the review of exchange offering prospectuses will be governed by a new delegation agreement.

Interpretation Notes

As part of the Commission's program to attack promotional abuses, the Commission will issue Interpretation Notes setting out the disclosure and registration requirements applicable to promotional and investor relations activities and setting out fair trading practices that should be followed by all market participants.

Enhanced Insider Trading Reporting

The Commission will be taking several steps to enhance the reporting and disclosure of trading by insiders. The Commission proposes to offer electronic access to insider reports via commercial information systems and will issue a request for proposal. The Commission has developed, in conjunction with other jurisdictions, a new insider reporting form to correct deficiencies in the existing national form. Finally, the Commission will issue a notice to stimulate discussion and analysis of options for accelerating the reporting of trading by insiders through the use of electronic systems.

Additional Copies

Additional copies of the Weekly Summary supplement are available from the Commission's 11th floor receptionist.

DATED at Vancouver, British Columbia, on October 5, 1994.

Douglas M. Hyndman
Chair

REF: NIN#94/14
         NIN#94/15
         NIN#94/16
         NIN#94/17
         NIN#94/18

NIN#94/14

NOTICE

PROPOSED AMENDMENTS TO THE SECURITIES ACT

A package of proposed amendments to the *Securities Act* is being published for public comment. These proposed amendments implement part of the Government's response to the Matkin Report. These amendments are intended

- to strengthen the regulation of underwriting and promotional activity (see ss. 1(1) - "investor relations activities", 35, 36.1, 48.1 and 144)

- to authorize the Commission to conduct compliance reviews of self regulatory bodies (see s. 15.1)

Section 25 of the *Securities Amendment Act, 1990*, which amends section 35 of the *Securities Act*, has not yet been proclaimed. As section 35 is now proposed to be subject to further amendment, the text of the unproclaimed amendment is shown in italics.

Request for Comments

Direct written comments by November 17, 1994 to:

Susan Adams
A/Director
Policy and Legislation
British Columbia Securities Commission
1100 - 865 Hornby Street
Vancouver, B.C. V6Z 2H4

Comment letters submitted in response to Requests for Comment are placed in the public file and form part of the public record, unless confidentiality is requested. Although comment letters requesting confidentiality will not be placed on the public file, freedom of information legislation may require the Commission to make comment letters available. Persons submitting comment letters should therefore be aware that the press and members of the public may be able to obtain access to any comment letter.

DATED at Vancouver, British Columbia, on October 5, 1994.

Douglas M. Hyndman
Chair

Attachment

NIN#94/15

NOTICE

PROPOSED AMENDMENTS
TO THE SECURITIES REGULATION

The Commission is publishing for comment a significant package of proposed amendments to the Securities Regulation. Some of these proposed amendments implement part of the Government's response to the Matkin Report. Others are proposed by the Commission. The amendments are the culmination of a lengthy process beginning with the passage of the *Securities Amendment Act, 1990*.

The amendments are consequential to the *Securities Amendment Act, 1990* and *Securities Amendment Act, 1992*; address abuses and inequities in the market; simplify the regulatory regime through reorganizing some provisions and repealing others; codify existing practices; and incorporate plain language.

The proposed amendments can be grouped into a number of areas:

Exchange Contracts

The *Securities Act* was amended by the *Securities Amendment Act, 1990*, S.B.C. 1990, c. 25, to incorporate provisions regulating the trading of exchange contracts, which are defined to include futures and options. These amendments are not yet in force and trading in futures and options continues to be regulated under the *Commodity Contract Act*, R.S.B.C. 1979, c. 56. The proposed amendments to the Securities Regulation dealing with exchange contracts are consequential to the *Securities Amendment Act, 1990* and will facilitate bringing the regulation of exchange contracts under the *Securities Act*. See particularly Part 4 of the Securities Regulation, which provides for a number of new registration categories relating to exchange contracts.

Financial Reporting

The amendments clarify the financial reporting provisions and make them consistent, where appropriate, with national policies concerning mutual funds and future oriented financial information. One amendment prohibits issuers, during a distribution, from using "future oriented financial information", defined more broadly than "forecast", unless the future oriented financial information is contained in a prospectus. A second amendment requires foreign issuers to obtain the consent of the Superintendent (executive director) to use non-Canadian and non-United States generally accepted accounting principles ("GAAP"), with respect to financial statements included in a prospectus, and requires foreign issuers to reconcile their continuous disclosure material, as well as any financial statements filed with a prospectus, to Canadian GAAP.

Registration

The Commission proposes a rewrite of Part 4 of the Securities Regulation to codify existing practices; simplify the record keeping requirements; increase capital requirements for registrants; rationalize categories of registration (e.g., by the creation of a new category of "advising employee"); and move certain provisions from Part 6 into Part 4 of the Securities Regulation. The proposed amendments also impose a requirement for separate registration of underwriters, that is, a broker, investment dealer or securities dealer will no longer be deemed to have been granted registration as an underwriter. Under the proposed amendments, an underwriter must be a member of a self regulatory body or exchange in Canada.

The Commission is issuing for comment, under cover of a separate notice, draft amendments to Local Policy Statement 3-22. This draft policy contains specific proficiency and qualification requirements to replace those proposed to be deleted from Division 7 of Part 4 of the Securities Regulation.

Prospectus Renewals

The proposed amendments contain a new Division 4 of Part 7 which, together with section 7 of the *Securities Amendment Act, 1992*, clarifies the existing rules for prospectus renewals. By moving many of the substantive requirements into the Securities Regulation, the Commission can move to a more streamlined procedure in the future at the same time as other Canadian jurisdictions.

Exemptions

The proposed amendments to Parts 5 and 8 of the Securities Regulation tighten the existing rules for exempt market transactions, clarify drafting and simplify the resale rules. Among other things, these proposed amendments would:

(a)   define sophisticated purchaser with a "bright line" test;

(b)   remove certain exemptions the Commission no longer considers appropriate;

(c)   impose hold periods on securities issued by exchange issuers under a number of exemptions to which hold periods do not currently apply; and

(d)   restrict trades by insiders during periods of unusual promotional activity.

Miscellaneous

The most significant series of miscellaneous amendments concern the proposal of the Canadian Securities Administrators to facilitate electronic filing of records under the *Securities Act* and Securities Regulation. These amendments address signatures, "red herrings", graphs and photographs, and multiple copies. Some amendments to the *Securities Act* will also be required to facilitate electronic filing.

Another significant proposed amendment is the requirement for a person holding securities of a reporting issuer on behalf of another person to disclose to the issuer the name, address and holdings of the person, except where the person has given instructions to the contrary and in accordance with any requirements that the Commission may impose. This proposal is intended to facilitate communication by a reporting issuer to non-registered holders of its securities.

The proposed amendments also exempt individual security holders from filing an insider report where the transaction affects the security holders as a class and an officer of the issuer files written notice within ten days. Examples of affected transactions include stock dividends, stock splits, consolidations, amalgamations, reorganizations and mergers.

The Commission has not proposed any amendments to Part 2 of the Securities Regulation at this time. However, it anticipates that it will propose amendments to this Part in the near future.

Proposed amendments to the Registration Transfer Regulation, B.C. Reg. 286/86, made under section 159(2) of the *Securities Act*, to Form 20A and to the form of demand for production under section 128 of the *Securities Act* are also being released for comment as part of the package of proposed amendments.

Request for Comments

Direct written comments by November 17, 1994 to:

Susan Adams
A/Director
Policy and Legislation
British Columbia Securities Commission
1100 - 865 Hornby Street
Vancouver, B.C. V6Z 2H4

Comment letters submitted in response to Requests for Comment are placed in the public file and form part of the public record, unless confidentiality is requested. Although comment letters requesting confidentiality will not be placed on the public file, freedom of information legislation may require the Commission to make comment letters available. Persons submitting comment letters should therefore be aware that the press and members of the public may be able to obtain access to any comment letter.

Due to the extensive nature of the amendments proposed to the Securities Regulation, there is no black-lined draft of the proposed amendments. Instead, refer to the explanatory notes that accompany the proposed amendments in order to identify changes.

DATED at Vancouver, British Columbia, on October 5, 1994.

Douglas M. IIyndman
Chair

Attachment

NIN#94/16

NOTICE

DRAFT AMENDED LOCAL POLICY STATEMENT 3-22
REGISTRATION REQUIREMENTS

The Commission is publishing for comment draft amended Local Policy Statement 3-22, "Registration Requirements" (the "Draft Policy"). This notice provides background to the Draft Policy, which is intended to replace Interim Local Policy Statement 3-22, "Requirements for Registration for Trading in Securities", adopted by the Commission on February 10, 1989.

The Draft Policy sets out, in plain language and convenient form, the principal requirements for registration in British Columbia as a dealer, underwriter or adviser and for registration as an individual acting on behalf of a dealer or adviser.

The Commission is also publishing for comment, under cover of a separate notice, proposed amendments to the Securities Regulation (the "Draft Regulation") that relate, in part, to registration issues. The Draft Policy restates many of the provisions set out in the Draft Regulation as if those provisions were in force, and cites references to both the Draft Policy and to the *Securities Act* as authority for various registration requirements. The references are for convenience only.

Categories of Registration and Proficiency Requirements

The Draft Regulation has created a new category of registration, "exchange contracts dealer" (discussed in the next section), and the Draft Policy reflects this change. The existing categories of registration of mutual fund dealer, security issuer, real estate securities dealer and scholarship plan dealer, together with exchange contracts dealer, have been grouped under a new general category of "limited dealer". The existing categories of underwriter, portfolio manager, investment counsel and securities adviser remain. Because the Draft Regulation does not set out education and experience requirements for individuals acting on behalf of each category of registration, these are now set out in detail in the Draft Policy.

Exchange Contracts

The *Securities Act* was amended by the *Securities Amendment Act, 1990,* to incorporate provisions, not yet in force, regulating the trading of exchange contracts, which are defined to include futures and options and are now regulated under the *Commodity Contract Act.* In anticipation of these provisions coming into force, the Draft Policy incorporates registration requirements for persons that trade in, or advise on, exchange contracts.

For example, the Draft Policy sets out registration requirements for a new category of registrant, limited dealer - exchange contracts dealer, that is authorized to trade in any combination of exchange contracts or forward contracts. Similarly, the Draft Policy sets out registration requirements for portfolio managers, investment counsel and securities advisers that advise on exchange contracts or forward contracts.

Underwriting

The Draft Regulation imposes a requirement for separate registration of underwriters, that is, a broker, investment dealer or securities dealer would no longer be deemed to have been granted registration as an underwriter. As a consequence, the Draft Policy establishes registration requirements for underwriters, including proficiency requirements for an underwriter's compliance officer. An underwriter must be a member of a self regulatory body or exchange in Canada. The Draft Regulation also imposes an obligation on an underwriter to conduct due diligence reviews of distributions that it underwrites and the Draft Policy sets out guidelines on how an underwriter may discharge that obligation.

Capital Requirements and Financial Reporting Requirements

The Draft Policy, conforming to the Draft Regulation, sets out increased capital requirements. For example, it is proposed that a securities dealer be required to maintain excess risk adjusted capital on the basis of a minimum capital requirement of $100,000 (up from $50,000) and a limited dealer - mutual fund dealer be required to maintain working capital of at least $75,000 (up from $25,000).

Section 19 of the *Securities Act* was repealed by provisions of the *Securities Amendment Act, 1989*, not yet in force. As a consequence, financial reporting requirements have been moved to, and clarified in, the Draft Regulation. The Draft Policy sets out the requirement for a registered dealer (except a security issuer), underwriter or adviser to file audited annual financial statements and for a registered dealer (except a broker, investment dealer or security issuer), underwriter or adviser to file quarterly, and in some cases monthly, unaudited financial statements.

Request for Comments

Direct written comments by November 17, 1994 to:

> Susan Adams
> A/Director
> Policy and Legislation
> British Columbia Securities Commission
> 1100 - 865 Hornby Street
> Vancouver, B.C. V6Z 2H4

Comment letters submitted in response to Requests for Comment are placed in the public file and form part of the public record, unless confidentiality is requested. Although comment letters requesting confidentiality will not be placed on the public file, freedom of information legislation may require the Commission to make comment letters available. Persons submitting comment letters should therefore be aware that the press and members of the public may be able to obtain access to any comment letter.

DATED at Vancouver, British Columbia, on October 5, 1994.

> Douglas M. Hyndman
> Chair

Attachment

NIN#94/17

NOTICE

FORM 12A - PROSPECTUS FOR A JUNIOR INDUSTRIAL ISSUER,
INTERIM LOCAL POLICY STATEMENT 3-17 -
REGISTRANT DUE DILIGENCE
AND RELATED DISCLOSURE INITIATIVES

The British Columbia Securities Commission is publishing Form 12A - Prospectus for a Junior Industrial Issuer, Interim Local Policy Statement 3-17 - Registrant Due Diligence ("Interim LPS#3-17") and Form 12A Summary Prospectus. This Notice provides background to Form 12A and Interim LPS#3-17 and discusses the Commission's other related disclosure initiatives.

Form 12A - Prospectus for a Junior Industrial Issuer

In NIN#94/18, the Superintendent of Brokers specifies Form 12A as the required form of prospectus for a junior industrial issuer where, under Interim LPS#3-17, an underwriter must obtain an assessment report. Although the effective date for Form 12A is January 6, 1995, issuers and their underwriters are encouraged to use Form 12A and Interim LPS#3-17 for prospectuses filed prior to that date.

Form 12A is expected to reduce the time and expense to issuers for staff's review of a prospectus of a junior industrial issuer by:

1. providing a comprehensive guide to the disclosure requirements for junior industrial issuers including cross references to, and excerpts from, the *Securities Act*, the Securities Regulation and relevant policies and notices;

2. incorporating in the prospectus, instead of the technical report, disclosure about the junior industrial issuer's business; and

3. incorporating in Form 12A deficiencies in disclosure that staff routinely raise.

Staff have revised Draft Form 12A, which was published for comment in July 1992, to reflect comments received from industry participants and further analysis by Commission staff. Form 12A contains a number of additional disclosure requirements and a substantial number of drafting changes from the prior published draft.

Significant changes from Draft Form 12A include:

• **Summary and Analysis of Financial Operations** - A table summarizing key financial results for investors has been added. Disclosure must now be made of the issuer's liquidity and of variations arising from a significant or material change in the issuer's operations from the date of the information in the table. (See section 5.2 of Form 12A.)

• **Marketing Plans and Strategies** - Staff have accepted concerns that disclosure of certain business information could adversely affect issuers' competitive positions. Staff have therefore deleted the requirement to disclose the issuer's selling price and direct cost per unit. (Section 5.13)

• **Funds Available and Principal Purposes** - Disclosure is now required of any funds paid to insiders or used to reduce indebtedness and of the use of proceeds raised in any special warrant transactions. (Item 6)

• **Risk Factors** - A requirement has been added to rank the risks relating to the nature of issuer's business. (Item 7)

• **Share Capital** - Items 10 to 14 of Draft Form 12A have been significantly revised. (Item 11)

• **Relationship Between the Issuer and Professional Persons** - A new item has been added to require the disclosure of any direct or indirect interest in securities or property of, or position with, the issuer, or an associate or affiliate of the issuer, held by a professional person referred to in section 99 of the Securities Regulation or any associate of the professional person. (Item 17)

Interim LPS#3-17 - Registrant Due Diligence

In conjunction with Form 12A, the Commission is adopting, on an interim basis a new policy, Interim LPS#3-17, to provide guidelines and reporting requirements for registrant due diligence in respect of prospectuses for junior issuers. Effective January 6, 1995, Interim LPS#3-17 will replace Local Policy Statement 3-04 ("LPS#3-04"). LPS#3-04 is rescinded effective January 6, 1995.

In May 1990, the Commission published for comment Draft LPS#3-04, which was prepared in consultation with an industry committee. In July 1992, the Commission published for comment a revised Draft LPS#3-04, which incorporated comments received on the first published draft. This second published draft has been reconsidered in light of comments received from industry participants and Commission staff.

The Commission has made a number of substantive changes to the requirement to file assessment reports. Interim LPS#3-17 continues to require an independent qualified consultant to investigate and review the junior industrial issuer's business, including the risks associated with the business, and the management of the issuer. However, Interim LPS#3-17 requires the underwriter, and not the issuer, to retain the independent consultant to prepare the assessment report. This is intended to assist the underwriter in determining whether to proceed with the distribution and to assess the proposed disclosure in the preliminary prospectus. Because Form 12A now requires the disclosure of information relevant to investors, which was previously disclosed in the technical report filed under LPS#3-04, Interim LPS#3-17 does not require the assessment report to be filed or made public.

An underwriter plays an important role in protecting the public interest and the integrity of the local capital market. Interim LPS#3-17 is intended to improve and to document the due diligence of underwriters. Interim LPS#3-17 therefore requires underwriters to prepare and retain a due diligence report in respect of prospectuses for junior issuers.

As LPS#3-17 is being adopted by the Commission on an interim basis, the Commission encourages industry participants to comment on the ongoing operation of Interim LPS#3-17 and the effect it will have on the business of underwriting in the Province. The Commission is also seeking comment on whether the due diligence report should be made public.

Other Related Disclosure Initiatives

Form 12A and Interim LPS#3-17 are the first in a series of initiatives aimed at improving disclosure and streamlining the offering process for junior issuers. Other initiatives include:

Junior POP System and Form 12A Summary Prospectus Disclosure System

Under NIN#92/21, in July 1992, the Commission published for comment a proposal for a Junior POP system. The Commission was encouraged to proceed with this initiative. The Form 12A Summary Prospectus Disclosure System ("the System") is being introduced to make available to junior issuers certain features of the proposed Junior POP System. If the System proves to be successful, further features may be introduced later. The System provides investors with a shorter, user friendly prospectus and aims to make investors more informed about an issuer and its securities.

Junior industrial issuers required to file a prospectus in Form 12A may use the System. The System consists of a Form 12A Summary Prospectus, which in turn incorporates by reference a base disclosure document. The base disclosure document must be prepared in accordance with Form 12A. The System is similar in concept to the Simplified Prospectus Disclosure System for mutual funds under National Policy Statement No. 36 and the Prompt Offering Qualification System under National Policy Statement No. 47. The base disclosure document will be incorporated by reference in the Form 12A Summary Prospectus.

The Form 12A Summary Prospectus is a verbatim extract of a limited number of sections from the base disclosure document that contain the essential information necessary to make an investment decision. The Form 12A Summary Prospectus does not, of itself, meet the statutory standard of "full, true, and plain disclosure" of all material facts, which is and will continue to be satisfied in the base disclosure document.

Where a junior industrial issuer uses the System, the issuer must give the Form 12A Summary Prospectus to investors to satisfy section 66 of the *Securities Act*. Investors who wish to obtain from the issuer a copy of the base disclosure document will be entitled to do so at no cost.

The Commission will issue a blanket order to implement the System and will provide instructions on the use of the System in an amendment to Local Policy Statement 3-02 ("LPS#3-02"). Both the blanket order and amendment are anticipated to be published before Form 12A and Interim LPS#3-17 become effective. Industry participants that want to use the System before the blanket order is issued and the amendment to LPS#3-02 is made should apply for an exemption order from the Superintendent under section 59 of the *Securities Act*.

Form 14A - Prospectus for a Junior Natural Resource Issuer

Staff are preparing a new form of prospectus for junior natural resource issuers. Form 14A will be based on Form 12A but modified to recognize the different business of a natural resource issuer. Staff will publish this form for comment in the near future.

Exchange Offering Prospectus and Delegation Agreement

The *Securities Amendment Act, 1992* repeals the exemption for a statement of material facts contained in section 58(1)(c) of the *Securities Act*. The Commission recommended the repeal of the exemption because of technical problems associated with its use. The amendment will be brought into force once a form of exchange offering prospectus and a related policy, which will replace Local Policy Statement 3-26, are finalized for junior issuers. The delegation to the Vancouver Stock Exchange of the review of exchange offering prospectuses will be governed by a new delegation agreement.

Form 30 - Information Circular

Amendments will be made to ensure that prospectus-level disclosure is provided for certain transactions requiring security holder approval, including amalgamations, mergers, arrangements, reorganisations and reverse take-overs. Consideration will be given to whether amendments are necessary to other policies and forms. The Commission will publish for comment any proposed changes.

Form 61 - Quarterly Report

Amendments will be made to require, among other things, an ongoing reconciliation of corporate operations to the issuer's stated business objectives and proposed use of proceeds, and to require the Management Discussion and Analysis section of the report to provide enhanced discussion of investor relations activities engaged in by or on behalf of an issuer. Before implementation, the Commission will publish for comment any changes.

Request for Comment

The Commission is requesting written comment on the ongoing operation of Interim LPS#3-17, the effect Interim LPS#3-17 will have on the business of underwriting in the Province, whether the due diligence report should be made public and on the other initiatives discussed in this Notice.

Comment letters should be submitted to:

> Susan Adams
> A/Director, Policy & Legislation
> British Columbia Securities Commission
> 1100 - 865 Hornby Street
> Vancouver, B.C.
> V6Z 2H4

Comment letters submitted in response to Requests for Comment are placed in the public file and form part of the public record, unless confidentiality is requested. Although comment letters requesting confidentiality will not be placed on the public file, freedom of information legislation may require the Commission to make comment letters available. Persons submitting comment letters should therefore be aware that the press and members of the public may be able to obtain access to any comment letter.

DATED at Vancouver, British Columbia, on October 5, 1994.

> Douglas M. Hyndman
> Chair

Attachments

References: LPS#3-04
LPS#3-17
Form 12A
Form 12A Summary Prospectus
NIN#90-14
NIN#92-19
NIN#92-20
NIN#92-21
NIN#94-18

NIN#94/18

NOTICE

FORM 12A - PROSPECTUS FOR A JUNIOR INDUSTRIAL ISSUER

Effective January 6, 1995, in accordance with section 158 of the *Securities Act*, the Superintendent of Brokers specifies Form 12A as the required form of prospectus for a junior industrial issuer where, under Interim Local Policy Statement 3-17, the underwriter must obtain an assessment report, or would have been required to obtain an assessment report if the Superintendent had not waived the requirement.

Prior to January 6, 1995, industry participants may prepare and file a preliminary prospectus in accordance with Form 12A.

DATED at Vancouver, British Columbia, on October 5, 1994.

Dean E. Holley
Superintendent of Brokers

Reference: NIN#94/17
              LPS#3-17

NIN#94/19

NOTICE
DRAFT AMENDED NATIONAL POLICY STATEMENT NO. 41
SECURITY HOLDER COMMUNICATION

Introduction

The Canadian Securities Administrators ("CSA") are publishing for comment Draft Amended National Policy Statement No. 41 (the "Draft Policy"). The Draft Policy, like the existing policy on which it is modelled, recognizes the right of non-registered holders of securities to receive the security holder materials and voting rights that reporting issuers are currently required, under corporate law and securities legislation, to provide to registered holders and to exercise the voting rights attached to the securities they own.

The Draft Policy provides a procedure to enable a reporting issuer to send proxy-related materials and audited annual financial statements or annual reports to non-registered holders of its voting securities, and imposes obligations on various parties in the security holder communication process.

Most of the substantive provisions set out in the Draft Policy are derived from National Policy Statement No. 41 (the "Current Policy"), the CSA's existing policy on shareholder (security holder) communication. However, unlike its antecedent, the Draft Policy gives a reporting issuer the right, subject to certain restrictions, to obtain from an intermediary the names, addresses, holdings and preferred language of communication of the non-registered holders of the issuer's securities, where the holders have not given contrary instructions. This change is intended to give reporting issuers greater control over the security holder communication process, including cost, by allowing issuers to communicate directly with non-registered holders of their securities.

Background

The CSA approved the Current Policy on October 28, 1987. The Current Policy was based upon the recommendations of the Joint Regulatory Task Force on Shareholder Communication. The Task Force was comprised of: securities regulatory authorities from Québec, Ontario and British Columbia; corporate law administrators from Ontario and the federal Corporations Branch; the Toronto and Vancouver Stock Exchanges; and representatives from each of the Canadian Depository for Securities Limited ("CDS"), the Vancouver Stock Exchange Service Corp. (now West Canada Depository Trust Company ("WCDTC")), the Investment Dealers Association of Canada ("IDA") (Québec and Ontario), the Canadian Bankers Association ("CBA"), the Trust Companies Association, the Investment Funds Institute of Canada and the Canadian Corporate Shareholder Services Association ("CCSSA").

The Current Policy was amended in the summer of 1988 by Addendum "A" (now Part XII of the Current Policy) to deal with certain matters, including applications for waivers and exemptions.

An Industry Implementation and Monitoring Committee ("IIMC") was formed in 1988 to assess the implementation of the Current Policy. The IIMC is currently comprised of senior representatives of industry associations, namely the IDA, the CBA, depositories (CDS and WCDTC), the Securities Transfer Association of Canada, the Canadian Group of Thirty, the CCSSA, the Securities Trust Industry Committee, stock exchanges (Montréal Exchange, Toronto Stock Exchange, Alberta Stock Exchange and Vancouver Stock Exchange), the Institute of Chartered Secretaries and Administrators, the Canadian Investor Relations Institute and the Pension Investment Association of Canada. In addition, the IIMC includes a representative from ADP

Independent Investor Communications Corporation and the CSA National Policy 41 Committee ("CSA NP 41 Committee").

IIMC Survey, CSA Request for Comments and IIMC Report

In late 1991, the IIMC circulated a questionnaire about the Current Policy to approximately 100 reporting issuers and received 60 responses. The IIMC subsequently developed separate intermediary and non-registered holder questionnaires for distribution. Of 6,325 questionnaires sent to non-registered holders of six reporting issuers, 927 (15%) were returned. Of the non-registered holders that responded, a majority indicated that they valued the right to receive proxy-related materials (73%) and to vote their securities (65%). Most holders that responded (81%) claimed to return proxies sent with meeting material, always (43%) or at least sometimes (38%).

In November 1992, the CSA published a notice that included all three questionnaires and requested comments. Reporting issuers, non-registered holders, intermediaries, depositories and other interested parties were asked to provide specific comments as to deficiencies with the Current Policy, together with proposed solutions. The notice set out a number of issues that had generated greater discussion at the IIMC than others and described the potential for the creation of a single list of beneficial shareholders as being of particular interest to the CSA.

Only a limited number of questionnaires were returned to the CSA in response to the CSA notice. However, general comments that were received included submissions by industry groups representing issuers, intermediaries and others. The CSA would like to thank all persons, companies and industry groups that responded to the IIMC surveys or to the CSA request for comments.

In April of this year, the IIMC reported to the CSA with a list of ten recommended changes to the Current Policy. The CSA conditionally adopted most of the recommendations. The IIMC report also set out five issues on which the IIMC had been unable to reach consensus, and presented alternative solutions. The CSA conditionally adopted a position on each of the issues.

At the request of the CSA, the CSA NP 41 Committee invited members of the IIMC to comment on the CSA's conditional decisions. Comments were received, as late as the third week of June, from the majority of IIMC members or their organizations. A summary of comments that directly related to the conditional positions taken by the CSA was directed to the CSA, with recommendations from the CSA NP 41 Committee where appropriate. The CSA NP 41 Committee obtained further direction from the CSA. The CSA National Policy 41 Committee, comprised of staff from the securities regulatory authorities of Québec, Ontario, Alberta and British Columbia, then undertook to draft amendments to the Current Policy, resulting in the Draft Policy.

Right to list of non-objecting holders

The principal substantive change from the Current Policy is the express right set out in the Draft Policy for a reporting issuer, subject to certain restrictions, to obtain from an intermediary a list of the names, addresses, holdings and preferred language of communication of the non-registered holders of the issuer's securities, where the holders do not object to disclosure of such information (that is, non-objecting holders). Part X of the Current Policy permits a reporting issuer the alternative of delivering security holder materials itself, or through its transfer agent, if it can do so on a less costly basis, and invites the issuer to make arrangements with intermediaries to use this option. In practice, this option has not been freely available to issuers. The CSA have attempted to address this in the Draft Policy.

Confidentiality

The CSA recognize that intermediaries may feel constrained, in the absence of written instruction from their clients, from providing to a reporting issuer the names, addresses, holdings and preferred language of communication of clients that are non-responsive holders of securities of the issuer. A requirement for confidentiality of client information may arise under statute, Civil Code (Québec), common law, contract, trust agreement or otherwise. The ability of a reporting issuer to receive a list of the names and other information about the non-registered holders of its securities under the Draft Policy is made subject to confidentiality requirements imposed upon the intermediary by law.

The reporting issuer's right to receive information from an intermediary about the intermediary's clients that are non-registered holders of its securities is also subject to any contrary written instructions that an intermediary may have received from the client concerning release of information. The CSA expect that intermediaries will make vigorous efforts to receive instructions from their clients with respect to confidentiality. Forms B and C to the Current Policy are restated in plain language in Appendix A. Where no instructions are received from a non-registered holder of securities of a reporting issuer, the Draft Policy contemplates that, in Canadian jurisdictions other than the Province of Québec, the holder does not object to disclosure of the holder's name, address and holdings to the issuer (that is, the holder is a non-objecting holder). The holder's preferred language of communication, English or French, would also be disclosed to the issuer. This is consistent with Part V, section 3, of the Current Policy. Where a non-objecting holder is a resident of the Province of Québec, an intermediary may not disclose to the issuer the holder's name, address or holdings without the holder's express authority.

The CSA support the introduction of legislative provisions to expressly permit intermediaries to disclose to a reporting issuer the names, addresses, holdings and preferred language of communication of non-responsive holders of the issuer's securities, except where the holder has given written instructions to the contrary.

Fees and costs

The fees and costs set out in Appendix D to the Draft Policy reflect the view of the CSA that a reporting issuer should generally bear the basic cost of communicating with non- registered holders of its securities, including costs incurred by an intermediary, except for any costs associated with protecting the confidentiality of the client-intermediary relationship. These costs should be borne by the intermediary and client. This is consistent with the principles set out in the first paragraph of Part X of the Current Policy.

Election to receive security holder materials

Appendix A of the Draft Policy, like Forms B and C in the Current Policy, contemplate that a non-registered holder may elect to receive or not to receive security holder materials from reporting issuers. Where no instructions are received, the Draft Policy contemplates that a non-registered holder does not wish to receive security holder materials.

The CSA recognize that registered holders of securities of an issuer may not have the option, under applicable corporate legislation, to waive delivery of security holder materials. The CSA support amendment of corporate legislation to allow registered holders the option to not receive security holder materials.

Over-voting

Under corporate legislation in most jurisdictions, the right of a security holder to vote at a meeting of security holders may not be restricted to holders as of a record date for the meeting. With limited exception, corporate legislation in Canada does not fix a record date for voting purposes. The absence of a legislated record date may create the potential for over-voting.

For example, under the Canada Business Corporations Act and legislation modelled after it, a security holder that acquires securities after the rècord date for a meeting may be entitled to vote where the security holder provides evidence of ownership not less than ten days prior to the date of the meeting. Where securities are held in non-registered form, the opportunity for over-voting will occur if both the non-registered holder, as of the record date, and the non-registered holder, post-record date, vote.

Over-voting problems that originate in corporate legislation are outside the jurisdiction of securities regulatory authorities. The CSA support efforts to address these problems through appropriate amendments to corporate legislation.

A potential for over-voting may also arise in circumstances where securities are lent, if the agreement under which the securities are lent does not specify which of the lender or borrower is entitled to voting rights attaching to the lent securities. The CSA understand that the problem may be complicated by the fact that, for the purposes of the Income Tax Act (Canada), a lender of securities may be deemed to have disposed of the lent securities if it expressly gives up the right to vote the securities. While the CSA take no position on which party, the lender or borrower, has or should have the right to vote in respect of lent securities, as a practical measure, the CSA recommend that all parties strive to ensure that proxies or voting instructions not be issued for more than the total number of shares registered on the record date and evidenced by any omnibus proxy.

Request for comments

Written comment on any aspect of the Draft Policy is invited and may be forwarded to the attention of:

> CSA National Policy 41 Committee
> c/o Robert Hudson
> Policy Advisor
> British Columbia Securities Commission
> 1100 - 865 Hornby Street
> Vancouver, British Columbia
> V6Z 2H4

> (Facsimile: (604) 660-2688)

Comment letters should be submitted prior to **December, 14, 1994**. Five copies should accompany the original letter.

In addition to general comment on the Draft Policy, the CSA is seeking specific comment on the following:

(a) Permitted uses by a reporting issuer of the list of names, addresses, holdings and preferred language of communication of its non-registered holders - The Draft Policy restricts this use to mailing proxy-related materials and audited annual financial statements or annual reports. The CSA request comment on the issue of extending use of the list to "corporate governance" purposes.

(b) Fees and costs - The fees set out in Appendix D to the Draft Policy include a fee for obtaining a list containing information about non-objecting holders. The fee does not distinguish between the use of the list for mailing of security holder materials that include proxy-related materials or the use of such a list for other than a proxy mailing (e.g., where audited annual financial statements or an annual report are sent separately from proxy-related materials).

The CSA request comment on whether the fees set out in Appendix D to the Draft Policy should differentiate between proxy and non-proxy mailings, with the former being set at a higher level than the latter.

(c) Format of communication - The Draft Policy does not mandate a format for electronic communication from an intermediary to a reporting issuer of the list of names, addresses, holdings and preferred language of communication of non-registered holders of securities of the issuer. Although the CSA encourage all parties to develop and use a standard industry format, the Draft Policy does not require any particular format. The CSA request comment on whether a format should be mandated and, if so, who should develop that format.

(d) Application where non-registered holders reside outside of Canada - The Draft Policy, like the Current Policy, contemplates that a reporting issuer will send security holder materials to non-registered holders of their securities wherever they reside. Where CDS and WCDTC, in response to an early search, provide a reporting issuer with the names of participants, intermediaries or nominees of intermediaries that have an address outside of Canada, the issuer is required to deliver search cards to those participants, intermediaries and nominees.

Although such participants, intermediaries or nominees may follow the requirements of the Draft Policy, the Draft Policy may not by its terms be directly applicable. The CSA are seeking comment on how to encourage communication with non-registered holders that are resident in the United States or elsewhere outside of Canada.

(e) Reasonableness of April 1, 1995 implementation date - The Draft Policy establishes an implementation date of April 1, 1995, based on the latest date that a reporting issuer may file its notice of meeting and record dates. The CSA are seeking comment on the reasonableness of the proposed implementation date.

Where they are able to, commentators are encouraged to provide draft wording for any change that they may suggest be made to the Draft Policy.

Comment letters submitted in response to this request will be placed in the public file in certain jurisdictions and form part of the public record unless confidentiality is

Notices

requested. Comment letters will be circulated among the securities regulatory authorities for purposes of finalizing the Draft Policy whether or not confidentiality is requested. Accordingly, although comment letters for which confidentiality is requested will not be placed on the public file, freedom of information legislation may require the securities regulatory authorities in certain jurisdictions to make the comment letters available. Persons submitting comment letters should be aware that the press and members of the public may be able to obtain access to any comment letter.

For further information please contact any of the following:

Diane Joly
Chef du service de
  l'information continue
Commission des valeurs
  mobilières du Québec
(514) 873-5326

Robert F. Kohl
Solicitor, Capital Markets
Ontario Securities Commission
(416) 593-8233

Glenda A. Campbell
Senior Legal Counsel
Alberta Securities Commission
(403) 427-5201

Robert Hudson
Policy Advisor
British Columbia Securities
  Commission
(604) 660-4883

DATED at Vancouver, British Columbia, on October 12, 1994.

Douglas M. Hyndman
Chair

Attachment

NIN#94/20

NOTICE

DRAFT NATIONAL POLICY STATEMENT NO. 43
ADVERTISEMENTS OF SECURITIES AND RELATED SALES PRACTICES

The Canadian Securities Administrators (the "CSA") are publishing for comment Draft National Policy Statement No. 43 (the "Draft Policy"). The Draft Policy establishes minimum national standards for advertisements of securities.

Background

In May, 1987 the Ontario Securities Commission formed a private sector industry committee to examine advertising of securities and recommend changes to existing policy on advertising. In response to that Committee's recommendations, the CSA formed a committee in the fall of 1988 to draft a national policy on advertising. The CSA published for comment a draft policy in November, 1989.

The CSA received extensive comment on the draft policy, and has considered and incorporated many of those comments when preparing the Draft Policy.

In preparing the Draft Policy, the CSA considered a number of issues which, in its experience, have been a cause for concern with advertisements for securities. Although many of these concerns have been addressed directly in the Draft Policy, the CSA decided not to deal specifically with its concerns regarding advertised private placements. For instance, the CSA considered including a provision in the Draft Policy which would require an issuer or selling securityholder to afford a purchaser the right, in the agreement of purchase and sale for the advertised private placement, to disclaim the agreement within two business days following execution of the agreement. Consideration was also given to whether the agreement of purchase and sale should include representations regarding the materials that the investor has been provided with and disclosure regarding restrictions attached to the securities regulatory authorities. Accordingly, in addition to any specific or general comments you may have on the Draft Policy, the CSA asks that you provide specific comments on these issues.

Comments Requested

The CSA invite comment on the Draft Policy. Please submit 6 copies of any comment letter by January 16, 1995 to:

Director, Policy and Legislation
British Columbia Securities Commission
1100 - 865 Hornby Street
Vancouver, British Columbia
V6Z 2H4

Comment letters submitted in response to requests for comments are placed in the public file in certain jurisdictions and form part of the public record unless confidentiality is requested. Comment letters will be circulated among the securities regulatory authorities for purposes of finalizing the Draft Policy whether or not confidentiality is requested.

Accordingly, although letters for which confidentiality is requested will not be placed in the public file, freedom of information legislation may require the securities regulatory authorities in certain jurisdictions to make the comment letters available. Persons submitting comment letters should be aware that the press and members of the public may be able to obtain access to any comment letter.

DATED at Vancouver, British Columbia, on October 14, 1994.

Douglas M. Hyndman
Chair

Attachment

REF: NIN#89/37

NIN#94/21

NOTICE

EXPEDITED REVIEW OF SHORT FORM PROSPECTUSES AND RENEWAL AIFS

To expedite the review and receipt of short form prospectuses and the review and acceptance of renewal annual information forms ("Renewal AIFs") filed under the prompt offering qualification system (the "POP System") in more than one province or territory and to provide for continuing uniformity of administration of securities legislation, the following securities regulatory authorities (the "Participating Jurisdictions") have entered into a Memorandum of Understanding (the "Memorandum of Understanding") setting out the procedures to be followed by an eligible issuer or selling security holder (the "Issuer") to obtain a preliminary and final receipt for a short form prospectus or acceptance of a Renewal AIF on an expedited basis ("Expedited Review"):

- Alberta Securities Commission
- British Columbia Securities Commission
- Manitoba Securities Commission
- Nova Scotia Securities Commission
- Office of the Administrator of Securities, New Brunswick
- Ontario Securities Commission
- Registrar under the Prince Edward Island Securities Act
- Registrar of Securities under the Securities Act, Northwest Territories
- Registrar of Securities under the Yukon Territory Securities Act
- Saskatchewan Securities Commission
- Securities Commission of Newfoundland

The British Columbia Securities Commission is publishing the Memorandum of Understanding to facilitate the use of Expedited Review in British Columbia in the Weekly Summary of November 4, 1994. Other Participating Jurisdictions are taking equivalent steps.

The Memorandum of Understanding is substantially the same as the proposal (the "Proposal") for Expedited Review that the Canadian Securities Administrators (the "CSA") published for comment in August, 1994 but reflects, as discussed below, many of the comments received by the CSA on the Proposal. The Memorandum of Understanding takes effect on November 15, 1994.

Notices

The Commission is concurrently publishing in the Weekly Summary NIN#94/22, a permission granted by the Superintendent of Brokers under section 35(1)(c) of the Securities Act to facilitate Expedited Review by permitting representations as to the listing or quotation of securities on a stock exchange or an automatic quotation system provided certain conditions are met.

Each Participating Jurisdiction expects Issuers to comply with all local requirements of each province or territory in which they propose to distribute securities under Expedited Review.

COORDINATION WITH THE COMMISSION DES VALEURS MOBILIÈRES DU QUÉBEC

The Commission des valeurs mobilières du Québec (the "CVMQ") has participated in the discussions relating to the Memorandum of Understanding and agrees with its basic purpose and intent. However, the CVMQ is not currently in a position to become a Participating Jurisdiction under the Memorandum of Understanding.

An Issuer filing a preliminary short form prospectus or short form prospectus with Participating Jurisdictions and the CVMQ may nonetheless elect Expedited Review and file under National Policy Statement No. 1 ("NPS 1") provided it selects its Designated Jurisdiction under Expedited Review as its Principal Jurisdiction for the purposes of NPS 1. In these circumstances, the issuer will be dealing only with its Designated Jurisdiction and the CVMQ, unless one or more Participating Jurisdictions opts out of Expedited Review. The CVMQ has generally agreed to review any preliminary short form prospectus filed under Expedited Review within three working days.

Alternatively, an Issuer wishing to offer securities throughout Canada can file its preliminary short form prospectus under NPS 1 and the review process will be conducted in the same manner as prior to the implementation of Expedited Review. If it does so, it may select any province that is prepared to act in such capacity as its Principal Jurisdiction for the purposes of NPS 1. The Issuer may elect to receive a National Policy No. 1 Receipt that will have the same effect as prior to the implementation of Expedited Review.

DISCUSSION OF COMMENTS

Eight comment letters were received in response to the Request for Comments which accompanied the Proposal. Copies of these comment letters, other than those regarding which confidentiality was specifically requested, are available for inspection through the public filing system maintained by or on behalf of the British Columbia, Alberta and Ontario Securities Commissions.

Commentators were generally supportive of the Proposal. Some commentators requested that the procedures be extended to apply to renewal simplified prospectuses and annual information forms filed by mutual funds under National Policy Statement No. 36 or Initial AIFs. Other commentators suggested technical changes to clarify the application and effect of Expedited Review.

The Request for Comments published along with the Proposal indicated that the CVMQ was not a Participating Jurisdiction under the Proposal and contained alternative procedures under which the CVMQ was likely to agree to participate in a system of expedited review for short form prospectuses. Several of the commentators expressed concern that the CVMQ was not a Participating Jurisdiction under the Proposal.

The Memorandum of Understanding takes into account many of the comments received concerning the Proposal. This notice discusses the significant comments received on, and changes made to the Proposal. Issuers and their advisors are encouraged to review the Memorandum of Understanding in its entirety.

Eligibility

The Participating Jurisdictions recognize that it may be appropriate to extend the procedures implemented under Expedited Review to other issuers and types of distributions, but wish to defer any expansion of the eligibility criteria until Expedited Review has been operating long enough to allow them to take their experience with Expedited Review into consideration when examining whether or not to extend it.

After considering comments received, it was decided not to extend the availability of Expedited Review to renewal simplified prospectuses and annual information forms filed by mutual fund issuers for the reason stated above and to allow consideration of this issue in light of any proposal for change that might result from the overall review of the investment funds industry currently under way in Ontario.

The Participating Jurisdictions also decided not to extend the availability of Expedited Review to Initial AIFs or the situation where an Issuer files a Renewal AIF in a Participating Jurisdiction in which it has never filed an Initial AIF because some of the Participating Jurisdictions wish to retain their individual review procedures in recognition of the fact that the Initial AIF is the foundation for entry into the POP System in a particular Jurisdiction. For similar reasons, one commentator's suggestion that a waiver under section 4.5 of National Policy Statement No. 47 ("NPS 47") be considered by only the Designated Jurisdiction was not adopted. Such a waiver if granted amounts to a variation of NPS 47 for the particular Issuer and although certain waivers may be technical in nature, others may raise substantive issues.

The Proposal provided that Expedited Review would not be available for distributions of derivative securities. In view of concerns expressed as to the meaning of derivative securities, the Memorandum of Understanding includes a definition of derivative securities.

Effect of Opting Out by a Participating Jurisdiction

Some commentators were concerned about the ability of Participating Jurisdictions to opt out of Expedited Review. The Participating Jurisdictions reasonably expect that any uncertainty created by the opting out provisions will be reduced over time as Issuers gain experience with the limited circumstances under which the opting out provisions are used.

In response to comments received, the Memorandum of Understanding clarifies that where a Participating Jurisdiction opts out of Expedited Review for a particular preliminary short form prospectus, the preliminary expedited review receipt document remains effective for the preliminary short form prospectus filed in that Participating Jurisdiction. It also clarifies that where a Participating Jurisdiction opts out of Expedited Review the Issuer must file, as soon as is possible, the usual preliminary materials with the Participating Jurisdiction opting out. That Participating Jurisdiction will then conduct its own review of the particular short form prospectus in accordance with procedures under NPS 1.

Application of Expedited Review to Other Policy Statements

The Memorandum of Understanding clarifies that the filing procedures for a preliminary short form prospectus and short form prospectus set out in Section 6.3 of NPS 47 are subject to the filing procedures provided under the Memorandum of Understanding for Issuers electing Expedited Review.

Fees

One commentator suggested that the fees payable to Participating Jurisdictions other than the Designated Jurisdiction be reduced. Since the fees payable by a particular Issuer are designed to support the overall securities regulatory system for the benefit of the Issuer, the Issuer's security holders and other capital market participants and are not related to the workload associated with the review of a particular preliminary short form prospectus or Renewal AIF, this comment was not adopted.

Designated Jurisdiction

Schedule "A" has been updated to show the Designated Jurisdiction assigned to Issuers as at October 1, 1994.

SELECTIVE REVIEW

In the Memorandum of Understanding the Participating Jurisdictions acknowledge that a Participating Jurisdiction may adopt and implement a system of selective review of filings that would apply to preliminary short form prospectuses under Expedited Review. The Memorandum of Understanding provides that any Participating Jurisdiction adopting a system of selective review will agree to notify the other Participating Jurisdictions if and when it adopts a system of selective review and will provide sufficient information to those Participating Jurisdictions for them to assess the scope of review under the system of selective review.

The Ontario Securities Commission and its Director have adopted a system of selective review which came into effect on October 3, 1994 and which the Participating

Jurisdictions acknowledge will be applied to preliminary short form prospectuses and Renewal AIFs filed under Expedited Review. This selective review system is described in a notice entitled "Selective Review System" published in the OSC Bulletin dated September 16, 1994 at (1994), 17 OSCB 4387.

Responsibility for compliance with applicable securities legislation, policies and practices remains with Issuers and their advisors. The fact that a document is not selected for review in no way detracts from such responsibility. Issuers are cautioned that it may not be appropriate to rely on a short form prospectus or a Renewal AIF as a precedent notwithstanding that the Ontario Securities Commission, as the Issuer's Designated Jurisdiction, has issued an expedited review receipt document for it or accepted it as a Renewal AIF since not all preliminary short form prospectuses and Renewal AIFs are reviewed in the selective review system.

For information, please contact any of the following:

Glenda A. Campbell   Louyse Gauvin
Senior Legal Counsel   Policy Advisor
Alberta Securities Commission   British Columbia
                                          Securities Commission
(403) 427-5201
                                          (604) 660-4800
Susan I. McCallum
Policy Advisor to the Chairman
Ontario Securities Commission

(416) 593-8248

DATED at Vancouver, British Columbia, on November 3, 1994.

Douglas M. Hyndman
Chair

MEMORANDUM OF UNDERSTANDING
FOR EXPEDITED REVIEW OF SHORT FORM
PROSPECTUSES AND RENEWAL AIFS

1. PURPOSE

The Participating Jurisdictions recognize the ongoing need to improve the efficiency of the Canadian capital markets by speeding up the prospectus review process and by reducing costs for senior issuers. The Participating Jurisdictions are especially cognizant of the timing difficulties encountered by Issuers accessing public capital markets when required to deal with the various jurisdictions involved in securities regulation across Canada. In response, the Participating Jurisdictions have agreed to expedite the review and receipt of short form prospectuses and review and acceptance of Renewal AIFs filed under the prompt offering qualification system in more than one Canadian jurisdiction and have reached the following understanding with respect to the procedure to be followed by the Participating Jurisdictions. The Participating Jurisdictions believe that Expedited Review represents a step towards increased harmonization and the elimination of duplication in the current securities regulatory system.

2. INTERPRETATION

Capitalized terms have the meaning assigned to them in NPS 47 unless defined below:

"Designated Jurisdiction" means the Securities Regulatory Authority or Applicable Regulator, as the context requires, of the province or territory assigned to each Issuer eligible to use the POP System as at October 1, 1994 as set out in Schedule "A", as amended from time to time, or as communicated to the Issuer at the time of acceptance of its Initial AIF;

"Expedited Review" means the expedited review system and procedures provided for under this Memorandum of Understanding;

"Expedited Review Committee" means the working committee established by the Participating Jurisdictions;

"Facsimile" means a facsimile or other form of electronic communication;

"Final Filing Materials" means:

(a)   the documents and fees that are required to be filed with the various provinces and territories in connection with a preliminary short form prospectus and short form prospectus as specified in the "Table of Documents to be filed in respect of the Clearance of National Issues" forming part of NPS 1; and

(b)   all comment letters issued by the Designated Jurisdiction and responses thereto;

"Issuer" means issuer or selling security holder, as the context requires;

"NPS 1" means National Policy Statement No. 1, as amended from time to time;

"NPS 47" means National Policy Statement No. 47, as amended from time to time;

"Non-Participating Jurisdiction" means a Securities Regulatory Authority or Applicable Regulator, as the context requires, of a province or territory that is not a Participating Jurisdiction;

"Participating Jurisdiction" means:

(a)   a Securities Regulatory Authority or Applicable Regulator, as the context requires, of a province or territory that has agreed to participate in Expedited Review; or

(b)   any other Securities Regulatory Authority or Applicable Regulator, as the context requires, of a province or territory that becomes a participant in the manner set out in 4 below;

"Preliminary Materials" means the documents and fees that are required to be filed with the various provinces and territories with a preliminary short form prospectus as specified in the "Table of Documents to be filed in respect of the Clearance of National Issues" forming part of NPS 1;

"POP System" means the prompt offering qualification system for the distribution by an Issuer of securities of an Issuer by means of a short form prospectus as contemplated in NPS 47 or the Québec Securities Act and Securities Regulation;

"Undertaking" means the undertaking addressed to each of the Participating Jurisdictions other than the Designated Jurisdiction to file the Final Filing Materials within three working days following the date of the final expedited review receipt document.

3.   RETENTION OF DISCRETION

Expedited Review involves no surrender of jurisdiction by any Participating Jurisdiction. Each of the Participating Jurisdictions retains the statutory discretion to review and receipt or refuse to issue a receipt for a particular short form prospectus.

4.   SCOPE

This Memorandum of Understanding sets out the procedures agreed to by each of the Participating Jurisdictions governing the implementation and operation of Expedited Review.

At any time after the effective date of the Memorandum of Understanding, any Non-Participating Jurisdiction may become a Participating Jurisdiction by giving notice of its desire to participate in Expedited Review and executing a counterpart of the Memorandum of Understanding.

5.   ELIGIBILITY

An Issuer will be eligible to elect Expedited Review for:

(a)   distributions of its securities unless those securities are derivative securities[1] in more than one Participating Jurisdiction under the POP System; and

(b)   Renewal AIFs filed in more than one Participating Jurisdiction under NPS 47.

Notices

6. CONSULTATION

Each of the Participating Jurisdictions may appoint one representative to the Expedited Review Committee. The Expedited Review Committee will be responsible for ensuring consistency of review of filings and coordinating any changes or amendments to and otherwise monitoring Expedited Review.

7. DESIGNATED JURISDICTION

The Expedited Review Committee will assign a Designated Jurisdiction to each Issuer eligible to participate in the POP System. All decisions of the Expedited Review Committee will be based on its view of what is most administratively efficient and will be final. Each of the Securities Regulatory Authorities of Alberta, British Columbia, Manitoba, Nova Scotia, Ontario and Saskatchewan have agreed to act as Designated Jurisdictions. Designated Jurisdictions of Issuers eligible to participate in the POP System as at October 1, 1994 are set out in Schedule "A".

Any Issuer becoming eligible to use the POP System after October 1, 1994 will be assigned a Designated Jurisdiction by the Expedited Review Committee prior to acceptance of the Issuer's Initial AIF. The Designated Jurisdiction will notify the Issuer that it is the Issuer's Designated Jurisdiction at the time of acceptance of the Issuer's Initial AIF.

Schedule "A" will be amended and republished from time to time.

An Issuer electing Expedited Review is required to use the Designated Jurisdiction assigned to that Issuer. An Issuer filing a preliminary short form prospectus or short form prospectus with a Non-Participating Jurisdiction may, nonetheless, elect Expedited Review and file under NPS 1, provided it selects the Issuer's Designated Jurisdiction as its Principal Jurisdiction for the purposes of NPS 1.[2]

8. EXPEDITED REVIEW PROCESS FOR SHORT FORM PROSPECTUSES

8.1 Applications for Relief

The Issuer is responsible for making application for any exemptive relief which may be needed from any Participating Jurisdiction. Application should be made prior to filing Preliminary Materials in the Designated Jurisdiction under Expedited Review. Where an application cannot be made prior to the filing of the Preliminary Materials, it must be made contemporaneously with the filing.

If relief has not been obtained within the time for opting out of Expedited Review, the issuance of a final expedited review receipt document may be delayed or the Participating Jurisdiction (in which the relief is required) may opt out for the particular filing.

8.2 Filing Procedures for Preliminary Materials

The Issuer must indicate in the covering letter filed with the preliminary short form prospectus that it is electing Expedited Review and identify the provinces and territories in which the preliminary short form prospectus is being filed.

The Issuer shall file the Preliminary Materials with the Designated Jurisdiction only and, on the same day, send a Facsimile of the covering letter, preliminary short form prospectus and Undertaking to each of the other Participating Jurisdictions in which the Issuer proposes to distribute securities.

8.3 Preliminary Expedited Review Receipt Document

If the Preliminary Materials are acceptable, the Designated Jurisdiction will issue the preliminary expedited review receipt document. Immediately after its issuance, the Designated Jurisdiction will send, by Facsimile, the preliminary expedited review receipt document to each Participating Jurisdiction where the preliminary short form prospectus was filed.

The preliminary expedited review receipt document evidences that a preliminary receipt has been issued by each Participating Jurisdiction in which the preliminary short form prospectus was filed, including those that have opted out.

The preliminary expedited review receipt document will bear on its face the following legend:

> "This preliminary expedited review receipt document confirms that preliminary receipts of (name each Participating Jurisdiction in which the preliminary short form prospectus was filed) have been issued".

Certain jurisdictions will support the statements in the preliminary expedited review receipt document by in fact issuing a local preliminary receipt. In those jurisdictions a filing under Expedited Review will be treated as a request to hold the local preliminary receipt on behalf of the Issuer unless the Issuer requests physical possession of the preliminary receipts from those jurisdictions.

8.4   Review

A Participating Jurisdiction will have two working days following the date of the preliminary expedited review receipt document to conduct such review as it considers appropriate to determine whether it wishes to opt out of Expedited Review for that particular filing (see section 8.6 – Opting Out Procedures). In most cases, this review of the preliminary short form prospectus will be restricted to identifying any specific concerns with the transaction, the related disclosure or any other special circumstances.

Unless a Participating Jurisdiction notifies, by Facsimile, the Designated Jurisdiction otherwise within the two working days, it will, by its silence, have confirmed its participation in Expedited Review.

The Participating Jurisdictions acknowledge that a Participating Jurisdiction may adopt and implement a system of selective review of filings that would apply to preliminary short form prospectuses under Expedited Review. Any Participating Jurisdiction adopting a system of selective review will agree to notify the other Participating Jurisdictions if and when it adopts a system of selective review and will provide sufficient information to those Participating Jurisdictions for them to assess the scope of review under the system of selective review.

The Designated Jurisdiction is responsible for issuing comments to the Issuer arising out of its review. The comment letter will identify any Participating Jurisdictions that have opted out of Expedited Review. Comments will be issued within three working days following the date of filing of the preliminary short form prospectus unless, in the opinion of the Designated Jurisdiction, the proposed offering is too complex to be reviewed adequately within the three working days.[3] In the these circumstances, the Designated Jurisdiction will, by the end of the first working day following the date of the preliminary expedited review receipt document, notify the Issuer and the other Participating Jurisdictions by Facsimile that the time period will be extended to that applicable to prospectuses (other than short form prospectuses) and AIFs under NPS 1. Responses to comments should be in writing addressed to and will be resolved by the Designated Jurisdiction.

If the Designated Jurisdiction determines that it is not prepared to recommend that a final expedited review receipt document be issued for a particular short form prospectus, it will notify the Issuer and each of the Participating Jurisdictions that has not opted out of Expedited Review of its decision. At that point, the Issuer is obliged to co-ordinate the review process with each Participating Jurisdiction and Expedited Review is no longer applicable to this filing. Each of the Participating Jurisdictions will determine in accordance with its normal procedure whether or not to issue a final receipt for the short form prospectus.

8.5   Final Expedited Review Receipt Document

Designated Jurisdiction

The Designated Jurisdiction will issue the final expedited review receipt document if:

(a)   at least two working days have elapsed following the date of the preliminary expedited review receipt document;

(b)   all comments have been resolved with the Designated Jurisdiction; and

(c)   the Designated Jurisdiction has received, in acceptable form, the documents and fees that are required to be filed in that province in connection with a short form prospectus as specified in the "Table of Documents to be filed in respect of the Clearance of National Issues" forming part of NPS 1.

The issuance of the final expedited review receipt document by the Designated Jurisdiction will evidence that a final receipt has been issued by each Participating Jurisdiction in which the preliminary short form prospectus was filed other than those that have opted out of Expedited Review.

The final expedited review receipt document will bear on its face the following legend:

"This final expedited review receipt document confirms that receipts of (name each Participating Jurisdiction in which the preliminary short form prospectus was filed [except any that have opted out]) have been issued."

The Designated Jurisdiction will send, by Facsimile, the final expedited review receipt document immediately after its issuance to each Participating Jurisdiction in which the preliminary short form prospectus was filed other than those that have opted out of Expedited Review.

Certain jurisdictions will support the statements in the final expedited review receipt document by in fact issuing a local final receipt. In those jurisdictions a filing under Expedited Review will be treated as a request to hold the local final receipt on behalf of the Issuer unless the Issuer requests physical possession of the final receipts from those jurisdictions.

Participating Jurisdictions Other Than the Designated Jurisdiction

The Issuer, in accordance with its Undertaking, will file with the Participating Jurisdictions, other than the Designated Jurisdiction and those Participating Jurisdictions that have opted out of Expedited Review, the Final Filing Materials before the end of the third working day following the date of the final expedited review receipt document.

If the final expedited review receipt document is not issued in respect of a Participating Jurisdiction, the Undertaking is of no effect for that Participating Jurisdiction, except for fees. For greater certainty, Issuers will always be required to pay the relevant filing fees incurred in the Participating Jurisdictions in which the preliminary short form prospectus or short form prospectus was filed.

8.6   Opting Out Procedures

Each Participating Jurisdiction is entitled to opt out of Expedited Review for any particular preliminary short form prospectus. Any Participating Jurisdiction choosing to opt out of Expedited Review for a particular preliminary short form prospectus will notify the Issuer, the Designated Jurisdiction and all other Participating Jurisdictions, by Facsimile, before the end of the second working day following the date of the preliminary expedited review receipt document.

If a Participating Jurisdiction opts out of Expedited Review for a particular preliminary short form prospectus, the procedures set out in NPS 1 apply regarding that particular preliminary short form prospectus in that jurisdiction.

Immediately upon receipt of notification from a Participating Jurisdiction that it has opted out of Expedited Review with respect to a particular preliminary short form prospectus filing, the Issuer shall file Preliminary Materials with that Participating Jurisdiction. Notwithstanding the time periods provided for short form prospectuses in NPS 1, if the Preliminary Materials are not filed expeditiously with the Participating Jurisdiction opting out, the time periods provided for under NPS 1 may not be met by the Participating Jurisdiction opting out of Expedited Review.

A Participating Jurisdiction that has opted out of Expedited Review for a particular filing may opt back in at any time prior to the issuance of the final expedited review receipt document by notifying the Designated Jurisdiction, the other Participating Jurisdictions and the Issuer, by Facsimile. It is the responsibility of that Participating Jurisdiction to ensure that the final expedited review receipt document has not been issued prior to its opting back into Expedited Review.

9. EXPEDITED REVIEW PROCESS FOR RENEWAL AIFS

9.1 Filing Procedures

As an alternative to the Renewal AIF review procedure set out in section 5.2 of NPS 47, an Issuer may elect Expedited Review of its Renewal AIF filed with more than one Participating Jurisdiction. Where an Issuer elects Expedited Review, the procedures set out in section 5.2 of NPS 47 apply mutatis mutandis to the acceptance of a Renewal AIF under Expedited Review subject to the modifications described below.

The Issuer must indicate in the covering letter filed with its Renewal AIF that it is electing Expedited Review and must identify each province or territory in which its Renewal AIF is being filed.

If the Issuer is filing its Renewal AIF in more than one Participating Jurisdiction and in a Non-Participating Jurisdiction, it may nonetheless elect Expedited Review and be subject to selective review under section 5.2(6). In this case, the Designated Jurisdiction shall be the only Participating Jurisdiction to select the Issuer's Renewal AIF for review under section 5.2(6)(a) of NPS 47 and the Participating Jurisdictions anticipate the procedures set forth in section 5.2(6)(b), (d), (e) and (f) of NPS 47 will be followed by each Non-Participating Jurisdiction in which the Renewal AIF is filed.

The Issuer shall file the covering letter, Renewal AIF and supporting documents, in the number of copies specified for each province and territory in the "Table of Documents to be filed in respect of the Clearance of National Issues" forming part of NPS 1, with the Designated Jurisdiction and each Participating Jurisdiction in which its Renewal AIF is being filed.

9.2 Expedited Notice of Acceptance

The Designated Jurisdiction shall immediately accept for filing a Renewal AIF filed in accordance with section 5.2(1) of NPS 47 and shall forward to the Issuer an expedited notice of acceptance document of its Renewal AIF. Immediately after its issuance, the Designated Jurisdiction will send, by Facsimile, the expedited notice of acceptance to each Participating Jurisdiction where the Renewal AIF has been filed.

The expedited notice of acceptance document will evidence that the Renewal AIF has been accepted by each Participating Jurisdiction in which the Renewal AIF was filed.

The expedited notice of acceptance document will state the following:

"This expedited notice of acceptance confirms that the renewal annual information form of (name the Issuer) dated — has been accepted under National Policy Statement No. 47 by (name the Participating Jurisdictions in which the Renewal AIF has been filed)."

Issuers will not have to obtain a separate notice of acceptance from each of the Participating Jurisdictions.

9.3 Review of Renewal AIFs

Where an Issuer has elected Expedited Review for its Renewal AIF filed under section 5.2(1) of NPS 47, the Renewal AIF is only subject to selective review under section 5.2(6) of NPS 47 by the Designated Jurisdiction and any Non-Participating Jurisdiction.

Where an Issuer files its Renewal AIF and supporting documents in the circumstances described in either section 5.2(2) or 5.2(3) of NPS 47 and elects Expedited Review, the Renewal AIF shall only be subject to the review procedures referred to in section 5.1 of NPS 47 by the Designated Jurisdiction and any Non-Participating Jurisdiction.

Notices

Where the Designated Jurisdiction either reviews under section 5.2(2) or 5.2(3) or selects an Issuer's Renewal AIF for review under section 5.2(6) of NPS 47, no other Participating Jurisdiction will conduct a review of the Renewal AIF.

For the purposes of section 5.2(6)(a) of NPS 47, the Designated Jurisdiction shall forward, within 10 days of its acceptance of the Renewal AIF, by Facsimile, a notice to the Issuer, the other Participating Jurisdictions and any Non-Participating Jurisdiction in which the Renewal AIF was filed, stating that the Issuer's Renewal AIF will reviewed.

During any review period, all copies of the Renewal AIF provided to any Person by the Issuer shall have in bold faced type[4] on the outside front cover page the following statement or any variation that the Issuer's Designated Jurisdiction may permit:

> "This annual information form has been accepted for filing in (name of each Participating or Non-Participating Jurisdiction in which the Renewal AIF has been filed) but is currently subject to review by securities regulatory authorities of one or more provinces or territories of Canada. Information contained herein is subject to change."

As soon as practical after the completion of any review, or upon the Issuer filing a Revised AIF, if necessary, the Designated Jurisdiction shall issue a document stating that the review is completed and that either the Renewal AIF as filed or the Revised AIF, if any, is satisfactory to the Designated Jurisdiction. This document shall be sent to the Issuer with a copy to any other province or territory in which the Renewal AIF was filed.

Upon receipt of the document(s) referred to above from the Designated Jurisdiction and any Non-Participating Jurisdiction reviewing the Issuer's Renewal AIF, the Issuer shall promptly

(a)   if revisions were necessary, file the Revised AIF with all provinces and territories in which the Renewal AIF was filed and forward a copy of the Revised AIF to any Person who received a legended Renewal AIF and,

(b)   if revisions were not necessary, forward a notice that the review of the Renewal AIF is completed and that no revisions were necessary to any Person who received a legended Renewal AIF.

If a Revised AIF is filed, it shall be identified as such.

An Issuer shall not be entitled to a receipt for a final prospectus either evidenced by a final expedited review receipt document or otherwise until the Issuer notifies the Designated Jurisdiction that a Revised AIF, if any, has been filed with all the provinces and territories in which its Renewal AIF was filed.

Where an Issuer falls within the circumstances described in either sections 5.2(7) or 5.2(8) of NPS 47, the Issuer's preliminary short form prospectus and Renewal AIF will be reviewed at the same time within the time limits referred to in section 8, entitled "Expedited Review Process For Short Form Prospectuses", and the issuance of the expedited review receipt document for the short form prospectus will be subject in either case to the same condition as set out in section 5.2(7) of NPS 47.

10. IMPACT OF MEMORANDUM OF UNDERSTANDING

Where an Issuer has elected Expedited Review and follows the procedures set out herein for filing a preliminary short form prospectus and short form prospectus, the filing procedures for a preliminary short form prospectus and short form prospectus provided in section 6.3 of NPS 47 shall be subject to the filing procedures provided for under this Memorandum of Understanding.

The procedures for clearing short form prospectuses or Renewal AIFs under NPS 1 and NPS 47 used by any Non-Participating Jurisdiction will not be affected by Expedited Review.

Where a Non-Participating Jurisdiction is selected as Principal Jurisdiction by an Issuer, Expedited Review is not available and the procedures provided under NPS 47 will be followed.

11. CHRONOLOGY

Attached as Schedule "B" is a chronology which illustrates Expedited Review.

12. COUNTERPARTS

This Memorandum of Understanding may be executed in several counterparts, each of which so executed shall be deemed to be an original, and such counterparts together shall constitute one and the same instrument.

This Memorandum Of Understanding is effective as of this 15th day of November, 1994.

William L. Hess

Robert B. MacLellan

William L. Hess, Q.C.
Chairman of the Board
Alberta Securities Commission

Robert B. MacLellan, Chairman
Nova Scotia Securities Commission

Douglas M. Hyndman

Edward J. Waitzer

Douglas M. Hyndman, Chair
British Columbia Securities
Commission

Edward J. Waitzer, Chair
Ontario Securities Commission

Jocelyn Samson

Edison Shea

Jocelyn Samson, Chairman of the
Commission
Manitoba Securities Commission

Edison Shea, Registrar of Securities
Department of Provincial Affairs
and Attorney General
Prince Edward Island

Donne W. Smith Jr.

Marcel de la Gorgendiere

Donne W. Smith Jr., Administrator
Office of the Administrator of
Securities
New Brunswick

Marcel de la Gorgendiere, Chairman
Saskatchewan Securities Commission

George F. Kennedy

M. Richard Roberts

George F. Kennedy, Director of
Securities
Department of Justice
Government of Newfoundland and
Labrador

M. Richard Roberts
Registrar of Securities
Government of Yukon

Gary I. MacDougall

Gary I. MacDougall, Registrar of
Securities
Government of Northwest Territories

ENDNOTES

1. Derivative securities generally include securities the value of which, or the return from, is based upon the market price, value or return of one or more underlying securities or commodities or upon the level of one or more financial benchmarks such as interest rates, foreign exchange rates or stock market indices. For the purposes of this Memorandum of Understanding, derivative securities do not include warrants or other securities exchangeable for, or convertible into, securities issued by the issuer or an affiliate of the issuer.

2. For example, if a POP issuer wishes to offer securities throughout Canada, it should file a preliminary short form prospectus under NPS 1, and may, provided it selects its Designated Jurisdiction as its Principal Jurisdiction for the purposes of NPS 1, elect Expedited Review. In this case, the Designated Jurisdiction will act as the Principal Jurisdiction under NPS 1 and the Designated Jurisdiction under Expedited Review.

On receipt of acceptable materials, the Designated Jurisdiction will issue a preliminary expedited review receipt document that will evidence the issuance of a preliminary receipt by each of the Participating Jurisdictions. Any Non-Participating Jurisdiction will issue a separate preliminary receipt document.

The Designated Jurisdiction will review the preliminary short form prospectus and issue comments to the issuer and any Non-Participating Jurisdiction within three working days following the receipt of the preliminary short form prospectus. Any Non-Participating Jurisdiction will send its comments, if any, to the issuer and the Designated Jurisdiction, as Principal Jurisdiction, on or before the end of the second working day following the date of receipt of the Designated Jurisdiction's comments.

Prior to the issuance of comments from the Designated Jurisdiction, a Non-Participating Jurisdiction may, if it wishes, send its comments or notify the issuer and the Designated Jurisdiction that it has no comments on the preliminary short form prospectus. This practice would ensure that the Non-Participating Jurisdiction's comments, if any, are incorporated in the comment letter to be issued by the Designated Jurisdiction before the conclusion of the third working day following the filing of the preliminary short form prospectus.

Provided acceptable final materials have been received and comments from all Non-Participating Jurisdictions have been resolved, the Designated Jurisdiction will issue a final expedited review receipt document that will evidence the issuance of a final receipt by each Participating Jurisdiction that had not opted out of Expedited Review and, in its capacity as Principal Jurisdiction under NPS 1, will notify any Non-Participating Jurisdiction that it has done so. The Non-Participating Jurisdiction will then, if it considers it appropriate, issue a local final receipt.

Alternatively, an issuer wishing to offer securities throughout Canada can file its preliminary short form prospectus and supporting materials under NPS 1 and the review process will be conducted in the same manner as prior to the implementation of Expedited Review. If it does so, it may select any province that is prepared to act in such capacity as its Principal Jurisdiction for the purposes of NPS 1. The issuer may elect to receive a National Policy No. 1 Receipt that will have the same effect as prior to the implementation of Expedited Review.

3.   Issuers are reminded that if they are concerned that a proposed offering may be too complex to be reviewed within three working days they should discuss the proposed offering with the Designated Jurisdiction on a pre-filing basis.

4.   The statement required to be in bold faced type on the outside front cover of an issuer's Renewal AIF during a review period may be added by way of stamp, sticker or other method that will ensure that the statement may not be deleted or removed from the issuer's Renewal AIF.

SCHEDULE "A"

NAME OF POP ISSUER	DESIGNATED JURISDICTION
A.G.F. Management Limited	Ontario
AUR Resources Inc.	Ontario
Abitibi-Price Inc.	Ontario
Acklands Limited	Ontario
Agnico-Eagle Mines Limited	Ontario
Agra Industries Limited	Ontario
Air Canada	Ontario
Alberta Energy Company Ltd.	Alberta
Alberta Natural Gas Company Ltd.	Alberta
Alcan Aluminum Limited	Ontario
Alliance Communications Corporation	Ontario
American Barrick Resources Corporation	Ontario
Amoco Canada Petroleum Company Ltd.	Alberta
Anderson Exploration Ltd.	Alberta
Archer Resources Ltd.	Alberta

SCHEDULE "A"

NAME OF POP ISSUER	DESIGNATED JURISDICTION
Astral Communications Inc.	Ontario
Atco Ltd.	Alberta
Atcor Resources Ltd.	Alberta
Ault Foods Limited	Ontario
Avco Financial Services Canada Limited	Ontario
Avenor Inc.	Ontario
BC Gas Inc.	B.C.
BC Gas Utility Ltd.	B.C.
BC Sugar Refinery, Limited	B.C.
BC Tel	B.C.
BC Telecom Inc.	B.C.
BCE Inc.	Ontario
BCE Mobile Communications Inc.	Ontario
BGR Previous Metals Inc.	Ontario
Banister Inc.	Ontario
Bank of Montreal	Ontario
Bank of Nova Scotia, The	Ontario
Barrington Petroleum Ltd.	Alberta
Beau Canada Exploration Ltd.	Alberta
Bell Canada	Ontario
Beneficial Canada Inc.	Ontario
Biomira Inc.	Alberta
Bombardier Inc.	Ontario
Bow Valley Energy Ltd.	Alberta
Bracknell Corporation	Ontario
Bramalea Limited	Ontario
Brascan Limited	Ontario
British Petroleum Company plc, The	Ontario
Bruncor Inc.	Ontario
CAE Inc.	Ontario
CCL Industries Inc.	Ontario
CFCF Inc.	Ontario
C-MAC Industries Inc.	Ontario
CS Resources Inc.	Ontario
CT Financial Services Inc.	Ontario
Call-Net Enterprises Inc.	Ontario
Cambior Inc.	Ontario
Cambridge Shopping Centres Limited	Ontario
Cameco Corporation	Saskatchewan
Campbell Resources Inc.	Ontario
Canada Malting Co. Limited	Ontario
Canada Trustco Mortgage Company	Ontario
Canadian Imperial Bank of Commerce	Ontario
Canadian National Railway Company	Ontario
Canadian Natural Resources Limited	Alberta
Canadian Occidental Petroleum Ltd.	Alberta
Canadian Pacific Enterprises Limited	Ontario
Canadian Pacific Forest Products Limited	Ontario
Canadian Pacific Limited	Ontario
Canadian Pacific Securities Limited	Ontario
Canadian Tire Corporation, Limited	Ontario
Canadian Utilities Limited	Alberta
Canfor Corporation	B.C.
Carena Developments Limited	Ontario
Cascades Inc.	Ontario
Cascades Paperboard International Inc.	Ontario
Centra Gas Ontario Inc.	Ontario
Central Fund of Canada Limited	Ontario
Chancellor Energy Resources Inc.	Alberta
Chauvco Resources Ltd.	Alberta
Chieftain International Inc.	Alberta
Chrysler Credit Canada Ltd.	Ontario
Cineplex Odeon Corporation	Ontario
Cogeco Inc.	Ontario

Notices

SCHEDULE "A"

NAME OF POP ISSUER	DESIGNATED JURISDICTION
Co-Steel Inc.	Ontario
Cominco Fertilizers Ltd.	Alberta
Cominco Ltd.	B.C.
Consumers' Gas Company Ltd., The	Ontario
Conwest Exploration Company Limited	Alberta
Cott Corporation	Ontario
Crestar Energy Inc.	Alberta
Crown Life Insurance Company	Saskatchewan
Crownx Inc.	Ontario
Czar Resources Ltd.	Alberta
Delrina Corporation	Ontario
Derlan Industries Limited	Ontario
Discovery West Corp.	Ontario
Dofasco Inc.	Ontario
Doman Industries Limited	B.C.
Dominion Textile Inc.	Ontario
Domtar Inc.	Ontario
Donohue Inc.	Ontario
Dorset Exploration Ltd.	Alberta
Dreco Energy Services Ltd.	Alberta
Dundee Bancorp Inc.	Ontario
Du Pont Canada Inc.	Ontario
Dylex Limited	Ontario
Echo Bay Mines Ltd.	Alberta
Eden Roc Mineral Corp.	Ontario
Elan Energy Inc.	Alberta
Emco Limited	Ontario
Empire Company Limited	Nova Scotia
Enserv Corporation	Alberta
Euro-Nevada Mining Corporation Limited	Ontario
Excel Energy Inc.	Alberta
Fairfax Financial Holdings Limited	Ontario
Federal Industries Ltd.	Ontario
Finning Ltd.	B.C.
First Marathon Inc.	Ontario
Fletcher Challenge Canada Limited	B.C.
Ford Credit Canada Limited	Ontario
Fortis Inc.	Ontario
Four Seasons Hotels Inc.	Ontario
Franco-Nevada Mining Corporation Limited	Ontario
Future Shop Ltd.	B.C.
G.T.C. Transcontinental Group Ltd.	Ontario
Gaz Metropolitain Company, Limited Partnership	Ontario
Gaz Metropolitain Inc.	Ontario
General Motors Acceptance Company of Canada, Limited	Ontario
George Weston Limited	Ontario
Glamis Gold Inc.	B.C.
Golden Star Resources Ltd.	Ontario
Great Lakes Power Inc.	Ontario
Great-West Life Assurance Company, The	Manitoba
Great-West Lifeco Inc.	Manitoba
Gulf Canada Resources Limited	Ontario
Hammerson Property Investment and Development Corporation plc, The	Ontario
Hayes-Dana Inc.	Ontario
Hees International Bancorp Inc.	Ontario
Hemlo Gold Mines Inc.	Ontario
Hillcrest Resources Ltd.	Alberta
Hollinger Inc.	Ontario
Home Oil Company Limited	Alberta
Horsham Corporation, The	Ontario
Household Financial Corporation Limited	Ontario
Hudson's Bay Company	Ontario
Imasco Limited	Ontario

SCHEDULE "A"

NAME OF POP ISSUER	DESIGNATED JURISDICTION
Imperial Life Assurance Company of Canada, The	Ontario
Imperial Oil Limited	Ontario
Inco Limited	Ontario
Intertape Polymer Group Inc.	Ontario
Intensity Resources Ltd.	Alberta
International Colin Energy Corporation	Alberta
International Forest Products Limited	B.C.
International Semi-Tech Microelectronics Inc.	Ontario
Interprovincial PipeLine Inc.	Alberta
Interprovincial Pipe Line System Inc.	Alberta
Intrawest Corporation	B.C.
Inverness Petroleum Ltd.	Alberta
Investors Group Inc.	Manitoba
IPSCO Inc.	Saskatchewan
Ivaco Inc.	Ontario
Jannock Limited	Ontario
John Labatt Limited	Ontario
Jordan Petroleum Ltd.	Alberta
Kinross Gold Corporation	Ontario
La Caisse Centrale Desjardins Du Quebec	Ontario
LAC Minerals Ltd.	Ontario
Laidlaw Inc.	Ontario
Laurentian Bank of Canada	Ontario
Linamar Corporation	Ontario
Live Entertainment of Canada Ltd.	Ontario
Loblaw Companies Limited	Ontario
Loewen Group Inc., The	B.C.
London Insurance Group Inc.	Ontario
MDS Health Group Limited	Ontario
Mackenzie Financial Corporation	Ontario
MacMillan Bloedel Limited	B.C.
Magna International Inc.	Ontario
Malette Inc.	Ontario
Mannville Oil & Gas Ltd.	Alberta
Maple Leaf Foods Inc.	Ontario
Maritime Telegraph and Telephone Company, Limited	Nova Scotia
Maritime Tel & Tel Limited	Nova Scotia
Mark Resources Inc.	Alberta
Markborough Properties Inc.	Ontario
Meridian Technologies Inc.	Ontario
Metall Mining Corporation	Ontario
Methanex Corporation	B.C.
Metro-Richelieu Inc.	Ontario
Midland Walwyn Inc.	Ontario
Mitel Corporation	Ontario
Molson Companies Limited, The	Ontario
Montreal Trustco Inc.	Ontario
Moore Corporation Limited	Ontario
Morgan Hydrocarbons Inc.	Alberta
Morrison Petroleums Ltd.	Alberta
National Bank of Canada	Ontario
National Trustco Inc.	Ontario
New Brunswick Telephone Company Limited, The	Ontario
Newbridge Networks Corporation	Ontario
Newfoundland Light & Power Co. Limited	Ontario
Newfoundland Telephone Company Limited	Ontario
Newtel Enterprises Limited	Ontario
Noma Industries Limited	Ontario
Noranda Forest Inc.	Ontario
Noranda Inc.	Ontario
Norcen Energy Resources Limited	Alberta
North Canadian Oils Limited	Alberta
Northern Telecom Limited	Ontario
Northrock Resources Ltd.	Alberta

Notices

SCHEDULE "A"

NAME OF POP ISSUER	DESIGNATED JURISDICTION
Northstar Energy Corporation	Alberta
NOVA Corporation	Alberta
Nova Gas Transmission Ltd.	Alberta
Nova Scotia Power Inc.	Nova Scotia
Nowsco Well Services Ltd.	Alberta
Numac Energy Inc.	Alberta
Ocelot Energy Inc.	Alberta
Ondaatje Corporation, The	Ontario
Onex Corporation	Ontario
Oshawa Group Ltd., The	Ontario
Pagurian Corporation Limited, The	Ontario
PanCanadian Petroleum Limited	Alberta
Pegasus Gold Inc.	B.C.
Pengrowth Gas Income Fund	Alberta
Petro-Canada	Alberta
Petromet Resources Limited	Ontario
Philip Environmental Inc.	Ontario
Pinnacle Resources Ltd.	Alberta
Placer Dome Inc.	B.C.
POCO Petroleums Ltd.	Alberta
Potash Corporation of Saskatchewan Inc.	Saskatchewan
Power Corporation of Canada	Ontario
Power Financial Corporation	Ontario
Premdor Inc.	Ontario
Prime Resources Group Inc.	B.C.
Quadra Logic Technologies Inc.	B.C.
Quebec-Telephone	Ontario
Quebecor Inc.	Ontario
Quebecor Printing Inc.	Ontario
Quno Corporation	Ontario
Ranchmen's Resources Ltd.	Alberta
Ranger Oil Limited	Alberta
Rayrock Yellowknife Resources Inc.	Ontario
Renaissance Energy Ltd.	Alberta
Repap Enterprises Inc.	Ontario
Revenue Properties Company Limited	Ontario
Rigel Energy Corporation	Alberta
Rio Algom Limited	Ontario
Rio Alto Exploration Ltd.	Alberta
Riverside Forest Products Limited	B.C.
Rogers Cantel Mobile Communications Inc.	Ontario
Rogers Communications Inc.	Ontario
Rolland Inc.	Ontario
Royal Bank of Canada	Ontario
Royal Oak Mines Inc.	B.C.
SHL Systemhouse Inc.	Ontario
SNC Group Inc.	Ontario
SR Telecom Inc.	Ontario
Sceptre Resources Limited	Alberta
Scott's Hospitality Inc.	Ontario
Seagram Company Ltd., The	Ontario
Sears Acceptance Company Inc.	Ontario
Sears Canada Inc.	Ontario
Shaw Communications Inc.	Alberta
Shell Canada Limited	Alberta
Sherritt Inc.	Ontario
Slocan Forest Products Ltd.	B.C.
Southam Inc.	Ontario
Spar Aerospace Limited	Ontario
St. Lawrence Cement Inc.	Ontario
Stelco Inc.	Ontario
Stone-Consolidated Corporation	Ontario
Summit Resources Limited	Alberta
Suncor Inc.	Alberta

SCHEDULE "A"

NAME OF POP ISSUER	DESIGNATED JURISDICTION
TVX Gold Inc.	Ontario
Talisman Energy Inc.	Alberta
Tarragon Oil and Gas Limited	Alberta
Teck Corporation	B.C.
Teleglobe Inc.	Ontario
TELUS Corporation	Alberta
Tembec Inc.	Ontario
Thomson Corporation, The	Ontario
Toronto-Dominion Bank, The	Ontario
Torstar Corporation	Ontario
Total Petroleum (North America) Ltd.	Ontario
TransAlta Corporation	Alberta
TransAlta Utilities Corporation	Alberta
TransCanada PipeLines Limited	Alberta
Transwest Energy Inc.	Alberta
Tri Link Resources Ltd.	Alberta
Trilon Financial Corporation	Ontario
Trimac Limited	Alberta
Trimark Financial Corporation	Ontario
Trizec Corporation Ltd.	Alberta
Truscan Realty Limited	Ontario
Ulster Petroleums Ltd.	Alberta
Unican Security Systems Ltd.	Ontario
Union Gas Limited	Ontario
United Dominion Industries Limited	Ontario
United Westburne Inc.	Ontario
Univa Inc.	Ontario
Venezuelan Goldfields Ltd.	Ontario
Vicroy Resource Corporation	Ontario
Wascana Energy Inc.	Saskatchewan
West Fraser Timber Co. Ltd.	B.C.
Westcoast Energy Inc.	B.C.
WIC Western International Communications Ltd.	B.C.
Xerox Canada Inc.	Ontario
Xerox Canada Finance Inc.	Ontario

Schedule "B"

CHRONOLOGY

The following chronology illustrates the procedures for clearing a short form prospectus under Expedited Review:

Time Zone of Designated Jurisdiction:

Day 1   Preliminary Materials, including the preliminary short form prospectus, are filed in the Designated Jurisdiction and a Facsimile of the covering letter, preliminary short form prospectus and Undertaking (as defined below) is filed in each of the other Participating Jurisdictions in which the issuer proposes to distribute securities. Covering letter indicates election of Expedited Review and those provinces and territories in which the issuer proposes to distribute securities.

Issuer provides an undertaking to each Participating Jurisdiction other than the Designated Jurisdiction to file the Final Filing Materials before the end of the 3rd working day following the date of issuance of the final expedited review receipt document by the Designated Jurisdiction ("Undertaking"). If no final expedited review receipt document is issued in respect of a Participating Jurisdiction, the Undertaking is of no effect for that Participating Jurisdiction except with respect to fees.

The preliminary expedited review receipt document is issued by the Designated Jurisdiction.

The Designated Jurisdiction sends a Facsimile of the preliminary expedited review receipt document to each Participating Jurisdiction where the preliminary short form prospectus was filed.

Time Zone of most westerly Participating Jurisdiction in which the issuer has filed

Day 2   Review

Day 3   "Opting Out" Facsimile, if any, sent to Designated Jurisdiction, all other Participating Jurisdictions and the issuer before the end of the working day.

As part of its participation in Expedited Review, each Participating Jurisdiction has agreed that, unless the Designated Jurisdiction is advised otherwise within two working days following the date of the preliminary expedited review receipt document, silence will confirm to the Designated Jurisdiction the participation in Expedited Review by the Participating Jurisdiction.

Day 4   Comment letter sent by Facsimile to the issuer by the Designated Jurisdiction, including notation "Expedited Review filing" or equivalent.

Day X   Issuer files in the Designated Jurisdiction the documents and fees that are required to be filed in that province in connection with a short form prospectus as specified in the "Table of Documents to be filed in respect of the Clearance of National Issues" forming part of NPS 1.

The Designated Jurisdiction issues the final expedited review receipt document that evidences a final receipt has been issued by each Participating Jurisdiction in which the preliminary short form prospectus was filed other than those that have opted out of Expedited Review.

The Designated Jurisdiction notifies each Participating Jurisdiction other than those that have opted out, by Facsimile, that the final expedited review receipt document has been issued.

Distribution begins in the Designated Jurisdiction and each of the other Participating Jurisdictions.

Day X+3 Issuer files the Final Filing Materials (which include appropriate fees where required), in compliance with its Undertaking, in each Participating Jurisdiction other than the Designated Jurisdiction and those that have opted out of Expedited Review.

Day X+Y Issuer completes distribution and pays the additional fee where required to do so.

NIN#94/22

NOTICE

PERMISSION UNDER
SECTION 35(1)(c) OF THE SECURITIES ACT

Concurrently with this Notice, the British Columbia Securities Commission is publishing NIN#94/21 and the Memorandum of Understanding for Expedited Review of Short Form Prospectuses and Renewal AIFs (the "MOU"). The MOU sets out the procedures to be followed to obtain a preliminary and final receipt for a short form prospectus or acceptance of a renewal annual information form on an expedited basis ("Expedited Review") and is effective November 15, 1994. Capitalized terms not defined in this Notice have the same meaning as in the MOU.

Section 35(1)(c) of the Securities Act, S.B.C. 1985, c.83 ("the Act") prohibits any representation, written or oral, that a security will be listed or posted for trading on a stock exchange or that application has been made or will be made to list or post for trading the security on any stock exchange, except with the written permission of the Superintendent.

In order to facilitate the use of Expedited Review in British Columbia, the Superintendent hereby gives permission under section 35(1)(c) of the Act to make oral or written representations as to the listing and posting for trading or quotation, or an application to list and post for trading or quote, the securities being offered (or the securities underlying the securities being offered) on one or more stock exchanges or automated quotation systems, provided

(a)   the representations are made with respect to securities for which at least a preliminary short form prospectus has been filed with the Superintendent under the POP System in accordance with the Expedited Review procedures set out in the MOU;

(b)   an application to list and post for trading, or to quote, the securities has been made to the relevant stock exchange or automated quotation system;

(c)   disclosure is made that the listing and posting for trading, or quotation, of the securities is subject to fulfilling the requirements of the relevant stock exchange or automated quotation system or these requirements have been satisfied; and

(d)   where the stock exchange or automated quotation system prescribes that the disclosure required in (c) be made in a specified form or in specific language, the disclosure is made in the specified form or specific language.

An issuer is expected to file with the Superintendent written confirmation from the relevant stock exchange or automated quotation system of the application to list and post for trading or to quote or, with respect to an application to list and post for trading or quote on a stock exchange or automated quotation system located outside Canada, evidence satisfactory to the Designated Jurisdiction that confirmation or consent to refer to the making of an application is not normally provided by that stock exchange or automated quotation system,

(a)   if British Columbia is the issuer's Designated Jurisdiction

     (i)   prior to the issuance of the preliminary expedited review receipt document, where any representation is made in, or in connection with, the issuer's preliminary short form prospectus, or

     (ii)   prior to the issuance of the final expedited review receipt document, where any representation is made in, or in connection with, the issuer's short form prospectus, or

(b)   if British Columbia is not the issuer's Designated Jurisdiction, together with the Final Filing Materials in accordance with the Issuer's Undertaking under the MOU.

This permission is effective November 15, 1994.

DATED at Vancouver, British Columbia, on November 1, 1994.

Dean E. Holley
Superintendent of Brokers

NIN#94/24

NOTICE

PART XIII OF THE REGULATION TO THE SECURITIES ACT (ONTARIO) CONFLICTS OF INTEREST: RELATED AND CONNECTED ISSUERS

A Request for Comments and Ontario Securities Commission ("OSC") staff discussion paper regarding the conflicts of interest regime set out in Part XIII of the Regulation to the Securities Act (Ontario) and the equivalent provisions in the legislation of Alberta, British Columbia, Québec and Nova Scotia is published in the OSC Bulletin and the Alberta Securities Commission Summary. It will also be available for distribution at the offices of the securities administrators in British Columbia and Québec. The discussion paper provides background regarding this conflicts regime and alternative instruments which are available for the regulation of such conflicts.

Because of the number of issues that a detailed review of the conflict regime encompasses, OSC staff expects that once an overall policy direction is established, individual concerns will be addressed in sequence, with more pressing problems being given priority. As the Part XIII rule which has given rise to the greatest number of comments and applications since the imposition of Part XIII in 1987 relates to underwriting, those issues will be addressed first.

The deadline for responses to the Request for Comments is January 31, 1995.

As part of the consultative process, the Canadian Securities Administrators ("CSA") has established a committee to make recommendations regarding conflicts of interest arising out of the deregulation of the ownership rules in the securities industry. The first topic to be addressed by the committee will be the provisions applicable to underwriting conflicts of interest. This committee will be chaired by a representative of the CSA and be made up of CSA representatives and senior representatives from various market participant groups. The CSA will publish the list of committee members once the membership has been finalized.

The committee's initial report is expected to be published by the end of February, 1995. Staff expects to have formulated specific proposals for reform of Part XIII prior to the spring meeting of the CSA (in April, 1995).

Any questions regarding the Request for Comments may be addressed to:

> Tanis MacLaren
> Deputy Director,
> Capital markets/International Markets
> Ontario Securities Commission
> 20 Queen Street West
> Toronto, Ontario
> M5H 3S8
>
> Phone: (416) 593-8259
> Fax: (416) 593-8283

A limited number of copies of the discussion paper are available for pick up, upon request. Requests should be directed to:

> Shandie Hertslet
> Information Distribution Officer
> British Columbia Securities Commission
> 1100 - 865 Hornby Street
> Vancouver, B.C.
> V6Z 2H4
>
> Phone: (604) 660-4844
> Fax: (604) 660-2688

DATED at Vancouver, British Columbia, on November 9, 1994.

> Douglas M. Hyndman
> Chair

NIN#94/25

NOTICE

AMENDMENTS TO SECURITIES ACT

A number of amendments to the Securities Act (the "Act") and consequential amendments to the Securities Regulation (the "Regulation") were brought into force on November 17, 1994.

The Securities Amendment Act, 1992, S.B.C., 1992, c. 52 (the "Amendment Act") received royal assent on June 23, 1992. Certain sections of the Amendment Act were brought into force, effective July 24, 1992, by B.C. Reg. 289/92. A copy of the Amendment Act was attached to NIN#92/15 and a copy of the B.C. Reg. 289/92 was attached to NIN#92/24.

Additional sections of the Amendment Act were brought into force, effective November 17, 1994, by B.C. Reg. 418/94. An extract of the relevant sections of the Amendment Act is attached to this Notice. Consequential amendments to the Regulation were also brought into force, effective November 17, 1994 by B.C. Reg. 417/94. Copies of B.C. Reg. 417/94 and B.C. Reg 418/94 are attached to this Notice.

The amendments:

1. require that a specified form of information statement be delivered to purchasers and filed with the Commission no later than 10 days after a trade under section 32(g) of the Act;

2. harmonize the wording of the discretionary exempting powers in section 33 and 59 of the Act, establish consistent thresholds for granting exemptions and allow the Commission and the Superintendent greater flexibility to specify the individual requirements of the Act or Regulation that should be waived in particular circumstances;

3. narrow the wording of the certificate issued under section 60 of the Act to refer to not being in default of filing financial statements and fees; and

4. improve administrative efficiency under section 146 of the Act when issuing cease trade orders for failure to file records completed in accordance with the Act or Regulation.

In NIN#94/26 published concurrently with this Notice, the Superintendent is specifying, under section 158 of the Act, Form 58 as the form of information statement for the purpose of section 32(g) of the Act. In addition, sections 78.1 and 119.1 have been added to the Regulation as authority for the disclosure required in item 8 of Form 58 and to require a security holder to provide to a subsequent purchaser any disclosure that the issuer provided to the security holder under the information statement within the past two years.

The remaining amendments contained in the Amendment Act require the preparation of supporting material, such as amendments to the Regulation or forms, and will not be proclaimed until that material has been finalized. The Commission will issue a notice to advise of the proclamation of these amendments.

DATED at Vancouver, British Columbia, on November 23, 1994.

Douglas M. Hyndman
Chair

Attachments

References: NIN#92/15
                NIN#92/24
                NIN#94/26
                NIN#94/27

NIN#94/26

NOTICE

REQUIRED FORM UNDER SECTION 32(g) OF THE SECURITIES ACT

Section 5 of the Securities Amendment Act, 1992, S.B.C., 1992, c. 52, brought into force, effective November 17, 1994 by B.C. Reg. 418/94 (see NIN#94/25), amends section 32(g) of the Securities Act ("the Act") by requiring that a specified form of information statement be delivered to purchasers before an agreement of purchase and sale is entered into.

Effective November 23, 1994, the Superintendent specifies, in accordance with section 158 of the Act, Form 58 attached to this Notice as the required form of information statement for the purpose of section 32(g) of the Act.

DATED at Vancouver, British Columbia, on November 23, 1994.

Dean E. Holley
Superintendent of Brokers

Attachment

Reference: NIN#92/15
                NIN#92/24
                NIN#94/25

NIN#94/27

NEW FORM OF CERTIFICATE UNDER
SECTION 60(3) OF THE SECURITIES ACT

Section 11 of the Securities Amendment Act, 1992, S.B.C., 1992, c. 52 (the "Amendment Act"), brought into force effective November 17, 1994 by B.C. Reg. 418/94 (see NIN#94/25), amends section 60(3) of the Securities Act (the "Act") by narrowing the language of the certificate that the Superintendent may issue under that section to refer to not being in default of filing financial statements and fees.

Before the implementation of section 11 of the Amendment Act, the Superintendent had already indicated in NIN#93/19 that he was no longer prepared to exercise his discretion to issue a certificate that an issuer is not in default of any requirement of the Act or Regulation as was then possible under section 60(3) of the Act.

Notices

Effective November 23, 1994, the Superintendent will, in appropriate circumstances, issue the form of certificate attached to this Notice under section 60(3) of the Act.

DATED at Vancouver, British Columbia, on November 23, 1994.

Dean E. Holley
Superintendent of Brokers

Attachment

REF: NIN#92/15   NIN#92/24
          NIN#93/19   NIN#94/25

CERTIFICATE

under section 60(3) of the Securities Act

[Date]

Re: [Issuer name] (the "Reporting Issuer")
     File # _____

I certify that on this date the information on file with the British Columbia Securities Commission indicates that the Reporting Issuer is not in default of filing financial statements required by the Securities Act, S.B.C. 1985, c. 83, or the Securities Regulation, B.C. Reg. 270/86 or paying fees and charges prescribed by the Securities Regulation relating to those filings.

_____
Deputy Superintendent of Brokers
Corporate Finance

NIN#94/28

NOTICE

PROPOSED AMENDMENTS TO THE SECURITIES ACT

Six amendments to the *Securities Act*, which would implement part of the Government's response to the Matkin Report, were published for comment in a Special Supplement to the Weekly Summary for the week ending October 7, 1994. These proposed amendments would strengthen the regulation of underwriting and promotional activity and authorize the Commission to conduct compliance reviews of self regulatory bodies. See NIN#94/14.

The Commission is now publishing for comment further amendments that are not related to the Government's response to the Matkin Report. For convenience, the six amendments previously published are included in this package. The specific purposes of these amendments are:

•   to strengthen the Commission's investigative and enforcement powers

•   to provide authority for certain elements of a proposed package of amendments to the Securities Regulation

•   to accommodate a system of electronic filing of documents, an initiative being carried out by securities regulatory authorities across Canada

•   to clarify that the Commission can disclose certain personal information about registrants, directors, officers, promoters and control persons

•   to make housekeeping amendments to maintain the currency of the legislation

•   to maintain the uniformity of certain provisions of the legislation with the Ontario *Securities Act*

Request for Comments

Direct written comments by January 15, 1995 to:

Susan Adams
A/Director
Policy and Legislation
British Columbia Securities Commission
1100 - 865 Hornby Street
Vancouver, B.C. V6Z 2H4

Comment letters submitted in response to Requests for Comment are placed in the public file and form part of the public record, unless confidentiality is requested. Although comment letters requesting confidentiality will not be placed on the public file, freedom of information legislation may require the Commission to make comment letters available. Persons submitting comment letters should therefore be aware that the press and members of the public may be able to obtain access to any comment letter.

Certain other amendments to the *Securities Act* are being developed to implement other parts of the Government's response to the Matkin report and are expected to be published for comment in the near future. These amendments include:

- increasing the number of commissioners from 9 to 11

- expanding the civil remedies in the Act to provide a right of action for mis-representations in press releases and letters to shareholders

- granting the Commission the power to apply to court for disgorgement orders

- confirming the Commission's power to make policy statements

- granting the Commission power to make legally binding rules

DATED at Vancouver, British Columbia, on November 23, 1994.

Douglas M. Hyndman
Chair

Attachment

Reference: NIN#94/14

NIN#94/29

NOTICE

TRANSITIONAL RELIEF
INTERIM LOCAL POLICY STATEMENT NO. 3-17
REGISTRANT DUE DILIGENCE

By NIN#94/17, the Commission replaced Local Policy Statement No. 3-04 with Interim Local Policy Statement No. 3-17 - Registrant Due Diligence, effective January 6, 1995. The Commission has received submissions from various industry participants requesting transitional relief from the effective date of Interim LPS#3-17.

The Commission has determined that it is appropriate to provide additional time for registrants to implement procedures to address the new requirement that the registrant retain the consultant. Accordingly, pursuant to section 6.2 of Interim LPS#3-17, the Superintendent waives the requirement imposed on junior issuer under-writers to obtain an assessment report and file the certificate(s) required under Part 9 of Interim LPS#3-17 where the junior industrial issuer prepares and files a technical report in accordance with LPS#3-04.

This waiver expires on February 28, 1995 for all preliminary prospectuses filed by or on behalf of junior industrial issuers on or after that date.

The obligations with respect to the due diligence reports under Interim LPS#3-17 are effective for preliminary prospectuses filed on or after January 6, 1995.

DATED at Vancouver, British Columbia, on December 22, 1994.

Dean E. Holley
Superintendent of Brokers

References: NIN#94/17
Interim LPS#3-17
LPS#3-04

Notices

NOTICE

AMENDMENTS TO LOCAL POLICY STATEMENT 3-02
BLANKET ORDER #95/1
FORM 12A SUMMARY PROSPECTUS DISCLOSURE SYSTEM

The Commission is publishing amendments to Local Policy Statement 3-02 and Blanket Order #95/1. This Notice provides background to the LPS 3-02 amendment and BOR#95/1.

The amendments to LPS 3-02 and BOR#95/1 implement the Form 12A Summary Prospectus Disclosure System as described in NIN#94/17. This system is available for use by junior industrial issuers required to file on Form 12A - Information Required in Prospectus of Junior Industrial Issuer.

The Form 12A Summary Prospectus Disclosure System consist of a summary prospectus prepared in accordance with the requirements set out in the Form 12A summary prospectus and a base disclosure document prepared in accordance with the requirements set out in Form 12A. The base disclosure document is incorporated by reference into and deemed to form part of the summary prospectus.

The amendments to LPS 3-02 consist of a new Part 11 that sets out the rules for the use of the Form 12A Summary Prospectus Disclosure System. BOR#95/1 permits the use of a summary prospectus and base disclosure document prepared in accordance with the amendments to LPS 3-02.

DATED at Vancouver, British Columbia, on January 5, 1995.

Douglas M. Hyndman
Chair

Attachments

References:　　NIN#94/17
　　　　　　　　LPS 3-02
　　　　　　　　BOR#95/1
　　　　　　　　FORM 12A

NOTICE

PRINCIPLES OF FAIR TRADING

This Notice provides general guidance about activities that the British Columbia Securities Commission considers to be contrary to the principles of fair trading.

Public participation in any securities marketplace depends, to a great degree, on the confidence of investors and potential investors in the fairness and integrity of the system of securities trading. Some of the most fundamental principles of fair trading are set out in the following:

"When investors and potential investors see activity they are entitled to assume that it is real activity. They are entitled to assume that the prices they pay and receive are determined by the unimpeded interaction of real supply and real demand so that those prices are the collective marketplace judgments that they purport to be."[1]

Clearly, any attempt to interfere with the normal forces of supply and demand in the marketplace, or any attempt to create a misleading appearance with respect to the price of a security or its trading volume, is contrary to these fundamental principles and undermines public confidence in the market.

To ensure that trading practices are fair and equitable, stock exchanges in every major jurisdiction, including British Columbia, have developed comprehensive rules and policies to prohibit their members from engaging in practices or schemes that

---

[1]　re: *Edward J. Mawod & Co.*, 46 S.E.C. 865, 871-872 (1977), *aff'd*, 591 F.2d 588 (10th Cir. 1979).

might create misleading appearances of trading activity or artificial prices for securities.

The securities legislation in British Columbia contains a number of provisions that require that the principles of fair trading be observed by all market participants - registrants, insiders, issuers and public investors. Section 41.1(a) of the Securities Act, for example, prohibits transactions or schemes that create or result in a misleading appearance of trading activity in, or an artificial price for, any security listed on a stock exchange. In addition, the Criminal Code of Canada contains provisions relating to fraudulent manipulation of stock exchange transactions and fraud affecting the public markets.

Those who are active in the securities markets, particularly insiders, control persons, promoters and market makers, and those who are in the business of trading or advising others with respect to trading, must be aware of the legislation and the exchange rules, by-laws and policies governing trading practices. Those who engage in abusive, manipulative or deceptive trading practices expose themselves to serious administrative and criminal sanctions.

Abusive Trading Practices

Without limiting the generality of section 41.1 of the Act, the following activities could reasonably be expected to create or result in a misleading appearance of trading activity in, or an artificial price for, securities listed on a stock exchange:

(a) executing any transaction in a security, through the facilities of a stock exchange, where the transaction does not involve a change in beneficial ownership;

(b) effecting, alone or with others, a transaction or series of transactions in a security for the purpose of inducing others to purchase or sell the same, or a related security;

(c) effecting, alone or with others, a transaction or series of transactions that has the effect of artificially raising, lowering or maintaining the price of a security;

(d) entering one or more orders for the purchase or sale of a security that have the effect of artificially raising, lowering or maintaining the bid or offering prices of the security;

(e) entering one or more orders that could reasonably be expected to create an artificial appearance of investor participation in the market;

(f) executing, through the facilities of an exchange, a prearranged transaction in a security that has the effect of creating a misleading appearance of active public trading or that has the effect of improperly excluding other market participants from the transaction;

(g) purchasing or making offers to purchase a security at successively higher prices, or selling or making offers to sell a security at successively lower prices, if the transactions or offers create a misleading appearance of trading or an artificial market price for the security;

(h) effecting, alone or with others, one or a series of transactions through the facilities of an exchange where the purpose of the transaction is to defer payment for the security traded;

(i) entering an order to purchase a security without the ability and the bona fide intention to make the payments necessary to properly settle the transaction;

(j) entering an order to sell a security, except for a security sold short in accordance with the provisions of section 41 of the Act, without the ability and the bona fide intention to deliver the security necessary to properly settle the transaction; and

(k) engaging, alone or with others, in any transaction, practice or scheme that unduly interferes with the normal forces of demand for or supply of a security or that artificially restricts or reduces the public float of a security in a way that could reasonably be expected to result in an artificial price for the security.

Over the past few years, Commission staff have initiated a substantial number of enforcement proceedings based on manipulative and deceptive trading practices. Too often, the respondents in these cases have sought to defend their trading practices as "market making", despite the fact that their activities included a number of the abusive practices referred to above. Those who intend to engage in market making

Notices

activities are expected to be fully aware of the principles of fair trading and should seriously consider conducting their trading through a single brokerage account and with the ongoing advice and guidance of a registrant.

The Role of Registrants

Registrants have a responsibility to stock exchanges, to their clients and to the market place generally to ensure that their activities are carried out responsibly and in compliance with the letter and spirit of the legislation and exchange rules and by-laws. The following are examples of some of the activities that are expressly prohibited by exchanges and do not comply with the principles of fair trading:

(a) making a fictitious transaction;

(b) giving or accepting an order which a person knows or ought to know does not involve a change of ownership of the securities in question;

(c) purchasing, selling, or offering to purchase or sell securities where the person knows or ought to know that the effect of such a purchase or sale would be to unduly disturb the normal position of the market or to create an abnormal market condition in which market prices do not fairly reflect current market values, or being a party to any plan or scheme to do so;

(d) confirming a transaction when no trade has been executed;

(e) indiscriminate or improper solicitation of orders either by telephone or otherwise;

(f) high pressure or other trading tactics of a character considered undesirable;

(g) using or participating in the use of any manipulative or deceptive method of trading where the person knows or ought to know the nature of the method; and

(h) violation of any statute applicable to trading in securities.

Even if a registrant is not directly involved in an unfair or inequitable activity, the registrant is expected to be inquisitive and pro-active in dealing with such activities that are carried on by others and of which the registrant is or should be aware. Registrants should refuse to accept instructions from clients who, in the registrants' judgment, are engaged in illegal, unfair or abusive trading activities. All such instructions or orders should be reported immediately to the registrant's senior management. Senior management are expected to bring matters concerning serious misconduct in the markets to the attention of the stock exchange or the Compliance and Enforcement Division of the Commission.

DATED at Vancouver, British Columbia, on January 4, 1995.

Dean E. Holley
Superintendent of Brokers

NIN#95/6

NOTICE

DRAFT AMENDMENTS TO FORM 30
AND ADDITIONAL
DRAFT AMENDMENTS TO SECTION 146 OF THE SECURITIES REGULATION

The British Columbia Securities Commission is publishing for comment draft amendments to Form 30 (information circular) and additional draft amendments to section 146 of the Securities Regulation. Earlier draft amendments to section 146 were published on October 7, 1994 under NIN#94/15 as part of the Commission's package of proposed amendments to the Securities Regulation.

Background

The draft amendments to Form 30 are published in response to the findings of the Matkin Report on reverse takeover transactions. A reverse takeover ("RTO") is a transaction or series of transactions through which a private company is acquired by a listed company in a way that results in the shareholders of the private company controlling the listed company.

The Matkin Report concluded that RTOs are "back-door" listings which are particularly vulnerable to abuse in a junior venture market and should, therefore, be subject to the same standards of public disclosure and review that are applied to initial public offerings.

In response to the Report, the Commission announced that it would require the Vancouver Stock Exchange ("VSE") to impose prospectus level disclosure and review on RTOs and that it would amend Form 30 to ensure that prospectus level disclosure is provided where shareholders are asked to approve an RTO.

The VSE is currently finalizing its revised policy on RTO transactions. The policy will ensure that there is prospectus level disclosure in the Statement of Material Facts ("SMF") relating to an RTO and, when an SMF is not being filed, will require prospectus level disclosure in the Filing Statement relating to the RTO. The Filing Statement is a disclosure document filed with the VSE disclosing material changes in the affairs of the issuer. Under the Policy, the Filing Statement on SMF must provide full, true and plain disclosure of all material facts relating to the RTO, the listed issuer and the non-reporting issuer or the business to be acquired.

In addition, the VSE policy will require the listed issuer to issue a news release disclosing that a Filing Statement or SMF concerning the RTO has been filed with the VSE and placed in the public file of the issuer. The news release will also summarize the information contained in the Filing Statement or the SMF, and advise that the issuer will provide interested parties with a copy of the relevant document free of charge upon request.

Draft Amendments to Form 30

Several concerns have been identified with extending prospectus level disclosure requirements to information circulars. The information circular must be finalized earlier in the RTO process than the Filing Statement or SMF to satisfy corporate and securities law requirements relating to meetings of shareholders, including the requirements relating to shareholder communication. As a result, the information circular may contain information about the RTO that is ultimately incomplete or inaccurate. The solution to this problem would be to require the listed issuer to wait until the terms of the RTO are finalized before completing the information circular. This, however, would cause additional delays in the transaction. As well, the information circular is prepared for the benefit of the existing shareholders of the listed issuer, arguably a group of shareholders that is less in need of the protection of the Securities Act than the shareholders who will acquire securities of the listed issuer in the secondary market on the basis of the proposed RTO.

In light of these concerns and of the VSE's revised policy on RTOs, which will result in prospectus level disclosure being provided in the Filing Statement or SMF, the Commission concluded that it may not be necessary or appropriate to impose the same requirement in the information circular prepared in connection with a meeting of shareholders called to approve the RTO. The Commission is instead proposing to amend item 11 of Form 30 to require disclosure of certain specific information required by the form of prospectus applicable to the non-reporting issuer (private company) or business to be acquired through the RTO (Form 12A, if a junior industrial issuer and Form 14A, if a junior natural resource issuer). The Commission believes that this disclosure will provide sufficient information for shareholders to form a reasoned judgement on the proposed RTO.

In addition, the Commission is proposing to amend item 11 of Form 30 to require the listed issuer to disclose in its information circular that a Filing Statement or a SMF with respect to the RTO will be filed with the VSE. The information circular will also have to disclose that a news release will be issued

- confirming that a Filing Statement or a SMF has been filed with the VSE with respect to the RTO and placed in the public file of the issuer,

- summarizing the information contained in the Filing Statement or the SMF, and

- advising that a copy of the Filing Statement or SMF may be obtained free of charge from the listed issuer.

The Commission believes that this additional disclosure in the information circular and the actual issuance of the news release and availability of the Filing Statement or SMF will give existing as well as prospective shareholders of the listed issuer access to prospectus level disclosure about the proposed RTO.

Draft Amendments to Section 146

To ensure that the Commission's continuous disclosure record is complete, and to ensure that representations to the public are subject to the full range of enforcement provisions of the Act, the Commission proposes to seek a further amendment to section

146 of the Regulation to require the filing of the final version of any disclosure record not already filed with the Commission but filed with an exchange under the bylaws, rules or regulations of that exchange.

Other Proposed Amendments to Form 30

The Commission is also proposing to update the disclosure required under item 11 of Form 30 where shareholder approval is required for an amalgamation, merger, arrangement or reorganization. This proposed change would bring British Columbia's disclosure requirements in this area in line with those of the Ontario Securities Commission.

Request for Comment

The Commission is requesting written comment on the draft amendments to item 11 of Form 30 and to section 146 of the Regulation.

Comment letters should be submitted by February 28, 1995 to:

> Brenda J. Benham
> A/Director, Policy & Legislation
> British Columbia Securities Commission
> 100-865 Hornby Street
> Vancouver, B.C.
> V6Z 2H4

Comment letters submitted in response to Requests for Comment are placed in the public file and form part of the public record, unless confidentiality is requested. Although comment letters requesting confidentiality will not be placed on the public file, freedom of information legislation may require the Commission to make comment letters available. Persons submitting comment letters should therefore be aware that the press and members of the public may be able to obtain access to any comment letter.

DATED at Vancouver, British Columbia, on January 12, 1995.

> Douglas M. Hyndman
> Chair

Attachments

References: NIN#94/13
               NIN#94/15

NIN#95/7

NOTICE

DUTIES OF REGISTRANTS IN THE SUPERVISION OF ACCOUNTS OPERATING UNDER POWERS OF ATTORNEY OR TRADING AUTHORITIES

This Notice sets out the position of the Superintendent of Brokers on the duties of registrants when supervising and executing orders for client accounts operated under powers of attorney or trading authorities granted by the client.

Execution of unlawful advice through a registered dealer

When someone provides services in the province as a portfolio manager or investment counsel, they must, except under certain limited exemptions, register as an adviser under the Securities Act, S.B.C. 1985, c. 83. These registration requirements are intended to ensure that public investors are able to base investment decisions on the advice of people who are qualified and properly licensed.

In the past, enforcement staff have become aware of several situations in which individuals were acting as portfolio managers or investment counsel without registration and were directing trades based on this unlawful activity through a power of attorney (PA) or trading authority (TA) over the accounts of clients at registered dealers. Registered dealers are expected to be mindful of this problem and aware of the risks posed to their clients and the investing public by unqualified and unlicensed advisers. If dealers are vigilant, they can be of great assistance to the Commission in reducing these abuses by refusing to execute orders placed by unregistered advisers acting under PAs or TAs.

It would be unreasonable to expect dealers to monitor, in an absolute way, the use of PAs and TAs to determine if these instruments are being used to circumvent the requirements of the Act. However, dealers and individual registrants are expected to exercise considerable care and diligence in supervising and accepting orders for accounts operated under PAs and TAs.

A registrant presented with a PA or TA should first determine whether the person with authority over the account - the attorney - is a registered portfolio manager or investment counsel. If the attorney is not registered in that capacity, the dealer should inquire further about the relationship between the attorney and the client and should determine, for example, whether the attorney receives compensation for any investment advice given.

If the attorney is not registered but appears to be in the business of advising in securities, the registrant should alert the client and the attorney to the registration requirements of the Act and seek further comfort that the registration requirements are not being violated (e.g., whether an exemption from the adviser registration requirements is available). If the registrant knows or, after making inquiries, has reasonable concerns that the attorney is unlawfully acting as an adviser, the registrant should not take instructions from the attorney unless the dealer is of the opinion that its own legal position would be in jeopardy by failure to execute a particular order. In any case, the registrant should bring the matter to the attention of senior management who, in turn, should consider whether a referral to the Commission's Compliance and Enforcement Division is warranted.

The Abusive Operation of Nominee Accounts

Diligent monitoring of PAs and TAs will also enable dealers and individual registrants to better identify client accounts that are being used inappropriately, as nominee accounts, to hide or disguise abusive trading. Registrants should be particularly wary in situations in which a non-registrant has trading authority over several accounts or when trading authority is held by a corporate insider or control person who may be using the account(s) to avoid reporting requirements or resale restrictions. In such cases, registrants should make appropriate inquiries of the client to confirm the nature, purpose and true ownership of the account and should decline to execute trades through the account if the registrant knows or believes that the account is being utilized to execute illegal trades or evade other legal obligations.

Duties of Registrants

The Superintendent considers each registrant to have a duty to assist in maintaining the integrity of the capital markets by not participating in conduct which the registrant knows, or ought reasonably to know, violates the securities legislation. In addition, every registrant has a duty to deal fairly, honestly and in good faith with clients.

Registrants who knowingly participate or acquiesce in the activities of people providing unlawful advice or in the use of nominee accounts to conduct illegal or abusive trading do a serious disservice both to the market and to their clients. In addition to possible enforcement action against an unregistered adviser or the operator of the nominee account, Commission staff will seriously consider enforcement proceedings against the registrants involved, particularly in cases where the interests of clients or the integrity of the market have been jeopardized.

DATED at Vancouver, British Columbia, on January 12, 1995.

Dean E. Holley
Superintendent of Brokers

NIN#95/8

Notices

NOTICE

*TASK FORCE ON OPERATIONAL EFFICIENCIES IN THE
ADMINISTRATION OF SECURITIES REGULATION – INTERIM REPORT*

In NIN#94/7, the British Columbia Securities Commission announced that the Canadian Securities Administrators ("CSA") had agreed to encourage the formation of a task force to maximize operational efficiencies in the administration of securities regulation (the "Task Force"). The Task Force has prepared an Interim Report. The Commission is publishing the Interim Report of the Task Force in this edition of the Weekly Summary.

The Task Force has released the interim report with a view to encouraging public discussion, consultation and further input from concerned members of industry and the investing public.

The Task Force invites additional submissions with suggestions as to practical steps that can be taken by Canadian securities regulatory authorities, under existing laws, to render securities regulation more consistent, more predictable, more cost-effective and more timely. All submissions should be sent to:

> William L. Hess, Q.C.
> Chair, Task Force on Operational Efficiencies in the
>   Administration of Securities Regulation
> c/o McCarthy Tetrault
> Suite 3200, 421 - 7th Avenue S.W.
> Calgary, Alberta
> T2P 4K9
> Telecopier: (403)260-3501

Submissions must be received by March 15, 1995.

DATED at Vancouver, British Columbia, on July 20, 1995.

> Douglas M. Hyndman
> Chair

Ref: NIN#94/7

Attachment

NIN#95/9

NOTICE

GOVERNMENT STRIP BONDS - INFORMATION STATEMENT
LOCAL POLICY STATEMENT 3-43
BLANKET ORDER #91/12

Local Policy Statement 3-43 and Blanket Order #91/12 permit trades in government strip bonds to first time purchasers only if an information statement approved by the Commission or Superintendent is delivered to such purchasers.

On February 1, 1995, the Commission approved the attached revised information statement filed on behalf of the Investment Dealers Association of Canada (the "IDA") for use by IDA members in respect of trades in government strip bonds as defined in LPS 3-43 and BOR#91/12. At the same time the Commission revoked the approval granted in respect of the information statement previously filed by the IDA for trades in government strip bonds made by IDA members on or after February 20, 1995.

The Commission hereby approves the use of an information statement that does not differ in any material way from the revised information statement approved on behalf of the IDA. The approval granted in Part 4 of LPS 3-43 in respect of the information statement previously filed and set out in Appendix A of LPS 3-43 is hereby revoked for all trades in government strip bonds made on or after February 20, 1995. The Commission will be revising LPS 3-43 to replace the information statement set out in Appendix A with the revised information statement.

BOR#91/12 contains registration and prospectus exemptions for trading and distribution of government strip bonds. In NIN#91/23, the Commission requested comment on its proposal to remove the registration exemption. The Commission has determined that government strip bonds are sufficiently complex that only persons who are subject to the educational, suitability and other requirements imposed on registrants should be permitted to trade government strip bonds. As the Commission has not received any negative comments with respect to its proposal to remove the registration exemption, the Commission will be revising LPS 3-43 and replacing BOR#91/12 to implement its proposal. Interested persons that may be adversely affected by this proposal are requested to advise Brenda Benham, A/Director, Policy & Legislation by facsimile at (604) 660 - 2688 as soon as possible.

DATED at Vancouver, British Columbia on February 8, 1995.

> Douglas M. Hyndman
> Chair

Attachment

References: BOR#91/12   LPS 3-43
                     NIN#91/23

INVESTMENT DEALERS ASSOCIATION OF CANADA
STRIP BONDS AND STRIP BOND PACKAGES
INFORMATION STATEMENT

This Information Statement is being provided as required by securities regulatory authorities in Canada to describe certain attributes of "strip bonds" and "strip bond packages".

Strip Bonds and Strip Bond Packages

In this Information Statement the term "strip bond" refers to an interest in either (i) the amount payable on account of principal, or (ii) an amount payable on account of interest, in respect of one or more "Underlying Bonds". An Underlying Bond is a debt security issued or guaranteed by the government of Canada, a province of Canada or a foreign country or political division thereof and which pays interest at a fixed rate and at regular intervals. (Please note that: in New Brunswick and Quebec, only strip bonds in respect of Underlying Bonds issued or guaranteed by the government of Canada or a province of Canada are eligible for exemption from the registration and prospectus requirements of the applicable securities legislation; in Manitoba the exemption is limited to Underlying Bonds described in Section 19(2)a of the *Securities Act* (Manitoba); and in British Columbia the exemption is limited to Underlying Bonds of or guaranteed by the government of Canada or a province of Canada or a country or political subdivision of a country recognized by the British Columbia Securities Commission in an order made under section 32(a)(i.1) of the *Securities Act* (British Columbia).)

A strip bond entitles the holder to a single payment of a fixed amount in the future without the payment of any interest in the interim. The purchase price or present value of a strip bond is determined by discounting the amount of the payment to be received on the payment or maturity date of the strip bond by the appropriate interest rate or yield factor. Strip bonds are therefore different from conventional interest-bearing debt securities and purchasers of strip bonds should be aware of the special attributes of strip bonds as described in this Information Statement. Strip bonds may be purchased in various different forms as described below under "Custodial Arrangements".

In this Information Statement the term "strip bond package" refers to a security comprised of two or more strip bonds which are combined to make up a "bond-like" strip bond package or an "annuity-like" strip bond package. A bond-like strip bond package consists of an interest in the principal amount payable in respect of one or more Underlying Bonds, together with one or more interests in the interest payments to be made on one or more Underlying Bonds, thereby creating an instrument that resembles, in its payment characteristics, a conventional bond. An annuity-like strip bond package differs from a bond-like strip bond package only to the extent that it does not include an interest in the principal amount payable in respect of one or more Underlying Bonds. Strip bond packages may be purchased in the form of several separate strip bonds or as one security in one of the forms described below under "Custodial Arrangements".

Price Volatility

As with conventional interest-bearing debt securities, the market price of strip bonds and strip bond packages will fluctuate with prevailing interest rates. Generally, the market price of conventional interest-bearing debt securities and of strip bonds and strip bond packages will fluctuate in the same direction: when prevailing interest rates rise above the yield of these instruments, their market price will tend to fall; conversely, when prevailing interest rates fall below the yield of these instruments, their market price will tend to rise.

However, the market price of a strip bond will be significantly more volatile than the price of a conventional interest-bearing debt security with the same credit risk and term to maturity. When prevailing interest rates rise, the market price of a strip bond will tend to fall to a greater degree than the market price of a conventional interest-bearing debt security with the same credit risk and term to maturity. Conversely, when prevailing interest rates fall, the market price of a strip bond will tend to rise to a greater degree than the market price of a conventional interest-bearing debt security with the same credit risk and term to maturity. The primary reason for such volatility is the fact that no interest is paid in respect of a strip bond prior to its maturity. There is, therefore, no opportunity to reinvest interest payments at prevailing rates of interest prior to maturity.

The table below compares changes in the prices of conventional interest-bearing debt securities and strip bonds. The table shows, on a hypothetical basis, the difference in price fluctuation as a result of fluctuations in prevailing interest rates between, on the one hand, 5-year and 20-year $1,000 face amount conventional bonds bearing interest at 10% payable semi-annually, and, on the other hand, 5-year and 20-year $1,000 face amount strip bonds priced to yield 10%. It will be noted that the longer the term to maturity of the bond or the strip bond, the more volatile its market price will be.

	Market Price	Market Yield	Price with Rate Drop to 7%	% Price Change	Price Rate Increase to 13%	% Price Change
	Market Price Volatility (expressed as a percentage of face amount)					
10% 5 Year Bond	$100.00	10.00%	$112.47	+12.47%	$89.22	-10.78%
5 Year Strip Bond	61.39	10.00	70.89	+15.47	53.27	-13.23
10% 20 Year Bond	100.00	10.00	132.03	+32.03	78.78	-21.22
20 Year Strip Bond	14.20	10.00	25.26	+77.89	8.05	-43.30

In contrast to strip bonds, the income stream received on a strip bond package prior to maturity or the final payment date may be reinvested at the then prevailing interest rates. Therefore, the market price of a strip bond package will not be as volatile as the market price of a strip bond with the same credit risk and term to maturity or final payment date. However, it may be more volatile than the market price of a conventional interest-bearing debt security with the same credit risk and term to maturity.

Secondary Market and Liquidity

Strip bonds and strip bond packages do not trade in Canada in an auction market similar to that for shares listed on a stock exchange. Instead, strip bonds and strip bond packages trade in dealer or over-the-counter markets similar to those for most conventional debt securities. Certain strip bonds and strip bond packages that are available in Canada are offered by groups of investment dealers or financial institutions which may make markets for the strip bonds and strip bond packages they offer, although they are not obligated to do so. **There can be no assurance that a market for particular strip bonds or strip bond packages will be available at any given time.** In such circumstances, purchasers may have to hold their strip bonds and strip bond packages to maturity or final payment date in order to realize their investment.

Custodial Arrangements

Purchasers may purchase strip bonds and strip bond packages in four forms:

- A deposit receipt or certificate issued by a custodian where the receipt or certificate represents the relevant segregated underlying interest coupon(s) or principal residue(s) held by the custodian (alter-ego receipt).

- A deposit receipt or certificate issued by a custodian where the receipt or certificate represents an undivided interest in a pool of coupons or residues held by the custodian or in interest or principal payments to be made in respect of one or more Underlying Bonds held by the custodian (non alter-ego receipts).

- A book-entry position created by The Canadian Depository for Securities Limited (CDS) which represents an undivided interest in the relevant interest or principal payment(s) to be made in respect of one or more Underlying Bonds held by CDS.

- In limited circumstances, physical delivery of the actual coupon(s) or residue(s) (in specie).

Each of these forms has different characteristics:

- Alter-ego receipts may entitle the holder to take physical delivery of the under-lying coupon(s) or residue(s). If the holder decides to take physical delivery, the holder should be aware of the high risks associated with holding a bearer security which cannot be replaced. The holder also should be aware that the secondary market for physical strip bonds may be more limited than for other forms of strip bonds and strip bond packages, due to the risks involved.

- For alter-ego receipts and non alter-ego receipts, registered certificates may be available to the holder on request. Where registered certificates are not available under the custodial arrangements for the strip bond or the strip bond package, the holder will receive periodic statements showing the security position from his or her investment dealer or other financial institution.

- Holders of non alter-ego receipts and book-entry positions are not entitled to take physical delivery of the underlying coupon(s) or residue(s), except in cases where specifically allowed by the custodial arrangements or the rules of CDS, as the case may be.

- Holders of alter-ego receipts, non alter-ego receipts and book-entry positions, and holders of physical coupons(s) and residue(s), may be limited in their right to enforce the terms of the Underlying Bond(s) directly against the issuer. Further, such holders may have their rights under applicable custodial arrangements and in respect of the Underlying Bond(s) affected by a specified majority of such holders. Voting rights may be allocated to holders of strip bonds and strip bond packages based on a formula specified as part of the relevant custodial arrange-ment or as specified in the terms of the Underlying Bond(s). Each purchaser should review the relevant custodial arrangements and the purchaser's rights thereunder.

The facilities of CDS are available for custody and settlement of strip bonds and strip bond packages for any CDS participant which has deposited its Underlying Bonds with CDS or has taken delivery of them through CDS.

In some cases the Underlying Bonds are redeemable or callable prior to maturity. Purchasers of strip bonds or strip bond packages relating to interest payments to be made in respect of Underlying Bonds that are redeemable or callable should satisfy themselves that such interest payments do not relate to interest payment dates that may occur after the Underlying Bond's earliest call or redemption date.

Canadian Income Tax Summary

The Canadian federal income tax consequences of purchasing strip bonds and strip bond packages are complex. Purchasers of strip bonds and strip bond packages should consult their own tax advisors for advice relating to their particular circumstances. The following summary is intended to be a general commentary on the attributes of strip bonds and strip bond packages under the *Income Tax Act* (Canada) ("Tax Act") and the regulations there-under ("Regulations") for purchasers who hold their strip bonds and strip bond packages as capital property for purposes of the Tax Act.

Qualified Investments

Strip bonds and strip bond packages relating to Underlying Bonds that are issued or guaranteed by the government of Canada or issued by a province of Canada are "qualified investments" eligible for purchase by trusts governed by registered retire-ment savings plans ("RRSPs"), registered retirement income funds ("RRIFs") and deferred profit sharing plans ("DPSPs").

Annual Taxation of Strip Bonds

Revenue Canada has indicated that purchasers of strip bonds will be treated as having purchased a "prescribed debt obligation" within the meaning of the Regula-tions. Accordingly, a purchaser will be required to include in income in each year a notional amount of interest, notwithstanding that no interest will be paid or received in the year (see example below). Therefore, these instruments may be more attractive to non-taxable accounts, such as self-directed RRSPs, RRIFs, DPSPs, pension funds and charities, than to taxable accounts.

In general terms, the amount of notional interest deemed to accrue each year will be determined by using that interest rate which, when applied to the original purchase price and compounded at least annually, will result in a cumulative accrual of notional interest from the date of purchase to the date of maturity equal to the amount of the discount from face value at which the strip bond was purchased.

For individuals and certain trusts, the required accrual of notional interest in each year is generally only up to the anniversary date of the issuance of the Underlying Bond. For example, if a strip bond is purchased on February 1 of a year and the anniversary date of the issuance of the Underlying Bond is June 30, only five months of notional interest accrual will be required in the year of purchase. However, in each subsequent year, notional interest will be required to be accrued from July 1 of the previous year to June 30 of the subsequent year.

The table below sets out the income tax treatment of a taxable individual investor resident in Canada who purchases a $5,000 strip bond on February 1, 1995 at a cost of $3,256.69. The anniversary date of the issuance of the Underlying Bond is June 30. The strip bond is due on June 30, 2000 (i.e. 5 years and 5 months later) and the investor holds it to maturity. Thus, the effective interest rate on the strip bond for purposes of the interest accrual rules will be 8.25%. The investor's marginal tax rate is assumed to be 53%.

	Base for interest compounding (i.e. purchase price plus previously accrued notional interest)	Accrued notional interest for year (i.e. 8.25% of the base for interest compounding except in the first year)	Tax Liability at 53%
1995	$3,256.69	$107.11*	$ 56.77
1996	3,363.80	277.51	147.08
1997	3,641.32	300.41	159.22
1998	3,941.72	325.19	172.35
1999	4,266.92	352.02	186.57
2000	4,618.94	381.06	201.96
		$1,743.30	

* $[(1.0825)^{149/365} \times \$3,256.69] - \$3,256.69$

Note: February 1, 1995 to June 30, 1995 = 149 days

because the investor is not credited with interest for the day of purchase

In some circumstances the anniversary date of the issuance of the Underlying Bond may not be readily determinable. In these circumstances individual investors may wish to consider accruing notional interest each year to the end of the year.

A corporation, partnership, unit trust or any trust of which a corporation or partnership is a beneficiary is required for each taxation year to accrue notional interest to the end of the taxation year and not just to an earlier anniversary date in the taxation year.

Disposition of Strip Bonds Prior To Maturity

Upon the disposition of a strip bond prior to maturity, purchasers will be required to include in their income for the year of disposition notional interest to the date of disposition. If the amount received on such a disposition exceeds the total of the purchase price and the amount of all notional interest accrued and included in income, the excess will be treated as a capital gain. If the amount received on disposition is less than the total of the purchase price and the amount of all notional interest accrued and included in income, the difference will be treated as a capital loss. As of the date of this Information Statement, a taxpayer was required to take into account three quarters of the capital gain or loss in determining taxable income.

The table below sets out the income tax treatment for the individual investor in the previous example where the investor sells the strip bond on September 30, 1997 for an assumed sale price of $4,321.26.

Proceeds of disposition		$4,321.26
Base for calculation of capital gain		
• initial cost	$3,256.69	
• accrued income for 1995 (see previous table)	107.11	
• accrued income for 1996 (see previous table)	107.11	
• accrued income for 1997		
• to anniversary date (see previous table)	300.41	
• to September 30	73.49*	4,015.21
Capital gain		306.05
Taxable capital gain (3/4 of capital gain)		229.54
* [(1.0825) $^{92/365}$ x $3,641.32] - $3,641.32		

Strip Bond Packages

Because a strip bond package consists for tax purposes of a series of separate strip bonds, the interest inclusion rules will be satisfied if an annual notional interest inclusion is determined in respect of each separate strip bond as outlined above. However, the calculation of such annual notional interest inclusion may be very complex. In addition, the calculation may be impossible to perform for individual purchasers to the extent that the anniversary dates of the Underlying Bonds are unknown.

As an alternative, purchasers of strip bond packages may wish to consider accruing notional interest to the end of each year at the internal rate of return or yield of the strip bond package determined in respect of the purchaser on the assumption that the strip bond package is held to maturity or final payment date. The use of this method may in some circumstances result in a marginally less favourable income tax result to an individual purchaser than the calculation of an annual notional interest inclusion in respect of each separate strip bond comprising the strip bond package.

Upon the disposition of a strip bond package prior to maturity, purchasers will be required to include in their income for the year of disposition notional interest to the date of disposition. If the amount received on such a disposition exceeds the total of the purchase price and the amount of all notional interest accrued and included in income, the excess will be treated as a capital gain. If the amount received on disposition is less than the total of the purchase price and the amount of all notional interest accrued and included in income, the difference will be treated as a capital loss. As of the date of this Information Statement, a taxpayer was required to take into account three quarters of the capital gain or loss in determining taxable income.

Non-Residents of Canada

Non-residents of Canada for the purposes of the Tax Act who purchase strip bonds or strip bond packages relating to Underlying Bonds issued or guaranteed by the government of Canada or issued by a province of Canada and which were issued after April 15, 1966 will not be liable for income tax in Canada (including withholding tax) on any amounts paid or credited with respect to the strip bonds or strip bond packages if such purchasers do not use or hold the strip bonds or strip bond packages in carrying on business in Canada and their sole connection with Canada is the acquisition and ownership of the strip bonds or strip bond packages.

January 1995.

NIN#95/10

NOTICE

*PROPOSED AMENDMENTS TO THE SECURITIES ACT,
SECURITIES REGULATION AND VANCOUVER STOCK EXCHANGE ACT*

The Commission is publishing for comment, on behalf of the Ministry of Finance and Corporate Relations, a package of proposed amendments to the *Securities Act*, Securities Regulation and the *Vancouver Stock Exchange Act* for introduction in the Spring 1995 legislative session. The Commission prepared and published, on October 7, 1994, a first set of proposed amendments to the *Securities Act* (see NIN#94/14), which implemented part of the Government's response to the Matkin Report, and on November 25, 1995, a second set of amendments to the *Securities Act* that were unrelated to the Government's response to the Matkin Report (see NIN#94/28).

This third set of amendments is part of the Government's response to the Matkin Report. The amendments were prepared by the Policy and Legislation Branch of the Ministry of Finance and Corporate Relations. Any questions about the proposed amendments should be directed to Carol Anne Rolf, Acting Director, Policy and Legislation Branch at 387-1269.

The Commission strongly encourages comment on the proposed amendments.

DATED at Vancouver, British Columbia, on February 9, 1995.

Douglas M. Hyndman
Chair

REF: NIN#94/14
NIN#94/28

Summary of Legislative Initiatives

This is the third in a series of proposed legislative amendments to implement the Government's response to the Matkin Report as announced by the Honourable Elizabeth Cull, Minister of Finance and Corporate Relations.

Proposed Amendments to the Securities Act

The proposed amendments to the *Securities Act* are intended to:

- increase the number of commissioners and create a position of second vice-Chair (see sections 4(2), (4), (7) and (9));

- provide for the establishment of a Securities Policy Advisory Committee (see section 8.1);

- create a statutory civil cause of action for misrepresentations in press releases and letters to shareholders (see section 115.1);

- enable the Commission to apply to the Supreme Court for an order for disgorgement (see section 144.3); and

- provide the Commission with rule-making authority (see section 159.1). A proposed new regulation sets out the requirements (including ministerial approval, and public notice and consultation), which the Commission must comply with prior to the exercise of its new rule-making powers.

Proposed Amendments to the Vancouver Stock Exchange Act

The proposed amendments to the *Vancouver Stock Exchange Act* are intended to:

- provide that the Vancouver Stock Exchange Board of Governors (VSE Board) be comprised of 21 members, 7 of whom would be public governors appointed by the Lieutenant Governor in Council;

- require that the VSE Board elect one of the public governors as chair; and

- remove the requirement that one public governor be a member in good standing of the Law Society of British Columbia and that one public governor be a member in good standing of the Institute of Chartered Accountants of British Columbia.

Request for Comments

Written comments should be directed by March 24, 1995 to:

Carol Anne Rolf
A/Director
Policy and Legislation Branch
Ministry of Finance and Corporate Relations
Room 201, 553 Superior Street
Victoria, British Columbia
V8V 1X4

Comment letters submitted in response to Requests for Comment are placed on the public file and form part of the public record, unless confidentiality is requested. Although comment letters requesting confidentiality will not be placed on the public file, freedom of information legislation may require the Ministry of Finance and Corporate Relations to make comment letters available. Persons submitting comment letters should therefore be aware that the press and members of the public may be able to obtain access to any comment letter.

NIN#95/11

NOTICE

PROPOSED AMENDMENTS TO THE SECURITIES ACT
CONCERNING RELATED PARTY TRANSACTIONS INVOLVING MUTUAL FUNDS

The Commission is publishing for comment proposed amendments to the Securities Act that are intended to prohibit certain related party transactions involving mutual funds. This notice provides background to the proposed amendments.

In the Weekly Summary for the week ending November 25, 1995, the Commission published for comment in NIN#94/28, a number of proposed amendments to the Securities Act unrelated to the Government's response to the Matkin Report. Included in that request for comment were drafting instructions for a new provision, section 110.1. The actual proposed provision, together with related provisions and a proposed draft blanket order, are attached to this NIN.

Proposed section 110.1 would (1) restrict a mutual fund from investing in certain issuers in which a responsible person of the mutual fund is a director, officer or partner, (2) prohibit principal transactions between a mutual fund and a responsible person, and (3) prohibit loans from a mutual fund to a responsible person. The proposed provision is similar to section 118 of the Ontario Securities Act. However, unlike section 118, the definition of "responsible person" covers a broader range of related parties to a mutual fund. The broader range of related parties included in the definition of responsible person is intended to address the changes in the mutual fund industry that have occurred since the removal of the ownership restrictions previously imposed on financial institutions. These changes have created increased potential for conflicts of interest. The definition of responsible persons includes a person responsible for managing the mutual fund or its portfolio, a person responsible for advising the mutual fund with respect to its portfolio, associates and affiliates of such persons and related mutual funds.

The Commission recognizes that, provided there are adequate investor protection safeguards in place to address potential conflicts, principal trading transactions between the mutual fund and the responsible person with respect to debt securities issued by certain issuers may be beneficial to the mutual fund, on the basis that such trading may

(a) increase the market available to the mutual fund for its purchases or sales of debt securities, and

(b) facilitate access to trading strategies formulated by related parties that may enhance the performance of the mutual fund.

Accordingly, the Commission is considering providing blanket relief from the proposed section 110.1(1)(b) with respect to certain principal transactions between a responsible person and a mutual fund. The relief being contemplated is similar to that considered by the Canadian Securities Administrators with respect to certain provisions of National Policy Statement No. 39. (See NIN#92/30.) However, the proposed relief is restricted to purchases and sales in debt securities:

(i) issued or guaranteed by the federal or provincial government,

(ii) issued by a municipal government of Canada, and

(iii) issued or guaranteed by those governments recognized by the Commission for the purposes of section 32(a)(i.1) of the Act,

provided the debt meets specified rating requirements.

Under the proposed relief, a purchase or sale of debt securities by the mutual fund is required to meet certain conditions, including conditions related to pricing. The purchase or sale of debt securities by the mutual fund continues to be subject to the applicable investment restrictions and practices set out in NP 39. Further, the purchase or sale of debt securities by the mutual fund must be consistent with the fundamental investment objectives of the mutual fund and be in the best interest of the mutual fund.

The Commission is requesting comments on the proposed amendment and blanket relief. Comments are specifically requested on the following:

(a) whether the definition of responsible person is appropriate,

(b) what types of transactions currently being undertaken by mutual funds would be affected by the proposed provision and whether any transitional relief is required,

(c) whether the relief proposed should be made available to all of the parties,

(d) the adequacy or appropriateness of the conditions, including the pricing requirements, imposed under the draft BOR,

(e) the appropriateness of the ratings specified in Appendix "A" to the draft BOR,

(f) whether the relief proposed under the draft BOR should cover highly rated corporate debt or equity securities issued by substantial issuers, and

(g) whether relief from section 111 of the Act is also required.

Interested persons are invited to provide comments on the proposed amendments and draft BOR. Comment letters should be submitted by March 24, 1995 to:

> Brenda Benham
> A/Director, Policy & Legislation
> British Columbia Securities Commission
> 1100 - 865 Hornby Street
> Vancouver, B.C.
> V6Z 2H4

Comment letters submitted in response to Requests for Comment are placed on the public file and form part of the public record, unless confidentiality is requested. Although comment letters requesting confidentiality will not be placed on the public file, freedom of information legislation may require the Commission to make comment letters available. Persons submitting comment letters should therefore be aware that the press and members of the public may be able to obtain access to any comment letter.

The Commission will be considering the comments received on the proposed relief set out in the draft BOR together with the comments made by Ontario Securities Commissioner Glorianne Stromberg in her report on the investment industry, entitled "Regulatory Strategies for the MID-90's: Recommendations for Regulating Investment Funds in Canada" and the position of other CSA members with respect to the relief being considered under NP 39.

DATED at Vancouver, British Columbia, on February 16, 1995.

> Douglas M. Hyndman
> Chair

References: NIN#94/28
                  NIN#92/30

NIN#95/12

NOTICE

EXECUTIVE COMPENSATION AND INDEBTEDNESS DISCLOSURE - ONTARIO STAFF REPORT

A staff report on Ontario Regulation 638/93, which amended the requirements in respect of the disclosure of executive compensation and indebtedness of directors, executive officers and senior officers, was published in the Ontario Securities Commission Bulletin of February 17, 1995.

Staff of the Corporate Finance Branch of the Ontario Securities Commission ("OSC staff") conducted a selective review of the executive compensation and indebtedness disclosure contained in approximately 75 information circulars filed with the Ontario Securities Commission since the coming into force of the Ontario Regulation in October 1993.

The staff report addresses the interpretation issues that arose during the course of the review as well as those that arose through public inquiries received by OSC staff. In addition, the report includes a discussion of special areas of application of the Ontario Regulation, including reorganizations and management services agreements. For the most part, the report contains the responses that were given to those who sought assistance from OSC staff. The report provides information that will assist issuers in complying with the Ontario Regulation, identifies common deficiencies and provides guidance for improving the quality of the required disclosure.

The British Columbia Securities Commission amended Form 41 and the relevant portions of Forms 12, 13, 14, 15, 28 and 30 in December 1993 to require the same disclosure of executive compensation and indebtedness as that required by the Ontario Regulation. Accordingly, reporting issuers in British Columbia may benefit from the guidance provided by the OSC staff report.

Copies of the OSC staff report are available for pick up upon request. Requests should be directed to:

> Shandie Hertslet
> Information Distribution Officer
> British Columbia Securities Commission
> 1100 - 865 Hornby Street
> Vancouver, B.C.
> V6Z 2H4
>
> Telephone: (604) 660-4800

DATED at Vancouver, British Columbia, on March 1, 1995.

> Douglas M. Hyndman
> Chair

NIN#95/13

NOTICE

AMENDMENTS TO THE SECURITIES REGULATION
RELATING TO FILING REQUIREMENTS AND FEES APPLICABLE TO
CERTAIN MUTUAL FUNDS

Two amendments to the Securities Regulation were brought into force on March 9, 1995 by B.C. Reg. 97/95. A copy of B.C. Reg. 97/95 is attached to this Notice. The amendments address certain anomalies in the legislation and are housekeeping in nature.

Section 132 of the Securities Regulation requires issuers who distribute securities under certain exemptions from prospectus requirements to file a form within a specified time period. For most exemptions, the form must be filed within 10 days after the distribution. Annual filings are, however, permitted for certain exemptions that involve distributions made on a regular or automatic basis. The amendment to section 132 permits mutual funds that rely on section 55(2)(19) of the Act to file on an annual basis within 10 days after the end of the calendar year in which the distribution took place rather than within 10 days after each distribution. This amendment reduces the administrative burden imposed on mutual funds that rely on section 55(2)(19) of the Act.

The amendment to item 22 of section 183(1) of the Securities Regulation reduces the fee for exempt offerings of securities by money market mutual funds. Previously the fee for exempt offerings by money market mutual funds was higher than the fee for public offerings by money market mutual funds. The amendment removes this anomaly.

DATED at Vancouver, British Columbia, on March 16, 1995.

> Douglas M. Hyndman
> Chair

Attachment

Notices

NOTICE
AMENDMENTS TO THE INSIDER REPORT FORM (FORM 36)

Section 70(2) of the *Securities Act* requires that an insider of a reporting issuer file an insider report in the required form disclosing any direct or indirect beneficial ownership of, or control or direction over, securities of the reporting issuer.

Effective April 17, 1995, in accordance with section 158 of the Act, Form 36, attached to this Notice, is specified as the required form of insider report for the purposes of section 70(2) and (4) of the Act and section 130 of the Regulation.

Background

In December 1993, the Canadian Securities Administrators began to consider amending the insider report. Comments on the proposed amendments were incorporated from a variety of sources. The amendments are part of the Commission's efforts to make it easier for insiders to fulfill their reporting obligations under the legislation.

Amendments

The most significant amendments to the Form are to provide, in Box 5(E), a place for insiders to report control or direction over securities of the reporting issuer and, in Box 5(F), a place for insiders to identify the registered holder where control or direction is exercised. The amendments also improve the readability of the Form, incorporate references to other legislation, including freedom of information legislation, and make the Form uniform for filing under federal and provincial laws.

The CSA have agreed to implement this Form across the country effective April 17, 1995. In those jurisdictions in which the Form is part of a regulation, the securities regulatory authorities of those jurisdictions are taking whatever steps are necessary to amend the regulation. If any required amendments are not made before April 17, 1995, the securities regulatory authorities in those jurisdictions have agreed to accept the filing of the Form attached to this Notice as satisfying the filing requirements of the securities legislation.

To assist insiders and their professional advisers to complete Form 36, an example of how to complete the Form is attached that shows how balances are to be carried forward from month to month. The Commission is also mailing the Form, this Interpretation Note and NIN#95/15 to exchange issuers, brokers, investment dealers, mutual fund dealers, securities dealers and securities lawyers and accountants. The Form may also be obtained from the Commission's 11th floor receptionist.

DATED at Vancouver, British Columbia, on March 23, 1995.

Dean E. Holley
Superintendent of Brokers

REF: NIN#95/15

Attachments (3)

EXAMPLE (page 1 of 2)

INSIDER REPORT

(See instructions on the back of this report)

Where freedom of information legislation is in force in the jurisdiction where this form is filed: The personal information requested on this form is collected under the authority and used for the purposes of administering the provincial securities Acts, Bank Act, Cooperative Credit Associations Act, Insurance Companies Act, Trust and Loan Companies Act and Canada Business Corporations Act. Under the CBCA the information provided satisfies the disclosure requirements of section 127. While the federal Privacy Act protects personal information provided, it also permits public disclosure pursuant to section 266 of the CBCA. All information contained in this form will be made available to the public. Known as the Freedom of Information records stored in personal information bank number CCAP-PU-082. In British Columbia, if you have questions about how the Freedom of Information legislation applies to the personal information collected on this form, call the Manager, Public Information and Records at (604) 660-4627 or write the Manager, 1100-865 Hornby Street, Vancouver, B.C. V6Z 2H4.

BOX 1. NAME OF THE REPORTING ISSUER (BLOCK LETTERS)

REPORTING ISSUER INC.

BOX 2. INSIDER DATA

RELATIONSHIP(S) TO REPORTING ISSUER

[4] [5]

DATE OF LAST REPORT FILED — DAY MONTH YEAR — 0 4 | 0 1 | 9 5

CHANGE IN RELATIONSHIP FROM LAST REPORT [ ] YES [X] NO

IF INITIAL REPORT, DATE ON WHICH YOU BECAME AN INSIDER — DAY MONTH YEAR

BOX 3. NAME, ADDRESS AND TELEPHONE NUMBER OF THE INSIDER (BLOCK LETTERS)

FAMILY NAME OR CORPORATE NAME: DOE

GIVEN NAMES: JOHN

NO. 123   STREET: MAIN STREET   APT.

CITY: VANCOUVER   PROV: BRITISH COLUMBIA   POSTAL CODE: A 1 B 2 C 3

BUSINESS TELEPHONE NUMBER: 6 0 4 - 1 2 3 - 4 5 6 7

BUSINESS FAX NUMBER: 6 0 4 - 7 6 5 - 4 3 2 1

CHANGE IN NAME, ADDRESS OR TELEPHONE NUMBER FROM LAST REPORT [ ] YES [X] NO

BOX 4. JURISDICTION(S) WHERE THE ISSUER IS A REPORTING ISSUER OR THE EQUIVALENT

[ ] ALBERTA   [ ] NEWFOUNDLAND
[X] BRITISH COLUMBIA   [ ] NOVA SCOTIA
[ ] FEDERAL   [ ] ONTARIO
   [ ] BANK ACT   [ ] QUEBEC
   [ ] CCAA
   [ ] ICA   [ ] SASKATCHEWAN
   [ ] TLCA
   [ ] CBCA   [ ] UNITED STATES
[ ] MANITOBA   [ ] NASDAQ
     [ ] SEC

BOX 5. INSIDER HOLDINGS AND CHANGES (IF INITIAL REPORT, COMPLETE SECTIONS (A) (B) (C) ONLY. SEE ALSO INSTRUCTIONS TO BOX 5)   (A) AMD   (P)

(A) DESIGNATION OF CLASS OF SECURITIES	(B) BALANCE OF CLASS OF SECURITIES ON LAST REPORT	(C) DATE DAY MONTH YEAR	NATURE	(D) TRANSACTIONS NUMBER/VALUE ACQUIRED	(E) NUMBER/VALUE DISPOSED OF	(F) UNIT PRICE/ EXERCISE PRICE	$ US	(G) PRESENT BALANCE OF CLASS OF SECURITIES HELD	(H) DIRECT/INDIRECT OWNERSHIP CONTROL, OR DIRECTION	(I) IDENTIFY THE REGISTERED HOLDER WHERE OWNERSHIP OF ISSUER OR INDIRECT OR WHERE CONTROL OR DIRECTION IS EXERCISED
COMMON	60,000	0 6 0 1 9 5	1 0	5,000		2.10		65,000	0	
		1 6 0 1 9 5	5 5	30,000				95,000	0	
		1 8 0 1 9 5	1 0		20,000	2.15		75,000	1	ABC COMPANY
COMMON	50,000	2 2 0 1 9 5	1 0	10,000		2.10		60,000	1	DEF COMPANY
COMMON	100,000							100,000	2	DEF COMPANY

BOX 6. REMARKS

The undersigned certifies that the information given in this report is true and complete in every respect. It is an offence to file a report that, at the time and in the light of the circumstances in which it is made, contains a misrepresentation.

BOX 7. SIGNATURE

NAME (BLOCK LETTERS): JOHN DOE

SIGNATURE: John Doe

DATE OF THE REPORT — DAY MONTH YEAR — 1 0 | 0 1 | 9 5

ATTACHMENT [ ] YES [X] NO

This form is used as a uniform report for the insider reporting requirements under all provincial securities Acts, Bank Act, Cooperative Credit Associations Act, Insurance Companies Act, Trust and Loan Companies Act and Canada Business Corporations Act. The terminology used is generic to accommodate the various Acts.

CORRESPONDENCE [X] ENGLISH [ ] FRENCH

KEEP A COPY FOR YOUR FILE

FIN 2036 Rev. 05/2/22 HS — 94   VERSION FRANÇAISE DISPONIBLE SUR DEMANDE

EXAMPLE (page 2 of 2)

INSIDER REPORT
(See instructions on the back of this report)

Where *Freedom of Information legislation is in force in the jurisdiction where this form is filed:* The personal information requested on this form is collected under the authority and used for the purposes of administering the provincial securities Acts, Bank Act, Cooperative Credit Associations Act, Insurance Companies Act, Trust and Loan Companies Act and Canada Business Corporations Act. Under the CBCA the information provided satisfies the disclosure requirements of section 127. While the federal *Privacy Act* protects personal information provided, it also permits public disclosure pursuant to section 266 of the CBCA. All information contained in this form will be made available to the public. Federally, this information will be stored in personal information bank number CCAAF-PU-062. In British Columbia, if you have questions about how the freedom of information legislation applies to the personal information collected on this form, call the Manager, Public Information and Records at (604) 660-4827 or write the Manager, 1100-865 Hornby Street, Vancouver, B.C. V6Z 2H4.

BOX 1. NAME OF THE REPORTING ISSUER (BLOCK LETTERS)

REPORTING ISSUER INC.

BOX 2. INSIDER DATA

	DAY / MONTH / YEAR
DATE OF LAST REPORT FILED	0 8 / 0 2 / 9 5
OR	DAY / MONTH / YEAR
IF INITIAL REPORT, DATE ON WHICH YOU BECAME AN INSIDER	

RELATIONSHIP(S) TO REPORTING ISSUER: 4 5

CHANGE IN RELATIONSHIP FROM LAST REPORT: ☐ YES ☒ NO

BOX 3. NAME, ADDRESS AND TELEPHONE NUMBER OF THE INSIDER (BLOCK LETTERS)

FAMILY NAME OR CORPORATE NAME: DOE
GIVEN NAMES: JOHN
NO.: 123 STREET: MAIN STREET APT:
CITY: VANCOUVER PROV.: BRITISH COLUMBIA POSTAL CODE: A1B 2C3
BUSINESS TELEPHONE NUMBER: 604 - 123 - 4567
BUSINESS FAX NUMBER: 604 - 765 - 4321

CHANGE IN NAME, ADDRESS OR TELEPHONE NUMBER FROM LAST REPORT: ☐ YES ☒ NO

BOX 4. JURISDICTION(S) WHERE THE ISSUER IS A REPORTING ISSUER OR THE EQUIVALENT

☐ ALBERTA
☒ BRITISH COLUMBIA
☐ FEDERAL
  ☐ BANK ACT
  ☐ CCAA
  ☐ ICA
  ☐ TLCA
  ☐ CBCA
☐ MANITOBA
☐ NEWFOUNDLAND
☐ NOVA SCOTIA
☐ ONTARIO
☐ QUEBEC
☐ SASKATCHEWAN
☐ UNITED STATES
  ☐ NASDAQ
  ☐ SEC

BOX 5. INSIDER HOLDINGS AND CHANGES (IF INITIAL REPORT, COMPLETE SECTIONS (A) (D) (E) (F) ONLY. SEE ALSO INSTRUCTIONS TO BOX 5)

(A) DESIGNATION OF CLASS OF SECURITIES	(B) BALANCE OF CLASS OF SECURITIES ON LAST REPORT	(C) TRANSACTIONS DATE DAY/MONTH/YEAR	(C) NATURE	(C) NUMBER/VALUE ACQUIRED	(C) NUMBER/VALUE DISPOSED OF	(C) UNIT PRICE/ EXERCISE PRICE	(C) $ US	(D) PRESENT BALANCE OF CLASS OF SECURITIES HELD	(E) DIRECT/INDIRECT OWNERSHIP CONTROL OR DIRECTION	(F) IDENTIFY THE REGISTERED HOLDER WHERE OWNERSHIP IS INDIRECT OR WHERE CONTROL OR DIRECTION IS EXERCISED
COMMON	75,000	06/02/95	10		25,000	2.25		50,000	0	
COMMON	60,000	15/02/95	10	20,000		2.50		40,000	1	ABC COMPANY
COMMON	100,000							100,000	2	DEF COMPANY

BOX 6. REMARKS

The undersigned certifies that the information given in this report is true and complete in every respect. It is an offence to file a report that, at the time and in the light of the circumstances in which it is made, contains a misrepresentation.

BOX 7. SIGNATURE

NAME (BLOCK LETTERS): JOHN DOE
SIGNATURE: *John Doe*
DATE OF THE REPORT: DAY 1 / MONTH 0 / YEAR 0 3 9 5

ATTACHMENT ☐ YES ☒ NO

This form is used as a uniform report for the insider reporting requirements under all provincial securities Acts, Bank Act, Cooperative Credit Associations Act, Insurance Companies Act, Trust and Loan Companies Act and Canada Business Corporations Act. The terminology used is generic to accommodate the various Acts.

CORRESPONDENCE ☒ ENGLISH ☐ FRENCH

KEEP A COPY FOR YOUR FILE

FIN 2036 Rev. 91 / 2 / 22 HB —/94   VERSION FRANÇAISE DISPONIBLE SUR DEMANDE

INTERPRETATION NOTE

DISCLOSURE OF SECURITIES UNDER "CONTROL OR DIRECTION"

Effective April 17, 1995, the Superintendent of Brokers, along with the securities regulators in the other provinces and territories of Canada, the Office of the Superintendent of Financial Institutions and Industry Canada Corporations Directorate, will specify a new insider reporting Form (Form 36). The new Form is intended to improve readability and to assist insiders to comply with their reporting obligations. The new Form will be accepted for filing in all Canadian jurisdictions, both federal and provincial.

The most significant amendments to the Form are to provide, in Box 5(E), a place for insiders to more easily and clearly disclose changes in the securities over which they have control or direction and, in Box 5(F), a place for insiders to identify the registered holder where control or direction is exercised. The British Columbia *Securities Act* and securities legislation elsewhere has, for years, required that insiders disclose not only changes in securities directly or indirectly beneficially owned, but also securities over which the insider has control or direction. See NIN#95/14.

The purpose of this Interpretation Note is to clarifys the meaning of the words "control or direction" over securities in the definition of insider in section 1(1) and in section 70 of the *Securities Act*.

A person with "control or direction" over securities includes any person, including a portfolio manager, who, directly or indirectly, through any contract, arrangement, understanding, relationship or otherwise has or shares:

a)   voting power, which includes the power to vote, or to direct the voting of, such securities, and/or

b)   investment power, which includes the power to acquire or dispose, or to direct the acquisition or disposition of, such securities.

A person other than the beneficial owner of the securities may hold this power through a power of attorney, grant of limited trading authority, or management agreement. For example, a portfolio manager may hold this power over the securities of clients where the clients have assigned discretionary trading authority to the portfolio manager. A director of an issuer may have been granted trading authority over the securities held by family members or associates. A director or owner of a private company may have direction or control over the securities held by the private company.

Regardless of how the authority to exercise control or direction over the securities is conveyed, where the aggregate securities under a person's control or direction exceeds 10% of the voting securities of a reporting issuer that person is an insider of the reporting issuer within the meaning of section 1(1) of the Act and must comply with the provisions of section 70 concerning the filing of insider reports on an initial and then monthly basis.

For example, portfolio managers for a number of clients may find that they have no single client that holds securities carrying more than 10% of the voting rights attached to all the outstanding voting securities in a specific reporting issuer. However, when the holdings of all of the portfolio manager's clients are aggregated, the portfolio manager may have direction over more than 10% of the voting securities of the reporting issuer. In this case, the portfolio manager must comply with section 70 of the Act and file an insider report. Similarly, a management company in a family or group of mutual funds would also have to consider whether it had control or direction over the portfolio securities of the family or group of mutual funds.

In the OSC Bulletin of September 16, 1994, the Ontario Securities Commission published a discussion paper [(1994), 17 *OSC Bulletin* 4437] concerning several issues related to a proposed refinement of the early warning regime and the rules regarding insider reporting, take-over bids and control block distributions. One of the issues raised in that paper was the potential difficulty faced by at least some portfolio and mutual fund managers in trying to comply with the reporting obligations that flow from having "control or direction" over securities. Alternatives to the current reporting requirements are under consideration and may be implemented in one or all Canadian jurisdictions.

In British Columbia, the insider reporting requirements are clearly set out in the *Securities Act*. The Commission expects all insiders to comply, on a timely basis, with the legislation. In addition to the circumstances set out in LPS#3-14 - Applications for Insider Reporting Exemptions, in certain isolated circumstances, the Commission may consider applications under section 152.2(b) of the Securities Regulation for discretionary relief from the insider reporting requirements. To grant the relief, the Commission or Superintendent must be satisfied in the circumstances that there is adequate justification for so doing and that it would not be prejudicial to the public interest to do so.

DATED at Vancouver, British Columbia, on March 23, 1995.

Joyce C. Maykut, Q.C.
Vice Chair

REF: NIN#95/14
         LPS#3-14

NIN#95/16

NOTICE

AMENDMENTS TO FORM 30 (INFORMATION CIRCULAR)

The British Columbia Securities Commission is publishing amendments to Form 30 (Information Circular) to require improved disclosure by reporting issuers when preparing information circulars concerning reverse take-overs ("RTOs"), amalgamations, mergers, arrangements and reorganizations. These amendments, particularly those concerning RTO disclosure, are intended to ensure that security holders receive sufficient information to make reasoned judgments on issues brought before meetings of security holders. The amendments concerning amalgamations, mergers, arrangements and reorganizations bring British Columbia's disclosure requirements in line with those of Ontario.

The Superintendent of Brokers specifies, in accordance with section 158 of the Securities Act (the "Act"), amendments to item 11 of Form 30 to implement the new requirements. The amended item 11 of Form 30 is attached to this Notice.

Background

In January 1995, the Commission published for comment NIN#95/6 entitled "Draft Amendments to Form 30 and Additional Draft Amendments to Section 146 of the Securities Regulation". The Commission received three comment letters in response.

Section 146

In addition to comments on NIN#95/6, comments had also been received on section 146 in response to the Commission's package of proposed amendments to the Securities Regulation published on October 7, 1994. Amendments to section 146 are currently being examined in light of all comments received.

Form 30

The amendments to item 11 of Form 30 have been revised from the NIN#95/6 draft to reflect some of the comments received and to clarify certain provisions. Other areas of concern raised in the comment letters are discussed below.

The requirements concerning RTOs have been revised to require that the financial statements included in the information circular be approved by the directors, partners or the sole proprietor of the non-reporting issuer or of the vendor of the business to be acquired in the RTO. In addition, drafting changes were made to the section dealing with interim financial statements to make it easier to read. Drafting changes were also made to clarify the type of information that must be summarized in the press release to be issued by the reporting issuer once it has filed its Filing Statement or Statement of Material Facts with the Vancouver Stock Exchange ("VSE").

The requirements relating to amalgamations, mergers, arrangements or reorganizations have been revised to clarify that they apply only where the matter is submitted to security holder approval as a result of applicable corporate legislation. A reporting issuer undergoing a "reorganization" or "change of business", as defined in the VSE listings policies, would not be subject to these specific requirements unless that "reorganization" or "change of business" involved a corporate law transaction that would require such disclosure. Note, however, that the general rule set out in item 11, that matters submitted to a meeting of security holders must be described in sufficient detail to permit security holders to form a reasoned judgment concerning the matter, still applies to information circulars prepared in connection with such a "reorganization" or "change of business". Guidance as to what Commission staff will generally consider to be appropriate disclosure in this context can be found in the specific disclosure requirements relating to RTOs in item 11 of Form 30.

Some commentators expressed concern about having to prepare the information circular for a meeting of shareholders to approve an RTO or other corporate trans-action at a relatively early stage in the transaction. General instruction one of the Form requires that the information contained in an information circular be as of a specified date, not be more than 30 days before the information is first sent to any security holder. As of that date, the information contained in the circular must be accurate and complete. Staff acknowledge that, because the transaction will still be subject to regulatory approval by the VSE, certain of the information ultimately contained in the Filing Statement or Statement of Material Facts may vary from the information included earlier in the circular. The critical requirement for the reporting issuer is that the information circular must not contain any statement that is a misrepresentation, at the time and in light of the circumstances under which it is made.

A concern had also been raised about potential timing difficulties for information circulars concerning RTOs given the requirements of National Policy Statement No. 41 ("NPS 41"). Staff believe that the nature of the RTO disclosure required in the amended Form 30, and the relief and waiver options available under NPS 41, minimize the likelihood of any serious timing problems.

Implementation

The amendments to item 11 of Form 30 are effective for information circulars dated on or after July 1, 1995. An information circular dated prior to July 1, 1995 may comply with either the current or the amended form.

Any amendments to section 146 will be implemented in conjunction with the Commission's package of proposed amendments to the Securities Regulation. The Commission intends to recommend to the government that section 146 be amended to require reporting issuers to file with the Commission a copy of any Filing Statement filed with the VSE in connection with an RTO. Reporting issuers are invited to file a copy of any RTO Filing Statement with the Commission before the amendments to section 146 are implemented.

DATED at Vancouver, British Columbia, on April 20, 1995.

> Dean E. Holley
> Superintendent of Brokers

Attachment

REF: NIN#94/15
       NIN#95/6

NIN#95/17

Notices

NOTICE

FORM 14A - INFORMATION REQUIRED IN PROSPECTUS OF A NATURAL RESOURCE ISSUER

Form 14A - Information required in Prospectus of a Natural Resource Issuer is published in the Weekly Summary for the week ending April 21, 1995. This Notice provides background to, and specifies, the new form.

A request for comment on Draft Form 14A was issued under NIN#95/3. The comments received have been reviewed and where appropriate incorporated in Form 14A. A number of drafting changes were also made to the published draft. In response to comments received, Form 14A will be made available for all natural resource issuers and the Draft Form 14A has accordingly been revised to modify in certain items the disclosure requested for senior issuers (see General Instructions 10 and 12, and Sections 1.6, 5.2, 6.1, 6.2, 6.6, 6.7, 6.13, 7, 8.2, 12.1 - 12.3, 13.1, 13.2, 14, 15 and 17.1).

The reference to "major properties" in the definition of "principal properties" has been deleted (see General Instruction 12). The disclosure of interest held in the issuer by a responsible solicitor and certain related parties that was required in the published draft has been narrowed (see Item 21). The comments received with respect to requiring title opinions and expertising the differences in corporate laws will be considered and addressed in revisions to Local Policy Statements 3-02 and 3-03.

Effective August 1, 1995, in accordance with section 158 of the *Securities Act*, the Superintendent of Brokers specifies Form 14A as the required form of prospectus for a natural resource issuer where, (1) the issuer intends to distribute the securities solely in British Columbia, or (2) the issuer intends to distribute securities in British Columbia and does not meet the minimum listing requirements for the senior board of the Vancouver Stock Exchange. All other natural resource issuers are permitted and encouraged to use Form 14A.

Prior to August 1, 1995, natural resource issuers may prepare and file a preliminary prospectus in accordance with Form 14A.

As noted in NIN#95/3, a Form 14A Summary Prospectus Disclosure System will also be available once an amendment to Part 11 of Local Policy Statement 3-02 and a blanket order have been finalized. Both the amendment and the blanket order are anticipated to be published before Form 14A becomes effective. The Form 14A Summary Prospectus Disclosure System will make available to natural resource issuers filing on Form 14A the use of a summary prospectus and base disclosure document in the same manner as the Form 12A Summary Prospectus Disclosure System. (For a description of the Form 12A Summary Prospectus Disclosure System refer to NIN#94/17 and NIN#95/4.)

DATED at Vancouver, British Columbia, on April 20, 1995.

Dean E. Holley
Superintendent of Brokers

Reference: Form 14A
               NIN#94/17
               NIN#95/3
               NIN#95/4
               LPS#3-02
               LPS#3-03

NIN#95/18

NOTICE

DRAFT NATIONAL POLICY STATEMENT NO. 54
EXPEDITED REGISTRATION SYSTEM FOR ADVISERS

The Canadian Securities Administrators (the "CSA") are publishing for comment Draft National Policy Statement No. 54 (the "Draft Policy"). The purpose of the Draft Policy is to simplify the process for registration as an adviser in more than one province or territory. It applies to both corporate and individual advisers.

The Draft Policy proposes a system whereby an applicant could apply for registration in more than one province or territory by using the forms and meeting the requirements of the securities regulatory authority in its principal jurisdiction. The applicant must also comply with all the initial requirements in Québec. The principal jurisdiction is the province or territory in which the adviser has its principal place of business.

The securities regulatory authority of a non-principal jurisdiction could opt out of the expedited registration process for a specific application. This would likely occur only where the jurisdiction had concerns about the applicant or the application.

On completion of registration procedures, the securities regulatory authority in the principal jurisdiction would issue an expedited registration document as evidence that the applicant has been registered in the principal jurisdiction and most non-principal jurisdictions. The securities regulatory authorities in the Northwest Territories and Québec would issue their own registration certificates within a short period after the expedited registration document is issued.

The expedited registration process would apply to renewals of registration as well as to amendments of registration, except in the Northwest Territories. Advisers would have the same anniversary date in each jurisdiction, and could renew their registration in each jurisdiction at the same time.

After becoming registered under the Draft Policy, advisers could, with certain exceptions, satisfy the requirements of all jurisdictions by complying with the requirements of the securities regulatory authority of the principal jurisdiction. Advisers must comply with conflict of interest rules of the jurisdictions that have such rules. Advisers registered in Québec must comply with all local requirements.

The Draft Policy waives, on certain conditions, the office, residency and records requirements of the securities regulatory authorities in non-principal jurisdictions other than Québec.

The Ontario Securities Commission has recently acquired the authority to make rules. Other securities regulatory authorities are seeking similar authority. Because certain procedures must be followed when making rules, those securities regulatory authorities with rule-making power may have to redraft certain parts of the Draft Policy into a new format and republish for comment. Until this rule-making process is complete, the Draft Policy cannot be implemented in Ontario.

Request for Comments

The CSA invite comment on the Draft Policy. Please submit 12 copies of any comment letter by **June 30, 1995** to:

> Capital Markets Committee
> c/o Barbara Shourounis
> Saskatchewan Securities Commission
> 850 - 1914 Hamilton Street
> Regina, Saskatchewan
> S4P 3V7

Comment letters submitted in response to requests for comments are placed in the public file in certain jurisdictions. They form part of the public record unless confidentiality is requested. Comment letters will be circulated among the securities regulatory authorities for purposes of finalizing the Draft Policy whether or not confidentiality is requested.

Accordingly, although letters for which confidentiality is requested will not be placed in the public file, freedom of information legislation may require the securities regulatory authorities in certain jurisdictions to make the comment letters available. Persons submitting comment letters should be aware that the press and members of the public may be able to obtain access to any comment letter.

For further information please contact any of the following:

Barbara Shourounis
Saskatchewan Securities Commission
(306) 787-5842

Ross McLennan
British Columbia Securities Comission
(604) 660-0001 (Greater Vancouver)
1-800-373-6393 (all other regions of
British Columbia)

Daniel Laurion
Commision des valeurs mobilières du
Québec
(514) 873-5009 extension 266

DATED at Vancouver, British Columbia, on April 20, 1995.

> Douglas M. Hyndman
> Chair

NIN#95/19

NOTICE

FORM 61 - QUARTERLY REPORT

A revised Form 61 - Quarterly Report is published in the Weekly Summary for the week ending April 21, 1995. This Notice provides background to, and specifies, the revised form.

Staff's ongoing review of quarterly reports filed by exchange issuers has revealed a number of recurring deficiencies in the quality and scope of disclosure provided to the public. The purpose of this Notice is to flag those deficiencies and to discuss the revisions made to Form 61 to specifically highlight the areas where enhanced disclosure is required.

The quarterly report and, specifically, management's discussion of the issuer's operations under Schedule C of the report, has frequently not provided the level of meaningful disclosure expected by the investing public. In particular, many exchange issuers have filed quarterly reports in which they do not:

- state the aggregate amount of expenditures made to parties not at arm's length from the issuer during the quarter,

- provide a discussion of material expenditures that have been made during the quarter,

- reconcile the previously disclosed intended use of proceeds with the actual use of proceeds, and

- provide any meaningful discussion of investor relation activities that have been undertaken by or on behalf of the issuer during the quarter.

Staff is of the view that these are all disclosure topics important to investors, particularly in the case of venture companies.

Staff have, in the past, issued deficiency letters requesting that quarterly reports be revised to incorporate meaningful discussions of issuers' operations during the period. In several instances, the disclosure provided in quarterly reports has been so deficient as to warrant the issuance of a cease trade order. Exchange issuers are reminded of the need to provide meaningful management discussion in quarterly reports and are expected, in particular, to include discussion of the items noted above.

Schedule C of Form 61 has been revised to specifically refer to material expenditures, use of proceeds reconciliation and investor relations activities. The changes have been blacklined in the revised Form 61.

Effective for all quarterly reports filed after July 31, 1995, the Superintendent specifies, pursuant to section 158 of the *Securities Act*, the revised Form 61 as the required form of quarterly report to be filed by exchange issuers under section 145 of the Regulation. The specification of the prior quarterly report, set out in NIN#89/5, is revoked for all quarterly reports filed after July 31, 1995.

Staff will continue reviewing quarterly reports and will consider the issuance of cease trade orders in circumstances where there is inadequate disclosure provided in the report. Issuers who require guidance in the preparation of their quarterly reports are encouraged to contact the Corporate Finance Division of the Commission.

DATED at Vancouver, British Columbia, on April 20, 1995.

Dean E. Holley
Superintendent of Brokers

Reference: NIN#89/5

NIN#95/20

NOTICE

DRAFT FORMS 12B AND 14B -
INFORMATION REQUIRED IN EXCHANGE OFFERING PROSPECTUS
OF AN INDUSTRIAL ISSUER AND INFORMATION REQUIRED IN
EXCHANGE OFFERING PROSPECTUS OF A NATURAL RESOURCE ISSUER

The Commission is publishing for comment Draft Form 12B - Information Required in Exchange Offering Prospectus of an Industrial Issuer and Draft Form 14B - Information Required in Exchange Offering Prospectus of a Natural Resource Issuer. This Notice provides background to the Draft EOP Forms and invites comments on specific issues.

As noted in NIN#94/17, the amendment repealing the statement of material facts exemption contained in section 58(1)(c) of the Securities Act will be brought into force once the exchange offering prospectus forms and the circumstances under which they will be used has been finalized.

Draft Form 12B is based on Form 12A - Information Required in Prospectus of a Junior Industrial Issuer and Draft Form 14B is based on Form 14A - Information Required in Prospectus of a Natural Resource Issuer. The disclosure requirements have been modified to recognize that issuers using the EOP Forms are reporting issuers listed on the Vancouver Stock Exchange and that senior issuers may use the EOP Forms.

The Commission anticipates that the EOP Forms will be made available for all distributions of securities made on or through the facilities of the Vancouver Stock Exchange provided the distribution is not an initial public offering. Accordingly, the use of the EOP Forms will be available to all issuers listed on the VSE and will not be restricted to issuers who are subject to the assessment report requirement under Local Policy Statement 3-17.

The Commission is requesting comment on the Draft EOP Forms. Specific comment is requested with respect to the following items:

- Is the extent of disclosure required under the EOP Forms appropriate for all issuers permitted to use the EOP Forms? Should a distinction be made between issuers listed on the venture board and issuers listed on the senior board, i.e., should an issuer listed on the senior board be permitted to omit certain of the detailed disclosure requirements (beyond those already permitted) of the EOP Forms and, if so, which requirements and why?

- Is the time period over which disclosure is required appropriate for distributions by issuers after their initial public offering and, if not, what is the appropriate time period and why?

- Is there additional disclosure that should be added and, if so, what disclosure and why?

Consistent with the Summary Prospectus Disclosure System available for junior industrial issuers filing on a Form 12A and natural resource issuers filing on a Form 14A, an EOP Summary Prospectus Disclosure System will also be introduced upon finalization of the EOP Forms. The EOP Summary Prospectus Disclosure System will make available to issuers filing an EOP the use of a summary prospectus and base disclosure document in the same manner as the Form 12A Summary Prospectus Disclosure System. (For a description of the Form 12A Summary Prospectus Disclosure System, please refer to NIN#94/17 and NIN#95/4.)

Request for Comment

The Commission is requesting written comment on the Draft EOP Forms. Comment letters should be submitted by June 16, 1995 to:

> Brenda J. Benham
> Director, Policy & Legislation
> British Columbia Securities Commission
> 1100 - 865 Hornby Street
> Vancouver, B.C.
> V6Z 2H4

Comment letters submitted in response to Requests for Comment are placed on the public file and form part of the public record, unless confidentiality is requested. Although comment letters requesting confidentiality will not be placed on the public file, freedom of information legislation may require the Commission to make comment letters available. Persons submitting comment letters should therefore be aware that the press and members of the public may be able to obtain access to any comment letter.

DATED at Vancouver, British Columbia, on April 26, 1995.

> Dean E. Holley
> Superintendent of Brokers

References: NIN#94/17
                NIN#95/4
                Form 12A
                Form 14A
                LPS#3-17

Notices

NIN#95/21

NOTICE

DECISIONS OF THE BRITISH COLUMBIA SECURITIES COMMISSION

This notice is accompanied by a list of the decisions issued by the British Columbia Securities commission from April 1987 through April 1995.

The list, which is intended as a reference guide, provides the dates when the decisions were issued, the names of the respondents or applicants, and the dates and edition numbers of the Weekly summary in which the decisions were published.

DATED at Vancouver, British Columbia, on May 11, 1995.

Douglas M. Hyndman
Chair

INDEX OF DECISIONS OF THE
BRITISH COLUMBIA SECURITIES COMMISSION

Date Decision Issued (mm/dd/yy)	In the Matter of:	Date of Weekly Summary (mm/dd/yy)	Ed. W.S.
04/14/87	PEMGOLD RESOURCES INC.	05/01/87	87:17
06/09/87	CAROLIN MINES LTD.	06/12/87	87:23
06/22/87	EQUINOX RESOURCES LTD., Equinox Entertainment Corp., Vancouver Stock Exchange	06/26/87	87:25
10/05/87	ARGONAUT RESOURCES LTD., Vancouver Stock Exchange	10/06/87	87:45
12/17/87	BANCO RESOURCES LTD., Eurell Verster Potts, Anton Johann Drescher, Donald Edward Cameron, Arthur Leonard Cameron	12/18/87	87:51
01/21/88	CENTRAL TRUST COMPANY, Guaranty Trust Company of Canada, Yorkshire Trust Company	01/22/88	88:55
01/21/88	TECHNIGEN CORPORATION, David Charles Stuart, Corporacion Relacio, S.A.	01/22/88	88:55
02/02/88	DONALD A. LYONS	02/05/88	88:57
02/03/88	PAC INDUSTIRES, INC.	02/12/88	88:58
02/25/88	ALEXANDER LINDSAY LAXTON, Vancouver Stock Exchange	02/26/88	88:60
03/16/88	KELVIN ENERGY LTD., Asiamerica Capital Ltd., Asiamerica Equities Ltd., Industrial Equity (Pacific) Limited Wilbur Enterprises Limited, Industrial Equity Limited, Citizens & Grazier Assurance Co Ltd., Brierley Investments Co., Limited, Can-Kor Development (Far East) Ltd., I.E.J.W. Joint Venture	03/18/88	88:63
04/08/88	WESTERN CORPORATE ENTERPRISES INC., 1710 Holdings Ltd.	04/15/88	88:66
07/04/88	WILLIAM F. ROBERTSON	07/08/88	88:78
09/15/88	SUNSHINE ORANGE GROVES INC., Trans-Globe Financial Corporation, L.R.D. Associates, John Edwards & Company, John Edwards, Roland (Ron) Lemay	09/30/88	88:89

Date Decision Issued (mm/dd/yy)	In the Matter of:	Date of Weekly Summary (mm/dd/yy)	Ed. W.S.
09/21/88	CAPITAL RESERVE INC., Jerome Rak, Maureen Macneill, Christopher Bass, Donald R. Stratton, Leif Ostensoe, Alan Charuk, Wayne Wile, Belmont Capital Corporation, Prairie Pacific Capital Inc.	09/30/88	88:89
09/30/88	GORDON STANLEY LACKENBAUER, Kenneth George Copland, Terry Alan Jackson, Vancouver Stock Exchange	10/07/88	88:90
10/17/88	C.E.L. INDUSTRIES LIMITED, Handart Services Limited, Week Securities Limited, Certac International Limited	10/21/88	88:92
11/25/88	CAPITAL RESERVE INC., Jerome Rak, Maureen Macneill, Christopher Bass, Donald R. Stratton, Leif Ostensoe, Alan Charuk, Wayne Wile, Belmont Capital Corporation, Prairie Pacific Capital Inc.	12/02/88	88:98
12/05/88	DUCK BOOK COMMUNICATIONS LIMITED	12/09/88	88:99
12/15/88	RONALD BRUCE BIEBER, Vancouver Stock Exchange, Bankit Resource Corporation, Caliente Resources Ltd., Draw International Resources Corp., Flow Resources Ltd., High Rise Resources Ltd., Longboat Resources Inc., Midnapore (1979) Resources Inc., Nu-Start Resource Corp., Shallow Resources Inc.	12/23/88	88:101
01/09/89	FIRST VANCOUVER SECURITIES INC., Vancouver Stock Exchange	01/13/89	89:103
02/02/89	MORGAN-TAYLOR INTERNATIONAL INC., Paul Kevin Groat and James Morris Durward	02/10/89	89:107
03/10/89	MARATHON MINERALS INC., Earl MacRae, J. Keith Judd, Michael D. Judd, Neil W. Humphrey, Cathryn J. Garcia, BJ Illingby, Marvin L. Judd, Buxton Placer Exploration Ltd., Douglas R.G. Harris, George Krueckl, Corcoran & Company Limited Partnership, Piers Vanziffle	03/17/89	89:112
03/23/89	MUREX CLINICAL TECHNOLOGIES CORPORATION, Hubert Barry Hemsworth, David John Kotula, Vancouver Stock Exchange	03/31/89	89:113
06/19/89	GREENWELL RESOURCES CORPORATION, Harold Dale Baker, Thomas Rodney Irving	03/31/89	89:125
07/17/89	CHROMEX NICKEL MINES LTD., Kleena Kleene Gold Mines Ltd.	07/21/89	89:129
07/24/89	PHILIP LIEBERMAN	07/28/89	89:130
08/31/89	LESLIE PHILIP PRICE, Brian Edward Stanford, William Thomas Lightbody	09/08/89	89:136
09/18/89	GERALD EMILE SKLAR	09/22/89	89:138
12/05/89	STEPHEN ROSS GOODER	12/08/89	89:149
12/11/89	ROBERT JOHN CHAPMAN	12/15/89	89:150

Notices

Date Decision Issued (mm/dd/yy)	In the Matter of:	Date of Weekly Summary (mm/dd/yy)	Ed. W.S.
12/19/89	O.E.X. ELECTROMAGNETIC INC., Four Star Management Ltd., Byron Leslie Williams, Montague Simons, Elford Scott, Gregory Shafransky, Gary Wayne Cooper, Mark Stephen Wilson	12/22/89	89:151
01/12/90	ATHENA GOLD CORPORATION, Serona Resource Corporation, Vancouver Stock Exchange	01/19/90	90:3
06/13/90	PRIME RESOURCES CORPORATION, now known as Prime Resources Group Inc., Murray Pezim, Lawrence Page, John Ivany	06/15/90	90:23
07/12/90	RICHMOND CABS LTD. Gill And Others	07/13/90	90:27
07/17/90	ROBERT THEODORE SLAVIK	07/20/90	90:28
07/10/90	SEVEN MILE HIGH GROUP INC. Maurice Hamelin, Craig Harrison, Mervyn Weiss		
07/27/90	SEVEN MILE HIGH GROUP INC. Maurice Hamelin, Craig Harrison, Mervyn Weiss	08/03/90	90:30
09/04/90	SEVEN MILE HIGH GROUP INC., Maurice Hamelin, Craig Harrison, Mervyn Weiss	09/07/90	90:35
09/11/90	GEORGE DENGIN, Vancouver Stock Exchange	09/14/90	90:36
11/17/90	PRIME RESOURCES CORPORATION, now known as Prime Resources Group Inc., Murray Pezim, Lawrence Page, John Ivany	11/16/90	90:45
12/17/90	PRIME RESOURCES CORPORATION, now know as Prime Resources Group Inc., Murray Pezim, Lawrence Page, John Ivany	12/21/90	90:50
12/21/90	JAMES ELIAS RYAN	12/21/90	90:50
02/25/91	INTERNATIONAL MUREX TECHNOLOGIES CORPORATION Hubert Barry Hemsworth and David John Kotula	03/01/91	91:09
05/21/91	CAM-NET COMMUNICATIONS NETWORK INC., Elford Scott, Byron Williams 308742 B.C. Ltd.	05/24/91	91:20
06/14/91	CAM-NET COMMUNICATIONS NETWORK INC., Elford Scott, Byron Williams 308742 B.C. Ltd.	06/21/91	91:24
06/10/91	CHROMEX NICKEL MINES LTD., Kleena Kleene Gold Mines Ltd., Michael Hretchka	07/26/91	91:29 Page 9
07/25/91	TOODOGGONE GOLD INC., Algo Resources Limited Errol Hemingson, Margaret Alexa Hemingson and Aggressive Resource Management Ltd.	07/26/91	91:29 Page 24
09/17/91	INTERNATIONAL MUREX TECHNOLOGIES CORPORATION, Hubert Barry Hemsworth, David John Kotula	09/20/91	91:37 Page 4
10/04/91	EUGENO SIRIANNI, Francesco Sirianni, Montreux Development Corporation	10/11/91	91:40 Page 7
11/20/91	INVESTORS SYNDICATE LTD.	11/22/91	91:46 Page 4

Date Decision Issued (mm/dd/yy)	In the Matter of:	Date of Weekly Summary (mm/dd/yy)	Ed. W.S.
11/22/91	SEVEN MILE HIGH GROUP INC. Maurice Hamelin, Craig Harrison	11/29/91	91:47 Page 7
01/15/92	AATRA RESOURCES LTD., Victor J. Meunier, Joanne S. McClusky, Paul A. Quinn, Ralph A.A. Simpson, Joel Machtinger, Henry P.M. Huber, Alex Pancer, David J. Foster and Durham Securities Corporation Limited	01/17/92	92:03 Page 16
02/06/92	AMSWISS SCIENTIFIC INC., Ramcross Capital Corporation, 345397 B.C. Limited, Geneva Capital Corporation, Robert Andrew McNeilly, Toni Cross, Robert W. Dingee, Robin Wakefield and Steven Simonyi-Gindele	02/14/92	92:07 Page 12
02/14/92	GREENWELL RESOURCES CORPORATION, and Supreme Resources Inc., Advance Capital Services Corporation Jason Dallas, Robert Palm, Michael Doherty and David Lyon	02/21/92	92:08 Page 5
03/04/92	RUSSELL JAMES BENNETT, William Richards Bennett and Harbanse Singh Doman	03/13/92	92:11 Page 6
03/12/92	C. PHILIP YEANDLE	03/20/92	92:12 Page 10
03/13/92	TOODOGGONE GOLD INC., Algo Resources Limited, Errol Hemingson, Margaret Alexa Hemingson and Aggressive Resource Management Ltd.	03/20/92	92:12 Page 12
04/10/92	AATRA RESOURCES LTD., Victor J. Meunier, Joanne S. McClusky, Paul A. Quinn, Ralph A.A. Simpson, Joel Machtinger, Henry P.M. Huber, Alex Pancer, David J. Foster and Durham Securities Corporation Limited	04/24/92	92:16 Page 64
04/23/92	IRVING S. LINDZON International Serling Holdings Inc.	05/01/92	92:17 Page 7
04/28/92	PUBLIC PETROLEUM LTD., Elmer Patrick Ayers and Frederick David Helsel	05/01/92	92:17 Page 14
04/29/92	RAINFOREST MUSHROOMS LTD., G. Gerry Hargitai and John Czinege	05/01/92	92:17 Page 17
04/30/92	ANDREW JAMES BRASS, Tri-star International Inc., Crown Securities	05/08/92	92:18 Page 9
05/13/92	AATRA RESOURCES LTD., Victor J. Meunier, Paul A. Quinn, Ralph A.A. Simpson, Joel Machtinger, Henry P.M. Huber, Alex Pancer, David J. Foster and Durham Securities Corporation Limited	05/15/92	92:19 Page 151
05/14/92	GROWTH CAPITAL SECURITIES INC., Gary George Anderson, Elizabeth Anne Morgan and Michael McLoughlin	05/15/92	92:19 Page 154
07/07/92	C. PHILIP YEANDLE	07/10/92	92:27 Page 12

Notices

Date Decision Issued (mm/dd/yy)	In the Matter of:	Date of Weekly Summary (mm/dd/yy)	Ed. W.S.
07/07/92	INTERNATIONAL SWISS IN- VESTMENST CORP., The Leverage Fund, The Sulphur Fund, Leonard Charles Zrnic and Jana Lee Whyman, aka Mrs. Leonard Charles Zrnic	07/10/92	92:27 Page 14
07/07/92	GHZ RESOURCES CORPORATION Van- couver Stock Exchange	07/10/92	92:27 Page 18
07/29/92	METAXA RESOURCES LTD., Bu-Max Gold Corp., Francis D. Balfour, Gordon Cor- mack, Leonard E. Tinkler, Denise Spitz, Bradley J. Orloski, G. Brent Pierce, Venessa L. Ellwyn and Peter Cox	07/31/92	92:30 Page 8
08/12/92	CAPITAL RESERVE INC., Jerome Rak, Maureen MacNeil, Christopher Bass, Donald R. Stratton, Leif Ostensoe, Alan Charuk, Wayne Wile, Belmont Capital Cor- poration and Prairie Pacific Capital Inc.	08/14/92	92:32 Page 5
08/12/92	O.E.X. ELECTROMAGNETIC INC., Four Star Management Ltd., Byron Leslie Wil- liams, Montague Simons, Elford Scott, Greogry Sharfransky, Gary Wayne Cooper and Mark Stephen Wilson	O8/14/92	92:32 Page 6
08/25/92	PUBLIC PETROLEUM LTD	09/04/92	92:35 Page 10
09/03/92	INTERNATIONAL SHASTA RESOURCES LTD., Peter Hunton Blanchet	09/04/92	92:35 Page 17
10/02/92	CHROMEX NICKEL MINES LTD., Kleena Kleen Gold Mines Ltd., Michael Hretchka	10/09/92	92:40 Page 14
10/02/92	GERALD EMILE SKLAR	10/09/92	92:40 Page 15
10/02/92	NORTHRIDGE ENERGY OPTIMIZER CORPORATION Roy Carter, David Tang	10/09/92	92:40 Page 16
10/09/92	INTERNATIONAL TRADING INC., Valeria Deyong	10/16/92	92:41 Page 5
10/13/92	THE ATLANTIC TRUST MANAGEMENT GROUP Richard Frank John Newsom, Douglas Newsom, Donald Newsom, Nor- man John Newsom, Laurence Newsom, Tatjana Pessl, David V. Ellison, David J. Ellison, Michael Jolly, Shane Chambers	10/23/92	92:42 Page 5
11/10/92	ROBERT G. REID	11/13/92	92:45 Page 9
12/14/92	HARVEY S. WISH	12/18/92	92:50 Page 28
02/24/93	INGOT GROUP HOLDINGS INC.	02/26/93	93:8 Page 5
03/15/93	KASTLEKEEP SAVINGS AND MORT- GAGE FUND	03/19/93	93:11 Page 1
04/15/93	KIRBY, EDWARD JOSEPH	04/16/93	93:14 Page 6
04/30/93	MUSEWALD, DETLEF	05/07/93	93:17 Page 5

Date Decision Issued (mm/dd/yy)	In the Matter of:	Date of Weekly Summary (mm/dd/yy)	Ed. W.S.
05/13/93	BERINGER PROPERTIES INC., Beringer Acquisitions Ltd., Parallel Research Inc., Sean Francis Kehoe, James Morris Durward, Trian Equities Ltd.	05/14/93	93:18 Page 18
05/17/93	CRAVEN VENTURES INC., James V. De Santo	05/21/93	93:19 Page 14
05/26/93	FAULKNER, HARRY CLAUDE, International Shasta	06/04/93	93:21 Page 17
06/04/93	AATRA RESOURCES LTD., Victor J. Meunier, Paul A. Quinn, Ralph A.A. Simpson, Joel Machtinger, Henry P.M. Huber, Alex Pancer, David J. Foster, Durham Securities Corporation Limited	06/11/93	93:22 Page 37
06/25/93	AXAGON RESOURCES LTD., Steven Jeffrey Greenwald, Jay Robin Greenwald	07/02/93	93:25 Page 34
06/25/93	METAXA RESOURCES LTD., Bu-Max Gold Corp. Francis D. Balfour, Leonard E. Tinkler, Peter Cox	07/02/93	93:25 Page 46
06/28/93	NICHOLAS MICHAEL ROSS	07/02/93	93:25 Page 50
06/28/93	ROBERT G. REID	07/02/93	93:25 Page 52
07/20/93	MERVIN DERRICK HOLOBOFF (AKA Derrick Mervin Constance Holoboff) Jane Elizabeth Holoboff Katheryn Elizabeth Louise Mckinney	07/30/93	93:29 Page 7
07/28/93	PLC SYSTEMS INC., Logan Anderson, Harry C. Moll, Derek Van Laare	07/30/93	93:29 Page 14
08/13/93 06/04/93	INGOT GROUP HOLDINGS INC.	09/10/93	93:35 Page 16
09/20/93	AATRA RESOURCES LTD., Victor J. Meunier, Paul A. Quinn, Ralph A.A. Simpson, Joel Machtinger, Henry P.M. Huber, Alex Pancer, David J. Foster, Durham Securities Corporation Limited	09/24/93	93:37 Page 11
09/23/93	D.N.I. HOLDINGS INC., Gino Cicci	10/01/93	93:38 Page 6
10/29/93	RUSSELL JAMES BENNETT, William Richards Bennett, Harbanse Singh Doman	11/05/93	93:43 Page 4
11/10/93	RODGER LUTZ	11/12/93	93:44 Page 7
11/13/93	CANADA ORIENT RESOURCES INC., Joseph Ernest Hooi, Robert Mah Shing Voong, Edward Clive Ashworth, James Arthur Barnes, Donald Lynn Whorley	11/19/93	93:45 Page 11
03/03/94	KEYWEST RESOURCES LTD.	03/04/94	94:9 Page 18
03/16/94	PHILIP LIEBERMAN	03/18/94	94:11 Page 9

Notices

Date Decision Issued (mm/dd/yy)	In the Matter of:	Date of Weekly Summary (mm/dd/yy)	Ed. W.S.
04/22/94	MARINO JOHN INGATIUS SPECOGNA Efrem Mario Maurizio Specogna, Lucia Specogna, Specogna Minerals Corporation	04/29/94	94:16 Page 3
05/27/94	HARRY CLAUDE FAULKNER	07/10/94	94:22 Page 18
05/30/94	DR. WILLIAM H. PATMORE Leisureways Marketing Ltd	07/10/94	94:22 Page 37
07/08/94	INTER CABLE COMMUNICATIONS INC	07/22/94	94:28 Page 5
07/22/94	NORTHRIDGE ENERGY OPTIMIZER CORP. Roy Carter, David Tang	07/29/94	94:29 Page 13
08/01/94	MERLIN RESOURCES INC.	08/05/94	94:30 Page 6
01/10/95	SLOCAN FOREST PRODUCTS LTD Canfor Corporation	01/13/95	95:2 Page 26
01/27/95	RUSSELL JAMES BENNETT, William Richards Bennett, Harbanse Singh Doman	02/03/95	95:05 Page 13
02/01/95	ALEXANDER DICIMBRIANI (a.k.a. Ralph Sims), William David Bunt, W.B. Investments, Inc.	02/03/95	95:05 Page 4
04/04/95	KEYWEST RESOURCES LTD. John Walter Scott Roeder, William Gordon Buchanan, Veryan Elizabeth Thompson, Bernard E. Stang	04/07/95	95:14 Page 9
04/04/95	ROBERT ANTHONY DONAS	04/07/95	95:14 Page 39
04/04/95	ATLANTIC TRUST MANAGEMENT GROUP Richard Frank John Newsom, Douglas Newsom, Donald Newsom	04/07/95	95:14 Page 54
04/21/95	Metaxa Resources Ltd. BU-MAX GOLD CORP. Francis D. Balfour, Leonard E. Tinkler, Peter Cox	04/28/95	95:16 Page 115

NIN#95/22

NOTICE

RELEASE OF IOSCO / BIS JOINT REPORT ON THE FRAMEWORK FOR SUPERVISORY INFORMATION ABOUT THE DERIVATIVES ACTIVITIES OF BANKS AND SECURITIES FIRMS

The British Columbia Securities Commission is publishing a press communiqué issued jointly by the Basle Committee on Banking Supervision and the Technical Committee of the International Organisation of Securities Commissions ("IOSCO"). The communiqué announces the publication of a joint report entitled "Framework for supervisory information about the derivatives activities of banks and securities firms".

The purpose of the paper is to provide bank and securities firm regulators and self regulatory organisations with a framework for supervisory information about the derivatives activities of banks and securities firms. The Commission encourages industry participants to review and consider the framework set out in the paper.

A limited number of copies of the full report (44 pages) are available for pick-up from the Commission, upon request. Requests should be directed to:

> Shandie Hertslet
> Information Distribution Officer
> 1100 - 865 Hornby Street
> Vancouver, British Columbia V6Z 2H4
> Tel: (604) 660-4844
> Fax: (604) 660-2688

DATED at Vancouver, British Columbia, on June 1, 1995.

> Douglas M. Hyndman
> Chair

NIN#95/23

NOTICE

SECURITIES AMENDMENT ACT (NO. 1), 1995,

The Securities Amendment Act (No. 1), 1995, S.B.C. 1995, c. 15 (the "Amendment Act") received Royal Assent on June 8, 1995. The Amendment Act is now in effect, retroactive to the end of March 31, 1995.

Amendments

The Amendment Act is intended to make the Commission more financially autonomous. The British Columbia Securities Commission is continued as a corporation and is no longer subject to the requirements imposed on government ministries by the Public Service Act and the Financial Administration Act. As a crown agency, the Commission will have more flexibility in financial and personnel management and more certainty in planning for long term expenditures. A copy of the Amendment Act is attached to this notice.

Under the Amendment Act the Commission will appoint officers and employees of the Commission as necessary to enable the Commission and Superintendent to perform their duties and exercise their powers under the Securities Act. Employee classification and remuneration will still be subject to the prior approval of the Treasury Board. Revenue received under the Securities Act including administrative penalties and cost recoveries will be paid to the Commission and with the exception noted below, money received by the Commission may be expended for costs involved in the administration and enforcement of the Securities Act. The exception to this is that revenue from administrative penalties under section 144.1 of the Act may be expended only for the purpose of educating participants in the market (as is currently the case under section 9.1(5) of the Securities Act).

At least once every fiscal year the Commission will be responsible to provide Treasury Board with a business plan and to submit to the Minister within 90 days of each fiscal year end an annual report containing a summary of the Commission's operations for the fiscal year of the report, a financial statement, and any other information that the Minister may specify.

Other Legislative Initiatives

The Vancouver Stock Exchange Amendment Act, 1995, S.B.C. 1995, c. 17 (the "VSE Act") received Royal Assent on June 8, 1995. The Securities Amendment Act (No.2), 1995 ("Bill 44") received second reading on June 5, 1995.

The VSE Act requires that one-third of the Vancouver Stock Exchange's Board of Governors be public governors and requires the VSE board to elect one of these public governors as its chair. The amendments also define the purpose of the VSE as being to contribute to the provincial economy and requires the VSE to file an annual report with the Minister to be tabled in the Legislature.

Bill 44 contains a number of significant changes to the Securities Act, including those required to implement the government's response to the Matkin Commission report.

Major elements of Bill 44 include:

- an increase to the size of the commission from 9 to 11 members, provision for a second vice-chair and provision of statutory authority for the appointment of the new Securities Policy Advisory Committee;

- power for the Commission to enact binding rules which have the same force and effect as regulations enacted by the lieutenant governor in council;

- strengthening the regulation of investor relations activity;

- additional powers to compel production of documents and to conduct searches;

- power to conduct on-site audits of self-regulatory organizations and registrants;

- power to seek the court-ordered forfeiture of ill-gotten gains;

- power to make enforcement orders prohibiting a person from purchasing securities and prohibiting a person from engaging in investor relations activities;

- some tightening and clarification of the scope of registration exemptions for trading and advising, including removing the exemption for the sale of short term promissory notes and commercial paper to individuals (as recommended in the Ombudsman's report on the Principal Group promissory notes), and

- tighter rules for related party transactions of mutual funds.

Bill 44 does not include the imposition of a statutory obligation for registrants and directors of issuers to conduct due diligence nor any changes to statutory civil remedies. Proposals previously made in these areas raised significant concerns about their effect on the industry and about the risks of departing from a uniform national approach. While the government did not proceed with the imposition of a positive due diligence obligation on registrants or directors of issuers, the Commission will be working with the self regulatory organizations to develop by-laws or rules that balance the concerns with the adequacy of due diligence with the concerns of underwriters about non-uniformity and non-competitiveness. In addition, the Commission recently adopted Local Policy Statement 3-17, which has as its stated purpose the improvement of and documentation of the due diligence process of underwriters in respect of offerings of junior issuers. Changes to statutory civil remedies have been deferred pending further study and consultation. The Government announced in its 6 month report on its response to the Matkin Commission recommendations that it would be publishing revised draft legislation for comment in October.

The Commission anticipates that Bill 44 will come into force later this year, concurrently with an amendment package to the Securities Regulation. The Commission is still considering the vast number of comments received on the proposed regulation amendments that were published for comment in October 1994 and is working with legislative counsel to finalize the draft regulations. The regulations will be published when they have received cabinet approval but with a transition period before they become effective. Immediately prior to proclamation of Bill 44, all unproclaimed sections of the Securities Amendment Act, 1990 (except section 34, which Bill 44 repeals) and the Securities Amendment Act, 1992 will be proclaimed. The Securities Amendment Act, 1990 generally incorporates provisions dealing with exchange contracts into the Securities Act and repeals the Commodity Contract Act. The unproclaimed sections of the Securities Amendment Act, 1992 include significant amendments to the provisions dealing with prospectus renewals and deletion of the prospectus exemption for statements of material facts (to be replaced by exchange offering prospectuses).

The Commission will issue a further notice when Bill 44 receives Royal Assent and another notice when Bill 44 is proclaimed in force.

DATED at Vancouver, British Columbia, on June 14, 1995.

Douglas M. Hyndman
Chair

NOTICE

FEE PAYMENTS UNDER THE SECURITIES ACT AND THE COMMODITY CONTRACT ACT

The Securities Amendment Act (No. 1), 1995, S.B.C. 1995, c. 15 received Royal Assent on June 8, 1995. The Amendment Act is now in effect, retroactive to March 31, 1995. As a consequence of the Amendment Act, the Commission is now a government corporation rather than part of the government itself. See NIN#95/23.

Effective July 10, 1995 filing fees payable under the Securities Act and Commodity Contract Act should be made payable to the "British Columbia Securities Commission". Issuers and their professional advisers should advise their accounts payable departments of this change. Any references, in policy statements and the fee checklist, to making cheques payable to the "Minister of Finance" should be read as making cheques payable to the "British Columbia Securities Commission". Such references, and the Commission's fee checklists, will be amended in due course.

Filing fees filed before July 10, 1995 may be made payable to either the Minister of Finance or the British Columbia Securities Commission.

DATED at Vancouver, British Columbia, on June 22, 1995.

Douglas M. Hyndman
Chair

NOTICE

REVOCATION OF BLANKET ORDER #87/18

BOR#87/18, issued on March 23, 1987, exempts trades in and distributions of certain deposit receipts or other certificates ("Certificates") representing undivided interests in pools of bonds, debentures or other evidences of indebtedness of or guaranteed by the Government of Canada or a province of Canada from the registration and prospectus requirements of the Securities Act, subject to specified conditions, including the requirement that an information document satisfactory to the Superintendent of Brokers be furnished to each first time purchaser of the Certificates.

Staff has received applications from persons proposing to rely on BOR#87/18 in circumstances in which staff considers such reliance would not be in the public interest. Staff is of the view that certain of the offerings that could be made in reliance upon BOR#87/18 would be better dealt with on a case by case basis so that appropriate conditions can be imposed on each offering. As a result of such applications and consistent with the revocation of the Synthetic Securities Blanket Ruling (BOR#88/1) on October 12, 1990, staff has recommended to the Superintendent of Brokers that BOR#87/18 be revoked.

No comments were received in response to the request for comment issued under NIN#95/2. Accordingly, the Superintendent of Brokers has issued a revocation order, BOR#95/2, which revokes BOR#87/18 effective July 4, 1995.

DATED at Vancouver, British Columbia, on June 22, 1995.

Dean E. Holley
Superintendent of Brokers

References   BOR#87/18
                BOR#88/1
                BOR#95/2

Notices & Interpretation Notes

NOTICE

REPORT OF COMMITTEE ON UNDERWRITING CONFLICTS OF INTEREST
REQUEST FOR COMMENT

In the late 1980s, Alberta, British Columbia, Nova Scotia, Ontario and Québec introduced provisions to address potential new conflicts of interest that were expected following deregulation of ownership of the securities industry participants.

In the light of the industry's and regulators' experience with the application and operation of this conflict regime and the profound changes that the Canadian securities markets have undergone, the Canadian Securities Administrators ("CSA") undertook a detailed review of the issues and a reassessment of the manner and extent to which this conflict regime regulates conflicts of interest in the securities industry.

The first step in the CSA review process was the publication of a discussion paper setting out a summary of the issues and possible alternative regulatory responses available (see NIN#94/24). The CSA invited public comment on the correct range of conflicts of interest that should be addressed by the conflict regime and the appropriate regulatory mechanisms to accomplish this control.

The second stage was the establishment by the CSA of a committee to assist in the development of recommendations regarding underwriting conflicts of interest, as these were viewed as the area where there were the greatest number of concerns. The committee was chaired by a Vice-Chair of the Ontario Securities Commission and was made up of CSA appointees from Alberta, Ontario and Québec and senior representatives from various market participant groups, including dealers, issuers and institutional investors.

The committee's report, and the minority report of one of its members, have now been finalized and will be published for comment in the OSC Bulletin shortly. These have not yet been considered by the CSA, and do not necessarily represent the views of the members of the CSA.

The CSA are soliciting public comment on the recommendations contained in the report. Please submit 5 copies of any comment letter on or before September 15, 1995 at the following address:

> The Secretary
> Ontario Securities Commission
> 20 Queen Street West
> Toronto, Ontario
> M5H 3S8

Comment letters submitted in response to a request for comment are placed in the public file in certain jurisdictions. They form part of the public record unless confidentiality is requested. Comment letters will be circulated among the securities regulatory authorities for the purposes of discussion whether or not confidentiality is requested.

Accordingly, although letters for which confidentiality is requested will not be placed in a public file, freedom of information legislation may require the securities regulatory authorities in certain jurisdictions to make the comment letter available. Persons submitting comment letters should be aware that the press and members of the public may be able to obtain access to any comment letter.

Questions may be directed to:

> Tanis MacLaren
> Ontario Securities Commission
> Phone: (416) 593-8259
> Fax: (416) 593-8283

> Joëlle Saint Arnault
> Commission des valeurs mobilières du Québec
> Phone: (514) 873-5009 ext. 237
> Fax: (514) 873-6155

A limited number of copies of both the majority and minority reports are available for pick up upon request. Requests should be directed to:

Shandie Hertslet
Information Distribution Officer
British Columbia Securities Commission
1100 - 865 Hornby Street
Vancouver, B.C.
V6Z 2H4
Phone: (604) 660-4844 (Greater Vancouver and outside British
Columbia)
1-800-373-6393 (All other regions of British Columbia)
Fax: (604) 660-2688

DATED at Vancouver, British Columbia, on June 28, 1995.

Douglas M. Hyndman
Chair

REFERENCE: NIN#94/24

NIN#95/27

NOTICE

REVISED INDICES OF NOTICES AND INTERPRETATION NOTES, BLANKET
ORDERS AND RULINGS,
LOCAL POLICY STATEMENTS AND FORMS UNDER THE SECURITIES ACT
AND SECURITIES REGULATION

Effective June 30, 1995, the Commission is rescinding the indices dated effective January 6, 1995 of the Notices and Interpretation Notes, Blanket Orders and Rulings, Local Policy Statements and Forms under the Securities Act and Securities Regulation and substituting the indices attached to this Notice.

The NIN index contains only the NINs that are in effect and that have been lapsed since the publication of the previous index. The lapsing of a particular Notice does not imply that any material introduced or referred to in the Notice is no longer in effect. The index of BORs contains only the BORs that are in effect.

DATED at Vancouver, British Columbia, on June 29, 1995.

Douglas M. Hyndman
Chair

INDEX OF CANADIAN SECURITIES ADMINISTRATORS' NOTICES

Effective July 1, 1995

CSA#	Date of CSAN (mm/dd/yy)	Description	Status (mm/dd/yy)
90/1	10/19/90	Audit committees	in effect
90/2	10/23/90	Rates of return on money market mutual funds	lapsed
91/1	01/31/91	Advertising by money market mutual funds that have not offered their securities to the public for a full year	lapsed
92/1	06/10/92	Soft dollar transactions	in effect
92/2	07/09/92	Applications for discretionary orders	in effect
92/3	08/06/92	Bought deal financings	in effect
92/4	11/20/92	Review of National Policy Statement No. 41	in effect
93/1	01/20/93	Mutual fund sales incentives	in effect
93/2	06/11/93	Bought deals	in effect
93/3	06/11/93	Pre-marketing activities in the context of bought deals	in effect
93/5	12/03/93	Sales communications	in effect
94/1	06/15/94	An electronic system for securities filings	in effect
95/1	01/12/95	Conflicts of interest	in effect
95/2	01/13/95	Mutual fund sales incentives – Point-of-sale disclosure statement	in effect
95/3	04/21/95	SEDAR	in effect
95/4	04/28/95	Proposed Foreign Issuer Prospectus and Continuous Disclosure System (Draft National Policy Statement No. 53)	in effect

CANADIAN SECURITIES ADMINISTRATORS NOTICE

AUDIT COMMITTEES

INTRODUCTION

1. Increasingly the Canadian Securities Administrators are being asked their views concerning the role and the responsibilities that should be adopted by audit committees. The Administrators strongly support the efforts of audit committees which significantly improve the quality of financial reporting. This notice sets out certain practice standards which should be followed if an audit comittee is to discharge its responsibilities in an effective way.

2. An audit committee is a committee of the board of directors to which the board delegates its responsibility for oversight of the financial reporting process.

3. The objectives of an audit committee, as stated in a research study published by the Canadian Institute of Chartered Accountants, are as follows:

  (a) to help directors meet their responsibilities, especially for accountability;

  (b) to provide better communication between directors and external auditors;

  (c) to enhance the external auditor's independence;

  (d) to increase the credibility and objectivity of financial reports; and

  (e) to strengthen the role of the outside directors by facilitating in depth discussions between directors on the committee, management and external auditors.

4. A number of recent reports, such as the Report of the Commission to Study the Public's Expectations of Audits (the MacDonald Commission), have concluded that an audit committee can make a major contribution towards improving the quality of financial reporting. This relates to a fundamental requirement of securities regulation and the Administrators agree with this conclusion.

5. Audit committees are a relatively recent development and it is emphasized that their role is continuing to evolve. Boards of directors of reporting issuers should adapt the responsibilities of their audit committees to their particular circumstances. It is also emphasized that no published set of practices can substitute for the active commitment to high standards by every party having responsibility for the corporate disclosure system.

6. The practices outlined in this notice complement the requirements for audit committees set out in the corporate law statutes and, in the view of the Administrators, can be followed without conflict with those requirements.

7. The Administrators consider that fulfilment of the responsibilities set out in this notice will result in an audit committee becoming more informed, vigilant and effective.

8. Boards of directors of reporting issuers are encouraged to incorporate these matters in the terms of reference for their audit committees. Consideration should be given to disclosing the terms of reference to shareholders annually.

INTERIM FINANCIAL STATEMENTS

9. The Administrators gave particular consideration to the matter of audit committee review of interim financial statements. Financial statement users rely heavily on interim financial statements but interim reporting is subject to fewer controls than annual reporting. While the external auditor may review quarterly results, any such review is frequently part of the annual audit which is conducted after the end of the fiscal year, at which time it is too late to take corrective action.

10. The Administrators recommend that audit committees review interim financial information before it is released to the public.

MEMBERSHIP OF AUDIT COMMITTEES

11. The Administrators strongly encourge boards of directors of reporting issuers to select independent directors as members of audit committees and to limit membership to such directors whenever possible.

12. The chairperson of the audit committee should be an independent director.

13. An audit committe should normally consist of no fewer than three persons.

MEETINGS

14. Meetings of the audit committee should be scheduled to take place on a regular basis.

15. Opportunities should be afforded periodically to the external auditor, the internal auditor and to senior management to meet separately with the independent members of the audit committee.

16. Minutes should be kept of all meetings of the audit committee.

RESPONSIBILITIES OF AUDIT COMMITTEES

17. The audit committee should periodically report the results of reviews undertaken and any associated recommendations to the board of directors.

18. Audit committee practices intended to preserve the independence of the external auditor should include the following:

    (a)   review management's recommendations for the appointment of an external auditor;

    (b)   review the terms of the external auditor's engagement, the appropriateness and reasonableness of the proposed audit fees and any unpaid fees;

    (c)   when there is to be a change of auditor, review all issues related to the change, including the information to be included in the notice of change of auditor called for under National Policy 31, and the planned steps for an orderly transition;

    (d)   review all reportable events, including disagreements, unresolved issues and consultations, as defined in National Policy 31, on a routine basis, whether or not there is to be a change of auditor; and

    (e)   review any engagements for non-audit services to be provided by the external auditor's firm or its affiliates, together with estimated fees, and consider the impact on the independence of the external auditor.

19. Audit committee practices related to audits and financial reporting should include the following:

    (a)   review the audit plan with the external auditor and with management;

    (b)   review with management and with the external auditor any proposed changes in major accounting policies, the presentation and impact of significant risks and uncertainties, and key estimates and judgements of management that may be material to financial reporting;

    (c)   question management and the external auditor regarding significant financial reporting issues discussed during the fiscal period and the method of resolution;

    (d)   review any problems experienced by the external auditor in performing the audit, including any restrictions imposed by management or significant accounting issues on which there was a disagreement with management;

    (e)   review audited annual financial statements, in conjunction with the report of the external auditor, and obtain an explanation from management of all significant variances between comparative reporting periods;

    (f)   review the post-audit or management letter, containing the recommendations of the external audit, and management's response and subsequent follow-up to any identified weaknesses;

    (g)   review interim unaudited financial statements before release to the public;

    (h)   review all public disclosure documents containing audited or unaudited financial information before release, including any prospectus, the annual report, the annual information form and management's discussion and analysis;

    (i)   review the evaluation of internal controls by the external auditor, together with management's response;

    (j)   review the terms of reference of the internal auditor;

    (k)   review the reports issued by the internal auditor and management's response and subsequent follow-up to any identified weaknesses; and

    (l)   review the appointments of the chief financial officer and any key financial executives involved in the financial reporting process.

20. The responsibilities outlined in this notice are not intended to be comprehensive. Boards of directors of reporting issuers should consider any additional areas which may require oversight when determining the responsibilities to be assigned to the audit committee.

January 31, 1991

CSA#92/1

CANADIAN SECURITIES ADMINISTRATORS NOTICE

SOFT DOLLAR TRANSACTIONS

Introduction

As a result of recent submissions, the Canadian Securities Administrators (the "CSA") have concluded that certain concerns in connection with "soft dollar" or "soft commission" transactions should be investigated to determine whether changes to the existing regulatory regime relating to these transactions are necessary or whether an alternative regulatory reponse is required. Consequently, the CSA are issuing this Request for Comments.

By way of background, in 1986, the Ontario Securities Commission (the "OSC") and the Commission des valeurs mobilières du Québec (the CVMQ) adopted OSC Policy Statement No. 1.9 ("OSC Policy 1.9") and CVMQ Policy Statement No. Q-20, respectively (collectively, the "Soft Dollar Policies"). Although these policies were discussed by the CSA at the time they were adopted, a National Policy Statement on soft dollar transactions was never formally adopted. If, following an analysis of the responses to their Request for Comments, the CSA consider it advisable to adopt a National Policy Statement, such a policy could adopt the approach taken in the Soft Dollar Policies (which staff of the OSC and the CVMQ believe have proved effective within their scope), with such amendments as the CSA consider necessary to address current concerns.

The CSA consider soft dollar or soft commission transactions as being those which involve the payment by a portfolio/fund manager or adviser to a dealer of commissions in circumstances where a percentage of the commissions are used by the dealer to fund or pay for goods and services. These goods and services may be provided by the dealer or by third parties to the manager, the adviser, the sponsor or the portfolio/fund beneficiaries. As well, soft commissions may take the form of reciprocal commissions, which are discussed in further detail below.

Background

Soft dollar transactions may arise in a variety of circumstances. The conventional situation is where commissions are paid by a portfolio manager to a dealer in return for investment decision-making and order execution services which are provided by the dealer to the manager.

One use of soft dollars which has been a cause for concern to some capital market participants involves the triangular relationship established when a fund or pension plan sponsor requires the fund or pension plan manager to direct brokerage transactions to a particular dealer. That dealer in turn is required to use a portion of the commission income from the brokerage transaction to fund the provision to the sponsor of goods and/or services. One example of this practice is the payment by a dealer out of commission revenues to a third party performance measurement firm of amounts in return for the provision of reports and information directly to the sponsor. Another example of the use of soft dollars is where a "reciprocal commission" is paid, i.e. where execution business providing a brokerage commission is directed by a mutual fund manager or adviser to a dealer as compensation for sales of the mutual fund's units. A further example is where soft commissions are used to fund other non-conventional services, such as dealer advertising with respect to a particular mutual fund.

Each of the Soft Dollar Policies states that the negotiation of commissions is governed by the general obligation of the manager to act in the best interests of the beneficiaries of the portfolio or fund and that, consequently, commissions must only be used as payment for goods and services which are for the benefit of the beneficiaries, and should not be used as payment for goods and services which are for the benefit of the manager.

The Soft Dollar Policies recognize the utility to beneficiaries of "investment decision-making" and "order execution" services (both of which phrases are broadly defined) provided to the manager, and state that such services may legitimately be provided in return for soft dollars. In respect of other goods and services, the Director of the OSC, in a notice published in November 1987, which dealt specifically with the question of whether it was appropriate for shareholder litigation to be funded through soft dollars, stated that the Director (now the Executive Director) will exempt similar soft dollar transactions on a case-by-case basis where benefits are clearly intended to accrue to shareholders, as opposed to solely the manager or the plaintiff, and all commissions on the directed trades are at competitive levels.

With respect to reciprocal commissions in the mutual fund context, the Soft Dollar Policies provide that these are permissible if the commission rates charged are equivalent to those which would have been normally charged by the dealer if the dealer did not distribute units of the mutual fund and if certain disclosure requirements are met.

During the six years since the adoption of OSC Policy 1.9, staff of the OSC have received very few requests for relief or exemption from the provisions of that policy. While staff of the OSC believe that OSC Policy 1.9 has proved effective within its scope, they recognize that there may be instances of abuse which may not have been adequately provided for in that policy. The experience of CVMQ staff is comparable. Accordingly, the CSA are issuing this Request for Comments.

Request For Comments

The responses provided in connection with this Request for Comments will supply the information necessary for a comprehensive analysis of whether and to what extent changes should be made to the Soft Dollar Policies (whether in connection with the adoption of a National Policy Statement or otherwise) or compliance actions should be implemented or increased. Comments are sought with respect to the implications, both positive and negative, of soft dollar arrangements for the health of the capital markets generally. In this regard, dealers, fund and portfolio managers and advisers, investors and other interested persons are asked to provide a description of soft dollar arrangements in the marketplace of which they are aware, with particulars relating to all aspects of these arrangements. The business of the parties involved, the benefits which accrue to them and the relationship between them are of particular interest. It will be helpful if the responses provide specific details with respect to the volume and dollar value of soft dollar transactions engaged in, together with a breakdown of the types of goods and services for which payment is being made through soft dollars. In addition, comments are sought in respect of the conflict of interest implications of soft dollar arrangements.

In connection with the use of reciprocal commissions in the mutual fund industry, in August 1991, The Investment Funds Institute for Canada ("IFIC") issued its report on mutual fund sales incentives. The code of conduct (the "IFIC Code") for IFIC members which resulted from that report prohibited the direction of brokerage commissions to a dealer as compensation for anything other than investment decision-making services or order execution services (as defined in OSC Policy 1.9). In November 1991, the CSA published a notice which stated, among other things, that the CSA had noted the recommendations in the report with respect to reciprocal commissions and that they intended to consider these recommendations further. The CSA also stated that, pending discussion, they expected that the mutual fund industry would follow the IFIC Code.

Following the publication of the IFIC Code, there has been considerable debate with respect to the advisability of reciprocal commissions. As a result, and as part of this initiative, the CSA are requesting specific submissions relating to the public interest and other implications (including the potential benefits to unitholders and the impact on the competitive position of particular segments of the mutual fund industry) of reciprocal commission arrangements made to compensate dealers and their sales staff for mutual fund sales, advertising expenses incurred to promote mutual fund sales and other marketing related matters.

The CSA understand that persons submitting responses may be concerned from a confidentiality perspective as a result of competitive, commercial or economic considerations. Accordingly, responses will, upon request, be treated as confidential and will not be placed on the public files of the securities regulatory authorities. Public access to such responses will not be permitted except as may be required by law. However, copies of all responses will be circulated among and reviewed and considered by the CSA in connection with this initiative.

Comments should be in writing only, and twelve copies of each comment letter should be delivered to the attention of the CSA. Comments relating to reciprocal commissions in connection with mutual funds should be submitted no later than July 31, 1992, and all other comments should be submitted on or before September 25, 1992. All comment letters should be delivered to the following address:

Canadian Securities Administrators
c/o Secretary, Ontario Securities Commission
8th Floor
20 Queen Street West
Toronto, Ontario
M5H 3S8

Questions may be referred to:

Susan McCallum
Director, Corporate Finance
Ontario Securities Commission
(416) 593-8248

Rahul Suri
Special Assistant, Legal and Policy
Office of the Executive Director
Ontario Securities Commission
(416) 593-8137

June 10, 1992

CSA#92/2

CANADIAN SECURITIES ADMINISTRATORS NOTICE

APPLICATIONS FOR DISCRETIONARY ORDERS

The Canadian Securities Administrators (the "CSA") are concerned about the procedures followed by many applicants for discretionary orders where applications are made in more than one Canadian jurisdiction. Where an application is not made simultaneously to all of the jurisdictions in question, the securities regulatory authorities in those jurisdictions may not have sufficient time to consider the application and to coordinate their response. Jurisdictions have frequently been asked to consider at the last minute an application that another jurisdiction has been considering for some time or in respect of which that other jurisdiction has already issued an order. This can cause problems for both the applicant and the securities regulatory authorities.

The CSA have concluded that where an application for a discretionary order is to be made in more than one Canadian jurisdiction, that application should be made simultaneously in all the jurisdictions in question. The covering letter for the application should identify all of the Canadian jurisdictions in which applications are being made. This procedure will increase the efficiency of securities regulatory authorities in dealing with applications for discretionary orders.

July 9, 1992

CANADIAN SECURITIES ADMINISTRATORS NOTICE
BOUGHT DEAL FINANCINGS

Introduction

Over the past decade a financing technique known as the "bought deal" has emerged and has become the principal means by which issuers eligible to use the prompt offering qualification system (the "POP System") have raised capital in the Canadian capital markets. A bought deal may be characterized as a public offering of securities in Canada where the issuer and underwriter enter into an underwriting agreement prior to, or contemporaneously with, the filing of a preliminary prospectus. Bought deals have become increasingly common over the past number of years and are said to currently account for the majority of debt and equity offerings of issuers eligible to use the POP System. However, certain concerns have been expressed in respect of bought deals and the Canadian Securities Administrators (the "CSA") have resolved to examine these concerns in order to determine whether: (i) regulatory changes should be made to eliminate bought deals, (ii) changes should be made to the regulatory regime in respect of bought deals, or (iii) no changes to the current regulatory regime should be made. Consequently, the CSA are issuing this Request for Comments.

Background

Prior to the emergence of bought deals in the early 1980s, an underwriter would not enter into a firm commitment to purchase securities from an issuer until it had "pre-marketed" the issue after the filing of a preliminary prospectus. In contrast to a bought deal, the prospective issue was disclosed to the market prior to the time when the underwriter entered into an underwriting agreement with the issuer. The underwriter determined the appropriate size and price of a prospective offering at the conclusion of a pre-marketing period, which occurred after the filing of a preliminary prospectus, and based its underwriting commitment on that information.

With the advent of the bought deal, the underwriter committed its capital prior to, or contemporaneously with, the filing of a preliminary prospectus. It has been expressed to the CSA that while this financing technique enables issuers to obtain a firm price and satisfaction of its financing needs with a minimum of risk and delay, it also increases an underwriter's risk, relative to traditional underwritings, due to the lack of a pre-marketing period prior to the entering into an underwriting agreement.

In 1986, blanket rulings (the "Blanket Rulings") were issued by several provincial securities regulatory authorities. Generally, the Blanket Rulings permit the solicitation of expressions of interest from investors two business days prior to the filing of a preliminary short form prospectus provided that an underwriting agreement has been entered into which requires, among other things, that a preliminary short form prospectus be filed with a securities regulatory authority within two business days of the entering into of such underwriting agreement.

Request for Comments

Various concerns have been expressed by the CSA with respect to certain aspects of bought deals, which include, but are not limited to, retail participation, underwriting risks and pre-marketing practices. The Corporate Finance Committee of the Investment Dealers Association of Canada has, over the past number of months, reviewed the practices relating to bought deals and has now provided the CSA with specific proposals to modify the bought deal financing technique (the "IDA Proposals"), in order to address some of these same concerns. The IDA Proposals are being published along with this Request for Comments in order to facilitate and generate comment from interested parties concerning bought deals in general, and the IDA Proposals in particular.

The CSA have neither accepted nor rejected the IDA Proposals and the publication of such proposals should not be viewed as an endorsement of them, but merely as publication for the purpose of soliciting comments. In addition, the fact that the CSA have determined that it is appropriate to examine concerns expressed by various parties regarding bought deals should not be taken as indicating that the CSA have in any respect determined that bought deals, as they currently exist, are prejudicial to investor protection or the effective operation of the Canadian capital markets.

It would be helpful to the CSA in conducting their examination of bought deals to have the benefit of the views of issuers, dealers, retail, mutual fund and institutional investors and other interested parties. Where appropriate, interested parties are strongly encouraged to provide, if at all possible, statistical information which addresses various issues related to bought deals and, in particular, statistical information relating to the impact that bought deals have had on the retail investor and the cost of capital to issuers.

It has been expressed to the CSA that a number of the concerns relating to bought deals stem from the desire of underwriters to reduce their underwriting risk in such transactions. Comment is requested on the concerns set out below and, in addition, the CSA seek comment on the relationship between these concerns and the underwriting risk associated with bought deals. The following is not intended to set out all of the concerns related to bought deals, but rather to highlight certain concerns which have been expressed for the purpose of eliciting public comment. Comment need not be restricted to the matters set out below.

The issue of greatest interest to the CSA is the impact of bought deals on the overall structure of the capital markets in Canada and the way that such markets are perceived. The CSA seek comment as to whether bought deals have "institutionalized" capital formation in Canada and, if this has occurred, whether this change may be negatively impacting certain investors and the integrity and efficiency of the capital markets.

It has been suggested that the perception that there exists a lack of retail participation in bought deals, whether accurate or not, erodes retail investor confidence. In addition, concern has been expressed to the CSA that retail investors do not have an opportunity to purchase securities in certain bought deals at an offering price which reflects a discount from the then current market price in the same manner as institutional investors and that this further erodes retail investor confidence. With respect to existing individual shareholders, it has been stated that such investors should have the opportunity to participate in new offerings of the issuers in which they already own securities, so that their ownership interests are not diluted without them having the opportunity to preserve those interests, and that such shareholders would have that opportunity were retail participation in bought deals increased. It has also been stated that the apparent exclusion of smaller institutional investors from greater participation in bought deals results in a two-tier institutional investor structure that negatively impacts the marketplace. Comment is requested regarding the impact on primary and secondary markets of perceived or actual reduced retail, existing individual shareholder and smaller institutional participation in bought deals.

The IDA Proposals would introduce a "delay period" commencing after the earlier of the filing of a preliminary prospectus and the issuance of a press release. Prior to the delay period, no pre-marketing activities (as defined) may be conducted by dealers. The stated objective of the delay period is to provide dealers with the opportunity to make an informed decision about the size and price of the offering prior to entering into an underwriting agreement. Retail demand is to be canvassed through contact with the dealers' retail distribution networks. The IDA Proposals indicate that the delay period is intended to provide an improved opportunity for retail investors to participate in bought deals. Comment is specifically requested as to whether the proposed delay period would achieve this purpose and/or whether it may lead to other problems.

Comment is also sought on a number of other issues relating to the delay period contemplated in the IDA Proposals. Many of the securities which are the subject of bought deals are of issuers whose securities are inter-listed on foreign exchanges. Since the delay period contained within the IDA Proposals is based upon domestic stock exchange trading hours, comment is requested as to the impact on domestic markets and the bought deals of such issuers of trading which may occur on foreign markets during the delay period. Comment is requested as to whether the filing of a preliminary prospectus is an acceptable alternative to the filing of a press release for the purpose of determining the commencement of the delay period. In addition, comment is requested as to whether the required contents of a press release contemplated under the IDA Proposals are appropriate.

Concern has been expressed to the CSA about the potential systemic risk that bought deals represent for the Canadian capital markets as a result of the capital risk faced by individual underwriters that participate in such deals. It has been suggested to the CSA that the reduced use of "market out" clauses in underwriting agreements used in bought deals compounds the risks associated with the early commitment of capital by dealers in such financings.

The IDA Proposals indicate that the ability to assess market demand during the delay period will improve the likelihood that an offering will be sold successfully at an attractive price to the issuer; thereby reducing the risk that an underwriter will be forced to absorb losses by selling the offered securities at prices below the initial offering price. Comment is specifically requested on whether bought deals have created undue risk to Canadian underwriters and whether this risk is destabilizing to the Canadian capital markets and/or adversely effects competition. In addition comment is specifically requested as to whether, and to what degree, the IDA Proposals will reallocate market risks between underwriters and issuers and what the effect on the Canadian capital markets might be of any such reallocation of risk.

It has been suggested to the CSA that underwriters are unable to perform adequate due diligence within the time-frame of a bought deal. Comment is specifically requested on this issue.

Having regard to the efficiency of raising capital in the Canadian marketplace and the concerns expressed regarding retail participation, systemic risk to the Canadian capital markets and due diligence, comment is requested as to whether the suggested delay period in the IDA Proposals is appropriate, and if not, whether it should be shorter or longer. In addition, comment is requested as to whether there should be a maximum length of time for any delay period.

Concerns have been expressed to the CSA that pre-marketing activities, contrary to the Blanket Rulings, are being carried on prior to the entering into of an underwriting agreement. A related issue is that insider information may be being divulged unintentionally or otherwise. The IDA Proposals restrict marketing activities to the period after the earlier of the issuance of a press release and the filing of a preliminary prospectus. The stated intent of these proposals is that there be no pre-marketing activities conducted prior to information about the offering being made public.

The restrictions on pre-marketing activities contained within the IDA Proposals hinge upon the definition proposed for the term "pre-marketing". The term "pre-marketing" is defined in the IDA Proposals as "the imparting of information on an issuer's ... intentions in relation to an issue ... of [e]quity [s]ecurities ..." to a prospective investor. Comment is requested as to whether this definition is appropriate. Comment is specifically sought as to whether the focus on the "imparting" of an issuer's intention contained within the proposed definition creates problems for the general application of the pre-marketing restrictions. Comment is further sought as to whether the focus on an issuer's "intention" contained within the proposed definition creates similar problems. Comment is also requested on whether the definition should be expanded to include the imparting of information on the dealer's intention so as to restrict a dealer advising others that it is contemplating making a specific financing proposal to a particular issuer. In addition, the pre-marketing restrictions contained in the IDA Proposals do not appear to relate to general discussions that dealers may have with their clients in order to broaden their understanding of market developments and client needs. Comment is generally sought on the implications of the proposed pre-marketing restrictions and the exceptions outlined in the IDA Proposals.

There are two ways in which bought deals may be initiated. Either the offerings are initiated by the issuer (solicited bought deals) or they are initiated by the dealer (unsolicited bought deals). Comment is requested on the differing impact, if any, of the IDA Proposals on unsolicited bought deals in general, and the pre-marketing of such deals in particular.

It has been suggested to CSA that innovative terms and financing techniques in securities financings are encouraged by bought deals because underwriters are able to enter into underwriting agreements prior to information relating to the financing entering the public domain. Comment is requested on the impact of bought deals, generally, and the IDA Proposals, in particular, on innovation in the Canadian capital markets and on competition among underwriters.

Comment is also requested on the impact that bought deals have had on Canadian issuers in terms of cost of capital, access to capital, financing risk and the competitiveness of Canadian capital markets to satisfy the needs of such issuers. Comment is further requested on the probable impact that the IDA Proposals would have on these factors.

Market stabilization rules set out restrictions on secondary market trading by issuers, underwriters and certain other distribution participants during a prospectus distribution of exchange listed securities. Connected and related issuer rules restrict the portion of a distribution that may be underwritten by dealers that are "connected" or "related" to an issuer. Comment is sought as to the effect that these rules have had on bought deals and whether implementation of the IDA Proposals would require changes to the foregoing rules.

Comment is sought as to the extent to which any of the foregoing concerns relate to bought deals for debt securities or preferred shares and, since the IDA Proposals deal only with equity securities and securities convertible into such securities, whether any regulatory response is necessary with respect to bought deals for debt securities or preferred shares.

The CSA understand that persons submitting responses may be concerned from a confidentiality perspective as a result of competitive, commercial or economic considerations. Accordingly, responses will, upon request, be treated as confidential and will not be placed on the public files of the securities regulatory authorities. Public access to such responses will not be permitted except as may be required by law. However, copies of all responses will be circulated among and reviewed and considered by the CSA in connection with this initiative.

Comments should be in writing and should be delivered to the address indicated below on or before October 30, 1992.

> Canadian Securities Administrators
> Corporate Finance Committee
> c/o Secretary, Ontario Securities Commission
> Ontario Securities Commission
> Suite 800, Box 55
> 20 Queen Street West
> Toronto, Ontario
> M5H 3S8

Questions may be referred to:

> Susan I. McCallum
> Director, Corporate Finance
> Ontario Securities Commission
> (416) 593-8248

> Arnold Hochman
> Deputy Director, Policy
> Corporate Finance
> Ontario Securities Commission
> (416) 593-8247

August 7, 1992

CSA#92/4

CANADIAN SECURITIES ADMINISTRATORS NOTICE
REVIEW OF NATIONAL POLICY STATEMENT No. 41

Introduction

National Policy Statement 41 ("NP 41") provides a procedure to enable issuers to communicate with non-registered holders. Among other things, NP 41 is designed to ensure that proxy-related meeting materials, audited annual financial statements and interim financial statements are sent to non-registered holders of securities. The Canadian Securities Administrators ("CSA") have been monitoring NP 41 since its introduction and over the past few years a number of issues have arisen. The CSA have determined that it is advisable to undertake a review of NP 41 at this time.

Background

NP 41 was approved by the CSA on October 28, 1987. NP 41 was based upon the recommendations of the Joint Regulatory Task Force on Shareholder Communication. That task force was comprised of securities regulators from Ontario, Québec and British Columbia, corporate administrators from Ontario and the federal Corporations Branch, the Toronto and Vancouver Stock Exchanges, representatives from the Canadian Depository for Securities Limited, the Vancouver Stock Exchange Service Corp. (now West Canada Depository Trust Company), the Investment Dealers Association

(Québec and Ontario), the Canadian Bankers Association, the Trust Companies Association, the Investment Funds Institute of Canada and the Canadian Corporate Shareholder Services Association (the "CCSSA"). In addition, the views of many other individuals were solicited, and considered, by the CSA when formulating NP 41.

NP 41 recognizes the right of non-registered holders to receive the materials and voting rights that reporting issuers are currently required by corporate and securities legislation to provide to registered shareholders.

NP 41 imposes obligations on various parties within the shareholder communication process. The obligations are imposed within a framework of various time frames, the most important of which is the requirement for a minimum of 25 days between the time of mailing materials by intermediaries to non-registered holders and the meeting in question.

NP 41 was amended in the summer of 1988 by Addendum "A" (Part XII of NP 41) to deal with certain matters, including applications for waivers and exemptions. To date, most applications have involved waivers of time periods as a result of difficulty in meeting the timing requirements of NP 41.

The Industry Implementation and Monitoring Committee

The Industry Implementation and Monitoring Committee (the "IIMC") was formed in 1988 to track the implementation of NP 41. Currently, the IIMC is co-chaired by Mr. Arden Cornford (Assistant to the Corporate Secretary, Dofasco Inc., and President of the CCSSA) and Ms. Cecilia Widup (Assistant Secretary, Inco Limited, and Past President of the CCSSA). The IIMC includes representatives from intermediaries (trust companies, banks, dealers and a third party service company), transfer agents, reporting issuers, depositories and regulators (securities commissions and exchanges).

In late 1991, the IIMC circulated a questionnaire to approximately 100 reporting issuers, including junior issuers, and received 60 responses. The IIMC has also developed separate intermediary and non-registered holder questionnaires for distribution. Copies of all three questionnaires are attached. **The CSA encourage reporting issuers, intermediaries and non-registered holders to participate in the IIMC's research by completing the appropriate questionnaire and returning same to the IIMC, care of the address shown at the end of this notice.**

The intermediary questionnaire may also be distributed by certain industry groups, including the Canadian Bankers Association. Members of these groups, rather than returning questionnaires to the address shown at the end of this notice, may return completed questionnaires to their respective industry group.

The concerns and potential solutions identified to date have been raised with the IIMC primarily by issuers. The IIMC is continuing to seek input from all interested parties and the full committee of the IIMC has not endorsed any particular solutions advanced to date. Certain issues have, however, generated greater discussion than others. Included among those issues are:

- prescribed fees and other costs of compliance with NP 41 (e.g., should prescribed fees be removed and fees left open to negotiation)

- conflicts between corporate law and NP 41 (e.g., the ability under the British Columbia *Company Act* to nominate directors up to 35 days before a meeting)

- clarification of non-registered holder voting rights (e.g., where a non-registered holder wishes to attend and vote at a meeting, rather than complete and return a proxy in advance as contemplated under NP 41)

- overall clarification and simplification of NP 41 (including the need for waivers or exemptions and the possible elimination of Forms B and C).

Request for Comments

These preliminary concerns underscore the need for a review of NP 41 at this time. Accordingly, the CSA are seeking the information necessary for a comprehensive analysis of whether, and to what extent, changes should be made to NP 41.

In this regard, reporting issuers, non-registered holders, intermediaries, depositories and other interested parties are asked to provide specific comments as to deficiencies with NP 41, together with proposed solutions. Comment on the preliminary issues highlighted above, including costs, as well as on the potential for the creation of a single list of beneficial shareholders, is of particular interest to the CSA.

CSA
Notices

Commentators should bear in mind the fundamental premise underlying NP 41 and supported by the CSA, namely that non- registered holders are entitled to:

(a) receive proxy-related materials and audited annual financial statements in a timely manner prior to a meeting,

(b) vote at a meeting, and

(c) receive interim financial statements, where so elected.

Commentators should also consider that the trend toward lodging securities with a depository and registering securities in the name of the depository's nominee is likely to increase, with a concomitant increase in the number of non-registered holders.

The CSA understand that persons submitting responses may be concerned from a confidentiality perspective as a result of competitive, commercial or economic considerations. Accordingly, responses will, upon request, be treated as confidential and will not be placed on the public files of the securities regulatory authorities. Public access to such responses will not be permitted except as may be required by law. However, copies of all responses will be circulated among and reviewed and considered by the CSA in connection with this initiative.

Comments should be in writing only, and twelve copies of each comment letter should be delivered to the attention of the CSA. Comments should be submitted on or before January 15, 1993. All comment letters should be delivered to the following address:

Canadian Securities Administrators
c/o Policy and Legislation
British Columbia Securities Commission
1100 - 865 Hornby Street
Vancouver, B.C.
V6Z 2H4

Completed questionnaires may also be delivered to the above address. No additional copies of the questionnaires are required.

Questions may be referred to Robert Hudson, Policy Advisor, Policy and Legislation, British Columbia Securities Commission (telephone: 604-660-4883).

Enclosures (3)

November 20, 1992

CSA#93/1

CANADIAN SECURITIES ADMINISTRATORS' NOTICE

MUTUAL FUND SALES INCENTIVES

In August 1991, The Investment Funds Institute of Canada ("IFIC") issued a report on mutual fund sales incentives. That report was followed, in October 1991, by a Code of Conduct (the "IFIC Code") dealing with sales incentives.

In November 1991, the Canadian Securities Administrators (the "CSA") published a notice relating to the IFIC Code. The CSA notice stated that the CSA accepted the recommendations made by IFIC with respect to domestic and foreign trips. The CSA noted the balance of the recommendations made in the IFIC Code and indicated that they intended to give these recommendations, particularly the recommendations related to soft dollar/reciprocal commission transactions and service fees (trailer commissions), further consideration. Pending such consideration, the CSA stated that they expected the mutual fund industry to follow the IFIC Code. Finally, the CSA stated that the appropriate securities regulatory authorities would consider each lack of compliance with the IFIC Code by the mutual fund industry on a case-by-case basis and would take any action they considered appropriate in the circumstances.

The IFIC Code requires improved prospectus disclosure of sales incentives. It also requires that investors in mutual funds be provided with a separate "point-of-sale" disclosure document at the time of purchasing mutual fund securities advising them of the type of sales incentives applicable with respect to the purchase. The IFIC Code also restricts domestic and foreign conference trips to locations in Canada and the continental United States; permits the payment of service fees (trailer commissions) and the costs of co- operative marketing programs; restricts merchandise awards or gifts paid to a sales representative in a non-affiliated dealer organization to a maximum of $750 in any calendar year; prohibits the direction of brokerage commissions as compensation for mutual fund sales; prohibits the selection of underwriting or selling group participants in public securities offerings and private placements exclusively on the basis of mutual fund sales; and sets out procedures for IFIC to enforce the IFIC Code.

It is the general policy of the CSA not to regulate the compensation of salespersons but to focus upon those matters which promote sufficient disclosure to be made in order that investors are able to make informed investment decisions.

During the past year, the CSA have been monitoring the effectiveness of the IFIC Code and have concluded that all of the disclosure of sales incentives required by the IFIC Code has been effective in alleviating regulatory concerns. Therefore, the CSA have determined that, at present, it is not necessary to take further regulatory action other than implementing, through amendments to policy statements and regulations, the recommendations made by IFIC concerning disclosure of sales incentives in a mutual fund's prospectus and in a point-of-sale disclosure document.

The CSA in analyzing sales incentives, addressed the potential conflict of interest that might occur where domestic and foreign trips are offered to mutual fund salespersons. It has been argued that a conflict of interest occurs between a salesperson's duty to recommend the most appropriate investment for a particular investor and the desire to recommend an investment that leads to earning a domestic or foreign trip, particularly one outside of Canada or the continental United States. The same argument concerning a conflict of interest has also been made with respect to other types of sales incentives.

The CSA have determined that the perceived potential for conflict of interest is best addressed through disclosure of all material facts relating to the granting of sales incentives. The CSA have noted that it is inappropriate to restrict a single form of compensation, such as domestic and foreign trips, where they do not regulate overall levels of compensation. In this regard, the CSA note that the overall levels of sales compensation differ as between similar types of mutual funds under different management and as between different types of mutual funds under the same management. In all cases, investors and the marketplace in general determine acceptable levels of overall sales compensation. Similarly, the full disclosure of sales incentives should, given competitive market forces, allow investors and the marketplace in general to monitor sales incentives and to determine acceptable practices.

The disclosure requirements for sales incentives will be implemented through amendments to National Policy Statement Nos. 36 and 39 and regulations. All dealers, including investment dealers, mutual fund dealers and others, distributing mutual fund securities will be required to provide a point-of-sale disclosure document to investors at the time of their purchase of mutual fund securities, advising them of the type of sales incentives applicable with respect to the purchase. This disclosure document will also be required to refer investors to the mutual fund prospectus for additional information and invite them to discuss sales incentives with their salesperson.

The above-described amendments will require a summary of the sales incentives offered by managers to dealers with respect to the mutual fund securities being distributed under the prospectus to be set out on the inside front cover page of the mutual fund prospectus under the heading "Summary of Dealer Compensation". A complete description of such sales incentives will be required in the body of the prospectus in a separate section entitled "Dealer Compensation". Specifically, with respect to domestic and foreign conference trips offered by managers to dealers as sales incentives, the prospectus will be required to disclose the location of the conference and its approximate cost per attendee if the conference would not comply with the restrictions in the IFIC Code.

With respect to soft dollar/reciprocal commission transactions, substantial comments have been received in response to the CSA request for comments concerning soft dollars published in June 1992. The issues raised by soft dollars generally are currently being considered by the CSA. The CSA have determined that the ultimate resolution of the issue of soft dollar/reciprocal commission transactions should be deferred until the issue of soft dollars generally is resolved. In the interim, the CSA have determined to require enhanced disclosure of these transactions.

CSA Notices

Until such time as the amendments to the policy statements are implemented, the CSA will not take any action in respect of any non-compliance with the IFIC Code by industry participants regarding compensation paid for mutual fund sales made on or after January 1, 1993, except with respect to the disclosure requirements relating to the prospectus and the requirements regarding delivery of a point-of-sale disclosure document.

This notice revokes and replaces the prior CSA notices dealing with mutual fund sales incentives dated December 20, 1990 and November 8, 1991.

For further information please contact any of:

Robert Bouchard
Deputy Director
Corporate Finance
The Manitoba Securities
Commission
(204) 945-2548

Susan I. McCallum
Director
Corporate Finance
Ontario Securities
Commission
(416) 593-8248

Arnold Hochman
Deputy Director, Policy
Corporate Finance
Ontario Securities
Commission
(416) 593-8247

Anna Drummond
Solicitor, Policy
Corporate Finance
Ontario Securities
Commission
(416) 593-8192

Johanne Duchesne
Deputy Director,
Financial Operations
Commission des Valeurs
Mobilières du Quebec
(514) 873-5326

Wayne Redwick
Deputy Superintendent
Corporate Finance
British Columbia
Securities Commission
(604) 660-4800

Ron Sczinski
Director, Securities Analysis
Alberta Securities Commission
(403) 427-5201

January 20, 1993

CSA#93/2

CANADIAN SECURITIES ADMINISTRATORS' NOTICE

BOUGHT DEALS

In July 1992, the Corporate Finance Committee of the Investment Dealers Association of Canada (the "IDA") provided the Canadian Securities Administrators (the "CSA") with specific proposals to modify the bought deal financing technique (the "IDA Proposals"). The CSA published the IDA Proposals in August 1992, together with a CSA Notice requesting comments on bought deal financings (the "Request for Comments"). The Request for Comments indicated that it would be helpful for the CSA in conducting their examination of bought deals to have the benefit of the views of issuers, dealers, retail, institutional and mutual fund investors and other interested parties on bought deals, in general, and on the IDA Proposals, in particular. In addition, commentators were strongly encouraged to provide, if at all possible, statistical information relating to bought deals. The CSA received 46 comment letters in response to the Request for Comments, however, they received virtually no comment letters from institutional investors, mutual funds and retail investors. In addition, the CSA received very little statistical information from commentators concerning various issues related to bought deals, including retail participation and the cost of capital to issuers.

At this stage of their review of bought deal financings, staff of each of the CSA (collectively, "staff") have determined that it is important to clarify whether certain activities that may be undertaken to facilitate the distribution of securities and limit underwriting risk ("pre-marketing activities") are contrary to or inconsistent with the provisions of securities legislation of each of the provinces and territories of Canada ("securities legislation"). Accordingly, to address the uncertainties of market participants with respect to pre-marketing activities in the context of bought deals, the

CSA are publishing contemporaneously with this notice a CSA notice regarding such pre-marketing activities (the "Pre-Marketing Notice"). The Pre-Marketing Notice summarizes staff's conclusions[1] as to the legality of pre-marketing activities in the context of bought deals. The CSA are of the view that dealers should develop, implement, maintain and enforce procedures to ensure that pre-marketing activities that are contrary to securities legislation are not engaged in by their directors, officers, employees and agents. The CSA understand that staff are considering a compliance mechanism for monitoring compliance with the Pre-Marketing Notice.

The CSA understand that staff will not consider the marketing activities of dealers in the context of special warrant transactions to be inappropriate if such activities are not altered from current practice. This would not be the case if the private placement of the warrants and the exercise of the warrants occur in such close proximity that it could reasonably be considered that the special warrant offering is a public distribution of the securities into which the special warrants are convertible.

In light of staff's legal conclusions regarding pre- marketing activities set out in the Pre-Marketing Notice, which may affect the views of interested parties on the IDA Proposals, the CSA are offering interested parties a further opportunity to comment on the IDA Proposals, and in particular on the necessity or desirability for the six hour delay period proposed by the IDA, before the CSA complete their review of bought deals. Comments should be in writing and should be submitted to the address indicated below on or before July 31, 1993.

>Canadian Securities Administrators
>Corporate Finance Committee
>c/o Secretary, Ontario Securities Commission
>Ontario Securities Commission
>Suite 800, Box 55
>20 Queen Street West
>Toronto, Ontario
>M5H 3S8

Comment letters submitted in response to this CSA Notice will be placed in the public file in certain jurisdictions and form part of the public record, unless confidentiality is requested. Comment letters will be circulated among the securities regulatory authorities whether or not confidentiality is requested. Accordingly, although comment letters requesting confidentiality will not be placed in the public file, freedom of information legislation may require the securities regulatory authorities in certain jurisdictions to make comment letters available. Persons submitting comment letters should therefore be aware that the press and members of the public may be able to obtain access to any comment letter.

June 11, 1993

CSA#93/3

CANADIAN SECURITIES ADMINISTRATORS' NOTICE
PRE-MARKETING ACTIVITIES IN THE CONTEXT OF BOUGHT DEALS

Background

For some time, there has been debate as to whether certain activities that may be undertaken to facilitate the distribution of securities and limit underwriting risk are contrary to, or inconsistent with, the provisions of the securities legislation of each of the provinces and territories of Canada (collectively, "securities legislation"). The debate has become more focused with the proposals made in 1992 by the Investment Dealers Association of Canada (the "IDA") to modify "bought deals".

Summary

This notice summarizes the conclusions of staff of each of the Canadian Securities Administrators (collectively "staff") on the legality of "pre-marketing" activities in the

---

[1]   In the Pre-Marketing Notice, the staff of each province and territory set out their views with respect to the securities legislation of their own jurisdiction only.

context of bought deals.[2] These conclusions are set out under the heading "Permitted and Prohibited Pre-Marketing" below.

What is Pre-Marketing?

The term "pre-marketing" has no legal meaning. In the context of a bought deal, pre-marketing is understood generally to include communications by a dealer, directly or with any person or company (other than another dealer) for the purpose of obtaining from that person or company information as to the interest that it, or any person or company that it represents, may have in purchasing securities of the type that are proposed to be distributed, prior to a preliminary prospectus relating to those securities being filed with the relevant securities regulatory authorities. In this notice, "pre-marketing" will be used to denote this range of activities.

Legislative Framework

The provisions of securities legislation that circumscribe pre-marketing activities are:

– those dealing with distributions of securities that circumscribe generally the manner in which information may be communicated in furtherance of a distribution of securities, and

– those dealing with continuous disclosure obligations of reporting issuers and with tipping, insider trading and self dealing, that proscribe the dissemination of previously undisclosed material information and trading on the basis of such information by persons in a special relationship with a reporting issuer.

This notice focuses on the extent to which pre-marketing may be undertaken by dealers within the rules applicable to the distribution of securities under securities legislation. The notice does not discuss the application of the tipping and insider trading provisions of securities legislation as these provisions are very much fact specific, involving the question of whether an undisclosed material fact or material change has been used or communicated other than in the necessary course of business. As the current legal regime, insofar as it relates to tipping and insider trading, will continue to apply, compliance with this notice will not affect a legal determination that tipping or insider trading has occurred nor will it affect any action that securities regulatory authorities would take in respect of such activities.

Pre-Marketing under the Rules Governing the Distribution of Securities

Securities legislation provides generally that no one may trade in a security where that trade would be a distribution unless a preliminary prospectus and (final) prospectus have been filed and the necessary receipts obtained from the relevant securities regulatory authority. This requirement does not extend to distributions that are specifically exempt from these requirements under securities legislation.

The analysis of whether particular pre-marketing activities may or may not be carried out under this regime turns largely on whether such pre-marketing activities constitute a trade and, if so, whether such a trade would constitute a distribution that is not exempt from the prospectus requirements of securities legislation (a "non-exempt distribution").

In the Province of Quebec, since securities legislation has been designed without the notion of a "trade", the analysis is dependent solely on whether the pre-marketing activities constitute a distribution.

Does Pre-Marketing Constitute a "Trade"?

Securities legislation (other than the securities legislation of Quebec) defines a "trade" in a non-exhaustive manner to include, among other things:

– any sale or disposition of a security for valuable consideration,

– any receipt by a registrant of an order to buy or sell a security, and

– any act, advertisement, solicitation, conduct or negotiation directly or indirectly in furtherance of any of the foregoing.

---

2   In this notice, the staff of each province and territory set out their views with respect to the securities law of their own jurisdiction only.

Pre-marketing activities are, at a minimum, "conduct directly or indirectly in furtherance" of the sale of a security and therefore fall within the definition of a trade.

Does Pre-Marketing Constitute a Non-Exempt Distribution?

Even though pre-marketing activities constitute a "trade" for the purposes of securities legislation (other than the securities legislation of Quebec), they would be prohibited only if they also constituted a distribution under securities legislation. Securities legislation (other than the securities legislation of Quebec) defines a distribution to include a "trade" in, among other things, previously unissued securities and securities that form part of a control block.

The definition of distribution under the securities legislation of Quebec includes the endeavour to obtain or the obtaining, by an agent, of subscribers or purchasers of securities being distributed.

The definitions of trade, and in the Province of Quebec the definition of distribution, are so broad as to include potentially every activity, however remote from the actual sale of a security, within the securities legislation prohibition on trading or distributing securities absent a preliminary prospectus or (final) prospectus having been filed. Staff, however, believe that such an interpretation is incorrect. For communications to form part of a distribution, it is staff's view that they must be undertaken within the context of the distribution.

The view that pre-marketing undertaken in the period between the execution of an underwriting agreement and the filing of a preliminary short form prospectus forms part of the distribution is implicit in blanket rulings or orders issued by the Alberta, British Columbia, Ontario, Manitoba, Quebec and Saskatchewan securities commissions. The blanket rulings should not, however, be interpreted as implying that pre-marketing undertaken in advance of the execution of an underwriting agreement is not part of a distribution. Staff believe that such an interpretation is too restrictive.

Permitted and Prohibited Pre-Marketing

It is the view of staff that a distribution commences at the time (the "Commencement of Distribution") when:

– a dealer has had discussions with an issuer or a selling security holder, or with another dealer that has had discussions with an issuer or a selling security holder about a distribution of securities ("Distribution Discussions"), and

– those Distribution Discussions are of sufficient specificity that it is reasonable to expect that the dealer (alone or together with other dealers) will propose an underwriting of the securities to the issuer or the selling security holder, as the case may be.

Staff understand that many dealers communicate on a regular basis with clients and prospective clients concerning their interest in various securities. Staff do not believe that such ordinary course communications generally are made in furtherance of a distribution. However, from the Commencement of Distribution, communications by the dealer, with a person or company designed to have the effect of determining the interest that it, or any person or company that it represents, may have in purchasing securities of the type that are the subject of the Distribution Discussions, that are undertaken by any director, officer, employee or agent of the dealer:

(i) who participated in or had actual knowledge of the Distribution Discussions, or

(ii) whose communications were directed, suggested or induced by a person referred to in (i) or another person acting directly or indirectly at or upon the direction, suggestion or inducement of a person referred to in (ii),

are, in staff's view, in furtherance of the distribution and contrary to securities legislation. Therefore, from the Commencement of Distribution until the earliest of:

– the issuance of a receipt for a preliminary prospectus in respect of the distribution,

– the time at which a press release that announces the entering into of an enforceable agreement in respect of a bought deal is issued and filed in accordance with any blanket ruling or order, or notice made pursuant to an existing blanket ruling or order, of a securities regulatory authority of a province or territory of Canada, and provided that all of the conditions set forth in such blanket ruling or order or such notice and its related blanket ruling or order are met, and

–   the time at which the dealer determines not to pursue the distribution,

no such communications are permitted.

Market making and other principal trading activities in securities of the type that are the subject of the Distribution Discussions would be similarly prohibited if engaged in from the Commencement of Distribution until the earliest of the points in times indicated above, by a person referred to in (i), above, or at or upon the direction, suggestion or inducement of a person or persons referred to in (i) or (ii), above.

Are Prospectus Exemptions Available?

It has been suggested by some that, even if clearly made in furtherance of a distribution, pre-marketing could be undertaken in certain circumstances. Specifically, it has been suggested that if an exemption from the prospectus requirements would be available in respect of a specific distribution, pre-marketing of such distribution is exempt from the prospectus requirements.

This analysis is premised on an argument that the pre- marketing constitutes one distribution that is exempt from the prospectus requirements while the actual sale of the security to the purchaser constitutes a second discrete distribution effected pursuant to the prospectus. Staff are of the view that this analysis is contrary to securities legislation. It is staff's view that, in these circumstances, the distribution in respect of which the pre- marketing activity is undertaken is the distribution pursuant to the anticipated prospectus. The pre-marketing activity must be viewed in the context of the prospectus offering and as an activity in furtherance of that distribution. If it were otherwise, the overriding concerns implicit and explicit in securities legislation regarding equal access to information, conditioning of the market, tipping and insider trading, and the provisions of the legislation designed to ensure such access to information and curb such abuses, could be easily circumvented.

Staff recognize that an issuer and a dealer may have a demonstrable bona fide intention to effect an exempt distribution and this distribution may be abandoned in favour of a prospectus offering. In these limited circumstances, in the view of staff, there are two separate distributions.

From the time when it is reasonable for a dealer to expect that a bona fide exempt distribution will be abandoned in favour of a prospectus offering, the rules relating to pre-marketing outlined above apply.

Compliance

Staff are of the view that dealers should develop, implement, maintain and enforce procedures to ensure that pre-marketing activities that are contrary to securities legislation are not engaged in by their directors, officers, employees and agents. The selection and implementation of appropriate procedures is the responsibility of each dealer.

Reference:

For further information, please contact any of the following:

Brenda Benham
Acting Executive Director
Policy and Legislation
British Columbia
Securities Commission
(604) 660-4800

Louyse Gauvin
Policy Advisor
British Columbia
Securities Commission
(604) 660-4800

Anna Drummond
Corporate Finance
Solicitor, Policy
Ontario Securities
Commission
(416) 593-8192

Arnold Hochman
Deputy Director, Policy
Ontario Securities
Commission
(416) 593-8247

Rosetta Gagliardi
Policy Coordinator
Commission des valeurs
mobilières du Québec
(514) 873-5326

Susan McCallum
Director, Corporate Finance
Ontario Securities
Commission
(416) 593-8248

Robert Garneau
Directeur des Opérations
financières et de
l'Information continue
Commission des valeurs
mobilières du Québec
(514) 873-5326

Ron Sczinski
Director of Securities
Analysis
Alberta Securities
Commission
(403) 427-5201

June 11, 1993

CSA #93/5

CANADIAN SECURITIES ADMINISTRATORS' NOTICE

NATIONAL POLICY STATEMENT NO. 39 – MUTUAL FUNDS
SECTION 16 – SALES COMMUNICATIONS

The Canadian Securities Administrators (the "CSA") published amendments to National Policy Statement No. 39 ("N.P. 39") which resulted in section 16 of N.P. 39 being deleted in its entirety and being replaced with a revised section 16 (the "Revised Section 16") which establishes guidelines regarding mutual fund sales communications. The effective date of the Revised Section 16 was August 1, 1992.

In the Revised Section 16, sales communication is defined, in part, as any oral or written communication used to induce the purchase of securities issued by a mutual fund. The Revised Section 16 requires that most sales communications, including broadcast television and radio advertisements, include certain warnings as set out in section 16.06 of N.P. 39 ("Warnings").

Since the Revised Section 16 became effective, various mutual fund industry participants have raised the question of whether "image advertisements" which are intended to promote a corporate identity or the expertise of a mutual fund manager must contain Warnings. The CSA are of the view that, where an advertisement or other communication does not refer to a specific mutual fund or funds and does not promote any particular investment portfolio or strategy, such an advertisement or other communication is not a "sales communication" as defined in subsection 16.01(a) of N.P. 39 because it cannot be said to "induce the purchase of securities issued by a mutual fund" and therefore need not contain Warnings. This applies to both print and broadcast (radio or television) advertisements or other communications.

For further information or clarification please contact any of:

Robert Bouchard
Deputy Director,
Corporate Finance
The Manitoba Securities
Commission
(204) 945-2548

Susan I. McCallum
Director, Corporate Finance
Ontario Securities Commission
(416) 593-8248

Johanne Duchesne
Deputy Director,
Financial Operations
Commission des Valeurs
Mobilières du Québec
(514) 873-5326

Wayne Redwick
Deputy Superintendent
Corporate Finance
British Columbia
Securities Commission
(604) 660-4800

Susan Wolburgh Jenah
Deputy Director, Policy
Ontario Securities
Commission
(416) 593-8245

Ron Sczinski
Chief of Securities
Administration
Alberta Securities Commission
(403) 427-5201

December 3, 1993

CANADIAN SECURITIES ADMINISTRATORS' NOTICE
AN ELECTRONIC SYSTEM FOR SECURITIES FILINGS

Introduction

In the Spring of 1990, the Canadian Securities Administrators ("CSA") began developing an electronic filing system for all required securities filings. The system, called SEDAR (System for Electronic Document Analysis and Retrieval/Système électronique de document d'analyse et de recherche), is scheduled for implementation during 1995. It will ultimately permit electronic filing of required public securities filings and create a remotely accessible electronic database of all publicly available information regarding those issuers using the system. It will also provide the means to electronically link all participants in the securities markets in the country.

CSA decided to pursue electronic filing for a number of reasons. Currently, most securities filings are prepared on computers and printed on paper. Copies are made and sent, usually by courier, to multiple jurisdictions and stock exchanges, each of which must maintain bulky paper records. The paper records are difficult for both regulators and market participants to search. Electronic filing will permit a single electronically filed package to satisfy the filing requirements of all 12 CSA jurisdictions and, it is expected, some or all of the Canadian stock exchanges. The maintenance of securities filings in electronic form will permit much faster and better access by more market participants to more information.

The use of technology will also facilitate regulatory harmonization at an international level. The Securities and Exchange Commission of the United States (the "SEC") is implementing the Electronic Data Gathering and Retrieval system ("EDGAR"). This system mandates electronic filing for the vast majority of U.S. issuers. The North American Securities Administrators Association is developing the Securities Registration Depository to link to EDGAR and facilitate state filings. The Multijurisdictional Disclosure System has been in place for over two years. Securities markets in North America have become increasingly interdependent. CSA has concluded that an electronic system for regulatory filings is needed to improve the efficiency and ensure the continued competitiveness of the Canadian markets.

This notice is being published to provide the securities community with the opportunity to comment on SEDAR. The notice includes preliminary information with respect to systems requirements, certain legal and procedural issues and implementation. The introduction of SEDAR will change the manner in which filings are made with securities commissions in Canada. CSA appreciates the time that commenters have given and will give to this project.

Systems Requirements

SEDAR has been developed with significant input from the securities filing community. Care has been taken to ensure that the final system will be easy to use and accommodate systems in use by the majority of filers.

SEDAR is a network with electronic mail capability and a database. IBM Canada Ltd. ("IBM") will develop and initially manage both. Filings will be sent by the filer electronically to the SEDAR main computer via the IBM Information Network. Required filing fees will also be remitted electronically. Those securities commissions or exchanges designated by the filer to receive the submission will receive an electronic message that the submission has been made. If a securities commission or exchange wishes to review the submission, it will download the submission to its local computer facility. Through use of the system, the filer will be able to monitor the status of the filing. Interaction between the regulator and the filer (e.g., the issuance of prospectus comment letters and responses to them, and the issuance of receipts) will be accommodated through the system.

The network will be "distance insensitive". Whether a filing is made with a securities commission 100 or 1000 miles away will be irrelevant; the system access charges will remain the same. System access charges (those charges paid to IBM to file the material electronically) are being developed in consultation with the filing community and CSA, with a view to ensuring that on a system wide basis the cost of using SEDAR will be less than the costs that are being displaced by SEDAR. In other words, in most cases, use of the system should cost less than the copying, courier, mailing and other costs that will be eliminated in an electronic environment.

For example, on a national prospectus filing, filers must prepare at least one and sometimes multiple copies of all material for filing in 12 jurisdictions. The packages must be physically assembled and placed into courier packages. It then takes 24 to 48 hours to have those packages couriered to each of the jurisdictions. With SEDAR, one electronic package will be prepared and electronically delivered immediately to all 12 jurisidictions.

CSA has chosen to develop SEDAR with certain systems requirements. These requirements were set following informal surveys of the filing community. CSA recognizes that some filers may not have systems able to meet all of the system requirements. However, the cost of making the required acquisitions is minimal compared to the ongoing costs that would have been incurred with a more generic model.

CSA wanted to avoid the complexity and cost of a generic model and chose to simplify the structure throught the use of readily available software packages. In order to access SEDAR using a standard application developed by IBM, filers will need an IBM compatible computer with the following software:

1. *Windows 3.1*

Of utmost importance to CSA was "ease of use". CSA made it clear to the developers that, while third parties might want to involve themselves in the filing process, generally speaking, the system should be capable of being used by anyone with general computer skills. This necessitated the use of an "intuitive" operating system and the surveys indicated that Microsoft Windows was the most commonly used program of this type within the filing community.

2. *WordPerfect 5.1 or 5.2*

Only documents submitted in IBM compatible WordPerfect 5.1 or 5.2 will be accepted by SEDAR. Informal surveys have indicated that WordPerfect is in wide use in the legal and accounting community. Acceptance of more than one wordprocessing format would have caused considerable concern with respect to the integrity of the SEDAR database. The ready availability of translation software will allow filers or third parties to convert documents prepared using word processing software other than IBM comptaible WordPerfect 5.1 or 5.2.

Legal and Procedural Issues

Signatures

The signing of documents filed electronically is a key issue that must be resolved to permit SEDAR to operate efficiently.

Courts in England and Canada have held that the primary purpose of requiring a signature manually or otherwise is to authenticate the document by ensuring that the person signing has given personal attention to the document and assumed responsibility for its contents. The rules adopted by the SEC in connection with EDGAR provide that the electronic entry of a typed name satisfies the signature requirement for all documents filed through EDGAR. According to SEC publications, commenters who addressed the issue of signatures in the United States strongly supported the view that filers should be able to satisfy signature requirements by reproducing the signatory's name in typed form. The following are the rules contained in Regulation S-T, the general regulation for filing under EDGAR.

Reg. 232.302.

(a) Signatures to or within any electronic submission shall be in typed form rather than manual format. When used in connection with an electronic filing, the term "signature" means an electronic entry in the form of a magnetic impulse or other form of computer data compilation of any letter or series of letters comprising a name, executed, adopted or authorized as a signature.

(b) A manually signed signature page or other document authenticating, acknowledging or otherwise adopting the signatures that appear in typed form within an electronic filing shall be executed before or at the time the electronic filing is made and shall be retained by the filer for a period of five years. Upon request, an electronic filer shall furnish to the Commission or its staff a copy of any or all documents retained pursuant to this section.

CSA is considering a similar approach with respect to electronic signatures. However, in place of the EDGAR requirements for retention of signature pages found in Reg. 232.302(b), CSA will require that one manually signed document entitled "Certificate of Authority to File" be submitted within a prescribed period of time following the electronic submission. This Certificate will be signed by all persons who would otherwise have been required to sign the paper filing.

Acceptance of Graphic and Other Material

Certain material required to be filed with a securities commission does not lend itself, at present, to easy and inexpensive electronic transmission and storage.

This material falls generally into three categories:

1.　graphic material incorporated directly into filings (e.g., photographs, maps, graphs, etc.);

2.　material prepared in a non-electronic environment that is required to be filed in support of a filing (e.g., old trust deeds, contracts prepared by third parties, etc.); and

3.　material prepared in an electronic environment by third parties (e.g., consent letters, financial statements).

Here again, CSA is proposing to borrow from the procedures put in place by the SEC for EDGAR. With respect to material falling into the first category, there will be a requirement that the electronic submission contain an accurate and complete textual description of the graphic material that would otherwise be included. The hard copy of the material that is included in the commercial copies of the submission will be incorporated by reference into the electronic copy. The filer will be required to forward, on request, any of this graphic material to any securities commission that requests it.

Material falling into the second category will be reproduced electronically in a WordPerfect file by the filer and filed together with certification in electronic form that the electronically filed material accurately reflects the content of the original material maintained by the filer.

Material included in the third category will generally be required to be filed electronically by the filer following conversion by the filer or the third party into IBM compatible WordPerfect format.

Mandating

The SEC is mandating electronic filings through EDGAR. A number of representatives of the Canadian filing community have submitted that CSA consider mandating SEDAR.

There are some practical reasons to consider mandating of electronic filings once CSA is satisfied with the viability of the system. Requiring use of SEDAR should permit each of the jurisdictions and all filers to reduce costs in a number of areas. Mandating would also create a complete electronic record with respect to all issuers. CSA invites particular comment on this issue.

Conclusion

SEDAR is scheduled for implementation during 1995. Testing of the system by all types of issuers is expected to be conducted during 1994 and early 1995.

The introduction of SEDAR is a major step by CSA toward making compliance with Canadian securities regulatory requirements easier and more efficient. Implementation will require the cooperation and assistance of all participants in the securities markets. While the filing community has already played a significant role in the development of SEDAR, CSA encourages market participants to provide further comment.

Comment letters submitted in response to this notice will be placed in the public file in certain jurisdictions and form part of the public record unless confidentiality is requested. Comment letters will be circulated among the securities regulatory authorities for purposes of preparing draft procedures for SEDAR whether or not confidentiality is requested. Accordingly, although comment letters for which confidentiality is requested will not be placed in the public file, freedom of information legislation may require the securities regulatory authorities in certain jurisdictions to make the comment letters available. Persons submitting comment letters should be aware that the press and members of the public may be able to obtain access to any comment letter.

Comments should be in writing only and should be delivered to the attention of CSA. Comments should be submitted on or before August 15, 1994. All comment letters should be delivered to the following address:

> Canadian Securities Administrators
> SEDAR Working Committee
> c/o Secretary
> British Columbia Securities Commission
> 1100 - 865 Hornby Street
> Vancouver, B.C.
> V6Z 2H4

Questions may be referred to:

> Wade D. Nesmith
> Lang Michener Lawrence & Shaw
> Barristers and Solicitors
> (604) 691-7415

> Mark DesLauriers
> Osler, Hoskin & Harcourt
> Barristers and Solicitors
> (416) 862-5914

> Karen Eby
> Ontario Securities Commission
> (416) 593-8242

> Pascale Mercier
> Lavery, de Billy
> Barristers and Solicitors
> (514) 871-1522

> Richard Proulx
> Commission des valeurs mobilières du Québec
> (514) 873-5326

June 15, 1994

CSA#95/1

CANADIAN SECURITIES ADMINISTRATORS' NOTICE

CONFLICTS OF INTEREST

The Canadian Securities Administrators ("CSA") are undertaking a review of the conflict of interest regimes that were instituted in Alberta, British Columbia, Nova Scotia, Ontario and Québec at the time ownership of the securities industry was deregulated. This review consists of two concurrent approaches. In November, a Request for Comments and staff discussion paper were published in the Alberta Securities Commission Summary and the Ontario Securities Commission Bulletin and made available for distribution at the offices of the securities administrators in British Columbia and Québec (see NIN#94/24). The deadline for submissions to the Request for Comments is January 31, 1995. Submissions should be sent to:

> The Secretary
> Ontario Securities Commission
> 20 Queen Street West
> Toronto, Ontario
> M5H 3S8

In addition, the CSA has established a consultative committee to assist in the formulation of recommendations regarding underwriting conflicts of interest. Submissions, when received in response to the Request for Comments, will be considered by the committee. Accordingly, early responses to the Request would be greatly appreciated.

The committee is chaired by a representative of the CSA and is made up of CSA appointees and senior representatives from various market participant groups including dealers, issuers and investors.

The committee members are:

CSA Representatives:

John A. Geller (Chair)	Vice-Chair, Ontario Securities Commission
William L. Hess	Chair, Alberta Securities Commission
Tanis J. MacLaren	Deputy Director, Capital Markets/International Markets, Ontario Securities Commission
Joëlle St. Arnault	Legal Counsel, Québec Securities Commission

Issuer Representatives:

Robert H. Kidd	Senior Vice-President & CFO, George Weston Limited
Gordon W. Steele	Chairman, President & CEO, Riverside Forest Products Limited

Investor Representatives:

Henry Rachfalowski	Vice-President, Portfolio Management, Ontario Municipal Employees Retirement System
Donald Walcot	Chief Investment Officer, Bimcor Inc.

Securities Industry Representatives:

James T. Kiernan	President, Goldman Sachs Canada
Joseph J. Oliver	Vice-President & Director, Investment Banking, First Marathon Securities Limited
R. Jeffrey Orr	Executive Vice-President & Director, Investment Banking, Nesbitt Burns Inc.
Daniel F. Sullivan	Deputy-Chairman, ScotiaMcLeod Inc.

The committee's initial report is expected to be published by the end of February, 1995.

REF: NIN#94/24

January 12, 1995

CSA#95/2

CANADIAN SECURITIES ADMINISTRATORS' NOTICE

MUTUAL FUND SALES INCENTIVES
POINT-OF-SALE DISCLOSURE STATEMENT

In August 1991, the Investment Funds Institute of Canada ("IFIC") issued its report on mutual fund sales incentives (the "IFIC Report"). The IFIC Report was followed by the release, in October 1991, of the IFIC Code of Conduct (the "IFIC Code") dealing with sales incentives.

The IFIC Code required enhanced disclosure of sales incentives offered as compensation for sales of mutual fund securities by way of a summary on the inside front cover of the fund prospectus and a full and complete description of all sales incentives in the body of the prospectus, indexed for reference purposes in the prospectus table of contents. The IFIC Code also required that investors in mutual funds be provided with a separate "point-of-sale" disclosure statement at the time of purchase of mutual fund securities advising investors of the type of sales incentives applicable with respect to the purchase.

Subsequently, the Canadian Securities Administrators (the "CSA") published a notice dated January 29, 1993 (the "January Notice") in which the CSA said that they planned to implement the requirements established in the IFIC Code with respect to sales incentive disclosure by way of amendments to the relevant policy statements. The January Notice indicated the CSA's expectation that industry participants would comply with the recommendations in the IFIC Code relating to enhanced prospectus disclosure of sales incentives and delivery of a point-of-sale disclosure statement.

The CSA are of the view that the generic nature of the point-of-sale disclosure statements which have been provided by industry participants to date does not convey sufficient meaningful information to the investor to justify the additional level of expense in the distribution process. Therefore, the CSA wish to announce that, pending the completion of the overall review of the regulation of investment funds, which was announced by the Chairman of the OSC in February 1994, the CSA do not expect industry participants to provide a point-of-sale disclosure statement as originally contemplated in the January Notice.

For further information, please contact any of:

Robert Bouchard
Deputy Director, Corporate Finance
The Manitoba Securities Commission
(204) 945-2548

Marguerite Child
Senior Financial Policy Analyst
Policy Department
Alberta Securities Commision
(403) 427-5201

Susan Wolburgh Jenah
Deputy Director, Policy
Corporate Finance
Ontario Securities Commission
(416) 593-8245

Wayne Redwick
Deputy Superintendent
Corporate Finance
British Columbia Securities Commission
(604) 660-4800

Johanne Duchesne
Deputy Director, Financial Operations
Commission des Valeurs
Mobilieres du Quebec
(514) 873-5326

Lata Casciano
Policy Advisor
Policy and Legislation
British Columbia Securities Commission
(604) 660-4800

January 13, 1995

CSA#95/3

CANADIAN SECURITIES ADMINISTRATORS' NOTICE

SEDAR

On June 15, 1994, the Canadian Securities Administrators ("CSA") published CSA Notice #94/1 (the "Notice") entitled "An Electronic System for Securities Filings. The Notice introduced SEDAR (System for Electronic Document Analysis and Retrieval/Système électronique de document d'analyse et de recherche). This notice is designed to update the filing community on the progress of the development of SEDAR.

General

Following the publication of the Notice, the CSA committee charged with responsibility for the development of SEDAR continued to work with IBM as IBM developed the SEDAR application. The first version of the application was delivered to CSA in October, 1994 and since that time it has been subjected to rigorous testing by the securities commissions in Quebec, Ontario and British Columbia. As a result of that testing, a number of issues were identified and a new interim version of the application is due to be delivered in July, 1995. Introduction of SEDAR as the method for filing securities documents is now scheduled for early 1996.

CDS

The major development in the SEDAR project has been the introduction of the Canadian Depository for Securities Ltd. ("CDS"). CDS is a privately held corporation owned by members of the Investment Dealers' Association of Canada, the Montreal and Toronto stock exchanges and a number of the larger Canadian banks and trust companies. In December, 1994, CDS purchased the SEDAR application from IBM. Under the terms of the agreement with IBM, CDS will ultimately assume responsibility for the operations and management for SEDAR. IBM will complete the application development and Advantis Canada, an IBM affiliate, will provide the network upon which SEDAR will run.

CDS has, for a number of years, played a key role in the Canadian securities markets, acting as the depository for the majority of equity securities held in this country. That important role will now be expanded with its management of SEDAR.

CSA
Notices

WordPerfect / MicroSoft Word

In the Notice, CSA announced its preliminary decision to require the use of IBM compatible WordPerfect 5.1 or 5.2 as the standard for use in SEDAR. This proposal has generated more comment from the filing community than any other. In the result, CSA has consulted with IBM and CDS and come to the conclusion that, on balance, it is preferable to include the use of WordPerfect and MicroSoft Word as the two wordprocessing formats to be accepted. The required version of each of WordPerfect and MicroSoft Word will be determined in the near future and announced in a subsequent CSA notice.

Mandating

Use of the EDGAR electronic filing system of the Securities and Exchange Commission of the United States is mandated for most U.S. securities filers. CSA has considered the comments received in response to the Notice and has consulted with the filing community. CSA has come to the conclusion that, subject to the successful testing of SEDAR, each CSA jurisdiction will take those steps within its power to require the use of SEDAR for at least those issuers who file nationally. A decision with respect to filers who file in only one jurisdiction will be made at a later date.

The process through which SEDAR will be mandated will vary by jurisdiction. In certain jurisdictions, it may be accomplished by changes to policy or the introduction of rules. In others, it may require legislative change. Not all national filers will be mandated to use SEDAR at the same time. Mandating will occur according to a schedule, to be published in a subsequent CSA notice, that will add identifiable filer groups one at a time.

Conclusion

SEDAR is progressing toward implementation. The addition of CDS marks a significant step in SEDAR's development.

Questions may be referred to:

Wade D. Nesmith	Pascal Mercier
Lang Michener Lawrence & Shaw	Lavery, de Billy
Barristers and Solicitors	Barristers and Solicitors
(604) 691-7415	(514) 871-1522
Mark DesLauriers	Richard Proulx
Osler, Hoskin & Harcourt	Commission des Valeurs
Barristers and Solicitors	Mobilieres du Quebec
(416) 862-5914	(514) 873-5009
Karen Eby	Sandy MacDonald
Ontario Securities Commission	British Columbia Securities Commission
(416) 593-8242	(604) 660-4800

April 21, 1995

CSA#95/4

CANADIAN SECURITIES ADMINISTRATORS' NOTICE

PROPOSED FOREIGN ISSUER PROSPECTUS AND CONTINUOUS DISCLOSURE SYSTEM (DRAFT NATIONAL POLICY STATEMENT NO. 53)

Background

In August 1993, the Canadian Securities Administrators ("CSA") published a Request for Comments outlining proposed draft National Policy Statement No. 53, which was entitled the "Foreign Issuer Prospectus and Continuous Disclosure System" ("FIPS") and was designed to facilitate world-class foreign issuers offering securities in Canada as part of an international offering. Since that time, various factors have led to significant changes in the underlying approach, which is described below.

The CSA will be publishing for comment the revised FIPS, which will be a draft rule in Ontario and is expected to take the form of a policy statement in other participating Canadian provinces and territories. It is contemplated that FIPS would, among other things, permit offerings of securities of major foreign issuers to be made in Canada on a basis that would be exempt from most Canadian disclosure requirements, including Canadian GAAP reconciliation requirements. FIPS would be available for offerings which are also being made on a registered basis pursuant to United States federal securities laws and which meet certain eligibility requirements. FIPS would also provide for exemptions from certain Canadian continuous disclosure requirements.

In response to certain inquiries, staff of the various provincial and territorial securities regulatory authorities wish to advise that they are willing to consider recommending relief on a case-by-case basis to permit offerings along the lines of FIPS prior to the formal implementation of FIPS.

FIPS

General

The purpose of FIPS is to facilitate certain offerings of securities of foreign issuers in Canada while seeking to ensure that Canadian investors remain adequately protected. This is expected to enable Canadian dealers and retail investors to participate directly in global securities offerings, including foreign privatizations.

FIPS will be limited to major issuers whose securities can be expected to be liquid and to have a significant market following. Offerings made pursuant to FIPS in Canada will be completed by way of a prospectus on the basis of documents prepared in accordance with U.S. federal securities legislation (with certain additional Canadian disclosure), thus preserving traditional civil liability remedies for Canadian investors.

FIPS is designed to permit eligible transactions to occur in Canada with minimal review on the basis of disclosure documents prepared in accordance with United States federal securities laws and regulations, and builds on the mechanisms set forth in existing Canada-U.S. Multijurisdictional Disclosure System contained in National Policy Statement No. 45 ("NP 45"). However, unlike MJDS, FIPS will not be reciprocal, i.e. Canadian issuers will not receive similar treatment in any jurisdiction outside of Canada. Although in most cases there will be minimal review, the substance of the disclosure documents will be reviewed in the unusual case where, through monitoring of the materials or otherwise, the Canadian securities regulatory authorities have reason to believe that there may be a problem with a transaction or the related disclosure or other special circumstances exist. In addition, eligible foreign issuers will not be required to provide Canadian GAAP information (provided that U.S. GAAP information is included, directly or by reconciliation).

The requirements and exemptions available under FIPS for offerings of securities of eligible foreign issuers that are not being concurrently made on a registered basis in the U.S. will be determined on a case-by-case basis.

While FIPS will not be available for business combinations, consideration is being given to extending FIPS to certain take-over bids and issuer bids, including securities exchange offerings made in respect of foreign issuers.

Eligibility Requirements

FIPS will be available for offerings of equity, debt and other securities (subject to certain exclusions, such as derivative securities) of or by foreign issuers (i) having a market value and public float (being the market value held by non-affiliates and non-associates), on a post-offering basis, of Cdn. $3 billion and Cdn. $1 billion, respectively, (ii) which are being offered in the U.S. and registered contemporaneously with the U.S. Securities and Exchange Commission, and (iii) where the securities proposed to be distributed in Canada represent 10% or less of the securities to be distributed worldwide (including Canada).

The foreign issuer must not be a commodity pool issuer, collective investment program, mutual fund or investment company within the meaning of the U.S. Investment Company Act of 1940.

In addition, certain debt or preferred shares of majority-owned subsidiaries of eligible foreign issuers which are guaranteed by the latter may also be offered under FIPS, provided that they are non-convertible or convertible only into securities of the eligible foreign issuer and provided that the guarantor signs a prospectus certificate.

Procedures

The procedures for completing a prospectus offering under FIPS will be substantially similar to those under NP 45. Certain minimal legends will be required, but, as noted above, Canadian GAAP information will not be required if U.S. GAAP information is provided, either directly or by reconciliation. Canadian forms of certificates of issuers and underwriters will be required.

It is anticipated that shelf and post-receipt pricing procedures will be available, including unallocated shelf procedures to the extent available in the United States.

Continuous Disclosure, Proxy Solicitation, Etc.

Continuous disclosure and proxy solicitation requirements for eligible foreign issuers that are U.S. companies or entities will generally be those applicable in the U.S., provided that all such documents are filed promptly in Canada and, if applicable, made available to Canadian resident securityholders in the same manner and time as required under U.S. law. However, as under NP 45, Canadian early warning requirements will continue to apply. There will be no requirement to file insider reports in Canada so long as U.S. rules are complied with.

Guaranteed securities will be subject to the requirement to file and deliver to securityholders the guarantor's financial statements at the same time as in the U.S.

The continuous disclosure and insider reporting requirements applicable to non-U.S. eligible foreign issuers that are U.S. registrants will be those applicable in the U.S., again with certain filing and delivery requirements applicable in Canada. For greater certainty, such issuers will be exempt from Canadian proxy solicitation requirements. However, U.S. eligible and non-U.S. eligible foreign issuers will deliver to Canadian security holders any documents that they deliver to U.S. security holders and in the same manner.

The continuous disclosure and insider reporting requirements and exemptions applicable to non-U.S. eligible foreign issuers that are not U.S. registrants will be determined on a case-by-case basis.

Continuous disclosure relief will also be available on similar terms for eligible issuers that have not completed an offering under FIPS but are reporting issuers in Canada for other reasons.

Foreign Dealers' Participation

Dealers registered as international dealers in Ontario will be able to distribute securities offered under FIPS to designated institutions (as defined in the Regulation) in Ontario. Certain other jurisdictions are considering whether they should allow foreign dealers to offer securities under FIPS to institutions and other sophisticated investors. Consideration is also being given by certain jurisdictions to whether international dealers should be permitted to sign the Underwriter's Certificate in a FIPS prospectus.

Case-By-Case Relief

Persons wishing to seek relief necessary to accomplish a transaction that is contemplated by FIPS prior to FIPS being implemented are invited to contact Commission Staff of the applicable regulatory authorities to discuss how this can best be achieved.

For further information, please contact:

Alberta Securities Commission
Ron Sczinski
Chief of Securities Administration
(403) 427-5201

British Columbia Securities Commission
Louyse Gauvin
Policy Advisor, Policy & Legislation
(604) 660-4491

Ontario Securities Commission
Randee Pavalow
Senior Counsel, International Markets Branch
(416) 593-8257

Veronica Wessels
Deputy Director, Legal, Corporate Finance Branch
(416) 593-8114

Simon Romano
Special Counsel
(416) 593-8161

Commission des valeurs mobilières du Québec
Robert Garneau
Director of Corporate Finance and Continuous Disclosure
(514) 873-5009 ext. 224

Rosetta Gagliardi
Policy Adviser
(514) 873-5009 ext. 252

Saskatchewan Securities Commission
Ian McIntosh
Deputy Director, Corporate Finance
(306) 787-5687

April 28, 1995

Index

References are to page numbers and the following:

Accountants
acting as advisers, s30
defined, s30(1)
exemption from registration, s30(3)

Acquisitions
direct or indirect, s79
during bid, s94(1)
  further press releases, s94(2), Reg 163.2
press release, s93(1)
  acquisition by offeror, Reg 163.1
  person other than offeror, by, Reg 163.2
reports of, s93(1)
  exception, s93(4)
  restrictions on, s93(3)
restrictions on
  during issuer bid, s84
  during take-over bid, s83, Reg 156
  pre-bid and post-bid, s85, Reg 157

Act
defined, Reg 1

Acting jointly or in concert, s 78(1)
limitation, s78(2)

Administrator
individuals, exclusion from
  definition, s1(1)
registration for trades,
  exemptions, s31(2)*(1)*(i)
take over bids, exemptions, s80(2)(a)

Advertising.
(see generally Securities Act, ss20, 30,
  35, 37-40; Securities Regulation,
  Regs 87, 127; LPS 3-39; NPS 21, 22,
  25, 42; NIN#92/14; UAP No. 2-13;
  CSA#91/1, #93/5)
approval by Commission, s40
guidelines LPS 3-39, 4-125
offering memorandum, Reg 127
representation of registration, ss38, 39
submission of, Reg 87
use of name of another registrant
  in, s37

Adviser
accountant, barrister and
  solicitor, s30(2)
business procedures, Reg 40
categories, Reg 14
  investment counsel, Regs 14(a), 61
  portfolio manager, Regs 14(b), 61
  securities adviser, Regs 14(c), 60

defined, s1(1)
Federal Business Development
  Bank, s30(2)(b)
insurer, s30(2)(a)
jurisdiction of incorporation, Reg 16.1
limitations on, Reg 167.7
minimum free capital, Reg 21
registration
  application for, Form 3, 3-7
  application for amendment of, Form
    7, 3-28
  application for transfer/change of
    status, Form 7A, 3-30
  exemptions from, s30, Regs 73, 74,
    76-78
  granting, s21
  notice of change, s28(2), Reg 69
  requirement of, s20
registered advisers, filings, s28(2)
registered dealer, s30(e)
savings institution, s30(2)(a)
securities adviser, defined, Reg 14

Affidavit
superintendent may require, s24(b)

Agreement
defined, Reg 184
filing, Reg 188
receipt for, Reg 187
safekeeping agreement, Reg 51
subordination agreement, Reg 26
  Form 60, 3-285
terms of, Reg 186

Appeals
B.C. Securities Commission,
  decisions, s149
Court of Appeal, to, s149
designated organization, decision, s148
regulations, s159(1)*(28)*
superintendent, decision, s147

Associate
accountability for gain, s119(5)
associate of offeror, s78(1)
defined, s1(1)

Associated party of the registrant
defined, Reg 167.1(1)

Audit
B.C.S.C. Notices & Interpretation Notes
  auditor's report on comparative finan-
    cial statements NIN#91/18, 8-69
  comparative interim financial state-
    ments NIN#91/20, 8-70

Dealer ownership restrictions
exemptions, Reg 72.4
interpretation, Reg 72.1
notice of diversification, Reg 72.3
notice of ownership, Reg 72.2

Debt security
defined, Reg 1

Decision
defined, s1(1)

Designated organization
defined, s1(1)
immunity of, s152
party to hearing, s147(7)
regulation, s159(1)*(30)*
review of decision by, s148
revocation and variation of
    decision, s153

Designated security
defined, s1(1)

Director
alternate signing authority, Reg 163.6
appointment by court, s140(2)(d)
certificate of issuer, s49
circular. *see* **Directors' circular**
costs of action, s121(3)
deemed commission of offence, s138(3)
deemed insider, s2(1)-(3)
defined, s1(1)
enforcement order, s144(1)
    resignation under, s144(1)(d)
filing, change of, s28, Reg 69
financial statements, approval of, Reg
    112
individual director circular, s91(3)
insider report for reporting issuer, s70
liability for misrepresentation
    circular, in, s115
    prospectus, in, s114
personal information filing, s73.1
    Form 4B, 3-23
    NIN#92/18, 8-85

Directors' circular
delivery, s92(2), (3)
disclosure in, Reg 163.5
filing, Reg 163.7
Form 34, 3-206
individual director circular, s91(3)
    Form 35, 3-209
liability for misrepresentation
    in, s115(3), (9), (10)
notice of change or variation, s91(6)
statement of rights, Reg 163.4
take-over bid, s91

Disclosure. *see also* **Continuous disclosure**
experience of directors, officers,
    promoters and control persons, of
    NIN#89/36, 8-53
filing of, Regs 144-147
financial, Regs 135-143
insider reporting, Regs 148-152.3
    Form 36, 3-211
material change report, Form 27, 3-180

multijurisdictional disclosure system
    BOR#91/7, 7-18
    NPS 45, 5-201
    guide to NIN#91/22, 8-74
promotional or investor relations ar-
    rangements, of NIN#89/35, 8-52
timely NPS 40, 5-144

Distributing firm
defined, Reg 109

Distribution
continuing after lapse, s51(4)
deemed
    exchange issuer, Reg 134
    other than exchange issuer, Reg 133
defined, s1(1)
exemptions from prospectus
    requirements, ss55(2), 58
    call option contract, Form 26, 3-179
    form of report, Form 20, 3-164
    objection by Superintendent, s55(3)
    prescribed amounts for, Reg 118
    put option contract, Form 25, 3-178
    statement of material facts, Reg 121
        Form 24, 3-170
    Superintendent orders re, s59
list, s63
material given on, s65
preliminary prospectus, of, s62
report on, Reg 132
    Form 20, 3-164
Superintendent orders re, s52
venture capital issuer LPS 3-13, 4-53
waiting period limitations, s61

Distribution contract
defined, s1(1)

Documents
action for failure to deliver, s118
execution and certification of, Reg 182

Enforcement
commission order, s144.2
order, general, s144
    notice of hearing, s144(4)
    temporary order, s144(2), (3)

Equity security
defined, s74(1)

Escrow agreement
agent of, Reg 181
B.C.S.C. Blanket Orders and Rulings
    trades in securities held subject to an
        escrow or pooling agreement
        BOR#89/5, 7-10
Form 16, 3-159
regulations, s159(1)*(15)*

Evidence
certified statement as, s150
confidential, s132
damage of, s137(3)
Evidence Act, s128(2)
expert examination of, s9(2)
reviews and appeals, rules of, s154.1,
    Reg 175